BLACK'S LAW DICTIONARY

Second
Pocket Edition

BRYAN A. GARNER
Editor in Chief

A THOMSON COMPANY

ST. PAUL, MINN., 2001

ISBN 0-314-25791-8

Preface to the Second Edition

If dictionaries can be said to lead interesting lives, this one certainly has had one.

It began in 1994 as a book that two colleagues and I began writing from scratch, using modern lexicographic techniques. When that book was published in 1996, I began working on the unabridged *Black's Law Dictionary* (7th ed.), again with lawyers that I had trained in legal lexicography. We used the 1996 pocket edition as the starting point for that book and added thousands of new entries, which we drafted with an eye to earlier editions of *Black's*—but we drafted them essentially anew. While adding all these new terms, we inevitably improved many of the definitions from the earlier pocket edition. The seventh edition appeared in August 1999.

Then the West Group asked me to abridge the seventh edition, to replace the old paperback abridgment of the sixth edition. (For many years, *Black's* has been out in several editions—deluxe, standard, abridged, and from 1996 on, the pocket.) The new abridged edition appeared in June 2000.

The last step in the cycle, at least for now, was to produce a new pocket edition. This meant abridging the abridged edition by more than half, while keeping an eye on which terms appeared in the first pocket edition. The result, as anyone will see who bothers to compare the editions, is a textually distinct book—and, I think, much improved.

Perhaps the most important innovation is that my colleagues and I have managed to fit more than 2,000 additional entries into the book, mainly by minimizing the kinds of cross-references that can so easily fit into a bigger dictionary. So while the first pocket edition had some 7,500 main headwords, this one has more than 10,000—and the text itself is only 85 pages longer. To make this possible, we excluded most of the variants for legal terms. For those, you'll need to consult the unabridged or even the abridged seventh edition. The more useful function here, we thought, would be to include additional entries—not to list secondary variants that take up precious space.

Everyone who has worked on this project has shared a goal: to produce the most accurate, readable, and comprehensive small law dictionary ever published. Though we doubtless could have done better here and there, we think we have met our goal. We hope it meets your needs.

BRYAN A. GARNER

Dallas, Texas
February 2001

Preface to the First Edition

Every subject has its seminal reference book—the one that becomes a household word. When you think of world records, you think of *Guinness*; of encyclopedias, *Britannica*; of anatomy, *Gray's*; of music dictionaries, *Grove's*; of English-language dictionaries, *Webster* (in the U.S.) and *Oxford* (in the U.K.).

And whenever somebody thinks of law dictionaries, *Black's* seems inevitably to come to mind. Henry Campbell Black (1860–1927) first published his magnum opus in 1891, and his achievement might easily be taken for granted today. He entered a crowded field, for there were many law dictionaries then in print—several more major ones, in fact, than there are today. But who today, apart from the specialist, remembers the names of Anderson, Burrill, English, Kinney, Lawson, Rapalje, Sweet, Wharton, or even the better-known Bouvier?

What happened is that Henry Campbell Black's dictionary took the field and became incontestably supreme, partly because of his comprehensiveness, partly because of his academic standing, and partly because he had the good fortune of publishing his work with West Publishing Company.

Black's Law Dictionary has evolved over its six unabridged editions. And this pocket edition continues that evolution. Indeed, because it was compiled on modern lexicographic principles, the book you're holding is something of a radical leap forward in the evolutionary line.

Lexicographic Methods and Features

Little is known about exactly how Black and his contemporaries worked, but one thing is certain to anyone who has spent any time examining 19th-century and early-20th-century law dictionaries: a great deal of the "work" was accomplished through wholesale borrowing from other dictionaries. To cite but one example, in Bouvier (1839), Anderson (1890), Black (1891), Kinney (1893), Shumaker & Longsdorf (1901), and several other law dictionaries of the period, the phrase *disorderly house* is defined in the following word-for-word sequence: a "house the inmates of which behave so badly as to become a nuisance to the neighborhood." Hundreds of other definitions are virtually verbatim from book to book.

Although this practice of heavy borrowing is suspect today, it may be wrong to judge these early lexicographers by modern standards. They might have copied for various reasons. First, even nonspecialist lexicographers of the time commonly borrowed from each other; that is, apart from a few notable exceptions such as Samuel Johnson (1709–1784), Noah Webster (1758–1843), and James A.H. Murray (1837–1915—the first editor of the *Oxford English Dictionary*), a high percentage of entries in early English-language dictionaries were directly traceable to even earlier dictionaries. Second, dictionary editors in the legal field were trained as common-law lawyers, under the Anglo-American system of precedent. As a result, they might have thought that accuracy precluded a reconsideration of their predecessors' words—especially if the earlier dictionary-maker cited caselaw in support of a definition. And third, notions of plagiarism were much less well defined than they are today (and, in any event, have always been looser in lexicography than elsewhere).

But the result of all this is that, as the legal language has grown, law dictionaries have generally strayed further and further afield from actual legal usage. Instead of monitoring legal language for new entries—words that emerge in a given practice area, legal slang that crops up in a certain context, words that take on meanings different from their traditional ones—compilers of law dictionaries have tended to look too much at their forerunners.

This book, however, represents a stem-to-stern (very stern) reconsideration of legal terms—an entirely fresh edition of

PREFACE TO THE FIRST EDITION

Black's Law Dictionary compiled on modern lexicographic methods. This means that my colleagues and I have done several things. We have:

- Attempted a thorough marshaling of the language of the law from original sources. Many terms make their "debut" in this edition.
- Examined the writings of specialist scholars rather than looking only at judicial decisions.
- Considered entries entirely anew rather than merely accepting what previous editions have said. We have often checked Westlaw and other sources when trying to decide which of two competing forms now predominates in legal usage.
- Imposed analytical rigor on entries by avoiding duplicative definitions and by cataloguing and numbering senses.
- Shown pronunciations that reflect how American lawyers actually say the words and phrases—not how English lawyers used to say them (and not how Latin teachers would have us say them).
- Recorded cognate forms—for example, the verb and adjective corresponding to a given noun.
- Ensured that specialized vocabularies are included—from bankruptcy to securities law, from legal realism to critical legal studies.

As a result, this book represents a balanced and up-to-date treatment of legal terms—even within the strict confines of a "pocket" dictionary.

BRYAN A. GARNER

Dallas, Texas
May 1996

*

Acknowledgments

There are many people to thank. My primary helpers on this second pocket edition were Tiger Jackson and Jeffrey Newman. Tiger worked for more than seven weeks refining the cuts I had made to the abridged edition and editing the text—not to mention supplying the cross-references. She read and marked the entire text with great skill, as did Jeff (during his first month on the job—a daunting task). And Karen Magnuson, as with all my other recent books, meticulously proofread the entire text with great skill.

Thanks are also due to the many people who have helped on other editions of *Black's Law Dictionary* since it has been under my editorship. Their contributions are noted in the various editions. In particular, though, I thank the following people for outstanding contributions: Michael L. Atchley, Hans W. Baade, Beverly Ray Burlingame, Charles Dewey Cole Jr., Lance A. Cooper, Charles Harrington Elster, Herbert J. Hammond, Tony Honoré, Cynde L. Horne, Elizabeth S. Kerr, Becky McDaniel, Sir Robert Megarry, Roy M. Mersky, Elizabeth C. Powell, David W. Schultz, Ann Taylor Schwing, Joseph F. Spaniol Jr., David M. Walker, Sir David Williams, and the late Charles Alan Wright.

My wife, Pan Garner, brought tenacity and flair to the project. As the chief administrator of LawProse, Inc.—which has housed the *Black's Law Dictionary* projects since 1994—she has made the day-to-day operations run smoothly.

At the West Group, I thank David J. Oliveiri, John Perovich, Doug Powell, Pamela Siege, and Kathy Walters. I very much appreciate their dedication to quality in the production of the *Black's Law Dictionary* series.

B.A.G.

*

GUIDE TO THE DICTIONARY

1. Alphabetization

All headwords, including abbreviations, are alphabetized letter by letter, not word by word. For example:

per annum
P/E ratio
per capita
percentage lease
per diem
peremptory

Numerals included in a headword precede the letter "a" and are arranged in ascending numerical order:

Rule 10b–5
Rule 11
rule absolute
rulemaking
rule of 72
rule of 78

Numerals at the beginning of a headword are alphabetized as if the numeral were spelled out:

Eighth Amendment
eight-hour law
8–K
ejection

Commas break the letter-by-letter alphabetization:

at the bar
attorney
attorney, power of
attorney-at-law
attorney-client privilege

2. Pronunciation

A word may have more than one acceptable pronunciation. When that is so, the preferred pronunciation appears first. For variably pronounced syllables, only the changed syllables are generally included. Boldface syllables receive primary stress. For example:

> **oligopoly** (ol-ə-**gop**-ə-lee *or* ohl-), *n.*

Brackets in pronunciations indicate either an optional sound, as in *inure* (i-**n[y]oor**), or a soft schwa sound, as in *patent* (**pa**-t[ə]nt).

For quick reference, the pronunciation guide is located inside the front cover.

3. Style and Usage Tags

Archaic = old-fashioned and declining in use
Slang = very informal
Jargon = typical of stilted legal writing and easily simplified
pl. = plural
cap. = capitalized

4. Angle Brackets

Contextual illustrations of a headword are given in angle brackets:

> **avail,** *n.* **1.** Use or advantage <of little or no avail>. **2.** (*pl.*) Profits or proceeds, esp. from a sale of property <the avails of the trust fund>.

5. Cognate Forms

This dictionary lists corresponding parts of speech. For example, under the definition of *confirmation,* the corresponding verb (*confirm*) and adjective (*confirmatory*) are listed.

Agent nouns are included only if they are irregularly formed—that is, do not end in *-er.* But agent nouns ending in *-er* are included if there is more than one acceptable form, such as *abettor* and *abetter.* Also, if the corresponding form ending in *-ee* is defined, then the agent noun ending in *-er* or *-or* is included as a separate headword. For example, *garnisher* and *garnishee* are defined at separate entries.

Adjectives ending in *-able* are included only if they are irregularly formed—for example, *abdicable.*

If a cognate form applies to only one sense of a headword, that form is denoted as follows:

> **construction,** *n.* **1.** The act of building by combining or arranging parts or elements; the thing so built. **2.** The act or process of interpreting or explaining the sense or intention of something (such as a statute, opinion, or instrument).—**construct** (for sense 1), *vb.*—**construe** (for sense 2), *vb.*

6. Cross-references

a. See

The signal "See" is used in three ways:

(1) To indicate that the definition is at another location in the dictionary. For example:

> **call loan.** See LOAN.
>
> **perpetuities, rule against.** See RULE AGAINST PERPETUITIES.

(2) To refer to closely related terms:

> **checks and balances.** The theory of governmental power and functions whereby each branch of government has the ability to counter the actions of any other branch, so that no single branch can control the entire government; for example, the executive can check the legislature by exercising its veto power, but the legislature can, by a sufficient majority, override any veto. See SEPARATION OF POWERS.

cognovit (kog-**noh**-vit). [Latin "the person has conceded (a debt or an action)"] An acknowledgment of debt or liability in the form of a confessed judgment; formerly, credit contracts often included a cognovit clause in which consumers agreed in advance that, if they were sued for nonpayment, they had relinquished any right to be notified of court hearings—but such clauses are generally illegal today. See *confession of judgment* under JUDGMENT.

(3) To refer to a synonymous subentry:

binding instruction. See *mandatory instruction* under JURY INSTRUCTION.

b. Cf.

"Cf." is used to refer to related but distinguishable terms. For example:

bigamy, *n.* The act of marrying one person while legally married to another; bigamy is a criminal offense if it is committed knowingly.—**bigamous,** *adj.*—**bigamist,** *n.* Cf. POLYGAMY; MONOGAMY.

c. Also termed

The phrase "also termed" at the end of an entry signals a synonymous word or phrase. Variations on "also termed" include "formerly also termed," "also spelled," and "often shortened to."

d. Terms with multiple senses

If the cross-referenced term has multiple senses, the particular sense referred to is indicated in parentheses:

delivery bond. See BOND (2).

collateral fraud. See *extrinsic fraud* (1) under FRAUD.

7. Subentries

Many terms in this dictionary are collected by topic. For example, the different types of contracts, such as *bilateral contract* and *gratuitous contract,* are defined under the main term *contract.* If a term has more than one sense, then the corresponding subentries are placed under the appropriate sense of that term.

8. Typefaces

Most of the typefaces used in this dictionary are self-explanatory. For instance, all headwords and cognate forms are in boldface type and all subentries are italicized. As for headwords of foreign origin, those that are fully naturalized are in boldface roman type, while those that are not fully naturalized are in boldface italics. Generally, small caps are used with "See" and "Cf." cross-references. There are, however, three other uses of small caps deserving special mention:

a. Small caps refer to a synonymous headword. In the following example, the small caps suggest that you review the definition at *contiguous* for further information:

> **adjoining, *adj.*** Touching; sharing a common boundary; CONTIGUOUS.—**adjoin,** *vb.* Cf. ADJACENT.

b. Small caps also refer to the predominant form when it may be phrased or spelled in more than one way. For example, the following uses of small caps direct you to the entries at *perjury* and *payor:*

> **false swearing.** PERJURY.

> **payer.** PAYOR.

c. Small caps also refer to the spelled-out form of abbreviations (the term is defined at the spelled-out headword, not the abbreviated form). For example:

> **FDIC.** *abbr.* FEDERAL DEPOSIT INSURANCE CORPORATION.

> **Federal Deposit Insurance Corporation.** An independent governmental agency that insures bank deposits up to a statutory amount per depositor at each participating bank; the insurance fund is financed by a small fee paid by the participating banks.—*Abbr.* FDIC.

*

CONTENTS

*

BLACK'S LAW DICTIONARY

Second
Pocket Edition

*

A

A. **1.** (*usu. cap.* & *often ital.*) A hypothetical person <A deeds Blackacre to B>. **2.** [Latin] From; by; in; on; of; at. **3.** [Law Latin] With. **4.** [Law French] Of; at; to; for; in; with. **5.** (*cap.*) *abbr.* ATLANTIC REPORTER.

A.2d. *abbr. Atlantic Reporter Second Series*. See ATLANTIC REPORTER.

AAA. *abbr.* AMERICAN ARBITRATION ASSOCIATION.

AALS. *abbr.* ASSOCIATION OF AMERICAN LAW SCHOOLS.

ABA. *abbr.* AMERICAN BAR ASSOCIATION.

abandoned property. See PROPERTY.

abandonee (ə-ban-də-**nee**). One to whom property rights are relinquished; one to whom something is formally or legally abandoned.

abandonment, *n.* **1.** The relinquishing of a right or interest with the intention of never again claiming it. **2.** *Family law*. The act of leaving a spouse or child willfully and without an intent to return. Cf. DESERTION. **3.** *Criminal law*. RENUNCIATION (2). **4.** *Contracts*. RESCISSION (2). — **abandon,** *vb.*

abatable nuisance. See NUISANCE.

abatement (ə-**bayt**-mənt), *n.* **1.** The act of eliminating or nullifying. **2.** The suspension or defeat of a pending action for a reason unrelated to the merits of the claim. See *plea in abatement* under PLEA. **3.** The act of lessening or moderating; diminution in amount or degree. **4.** The reduction of a legacy, general or specific, as a result of the estate's being insufficient to pay all debts and legacies. — **abate,** *vb.* — **abatable,** *adj.*

abatement clause. A lease provision that releases the tenant from the rent obligation when an act of God precludes occupancy.

abator (ə-**bay**-tər *or* -tor). A person who eliminates a nuisance. See ABATEMENT (1).

abduction (ab-**dək**-shən), *n.* The act of leading someone away by force or fraudulent persuasion. • Some jurisdictions have added various elements to this basic definition, such as that the abductor must have the intent to marry or defile the person, that the abductee must be a child, or that the abductor must intend to subject the abductee to concubinage or prostitution. — **abduct,** *vb.* — **abductor,** *n.* — **abductee,** *n.* See KIDNAPPING.

aberrant behavior (a-**ber**-ənt). A single act of unplanned or thoughtless criminal behavior.

abet (ə-**bet**), *vb.* **1.** To aid, encourage, or assist (someone), esp. in the commission of a crime. **2.** To support (a crime) by active assistance. — **abetment,** *n.* — **abettor,** *n.* See AID AND ABET. Cf. INCITE.

abeyance (ə-**bay**-ənts), *n.* **1.** Temporary inactivity; suspension. **2.** *Proper-*

ty. A lapse in succession during which no person is vested with title. — **abeyant,** *adj.*

abide, *vb.* **1.** To tolerate or withstand. **2.** To obey. **3.** To await. **4.** To perform or execute (an order or judgment). **5.** To stay or dwell.

ability. The capacity to perform an act or service; esp., the power to carry out a legal act.

ab initio (ab i-**nish**-ee-oh), *adv.* [Latin] From the beginning.

abnormally dangerous activity. An undertaking that cannot be performed safely even if reasonable care is used, and for which the actor may face strict liability for any harm caused; esp., an activity (such as dynamiting) for which the actor is held strictly liable because the activity (1) involves the risk of serious harm to persons or property, (2) cannot be performed without this risk, regardless of the precautions taken, and (3) does not ordinarily occur in the community. See *strict liability* under LIABILITY.

abode. A home; a fixed place of residence. See DOMICILE.

abolition. 1. The act of abolishing. **2.** The state of being annulled or abrogated. **3.** (*usu. cap.*) The legal termination of slavery in the United States. — **abolish,** *vb.*

abortion, *n.* **1.** An artificially induced termination of a pregnancy for the purpose of destroying an embryo or fetus. ● In *Roe v. Wade*, the Supreme Court first recognized a woman's right to choose to end her pregnancy as a privacy right stemming from the Due Process Clause of the 14th Amendment. 410 U.S. 113, 93 S.Ct. 705 (1973). **2.** The spontaneous expulsion of an embryo or fetus before viability; MISCARRIAGE. — **abort,** *vb.* — **abortionist,** *n.*

above, *adv.* (Of an appellate court) having dealt with an appeal in the case at issue; having the power to review the case at issue. Cf. BELOW.

above-the-line, *adj.* (Of a deduction) taken after calculating gross income and before calculating adjusted gross income. Cf. BELOW-THE-LINE.

abridge, *vb.* **1.** To reduce or diminish. **2.** To condense (as a book or other writing). — **abridgment,** *n.*

abrogate (**ab**-rə-gayt), *vb.* To abolish (a law or custom) by formal or authoritative action; to annul or repeal. — **abrogation,** *n.* Cf. OBROGATE.

abscond (ab-**skond**), *vb.* **1.** To depart secretly or suddenly, esp. to avoid arrest, prosecution, or service of process. **2.** To leave a place, usu. hurriedly, with another's money or property. — **abscondence** (ab-**skon**-dənts), *n.*

absconding debtor. See DEBTOR.

absentee, *n.* **1.** A person who is away from his or her usual residence; a person who is absent. **2.** A person who is not present where expected. — **absentee,** *adj.* — **absentee,** *adv.*

absentee voting. See VOTING.

absolute, *adj.* **1.** Free from restriction, qualification, or condition <absolute ownership>. **2.** Conclusive and not liable to revision <absolute delivery>. **3.** Unrestrained in the exercise of governmental power <absolute monarchy>.

absolute covenant. See COVENANT (1).

absolute deed. See DEED.

absolute delivery. See DELIVERY.

absolute disparity. *Constitutional law.* The difference between the percentage of a group in the general population and the percentage of that group in the pool of prospective jurors on a venire. See FAIR-CROSS-SECTION REQUIREMENT; DUREN TEST; STATISTICAL-DECISION THEORY. Cf. COMPARATIVE DISPARITY.

absolute duty. See DUTY.

absolute guaranty. See GUARANTY.

absolute immunity. See IMMUNITY (1).

absolute interest. See INTEREST (2).

absolute law. A supposed law of nature thought to be unchanging in principle, although circumstances may vary the way in which it is applied. See NATURAL LAW.

absolute nuisance. See NUISANCE.

absolute obligation. See OBLIGATION.

absolute privilege. See PRIVILEGE (1).

absolute title. See TITLE (2).

absolute veto. See VETO.

absolve (ab- *or* əb-**zolv**), *vb.* **1.** To release from an obligation, debt, or responsibility. **2.** To free from the penalties for misconduct. — **absolution** (ab-sə-**loo**-shən), *n.*

absorption, *n.* **1.** The act or process of including or incorporating a thing into something else; esp., the application of rights guaranteed by the U.S. Constitution to actions by the states. **2.** *Labor law.* In a postmerger collective-bargaining agreement, a provision allowing seniority for union members in the resulting entity. **3.** *Real estate.* The rate at which property will be leased or sold on the market at a given time. **4.** *Commercial law.* A sales method by which a manufacturer pays the seller's freight costs, which the manufacturer accounts for before quoting the seller a price. — **absorb,** *vb.*

abstention. 1. The act of withholding or keeping back (something or oneself); esp., the withholding of a vote. **2.** A federal court's relinquishment of jurisdiction when necessary to avoid needless conflict with a state's administration of its own affairs. **3.** The legal principle underlying such a relinquishment of jurisdiction. Cf. COMITY. — **abstain,** *vb.*

Burford abstention. A federal court's refusal to review a state court's decision in cases involving a complex regulatory scheme and sensitive areas of state concern. *Burford v. Sun Oil Co.*, 319 U.S. 315, 63 S.Ct. 1098 (1943).

Colorado River abstention. A federal court's decision to abstain while relevant and parallel state-court proceedings are underway. *Colorado River Water Conservation Dist. v. United States*, 424 U.S. 800, 96 S.Ct. 1236 (1976).

Pullman abstention. A federal court's decision to abstain so that state courts will have an opportunity to settle an underlying state-law question whose resolution may avert the need to decide a federal constitutional question. *Railroad*

Comm'n v. Pullman Co., 312 U.S. 496, 61 S.Ct. 643 (1941).

Thibodaux abstention (**tib**-ə-doh). A federal court's decision to abstain so that state courts can decide difficult issues of public importance that, if decided by the federal court, could result in unnecessary friction between state and federal authorities. *Louisiana Power & Light Co. v. City of Thibodaux*, 360 U.S. 25, 79 S.Ct. 1070 (1959).

Younger abstention. **1.** A federal court's decision not to interfere with an ongoing state criminal proceeding by issuing an injunction or granting declaratory relief, unless the prosecution has been brought in bad faith or merely as harassment. *Younger v. Harris*, 401 U.S. 37, 91 S.Ct. 746 (1971). **2.** By extension, a federal court's decision not to interfere with a state-court civil proceeding used to enforce the criminal law, as to abate an obscene nuisance. See OUR FEDERALISM.

abstract, *n.* A concise statement of a text, esp. of a legal document; a summary. See ABSTRACT OF JUDGMENT; ABSTRACT OF TITLE.

abstraction (ab- *or* əb-**strak**-shən), *n.* **1.** The mental process of considering something without reference to a concrete instance. **2.** A theoretical idea not applied to any particular instance. **3.** The summarizing and recording of a legal instrument in public records. **4.** The act of taking with the intent to injure or defraud. — **abstract** (ab-**strakt**), *vb.*

abstract of judgment. A copy or summary of a judgment that, when filed with the appropriate public office, creates a lien on the judgment debtor's nonexempt property.

abstract of title. A concise statement, usu. prepared for a mortgagee or purchaser of real property, summarizing the history of a piece of land, including all conveyances, interests, liens, and encumbrances that affect title to the property.

abuse (ə-**byoos**), *n.* **1.** A departure from legal or reasonable use; misuse. **2.** Physical or mental maltreatment, often resulting in mental, emotional, sexual, or physical injury. — **abusive** (ə-**byoo**-siv), *adj.* — **abusively,** *adv.*

abuse of the elderly. Abuse of a senior citizen by a caregiver. • Examples include deprivation of food or medication, beatings, oral assaults, and isolation.

child abuse. **1.** Intentional or neglectful physical or emotional harm inflicted on a child, including sexual molestation; esp., a parent's or caregiver's act or failure to act that results in a child's exploitation, serious physical or emotional injury, sexual abuse, or death. **2.** An act or failure to act that presents an imminent risk of serious harm to a child. See BATTERED-CHILD SYNDROME. Cf. CHILD NEGLECT.

sexual abuse. **1.** An illegal sex act, esp. one performed against a minor by an adult. **2.** RAPE (2).

spousal abuse. Physical, sexual, or psychological abuse inflicted by one spouse on the other spouse. See BATTERED-WOMAN SYNDROME.

abuse (**ə-byooz**), *vb.* **1.** To damage (a thing). **2.** To depart from legal or reasonable use in dealing with (a person or thing); to misuse. **3.** To injure (a person) physically or mentally. **4.** In the context of child welfare, to hurt or injure (a child) by maltreatment.

abuse excuse. *Criminal law.* The defense that a defendant is unable to tell right from wrong because of physical or mental abuse suffered as a child. • Like the traditional excuse of insanity, the abuse excuse is asserted by a defendant in an effort to avoid all culpability for the crime charged.

abuse of discretion. **1.** An adjudicator's failure to exercise sound, reasonable, and legal decision-making. **2.** An appellate court's standard for reviewing a decision that is asserted to be grossly unsound, unreasonable, or illegal. See DISCRETION.

abuse of process. The improper and tortious use of a legitimately issued court process to obtain a result that is either unlawful or beyond the process's scope. Cf. MALICIOUS PROSECUTION.

abuse of the elderly. See ABUSE.

abuse-of-the-writ doctrine. *Criminal procedure.* The principle that a petition for a writ of habeas corpus may not raise claims that should have been, but were not, asserted in a previous petition. Cf. SUCCESSIVE-WRIT DOCTRINE.

abut (**ə-bət**), *vb.* To join at a border or boundary; to share a common boundary with. — **abutment** (**ə-bət-mənt**), *n.*

abuttals (**ə-bət-əlz**). Land boundaries; the boundary lines of a piece of land in relation to other contiguous lands.

a/c. *abbr.* ACCOUNT (1).

ACA. *abbr.* ASSIMILATIVE CRIMES ACT.

academic freedom. The right (esp. of a university teacher) to speak freely about political or ideological issues without fear of loss of position or other reprisal.

accelerated depreciation method. See DEPRECIATION METHOD.

accelerated remainder. See REMAINDER.

acceleration, *n.* **1.** The advancing of a loan agreement's maturity date so that payment of the entire debt is due immediately. **2.** The shortening of the time for vesting in possession of an expectant interest. **3.** *Property.* The hastening of an owner's time for enjoyment of an estate because of the failure of a preceding estate. — **accelerate,** *vb.*

acceleration clause. A loan-agreement provision that requires the debtor to pay off the balance sooner than the due date if some specified event occurs, such as failure to pay an installment or to maintain insurance. Cf. INSECURITY CLAUSE.

acceptance, *n.* **1.** An agreement, either by express act or by implication from conduct, to the terms of an offer so that a binding contract is formed. • If an acceptance modifies the terms or adds new ones, it generally operates as a counteroffer. Cf. OFFER. **2.** A buyer's assent that the goods are to be taken in performance of a contract for sale. **3.** The formal receipt of and agreement to pay a negotiable instrument. **4.** A negotiable instrument, esp. a bill of exchange, that has been accepted for payment. — **accept,** *vb.*

accommodation acceptance. The acceptance of an offer to buy goods for current or prompt shipment by shipping nonconforming goods after notifying the buyer that the shipment is intended as an accommodation. • This type of "acceptance" is not truly an acceptance under contract law, but operates instead as a counteroffer if the buyer is duly notified.

acceptance-of-the-benefits rule. The doctrine that a party may not appeal a judgment after having voluntarily and intentionally received the relief provided by it.

access easement. See EASEMENT.

accession (ak-**sesh**-ən). **1.** The act of acceding or agreeing. **2.** A coming into possession of a right or office. **3.** The acquisition of title to personal property by bestowing labor on a raw material to convert it to another thing. **4.** A property owner's right to all that is added to the land, naturally or by labor, including land left by floods and improvements made by others. Cf. ANNEXATION. **5.** An improvement to existing personal property, such as new shafts on golf clubs.

accessory (ak-**ses**-ə-ree), *n.* **1.** Something of secondary or subordinate importance. **2.** A person who aids or contributes in the commission or concealment of a crime. • An accessory is usually liable only if the crime is a felony. — **accessory,** *adj.* — **accessoryship,** *n.* Cf. PRINCIPAL (2).

accessory after the fact. An accessory who was not at the scene of the crime but knows that a crime has been committed and who helps the offender try to escape arrest or punishment. • An accessory after the fact may be prosecuted for obstructing justice.

accessory before the fact. An accessory who assists or encourages another to commit a crime but who is not present when the offense is actually committed. • Most jurisdictions have abolished this category of accessory and instead treat such an offender as an accomplice. See ACCOMPLICE.

accessory obligation. See OBLIGATION.

accident, *n.* **1.** An unintended and unforeseen injurious occurrence; something that does not occur in the usual course of events or that could not be reasonably anticipated. **2.** *Equity practice*. An unforeseen and injurious occurrence not attributable to mistake, neglect, or misconduct. — **accidental,** *adj.*

accidental injury. See INJURY.

accidental killing. Homicide resulting from a lawful act performed in a lawful manner under a reasonable belief that no harm could occur. See *justifiable homicide* under HOMICIDE. Cf. *involuntary manslaughter* under MANSLAUGHTER.

accommodation, *n.* **1.** A loan or other financial favor. **2.** The act of signing an accommodation paper as surety for another. See ACCOMMODATION PAPER. **3.** The act or an instance of making a change or provision for someone or something; an adaptation or adjustment. See PUBLIC ACCOMMODATION; REASONABLE ACCOMMODATION.

accommodation acceptance. See ACCEPTANCE.

accommodation indorsement. See INDORSEMENT.

accommodation indorser. See INDORSER.

accommodation land. See LAND.

accommodation loan. See LOAN.

accommodation maker. See MAKER.

accommodation paper. A negotiable instrument that one party cosigns, without receiving any consideration, as surety for another party who remains primarily liable. • An accommodation paper is typically used when the cosigner is more creditworthy than the principal debtor.

accommodation party. A person who, without recompense or other benefit, signs a negotiable instrument for the purpose of being a surety for another party (called the *accommodated party*) to the instrument. • The accommodation party can sign in any capacity (i.e., as maker, drawer, acceptor, or indorser). An accommodation party is liable to all parties except the accommodated party, who impliedly agrees to pay the note or draft and to indemnify the accommodation party for all losses incurred in having to pay it. See SURETY.

accomplice (ə-**kom**-plis). **1.** A person who is in any way involved with another in the commission of a crime, whether as a principal in the first or second degree or as an accessory. • Although the definition includes an accessory before the fact, not all authorities treat this term as including an accessory after the fact. **2.** A person who knowingly, voluntarily, and intentionally unites with the principal offender in committing a crime and thereby becomes punishable for it. See ACCESSORY. Cf. PRINCIPAL (2).

accomplice liability. See LIABILITY.

accomplice witness. See WITNESS.

accord, *n.* **1.** An offer to give or to accept a stipulated performance in the future to satisfy an obligor's existing duty, together with an acceptance of that offer. • The performance becomes what is known as a *satisfaction*. See ACCORD AND SATISFACTION; SATISFACTION. Cf. NOVATION. **2.** A signal used in a legal citation to introduce a case clearly supporting a proposition for which another case is being quoted directly.

accord and satisfaction. An agreement to substitute for an existing debt some alternative form of discharging that debt, coupled with the actual discharge of the debt by the substituted performance. • The new agreement is called the *accord*, and the discharge is called the *satisfaction*. Cf. NOVATION; SETTLEMENT.

account, *n.* **1.** A detailed statement of the debits and credits between parties to a contract or to a fiduciary relationship; a reckoning of monetary dealings. — Abbr. acct.; a/c. **2.** A course of business dealings or other relations for which records must be kept. **3.** ACCOUNTING (3). **4.** ACCOUNTING (4). **5.** A statement by which someone seeks to explain an event.

account payable. (*usu. pl.*) An account reflecting a balance owed to a creditor; a debt owed by an enterprise in the normal course of business dealing. Pl. *accounts payable*.

account receivable. (*usu. pl.*) An account reflecting a balance owed by a debtor; a debt owed by a customer to an enterprise for goods or services. Pl. *accounts receivable*.

account stated. **1.** A balance that parties to a transaction or settlement agree on, either expressly or by implication. • The phrase also refers to the agreement itself or to the assent giving rise to the agreement. **2.** A plaintiff's claim in a suit for such a balance. **3.** *Equity practice*. A defendant's plea in response to an action for an accounting. • The defendant states that the balance due on the statement of the account has been discharged and that the defendant holds the plaintiff's release.

joint account. A bank or brokerage account opened by two or more people, by which each party has a present right to all funds in the account and, upon the death of one party, the survivors become the owners of the account, with no right of the deceased party's heirs or devisees to share in it.

open account. **1.** An unpaid or unsettled account. **2.** An account that is left open for ongoing debit and credit entries and that has a fluctuating balance until either party finds it convenient to settle and close, at which time there is a single liability.

running account. An open, unsettled account that exhibits the reciprocal demands between the parties.

accountable, *adj.* Responsible; answerable <the company was held accountable for the employee's negligence>. — **accountability,** *n.*

accountant–client privilege. See PRIVILEGE (3).

account debtor. See DEBTOR.

account for. 1. To furnish a good reason or convincing explanation for; to explain the cause of. **2.** To render a reckoning of (funds held, esp. in trust). **3.** To answer for (conduct).

accounting. 1. The act or a system of establishing or settling financial accounts; esp., the process of recording transactions in the financial records of a business and periodically extracting, sorting, and summarizing the recorded transactions to produce a set of financial records. Cf. BOOKKEEPING. **2.** A rendition of an account, either voluntarily or by court order. • The term frequently refers to the report of all items of property, income, and expenses prepared by a personal representative, trustee, or guardian and given to heirs, beneficiaries, and the probate court. **3.** A legal action to compel a defendant to account for and pay over money owed to the plaintiff but held by the defendant (often the plaintiff's agent); ACCOUNTING FOR PROFITS. **4.** More broadly, an action for the recovery of money for services performed, property sold and delivered, money loaned, or damages for the nonperformance of simple contracts. • Such an action is available when the rights of parties will be adequately protected by the payment of money. **5.** *Commercial law*. An equitable proceeding for a complete settlement of all partnership affairs, usu. in connection with partner misconduct or with a winding up. See WINDING UP. **6.** *Secured transactions*. A record that (1) is authenticated by a secured party, (2) indicates the aggregate unpaid secured obligation as of a date no more than 35 days before or after the date of the record, and (3) identifies the components of the obligations in reasonable detail. UCC § 9–102(a)(2).

accounting for profits. An action for equitable relief against a person in a fiduciary relationship to recover profits taken in a breach of the relationship.

accounting method. A system for determining income and expenses for tax purposes.

accrual accounting method (ə-**kroo**-əl). An accounting method that records entries of debits and credits when the liability arises, rather than when the income or expense is received or disbursed.

cash-basis accounting method. An accounting method that considers only cash actually received as income and cash actually paid out as an expense.

installment accounting method. A method by which a taxpayer can spread the recognition of gains from a sale of property over the payment period by computing the gross-profit percentage from the sale and applying it to each payment.

accounting period. A regular span of time used for accounting purposes; esp., a period used by a taxpayer in determining income and related tax liability.

account payable. See ACCOUNT.

account receivable. See ACCOUNT.

accredited law school. See LAW SCHOOL.

accredited representative. See REPRESENTATIVE.

accretion (ə-**kree**-shən). The gradual accumulation of land by natural forces, esp. as alluvium is added to land situated on the bank of a river or on the seashore. Cf. ALLUVION; AVULSION (2); DELICTION; EROSION.

accroach (ə-**krohch**), *vb.* To exercise power without authority; to usurp. — **accroachment** (ə-**krohch**-mənt), *n.*

accrual accounting method. See ACCOUNTING METHOD.

accrue (ə-**kroo**), *vb.* **1.** To come into existence as an enforceable claim or right; to arise <the plaintiff's cause of action for silicosis did not accrue until the plaintiff knew or had reason to know of the disease>. **2.** To accumulate periodically <the savings-account interest accrues monthly>. — **accrual,** *n.*

accrued compensation. See COMPENSATION.

accrued expense. See EXPENSE.

accrued income. See INCOME.

accrued interest. See INTEREST (3).

accrued liability. See LIABILITY.

accrued tax. See TAX.

acct. *abbr.* ACCOUNT (1).

accumulated depreciation. See DEPRECIATION.

accumulated-earnings tax. See TAX.

accumulated legacy. See LEGACY.

accumulations, rule against. A rule rendering void any accumulation of income beyond the period of perpetuities.

accumulative judgment. See JUDGMENT.

accusation, *n.* **1.** A formal charge of criminal wrongdoing. • The accusation is usually presented to a court or magistrate having jurisdiction to inquire into the alleged crime. **2.** An informal statement that a person has engaged in an illegal or immoral act. — **accusatory** (ə-**kyoo**-zə-tor-ee), *adj.* — **accuse,** *vb.*

accusatory body. A body (such as a grand jury) that hears evidence and determines whether a person should be charged with a crime.

accusatory pleading. See PLEADING (1).

accusatory stage. *Criminal procedure.* The point in a criminal proceeding when the suspect's right to counsel attaches. • This occurs usually after arrest and once interrogation begins. Cf. CRITICAL STAGE.

accuse, *vb.* To charge (a person) judicially or publicly with an offense; to make an accusation against.

accused, *n.* A person who has been blamed for wrongdoing; esp., a person who has been arrested and brought before a magistrate or who has been formally charged with a crime (as by indictment or information).

acknowledge, *vb.* **1.** To recognize (something) as being factual. **2.** To show that one accepts responsibility for (someone or something). **3.** To make known the receipt of (something). **4.** To confirm as genuine before an authorized officer <acknowledged before a notary public>. **5.** (Of a notary public or other officer) to certify as genuine.

acknowledgment. **1.** A recognition of something as being factual. **2.** An acceptance of responsibility. **3.** The act of making it known that one has received something. **4.** A formal declaration made in the presence of an authorized officer, such as a notary public, by someone who signs a document and confirms that the signature is authentic. • In most states, the officer certifies that (1) he or she personally knows the document signer or has established the signer's identity through satisfactory evidence, (2) the signer appeared before the officer on the date and in the place (usually the county) indicated, and (3) the signer acknowledged signing the document freely. Cf. VERIFICATION (1). **5.** The officer's certificate that is affixed to the document. — **acknowledge,** *vb.* See PROOF OF ACKNOWLEDGMENT.

ACLU. *abbr.* AMERICAN CIVIL LIBERTIES UNION.

acquaintance rape. See RAPE.

acquiescence (ak-wee-**es**-ənts). A person's tacit or passive acceptance; implied consent to an act. — **acquiesce** (ak-wee-**es**), *vb.* — **acquiescent,** *adj.*

acquired servitude. See SERVITUDE (1).

acquisition, *n.* **1.** The gaining of possession or control over something. **2.** Something acquired.

acquisition cost. See COST.

acquisitive offense. See OFFENSE.

acquit, *vb.* **1.** To clear (a person) of a criminal charge. **2.** To pay or discharge (a debt or claim).

acquittal, *n.* **1.** The legal certification, usu. by jury verdict, that an accused person is not guilty of the charged offense.

acquittal in fact. An acquittal by a jury verdict of not guilty.

acquittal in law. An acquittal by operation of law, as of someone who has been charged merely as an accessory after the principal has been acquitted.

implied acquittal. An acquittal in which a jury convicts the defendant of a lesser-included offense without commenting on the greater offense. • Double jeopardy bars the retrial of a defendant who has received an implied acquittal.

2. *Contracts.* A release or discharge from debt or other liability; ACQUITTANCE.

acquittance, *n.* A document by which one is discharged from a debt or other obligation; a receipt or release indicating payment in full. — **acquit,** *vb.*

act, *n.* **1.** Something done or performed, esp. voluntarily; a deed. **2.** The process of doing or performing; an occurrence that results from a person's will being exerted on the external world; ACTION (1).

act in pais (in **pay**). [Law French] An act performed out of court, such as a deed made between two parties on the land being transferred. See IN PAIS.

act in the law. An act that is intended to create, transfer, or extinguish a right and that is effective in law for that purpose; the exercise of a legal power.

act of omission. See *negative act.*

act of the law. The creation, extinction, or transfer of a right by the operation of the law itself, without any consent on the part of the persons concerned.

administrative act. An act made in a management capacity; esp., an act made outside the actor's usual field (as when a judge supervises court personnel). • An administrative act is often subject to a greater risk of liability than an act within the actor's usual field. See IMMUNITY (1).

bilateral act. An act that involves the consenting wills of two or more distinct parties, as with a contract, a conveyance, a mortgage, or a lease; AGREEMENT (1).

external act. An act involving bodily activity, such as speaking.

intentional act. An act resulting from the actor's will directed to that end. • An act is intentional when it is foreseen and desired by the doer, and this foresight and desire resulted in the act through the operation of the will.

internal act. An act of the mind, such as thinking.

judicial act. An act involving the exercise of judicial power.

jural act (**joor**-əl). An act taken in the context of or in furtherance of a society's legal system.

negative act. The failure to do something that is legally required; a nonoccurrence that involves the breach of a legal duty to take positive action. • This takes the form of either a forbearance or an omission.

unilateral act. An act in which there is only one party whose will operates, as in a testamentary disposition, the exercise of a power of appointment, or the voidance of a voidable contract.

unintentional act. An act not resulting from the actor's will toward what actually takes place.

verbal act. An act performed through the medium of words, either spoken or written.

3. The formal product of a legislature or other deliberative body; esp., STATUTE.

acting, *adj.* Holding an interim position; serving temporarily <an acting director>.

acting executor. See EXECUTOR.

action. 1. The process of doing something; conduct or behavior; ACT (2). **2.** A thing done; ACT (1). **3.** A civil or criminal judicial proceeding.

action in equity. An action that seeks equitable relief, such as an injunction or specific performance, as opposed to damages.

action in personam (in pər-**soh**-nəm). An action determining the rights and interests of the parties themselves in the subject matter of the case. See IN PERSONAM.

action in rem (in **rem**). An action determining the title to property and the rights of the parties, not merely among themselves, but also against all persons at any time claiming an interest in that property. See IN REM.

action quasi in rem (**kway**-sɪ in **rem** *or* **kway**-zɪ). An action brought against the defendant personally, with jurisdiction based on an interest in property, the objective being to deal with the particular property or to subject the property to the discharge of the claims asserted. See *quasi in rem* under IN REM.

action to quiet title. A proceeding to establish a plaintiff's title to land by compelling the adverse claimant to establish a claim or be forever estopped from asserting it.

civil action. An action brought to enforce, redress, or protect a private or civil right; a noncriminal litigation.

collusive action. An action between two parties who have no actual controversy, being merely for the purpose of determining a legal question or receiving a precedent that might prove favorable in related litigation.

criminal action. An action instituted by the government to punish offenses against the public.

penal action. **1.** A criminal prosecution. **2.** A civil proceeding in which either the state or a common informer sues to recover a penalty from a defendant who has violated a statute. See COMMON INFORMER. **3.** A civil lawsuit by an aggrieved party seeking recovery of a statutory fine or a penalty, such as punitive damages.

personal action. **1.** An action brought for the recovery of debts, personal property, or damages arising from any cause. **2.** See *action in personam.*

petitory action (**pet**-ə-tor-ee). An action to establish and enforce title to property independently of the right to possession.

plenary action (**plee**-nə-ree *or* **plen**-ə-). A full hearing or trial on the merits, as opposed to a summary proceeding. Cf. *summary proceeding* under PROCEEDING.

possessory action (pə-**zes**-ə-ree). An action to obtain, recover, or maintain possession of property but not title to it, such as an action to evict a nonpaying tenant.

real action. An action brought for the recovery of land or other real property; specif., an action to recover the possession of a freehold estate in real property, or seisin. See SEISIN.

separate action. An action brought alone by each of several complainants who are all involved in the same transaction but cannot legally join the suit.

third-party action. An action distinct from the main claim, whereby the defendant brings in an entity that is not directly involved in the lawsuit but that may be liable to the defendant for all or part of the plaintiff's claim. • A common example is an action for indemnity or contribution.

actionable, *adj.* Furnishing the legal ground for a lawsuit or other legal action <intentional interference with contractual relations is an actionable tort>.

active case. See CASE.

active concealment. See CONCEALMENT.

active income. See INCOME.

active negligence. See NEGLIGENCE.

act of Congress. A law that is formally enacted in accordance with the legislative power granted to Congress by the U.S. Constitution.

act of God. An overwhelming, unpreventable event caused exclusively by forces of nature, such as an earthquake, flood, or tornado. • The definition has been statutorily broadened to include all natural phenomena that are exceptional, inevitable, and irresistible, the effects of which could not be prevented or avoided by the exercise of due care or foresight. 42 USCA § 9601(1).

act of possession. Conduct indicating an intent to claim the property in question as one's own; esp., conduct that supports a claim of adverse possession.

actual, *adj.* Existing in fact; real <actual malice>. Cf. CONSTRUCTIVE.

actual agency. See AGENCY (1).

actual authority. See AUTHORITY (1).

actual bailment. See BAILMENT.

actual damages. See DAMAGES.

actual delivery. See DELIVERY.

actual eviction. See EVICTION.

actual force. See FORCE.

actual fraud. See FRAUD.

actual innocence. See INNOCENCE.

actual knowledge. See KNOWLEDGE (1).

actual loss. See LOSS.

actually litigated. (Of a claim that might be barred by collateral estoppel) properly raised in an earlier lawsuit, submitted to the court for a determination, and determined.

actual malice. See MALICE.

actual notice. See NOTICE.

actual physical control. Direct bodily power over something, esp. a vehicle. • Many jurisdictions require a showing of "actual physical control" of a vehicle by a person charged with driving while intoxicated.

actual possession. See POSSESSION.

actual taking. See TAKING (2).

actus reus (**ak**-təs **ree**-əs *also* **ray**-əs). [Law Latin "guilty act"] The wrongful deed that comprises the physical components of a crime and that generally must be coupled with *mens rea* to establish criminal liability; a forbidden act. See CORPUS DELICTI. Cf. MENS REA.

ADA. *abbr.* AMERICANS WITH DISABILITIES ACT.

***ad damnum* clause** (ad **dam**-nəm). [Latin "to the damage"] A clause in a prayer for relief stating the amount of damages claimed. See PRAYER FOR RELIEF.

addendum (ə-**den**-dəm). Something to be added, esp. to a document; a supplement.

addition. A structure that is attached to or connected with another building that predates the structure; an extension or annex.

additional instruction. See JURY INSTRUCTION.

additional insured. See INSURED.

additional servitude. See SERVITUDE (1).

additional standard deduction. See DEDUCTION.

additional term. See TERM (5).

additur (**ad**-ə-tur). [Latin "it is added to"] A trial court's order, issued usu. with the defendant's consent, that increases the damages awarded by the jury to avoid a new trial on grounds of inadequate damages. • The term may also refer to the increase itself, the procedure, or the court's power to make the order. Cf. REMITTITUR.

add-on clause. An installment-contract provision that converts earlier purchases into security for new purchases.

add-on interest. See INTEREST (3).

add-on loan. See LOAN.

adduce (ə-**d[y]oos**), *vb.* To offer or put forward for consideration (something) as evidence or authority <adduce the engineer's expert testimony>. — **adduction** (ə-**dək**-shən), *n.* — **adducible** (ə-**d[y]oo**-sə-bəl), *adj.*

ADEA. *abbr.* AGE DISCRIMINATION IN EMPLOYMENT ACT.

ademption (ə-**demp**-shən), *n. Wills & estates.* The destruction or extinction of a testamentary gift by reason of a bequeathed asset's ceasing to be part of the estate at the time of the testator's death; a beneficiary's forfeiture of a legacy or bequest that is no longer operative. — **adeem** (**ə-deem**), *vb.* Cf. ABATEMENT; ADVANCEMENT; LAPSE (2).

ademption by extinction. An ademption that occurs because the unique property that is the subject of a specific bequest has been sold, given away, or destroyed, or is not otherwise in existence at the time of the testator's death.

ademption by satisfaction. An ademption that occurs because the testator, while alive, has already given property to the beneficiary in lieu of the testamentary gift.

adequate consideration. See CONSIDERATION.

adequate provocation. See PROVOCATION.

adequate remedy at law. See REMEDY.

adequate representation. A close alignment of interests between actual parties and potential parties in a lawsuit, so that the interests of potential parties are sufficiently protected by the actual parties. • The concept of adequate representation is often used in procedural contexts. For example, if a case is to be certified as a class action, there must be adequate representation by the named plaintiffs of all the potential class members. Fed. R. Civ. P. 23(a)(4). And if a nonparty is to intervene in a lawsuit, there must not already be adequate representation of the nonparty by an existing party. Fed. R. Civ. P. 24(a)(2).

adequate-state-grounds doctrine. A judge-made principle that prevents the Supreme Court from reviewing a state-court decision based partially on state law if a decision on a federal issue would not change the result.

adequate warning. *Products liability.* Notice of the potential dangers involved in using a product, provided in a way that is reasonably calculated to reach the product's consumers and to catch their attention, and written so that it is comprehensible to the average user of the product and fairly conveys the nature and extent of any danger involved in using the product and the way to avoid the danger. Restatement (Third) of Torts: Products Liability § 2(c) cmt. i (1998).

adhesion contract. See CONTRACT.

ad hoc (ad **hok**), *adj.* [Latin "for this"] Formed for a particular purpose <the board created an ad hoc committee to discuss funding for the new arena>. — **ad hoc,** *adv.*

ad hoc arbitration. See ARBITRATION.

ad hominem (ad **hom**-ə-nəm), *adj.* [Latin "to the person"] Appealing to personal prejudices rather than to reason; attacking an opponent's character rather than the opponent's assertions. — **ad hominem,** *adv.*

adjacent, *adj.* Lying near or close to, but not necessarily touching. Cf. ADJOINING.

adjective law (**aj**-ik-tiv). The body of rules governing procedure and practice; PROCEDURAL LAW.

adjoining (**ə-joyn**-ing), *adj.* Touching; sharing a common boundary; CONTIG-

UOUS. — **adjoin** (ə-**joyn**), *vb.* Cf. ADJACENT.

adjoining owner. See OWNER.

adjourn (ə-**jərn**), *vb.* To recess or postpone. — **adjournment** (ə-**jərn**-mənt), *n.*

adjourned term. See TERM (5).

adjudge (ə-**jəj**), *vb.* **1.** To rule upon judicially. **2.** To deem or pronounce to be. **3.** To award judicially.

adjudication (ə-joo-di-**kay**-shən), *n.* **1.** The legal process of resolving a dispute; the process of judicially deciding a case. **2.** JUDGMENT. — **adjudicate** (ə-**joo**-di-kayt), *vb.* — **adjudicative** (ə-**joo**-di-kə-tiv), *adj.*

adjudicative-claims arbitration. See ARBITRATION.

adjudicative fact. See FACT.

adjudicatory hearing. See HEARING.

adjunct (**aj**-əngkt), *adj.* Added as an accompanying object or circumstance; attached in a subordinate or temporary capacity <an adjunct professor>. — **adjunct,** *n.*

adjure (ə-**juur**), *vb.* To charge or entreat solemnly. — **adjuration** (aj-ə-**ray**-shən), *n.* — **adjuratory** (ə-**juur**-ə-tor-ee), *adj.* — **adjurer, adjuror** (ə-**juur**-ər), *n.*

adjusted basis. See BASIS.

adjusted cost basis. See BASIS.

adjusted gross income. See INCOME.

ad litem (ad **lı**-tem *or* -təm). [Latin "for the suit"] For the purposes of the suit; pending the suit. See *guardian ad litem* under GUARDIAN.

admeasurement (ad-**mezh**-ər-mənt), *n.* **1.** Ascertainment, assignment, or apportionment by a fixed quantity or value, or by certain limits. **2.** A writ obtained for purposes of ascertaining, assigning, or apportioning a fixed quantity or value or to establish limits; esp., a writ available against persons who usurp more than their rightful share of property. — **admeasure** (ad-**mezh**-ər), *vb.*

administration, *n.* **1.** The management or performance of the executive duties of a government, institution, or business. **2.** In public law, the practical management and direction of the executive department and its agencies. **3.** A judicial action in which a court undertakes the management and distribution of property. **4.** The management and settlement of the estate of an intestate decedent, or of a testator who has no executor, by a person legally appointed and supervised by the court. — **administer,** *vb.* — **administrative,** *adj.*

administration cum testamento annexo (kəm tes-tə-**men**-toh ə-**nek**-soh). [Latin "with the will annexed"] An administration granted when (1) a testator's will does not name any executor or when the executor named is incompetent to act, is deceased, or refuses to act, and (2) no successor executor has been named or is qualified to serve. — Abbr. c.t.a. — Also termed *administration with the will annexed*.

administration de bonis non (dee **boh**-nis **non**). [Latin "of the goods not administered"] An administration granted for the purpose of settling the remainder of an intestate estate that was not administered by the former administrator. — Abbr. d.b.n.

administration de bonis non cum testamento annexo (de **boh**-nis non kəm tes-tə-**men**-toh ə-**nek**-soh). An administration granted to settle the remainder of a testate estate not settled by a previous administrator or executor. • This type of administration arises when there is a valid will, as opposed to an *administration de bonis non*, which is granted when there is no will. — Abbr. d.b.n.c.t.a.

administration durante absentia (d[y]uu-**ran**-tee ab-**sen**-shee-ə). An administration granted during the absence of either the executor or the person who has precedence as administrator.

administration durante minore aetate (d[y]uu-**ran**-tee mi-**nor**-ee ee-**tay**-tee). An administration granted during the minority of either a child executor or the person who has precedence as administrator.

administration pendente lite (pen-**den**-tee **lɪ**-tee). An administration granted during the pendency of a suit concerning a will's validity. See PENDENTE LITE.

ancillary administration (**an**-sə-ler-ee). An administration that is auxiliary to the administration at the place of the decedent's domicile, such as one in another state. • The purpose of this process is to collect assets, to transfer and record changed title to real property located there, and to pay any debts in that locality.

caeterorum administration (set-ə-**ror**-əm). [Latin "of the rest"] An administration granted when limited powers previously granted to an administrator are inadequate to settle the estate's residue.

domiciliary administration (dom-ə-**sil**-ee-er-ee). The handling of an estate in the state where the decedent was domiciled at death.

general administration. An administration with authority to deal with an entire estate. Cf. *special administration*.

limited administration. An administration for a temporary period or for a special purpose.

public administration. In some jurisdictions, an administration by an officer appointed to administer for an intestate who has left no person entitled to apply for letters (or whose possible representatives refuse to serve).

special administration. **1.** An administration with authority to deal with only some of a decedent's property, as opposed to administering the whole estate. **2.** See *administration pendente lite*.

temporary administration. An administration in which the court appoints a fiduciary to administer the affairs of a decedent's estate for a short time before an administrator or executor can be appointed and qualified.

administrative act. See ACT.

administrative crime. See CRIME.

administrative law. The law governing the organization and operation of the executive branch of government (including independent agencies) and the relations of the executive with the legislature, the judiciary, and the public. • Administrative law is divided into three parts: (1) the statutes endowing agencies with powers and establishing rules of substantive law relating to those powers; (2) the body of agency-made law, consisting of administrative rules, regulations, reports or opinions containing findings of fact, and orders; and (3) the legal principles governing the acts of public agents when those acts conflict with private rights.

administrative-law judge. An official who presides at an administrative hearing and who has the power to administer oaths, take testimony, rule on questions of evidence, and make factual and legal determinations. 5 USCA § 556(c). — Abbr. ALJ.

administrative proceeding. A hearing, inquiry, investigation, or trial before an administrative agency, usu. adjudicatory in nature but sometimes quasi-legislative.

administrative remedy. See REMEDY.

administrative review. See REVIEW.

administrative rule. A broadly applicable agency statement that interprets a law or policy or describes the agency's requirements.

administrative search. See SEARCH.

administrative warrant. See WARRANT (1).

administrator (ad-**min**-ə-stray-tər). **1.** A person who manages or heads a business, public office, or agency. **2.** A person appointed by the court to manage the assets and liabilities of an intestate decedent. • This term once referred to males only (as opposed to *administratrix*), but legal writers now generally use *administrator* to refer to someone of either sex. Cf. EXECUTOR (2).

administrator ad litem (ad **lɪ**-tem *or* -təm). A special administrator appointed by the court to represent the estate's interest in an action usu. either because there is no administrator of the estate or because the current administrator has an interest in the action adverse to that of the estate.

administrator ad prosequendum (ad prahs-ə-**kwen**-dəm). An administrator appointed to prosecute or defend a certain action or actions involving the estate.

administrator cum testamento annexo (kəm tes-tə-**men**-toh ə-**nek**-soh). An administrator appointed by the court to carry out the provisions of a will when the testator has named no executor, or the executors named refuse, are incompetent to act, or have died before performing their duties. — Abbr. *administrator c.t.a.*

administrator de bonis non (dee **boh**-nis **non**). An administrator appointed by the court to administer the decedent's goods that were not administered by an earlier administrator or executor. • If there is no will, the administrator bears the name *administrator de bonis non* (abbr. *administrator d.b.n.*), but if there is a will, the full name is *administrator de bonis non cum testamento annexo* (abbr. *administrator d.b.n. c.t.a.*).

administrator pendente lite. See *special administrator.*

administrator with the will annexed. See *administrator cum testamento annexo.*

ancillary administrator (**an**-sə-ler-ee). A court-appointed administrator who oversees the distribution of the part of a decedent's estate located in a jurisdiction other than where the decedent was domiciled (the place of the main administration).

general administrator. A person appointed to administer an intestate decedent's entire estate.

public administrator. A state-appointed officer who administers intestate estates that are not administered by the decedent's relatives. • This officer's right to administer is usually subordinate to the rights of creditors, but in a few jurisdictions the creditors' rights are subordinate.

special administrator. **1.** A person appointed to administer only a specific part of an intestate decedent's estate. **2.** A person appointed to serve as administrator of an estate solely because of an emergency or an unusual situation, such as a will contest. — Also termed (in sense 2) *administrator pendente lite.*

administratrix. See ADMINISTRATOR (2).

admissibility (ad-mis-ə-**bil**-ə-tee), *n.* The quality or state of being allowed to be entered into evidence in a hearing, trial, or other proceeding.

conditional admissibility. The evidentiary rule that when a piece of evidence is not itself admissible, but is admissible if certain other facts make it relevant, the evidence becomes admissible on condition that counsel later introduce the connecting facts.

curative admissibility. The rule that an inadmissible piece of evidence may be admitted if offered to cure or counteract the effect of some similar piece of the opponent's evidence that itself should not have been admitted.

limited admissibility. The principle that testimony or exhibits may be admitted into evidence for a restricted purpose.

multiple admissibility. The evidentiary rule that, although a piece of evidence is inadmissible under one rule for the purpose given in offering it, it is nevertheless admissible if relevant and offered for some other purpose not forbidden by the rules of evidence.

admissible (ad-**mis**-ə-bəl), *adj.* **1.** Capable of being legally admitted; allowable; permissible. **2.** Worthy of gaining entry or being admitted.

admissible evidence. See EVIDENCE.

admission (ad-**mish**-ən), *n.* **1.** Any statement or assertion made by a party to a case and offered against that party; an acknowledgment that facts are true. — **admit,** *vb.* Cf. CONFESSION.

admission against interest. A person's statement acknowledging a fact that is harmful to the person's position as a litigant.

admission by party-opponent. An opposing party's admission, which is not considered hearsay if it is offered against that party and is (1) the party's own statement, in either an individual or a representative capacity; (2) a statement of which the party has manifested an adoption or belief in its truth; (3) a statement by one authorized by the party to make such a statement; (4) a statement by the party's agent concerning a matter within the scope of the agency or employment and made during the existence of the relationship; or (5) a statement by a coconspirator of the party during the course of and in furtherance of the conspiracy. Fed. R. Evid. 801(d)(2).

admission by silence. The failure of a party to speak after another party's assertion of fact that, if untrue, would naturally compel a person to deny the statement.

adoptive admission. An action by a party that indicates approval of a statement made by another, and thereby acceptance that the statement is true.

extrajudicial admission. An admission made outside court proceedings.

implied admission. An admission reasonably inferable from a party's action or statement, or a party's failure to act or speak.

judicial admission. A formal waiver of proof that relieves an opposing party from having to prove the admitted fact and bars the party who made the admission from disputing it.

quasi-admission. An act or utterance, usu. extrajudicial, that creates an inconsistency with and discredits, to a greater or lesser degree, a present claim or other evidence of the person creating the inconsistency.

2. Acceptance of a lawyer by the established licensing authority, such as a state bar association, as a member of the practicing bar, usu. after the lawyer passes a bar examination and supplies adequate character references.

admonition (ad-mə-**nish**-ən), *n.* **1.** Any authoritative advice or caution from the court to the jury regarding their duty as jurors or the admissibility of evidence for consideration. **2.** A reprimand or cautionary statement addressed to counsel by a judge. — **admonish** (ad-**mon**-ish), *vb.* — **admonitory** (ad-**mon**-ə-tor-ee), *adj.*

adoption, *n.* **1.** *Family law.* The creation of a parent–child relationship by judicial order between two parties who usu. are unrelated. • This is accomplished only after a determination that the child is an orphan or has been abandoned, or that the parents' parental rights have been terminated by court order.

adoption by estoppel. **1.** An equitable adoption of a child by a person's promises and acts that preclude the person and his or her estate from denying adopted status to the child. **2.** An adoption decree formerly conferred by a court of equity or, today, by a court exercising equitable powers, treating as done that which ought to have been done.

private adoption. An adoption that occurs independently between the biological mother (and sometimes the biological father) and the adoptive parents without the involvement of an agency. — Also termed *private-placement adoption.*

2. *Contracts.* The process by which a person agrees to assume a contract previously made for that person's benefit, such as a newly formed corporation's acceptance of a preincorporation contract. — **adopt,** *vb.* — **adoptive,** *adj.*

adoptive-admissions rule. *Evidence.* The principle that a statement offered against an accused is not inadmissible hearsay if the accused is aware of the statement and has, by words or conduct, indicated acceptance that the statement is true. See *adoptive admission* under ADMISSION.

adoptive parent. See PARENT.

ADR. *abbr.* ALTERNATIVE DISPUTE RESOLUTION.

adult (ə-**dəlt** *or* **ad**-əlt), *n.* A person who has attained the legal age of majority, generally 17 in criminal cases and 18 for other purposes. — **adult** (ə-**dəlt**), *adj.*

adultery (ə-**dəl**-tə-ree), *n.* Voluntary sexual intercourse between a married person and someone other than that person's spouse. • Adultery is variously defined and punished in some state statutes, but it is seldom prosecuted. — **adulterous,** *adj.* Cf. FORNICATION; INFIDELITY.

adult offender. See OFFENDER.

ad valorem tax. See TAX.

advance, *n.* **1.** The furnishing of money or goods before any consideration is received in return. **2.** The money or goods furnished.

advance directive. **1.** A durable power of attorney that takes effect upon one's incompetency and designates a surrogate decision-maker for health-care matters. See POWER OF ATTORNEY. **2.** A legal document explaining one's wishes about medical treatment if one becomes incompetent or unable to communicate. Cf. LIVING WILL.

advancement, *n.* A payment or gift to an heir (esp. a child) during one's lifetime as an advance share of one's estate, with the intention of extinguishing or diminishing the heir's claim to the estate under intestacy laws. — **advance,** *vb.* See SATISFACTION (4). Cf. ADEMPTION.

advance payment. See PAYMENT.

advance sheets. A softcover pamphlet containing recently reported opinions by a court or set of courts. • Advance sheets are published during the interim between an opinion's announcement and its inclusion in a bound volume of law reports. Cf. *slip opinion* (1) under OPINION (1); REPORT (3).

adventure. A commercial undertaking that has an element of risk; a venture. Cf. JOINT VENTURE.

adversary (**ad**-vər-ser-ee), *n.* An opponent; esp., opposing counsel. — **adversary, adversarial,** *adj.*

adversary proceeding. A hearing involving a dispute between opposing parties.

adversary system. A procedural system, such as the Anglo-American legal system, involving active and unhindered parties contesting with each other to put forth a case before an independent decision-maker. — Also termed *adversary procedure*.

adverse authority. See AUTHORITY (4).

adverse enjoyment. See ENJOYMENT.

adverse interest. An interest that is opposed or contrary to that of someone else.

adverse-interest rule. The principle that if a party fails to produce a witness who is within its power to produce and who should have been produced, the judge may instruct the jury to infer that the witness's evidence is unfavorable to the party's case.

adverse party. See PARTY (2).

adverse possession. A method of acquiring title to real property by possession for a statutory period under certain conditions, esp. a nonpermissive use of the land with a claim of right when that use is continuous, exclusive, hostile, open, and notorious. Cf. PRESCRIPTION (2).

> ***constructive adverse possession.*** Adverse possession in which the claim arises from the claimant's payment of taxes under color of right rather than by actual possession of the land.

adverse title. See TITLE (2).

advertent negligence. See NEGLIGENCE.

advice of counsel. **1.** The guidance given by lawyers to their clients. **2.** In a malicious-prosecution lawsuit, a defense requiring both a complete presentation of facts by the defendant to his or her attorney and honest compliance with the attorney's advice. **3.** A defense in which a party seeks to avoid liability by claiming that he or she acted reasonably and in good faith on the attorney's advice. • Such a defense usually requires waiver of the attorney–client privilege, and the attorney cannot have knowingly participated in implementing an illegal plan.

advisement (ad-**vɪz**-mənt). Careful consideration; deliberation <the judge took the matter under advisement and promised a ruling by the next day>.

advisory jury. See JURY.

advisory opinion. See OPINION (1).

advocate (**ad**-və-kit), *n.* A person who assists, defends, pleads, or prosecutes for another.

aff'd. *abbr.* Affirmed.

affects doctrine. *Constitutional law.* The principle allowing Congress to regulate intrastate activities that have a substantial effect on interstate commerce. • The doctrine is so called because the test is whether a given activity "affects" interstate commerce.

aff'g. *abbr.* Affirming.

affiant (ə-**fɪ**-ənt). **1.** One who makes an affidavit. **2.** COMPLAINANT (2).

affidavit (af-ə-**day**-vit). A voluntary declaration of facts written down and sworn to by the declarant before an officer authorized to administer oaths, such as a notary public. Cf. DECLARATION (8).

> ***affidavit of inquiry.*** An affidavit, required in certain states before sub-

stituted service of process on an absent defendant, in which the plaintiff's attorney or a person with knowledge of the facts indicates that the defendant cannot be served within the state.

affidavit of service. An affidavit certifying the service of a notice, summons, writ, or process.

poverty affidavit. An affidavit made by an indigent person seeking public assistance, appointment of counsel, waiver of court fees, or other free public services. 28 USCA § 1915.

self-proving affidavit. An affidavit attached to a will and signed by the testator and witnesses certifying that the statutory requirements of due execution of the will have been complied with. • The affidavit, which recites the facts of the will's proper execution, permits the will to be probated without the necessity of having the witnesses appear and prove due execution by their testimony.

affiliate (ə-**fil**-ee-it), *n.* A corporation that is related to another corporation by shareholdings or other means of control; a subsidiary, parent, or sibling corporation. — **affiliate** (ə-**fil**-ee-ayt), *vb.* — **affiliation** (ə-fil-ee-**ay**-shən), *n.*

affinity (ə-**fin**-ə-tee). **1.** A close agreement. **2.** The relation that one spouse has to the blood relatives of the other spouse; relationship by marriage. **3.** Any familial relation resulting from a marriage. — **affine** (ə-**fin**) (for sense 3), *n.* Cf. CONSANGUINITY.

affirm, *vb.* **1.** To confirm (a judgment) on appeal. **2.** To solemnly declare rather than swear under oath.

affirmance, *n.* **1.** A ratification, reacceptance, or confirmation. **2.** The formal approval by an appellate court of a lower court's judgment, order, or decree.

affirmation, *n.* A pledge equivalent to an oath but without reference to a supreme being or to "swearing." • While an oath is "sworn to," an affirmation is merely "affirmed," but either type of pledge may subject the person making it to the penalties for perjury. — **affirm,** *vb.* — **affirmatory,** *adj.* Cf. OATH.

affirmative, *adj.* **1.** Supporting the existence of certain facts <affirmative evidence>. **2.** Involving or requiring effort <an affirmative duty>.

affirmative action. A set of actions designed to eliminate existing and continuing discrimination, to remedy lingering effects of past discrimination, and to create systems and procedures to prevent future discrimination. See *reverse discrimination* under DISCRIMINATION.

affirmative converse instruction. See JURY INSTRUCTION.

affirmative defense. See DEFENSE (1).

affirmative easement. See EASEMENT.

affirmative instruction. See JURY INSTRUCTION.

affirmative misconduct. See MISCONDUCT.

affirmative pregnant. A positive statement that ambiguously implies a negative; a statement that does not explicitly deny a charge, but instead answers an unasked question and thereby implies culpability, as when a person says "I returned your car yesterday" to the charge "You stole my car!" Cf. NEGATIVE PREGNANT.

affirmative proof. See PROOF.

affirmative relief. See RELIEF.

affirmative representation. See REPRESENTATION.

affirmative statute. See STATUTE.

affirmative testimony. See TESTIMONY.

affix (ə-**fiks**), *vb.* To attach, add to, or fasten on permanently. — **affixation** (af-ik-**say**-shən), *n.* See FIXTURE.

affray (ə-**fray**). The fighting, by mutual consent, of two or more persons in some public place, to the terror of onlookers. • The fighting must be mutual. If one person unlawfully attacks another who resorts to self-defense, the first is guilty of assault and battery, but there is no affray. Cf. RIOT; *unlawful assembly* under ASSEMBLY; ROUT.

AFL–CIO. *abbr.* AMERICAN FEDERATION OF LABOR AND CONGRESS OF INDUSTRIAL ORGANIZATIONS.

aforesaid (ə-**for**-sed), *adj. Jargon.* Mentioned above; referred to previously.

aforethought (ə-**for**-thawt), *adj.* Thought of in advance; deliberate; premeditated. See MALICE AFORETHOUGHT.

a fortiori (ay for-shee-**or**-I *or* ah for-shee-**or**-ee), *adv.* [Latin] By even greater force of logic; even more so <if a 14-year-old child cannot sign a binding contract, then, *a fortiori*, a 13-year-old cannot>. Cf. A MULTO FORTIORI.

after-acquired domicile. See DOMICILE.

after-acquired title. See TITLE (2).

after-acquired-title doctrine. The principle that title to property automatically vests in a person who bought the property from a seller who acquired title only after purporting to sell the property to the buyer.

after-born child. See CHILD.

after-born heir. See HEIR.

after the fact. Subsequent to an event of legal significance.

AG. *abbr.* ATTORNEY GENERAL.

against the form of the statute. Contrary to the statutory requirements. • This formal phrase, which traditionally concludes an indictment, indicates that the conduct alleged contravenes the cited statute and therefore constitutes a criminal offense. In modern contexts, the full conclusion often reads: "against the form of the statute in such case made and provided."

against the peace and dignity of the state. A concluding phrase in an indictment, used to condemn the offending conduct generally (as opposed to the specific charge of wrongdoing contained in the body of the instrument).

against the weight of the evidence. (Of a verdict or judgment) contrary to the credible evidence; not sufficiently supported by the evidence in the record. See WEIGHT OF THE EVIDENCE.

against the will. Contrary to a person's wishes. • Indictments use this phrase to indicate that the defendant's conduct was without the victim's consent.

age, *n.* A period of time; esp., a period of individual existence or the duration of a person's life.

age of capacity. The age, usu. defined by statute as 18 years, at which a person is legally capable of agreeing to a contract, executing a will, maintaining a lawsuit, or the like. See CAPACITY.

age of consent. The age, usu. defined by statute as 16 years, at which a person is legally capable of agreeing to marriage (without parental consent) or to sexual intercourse. See CONSENT.

age of majority. **1.** The age, usu. defined by statute as 18 years, at which a person attains full legal rights, esp. civil and political rights such as the right to vote. **2.** See *age of capacity.*

age of reason. The age at which a person becomes able to distinguish right from wrong and is thus legally capable of committing a crime or tort.

Age Discrimination in Employment Act. A federal law prohibiting job discrimination based on a person's age, esp. unfair and discriminatory employment decisions that negatively affect someone who is 40 years old or older. 29 USCA §§ 621–634. — Abbr. ADEA.

agency. 1. A fiduciary relationship created by express or implied contract or by law, in which one party (the *agent*) may act on behalf of another party (the *principal*) and bind that other party by words or actions. See AUTHORITY (1).

actual agency. An agency in which the agent is in fact employed by a principal.

agency by estoppel. An agency created by operation of law and established by a principal's actions that would reasonably lead a third person to conclude that an agency exists.

agency coupled with an interest. An agency in which the agent is granted not only the power to act on behalf of a principal but also a legal interest in the estate or property involved. See *power coupled with an interest* under POWER.

exclusive agency. The right to represent a principal — esp. either to sell the principal's products or to act as the seller's real-estate agent — within a particular market free from competition.

express agency. An actual agency arising from the principal's written or oral authorization of a person to act as the principal's agent. Cf. *implied agency.*

general agency. A principal's delegation to an agent, without restriction, to take any action connected with a particular trade, business, or employment.

implied agency. An actual agency arising from the conduct by the principal that implies an intention to create an agency relationship. Cf. *express agency.*

special agency. An agency in which the agent is authorized only to conduct a single transaction or a series of transactions not involving continuous service.

undisclosed agency. An agency relationship in which an agent deals with a third party who has no knowledge that the agent is acting on a principal's behalf. • The fact that the agency is undisclosed does not prohibit the third party from seeking redress from the principal or the agent.

2. An agent's place of business. **3.** A governmental body with the authority to implement and administer particular legislation.

federal agency. A department or other instrumentality of the executive branch of the federal government, including a government corporation and the Government Printing Office. 5 USCA § 551.

independent agency. A federal agency, commission, or board that is not under the direction of the executive, such as the Federal Trade Commission or the National Labor Relations Board.

quasi-governmental agency. A government-sponsored enterprise or corporation, such as the Federal National Mortgage Corporation.

agent. 1. One who is authorized to act for or in place of another; a representative <a professional athlete's agent>. Cf. PRINCIPAL (1); EMPLOYEE. **2.** Something that produces an effect <an intervening agent>. See CAUSE (1).

apparent agent. A person who reasonably appears to have authority to act for another, regardless of whether actual authority has been conferred.

corporate agent. An agent authorized to act on behalf of a corporation; broadly, all employees and officers who have the power to bind the corporation.

del credere agent (del **kred**-ə-ray *or* **kray**-də-ray). An agent who guarantees the solvency of the third party with whom the agent makes a contract for the principal.

general agent. An agent authorized to transact all the principal's business of a particular kind or in a particular place.

government agent. **1.** An employee or representative of a governmental body. **2.** A law-enforcement official, such as a police officer or an FBI agent. **3.** An informant, esp. an inmate, hired by law enforcement to obtain incriminating statements from another inmate.

independent agent. An agent who exercises personal judgment and is subject to the principal only for the results of the work performed.

managing agent. A person with general power involving the exercise of judgment and discretion, as opposed to an ordinary agent who acts under the direction and control of the principal.

process agent. A person authorized to accept service of process on behalf of another.

registered agent. A person authorized to accept service of process for another person, esp. a corporation, in a particular jurisdiction.

statutory agent. An agent designated by law to receive litigation documents and other legal notices for a nonresident corporation. • In most states, the secretary of state is the statutory agent for such corporations.

undercover agent. **1.** An agent who does not disclose his or her role as an agent. **2.** A police officer who gathers evidence of criminal activity without disclosing his or her identity to the suspect.

universal agent. An agent authorized to perform all acts that the principal could personally perform.

agent provocateur (**ay**-jənt prə-vok-ə-**tər** *or* **a**-zhaw*n* praw-vaw-kə-**tuur**), *n.* **1.** An undercover agent who instigates or participates in a crime, often by infiltrating a group involved in suspected illegal conduct, to expose and punish criminal activity. **2.** A person who entraps another, or entices another to break the law, and then informs against the other as a lawbreaker.

age of capacity. See AGE.

age of consent. See AGE.

age of majority. See AGE.

age of reason. See AGE.

aggravated, *adj.* **1.** (Of a crime) made worse or more serious by circumstances such as violence, the presence of a deadly weapon, or the intent to commit another crime <aggravated robbery>. Cf. SIMPLE (1). **2.** (Of a tort) made worse or more serious by circumstances such as intention to cause harm or reckless disregard for another's safety <the defendant's negligence was aggravated by malice>. **3.** (Of an injury) harmful to a part of the body previously injured or debilitated <an aggravated bone fracture>.

aggravated assault. See ASSAULT.

aggravated battery. See BATTERY.

aggravated kidnapping. See KIDNAPPING.

aggravated larceny. See LARCENY.

aggravated robbery. See ROBBERY.

aggravated sodomy. See SODOMY.

aggravating circumstance. See CIRCUMSTANCE.

aggregate (**ag**-rə-gayt), *vb.* To collect (separate things) into a whole <aggregate the claims>. — **aggregate** (**ag**-rə-git), *adj.*

aggregate income. See INCOME.

aggregate sentence. See SENTENCE.

aggregate theory of partnership. The theory that a partnership does not have a separate legal existence (as does a corporation), but rather is only the totality of the partners who make it up. Cf. ENTITY THEORY OF PARTNERSHIP.

aggregation doctrine. The rule that precludes a party from totaling all claims for purposes of meeting the minimum amount necessary to give rise to federal diversity jurisdiction under the amount-in-controversy requirement. See *diversity jurisdiction* under JURISDICTION; AMOUNT IN CONTROVERSY.

aggressor doctrine. *Civil law.* The principle precluding tort recovery for a plaintiff who acts in a way that would provoke a reasonable person to use physical force for protection, unless the defendant uses excessive force to repel the plaintiff.

aggrieved party. See PARTY (2).

agnate, *n.* A blood relative whose connection is through the male line. — **agnatic,** *adj.* Cf. COGNATE.

agreed-boundary doctrine. The principle that owners of contiguous land may agree on the boundary between the parcels, as long as the actual boundary is uncertain, there is agreement between the two owners about the boundary line, there is acquiescence in the agreed line for a time exceeding the statute of limitations, and the agreed boundary is identifiable on the ground.

agreed judgment. See JUDGMENT.

agreement. 1. A mutual understanding between two or more persons about their relative rights and duties regarding past or future performances; a manifestation of mutual assent by two or more persons. **2.** The parties' actual bargain as found in their language or by implication from other circumstances, including course of dealing, usage of trade, and course of performance. UCC § 1–201(3).

binding agreement. An enforceable contract. See CONTRACT.

formal agreement. An agreement in which the law requires not only the consent of the parties but also a manifestation of the agreement in some particular form, in default of which the agreement is null.

simple agreement. An agreement in which the law requires nothing for its effective operation beyond some manifestation that the parties have consented.

unconscionable agreement (ən-**kon**-shə-nə-bəl). An agreement that no promisor with any sense, and not under a delusion, would make, and that no honest and fair promisee would accept.

AICPA. *abbr.* American Institute of Certified Public Accountants.

aid and abet, *vb.* To assist or facilitate the commission of a crime, or to promote its accomplishment. • Aiding and abetting is a crime in most jurisdictions. — **aider and abettor,** *n.*

aider by pleading over. The cure of a pleading defect by an adversary's answering the pleading without an objection, so that the objection is waived.

aider by verdict. The cure of a pleading defect by a trial verdict, based on the presumption that the record contains adequate proof of the necessary facts even if those facts were not specifically alleged.

air piracy. See PIRACY.

air right. The right to use all or a portion of the airspace above real property.

a.k.a. *abbr.* Also known as.

aleatory (**ay**-lee-ə-tor-ee), *adj.* Dependent on uncertain contingencies.

aleatory contract. See CONTRACT.

alegal, *adj.* Outside the sphere of law; not classifiable as being legal or illegal. — **alegality,** *n.*

***Alford* plea.** A guilty plea that a defendant enters as part of a plea bargain, without actually admitting guilt. *North Carolina v. Alford*, 400 U.S. 25, 91 S.Ct. 160 (1970).

ALI. *abbr.* AMERICAN LAW INSTITUTE.

alias, *n.* An assumed or additional name that a person has used or is known by.

alias subpoena. See SUBPOENA.

alias writ. See WRIT.

alibi (**al**-ə-bɪ), *n.* [Latin "elsewhere"] **1.** A defense based on the physical impossibility of a defendant's guilt by placing the defendant in a location other than the scene of the crime at the relevant time. Fed. R. Crim. P. 12.1. **2.** The fact or state of having been elsewhere when an offense was committed. — **alibi,** *vb.*

alibi witness. See WITNESS.

alien (**ay**-lee-ən *or* **ayl**-yən), *n.* A person who resides within the borders of a country but is not a citizen or subject of that country; a person not owing allegiance to a particular nation.

illegal alien. An alien who enters a country at the wrong time or place, eludes an examination by officials, obtains entry by fraud, or enters into a sham marriage to evade immigration laws.

nonresident alien. A person who is neither a resident nor a citizen of the United States.

resident alien. An alien who has a legally established domicile in the United States. See NATURALIZATION.

alien, *vb.* See ALIENATE.

alienate (**ay**-lee-ə-nayt *or* **ayl**-yə-nayt), *vb.* To transfer or convey (property or a property right) to another. — **alienable,** *adj.* — **alienability,** *n.*

alienation (ay-lee-ə-**nay**-shən *or* ayl-yə-**nay**-shən), *n.* **1.** Withdrawal from former attachment; estrangement <alienation of affections>. **2.** Conveyance or transfer of property to another <alienation of one's estate>. — **alienative** (**ay**-lee-ə-nay-tiv), *adj.*

alienation clause. 1. A deed provision that either permits or prohibits the further conveyance of the property. **2.** A clause in an insurance policy voiding coverage if the policyholder alienates the insured property.

alienation of affections. A tort claim for willful or malicious interference with a marriage by a third party without justification or excuse. • The tort has been abolished in most states. See CONSORTIUM.

alienee (ay-lee-ə-**nee** *or* ayl-yə-**nee**), *n.* One to whom property is transferred or conveyed.

alienist. *Archaic.* A psychiatrist, esp. one who assesses a criminal defendant's sanity or capacity to stand trial.

alienor (**ay**-lee-ə-nər *or* -nor), *n.* One who transfers or conveys property to another.

alimony (**al**-ə-moh-nee). A court-ordered allowance that one spouse pays to the other spouse for maintenance and support while they are separated, while they are involved in a matrimonial lawsuit, or after they are divorced. Cf. CHILD SUPPORT.

aliquot (**al**-ə-kwot), *adj.* Contained in a larger whole an exact number of times; fractional <5 is an aliquot part of 30>.

aliquot-part rule. The principle that a person must intend to acquire a fractional part of the ownership of property before a court can declare a resulting trust in the person's favor.

aliunde (ay-lee-**yən**-dee), *adj.* [Latin] *Jargon.* From another source; from elsewhere. See *extrinsic evidence* under EVIDENCE.

aliunde rule. *Evidence.* The doctrine that a verdict may not be impeached by a juror's testimony unless a foundation for the testimony is first made by competent evidence from another source.

ALJ. *abbr.* ADMINISTRATIVE-LAW JUDGE.

all and singular. *Jargon.* Collectively and individually.

allegation, *n.* **1.** The act of declaring something to be true. **2.** Something declared or asserted as a matter of fact, esp. in a legal pleading; a party's formal statement of a factual matter as being true or provable, without its having yet been proved. — **allege,** *vb.*

disjunctive allegation. A statement in a pleading or indictment that expresses something in the alternative, usu. with the conjunction "or" <a charge that the defendant murdered or caused to be murdered is a disjunctive allegation>.

material allegation. In a pleading, an assertion that is essential to the claim or defense <a material allegation in a battery case is harmful or offensive contact with a person>.

primary allegation. The principal charge made against an adversary in a legal proceeding.

alleged (**ə-lejd**), *adj.* **1.** Asserted to be true as described <alleged offenses>. **2.** Accused but not yet tried <alleged murderer>.

***Allen* charge.** *Criminal procedure.* A supplemental jury instruction given by the court to encourage a deadlocked jury, after prolonged deliberations, to reach a verdict. *Allen v. United States*, 164 U.S. 492, 17 S.Ct. 154 (1896). — Also termed *dynamite charge.*

all-events test. *Tax.* A requirement that all events fixing an accrual-method taxpayer's right to receive income or incur expense must occur before the taxpayer can report an item of income or expense.

all fours. See ON ALL FOURS.

allied offense. See OFFENSE.

allocation, *n.* A designation or apportionment for a specific purpose; esp., the crediting of a receipt or the charging of a disbursement to an account <allocation of funds>. — **allocate,** *vb.* — **allocable,** *adj.* — **allocator,** *n.*

allocution (al-ə-**kyoo**-shən), *n. Criminal procedure.* **1.** A trial judge's formal address to a convicted defendant, asking him or her to speak in mitigation of the sentence to be imposed. • This address is required under Fed. R. Crim. P. 32(c)(3)(C). **2.** An unsworn statement from a convicted defendant to the sentencing judge or jury in which the defendant can ask for mercy, explain his or her conduct, apologize for the crime, or say anything else in an effort to lessen the impending sentence. • This statement is not subject to cross-examination. — **allocute** (**al**-ə-kyoot), *vb.* — **allocutory** (ə-**lok**-yə-tor-ee), *adj.*

allodial (ə-**loh**-dee-əl), *adj.* Held in absolute ownership; pertaining to an allodium. — **allodially,** *adv.*

allodium (ə-**loh**-dee-əm), *n.* An estate held in fee simple absolute.

allograph (**al**-ə-graf). An agent's writing or signature for the principal.

allonge (a-**law*n*zh**). A slip of paper sometimes attached to a negotiable instrument for the purpose of receiving further indorsements when the original paper is filled with indorsements.

all-or-nothing rule. A gloss on the rule against perpetuities holding that a class gift is invalid in its entirety if it is invalid in part. • The effect is to invalidate a class member's interest even if it vests within the period of the rule because it may be subject to partial divestment by the remote interest of another class member.

allotment, *n.* **1.** A share or portion of something, such as property previously held in common or shares in a corporation. **2.** In American Indian law, the selection of specific land awarded to an individual allottee from a common holding. — **allot,** *vb.*

allowance. 1. A share or portion, esp. of money that is assigned or granted.

family allowance. A portion of a decedent's estate set aside by statute for a surviving spouse, children, or parents, regardless of any testamentary disposition or competing claims.

spousal allowance. A portion of a decedent's estate set aside by statute for a surviving spouse, regardless of any testamentary disposition or competing claims.

2. The sum awarded by a court to a fiduciary as payment for services. **3.** A deduction.

allurement. *Torts.* An attractive object that tempts a trespassing child to meddle when the child ought to abstain. See ATTRACTIVE-NUISANCE DOCTRINE.

alluvial mining. The practice of removing sand and gravel from a riverbed.

alluvion (ə-**loo**-vee-ən). [fr. Latin *alluvio* "flood"] *Roman & civil law.* **1.** Strictly, the flow or wash of water against a shore or riverbank. **2.** A deposit of soil, clay, or other material caused by running water; esp., in land law, an addition of land caused by the buildup of deposits from running water, the added land then belonging to the owner of the property to which it is added. Cf. ACCRETION; AVULSION (2); DELICTION; EROSION.

All Writs Act. A federal statute that gives the U.S. Supreme Court and all courts established by Congress the power to issue writs in aid of their jurisdiction and in conformity with the usages and principles of law. 28 USCA § 1651(a).

ALTA. *abbr.* American Land Title Association.

alteration. 1. A substantial change to real estate, esp. to a structure, not involving an addition to or removal of the exterior dimensions of a building's structural parts.

structural alteration. A significant change to a building or other structure, essentially creating a different building or structure.

2. An act done to an instrument, after its execution, whereby its meaning or language is changed; esp., the changing of a term in a negotiable instrument without the consent of all parties to it. • Material alterations void an instrument, but immaterial ones do not.

material alteration. **1.** A significant change in something; esp., a change in a legal instrument sufficient to alter the instrument's legal meaning or effect. **2.** An unauthorized change in an instrument or an addition to an incomplete instrument resulting in the modification of a party's obligations. UCC § 3–407.

alter ego. A corporation used by an individual in conducting personal business, the result being that a court may impose liability on the individual by piercing the corporate veil when fraud has been perpetrated on someone dealing with the corporation. See PIERCING THE CORPORATE VEIL.

alter-ego rule. 1. *Criminal law.* The principle that one who defends another against attack stands in the position of that other person and can use only the amount of force that the other person could use under the circumstances. **2.** *Corporate law.* The doctrine that shareholders will be treated as the owners of a corporation's property, or as the real parties in interest, whenever it is necessary to do so to prevent fraud or to do justice.

alternative contract. See CONTRACT.

alternative dispute resolution. A procedure for settling a dispute by means other than litigation, such as arbitration, mediation, or minitrial. — Abbr. ADR.

alternative legacy. See LEGACY.

alternative liability. See LIABILITY.

alternative-means doctrine. *Criminal law.* The principle that when a crime may be committed in more than one way, the jury must be unanimous on the defendant's guilt but need not be unanimous on the possible different methods of committing the crime, as long as each possible method is supported by substantial evidence.

alternative minimum tax. See TAX.

alternative obligation. See OBLIGATION.

alternative pleading. See PLEADING (2).

alternative promise. See PROMISE.

alternative relief. See RELIEF.

alternative remainder. See REMAINDER.

alternative sentence. See SENTENCE.

alternative writ. See WRIT.

AMA. *abbr.* American Medical Association.

amalgamation (ə-mal-gə-**may**-shən), *n.* The act of combining or uniting; consolidation. — **amalgamate,** *vb.* — **amalgamator,** *n.* See MERGER.

ambiguity (am-bi-**gyoo**-ə-tee), *n.* An uncertainty of meaning or intention, as in a contractual term or statutory provision. — **ambiguous** (am-**big**-yoo-əs), *adj.*

latent ambiguity. An ambiguity that does not readily appear in the language of a document, but instead arises from a collateral matter when the document's terms are applied or executed <the contract contained a latent ambiguity: the shipping terms stated that the goods would arrive on the *Peerless*, but two ships have that name>.

patent ambiguity (**payt**-ənt). An ambiguity that clearly appears on the face of a document, arising from the language itself <the nonperformance was excused because the two different prices expressed in the contract created a patent ambiguity>.

ambit (**am**-bit). **1.** A boundary line or limit; esp., the scope of a statute or regulation, or the sphere of influence and authority of an agency, committee, department, or the like. **2.** A space surrounding a house or town.

ambulatory (**am**-byə-lə-tor-ee), *adj.* **1.** Able to walk. **2.** Capable of being altered or revised.

ambulatory will. See WILL.

ameliorate (ə-**meel**-yə-rayt), *vb.* **1.** To make better. **2.** To become better. — **amelioration,** *n.* — **ameliorative,** *adj.*

ameliorating waste. See WASTE (1).

amenable (ə-**mee**-nə-bəl *or* -**men**-ə-), *adj.* Legally answerable; liable to being brought to judgment. — **amenability,** *n.*

amend, *vb.* **1.** To make right; to correct or rectify. **2.** To change the wording of; specif., to alter (a statute, constitution, etc.) formally by adding or deleting a provision or by modifying the wording. — **amendatory** (ə-**men**-də-tor-ee), *adj.*

amended complaint. See COMPLAINT.

amended pleading. See PLEADING (1).

amended return. See TAX RETURN.

amendment. 1. A formal revision or addition proposed or made to a statute, constitution, or other instrument. **2.** The process of making such a revision. **3.** A change made by addition, deletion, or correction; an alteration in wording. — Abbr. amend.

amendment of indictment. The alteration of the charging terms of an indictment, either literally or in effect, after the grand jury has made a decision on it. • The indictment usually cannot be amended at trial in a way that would prejudice the defendant by having a trial on matters that were not contained in the indictment. To do so would violate the defendant's Fifth Amendment right to indictment by grand jury.

a mensa et thoro (ay **men**-sə et **thor**-oh). [Latin "from board and hearth"] (Of a divorce decree) effecting a separation of the parties rather than a dissolution of the marriage. See *divorce a menso et thoro* under DIVORCE; SEPARATION; A VINCULO MATRIMONII.

amercement (ə-**mərs**-mənt), *n.* [fr. Law French *estre à merci* "to be at the mercy (of another)," fr. Latin *merces* "payment"] **1.** The imposition of a discretionary fine or penalty by a court, esp. on an official for misconduct. **2.** The fine or penalty so imposed. — **amerce** (ə-**mərs**), *vb.* — **amerceable** (ə-**mər**-sə-bəl), **amerciable** (ə-**mər**-see-ə-bəl), *adj.*

American Arbitration Association. A national organization that maintains a panel of arbitrators to hear labor and commercial disputes. — Abbr. AAA.

American Bar Association. A voluntary national organization of lawyers. • Among other things, it participates in law reform, law-school accreditation, and continuing legal education in an effort to improve legal services and the administration of justice. — Abbr. ABA.

American Bar Foundation. An outgrowth of the American Bar Association involved with sponsoring and funding projects in law-related research, education, and social studies.

American Civil Liberties Union. A national organization whose primary purpose is to help enforce and preserve individual rights and liberties guaranteed by federal and state constitutions. — Abbr. ACLU.

American Federation of Labor and Congress of Industrial Organizations. A voluntary affiliation of more than 100 labor unions that operate autonomously yet benefit from the affiliation's political activities and its establishment of broad policies for the national labor movement. — Abbr. AFL–CIO.

American Law Institute. An organization of lawyers, judges, and legal scholars who promote consistency and simplification of American law by publishing restatements of the law and other model codes and treatises, as well as promoting continuing legal education. — Abbr. ALI.

American rule. 1. The general policy that all litigants must bear their own attorney's fees, including the prevailing party. • The rule is subject to bad-faith and other statutory and contractual exceptions. **2.** The doctrine that a witness cannot be questioned on cross-examination about any fact or circumstance not connected with the matters brought out in the direct examination.

American Stock Exchange. An organized stock exchange and self-regulating organization under the Securities Exchange Act of 1934, located in New York City and engaged in national trading of corporate stocks. • It often trades in the securities of young or small companies because its listing requirements are less strict than those of the New York Stock Exchange. — Abbr. AMEX; ASE.

Americans with Disabilities Act. A federal statute that prohibits discrimination — in employment, public services, and public accommodations — against any person with a disability ("a physical or mental impairment that substantially limits one or more of the major life activities"). 42 USCA §§ 12101–12213. • Under the ADA, major life activities include any activity that an average person in the general population can perform with little or no difficulty, such as seeing, hearing, sleeping, eating, walking, traveling, and working. The statute applies to both private and governmental entities. — Abbr. ADA.

AMEX (**am**-eks). *abbr.* AMERICAN STOCK EXCHANGE.

amicable action. See *test case* under CASE.

amicable suit. See *test case* under CASE.

amicus curiae (ə-**mee**-kəs **kyoor**-ee-I *or* ə-**mI**-kəs **kyoor**-ee-ee *also* **am**-i-kəs). [Latin "friend of the court"] A person who is not a party to a lawsuit but who petitions the court or is requested by the court to file a brief in the action because that person has a strong interest in the subject matter. Pl. **amici curiae** (ə-**mee**-kee *or* ə-**mI**-sI *or* ə-**mI**-kI).

amnesty, *n.* A pardon extended by the government to a group or class of persons, usu. for a political offense; the act of a sovereign power officially forgiving certain classes of persons who are subject to trial but have not yet been convicted. — **amnesty,** *vb.* See PARDON.

amortization (am-ər-tə-**zay**-shən), *n.* **1.** The act or result of gradually extinguishing a debt, such as a mortgage, usu. by contributing payments of principal each time a periodic interest payment is due.

> ***negative amortization.*** An increase in a loan's principal balance caused by monthly payments insufficient to pay accruing interest.

2. The act or result of apportioning the initial cost of a usu. intangible asset, such as a patent, over the asset's useful life. Cf. DEPRECIATION.

amortize, *vb.* **1.** To extinguish (a debt) gradually, often by means of a sinking fund. **2.** To arrange to extinguish (a debt) by gradual increments.

amortized loan. See LOAN.

amotion. 1. A turning out, as the eviction of a tenant or the removal of a person from office. **2.** The common-law procedure available to shareholders to remove a corporate director for cause. **3.** The wrongful moving or carrying away of another's personal property.

amount in controversy. The damages claimed or relief demanded by the injured party in a lawsuit. • For a federal court to have diversity jurisdiction, the amount in controversy must exceed $75,000. 28 USCA § 1332(a). See DIVERSITY OF CITIZENSHIP; AGGREGATION DOCTRINE.

amount realized. *Tax.* The amount received by a taxpayer for the sale or exchange of an asset, such as cash, property, services received, or debts assumed by a buyer. Cf. GAIN (3); LOSS (4).

a multo fortiori (ay **məl**-toh for-shee-**or**-I). [Latin] By far the stronger reason. Cf. A FORTIORI.

analytical jurisprudence. See JURISPRUDENCE.

anarchist, *n.* One who advocates the overthrow of organized government by force or who believes in the absence of government as a political ideal. — **anarchism** (the philosophy), *n.*

anarchy, *n.* Absence of government; lawlessness. — **anarchic,** *adj.*

anatomical gift. See GIFT.

ancestry. A line of descent; lineage.

ancient, *adj. Evidence.* Existing for a long time, usu. at least 20 to 30 years. • Ancient items are usually presumed to be valid even if proof of validity cannot be made. Fed. R. Evid. 901(b)(8).

ancient document. See DOCUMENT.

ancillary (**an**-sə-ler-ee), *adj.* Supplementary; subordinate. — **ancillarity** (an-sə-**la[i]r**-ə-tee), *n.*

ancillary administration. See ADMINISTRATION.

ancillary administrator. See ADMINISTRATOR.

ancillary claim. A claim that is collateral to, dependent on, or auxiliary to another claim, such as a state-law claim that is sufficiently related to a federal claim to permit federal jurisdiction over it. • The concept of ancillary federal jurisdiction is now contained in the supplemental-jurisdiction statute, 28 USCA § 1367. See *ancillary jurisdiction* and *supplemental jurisdiction* under JURISDICTION.

ancillary jurisdiction. See JURISDICTION.

ancillary legislation. See LEGISLATION.

ancillary suit. See SUIT.

Anders **brief.** *Criminal procedure.* A brief filed by a court-appointed defense attorney who wants to withdraw from the case on appeal based on a belief that the appeal is frivolous. • In an *Anders* brief, the attorney seeking to withdraw must identify anything in the record that might arguably support the appeal. The court then decides whether the appeal is frivolous and whether the attorney should be permitted to withdraw. *Anders v. California*, 386 U.S. 738, 87 S.Ct. 1396 (1967).

animus (**an**-ə-məs). [Latin] **1.** Ill will; animosity. **2.** Intention.

annex, *n.* Something that is attached, such as a document to a report or an addition to a building.

annexation, *n.* **1.** The act of attaching; the state of being attached. **2.** *Property.* The point at which a fixture becomes a part of the realty to which it is attached. **3.** A formal act by which a nation, state, or municipality incorporates land within its dominion. **4.** The annexed land itself. — **annex,** *vb.* Cf. ACCESSION (5).

annotation (an-ə-**tay**-shən), *n.* **1.** A brief summary of the facts and decision in a case, esp. one involving statutory interpretation. **2.** A note that explains or criticizes a source of law, usu. a case. • Annotations appear, for example, in the *United States Code Annotated* (USCA). **3.** A volume containing such explanatory or critical notes. — **annotate** (**an**-ə-tayt), *vb.* — **annotative** (**an**-ə-tay-tiv), *adj.* — **annotator** (**an**-ə-tay-tər), *n.* Cf. NOTE (2).

annual depreciation. See DEPRECIATION.

annual exclusion. See EXCLUSION.

annual percentage rate. See INTEREST RATE.

annuitant (ə-**n[y]oo**-ə-tənt), *n.* A beneficiary of an annuity.

annuity (ə-**n[y]oo**-ə-tee). **1.** An obligation to pay a stated sum, usu. monthly or annually, to a stated recipient. **2.** A fixed sum of money payable periodically. **3.** A right, often acquired under a life-insurance contract, to receive fixed payments periodically for a specified duration. Cf.

PENSION. **4.** A savings account with an insurance company or investment company, usu. established for retirement income.

annulment (ə-**nəl**-mənt), *n.* **1.** The act of nullifying or making void. **2.** A judicial or ecclesiastical declaration that a marriage is void. • Unlike a divorce, an annulment establishes that the marriage never existed in law. — **annul** (ə-**nəl**), *vb.* Cf. DIVORCE.

anomalous jurisdiction. See JURISDICTION.

anomalous plea. See PLEA (3).

anomalous pleading. See PLEADING (1).

anonymous, *adj.* Not named or identified. — **anonymity** (an-ə-**nim**-ə-tee), *n.*

answer, *n.* A defendant's first pleading that addresses the merits of the case, usu. by denying the plaintiff's allegations. • An answer usually sets forth the defendant's defenses and counterclaims.

answer, *vb.* **1.** To respond to a pleading or a discovery request <the company failed to answer the interrogatories within 30 days>. **2.** To assume the liability of another <a guarantor answers for another person's debt>. **3.** To pay (a debt or other liability) <she chose to promise to answer damages out of her own estate>.

answer day. See DAY.

ante (**an**-tee), *prep.* [Latin] Before. Cf. POST.

antecedent (an-tə-**seed**-ənt), *adj.* Earlier; preexisting; previous. — **antecedent** (preceding thing), *n.* — **antecedence** (quality or fact of going before), *n.*

antedate (**an**-ti-dayt), *vb.* **1.** To affix with a date earlier than the true date; BACKDATE (1). **2.** To precede in time. — **antedate,** *n.* Cf. POSTDATE.

anticipatory breach. See BREACH OF CONTRACT.

anticipatory repudiation. See REPUDIATION.

anticipatory search warrant. See SEARCH WARRANT.

Anti-Injunction Act. A federal statute providing that a federal court may not enjoin state-court proceedings unless an injunction is (1) expressly authorized by Congress, (2) necessary for the federal court's in rem jurisdiction, or (3) necessary to prevent relitigation of a judgment rendered by the federal court. 28 USCA § 2283. — Abbr. AIA.

anti-john law. A criminal-law statute punishing prostitutes' customers.

antilapse statute. *Wills & estates.* A statute that substitutes certain heirs of some types of testamentary beneficiaries when the beneficiary has predeceased the testator and permits them to take the gift, which would otherwise fail and thus pass to the residuary beneficiary (if any) or to the intestate heirs.

antinomy (an-**tin**-ə-mee), *n.* A contradiction in law or logic; esp., a conflict of authority, as between two decisions. — **antinomic** (an-ti-**nom**-ik), *adj.*

antitrust law. The body of law designed to protect trade and commerce from restraints, monopolies, price-fixing, and price discrimination. • The principal federal antitrust laws are the Sherman Act (15 USCA §§ 1–7) and the Clayton Act (15 USCA §§ 12–27).

apex deposition. See DEPOSITION.

a posteriori (ay pos-teer-ee-**or**-I *or* ah pos-teer-ee-**or**-ee), *adv.* [Latin "from what comes after"] Inductively; from the particular to the general, or from known effects to their inferred causes <as a legal analyst, she reasoned a posteriori — from countless individual cases to generalized rules that she finally applied>. — **a posteriori,** *adj.* Cf. A PRIORI.

apparent, *adj.* Visible; manifest; obvious.

apparent agent. See AGENT.

apparent authority. See AUTHORITY (1).

apparent danger. See DANGER.

apparent easement. See EASEMENT.

apparent servitude. See SERVITUDE (1).

appeal, *n.* A proceeding undertaken to have a decision reconsidered by bringing it to a higher authority; esp., the submission of a lower court's or agency's decision to a higher court for review and possible reversal. — **appeal,** *vb.* — **appealability,** *n.* Cf. CERTIORARI.

appeal by right. An appeal to a higher court from which permission need not be first obtained.

consolidated appeal. An appeal in which two or more parties, whose interests were similar enough to make a joinder practicable, proceed as a single appellant.

cross-appeal. An appeal by the appellee, usu. heard at the same time as the appellant's appeal.

direct appeal. An appeal from a trial court's decision directly to the jurisdiction's highest court, thus bypassing review by an intermediate appellate court.

interlocutory appeal. An appeal that occurs before the trial court's final ruling on the entire case. • Some interlocutory appeals involve legal points necessary to the determination of the case, while others involve collateral orders that are wholly separate from the merits of the action. Cf. FINAL-JUDGMENT RULE.

limited appeal. An appeal from only certain portions of a decision, usu. only the adverse or unfavorable portions.

appealable decision. See DECISION.

appeal bond. See BOND (2).

appeal by right. See APPEAL.

appearance, *n. Procedure.* A coming into court as a party or interested person, or as a lawyer on behalf of a party or interested person. — **appear,** *vb.*

compulsory appearance. An appearance by one who is required to appear by having been served with process.

general appearance. A general-purpose appearance that waives a party's ability later to dispute the court's authority to enter a binding judgment against him or her.

initial appearance. A criminal defendant's first appearance in court to hear the charges read, to be advised of his or her rights, and to have bail determined. See ARRAIGNMENT.

special appearance. **1.** A defendant's pleading that either claims that the court lacks personal jurisdiction over the defendant or objects to improper service of process. **2.** A defendant's showing up in court for the sole purpose of contesting the court's assertion of personal jurisdiction over the defendant.

appearance docket. See DOCKET (1).

appearance doctrine. In the law of self-defense, the rule that a defendant's use of force is justified if the defendant reasonably believed it to be justified.

appellant (ɔ-**pel**-ənt). A party who appeals a lower court's decision, usu. seeking reversal of that decision. Cf. APPELLEE.

appellate (ə-**pel**-it), *adj.* Of or relating to an appeal or appeals generally.

appellate counsel. See COUNSEL.

appellate court. See COURT.

appellate division. A department of a superior court responsible for hearing appeals; an intermediate appellate court in some states, such as New York and New Jersey.

appellate jurisdiction. See JURISDICTION.

appellate review. See REVIEW.

appellate rules. A body of rules governing appeals from lower courts.

appellee (ap-ə-**lee**). A party against whom an appeal is taken and whose role is to respond to that appeal, usu. seeking affirmance of the lower court's decision. Cf. APPELLANT.

appendant (ə-**pen**-dənt), *adj.* Attached or belonging to property as an additional but subsidiary right. — **appendant,** *n.*

appendant power. See POWER.

appendix, *n.* A supplementary document attached to the end of a writing. Pl. **appendixes, appendices.**

applicant. One who requests something; a petitioner, such as a person who applies for letters of administration.

application. 1. MOTION. **2.** *Bankruptcy.* A request for an order not requiring advance notice and an opportunity for a hearing before the order is issued.

application for leave to appeal. A motion requesting an appellate court to hear a party's appeal from a judgment when the party has no appeal by right or when the party's time limit for an appeal by right has expired. • The reviewing court has discretion whether to grant or reject such a motion.

apply, *vb.* **1.** To make a formal request or motion <apply for injunctive relief>. **2.** To employ for a limited purpose <apply payments to a reduction in interest>. **3.** To put to use with a particular subject matter <apply the law to the facts>.

appointee. 1. One who is appointed. **2.** One who receives the benefit of a power of appointment. See POWER OF APPOINTMENT.

appointment, *n.* **1.** The designation of a person for a job or duty; esp., the naming of someone to a nonelected public office. **2.** An office occupied by someone who has been appointed. **3.** The act of disposing of property, in exercise of a power granted for that purpose. See POWER OF APPOINTMENT. — **appoint,** *vb.* — **appointer** (for senses 1 & 2), *n.* — **appointor** (for sense 3), *n.*

Appointments Clause. The clause of the U.S. Constitution giving the President the power to nominate federal judges and various other officials. U.S. Const. art. II, § 2.

apportionment, *n.* **1.** Division into proportionate shares. **2.** The act of allocating or attributing moneys or expenses in a given way, as when a taxpayer allocates part of profits to a particular tax year or part of the use of a personal asset to a business. **3.** Distribution of legislative seats among districts; esp., the allocation of congressional representatives among the states based on population, as required by the 14th Amendment. See REAPPORTIONMENT. **4.** The division (by statute or by the testator's instruction) of an estate-tax liability among persons interested in an estate. — **apportion,** *vb.*

apportionment of liability. *Torts.* The parceling out of liability for an injury among multiple tortfeasors, and possibly the plaintiff as well. • Apportionment of liability encompasses such legal doctrines as joint and several liability, comparative responsibility, indemnity, and settlements. See Restatement (Third) of Torts: Apportionment of Liability (1999).

appraisal, *n.* **1.** The determination of what constitutes a fair price; valuation; estimation of worth. **2.** The report of such a determination. — **appraise,** *vb.* — **appraiser,** *n.* Cf. ASSESSMENT (3).

appraisement. **1.** APPRAISAL. **2.** An ADR method used for resolving the amount or extent of liability on a contract when the issue of liability itself is not in dispute. • Unlike arbitration, appraisement is not a quasi-judicial proceeding but instead an informal determination of the amount owed on a contract.

appreciation, *n.* **1.** An increase in an asset's value, usu. because of inflation. Cf. DEPRECIATION. **2.** The understanding of the significance, meaning, or value of something. — **appreciate,** *vb.* — **appreciable,** *adj.*

appreciation test. *Criminal law.* A test for the insanity defense requiring proof by clear and convincing evidence that at the time of the crime, the defendant suffered from a severe mental disease or defect preventing him or her from appreciating the wrongfulness of the conduct. 18 USCA § 17. See INSANITY DEFENSE.

apprehension, *n.* **1.** Seizure in the name of the law; arrest. **2.** Perception; comprehension. **3.** Fear; anxiety. — **apprehend,** *vb.*

appropriation, *n.* **1.** The exercise of control over property; a taking of possession. **2.** A legislative body's act of setting aside a sum of money for a public purpose. **3.** The sum of money so voted. **4.** *Torts.* An invasion of privacy whereby one person takes the name or likeness of another for commercial gain. — **appropriate,** *vb.* —

appropriable, *adj.* — **appropriator,** *n.* Cf. EXPROPRIATION; MISAPPROPRIATION.

appropriation bill. See APPROPRIATION.

approximation, doctrine of. See DOCTRINE OF APPROXIMATION.

appurtenance (ə-**pərt**-[ə-]nənts), *n.* Something that belongs or is attached to something else <the garden is an appurtenance to the land>.

appurtenant, *adj.* Annexed to a more important thing.

à prendre (ah **prawn**-drə *or* -dər). [French] For taking; for seizure. See PROFIT À PRENDRE.

a priori (ay prI-**or**-I *or* ah pree-**or**-ee), *adv.* [Latin "from what is before"] Deductively; from the general to the particular <as an analyst, he reasoned a priori — from seemingly self-evident propositions to particular conclusions>. — **a priori,** *adj.* Cf. A POSTERIORI.

arable land. See LAND.

arbiter (**ahr**-bə-tər). One with the power to decide disputes, such as a judge. Cf. ARBITRATOR.

arbitrament (ahr-**bi**-trə-mənt). **1.** The power to decide for oneself or others; the power to decide finally and absolutely. **2.** The act of deciding or settling a dispute that has been referred to arbitration. **3.** AWARD.

arbitrary, *adj.* **1.** Depending on individual discretion; specif., determined by a judge rather than by fixed rules, procedures, or law. **2.** (Of a judicial decision) founded on prejudice or preference rather than on reason or fact. • This type of decision is often termed *arbitrary and capricious.* Cf. CAPRICIOUS.

arbitration, *n.* A method of dispute resolution involving one or more neutral third parties who are usu. agreed to by the disputing parties and whose decision is binding. — **arbitrate,** *vb.* — **arbitral,** *adj.* Cf. MEDIATION.

ad hoc arbitration. Arbitration of only one issue.

adjudicative-claims arbitration. Arbitration designed to resolve matters usu. handled by courts (such as a tort claim), in contrast to arbitration of labor issues, international trade, and other fields traditionally associated with arbitration.

compulsory arbitration. Arbitration required by law or forced by law on the parties.

final-offer arbitration. Arbitration in which both parties are required to submit their "final offer" to the arbitrator, who may choose only one.

voluntary arbitration. Arbitration by the agreement of the parties.

arbitration act. A federal or state statute providing for the submission of disputes to arbitration.

arbitration clause. A contractual provision mandating arbitration — and thereby avoiding litigation — of disputes about the contracting parties' rights, duties, and liabilities.

arbitrator, *n.* A neutral person who resolves disputes between parties, esp. by means of formal arbitration. **arbitratorship,** *n.* Cf. ARBITER.

arguendo (ahr-gyoo-**en**-doh). [Latin "in arguing"] *Jargon.* **1.** For the sake of argument <assuming arguendo that discovery procedures were correctly followed, the court still cannot grant the defendant's motion to dismiss>. **2.** During the course of argument <counsel mentioned arguendo that the case has been followed in three other decisions>.

argument. 1. A statement that attempts to persuade; esp., the remarks of counsel in analyzing and pointing out or repudiating a desired inference, for the assistance of a decision-maker. **2.** The act or process of attempting to persuade. See ORAL ARGUMENT; CLOSING ARGUMENT.

argumentative, *adj.* **1.** Of or relating to argument or persuasion. **2.** Stating not only facts, but also inferences and conclusions drawn from facts.

argumentative instruction. See JURY INSTRUCTION.

arise, *vb.* **1.** To originate; to stem (from) <a federal claim arising under the U.S. Constitution>. **2.** To result (from) <litigation routinely arises from such accidents>. **3.** To emerge in one's consciousness; to come to one's attention <the question of appealability then arose>.

armed robbery. See ROBBERY.

arm-in-arm, *adj.* Of, relating to, or involving a transaction between parties whose personal interests are involved. Cf. ARM'S-LENGTH.

arm of the state. An entity created by a state and operating as an alter ego or instrumentality of the state, such as a state university or a state department of transportation. • The 11th Amendment of the U.S. Constitution generally bars suits in federal court by individuals against states. The Amendment has been interpreted as protecting arms of the state as well as the state itself.

arm's-length, *adj.* Of or relating to dealings between two parties who are not related or not on close terms and who are presumed to have roughly equal bargaining power; not involving a confidential relationship. Cf. ARM-IN-ARM.

arraignment, *n.* The initial step in a criminal prosecution whereby the defendant is brought before the court to hear the charges and to enter a plea. — **arraign,** *vb.* Cf. PRELIMINARY HEARING; *initial appearance* under APPEARANCE.

array, *n.* **1.** A panel of potential jurors; VENIRE (1). **2.** The jurors actually empaneled. **3.** A list or roster of empaneled jurors. **4.** Order; arrangement.

array, *vb.* **1.** To empanel a jury for trial. **2.** To call out the names of jurors, one by one, as they are empaneled.

arrear, *n.* (*usu. pl.*) **1.** The state of being behind in the payment of a debt or the discharge of an obligation. **2.** An unpaid or overdue debt. **3.** An unfinished duty. See IN ARREARS.

arrest, *n.* **1.** A seizure or forcible restraint. **2.** The taking or keeping of a person in custody by legal authority, esp. in response to a criminal charge. — **arrest,** *vb.*

citizen's arrest. An arrest of a private person by another private person on grounds that (1) a public offense was committed in the arrester's presence, or (2) the arrester has reasonable cause to believe that the arrestee has committed a felony.

false arrest. An arrest made without proper legal authority. Cf. FALSE IMPRISONMENT.

lawful arrest. The taking of a person into legal custody either under a valid warrant or on probable cause that the person has committed a crime.

malicious arrest. An arrest made without probable cause and for an improper purpose; esp., an abuse of process by which a person procures the arrest (and often the imprisonment) of another by means of judicial process, without any reasonable cause. • Malicious arrest can be grounds for an action for abuse of process, false imprisonment, or malicious prosecution.

parol arrest (pə-**rohl** *or* **par**-əl). An arrest ordered by a judge or magistrate from the bench, without written complaint, and executed immediately, such as an arrest of a person who breaches the peace in open court. See CONTEMPT.

pretextual arrest. An arrest of a person for a minor offense for the opportunity to investigate the person's involvement in a more serious offense for which there are no lawful grounds to make an arrest.

warranted arrest. An arrest made under authority of a warrant.

warrantless arrest. An arrest, without a warrant, based on probable cause of a felony, or for a misdemeanor committed in a police officer's presence. See WARRANT.

arrestee. A person who has been taken into custody by legal authority; a person who has been arrested.

arrest of judgment. The staying of a judgment after its entry; esp., a court's refusal to render or enforce a judgment because of a defect apparent from the record.

arrest record. 1. A form completed by a police officer when a person is arrested. **2.** A cumulative list of the instances when a person has been arrested.

arrest warrant. See WARRANT (1).

arrogation (ar-ə-**gay**-shən), *n.* The act of claiming or taking something without the right to do so <some commentators argue that limited military actions unilaterally ordered by the President are an arrogation of Congress's exclusive power to declare war>. — **arrogate,** *vb.*

arson, *n.* **1.** At common law, the malicious burning of someone else's dwelling house or outhouse that is either appurtenant to the dwelling house or within the curtilage. **2.** Under modern statutes, the intentional and wrongful burning of someone else's property (as to destroy a building) or one's own property (as to fraudulently collect insurance). See Model Penal Code § 220.1(1). — **arsonous,** *adj.* Cf. HOUSEBURNING; CRIMINAL DAMAGE TO PROPERTY.

arsonable, *adj.* (Of property) of such a nature as to give rise to a charge of arson if maliciously burned. • Only real property, and not personal property, is arsonable.

arsonist. One who commits arson; INCENDIARY (1).

art. 1. The methodical application of knowledge or skill in creating something. **2.** An occupation or business that requires skill; a craft.

artful pleading. See PLEADING (2).

article, *n.* **1.** Generally, a particular item or thing. **2.** A separate and distinct part (as a clause or stipulation) of a writing, esp. in a contract, statute, or constitution. **3.** (*pl.*) An instrument containing a set of rules or stipulations. **4.** A nonfictional literary composition forming an independent part of a publication, such as a law review or journal.

Article I court. See *legislative court* under COURT.

Article II judge. A U.S. bankruptcy judge or magistrate judge appointed for a term of years as authorized by Congress under Article II of the U.S. Constitution. 28 USCA §§ 151 et seq., 631 et seq.

Article III court. A federal court that, deriving its jurisdiction from U.S. Const. art. III, § 2, hears cases arising under the Constitution and the laws and treaties of the United States, cases in which the United States is a party, and cases between the states and between citizens of different states.

Article III judge. A U.S. Supreme Court, Court of Appeals, or District Court judge appointed for life under Article III of the U.S. Constitution.

articles of amendment. A document filed to effectuate an amendment or change to a corporation's articles of incorporation.

articles of association. 1. ARTICLES OF INCORPORATION. **2.** A document — similar to articles of incorporation — that legally creates a nonstock or nonprofit organization.

articles of dissolution. A document that a dissolving corporation must file with the appropriate governmental agency, usu. the secretary of state, after the corporation has settled all its debts and distributed all its assets.

articles of impeachment. A formal document alleging the specific charges against a public official and the reasons for removing that official from office. See IMPEACHMENT.

articles of incorporation. A document that sets forth the basic terms of a corporation's existence, including the number and classes of shares and the purposes and duration of the corporation. Cf. BYLAW (1); CHARTER (2).

articulated pleading. See PLEADING (1).

artificial person. See PERSON.

as-applied challenge. See CHALLENGE (1).

ascendant (ə-**sen**-dənt), *n.* One who precedes in lineage, such as a parent or grandparent. — **ascendant,** *adj.* Cf. DESCENDANT.

collateral ascendant. Loosely, an aunt, uncle, or other relative who is not strictly an ancestor.

ascent. The passing of an estate upwards to an heir in the ascending line. Cf. DESCENT.

ASE. *abbr.* AMERICAN STOCK EXCHANGE.

Ashwander **rules.** A set of principles outlining the U.S. Supreme Court's policy of deciding constitutional questions only when necessary, and of avoiding a constitutional question if the case can be decided on the basis of another issue. • These rules were outlined in Justice Brandeis's concurring opinion in *Ashwander v. Tennessee Valley Authority*, 297 U.S. 288, 56 S.Ct. 466 (1936).

as is, *adv. & adj.* In the existing condition without modification. • Under UCC § 2–316(3)(a), a seller can disclaim all implied warranties by stating that the goods are being sold "as is" or "with all faults." Generally, a sale of property "as is" means that the property is sold in its existing condition, and use of the phrase *as is* relieves the seller from liability for defects in that condition.

as-is warranty. See WARRANTY (2).

as of. On; at. • This is often used to signify the effective legal date of a document, as when the document is backdated or the parties sign at different times <the lease commences as of June 1>.

as of right. By virtue of a legal entitlement <the case is not one triable to a jury as of right>.

as per. *Jargon.* In accordance with; PER (3). • This phrase has traditionally been considered a barbarism, *per* being the preferred form in commercialese <per your request>. But even *per* can be improved on <as you requested>.

asportation (as-pər-**tay**-shən), *n.* The act of carrying away or removing (property or a person). • Asportation is a necessary element of larceny. — **asport,** *vb.* — **asportative,** *adj.* See LARCENY.

assailant. 1. One who physically attacks another; one who commits an assault. **2.** One who attacks another using nonphysical means; esp., one who attacks another's position or feelings, as by criticism, argument, or abusive language. — **assail,** *vb.*

assassination, *n.* The act of deliberately killing someone, esp. a public figure, usu. for hire or for political reasons. — **assassinate,** *vb.* — **assassin,** *n.*

assault, *n.* **1.** *Criminal & tort law.* The threat or use of force on another that causes that person to have a reasonable apprehension of imminent harmful or offensive contact; the act of putting another person in reasonable fear or apprehension of an immediate battery by means of an act amounting to an attempt or threat to commit a battery. **2.** *Criminal law.* An attempt to commit battery, requiring the specific intent to cause physical injury. **3.** Loosely, a battery. **4.** Popularly, any attack. — **assault,** *vb.* — **assaultive,** *adj.* Cf. BATTERY.

aggravated assault. Criminal assault accompanied by circumstances that make it more severe, such as the intent to commit another crime or the intent to cause serious bodily injury, esp. by using a deadly weapon. See Model Penal Code § 211.1(2).

assault with a deadly weapon. An aggravated assault in which the defendant, using a deadly weapon, threatens the victim with death or serious bodily injury.

assault with intent. Any of several assaults that are carried out with an additional criminal purpose in mind, such as assault with intent to murder, assault with intent to rob, assault with intent to rape, and assault with intent to inflict great bodily injury.

attempted assault. An attempt to commit an assault; an attempted battery that has not progressed far enough to be an assault, as when a person intends to harm someone physically but is captured after trying to locate the intended victim in his or her place of employment.

civil assault. An assault considered as a tort and not as a crime. • Although the same assaultive conduct can be both a tort and a crime, this term isolates the legal elements that give rise to civil liability.

conditional assault. An assault expressing a threat on condition, such as "your money or your life."

criminal assault. An assault considered as a crime and not as a tort. • This term isolates the legal elements that give rise to criminal liability even though the act might also have been tortious.

sexual assault. **1.** Sexual intercourse with another person who does not consent. • Several state statutes have abolished the crime of rape and replaced it with the offense of sexual assault. **2.** Offensive sexual contact with another person, exclusive of rape. Cf. RAPE.

assault and battery. Loosely, a criminal battery. See BATTERY.

assembly. 1. A group of persons organized and united for some common purpose.

unlawful assembly. A meeting of three or more persons who intend either to commit a violent crime or to carry out some act, lawful or unlawful, that will constitute a breach of the peace. Cf. RIOT.

2. In many states, the lower house of a legislature.

assent, *n.* Agreement, approval, or permission. — **assent,** *vb.* See CONSENT.

constructive assent. Assent imputed to someone based on conduct.

express assent. Assent that is clearly and unmistakably communicated.

implied assent. Assent inferred from one's conduct rather than from direct expression.

assenting-silence doctrine. *Criminal law.* The principle that an accusation will be taken as true, despite silence by the accused, if the accusation was made under circumstances in which silence can be fairly said to be an agreement.

assertion, *n.* A declaration or allegation. — **assert,** *vb.* — **assertor,** *n.*

assertive conduct. See CONDUCT.

assertory oath. See OATH.

assessed valuation. See VALUATION.

assessment, *n.* **1.** Determination of the rate or amount of something, such as a tax or damages. **2.** Imposition of something, such as a tax or fine, according to an established rate; the tax or fine so imposed. **3.** Official valuation of property for purposes of taxation. Cf. APPRAISAL. **4.** An audit or review. — **assess,** *vb.*

assessor. 1. One who evaluates or makes assessments, esp. for purposes of taxation. **2.** A person who advises a judge or magistrate about scientific or technical matters during a trial. See MASTER (2). — **assessorial** (as-ə-**sor**-ee-əl), *adj.* — **assessorship,** *n.*

asset. 1. An item that is owned and has value. **2.** (*pl.*) The entries on a balance sheet showing the items of property owned, including cash, inventory, equipment, real estate, accounts receivable, and goodwill. **3.** (*pl.*) All the property of a person (esp. a bankrupt or deceased person) available for paying debts or for distribution.

asset-depreciation range. The IRS's range of depreciation lifetimes allowed for assets placed in service. — Abbr. ADR. See MODIFIED ACCELERATED COST RECOVERY SYSTEM.

asseverate (ə-**sev**-ə-rayt), *vb.* To state solemnly or positively; to aver. — **asseveration** (ə-sev-ə-**ray**-shən), *n.* See AVERMENT.

assignable, *adj.* Capable of being assigned; transferable from one person to another, so that the transferee has the same rights as the transferor had. Cf. NEGOTIABLE.

assignable lease. See LEASE.

assigned counsel. See COUNSEL.

assignee (ə-SI-**nee** *or* as-ə-**nee**). One to whom property rights or powers are transferred by another. • Use of the term is so widespread that it is difficult to ascribe positive meaning to it with any specificity. Courts often look to the intent of the assignor and assignee in making the assignment — rather than to the formality of the use of the term *assignee* — in defining rights and responsibilities.

assignee clause. A provision of the Judiciary Act of 1789 that prevented a litigant without diversity of citizenship from assigning a claim to another who did have the required diversity. • In 1948 the assignee clause was replaced by 28 USCA § 1359, which denies federal jurisdiction when a party is improperly or collusively joined, by assignment or otherwise, merely to invoke jurisdiction.

assignment, *n.* **1.** The transfer of rights or property. **2.** The rights or property so transferred. **3.** The instrument of transfer. **4.** A task, job, or appointment. **5.** In litigation practice, a point that a litigant advances.

assignment for the benefit of creditors. Assignment of a debtor's property to another person in trust so as to consolidate and liquidate the debtor's assets for payment to creditors, any surplus being returned to the debtor. • This procedure serves as a state-law substitute for federal bankruptcy proceedings. The debtor is not discharged from unpaid debts by this procedure since creditors do not agree to any discharge.

assignment of error. A specification of the trial court's alleged errors on which the appellant relies in seeking an appellate court's reversal, vacation, or modification of an adverse judgment. Pl. **assignments of error.** See ERROR. Cf. WRIT OF ERROR.

assignment of rights. *Contracts.* The transfer of rights, esp. contractual rights, from one party to another.

assignor (as-ə-**nor** *or* ə-sɪ-nər *or* ə-sɪ-**nor**). One who transfers property rights or powers to another.

Assimilative Crimes Act. A federal statute providing that state law applies to a crime committed within a federal enclave in that state (such as a reservation or military installation) if the crime is not punishable under federal law. 18 USCA § 13. — Abbr. ACA.

assistance of counsel. Representation by a lawyer, esp. in a criminal case. See RIGHT TO COUNSEL.

effective assistance of counsel. A conscientious, meaningful legal representation, whereby the defendant is advised of all rights and the lawyer performs all required tasks reasonably according to the prevailing professional standards in criminal cases. See Fed. R. Crim. P. 44; 18 USCA § 3006A.

ineffective assistance of counsel. A representation in which the defendant is deprived of a fair trial because the lawyer handles the case unreasonably, usu. either by performing incompetently or by not devoting full effort to the defendant, esp. because of a conflict of interest. • In determining whether a criminal defendant received ineffective assistance of counsel, courts generally consider several factors, including: (1) whether the lawyer had previously handled criminal cases; (2) whether strategic trial tactics were involved in the allegedly incompetent action; (3) to what extent the defendant was prejudiced as a result of the lawyer's alleged ineffectiveness; and (4) whether the ineffectiveness was due to matters beyond the lawyer's control.

assisted suicide. See SUICIDE.

assize (ə-**sɪz**), *n.* **1.** A session of a court or council. **2.** A law enacted by such a body, usu. one setting the measure, weight, or price of a thing. **3.** The procedure provided for by such an enactment. **4.** The court that hears cases involving that procedure. **5.** A jury. **6.** A jury trial. **7.** A jury's finding. **8.** A writ.

associate, *n.* **1.** A colleague or companion. **2.** A junior member of an organization or profession; esp., a lawyer in a law firm, usu. with fewer than a certain number of years in practice, who may, upon achieving the requisite seniority, receive an offer to become a partner or shareholder.

associate judge. See JUDGE.

associate justice. See JUSTICE (2).

association. **1.** The process of mentally collecting ideas, memories, or sensations. **2.** A gathering of people for a common purpose; the persons so joined. **3.** An unincorporated business organization that is not a legal entity separate from the persons who compose it. • If an association has sufficient corporate attributes, such as centralized management, continuity of existence, and limited liability, it may be classified and taxed as a corporation.

professional association. **1.** A group of professionals organized to practice their profession together, though not necessarily in corporate or partnership form. **2.** A group of professionals organized for education, social activity, or lobbying, such as a bar association. — Abbr. P.A.

trade association. An association of business organizations having similar concerns and engaged in similar fields, formed for mutual protection, the interchange of ideas and statistics, and the establishment and maintenance of industry standards.

Association of American Law Schools. An organization of law schools that have each graduated at least three annual classes of students. — Abbr. AALS.

assumed name. **1.** ALIAS (1). **2.** The name under which a business operates or by which it is commonly known. See D/B/A.

assumpsit (ə-**səm**[**p**]-sit). [Law Latin "he undertook"] **1.** An express or implied promise, not under seal, by which one person undertakes to do some act or pay something to another. **2.** A common-law action for breach of such a promise or for breach of a contract.

general assumpsit. An action based on the defendant's breach of an implied promise to pay a debt to the plaintiff.

assumption, *n.* **1.** A fact or statement taken for granted; a supposition. **2.** The act of taking (esp. someone else's debt or other obligation) for or on oneself; the agreement to so take. — **assume,** *vb.*

implied assumption. The imposition of personal liability on a land purchaser who buys subject to a mortgage and who deducts the mortgage amount from the purchase price, so that the purchaser is treated as having assumed the debt.

assumption of the risk. *Torts.* **1.** The act or an instance of a prospective plaintiff's taking on the risk of loss, injury, or damage. **2.** The principle that one who takes on the risk of loss, injury, or damage cannot maintain an action against a party that causes the loss, injury, or damage. • Assumption of the risk was originally an affirmative defense, but in most jurisdictions it has now been wholly or largely subsumed by the doctrines of contributory and comparative negligence.

assurance, *n.* **1.** Something that gives confidence; the state of being confident or secure. **2.** A pledge or guarantee. **3.** The act of transferring real property; the instrument by which it is transferred. — **assure,** *vb.*

further assurance. A covenant contained in a warranty deed whereby the grantor promises to execute any document that might be needed in the future to perfect the title that the original deed purported to transfer.

asylum. **1.** A sanctuary or shelter. **2.** Protection of usu. political refugees from arrest by a foreign jurisdiction; a nation or embassy that affords such protection. **3.** An institution for the protection and relief of the unfortunate, esp. the mentally ill.

at bar. Now before the court <the case at bar>.

at equity. According to equity; by, for, or in equity.

at issue. Taking opposite sides; under dispute; in question <the federal appeals courts are at issue over a question of law>.

at-issue waiver. An exemption from the attorney–client privilege, whereby a litigant is considered to have waived the privilege by taking a position that cannot be effectively challenged without analyzing privileged information. Cf. OFFENSIVE-USE WAIVER.

***Atlantic Reporter*.** A set of regional lawbooks that, being part of the West Group's National Reporter System, contain every published decision from Connecticut, Delaware, Maine, Maryland, New Hampshire, New Jersey, Pennsylvania, Rhode Island, and Vermont, as well as the decisions of the District of Columbia Municipal Court of Appeals, from 1885 to date. • The first series ran from 1885 to 1938; the second series is the current one. — Abbr. A.; A.2d.

at large. 1. Free; unrestrained; not under control <the suspect is still at large>. **2.** Not limited to any particular place, person, matter, or question <at-large election>. **3.** Chosen by the voters of an entire political entity, such as a state, county, or city, rather than from separate districts within the entity <councilmember at large>. **4.** Not ordered in a topical way; at random <statutes at large>. **5.** Fully; in detail; in an extended form <there wasn't time to discuss the issue at large>.

at law. According to law; by, for, or in law.

at-risk rules, *n. pl.* Statutory limitations of a taxpayer's deductible losses to the amount the taxpayer could actually lose, to prevent the taxpayer from sheltering income.

atrocious felony. See FELONY.

ATS. *abbr.* At the suit of.

attach, *vb.* **1.** To annex, bind, or fasten <attach the exhibit to the pleading>. **2.** To take or seize under legal authority <attach the debtor's assets>. **3.** To become attributed; to adhere <jeopardy attaches when the jury is sworn>.

attachment. 1. The seizing of a person's property to secure a judgment or to be sold in satisfaction of a judgment. Cf. GARNISHMENT; SEQUESTRATION (1). **2.** The arrest of a person who either is in contempt of court or is to be held as security for the payment of a judgment. **3.** A writ ordering legal seizure of property (esp. to satisfy a creditor's claim) or of a person. **4.** The creation of a security interest in property, occurring when the debtor agrees to the security, receives value from the secured party, and obtains rights in the collateral. UCC § 9–203. Cf. PERFECTION. **5.** The act of affixing or connecting; something (as a document) that is affixed or connected to something else.

attachment of risk. The point when the risk of loss of purchased goods passes from the seller to the buyer. UCC § 2–509.

attainder (ə-**tayn**-dər), *n.* At common law, the act of extinguishing a person's civil rights when that person is sentenced to death or declared an outlaw for committing a felony or treason. — **attaint** (ə-**taynt**), *vb.* See BILL OF ATTAINDER.

attaint (ə-**taynt**), *adj.* Maligned or tarnished reputationally; under an attainder for crime.

attempt, *n.* **1.** The act or an instance of making an effort to accomplish something, esp. without success. **2.** *Criminal law.* An overt act that is done with the intent to commit a crime but that falls short of completing the crime. • Attempt is an inchoate offense distinct from the attempted crime. Under the Model Penal Code, an attempt includes any act that is a substantial step toward commission of a crime, such as enticing, lying in wait for, or following the intended victim or unlawfully entering a building where a crime is expected to be committed. Model Penal Code § 5.01. See DANGEROUS-PROXIMITY TEST; INDISPENSABLE-ELEMENT TEST; LAST-PROXIMATE-ACT TEST; PHYSICAL-PROXIMITY TEST; PROBABLE-DESISTANCE TEST; RES IPSA LOQUITUR TEST. Cf. CONSPIRACY; SOLICITATION (2); PREPARATION; SUBSTANTIAL-STEP TEST. — **attempt,** *vb.*

attempted assault. See ASSAULT.

attempted suicide. See SUICIDE.

attempt to attempt. A first step made toward a criminal attempt of some sort, such as a failed effort to mail someone a note inciting that person to engage in criminal conduct. • As a general rule, courts do not recognize an attempt to commit a crime that is itself an attempt. But some jurisdictions recognize this offense, especially when the attempted crime is defined to be an independent substantive crime.

attendant, *adj.* Accompanying; resulting <attendant circumstances>.

attendant term. See TERM (4).

attenuation doctrine (ə-ten-yə-**way**-shən). *Criminal procedure.* The rule providing that evidence obtained by illegal means may nonetheless be admissible if the connection between the evidence and the illegal means is sufficiently remote. • This is an exception to the fruit-of-the-poisonous-tree doctrine. See FRUIT-OF-THE-POISONOUS-TREE DOCTRINE.

attest (ə-**test**), *vb.* **1.** To bear witness; testify. **2.** To affirm to be true or genuine; to authenticate by signing as a witness. — **attestation** (a-te-**stay**-shən), *n.* — **attestative** (ə-**tes**-tə-tiv), *adj.*

attestation clause. A provision at the end of an instrument (esp. a will) that is signed by the instrument's witnesses and that recites the formalities required by the jurisdiction in which the instrument might take effect (such as where the will might be probated). • The attestation strengthens the presumption that all the statutory requirements for executing the will have been satisfied. Cf. TESTIMONIUM CLAUSE.

attesting witness. See WITNESS.

attorn (ə-**tərn**), *vb.* **1.** To agree to be the tenant of a new landlord. **2.** To transfer (money, goods, etc.) to another.

attorney. 1. Strictly, one who is designated to transact business for another; a legal agent. **2.** A person who practices law; LAWYER. Cf. COUNSEL. — Abbr. att'y. Pl. **attorneys.**

attorney–client privilege. See PRIVILEGE (3).

attorney general. The chief law officer of a state or of the United States, responsible for advising the government on legal matters and representing it in litigation. — Abbr. AG. Pl. **attorneys general.**

attorney general's opinion. 1. An opinion furnished by the U.S. Attorney General to the President or another executive official on a request concerning a question of law. **2.** A written opinion by a state attorney general, usu. given at the request of a public official, interpreting a legal provision.

attorney's fees. The charge to a client for services performed for the client, such as an hourly fee, a flat fee, or a contingent fee. Cf. RETAINER (2).

attornment (ə-**tərn**-mənt), *n.* **1.** A tenant's agreement to hold the land as the tenant of a new landlord. **2.** A constructive delivery involving the transfer of mediate possession while a third person has immediate possession; esp., a bailee's acknowledgment that he or she will hold the goods on behalf of someone other than the bailor. — **attorn,** *vb.*

attractive nuisance. See NUISANCE.

attractive-nuisance doctrine. *Torts.* The rule that a person who owns property on which there is a dangerous thing or condition that will foreseeably lure children to trespass is under a duty to protect those children from the danger. See ALLUREMENT; DANGEROUS INSTRUMENTALITY.

attribution, *n.* The process — outlined in the Internal Revenue Code — by which a person's or entity's stock ownership is assigned to a related family member or entity for tax purposes. — **attribute,** *vb.* — **attributive,** *adj.*

att'y. *abbr.* ATTORNEY.

at will. Subject to one's discretion; as one wishes or chooses; esp. (of a legal relationship), able to be terminated or discharged by either party without cause <employment at will>.

auction, *n.* A sale of property to the highest bidder. • Under the UCC, a sale at auction is complete when the auctioneer so announces in a customary manner, as by pounding a hammer. — **auction,** *vb.* — **auctioneer,** *n.*

audit, *n.* A formal examination of an individual's or organization's accounting records, financial situation, or compliance with some other set of standards. — **audit,** *vb.* — **auditor,** *n.* See GENERALLY ACCEPTED AUDITING STANDARDS.

audit trail. The chain of evidence connecting account balances to original transactions and calculations.

aural acquisition. *Criminal law.* Under the Federal Wiretapping Act, hearing or tape-recording a communication, as opposed to tracing its origin or destination. 18 USCA § 2510(4).

authentication, *n.* **1.** Broadly, the act of proving that something (as a document) is true or genuine, esp. so that it may be admitted as evidence; the condition of being so proved. **2.** Specif., the assent to or adoption of a writing as one's own. — **authenticate,** *vb.*

self-authentication. Authentication without extrinsic evidence of truth or genuineness. • In federal courts, certain writings, such as notarized documents and certified copies of public records, may be admitted into evidence by self-authentication. Fed. R. Evid. 902.

authentic interpretation. See INTERPRETATION.

authority. 1. The right or permission to act legally on another's behalf; the power delegated by a principal to an agent. See AGENCY (1).

actual authority. Authority that a principal intentionally confers on an agent, including the authority that the agent reasonably believes he or she has as a result of the agent's dealings with the principal. • Actual authority can be either express or implied.

apparent authority. Authority that a third party reasonably believes an agent has, based on the third party's dealings with the principal. • Apparent authority can be created by law even when no actual authority has been conferred.

authority coupled with an interest. Authority given to an agent for valuable consideration. • This authority cannot be unilaterally terminated by the principal.

constructive authority. Authority that is inferred because of an earlier grant of authority.

express authority. Authority given to the agent by explicit agreement, either orally or in writing.

general authority. A general agent's authority, intended to apply to all matters arising in the course of business.

implied authority. Authority given to the agent as a result of the principal's conduct, such as the principal's earlier acquiescence to the agent's actions.

incidental authority. Authority needed to carry out actual or apparent authority. • For example, the actual authority to borrow money includes the incidental authority to sign commercial paper to bring about the loan.

inherent authority. Authority of an agent arising from the agency relationship.

naked authority. Authority delegated solely for the principal's benefit, without giving any consideration to the agent. • This authority can be revoked by the principal at any time.

special authority. Authority limited to an individual transaction.

2. Governmental power or jurisdiction. **3.** A governmental agency or corporation that administers a public enterprise. **4.** A legal writing taken as definitive or decisive.

adverse authority. Authority that is unfavorable to an advocate's position.

persuasive authority. Authority that carries some weight but is not binding on a court.

primary authority. Authority that issues directly from a law-making body; legislation and the reports of litigated cases.

secondary authority. Authority that explains the law but does not itself establish it, such as a treatise, annotation, or law-review article.

5. A source, such as a statute, case, or treatise, cited in support of a legal argument.

authorize, *vb.* **1.** To give legal authority; to empower. **2.** To formally approve; to sanction. — **authorization,** *n.*

autocracy (aw-**tok**-rə-see), *n.* Government by one person with unlimited power and authority; unlimited monarchy. — **autocratic** (aw-tə-**krat**-ik), *adj.* — **autocrat (aw**-tə-krat), *n.*

automated transaction. A contract formed or performed, in whole or in part, by electronic means or by electronic messages in which either party's electronic actions or messages establishing the contract are not intended to be reviewed in the ordinary course by an individual. UCC § 2A–102(a)(3).

automatism (aw-**tom**-ə-tiz-əm), *n.* **1.** Action or conduct occurring without will, purpose, or reasoned intention, such as sleepwalking; behavior carried out in a state of unconsciousness or mental dissociation without full awareness. • Automatism may be asserted as a defense to negate the requisite mental state of voluntariness for commission of a crime. **2.** The state of a person who, though capable of action, is not conscious of his or her actions. — **automaton,** *n.*

automobile exception. An exception to the warrant requirement in Fourth Amendment search-and-seizure law, holding that the police may, without a warrant, thoroughly search a movable vehicle for which the individual has a lessened expectation of privacy (such as a car or boat) if probable cause exists. • For purposes of this doctrine, exigent circumstances are presumed to exist. Once the right to conduct a warrantless search arises, the actual search may take place at a later time. *Carroll v. United States*, 267 U.S. 132, 45 S.Ct. 280 (1925); *California v. Acevedo*, 500 U.S. 565, 111 S.Ct. 1982 (1991). See *exigent circumstances* under CIRCUMSTANCE.

autonomic law (aw-tə-**nom**-ik). The type of enacted law that has its source in various forms of subordinate and restricted legislative authority possessed by private persons and bodies of persons. • Examples are corporate bylaws, university regulations, and the rules of the International Monetary Fund.

autonomy (aw-**tahn**-ə-mee), *n.* **1.** The right of self-government. **2.** A self-governing state. — **autonomous** (aw-**tahn**-ə-məs), *adj.*

autopsy (aw-top-see). **1.** An examination of a dead body to determine the cause of death, esp. in a criminal investigation. **2.** The evidence of one's own senses.

autre vie (**oh**-trə **vee**). [Law French] Another's life. See PUR AUTRE VIE; VIE.

avail, *n.* **1.** Use or advantage <of little or no avail>. **2.** (*pl.*) Profits or proceeds, esp. from a sale of property <the avails of the trust fund>.

availment, *n.* The act of making use or taking advantage of something for oneself <availment of the benefits of public office>. — **avail,** *vb.*

aver (ə-**vər**), *vb.* To assert positively, esp. in a pleading; to allege.

average tax rate. See TAX RATE.

averment (ə-**vər**-mənt), *n.* A positive declaration or affirmation of fact; esp., an assertion or allegation in a pleading. Cf. ASSEVERATE.

immaterial averment. An averment that alleges something in needless detail; a statement that goes far beyond what is in issue. • This type of averment may be ordered struck from the pleading.

negative averment. An averment that is negative in form but affirmative in substance and that must be proved by the alleging party. • An example is the statement "she was not old enough to enter into the contract," which is more than just a simple denial. Cf. TRAVERSE.

a vinculo matrimonii (ay **ving**-kyə-loh ma-trə-**moh**-nee-ɪ). [Latin] From the bond of matrimony. See *divorce a vinculo matrimonii* under DIVORCE.

avoid, *vb. Jargon.* To render void. • Because this legal use of *avoid* can be easily confused with the ordinary sense of the word, the verb *to void* is preferable.

avoidance, *n.* **1.** The act of evading or escaping. See TAX AVOIDANCE. **2.** The act of refraining from (something). **3.** *Jargon.* VOIDANCE. **4.** CONFESSION AND AVOIDANCE.

avulsion (ə-**vəl**-shən), *n.* **1.** A forcible detachment or separation. **2.** A sudden removal of land caused by change in a river's course or by flood. • Land removed by avulsion remains the property of the original owner. Cf. ALLUVION; ACCRETION; DELICTION; EROSION. **3.** A tearing away of a body part surgically or accidentally. — **avulse,** *vb.*

award, *n.* A final judgment or decision, esp. one by an arbitrator or by a jury assessing damages.

award, *vb.* To grant by formal process or by judicial decree.

AWOL. *abbr.* Absent without leave; missing without notice or permission.

axiom (**ak**-see-əm), *n.* An established principle that is universally accepted within a given framework of reasoning or thinking <"innocent until proven guilty" is an age-old axiom of criminal law>. — **axiomatic** (ak-see-ə-**mat**-ik), *adj.*

B

Baby Doe. A generic pseudonym for a very young child involved in litigation, esp. in the context of medical care.

Baby FTC Act. A state statute that, like the Federal Trade Commission Act, outlaws deceptive and unfair trade practices.

BAC. *abbr.* BLOOD ALCOHOL CONTENT.

back, *vb.* **1.** To indorse; to sign the back of an instrument. **2.** To sign so as to show acceptance or approval. **3.** To sign so as to indicate financial responsibility for.

backdate, *vb.* **1.** To put a date earlier than the actual date on (something, as an instrument); ANTEDATE (1). • Under UCC § 3–113(a), backdating does not affect an instrument's negotiability. Cf. POSTDATE. **2.** To make (something) retroactively valid.

backing. Endorsement, esp. of a warrant by a magistrate.

back lands. Generally, lands lying away from — not next to — a highway or a watercourse.

bad character. A person's predilection toward evil. • In limited circumstances, proof of bad character may be introduced into evidence to discredit a witness. Fed. R. Evid. 608, 609. See *character evidence* under EVIDENCE.

bad check. See CHECK.

bad faith, *n.* Dishonesty of belief or purpose. — **bad-faith,** *adj.* Cf. GOOD FAITH.

badge of fraud. A circumstance that the courts generally interpret as a reliable indicator that a party to a transaction was trying to hinder or defraud the other party, such as a transfer in anticipation of litigation, a transaction outside the usual course of business, or a false statement. See FRAUD.

badge of slavery. 1. Strictly, a legal disability suffered by a slave, such as the inability to vote or to own property. **2.** Broadly, any act of racial discrimination — public or private — that Congress can prohibit under the 13th Amendment.

badger game. A scheme to extort money or some other benefit by arranging to catch someone in a compromising position and then threatening to make that person's behavior public.

bad-man theory. The jurisprudential doctrine or belief that a bad person's view of the law represents the best test of what the law actually is because that person will carefully calculate precisely what the rules allow and operate up to the rules' limits. • This theory was first espoused by Oliver Wendell Holmes in his essay *The Path of the Law*, 10 Harv. L. Rev. 457 (1897). See LEGAL REALISM.

bad motive. See MOTIVE.

bad title. **1.** See *defective title* under TITLE (2). **2.** See *unmarketable title* under TITLE (2).

bagman. A person who collects and distributes illegally obtained money; esp., an intermediary who collects a bribe for a public official.

bail, *n.* **1.** A security such as cash or a bond; esp., security required by a court for the release of a prisoner who must appear at a future time. Cf. RECOGNIZANCE.

excessive bail. Bail that is unreasonably high considering both the offense with which the accused is charged and the risk that the accused will not appear for trial. • The Eighth Amendment prohibits excessive bail.

2. Release of a prisoner on security for a future appearance. **3.** One or more sureties for a criminal defendant. See BAILER (1).

bail, *vb.* **1.** To obtain the release of (oneself or another) by providing security for future appearance. **2.** To release (a person) after receiving such security. **3.** To place (personal property) in someone else's charge or trust. — **bailable,** *adj.*

bailable offense. See OFFENSE.

bail bond. See BOND (2).

bailee. A person who receives personal property from another as a bailment. See BAILMENT.

bailer. **1.** One who provides bail as a surety for a criminal defendant's release. **2.** BAILOR (1).

bailiff. **1.** A court officer who maintains order during court proceedings. **2.** A sheriff's officer who executes writs and serves processes.

bail-jumping, *n.* The criminal offense of defaulting on one's bail. See Model Penal Code § 242.8. — **bail-jumper,** *n.* See JUMP BAIL.

bailment. **1.** A delivery of personal property by one person (the *bailor*) to another (the *bailee*) who holds the property for a certain purpose under an express or implied-in-fact contract. • Unlike a sale or gift of personal property, a bailment involves a change in possession but not in title. Cf. PAWN.

actual bailment. A bailment that arises from an actual or constructive delivery of property to the bailee.

bailment for hire. A bailment for which the bailee is compensated, as when one leaves a car with a parking attendant.

bailment for mutual benefit. A bailment for which the bailee is compensated and from which the bailor receives some additional benefit, as when one leaves a car with a parking attendant who will also wash the car while it is parked.

constructive bailment. A bailment that arises when the law imposes an obligation on a possessor of personal property to return the property to its rightful owner, as with an involuntary bailment.

gratuitous bailment. A bailment for which the bailee receives no compensation, as when one borrows a friend's car. • A gratuitous bailee is liable for loss of the property only if the loss is caused by the bailee's gross negligence.

involuntary bailment. A bailment that arises when a person accidentally, but without any negligence, leaves personal property in another's possession. • An involuntary bailee who refuses to return the property to the owner can be liable for conversion. See *abandoned property*, *lost property*, *mislaid property* under PROPERTY.

2. The personal property delivered by the bailor to the bailee. **3.** The contract or legal relation resulting from such a delivery. **4.** The act of posting bail for a criminal defendant. **5.** The documentation for the posting of bail for a criminal defendant.

bailor (bay-**lor** *or* **bay**-lər). **1.** A person who delivers personal property to another as a bailment. **2.** BAILER (1).

bail-point scale. A system for determining a criminal defendant's eligibility for bail, whereby the defendant either will be released on personal recognizance or will have a bail amount set according to the total number of points given, based on the defendant's background and behavior.

bail revocation. The court's cancellation of bail granted previously to a criminal defendant.

bait and switch. A sales practice whereby a merchant advertises a low-priced product to lure customers into the store only to induce them to buy a higher-priced product. • Most states prohibit the bait and switch when the original product is not actually available as advertised.

balance, *vb.* **1.** To compute the difference between the debits and credits of (an account). **2.** To equalize in number, force, or effect; to bring into proportion. **3.** To measure competing interests and offset them appropriately. — **balance,** *n.*

balance of sentence suspended. A sentencing disposition in which a criminal defendant is sentenced to jail but credited with the time already served before trial, resulting in a suspension of the remaining sentence and release of the defendant from custody. Cf. SENTENCED TO TIME SERVED.

balance sheet. A statement of an entity's current financial position, disclosing the value of the entity's assets, liabilities, and owners' equity. Cf. INCOME STATEMENT.

balancing test. A judicial doctrine, used esp. in constitutional law, whereby a court measures competing interests — as between individual rights and governmental powers, or between state authority and federal supremacy — and decides which interest should prevail.

ballistics. **1.** The science of the motion of projectiles, such as bullets. **2.** The study of a weapon's firing characteristics, esp. as used in criminal cases to determine a gun's firing capacity and whether a particular gun fired a given bullet.

balloon payment. See PAYMENT.

B and E. *abbr.* Breaking and entering. See BURGLARY (2).

bank. 1. A financial establishment for the deposit, loan, exchange, or issue of money and for the transmission of funds; esp., a member of the Federal Reserve System. • Under securities law, a bank includes any banking institution, whether or not incorporated, doing business under federal or state law, if a substantial portion of the institution's business consists of receiving deposits or exercising fiduciary powers similar to those permitted to national banks and if the institution is supervised and examined by a state or federal banking authority; or a receiver, conservator, or other liquidating agent of any of the above institutions. 15 USCA § 78c(a)(6). **2.** The office in which such an establishment conducts transactions.

collecting bank. In the check-collection process, any bank handling an item for collection, except for the payor bank or the depository bank. UCC § 4–105(5).

commercial bank. A bank authorized to receive both demand and time deposits, to engage in trust services, to issue letters of credit, to rent time-deposit boxes, and to provide similar services.

depositary bank. The first bank to which an item is transferred for collection. UCC § 4–105(2).

drawee bank. See *payor bank.*

intermediary bank. A bank to which an item is transferred in the course of collection, even though the bank is not the depositary or payor bank. UCC § 4–105(4).

payor bank. A bank that is requested to pay the amount of a negotiable instrument and, on the bank's acceptance, is obliged to pay that amount; a bank by which an item is payable as drawn or accepted. UCC § 4–105(3).

presenting bank. A nonpayor bank that presents a negotiable instrument for payment. UCC § 4–105.

savings-and-loan bank. See SAVINGS-AND-LOAN ASSOCIATION.

savings bank. A bank that receives deposits, pays interest on them, and makes certain types of loans, but does not provide checking services.

bank, *vb.* **1.** To keep money at <he banks at the downtown branch>. **2.** To deposit (funds) in a bank <she banked the prize money yesterday>. **3.** *Slang.* To loan money to facilitate (a transaction) <who banked the deal?>. • The lender's consideration usually consists of a fee or an interest in the property involved in the transaction.

bank draft. See DRAFT.

banking day. 1. Banking hours on a day when a bank is open to the public for carrying on substantially all its banking functions. • Typically, if the bookkeeping and loan departments are closed by a certain hour, the remainder of that day is not part of that bank's banking day. **2.** A day on which banks are open for banking business.

Bankr. Rep. *abbr.* Bankruptcy Reporter.

bankrupt, *n.* **1.** A person who cannot meet current financial obligations; an insolvent person. **2.** DEBTOR (2). — **bankrupt,** *adj.* — **bankrupt,** *vb.*

bankruptcy. 1. The statutory procedure, usu. triggered by insolvency, by which a person is relieved of most debts and undergoes a judicially supervised reorganization or liquidation for the benefit of that person's creditors. • For various types of bankruptcy under federal law, see the entries at CHAPTER.

involuntary bankruptcy. A bankruptcy proceeding initiated by creditors (usu. three or more) to force the debtor to declare bankruptcy or be legally declared bankrupt. 11 USCA § 303(b).

voluntary bankruptcy. A bankruptcy proceeding initiated by the debtor. 11 USCA § 301.

2. The fact of being financially unable to pay one's debts and meet one's obligations; insolvency. **3.** The status of a party who has declared bankruptcy under a bankruptcy statute. **4.** The fact of having declared bankruptcy under a bankruptcy statute. **5.** The field of law dealing with the rights and entitlements of debtors and creditors in bankruptcy.

Bankruptcy Act. *Hist.* The Bankruptcy Act of 1898, which governed bankruptcy cases filed before October 1, 1979.

Bankruptcy Code. The Bankruptcy Reform Act of 1978 (as amended and codified in 11 USCA), which governs bankruptcy cases filed on or after October 1, 1979.

Bankruptcy Court. 1. A U.S. district court that is exclusively concerned with administering bankruptcy proceedings. **2.** The bankruptcy judges within a given district, considered as making up a court that is a subunit of a U.S. district court.

bankruptcy fraud. See FRAUD.

bankruptcy judge. A judicial officer appointed by a U.S. Court of Appeals to preside over a bankruptcy court in a designated judicial district for a term of 14 years. • A bankruptcy judge is called an Article II judge. 28 USCA §§ 151 et seq. See ARTICLE II JUDGE.

bankruptcy plan. A detailed program of action formulated by a debtor or its creditors to govern the debtor's rehabilitation, continued operation or liquidation, and payment of debts. • The bankruptcy court and creditors must approve the plan before it is implemented.

bankruptcy proceeding. 1. BANKRUPTCY (1). **2.** Any judicial or procedural action (such as a hearing) related to a bankruptcy.

bankruptcy trustee. The person appointed by the U.S. Trustee and approved by the bankruptcy court to take charge of and administer the debtor's estate during bankruptcy proceedings.

Bank Secrecy Act. A federal statute that requires banks and other financial institutions to maintain records of customers' transactions and to report certain domestic and foreign transactions. • This act, passed by Congress in 1970, is designed to help the federal government in criminal, tax, and other regulatory investigations. 12 USCA § 1829b; 31 USCA § 5311.

bank-statement rule. *Commercial law.* The principle that if a bank customer fails to examine a bank statement within a reasonable time (usu. no more than a year for a forged drawer's signature or alteration, and no more than three years for a forged indorsement), the customer is precluded from complaining about a forgery or material alteration. UCC § 4–406.

bar, *n.* **1.** In a courtroom, the railing that separates the front area, where the judge, court personnel, lawyers, and witnesses conduct court business, from the back area, which provides seats for observers; by extension, a similar railing in a legislative assembly. **2.** The whole body of lawyers qualified to practice in a given court or jurisdiction; the legal profession, or an organized subset of it. See BAR ASSOCIATION. **3.** A particular court or system of courts. **4.** BAR EXAMINATION. **5.** A preventive barrier to or the destruction of a legal action or claim; the effect of a judgment for the defendant. Cf. MERGER (5). **6.** A plea arresting a lawsuit or legal claim. See PLEA IN BAR.

bar, *vb.* To prevent, esp. by legal objection.

bar association. An organization of members of the legal profession. See BAR (2).

integrated bar. A bar association in which membership is a statutory requirement for the practice of law.

specialty bar. A voluntary bar association for lawyers with special interests, specific backgrounds, or common practices.

state bar association. An association or group of attorneys that have been admitted to practice law in a given state. • State bar associations are usually created by statute, and membership is often mandatory for those who practice law in the state. Unlike voluntary, professional-development bar associations such as the American Bar Association, state bar associations often have the authority to regulate the legal profession, by undertaking such matters as disciplining attorneys and bringing lawsuits against those who participate in the unauthorized practice of law.

voluntary bar. A bar association that lawyers need not join to practice law.

barebones indictment. See INDICTMENT.

bare license. See LICENSE.

bare licensee. See LICENSEE.

bar examination. A written test that a person must pass before being licensed to practice law. • The content and format of bar examinations vary from state to state.

Multistate Bar Examination. A part of every state's bar examination given in the form of a multiple-choice test covering broad legal subjects, including constitutional law, contracts, criminal law, evidence, property, and torts. — Abbr. MBE.

bar examiner. One appointed by the state to test applicants (usu. law graduates) by preparing and administering the bar examination.

bargain, *n.* An agreement between parties for the exchange of promises or performances. • A bargain is not necessarily a contract because the consideration may be insufficient or the transaction may be illegal. —**bargain,** *vb.*

bargain and sale. A written agreement for the sale of land whereby the buyer would give valuable consideration (recited in the agreement) without having to enter the land and perform livery of seisin, so that the parties equitably "raised a use" in the buyer. • The result of the bargain and sale was to leave the legal estate in fee simple in the seller and to create an equitable estate in fee simple in the buyer.

bargain-and-sale deed. See DEED.

bargain sale. A sale of property for less than its fair market value. • For tax purposes, the difference between the sale price and the fair market value must be taken into account. And bargain sales between family members may lead to gift-tax consequences.

bargain theory of consideration. The theory that a promise in exchange for a promise is sufficient consideration for a contract. • This theory underlies all bilateral contracts. See *bilateral contract* under CONTRACT.

barratry (bar-ə-tree *or* **bair-**), *n.* Vexatious incitement to litigation, esp. by soliciting potential legal clients. • Barratry is a crime in most jurisdictions. — **barratrous (bar**-ə-trəs), *adj.*

barring of entail. The freeing of an estate from the limitations imposed by an entail and permitting its free disposition. • This was anciently done by means of a fine or common recovery, but later by deed in which the tenant and next heir join. See ENTAIL.

barter, *n.* The exchange of one commodity for another without the use of money. — **barter,** *vb.*

base fee. See FEE (2).

basement court. *Slang.* A low-level court of limited jurisdiction, such as a police court, traffic court, municipal court, or small-claims court.

basic-form policy. See INSURANCE POLICY.

basis. 1. A fundamental principle; an underlying condition. **2.** *Tax.* The value assigned to a taxpayer's investment in property and used primarily for computing gain or loss from a transfer of the property. • When the assigned value represents the cost of acquiring the property, it is also called *cost basis*. Pl. **bases.**

adjusted basis. Basis increased by capital improvements and decreased by depreciation deductions.

adjusted cost basis. Basis resulting from the original cost of an item plus capital additions minus depreciation deductions.

carryover basis. The basis of property transferred by gift or in trust, equaling the transferor's basis.

stepped-up basis. The basis of property transferred by inheritance. • Stepped-up basis equals the fair market value of property on the date of the decedent's death (or on the alternate valuation date).

substituted basis. **1.** The basis of property transferred in a tax-free exchange or other specified transaction. **2.** See *carryover basis*.

bastard. 1. See *illegitimate child* under CHILD. **2.** A child born to a married woman whose husband could not be or is otherwise proved not to be the father. • Because the word is most commonly used as a slur, its use in family-law contexts is much in decline.

batable ground (bay-tə-bəl). Land of uncertain ownership.

***Batson* challenge.** See CHALLENGE (1).

battered-child syndrome. *Family law.* A constellation of medical and psychological conditions of a child who has suffered continuing injuries that could not be accidental and are therefore presumed to have been inflicted by someone close to the child, usu. a caregiver.

battered-woman syndrome. The medical and psychological condition of a woman who has suffered physical, sexual, or emotional abuse at the hands of a spouse or partner. • This syndrome is sometimes proposed as a defense to justify a woman's killing of a man.

battery, *n.* **1.** *Criminal law.* The use of force against another, resulting in harmful or offensive contact. • Battery is a misdemeanor under most modern statutes.

aggravated battery. A criminal battery accompanied by circumstances that make it more severe, such as the use of a deadly weapon or the fact that the battery resulted in serious bodily harm.

sexual battery. The forced penetration of or contact with another's sexual organs or the sexual organs of the perpetrator. See RAPE.

simple battery. A criminal battery not accompanied by aggravating circumstances and not resulting in serious bodily harm.

2. *Torts.* An intentional and offensive touching of another without lawful justification. — **batter,** *vb.* Cf. ASSAULT.

battle of the forms. The conflict between the terms of standard forms exchanged between a buyer and a seller during contract negotiations. • UCC § 2–207 attempts to resolve battles of the forms by abandoning the common-law requirement of mirror-image acceptance and providing that an acceptance with additional terms is normally valid. See MIRROR-IMAGE RULE.

bearer. One who possesses a negotiable instrument marked "payable to bearer" or indorsed in blank.

bearer bond. See BOND (3).

before the fact. Prior to an event of legal significance.

belief–action distinction. *Constitutional law.* In First Amendment law, the Supreme Court's distinction between allowing a person to follow any chosen belief and allowing the state to intervene if necessary to protect others from the practices of that belief.

below, *adj. & adv.* (Of a lower court) having heard the case at issue; having the power to hear the case at issue. Cf. ABOVE.

below-the-line, *adj.* (Of a deduction) taken after calculating adjusted gross income and before calculating taxable income. Cf. ABOVE-THE-LINE.

bench. 1. The raised area occupied by the judge in a courtroom. **2.** The court considered in its official capacity. **3.** Judges collectively. **4.** The judges of a particular court.

bench memo. 1. A short brief submitted by a lawyer to a trial judge, often at the judge's request. **2.** A legal memorandum prepared by an appellate judge's law clerk to help the judge in preparing for oral argument and perhaps in drafting an opinion. • A trial-court judge may similarly assign a bench memo to a law clerk, for use in preparing for hearing or trial or in drafting an opinion.

bench probation. See PROBATION.

bench ruling. An oral ruling issued by a judge from the bench.

bench trial. See TRIAL.

bench warrant. See WARRANT.

beneficial, *adj.* **1.** Favorable; producing benefits. **2.** Consisting in a right that derives from something other than legal title.

beneficial enjoyment. See ENJOYMENT.

beneficial interest. A right or expectancy in something (such as a trust or an estate), as opposed to legal title to that thing. • For example, a person with a beneficial interest in a trust receives income from the trust but does not hold legal title to the trust property.

beneficial owner. See OWNER.

beneficial ownership. See OWNERSHIP.

beneficial power. See POWER.

beneficiary (ben-ə-**fish**-ee-er-ee *or* ben-ə-**fish**-ə-ree), *n.* A person who is designated to benefit from an appointment, disposition, or assignment (as in a will, insurance policy, etc.); one designated to receive something as a result of a legal arrangement or instrument. — **beneficiary,** *adj.*

contingent beneficiary. **1.** A person designated in a life-insurance policy to receive the proceeds if the primary beneficiary is unable to do so. **2.** A person designated by the testator to receive a gift if the primary beneficiary is unable or unwilling to take the gift.

creditor beneficiary. A third-party beneficiary who is owed a debt that is to be satisfied by performing the contract.

donee beneficiary. A third-party beneficiary who is intended to receive the benefit of the contract's performance as a gift from the promisee.

incidental beneficiary. A third-party beneficiary who is not intended to benefit from a contract and thus does not acquire rights under the contract. Cf. *intended beneficiary.*

income beneficiary. A person entitled to income from property; esp., a person entitled to receive trust income.

intended beneficiary. A third-party beneficiary who is intended to benefit from a contract and thus acquires rights under the contract as well as the ability to enforce the contract once those rights have vested. Cf. *incidental beneficiary.*

primary beneficiary. The person designated in a life-insurance policy to receive the proceeds when the insured dies.

third-party beneficiary. A person who, though not a party to a contract, stands to benefit from the contract's performance. • For example, if Ann and Bob agree to a contract under which Bob will render some performance to Chris, then Chris is a third-party beneficiary.

benefit, *n.* **1.** Advantage; privilege. **2.** Profit or gain.

fringe benefit. A benefit (other than direct salary or compensation) received by an employee from an employer, such as insurance, a company car, or a tuition allowance.

general benefit. Eminent domain. The whole community's benefit as a result of a taking. • It cannot be considered to reduce the compensation that is due the condemnee.

pecuniary benefit. A benefit capable of monetary valuation.

special benefit. Eminent domain. A benefit that accrues to the owner of the land in question and not to any others. • Any special benefits justify a reduction in the amount of damages payable to the owner of land that is partially taken by the government during a public project.

3. Financial assistance that is received from an employer, insurance, or a public program (such as social security) in time of sickness, disability, or unemployment. — **benefit,** *vb.*

benefit-of-the-bargain damages. See DAMAGES.

benefit-of-the-bargain rule. 1. The principle that a party who breaches a contract must provide the aggrieved party everything the aggrieved party would have received, including profits, had the contract been fully performed. **2.** The principle that a defrauded buyer may recover from the seller as damages the difference between the misrepresented value of the property and the actual value received. Cf. OUT-OF-POCKET RULE.

bequeath (bə-**kweeth**), *vb.* To give property (usu. personal property) by will.

bequest (bə-**kwest**), *n.* **1.** The act of giving property (usu. personal property) by will. **2.** Property (usu. personal property other than money) disposed of in a will. Cf. DEVISE; LEGACY.

charitable bequest. A bequest given to a philanthropic organization. See CHARITABLE ORGANIZATION.

conditional bequest. A bequest whose effectiveness or continuation depends on the occurrence or nonoccurrence of some particular event.

demonstrative bequest. A bequest that, by its terms, must be paid out of a specific source, such as a stock fund.

executory bequest. A bequest of a future, deferred, or contingent interest in personalty.

general bequest. **1.** A bequest of a general benefit, rather than a particular asset, such as a gift of money or a gift of all the testator's stocks. **2.** A bequest payable out of the general assets of the estate.

pecuniary bequest. A testamentary gift of money; a legacy.

residuary bequest. A bequest of the remainder of the testator's estate, after the payment of the debts, legacies, and specific bequests.

specific bequest. A bequest of a specific or unique item of property, such as any real estate or a particular piece of furniture.

***Berry* rule.** The doctrine that a defendant seeking a new trial on grounds of newly discovered evidence must show that (1) the evidence is newly discovered and was unknown to the defendant at the time of trial; (2) the evidence is material rather than merely cumulative or impeaching; (3) the evidence will probably produce an acquittal; and (4) the failure to learn of the evidence was not due to the defendant's lack of diligence. *Berry v. State*, 10 Ga. 511 (1851).

best efforts. Diligent attempts to carry out an obligation. • As a standard, a best-efforts obligation is stronger than a good-faith obligation. Cf. *due diligence* (1) under DILIGENCE; GOOD FAITH.

best evidence. See EVIDENCE.

best-evidence rule. The evidentiary rule providing that, to prove the contents of a writing (or a recording or photograph), a party must produce the original writing (or a mechanical, electronic, or other familiar duplicate, such as a photocopy) unless it is unavailable, in which case secondary evidence — the testimony of the drafter or a person who read the document — may be admitted. Fed. R. Evid. 1001–1004.

bestiality (bes-chee-**al**-ə-tee). Sexual activity between a human and an animal. • Some authorities restrict the term to copulation between a human and an animal of the opposite sex. See SODOMY.

bestow, *vb.* To convey as a gift <bestow an honor on another>. —**bestowal,** *n.*

betterment. An improvement that increases the value of real property. See IMPROVEMENT.

betterment act. A statute requiring a landowner to compensate an occupant who improves the land under a mistaken belief that the occupant is the real owner. • The compensation usually equals the increase in the land's value generated by the improvements.

beyond seas. (Of a person) being absent from a jurisdiction or nation. • Some jurisdictions toll the statute of limitations during a defendant's absence.

BFOQ. *abbr.* BONA FIDE OCCUPATIONAL QUALIFICATION.

BFP. See *bona fide purchaser* under PURCHASER (1).

bias, *n.* Inclination; prejudice. — **bias,** *vb.* — **biased,** *adj.*

bid, *n.* **1.** A buyer's offer to pay a specified price for something that may or may not be for sale. **2.** A submitted price at which one will perform work or supply goods. — **bid,** *vb.* See BID-SHOPPING.

firm bid. A bid that, by its terms, remains open and binding until accepted or rejected. • A firm bid usually contains no unusual conditions that might defeat acceptance.

open bid. A bid that the bidder may alter after submission so as to meet competing bids.

sealed bid. A bid that is not disclosed until all submitted bids are opened and considered simultaneously.

bidding up. The act or practice of raising the price for an auction item by making a series of progressively higher bids. • *Bidding up* is unlawful if the bids are made collusively by persons with an interest in raising the bids. Cf. BY-BIDDING.

bid-shopping. A general contractor's effort — after being awarded a contract — to reduce its own costs by finding a subcontractor that will submit a lower bid than that used in calculating the total contract price. • If a lower bid is secured, the general contractor will receive a windfall profit because the savings are usually not passed on to the property owner. The subcontractor whose bid is used in the initial proposal can seek to avoid bid-shopping by insisting that it be irrevocably named in the contract as the project's subcontractor.

biennial session. See SESSION.

bifurcated trial. See TRIAL.

bigamy, *n.* The act of marrying one person while legally married to another. • Bigamy is a criminal offense if it is committed knowingly. See Model Penal Code § 230.1(1). — **bigamous (big-ə-məs),** *adj.* — **bigamist,** *n.* Cf. POLYGAMY; MONOGAMY.

bilateral, *adj.* Affecting or obligating both parties. See RECIPROCAL.

bilateral act. See ACT.

bilateral contract. See CONTRACT.

bill, *n.* **1.** A formal written complaint, such as a court paper requesting some specific action for reasons alleged. **2.** An equitable pleading by which a claimant brings a claim in a court of equity. • Before the merger of law and equity, the bill in equity was analogous to a declaration in law. See DECLARATION (7).

bill of certiorari. A bill in equity seeking removal of an action to a higher court. See CERTIORARI.

bill of costs. A certified, itemized statement of the amount of costs owed by one litigant to another.

bill of discovery. A bill in equity seeking disclosure of facts within the adverse party's knowledge. See DISCOVERY.

bill of exceptions. **1.** A formal written statement — signed by the trial judge and presented to the appellate court — of a party's objections or exceptions taken during trial and the grounds on which they are founded. • These bills have largely been replaced by straight appeals under the Federal Rules of Civil Procedure. See EXCEPTION (1). **2.** In some jurisdictions, a record made to preserve error after the judge has excluded evidence.

bill of peace. An equitable bill filed by one who is threatened with multiple suits involving the same right, or with recurrent suits on the same right, asking the court to determine the question once and for all, and to enjoin the plaintiffs from proceeding with the threatened litigation.

bill of review. A bill in equity requesting that a court reverse or revise a prior decree.

bill of revivor. A bill filed for the purpose of reviving and continuing a suit in equity when there has been an abatement of the suit before final consummation. • The most common cause of such an abatement is the death of either the plaintiff or the defendant.

bill to perpetuate testimony. An original bill to preserve the testimony of a material witness who may die or leave the jurisdiction before a suit is commenced, or to prevent or avoid future litigation.

3. A legislative proposal offered for debate before its enactment.

appropriation bill. A bill that authorizes governmental expenditures. • The federal government cannot spend money unless Congress has appropriated the funds. U.S. Const. art. I, § 9, cl. 7. See APPROPRIATION (2), (3).

engrossed bill. A bill passed by one house of the legislature.

enrolled bill. A bill passed by both houses of the legislature and signed by their presiding officers. See ENROLLED-BILL RULE.

house bill. (*often cap.*) A legislative bill being considered by a house of representatives. — Abbr. H.B.

omnibus bill. **1.** A single bill containing various distinct matters, usu. drafted in this way to force the executive either to accept all the unrelated minor provisions or to veto the major provision. **2.** A bill that deals with all proposals relating to a particular subject, such as an "omnibus judgeship bill" covering all proposals for new judgeships or an "omnibus crime bill" dealing with different subjects such as new crimes and grants to states for crime control.

public bill. A bill relating to public policy in the whole community.

revenue bill. A bill that levies or raises taxes. • Federal revenue bills must originate in the House of Representatives. U.S. Const. art. I, § 7, cl. 1.

senate bill. (*often cap.*) A legislative bill being considered by a senate. — Abbr. S.B.

4. An enacted statute. **5.** An itemized list of charges; an invoice. **6.** A bill of exchange; a draft. See DRAFT (1). **7.** A formal document or note; an instrument. **8.** A piece of paper money. **9.** A promissory note.

billable hour. A unit of time used by an attorney or paralegal to account for work performed and chargeable to a client. • Billable hours are usually divided into quarters or tenths of an hour.

billable time. An attorney's or paralegal's time that is chargeable to a client. Cf. NONBILLABLE TIME.

bill of attainder. 1. *Archaic.* A special legislative act that imposes a death sentence on a person without a trial. **2.** A special legislative act prescribing punishment, without a trial, for a specific person or group. • Bills of attainder are prohibited by the U.S. Constitution (art. I, § 9, cl. 3; art. I, § 10, cl. 1). See ATTAINDER; BILL OF PAINS AND PENALTIES.

bill of certiorari. See BILL (2).

bill of costs. See BILL (2).

bill of discovery. See BILL (2).

bill of exceptions. See BILL (2).

bill of indictment. An instrument presented to a grand jury for the jury's determination whether sufficient evidence exists to formally charge the accused with a crime. See INDICTMENT; NO BILL; TRUE BILL.

bill of lading (layd-ing). A document of title acknowledging the receipt of goods by a carrier or by the shipper's agent; a document that indicates the receipt of goods for shipment and that is issued by a person engaged in the business of transporting or forwarding goods. • An airbill is usually included within the definition of the term. — Abbr. B/L.

bill of pains and penalties. A legislative act that, though similar to a bill of attainder, prescribes punishment less severe than capital punishment. • Bills of pains and penalties are included within the U.S. Constitution's ban of bills of attainder. U.S. Const. art I, § 9.

bill of particulars. A formal, detailed statement of the claims or charges brought by a plaintiff or a prosecutor, usu. filed in response to the defendant's request for a more specific complaint. See MOTION FOR MORE DEFINITE STATEMENT.

bill of peace. See BILL (2).

bill of review. See BILL (2).

bill of revivor. See BILL (2).

bill of rights. (*usu. cap.*) A section or addendum, usu. in a constitution, defining the situations in which a politically organized society will permit free, spontaneous, and individual activity, and guaranteeing that governmental powers will not be used in certain ways; esp., the first ten amendments to the U.S. Constitution.

bill of sale. An instrument for the conveyance of title to personal property, absolutely or by way of security. Cf. DEED.

bill to perpetuate testimony. See BILL (2).

bind, *vb.* To impose one or more legal duties on (a person or institution). — **binding,** *adj.* — **bindingness,** *n.*

binder. 1. A document in which the buyer and the seller of real property declare their common intention to bring about a transfer of ownership, usu. accompanied by the buyer's initial payment. **2.** Loosely, the buyer's initial payment in the sale of real property. Cf. EARNEST MONEY. **3.** An insurer's memorandum giving the insured temporary coverage while the application for an insurance policy is being processed or while the formal policy is being prepared.

binding, *adj.* **1.** (Of an agreement) that binds. **2.** (Of an order) that requires obedience.

binding agreement. See AGREEMENT.

binding precedent. See PRECEDENT.

bind over, *vb.* **1.** To put (a person) under a bond or other legal obligation to do something, esp. to appear in court. **2.** To hold (a person) for trial; to turn (a defendant) over to a sheriff or warden for imprisonment pending further judicial action. — **binding over,** *n.* — **bindover,** *adj.*

biological mother. See MOTHER.

bipartite, *adj.* (Of an instrument) executed in two parts by both parties.

birth mother. See MOTHER.

birth records. Statistical data kept by a governmental entity concerning people's birthdates, birthplaces, and parentage.

***Bivens* action.** A lawsuit brought to redress a federal official's violation of a constitutional right. *Bivens v. Six Unknown Named Agents of the Federal Bureau of Narcotics*, 403 U.S. 388, 91 S.Ct. 1999 (1971). • A *Bivens* action allows federal officials to be sued in a manner similar to that set forth at 42 USCA § 1983 for state officials who violate a person's constitutional rights under color of state law.

B/L. *abbr.* BILL OF LADING.

Blackacre. A fictitious tract of land used in legal discourse (esp. law-school hypotheticals) to discuss real-property issues. • When another tract of land is needed in a hypothetical, it is often termed "Whiteacre."

blackletter law. One or more legal principles that are old, fundamental, and well settled. • The term refers to the law printed in books set in Gothic type, which is very bold and black.

blacklist, *vb.* To put the name of (a person) on a list of those who are to be boycotted or punished. — **blacklist,** *n.*

blackmail, *n.* A threatening demand made without justification; EXTORTION. — **blackmail,** *vb.* Cf. GRAYMAIL; GREENMAIL; FEEMAIL.

blackmail suit. See SUIT.

blank check. See CHECK.

blanket policy. See INSURANCE POLICY.

blanket search warrant. See SEARCH WARRANT.

blank indorsement. See INDORSEMENT.

blasphemy (**blas**-fə-mee), *n.* Irreverence toward God, religion, a religious icon, or something else considered sacred. • Blasphemy was a crime at common law and remains so in some U.S. jurisdictions, but it is rarely if ever enforced because of its questionable constitutionality under the First Amendment. — **blaspheme** (blas-**feem** *or* **blas**-feem), *vb.* — **blasphemous** (**blas**-fə-məs), *adj.* — **blasphemer** (**blas**-fee-mər), *n.*

blended family. See FAMILY.

blending clause. A provision in a will disposing of both the testator's own property and the property over which the testator has a power of appointment, so that the two types of property are treated as a unit.

blind plea. See PLEA (1).

blind selling. The sale of goods without giving a buyer the opportunity to examine them.

blind trust. See TRUST.

bloc. A group of persons or countries aligned with a common interest or purpose, even if only temporarily <voting bloc>.

block, *n.* **1.** A municipal area enclosed by streets. See LOT (1). **2.** A quantity of things bought or sold as a unit.

blockbusting. The act or practice, usu. by a real-estate broker, of persuading one or more property owners to sell their property quickly, and often at a loss, to avoid an imminent influx of minority groups. • Blockbusting is illegal in many states.

blood. A relationship between persons arising by descent from a common ancestor. See RELATIVE.

full blood. The relationship existing between persons having the same two parents; unmixed ancestry.

half blood. The relationship existing between persons having the same father or mother, but not both parents in common.

mixed blood. The relationship between persons whose ancestors are of different races or nationalities.

blood alcohol content. The concentration of alcohol in one's bloodstream, expressed as a percentage. • Blood alcohol content is used to determine whether a person is legally intoxicated, esp. under a driving-while-intoxicated law. — Abbr. BAC. See DRIVING UNDER THE INFLUENCE; DRIVING WHILE INTOXICATED.

blood-grouping test. A test used in paternity and illegitimacy cases to determine whether a particular man could be the father of a child. • The test does not establish paternity; rather, it eliminates men who could not be the father. See PATERNITY TEST.

blood relative. See RELATIVE.

Blue Book. 1. A compilation of session laws. See SESSION LAWS (2). **2.** A volume formerly published to give parallel citation tables for a volume in the National Reporter System.

Bluebook. The citation guide — formerly titled *A Uniform System of Citation* — that is generally considered the authoritative reference for American legal citations. • The book's complete title is *The Bluebook: A Uniform System of Citation*. It is compiled by the editors of the *Columbia Law Review*, the *Harvard Law Review*, the *University of Pennsylvania Law Review*, and *The Yale Law Journal*.

blue law. A statute regulating or prohibiting commercial activity on Sundays. • Although blue laws were formerly common, they have declined since the 1980s, when many courts held them invalid because of their origin in religion (i.e., Sunday being the Christian Sabbath). Blue laws usually pass constitutional challenge if they are enacted to support a nonreligious purpose, such as a day of rest for workers.

blue-pencil test. A judicial standard for deciding whether to invalidate the whole contract or only the offending words. • Under this standard, only the offending words are invalidated if it would be possible to delete them simply by running a blue pencil through them, as opposed to changing, adding, or rearranging words.

blue-ribbon jury. See JURY.

blue-sky, *vb.* To approve (the sale of securities) in accordance with blue-sky laws.

blue-sky, *adj.* (Of a security) having little value.

blue-sky law. A state statute establishing standards for offering and selling securities, the purpose being to protect citizens from investing in fraudulent schemes or unsuitable companies.

board-certified, *adj.* (Of a professional) recognized by an official body as a specialist in a given field of law or medicine. See BOARD OF LEGAL SPECIALIZATION.

board of directors. 1. The governing body of a corporation, elected by the shareholders to establish corporate policy, appoint executive officers, and make major business and financial decisions. See DIRECTOR. **2.** The governing body of a partnership, association, or other unincorporated group.

Board of Immigration Appeals. The highest administrative tribunal for matters arising under U.S. immigration law, charged with hearing appeals from the Immigration and Naturalization Service.

board of legal specialization. A body, usu. an arm of a state bar association, that certifies qualified lawyers as specialists within a given field. • Typically, to qualify as a specialist, a lawyer must meet a specified level of experience, pass an examination, and provide favorable recommendations from peers.

board of pardons. A state agency, of which the governor is usu. a member, authorized to pardon persons convicted of crimes.

bodily harm. See HARM.

bodily injury. See INJURY.

body. 1. The main part of a written instrument. **2.** A collection of laws. See CORPUS JURIS. **3.** An artificial person created by a legal authority. See CORPORATION. **4.** An aggregate of individuals or groups.

body politic. A group of people regarded in a political (rather than private) sense and organized under a single governmental authority.

boilerplate, *n.* **1.** Ready-made or all-purpose language that will fit in a variety of documents. **2.** Fixed or standardized contractual language that the proposing party views as relatively nonnegotiable. —**boilerplate,** *adj.*

boiler-room transaction. *Slang.* A high-pressure telephone sales pitch, often of a fraudulent nature.

bolster, *vb.* To enhance (unimpeached evidence) with additional evidence. • This practice is often considered improper when lawyers seek to enhance the credibility of their own witnesses.

bona fide (**boh**-nə fid *or* **boh**-nə fi-dee), *adj.* [Latin "in good faith"] **1.** Made in good faith; without fraud or deceit. **2.** Sincere; genuine. See GOOD FAITH. — **bona fide,** *adv.*

bona fide occupational qualification. An employment qualification that, although it may discriminate against a protected class (such as one based on sex, religion, or national origin), relates to an essential job duty and is considered reasonably necessary to the operation of the particular business. • Such a qualification is not illegal under federal employment-discrimination laws. —Abbr. BFOQ.

bona fide possession. See POSSESSION.

bona fide purchaser. See PURCHASER.

bona fides (**boh**-nə fı-deez), *n.* [Latin] See GOOD FAITH.

bond, *n.* **1.** An obligation; a promise. **2.** A written promise to pay money or do some act if certain circumstances occur or a certain time elapses; a promise that is defeasible upon a condition subsequent.

appeal bond. A bond that an appellate court may require from an appellant in a civil case to ensure payment of the costs of appeal; a bond required as a condition to bringing an appeal or staying execution of the judgment appealed from. Fed. R. App. P. 7. Cf. *supersedeas bond.*

bail bond. A bond given to a court by a criminal defendant's surety to guarantee that the defendant will duly appear in court in the future and, if the defendant is jailed, to obtain the defendant's release from confinement. See BAIL.

discharging bond. A bond that both permits a defendant to regain possession of attached property and releases the property from the attachment lien.

fiduciary bond. A type of surety bond required of a trustee, administrator, executor, guardian, conservator, or other fiduciary to ensure the proper performance of duties.

judicial bond. A bond to indemnify an adverse party in a lawsuit against loss occasioned by delay or by deprivation of property resulting from the lawsuit.

payment bond. A bond given by a surety to cover any amounts that, because of the general contractor's default, are not paid to a subcontractor or materialman.

peace bond. A bond required by a court from a person who has breached or threatened to breach the peace. See BREACH OF THE PEACE.

penal bond. A bond requiring the obligor to pay a specified sum as a penalty if the underlying obligation is not performed.

registered bond. A governmental or corporate obligation to pay money, represented by a single certificate delivered to the creditor.

straw bond. A bond, usu. a bail bond, that carries either a fictitious name or the name of a person who is unable to pay the sum guaranteed; a worthless or inadequate bond.

supersedeas bond (soo-pər-see-dee-əs). An appellant's bond to stay execution on a judgment during the pendency of the appeal. Fed. R. Civ. P. 62(d); Fed. R. App. P. 8(b). See SUPERSEDE (2). Cf. *appeal bond.*

3. A long-term, interest-bearing debt instrument issued by a corporation or governmental entity, usu. to provide for a particular financial need; esp., such an instrument in which the debt is secured by a lien on the issuer's property. Cf. DEBENTURE.

bearer bond. A bond payable to the person holding it. • The transfer of possession transfers the bond's ownership. Cf. *registered bond.*

callable bond. A bond that the issuer may call for payment.

convertible bond. A bond that can be exchanged for stock shares in the corporation that issued the bond.

discount bond. A bond sold at its current market value, which is less than its face value.

junk bond. A high-risk, high-yield subordinated bond issued by a corporation with a below-standard industry rating.

municipal bond. A bond issued by a nonfederal government or governmental unit, such as a state bond to finance local improvements. • The interest received from a municipal bond may be exempt from federal, state, and local taxes.

premium bond. A bond with a selling price above face or redemption value.

savings bond. A nontransferable bond issued by the U.S. government.

secured bond. A bond backed by some type of security. Cf. DEBENTURE (2).

serial bond. A bond issued concurrently with other bonds having different maturity dates.

series bonds. A group of bonds issued under the authority of the same indenture, but offered publicly at different times and with different maturity dates and interest rates.

zero-coupon bond. A bond paying no interest. • It is sold at a discount price and later redeemed at face value, the profit being the difference.

bond, *vb.* **1.** To secure payment by providing a bond. **2.** To provide a bond for (a person).

bonded, *adj.* (Of a person or entity) acting under, or placed under, a bond.

bond indenture. 1. A contract between a bond issuer and a bondholder outlining a bond's face value, interest rate, maturity date, and other features. **2.** A mortgage held on specified corporate property to secure payment of the bond.

bond retirement. The cancellation of a bond that has been called or paid.

bondsman. One who guarantees a bond; a surety.

bonus. A premium paid in addition to what is due or expected. • In the employment context, workers' bonuses are not a gift or gratuity; they are paid for services or on consideration in addition to or in excess of the compensation that would ordinarily be given.

book, *vb.* **1.** To record the name of (a person arrested) in a sequential list of police arrests, with details of the person's identity (usu. including a photograph and a fingerprint), particulars about the alleged offense, and the name of the arresting officer. **2.** To engage (someone) contractually as a performer or guest.

book entry. 1. A notation made in an accounting journal. **2.** The method of reflecting ownership of publicly traded securities whereby a customer of a brokerage firm receives confirmations of transactions and monthly statements, but not stock certificates.

bookkeeping, *n.* The mechanical recording of debits and credits or the summarizing of financial information, usu. about a business enterprise. Cf. ACCOUNTING.

book value. The value at which an asset is carried on a balance sheet.

boot, *n.* **1.** *Tax.* Supplemental money or property subject to tax in an otherwise tax-free exchange. **2.** *Corporations.* In a corporate reorganization, anything received other than the stock or securities of a controlled corporation. **3.** *Commercial law.* Cash or other consideration used to balance an otherwise unequal exchange.

boot camp. 1. A camp for basic training of Navy or Marine Corps recruits. **2.** A military-like facility esp. for juvenile offenders. • Boot camps are specialized programs for offenders who are generally nonviolent males from 17 to 25 years old. While proponents applaud the success of these programs, others find their long-term success limited at best.

bootleg, *vb.* To manufacture, reproduce, or distribute (something) illegally or without authorization. — **bootlegger,** *n.*

bootstrap, *vb.* **1.** To succeed despite sparse resources. **2.** To reach an unsupported conclusion from questionable premises.

bootstrap doctrine. *Conflict of laws.* The doctrine that forecloses collateral attack on the jurisdiction of another state's court that has rendered final judgment. • The doctrine, however, cannot give effectiveness to a judgment by a court that had no subject-matter jurisdiction. For example, parties cannot, by appearing before a state court, "bootstrap" that court into having jurisdiction over a federal matter.

border search. See SEARCH.

bork (bork), *vb. Slang.* **1.** (Of the U.S. Senate) to reject a nominee, esp. for the U.S. Supreme Court, on grounds of the nominee's unorthodox political and legal philosophy. • The term derives from the name of Robert Bork, President Ronald Reagan's unsuccessful nominee for the Supreme Court in 1987. **2.** (Of political and legal activists) to embark on a media campaign to pressure U.S. Senators into rejecting a President's nominee. **3.** Generally, to smear a political opponent.

borrowed employee. See EMPLOYEE.

borrowing statute. A legislative exception to the conflict-of-laws rule holding that a forum state must apply its own statute of limitations. • A borrowing statute specifies the circumstances in which a forum state will apply another state's statute of limitations.

bottomland. Low-lying land, often located in a river's floodplain.

bound, *adj.* **1.** Constrained by a contractual or other obligation. **2.** (Of a court) constrained to follow a precedent.

bound, *n.* (*usu. pl.*) **1.** BOUNDARY. **2.** A limitation or restriction on action.

bound, *vb.* To delineate a property boundary.

boundary. A natural or artificial separation that delineates the confines of real property. See METES AND BOUNDS.

bounty. 1. A premium or benefit offered or given, esp. by a government, to induce someone to take action or perform a service. **2.** A gift, esp. in a will; generosity in giving.

bounty hunter. A person who for a fee pursues someone charged with or suspected of a crime; esp., a person hired by a bail-bond company to find and arrest a criminal defendant who has breached the bond agreement by failing to appear in court as ordered.

boutique (boo-**teek**). A small specialty business; esp., a small law firm specializing in one particular aspect of law practice <a tax boutique>.

boycott, *n.* **1.** An action designed to achieve the social or economic isolation of an adversary. **2.** A concerted refusal to do business with a party to express disapproval of that party's practices. — **boycott,** *vb.* Cf. PICKETING; STRIKE.

consumer boycott. A boycott by consumers of products or services to show displeasure with the manufacturer, seller, or provider.

primary boycott. A boycott by union members who stop dealing with a former employer.

secondary boycott. A boycott of the customers or suppliers of a business so that they will withhold their patronage from that business.

B.R. *abbr.* Bankruptcy Reporter. — Also abbreviated *Bankr. Rep.*

bracket creep. The process by which inflation or increased income pushes individuals into higher tax brackets.

Brady Act. A federal law establishing a national system for quickly checking the background of a prospective handgun purchaser. 18 USCA §§ 921–930.

Brady material. *Criminal procedure.* Information or evidence that is favorable to a defendant's case and that the prosecution has a duty to disclose. • The prosecution's withholding of such information violates the defendant's due-process rights. *Brady v. Maryland*, 373 U.S. 83, 83 S.Ct. 1194 (1963). Cf. JENCKS MATERIAL.

brain death. See DEATH.

branch. 1. An offshoot, lateral extension, or division of an institution. **2.** A line of familial descent stemming from a common ancestor.

Brandeis brief (**bran**-dɪs). A brief, usu. an appellate brief, that makes use of social and economic studies in addition to legal principles and citations. • The brief is named after Supreme Court Justice Louis D. Brandeis, who as an advocate filed the most famous such brief in *Muller v. Oregon*, 208 U.S. 412, 28 S.Ct. 324 (1908), in which he persuaded the Court to uphold a statute setting a maximum ten-hour workday for women.

breach, *n.* A violation or infraction of a law or obligation. — **breach,** *vb.*

breach of close. The unlawful or unauthorized entry on another person's land; a common-law trespass. See CLOSE.

breach of contract. Violation of a contractual obligation, either by failing to perform one's own promise or by interfering with another party's performance.

anticipatory breach. A breach of contract caused by a party's anticipatory repudiation, i.e., unequivocally indicating that the party will not perform when performance is due. • Under these circumstances, the nonbreaching party may elect to treat the repudiation as an immediate breach and sue for damages. See REPUDIATION.

continuing breach. A breach of contract that endures for a considerable time or is repeated at short intervals.

efficient breach. An intentional breach of contract and payment of damages by a party who would incur greater economic loss by performing under the contract. See EFFICIENT-BREACH THEORY.

immediate breach. A breach that entitles the nonbreaching party to sue for damages immediately.

material breach. A substantial breach of contract, usu. excusing the aggrieved party from further performance and affording it the right to sue for damages.

partial breach. A breach of contract that is less significant than a material breach and that gives the aggrieved party a right to damages, but does not usu. excuse that party from performance.

total breach. A material breach of contract that gives rise to a claim for damages based on the injured party's remaining rights to performance under the contract.

breach of covenant. The violation of an express or implied promise, usu. in a contract, either to do or not to do an act. See COVENANT.

breach of duty. The violation of a legal or moral obligation; the failure to act as the law obligates one to act. See NEGLIGENCE.

breach of the peace. The criminal offense of creating a public disturbance or engaging in disorderly conduct, particularly by making an unnecessary or distracting noise. See *disorderly conduct* under CONDUCT.

breach of trust. A trustee's violation of either the trust's terms or the trustee's general fiduciary obligations; the violation of a duty that equity imposes on a trustee, whether the violation was willful, fraudulent, negligent, or inadvertent. • A breach of trust subjects the trustee to removal and creates personal liability.

breach of warranty. A breach of an express or implied warranty relating to the title, quality, content, or condition of goods sold. UCC § 2–312.

break, *vb.* **1.** To violate or disobey (a law). **2.** To nullify (a will) by court proceeding. **3.** To escape from (a place of confinement) without permission. **4.** To open (a door, gate, etc.) and step through illegally.

breakage. An allowance given by a manufacturer to a buyer for goods damaged during transit or storage.

breaking, *n. Criminal law.* In the law of burglary, the act of entering a building without permission.

breaking a case. **1.** The voicing by one appellate judge to another judge on the same panel of a tentative view on how a case should be decided. • These informal expressions assist the judges in ascertaining how close they are to agreement. **2.** The solving of a case by the police.

breaking bulk, *n.* **1.** The act of dividing a large shipment into smaller units. **2.** Larceny by a bailee, esp. a carrier, who opens containers, removes items from them, and converts the items to personal use. — **break bulk,** *vb.*

Breathalyzer. A device used to measure the blood alcohol content of a person's breath, esp. when the police suspect that the person was driving while intoxicated. • Breathalyzer test results are admissible as evidence if the test was properly administered. — **breathalyze,** *vb.* See BLOOD ALCOHOL CONTENT.

breathing room. *Slang.* The postbankruptcy period during which a debtor may formulate a debt-repayment plan without harassment or interference by creditors.

bribe, *n.* A price, reward, gift, or favor bestowed or promised with a view to pervert the judgment of or influence the action of a person in a position of trust.

bribery, *n.* The corrupt payment, receipt, or solicitation of a private favor for official action. • Bribery is a felony in most jurisdictions. See Model Penal Code § 240.1. — **bribe,** *vb.* Cf. KICKBACK.

commercial bribery. **1.** The knowing solicitation or acceptance of a benefit in exchange for violating an oath of fidelity, such as that owed by an employee, partner, trustee, or attorney. Model Penal Code § 224.8(1). **2.** A supposedly disinterested appraiser's acceptance of a benefit that influences the appraisal of goods or services. Model Penal Code § 224.8(2). **3.** Corrupt dealing with the agents or employees of prospective buyers to secure an advantage over business competitors.

bridge loan. See LOAN.

brief, *n.* A written statement setting out the legal contentions of a party in litigation, esp. on appeal; a document prepared by counsel as the basis for arguing a case, consisting of legal and factual arguments and the authorities in support of them.

proof brief. A preliminary appellate brief to be reviewed by the clerk of the court for compliance with applicable rules. • Proof briefs are required by local rules of the U.S. Court of Appeals for the Sixth Circuit.

reply brief. A brief that responds to issues and arguments raised in the brief previously filed by one's opponent.

trial brief. Counsel's written submission, usu. just before trial, outlining the legal issues before the court and arguing one side's position.

brief-writing. The art or practice of preparing legal briefs.

bright-line rule. A judicial rule of decision that tends to resolve issues, esp. ambiguities, simply and straightforwardly, sometimes sacrificing equity for certainty.

bring to book. To arrest and try (an offender).

broad-form insurance. See INSURANCE.

broad-form policy. See INSURANCE POLICY.

broker, *n.* An agent who acts as an intermediary or negotiator, esp. between prospective buyers and sellers; a person employed to make bargains and contracts between other persons in matters of trade, commerce, and navigation. — **broker,** *vb.* Cf. FACTOR.

brokerage. 1. The business or office of a broker. **2.** A broker's fee.

Bruton **error (broot-ən).** The violation of a criminal defendant's constitutional right of confrontation by admitting into evidence a nontestifying codefendant's confession that implicates a defendant who claims innocence. *Bruton v. United States*, 391 U.S. 123, 88 S.Ct. 1620 (1968).

BTA. *abbr.* Board of Tax Appeals. See TAX COURT, U.S.

bubble. *Slang.* A dishonest or insubstantial business project, generally founded on a fictitious or exaggerated prospectus, designed to ensnare unwary investors.

budget. 1. A statement of an organization's estimated revenues and expenses for a specified period, usu. a year. **2.** A sum of money allocated to a particular purpose or project.

buffer zone. *Land-use planning.* An area of land separating two different zones or areas to help each blend more easily with the other, such as a strip of land between industrial and residential areas.

buggery, *n.* Sodomy or bestiality. — **bugger,** *vb.* — **bugger,** *n.* See SODOMY.

bugging, *n.* A form of electronic surveillance by which conversations may be electronically intercepted, overheard, and recorded, usu. covertly; eavesdropping by electronic means. See WIRETAPPING.

building-and-loan association. A quasi-public corporation that accumulates funds through member contributions and lends money to the members buying or building homes. Cf. SAVINGS-AND-LOAN ASSOCIATION.

building line. A boundary drawn along a curb or the edge of a municipality's sidewalks to establish how far a building must be set away from the street to maintain a uniform appearance. • This is often referred to as a setback requirement.

bulk sale. A sale of a large quantity of inventory outside the ordinary course of the seller's business. • Bulk sales are regulated by Article 6 of the UCC, which is designed to prevent sellers from defrauding unsecured creditors by making these sales and then dissipating the sale proceeds.

bullpen. *Slang.* **1.** An area in a prison where inmates are kept in close confinement. **2.** A detention cell where prisoners are held until they are brought into court.

bumping. 1. Displacement of a junior employee's position by a senior employee. **2.** An airline-industry practice of denying seats to passengers because of overbooking.

bunco. A swindling game or scheme; any trick or ploy calculated to win a person's confidence in an attempt to deceive that person.

bundle, *vb.* To sell related products or services in one transaction at an all-inclusive price.

burden, *n.* **1.** A duty or responsibility. **2.** Something that is oppressive. **3.** A restriction on the use or value of land; an encumbrance. — **burden,** *vb.* — **burdensome,** *adj.*

burden of allegation. A party's duty to plead a matter in order for that matter to be heard in the lawsuit.

burden of persuasion. A party's duty to convince the fact-finder to view the facts in a way that favors that party. • In civil cases, the plaintiff's burden is usually "by a preponderance of the evidence," while in criminal cases the prosecution's burden is "beyond a reasonable doubt."

burden of production. A party's duty to introduce enough evidence on an issue to have that issue decided by the fact-finder, rather than decided against the party in a peremptory ruling such as a summary judgment or a directed verdict.

burden of proof. **1.** A party's duty to prove a disputed assertion or charge. • The burden of proof includes both the *burden of persuasion* and the *burden of production*. **2.** Loosely, BURDEN OF PERSUASION.

Bureau of Prisons. A federal agency that oversees all federal penal and correctional facilities, assists states and local governments in improving their correctional facilities, and provides notice of prisoner releases. 18 USCA §§ 4041 et seq. • The Bureau of Prisons falls within the purview of the U.S. Attorney General. See NATIONAL INSTITUTE OF CORRECTIONS.

***Burford* abstention.** See ABSTENTION.

burglar, *n.* One who commits burglary.

burglary, *n.* **1.** The common-law offense of breaking and entering another's dwelling at night with the intent to commit a felony. **2.** The modern statutory offense of breaking and entering any building — not just a dwelling, and not only at night — with the intent to commit a felony. • Some statutes make petit larceny an alternative to a felony for purposes of proving burglarious intent. — **burglarize, burgle,** *vb.* — **burglarious** (bər-**glair**-ee-əs), *adj.* — **burglariously,** *adv.* Cf. ROBBERY.

burglary tool. (*often pl.*) An implement designed to assist a person in committing a burglary. • In many jurisdictions, it is illegal to possess such a tool if the possessor intends to commit a burglary.

bursting-bubble theory. *Evidence.* The principle that a presumption disappears once the presumed facts have been contradicted by credible evidence.

business court. See COURT.

business enterprises. The field of law dealing with various forms of business, such as corporations, limited-liability companies, and partnerships.

business expense. See EXPENSE.

business guest. See INVITEE.

business homestead. See HOMESTEAD.

business-judgment rule. *Corporations.* The presumption that in making business decisions not involving direct self-interest or self-dealing, corporate directors act on an informed basis, in good faith, and in the honest belief that their actions are in the corporation's best interest. • The rule shields directors and officers from liability for unprofitable or harmful corporate transactions if the transactions were made in good faith, with due care, and within the directors' or officers' authority.

business plan. A written proposal explaining a new business or business idea and usu. covering financial, marketing, and operational plans.

business-purpose doctrine. *Tax.* The principle that a transaction must serve a bona fide business purpose (i.e., not just for tax avoidance) to qualify for beneficial tax treatment.

business-records exception. *Evidence.* A hearsay exception allowing business records (such as reports or memoranda) to be admitted into evidence if they were prepared in the ordinary course of business. Fed. R. Evid. 803(6).

but-for cause. See CAUSE (1).

but-for test. *Tort & criminal law.* The doctrine that causation exists only when the result would not have occurred without the party's conduct. See *but-for cause* under CAUSE (1). Cf. SUBSTANTIAL-FACTOR TEST.

buyer. One who makes a purchase. See PURCHASER.

buyer in ordinary course of business. A person who — in good faith and without knowledge that the sale violates a third party's ownership rights or security interest in the goods — buys from a person regularly engaged in the business of selling goods of that kind. • Pawnbrokers are excluded from the definition. UCC § 1–201(9).

buying in, *n.* The purchase of property by the original owner or an interested party at an auction or foreclosure sale. — **buy in,** *vb.*

buyout, *n.* The purchase of all or a controlling percentage of the assets or shares of a business. — **buy out,** *vb.* Cf. MERGER (7).

leveraged buyout. The purchase of a publicly held corporation's outstanding stock by its management or outside investors, financed mainly with funds borrowed from investment bankers or brokers and usu. secured by the corporation's assets.

management buyout. **1.** A buyout of a corporation by its own directors and officers. **2.** A leveraged buyout of a corporation by an outside entity in which the corporation's management has a material financial interest.

buy–sell agreement. **1.** An arrangement between owners of a business by which the surviving owners agree to purchase the interest of a withdrawing or deceased owner. Cf. CONTINUATION AGREEMENT. **2.** *Corporations.* A share-transfer restriction that commits the shareholder to sell, and the corporation or other shareholders to buy, the shareholder's shares at a fixed price when a specified event occurs.

by-bidding. The illegal practice of employing a person to bid at an auction for the sole purpose of stimulating bidding on the seller's property. — **by-bidder,** *n.* Cf. BIDDING UP.

bylaw. 1. A rule or administrative provision adopted by an association or corporation for its internal governance. See ARTICLES OF INCORPORATION. **2.** ORDINANCE. — Sometimes spelled *by-law*; *byelaw*.

bypass trust. See TRUST.

bystander. One who is present when an event takes place, but who does not become directly involved in it.

C

c. *abbr.* **1.** CIRCA. **2.** COPYRIGHT.

ca. *abbr.* CIRCA.

cabinet. (*often cap.*) The advisory council to an executive officer, esp. the President.

caeterorum administration. See ADMINISTRATION.

calendar, *n.* **1.** A court's list of civil or criminal cases. **2.** A list of bills reported out of a legislative committee for consideration by the entire legislature.

calendar, *vb.* **1.** To place an important event on a calendar, esp. so that the event will be remembered. **2.** To place a case on a calendar.

calendar call. A court session in which the judge calls each case awaiting trial, determines its status, and assigns a trial date.

calendar motion. See MOTION.

call, *n.* **1.** A request or command to come or assemble; an invitation or summons. **2.** A demand for payment of money. **3.** A demand for the presentation of a security (esp. a bond) for redemption before the maturity date. **4.** A landmark designating a property boundary. See METES AND BOUNDS.

call, *vb.* **1.** To summon. **2.** To demand payment of money. **3.** To redeem (a bond) before maturity. (for sense 3) — **callable,** *adj.* See REDEMPTION.

callable bond. See BOND (3).

call loan. See LOAN.

calumny (kal-əm-nee), *n. Archaic.* **1.** The act of maliciously misrepresenting someone's words or actions in a way that is calculated to injure that person's reputation. See OBLOQUY. **2.** A false charge or imputation. — **calumniate** (kə-**ləm**-nee-ayt), *vb.* — **calumnious** (kə-**ləm**-nee-əs), *adj.* — **calumniator** (kə-**ləm**-nee-ay-tər), *n.*

can, *vb.* **1.** To be able to do something. **2.** To have permission (as often interpreted by courts); MAY.

canceled check. See CHECK.

cancellation, *n.* **1.** The act of defacing or obliterating a writing (as by marking lines across it), thereby rendering it void. **2.** An annulment or termination of a promise or an obligation. **3.** An equitable remedy by which courts call in and annul outstanding void or rescinded instruments because they may either spawn vexatious litigation or cloud someone's title to property. — **cancel,** *vb.* — **cancelable,** *adj.*

canon (kan-ən), *n.* **1.** A rule or principle, esp. one accepted as fundamental. **2.** (*usu. cap.*) A maxim stating in general terms the standards of professional conduct expected of lawyers. • The Model Code of Judicial Conduct (1990) contains five canons and hundreds of specific rules. **3.** A corpus of writings. — **canonical** (kə-non-ə-kəl), *adj.* — **canonist** (**kan**-ən-ist), *n.*

canvass, *vb.* **1.** To examine in detail; scrutinize. **2.** To solicit political support from voters or a voting district; to take stock of public opinion. — **canvass,** *n.*

cap, *n.* An upper limit, such as a statutory limit on the recovery in a tort action or on the interest a bank can charge. — **cap,** *vb.*

capacitate (kə-**pas**-ə-tayt), *vb.* To qualify; to make legally competent. — **capacitation** (kə-pas-ə-**tay**-shən), *n.*

capacity. 1. The role in which one performs an act. **2.** A legal qualification, such as legal age, that determines one's ability to sue or be sued, to enter into a binding contract, and the like. **3.** The mental ability to understand the nature and effect of one's acts. See COMPETENCY.

criminal capacity. The mental ability that a person must possess to be held accountable for a crime; the ability to understand right from wrong. See INSANITY; INFANCY.

diminished capacity. An impaired mental condition — short of insanity — that is caused by intoxication, trauma, or disease and that prevents the person from having the mental state necessary to be held responsible for a crime. • In some jurisdictions, a defendant's diminished capacity can be used to determine the degree of the offense or the severity of the punishment. Cf. INSANITY.

testamentary capacity. The mental ability a person must have to prepare a valid will. • This capacity is often described as the ability to recognize the natural objects of one's bounty, the nature and extent of one's estate, and the fact that one is making a plan to dispose of the estate after death.

capacity defense. See DEFENSE (1).

capias (**kay**-pee-əs *or* **kap**-ee-əs). [Latin "that you take"] Any of various types of writs that require an officer to take a named defendant into custody.

capital, *adj.* **1.** Of or relating to economic or financial capital <capital market>. **2.** Punishable by execution; involving the death penalty <a capital offense>.

capital, *n.* **1.** Money or assets invested, or available for investment, in a business. **2.** The total assets of a business, esp. those that help generate profits. **3.** The total amount or value of a corporation's stock; corporate equity.

capital expenditure. An outlay of funds to acquire or improve a fixed asset.

capital expense. See EXPENSE.

capital gain. See GAIN (3).

capital-gains tax. See TAX.

capitalism, *n.* An economic system that depends on the private ownership of the means of production and on competitive forces to determine what is produced. — **capitalist,** *adj.* & *n.*

capital leverage. The use of borrowed funds in a business to obtain a return greater than the interest rate.

capital loss. See LOSS.

capital offense. See OFFENSE.

capital outlay. 1. CAPITAL EXPENDITURE. **2.** Money expended in acquiring, equipping, and promoting a business.

capital recovery. The collection of charged-off bad debt that has been previously written off against the allowance for doubtful accounts.

capital structure. The mix of debt and equity by which a business finances its operations; the relative proportions of short-term debt, long-term debt, and capital stock.

capitulation (kə-pich-ə-**lay**-shən), *n.* The act of surrendering or giving in. — **capitulate,** *vb.* — **capitulatory,** *adj.*

capricious (kə-**prish**-əs), *adj.* **1.** (Of a person) characterized by or guided by unpredictable or impulsive behavior. **2.** (Of a decree) contrary to the evidence or established rules of law. Cf. ARBITRARY.

caption. 1. The introductory part of a court paper stating the names of the parties, the name of the court, the docket or file number, and the title of the action. **2.** The arrest or seizure of a person by legal process.

care, *n.* **1.** Serious attention; heed. **2.** Under the law of negligence, the conduct demanded of a person in a given situation. • Typically, this involves a person's giving attention both to possible dangers, mistakes, and pitfalls and to ways of ensuring that these risks do not materialize. See DEGREE OF CARE; REASONABLE PERSON.

***great care.* 1.** The degree of care that a prudent person exercises in dealing with very important personal affairs. **2.** The degree of care exercised in a given situation by the person most competent to deal with the situation.

reasonable care. As a test of liability for negligence, the degree of care that a prudent and competent person engaged in the same line of business or endeavor would exercise under similar circumstances. See REASONABLE PERSON.

slight care. The degree of care a person gives to matters of minor importance; the degree of care given by a person of limited accountability.

career offender. See OFFENDER.

careless, *adj.* (Of an action or behavior) engaged in without reasonable care. Cf. RECKLESS.

carelessness, *n.* **1.** The fact, condition, or instance of a person's either not having done what he or she ought to have done, or having done what he or she ought not to have done. **2.** A person's general disposition not to do something that ought to be done.

carnal knowledge. Sexual intercourse, esp. with an underage female.

carrier. 1. An individual or organization (such as a railroad or an airline) that transports passengers or goods for a fee.

common carrier. A carrier that is required by law to transport passengers or freight, without refusal, if the approved fare or charge is paid.

private carrier. A carrier that is not bound to accept business from the general public and is therefore not considered a common carrier.

2. INSURER.

carryback. *Tax.* An income-tax deduction (esp. for a net operating loss) that cannot be taken entirely in a given period but may be taken in an earlier period (usu. the previous three years). Cf. CARRYOVER.

carryover. An income-tax deduction (esp. for a net operating loss) that cannot be taken entirely in a given period but may be taken in a later period (usu. the next five years). Cf. CARRYBACK.

carryover basis. See BASIS.

cartel (kahr-**tel**), *n.* **1.** A combination of producers or sellers that join together to control a product's production or price. **2.** An association of firms with common interests, seeking to prevent extreme or unfair competition, allocate markets, or share knowledge. — **cartelize** (**kahr**-tə-lIz *or* kahr-**tel**-Iz), *vb.*

carveout, *n.* **1.** An explicit exception to a broad rule. **2.** *Tax.* For tax purposes, the separation from property of the income derived from the property. — **carve out,** *vb.*

case. 1. A proceeding, action, suit, or controversy at law or in equity.

active case. A case that is still pending.

case at bar. A case under the immediate consideration of the court. — Also termed *instant case*; *present case.*

case of first impression. A case that presents the court with issues of law that have not previously been decided in that jurisdiction.

case reserved. A written statement of the facts proved at trial and drawn up and stipulated to by the parties, so that certain legal issues can be decided by an appellate court. — Also termed *case made*; *special case.*

case stated. A formal written statement of the facts in a case, submitted to the court jointly by the parties so that a decision may be rendered without trial.

inactive case. A pending case that is not proceeding toward resolution. • This may occur for several reasons, such as nonservice, want of prosecution, or (in a criminal case) the defendant's having absconded.

instant case. See *case at bar.*

present case. See *case at bar.*

special case. See *case reserved.*

test case. **1.** A lawsuit brought to establish an important legal principle or right. • Such an action is frequently brought by the parties' mutual consent on agreed facts — when that is so, a test case is also sometimes termed *amicable action* or *amicable suit.* **2.** An action selected from several suits that are based on the same facts and evidence, raise the same question of law, and have a common plaintiff or a common defendant. • Sometimes, when all parties agree, the court orders a consolidation and all parties are bound by the decision in the test case. — Also termed *test action*.

2. A criminal investigation. **3.** An individual suspect or convict in relation to any aspect of the criminal-justice system. **4.** An argument. **5.** An instance, occurrence, or situation. **6.** See *trespass on the case* under TRESPASS.

casebook. A compilation of extracts from instructive cases on a particular subject, usu. with commentary and questions about the cases, designed as a teaching aid. Cf. HORNBOOK.

casebook method. An inductive system of teaching law in which students study specific cases to learn general legal principles. Cf. HORNBOOK METHOD.

caseflow. 1. The movement of cases through the judicial system, from the initial filing to the final appeal. **2.** An analysis of that movement.

case-in-chief. 1. The evidence presented at trial by the party with the burden of proof. **2.** The part of a trial in which a party presents evidence to support its claim or defense. Cf. REBUTTAL.

caselaw. The law to be found in the collection of reported cases that form the body of law within a given jurisdiction. — Also written *case law*.

caseload. The volume of cases assigned to a given court, agency, officer, judge, law firm, or lawyer.

case made. See *case reserved* under CASE.

case of first impression. See CASE.

case-or-controversy requirement. The constitutional requirement that, for a federal court to hear a case, the case must involve an actual dispute. See CONTROVERSY (3).

case reserved. See CASE.

case stated. See CASE.

cash, *n.* **1.** Money or its equivalent. **2.** Currency or coins, negotiable checks, and balances in bank accounts. — **cash,** *vb.*

cash-basis accounting method. See ACCOUNTING METHOD.

cash discount. See DISCOUNT.

cash equivalent. A short-term security that is liquid enough to be considered equivalent to cash.

cash flow. 1. The movement of cash through a business, as a measure of profitability or liquidity. **2.** The cash generated from a business or transaction. **3.** Cash receipts minus cash disbursements for a given period. — Sometimes spelled *cashflow*.

cashier, *vb.* To dismiss from service dishonorably <after three such incidents, Jones was cashiered>.

cashier's check. See CHECK.

cashout, *n.* An arrangement by a seller to receive the entire amount of equity in cash rather than retain an interest in the property. — **cash out,** *vb.*

castle doctrine. *Criminal law.* An exception to the retreat rule allowing the use of deadly force by a person who is protecting his or her home and its inhabitants from attack, esp. from a trespasser who intends to commit a felony or inflict serious bodily harm. See RETREAT RULE.

casualty. 1. A serious or fatal accident. **2.** A person or thing injured, lost, or destroyed.

casualty loss. See LOSS.

casualty pot. *Tax.* A step in evaluating tax liability in which casualty gains and losses are compared to determine whether a net loss or gain has occurred. Cf. MAIN POT.

casus omissus (**kay**-səs ə-**mis**-əs). [Latin "case omitted"] A situation not provided for by a statute or contract, and therefore governed by caselaw or new judge-made law. Pl. ***casus omissi.***

categorical question. See QUESTION.

caucus (**kaw**-kəs), *n.* **1.** Representatives from a political party who assemble to nominate candidates and decide party policy. **2.** A meeting of a group of people to formulate a policy or strategy. — **caucus,** *vb.*

causal (**kaw**-zəl), *adj.* **1.** Of, relating to, or involving causation. **2.** Arising from a cause.

causality (kaw-**zal**-ə-tee), *n.* The principle of causal relationship; the relation between cause and effect. — **causal,** *adj.*

causa mortis (**kaw**-zə **mor**-tis), *adj.* Done or made in contemplation of one's own death. See *gift causa mortis* under GIFT.

causation (kaw-**zay**-shən). **1.** The causing or producing of an effect. **2.** CAUSALITY.

cause, *n.* **1.** Something that produces an effect or result. — **cause,** *vb.* — **causative** (**kaw**-zə-tiv), *adj.*

but-for cause. The cause without which the event could not have occurred.

concurrent cause. **1.** One of two or more causes that simultaneously create a condition that no single cause could have brought about. **2.** One of two or more causes that simultaneously create a condition that any one cause could have created alone.

immediate cause. The last event in a chain of events, though not necessarily the proximate cause of what follows.

intervening cause. An event that comes between the initial event in a sequence and the end result, thereby altering the natural course of events that might have connected a wrongful act to an injury. • If the intervening cause is strong enough to relieve the wrongdoer of any liability, it becomes a *superseding cause.* A *dependent intervening cause* is one that is not an act and is never a superseding cause. An *independent intervening cause* is one that operates on a condition produced by an antecedent cause but in no way resulted from that cause. See *superseding cause.*

proximate cause. **1.** A cause that is legally sufficient to result in liability. **2.** A cause that directly produces an event and without which the event would not have occurred.

remote cause. A cause that does not necessarily or immediately produce an event or injury.

sole cause. The only cause that, from a legal viewpoint, produces an event or injury. • If it comes between a defendant's action and the event or injury at issue, it is treated as a *superseding cause*.

superseding cause. An intervening act that the law considers sufficient to override the cause for which the original tortfeasor was responsible, thereby exonerating that tortfeasor from liability. Cf. *intervening cause*.

2. A ground for legal action.

good cause. A legally sufficient reason. • Good cause is often the burden placed on a litigant (usually by court rule or order) to show why a request should be granted or an action excused.

3. A lawsuit; a case.

cause-and-prejudice rule. *Criminal law*. The doctrine that a prisoner attacking the conviction or sentence — as by a petition for writ of habeas corpus — on the basis of a constitutional challenge that was not presented to the trial court, must show good cause for failing to preserve the objection at trial, and must show that the trial court's error resulted in actual prejudice to the defendant. • The cause-and-prejudice rule creates a higher burden than the defendant would face in a direct appeal. It is intended to provide protection from fundamental miscarriages of justice, not every trial-court error. But in death-penalty cases in which the defendant proves actual innocence, the court may grant relief even when the standards of the cause-and-prejudice rule have not been met. See *actual innocence* under INNOCENCE.

cause célèbre (kawz sə-leb *or* **kawz** say-**leb**-rə). [French "celebrated case"] A trial or decision in which the subject matter or the characters are unusual or sensational.

cause of action. 1. A group of operative facts giving rise to one or more bases for suing; a factual situation that entitles one person to obtain a remedy in court from another person; CLAIM (4). **2.** A legal theory of a lawsuit. Cf. RIGHT OF ACTION. **3.** Loosely, a lawsuit.

cautionary instruction. See JURY INSTRUCTION.

caveat (kav-ee-aht *or* **kay**-vee-at *or* **kav**-ee-at). [Latin "let him or her beware"] **1.** A warning or proviso. **2.** A formal notice or warning given by a party to a court or court officer requesting a suspension of proceedings. **3.** *Property*. Under the Torrens system of land titles, a formal notice of an unregistered interest in land. • Once lodged with the register of deeds, this notice prevents the register from recording any dealing affecting the estate or the interest claimed. See TORRENS SYSTEM. — **caveat,** *vb.*

CBOE. *abbr.* CHICAGO BOARD OPTIONS EXCHANGE.

CBOT. *abbr.* CHICAGO BOARD OF TRADE.

CBT. *abbr.* CHICAGO BOARD OF TRADE.

C.C. *abbr.* **1.** Circuit, city, civil, or county court. **2.** Chancery, civil, criminal, or Crown cases. **3.** CIVIL CODE.

C corporation. See CORPORATION.

CCPA. *abbr.* CONSUMER CREDIT PROTECTION ACT.

CD. *abbr.* CERTIFICATE OF DEPOSIT.

cease-and-desist order. A court's or agency's order prohibiting a person from continuing a particular course of conduct. See INJUNCTION; RESTRAINING ORDER.

cede (seed), *vb.* **1.** To surrender or relinquish. **2.** To assign or grant. — **cession** (**sesh**-ən), *n.* — **cessionary** (**sesh**-ən-er-ee), *adj.*

censor, *vb.* To officially inspect (esp. a book or film) and delete material considered offensive.

censure (**sen**-shər), *n.* An official reprimand or condemnation; harsh criticism. — **censure,** *vb.* — **censorious,** *adj.*

census. The official counting of people to compile social and economic data for the political subdivision to which the people belong. Pl. **censuses.**

Central Intelligence Agency. A U.S. federal agency responsible for gathering, analyzing, and sometimes acting on information relating to national security, esp. foreign intelligence and counterintelligence activities. — Abbr. CIA.

CEO. *abbr.* CHIEF EXECUTIVE OFFICER.

CERCLA (**sər**-klə). *abbr.* Comprehensive Environmental Response, Compensation, and Liability Act of 1980. • This statute holds responsible parties liable for the cost of cleaning up hazardous-waste sites. 42 USCA §§ 9601 et seq. See SUPERFUND.

ceremonial marriage. See MARRIAGE (2).

cert. *abbr.* CERTIORARI.

certain contract. See CONTRACT.

certificate, *n.* **1.** A document in which a fact is formally attested. **2.** A document certifying the bearer's status or authorization to act in a specified way. **3.** A notice by one court to another court of the action it has taken.

certificate of authority. 1. A document authenticating a notarized document that is being sent to another jurisdiction. **2.** A document issued by a state agency, usu. the secretary of state, granting an out-of-state corporation the right to do business in the state.

certificate of conference. A section of a pleading or motion filed with the court, usu. contained separately on a page near the end of the document, whereby the party filing the pleading or motion certifies to the court that the parties have attempted to resolve the matter, but that a judicial determination is needed because an agreement could not be reached.

certificate of deposit. 1. A banker's certificate acknowledging the receipt of money and promising to repay the depositor. **2.** A bank document showing the existence of a time deposit, usu. one that pays interest. — Abbr. CD.

certificate of incorporation. 1. A document issued by a state authority (usu. the secretary of state) granting a corporation its legal existence and the right to function as a corporation. **2.** ARTICLES OF INCORPORATION.

certificate of service. A section of a pleading or motion filed with the court, usu. contained separately on the last page, whereby the party filing the pleading or motion certifies to the court that a copy has been sent to the opposing party. Fed. R. Civ. P. 5(d).

certificate of title. A document indicating ownership of real or personal property. • This document usually identifies any liens or other encumbrances.

certification, *n.* **1.** The act of attesting. **2.** The state of having been attested. **3.** An attested statement. **4.** The writing on the face of a check by which it is certified. **5.** A procedure by which a federal appellate court asks the U.S. Supreme Court or the highest state court to review a question of law arising in a case pending before the appellate court and on which it needs guidance.

certified check. See CHECK.

certified copy. See COPY.

certified juvenile. See JUVENILE.

certified mail. Mail for which the sender requests proof of delivery in the form of a receipt signed by the addressee.

certified question. A point of law on which a federal appellate court seeks guidance from either the U.S. Supreme Court or the highest state court by the procedure of certification.

certify, *vb.* **1.** To authenticate or verify in writing. **2.** To attest as being true or as meeting certain criteria. **3.** (Of a court) to issue an order allowing a class of litigants to maintain a class action; to create (a class) for purposes of a class action. See CERTIFICATION. Cf. DECERTIFY.

certiorari (sər-shee-ə-**rair**-ɪ *or* **-rair**-ee *or* **-rah**-ree). [Law Latin "to be more fully informed"] An extraordinary writ issued by an appellate court, at its discretion, directing a lower court to deliver the record in the case for review. • The U.S. Supreme Court uses certiorari to review most of the cases that it decides to hear. — Abbr. cert. Cf. CERTIFICATION (5).

certworthy, *adj. Slang.* (Of a case or issue) deserving of review by writ of certiorari. — **certworthiness,** *n.*

cession (**sesh**-ən). **1.** The act of relinquishing property rights. **2.** The relinquishment or transfer of land from one nation to another, esp. after a war as part of the price of peace. **3.** The land so relinquished or transferred.

cestui (**set**-ee *or* **ses**-twee). [French "he who"] *Archaic.* A beneficiary.

cestui que trust (**set**-ee [*or* **ses**-twee] kee [*or* kə] **trəst**). [Law French] *Archaic.* One who possesses equitable rights in property and receives the rents, issues, and profits from it; BENEFICIARY. Pl. **cestuis que trust** or (erroneously) **cestuis que trustent.**

cestui que use (**set**-ee [*or* **ses**-twee] kee [*or* kə] **yoos**). *Archaic.* The person for whose use and benefit property is being held by another, who holds the legal title to the property. Pl. **cestuis que use** or (erroneously) **cestuis que usent.**

cestui que vie (**set**-ee [*or* **ses**-twee] kee [*or* kə] **vee**). The person whose life measures the duration of a trust, gift, estate, or insurance contract.

cf. *abbr.* [Latin *confer*] Compare. • As a citation signal, Cf. directs the reader's attention to another authority or section of the work in which contrasting, analogous, or explanatory statements may be found.

CFR. *abbr.* CODE OF FEDERAL REGULATIONS.

chain-certificate method. The procedure for authenticating a foreign official record by the party seeking to admit the record as evidence at trial. See Fed. R. Civ. P. 44.

chain conspiracy. See CONSPIRACY.

chain of causation. **1.** A series of events each caused by the previous one. **2.** The causal connection between a cause and its effects. Cf. CAUSATION.

chain of custody. **1.** The movement and location of real evidence from the time it is obtained to the time it is presented in court. **2.** The history of a chattel's possession.

chain of title. **1.** The ownership history of a piece of land, from its first owner to the present one. **2.** The ownership history of commercial paper, traceable through the indorsements. • For the holder to have good title, every prior negotiation must have been proper. If a necessary indorsement is missing or forged, the chain of title is broken and no later transferee can become a holder.

challenge, *n.* **1.** An act or instance of formally questioning the legality or legal qualifications of a person, action, or thing. — **challenge,** *vb.*

as-applied challenge. A lawsuit claiming that a law or governmental policy, though constitutional on its face, is unconstitutional as applied, usu. because of a discriminatory effect; a claim that a statute is unconstitutional on the facts of a particular case or to a particular party.

Batson challenge. *Criminal procedure.* A defendant's objection that the prosecution has used peremptory challenges to exclude potential jurors on the basis of race, ethnicity, or gender. • It was named for *Batson v. Kentucky*, 476 U.S. 79, 106 S.Ct. 1712 (1986) and was extended to civil cases by *Edmonson v. Leesville Concrete Co.*, 500 U.S. 614, 111 S.Ct. 2077 (1991).

constitutional challenge. A lawsuit claiming that a law or governmental action is unconstitutional.

facial challenge. A claim that a statute is unconstitutional on its face — that is, that it always operates unconstitutionally.

2. A party's request that a judge disqualify a potential juror or an entire jury panel. — **challenge,** *vb.*

challenge for cause. A party's challenge supported by a specified reason, such as bias or prejudice, that would disqualify that potential juror.

challenge to the array. A legal challenge to the manner in which the entire jury panel was selected, usu. for a failure to follow prescribed procedures designed to produce impartial juries.

peremptory challenge. One of a party's limited number of challenges that need not be supported by any reason, although a party may not use such a challenge in a way that discriminates on the basis of race, ethnicity, or gender. See STRIKE (2).

chamber, *n.* **1.** A room or compartment. **2.** A legislative or judicial body; the hall or room where such a body conducts business. — **chamber,** *adj.*

judge's chamber. (*usu. pl.*) **1.** The private room or office of a judge. **2.** Any place that a judge transacts official business when not holding a session of the court. See IN CAMERA.

lower chamber. In a bicameral legislature, the larger of the two legislative bodies, such as the House of Representatives or the House of Commons.

upper chamber. In a bicameral legislature, the smaller of the two legislative bodies, such as the Senate or the House of Lords.

chamber, *vb.* (Of a judge) to sit in one's chambers at a given location <Chief Judge Kaye chambers sometimes in New York City and sometimes in Albany>.

chamber business. A judge's official business that is conducted outside the courtroom.

champerty (**cham**-pər-tee), *n.* **1.** An agreement between a stranger to a lawsuit and a litigant by which the stranger pursues the litigant's claim as consideration for receiving part of any judgment proceeds. **2.** The act or fact of maintaining, supporting, or promoting another person's lawsuit. Cf. MAINTENANCE (6). — **champertous** (**cham**-pər-təs), *adj.* — **champertor** (**cham**-pər-tər), *n.*

chance, *n.* **1.** A hazard or risk. **2.** The unforeseen, uncontrollable, or unintended consequences of an act. **3.** An accident. **4.** Opportunity; hope.

chancellor, *n.* **1.** A judge serving on a court of chancery. **2.** A university president or CEO of an institution of higher education. — **chancellorship,** *n.*

chance-of-survival doctrine. The principle that a wrongful-death plaintiff need only prove that the defendant's conduct was a substantial factor in causing the death — that is, that the victim might have survived but for the defendant's conduct.

chancery (**chan**-sər-ee). **1.** A court of equity; collectively, the courts of equity. **2.** The system of jurisprudence administered in courts of equity. See EQUITY.

chance verdict. See VERDICT.

change in circumstances. A modification in the physical, emotional, or financial condition of one or both parents, used to show the need to modify a custody or support order; esp., an involuntary occurrence that, if it had been known at the time of the divorce decree, would have resulted in the court's issuing a different decree, as when an involuntary job loss creates a need to modify the decree to provide for reduced child-support payments.

change of venue. **1.** The transfer of a lawsuit from one locale to another. **2.** The transfer of a lawsuit begun in one court to another court in the same district, usu. because of questions of fairness. See VENUE.

channel. 1. The bed of a stream of water; the groove through which a stream flows. **2.** The line of deep water that shipping vessels follow. **3.** A water route between two islands or an island and a continent. **4.** A mode of transmitting something.

Chapter 7. 1. The chapter of the Bankruptcy Code allowing a trustee to collect and liquidate a debtor's property, either voluntarily or by court order, to satisfy creditors. **2.** A bankruptcy case filed under this chapter. • An individual debtor who undergoes this type of liquidation (the most common type of bankruptcy) usually gets a fresh financial start by receiving a discharge of all debts.

Chapter 9. 1. The chapter of the Bankruptcy Code governing the adjustment of a municipality's debts. **2.** A bankruptcy case filed under this chapter.

Chapter 11. 1. The chapter of the Bankruptcy Code allowing an insolvent business, or one that is threatened with insolvency, to reorganize itself under court supervision while continuing its normal operations and restructuring its debt. • The vast majority of Chapter 11 cases involve business debtors. **2.** A business reorganization conducted under this chapter.

Chapter 12. 1. The chapter of the Bankruptcy Code providing for a court-approved debt-payment relief plan for family farmers with a regular income. **2.** A bankruptcy case filed under this chapter.

Chapter 13. 1. The chapter of the Bankruptcy Code allowing a person's future earnings to be collected by a trustee and paid to unsecured creditors. • A plan filed under Chapter 13 is sometimes called a *wage-earner's plan*, a *wage-earner plan*, or an *income-based plan*. A Chapter 13 debtor does not receive a discharge of debts; rather, Chapter 13 allows the debtor to propose a plan of rehabilitation to extend or reduce the balance of any obligations. **2.** A bankruptcy case filed under this chapter.

character evidence. See EVIDENCE.

characterization. 1. *Conflict of laws.* The classification, qualification, and interpretation of laws that apply to the case. **2.** The process of classifying property accumulated by spouses as either separate or marital property (or community property).

character witness. See WITNESS.

charge, *n.* **1.** A formal accusation of a crime as a preliminary step to prosecution. **2.** An instruction or command. **3.** JURY CHARGE. **4.** An assigned duty or task; a responsibility. **5.** An encumbrance, lien, or claim. **6.** A person or thing entrusted to another's care. **7.** Price, cost, or expense. — **charge,** *vb.* — **chargeable,** *adj.*

charge bargain. See PLEA BARGAIN.

charge conference. A meeting between a trial judge and the parties' attorneys to develop a jury charge.

charging instrument. A formal document — usu. either an indictment or an information — that sets forth an accusation of a crime.

charging order. *Partnership.* A statutory procedure whereby an individual partner's creditor can satisfy its claim from the partner's interest in the partnership.

charitable bequest. See BEQUEST.

charitable contribution. 1. A contribution of money or property to an organization engaged in charitable activities. **2.** A contribution to a qualified nonprofit charitable organization. • Charitable contributions are deductible for certain tax purposes.

charitable corporation. See CORPORATION.

charitable deduction. See DEDUCTION.

charitable immunity. See IMMUNITY (2).

charitable organization. *Tax.* A tax-exempt organization that (1) is created and operated exclusively for religious, scientific, literary, educational, athletic, public-safety, or community-service purposes, (2) does not distribute earnings for the benefit of private individuals, and (3) does not interfere in any way with political campaigns and decision-making processes. IRC (26 USCA) § 501(c)(3).

charitable purpose. *Tax.* The purpose for which an organization must be formed so that it qualifies as a charitable organization under the Internal Revenue Code.

charitable remainder. See REMAINDER.

charitable trust. See TRUST.

charlatan (**shahr**-lə-tən), *n.* A person who pretends to have more knowledge or skill than he or she actually has; a quack or faker. — **charlatanism, charlatanry,** *n.*

charter, *n.* **1.** An instrument by which a municipality is incorporated, specifying its organizational structure and its highest laws. **2.** The organic law of an organization; loosely, the highest law of any entity. Cf. ARTICLES OF INCORPORATION. **3.** A legislative act that creates a business or defines a corporate franchise. **4.** The leasing or hiring of an airplane, ship, or other vessel. — **charter,** *vb.*

charterparty. A contract by which a ship, or a principal part of it, is leased by the owner, esp. to a merchant for the conveyance of goods on a predetermined voyage to one or more places; a special contract between the shipowner and charterer, esp. for the carriage of goods at sea.

chattel (**chat**-əl). (*usu. pl.*) Movable or transferable property; esp., personal property.

chattel personal. A tangible good or an intangible right (such as a patent).

chattel real. A real-property interest that is less than a freehold or fee, such as a leasehold estate. • The most important chattel real is an estate for years in land, which is considered a chattel because it lacks the indefiniteness of time essential to real property.

chattel paper. A writing that shows both a monetary obligation and a security interest in or a lease of specific goods. • Chattel paper is generally used in a consumer transaction when the consumer buys goods on credit. The consumer typically promises to pay for the goods by executing a promissory note, and the seller retains a security interest in the goods.

electronic chattel paper. Chattel paper evidenced by a record or records consisting of information stored in an electronic medium and retrievable in perceivable form. UCC § 9–102(a)(22).

tangible chattel paper. Chattel paper evidenced by a record or records consisting of information that is inscribed on a tangible medium. UCC § 9–102(a)(54).

cheating. The fraudulent obtaining of another's property by means of a false symbol or token, or by other illegal practices. See FRAUD.

cheating by false pretenses. The act of purposely obtaining both the possession and ownership of money, goods, wares, or merchandise by means of misrepresentations, with the intent to defraud. See FALSE PRETENSES. Cf. *larceny by trick* under LARCENY.

check, *n.* A draft signed by the maker or drawer, drawn on a bank, payable on demand, and unlimited in negotiability. • Under UCC § 3–104(4), an instrument may be a check even though it is described on its face by another term, such as "money order." See DRAFT.

bad check. A check that is not honored because the account either contains insufficient funds or does not exist.

blank check. A check signed by the drawer but left blank as to the payee or the amount, or both.

canceled check. A check bearing a notation that it has been paid by the bank on which it was drawn.

cashier's check. A check drawn by a bank on itself, payable to another person, and evidencing the payee's authorization to receive from the bank the amount of money represented by the check; a draft for which the drawer and drawee are the same bank, or different branches of the same bank.

certified check. A depositor's check drawn on a bank that guarantees the availability of funds for the check. • The guarantee may be by the drawee's signed agreement to pay the draft or by a notation on the check that it is certified.

depository-transfer check. An unsigned, nonnegotiable check that is used by a bank to transfer funds from its branch to the collection bank.

raised check. A check whose face amount has been increased, usu. without the knowledge of the issuer — an act that under the UCC is considered a material alteration. UCC § 3–407. See RAISING AN INSTRUMENT.

stale check. A check that has been outstanding for an unreasonable time — more than six months under the UCC. • Banks in jurisdictions adopting the UCC may choose not to honor such a check. UCC § 4–404.

check, *vb.* **1.** To control or restrain <handcuffs checked the defendant's movement>. **2.** To verify or audit <an accountant checked the in-

voices>. **3.** To investigate <the police checked up on the suspect>.

check-kiting. The illegal practice of writing a check against a bank account with insufficient funds to cover the check, in the hope that the funds from a previously deposited check will reach the account before the bank debits the amount of the outstanding check.

checkpoint search. See SEARCH.

checks and balances. The theory of governmental power and functions whereby each branch of government has the ability to counter the actions of any other branch, so that no single branch can control the entire government. See SEPARATION OF POWERS.

Chicago Board of Trade. The commodities exchange where futures contracts in a large number of agricultural products are made. — Abbr. CBT; CBOT.

Chicago Board Options Exchange. The predominant organized marketplace in the United States for trading options. — Abbr. CBOE.

chicanery (shi-**kay**-nər-ee), *n.* Trickery; deception. — **chicanerous,** *adj.*

chief executive. See EXECUTIVE (1).

chief executive officer. A corporation's highest-ranking administrator, who manages the firm day by day and reports to the board of directors. — Abbr. CEO.

chief judge. See JUDGE.

chief justice. See JUSTICE (2).

child. 1. A person under the age of majority. **2.** *Hist.* At common law, a person who has not reached the age of 14. **3.** A boy or girl; a young person. **4.** A son or daughter. **5.** A baby or fetus. See JUVENILE; MINOR.

afterborn child. A child born after execution of a will or after the time in which a class gift closes. See *afterborn heir* under HEIR.

delinquent child. A child who has committed an offense that would be a crime if committed by an adult. • A delinquent child may not be subject to the jurisdiction of the juvenile court if the child is under a statutory age. Cf. JUVENILE DELINQUENT.

foster child. A child whose care and upbringing are entrusted to an adult other than the child's natural or adoptive parents, usu. by an agency. See *foster parent* under PARENT.

illegitimate child. A child who was not conceived or born in lawful wedlock, nor later legitimated.

incorrigible child. A child who refuses to obey his or her parents or guardians.

***legitimate child.* 1.** At common law, a child conceived or born in lawful wedlock. **2.** Modernly, a child conceived or born in lawful wedlock, or legitimated either by the parents' later marriage or by a declaration or judgment of legitimation.

***natural child.* 1.** A child by birth, as distinguished from an adopted child. **2.** A child that is genetically related to the mother and father as opposed to a child conceived by donor insemination or by egg donation. **3.** *Archaic.* An illegitimate child.

neglected child. **1.** A child whose parents or legal custodians are unfit to care for him or her because of cruelty, immorality, or incapacity. **2.** A child whose parents or legal custodians refuse to provide the necessary care and medical services for the child.

posthumous child. A child born after a parent's death. • Ordinarily, the phrase *posthumous child* suggests one born after the father's death. But in at least one case, a legally dead pregnant woman was kept on life-support machines until the child could be safely delivered; so it is possible for a mother's posthumous child to be born.

child abuse. See ABUSE.

child- and dependent-care tax credit. See TAX CREDIT.

child endangerment. The placing of a child in a place or position that exposes him or her to danger to life or health.

child-kidnapping. See KIDNAPPING.

child-labor law. A state or federal statute that protects children by prescribing the necessary working conditions for children in a workplace.

child molestation. See MOLESTATION.

child neglect. The failure of a person responsible for a minor to care for the minor's emotional or physical needs. Cf. CHILD ABUSE.

child pornography. See PORNOGRAPHY.

child support. *Family law.* **1.** A parent's legal obligation to contribute to the economic maintenance and education of a child until the age of majority, the child's emancipation before reaching majority, or the child's completion of secondary education. • The obligation is enforceable both civilly and criminally. **2.** In a custody or divorce action, the money legally owed by one parent to the other for the expenses incurred for children of the marriage. Cf. ALIMONY.

chill, *vb.* To inhibit or discourage <chill one's free-speech rights>.

chilling a sale. The act of bidders or others who combine or conspire to discourage others from attempting to buy an item so that they might buy the item themselves for a lower price.

chilling effect. **1.** *Constitutional law.* The result of a law or practice that seriously discourages the exercise of a constitutional right, such as the right to appeal or the right of free speech. **2.** Broadly, the result when any practice is discouraged.

Chinese wall. See ETHICAL WALL.

chit. **1.** A signed voucher for money received or owed, usu. for food, drink, or the like. **2.** A slip of paper with writing on it.

choate (**koh**-it), *adj.* **1.** Complete in and of itself. **2.** Having ripened or become perfected. — **choateness,** *n.* Cf. INCHOATE.

choice of law. The question of which jurisdiction's law should apply in a given case. See CONFLICT OF LAWS.

choice-of-law clause. A contractual provision by which the parties designate the jurisdiction whose law will govern any disputes that may arise between the parties. Cf. FORUM-SELECTION CLAUSE.

chose (shohz), *n.* [French] A thing, whether tangible or intangible; a personal article; a chattel. See THING.

chose in action. **1.** A proprietary right in personam, such as a debt owed by another person, a share in a joint-stock company, or a claim for damages in tort. **2.** The right to bring an action to recover a debt, sum of money, or thing. **3.** Personal property that one person owns but another person possesses, the owner being able to regain possession through a lawsuit.

churning, *n. Securities.* A stockbroker's excessive trading of a customer's account to earn more commissions rather than to further the customer's interests; an abuse of a customer's confidence for personal gain by frequent and numerous transactions, disproportionate to the size and nature of the customer's account. • Under securities laws, the practice is illegal — a violation of section 10(b) of the Securities Exchange Act of 1934 (15 USCA § 78j(b)). But because the fraud is the activity as a whole and there is no communication between the broker and the customer about a specific sale of securities, there is not normally a right of action for fraud based on churning. — **churn,** *vb.*

CIA. *abbr.* CENTRAL INTELLIGENCE AGENCY.

circa (**sər**-kə), *prep.* [Latin] About or around (a date, esp. an ancient one); approximately. — Abbr. ca.; c.

circuit, *n.* **1.** A judicial division in which hearings occur at several locations, as a result of which judges often travel to different courthouses. **2.** A judicial division of the United States — that is, one of the 13 circuits where the U.S. courts of appeals sit.

circuit court. See COURT.

circuit judge. See JUDGE.

circuit justice. See JUSTICE (2).

circuity of action. A procedure allowing duplicative lawsuits, leading to unnecessarily lengthy and indirect litigation, as when a defendant fails to bring a counterclaim, but later brings a separate action to recover what could have been awarded in the original lawsuit. • Civil-procedure rules have eliminated many problems associated with circuity of action.

circumstance, *n.* (*often pl.*) An accompanying or accessory fact, event, or condition, such as a piece of evidence that indicates the probability of an event. — **circumstantial,** *adj.*

aggravating circumstance. **1.** A fact or situation that increases the degree of liability or culpability for a criminal act. **2.** A fact or situation that relates to a criminal offense or defendant and that is considered by the court in imposing punishment (esp. a death sentence).

exigent circumstances. **1.** A situation that demands unusual or immediate action and that may allow people to circumvent usual procedures, as when a neighbor breaks through a window of a burning house to save someone inside. **2.** A situation in which a police officer must take immediate action to effectively make an arrest, search, or seizure for which probable cause exists, and thus may do so without first obtaining a warrant. • Exigent circumstances may exist if (1) a person's life or safety is threatened, (2) a suspect's escape is imminent, or (3) evidence is about to be removed or destroyed.

extraordinary circumstances. A highly unusual set of facts that are not commonly associated with a particular thing or event.

incriminating circumstance. A fact or situation showing either that a crime was committed or that a particular person committed it.

mitigating circumstance. **1.** A fact or situation that does not justify or excuse a wrongful act or offense but that reduces the degree of culpability and thus may reduce the damages (in a civil case) or the punishment (in a criminal case). **2.** A fact or situation that does not bear on the question of a defendant's guilt but that is considered by the court in imposing punishment and esp. in lessening the severity of a sentence. **3.** *Contracts.* An unusual or unpredictable event that prevents performance, such as a labor strike.

circumstantial evidence. See EVIDENCE.

citation, *n.* **1.** A court-issued writ that commands a person to appear at a certain time and place to do something demanded in the writ, or to show cause for not doing so. **2.** A police-issued order to appear before a judge on a given date to defend against a stated charge, such as a traffic violation. **3.** A reference to a legal precedent or authority, such as a case, statute, or treatise, that either substantiates or contradicts a given position. — **citational,** *adj.*

parallel citation. An additional reference to a case that has been reported in more than one reporter. • For example, whereas a *Bluebook* citation reads "*Morgan v. United States*, 304 U.S. 1 (1938)," the same reference including parallel citations reads "*Morgan v. United States*, 304 U.S. 1, 58 S.Ct. 773, 82 L.Ed. 1129 (1938)," in which the main citation is to the *U.S. Reports* and the parallel citations are to the *Supreme Court Reporter* and to the *Lawyer's Edition*.

pinpoint citation. The page on which a quotation or relevant passage appears, as opposed to the page on which a case or article begins. • For example, the number 217 is the pinpoint citation in *Baker v. Carr*, 369 U.S. 186, 217 (1962).

citation order. The appropriate ranking of the various authorities marshaled in support of a legal proposition.

cite, *vb.* **1.** To summon before a court of law <the witness was cited for contempt>. **2.** To refer to or adduce as precedent or authority <counsel then cited the appropriate statutory provision>. **3.** To commend or honor <the soldier was cited for bravery>.

citizen, *n.* **1.** A person who, by either birth or naturalization, is a member of a political community, owing allegiance to the community and being entitled to enjoy all its civil rights and protections; a member of the civil state, entitled to all its privileges. Cf. RESIDENT; DOMICILIARY. **2.**

For diversity-jurisdiction purposes, a corporation that was incorporated within a state or has its principal place of business there.

citizen's arrest. See ARREST.

Citizenship Clause. The clause of the U.S. Constitution providing that all persons born or naturalized in the United States are citizens of the United States and the state they reside in. U.S. Const. art. XIV, § 1, cl. 1.

city attorney. An attorney employed by a city to advise it and represent it in legal matters.

civ. ct. *abbr.* See *civil court* under COURT.

civic, *adj.* **1.** Of or relating to citizenship or a particular citizen <civic responsibilities>. **2.** Of or relating to a city <civic center>.

civil, *adj.* **1.** Of or relating to the state or its citizenry. **2.** Of or relating to private rights and remedies that are sought by action or suit, as distinct from criminal proceedings. **3.** Of or relating to any of the modern legal systems derived from Roman law.

civil action. See ACTION.

civil assault. See ASSAULT.

Civil Code. 1. The code that embodied the law of Rome. **2.** The code that embodies the law of France, from which a great part of the Louisiana Civil Code is derived. — Abbr. C.C. See NAPOLEONIC CODE. **3.** A codification of noncriminal statutes.

civil commitment. See COMMITMENT.

civil commotion. A public uprising by a large number of people who, acting together, cause harm to people or property. • A civil commotion usually involves many more people than a riot. Cf. RIOT.

civil conspiracy. See CONSPIRACY.

civil contempt. See CONTEMPT.

civil court. See COURT.

civil disability. See DISABILITY (2).

civil disobedience. A deliberate but nonviolent act of lawbreaking to call attention to a particular law or set of laws of questionable legitimacy or morality.

civil disorder. A public disturbance involving three or more people who commit violent acts that cause immediate danger or injury to people or property. See RIOT.

civil forfeiture. See FORFEITURE.

civil fraud. See FRAUD.

civil injury. See INJURY.

civilization. The transformation of a criminal matter to a civil one by law or judgment. Cf. CRIMINALIZATION.

civil justice. The methods by which a society redresses civil wrongs. Cf. CRIMINAL JUSTICE (1).

civil law. 1. (*usu. cap.*) One of the two prominent legal systems in the Western World, originally administered in the Roman Empire and still influential in continental Europe, Latin America, Scotland, and Louisiana, among other parts of the world. Cf. COMMON LAW (2). **2.** ROMAN LAW (1). **3.** The body of law imposed by the state, as opposed to moral law. **4.** The law of civil or private rights, as opposed to criminal law or administrative law. — Abbr. CL.

civil liability. See LIABILITY.

civil liberty. (*usu. pl.*) Freedom from undue governmental interference or restraint. • This term usually refers to freedom of speech or religion.

civil marriage. See MARRIAGE (2).

civil penalty. See PENALTY.

civil procedure. **1.** The body of law — usu. rules enacted by the legislature or courts — governing the methods and practices used in civil litigation. **2.** A particular method or practice used in carrying on civil litigation.

civil right. (*usu. pl.*) **1.** The individual rights of personal liberty guaranteed by the Bill of Rights and by the 13th, 14th, 15th, and 19th Amendments, as well as by legislation such as the Voting Rights Act. • Civil rights include especially the right to vote, the right of due process, and the right of equal protection under the law. **2.** CIVIL LIBERTY.

civil-rights act. One of several federal statutes enacted after the Civil War (1861–1865) and, much later, during and after the civil-rights movement of the 1950s and 1960s, for the purpose of implementing and giving further force to the basic rights guaranteed by the Constitution, and esp. prohibiting discrimination in employment and education on the basis of race, sex, religion, color, or age.

civil-rights removal. See REMOVAL.

civil wrong. See WRONG; TORT.

C.J. *abbr.* **1.** See *chief justice* under JUSTICE (2). **2.** See *chief judge* under JUDGE. **3.** See *circuit judge* under JUDGE. **4.** CORPUS JURIS.

CJE. CONTINUING JUDICIAL EDUCATION.

C.J.S. *abbr. Corpus Juris Secundum.*

CL. *abbr.* CIVIL LAW.

Claflin-trust principle. The doctrine that a trust cannot be terminated by the beneficiaries if the termination would defeat one of the settlor's material purposes in establishing the trust.

claim, *n.* **1.** The aggregate of operative facts giving rise to a right enforceable by a court. **2.** The assertion of an existing right; any right to payment or to an equitable remedy, even if contingent or provisional. **3.** A demand for money or property to which one asserts a right. **4.** An interest or remedy recognized at law; the means by which a person can obtain a privilege, possession, or enjoyment of a right or thing; CAUSE OF ACTION (1). **5.** A right to payment or to an equitable remedy for breach of performance if the breach gives rise to a right to payment.

claim and delivery. A claim for the recovery of specific personal property wrongfully taken or detained, as well as for any damages caused by the taking or detention.

claimant, *n.* One who asserts a right or demand, esp. formally.

claim for relief. The part of a complaint in a civil action specifying what relief the plaintiff asks of the court.

claim of ownership. **1.** The possession of a piece of property with the intention of claiming it in hostility to the true owner. **2.** A party's manifest intention to take over land, regardless of title or right.

claims-made policy. See INSURANCE POLICY.

clandestine (klan-**des**-tin), *adj.* Secret or concealed, esp. for illegal or unauthorized purposes.

class, *n.* **1.** A group of people, things, qualities, or activities that have common characteristics or attributes. **2.** The order or rank that people or things are arranged in. **3.** A group of people, uncertain in number.

testamentary class (tes-tə-**men**-tə-ree *or* -tree). A group of beneficiaries who are uncertain in number but whose number will be ascertainable in the future, when each will take an equal or other proportionate share of the gift.

4. *Civil procedure.* A group of people who have a common legal position, so that all their claims can be efficiently adjudicated in a single proceeding.

settlement class. Numerous similarly situated people for whom a claimant's representative and an adversary propose a contract liquidating the claims of all class members. • During the 1980s and 1990s, mass-tort defendants began using settlement classes as a means of foreclosing claims by some unknown number of future claimants.

class action. A lawsuit in which a single person or a small group of people represents the interests of a larger group. • Federal procedure has several requirements for maintaining a class action: (1) the class must be so large that individual suits would be impracticable, (2) there must be legal or factual questions common to the class, (3) the claims or defenses of the representative parties must be typical of those of the class, and (4) the representative parties must adequately protect the interests of the class. Fed. R. Civ. P. 23.

hybrid class action. A type of action in which the rights to be enforced are several and varied, but the object is to adjudicate claims that do or may affect the specific property in the action.

class gift. See GIFT.

class-one insured. See INSURED.

class representative. See REPRESENTATIVE.

class-two insured. See INSURED.

class voting. See VOTING.

clause, *n.* **1.** A distinct section or provision of a legal document or instrument. **2.** ITEM (2). — **clausal,** *adj.*

clawback, *n.* **1.** Money taken back. **2.** The retrieval or recovery of tax allowances by additional forms of taxation. — **claw back,** *vb.*

Clayton Act. A federal statute — enacted in 1914 to amend the Sherman Act — that prohibits price discrimination, tying arrangements, and exclusive-dealing contracts, as well as mergers and interlocking directorates, if their effect might substantially lessen competition or create a monopoly in any line of commerce. 15 USCA §§ 12–27.

CLE. *abbr.* CONTINUING LEGAL EDUCATION.

clean-hands doctrine. The principle that a party cannot seek equitable relief or assert an equitable defense if that party has violated an equitable principle, such as good faith. • Such a party is described as having "unclean hands."

clear, *vb.* **1.** To acquit or exonerate. **2.** (Of a drawee bank) to pay (a check or draft) out of funds held on behalf of the maker. **3.** (Of a check or draft) to be paid by the drawee bank out of funds held on behalf of the maker.

clear and convincing evidence. See EVIDENCE.

clear-and-present-danger test. *Constitutional law.* The doctrine allowing the government to restrict the First Amendment freedoms of speech and press if necessary to prevent immediate and severe danger to interests that the government may lawfully protect. • This test was formulated by Justice Oliver Wendell Holmes in *Schenck v. United States*, 249 U.S. 47, 39 S.Ct. 247 (1919).

clear error. See ERROR (2).

***Clearfield Trust* doctrine.** The doctrine describing the federal courts' power to make federal common law when there is both federal lawmaking power to do so and a strong federal interest in a nationally uniform rule. *Clearfield Trust Co. v. United States*, 318 U.S. 363, 63 S.Ct. 573 (1943). Cf. ERIE DOCTRINE.

clearinghouse. 1. A place where banks exchange checks and drafts and settle their daily balances; an association of banks or other payors regularly clearing items. See UCC § 4–104(a)–(d). **2.** A stock-and-commodity exchange where the daily transactions of the brokers are cleared. **3.** Any place for the exchange of specialized information.

clearly-erroneous standard. The standard of review that an appellate court usu. applies in judging a trial court's treatment of factual issues. • Under this standard, a judgment will be upheld unless the appellate court is left with the firm conviction that an error has been committed.

clear-reflection-of-income standard. *Tax.* An income-accounting method that the IRS can force on a taxpayer if the method used does not clearly reflect income. IRC (26 USCA) § 446(b).

clear title. See TITLE (2).

clemency (**klem**-ən-see), *n.* Mercy or leniency; esp., the power of the President or a governor to pardon a criminal or commute a criminal sentence. — **clement** (**klem**-ənt), *adj.* See PARDON; COMMUTATION.

clerical error. See ERROR (2).

clerical misprision. See MISPRISION.

clerk, *n.* **1.** A public official whose duties include keeping records or accounts. **2.** A court officer responsible for filing papers, issuing process, and keeping records of court proceedings as generally specified by rule or statute. **3.** A law student who assists a lawyer or judge with legal research, writing, and other tasks. See INTERN. **4.** A lawyer who assists a judge with research, writing, and case management.

clerkship. A type of internship in which a law student or recent law-school graduate assists a lawyer or judge with legal writing, research, and other tasks. — **clerk,** *vb.*

client, *n.* A person or entity that employs a professional for advice or help in that professional's line of work. — **cliental,** *adj.*

***Clifford* trust.** See TRUST.

clinical legal studies. Law-school training in which students participate in actual cases under the supervision of a practicing attorney or law professor.

close, *n.* **1.** An enclosed portion of land. **2.** The interest of a person in a particular piece of land, enclosed or not. **3.** The final price of a stock at the end of the exchange's trading day.

close, *vb.* **1.** To conclude; to bring to an end. **2.** To conclude discussion or negotiation about. See CLOSING.

close corporation. See CORPORATION.

closed, *adj.* **1.** (Of a class or organization) confined to a limited number <a closed mass-tort class>. **2.** (Of a proceeding or gathering) conducted in secrecy <a closed hearing>.

closed policy. See INSURANCE POLICY.

closed session. See SESSION.

closed transaction. See TRANSACTION.

closing. 1. *Real estate.* The final meeting between the parties to a transaction, at which the transaction is consummated; esp., in real estate, the final transaction between the buyer and seller, whereby the conveyancing documents are concluded and the money and property transferred. **2.** *Wills & estates.* The completion of the administration of a decedent's estate, brought about by the administrator's distribution of estate assets, payment of taxes, and filing of necessary accounts with the probate court.

closing argument. In a trial, a lawyer's final statement to the judge or jury before deliberation begins, in which the lawyer requests the judge or jury to consider the evidence and to apply the law in his or her client's favor.

closing statement. 1. CLOSING ARGUMENT. **2.** A written breakdown of the costs involved in a particular real-estate transaction, usu. prepared by a lender or an escrow agent.

cloture (**kloh**-chər), *n.* The procedure of ending debate in a legislative body and calling for an immediate vote. — **cloture,** *vb.*

cloud on title. A defect or potential defect in the owner's title to a piece of land arising from some claim or encumbrance, such as a lien, an easement, or a court order. See *action to quiet title* under ACTION.

CLS. *abbr.* CRITICAL LEGAL STUDIES.

CLSer. See CRIT.

CMR. *abbr.* **1.** COURT-MARTIAL REPORTS. **2.** See *court of military review* under COURT OF CRIMINAL APPEALS.

CN. *abbr.* Code Napoléon. See NAPOLEONIC CODE (1).

coadjutor (koh-ə-**joo**-tər *or* koh-**aj**-ə-tər), *n.* A coworker or assistant. — **coadjutor,** *adj.*

Coase Theorem (kohs). An economic proposition describing the relationship between legal rules about entitlements and economic efficiency. • The theorem, innovated by Ronald Coase, holds that if there are no transaction costs — such as the costs of bargaining or acquiring information — then any legal rule will produce an efficient result.

COBRA (koh-brə). *abbr.* CONSOLIDATED OMNIBUS BUDGET RECONCILIATION ACT OF 1985.

coconspirator. A person who engages in a criminal conspiracy with another; a fellow conspirator. See CONSPIRATOR.

coconspirator's exception. An exception to the hearsay rule whereby one conspirator's acts and statements, if made during and in furtherance of the conspiracy, are admissible against a defendant even if the statements are made in the defendant's absence. See HEARSAY.

C.O.D. *abbr.* **1.** Cash on delivery; collect on delivery. **2.** Costs on delivery. **3.** Cash on demand.

code. A complete system of positive law, carefully arranged and officially promulgated; a systematic collection or revision of laws, rules, or regulations <the Uniform Commercial Code>. • Strictly, a code is a compilation not just of existing statutes, but also of much of the unwritten law on a subject, which is newly enacted as a complete system of law.

codefendant. One of two or more defendants sued in the same litigation or charged with the same crime. Cf. COPLAINTIFF.

Code Napoléon **(kohd** na-poh-lay-**awn).** See NAPOLEONIC CODE.

code of conduct. A written set of rules governing the behavior of specified groups, such as lawyers, government employees, or corporate employees.

Code of Federal Regulations. The annual collection of executive-agency regulations published in the daily Federal Register, combined with previously issued regulations that are still in effect. — Abbr. CFR.

Code of Professional Responsibility. See MODEL CODE OF PROFESSIONAL RESPONSIBILITY.

code pleading. See PLEADING (2).

codicil (kod-ə-səl *or* -sil). A supplement or addition to a will, not necessarily disposing of the entire estate but modifying, explaining, or otherwise qualifying the will in some way. • When admitted to probate, the codicil becomes a part of the will.

codification (kod-ə-fi-**kay**-shən), *n.* **1.** The process of compiling, arranging, and systematizing the laws of a given jurisdiction, or of a discrete branch of the law, into an ordered code. **2.** The code that results from this process. — **codify (kod-ə-fı)**, *vb.* — **codifier (kod-ə-fı-ər)**, *n.*

codifying statute. See STATUTE.

coemption (koh-**emp**-shən), *n.* The act of purchasing the entire quantity of any commodity. — **coemptional, coemptive,** *adj.*

coerced confession. See CONFESSION.

coercion (koh-**ər**-shən), *n.* **1.** Compulsion by physical force or threat of physical force. • An act such as signing a will is not legally valid if done under coercion. See DURESS; UNDUE

INFLUENCE. **2.** Conduct that constitutes the improper use of economic power to compel another to submit to the wishes of one who wields it. — **coerce** (koh-**ərs**), *vb.* — **coercive,** *adj.* — **coercer,** *n.*

coercive relief. See RELIEF.

cogent (**koh**-jənt), *adj.* Compelling or convincing. — **cogency,** *n.*

cognate, *n.* One who is kin to another. Cf. AGNATE.

cognate offense. See OFFENSE.

cognation (kog-**nay**-shən), *n.* Relationship by blood rather than by marriage; relationship arising through common descent from the same man and woman, whether the descent is traced through males or females. — **cognatic** (kog-**nat**-ik), *adj.*

cognitive test. *Criminal law.* A test of the defendant's ability to know certain things, specifically the nature of his or her conduct and whether the conduct was right or wrong. • This test is used in assessing whether a defendant may rely on an insanity defense.

cognizable (**kog**-ni-zə-bəl), *adj.* **1.** Capable of being known or recognized; esp., capable of being identified as a group because of a common characteristic or interest that cannot be represented by others. **2.** Capable of being judicially tried or examined before a designated tribunal; within the court's jurisdiction.

cognizance (**kog**-ni-zəns), *n.* **1.** The right and power to try and determine cases; JURISDICTION. **2.** The taking of judicial or authoritative notice. **3.** Acknowledgment or admission of an alleged fact. **4.** *Common-law pleading.* In a replevin action, a plea by the defendant that the goods are held in bailment for another.

cognovit (kog-**noh**-vit). [Latin "he has conceded (a debt or an action)"] An acknowledgment of debt or liability in the form of a confessed judgment. See CONFESSION OF JUDGMENT.

cognovit clause. A contractual provision by which a debtor agrees to jurisdiction in certain courts, waives notice requirements, and authorizes the entry of an adverse judgment in the event of a default or breach. • Cognovit clauses are outlawed or restricted in most states.

cohabitation (koh-hab-ə-**tay**-shən), *n.* The fact or state of living together, esp. as partners in life, usu. with the suggestion of sexual relations. — **cohabit** (koh-**hab**-it), *vb.* — **cohabitative** (koh-**hab**-ə-tay-tiv), *adj.* — **cohabitant** (koh-**hab**-ə-tənt), *n.*

illicit cohabitation. **1.** The condition of a man and a woman who, though not married, live together in circumstances that make the arrangement illegal. **2.** The offense committed by an unmarried man and woman who live together as husband and wife and engage in sexual intercourse. • This offense, where it still exists, is seldom prosecuted. — Also termed LASCIVIOUS COHABITATION.

notorious cohabitation. The act of a man and a woman who, though not married, live together openly under circumstances that make the arrangement illegal.

cohort analysis (**koh**-hort). A method of measuring racial discrimination in the workplace by comparing, at several points in time, the pay and promotions of employees of different races.

Coinage Clause. The provision in the U.S. Constitution (art. I, § 8, cl. 5) granting to Congress the power to coin money.

coinsurance. See INSURANCE.

cold blood. A killer's state of mind when committing a willful and premeditated homicide. See COOL BLOOD. Cf. HEAT OF PASSION.

collapsible corporation. See CORPORATION.

collapsible partnership. See PARTNERSHIP.

collateral (kə-**lat**-ər-əl), *adj.* **1.** Supplementary; accompanying, but secondary and subordinate to <whether the accident victim was wearing a seat belt is a collateral issue>. **2.** Not direct in line, but on a parallel or diverging line of descent <an uncle is in my collateral line of descent>. Cf. LINEAL. — **collaterality** (kə-lat-ər-**al**-ə-tee), *n.*

collateral (kə-**lat**-ər-əl), *n.* **1.** A person collaterally related to a decedent. **2.** Property that is pledged as security against a debt; the property subject to a security interest. See UCC § 9–102(a)(9).

collateral ascendant. See ASCENDANT.

collateral attack. An attack on a judgment entered in a different proceeding. • A petition for a writ of habeas corpus is one type of collateral attack. Cf. DIRECT ATTACK.

collateral consanguinity. See CONSANGUINITY.

collateral contract. See CONTRACT.

collateral-contract doctrine. The principle that in a dispute concerning a written contract, proof of a second (but oral) agreement will not be excluded under the parol-evidence rule if the oral agreement is independent of and not inconsistent with the written contract, and if the information in the oral agreement would not ordinarily be expected to be included in the written contract.

collateral estoppel (e-**stop**-əl). An affirmative defense barring a party from relitigating an issue determined against that party in an earlier action, even if the second action differs significantly from the first one. Cf. RES JUDICATA.

defensive collateral estoppel. Estoppel asserted by a defendant to prevent a plaintiff from relitigating an issue previously decided against the plaintiff and for another defendant.

offensive collateral estoppel. Estoppel asserted by a plaintiff to prevent a defendant from relitigating an issue previously decided against the defendant and for another plaintiff.

collateral heir. See HEIR.

collateral issue. See ISSUE (1).

collateralize (kə-**lat**-ər-əl-IZ), *vb.* **1.** To serve as collateral for. **2.** To make (a loan) secure with collateral. — **collateralization** (kə-lat-ər-əl-ə-**zay**-shən), *n.*

collateral line. See LINE.

collateral matter. *Evidence.* Any matter on which evidence could not have been introduced for a relevant purpose. • If a witness has erred in testifying about a detail that is collateral to the relevant facts, then another party cannot call witnesses to contradict that point — cross-examination alone must suffice.

collateral-negligence doctrine. The rule holding that one who engages an independent contractor is not liable for physical harm that the contractor causes if (1) the contractor's negligence consists solely of the improper manner in which the contractor's work is performed, (2) the risk of harm created is not normal to the work, and (3) the employer had no reason to contemplate the contractor's negligence when the contract was made.

collateral-order doctrine. A doctrine allowing appeal from an interlocutory order that conclusively determines an issue wholly separate from the merits of the action and effectively unreviewable on appeal from a final judgment. See *appealable decision* under DECISION.

collateral proceeding. See PROCEEDING.

collateral relative. See RELATIVE.

collateral-source rule. *Torts.* The doctrine that if an injured party receives compensation for the injuries from a source independent of the tortfeasor, the payment should not be deducted from the damages that the tortfeasor must pay. • Insurance proceeds are the most common collateral source.

collateral warranty. See WARRANTY (1).

collation (kə-**lay**-shən), *n.* **1.** The comparison of a copy with its original to ascertain its correctness; the report of the officer who made the comparison. **2.** The taking into account of the value of advancements made by an intestate to his or her children so that the estate may be divided in accordance with the intestacy statute. — **collate** (kə-**layt**), *vb.* — **collator** (kə-**lay**-tər), *n.*

collecting bank. See BANK.

collective mark. A trademark or servicemark used by an association, union, or other group either to identify the group's products or services or to signify membership in the group.

collective punishment. A penalty inflicted on a group of persons without regard to individual responsibility for the conduct giving rise to the penalty.

collective work. *Copyright.* **1.** A publication (such as a periodical issue, anthology, or encyclopedia) in which several contributions, constituting separate and independent works in themselves, are assembled into a copyrightable whole. **2.** A selection and arrangement of brief portions of different movies, television shows, or radio shows into a single copyrightable work. Cf. COMPILATION (1).

colloquium (kə-**loh**-kwee-əm). *Defamation.* **1.** The offer of extrinsic evidence to show that the alleged defamatory statement referred to the plaintiff even though it did not explicitly mention the plaintiff. **2.** The introductory averments in a plaintiff's pleading setting out all the special circumstances that make the challenged words defamatory. Pl. **collo-**

quiums, colloquia. Cf. INDUCEMENT (4); INNUENDO (2).

colloquy (**kol**-ə-kwee). Any formal discussion, such as an oral exchange between a judge, the prosecutor, the defense counsel, and a criminal defendant in which the judge ascertains the defendant's understanding of the proceedings and of the defendant's rights.

collusion (kə-**loo**-zhən), *n.* An agreement to defraud another or to do or obtain something forbidden by law. — **collude,** *vb.* — **collusive,** *adj.* — **colluder,** *n.*

collusive action. See ACTION.

collusive joinder. See JOINDER.

color, *n.* **1.** Appearance, guise, or semblance; esp., the appearance of a legal claim to a right, authority, or office. **2.** *Common-law pleading.* An apparent, but legally insufficient, ground of action, admitted in a defendant's pleading to exist for the plaintiff; esp., a plaintiff's apparent (and usu. false) right or title to property, the existence of which is pleaded by the defendant as a confession and avoidance to remove the case from the jury by turning the issue from one of fact to one of law. — **colorable,** *adj.*

colorable transaction. See TRANSACTION.

Colorado River **abstention.** See ABSTENTION.

color of law. The appearance or semblance, without the substance, of a legal right. • The term usually implies a misuse of power made possible because the wrongdoer is clothed with the authority of the state. *State action* is synonymous with *color of law* in the context of federal civil-rights statutes or criminal law. See STATE ACTION.

color of title. A written instrument or other evidence that appears to give title, but does not do so.

comes now. *Jargon.* Traditionally, the standard commencement in pleadings <Comes now the plaintiff, Gilbert Lewis, by and through his attorneys of record, and would show unto the court the following>. • For a plural subject, the phrase is *come now* <Come now the plaintiffs, Bob and Louise Smith>. — Also termed *now comes.*

comity (**kom**-ə-tee). Courtesy among political entities (as nations, states, or courts of different jurisdictions), involving esp. mutual recognition of legislative, executive, and judicial acts. Cf. ABSTENTION.

> ***judicial comity.*** The respect a court of one state or jurisdiction shows to another state or jurisdiction in giving effect to the other's laws and judicial decisions.

Comity Clause. The clause of the U.S. Constitution giving citizens of one state the right to all privileges and immunities enjoyed by citizens of the other states. U.S. Const. art. IV, § 2, cl. 1. See PRIVILEGES AND IMMUNITIES CLAUSE.

comm. *abbr.* COMMONWEALTH.

command. 1. An order; a directive. **2.** In legal positivism, the sovereign's express desire that a person act or refrain from acting a certain way, combined with the threat of punishment for failure to comply. — **command,** *vb.*

Commander in Chief Clause. The clause of the U.S. Constitution appointing the President as supreme commander of the military. U.S. Const. art. II, § 2, cl. 1.

comment, *n.* **1.** NOTE (2). **2.** An explanatory statement made by the drafters of a particular statute, code section, or rule. — **commentator,** *n.*

comment on the evidence. A statement made to the jury by the judge or by counsel on the probative value of certain evidence. • Most state-court judges are not permitted to make statements when examining a witness, instructing the jury, and the like (in which case the comment is sometimes termed an *impermissible comment on the evidence*).

commerce. The exchange of goods and services, esp. on a large scale involving transportation between cities, states, and nations.

interstate commerce. Trade and other business activities between those located in different states; esp., traffic in goods and travel of people between states.

intrastate commerce. Commerce that begins and ends entirely within the borders of a single state.

Commerce Clause. U.S. Const. art. I, § 8, cl. 3, which gives Congress the exclusive power to regulate commerce among the states, with foreign nations, and with Indian tribes.

Dormant Commerce Clause. The constitutional principle that the Commerce Clause prevents state regulation of interstate commercial activity even when Congress has not acted under its Commerce Clause power to regulate that activity.

commercial-activity exception. An exemption from the rule of sovereign immunity, permitting a claim against a foreign state if the claim arises from private acts undertaken by the foreign state, as opposed to the state's public acts.

commercial bank. See BANK.

commercial bribery. See BRIBERY.

commercial crime. See CRIME.

commercial domicile. See DOMICILE.

commercial frustration. See FRUSTRATION.

commercial impracticability. See IMPRACTICABILITY.

commercialized obscenity. See OBSCENITY.

commercial law. The substantive law dealing with the sale and distribution of goods, the financing of credit transactions on the security of the goods sold, and negotiable instruments. • Most American commercial law is governed by the Uniform Commercial Code.

commercial lease. See LEASE.

commercial loan. See LOAN.

commercially reasonable, *adj.* (Of a property sale) conducted in good faith and in accordance with commonly accepted commercial practice. • Under the UCC, a sale of collateral by a secured party must be done in a commercially reasonable manner, or the sale may be rescinded. UCC § 9–504.

commercial speech. See SPEECH.

commercial tort claim. A claim arising in tort when the claimant is either (1) an organization, or (2) an individual whose claim arose in the course of the claimant's business or profession, and the claim does not include damages arising out of personal injury or death. UCC § 9–102(a)(10).

commercial unit. A unit of goods that by commercial usage is a single whole for purposes of lease and whose division materially impairs its character or value in its market or in use. UCC § 2–102(a)(7). • Under the UCC, "a commercial unit may be a single article, such as a machine; a set of articles, such as a suite of furniture or a line of machinery; a quantity, such as a gross or carload; or any other unit treated in use or in the relevant market as a single whole." *Id.*

commingle (kə-**ming**-gəl), *vb.* To put together in one mass, as when one mixes separate funds or properties into a common fund. — **commingling** (kə-**ming**-gling), *n.*

commissary (**kom**-i-ser-ee), *n.* A person who is delegated or commissioned to perform some duty, usu. as a representative of a superior. — **commissary,** *adj.*

commission, *n.* **1.** A warrant or authority, from the government or a court, that empowers the person named to execute official acts. **2.** The authority under which a person transacts business for another. **3.** A body of persons acting under lawful authority to perform certain public services. **4.** The act of doing or perpetrating (as a crime). **5.** A fee paid to an agent or employee for a particular transaction, usu. as a percentage of the money received from the transaction.

commission del credere (del **kred**-ər-ay). The commission received by the seller's agent for guaranteeing a buyer's debt.

commissioner. 1. A person who directs a commission; a member of a commission. **2.** The administrative head of an organization, such as a professional sport.

commission plan. A form of municipal government whereby both legislative and executive power is vested in a small group of elected officials. • Today, commission plans are used in only a few cities.

commission to examine a witness. A judicial commission directing that a witness beyond the court's territorial jurisdiction be deposed. Cf. LETTER OF REQUEST.

commissive waste. See WASTE (1).

commit, *vb.* **1.** To perpetrate (a crime). **2.** To send (a person) to prison or to a mental health facility, esp. by court order.

commitment, *n.* **1.** An agreement to do something in the future, esp. to assume a financial obligation. **2.** The act of entrusting or giving in charge. **3.** The act of confining a person in a prison, mental hospital, or other institution. **4.** The order directing an officer to take a person to a penal or mental institution.

civil commitment. A commitment of a person who is ill, incompetent, drug-addicted, or the like, as contrasted with a criminal sentence.

diagnostic commitment. Presentencing confinement of an individual, usu. to determine the individual's competency to stand trial or to determine the appropriate sentence to be rendered.

mandatory commitment. An automatically required commitment for a defendant found not guilty by reason of insanity. • This type of commitment is required under federal law, but in only a minority of states.

committee. 1. (kə-**mit**-ee) A group of people appointed or elected to consider, determine, or manage a matter. **2.** (kom-i-**tee**) A person who is civilly committed, usu. to a psychiatric hospital. **3.** (kom-i-**tee**) The guardian for the person so committed.

committing magistrate. See MAGISTRATE.

commodity. 1. A tangible article of trade or commerce. **2.** An economic good, esp. a raw material or an agricultural product.

common, *n.* **1.** A legal right to use another person's property, such as an easement. See PROFIT À PRENDRE. **2.** A tract of land set aside for the general public's use.

commonality test. The principle that a group seeking to be certified as a class in a class-action suit must share at least one issue whose resolution will affect all or a significant number of the putative class members.

common area. 1. *Landlord–tenant law.* The realty that all tenants may use though the landlord retains control and responsibility over it. **2.** An area owned and used in common by the residents of a condominium, subdivision, or planned-unit development.

common-authority rule. The principle that a person may consent to a police officer's search of another person's property if both persons use, control, or have access to the property. • Under this rule, the consenting person must have been legally able to permit the search in his or her own right, and the defendant must have assumed the risk that a fellow occupant might permit a search. See THIRD-PARTY CONSENT.

common carrier. See CARRIER.

common-character requirement. The rule that for a group of persons to qualify as a class in a class-action lawsuit, the appointment of the class must achieve economies of time, effort, and expense, and must promote uniformity of decision for persons similarly situated in addition to sharing common questions of fact and law.

common design. 1. The intention by two or more people to join in committing an unlawful act. **2.** An intention to commit more than one crime. **3.** The general design or layout of plots of land surrounding a particular tract. See ZONING.

common disaster. An event that causes two or more persons with related property interests (such as an insured and the beneficiary) to die at very nearly the same time, with no way of telling who died first. See UNIFORM SIMULTANEOUS DEATH ACT.

common-disaster clause. A provision in a dispositive instrument, such as an insurance policy or a will, that seeks to cover the situation in which the transferor and transferee die in a common disaster.

common duty of care. A landowner's obligation to take reasonable care under the circumstances to see that a lawful visitor will be reasonably safe in using the premises for the purposes for which the visitor is permitted to be there.

common easement. See EASEMENT.

common-enemy doctrine. *Property.* The rule that a landowner may repel surface waters as necessary (as during a flood), without having to consider the consequences to other landowners. • The doctrine takes its name from the idea that the floodwater is every landowner's common enemy.

common error. *Copyright.* A mistake found both in a copyrighted work and in an allegedly infringing work, the mistake being persuasive evidence of unauthorized copying.

common informer. A person who sues to recover a penalty in a penal action. See INFORMER; *penal action* under ACTION.

common knowledge. A fact that is so generally known that a court may accept it as true without proof. See JUDICIAL NOTICE.

common-knowledge exception. The principle that lay testimony concerning routine or simple medical procedures is admissible to establish negligence in a medical-malpractice action.

common law, *n.* [fr. Law French *commen ley* "common law"] **1.** The body of law derived from judicial decisions, rather than from statutes or constitutions; CASELAW. Cf. STATUTORY LAW.

federal common law. The judge-made law of federal courts, excluding the law in all cases governed by state law; specif., the body of decisional law derived from federal courts adjudicating federal questions and other matters of federal concern, such as the law applying to disputes between two states, as well as foreign-relations law.

general federal common law. Hist. In the period before *Erie v. Tompkins*, 304 U.S. 64, 58 S.Ct. 817 (1938), the judge-made law developed by federal courts in deciding disputes in diversity cases. • Since *Erie* was announced in 1938, a federal court has been bound to apply, as a general matter, the law of the state in which it sits. Thus, although there is a "federal common law," there is no *general* federal common law applicable to all disputes heard in federal court.

2. The body of law based on the English legal system, as distinct from a civil-law system. Cf. CIVIL LAW (1). **3.** General law common to the country as a whole, as opposed to special law that has only local application. **4.** The body of law to which no constitution or statute applies.

common-law crime. See CRIME.

common-law dedication. See DEDICATION.

common-law lawyer. A lawyer who is versed in or practices under a common-law system.

common-law marriage. See MARRIAGE (1).

common-law rule. 1. A judge-made rule as opposed to a statutory one. **2.** A legal as opposed to an equitable rule. **3.** A general rule as opposed to one deriving from special law (such as a local custom or a rule of foreign law that, based on choice-of-law principles, is applied in place of domestic law).

common-law state. Any state that has not adopted a community-property regime. • The chief difference today between a community-property state and a common-law state is that in a common-law state, a spouse's interest in property held by the other spouse does not vest until (1) a divorce action has been filed, or (2) the death of the other spouse. Cf. COMMUNITY-PROPERTY STATE.

common-nucleus-of-operative-fact test. The doctrine that a federal court will have jurisdiction over state-law claims that arise from the same facts as the federal claims providing a basis for subject-matter jurisdiction.

common plea. See PLEA (3).

common property. See PROPERTY.

common-source doctrine. The principle that a defendant in a trespass-to-try-title action who claims under a source common to both the defendant and the plaintiff may not demonstrate title in a third source that is paramount to the common source because doing so amounts to an attack on the source under which the defendant claims title.

common thief. See THIEF.

common traverse. See TRAVERSE.

common trust fund. See TRUST FUND.

commonwealth. 1. A nation, state, or other political unit <the Commonwealth of Pennsylvania>. **2.** A political unit that has local autonomy but is voluntarily united with the United States <Puerto Rico is a commonwealth>. Cf. DEPENDENCY (1); TERRITORY (2). **3.** A loose association of countries that recognize one sovereign <the British Commonwealth>. — Abbr. Commw.; comm.

commune (kom-yoon), *n.* A community of people who share property.

communication. 1. The expression or exchange of information by speech, writing, or gestures. **2.** The information so expressed or exchanged.

conditionally privileged communication. A defamatory statement made in good faith by a person with an interest in a subject to someone who also has an interest in the subject, as an employer giving a poor but accurate job review of a former employee to a potential future employer. • The privilege may be lost on a showing of malice or bad faith.

confidential communication. A communication made within a certain protected relationship — such as husband–wife, attorney–client, or priest–penitent — and legally protected from forced disclosure.

privileged communication. A communication that is protected by law from forced disclosure. See PRIVILEGE (3).

community. **1.** A neighborhood, vicinity, or locality. **2.** A society or group of people with similar rights or interests. **3.** A collection of common interests that arise from an association.

community control. A criminal sentence consisting in intensive and strict supervision of an offender in the community, as by restricting the offender's movements, conducting electronic surveillance, and severely sanctioning the offender for violations of any of the sentence terms.

community lease. See LEASE.

community of interest. **1.** Participation in a joint venture characterized by shared liability and shared opportunity for profit. See JOINT VENTURE. **2.** A common grievance that must be shared by all class members to maintain the class action. See CLASS ACTION. **3.** *Labor law.* A criterion used by the National Labor Relations Board in deciding whether a group of employees should be allowed to act as a bargaining unit.

community policing. A law-enforcement technique in which police officers are assigned to a particular neighborhood or area to develop relationships with the residents for the purpose of enhancing the chances of detecting and thwarting criminal activity.

community property. Property owned in common by husband and wife as a result of its having been acquired during the marriage by means other than an inheritance or a gift to one spouse, each spouse holding a one-half interest in the property. • Only nine states have community-property systems: Arizona, California, Idaho, Louisiana, Nevada, New Mexico, Texas, Washington, and Wisconsin. See *marital property* under PROPERTY. Cf. SEPARATE PROPERTY.

community-property state. A state in which spouses hold property that is acquired during marriage (other than property acquired by inheritance or individual gift) as community property. See COMMUNITY PROPERTY. Cf. COMMON-LAW STATE.

commutation (kom-yə-**tay**-shən), *n.* **1.** An exchange or replacement. **2.** *Criminal law.* The executive's substitution in a particular case of a less severe punishment for a more severe one that has already been judicially imposed on the defendant. Cf. PARDON; REPRIEVE. **3.** *Commercial & civil law.* The substitution of one form of payment for the other. — **commute,** *vb.* — **commutative,** *adj.*

commutative justice. See JUSTICE (1).

commw. *abbr.* COMMONWEALTH.

compact (**kom**-pakt), *n.* An agreement or covenant between two or more parties, esp. between governments or states.

interstate compact. A voluntary agreement between states enacted into law in the participating states upon federal congressional approval. Cf. INTERSTATE AGREEMENT.

Compact Clause. U.S. Const. art. I, § 10, cl. 3, which disallows a state from entering into a contract with another state or a foreign country without congressional approval.

company. A corporation — or, less commonly, an association, partnership, or union — that carries on a commercial or industrial enterprise; a corporation, partnership, association, joint-stock company, trust, fund, or organized group of persons, whether incorporated or not, and (in an official capacity) any receiver, trustee in bankruptcy, or similar official, or liquidating agent, for any of the foregoing. Investment Company Act § 2(a)(8) (15 USCA § 80a–2(a)(8)). — Abbr. co.; com.

holding company. A company formed to control other companies, usu. confining its role to owning stock and supervising management.

joint-stock company. **1.** An unincorporated association of individuals possessing common capital, the capital being contributed by the members and divided into shares, of which each member possesses a number of shares proportionate to the member's investment. **2.** A partnership in which the capital is divided into shares that are transferable without the express consent of the partners.

limited company. A company in which the liability of each shareholder is limited to the amount individually invested. • A corporation is the most common example of a limited company.

limited-liability company. A company — statutorily authorized in certain states — that is characterized by limited liability, management by members or managers, and limitations on ownership transfer. — Abbr. L.L.C.

personal holding company. A holding company that is subject to special taxes and that usu. has a limited number of shareholders, with most of its revenue originating from passive income such as dividends, interest, rent, and royalties.

title company. A company that examines real-estate titles for any encumbrances, claims, or other flaws, and issues title insurance. See TITLE SEARCH.

trust company. A company that acts as a trustee for people and entities and that sometimes also operates as a commercial bank.

comparable (kom-pər-ə-bəl), *n.* (*usu. pl.*) A piece of property used as a comparison to determine the value of a similar piece of property.

comparable worth. **1.** The analogous value that two or more employees bring to a business through their work. **2.** The idea that employees who perform identical work should receive identical pay, regardless of their sex; the doctrine that men and women who perform work of equal value should receive comparable pay.

comparative disparity. *Constitutional law.* The percentage of underrepresentation of a particular group among potential jurors on a venire, in comparison with the group's percentage of the general population. See DUREN TEST; FAIR-CROSS-SECTION REQUIREMENT; STATISTICAL-DECISION THEORY. Cf. ABSOLUTE DISPARITY.

comparative-impairment test. *Conflict of laws.* A test that asks which of two or more forums would have its policies most impaired by not having its law applied in the case.

comparative interpretation. A method of statutory interpretation by which parts of the statute are compared to each other, and the statute as a whole is compared to other documents from the same source on a similar subject.

comparative jurisprudence. See JURISPRUDENCE.

comparative negligence. See NEGLIGENCE.

comparative-negligence doctrine. *Torts*. The principle that reduces a plaintiff's recovery proportionally to the plaintiff's degree of fault in causing the damage, rather than barring recovery completely. • Most states have statutorily adopted the comparative-negligence doctrine. See NEGLIGENCE. Cf. CONTRIBUTORY-NEGLIGENCE DOCTRINE.

comparative-rectitude doctrine. *Family law*. Before the advent of no-fault divorce, the rule providing that when both spouses show grounds for divorce, the party less at fault is granted the requested relief.

compel, *vb.* **1.** To cause or bring about by force or overwhelming pressure <a lawyer cannot be compelled to testify about a privileged communication>. **2.** (Of a legislative mandate or judicial precedent) to convince (a court) that there is only one possible resolution of a legal dispute <the wording of the statute compels us to affirm>. — **compellable,** *adj.*

compelling-state-interest test. *Constitutional law*. A method for determining the constitutional validity of a law, whereby the government's interest in the law is balanced against the individual's constitutional right to be free of the law. • Only if the government's interest is strong enough will the law be upheld. The compelling-state-interest test is used most commonly in equal-protection analysis when the disputed law requires strict scrutiny. See STRICT SCRUTINY.

compensable (kəm-**pen**-sə-bəl), *adj.* Able or entitled to be compensated for.

compensation (kom-pən-**say**-shən), *n.* **1.** Remuneration and other benefits received in return for services rendered; esp., salary or wages. **2.** Payment of damages, or any other act that a court orders to be done by a person who has caused injury to another and must therefore make the other whole. **3.** See SETOFF (2). — **compensatory** (kəm-**pen**-sə-tor-ee), *adj.* — **compensational** (kom-pən-**say**-shə-nəl), *adj.* — **compensate** (**kom**-pən-sayt), *vb.*

accrued compensation. Remuneration that has been earned but not yet paid.

deferred compensation. **1.** Payment for work performed, to be paid in the future or when some future event occurs. **2.** An employee's earnings that are taxed when received or distributed and not when earned, such as contributions to a qualified pension or profit-sharing plan.

just compensation. Under the Fifth Amendment, a fair payment by the government for property it has taken under eminent domain — usu.

the property's fair market value, so that the owner is no worse off after the taking.

unreasonable compensation. Under the Internal Revenue Code, pay that is out of proportion to the actual services rendered and is therefore not deductible as a business expense by the payor.

compensatory damages. See DAMAGES.

competence, *n.* **1.** A basic or minimal ability to do something; qualification, esp. to testify. **2.** The capacity of an official body to do something. **3.** Authenticity. — **competent,** *adj.* Cf. COMPETENCY.

competency, *n.* **1.** The mental ability to understand problems and make decisions. **2.** A criminal defendant's ability to stand trial, measured by the capacity to understand the proceedings, to consult meaningfully with counsel, and to assist in the defense. — **competent,** *adj.* See CAPACITY. Cf. COMPETENCE.

competency proceeding. See PROCEEDING.

competent evidence. 1. See *admissible evidence* under EVIDENCE. **2.** See *relevant evidence* under EVIDENCE.

competent witness. See WITNESS.

competition. The effort or action of two or more commercial interests to obtain the same business from third parties.

fair competition. Open, equitable, and just competition between business competitors.

horizontal competition. Competition between a seller and its competitors. • The Sherman Act prohibits unreasonable restraints on horizontal competition, such as price-fixing agreements between competitors.

vertical competition. Competition between participants at different levels of distribution, such as manufacturer and distributor.

compilation (kom-pə-**lay**-shən), *n.* **1.** *Copyright.* A collection of literary works arranged in an original way; esp., a work formed by collecting and assembling preexisting materials or data that are selected, coordinated, or arranged in such a way that the resulting product constitutes an original work of authorship. Cf. COLLECTIVE WORK; DERIVATIVE WORK. **2.** A collection of statutes, updated and arranged to facilitate their use. — **compile,** *vb.*

complainant (kəm-**playn**-ənt). **1.** The party who brings a legal complaint against another; esp., the plaintiff in a civil suit. **2.** A person who, under oath, signs a statement (called a "complaint") establishing reasonable grounds to believe that some named person has committed a crime.

complaint. 1. The initial pleading that starts a civil action and states the basis for the court's jurisdiction, the basis for the plaintiff's claim, and the demand for relief. • In some states, this pleading is called a *petition.* **2.** *Criminal law.* A formal charge accusing a person of an offense. Cf. INDICTMENT; INFORMATION.

amended complaint. A complaint that modifies and replaces the original complaint by adding relevant matters that occurred before or at the time the action began. • In some circumstances, a party must obtain the court's permission to amend its complaint.

preliminary complaint. A complaint issued by a court to obtain jurisdiction over a criminal suspect for a hearing on probable cause or on whether to bind the suspect over for trial.

supplemental complaint. An additional complaint that either corrects a defect in the original complaint or adds relevant matters that occurred after the action began. • Generally, a party must obtain the court's permission to file a supplemental complaint.

third-party complaint. A complaint filed by the defendant against a third party, alleging that the third party may be liable for some or all of the damages that the plaintiff is trying to recover from the defendant.

well-pleaded complaint. An original or initial pleading that sufficiently sets forth a claim for relief — by including the grounds for the court's jurisdiction, the basis for the relief claimed, and a demand for judgment — so that a defendant may draft an answer that is responsive to the issues presented. • A well-pleaded complaint must raise a controlling issue of federal law for a federal court to have federal-question jurisdiction over the lawsuit.

completed gift. See GIFT.

complete diversity. See DIVERSITY.

complete in itself, *adj.* (Of a legislative act) fully covering an entire subject.

complete integration. See INTEGRATION.

completely integrated contract. See INTEGRATED CONTRACT.

complete-preemption doctrine. The rule that a federal statute's preemptive force may be so extraordinary and all-encompassing that it converts an ordinary state-common-law complaint into one stating a federal claim for purposes of the well-pleaded-complaint rule.

complicity (kəm-**plis**-ə-tee), *n.* Association or participation in a criminal act; the act or state of being an accomplice. • Under the Model Penal Code, a person can be an accomplice as a result of either that person's own conduct or the conduct of another (such as an innocent agent) for which that person is legally accountable. Model Penal Code § 2.06. — **complicitous** (kəm-**plis**-ə-təs), *adj.* See ACCOMPLICE; *innocent agent* under AGENT.

composite work (kəm-**poz**-it). *Copyright.* An original publication that relates to a variety of subjects and that includes discrete selections from many authors. 17 USCA § 304(a).

composition, *n.* **1.** An agreement between a debtor and two or more creditors for the adjustment or discharge of an obligation for some lesser amount; an agreement among the debtor and two or more creditors that the debtor will pay the creditors less than their full claims in full satisfaction of their claims. **2.** The compensation paid as part of such an agreement. — **compose,** *vb.*

compos mentis (**kom**-pəs **men**-tis), *adj.* [Latin "master of one's mind"] Of sound mind; having use and control over one's own mental faculties. Cf. NON COMPOS MENTIS.

compound (kom- *or* kəm-**pownd**), *vb.* **1.** To put together, combine, or construct. **2.** To compute (interest) on the principal and the accrued interest. **3.** To settle (a matter, esp. a debt) by a money payment, in lieu of other liability; to adjust by agreement. **4.** To agree for consideration not to prosecute (a crime). **5.** Loosely, to aggravate; to make (a crime, etc.) more serious by further bad conduct.

compounder (kom- *or* kəm-**pown**-dər). **1.** One who settles a dispute; the maker of a composition. See COMPOSITION (1). **2.** One who knows of a crime by another and agrees, for a promised or received reward, not to prosecute.

compounding a crime. The offense of either agreeing not to prosecute a crime that one knows has been committed or agreeing to hamper the prosecution.

compound interest. See INTEREST (3).

comprehensive general liability policy. See INSURANCE POLICY.

comprehensive zoning plan. A general plan to control and direct the use and development of a large piece of property. See ZONING.

compromise, *n.* **1.** An agreement between two or more persons to settle matters in dispute between them. **2.** A debtor's partial payment coupled with the creditor's promise not to claim the rest of the amount due or claimed. — **compromise,** *vb.*

compromise verdict. See VERDICT.

comptroller (kən-**troh**-lər). An officer of a business or a private, state, or municipal corporation who is charged with duties usu. relating to fiscal affairs, including auditing and examining accounts and reporting the financial status periodically.

compulsion, *n.* **1.** The act of compelling; the state of being compelled. **2.** An uncontrollable inclination to do something. **3.** Objective necessity; duress. — **compel,** *vb.*

compulsory (kəm-**pəl**-sə-ree), *adj.* Compelled; mandated by legal process or by statute.

compulsory appearance. See APPEARANCE.

compulsory arbitration. See ARBITRATION.

compulsory condition. See CONDITION (2).

compulsory counterclaim. See COUNTERCLAIM.

compulsory insurance. See INSURANCE.

compulsory joinder. See JOINDER.

compulsory nonsuit. See NONSUIT.

Compulsory Process Clause. The clause of the Sixth Amendment to the U.S. Constitution giving criminal defendants the subpoena power for obtaining witnesses in their favor.

computer crime. See CRIME.

Comstock law (**kom**-stok). An 1873 federal statute that tightened rules against mailing "obscene, lewd, or lascivious" books or pictures, as well as "any article or thing designed for the prevention of conception or procuring of abortions." • Because of the intolerance that led to this statute, the law gave rise to an English word roughly equivalent to *prudery* — namely, *comstockery*.

con. *abbr.* **1.** Confidence <con game>. **2.** Convict <ex-con>. **3.** Contra <pros and cons>. **4.** (*cap.*) Constitutional <Con. law>.

concealed weapon. See WEAPON.

concealment, *n.* **1.** The act of refraining from disclosure; esp., an act by which one prevents or hinders the discovery of something. **2.** The act of removing from sight or notice; hiding. — **conceal,** *vb.*

active concealment. The concealment by words or acts of something that one has a duty to reveal.

fraudulent concealment. The affirmative suppression or hiding, with the intent to deceive or defraud, of a material fact or circumstance that one is legally (or, sometimes, morally) bound to reveal.

passive concealment. The act of maintaining silence when one has a duty to speak.

concealment rule. The principle that a defendant's conduct that hinders or prevents a plaintiff from discovering the existence of a claim tolls the statute of limitations until the plaintiff discovers or should have discovered the claim.

conception of invention. The formation in the inventor's mind of a definite and permanent idea of a complete invention that is thereafter applied in practice.

concerted action. An action that has been planned, arranged, and agreed on by parties acting together to further some scheme or cause, so that all involved are liable for the actions of one another.

concert-of-action rule. See WHARTON RULE.

concession, *n.* **1.** A government grant for specific privileges. **2.** The voluntary yielding to a demand for the sake of a settlement. **3.** A rebate or abatement. — **concede,** *vb.* — **concessive,** *adj.*

conciliation, *n.* **1.** A settlement of a dispute in an agreeable manner. **2.** A process in which a neutral person meets with the parties to a dispute (often labor) and explores how the dispute might be resolved; MEDIATION. — **conciliate,** *vb.* — **conciliative, conciliatory,** *adj.* — **conciliator,** *n.*

conclude, *vb.* **1.** To ratify or formalize (a treaty, convention, or contract). **2.** To bind; estop.

conclusion, *n.* **1.** The final part of a speech or writing (such as a jury argument or a pleading). **2.** A judgment arrived at by reasoning; an inferential statement. **3.** The closing, settling, or final arranging (as of a treaty or contract).

conclusion of fact. A factual deduction drawn from observed or proven facts; an evidentiary inference. Cf. FINDING OF FACT.

conclusion of law. An inference on a question of law, made as a result of a factual showing, no further evidence being required; a legal inference. Cf. FINDING OF FACT; LEGAL CONCLUSION.

conclusive, *adj.* Authoritative; decisive; convincing. Cf. CONCLUSORY.

conclusive evidence. See EVIDENCE.

conclusive presumption. See PRESUMPTION.

conclusory (kən-**kloo**-zə-ree *or* -sə-ree), *adj.* Expressing a factual inference without stating the underlying facts on which the inference is based. Cf. CONCLUSIVE.

concomitant (kən-**kom**-ə-tənt), *adj.* Accompanying; incidental <concomitant actions>. — **concomitant,** *n.*

concomitant evidence. See EVIDENCE.

concord (**kon**-kord *or* **kong**-), *n.* An amicable arrangement or settlement between parties, esp. between peoples or nations; a compact or treaty.

concubinage (kon-**kyoo**-bə-nij), *n.* **1.** The relationship of a man and woman who cohabit without the benefit of marriage. **2.** The state of being a concubine.

concur (kən-**kər**), *vb.* **1.** To agree; to consent. **2.** In a judicial opinion, to agree with the judgment in the case (usu. as expressed in the opinion of another judge), or the opinion of another judge, but often for different reasons or through a different line of reasoning.

concurrence. 1. Agreement; assent. **2.** A vote cast by a judge in favor of the judgment reached, often on grounds differing from those expressed in the opinion or opinions explaining the judgment. **3.** A separate written opinion explaining such a vote.

concurrent, *adj.* **1.** Operating at the same time; covering the same matters <concurrent sentence>. **2.** Having authority on the same matters <concurrent jurisdiction>.

concurrent cause. See CAUSE (1).

concurrent condition. See CONDITION (2).

concurrent covenant. See COVENANT (1).

concurrent estate. See ESTATE (4).

concurrent jurisdiction. See JURISDICTION.

concurrent lease. See LEASE.

concurrent negligence. See NEGLIGENCE.

concurrent policy. See INSURANCE POLICY.

concurrent power. See POWER.

concurrent remedy. See REMEDY.

concurrent resolution. See RESOLUTION.

concurrent-sentence doctrine. The principle that an appellate court affirming a conviction with a concurrent sentence need not hear a challenge to a conviction on another count if the conviction on the other count carries a sentence that is equal to or less than the affirmed conviction.

concurrent sentences. See SENTENCE.

concurrent tortfeasors. See TORTFEASOR.

condemn, *vb.* **1.** To judicially pronounce (someone) guilty. **2.** To determine and declare that certain property is assigned to public use. See EMINENT DOMAIN; APPROPRIATION

(1). **3.** To adjudge (a building) as being unfit for habitation. **4.** To adjudge (food or drink) as being unfit for human consumption.

condemnation (kon-dem-**nay**-shən), *n.* **1.** The act of judicially pronouncing someone guilty; conviction. **2.** The determination and declaration that certain property (esp. land) is assigned to public use, subject to reasonable compensation; the exercise of eminent domain by a governmental entity. See EMINENT DOMAIN.

excess condemnation. The taking of property beyond what is needed for public use.

inverse condemnation. An action brought by a property owner for compensation from a governmental entity that has taken the owner's property without bringing formal condemnation proceedings.

quick condemnation. The immediate taking of private property for public use, whereby the estimated reasonable compensation is placed in escrow until the actual amount of compensation can be established.

3. An official pronouncement that a thing (such as a building) is unfit for use or consumption; the act of making such a pronouncement.

condemnation money. 1. Damages that a losing party in a lawsuit is condemned to pay. **2.** Compensation paid by an expropriator of land to the landowner for taking the property.

condemnee (kon-dem-**nee**). One whose property is expropriated for public use or taken by a public-works project.

condemnor (kon-dem-**nor** *or* kən-**dem**-nər). A public or semipublic entity that expropriates property for public use.

condition, *n.* **1.** A future and uncertain event on which the existence or extent of an obligation or liability depends; an uncertain act or event that triggers or negates a duty to render a promised performance. **2.** A stipulation or prerequisite in a contract, will, or other instrument, constituting the essence of the instrument.

compulsory condition. A condition expressly requiring that a thing be done, such as a tenant's paying rent on a certain day.

concurrent condition. A condition that must occur or be performed at the same time as another condition, the performance by each party separately operating as a condition precedent; a condition that is mutually dependent on another, arising when the parties to a contract agree to exchange performances simultaneously.

condition precedent. An act or event, other than a lapse of time, that must exist or occur before a duty to perform something promised arises.

condition subsequent. A condition that, if it occurs, will bring something else to an end; an event the existence of which, by agreement of the parties, discharges a duty of performance that has arisen.

express condition. A condition that is explicitly stated in an instrument; esp., a contractual condition that the parties have reduced to writing.

implied condition. A condition that is not expressly mentioned, but is imputed by law from the nature of the transaction or the conduct of the parties to have been tacitly understood between them as a part of the agreement.

negative condition. A condition forbidding a party from doing a certain thing, such as prohibiting a tenant from subletting leased property; a promise not to do something, usu. as part of a larger agreement. See *negative easement* under EASEMENT.

3. Loosely, a term, provision, or clause in a contract. **4.** A qualification attached to the conveyance of property providing that if a particular event does or does not take place, the estate will be created, enlarged, defeated, or transferred. **5.** A state of being; an essential quality or status. — **condition,** *vb.* — **conditional,** *adj.*

dangerous condition. **1.** A property defect creating a substantial risk of injury when the property is used in a reasonably foreseeable manner. • A dangerous condition may result in waiver of sovereign immunity. **2.** A property risk that children, because of their immaturity, cannot appreciate or avoid.

conditional admissibility. See ADMISSIBILITY.

conditional assault. See ASSAULT.

conditional bequest. See BEQUEST.

conditional covenant. See COVENANT (1).

conditional delivery. See DELIVERY.

conditional devise. See DEVISE.

conditional guaranty. See GUARANTY.

conditional indorsement. See INDORSEMENT.

conditional legacy. See LEGACY.

conditional limitation. See LIMITATION.

conditionally privileged communication. See COMMUNICATION.

conditional obligation. See OBLIGATION.

conditional payment. See PAYMENT.

conditional promise. See PROMISE.

conditional proof. See PROOF.

conditional purpose. **1.** An intention to do something, conditions permitting. **2.** *Criminal law.* A possible defense against a crime if the conditions make committing the crime impossible (e.g., "I will steal the money if it's there," and the money is not there).

conditional release. See RELEASE.

conditional sentence. See SENTENCE.

condition of employment. A qualification or circumstance required for obtaining or keeping a job.

condition precedent. See CONDITION (2).

conditions of sale. The terms under which auctions are to be conducted.

condition subsequent. See CONDITION (2).

condominium (kon-də-**min**-ee-əm). **1.** Ownership in common with others. **2.** A single real-estate unit in a multiunit development in which a person has both separate ownership of a unit and a common interest, along with the development's other owners, in the common areas. Pl. (for sense 2) **condominiums.** Cf. COOPERATIVE (2).

condonation (kon-də-**nay**-shən), *n.* A victim's implied forgiveness of or excuse of an offense, esp. by treating the offender as if there had been no offense. — **condone** (kən-**dohn**), *vb.* — **condonable** (kən-**dohn**-ə-bəl), *adj.*

conduct, *n.* Personal behavior, whether by action or inaction; the manner in which a person behaves. — **conduct,** *vb.*

assertive conduct. Evidence. Nonverbal behavior that is intended to be a statement, such as pointing one's finger to identify a suspect in a police lineup. • Assertive conduct is a statement under the hearsay rule, and thus it is not admissible unless a hearsay exception applies. Fed. R. Evid. 801(a)(2).

disorderly conduct. Behavior that tends to disturb the public peace, offend public morals, or undermine public safety. See BREACH OF THE PEACE.

disruptive conduct. Disorderly conduct in the context of a governmental proceeding. See CONTEMPT.

nonassertive conduct. Evidence. Nonverbal behavior that is not intended to be a statement, such as fainting while being questioned as a suspect by a police officer. • Nonassertive conduct is not a statement under the hearsay rule, and thus it is admissible. Fed. R. Evid. 801.

outrageous conduct. Conduct so extreme that it exceeds all reasonable bounds of human decency. See EMOTIONAL DISTRESS.

unprofessional conduct. Behavior that is immoral, unethical, or dishonorable, either generally or when judged by the standards of the actor's profession.

confederacy, *n.* **1.** An association of two or more persons, usu. for unlawful purposes; CONSPIRACY. **2.** The fact or condition of being an ally or accomplice. — **confederate,** *n.*

confederation. A league or union of states or nations, each of which retains its sovereignty but also delegates some rights and powers to a central authority. Cf. FEDERATION.

confession, *n.* A criminal suspect's acknowledgment of guilt, usu. in writing and often including details about the crime. Cf. ADMISSION; STATEMENT. — **confess,** *vb.* — **confessor,** *n.*

coerced confession. A confession that is obtained by threats or force.

direct confession. A statement in which an accused person acknowledges having committed the crime.

extrajudicial confession. A confession made out of court, and not as a part of a judicial examination or investigation. • Such a confession must be corroborated by some other proof of the corpus delicti, or else it is insufficient to warrant a conviction. Cf. *judicial confession.*

interlocking confessions. Confessions by two or more suspects whose statements are substantially the same and consistent concerning the elements of the crime.

involuntary confession. A confession induced by the police or other law-enforcement authorities who coerce, deceive, or make promises to the suspect.

judicial confession. A plea of guilty or some other direct manifestation of guilt in court or in a judicial proceeding. Cf. *extrajudicial confession*.

naked confession. A confession unsupported by any evidence that a crime has been committed, and therefore usu. highly suspect.

plenary confession (**plee**-nə-ree *or* **plen**-ə-). A complete confession; one that is believed to be conclusive against the person who made it.

threshold confession. A spontaneous confession made promptly after arrest and without interrogation by the police.

confession and avoidance. A plea in which a defendant admits allegations but pleads additional facts that deprive the admitted facts of an adverse legal effect. • For example, a plea of contributory negligence (before the advent of comparative negligence) was a confession and avoidance.

confession of judgment. 1. A person's agreeing to the entry of judgment upon the occurrence or nonoccurrence of an event, such as making a payment. **2.** A judgment taken against a debtor by the creditor, based on the debtor's written consent. **3.** The paper on which the person so agrees, before it is entered. See COGNOVIT.

confidence. 1. Assured expectation; firm trust; faith. **2.** Reliance on another's discretion; a relation of trust. **3.** A communication made in trust and not intended for public disclosure; specif., a communication protected by the attorney–client or similar privilege. — **confide,** *vb.*

confidence game. A means of obtaining money or property whereby a person intentionally misrepresents facts to gain the victim's trust so that the victim will transfer money or property to the person.

confidential communication. See COMMUNICATION.

confidentiality, *n.* **1.** Secrecy; the state of having the dissemination of certain information restricted. **2.** The relation between lawyer and client or guardian and ward, or between spouses, with regard to the trust that is placed in the one by the other. — **confidential,** *adj.*

confidential source. A person who provides information to a law-enforcement agency or to a journalist on the express or implied guarantee of anonymity.

confinement, *n.* The act of imprisoning or restraining someone; the state of being imprisoned or restrained. — **confine,** *vb.*

confirmation, *n.* **1.** The act of giving formal approval. **2.** The act of verifying or corroborating; a statement that verifies or corroborates. **3.** The act of ratifying a voidable estate; a type of conveyance in which a voidable estate is made certain or a particular estate is increased. **4.** *Commercial law*. A bank's agreement to honor a letter of credit issued by another bank. — **confirm,** *vb.* — **confirmatory** (kən-**fər**-mə-tor-ee), *adj.* Cf. RATIFICATION.

confiscation (kon-fi-**skay**-shən), *n.* **1.** Seizure of property for the public treasury. **2.** Seizure of property by actual or supposed authority. — **confiscate** (**kon**-fə-skayt), *vb.* — **confiscatory** (kən-**fis**-kə-tor-ee), *adj.* — **confiscable** (kən-**fis**-kə-bəl *or* **kon**-fə-skə-bəl), *adj.* — **confiscator** (**kon**-fə-skay-tər), *n.*

conflicting evidence. See EVIDENCE.

conflicting presumption. See PRESUMPTION.

conflict of authority. 1. A disagreement between two or more courts, often courts of coordinate jurisdiction, on a point of law. **2.** A disagreement between two or more treatise authors or other scholars, esp. in an area in which scholarly authority is paramount, such as public or private international law.

conflict of interest. 1. A real or seeming incompatibility between one's private interests and one's public or fiduciary duties. **2.** A real or seeming incompatibility between the interests of two of a lawyer's clients, such that the lawyer is disqualified from representing both clients if the dual representation adversely affects either client or if the clients do not consent.

conflict of laws. 1. A difference between the laws of different states or countries in a case in which a transaction or occurrence central to the case has a connection to two or more jurisdictions. **2.** The body of jurisprudence that undertakes to reconcile such differences or to decide what law is to govern in these situations; the principles of choice of law.

conflict out, *vb.* To disqualify (a lawyer or judge) on the basis of a conflict of interest.

conformed copy. See COPY.

conforming, *adj.* Being in accordance with contractual obligations <conforming goods> <conforming conduct>. UCC § 2–102(a)(8).

conformity hearing. 1. A court-ordered hearing to determine whether the judgment or decree prepared by the prevailing party conforms to the decision of the court. **2.** A hearing before a federal agency or department to determine whether a state-submitted plan complies with the requirements of federal law. • This type of hearing is common in cases involving social services.

Confrontation Clause. The Sixth Amendment provision guaranteeing a criminal defendant's right to directly confront an accusing witness and to cross-examine that witness.

confusion of goods. The mixture of things of the same nature but belonging to different owners so that the identification of the things is no longer possible.

congeries (kon-**jeer**-eez *or* **kon**-jə-reez). A collection or aggregation.

conglomerate (kən-**glom**-ər-it), *n.* A corporation that owns unrelated enterprises in a wide variety of industries. — **conglomerate** (kən-**glom**-ə-rayt), *vb.* — **conglomerate** (kən-**glom**-ər-it), *adj.*

congress, *n.* **1.** A formal meeting of delegates or representatives. **2.** (*cap.*) The legislative body of the federal government, created under U.S. Const. art. I, § 1 and consisting of the Senate and the House of Representatives. — **congressional,** *adj.*

congressional district. See DISTRICT.

congressional immunity. See IMMUNITY (1).

Congressional Record. The published record of the daily proceedings in the U.S. Senate and House of Representatives.

conjectural choice, rule of. The principle that no basis for recovery is presented when all theories of causation rest only on conjecture.

conjecture (kən-**jek**-chər), *n.* A guess; supposition; surmise. — **conjecture** (kən-**jek**-chər), *vb.* — **conjectural** (kən-**jek**-chər-əl), *adj.*

conjoint (kən-**joynt**). A person connected with another in a joint interest, act, or obligation, such as a cotenant or spouse.

conjugal (**kon**-jə-gəl), *adj.* Of or relating to the married state, often with an implied emphasis on sexual relations between spouses <the prisoner was allowed a private bed for conjugal visits>.

conjugal rights. The rights and privileges arising from the marriage relationship, including the mutual rights of companionship, support, and sexual relations. • Loss of conjugal rights amounts to loss of consortium. See CONSORTIUM.

conjunctive denial. See DENIAL.

connecting factors. *Conflict of laws.* Factual or legal circumstances that help determine the choice of law by linking an action or individual with a state or jurisdiction. • An example of a connecting factor is a party's domicile within a state.

connecting-up doctrine. The rule allowing evidence to be admitted on condition that the party offering it will adduce other evidence to show relevance.

connivance (kə-**nI**-vənts), *n.* **1.** The act of promoting, encouraging, or setting up another's wrongdoing. **2.** *Family law.* As a defense to divorce, one spouse's corrupt consent, express or implied, to have the other commit adultery or some other act of sexual misconduct. • Consent is an essential element of connivance. The complaining spouse must have consented to the act complained of. — **connive** (kə-**nIv**), *vb.*

consanguinity (kon-sang-**gwin**-ə-tee), *n.* The relationship of persons of the same blood or origin. — **consanguineous,** *adj.* See *prohibited degree* under DEGREE. Cf. AFFINITY.

collateral consanguinity. The relationship between persons who have the same ancestor but do not descend or ascend from one another (for example, uncle and nephew, etc.).

lineal consanguinity. The relationship between persons who are directly descended or ascended from one another (for example, mother and daughter, great-grandfather and grandson, etc.).

conscience. **1.** The moral sense of right and wrong; esp., a moral sense applied to one's own judgment and actions. **2.** In law, the moral rule that requires justice and honest dealings between people.

conscience of the court. **1.** The court's equitable power to decide issues based on notions of fairness and justice. **2.** A standard applied by the court in deciding whether the parties or a jury has acted within limits. • Thus, in some cases, a jury's award of damages is upset because it is said to "shock the conscience of the court."

conscionable (**kon**-shə-nə-bəl), *adj.* Conforming with good conscience; just and reasonable <a conscionable bargain>. — **conscionableness, conscionability,** *n.* Cf. UNCONSCIONABLE.

consecutive sentences. See SENTENCE.

consecutive tortfeasors. See TORTFEASOR.

consent, *n.* Agreement, approval, or permission as to some act or purpose, esp. given voluntarily by a competent person. • Consent is an affirmative defense to assault, battery, and related torts, as well as such torts as defamation, invasion of privacy, conversion, and trespass. Consent may be a defense to a crime if the victim has the capacity to consent and if the consent negates an element of the crime or thwarts the harm that the law seeks to prevent. See Model Penal Code § 2.11. — **consent,** *vb.* — **consensual,** *adj.*

express consent. Consent that is clearly and unmistakably stated.

implied consent. Consent inferred from one's conduct rather than from one's direct expression.

informed consent. **1.** A person's agreement to allow something to happen, made with full knowledge of the risks involved and the alternatives. **2.** A patient's knowing choice about a medical treatment or procedure, made after a physician or other healthcare provider discloses whatever information a reasonably prudent provider in the medical community would give to a patient regarding the risks involved in the proposed treatment or procedure.

consent decree. See DECREE.

consent jurisdiction. See JURISDICTION.

consent search. See SEARCH.

consent to be sued. Agreement in advance to be sued in a particular forum. See COGNOVIT CLAUSE.

consent to notice. A provision stating that notice required by a document may be given beforehand or to a designated person.

consequential damages. See DAMAGES.

consequential loss. See LOSS.

conservator (kən-**sər**-və-tər *or* **kon**-sər-vay-tər), *n.* A guardian, protector, or preserver. — **conservatorship,** *n.*

managing conservator. **1.** A person appointed by a court to manage the estate or affairs of someone who is legally incapable of doing

SO; GUARDIAN (1). **2.** *Family law*. In the child-custody laws of some states, the parent who has primary custody of a child, with the right to establish the child's primary domicile. See CUSTODY.

possessory conservator. *Family law*. In the child-custody laws of some states, the parent who has visitation rights, but not the primary custody rights, of the child.

consideration, *n*. Something of value (such as an act, a forbearance, or a return promise) received by a promisor from a promisee. • Consideration, or a substitute such as promissory estoppel, is necessary for an agreement to be enforceable.

adequate consideration. Consideration that is fair and reasonable under the circumstances of the agreement. Cf. *sufficient consideration*.

fair consideration. **1.** Consideration that is equal in value to the thing being exchanged; consideration given for property or for an obligation in either of the following circumstances: (1) when given in good faith as an exchange for the property or obligation, or (2) when the property or obligation is received in good faith to secure a present advance or prior debt in an amount not disproportionately small as compared with the value of the property or obligation obtained. **2.** Consideration that is honest, reasonable, and free from suspicion, but not strictly adequate or full.

future consideration. **1.** Consideration to be given in the future; esp., consideration that is due after the other party's performance. **2.** Consideration that is a series of performances, some of which will occur after the other party's performance. **3.** Consideration the specifics of which have not been agreed on between the parties. Cf. *past consideration*.

good consideration. **1.** Consideration based on natural love or affection or on moral duty. **2.** Loosely, valuable consideration; consideration that is adequate to support the bargained-for exchange between the parties.

gratuitous consideration (**grə-t[y]oo-i-təs**). Consideration that, not being founded on any detriment to the party who gives it, will not support a contract; a performance for which a party was already obligated.

illegal consideration. Consideration that is contrary to the law or public policy, or prejudicial to the public interest. • Such consideration does not support a contract.

implied consideration. Consideration that is inferred by law from the parties' actions.

inadequate consideration. Consideration that does not involve an exchange of equal values.

invented consideration. Fictional consideration created by a court to prevent the invalidation of a contract that lacks consideration.

nominal consideration. Consideration that is so insignificant as to bear no relationship to the value of what is being exchanged (e.g., $10 for a piece of real estate). • Such consideration can be valid, since courts do not ordinarily examine the adequacy of consideration (although they do often inquire into such issues as fraud and duress).

other consideration. Additional things of value to be provided under a contract, usu. not specified in the contract because they are too numerous to conveniently list or because the parties want to keep secret the total amount of consideration.

past consideration. An act done or a promise given by a promisee before making a promise sought to be enforced. • Past consideration is not consideration for the new promise because it has not been given in exchange for this promise (although exceptions exist for new promises to pay debts barred by limitations or debts discharged in bankruptcy). See PREEXISTING-DUTY RULE. Cf. *future consideration.*

sufficient consideration. Enough consideration — as a matter of law — to support a contract. Cf. *adequate consideration.*

valuable consideration. Consideration that is valid under the law; consideration that either confers a pecuniarily measurable benefit on one party or imposes a pecuniarily measurable detriment on the other.

consideration, failure of. See FAILURE OF CONSIDERATION.

consideration, want of. See WANT OF CONSIDERATION.

consign (kən-**sɪn**), *vb.* **1.** To transfer to another's custody or charge. **2.** To give (goods) to a carrier for delivery to a designated recipient. **3.** To give (merchandise or the like) to another to sell, usu. with the understanding that the seller will pay the owner for the goods from the proceeds.

consignee (kon-sɪ-**nee** *or* kən-). One to whom goods are consigned.

consignment (kən-**sɪn**-mənt). **1.** The act of consigning goods for custody or sale. **2.** A quantity of goods delivered by this act, esp. in a single shipment. **3.** Under the UCC, a transaction in which a person delivers goods to a merchant for the purpose of sale, and (1) the merchant deals in goods of that kind under a name other than the name of the person making delivery, is not an auctioneer, and is not generally known by its creditor to be substantially engaged in selling others' goods, (2) with respect to each delivery, the aggregate value of the goods is $1,000 or more at the time of delivery, (3) the goods are not consumer goods immediately before delivery, and (4) the transaction does not create a security interest that secures an obligation. UCC § 9–102(a)(20).

consignor (kən-**sɪ**-nər *or* kon-sɪ-**nor**). One who dispatches goods to another on consignment.

consolidated appeal. See APPEAL.

Consolidated Omnibus Budget Reconciliation Act of 1985. A federal statute that requires employers who offer group health coverage to their employees to continue to do so for a prescribed period (usu. 18 to 36 months) after employment has terminated so that an employee can continue to benefit from group-health rates until becoming a member of another health-insurance plan. — Abbr. COBRA.

consolidated return. See TAX RETURN.

consolidating statute. See STATUTE.

consolidation, *n.* **1.** The act or process of uniting; the state of being united. **2.** *Corporations.* The unification of two or more corporations by dissolving the existing ones and creating a single new corporation. Cf. MERGER (7). **3.** *Civil procedure.* The court-ordered unification of two or more actions, involving the same parties and issues, into a single action resulting in a single judgment or, sometimes, in separate judgments. Cf. JOINDER. — **consolidate,** *vb.* — **consolidatory** (kən-sol-ə-day-tər-ee), *adj.*

consolidation loan. See LOAN.

consonant statement. See STATEMENT.

consortium (kən-sor-shee-əm). The benefits that one person, esp. a spouse, is entitled to receive from another, including companionship, cooperation, affection, aid, and (between spouses) sexual relations. See LOSS OF CONSORTIUM.

conspicuous, *adj.* (Of a term or clause) clearly visible or obvious.

conspicuous place. For purposes of posting notices, a location that is reasonably likely to be seen.

conspiracy, *n.* An agreement by two or more persons to commit an unlawful act; a combination for an unlawful purpose. See Model Penal Code § 5.03(7). — **conspire,** *vb.* — **conspiratorial,** *adj.* — **conspirator,** *n.* Cf. ATTEMPT (2); SOLICITATION (2).

chain conspiracy. A single conspiracy in which each person is responsible for a distinct act within the overall plan, such as an agreement to produce, import, and distribute narcotics in which each person performs only one function. • All participants are interested in the overall scheme and liable for all other participants' acts in furtherance of that scheme.

civil conspiracy. An agreement between two or more persons to commit an unlawful act that causes damage to a person or property.

seditious conspiracy. A criminal conspiracy to forcibly (1) overthrow or destroy the U.S. government, (2) oppose its authority, (3) prevent the execution of its laws, or (4) seize or possess its property. 18 USCA § 2384.

wheel conspiracy. A conspiracy in which a single member or group (the "hub") separately agrees with two or more other members or groups (the "spokes"). • The person or group at the hub is the only part liable for all the conspiracies.

conspirator, *n.* A person who takes part in a conspiracy.

unindicted conspirator. A person who has been identified by law enforcement as a member of a conspiracy, but who has not been named in the fellow conspirator's indictment. • Prosecutors typically name someone an unindicted conspirator because any statement that the unindicted conspirator has made in the course and furtherance of the conspiracy is admissible against the indicted defendants.

constable (**kon**-stə-bəl), *n.* A peace officer responsible for minor judicial duties, such as serving writs and warrants, but with less authority and smaller jurisdiction than a sheriff. — **constabulary** (kən-**stab**-yə-ler-ee), *adj.* — **constabulary** (body or force), *n.*

constituent, *adj.* **1.** (Of a component) that helps make up or complete a unit or a whole. **2.** (Of an assembly) able to frame or amend a constitution.

constituent, *n.* **1.** A person who gives another the authority to act as a representative; a principal who appoints an agent. **2.** Someone who is represented by a legislator or other elected official. **3.** One part of something that makes up a whole; an element. — **constituency,** *n.*

constitution. 1. The fundamental and organic law of a nation or state, establishing the conception, character, and organization of its government, as well as prescribing the extent of its sovereign power and the manner of its exercise. **2.** The written instrument embodying this fundamental law.

constitutional, *adj.* **1.** Of or relating to a constitution. **2.** Proper under a constitution. — **constitutionality,** *n.*

constitutional challenge. See CHALLENGE (1).

constitutional convention. An assembly of state or national delegates who meet to frame, amend, or revise their constitution.

constitutional court. See COURT.

constitutional freedom. A basic liberty guaranteed by the Constitution or Bill of Rights, such as the freedom of speech.

constitutional homestead. See HOMESTEAD.

constitutional immunity. See IMMUNITY (1).

constitutionalize, *vb.* **1.** To provide with a constitution. **2.** To make constitutional; to bring in line with a constitution. **3.** To make a constitutional question out of a question of law.

constitutional law. 1. The body of law deriving from the U.S. Constitution and dealing primarily with governmental powers, civil rights, and civil liberties. **2.** The body of legal rules that determine the make-up of a state or country with a flexible constitution. Cf. STATUTORY LAW; COMMON LAW.

constitutional limitation. A constitutional provision that restricts the powers of a governmental branch, department, agency, or officer.

constitutional question. A legal issue resolvable by the interpretation of a constitution, rather than a statute.

constitutional right. A right guaranteed by a constitution; esp., one guaranteed by the U.S. Constitution or by a state constitution.

constitutional tort. See TORT.

construction, *n.* **1.** The act of building by combining or arranging parts or elements; the thing so built. **2.** The act or process of interpreting or explaining the sense or intention of a writing (usu. a statute, opinion, or instrument). — **construct** (for sense 1), *vb.* — **construe** (for sense 2), *vb.*

liberal construction. An interpretation that applies a writing in light of the situation presented and that tends to effectuate the spirit and purpose of the writing.

strict construction. **1.** An interpretation that considers only the literal words of a writing. See STRICT CONSTRUCTIONISM. **2.** A construction that considers words narrowly, usu. in their historical context. • This type of construction treats statutory and contractual words with highly restrictive readings. **3.** The philosophy underlying strict interpretation of statutes; STRICT CONSTRUCTIONISM.

construction warranty. See WARRANTY (2).

constructive, *adj.* Legally imputed; having an effect in law though not necessarily in fact. • Courts usually give something a constructive effect for equitable reasons. See LEGAL FICTION. Cf. ACTUAL.

constructive adverse possession. See ADVERSE POSSESSION.

constructive assent. See ASSENT.

constructive authority. See AUTHORITY (1).

constructive bailment. See BAILMENT.

constructive custody. See CUSTODY (1).

constructive delivery. See DELIVERY.

constructive desertion. See DESERTION.

constructive discharge. See DISCHARGE.

constructive eviction. See EVICTION.

constructive force. See FORCE.

constructive fraud. See FRAUD.

constructive intent. See INTENT (1).

constructive knowledge. See KNOWLEDGE (1).

constructive larceny. See LARCENY.

constructive loss. See LOSS.

constructive notice. See NOTICE.

constructive payment. See PAYMENT.

constructive possession. See POSSESSION.

constructive-receipt doctrine. The rule that gross income under a taxpayer's control before it is actually received (such as accumulated interest income that has not been withdrawn) must be included by the taxpayer in gross income, unless the actual receipt is subject to significant constraints. IRC (26 USCA) § 451.

constructive service. See SERVICE.

constructive taking. See TAKING (1).

constructive transfer. See TRANSFER.

constructive trust. See TRUST.

construe (kən-stroo), *vb.* To analyze and explain the meaning of (a sentence or passage).

consultation, *n.* **1.** The act of asking the advice or opinion of someone (such as a lawyer). **2.** A meeting in which parties consult or confer. —

consult, *vb.* — **consulting, consultative,** *adj.*

consulting expert. See EXPERT.

consumable, *n.* A thing (such as food) that cannot be used without changing or extinguishing its substance. Cf. NONCONSUMABLE.

consumer. A person who buys goods or services for personal, family, or household use, with no intention of resale; a natural person who uses products for personal rather than business purposes. 40 CFR § 721(b)(1).

consumer boycott. See BOYCOTT.

consumer-contemplation test. A method of imposing product liability on a manufacturer if the evidence shows that a product's danger is greater than what a reasonable consumer would expect. Cf. RISK-UTILITY TEST.

Consumer Credit Protection Act. A federal statute that safeguards the consumer in connection with the use of credit by (1) requiring full disclosure of the terms of the loan agreement, including finance charges, (2) restricting the garnishment of wages, and (3) regulating the use of credit cards (15 USCA §§ 1601–1693). — Abbr. CCPA. See UNIFORM CONSUMER CREDIT CODE.

consumer-credit transaction. A transaction by which a person receives a loan for buying consumer goods or services.

consumer law. The area of law dealing with consumer transactions — that is, a person's obtaining credit, goods, real property, or services for personal, family, or household purposes.

consumer lease. See LEASE.

consumer loan. See LOAN.

consumer product. An item of personal property that is distributed in commerce and is normally used for personal, family, or household purposes. 15 USCA § 2301(1).

consumer-protection law. A state or federal statute designed to protect consumers against unfair trade and credit practices involving consumer goods, as well as to protect consumers against faulty and dangerous goods.

consummate (kon-sə-mayt), *vb.* **1.** To bring to completion; esp., to make (a marriage) complete by sexual intercourse. **2.** To achieve; fulfill. **3.** To perfect; carry to the highest degree. — **consummate** (kən-**səm**-it), *adj.*

consumption. The act of destroying a thing by using it; the use of a thing in a way that thereby exhausts it.

contemner (kən-**tem**-ər *or* -nər). A person who is guilty of contempt before an instrumentality of government, such as a court or legislature. — **contemn** (kən-**tem**), *vb.*

contemplation of death. The thought of dying, not necessarily from an imminent danger, but as the compelling reason to transfer property to another. See *gift causa mortis* under GIFT.

contemporaneous-construction doctrine. The rule that the initial interpretation of an ambiguous statute by an administrative agency or lower court is entitled to great deference if the interpretation has been used over a long period.

contemporaneous-objection rule. The doctrine that a proper objection to the admission of evidence must be made at trial for the issue of admissibility to be considered on appeal.

contemporary community standards. The gauge by which a fact-finder decides whether material is obscene, judging by its patent offensiveness and its pruriency in the locale at a given time. See OBSCENITY (1).

contempt, *n.* **1.** The act or state of despising; the condition of being despised. **2.** Conduct that defies the authority or dignity of a court or legislature. • Because such conduct interferes with the administration of justice, it is punishable, usually by fine or imprisonment. — **contemptuous,** *adj.*

civil contempt. The failure to obey a court order that was issued for another party's benefit. • A civil-contempt proceeding is coercive or remedial in nature. The usual sanction is to confine the contemner until he or she complies with the court order.

criminal contempt. An act that obstructs justice or attacks the integrity of the court. • A criminal-contempt proceeding is punitive in nature.

direct contempt. A contempt (such as an assault of a testifying witness) committed in the immediate vicinity of a court; esp., a contempt committed in a judge's presence.

indirect contempt. Contempt that is committed outside of court, as when a party disobeys a court order.

contempt power. The power of a public institution (as Congress or a court) to punish someone who shows contempt for the process, orders, or proceedings of that institution.

contempt proceeding. See PROCEEDING.

content-based restriction. *Constitutional law.* A restraint on the substance of a particular type of speech. • This type of restriction can survive a challenge only if it is based on a compelling state interest and its measures are narrowly drawn to accomplish that end. See SPEECH.

contest (kən-**test**), *vb.* **1.** To strive to win or hold; contend. **2.** To litigate or call into question; challenge. **3.** To deny an adverse claim or assert a defense to it in a court proceeding. — **contest** (**kon**-test), *n.*

contestant. One who contests the validity of a will.

context, *n.* **1.** The surrounding text of a word or passage, used to determine the meaning of that word or passage. **2.** Setting or environment. — **contextual,** *adj.*

contiguous (kən-**tig**-yoo-əs), *adj.* **1.** Touching at a point or along a boundary; ADJOINING. **2.** Near in time or sequence; successive. — **contiguity** (kon-ti-**gyoo**-ə-tee), *n.*

contingency (kən-**tin**-jən-see). **1.** An event that may or may not occur; a possibility. **2.** The condition of being dependent on chance; uncertainty. — **contingent** (kən-**tin**-jənt), *adj.*

contingent beneficiary. See BENEFICIARY.

contingent estate. See ESTATE (4).

contingent fee. A fee charged for a lawyer's services only if the lawsuit is successful or is favorably settled out of court.

contingent fund. See FUND.

contingent guaranty. See GUARANTY.

contingent interest. See INTEREST (2).

contingent legacy. See LEGACY.

contingent liability. See LIABILITY.

contingent ownership. See OWNERSHIP.

contingent remainder. See REMAINDER.

contingent use. See USE.

continuance, *n.* **1.** The act of keeping up, maintaining, or prolonging. **2.** Duration; time of continuing. **3.** *Procedure.* The adjournment or postponement of a trial or other proceeding to a future date. — **continue,** *vb.* Cf. RECESS (1).

continuation agreement. *Partnership.* An agreement among the partners that, in the event of dissolution, the business of the partnership can be continued without the necessity of liquidation. Cf. BUY-SELL AGREEMENT (1).

continuing, *adj.* **1.** (Of an act or event) that is uninterrupted <a continuing offense>. **2.** (Of status or power) that needs no renewal; enduring <continuing jurisdiction>.

continuing breach. See BREACH OF CONTRACT.

continuing guaranty. See GUARANTY.

continuing injury. See INJURY.

continuing judicial education. Continuing legal education for judges, usu. organized and sponsored by a governmentally subsidized body and often involving topics such as judicial writing, efficient decision-making, caseload management, and the like. — Abbr. CJE.

continuing jurisdiction. See JURISDICTION.

continuing-jurisdiction doctrine. 1. The rule that a court retains power to enter and enforce a judgment over a party even though that party is no longer subject to a new action. **2.** *Family law.* The rule that once a court has acquired jurisdiction over a child-custody or support case, that court continues to have jurisdiction to modify orders, even if the child or a parent moves to another state.

continuing legal education. 1. The process or system through which lawyers extend their learning beyond their law-school studies, usu. by attending seminars designed to sharpen lawyering skills or to provide updates on legal developments within particular practice areas. **2.** The enhanced skills or knowledge derived from this process. **3.** The business field in which educational providers supply the demand for legal seminars, books, audiotapes, and videotapes designed to further the education of lawyers. — Abbr. CLE.

continuing nuisance. See NUISANCE.

continuing objection. See OBJECTION.

continuing offense. See OFFENSE.

continuing wrong. See WRONG.

continuity of business enterprise. A doctrine covering acquisitive reorganizations whereby the acquiring corporation must continue the target corporation's historical business or must use a significant portion of the target's business assets in a new business to qualify the exchange as a tax-deferred transaction.

continuity of interest. **1.** A doctrine covering acquisitive reorganizations whereby a target corporation's shareholders must retain a share in the acquiring corporation to qualify the exchange as a tax-deferred transaction. **2.** A judicial requirement for divisive reorganizations whereby a target corporation's shareholders must retain an interest in both the distributing and the controlled corporations to qualify the exchange as a tax-deferred transaction.

continuity-of-life doctrine. The principle that the withdrawal, incapacity, bankruptcy, or death of the owner of an entity (esp. a corporation) does not end the entity's existence.

continuous-adverse-use principle. The rule that the uninterrupted use of land — along with the other elements of adverse possession — will result in a successful claim for adverse possession. See ADVERSE POSSESSION.

continuous crime. See CRIME.

continuous easement. See EASEMENT.

continuous-treatment doctrine. The principle that the limitations period for bringing a medical-malpractice action is tolled while the patient continues treatment that is related to the negligent act or omission.

contort (**kon**-tort), *n.* **1.** (*usu. pl.*) The overlapping domain of contract law and tort law. **2.** A specific wrong that falls within that domain.

contra (**kon**-trə), *prep.* Against or contrary to. • As a citation signal, *contra* denotes that the cited authority supports a contrary view.

contraband (**kon**-trə-band), *n.* **1.** Illegal or prohibited trade; smuggling. **2.** Goods that are unlawful to import, export, or possess. — **contraband,** *adj.*

contract, *n.* **1.** An agreement between two or more parties creating obligations that are enforceable or otherwise recognizable at law. **2.** The writing that sets forth such an agreement. **3.** Loosely, an unenforceable agreement between two or more parties to do or not to do a thing or set of things; a compact. **4.** A promise or set of promises by a party to a transaction, enforceable or otherwise recognizable at law; the writing expressing that promise or set of promises. **5.** Broadly, any legal duty or set of duties not imposed by the law of tort; esp., a duty created by a decree or declaration of a court. **6.** The body of law dealing with agreements and exchange. **7.** The terms of an agreement, or any particular term. — **contract,** *vb.* — **contractual,** *adj.*

adhesion contract. A standard-form contract prepared by one party, to be signed by the party in a weaker position, usu. a consumer, who has little choice about the terms.

aleatory contract (**ay**-lee-ə-tor-ee). A contract in which at least one party's performance depends on some uncertain event that is beyond the control of the parties involved. • Most insurance contracts are of this type. Cf. *certain contract.*

alternative contract. A contract in which the performing party may elect to perform one of two or more specified acts to satisfy the obligation; a contract that provides more than one way for a party to complete performance, usu. permitting that party to choose the manner of performance.

bilateral contract. A contract in which each party promises a performance, so that each party is an obligor on that party's own promise and an obligee on the other's promise.

certain contract. A contract that will be performed in a stipulated manner. Cf. *aleatory contract.*

collateral contract. A side agreement that relates to a contract, which, if unintegrated, can be supplemented by evidence of the side agreement; an agreement made before or at the same time as, but separately from, another contract. See COLLATERAL-CONTRACT DOCTRINE.

contract for deed. A conditional sales contract for the sale of real property.

contract for sale. **1.** A contract for the present transfer of property for a price. **2.** A contract to sell goods at a future time.

cost-plus contract. A contract in which payment is based on a fixed fee or a percentage added to the actual cost incurred.

destination contract. A contract in which a seller bears the risk of loss until the goods arrive at the destination. UCC § 2–509. Cf. *shipment contract.*

employment contract. A contract between an employer and employee in which the terms and conditions of employment are stated.

executed contract. **1.** A contract that has been fully performed by both parties. **2.** A signed contract.

executory contract (eg-**zek**-yə-tor-ee). A contract that remains wholly unperformed or for which there remains something still to be done on both sides, often as a component of a larger transaction and sometimes memorialized by an informal letter agreement, by a memorandum, or by oral agreement.

express contract. A contract whose terms the parties have explicitly set out. Cf. *implied contract.*

illegal contract. A promise that is prohibited because the performance, formation, or object of the agreement is against the law. • Technically speaking, an illegal contract is not a contract at all, so the phrase is a misnomer.

illusory contract. An agreement in which one party gives as consideration a promise that is so insubstantial as to impose no obligation. • The insubstantial promise renders the contract unenforceable.

implied contract. **1.** An implied-in-law contract. **2.** An implied-in-fact contract. Cf. *express contract.*

implied-in-fact contract. A contract that the parties presumably intended, either by tacit understanding or by the assumption that it existed.

implied-in-law contract. An obligation imposed by law because of the conduct of the parties, or some special relationship between them, or because one of them would otherwise be unjustly enriched. • An implied-in-law contract is not actually a contract, but instead a remedy that allows the plaintiff to recover a benefit conferred on the defendant. See UNJUST ENRICHMENT.

installment contract. A contract requiring or authorizing the delivery of goods in separate lots, or payments in separate increments, to be separately accepted.

output contract. A contract in which a buyer promises to buy all the goods or services that a seller can supply during a specified period and at a set price. • The quantity term is measured by the seller's output. Cf. *requirements contract.*

parol contract (pə-rohl *or* par-əl). **1.** A contract or modification of a contract that is not in writing or is only partially in writing. **2.** At common law, a contract not under seal, although it could be in writing. See PAROL-EVIDENCE RULE.

precontract. A contract that precludes a party from entering into a comparable agreement with someone else. Cf. LETTER OF INTENT.

quasi-contract. An obligation imposed by law because of the conduct of the parties, or some special relationship between them, or because one of them would otherwise be unjustly enriched. • An implied-in-law contract is not actually a contract, but instead a remedy that allows the plaintiff to recover a benefit conferred on the defendant.

requirements contract. A contract in which a seller promises to supply all the goods or services that a buyer needs during a specific period and at a set price, and in which the buyer promises (explicitly or implicitly) to obtain those goods or services exclusively from the seller. • The quantity term is measured by the buyer's requirements. Cf. *output contract.*

severable contract. A contract that includes two or more promises, each of which can be enforced separately, so that failure to perform one of the promises does not necessarily put the promisor in breach of the entire contract. See SEVERABILITY CLAUSE.

shipment contract. A contract in which a seller bears the risk of damage to the items sold only until they are brought to the place of shipment. • If a contract for the sale of goods does not address the terms of delivery, it is presumed to be a shipment contract. UCC §§ 2–319, 2–504, 2–509. Cf. *destination contract.*

standard-form contract. A usu. preprinted contract containing set clauses, used repeatedly by a business or within a particular industry with only slight additions or modifications to meet the specific situation.

subcontract. A contract made by a party to another contract for carrying out the other contract, or a part of it.

unilateral contract. A contract in which only one party makes a promise or undertakes a performance.

voidable contract. A contract that can be affirmed or rejected at the option of one of the parties; a contract that is void as to the wrongdoer but not void as to the party wronged, unless that party elects to treat it as void.

void contract. **1.** A contract that is of no legal effect, so that there is really no contract in existence at all. **2.** A contract that has been fully performed. **3.** Loosely, a voidable contract.

contract, freedom of. See FREEDOM OF CONTRACT.

contractor. **1.** A party to a contract. **2.** More specif., one who contracts to do work or provide supplies for another.

contract rate. See INTEREST RATE.

Contracts Clause. The clause of the U.S. Constitution prohibiting states from passing a law that would impair private contractual obligations. • The Supreme Court has generally interpreted this clause so that states can regulate private contractual obligations if the regulation is reasonable and necessary. U.S. Const. art. I, § 10, cl. 1.

contra non valentum. See DOCTRINE OF CONTRA NON VALENTUM.

contrary to law. **1.** (Of an act or omission) illegal. **2.** (Of a jury verdict) in conflict with established law.

contrary to the evidence. (Of an argument) that is counter to the weight of the evidence presented at a contested hearing.

contravene (kon-trə-**veen**), *vb.* **1.** To violate or infringe; to defy. **2.** To come into conflict with; to be contrary to. — **contravention** (kon-trə-**ven**-shən), *n.*

contravening equity. See EQUITY.

contributing to the delinquency of a minor. The offense of an adult's engaging in conduct involving a minor — or in the presence of a minor — likely to result in delinquent conduct. • Examples include encouraging a minor to shoplift, to lie under oath, or to commit vandalism. See JUVENILE DELINQUENCY. Cf. IMPAIRING THE MORALS OF A MINOR.

contribution. **1.** The right that gives one of several persons who are liable on a common debt the ability to recover ratably from each of the others when that one person discharges the debt for the benefit of all; the right to demand that another who is jointly responsible for a third party's injury supply part of what is required to compensate the third party. **2.** A tortfeasor's right to collect from others responsible for the same tort after the tortfeasor has paid more than his or her proportionate share, the shares being determined as a percentage of fault. **3.** The actual payment by a joint tortfeasor of a proportionate share of what is due. Cf. INDEMNITY.

contributory (kən-**trib**-yə-tor-ee), *adj.* **1.** Tending to bring about a result. **2.** (Of a pension fund) that receives contributions from both the employer and the employees.

contributory, *n.* **1.** One who contributes or who has a duty to contribute. **2.** A contributing factor.

contributory negligence. See NEGLIGENCE.

contributory-negligence doctrine. *Torts.* The principle that completely bars a plaintiff's recovery if the damage suffered is partly the plaintiff's own fault. See NEGLIGENCE. Cf. COMPARATIVE-NEGLIGENCE DOCTRINE.

control, *n.* The direct or indirect power to direct the management and policies of a person or entity, whether through ownership of voting securities, by contract, or otherwise; the power or authority to manage, direct, or oversee.

control, *vb.* **1.** To exercise power or influence over. **2.** To regulate or govern. **3.** To have a controlling interest in.

control group. The persons with authority to make decisions on a corporation's behalf.

control-group test. A method of determining whether the attorney–client privilege protects communications made by corporate employees, by providing that those communications are protected only if made by an employee who is a member of the group with authority to direct the corporation's actions as a result of that communication. • The U.S. Supreme Court rejected the control-group test in *Upjohn Co. v. United States*, 449 U.S. 383, 101 S.Ct. 677 (1981). Cf. SUBJECT-MATTER TEST.

controlled company. See COMPANY.

controlled substance. Any type of drug whose possession and use is regulated by law, including a narcotic, a stimulant, or a hallucinogen. See DRUG.

controlled-substance act. A federal or state statute that is designed to control the distribution, classification, sale, and use of certain drugs.

control theory. The theory that people will engage in criminal behavior unless certain personally held social controls (such as a strong investment in conventional, legitimate activities or a belief that criminal behavior is morally wrong) are in place to prevent them from doing so. Cf. ROUTINE-ACTIVITIES THEORY; RATIONAL-CHOICE THEORY; STRAIN THEORY.

controversy. 1. A disagreement or a dispute, esp. in public. **2.** A justiciable dispute. **3.** *Constitutional law.* A case that requires a definitive determination of the law on the facts alleged for the adjudication of an actual dispute, and not merely a hypothetical, theoretical, or speculative legal issue. See CASE-OR-CONTROVERSY REQUIREMENT.

controvert (**kon**-trə-vərt *or* kon-trə-**vərt**), *vb.* To dispute or contest; esp., to deny (as an allegation in a pleading) or oppose in argument.

contumacy (**kon**-t[y]uu-mə-see), *n.* Contempt of court; the refusal of a person to follow a court's order or direction. — **contumacious,** *adj.* See CONTEMPT.

convene, *vb.* **1.** To call together; to cause to assemble. **2.** *Civil law.* To bring an action.

convention. 1. An agreement or compact, esp. one among nations; a multilateral treaty. **2.** An assembly or meeting of members belonging to an organization or having a common objective. **3.** A generally accepted rule or practice; usage or custom. — **conventional,** *adj.*

conventional interest. See INTEREST (3).

conventionalism. A jurisprudential conception of legal practice and tradition holding that law is a matter of respecting and enforcing legal and social rules.

conventional law. A rule or system of rules agreed on by persons for the regulation of their conduct toward one another; law constituted by agreement as having the force of special law between the parties, by either supplementing or replacing the general law of the land.

conventional obligation. See OBLIGATION.

conversion, *n.* **1.** The act of changing from one form to another; the process of being exchanged. **2.** *Tort & criminal law.* The wrongful possession or disposition of another's property as if it were one's own; an act or series of acts of willful interference, without lawful justification, with an item of property in a manner inconsistent with another's right, whereby that other person is deprived of the use and possession of the property. — **convert,** *vb.*

convertible bond. See BOND (3).

convertible debenture. See DEBENTURE.

convertible insurance. See INSURANCE.

convertible subordinated debenture. See DEBENTURE.

convey, *vb.* To transfer or deliver (something, such as a right or property) to another, esp. by deed or other writing.

conveyance (kən-**vay**-ənts), *n.* **1.** The voluntary transfer of a right or of property. **2.** The transfer of a property right that does not pass by delivery of a thing or merely by agreement. **3.** The transfer of an interest in real property from one living person to another, by means of an instrument such as a deed. **4.** The document (usu. a deed) by which such a transfer occurs. **5.** A means of transport; a vehicle. See FRAUDULENT CONVEYANCE.

conveyancer (kən-**vay**-ən-sər). A lawyer who specializes in real-estate transactions.

conveyancing (kən-**vay**-ən-sing). The act or business of drafting and preparing legal instruments, esp. those (such as deeds or leases) that transfer an interest in real property.

conveyee (kən-vay-**ee**). One to whom property is conveyed.

conveyor (kən-**vay**-ər *or* -or). One who transfers or delivers title to another.

convict (**kon**-vikt), *n.* A person who has been found guilty of a crime and is serving a sentence of confinement for that crime; a prison inmate.

conviction (kən-**vik**-shən), *n.* **1.** The act or process of judicially finding someone guilty of a crime; the state of having been proved guilty. **2.** The judgment (as by a jury verdict) that a person is guilty of a crime. **3.** A strong belief or opinion. — **convict** (kən-**vikt**), *vb.*

conviction rate. Within a given area or for a given time, the number of convictions (including plea bargains) as a percentage of the total number of prosecutions undertaken.

cool blood. *Criminal law.* In the law of homicide, a condition in which the defendant's emotions are not in such an excited state that they interfere with his or her faculties and reason. See COLD BLOOD. Cf. HEAT OF PASSION.

***Cooley* doctrine.** *Constitutional law.* The principle that Congress has exclusive power under the Commerce Clause to regulate the national as well as the local aspects of national commercial matters, and that the states may regulate those aspects of interstate commerce so local in character as to require diverse treatment. • The Supreme Court has abandoned the *Cooley* doctrine in favor of a balancing test for Commerce Clause cases. *Cooley v. Port Bd. of Wardens*, 53 U.S. (12 How.) 299 (1851).

cooling-off period. 1. An automatic delay between a person's taking some legal action and the consequence of that action. **2.** A period during which a buyer may cancel a purchase. **3.** An automatic delay in some states between the filing of divorce papers and the divorce hearing. **4.** During a dispute, a period during which no action may be taken by either side.

cooling time. *Criminal law.* Time to recover cool blood after great excitement, stress, or provocation, so that one is considered able to contemplate, comprehend, and act with reference to the consequences that are likely to follow. See COOL BLOOD.

cooperative, *n.* **1.** An organization or enterprise (as a store) owned by those who use its services. **2.** A dwelling (as an apartment building) owned by its residents, to whom the apartments are leased. Cf. CONDOMINIUM (2).

cooperative federalism. Distribution of power between the federal government and the states in which each recognizes the powers of the other but shares those powers to jointly engage in governmental functions.

coowner, *n.* A person who is in concurrent ownership, possession, and enjoyment of property with one or more others; a tenant in common, a joint tenant, or a tenant by the entirety. — **coown,** *vb.* — **coownership,** *n.*

cop a plea, *vb. Slang.* (Of a criminal defendant) to plead guilty to a lesser charge as a means to avoid standing trial for a more serious offense. See PLEA BARGAIN.

coparcenary (koh-**pahr**-sə-ner-ee), *n.* An estate that arises when two or more persons jointly inherit from one ancestor, the title and right of possession being shared equally by all. — **coparcenary,** *adj.* — **coparcener** (koh-**pahr**-sə-nər), *n.*

coparty. A litigant or participant in a legal transaction who has a like status with another party; a party on the same side of a lawsuit. See CODEFENDANT; COPLAINTIFF.

coplaintiff. One of two or more plaintiffs in the same litigation. Cf. CODEFENDANT.

coprincipal. 1. One of two or more participants in a criminal offense who either perpetrate the crime or aid a person who does so. **2.** One of two or more persons who have appointed an agent whom they both have the right to control.

copy, *n.* An imitation or reproduction of an original. • In the law of evidence, a copy is generally admissible to prove the contents of a writing. Fed. R. Evid. 1003. See BEST-EVIDENCE RULE.

certified copy. A duplicate of an original (usu. official) document, certified as an exact reproduction usu. by the officer responsible for issuing or keeping the original.

conformed copy. An exact copy of a document bearing written explanations of things that were not or could not be copied, such as a note on the document indicating that it was signed by a person whose signature appears on the original.

copyright, *n.* **1.** A property right in an original work of authorship (such as a literary, musical, artistic, photographic, or film work) fixed in any tangible medium of expression, giving the holder the exclusive right to reproduce, adapt, distribute, perform, and display the work. **2.** The body of law relating to such works. • Federal copyright law is governed by the Copyright Act of 1976. 17 USCA §§ 101–1332. — Abbr. c. — **copyright,** *vb.* — **copyrighted,** *adj.*

Copyright Clause. U.S. Const. art. I, § 8, cl. 8, which gives Congress the power to secure to authors the exclusive rights to their writings for a limited time.

copyright notice. A notice that a work is copyright-protected, usu. placed in each published copy of the work. • Since March 1, 1989, such notice is not required for a copyright to be valid (although it continues to provide certain procedural advantages).

copyright owner. One who holds exclusive rights to copyrighted material. 17 USCA § 101.

corespondent. 1. A coparty who responds to a petition, such as a petition for a writ of certiorari. **2.** In some states, a coparty who responds to an appeal. **3.** *Family law.* In a divorce suit based on adultery, the person with whom the spouse is accused of having committed adultery. See RESPONDENT.

corollary (kor- *or* **kahr-**ə-ler-ee), *n.* A proposition that follows from a proven proposition with little or no additional proof; something that naturally follows.

coroner (kor- *or* **kahr-**ə-nər). A public official whose duty is to investigate the causes and circumstances of any death that occurs suddenly, suspiciously, or violently. See MEDICAL EXAMINER.

coroner's jury. See JURY.

corporal oath. See OATH.

corporal punishment. See PUNISHMENT.

corporate, *adj.* Of or relating to a corporation, esp. a business corporation.

corporate acquisition. The takeover of one corporation by another if both parties retain their legal existence after the transaction. Cf. MERGER (7).

corporate agent. See AGENT.

corporate authority. 1. The power rightfully wielded by officers of a corporation. **2.** In some jurisdictions, a municipal officer, esp. one empowered to represent the municipality in certain statutory matters.

corporate books. Written records of a corporation's activities and business transactions.

corporate citizenship. Corporate status in the state of incorporation, though a corporation is not a citizen for the purposes of the Privileges and Immunities Clause of the U.S. Constitution.

corporate crime. See CRIME.

corporate domicile. See DOMICILE.

corporate immunity. See IMMUNITY (2).

corporate-opportunity doctrine. The rule that a corporation's directors, officers, and employees are precluded from using information gained in corporate capacity to take personal advantage of any business opportunities that the corporation has an expectancy right or property interest in, or that in fairness should otherwise belong to the corporation. • In a partnership, the analogous principle is the *firm-opportunity doctrine*.

corporate purpose. The general scope of the business objective for which a corporation was created. • A statement of corporate purpose is commonly required in the articles of incorporation.

corporate seal. See SEAL.

corporate speech. See SPEECH.

corporate trustee. See TRUSTEE.

corporate veil. The legal assumption that the acts of a corporation are not the actions of its shareholders, so that the shareholders are exempt from liability for the corporation's actions. See PIERCING THE CORPORATE VEIL.

corporate welfare. See WELFARE (2).

corporation, *n.* An entity (usu. a business) having authority under law to act as a single person distinct from the shareholders who own it and having rights to issue stock and exist indefinitely; a group or succession of persons established in accordance with legal rules into a legal or juristic person that has legal personality distinct from the natural persons who make it up, exists indefinitely apart from them, and has the legal powers that its constitution gives it. — **incorporate,** *vb.* — **corporate,** *adj.* See COMPANY.

> ***C corporation.*** A corporation whose income is taxed through it rather than through its shareholders. • Any corporation not electing S-corporation tax status under the Internal Revenue Code is a C corporation by default. Cf. *S corporation*.
>
> ***charitable corporation.*** A nonprofit corporation that is dedicated to

benevolent purposes and thus entitled to special tax status under the Internal Revenue Code. See CHARITABLE ORGANIZATION.

close corporation. A corporation whose stock is not freely traded and is held by only a few shareholders (often within the same family). • The requirements and privileges of close corporations vary by jurisdiction.

collapsible corporation. A corporation formed to give a short-term venture the appearance of a long-term investment in order to portray income as capital gain, rather than profit. • The corporation is typically formed for the sole purpose of purchasing property. The corporation is usually dissolved before the property has generated substantial income. The Internal Revenue Service treats the income earned through a collapsible corporation as ordinary income rather than as capital gain. IRC (26 USCA) § 341(a). Cf. *collapsible partnership* under PARTNERSHIP.

domestic corporation. **1.** A corporation that is organized and chartered under the laws of a state. • The corporation is considered *domestic* by the chartering state. Cf. *foreign corporation*. **2.** *Tax.* A corporation created or organized in the United States or under federal or state law. IRC (26 USCA) § 7701(a)(4).

dummy corporation. A corporation whose only function is to hide the principal's identity and to protect the principal from liability.

foreign corporation. A corporation that was organized and chartered under the laws of another state, government, or country. Cf. *domestic corporation*.

nonprofit corporation. A corporation organized for some purpose other than making a profit, and usu. afforded special tax treatment.

parent corporation. A corporation that has a controlling interest in another corporation (called a *subsidiary corporation*), usu. through ownership of more than one-half the voting stock.

private corporation. A corporation founded by and composed of private individuals principally for a nonpublic purpose, such as manufacturing, banking, and railroad corporations (including charitable and religious corporations).

professional corporation. A corporation that provides services of a type that requires a professional license. • A professional corporation may be made up of architects, accountants, physicians, veterinarians, or the like. — Abbr. P.C.

public corporation. **1.** A corporation whose shares are traded to and among the general public. **2.** A corporation that is created by the state as an agency in the administration of civil government. **3.** A government-owned corporation that engages in activities that benefit the general public, usu. while remaining financially independent. • Such a corporation is managed by a publicly appointed board.

public-service corporation. A corporation whose operations serve a need of the general public, such as public transportation, communications, gas, water, or electricity. • This type of corporation is usually subject to extensive governmental regulation.

registered corporation. A publicly held corporation a security of which is registered under section 12 of the Securities Exchange Act of 1934. • The corporation is subject to the Act's periodic disclosure requirements and proxy regulations. 15 USCA § 78*l*.

S corporation. A corporation whose income is taxed through its shareholders rather than through the corporation itself. • Only corporations with a limited number of shareholders can elect S-corporation tax status under Subchapter S of the Internal Revenue Code.

shell corporation. A corporation that has no active business and usu. exists only in name as a vehicle for another company's business operations.

small-business corporation. **1.** A corporation having 75 or fewer shareholders and otherwise satisfying the requirements of the Internal Revenue Code provisions permitting a subchapter S election. IRC (26 USCA) § 1361. See *S corporation*. **2.** A corporation receiving money for stock (as a contribution to capital and paid-in surplus) totaling not more than $1 million, and otherwise satisfying the requirements of IRC § 1244(c), thereby enabling the shareholders to claim an ordinary loss on worthless stock.

subsidiary corporation. A corporation in which a parent corporation has a controlling share.

corporator (**kor**-pə-ray-tər). **1.** A member of a corporation. **2.** INCORPORATOR.

corporeal (kor-**por**-ee-əl), *adj.* Having a physical, material existence; tangible. — **corporeality,** *n.* Cf. INCORPOREAL.

corporeal ownership. See OWNERSHIP.

corporeal thing. See THING.

corpus (**kor**-pəs), *n.* [Latin "body"] **1.** An abstract collection or body. **2.** The property for which a trustee is responsible; the trust principal. **3.** Principal (as of a fund or estate), as opposed to interest or income. Pl. **corpora** (**kor**-pə-rə), **corpuses** (**kor**-pə-səz).

corpus delicti (**kor**-pəs də-**lik**-tɪ *or* -tee). [Latin "body of the crime"] **1.** The fact of a transgression; ACTUS REUS. **2.** Loosely, the material substance on which a crime has been committed; the physical evidence of a crime, such as the corpse of a murdered person.

***corpus delicti* rule.** *Criminal law.* The doctrine that prohibits a prosecutor from proving the corpus delicti based solely on a defendant's extrajudicial statements. • The prosecution must establish the *corpus delicti* with corroborating evidence to secure a conviction.

corpus juris (**kor**-pəs **joor**-is). [Latin "body of law"] The law as the sum or collection of laws <*Corpus Juris Secundum*>. — Abbr. C.J.

correction, *n.* **1.** Generally, the act or an instance of making right what is wrong <mark your corrections in red ink>. **2.** A change in business activity or market price following and counteracting an increase or decrease in the activity or price <the broker advised investors to sell before the inevitable stock-market correction>. **3.** (*usu. pl.*) The punishment and treatment of a criminal offender through a program of imprisonment, parole, and probation <Department of Corrections>. — **correct,** *vb.* — **corrective** (for senses 1 & 2), **correctional** (for sense 3), *adj.*

correlative (kə-**rel**-ə-tiv), *adj.* **1.** Related or corresponding; analogous. **2.** Having or involving a reciprocal or mutually interdependent relationship.

correlative-rights doctrine. *Water law.* The principle that adjoining landowners must limit their use of a common water source to a reasonable amount.

correspondent, *n.* **1.** The writer of a letter or letters. **2.** A person employed by the media to report on events. **3.** A securities firm or financial institution that performs services for another in a place or market that the other does not have direct access to. — **correspond,** *vb.*

corroborating evidence. See EVIDENCE.

corroborating witness. See WITNESS.

corroboration (kə-rob-ə-**ray**-shən), *n.* **1.** Confirmation or support by additional evidence or authority. **2.** Formal confirmation or ratification. — **corroborate,** *vb.* — **corroborative** (kə-**rob**-ə-rə-tiv), *adj.* — **corroborator** (kə-**rob**-ə-ray-tər), *n.*

corruption. 1. Depravity, perversion, or taint; an impairment of integrity, virtue, or moral principle; esp., the impairment of a public official's duties by bribery. **2.** The act of doing something with an intent to give some advantage inconsistent with official duty and the rights of others; a fiduciary's or official's use of a station or office to procure some benefit either personally or for someone else, contrary to the rights of others.

corruption of a minor. 1. The crime of engaging in sexual activity with a minor; specif., the offense of having sexual intercourse or engaging in sexual activity with a person who is not the actor's spouse and who (1) is under the legal age of consent, the actor being considerably older than the victim (usu. four or more years), or (2) is less than 21 years old (or other age established by the particular jurisdiction), the actor being the person's guardian or otherwise responsible for the victim's welfare. Model Penal Code § 213.3. • In some jurisdictions, the definition has been broadened to include aiding or encouraging a minor to commit a criminal offense. Cf. IMPAIRING THE MORALS OF A MINOR. **2.** A parent's or caregiver's act of stimulating or encouraging a child to engage in destructive antisocial behavior. — Also termed *corrupting*. Cf. CONTRIBUTING TO THE DELINQUENCY OF A MINOR.

corruptly, *adv.* In a corrupt or depraved manner; by means of corruption or bribery. • As used in criminal-law statutes, *corruptly* usually indicates a wrongful desire for pecuniary gain or other advantage.

corrupt-motive doctrine. *Criminal law.* The rule that conspiracy is punishable only if the agreement was entered into with an evil purpose, not merely with an intent to do the illegal act. • This doctrine has been rejected by the Model Penal Code.

corrupt-practices act. A federal or state statute that regulates campaign contributions and expenditures as well as their disclosure.

cosign, *vb.* To sign a document along with another person, usu. to assume obligations and to supply credit to the principal obligor. — **cosignature,** *n.* — **cosigner,** *n.*

cost, *n.* **1.** The amount paid or charged for something; price or expenditure. Cf. EXPENSE.

acquisition cost. An asset's net price; the original cost of an asset.

cost of completion. Contracts. A measure of damages based on the expense incurred by the party not in breach to finish the promised performance.

direct cost. The amount of money for material, labor, and overhead to produce a product.

fixed cost. A cost whose value does not fluctuate with changes in output or business activity; esp., overhead expenses such as rent, salaries, and depreciation.

indirect cost. A cost that is not specific to the production of a particular good or service, but that arises from production activity in general, such as overhead allocations for general and administrative activities.

marginal cost. The additional cost incurred in producing one more unit of output.

opportunity cost. The cost of acquiring an asset measured by the value of an alternative investment that is forgone.

replacement cost. The cost of acquiring an asset that is as equally useful or productive as an asset currently held.

sunk cost. A cost that has already been incurred and that cannot be recovered.

variable cost. The cost that varies in the short run in close relationship with changes in output.

2. (*pl.*) The charges or fees taxed by the court, such as filing fees, jury fees, courthouse fees, and reporter fees. **3.** (*pl.*) The expenses of litigation, prosecution, or other legal transaction, esp. those allowed in favor of one party against the other.

cost approach. A method of appraising real property, based on the cost of building a new property with the same utility, assuming that an informed buyer would pay no more for the property than it would cost to build a new property having the same usefulness. Cf. MARKET APPROACH; INCOME APPROACH.

cost basis. See BASIS (2).

cost-benefit analysis. An analytical technique that weighs the costs of a proposed decision, holding, or project against the expected advantages, economic or otherwise.

cost justification. Under the Robinson–Patman Act, an affirmative defense against a charge of price discrimination dependent on the seller's showing that it incurs lower costs in serving those customers who are paying less. 15 USCA § 13(a).

cost of completion. See COST.

cost-of-living clause. A provision (as in a contract or lease) that gives an automatic wage, rent, or benefit increase tied in some way to cost-of-living rises in the economy.

cost-plus contract. See CONTRACT.

costs of collection. Expenses incurred in receiving payment of a note; esp., attorney's fees created in the effort to collect a note.

cotenancy. See TENANCY.

coterminous (koh-**tər**-mə-nəs), *adj.* (Of ideas or events) coextensive in time or meaning.

council. 1. A deliberative assembly. **2.** An administrative or executive body.

councillor, *n.* A person who serves on a council, esp. at the local level. — **councillorship,** *n.*

counsel, *n.* **1.** Advice or assistance. **2.** One or more lawyers who represent a client. — In the singular, also termed *counselor*. Cf. ATTORNEY; LAWYER.

appellate counsel. A lawyer who represents a party on appeal. • The term is often used in contrast with *trial counsel*.

assigned counsel. An attorney appointed by the court to represent a person, usu. an indigent person.

general counsel. **1.** A lawyer or law firm that represents a client in all or most of the client's legal matters, but that sometimes refers extraordinary matters to other lawyers. **2.** The most senior lawyer in a corporation's legal department, usu. also a corporate officer.

independent counsel. An attorney hired to provide an unbiased opinion about a case or to conduct an impartial investigation; esp., an attorney appointed by a governmental branch or agency to investigate alleged misconduct within that branch or agency. See *special prosecutor* under PROSECUTOR. Cf. *special counsel*.

in-house counsel. One or more lawyers employed by a company.

lead counsel. The more highly ranked lawyer if two or more are retained; the lawyer who manages or controls the case or cases, esp. in class actions or multidistrict litigation.

of counsel. **1.** A lawyer employed by a party in a case; esp., one who — although not the principal attorney of record — is employed to assist in the preparation or management of the case or in its presentation on appeal. **2.** A lawyer who is affiliated with a law firm, though not as a member, partner, or associate.

special counsel. An attorney employed by the state or political subdivision to assist in a particular case when the public interest so requires. Cf. *independent counsel*.

trial counsel. A lawyer who represents a party at trial. • The term is often used in contrast with *appellate counsel*.

count, *n. Procedure*. **1.** The part of an indictment charging the suspect with a distinct offense. **2.** In a complaint or similar pleading, the statement of a distinct claim. Cf. DECLARATION (7).

general count. A count that states the plaintiff's claim without undue particularity.

multiple counts. Several separate causes of action or charged offenses contained in a single pleading or indictment.

separate count. One of two or more criminal charges contained in one indictment, each charge constituting a separate indictment for which the accused may be tried.

special count. A section of a pleading in which the plaintiff's claim is stated with great particularity — usu. employed only when the pleading rules require specificity.

count, *vb*. In pleading, to declare or state; to narrate the facts that state a claim.

counterclaim, *n*. A claim for relief asserted against an opposing party after an original claim has been made; esp., a defendant's claim in opposition to or as a setoff against the plaintiff's claim. — **counterclaim,** *vb*. — **counterclaimant,** *n*. Cf. CROSS-CLAIM.

compulsory counterclaim. A counterclaim that must be asserted to be cognizable, usu. because it relates to the opposing party's claim and arises out of the same subject matter. • If a defendant fails to assert a compulsory counterclaim in the original action, that claim may not be brought in a later, separate action (with some exceptions).

permissive counterclaim. A counterclaim that need not be asserted to be cognizable, usu. because it does not arise out of the same subject matter as the opposing party's claim or involves third parties over which the court does not have jurisdiction. • Permissive counterclaims may be brought in a later, separate action.

counterfeit, *vb*. To forge, copy, or imitate (something) without a right to do so and with the purpose of deceiving or defrauding; esp., to manufacture fake money (or other security) that might be used in place of the genuine article. • Manufacturing fake food stamps is considered counterfeiting. — **counterfeit,** *n*. — **counterfeiting,** *n*. — **counterfeit,** *adj*. — **counterfeiter,** *n*.

Counterfeit Access Device and Computer Fraud and Abuse Act of 1984. A federal statute that criminalizes various computer-related activities such as accessing without permission a computer system belonging to a bank or the federal government, or using that access to improperly obtain anything of value. 18 USCA § 1030.

countermand (**kown**-tər-mand), *n*. An action that has the effect of voiding something previously ordered; a revocation. — **countermand** (kown-tər-**mand** *or* **kown-**), *vb*.

counteroffer, *n. Contracts*. An offeree's new offer that varies the terms of the original offer and that therefore rejects the original offer. — **counteroffer,** *vb.* — **counterofferor,** *n.* See MIRROR-IMAGE RULE.

counterpart. 1. In conveyancing, a corresponding part of an instrument <the other half of the indenture — the counterpart — could not be found>. **2.** One of two or more copies or duplicates of a legal instrument <this lease may be executed in any number of counterparts, each of which is considered an original>.

counterpart writ. See WRIT.

counterpromise, *n.* A promise made in exchange for another party's promise. — **counterpromise,** *vb.*

countersign, *vb.* To write one's own name next to someone else's to verify the other signer's identity. — **countersignature,** *n.*

countervailing equity. See EQUITY.

county. The largest territorial division for local government within a state, generally considered to be a political subdivision and a quasi-corporation.

county court. See COURT.

county judge. See JUDGE.

course of business. The normal routine in managing a trade or business.

course of dealing. An established pattern of conduct between the parties to a particular transaction. • If a dispute arises, the parties' course of dealing can be used as evidence of how they intended to carry out the transaction. Cf. COURSE OF PERFORMANCE; *trade usage* under USAGE.

course of employment. Events that occur or circumstances that exist as a part of one's employment; esp., the time during which an employee furthers an employer's goals through employer-mandated directives.

course of performance. A sequence of previous performance by either party after an agreement has been entered into, when a contract involves repeated occasions for performance and both parties know the nature of the performance and have an opportunity to object to it. • A course of performance accepted or acquiesced in without objection is relevant to determining the meaning of the agreement. UCC §§ 2–208, 2A–301(a). Cf. COURSE OF DEALING; *trade usage* under USAGE.

court, *n.* **1.** A governmental body consisting of one or more judges who sit to adjudicate disputes and administer justice. **2.** The judge or judges who sit on such a governmental body. **3.** A legislative assembly. **4.** The locale for a legal proceeding. **5.** The building where the judge or judges convene to adjudicate disputes and administer justice.

appellate court. A court with jurisdiction to review decisions of lower courts or administrative agencies.

business court. A court that handles exclusively commercial litigation. • In the late 20th century, business courts emerged as a way to unclog the general dockets and to dispose of commercial cases more efficiently and consistently.

circuit court. A court usu. having jurisdiction over several counties, districts, or states, and holding sessions in all those areas; esp., UNITED STATES COURT OF APPEALS.

civil court. A court with jurisdiction over noncriminal cases. — Abbr. Civ. Ct.

constitutional court. A court named or described and expressly protected in a constitution.

county court. A court with powers and jurisdiction dictated by a state constitution or statute. • The county court may govern administrative or judicial matters, depending on state law.

court above. A court to which a case is appealed.

court below. A trial court or intermediate appellate court from which a case is appealed.

court of appeals. **1.** An intermediate appellate court. **2.** In New York and Maryland, the highest appellate court within the jurisdiction.

court of equity. A court that (1) has jurisdiction in equity, (2) administers and decides controversies in accordance with the rules, principles, and precedents of equity, and (3) follows the forms and procedures of chancery. Cf. *court of law*.

court of general jurisdiction. A court having unlimited or nearly unlimited trial jurisdiction in both civil and criminal cases.

court of last resort. The court having the authority to handle the final appeal of a case, such as the U.S. Supreme Court.

court of law. **1.** Broadly, any judicial tribunal that administers the laws of a state or nation. **2.** A court that proceeds according to the course of the common law, and that is governed by its rules and principles. Cf. *court of equity*.

court of limited jurisdiction. A court with jurisdiction over only certain types of cases, or cases in which the amount in controversy is limited.

court of original jurisdiction. A court where an action is initiated and first heard.

court of record. A court that is required to keep a record of its proceedings and that may fine and imprison people for contempt. See OF RECORD (2).

court of special session. A court that has no stated term and is not continuous, but is organized only for hearing a particular case.

district court. A trial court having general jurisdiction within its judicial district. — Abbr. D.C.

domestic court. **1.** A court having jurisdiction at the place of a party's residence or domicile. **2.** See *family court*.

examining court. A lower court (usu. presided over by a magistrate) that determines probable cause and sets bail at a preliminary hearing in a criminal case.

family court. A court having jurisdiction over matters involving divorce, child custody and support, paternity, domestic violence, and other family-law issues.

federal court. A court having federal jurisdiction, including the U.S. Supreme Court, courts of appeals, district courts, bankruptcy courts, and tax courts.

foreign court. **1.** The court of a foreign nation. **2.** The court of another state.

full court. A court session that is attended by all the court's judges; an en banc court.

hot court. A court, esp. an appellate court, that is familiar with the briefs filed in the case, and therefore with the issues, before oral argument. • Typically, a hot court controls the oral argument with its questioning, as opposed to listening passively to set presentations of counsel.

inferior court. **1.** Any court that is subordinate to the chief appellate tribunal within a judicial system. **2.** A court of special, limited, or statutory jurisdiction, whose record must show the existence of jurisdiction in any given case to give its ruling presumptive validity.

justice court. A court, presided over by a justice of the peace, that has jurisdiction to hear minor criminal cases, matters involving small amounts of money, or certain specified claims (such as forcible-entry-and-detainer suits).

juvenile court. A court having jurisdiction over cases involving children under a specified age, usu. 18.

kangaroo court. **1.** A self-appointed tribunal or mock court in which the principles of law and justice are disregarded, perverted, or parodied. **2.** A court or tribunal characterized by unauthorized or irregular procedures, esp. so as to render a fair proceeding impossible. **3.** A sham legal proceeding.

legislative court. A court created by a statute, as opposed to one authorized by a constitution.

magistrate's court (**maj**-i-strayts *or* -strits). **1.** A court with jurisdiction over minor criminal offenses. • Such a court also has the power to bind over for trial persons accused of more serious offenses. **2.** A court with limited jurisdiction over minor criminal and civil matters.

municipal court. A court having jurisdiction (usu. civil and criminal) over cases arising within the municipality in which it sits.

probate court. A court with the power to declare wills valid or invalid, to oversee the administration of estates, and in some states to appoint guardians and approve the adoption of minors. See PROBATE.

small-claims court. A court that informally and expeditiously adjudicates claims that seek damages below a specified monetary amount, usu. claims to collect small accounts or debts.

state court. A court of the state judicial system, as opposed to a federal court.

superior court. **1.** In some states, a trial court of general jurisdiction. **2.** In Pennsylvania, an intermediate court between the trial court and the chief appellate court.

trial court. A court of original jurisdiction where the evidence is first received and considered.

court calendar. A list of matters scheduled for trial or hearing; DOCKET (2).

courtesy supervision. Oversight of a parolee by a correctional agency located in a jurisdiction other than where the parolee was sentenced.

court for the trial of impeachments. A tribunal empowered to try a government officer or other person brought before it by the process of impeachment. • The U.S. Senate has this authority, as do the upper houses of most state legislatures.

court-martial, *n.* An ad hoc military court convened under military authority to try someone accused of violating the Uniform Code of Military Justice, particularly a member of the armed forces. Pl. **courts-martial. — court-martial,** *vb.*

Court-Martial Reports. A publication containing the opinions of the U.S. Court of Military Appeals and select decisions of the Courts of Military Review. • This publication appeared during the years 1951–1975. — Abbr. CMR.

court of appeals. See COURT.

Court of Civil Appeals. An intermediate appellate court in some states, such as Alabama and (formerly) Texas.

court of claims. 1. See COURT. **2.** (*cap.*) See UNITED STATES COURT OF FEDERAL CLAIMS.

Court of Common Pleas. 1. An intermediate-level court in some states, such as Arkansas. **2.** A trial court of general jurisdiction in some states, such as Ohio, Pennsylvania, and South Carolina. — Abbr. C.P.

Court of Criminal Appeals. 1. For each branch of the armed services, an intermediate appellate court that reviews court-martial decisions. 10 USCA §§ 859–876. **2.** In some jurisdictions, such as Texas and Oklahoma, the highest appellate court that hears criminal cases.

court of equity. See COURT.

court of general jurisdiction. See COURT.

court of last resort. See COURT.

court of law. See COURT.

court of limited jurisdiction. See COURT.

court of original jurisdiction. See COURT.

Court of Oyer and Terminer (oy-ər an[d] **tər**-mə-nər). In some states, a court of higher criminal jurisdiction.

court of record. See COURT.

court of special session. See COURT.

court papers. All documents that a party files with the court, including pleadings, motions, notices, and the like.

court recorder. See RECORDER.

court reporter. 1. A person who records testimony, stenographically or by electronic or other means, and when requested prepares a transcript. Cf. *court recorder* under RECORDER. **2.** REPORTER OF DECISIONS.

court rules. Regulations having the force of law and governing practice and procedure in the various courts, such as the Federal Rules of Civil Procedure, the Federal Rules of Criminal Procedure, the U.S. Supreme Court Rules, and the Federal

Rules of Evidence, as well as any local rules that a court promulgates.

covenant (**kəv**-ə-nənt), *n.* **1.** A formal agreement or promise, usu. in a contract.

absolute covenant. A covenant that is not qualified or limited by any condition. Cf. *conditional covenant.*

concurrent covenant. A covenant that requires performance by one party at the same time as another's performance.

conditional covenant. A covenant that is qualified by a condition. Cf. *absolute covenant.*

covenant not to compete. A contractual provision — typically found in employment, partnership, or sale-of-business agreements — in which one party agrees to refrain from conducting business similar to that of the other party. • Courts generally enforce these clauses for the duration of the original business relationship, but clauses extending beyond termination must usually be reasonable in time, scope, and territory.

covenant not to sue. A covenant in which a party having a right of action agrees not to assert that right in litigation.

express covenant. A covenant created by the words of the parties. Cf. *implied covenant.*

implied covenant. A covenant that can be inferred from the whole agreement and the conduct of the parties. Cf. *express covenant.*

implied covenant of good faith and fair dealing. An implied covenant to cooperate with the other party to an agreement so that both parties may obtain the full benefits of the agreement; an implied covenant to refrain from any act that would injure a contracting party's right to receive the benefit of the contract.

implied negative covenant. A covenant binding a grantor not to permit use of any reserved right in a manner that might destroy the benefits that would otherwise inure to the grantee.

negative covenant. A covenant that requires a party to refrain from doing something; esp., in a real-estate financing transaction, the borrower's promise to the lender not to encumber or transfer the real estate as long as the loan remains unpaid.

2. A common-law action to recover damages for breach of contract under seal. **3.** A promise made in a deed or implied by law; esp., an obligation in a deed burdening or favoring a landowner.

covenant against encumbrances. A grantor's promise that the property has no visible or invisible encumbrances. • In a special warranty deed, the covenant is limited to encumbrances made by the grantor.

covenant appurtenant (ə-**pər**-tə-nənt). A covenant that is connected with the grantor's land; a covenant running with the land. Cf. *covenant in gross.*

covenant for further assurances. A covenant to do whatever is reasonably necessary to perfect the title conveyed if it turns out to be imperfect. See *further assurance* under ASSURANCE.

covenant for quiet enjoyment. **1.** A covenant insuring against the consequences of a defective title or any other disturbance of the title. **2.** A covenant ensuring that the tenant will not be evicted or disturbed by the grantor or a person having a lien or superior title. • This covenant is sometimes treated as being synonymous with *covenant of warranty.*

covenant for title. A covenant that binds the grantor to ensure the completeness, security, and continuance of the title transferred. • This covenant usually includes the covenants for seisin, against encumbrances, for the right to convey, for quiet enjoyment, and of warranty.

covenant in gross. A covenant that does not run with the land. Cf. *covenant appurtenant.*

covenant of habitability (hab-ə-tə-**bil**-ə-tee). See *implied warranty of habitability* under WARRANTY (2).

covenant of nonclaim. A covenant barring a grantor or the grantor's heirs from claiming title in the conveyed land.

covenant of seisin (**see**-zin). A covenant, usu. appearing in a warranty deed, stating that the grantor has an estate, or the right to convey an estate, of the quality and size that the grantor purports to convey. • For the covenant to be valid, the grantor must have both title and possession at the time of the grant.

covenant of warranty. A covenant by which the grantor agrees to defend the grantee against any lawful or reasonable claims of superior title by a third party and to indemnify the grantee for any loss sustained by the claim. • This covenant is sometimes treated as being synonymous with *covenant for quiet enjoyment.* See WARRANTY (1).

covenant running with the land. A covenant that, because it relates to the land, binds successor grantees indefinitely. • The land cannot be conveyed without the covenant.

restrictive covenant. **1.** A private agreement, usu. in a deed or lease, that restricts the use or occupancy of real property, esp. by specifying lot sizes, building lines, architectural styles, and the uses to which the property may be put. **2.** See *covenant not to compete* under COVENANT (1).

special covenant against encumbrances. A grantor's promise that the property is free of encumbrances created by the grantor only, not the grantor's predecessors. See *special warranty deed* under DEED. Cf. *covenant against encumbrances.*

covenant, *vb.* To promise or undertake in a covenant; to agree formally.

covenantee (kəv-ə-nən-**tee**). The person to whom a promise by covenant is made; one entitled to the benefit of a covenant.

covenant marriage. See MARRIAGE (1).

covenantor (**kəv**-ə-nən-tər *or* kəv-ə-nən-**tor**). The person who makes a promise by covenant; one subject to the burden of a covenant.

coventurer (koh-**ven**-chər-ər). A person who undertakes a joint venture with one or more persons. Cf. JOINT VENTURE.

cover, *n.* The purchase on the open market, by the buyer in a breach-of-contract dispute, of goods to substitute for those promised but never delivered by the seller. • Under UCC § 2–712, the buyer can recover from the seller the difference between the cost of the substituted goods and the original contract price.

coverage, *n.* Inclusion of a risk under an insurance policy; the risks within the scope of an insurance policy. — **cover,** *vb.*

coverage ratio. A measurement of a firm's ability to cover its financing charges.

C.P. *abbr.* COURT OF COMMON PLEAS.

cracking, *n.* A gerrymandering technique in which a geographically concentrated political or racial group that is large enough to constitute a district's dominant force is broken up by district lines and dispersed throughout two or more districts. Cf. PACKING; STACKING.

cramdown, *n.* Court confirmation of a Chapter 11 bankruptcy plan despite the opposition of certain creditors. • Under the Bankruptcy Code, a court may confirm a plan — even if it has not been accepted by all classes of creditors — if the plan (1) has been accepted by at least one impaired class, (2) does not discriminate unfairly, and (3) is fair and equitable. 11 USCA § 1129(b). — **cram down,** *vb.* See IMPAIRMENT.

crashworthiness doctrine. *Products liability.* The principle that the manufacturer of a product will be held strictly liable for injuries occurring in a collision, even if the collision results from an independent cause, to the extent that a defect in the product causes injuries above and beyond those that would have occurred in the collision itself.

creature of statute. A doctrine, governmental agency, etc. that would not exist but for a legislative act that brought it into being.

credibility, *n.* The quality that makes something (as a witness or some evidence) worthy of belief. — **credible,** *adj.*

credible evidence. See EVIDENCE.

credible witness. See WITNESS.

credit, *n.* **1.** Belief; trust. **2.** One's ability to borrow money; the faith in one's ability to pay debts. **3.** The time that a seller gives the buyer to make the payment that is due. **4.** The availability of funds either from a financial institution or under a letter of credit. **5.** LETTER OF CREDIT. **6.** A deduction from an amount due; an accounting entry reflecting an addition to revenue or net worth. Cf. DEBIT. **7.** TAX CREDIT.

credit, *vb.* **1.** To believe. **2.** To enter (as an amount) on the credit side of an account.

credit bureau. An organization that compiles information on people's creditworthiness and publishes it in the form of reports that are used chiefly by merchants and service-providers who deal directly with customers. Cf. CREDIT-REPORTING BUREAU.

credit-card crime. The offense of using a credit card to purchase something with knowledge that (1) the card is stolen or forged, (2) the card has been revoked or canceled, or (3) the card's use is unauthorized.

credit freeze. See FREEZE.

creditor. 1. One to whom a debt is owed; one who gives credit for money or goods. **2.** A person or entity with a definite claim against another, esp. a claim that is capable of adjustment and liquidation. **3.** *Bankruptcy.* A person or entity having a claim against the debtor predating the order for relief concerning the debtor. Cf. DEBTOR.

creditor beneficiary. See BENEFICIARY.

creditor's bill. An equitable suit in which a judgment creditor seeks to reach property that cannot be reached by the process available to enforce a judgment.

creditors' committee. *Bankruptcy.* A committee comprising representatives of the creditors in a Chapter 11 proceeding, formed to negotiate the debtor's plan of reorganization. • Generally, a committee has no fewer than 3 and no more than 11 members and serves as an advisory body. 11 USCA § 1102.

credit-reporting bureau. An organization that, on request, prepares investigative reports not just on people's creditworthiness but also on personal information gathered from various sources, including interviews with neighbors, friends, and coworkers. • These reports are used chiefly by employers (for prospective employees), insurance companies (for applicants), and landlords (for prospective tenants). Cf. CREDIT BUREAU.

creditworthy, *adj.* (Of a borrower) financially sound enough that a lender will extend credit in the belief that the chances of default are slight; fiscally healthy. — **creditworthiness,** *n.*

crier (krɪ-ər). An officer of the court who makes public pronouncements as required by the court. See BAILIFF.

crime. A social harm that the law makes punishable; the breach of a legal duty treated as the subject matter of a criminal proceeding. See OFFENSE (1).

administrative crime. An offense consisting of a violation of an administrative rule or regulation that carries with it a criminal sanction.

commercial crime. A crime that affects commerce; esp., a crime directed toward the property or revenues of a commercial establishment. • Examples include robbery of a business, embezzlement, counterfeiting, forgery, prostitution, illegal gambling, and extortion. See 26 CFR § 403.38.

common-law crime. A crime that is punishable under the common law, rather than by force of statute. Cf. *statutory crime.*

computer crime. A crime requiring knowledge of computer technology, such as sabotaging or stealing computer data or using a computer to commit some other crime.

continuous crime. **1.** A crime that continues after an initial illegal act has been consummated; a crime that involves ongoing elements. • An example is illegal U.S. drug importation. The criminal act is completed not when the drugs enter the country, but when the drugs reach their final destination. **2.** A crime (such as driving a stolen vehicle) that continues over an extended period. Cf. *instantaneous crime*.

corporate crime. A crime committed either by a corporate body or by its representatives acting on its behalf. • Examples include price-fixing and consumer fraud.

crime of omission. An offense that carries as its material component the failure to act.

crime of passion. A crime committed in the heat of an emotionally charged moment, with no opportunity to reflect on what is happening. See HEAT OF PASSION.

hate crime. A crime motivated by the victim's race, color, ethnicity, religion, or national origin. • Certain groups have lobbied to expand the definition by statute to include a crime motivated by the victim's disability, gender, or sexual orientation. Cf. *hate speech* under SPEECH.

high crime. A crime that is offensive to public morality, though not necessarily a felony. • Under the U.S. Constitution, a government officer's commission of a "high crime" is, along with treason and bribery, grounds for removal from office. U.S. Const. art. II, § 4. See IMPEACHABLE OFFENSE.

infamous crime (**in**-fə-məs). **1.** At common law, a crime for which part of the punishment was infamy, so that one who committed it would be declared ineligible to serve on a jury, hold public office, or testify. • Examples are perjury, treason, and fraud. **2.** A crime punishable by imprisonment in a penitentiary. • The Fifth Amendment requires a grand-jury indictment for the prosecution of infamous (or capital) crimes, which include all federal felony offenses. See *indictable offense* under OFFENSE.

instantaneous crime. A crime that is fully completed by a single act, as arson or murder, rather than a series of acts. • The statute of limitations for an instantaneous crime begins to run with its completion. Cf. *continuous crime*.

quasi-crime. **1.** An offense not subject to criminal prosecution (such as contempt or violation of a municipal ordinance) but for which penalties or forfeitures can be imposed. **2.** An offense for which someone other than the actual perpetrator is held liable, the perpetrator being presumed to act on the command of the responsible party.

signature crime. A distinctive crime so similar in pattern, scheme, or modus operandi to previous crimes that it identifies a particular defendant as the perpetrator.

status crime. A crime of which a person is guilty by being in a certain condition or of a specific character, such as vagrancy.

statutory crime. A crime punishable by statute. Cf. *common-law crime.*

street crime. Crime generally directed against a person in public, such as mugging, theft, or robbery.

victimless crime. A crime that is considered to have no direct victim, usu. because only consenting adults are involved. • Examples are possession of illicit drugs and deviant sexual intercourse between consenting adults.

violent crime. A crime that has as an element the use, attempted use, threatened use, or substantial risk of use of physical force against the person or property of another. 18 USCA § 16.

crime-fraud exception. The doctrine that neither the attorney–client privilege nor the attorney-work-product privilege protects attorney–client communications that are in furtherance of a current or planned crime or fraud. *Clark v. United States*, 289 U.S. 1, 53 S.Ct. 465 (1933); *In re Grand Jury Subpoena Duces Tecum*, 731 F.2d 1032 (2d Cir. 1984).

crimes against persons. A category of criminal offenses in which the perpetrator uses or threatens to use force. • Examples include murder, rape, aggravated assault, and robbery. Cf. *offense against the person* under OFFENSE (1).

crimes against property. A category of criminal offenses in which the perpetrator seeks to derive an unlawful benefit from — or do damage to — another's property without the use or threat of force. • Examples include burglary, theft, and arson (even though arson may result in injury or death). Cf. *offense against property* under OFFENSE (1).

crime score. A number assigned from an established scale, indicating the relative seriousness of an offense based on the nature of the injury or the extent of property damage. Cf. DEFENDANT SCORE.

criminal, *adj.* **1.** Having the character of a crime; in the nature of a crime. **2.** Connected with the administration of penal justice.

criminal, *n.* **1.** One who has committed a criminal offense. **2.** One who has been convicted of a crime.

dangerous criminal. A criminal who has either committed a violent crime or used force in trying to escape from custody.

episodic criminal. **1.** A person who commits crimes sporadically. **2.** A person who commits crimes only during periods of intense stress, as in the heat of passion.

state criminal. **1.** A person who has committed a crime against the state (such as treason); a political criminal. **2.** A person who has committed a crime under state law.

criminal action. See ACTION.

criminal anarchy. The doctrine that advocates the violent overthrow of government. • To promote this doctrine is a criminal offense. 18 USCA § 2385.

criminal assault. See ASSAULT.

criminal capacity. See CAPACITY.

criminal contempt. See CONTEMPT.

criminal damage to property. 1. Injury, destruction, or substantial impairment to the use of property (other than by fire or explosion) without the consent of a person having an interest in the property. **2.** Injury, destruction, or substantial impairment to the use of property (other than by fire or explosion) with the intent to injure or defraud an insurer or lienholder. Cf. ARSON.

criminal desertion. See DESERTION.

criminal forfeiture. See FORFEITURE.

criminal fraud. See FRAUD.

criminal homicide. See HOMICIDE.

criminal instrument. 1. Something made or adapted for criminal use. Model Penal Code § 5.06(1)(a). **2.** Something commonly used for criminal purposes and possessed under circumstances showing an unlawful purpose. Model Penal Code § 5.06(1)(b).

criminal-instrumentality rule. The principle that when a criminal act is committed, that act — rather than the victim's negligence that made the crime possible — will be considered to be the crime's proximate cause.

criminal intent. See INTENT (1).

criminalistics (krim-ə-nə-**lis**-tiks), *n.* The science of crime detection, usu. involving the subjection of physical evidence to laboratory analysis, including ballistic testing, blood-fluid and tissue analysis, and other tests that are helpful in determining what happened. — **criminalist** (**krim**-ə-nəl-ist), *n.* Cf. CRIMINOLOGY.

criminality (krim-ə-**nal**-ə-tee). **1.** The state or quality of being criminal. **2.** An act or practice that constitutes a crime.

criminalization (**krim**-ə-nəl-ə-**zay**-shən), *n.* **1.** The act or an instance of making a previously lawful act criminal, usu. by passing a statute. — **criminalize** (**krim**-ə-nəl-IZ), *vb.* Cf. DECRIMINALIZATION; CIVILIZATION. **2.** The process by which a person develops into a criminal.

criminal jurisdiction. See JURISDICTION.

criminal justice. 1. The methods by which a society deals with those who are accused of having committed crimes. Cf. CIVIL JUSTICE. **2.** The field of study pursued by those seeking to enter law enforcement as a profession.

criminal-justice system. The collective institutions through which an accused offender passes until the accusations have been disposed of or the assessed punishment concluded.

criminal law. The body of law defining offenses against the community at large, regulating how suspects are investigated, charged, and tried, and establishing punishments for convicted offenders.

criminal lawyer. See LAWYER.

criminal libel. See LIBEL.

criminal negligence. See NEGLIGENCE.

criminal policy. The branch of criminal science concerned with limiting harmful conduct in society. • It draws on information provided by criminology, and its subjects for investigation are (1) the appropriate measures of social organization for preventing harmful activities, and (2) the treatment to be accorded to those who have caused harm, whether the offenders are to be given warnings, supervised probation, or medical treatment, or whether they are to suffer serious deprivations of life or liberty, such as capital punishment or imprisonment.

criminal possession. See POSSESSION.

criminal procedure. The rules governing the mechanisms under which crimes are investigated, prosecuted, adjudicated, and punished. • It includes the protection of accused persons' constitutional rights.

criminal proceeding. See PROCEEDING.

criminal protector. An accessory after the fact to a felony; one who aids or harbors a wrongdoer after the commission of a crime.

criminal sanction. See SANCTION.

criminal science. The study of crime with a view to discovering the causes of criminality, devising the most effective methods of reducing crime, and perfecting the means for dealing with those who have committed crimes. • The three main branches of criminal science are criminology, criminal policy, and criminal law.

criminal statute. See STATUTE.

criminology, *n.* The study of crime and criminal punishment as social phenomena; the study of the causes of crime, comprising (1) criminal biology, which examines causes that may be found in the mental and physical constitution of an offender (such as hereditary tendencies and physical defects), and (2) criminal sociology, which deals with inquiries into the effects of environment as a cause of criminality. — **criminological,** *adj.* — **criminologist,** *n.* Cf. CRIMINALISTICS; PENOLOGY.

crit. An adherent of critical legal studies.

critical evidence. See EVIDENCE.

critical legal studies. 1. A school of thought advancing the idea that the legal system's manipulative nature masks its true function, which, according to the predominant Marxist wing of this school, is to perpetuate the socioeconomic status quo. **2.** The body of work produced by adherents to this school of thought. — Abbr. CLS.

critical race theory. 1. A reform movement within the legal profession, particularly within academia, whose adherents believe that the legal system has disempowered racial minorities. • Critical race theorists observe that even if the law is couched in neutral language, it cannot be neutral because those who fashioned it had their own subjective perspectives that, once enshrined in law, have disadvantaged minorities and even perpetuated racism. **2.** The body of work produced by adherents to this theory. — Abbr. CRT.

critical stage. *Criminal procedure*. A point in a criminal prosecution when the accused's rights or defenses might be affected by the absence of legal representation. • Under the Sixth Amendment, a critical stage triggers the accused's right to appointed counsel. Examples of critical stages include preliminary hearings, jury selection, and (of course) trial. Cf. ACCUSATORY STAGE.

cross-appeal. See APPEAL.

cross-claim, *n.* A claim asserted between codefendants or coplaintiffs in a case and that relates to the subject of the original claim or counterclaim. — **cross-claim,** *vb.* — **cross-claimant,** *n.* Cf. COUNTERCLAIM.

cross-collateral. See COLLATERAL.

cross-collateral clause. An installment-contract provision allowing the seller, if the buyer defaults, to repossess not only the particular item sold but also every other item bought from the seller on which a balance remained due when the last purchase was made.

cross-collateralization. See *cross-collateral* (2) under COLLATERAL.

cross-complaint. 1. A claim asserted by a defendant against another party to the action. **2.** A claim asserted by a defendant against a person not a party to the action for a matter relating to the subject of the action.

cross-default. A provision under which default on one debt obligation triggers default on another obligation.

cross-demand. See DEMAND.

cross-error. See ERROR (2).

cross-examination, *n.* The questioning of a witness at a trial or hearing by the party opposed to the party who called the witness to testify. — **cross-examine,** *vb.* Cf. DIRECT EXAMINATION; RECROSS-EXAMINATION.

cross-interrogatory. See INTERROGATORY.

cross-offer, *n. Contracts.* An offer made to another in ignorance that the offeree has made the same offer to the offeror. — **cross-offer,** *vb.* — **cross-offeror,** *n.*

cross-question. See QUESTION.

cross-remainder. See REMAINDER.

CRT. *abbr.* CRITICAL RACE THEORY.

cruel and unusual punishment. See PUNISHMENT.

cruelty. The intentional and malicious infliction of mental or physical suffering on a living creature, esp. a human; abusive treatment; outrage.

extreme cruelty. As a ground for divorce, one spouse's physical violence toward the other spouse, or conduct that destroys or severely impairs the other spouse's mental health.

legal cruelty. Cruelty that will justify granting a divorce to the injured party; specif., conduct by one spouse that endangers the life, person, or health of the other spouse, or creates a reasonable apprehension of bodily or mental harm.

mental cruelty. As a ground for divorce, one spouse's course of conduct that creates such anguish that it endangers the life, physical health, or mental health of the other spouse. See EMOTIONAL DISTRESS.

physical cruelty. As a ground for divorce, actual personal violence committed by one spouse against the other.

Ct. Cl. *abbr.* Court of Claims. See UNITED STATES COURT OF FEDERAL CLAIMS.

culpable (**kəl**-pə-bəl), *adj.* **1.** Guilty; blameworthy. **2.** Involving the breach of a duty. — **culpability** (kəl-pə-**bil**-ə-tee), *n.*

culpable neglect. See NEGLECT.

culpable negligence. See NEGLIGENCE.

culprit. 1. A person accused or charged with the commission of a crime. **2.** A person who is guilty of a crime.

cumulative-effects doctrine. The rule that a transaction affecting interstate commerce in a trivial way may be taken together with other similar transactions to establish that the combined effect on interstate commerce is not trivial and can therefore be regulated under the Commerce Clause.

cumulative evidence. See EVIDENCE.

cumulative legacies. See LEGACY.

cumulative offense. See OFFENSE.

cumulative punishment. See PUNISHMENT.

cumulative remedy. See REMEDY.

cumulative testimony. See TESTIMONY.

cumulative traverse. See TRAVERSE.

cumulative voting. See VOTING.

curative admissibility. See ADMISSIBILITY.

curative-admissibility doctrine. The rule that otherwise inadmissible evidence will be admitted to rebut inadmissible evidence placed before the fact-finder by the adverse party. • The doctrine applies when a motion to strike cannot cure the prejudice created by the adverse party.

curative instruction. See JURY INSTRUCTION.

curator (**kyuur**-ə-tər *or* **kyuur**-ay-tər *or* kyuu-**ray**-tər), *n.* A temporary guardian or conservator appointed by a court to care for the property or person of a minor or incapacitated person.

curatorship. The office of a curator or guardian.

cure, *vb.* **1.** To remove legal defects or correct legal errors. • For example, curing title involves removing defects from title to unmarketable land so that title becomes marketable. **2.** The right of a seller under the UCC to correct a nonconforming delivery of goods, usu. within the contract period. — **curative,** *adj.*

currency. An item (such as a coin, government note, or banknote) that circulates as a medium of exchange. See LEGAL TENDER.

current-cost accounting. A method of measuring assets in terms of replacement cost. • This approach accounts for inflation by recognizing price changes in a company's assets and restating the assets in terms of their current cost.

current market value. The price at which an asset can be sold within the present accounting period.

current obligation. See OBLIGATION.

curtesy (**kər**-tə-see). At common law, a husband's right, upon his wife's death, to a life estate in the land that his wife owned during their marriage, assuming that a child was born alive to the couple. • This right has been largely abolished. Cf. DOWER.

curtilage (kər-tə-lij). The land or yard adjoining a house, usu. within an enclosure. • Under the Fourth Amendment, the curtilage is an area usually protected from warrantless searches. See OPEN-FIELDS DOCTRINE. Cf. MESSUAGE.

custodial interrogation. See INTERROGATION.

custodian, *n.* **1.** A person or institution that has charge or custody of property, papers, or other valuables; GUARDIAN. **2.** *Bankruptcy.* A prepetition agent who has taken charge of any asset belonging to the debtor. 11 USCA § 101(11). — **custodianship,** *n.*

custody, *n.* **1.** The care and control of a thing or person for inspection, preservation, or security.

constructive custody. Custody of a person (such as a parolee or probationer) whose freedom is controlled by legal authority but who is not under direct physical control.

physical custody. Custody of a person (such as an arrestee) whose freedom is directly controlled and limited.

preventive custody. Custody intended to prevent further dangerous or criminal behavior.

protective custody. The government's confinement of a person for that person's own security or well-being, such as a witness whose safety is in jeopardy or an incompetent person who may harm others.

2. *Family law.* The care, control, and maintenance of a child awarded by a court to a responsible adult. • Custody involves legal custody (decision-making authority) and physical custody (caregiving authority), and an award of custody usually grants both rights.

divided custody. An arrangement by which each parent has exclusive physical custody and full control of and responsibility for the child part of the time, with visitation rights in the other parent.

joint custody. An arrangement by which both parents share the responsibility for and authority over the child at all times, although one parent may exercise primary physical custody.

physical custody. **1.** The right to have the child live with the person awarded custody by the court. **2.** Possession of a child during visitation.

sole custody. An arrangement by which one parent has full control and sole decision-making responsibility — to the exclusion of the other parent — on matters such as health, education, religion, and living arrangements.

3. The detention of a person by virtue of lawful process or authority. — **custodial,** *adj.*

custody hearing. A judicial examination of the facts relating to parental custody in a divorce or separation proceeding.

custody of the law. The condition of property or a person being under the control of legal authority (as a court or law officer). See IN CUSTODIA LEGIS.

custom, *n.* **1.** A practice that by its common adoption and long, unvarying habit has come to have the force of law. See USAGE. **2.** (*pl.*) Duties imposed on imports or exports. **3.** (*pl.*) The agency or procedure for collecting these duties. — **customary** (for sense 1), *adj.*

custom and usage. General rules and practices that have become generally adopted through unvarying habit and common use. Cf. CUSTOM (1); USAGE.

customary, *n.* A record of all the established legal and quasi-legal practices within a community.

customary interpretation. See INTERPRETATION.

customary law. Law consisting of customs that are accepted as legal requirements or obligatory rules of conduct; practices and beliefs that are so vital and intrinsic a part of a social and economic system that they are treated as if they were laws.

cyberlaw (sɪ-bər-law). The field of law dealing with computers and the Internet, including such issues as intellectual-property rights, freedom of expression, and free access to information.

cybersquatting. The act of reserving a domain name on the Internet, esp. a name that would be associated with a company's trademark, and then seeking to profit by selling or licensing the name to the company that has an interest in being identified with it.

cyberstalking. The act of threatening, harassing, or annoying someone through multiple e-mail messages, as through the Internet, esp. with the intent of placing the recipient in fear that an illegal act or an injury will be inflicted on the recipient or a member of the recipient's family or household.

cybertheft. The act of using an online computer service, such as one on the Internet, to steal someone else's property or to interfere with someone else's use and enjoyment of property. • Examples of cybertheft are hacking into a bank's computer records to wrongfully credit one account and debit another, and interfering with a copyright by wrongfully sending protected material over the Internet.

cy pres (see **pray** *also* SI). [Law French "as near as"] The equitable doctrine under which a court reforms a written instrument with a gift to charity as closely to the donor's intention as possible, so that the gift does not fail. • Courts use *cy pres* especially in construing charitable gifts when the donor's original charitable purpose cannot be fulfilled. Cf. DOCTRINE OF APPROXIMATION.

D

D. *abbr.* **1.** DISTRICT. **2.** DEFENDANT. **3.** DIGEST.

D.A. *abbr.* DISTRICT ATTORNEY.

daily balance. The final daily accounting for a day on which interest is to be accrued or paid.

damage, *adj.* Of or relating to monetary compensation for loss or injury to a person or property. Cf. DAMAGES.

damage, *n.* Loss or injury to person or property.

damages, *n. pl.* Money claimed by, or ordered to be paid to, a person as compensation for loss or injury. — **damage,** *adj.*

actual damages. An amount awarded to a complainant to compensate for a proven injury or loss; damages that repay actual losses.

benefit-of-the-bargain damages. Damages that a breaching party to a contract must pay to the aggrieved party, equal to the amounts that the aggrieved party would have received, including profits, if the contract had been fully performed.

compensatory damages (kəm-**pen**-sə-tor-ee). **1.** Damages sufficient in amount to indemnify the injured person for the loss suffered. **2.** See *actual damages*.

consequential damages. Losses that do not flow directly and immediately from an injurious act, but that result indirectly from the act.

exemplary damages. See *punitive damages*.

expectation damages. Compensation awarded for the loss of what a person reasonably anticipated from a transaction that was not completed.

future damages. Money awarded to an injured party for an injury's residual or projected effects that reduce the person's ability to function. • Examples are expected pain and suffering, loss or impairment of earning capacity, and projected medical expenses.

general damages. Damages that the law presumes follow from the type of wrong complained of. • General damages do not need to be specifically claimed or proved to have been sustained.

hedonic damages (hi-**don**-ik). Damages that attempt to compensate for the loss of the pleasure of being alive. • Such damages are not allowed in most jurisdictions.

incidental damages. **1.** Losses reasonably associated with or related to actual damages. **2.** A seller's commercially reasonable expenses incurred in stopping delivery or in transporting and caring for goods after a buyer's breach. UCC § 2–710. **3.** A buyer's expenses reasonably incurred in caring for goods after a seller's breach. UCC § 2–715(1).

liquidated damages. An amount contractually stipulated as a reasonable estimation of actual damages to be recovered by one party if the other party breaches. • If the parties to a contract have agreed on liquidated damages, the sum fixed is the measure of damages for a breach, whether it exceeds or falls short of the actual damages. See LIQUIDATED-DAMAGES CLAUSE. Cf. *unliquidated damages*; PENALTY CLAUSE.

nominal damages. A trifling sum awarded when a legal injury is suffered but when there is no substantial loss or injury to be compensated.

pecuniary damages (pə-**kyoo**-nee-er-ee). Damages that can be estimated and monetarily compensated.

punitive damages. Damages awarded in addition to actual damages when the defendant acted with recklessness, malice, or deceit.

reliance damages. Damages awarded for losses incurred by the plaintiff in reliance on the contract.

restitution damages. Damages awarded to a plaintiff when the defendant has been unjustly enriched at the plaintiff's expense.

speculative damages. **1.** Damages that are so uncertain that they will not be awarded. **2.** See *punitive damages*.

treble damages. Damages that, by statute, are three times the amount that the fact-finder determines is owed.

unliquidated damages. Damages that have been established by a verdict or award but cannot be determined by a fixed formula, so they are left to the discretion of the judge or jury. Cf. *liquidated damages*.

damnify, *vb.* To cause loss or damage to; to injure <the surety was damnified by the judgment obtained against it>. — **damnification,** *n.*

damnum (**dam**-nəm), *n.* [Latin] A loss; damage suffered. Pl. **damna.** See AD DAMNUM CLAUSE.

damnum sine injuria (**dam**-nəm **sɪ**-nee in-**joor**-ee-ə *or* **sin**-ay). [Latin "damage without wrongful act"] Loss or harm for which there is no legal remedy. Cf. INJURIA ABSQUE DAMNO.

danger. 1. Peril; exposure to harm, loss, pain, or other negative result. **2.** A cause of peril; a menace.

apparent danger. **1.** Obvious danger; real danger. **2.** *Criminal law.* The danger resulting from a person's overt demonstration of the intent to seriously injure or kill another, making it necessary for the threatened person to kill the offender. See SELF-DEFENSE.

deterrent danger. An obvious danger that an occupier of land creates to discourage trespassers, such as a barbed-wire fence or spikes on the top of a wall.

imminent danger. **1.** An immediate, real threat to one's safety that justifies the use of force in self-defense. **2.** *Criminal law.* The danger that results from an immediate threatened injury sufficient to cause a reasonable and prudent person to defend himself or herself.

retributive danger. A concealed danger that an occupier of land creates to injure trespassers. • A retributive danger is lawful only to the extent that it could be justified if the occupier had inflicted the injury personally or directly to the trespasser. Thus, a spring gun or a land mine is an unlawful means of defending land against a trespasser.

unavoidable danger. **1.** Inescapable danger. **2.** A danger that is unpreventable, esp. by a person operating a vessel.

danger-creation doctrine. The theory that if a state's affirmative conduct places a person in jeopardy, then the state may be liable for the harm inflicted on that person by a third party. • This is an exception to the general principle that the state is not liable for an injury that a third party inflicts on a member of the public. Cf. SPECIAL-RELATIONSHIP DOCTRINE.

danger-invites-rescue doctrine. The principle holding a defendant liable not only for injuries to the person that the defendant has imperiled, but also for injuries that a third person receives while trying to rescue the imperiled person.

dangerous, *adj.* **1.** (Of a condition, situation, etc.) perilous; hazardous; unsafe. **2.** (Of a person, an object, etc.) likely to cause serious bodily harm.

dangerous condition. See CONDITION (5).

dangerous criminal. See CRIMINAL.

dangerous instrumentality. An instrument, substance, or condition so inherently dangerous that it may cause serious bodily injury or death without human use or interference. • It may serve as the basis for strict liability. See ATTRACTIVE-NUISANCE DOCTRINE. Cf. *deadly weapon* under WEAPON.

dangerous-proximity test. *Criminal law.* A common-law test for the crime of attempt, focusing on whether the defendant is dangerously close to completing the offense. • Factors include the gravity of the potential crime, the apprehension of the victim, and the uncertainty of the crime's occurrence. See ATTEMPT (2).

dangerous situation. Under the last-clear-chance doctrine, the circumstance in which a plaintiff operating a motor vehicle has reached a position (as in the path of an oncoming train) that cannot be escaped by the exercise of ordinary care. See LAST-CLEAR-CHANCE DOCTRINE.

dangerous-tendency test. A propensity of a person or animal to inflict injury. • The test is used, especially in dog-bite cases, to determine whether an owner will be held liable for injuries caused by the owner's animal.

dangerous weapon. See WEAPON.

***Darden* hearing.** *Criminal procedure.* An ex parte proceeding to determine whether disclosure of an informer's identity is pertinent to establishing probable cause when there is otherwise insufficient evidence to establish probable cause apart from the arresting officer's testimony about an informer's communications. • The defense attorney may be excluded from the hearing but can usually submit questions to be used by the judge in the examination. *People v. Darden*, 313 N.E.2d 49 (N.Y. 1974).

date certain. A fixed or appointed day; a specified day, esp. a date fixed by an instrument such as a deed.

date of bankruptcy. The date when a court declares a person to be bankrupt; the date of bankruptcy adjudication.

date of injury. The inception date of an injury; the date of an accident causing an injury.

date rape. See RAPE.

***Daubert* test.** A method that federal district courts use to determine whether expert testimony is admissible under Federal Rule of Evidence 702, which generally requires that expert testimony consist of scientific, technical, or other specialized knowledge that will assist the fact-finder in understanding the evidence or determining a fact in issue. *Daubert v. Merrell Dow Pharms., Inc.*, 509 U.S. 579, 113 S.Ct. 2786 (1993). The Supreme Court has held that similar scrutiny must be applied to nonscientific expert testimony. *Kumho Tire Co. v. Carmichael*, 526 U.S. 137, 119 S.Ct. 1167 (1999). Variations of the *Daubert* test are applied in the trial courts of most states.

Davis–Bacon Act. A federal law originally enacted in 1931 to regulate the minimum-wage rates payable to employees of federal public-works projects. 40 USCA § 276a.

day. 1. Any 24-hour period; the time it takes the earth to revolve once on its axis. **2.** The period between the rising and the setting of the sun. **3.** Sunlight. **4.** The period when the sun is above the horizon, along with the period in the early morning and late evening when a person's face is discernible. **5.** Any specified time period, esp. as distinguished from other periods. Cf. NIGHT.

answer day. The last day for a defendant to file and serve a responsive pleading in a lawsuit. • Under the Federal Rules of Civil Procedure, a defendant generally must serve an answer (1) within 20 days after being served with the summons and complaint, or (2) if a defendant timely waives service at the plaintiff's request, within 60 days after the request for waiver was sent. Fed. R. Civ. P. 4(d), 12(a).

juridical day (juu-**rid**-i-kəl). A day on which legal proceedings can be held. Cf. *nonjudicial day*; NONJURIDICAL.

nonjudicial day. A day when courts do not sit or when legal proceedings cannot be conducted, such as a Sunday or legal holiday. See LEGAL HOLIDAY. Cf. *juridical day*.

peremptory day. A day assigned for trial or hearing, without further opportunity for postponement.

return day. **1.** A day on which a defendant must appear in court (as for an arraignment). **2.** A day on which a defendant must file an answer. **3.** A day on which a proof of service must be returned to court. **4.** A day on which a writ of execution must be returned to court. **5.** A day specified by law for counting votes in an election.

day in court. 1. The right and opportunity, in a judicial tribunal, to litigate a claim, seek relief, or defend one's rights. **2.** The right to be notified and given an opportunity to appear and to be heard when one's case is called.

d/b/a. *abbr.* Doing business as. • The abbreviation usually precedes a person's or business's assumed name <Paul Smith d/b/a Paul's Dry Cleaners>.

d.b.e. *abbr.* DE BENE ESSE.

D.C. *abbr.* See *district court* under COURT.

deadbeat. *Slang.* A person who does not pay debts or financial obligations (such as child-support payments, fines, and legal judgments), usu. with the suggestion that the person is also adept or experienced at evading creditors.

deadbeat dad. *Slang.* A father who has not paid or who is behind in making child-support payments.

deadbeat mom. *Slang.* **1.** A mother who has not paid or who is behind in making child-support payments. **2.** An able-bodied mother whose income is derived from welfare payments, not from gainful employment.

deadhand control. The convergence of various legal doctrines that allow a decedent's control of wealth to influence the conduct of a living beneficiary; esp., the use of executory interests that vest at some indefinite and remote time in the future to restrict alienability and to ensure that property remains in the hands of a particular family or organization. • The rule against perpetuities restricts certain types of deadhand control, which is sometimes referred to either as the power of the *mortua manus* (dead hand) or as trying to retain property *in mortua manu*. See RULE AGAINST PERPETUITIES.

dead letter. 1. A law or practice that, although not formally abolished, is no longer used, observed, or enforced. **2.** A piece of mail that can be neither delivered nor returned because it lacks correct addresses for both the intended recipient and the sender.

deadly force. See FORCE.

deadly weapon. See WEAPON.

deadly weapon per se. See WEAPON.

dead man's statute. A law prohibiting the admission of a decedent's statement as evidence in certain circumstances, as when an opposing party or witness seeks to use the statement to support a claim against the decedent's estate.

dead time. See TIME.

deal, *n.* **1.** An act of buying and selling; the purchase and exchange of something for profit. **2.** An arrangement for mutual advantage. **3.** An indefinite quantity.

deal, *vb.* **1.** To distribute (something). **2.** To transact business with (a person or entity). **3.** To conspire with (a person or entity).

dealer, *n.* **1.** A person who purchases goods or property for sale to others; a retailer. **2.** A person or firm that buys and sells securities for its own account as a principal, and then sells to a customer. See DEAL, *n.* & *vb.*

death. The ending of life; the cessation of all vital functions and signs.

brain death. The bodily condition of showing no response to external stimuli, no spontaneous movements, no breathing, no reflexes, and a flat reading (usu. for a full day) on a machine that measures the brain's electrical activity.

immediate death. **1.** See *instantaneous death.* **2.** A death occurring within a short time after an injury or seizure, but not instantaneously.

instantaneous death. Death occurring in an instant or within an extremely short time after an injury or seizure.

natural death. **1.** Bodily death. **2.** Death from causes other than accident or violence; death from natural causes. Cf. *violent death.* See NATURAL-DEATH ACT.

presumptive death. Death inferred from proof of the person's long, unexplained absence, usu. after seven years.

simultaneous death. The death of two or more persons in the same mishap, under circumstances that make it impossible to determine who died first. See SIMULTANEOUS-DEATH ACT.

violent death. Death accelerated by human intervention and resulting from a sharp blow, explosion, gunfire, or the like. Cf. *natural death.*

death benefits. An amount paid to a beneficiary on the death of an insured.

death case. **1.** A criminal case in which the death penalty may be or has been imposed. **2.** WRONGFUL-DEATH ACTION.

death certificate. An official document issued by a public registry verifying that a person has died, with information such as the date and time of death, the cause of death, and the signature of the attending or examining physician.

death-knell doctrine. A rule allowing an interlocutory appeal if precluding an appeal until final judgment would moot the issue on appeal and irreparably injure the appellant's rights. • Once recognized as an exception to the final-judgment rule, the doctrine was limited by the U.S. Supreme Court in *Coopers & Lybrand v. Livesay,* 437 U.S. 463, 98 S.Ct. 2454 (1978). There, the Court held that the death-knell doctrine does not permit an immediate appeal of an order denying class certification. But the doctrine still applies in some contexts. For example, the doctrine allows an immediate appeal of the denial of a temporary restraining order when the lack of an appeal would leave nothing to be considered in the trial court. *Woratzeck v. Arizona Bd. of Executive Clemency,* 117 F.3d 400 (9th Cir. 1997). See FINAL-JUDGMENT RULE.

death penalty. **1.** A sentence imposing death as punishment for a serious crime. **2.** A penalty that makes a person or entity ineligible to participate in an activity that the person or entity previously participated in. **3.** See *death-penalty sanction* under SANCTION.

death-penalty sanction. See SANCTION.

death row. The area of a prison where those who have been sentenced to death are confined.

death sentence. See SENTENCE.

death statute. A law that protects the interests of a decedent's family and other dependents, who may recover in damages what they would reasonably have received from the decedent if the death had not occurred. Cf. SURVIVAL STATUTE.

death trap. 1. A structure or situation involving an imminent risk of death. **2.** A situation that, although seemingly safe, is actually quite dangerous.

death warrant. See WARRANT.

debarment, *n.* The act of precluding someone from having or doing something; exclusion or hindrance. — **debar,** *vb.*

debasement. 1. The act of reducing the value, quality, or purity of something; esp., the act of lowering the value of coins by either reducing the weight of gold and silver in the coins or increasing the coins' alloy amounts. **2.** Degradation. **3.** The state of being degraded.

de bene esse (dee **bee**-nee **es**-ee *also* day **ben**-ay **es**-ay), *adv.* [Law Latin "of well-being"] As conditionally allowed for the present; in anticipation of a future need <Willis's deposition was taken *de bene esse*>. — Abbr. *d.b.e.* — ***de bene esse, adj.***

debenture (di-**ben**-chər). **1.** A debt secured only by the debtor's earning power, not by a lien on any specific asset. **2.** An instrument acknowledging such a debt. **3.** A bond that is backed only by the general credit and financial reputation of the corporate issuer, not by a lien on corporate assets. Cf. BOND (3).

convertible debenture. A debenture that the holder may change or convert into some other security, such as stock.

convertible subordinated debenture. A debenture that is subordinate to another debt but can be converted into a different security.

sinking-fund debenture. A debenture that is secured by periodic payments into a fund established to retire long-term debt.

subordinate debenture. A debenture that is subject to the prior payment of ordinary debentures and other indebtedness.

debenture indenture. An indenture containing obligations not secured by a mortgage or other collateral.

debit. 1. A sum charged as due or owing. **2.** In bookkeeping, an entry made on the left side of a ledger or account, noting an increase in assets or a decrease in liabilities. **3.** An account balance showing that something remains due to the holder of the account. Cf. CREDIT (6).

debt. 1. Liability on a claim; a specific sum of money due by agreement or otherwise. **2.** The aggregate of all existing claims against a person, entity, or state. **3.** A nonmonetary thing that one person owes another, such as goods or services. **4.** A common-law writ by which a court adjudicates claims involving fixed sums of money.

debt instrument. A written promise to repay a debt, such as a promissory note, bill, bond, or commercial paper.

debtor. 1. One who owes an obligation to another, esp. an obligation to pay money. **2.** *Bankruptcy.* A person who files a voluntary petition or against whom an involuntary petition is filed. **3.** *Secured transactions.* A person who either (1) has a property interest — other than a security interest or other lien — in collateral, even if the person is not an obligor, or (2) is a seller of accounts, chattel paper, payment intangibles, or promissory notes. UCC § 9–102(a)(19). Cf. CREDITOR.

absconding debtor. A debtor who flees from creditors to avoid having to pay a debt.

account debtor. A person obligated on an account, chattel paper, or general intangible. • The UCC exempts from the definition of *account debtor* a person obligated to pay a negotiable instrument, even if the instrument constitutes chattel paper. UCC § 9–105(1)(a).

new debtor. Secured transactions. A person who becomes bound as a debtor under a security agreement previously entered into by another person. UCC §§ 9–102(a)(39), 9–203(c).

debtor-in-possession. *Bankruptcy.* A Chapter 11 or 12 debtor that continues to operate its business as a fiduciary to the bankruptcy estate. — Abbr. DIP.

debt pooling. An arrangement by which a person's debts are consolidated and creditors agree to accept lower monthly payments or to take less money.

debt ratio. A corporation's total long-term and short-term liabilities divided by the firm's total assets.

debt retirement. Repayment of debt; RETIREMENT (3).

debt service. 1. The funds needed to meet a long-term debt's annual interest expenses, principal payments, and sinking-fund contributions. **2.** Payments due on a debt, including interest and principal.

debt-to-equity ratio. A corporation's long-term debt divided by its owners' equity, calculated to assess its capitalization.

decedent (di-**see**-dənt), *n.* A dead person, esp. one who has died recently.

decedent's estate. See ESTATE (3).

deceit, *n.* **1.** The act of intentionally giving a false impression. **2.** A tort arising from a false representation made knowingly or recklessly with the intent that another person should detrimentally rely on it. **3.** See *fraudulent misrepresentation* under MISREPRESENTATION. — **deceive,** *vb.* See FRAUD; MISREPRESENTATION.

deceptive act. As defined by the Federal Trade Commission and most state statutes, conduct that is likely to deceive a consumer acting reasonably under similar circumstances.

deceptive warranty. See WARRANTY (2).

decertify, *vb.* **1.** To revoke the certification of. **2.** To remove the official status of (a labor union) by withdrawing the right to act as a collective-bargaining agent. **3.** (Of a court) to overrule a previous order that created a class for purposes of a class action; to officially undo (a class). — **decertification,** *n.* Cf. CERTIFY.

decision, *n.* A judicial determination after consideration of the facts and the law; esp., a ruling, order, or judgment pronounced by a court when considering or disposing of a case. — **decisional,** *adj.* See JUDGMENT; OPINION (1).

appealable decision. A decree or order that is sufficiently final to receive appellate review (such as an order granting summary judgment), or an interlocutory decree or order that is immediately appealable, usu. by statute (such as an order denying immunity to a police officer in a civil-rights suit).

declarant (di-**klair**-ənt), *n.* **1.** One who has made a statement. **2.** One who has signed a declaration, esp. one stating an intent to become a U.S. citizen.

declaration, *n.* **1.** A formal statement, proclamation, or announcement, esp. one embodied in an instrument.

declaration of dividend. A company's setting aside of a portion of its earnings or profits for distribution to its shareholders. See DIVIDEND.

declaration of homestead. A statement required to be filed with a state or local authority, to prove property ownership to claim homestead-exemption rights. See HOMESTEAD.

declaration of intention. An alien's formal statement resolving to become a U.S. citizen and to renounce allegiance to any other government or country.

declaration of legitimacy. A formal pronouncement that a child is legitimate.

declaration of trust. **1.** The act by which the person who holds legal title to property or an estate acknowledges that the property is being held in trust for another person or for certain specified purposes. **2.** The instrument that creates a trust.

2. A document that governs legal rights to certain types of real property, such as a condominium or a residential subdivision. **3.** A listing of the merchandise that a person intends to bring into the United States. **4.** *Evidence.* An unsworn statement made by someone having knowledge of facts relating to an event in dispute.

declaration against interest. A statement by a person who is not a party to a suit and is not available to testify at trial, discussing a matter that is within the declarant's personal knowledge and is adverse to the declarant's interest. • Such a statement is admissible into evidence as an exception to the hearsay rule. Fed. R. Evid. 804(b)(3). See *admission against interest* under ADMISSION.

declaration of pain. A person's exclamation of present pain, which operates as an exception to the hearsay rule. Fed. R. Evid. 803(3).

declaration of state of mind. A person's state-of-mind statement that operates as an exception to the hearsay rule. Fed. R. Evid. 803(3).

dying declaration. A statement by a person who believes that death is imminent, relating to the cause or circumstances of the person's impending death. • The statement is admissible in evidence as an exception to the hearsay rule.

self-serving declaration. An out-of-court statement made to benefit one's own interest.

5. *Common-law pleading.* The plaintiff's first pleading in a civil action. • In most American jurisdictions, it is called a *petition* or *complaint.* See COUNT (2). Cf. PLEA (2). **6.** A formal, written statement — resembling an affidavit but not notarized or sworn to — that attests, under penalty of perjury, to facts known by the declarant. Cf. AFFIDAVIT. **7.** See *declaratory judgment* under JUDGMENT. — **declare,** *vb.* — **declaratory,** *adj.*

declaration of estimated tax. A required IRS filing by certain individuals and businesses of current estimated tax owed, accompanied by periodic payments of that amount. IRC (26 USCA) §§ 6315, 6654.

declaration of rights. An action in which a litigant requests a court's assistance not because any rights have been violated but because those rights are uncertain. • Examples include suits for a declaration of legitimacy, of nullity of marriage, of the legality or illegality of the conduct of state officers, and of the authoritative interpretation of wills. See *declaratory judgment* under JUDGMENT.

Declaration of Taking Act. The federal law regulating the government's taking of private property for public use under eminent domain. 40 USCA § 258a.

declarator of trust (di-**klar**-ə-tər *or* di-**klair**-ə-tər *or* -tor). A common-law action against a trustee who holds property under a title *ex facie* for the trustee's own benefit.

declaratory judgment. See JUDGMENT.

declaratory-judgment act. A federal or state law permitting parties to bring an action to determine their legal rights and positions regarding a controversy not yet ripe for adjudication, as when an insurance company seeks a determination of coverage before deciding whether to cover a claim. See *declaratory judgment* under JUDGMENT.

declaratory part of a law. A portion of a law clearly defining rights to be observed or wrongs to be avoided.

declaratory precedent. See PRECEDENT.

declaratory statute. See STATUTE.

declaratory theory. The belief that judges' decisions never make law but instead merely constitute evidence of what the law is. • This antiquated view is no longer accepted.

declination (dek-lə-**nay**-shən). **1.** A deviation from proper course. **2.** An act of refusal. **3.** A document filed by a fiduciary who chooses not to serve. **4.** At common law, a plea to the court's jurisdiction by reason of the judge's personal interest in the lawsuit.

declining-balance depreciation method. See DEPRECIATION METHOD.

deconstruction, *n.* In critical legal studies, a method of analyzing legal principles or rules by breaking down the supporting premises to show that these premises might also advance the opposite rule or result. — **deconstructionist,** *adj.* & *n.*

decoy, *vb.* To entice (a person) without force; to inveigle. Cf. ENTRAPMENT.

decoy letter. A letter prepared and mailed to detect a criminal who has violated the postal or revenue laws.

decree, *n.* **1.** Traditionally, a judicial decision in a court of equity, admiralty, divorce, or probate — similar to a judgment of a court of law. **2.** Any court order, but esp. one in a matrimonial case. — **decretal** (di-**kree**-təl), *adj.* See JUDGMENT; ORDER (2); DECISION.

consent decree. A court decree that all parties agree to.

decree absolute. A ripened decree nisi; a court's decree that has become unconditional because the time specified in the decree nisi has passed.

decree nisi (NI-SI). A court's decree that will become absolute unless the adversely affected party shows the court, within a specified time, why it should be set aside. See NISI.

decree of distribution. An instrument by which heirs receive the property of a deceased person.

decree of insolvency. A probate-court decree declaring an estate's insolvency.

decree of nullity. A decree declaring a marriage to be void *ab initio.*

decree pro confesso (proh kən-**fes**-oh). *Equity practice.* A decree entered in favor of the plaintiff as a result of the defendant's failure to timely respond to the allegations in the plaintiff's bill.

decrepit (di-**krep**-it), *adj.* (Of a person) disabled; physically or mentally incompetent to such an extent that the individual would be helpless in a personal conflict with a person of ordinary health and strength.

decriminalization, *n.* The legislative act or process of legalizing an illegal act. — **decriminalize,** *vb.* Cf. CRIMINALIZATION (1).

decry (di-**krI**), *vb.* To speak disparagingly about (someone or something).

dedication, *n. Property.* The donation of land or creation of an easement for public use. — **dedicate,** *vb.* — **dedicatory,** *adj.*

common-law dedication. A dedication made without a statute, consisting in the owner's appropriation of land, or an easement in it, for the benefit or use of the public, and the acceptance, by or on behalf of the land or easement.

dedication by adverse user. A dedication arising from the adverse, exclusive use by the public with the actual or imputed knowledge and acquiescence of the owner.

express dedication. A dedication explicitly manifested by the owner.

implied dedication. A dedication presumed by reasonable inference from the owner's conduct.

statutory dedication. A dedication for which the necessary steps are statutorily prescribed, all of which must be substantially followed for an effective dedication.

tacit dedication. A dedication of property for public use arising from silence or inactivity and without an express agreement.

dedition (di-**dish**-ən), *n.* [fr. Latin *deditio* "give up"] A surrender of something, such as property.

deductible, *n.* **1.** Under an insurance policy, the portion of the loss to be borne by the insured before the insurer becomes liable for payment. **2.** The insurance-policy clause specifying the amount of this portion.

deduction, *n.* **1.** The act or process of subtracting or taking away. **2.** *Tax.* An amount subtracted from gross income when calculating adjusted gross income, or from adjusted gross income when calculating taxable income. — **deductible,** *adj.* Cf. EXEMPTION (3); TAX CREDIT.

additional standard deduction. The sum of the additional amounts that a taxpayer who turns 65 or becomes blind before the close of the taxable year is entitled to deduct.

charitable deduction. A deduction for a contribution to a charitable enterprise that has qualified for tax-exempt status in accordance with IRC (26 USCA) § 501(c)(3) and is entitled to be deducted in full by the donor from the taxable estate or from gross income. See CHARITABLE CONTRIBUTION (2); CHARITABLE ORGANIZATION.

deduction in respect of a decedent. A deduction that accrues to the point of death but is not recognizable on the decedent's final income-tax return because of the accounting method used, such as an accrued-interest expense of a cash-basis debtor.

itemized deduction. An expense (such as a medical expense, home-mortgage interest, or a charitable contribution) that can be subtracted from adjusted gross income to determine taxable income.

marital deduction. A federal tax deduction allowed for lifetime and testamentary transfers from one spouse to another. IRC (26 USCA) §§ 2056, 2523.

miscellaneous itemized deduction. Generally, an itemized deduction of job or investment expenses; a deduction other than those allowable in computing adjusted gross income, those enumerated in IRC (26 USCA) § 67(b), and personal exemptions.

standard deduction. A specified dollar amount that a taxpayer can deduct from adjusted gross income, instead of itemizing deductions, to determine taxable income.

3. The portion of a succession to which an heir is entitled before a partition. **4.** The act or process of reasoning from general propositions to a specific application or conclusion. Cf. INDUCTION (2). — **deduct** (for senses 1–3), *vb.* — **deduce** (for sense 4), *vb.*

deed, *n.* **1.** Something that is done or carried out; an act or action. **2.** A written instrument by which land is conveyed. **3.** At common law, any written instrument that is signed, sealed, and delivered and that conveys some interest in property. — **deed,** *vb.* Cf. CONVEYANCE; BILL OF SALE.

absolute deed. A deed that conveys title without condition or encumbrance.

bargain-and-sale deed. A deed that conveys property to a buyer for valuable consideration but that lacks any guarantee from the seller about the validity of the title. See BARGAIN AND SALE.

deed in fee. A deed conveying the title to land in fee simple, usu. with covenants.

deed in lieu of foreclosure. A deed by which a borrower conveys fee-simple title to a lender in satisfaction of a mortgage debt and as a substitute for foreclosure. • This deed is often referred to simply as "deed in lieu."

deed of covenant. A deed to do something, such as a document providing for periodic payments by one party to another (usu. a charity) for tax-saving purposes.

deed of gift. A deed executed and delivered without consideration.

deed of partition. A deed that divides land held by joint tenants, tenants in common, or coparceners.

deed of trust. A deed conveying title to real property to a trustee as security until the grantor repays a loan.

deed poll. A deed made by and binding on only one party, or on two or more parties having similar interests. • It is so called because, traditionally, the parchment was "polled" (that is, shaved) so that it would be even at the top (unlike an indenture). Cf. INDENTURE.

defeasible deed. A deed containing a condition subsequent causing title to the property to revert to the grantor or pass to a third party.

gift deed. A deed given for a nominal sum or for love and affection.

grant deed. A deed containing, or having implied by law, some but not all of the usual covenants of title; esp., a deed in which the grantor warrants that he or she (1) has not previously conveyed the estate being granted, (2) has not encumbered the property except as noted in the deed, and (3) will convey to the grantee any title to the property acquired after the date of the deed.

quitclaim deed. A deed that conveys a grantor's complete interest or claim in certain real property but that neither warrants nor professes that the title is valid. Cf. *warranty deed.*

special warranty deed. **1.** A deed in which the grantor covenants to defend the title against only those claims and demands of the grantor and those claiming by and under the grantor. **2.** In a few jurisdictions, a quitclaim deed. Cf. *warranty deed.*

statutory deed. A warranty-deed form prescribed by state law and containing certain warranties and covenants even though they are not included in the printed form.

title deed. A deed that evidences a person's legal ownership of property. See TITLE.

warranty deed. A deed containing one or more covenants of title; esp., a deed that expressly guarantees the grantor's good, clear title and that contains covenants concerning the quality of title, including warranties of seisin, quiet enjoyment, right to convey, freedom from encumbrances, and defense of title against all claims. See WARRANTY (1). Cf. *quitclaim deed*; *special warranty deed.*

wild deed. A recorded deed that is not in the chain of title, usu. because a previous instrument connected to the chain of title has not been recorded.

deem, *vb.* **1.** To treat (something) as if (1) it were really something else, or (2) it has qualities that it doesn't have <although the document was not in fact signed until April 21, it explicitly states that it must be deemed to have been signed on April 14>. **2.** To consider, think, or judge <she deemed it necessary>.

deemed transferor. *Tax.* A person who holds an interest in a generation-skipping trust on behalf of a beneficiary, and whose death will trigger the imposition of a generation-skipping transfer tax. IRC (26 USCA) §§ 2601–2663. See GENERATION-SKIPPING TRANSFER; *generation-skipping transfer tax* under TAX; *generation-skipping trust* under TRUST; SKIP PERSON; NONSKIP PERSON.

deep issue. See ISSUE (1).

deep pocket. 1. (*pl.*) Substantial wealth and resources. **2.** A person or entity with substantial wealth and resources against which a claim may be made or a judgment may be taken.

deface (di-**fays**), *vb.* **1.** To mar or destroy (a written instrument, signature, or inscription) by obliteration, erasure, or superinscription. **2.** To detract from the value of (a coin) by punching, clipping, cutting, or shaving. **3.** To mar or injure (a building, monument, or other structure). — **defacement,** *n.*

de facto (di **fak**-toh *also* dee *or* day), *adj.* [Law Latin "in point of fact"] **1.** Actual; existing in fact; having effect even though not formally or legally recognized <a de facto contract>. See EX FACTO. **2.** Illegitimate but in effect <a de facto government>. Cf. DE JURE.

de facto judge. See JUDGE.

de facto segregation. See SEGREGATION.

de facto taking. See TAKING (2).

defalcation (dee-fal-**kay**-shən), *n.* **1.** EMBEZZLEMENT. **2.** Loosely, the failure to meet an obligation; a nonfraudulent default. — **defalcate** (di-**fal**-kayt *or* dee-), *vb.* — **defalcator,** *n.*

defamacast (di-**fam**-ə-kast). *Slang.* Defamation by television or radio broadcast. See DEFAMATION.

defamation, *n.* **1.** The act of harming the reputation of another by making a false statement to a third person. • If the alleged defamation involves a matter of public concern, the plaintiff is constitutionally required to prove both the statement's falsity and the defendant's fault. **2.** A false written or oral statement that damages another's reputation. — **defame,** *vb.* See LIBEL; SLANDER. Cf. DISPARAGEMENT.

defamation per quod. Defamation that either (1) is not apparent but is proved by extrinsic evidence showing its injurious meaning or (2) is apparent but is not a statement that is actionable per se.

defamation per se. A statement that is defamatory in and of itself and is not capable of an innocent meaning.

defamatory, *adj.* (Of a statement or communication) tending to harm a person's reputation, usu. by subjecting the person to public contempt, disgrace, or ridicule, or by adversely affecting the person's business. • The statement is likely to lower that person in the estimation of reasonable people and in particular to cause that person to be regarded with feelings of hatred, contempt, ridicule, fear, or dislike.

default, *n.* The omission or failure to perform a legal or contractual duty; esp., the failure to pay a debt when due. — **default,** *vb.* — **defaulter,** *n.*

default judgment. 1. A judgment entered against a defendant who has failed to plead or otherwise defend against the plaintiff's claim, often by failing to appear at trial. **2.** A judgment entered as a penalty against a party who does not comply with an order, esp. an order to comply with a discovery request. See JUDGMENT.

nil-dicit default judgment (nil **dɪ**-sit). [Latin "he says nothing"] A judgment for the plaintiff entered after the defendant fails to file a timely answer, often after appearing in the case by filing a preliminary motion.

no-answer default judgment. A judgment for the plaintiff entered after the defendant fails to timely answer or otherwise appear.

post-answer default judgment. A judgment for the plaintiff entered after the defendant files an answer, but fails to appear at trial or otherwise provide a defense on the merits.

defeasance (di-**feez**-ənts), *n.* **1.** An annulment or abrogation; VOIDANCE. **2.** The fact or an instance of bringing an estate or status to an end, esp. by conditional limitation. **3.** A condition upon the fulfillment of which a deed or other instrument is defeated or made void; a contractual provision containing such a condition. — **defease,** *vb.*

defeasible, *adj.* (Of an act, right, agreement, or position) capable of being annulled or avoided. See *fee simple defeasible* under FEE SIMPLE.

defeasible deed. See DEED.

defeasible estate. See ESTATE.

defeasible remainder. See REMAINDER.

defeasible title. See TITLE (2).

defect, *n.* An imperfection or shortcoming, esp. in a part that is essential to the operation or safety of a product. — **defective,** *adj.*

design defect. A product imperfection occurring when the seller or distributor could have reduced or avoided a foreseeable risk of harm by adopting a reasonable alternative design, and when, as a result of not using the alternative, the product is not reasonably safe.

fatal defect. A serious defect capable of nullifying a contract.

hidden defect. A product imperfection that is not discoverable by reasonable inspection and for which a seller or lessor is generally liable if the flaw causes harm. • Upon discovering a hidden defect, a purchaser may revoke a prior acceptance. UCC § 2–608(1)(b).

manufacturing defect. An imperfection in a product that departs from its intended design even though all possible care was exercised in its assembly and marketing.

marketing defect. **1.** The failure to adequately warn of a potential risk of harm that is known or should have been known about a product or its forseeable use. **2.** The failure to adequately instruct the user about how to use a product safely.

patent defect. A defect that is apparent to a normally observant person, esp. a buyer on a reasonable inspection.

product defect. An imperfection in a product that has a manufacturing defect or design defect, or is faulty because of inadequate instructions or warnings.

defective, *adj.* **1.** (Of a position, right, act, or process) lacking in legal sufficiency. **2.** (Of a product) containing an imperfection or shortcoming in a part essential to the product's safe operation.

defective condition. An unreasonably dangerous state that might well cause physical harm beyond that contemplated by the ordinary user or consumer who purchases the product. See PRODUCTS LIABILITY.

defective performance. See PERFORMANCE.

defective pleading. See PLEADING (1).

defective product. See PRODUCT.

defective record. See RECORD.

defective title. See TITLE (2).

defective verdict. See VERDICT.

defect of form. An imperfection in the style, manner, arrangement, or nonessential parts of a legal document, as distinguished from a substantive defect. Cf. DEFECT OF SUBSTANCE.

defect of parties. A failure to include all necessary parties in a lawsuit.

defect of substance. An imperfection in the substantive part of a legal document, as by omitting an essential term. Cf. DEFECT OF FORM.

defend, *vb.* **1.** To deny, contest, or oppose (an allegation or claim). **2.** To represent (someone) as an attorney.

defendant (di-**fen**-dənt). A person sued in a civil proceeding or accused in a criminal proceeding. — Abbr. D. Cf. PLAINTIFF.

defendant in error. *Archaic.* In a case on appeal, the prevailing party in the court below. See APPELLEE; RESPONDENT (1).

defendant score. A number taken from an established scale, indicating the relative seriousness of the defendant's criminal history. Cf. CRIME SCORE.

defendant's gain. The amount of money or the value of property that a criminal defendant has obtained by committing a crime.

defenestration (dee-fen-ə-**stray**-shən). The act of throwing someone or something out a window. — **defenestrate,** *vb.*

defense (di-**fen[t]s**). **1.** A defendant's stated reason why the plaintiff or prosecutor has no valid case; esp., a defendant's answer, denial, or plea.

affirmative defense. A defendant's assertion raising new facts and arguments that, if true, will defeat the plaintiff's or prosecution's claim, even if all allegations in the complaint are true. • Examples of affirmative defenses include duress and contributory negligence (in a civil case) and insanity and self-defense (in a criminal case).

capacity defense. A defense based on the defendant's inability to be held accountable for an illegal act or the plaintiff's inability to prosecute a lawsuit (as when the plaintiff was a corporation, but has lost its corporate charter). See CAPACITY.

derivative defense. A defense that rebuts the criminal elements that a prosecutor must establish to justify the submission of a criminal case to a jury.

dilatory defense (**dil**-ə-tor-ee). A defense that temporarily obstructs or delays a lawsuit but does not address the merits.

equitable defense. A defense formerly available only in a court of equity but now maintainable in a court of law. • Examples include mistake, fraud, illegality, and failure of consideration.

frivolous defense. A defense that has no basis in fact or law.

imperfect defense. A defense that fails to meet all legal requirements and usu. results only in a reduction in grade or sentence rather than an acquittal, as when a defendant is charged with manslaughter rather than murder because the defendant, while defending another, used unreasonable force to repel the attack. See *imperfect self-defense* under SELF-DEFENSE. Cf. *perfect defense.*

inconsistent defense. A defense so contrary to another defense that the acceptance of one requires abandonment of the other. • A person accused of murder, for example, cannot claim both self-defense and the alibi of having been in a different city when the murder took place.

issuable defense. Common-law pleading. A plea on the merits setting forth a legal defense. Cf. *issuable plea* under PLEA.

legal defense. A complete and adequate defense in a court of law.

lesser-evils defense. The defense that, while the defendant may have caused the harm or evil that would ordinarily constitute a criminal offense, in the present case the defendant has not caused a net harm or evil because of justifying circumstances and therefore should be exculpated.

meritorious defense (mer-ə-**tor**-ee-əs). **1.** A defense that addresses the substance or essentials of a case rather than dilatory or technical objections. **2.** A defense that appears likely to succeed or has already succeeded.

partial defense. A defense going either to part of the action or toward mitigation of damages.

peremptory defense (pər-**emp**-tər-ee). A defense that questions the plaintiff's legal right to sue or contends that the right to sue has been extinguished.

perfect defense. A defense that meets all legal requirements and results in the defendant's acquittal. See *perfect self-defense* under SELF-DEFENSE. Cf. *imperfect defense*.

pretermitted defense (pree-tər-**mit**-id). A defense available to a party that must be pleaded at the right time or be waived.

sham defense. A fictitious, untrue defense, made in bad faith.

true defense. A defense admitting that a defendant committed the charged offense, but seeking to avoid punishment based on a legal excuse (such as insanity) or justification (such as self-defense).

2. A defendant's method and strategy in opposing the plaintiff or the prosecution; a doctrine giving rise to such a method or strategy. **3.** One or more defendants in a trial. **4.** *Commercial law*. A basis for avoiding liability on a negotiable instrument.

personal defense. An ordinary defense in a contract action — such as failure of consideration or nonperformance of a condition — that the maker or drawer of a negotiable instrument is precluded from raising against a person who has the rights of a holder in due course. • A personal defense can be asserted only against a transferee who is not a holder in due course.

real defense. A type of defense that is good against any possible claimant, so that the maker or drawer of a negotiable instrument can raise it even against a holder in due course. • The ten real defenses are (1) fraud in the factum, (2) forgery of a necessary signature, (3) adjudicated insanity that, under state law, renders the contract void from its inception, (4) material alteration of the instrument, (5) infancy, which renders the contract voidable under state law, (6) illegality that renders the underlying contract void, (7) duress, (8) discharge in bankruptcy, or any discharge known to the holder in due course, (9) a suretyship defense (for example, if the holder knew that one indorser was signing as a surety or accommodation party), and (10) a statute of limitations (generally three years after dishonor or acceptance on a draft and six years after demand or other due date on a note).

defense of others. A justification defense available if one harms or threatens another when defending a third person. See JUSTIFICATION (2).

defense of property. A justification defense available if one harms or threatens another when defending one's property. See JUSTIFICATION (2).

defensive collateral estoppel. See COLLATERAL ESTOPPEL.

defer, *vb.* **1.** To postpone; to delay. — **deferment,** *n.* **2.** To show deference to (another); to yield to the opinion of.

deferral state. Under the Age Discrimination in Employment Act (ADEA), a state that has its own antidiscrimination legislation and enforcement mechanism, so that the time to file a federal lawsuit under the ADEA is postponed until state remedies have been exhausted.

deferred charge. An expense not currently recognized on an income statement but carried forward on the balance sheet as an asset to be written off in the future.

deferred claim. A claim postponed to a future accounting period.

deferred compensation. See COMPENSATION.

deferred credit. A credit (such as a premium on an issued bond) that is required to be spread over later accounting periods.

deferred expense. See EXPENSE.

deferred income. See INCOME.

deferred judgment. See JUDGMENT.

deferred payment. A principal-and-interest payment that is postponed; an installment payment.

deferred sentence. See SENTENCE.

deficiency, *n.* **1.** A lack, shortage, or insufficiency. **2.** A shortfall in paying taxes; the amount by which the tax properly due exceeds the sum of the amount of tax shown on a taxpayer's return. **3.** The amount still owed when the property secured by a mortgage is sold at a foreclosure sale for less than the outstanding debt; esp., the shortfall between the proceeds from a foreclosure sale and an amount consisting of the principal debt plus interest plus the foreclosure costs. See *deficiency judgment* under JUDGMENT.

deficiency judgment. See JUDGMENT.

deficiency suit. An action to recover the difference between a mortgage debt and the amount realized on foreclosure. See *deficiency judgment* under JUDGMENT.

deficit. 1. A deficiency or disadvantage; a deficiency in the amount or quality of something. **2.** An excess of expenditures or liabilities over revenues or assets.

deficit spending. The practice of making expenditures in excess of income, usu. from borrowed funds rather than actual revenues or surplus.

defile (di-fıl), *vb.* **1.** To make dirty; to physically soil. **2.** To figuratively tarnish; to dishonor. **3.** To make ceremonially unclean; to desecrate. **4.** To morally corrupt (someone). — **defilement** (di-fıl-mənt), *n.*

defined term. In legal drafting, a word or phrase given a specific meaning for purposes of the document in which it appears; a definiendum.

definition. The meaning of a term as explicitly stated in a drafted document such as a contract, a corporate bylaw, an ordinance, or a statute; a definiens.

lexical definition. A dictionary-style definition of a word, purporting to give the full meaning of a term.

stipulative definition. A definition that, for purposes of the document in which it appears, arbitrarily clarifies a term with uncertain boundaries or that includes or excludes specified items from the ambit of the term.

deforce, *vb.* **1.** To keep (lands) from the true owner by means of force. **2.** To oust (another) from possession by means of force. **3.** To detain (a creditor's money) unjustly and forcibly. — **deforcement,** *n.* — **deforciant,** *n.*

defraud, *vb.* To cause injury or loss to (a person) by deceit. — **defraudation,** *n.* See FRAUD.

degradation (deg-rə-**day**-shən). **1.** A reduction in rank, degree, or dignity. **2.** A moral or intellectual decadence or degeneration; a lessening of a person's or thing's character or quality. **3.** A wearing down of something, as by erosion.

degree. 1. Generally, a classification or specification. **2.** An incremental measure of guilt or negligence; a level based on the seriousness of an offense. **3.** A stage in a process; a step in a series of steps toward an end. **4.** A stage in intensity. **5.** In the line of descent, a measure of removal determining the proximity of a blood or marital relationship. See AFFINITY (2); CONSANGUINITY.

equal degree. A relationship between two or more relatives who are the same number of steps away from a common ancestor.

prohibited degree. A degree of relationship so close (as between brother and sister) that marriage between the persons is forbidden by law.

6. A title conferred on a graduate of a school, college, or university after the completion of required studies, or on a person in honor of special achievements.

degree of care. A standard of care to be exercised in a given situation. See CARE.

highest degree of care. **1.** The degree of care exercised commensurate with the danger involved. **2.** The degree of care applied by people in the business or profession of dealing with the given situation.

degree of crime. 1. A division or classification of a single crime into several grades of guilt, according to the circumstances surrounding the crime's commission, such as aggravating factors present or the type of injury suffered. **2.** A division of crimes generally, such as felonies or misdemeanors. See GRADING.

degree of negligence. One of the varying levels of negligence typically designated as slight negligence, ordinary negligence, and gross negligence. See NEGLIGENCE.

dehors (də-**hor** *or* də-**horz**). [Law French] *Jargon.* Outside; beyond the scope of <the court cannot consider the document because it is dehors the record>.

de jure (di **juur**-ee *also* dee *or* day), *adj.* [Law Latin "as a matter of law"] Existing by right or according to law <de jure segregation during the pre-*Brown* era>. Cf. DE FACTO.

de jure segregation. See SEGREGATION.

delay, *n.* **1.** The act of postponing or slowing. **2.** An instance at which something is postponed or slowed. **3.** The period during which something is postponed or slowed.

delayed sentence. See SENTENCE.

del credere (del **kred**-ə-ray *or* **kray**-də-ray), *adj.* [Italian] Of belief or trust.

***del credere agent*.** See AGENT.

delegable duty. See DUTY.

delegate (del-ə-git), *n.* One who represents or acts for another person or a group.

delegatee (del-ə-gə-**tee**). An agent or representative to whom a matter is delegated.

delegation, *n.* **1.** The act of entrusting another with authority or empowering another to act as an agent or representative. **2.** A group of representatives. — **delegate (del**-ə-gayt) (for sense 1), *vb.* — **delegable (del**-ə-gə-bəl) (for sense 1), *adj.*

delegation doctrine. *Constitutional law.* The principle (based on the separation-of-powers concept) limiting Congress's ability to transfer its legislative power to another governmental branch, esp. the executive branch. • Delegation is permitted only if Congress prescribes an intelligible principle to guide an executive agency in making policy.

delegation of duties. *Contracts.* A transaction by which a party to a contract arranges to have a third party perform the party's contractual duties.

delegation of powers. A transfer of authority by one branch of government to another branch or to an administrative agency. See DELEGATION DOCTRINE.

deleterious (del-ə-**teer**-ee-əs), *adj.* **1.** Poisonous. **2.** Unwholesome; psychologically or physically harmful.

deliberate (di-**lib**-[ə]-rit), *adj.* **1.** Intentional; premeditated; fully considered. **2.** Unimpulsive; slow in deciding.

deliberate elicitation. The purposeful yet covert drawing forth of an incriminating response (usu. not during a formal interrogation) from a suspect whose Sixth Amendment right to counsel has attached but who has not waived that right. • Deliberate elicitation may occur, for example, when a police officer engages an arrested suspect in conversation on the way to the police station. Deliberate elicitation violates the Sixth Amendment. *Massiah v. United States*, 377 U.S. 201, 84 S.Ct. 1199 (1964). See MASSIAH RULE.

deliberate indifference. *Criminal law.* The careful preservation of one's ignorance despite awareness of circumstances that would put a reasonable person on notice of a fact essential to a crime. See JEWELL INSTRUCTION.

deliberate speed, with all. As quickly as the maintenance of law and order and the welfare of the people will allow, esp. with respect to the desegregation of public schools. *Brown v. Board of Educ.*, 347 U.S. 483, 74 S.Ct. 686 (1954).

deliberation, *n.* The act of carefully considering issues and options before making a decision or taking some action; esp., the process by which a jury reaches a verdict, as by analyzing, discussing, and weighing the evidence. — **deliberate** (di-**lib**-ə-rayt), *vb.*

deliberative privilege. See PRIVILEGE (1).

delict (di-**likt**), *n.* [Latin *delictum* "an offense"] A violation of the law; a tort; a wrong. — **delictual** (di-**lik**-chə-wəl), *adj.*

deliction (di-**lik**-shən). The loss of land by gradual, natural changes over time, such as erosion resulting from a change in the course of a river or stream. Cf. ACCRETION; ALLUVION; AVULSION (2); EROSION.

delimit (di-**lim**-it), *vb.* To mark (a boundary); to fix (a limit). — **delimitation,** *n.*

delinquency, *n.* **1.** A failure or omission; a violation of a law or duty. See JUVENILE DELINQUENCY. **2.** A debt that is overdue in payment.

delinquent, *adj.* **1.** (Of a person) failing to perform an obligation. **2.** (Of a person) guilty of serious antisocial or criminal conduct. **3.** (Of an obligation) past due or unperformed.

delinquent, *n.* **1.** A person who fails to perform an obligation. **2.** A person guilty of serious antisocial or criminal conduct. See JUVENILE DELINQUENT.

delinquent child. See CHILD.

delirium. **1.** A disordered mental state, often occurring during illness. **2.** Exaggerated excitement. **3.** A delusion; a hallucination.

deliverance. **1.** A jury's verdict. **2.** A judicial opinion or judgment. **3.** A court's order directing that a person in custody be released.

delivery, *n.* **1.** The formal act of transferring or conveying something, such as a deed; the giving or yielding possession or control of something to another. **2.** The thing so transferred or conveyed. — **deliver,** *vb.* Cf. LIVERY; NONDELIVERY.

absolute delivery. A delivery that is complete upon the actual transfer of the instrument from the grantor's possession.

actual delivery. The act of giving real and immediate possession to the buyer or the buyer's agent.

conditional delivery. A delivery that passes possession only upon the happening of a specified event.

constructive delivery. An act that amounts to a transfer of title by operation of law when actual transfer is impractical or impossible. • For example, the delivery of a deposit-box key by someone who is ill and immobile amounts to a constructive delivery of the box's contents even though the box may be miles away.

second delivery. A legal delivery by the depositary of a deed placed in escrow.

symbolic delivery. The constructive delivery of the subject matter of a sale by the actual delivery of an article that represents the item, that renders access to it possible, or that provides evidence of the purchaser's title to it, such as the key to a warehouse or a bill of lading for goods on shipboard.

unconditional delivery. A delivery that immediately passes both possession and title and that takes effect immediately.

delivery in escrow. The physical transfer of something to an escrow agent to be held until some condition is met, at which time the agent will release it. • This type of delivery creates immediate conditional rights in the promisee. See ESCROW.

delivery of deed. The placing of a deed in the grantee's hands or within the grantee's control. • By this act, the grantor shows an intention that the deed operates immediately as a conveyance.

demand, *n.* **1.** The assertion of a legal right.

cross-demand. A party's demand opposing an adverse party's demand. See COUNTERCLAIM; CROSS-CLAIM.

2. A request for payment of a debt or an amount due.

demand, *vb.* **1.** To claim as one's due; to require; to seek relief. **2.** To summon; to call into court.

demand clause. A provision in a note allowing the holder to compel full payment if the maker fails to meet an installment.

demand instrument. An instrument payable on demand, at sight, or on presentation, as opposed to an instrument that is payable at a set future date.

demand letter. A letter by which one party explains its legal position in a dispute and requests that the recipient take some action (such as paying money owed), or else risk being sued. • Under some statutes (especially consumer-protection laws), a demand letter is a prerequisite for filing a lawsuit.

demeanor. Outward appearance or behavior, such as facial expressions, tone of voice, gestures, and the hesitation or readiness to answer questions. • In evaluating a witness's credibility, the jury may consider the witness's demeanor.

demeanor evidence. See EVIDENCE.

demesne (di-**mayn** *or* di-**meen**), *n.* [French] **1.** At common law, land held in one's own right, and not through a superior. **2.** Domain; realm. — **demesnial** (di-**may**-nee-əl *or* di-**meen**-ee-əl), *adj.*

de minimis (də **min**-ə-mis), *adj.* [Latin "of the least"] **1.** Trifling; minimal. **2.** (Of a fact or thing) so insignificant that a court may overlook it in deciding an issue or case. **3.** DE MINIMIS NON CURAT LEX.

de minimis non curat lex (də **min**-ə-mis non **kyoor**-at **leks**). [Latin] The law does not concern itself with trifles.

demise (di-**mɪz**), *n.* **1.** The conveyance of an estate by will or lease <the demise of the land for one year>. **2.** The instrument by which such a conveyance is accomplished <the demise set forth the terms of the transfer>. **3.** The passing of property by descent or bequest <a testator's demise of $100,000 to charity>. **4.** The death of a person or (figuratively) of a thing <the corporation's untimely demise>. — **demise,** *vb.*

demonstrative bequest. See BEQUEST.

demonstrative evidence. See EVIDENCE.

demonstrative legacy. See LEGACY.

demur (di-**mər**), *vb.* To file a demurrer; to object to the legal sufficiency of a claim alleged in a pleading without admitting or denying the truth of the facts stated. See DEMURRER.

demurrable (di-**mər**-ə-bəl), *adj.* (Of a claim, pleading, etc.) subject to a demurrer. See DEMURRER.

demurrant (di-**mər**-ənt). A party who interposes a demurrer. See DEMURRER.

demurrer (di-**mər**-ər). [Law French *demorer* "to wait or stay"] A pleading stating that although the facts alleged in a complaint may be true, they are insufficient for the plaintiff to state a claim for relief and for the defendant to frame an answer. • In most jurisdictions, such a pleading is now termed a *motion to dismiss*, but the demurrer is still used in a few states, including California, Nebraska, and Pennsylvania. Cf. DENIAL (1).

speaking demurrer. A demurrer that cannot be sustained because it introduces new facts not contained in the original complaint.

special demurrer. An objection that questions the form of the pleading and states specifically the nature of the objection, such as that the pleading violates the rules of pleading or practice.

demurrer to evidence. A party's objection or exception that the evidence is legally insufficient to make a case. • Its effect, upon joinder in the demurrer by the opposite party, is that the jury is discharged and the demurrer is entered on record and decided by the court. A demurrer to evidence admits the truth of all the evidence and the legal deductions from that evidence.

demurrer to interrogatories. The objection or reason given by a witness for failing to answer an interrogatory.

denial, *n.* **1.** A refusal or rejection; esp., a court's refusal to grant a request presented in a motion or petition. **2.** A defendant's response controverting the facts that a plaintiff has alleged in a complaint; a repudiation. Cf. DEMURRER.

conjunctive denial. A response that controverts all the material facts alleged in a complaint.

disjunctive denial. A response that controverts the truthfulness of two or more allegations of a complaint in the alternative.

general denial. A response that puts in issue all the material assertions of a complaint or petition.

qualified general denial. A general denial of all the allegations except the allegations that the pleader expressly admits.

specific denial. A separate response applicable to one or more particular allegations in a complaint.

3. A refusal or rejection. 4. A deprivation or withholding. — **deny,** *vb.*

denizen (**den**-ə-zən). A person given certain rights in a foreign nation or living habitually in a foreign nation. — **denize** (**den**-ɪz *or* di-**nɪz**), *vb.* — **denization** (den-ə-**zay**-shən), *n.*

denomination. 1. An act of naming. **2.** A collective designation, esp. of a religious sect.

denounce, *vb.* **1.** To condemn openly, esp. publicly. **2.** To declare (an act or thing) to be a crime and prescribe a punishment for it. **3.** To accuse or inform against. — **denouncement,** *n.* — **denunciatory, denunciative,** *adj.*

de novo (di **noh**-voh *or* dee), *adj.* Anew.

de novo judicial review. See JUDICIAL REVIEW.

denumeration. An act of making a present payment.

department, *n.* **1.** A division of a greater whole; a subdivision. **2.** A country's division of territory, usu. for governmental and administrative purposes, as in the division of a state into counties. **3.** A principal branch or division of government ; specif., a division of the executive branch of the U.S. government, headed by a secretary who is a member of the President's cabinet. — **departmental,** *adj.*

Department of Defense. An executive department of the federal government, responsible for coordinating and overseeing military affairs and the agencies responsible for national security.

Department of Energy. A federal department that oversees a comprehensive national energy plan, including the research, development, and demonstration of energy technology; energy conservation; the nuclear-weapons program; and pricing and allocation. — Abbr. DOE.

Department of Justice. The federal executive division that is responsible for federal law enforcement and related programs and services. • The U.S. Attorney General heads this department, which has separate divisions for prosecuting cases under federal antitrust laws, tax laws, environmental laws, and criminal laws. The department also has a civil division that represents the U.S. government in cases involving tort claims and commercial litigation. — Abbr. DOJ.

Department of State. See STATE DEPARTMENT.

Department of the Interior. The federal executive division responsible for managing federally owned land and natural resources, and for overseeing American Indian reservations. • The department administers a number of agencies, including the Bureau of Land Management, the Bureau of Indian Affairs, the U.S. Fish and Wildlife Service, and the U.S. Geological Survey.

Department of Transportation. The federal executive division responsible for programs and policies concerning transportation. • Through a series of specialized agencies, this department oversees aviation, highways, railroads, mass transit, the U.S. merchant marine, and other programs. — Abbr. DOT.

departure, *n.* **1.** A deviation or divergence from a standard rule, regulation, measurement, or course of conduct.

downward departure. In the federal sentencing guidelines, a court's imposition of a sentence more lenient than the standard guidelines propose, as when the court concludes that a criminal's history is less serious than it appears.

forbidden departure. An impermissible deviation from the federal sentencing guidelines based on race, sex, national origin, creed, religion, or socioeconomic status.

lateral departure. In the federal sentencing guidelines, a sentence allowing a defendant to avoid incarceration through community or home confinement.

upward departure. In the federal sentencing guidelines, a court's imposition of a sentence harsher than the standard guidelines propose, as when the court concludes that a criminal's history did not take into account additional offenses committed while the prisoner was out on bail.

2. A variance between a pleading and a later pleading or proof. **3.** A party's desertion of the ground (either legal or factual) taken in the immediately preceding pleading and resort to another ground. — **depart,** *vb.*

dependency. 1. A land or territory geographically distinct from the country governing it, but belonging to the country and governed by its laws. Cf. COMMONWEALTH (2); TERRITORY (2). **2.** A relationship between two persons or things whereby one is sustained by the other or relies on the other for support or necessities.

dependency exemption. See EXEMPTION.

dependent, *n.* **1.** One who relies on another for support; one not able to exist or sustain oneself without the power or aid of someone else.

lawful dependent. **1.** One who receives an allowance or benefits from the public, such as social security. **2.** One who qualifies to receive a benefit from private funds as determined within the terms of the laws governing the distribution.

legal dependent. A person who is dependent according to the law; a person who derives principal support from another and usu. may invoke laws to enforce that support.

2. *Tax.* A relative, such as a child or parent, for whom a taxpayer may claim a personal exemption if the taxpayer provides more than half the person's support during the taxable year. — **dependent,** *adj.*

dependent intervening cause. See *intervening cause* under CAUSE (1).

dependent promise. See PROMISE.

dependent relative revocation. A common-law doctrine that operates to undo an otherwise sufficient revocation of a will when there is evidence that the testator's revocation was conditional rather than absolute. • Typically, the doctrine applies when a testator has physically revoked the will and believes that a new will is valid, although this belief is mistaken. The doctrine undoes only the revocation; it does not always accomplish the testator's intent or validate an otherwise invalid will.

depletion, *n.* An emptying, exhausting, or wasting of an asset, esp. of a finite natural resource such as oil. — **deplete,** *vb.* — **depletive,** *adj.*

deponent (di-**poh**-nənt), *n.* **1.** One who testifies by deposition. **2.** A witness who gives written testimony for later use in court; AFFIANT. — **depone,** *vb.*

deportation (dee-por-**tay**-shən), *n.* The act or an instance of removing a person to another country; esp., the expulsion or transfer of an alien from a country. — **deport,** *vb.* Cf. TRANSPORTATION (2).

depose (di-**pohz**), *vb.* **1.** To examine (a witness) in a deposition <the defendant's attorney will depose the plaintiff on Tuesday>. **2.** To testify; to bear witness <the affiant deposes and states that he is at least 18 years old>. **3.** To remove from office or from a position of power; dethrone <the rebels sought to depose the dictator>.

deposit, *n.* **1.** The act of giving money or other property to another who promises to preserve it or to use it and return it in kind; esp., the act of placing money in a bank for safety and convenience. **2.** The money or property so given. **3.** Money placed with a person as earnest money or security for the performance of a contract. • The money will be forfeited if the depositor fails to perform. **4.** *Copyright.* The placing of two copies of a published work with the Library of Congress within three months of publication. • This requirement is independent of copyright registration.

depositary. A person or institution that one leaves money or valuables with for safekeeping. • When a depositary is a company, it is often termed a *safe-deposit company.* Cf. DEPOSITORY.

depositary bank. See BANK.

deposit in court. The placing of money or other property that represents a person's potential liability in the court's temporary custody, pending the outcome of a lawsuit.

deposit insurance. See INSURANCE.

deposition (dep-ə-**zish**-ən). **1.** A witness's out-of-court testimony that is reduced to writing (usu. by a court reporter) for later use in court or for discovery purposes. **2.** The session at which such testimony is recorded.

apex deposition. The deposition of a person whose position is at the highest level of a company's hierarchy. • Courts often preclude an apex deposition unless (1) the person to be deposed has particular knowledge regarding the claim, and (2) the requesting party cannot obtain the requested — and discoverable — information by any less intrusive means.

deposition de bene esse (dee **bee**-nee **es**-ee *also* day **ben**-ay **es**-ay). A deposition taken from a witness who will likely be unable to attend a scheduled trial or hearing. • If the witness is not available to attend trial, the testimony is read at trial as if the witness were present in court. See *testimony de bene esse* under TESTIMONY.

deposition on written questions. A deposition given in response to a prepared set of written questions, as opposed to a typical oral deposition.

oral deposition. A deposition given in response to oral questioning by a lawyer.

30(b)(6) deposition. Under the Federal Rules of Civil Procedure, the deposition of an organization, through the organization's designated representative. • Under Rule 30(b)(6), a party may take the deposition of an organization, such as a corporation. The notice of deposition (or subpoena) may name the organization and may specify the matters to be covered in the deposition. The organization must then designate a person to testify about those matters on its behalf. Most states authorize a similar procedure under state-court procedural rules.

depository (di-**poz**-ə-tor-ee), *n.* A place where one leaves money or valuables for safekeeping. Cf. DEPOSITARY.

depository-transfer check. See CHECK.

Depository Trust Corporation. The principal central clearing agency for securities transactions on the public markets. — Abbr. DTC.

depraved, *adj.* **1.** (Of a person) corrupt; perverted. **2.** (Of a crime) heinous; morally horrendous.

depraved-heart murder. See MURDER.

depreciation (di-pree-shee-**ay**-shən), *n.* A decline in an asset's value because of use, wear, or obsolescence. — **depreciate,** *vb.* — **depreciable,** *adj.* Cf. APPRECIATION (1); AMORTIZATION (2); OBSOLESCENCE.

accumulated depreciation. The total depreciation currently recorded on an asset.

annual depreciation. The annual loss to property due to regular wear and tear.

functional depreciation. Depreciation that results from the replacement of equipment that is not yet worn out, but that is obsolete in light of a new invention or improved machinery allowing more efficient and satisfactory production.

depreciation method. A set formula used in estimating an asset's use, wear, or obsolescence over the asset's useful life. • This method is useful in calculating the allowable annual tax deduction for depreciation. See USEFUL LIFE.

accelerated depreciation method. A depreciation method that yields larger deductions in the earlier years of an asset's life and smaller deductions in the later years.

declining-balance depreciation method. A method of computing the annual depreciation allowance by multiplying the asset's undepreciated cost each year by a uniform rate that may not exceed double the straight-line rate or 150 percent.

double-declining depreciation method. A depreciation method that spreads over time the initial cost of a capital asset by deducting in each period twice the percentage recognized by the straight-line method and applying that double percentage to the undepreciated balance existing at the start of each period.

straight-line depreciation method. A depreciation method that writes off the cost or other basis of the asset by deducting the expected salvage value from the initial cost of the capital asset, and dividing the difference by the asset's estimated useful life.

depredation. The act of plundering; pillaging.

depression. A period of economic stress that persists over an extended period, accompanied by poor business conditions and high unemployment. Cf. RECESSION.

deprivation. 1. An act of taking away. **2.** A withholding of something. **3.** The state of being without something; wanting. **4.** A removal or degradation from office.

***Deprizio* doctrine.** *Bankruptcy.* The rule that a debtor's payment to an outside creditor more than 90 days before a bankruptcy filing is voidable as a preferential transfer if it benefits an inside creditor. *Levit v. Ingersoll Rand Fin. Corp.* (*In re V.N. Deprizio Constr. Co.*), 874 F.2d 1186 (7th Cir. 1989).

deputy, *n.* A person appointed or delegated to act as a substitute for another, esp. for an official. — **deputize, depute,** *vb.*

deregulation, *n.* The reduction or elimination of governmental control of business, esp. to permit free markets and competition. — **deregulate,** *vb.*

derelict (**der**-ə-likt), *adj.* **1.** Forsaken; abandoned; cast away <derelict property>. **2.** Lacking a sense of duty; in breach of a legal or moral obligation <the managers were derelict in their duties>.

derelict, *n.* **1.** Personal property abandoned or thrown away by the owner with an intent to no longer claim it, such as a ship deserted at sea. **2.** Land uncovered by water receding from its former bed. **3.** A street person or vagrant; a hobo.

dereliction (der-ə-**lik**-shən), *n.* **1.** Abandonment, esp. through neglect or moral wrong. **2.** An increase of land caused by the receding of a sea, river, or stream from its usual watermark. See RELICTION.

derivative action. 1. A suit by a beneficiary of a fiduciary to enforce a right belonging to the fiduciary; esp., a suit asserted by a shareholder on the corporation's behalf against a third party (usu. a corporate officer) because of the corporation's failure to take some action against the third party. Cf. DIRECT ACTION (3). **2.** A lawsuit arising from an injury to another person, such as a husband's action for loss of consortium arising from an injury to his wife caused by a third person.

derivative defense. See DEFENSE (1).

derivative estate. See ESTATE.

derivative evidence. See EVIDENCE.

derivative-jurisdiction doctrine. The principle that a case is not properly removable unless it is within the subject-matter jurisdiction of the state court from which it is removed.

derivative liability. See LIABILITY.

derivative possession. See POSSESSION.

derivative title. See TITLE (2).

derivative work. *Copyright.* A copyrightable creation that is based on a preexisting product, such as a translation, abridgment, musical arrangement, fictionalization, motion-picture version, or any other recast or adapted form, and that only the holder of the copyright on the original form can produce or give permission to another to produce. Cf. COMPILATION (1).

derogation (der-ə-**gay**-shən), *n.* **1.** The partial repeal or abrogation of a law by a later act that limits its scope or impairs its utility and force. **2.** Disparagement; depreciation in value or estimation. **3.** Detraction, prejudice, or destruction (of a grant or right). — **derogate** (**der**-ə-gayt), *vb.*

derogatory clause. *Wills & estates.* A clause that a testator inserts secretly in a will, containing a provision that any later will not having that precise clause is invalid. • A derogatory clause seeks to protect against a later will extorted by undue influence, duress, or violence.

descendant (di-**sen**-dənt), *n.* One who follows in lineage, in direct (not collateral) descent from a person. • Examples are children and grandchildren. — **descendant,** *adj.* Cf. ASCENDANT.

descendibility of future interests. The legal possibility that a future interest (such as a remainder or an executory interest) can legally pass by inheritance.

descendible, *adj.* (Of property) capable of passing by descent or being inherited.

descent, *n.* **1.** The acquisition of real property by law, as by inheritance; the passing of intestate real property to heirs. See SUCCESSION (2). Cf. ASCENT; DISTRIBUTION (1); PURCHASE (2). **2.** The fact or process of originating from a common ancestor. — **descend,** *vb.*

description. **1.** A delineation or explanation of something by an account setting forth the subject's characteristics or qualities. **2.** A representation by words or drawing of something seen or heard or otherwise experienced. **3.** An enumeration or specific identification of something. **4.** LEGAL DESCRIPTION.

desecrate, *vb.* To divest (a thing) of its sacred character; to defile or profane (a sacred thing).

desegregation, *n.* **1.** The abrogation of policies that separate people of different races into different institutions and facilities (such as public schools). **2.** The state of having had such policies abrogated. — **desegregate,** *vb.* Cf. INTEGRATION (3).

desertion, *n.* The willful and unjustified abandonment of a person's duties or obligations, esp. to military service or to a spouse or family. • In family law, the five elements of spousal desertion are (1) a cessation of cohabitation, (2) the lapse of a statutory period, (3) an intention to abandon, (4) a lack of consent from the abandoned spouse, and (5) a lack of spousal misconduct that might justify the abandonment. — **desert,** *vb.*

constructive desertion. One spouse's misconduct that forces the other spouse to leave the marital abode.

criminal desertion. One spouse's willful failure without just cause to provide for the care, protection, or support of the other spouse who is in ill health or needy circumstances.

design, *n.* **1.** A plan or scheme. **2.** Purpose or intention combined with a plan. **3.** The pattern or configuration of elements in something, such as a work of art. **4.** *Patents.* The drawing or the depiction of an original plan for a novel pattern, model, shape, or configuration that is chiefly decorative or ornamental. — **design,** *vb.*

designated public forum. See PUBLIC FORUM.

design defect. See DESIGN.

designedly, *adv.* Willfully; intentionally.

despoil (di-**spoil**), *vb.* To deprive (a person) of possessions illegally by violence or by clandestine means; to rob. — **despoliation** (di-spoh-lee-**ay**-shən), *n.* — **despoilment,** *n.*

despot (**des**-pət), *n.* **1.** A ruler with absolute power and authority. **2.** A tyrant. — **despotic** (di-**spot**-ik), *adj.*

despotism (**des**-pə-tiz-əm). **1.** A government by a ruler with absolute, unchecked power. **2.** Total power or controlling influence.

destination contract. See CONTRACT.

destitute (**des**-ti-t[y]oot), *adj.* Not possessing the necessaries of life; lacking possessions and resources; indigent.

destructibility, *n.* The capability of being destroyed by some action, turn of events, or operation of law. — **destructible,** *adj.*

destructibility of contingent remainders. *Property.* The common-law doctrine requiring a future interest to vest by the time it is to become possessory or else suffer total destruction (the interest then reverting to the grantor). • This doctrine has been abolished in all but a few American jurisdictions; the abolishing statutes are commonly termed *anti-destructibility statutes.*

destructible trust. See TRUST.

desuetude (**des**-wə-t[y]ood). **1.** Lack of use; obsolescence through disuse. **2.** The doctrine holding that if a statute or treaty is left unenforced long enough, the courts will no longer regard it as having any legal effect even though it has not been repealed.

detainer. 1. The action of detaining, withholding, or keeping something in one's custody.

unlawful detainer. The unjustifiable retention of the possession of real property by one whose original entry was lawful, as when a tenant holds over after lease termination despite the landlord's demand for possession.

2. The confinement of a person in custody. **3.** A writ authorizing a prison official to continue holding a prisoner in custody.

detention, *n.* The act or fact of holding a person in custody; confinement or compulsory delay. — **detain,** *vb.*

investigative detention. The holding of a suspect without formal arrest during the investigation of the suspect's participation in a crime. • Detention of this kind is constitutional only if probable cause exists.

pretrial detention. The holding of a defendant before trial on criminal charges either because the established bail could not be posted or because release was denied.

preventive detention. Confinement imposed usu. on a criminal defendant who has threatened to escape, poses a risk of harm, or has otherwise violated the law while awaiting trial, or on a mentally ill person who may cause harm.

detention hearing. See HEARING.

determinable, *adj.* **1.** Liable to end upon the happening of a contingency; terminable <fee simple determinable>. **2.** Able to be determined or ascertained <the delivery date is determinable because she kept the written invoice>.

determinable estate. See ESTATE.

determinate sentence. See SENTENCE.

determination, *n.* **1.** A final decision by a court or administrative agency. **2.** The ending or expiration of an estate or interest in property, or of a right, power, or authority. — **determine,** *vb.*

determination letter. A letter issued by the Internal Revenue Service in response to a taxpayer's request, giving an opinion about the tax significance of a specified transaction, such as whether a nonprofit corporation is entitled to tax-exempt status.

deterrence, *n.* The act or process of discouraging certain behavior, particularly by fear; esp., as a goal of criminal law, the prevention of criminal behavior by fear of punishment. — **deter,** *vb.* — **deterrent,** *adj.* Cf. REHABILITATION (1); RETRIBUTION (1).

general deterrence. A goal of criminal law generally, or of a specific conviction and sentence, to discourage people from committing crimes.

special deterrence. A goal of a specific conviction and sentence to dissuade the offender from committing crimes in the future.

deterrent, *n.* Something that impedes; something that prevents.

deterrent danger. See DANGER.

deterrent punishment. See PUNISHMENT.

detinue (**det**-i-n[y]oo). A common-law action to recover personal property wrongfully taken by another. Cf. REPLEVIN; TROVER.

detour, *n. Torts.* An employee's minor deviation from the employer's business for personal reasons. • Because a detour falls within the scope of employment, the employer is still vicariously liable for the employee's actions. Cf. FROLIC.

detraction, *n.* The removal of personal property from one state to another after transfer of title by a will or inheritance.

detriment. 1. Any loss or harm suffered by a person or property. **2.**

Contracts. The relinquishment of some legal right that a promisee would have otherwise been entitled to exercise.

detrimental reliance. See RELIANCE.

devastation. 1. An executor's squandering or mismanagement of the deceased's estate. **2.** An act of destruction.

development. 1. A human-created change to improved or unimproved real estate, including buildings or other structures, mining, dredging, filing, grading, paving, excavating, and drilling. **2.** An activity, action, or alteration that changes undeveloped property into developed property.

developmental disability. See DISABILITY (1).

deviance, *n.* The quality or state of departing from established norms, esp. in social customs. — **deviate** (**dee**-vee-ayt), *vb.* — **deviant,** *adj.* & *n.* — **deviate** (**dee**-vee-ət), *n.*

deviation doctrine. 1. A principle allowing variation from a term of a will or trust to avoid defeating the document's purpose. **2.** A principle allowing an agent's activity to vary slightly from the scope of the principal's permission.

device. 1. An invention or contrivance; any result of design. **2.** A scheme to trick or deceive; a stratagem or artifice, as in the law relating to fraud.

devisable, *adj.* **1.** Capable of being bequeathed by a will. **2.** Capable of being invented. **3.** Feigned.

devise (di-**vɪz**), *n.* **1.** The act of giving property (usu. real property) by will. **2.** The provision in a will containing such a gift. **3.** Property (usu. real property) disposed of in a will. **4.** A will disposing of real property. Cf. TESTAMENT (1). — **devise,** *vb.* Cf. BEQUEST; LEGACY.

conditional devise. A devise that depends on the occurrence of some uncertain event.

executory devise. An interest in land, created by will, that takes effect in the future and depends on a future contingency; a limitation, by will, of a future estate or interest in land when the limitation cannot, consistently with legal rules, take effect as a remainder. • An executory devise, which is a type of conditional limitation, differs from a remainder in three ways: (1) it needs no particular estate to support it, (2) with it a fee simple or lesser estate can be limited after a fee simple, and (3) with it a remainder can be limited in a chattel interest after a particular estate for life is created in that interest. See *conditional limitation* under LIMITATION.

general devise. **1.** A devise, usu. of a specific amount of money or quantity of property, that is payable from the estate's general assets. **2.** A devise that passes the testator's lands without specifically enumerating or describing them.

lapsed devise. A devise that fails because the devisor outlives the named recipient.

residuary devise. A devise of the remainder of the testator's real property left after other specific devises are taken.

specific devise. A devise that passes a particular piece of property.

devisee (dev-ə-**zee** *or* di-vɪ-**zee**). A recipient of property (usu. real property) by will.

deviser. One who invents or contrives <the deviser of these patents>.

devisor. One who disposes of property (usu. real property) in a will.

devolution (dev-ə-**loo**-shən), *n.* The act or an instance of transferring one's rights, duties, or powers to another; the passing of such rights, duties, or powers by transfer or succession. — **devolutionary,** *adj.*

devolve (di-**vahlv**), *vb.* **1.** To transfer (rights, duties, or powers) to another. **2.** To pass (rights, duties, or powers) by transmission or succession. See DEVOLUTION.

diagnosis (dɪ-əg-**noh**-sis). **1.** The determination of a medical condition (such as a disease) by physical examination or by study of its symptoms. **2.** The result of such an examination or study. Cf. PROGNOSIS.

diagnostic commitment. See COMMITMENT.

dialectic (dɪ-ə-**lek**-tik), *n.* **1.** A school of logic that teaches critical examination of the truth of an opinion, esp. by discussion or debate. **2.** An argument made by critically examining logical consequences. **3.** A logical debate. **4.** A disputant; a debater. Pl. **dialectics.**

dictum (**dik**-təm), *n.* **1.** A statement of opinion or belief considered authoritative because of the dignity of the person making it. **2.** A familiar rule; a maxim. **3.** OBITER DICTUM. Pl. **dicta.**

differential pricing. The setting of the price of a product or service differently for different customers. See PRICE DISCRIMINATION.

digest, *n.* An index of legal propositions showing which cases support each proposition; a collection of summaries of reported cases, arranged by subject and subdivided by jurisdiction and court. — Abbr. D.; Dig.

digital signature. See SIGNATURE.

dignatory tort. See TORT.

dilatory (**dil**-ə-tor-ee), *adj.* Tending to cause delay.

dilatory defense. See DEFENSE (1).

dilatory exception. See EXCEPTION (1).

dilatory motion. See MOTION.

dilatory plea. See PLEA (3).

diligence. 1. A continual effort to accomplish something. **2.** Care; caution; the attention and care required from a person in a given situation. — **diligent,** *adj.*

due diligence. **1.** The diligence reasonably expected from, and ordinarily exercised by, a person who seeks to satisfy a legal requirement or to discharge an obligation. **2.** *Corporations & securities.* A prospective buyer's or broker's investigation and analysis of a target company, a piece of property, or a newly issued security.

ordinary diligence. The diligence that a person of average prudence would exercise in handling his or her own property like that at issue.

reasonable diligence. A fair degree of diligence expected from someone of ordinary prudence under circumstances like those at issue.

slight diligence. The diligence that a person of less than common prudence takes with his or her own concerns.

dilution. 1. The act or an instance of diminishing a thing's strength or lessening its value. **2.** *Corporations.* The reduction in the monetary value or voting power of stock by increasing the total number of outstanding shares. **3.** *Constitutional law.* The limitation of the effectiveness of a particular group's vote by legislative reapportionment or political gerrymandering. **4.** *Trademarks.* The impairment of a trademark's strength or effectiveness caused by the use of the mark on an unrelated product, usu. blurring the trademark's distinctive character or tarnishing it with an unsavory association.

diminished capacity. See CAPACITY.

diminution (dim-ə-**n[y]oo**-shən), *n.* **1.** The act or process of decreasing, lessening, or taking away. **2.** An incompleteness or lack of certification in a court record sent from a lower court to a higher one for review. — **diminish** (for sense 1), *vb.*

diminution-in-value method. A way of calculating damages for breach of contract based on a reduction in market value that is caused by the breach.

DIP. *abbr.* DEBTOR-IN-POSSESSION.

diplomatic immunity. See IMMUNITY (1).

direct, *vb.* **1.** To aim (something or someone). **2.** To cause (something or someone) to move on a particular course. **3.** To guide (something or someone); to govern. **4.** To instruct (someone) with authority. **5.** To address (something or someone).

direct action. 1. A lawsuit by an insured against his or her own insurance company rather than against the tortfeasor and the tortfeasor's insurer. **2.** A lawsuit by a person claiming against an insured but suing the insurer directly instead of pursuing compensation indirectly through the insured. **3.** A lawsuit to enforce a shareholder's rights against a corporation. Cf. DERIVATIVE ACTION (1).

direct appeal. See APPEAL.

direct attack. An attack on a judgment made in the same proceeding as the one in which the judgment was entered. • Examples of direct attacks are appeals and motions for new trial. Cf. COLLATERAL ATTACK.

direct confession. See CONFESSION.

direct contempt. See CONTEMPT.

direct cost. See COST.

directed verdict. See VERDICT.

direct evidence. See EVIDENCE.

direct examination. The first questioning of a witness in a trial or other proceeding, conducted by the party who called the witness to testify. Cf. CROSS-EXAMINATION; REDIRECT EXAMINATION.

direct injury. See INJURY.

direct interest. See INTEREST (2).

direct line. See LINE.

direct loss. See LOSS.

direct notice. See NOTICE.

director (di-**rek**-tər). **1.** One who manages, guides, or orders; a chief administrator. **2.** A person appointed or elected to sit on a board that manages the affairs of a corporation or company by electing and exercising control over its officers. See BOARD OF DIRECTORS. Cf. OFFICER.

direct order of alienation. *Real estate.* The principle that a grantee who assumes the debt on a mortgaged property is required to pay the mortgage debt if the original mortgagor defaults.

directory call. *Property.* In a land description, a general description of the areas in which landmarks or other calls are found. See CALL (4); LOCATIVE CALLS.

directory requirement. A statutory or contractual instruction to act in a way that is advisable, but not absolutely essential — in contrast to a mandatory requirement. • A directory requirement is frequently introduced by the word *should* or, less frequently, *shall.*

directory statute. See STATUTE.

direct payment. See PAYMENT.

direct question. See QUESTION.

direct skip. *Tax.* A generation-skipping transfer of assets, either directly or through a trust. • A direct skip may be subject to a generation-skipping transfer tax — either a gift tax or an estate tax. IRC (26 USCA) §§ 2601–2602. See GENERATION-SKIPPING TRANSFER; *generation-skipping transfer tax* under TAX; SKIP PERSON.

direct tax. See TAX.

disability. **1.** The inability to perform some function; an objectively measurable condition of impairment, physical or mental <his disability entitled him to workers'-compensation benefits>.

developmental disability. An impairment of general intellectual functioning or adaptive behavior.

permanent disability. A disability that will indefinitely prevent a worker from performing some or all of the duties that he or she could do before an accident.

physical disability. An incapacity caused by a physical defect or infirmity, or by bodily imperfection or mental weakness.

temporary disability. A disability that exists until an injured worker is as far restored as the nature of the injury will permit.

total disability. A worker's inability to perform employment-related duties because of a physical or mental impairment.

2. Incapacity in the eyes of the law <most of a minor's disabilities are removed when he or she turns 18>.

civil disability. The condition of a person who has had a legal right or privilege revoked as a result of a criminal conviction, as when a person's driver's license is revoked after a DWI conviction.

disabled person. See PERSON.

disablement, *n.* **1.** The act of incapacitating or immobilizing. **2.** The imposition of a legal disability.

disabling restraints. Limits on the alienation of property. • These restraints are sometimes void as being against public policy.

disabling statute. See STATUTE.

disaffirm (dis-ə-**fərm**), *vb.* **1.** To repudiate; to revoke consent; to disclaim the intent to be bound by an earlier transaction. **2.** To declare (a voidable contract) to be void. — **disaffirmance** (dis-ə-**fərm**-ənts), *n.* — **disaffirmation,** *n*

disallow, *vb.* **1.** To refuse to allow (something). **2.** To reject (something).

disappeared person. A person who has been absent from home for at least seven continuous years and who, during that period, has not communicated with the person most likely to know his or her whereabouts. See SEVEN-YEARS'-ABSENCE RULE; MISSING PERSON.

disaster area. A region officially declared to have suffered a catastrophic emergency, such as a flood or hurricane, and therefore eligible for government aid.

disbarment, *n.* The action of expelling a lawyer from the bar or from the practice of law, usu. because of some disciplinary violation. — **disbar,** *vb.*

discharge (**dis**-chahrj), *n.* **1.** The payment of a debt or satisfaction of some other obligation. **2.** The release of a debtor from monetary obligations upon adjudication of bankruptcy; RELEASE (1). **3.** The dismissal of a case. **4.** The canceling or vacating of a court order. **5.** The release of a prisoner from confinement. **6.** The relieving of a witness, juror, or jury from further responsibilities in a case. **7.** The firing of an employee.

constructive discharge. A termination of employment brought about by making the employee's working conditions so intolerable that the employee feels compelled to leave.

retaliatory discharge. A discharge that is made in retaliation for the employee's conduct (such as reporting unlawful activity by the employer to the government) and that clearly violates public policy. • Most states have statutes allowing an employee who is dismissed by retaliatory discharge to recover damages.

unconditional discharge. **1.** A release from an obligation without any conditions attached. **2.** A release from confinement without any parole requirements to fulfill.

wrongful discharge. A discharge for reasons that are illegal or that violate public policy.

8. The dismissal of a member of the armed services from military service. — **discharge** (dis-**chahrj**), *vb.*

discharge in bankruptcy. **1.** The release of a debtor from personal liability for prebankruptcy debts. **2.** A bankruptcy court's decree releasing a debtor from that liability.

discharging bond. See BOND (2).

disciplinary proceeding. An action brought to reprimand, suspend, or expel a licensed professional or other person from a profession or other group because of unprofessional, unethical, improper, or illegal conduct.

disciplinary rule. (*often cap.*) A mandatory regulation stating the minimum level of professional conduct that a professional must sustain to avoid being subject to disciplinary action. • For lawyers, the disciplinary rules are found chiefly in the Model Code of Professional Responsibility. — Abbr. DR. Cf. ETHICAL CONSIDERATION.

disclaimer, *n.* **1.** A renunciation of one's legal right or claim. **2.** A repudiation of another's legal right or claim. **3.** A writing that contains such a renunciation or repudiation. — **disclaim,** *vb.*

disclaimer of warranty. An oral or written statement intended to limit a seller's liability for defects in the goods sold. • In some circumstances, printed words must be specific and conspicuous to be effective.

qualified disclaimer. A person's refusal to accept an interest in property so that he or she can avoid having to pay estate or gift taxes. • To be effective under federal tax law, the refusal must be in writing and must be executed no later than nine months from the time when the interest was created. IRC (26 USCA) § 2518.

disclosed principal. See PRINCIPAL (1).

disclosure, *n.* The act or process of making known something that was previously unknown; a revelation of facts. — **disclose,** *vb.* — **disclosural,** *adj.* See DISCOVERY; INITIAL DISCLOSURE.

discontinuance (dis-kən-**tin**-yoo-ənts), *n.* **1.** The termination of a lawsuit by the plaintiff; a voluntary dismissal or nonsuit. See DISMISSAL; NONSUIT. **2.** The termination of an estate tail by a tenant in tail who conveys a larger estate in the land than is legally allowed.

discontinuous easement. See EASEMENT.

discount, *n.* **1.** A reduction from the full amount or value of something, esp. a price. **2.** An advance deduction of interest when a person lends money on a note, bill of exchange, or other commercial paper, resulting in its present value. See PRESENT VALUE. — **discount,** *vb.*

cash discount. **1.** A seller's price reduction in exchange for an immediate cash payment. **2.** A reduction from the stated price if the bill is paid on or before a specified date.

trade discount. **1.** A discount from list price offered to all customers of a given type — for example, a discount offered by a lumber dealer to building contractors. **2.** The difference between a seller's list price and the price at which the dealer actually sells goods to the trade.

volume discount. A price decrease based on a large-quantity purchase.

discount bond. See BOND (3).

discount rate. See INTEREST RATE.

discoverable, *adj.* Subject to pretrial discovery.

discovery, *n.* **1.** The act or process of finding or learning something that was previously unknown. **2.** Compulsory disclosure, at a party's request, of information that relates to the litigation. • The primary discovery devices are interrogatories, depositions, requests for admissions, and requests for production. Although discovery typically comes from parties, courts also allow limited discovery from nonparties. **3.** The facts or documents disclosed. — **discover,** *vb.* — **discoverable,** *adj.*

postjudgment discovery. Discovery conducted after judgment has been rendered, usu. to determine the nature of the judgment debtor's assets or to obtain testimony for use in future proceedings.

pretrial discovery. Discovery conducted before trial to reveal facts and develop evidence.

discovery abuse. 1. The misuse of the discovery process, esp. by making overbroad requests for information that is unnecessary or beyond the scope of permissible disclosure. **2.** The failure to respond adequately to proper discovery requests.

discovery immunity. A (usu. statutory) prohibition that excludes certain documents or information from discovery.

discovery rule. *Civil procedure.* The rule that a limitations period does not begin to run until the plaintiff discovers (or reasonably should have discovered) the injury giving rise to the claim. • The discovery rule usually applies to injuries that are inherently difficult to detect, such as those resulting from medical malpractice. See STATUTE OF LIMITATIONS. Cf. OCCURRENCE RULE.

discredit, *vb.* To destroy or impair the credibility of (a witness, a piece of evidence, or a theory); to lessen the degree of trust to be accorded to (a witness or document). — **discredit,** *n.*

discretion (di-**skresh**-ən). **1.** A public official's power or right to act in certain circumstances according to personal judgment and conscience.

judicial discretion. The exercise of judgment by a judge or court based on what is fair under the circumstances and guided by the rules and principles of law; a court's power to act or not act when a litigant is not entitled to demand the act as a matter of right.

prosecutorial discretion. A prosecutor's power to choose from the options available in a criminal case, such as filing charges, prosecuting, plea-bargaining, and recommending a sentence to the court.

2. *Criminal & tort law.* The capacity to distinguish between right and wrong, sufficient to make a person responsible for his or her own actions. **3.** Wise conduct and management; cautious discernment; prudence.

discretion, abuse of. See ABUSE OF DISCRETION.

discretionary (di-**skresh**-ə-ner-ee), *adj.* (Of an act or duty) involving an exercise of judgment and choice, not an implementation of a hard-and-fast rule. • Such an act by a court may be overturned only after a showing of abuse of discretion.

discretionary act. A deed involving an exercise of personal judgment and conscience. See DISCRETION; ABUSE OF DISCRETION.

discretionary immunity. See IMMUNITY (1).

discretionary review. See REVIEW.

discretionary trust. See TRUST.

discrimination, *n.* **1.** The effect of a law or established practice that confers privileges on a certain class or that denies privileges to a certain class because of race, age, sex, nationality, religion, or handicap. **2.** Differential treatment; esp., a failure to treat all persons equally when no reasonable distinction can be found between those favored and those not favored. Cf. FAVORITISM.

invidious discrimination (in-**vid**-ee-əs). Discrimination that is offensive or objectionable, esp. because it involves prejudice or stereotyping.

reverse discrimination. Preferential treatment of minorities, usu. through affirmative-action programs, in a way that adversely affects members of a majority group. See AFFIRMATIVE ACTION.

3. The effect of state laws that favor local interests over out-of-state interests. • Such a discriminatory state law may still be upheld if it is narrowly tailored to achieve an important state interest. — **discriminate,** *vb.* — **discriminatory,** *adj.* Cf. FAVORITISM.

disenfranchise (dis-ən-**fran**-chɪz), *vb.* To deprive (a person) of the right to exercise a franchise or privilege, esp. to vote. — **disenfranchisement** (dis-ən-**fran**-chiz-mənt *or* -**fran**-chɪz-mənt), *n.*

disentailment (dis-ən-**tayl**-mənt), *n.* The act or process by which a tenant in tail bars the entail on an estate and converts it into a fee simple, thereby nullifying the rights of any later claimant to the fee tail. — **disentail,** *vb.*

disentitle (dis-ən-**tɪt**-əl), *vb.* To deprive (someone) of a title or claim.

disgorgement, *n.* The act of giving up something (such as profits illegally obtained) on demand or by legal compulsion. — **disgorge,** *vb.*

dishonor, *vb.* **1.** To refuse to accept or pay (a negotiable instrument) when presented. See NOTICE OF DISHONOR; WRONGFUL DISHONOR. **2.** To deface or defile (something, such as a flag). — **dishonor,** *n.*

disincentive, *n.* A deterrent (to a particular type of conduct), often created, intentionally or unintentionally, through legislation.

disinheritance, *n.* **1.** The act by which an owner of an estate deprives a would-be heir of the expectancy to inherit the estate. **2.** The state of being disinherited. — **disinherit,** *vb.*

disinter (dis-in-**tər**), *vb.* **1.** To exhume (a corpse). **2.** To remove (something) from obscurity. — **disinterment** (dis-in-**tər**-mənt), *n.*

disinterested, *adj.* Free from bias, prejudice, or partiality; not having a pecuniary interest.

disinterested witness. See WITNESS.

disinvestment, *n.* **1.** The consumption of capital. **2.** The withdrawal of investments, esp. on political grounds. — **disinvest,** *vb.*

disjoinder (dis-**joyn**-dər). The undoing of the joinder of parties or claims. See JOINDER. Cf. MISJOINDER; NONJOINDER.

disjunctive allegation. See ALLEGATION.

disjunctive denial. See DENIAL.

dismissal, *n.* **1.** Termination of an action or claim without further hearing, esp. before the trial of the issues involved.

dismissal for want of equity. A court's dismissal of a lawsuit on substantive, rather than procedural, grounds, usu. because the plaintiff's allegations are found to be untrue or because the plaintiff's pleading does not state an adequate claim.

dismissal for want of prosecution. A court's dismissal of a lawsuit because the plaintiff has failed to pursue the case diligently toward completion. — Abbr. DWOP.

dismissal without prejudice. A dismissal that does not bar the plaintiff from refiling the lawsuit within the applicable limitations period.

dismissal with prejudice. A dismissal, usu. after an adjudication on the merits, barring the plaintiff from prosecuting any later lawsuit on the same claim.

involuntary dismissal. A court's dismissal of a lawsuit because the plaintiff failed to prosecute or failed to comply with a procedural rule or court order. Fed. R. Civ. P. 41(b).

voluntary dismissal. A plaintiff's dismissal of a lawsuit at the plaintiff's own request or by stipulation of all the parties. Fed. R. Civ. P. 41(a).

2. A release or discharge from employment. See DISCHARGE (7). — **dismiss,** *vb.*

dismissal for cause. A dismissal of a contract employee for a reason that the law or public policy has recognized as sufficient to warrant the employee's removal.

disorder. 1. A lack of proper arrangement. **2.** An irregularity. **3.** A public disturbance; a riot. **4.** A disturbance in mental or physical health.

disorderly conduct. See CONDUCT.

disorderly house. 1. A dwelling where people carry on activities that are a nuisance to the neighborhood. **2.** A dwelling where people conduct criminal or immoral activities. • Examples are brothels and drug houses.

disorderly person. 1. A person guilty of disorderly conduct. **2.** A person who breaches the peace, order, decency, or safety of the public, as defined by statute.

disparagement (di-**spar**-ij-mənt), *n.* A false and injurious statement that discredits or detracts from the reputation of another's property, product, or business. • To recover in tort for disparagement, the plaintiff must prove that the statement caused a third party to take some action resulting in specific pecuniary loss to the plaintiff. Cf. DEFAMATION. — **disparage** (di-**spar**-ij), *vb.*

disparate impact (**dis**-pə-rit). The adverse effect of a facially neutral practice (esp. an employment practice) that nonetheless discriminates against persons because of their race, sex, national origin, age, or disability and that is not justified by business necessity. • Discriminatory intent is irrelevant in a disparate-impact claim.

disparate treatment. The practice, esp. in employment, of intentionally dealing with persons differently because of their race, sex, national origin, age, or disability. • To succeed on a disparate-treatment claim, the plaintiff must prove that the defendant acted with discriminatory intent or motive.

disparity (di-**spar**-ə-tee). Inequality; a difference in quantity or quality between two or more things.

display right. *Copyright.* A copyright holder's exclusive right to show or exhibit a copy of the protected work publicly, whether directly or by technological means. • For example, this right makes it illegal to transmit a copyrighted work over the Internet without permission.

disposable income. See INCOME.

Disposing Clause. The clause of the U.S. Constitution giving Congress the power to dispose of property belonging to the federal government. U.S. Const. art. IV, § 3, cl. 2.

disposition (dis-pə-**zish**-ən), *n.* **1.** The act of transferring something to another's care or possession, esp. by deed or will; the relinquishing of property. **2.** A final settlement or determination. **3.** Temperament or character; personal makeup. — **dispose,** *vb.* — **dispositive,** *adj.*

disposition hearing. See HEARING.

disposition without a trial. The final determination of a criminal case without a trial on the merits, as when a defendant pleads guilty or admits sufficient facts to support a guilty finding without a trial.

dispositive (dis-**poz**-ə-tiv), *adj.* Being a deciding factor; (of a fact or factor) bringing about a final determination.

dispositive fact. See FACT.

dispossession (dis-pə-**zesh**-ən), *n.* Deprivation of, or eviction from, possession of property; ouster. — **dispossess** (dis-pə-**zes**), *vb.* See DISSEISIN.

dispossess proceeding. A summary procedure initiated by a landlord to oust a defaulting tenant and regain possession of the premises. See FORCIBLE ENTRY AND DETAINER.

dispute, *n.* A conflict or controversy, esp. one that has given rise to a particular lawsuit. — **dispute,** *vb.*

disqualification, *n.* **1.** Something that makes one ineligible; esp., a bias or conflict of interest that prevents a judge or juror from impartially hearing a case, or that prevents a lawyer from representing a party. **2.** The act of making ineligible; the fact or condition of being ineligible. — **disqualify,** *vb.* Cf. RECUSAL.

vicarious disqualification. Disqualification of all the lawyers in a firm or in an office because one of the lawyers is ethically disqualified from representing the client at issue.

disruptive conduct. See CONDUCT.

disseisin (dis-**see**-zin), *n.* The act of wrongfully depriving someone of the freehold possession of property; DISPOSSESSION. — **disseise** (dis-**seez**), *vb.*

dissent (di-**sent**), *n.* **1.** A disagreement with a majority opinion, esp. among judges. **2.** See *dissenting opinion* under OPINION (1). **3.** A withholding of assent or approval. — **dissent** (di-**sent**), *vb.*

dissenting opinion. See OPINION (1).

dissipation. The use of an asset for an illegal or inequitable purpose, such as a spouse's use of community property for personal benefit when a divorce is imminent.

dissolution (dis-ə-**loo**-shən), *n.* **1.** The act of bringing to an end; termination. **2.** The cancellation or abrogation of a contract, with the effect of annulling the contract's binding force and restoring the parties to their original positions. See RESCISSION. **3.** The termination of a corporation's legal existence by expiration of its charter, by legislative act, by bankruptcy, or by other means; the event immediately preceding the liquidation or winding-up process. Cf. WINDING UP. **4.** The termination of a previously existing partnership upon the occurrence of an event specified in the partnership agreement, such as a partner's withdrawal from the partnership. Cf. WINDING UP. — **dissolve,** *vb.*

distinctiveness, *n.* The quality of a trademarked word, symbol, or device that identifies the goods of a particular merchant and distinguishes them from the goods of others. — **distinctive,** *adj.*

distinguish, *vb.* **1.** To note a significant factual, procedural, or legal difference in (an earlier case), usu. to minimize the case's precedential effect or to show that it is inapplicable. **2.** To make a distinction. — **distinction,** *n.* — **distinguishable,** *adj.*

distraction doctrine. The rule that a plaintiff may not be guilty of contributory negligence if the plaintiff's attention was diverted from a known danger by a sufficient cause. See *contributory negligence* under NEGLIGENCE.

distrain, *vb.* **1.** To force (a person, usu. a tenant), by the seizure and detention of personal property, to perform an obligation (such as paying overdue rent). **2.** To seize (goods) by distress. See DISTRESS.

distress, *n.* **1.** The seizure of another's property to secure the performance of a duty, such as the payment of overdue rent. **2.** The legal remedy authorizing such a seizure; the procedure by which the seizure is carried out. **3.** The property seized.

distressed property. See PROPERTY.

distress warrant. See WARRANT.

distributable net income. The amount of distributions from estates and trusts that the beneficiaries will have to include in income.

distributee (di-strib-yoo-**tee**), *n.* **1.** A beneficiary entitled to payment. **2.** An heir, esp. one who obtains personal property from the estate of an intestate decedent.

distribution, *n.* **1.** At common law, the passing of personal property to an intestate decedent's heirs. Cf. DESCENT (1). **2.** The act or process of apportioning or giving out. — **distribute,** *vb.*

distribution in kind. A transfer of property in its original state, such as a distribution of land instead of the proceeds of its sale.

distribution right. *Copyright.* A copyright holder's exclusive right to sell, lease, or otherwise transfer copies of the protected work to the public.

distributive clause. A will or trust provision governing the distribution of income and gifts.

distributive finding. A jury's decision partly in favor of one party and partly in favor of another.

distributive justice. See JUSTICE (1).

distributive share. **1.** The share that an heir or beneficiary receives from the legal distribution of an estate. **2.** The portion (as determined in the partnership agreement) of a partnership's income, gain, loss, or deduction that is passed through to a partner and reported on the partner's tax return. **3.** The share of assets or liabilities that a partner or partner's estate acquires after the partnership has been dissolved.

distributor. A wholesaler, jobber, or other manufacturer or supplier that sells chiefly to retailers and commercial users.

district. **1.** A territorial area into which a country, state, county, municipality, or other political subdivision is divided for judicial, political, electoral, or administrative purposes. **2.** A territorial area in which similar local businesses or entities are concentrated, such as a theater district or an arts district. — Abbr. D.

congressional district. A geographical unit of a state from which one member of the U.S. House of Representatives is elected.

legislative district. A geographical subdivision of a state for the purpose of electing legislative representatives.

municipal utility district. A publicly owned corporation, or a political subdivision, that provides the public with a service or services, such as water, electricity, gas, transportation, or telecommunications. — Abbr. MUD.

district attorney. A public official appointed or elected to represent the state in criminal cases in a particular judicial district; PROSECUTOR (1). — Abbr. D.A. Cf. UNITED STATES ATTORNEY.

district court. See COURT.

district-court magistrate. See MAGISTRATE.

district judge. See JUDGE.

disturbance, *n.* **1.** An act causing annoyance or disquiet, or interfering with a person's pursuit of a lawful occupation or the peace and order of a neighborhood, community, or meeting. **2.** At common law, a wrong done to an incorporeal hereditament by hindering the owner's enjoyment of it.

diversion, *n.* **1.** A deviation or alteration from the natural course of things; esp., the unauthorized alteration of a watercourse to the prejudice of a lower riparian owner, or the unauthorized use of funds. **2.** A distraction or pastime. — **divert,** *vb.*

diversion program. **1.** *Criminal law.* A program that refers certain criminal defendants before trial to community programs on job training, education, and the like, which if successfully completed may lead to the dismissal of the charges. Cf. *deferred judgment* under JUDGMENT. **2.** *Family law*. A community-based program or set of services designed to prevent the need for court intervention in matters of child neglect, minor juvenile delinquency, truancy, or incorrigibility.

diversity jurisdiction. See JURISDICTION.

diversity of citizenship. A basis for federal-court jurisdiction that exists when (1) a case is between citizens of different states, or between a citizen of a state and an alien, and (2) the matter in controversy exceeds a specific value (now $75,000). 28 USCA § 1332. • For purposes of diversity jurisdiction, a corporation is considered a citizen of both the state of incorporation and the state of its principal place of business. An unincorporated association, such as a partnership, is considered a citizen of each state where at least one of its members is a citizen. See *diversity jurisdiction* under JURISDICTION; AMOUNT IN CONTROVERSY.

***complete diversity*.** In a multiparty case, diversity between both sides to the lawsuit so that all plaintiffs have different citizenship from all defendants. • Complete diversity must exist for a federal court to have diversity jurisdiction over the matter. The rule of complete diversity was first laid down by Chief Justice Marshall in *Strawbridge v. Curtiss*, 7 U.S. (3 Cranch) 267 (1806).

***manufactured diversity*.** Improper or collusively created diversity of citizenship for the sole or primary purpose of creating federal jurisdiction. • Manufactured diversity is prohibited by 28 USCA § 1359.

divestiture (di-ves-tə-chər *or* dɪ-), *n.* **1.** The loss or surrender of an asset or interest. **2.** A court order to a party to dispose of assets or property. **3.** *Antitrust*. A court order to a defendant to rid itself of property, securities, or other assets to prevent a monopoly or restraint of trade. — **divest,** *vb.*

divestment, *n.* **1.** *Property*. The cutting short of an interest in property before its normal termination. **2.** The complete or partial loss of an interest in an asset, such as land or stock. **3.** DISINVESTMENT (2). — **divest,** *vb.*

divide-and-pay-over rule. *Wills & estates*. The principle that if the only provisions in a testamentary disposition are words ordering that payment be made at some time after the testator's death, time will be of the essence and the interest is future and contingent rather than vested and immediate.

divided court. An appellate court whose opinion or decision in a particular case is not unanimous, esp. when the majority is slim, as in a 5-to-4 decision of the U.S. Supreme Court.

divided custody. See CUSTODY (2).

dividend. A portion of a company's earnings or profits distributed pro rata to its shareholders, usu. in the form of cash or additional shares.

dividend income. See INCOME.

dividend-received deduction. A deduction allowed to a corporate shareholder for dividends received from a domestic corporation. IRC (26 USCA) §§ 243–247.

dividend-reinvestment plan. A company-sponsored program that enables common shareholders to reinvest their dividends, plus additional voluntary payments, into shares of the entity's common stock, usu. with no sales charge, and sometimes at a discount from the stock's market price.

divisible divorce. See DIVORCE.

divisible offense. See OFFENSE.

division of powers. The allocation of power between the national government and the states. • Under the Tenth Amendment, powers not delegated to the federal government are reserved to the states or to the people. But today the Tenth Amendment provides only a limited check on Congress's power to regulate the states. Cf. SEPARATION OF POWERS.

divorce. The legal dissolution of a valid marriage by a court. Cf. ANNULMENT.

divisible divorce. A divorce whereby the marriage itself is dissolved but the issues incident to the divorce, such as alimony, child custody, and visitation, are reserved until a later proceeding.

divorce a mensa et thoro (ay **men**-sə et **thor**-oh). [Latin "(divorce) from board and hearth"] *Hist.* A partial or qualified divorce by which the parties were separated and forbidden to live together, but remained technically married. • This type of divorce, abolished in England in 1857, was the forerunner of modern judicial separation.

divorce a vinculo matrimonii (ay **ving**-kyə-loh ma-trə-**moh**-nee-ɪ). [Latin "(divorce) from the chains of marriage"] A total divorce of husband and wife, dissolving the marriage tie and releasing the parties wholly from their matrimonial obligations. • This type of common-law divorce, which bastardizes any children from the marriage, is granted on grounds that existed before the marriage.

ex parte divorce (eks **pahr**-tee). A divorce proceeding in which only one spouse participates or appears in court.

foreign divorce. A divorce obtained outside the state or country in which one spouse resides.

limited divorce. **1.** A divorce that ends the legal relationship of marriage by court order but does not address financial support, property distribution, or care and custody of children. **2.** Loosely, a legal separation. **3.** See *divorce a mensa et thoro*.

mail-order divorce. *Slang.* A divorce obtained by parties who are not physically present or domiciled in the jurisdiction purporting to grant the divorce. • Such a divorce is not recognized in the United States because of the absence of the usual bases for jurisdiction.

migratory divorce. A divorce obtained in a jurisdiction other than the marital domicile; esp., a divorce obtained by a spouse who moves to, or temporarily resides in, another state or country to get the divorce.

no-fault divorce. A divorce in which the parties are not required to prove fault or grounds beyond a showing of the irretrievable breakdown of the marriage or irreconcilable differences.

DJIA. *abbr.* DOW JONES INDUSTRIAL AVERAGE.

DNA identification. A method of comparing a person's deoxyribonucleic acid (DNA) — a patterned chemical structure of genetic information — with the DNA in a biological specimen (such as blood, tissue, or hair) to determine whether the person is the source of the specimen. Cf. HLA TEST.

docket, *n.* **1.** A formal record in which a judge or court clerk briefly notes all the proceedings and filings in a court case.

appearance docket. A list of the parties and lawyers participating in an action, together with a brief abstract of the successive steps in the action.

judgment docket. A book that a court clerk keeps for the entry or recordation of judgments, giving official notice of existing judgment liens to interested parties.

2. A schedule of pending cases.

DWOP docket. A list of cases that the court has set for possible dismissal for want of prosecution.

preferred docket. A list of cases set for trial, arranged in order of priority. • Criminal cases are, for example, generally given precedence over civil cases on the preferred docket because of the constitutional right to a speedy trial.

3. DOCKET CALL. **4.** A written abstract that provides specific information (usu. about something attached); esp., a label.

docket, *vb.* **1.** To make a brief entry in the docket of the proceedings and filings in a court case. **2.** To abstract and enter in a book. **3.** To schedule (a case) for trial or some other event. See DOCKET, *n.*

docket call. A court session in which attorneys (and sometimes parties) appear in court to report the status of their cases. • For example, they may announce readiness for trial or report the suit's settlement.

docket fee. See FEE (1).

docket number. A number that the court clerk assigns to a case on the court's docket.

Doctor of Juridical Science. A graduate law degree, beyond the J.D. and the LL.M. — Abbr. S.J.D.; J.S.D.

doctor–patient privilege. See PRIVILEGE (3).

doctrine. A principle, esp. a legal principle, that is widely adhered to.

doctrine of approximation. A doctrine that authorizes a court to vary the details of a trust's administration to preserve the trust and to carry out the donor's intentions. Cf. CY PRES.

doctrine of *contra non valentem* (**kon**-trə non və-**len**-təm). The rule that a limitations or prescriptive period does not begin to run against a plaintiff who is unable to act, usu. because of the defendant's culpable act, such as concealing material information that would give rise to the plaintiff's claim.

doctrine of equivalents. *Patents.* A judicially created theory for finding patent infringement when the accused process or product falls outside the literal scope of the patent claims.

doctrine of necessaries. *Archaic.* The common-law rule holding a husband or father liable to one who sells goods to his wife or child if the goods are required for sustenance or support. See NECESSARIES.

doctrine of precedent. The rule that precedents not only have persuasive authority, but must be followed when similar circumstances arise. See STARE DECISIS.

doctrine of scrivener's error. A rule permitting a typographical error in a document to be reformed by parol evidence, if the evidence is precise, clear, and convincing. See *clerical error* under ERROR (2).

doctrine of worthier title. See WORTHIER-TITLE DOCTRINE.

document, *n.* **1.** Something tangible on which words, symbols, or marks are recorded. **2.** (*pl.*) The deeds, agreements, title papers, letters, receipts, and other written instruments used to prove a fact.

ancient document. Evidence. A document that is presumed to be authentic because its physical condition strongly suggests authenticity, it has existed for 20 or more years, and it has been maintained in proper custody (as by coming from a place where it is reasonably expected to be found). Fed. R. Evid. 901(b)(8).

foreign document. A document that originated in, or was prepared or executed in, a foreign state or country.

hot document. A document that directly supports a litigant's allegation.

public document. A document of public interest issued or published by a political body or otherwise connected with public business. Cf. *public record* under RECORD.

3. *Evidence.* Under the best-evidence rule, a physical embodiment of information or ideas, such as a letter, contract, receipt, account book, blueprint, or X-ray plate; esp., the original of such an embodiment.

document, *vb.* **1.** To support with records, instruments, or other evidentiary authorities <document the chain of custody>. **2.** To record; to create a written record of <document a file>.

documentary draft. See DRAFT.

documentary evidence. See EVIDENCE.

document of title. A written description, identification, or declaration of goods authorizing the holder (usu. a bailee) to receive, hold, and dispose of the document and the goods it covers. • Documents of title, such as bills of lading, warehouse receipts, and delivery orders, are generally governed by Article 7 of the UCC. See BAILMENT.

DOE. *abbr.* DEPARTMENT OF ENERGY.

DOJ. *abbr.* DEPARTMENT OF JUSTICE.

domain (doh-**mayn**), *n.* **1.** An estate in land. **2.** The complete and absolute ownership of land. See EMINENT DOMAIN; PUBLIC DOMAIN.

***Dombrowski* doctrine.** The rule entitling a person to a federal-court injunction to prevent prosecution under a broad or vague state statute that affects rights guaranteed by the First Amendment. *Dombrowski v. Pfister*, 380 U.S. 479, 85 S.Ct. 1116 (1965).

domestic, *adj.* **1.** Of or relating to one's own country. **2.** Of or relating to one's own jurisdiction. **3.** Of or relating to the family or the household.

domestic authority. A defense allowing a person responsible for another (such as a parent responsible for a child) to use nondeadly force when reasonably necessary to protect the person being cared for.

domestic corporation. See CORPORATION.

domestic court. See COURT.

domestic dispute. A disturbance, usu. at a residence and usu. within a family, involving violence and often resulting in a call to a law-enforcement agency.

domicile (**dom**-ə-sɪl), *n.* **1.** The place at which a person is physically present and that the person regards as home; a person's true, fixed, principal, and permanent home, to which that person intends to return and remain even though currently residing elsewhere. **2.** The residence of a person or corporation for legal purposes. — **domiciliate** (dom-ə-**sil**-ee-ayt), *vb.* Cf. ABODE; RESIDENCE; PLACE OF BUSINESS.

after-acquired domicile. A domicile established after the facts relevant to an issue arose. • An after-acquired domicile cannot be used to establish jurisdiction or choice of law.

commercial domicile. **1.** A domicile acquired by a nonresident corporation conducting enough activities to permit taxation of the corporation's property or activities located outside the bounds of the taxing state. **2.** A domicile acquired by a person or company freely residing or carrying on business in enemy territory or enemy-occupied territory.

corporate domicile. The place considered by law as the center of corporate affairs, where the corporation's functions are discharged; the legal home of a corporation, usu. its state of incorporation or the state in which it maintains its principal place of business. • For purposes of determining whether diversity jurisdiction exists in federal court, a corporation is considered a citizen of both its state of incorporation and the state of its principal place of business. See DIVERSITY OF CITIZENSHIP.

domicile of choice. **1.** A domicile established by physical presence within a state or territory, coupled with the intention to make it home. **2.** The domicile that a person chooses after reaching majority or being emancipated.

domicile of origin. The domicile of a person at birth, derived from the custodial parent or imposed by law.

domicile of succession. The domicile that determines the succession of a person's estate.

domiciliary (dom-ə-**sil**-ee-er-ee), *adj.* Of or relating to domicile.

domiciliary (dom-ə-**sil**-ee-er-ee), *n.* A person who resides in a particular place with the intention of making it a principal place of abode; one who is domiciled in a particular jurisdiction. Cf. RESIDENT; CITIZEN.

domiciliary administration. See ADMINISTRATION.

dominant estate. See ESTATE.

dominant-jurisdiction principle. The rule that the court in which a case is first filed maintains the suit, to the exclusion of all other courts that would also have jurisdiction.

dominate, *vb.* **1.** To master (someone or something); to control (someone or something). **2.** Predominate.

dominion. 1. Control; possession. **2.** Sovereignty.

donate, *vb.* To give (property or money) without receiving consideration for the transfer. — **donation,** *n.* — **donative** (**doh**-nə-tiv), *adj.*

donee (doh-**nee**). One to whom a gift is made.

donee beneficiary. See BENEFICIARY.

donee of power. The recipient of a power of appointment.

donor. 1. One who gives something without receiving consideration for the transfer. **2.** SETTLOR (1).

door-closing statute. A state law closing or denying access to local courts unless a plaintiff meets specified conditions; esp., a statute requiring a foreign corporation to "qualify" before doing business in the state, including registering with the secretary of state, paying a fee or tax, and appointing an agent to receive service of process.

doowop docket. *Slang.* See *DWOP docket* under DOCKET (2).

dormant (**dor**-mənt), *adj.* Inactive; suspended; latent. — **dormancy,** *n.*

dormant claim. A claim that is in abeyance.

Dormant Commerce Clause. See COMMERCE CLAUSE.

dormant judgment. See JUDGMENT.

dormant legislative intent. See LEGISLATIVE INTENT.

dormant title. See TITLE (2).

DOT. *abbr.* DEPARTMENT OF TRANSPORTATION.

double-declining depreciation method. See DEPRECIATION METHOD.

double-dipping, *n.* An act of seeking or accepting essentially the same benefit twice, either from the same source or from two different sources, as in simultaneously accepting retirement and unemployment benefits. — **double-dipper,** *n.*

double hearsay. See HEARSAY.

double indemnity. See INDEMNITY.

double insurance. See INSURANCE.

double jeopardy. The fact of being prosecuted twice for substantially the same offense. Cf. FORMER JEOPARDY.

Double Jeopardy Clause. The Fifth Amendment provision stating, "nor shall any person be subject for the same offence to be twice put in jeopardy of life or limb."

double plea. See PLEA (3).

double proof. See PROOF.

double recovery. See RECOVERY.

double standard. A set of principles permitting greater opportunity or greater lenience for one class of people than for another, usu. based on a difference such as gender or race. See DISCRIMINATION.

double taxation. See TAXATION.

doubtful title. See TITLE (2).

dower (**dow**-ər). At common law, the right of a wife, upon her husband's death, to a life estate in one-third of the land that he owned in fee. Cf. CURTESY.

Dow Jones Industrial Average. A stock-market-performance indicator that consists of the price movements in the stocks of 30 leading industrial companies in the United States. — Abbr. DJIA.

down payment. See PAYMENT.

downsizing. Reducing the number of employees, usu. to decrease labor costs and to increase efficiency.

downward departure. See DEPARTURE.

DR. *abbr.* DISCIPLINARY RULE.

draconian (dray- *or* drə-**koh**-nee-in), *adj.* (Of a law) harsh; severe.

draft, *n.* **1.** An unconditional written order signed by one person (the *drawer*) directing another person (the *drawee* or *payor*) to pay a certain sum of money on demand or at a definite time to a third person (the *payee*) or to bearer. • A check is the most common example of a draft. Cf. NOTE (1).

bank draft. A draft drawn by one financial institution on another.

documentary draft. A payment demand conditioned on the presentation of a document, such as a document of title, invoice, certificate, or notice of default.

share draft. A demand that a member draws against a credit-union share account, payable to a third party. • A share draft is similar to a check that is written to draw funds out of a checking account at a bank.

sight draft. A draft that is payable on the bearer's demand or on proper presentment to the drawer.

time draft. A draft that contains a specified payment date. UCC § 3–108.

2. The compulsory enlistment of persons into military service. **3.** An initial or preliminary version of a writing.

draft, *vb.* **1.** To write or compose. **2.** To recruit or select (someone).

drafter. A person who draws or frames a legal document, such as a will, contract, or legislative bill.

drafting. The practice, technique, or skill involved in preparing legal documents — such as statutes, rules, regulations, contracts, and wills — that set forth the rights, duties, liabilities, and entitlements of persons and legal entities.

dram-shop act. A statute allowing a plaintiff to recover damages from a commercial seller of alcoholic beverages for the plaintiff's injuries caused by a customer's intoxication.

dram-shop liability. Civil liability of a commercial seller of alcoholic beverages for personal injury caused by an intoxicated customer. • Claims based on a similar type of liability have been brought against private citizens for personal injury caused by an intoxicated social guest.

draw, *vb.* **1.** To create and sign (a draft) <draw a check to purchase goods>. **2.** To prepare or frame (a legal document) <draw up a will>. **3.** To take out (money) from a bank, treasury, or depository <she drew $6,000 from her account>. **4.** To select (a jury) <the lawyers began voir dire and had soon drawn a jury>.

drawee (draw-**ee**). The person or entity that a draft is directed to and that is requested to pay the amount stated on it. • The drawee is usually a bank that is directed to pay a sum of money on an instrument.

drawee bank. See *payor bank* under BANK.

drawer. One who directs a person or entity, usu. a bank, to pay a sum of money stated in an instrument — for example, a person who writes a check; the maker of a note or draft. See MAKER.

drawing lots. An act of selection or decision-making based on pure chance, with the result depending on the particular lot drawn.

driving under the influence. The offense of operating a motor vehicle in a physically or mentally impaired condition, esp. after consuming alcohol or drugs. • Generally, this is a lesser offense than driving while intoxicated. But in a few jurisdictions the two are synonymous. — Abbr. DUI. Cf. DRIVING WHILE INTOXICATED.

driving while intoxicated. 1. The offense of operating a motor vehicle in a physically or mentally impaired condition after consuming enough alcohol to raise one's blood alcohol content above the statutory limit (.08% in many states), or after consuming drugs. **2.** DRIVING UNDER THE INFLUENCE. — Abbr. DWI.

dropsy testimony. See TESTIMONY.

drug, *n.* **1.** A substance intended for use in the diagnosis, cure, treatment, or prevention of disease. **2.** A natural or synthetic substance that alters one's perception or consciousness. — **drug,** *vb.* See CONTROLLED SUBSTANCE.

drug-free zone. An area in which the possession or distribution of a controlled substance results in an increased penalty.

drug paraphernalia. Anything used, intended for use, or designed for use with a controlled substance.

dry, *adj.* **1.** Free from moisture; desiccated <dry land>. **2.** Unfruitful; destitute of profitable interest; nominal <a dry trust>. **3.** (Of a jurisdiction) prohibiting the sale or use of alcoholic beverages <a dry county>.

DTC. *abbr.* DEPOSITORY TRUST CORPORATION.

dual-capacity doctrine. The principle that makes an employer — who is normally shielded from tort liability by workers'-compensation laws — liable in tort to an employee if the employer and employee stand in a secondary relationship that confers independent obligations on the employer. Cf. DUAL-PURPOSE DOCTRINE.

dual distributor. A firm that sells goods simultaneously to buyers on two different levels of the distribution chain; esp., a manufacturer that sells directly to both wholesalers and retailers.

dual-persona doctrine (**d**[y]**oo**-əl pər-**soh**-nə). The principle that makes an employer (who is normally shielded from tort liability by workers'-compensation laws) liable in tort to an employee if the liability stems from a second persona unrelated to the employer's status as an employer.

dual-prosecution rule. The principle that the federal government and a state government may both prosecute a defendant for the same offense because both governments are separate and distinct entities. See DUAL-SOVEREIGNTY DOCTRINE.

dual-purpose doctrine. The principle that an employer is liable for an employee's injury that occurs during a business trip even though the trip also serves a personal purpose. Cf. DUAL-CAPACITY DOCTRINE.

dual-sovereignty doctrine. The rule that the federal and state governments may both prosecute someone for a crime, without violating the constitutional protection against double jeopardy, if the person's act violated both jurisdictions' laws. See DUAL-PROSECUTION RULE.

duces tecum (**d**[y]**oo**-səs **tee**-kəm *also* **tay**-kəm). [Latin] Bring with you. See *subpoena duces tecum* under SUBPOENA.

due, *adj.* **1.** Just, proper, regular, and reasonable <due care> <due notice>. **2.** Immediately enforceable <payment is due on delivery>. **3.** Owing or payable; constituting a debt <the tax refund is due>.

due-bill. See IOU.

due course, payment in. See PAYMENT IN DUE COURSE.

due-course holder. See HOLDER IN DUE COURSE.

due course of law. 1. The regular and customary administration of law through the legal system. **2.** DUE PROCESS.

due diligence. See DILIGENCE.

due influence. The sway that one person has over another, esp. as a result of persuasion, argument, or appeal to the person's affections. Cf. UNDUE INFLUENCE.

duel. A single combat; specif., a prearranged combat with deadly weapons fought between two or more persons under prescribed rules, usu. in the presence of at least two witnesses, to resolve a previous quarrel or avenge a deed. • In England and the United States, death resulting from a duel is treated as murder, and seconds may be liable as accessories. Cf. MUTUAL COMBAT.

due notice. See NOTICE.

due-on-encumbrance clause. A mortgage provision giving the lender the option to accelerate the debt if the borrower further mortgages the real estate without the lender's consent.

due-on-sale clause. A mortgage provision that gives the lender the option to accelerate the debt if the borrower transfers or conveys any part of the mortgaged real estate without the lender's consent.

due posting. **1.** The stamping and placing of letters or packages in the U.S. mail. **2.** The proper entry of an item into a ledger. **3.** Proper publication; proper placement of an item (such as an announcement) in a particular place, as on a particular wall.

due process. The conduct of legal proceedings according to established rules and principles for the protection and enforcement of private rights, including notice and the right to a fair hearing before a tribunal with the power to decide the case.

economic substantive due process. The doctrine that certain social policies, such as the freedom of contract or the right to enjoy property without interference by government regulation, exist in the Due Process Clause of the 14th Amendment, particularly in the words "liberty" and "property."

procedural due process. The minimal requirements of notice and a hearing guaranteed by the Due Process Clauses of the 5th and 14th Amendments, esp. if the deprivation of a significant life, liberty, or property interest may occur.

substantive due process. The doctrine that the Due Process Clauses of the 5th and 14th Amendments require legislation to be fair and reasonable in content and to further a legitimate governmental objective.

Due Process Clause. The constitutional provision that prohibits the government from unfairly or arbitrarily depriving a person of life, liberty, or property. • There are two Due Process Clauses in the U.S. Constitution, one in the 5th Amendment applying to the federal government, and one in the 14th Amendment applying to the states (although the 5th Amendment's Due Process Clause also applies to the states under the incorporation doctrine). Cf. EQUAL PROTECTION CLAUSE.

due-process rights. The rights (as to life, liberty, and property) so fundamentally important as to require compliance with due-process standards of fairness and justice. See DUE PROCESS; DUE PROCESS CLAUSE.

DUI. *abbr.* DRIVING UNDER THE INFLUENCE.

dummy, *adj.* Sham; make-believe; pretend.

dummy, *n.* **1.** A party who has no interest in a transaction, but participates to help achieve a legal goal. **2.** A party who purchases property and holds legal title for another.

dummy corporation. See CORPORATION.

dumping. **1.** The act of selling a large quantity of goods at less than fair value. **2.** Selling goods abroad at less than the market price at home. **3.** The disposal of waste matter into the environment.

dun (dən), *vb.* To demand payment from (a delinquent debtor). — **dun,** *n.*

Dunaway **hearing.** A hearing to determine whether evidence has been seized from an accused in violation of his or her Fourth Amendment rights, as by a search conducted without probable cause. *Dunaway v. New*

York, 442 U.S. 200, 99 S.Ct. 2248 (1979). See FOURTH AMENDMENT.

duplicate (d[y]oo-pli-kit), *n.* **1.** A reproduction of an original document having the same particulars and effect as the original. **2.** A new original, made to replace an instrument that is lost or destroyed. — **duplicate (d[y]oo-pli-kayt),** *vb.* — **duplicate (d[y]oo-pli-kit),** *adj.*

duplicate will. See WILL.

duplicitous indictment. See INDICTMENT.

duplicity (d[y]oo-**plis**-i-tee), *n.* **1.** Deceitfulness; double-dealing. **2.** The charging of the same offense in more than one count of an indictment. **3.** The pleading of two or more distinct grounds of complaint or defense for the same issue. • In criminal procedure, this takes the form of joining two or more offenses in the same count of an indictment. — **duplicitous** (d[y]oo-**plis**-i-təs), *adj.* Cf. *alternative pleading* under PLEADING (2); *double plea* under PLEA (3).

durable lease. See LEASE.

durable power of attorney. See POWER OF ATTORNEY.

duration. 1. The length of time something lasts. **2.** A length of time; a continuance in time.

durational-residency requirement. The requirement that one be a state resident for a certain time, such as one year, as a precondition to the exercise of a specified right or privilege. • When applied to voting, this requirement has been held to be an unconstitutional denial of equal protection because it burdens voting rights and impairs the fundamental personal right of travel.

***Duren* test.** *Constitutional law.* A test to determine whether a jury's composition violates the fair-cross-section requirement and a criminal defendant's Sixth Amendment right to an impartial jury. • Under the test, a constitutional violation occurs if (1) a distinctive group is not fairly and reasonably represented in the jury pool in relation to its population in the community, (2) the underrepresentation is the result of a systematic exclusion of the group from the jury-selection process, and (3) the government cannot reasonably justify the discrepancy. *Duren v. Missouri*, 439 U.S. 357, 99 S.Ct. 664 (1979). See FAIR-CROSS-SECTION REQUIREMENT; STATISTICAL-DECISION THEORY; ABSOLUTE DISPARITY; COMPARATIVE DISPARITY.

duress (d[y]uu-**res**). **1.** Strictly, the physical confinement of a person or the detention of a contracting party's property. • In the field of torts, duress is considered a species of fraud in which compulsion takes the place of deceit in causing injury. **2.** Broadly, the threat of confinement or detention, or other threat of harm, used to compel a person to do something against his or her will or judgment. **3.** The use or threatened use of unlawful force — usu. that a reasonable person cannot resist — to compel someone to commit an unlawful act. • Duress is a recognized defense to a crime, contractual breach, or tort. See Model Penal Code § 2.09. See COERCION; EXTORTION.

> ***economic duress.*** An unlawful coercion to perform by threatening financial injury at a time when one cannot exercise free will.

duty. 1. A legal obligation that is owed or due to another and that needs to be satisfied; an obligation for which somebody else has a corresponding right.

absolute duty. A duty to which no corresponding right attaches.

delegable duty. A duty that may be transferred to another to perform. See ASSIGNMENT.

duty to act. A duty to take some action to prevent harm to another, and for the failure of which one may be liable depending on the relationship of the parties and the circumstances.

duty to speak. A duty to say something to correct another's false impression.

legal duty. A duty arising by contract or by operation of law; an obligation the breach of which would be a legal wrong.

nondelegable duty (non-**del**-ə-gə-bəl). **1.** *Contracts.* A duty that cannot be delegated by a contracting party to a third party. • If the duty is transferred, the other contracting party can rightfully refuse to accept performance by the third party. **2.** *Torts.* A duty that may be delegated to an independent contractor by a principal, who retains primary (as opposed to vicarious) responsibility if the duty is not properly performed. • For example, a landlord's duty to maintain common areas, though delegated to a service contractor, remains the landlord's responsibility if someone is injured by improper maintenance.

preexisting duty. A duty that one is already legally bound to perform. See PREEXISTING-DUTY RULE.

2. Any action, performance, task, or observance owed by a person in an official or fiduciary capacity. **3.** *Torts.* A legal relationship arising from a standard of care, the violation of which subjects the actor to liability. **4.** A tax imposed on a commodity or transaction, esp. on imports. • A duty in this sense is imposed on things, not persons.

duty to mitigate (**mit**-i-gayt). *Contracts.* A nonbreaching party's duty to make reasonable efforts to limit losses resulting from the other party's breach. • Not doing so precludes the party from collecting damages that might have been avoided. See MITIGATION-OF-DAMAGES DOCTRINE.

dwell, *vb.* **1.** To remain; to linger. **2.** To reside in a place permanently or for some period.

dwelling-house. 1. The house or other structure in which a person lives; a residence or abode. **2.** *Real estate.* The house and all buildings attached to or connected with the house. **3.** *Criminal law.* A building, a part of a building, a tent, a mobile home, or another enclosed space that is used or intended for use as a human habitation. • The term has referred to connected buildings in the same curtilage but now typically includes only the structures connected either directly with the house or by an enclosed passageway.

DWI. *abbr.* DRIVING WHILE INTOXICATED.

DWOP. See *dismissal for want of prosecution* under DISMISSAL.

DWOP docket. See DOCKET (2).

dying declaration. See DECLARATION.

dynamite charge. See ALLEN CHARGE.

E

EAJA. *abbr.* EQUAL ACCESS TO JUSTICE ACT.

earned income. See INCOME.

earned-income credit. See TAX CREDIT.

earned time. See TIME.

earnest, *n.* **1.** A nominal payment or token act that serves as a pledge or a sign of good faith, esp. as the partial purchase price of property. **2.** EARNEST MONEY.

earnest money. A deposit paid (usu. in escrow) by a prospective buyer (esp. of real estate) to show a good-faith intention to complete the transaction, and ordinarily forfeited if the buyer defaults. Cf. BINDER (2); *down payment* under PAYMENT.

earning capacity. A person's ability or power to earn money, given the person's talent, skills, training, and experience. See LOST EARNING CAPACITY.

earnings. Revenue gained from labor or services, from the investment of capital, or from assets. See INCOME. Cf. PROFIT.

earnout agreement. An agreement for the sale of a business whereby the buyer first pays an agreed amount up front, leaving the final purchase price to be determined by the business's future profits.

earwitness. A witness who testifies about something that he or she heard but did not see. Cf. EYEWITNESS.

easement (**eez**-mənt). An interest in land owned by another person, consisting in the right to use or control the land, or an area above or below it, for a specific limited purpose (such as to cross it for access to a public road). • The land benefiting from an easement is called the *dominant estate*; the land burdened by an easement is called the *servient estate*. Unlike a lease or license, an easement may last forever, but it does not give the holder the right to possess, take from, improve, or sell the land. See SERVITUDE. Cf. PROFIT À PRENDRE.

access easement. An easement allowing one or more persons to travel across another's land to get to a nearby location, such as a road.

affirmative easement. An easement that forces the servient-estate owner to permit certain actions by the easement holder, such as discharging water onto the servient estate. Cf. *negative easement*.

apparent easement. A visually evident easement, such as a paved trail or a sidewalk.

common easement. An easement allowing the servient landowner to share in the benefit of the easement.

continuous easement. An easement that may be enjoyed by the party claiming it without interference. •

Examples are easements for drains, sewer pipes, lateral support of a wall, or light and air. Cf. *discontinuous easement*.

discontinuous easement. An easement that can be enjoyed only if the party claiming it interferes in some way with the servient estate. • An example is a right-of-way. Cf. *continuous easement*.

easement appurtenant. An easement created to benefit another tract of land, the use of the easement being incident to the ownership of that other tract. Cf. *easement in gross*.

easement by estoppel. A court-ordered easement created from a voluntary servitude after a person, mistakenly believing the servitude to be permanent, acted in reasonable reliance on the mistaken belief.

easement by necessity. An easement created by operation of law because the easement is indispensable to the reasonable use of nearby property, such as an easement connecting a parcel of land to a road.

easement in gross. An easement benefiting a particular person and not a particular piece of land. • The beneficiary need not, and usually does not, own any land adjoining the servient estate. Cf. *easement appurtenant*.

equitable easement. **1.** An implied easement created by equity when adjacent lands have been created out of a larger tract. **2.** See *restrictive covenant* (1) under COVENANT (3).

implied easement. An easement created by law after an owner of two parcels of land uses one parcel to benefit the other to such a degree that, upon the sale of the benefited parcel, the purchaser could reasonably expect the use to be included in the sale.

light-and-air easement. A negative easement preventing an adjoining landowner from constructing a building that would prevent light or air from reaching the dominant estate. See *negative easement*. Cf. *solar easement*.

negative easement. An easement that prohibits the servient-estate owner from doing something, such as building an obstruction. Cf. *affirmative easement*.

prescriptive easement. An easement created from an open, adverse, and continuous use over a statutory period.

solar easement. An easement created to protect the dominant estate's exposure to the direct rays of the sun. Cf. *light-and-air easement*.

EAT. *abbr.* Earnings after taxes.

eavesdropping. The act of secretly listening to the private conversation of others without their consent. Cf. BUGGING; WIRETAPPING.

ebb and flow. The coming in and going out of tide.

EBIT. *abbr.* Earnings before interest and taxes.

EC. *abbr.* European Community. See EUROPEAN UNION.

ECJ. *abbr.* European Court of Justice.

ECOA. EQUAL CREDIT OPPORTUNITY ACT.

e-commerce. The practice of buying and selling goods and services through online consumer services on the Internet. • The *e,* a shortened form of *electronic*, has become a popular prefix for other terms associated with electronic transactions. See ELECTRONIC TRANSACTION.

economic discrimination. Any form of discrimination within the field of commerce, such as boycotting a particular product or price-fixing. See BOYCOTT; PRICE DISCRIMINATION; PRICE-FIXING.

economic duress. See DURESS.

economic indicator. A statistical measure (such as housing starts) used to describe the state of the economy or to predict its direction.

economic life. The duration of an asset's profitability, usu. shorter than its physical life.

economic loss. A monetary loss such as lost wages or lost profits. • The term is usually used to refer to the damages recoverable in a lawsuit. For example, in a products-liability suit, economic loss includes the cost of repair or replacement of defective property, as well as commercial loss for the property's inadequate value and consequent loss of profits or use.

economic-loss rule. *Torts.* The principle that a plaintiff cannot sue in tort to recover for purely monetary loss — as opposed to physical injury or property damage — caused by the defendant. • Many states recognize an exception to this rule when the defendant commits fraud or negligent misrepresentation, or when a special relationship exists between the parties (such as an attorney–client relationship).

economic-realities test. A method by which a court determines the true nature of a business transaction or situation by examining the totality of the commercial circumstances.

economic substantive due process. See DUE PROCESS.

economy. 1. The management or administration of the wealth and resources of a community (such as a city, state, or country). **2.** The sociopolitical organization of a community's wealth and resources. **3.** Restrained, thrifty, or sparing use of resources; efficiency.

E.D. *abbr.* Eastern District, in reference to U.S. judicial districts.

EDI agreement. *abbr.* Electronic Data Interchange agreement; an agreement that governs the transfer or exchange of data, such as purchase orders, between parties by computer.

educational expense. See EXPENSE.

EEC. *abbr.* European Economic Community. See EUROPEAN UNION.

EEOC. *abbr.* EQUAL EMPLOYMENT OPPORTUNITY COMMISSION.

effect, *n.* **1.** That which is produced by an agent or cause; a result, outcome, or consequence. **2.** The result that an instrument between parties will produce on their relative rights, or that a statute will produce on existing law, as discovered from the language used, the forms employed, or other materials for construing it.

effect, *vb.* To bring about; to make happen.

effective assistance of counsel. See ASSISTANCE OF COUNSEL.

effective date. The date on which a statute, contract, insurance policy, or other such instrument becomes enforceable or otherwise takes effect, which sometimes differs from the date on which it was enacted or signed.

effective rate. See INTEREST RATE.

effects, *n. pl.* Movable property; goods <personal effects>.

efficient breach. See BREACH OF CONTRACT.

efficient-breach theory. *Contracts.* The view that a party should be allowed to breach a contract and pay damages, if doing so would be more economically efficient than performing under the contract. See BREACH OF CONTRACT.

effluent (**ef**-loo-ənt), *n.* Liquid waste that is discharged into a river, lake, or other body of water.

effluxion of time (i-**fluk**-shən). The expiration of a lease term resulting from the passage of time rather than from a specific action or event.

EFT. *abbr.* Electronic funds transfer.

e.g. *abbr.* [Latin *exempli gratia*] For example <an intentional tort, e.g., battery or false imprisonment>. Cf. I.E.

eggshell-skull rule. *Torts.* The principle that a defendant is liable for a plaintiff's unforeseeable and uncommon reactions to the defendant's negligent or intentional act. • Under this rule, for example, if one person negligently scrapes another who turns out to be a hemophiliac, the negligent defendant is liable for the full extent of the plaintiff's injuries even though the harm to another plaintiff would have been minor.

egregious (i-**gree**-jəs), *adj.* Extremely or remarkably bad; flagrant.

egress (**ee**-gres). **1.** The act of going out or leaving. **2.** The right or ability to leave; a way of exit. Cf. INGRESS.

Eighteenth Amendment. The constitutional amendment — ratified in 1919 and repealed by the 21st Amendment in 1933 — that prohibited the manufacture, sale, transportation, and possession of alcoholic beverages in the United States. See PROHIBITION (3).

Eighth Amendment. The constitutional amendment, ratified as part of the Bill of Rights in 1791, prohibiting excessive bail, excessive fines, and cruel and unusual punishment.

EIS. *abbr.* ENVIRONMENTAL-IMPACT STATEMENT.

eject, *vb.* **1.** To cast or throw out. **2.** To oust or dispossess; to put or turn out of possession. **3.** To expel or thrust out forcibly (e.g., disorderly patrons). — **ejector,** *vb.*

ejection, *n.* An expulsion by action of law or by actual or threatened physical force. See OUSTER.

ejectment. **1.** The ejection of an owner or occupier from property. **2.** A legal action by which a person wrongfully ejected from property seeks to recover possession and damages. • The essential allegations in an action for ejectment are that (1) the plaintiff has title to the land, (2) the plaintiff has been wrongfully dispossessed or ousted, and (3) the plaintiff has suffered damages. See FORCIBLE ENTRY AND DETAINER. Cf. EVICTION; OUSTER.

equitable ejectment. A proceeding brought to enforce specific performance of a contract for the sale of land and for other purposes. • Though in the form of an ejectment action, this proceeding is in reality a substitute for a bill in equity.

justice ejectment. A statutory proceeding to evict a tenant who has held over after termination of the lease or breach of its conditions.

ejectment bill. *Equity practice.* A bill in equity brought to recover real property and an accounting of rents and profits, without setting out a distinct ground of equity jurisdiction (and thus demurrable).

ejusdem generis (ee-**jəs**-dəm **jen**-ə-ris *also* ee-**joos**- *or* ee-**yoos**-). [Latin "of the same kind or class"] A canon of construction that when a general word or phrase follows a list of specific persons or things, the general word or phrase will be interpreted to include only persons or things of the same type as those listed. Cf. EXPRESSIO UNIUS EST EXCLUSIO ALTERIUS; NOSCITUR A SOCIIS.

elder law. The field of law dealing with the elderly, including such issues as estate planning, retirement benefits, social security, age discrimination, and healthcare.

election, *n.* **1.** The exercise of a choice; esp., the act of choosing from several possible rights or remedies in a way that precludes the use of other rights or remedies. See ELECTION OF REMEDIES. **2.** The doctrine by which a person is compelled to choose between accepting a benefit under a legal instrument or retaining some property right to which the person is already entitled; an obligation imposed on a party to choose between alternative rights or claims, so that the party is entitled to enjoy only one. See RIGHT OF ELECTION. **3.** The process of selecting a person to occupy a position or office, usu. a public office. — **elect,** *vb.* — **elective,** *adj.*

election, doctrine of. A doctrine holding that when a person has contracted with an agent without knowing of the agency and later learns of the principal's identity, the person may enforce the contract against either the agent or the principal, but not both. See ELECTION (1).

election contest. A challenge by an election's loser against the winner, calling for an analysis of the election returns, which may include reviewing voter qualifications or re-counting the ballots.

election dower. A name sometimes given to a law specifying a widow's statutory share of her deceased husband's estate if she chooses to reject her share under a will. See RIGHT OF ELECTION.

election fraud. Illegal conduct committed in an election, usu. in the form of fraudulent voting. • Examples include voting twice, voting under another person's name (usu. a deceased person), or voting while ineligible.

election of remedies. 1. A claimant's act of choosing between two or more concurrent but inconsistent remedies based on a single set of facts. **2.** The affirmative defense barring a litigant from pursuing a remedy inconsistent with another remedy already pursued, when that other remedy has given the litigant an advantage over, or has damaged, the opposing party. • This doctrine has largely fallen into disrepute and is now rarely applied. **3.** The affirmative defense that a claimant cannot simultaneously recover damages based on two different liability findings if the injury is the same for both claims, thus creating a double recovery. Cf. *alternative relief* under RELIEF.

elective share. *Wills & estates.* The percentage of a deceased spouse's estate, set by statute, that a surviving spouse (or sometimes a child) may choose to receive instead of taking under a will or in the event of being unjustifiably disinherited. See RIGHT OF ELECTION.

elector. 1. A member of the electoral college chosen to elect the President and Vice President. **2.** One who is qualified to vote; a voter. **3.** A person who chooses between alternative rights or claims.

electoral college. (*often cap.*) The body of electors chosen from each state to formally elect the U.S. President and Vice President by casting votes based on the popular vote.

electoral process. 1. A method by which a person is elected to public office. **2.** The taking and counting of votes.

electric chair. A chair that is wired so that electrodes can be fastened to a condemned person's head and one leg and a lethal charge passed through the body for the purpose of carrying out a death penalty.

electronic chattel paper. See CHATTEL PAPER.

electronic transaction. A transaction formed by electronic messages in which the messages of one or both parties will not be reviewed by an individual as an expected step in forming a contract. UCC § 2A-102(a)(16).

elements of crime. The constituent parts of a crime — usu. consisting of the actus reus, mens rea, and causation — that the prosecution must prove to sustain a conviction. • The term is more broadly defined by Model Penal Code § 1.13(9) to refer to each component of the actus reus, causation, the mens rea, any grading factors, and the negative of any defense.

Eleventh Amendment. The constitutional amendment, ratified in 1795, prohibiting a federal court from hearing an action between a state and a person who is not a citizen of that state. See *sovereign immunity* under IMMUNITY (1).

elisor (i-lɪ-zər). A person appointed by a court to assemble a jury, serve a writ, or perform other duties of the sheriff or coroner if either is disqualified.

Elkins Act. A 1903 federal law that strengthened the Interstate Commerce Act by prohibiting rebates and other forms of preferential treatment to large carriers. 49 USCA §§ 41–43 (superseded).

eloign (i-**loyn**), *vb.* **1.** To remove (a person or property) from a court's or sheriff's jurisdiction. **2.** To remove to a distance; conceal. — **eloigner,** *n.*

eloignment (i-**loyn**-mənt), *n.* The getting of a thing or person out of the way, or removing it to a distance, so as to be out of reach.

eluviation (i-loo-vee-**ay**-shən). Movement of soil caused by excessive water in the soil.

e-mail, *n.* A communication exchanged between people by computer, through either a local area network or the Internet. — **e-mail,** *vb.*

emancipate, *vb.* **1.** To set free from legal, social, or political restraint; esp., to free from slavery or bondage. **2.** To release (a child) from the control, support, and responsibility of a parent or guardian. — **emancipative,** *adj.* — **emancipatory,** *adj.* — **emancipator,** *n.*

emancipated minor. See MINOR.

emancipation. 1. The act by which one who was under another's power and control is freed. **2.** A surrender and renunciation of the correlative rights and duties concerning the care, custody, and earnings of a child; the act by which a parent (historically a father) frees a child and gives the child the right to his or her own earnings.

emancipation proclamation. (*usu. cap.*) An executive proclamation, issued by President Abraham Lincoln on January 1, 1863, declaring that all persons held in slavery in certain designated states and districts were freed.

embassy. 1. The building in which a diplomatic body is located; esp., the residence of the ambassador. **2.** A body of diplomatic representatives headed by an ambassador; a diplomatic mission on the ambassadorial level. **3.** The mission, business, and function of an ambassador.

embezzlement, *n.* The fraudulent taking of personal property with which one has been entrusted, esp. as a fiduciary. • The criminal intent for embezzlement — unlike larceny and false pretenses — arises after taking possession (not before or during the taking). — **embezzle,** *vb.* See LARCENY; FALSE PRETENSES.

emblem. 1. A flag, armorial bearing, or other symbol of a country, organization, or movement. **2.** Loosely, something that is used to symbolize something else.

emblements (**em**-blə-mənts). The growing crop annually produced by labor, as opposed to a crop occurring naturally.

embossed seal. See NOTARY SEAL.

embracery (im-**brays**-ə-ree), *n.* The attempt to corrupt or instruct a jury to reach a particular conclusion by means other than presenting evidence or argument in court, as by bribing or threatening jurors; a corrupt or wrongful attempt to influence a juror's vote on a verdict. Cf. JURY-FIXING; JURY-PACKING.

emendation (ee-men-**day**-shən). Correction or revision, esp. of a text. — **emend** (i-**mend**), *vb.*

Emergency Court of Appeals. A temporary court, established during World War II, whose purpose is to review wage- and price-control matters.

emergency doctrine. 1. A legal principle exempting a person from the ordinary standard of reasonable care if that person acted instinctively to meet a sudden and urgent need for aid. **2.** A legal principle by which consent to medical treatment in a dire situation is inferred when neither the patient nor a responsible party can consent but a reasonable person would do so. Cf. GOOD SAMARITAN DOCTRINE; RESCUE DOCTRINE. **3.** The principle that a police officer may conduct a search without a warrant if the officer has probable cause and reasonably believes that immediate action is needed to protect life or property. See *exigent circumstances* under CIRCUMSTANCE.

emergency search. See SEARCH.

emigrant (**em**-ə-grənt), *n.* One who leaves his or her country for any reason with the intent to establish a permanent residence elsewhere. Cf. IMMIGRANT.

emigration (em-ə-**gray**-shən), *n.* The act of leaving a country with the intent to not return and to maintain a residence elsewhere. — **emigrate,** *vb.* Cf. IMMIGRATION.

emigré (**em**-ə-gray *or* em-ə-**gray**), *n.* [French] One who is forced to leave his or her country for political reasons.

eminent domain. The inherent power of a governmental entity to take privately owned property, esp. land, and convert it to public use, subject to reasonable compensation for the taking. See CONDEMNATION (2); EXPROPRIATION; TAKING (2).

Eminent Domain Clause. The Fifth Amendment provision providing that private property cannot be taken for public use without just compensation.

emissary. One sent on a special mission as another's agent or representative, esp. to promote a cause or to gain information.

emit, *vb.* **1.** To give off or discharge into the air. **2.** To issue with authority. — **emission,** *n.*

emolument (i-**mol**-yə-mənt), *n.* (*usu. pl.*) Any advantage, profit, or gain received as a result of one's employment or one's holding of office.

Emolument Clause. The clause of the U.S. Constitution prohibiting both bestowal of American titles of nobility and the acceptance by public officeholders of any gift, title, or other benefit from a foreign power. U.S. Const. art. I, § 9, cl. 8.

emotional distress. A highly unpleasant mental reaction (such as anguish, grief, fright, humiliation, or fury) that results from another person's conduct; emotional pain and suffering. See INTENTIONAL INFLICTION OF EMOTIONAL DISTRESS; NEGLIGENT INFLICTION OF EMOTIONAL DISTRESS.

emotional insanity. See INSANITY.

empanel, *vb.* To swear in (a jury) to try an issue or case. — **empanelment,** *n.* — **empaneling,** *n.*

emphasis added. A citation signal indicating that the writer quoting another's words has italicized or otherwise emphasized some of them.

empirical (em-**pir**-i-kəl), *adj.* Of, relating to, or based on experience, experiment, or observation <the expert's theory was not supported by empirical data>.

employ, *vb.* **1.** To make use of. **2.** To hire. **3.** To use as an agent or substitute in transacting business. **4.** To commission and entrust with the performance of certain acts or functions or with the management of one's affairs.

employee. A person who works in the service of another person (the employer) under an express or implied contract of hire, under which the employer has the right to control the details of work performance. Cf. AGENT (1); INDEPENDENT CONTRACTOR.

> ***borrowed employee.*** An employee whose services are, with the employee's consent, lent to another employer who temporarily assumes control over the employee's work. See RESPONDEAT SUPERIOR.

employee benefit plan. A written stock-purchase, savings, option, bonus, stock-appreciation, profit-sharing, thrift, incentive, pension, or similar plan solely for employees, officers, and advisers of a company. • The term excludes any plan, fund, or program (other than an apprenticeship or training program) in which no employees are plan participants.

Employee Retirement Income Security Act. A federal statute that regulates private pension plans and employee benefit plans and that established the Pension Benefit Guaranty Corporation. 29 USCA §§ 1001 et seq. — Abbr. ERISA.

employer. A person who controls and directs a worker under an express or implied contract of hire and who pays the worker's salary or wages. See MASTER (1). Cf. PRINCIPAL (1).

employment. **1.** The act of employing; the state of being employed. **2.** Work for which one has been hired and is being paid by an employer.

employment contract. See CONTRACT.

empty-chair defense. A trial tactic in a multiparty case whereby one defendant attempts to put all the fault on a defendant who plea-bargained or settled before trial or on a person who was neither charged nor named as a party.

enabling clause. The part of a statute or constitution that gives governmental officials the power and authority to put the law into effect and enforce it. See ENACTING CLAUSE.

enabling statute. See STATUTE.

enact, *vb.* **1.** To make into law by authoritative act; to pass. **2.** (Of a statute) to provide. — **enactor,** *n.*

enacting clause. The part of a statute stating the legislative authority by which it is made and when it takes effect. • In codifications of statutes, enacting clauses generally appear not in the text of the statutes but in historical or legislative notes.

enactment, *n.* **1.** The action or process of making into law. **2.** A statute.

en banc (en **bangk** *or* on **bongk**), *adv.* & *adj.* [Law French "on the bench"]

With all judges present and participating; in full court.

en banc sitting. See SITTING.

enclosed land. See LAND.

enclosure. 1. Something enclosed in a parcel or envelope. **2.** Land surrounded by some visible obstruction; CLOSE (1). **3.** An artificial fence around one's estate.

encourage, *vb. Criminal law.* To instigate; to incite to action; to embolden; to help. See AID AND ABET.

encroach, *vb.* **1.** To enter by gradual steps or stealth into the possessions or rights of another; to trespass or intrude. **2.** To gain or intrude unlawfully upon another's lands, property, or authority.

encroachment, *n.* An infringement of another's rights or intrusion on another's property. See TRESPASS.

encumbrance, *n.* A claim or liability that is attached to property or some other right and that may lessen its value, such as a lien or mortgage; any property right that is not an ownership interest. • An encumbrance cannot defeat the transfer of possession, but it remains after the property or right is transferred. — **encumber,** *vb.*

encumbrancer. One having a legal claim, such as a lien or mortgage, against property.

endangerment, *n.* The act or an instance of putting someone or something in danger; exposure to peril or harm. — **endanger,** *vb.* See CHILD ENDANGERMENT; RECKLESS ENDANGERMENT.

endenizen (en-**den**-ə-zən), *vb.* To recognize as a legal resident; to naturalize.

endnote. A note that, instead of appearing at the bottom of the page (as a footnote does), appears at the end of the book, chapter, or paper.

endorsement, *n.* **1.** INDORSEMENT. **2.** An amendment to an insurance policy; a rider. — **endorse,** *vb.*

endowment. A gift of money or property to an institution (such as a university) for a specific purpose, esp. one in which the principal is kept intact indefinitely and only the interest income from that principal is used.

end position. One's legal and financial position on the signing of a contract, including the choices now available, such as renewal and renegotiation.

end user. See USER.

enfeoff (en-**fef** *or* en-**feef**), *vb.* To put (a person) in legal possession of a freehold interest; to transfer a fief to.

enfeoffment (en-**fef**-mənt *or* en-**feef**-), *n.* **1.** At common law, the act or process of transferring possession and ownership of an estate in land. **2.** The property or estate so transferred. **3.** The instrument or deed by which one obtains such property or estate.

Enforcement of Foreign Judgments Act. A uniform law, adopted by several states, that gives the holder of a foreign judgment essentially the same rights to levy and execute on the judgment as the holder of a domestic judgment. • The Act defines a *foreign judgment* as any judgment, decree, or order (of a court in the United States or of any other court) that is entitled to full faith and credit in the state. See FULL FAITH AND CREDIT.

enforcement power. The authority by which Congress may enforce a particular constitutional amendment's provisions by appropriate legislation. • Enforcement power is granted to Congress under the 13th, 14th, 15th, 19th, 23rd, 24th, and 26th Amendments.

enfranchise, *vb.* **1.** To grant voting rights or other rights of citizenship to (a person or class). **2.** To set free, as from slavery. — **enfranchisement** (en-**fran**-chiz-mənt *or* -chɪz-mənt), *n.*

engagement, *n.* **1.** A contract or agreement involving mutual promises. **2.** An agreement to marry; the period after which a couple has agreed to marry but before they do so.

engagement slip. A note sent by a lawyer to a court informing the court that the lawyer is professionally engaged in a second court on a given day and thus cannot appear before the first court on that day as scheduled.

engross, *vb.* **1.** To prepare a copy of (a legal document, such as a deed) for execution. **2.** To prepare a copy of (a bill or mandate) before a final legislative vote. **3.** To buy large quantities of (a stock or commodity) in an effort to corner the market and control the price. **4.** To absorb or fully occupy. — **engrossment,** *n.* Cf. ENROLL.

engrossed bill. See BILL (3).

enjoin, *vb.* **1.** To legally prohibit or restrain by injunction. **2.** To prescribe, mandate, or strongly encourage. — **enjoinment** (for sense 1), *n.* — **enjoinder** (for sense 2), *n.* — **enjoinable,** *adj.*

enjoy, *vb.* To have, possess, and use (something) with satisfaction; to occupy or have the benefit of (property).

enjoyment, *n.* **1.** Possession and use, esp. of rights or property. **2.** The exercise of a right.

adverse enjoyment. The possession or use of land under a claim of right against the owner of the property from which the easement derives.

beneficial enjoyment. The possession and benefit of property, but without legal title.

present enjoyment. The immediate possession and use of an estate.

quiet enjoyment. The possession of real property with the assurance that the possession will not be disturbed by a superior title. See *covenant for quiet enjoyment* under COVENANT (3).

enlarge, *vb.* **1.** To increase in size or extend in scope or duration. **2.** To free from custody or imprisonment. — **enlargement,** *n.*

enlargement of time. A usu. court-ordered extension of the time allowed to perform an action, esp. a procedural one.

en masse (en **mas**). [French] In a mass; in a large group all at once; all together.

Enoch Arden law (**ee**-nək **ahrd**-ən). A statute that grants a divorce or an exemption from liability so that a person can remarry when his or her spouse has been absent without explanation for a specified number of years (usu. five or seven). See *presumptive death* under DEATH; ABANDONMENT (2). Cf. SEVEN-YEARS'-ABSENCE RULE.

enroll, *vb.* **1.** To register or transcribe (a legal document, as a deed) into an official record on execution. **2.** To prepare (a bill passed by the legislature) for the executive's signature. — **enrollment,** *n.* — **enrolled,** *adj.* Cf. ENGROSS.

enrolled bill. See BILL (3).

enrolled-bill rule. The conclusive presumption that a statute, once formalized, appears precisely as the legislature intended, thereby preventing any challenge to the drafting of the bill.

entail, *n.* A fee abridged or limited to the owner's issue or class of issue rather than descending to all the heirs. — **entail,** *vb.* — **entailed,** *adj.* See BARRING OF ENTAIL; FEE TAIL.

enter, *vb.* **1.** To come or go into; esp., to go onto (real property) by right of entry so as to take possession <the landlord entered the defaulting tenant's premises>. **2.** To put formally before a court or on the record <the defendant entered a plea of no contest>. **3.** To become a party to <they entered into an agreement>. See ENTRY.

enterprise liability. See LIABILITY.

entertain, *vb.* **1.** To bear in mind or consider; esp., to give judicial consideration to. **2.** To amuse or please. **3.** To receive (a person) as a guest or provide hospitality to (a person).

entertainment law. The field of law dealing with the legal and business issues in the entertainment industry (such as film, music, and theater), and involving the representation of artists and producers, the negotiation of contracts, and the protection of intellectual-property rights.

entice, *vb.* To lure or induce; esp., to wrongfully solicit (a person) to do something. — **enticement,** *n.*

entire-contract clause. 1. INTEGRATION CLAUSE. **2.** A provision in an insurance contract stating that the entire agreement between the insured and insurer is contained in the contract, often including the application (if attached), declarations, insuring agreement, exclusions, conditions, and endorsements.

entire-controversy doctrine. The principle that a plaintiff or defendant who does not assert all claims or defenses related to the controversy in a legal proceeding is not entitled to assert those claims or defenses in a later proceeding. Cf. *compulsory counterclaim* under COUNTERCLAIM; RES JUDICATA (2).

entire interest. See INTEREST (2).

entire tenancy. See TENANCY.

entirety (en-tɪ-ər-tee). **1.** The whole, as opposed to a moiety or part. **2.** Something (such as certain judgments and contracts) that the law considers incapable of being divided into parts.

entire use. See USE.

entitlement. An absolute right to a (usu. monetary) benefit, such as social security, granted immediately upon meeting a legal requirement.

entity assumption. The presumption that a business is a unit separate from its owners and from other firms.

entity theory of partnership. The theory that a partnership is an entity with a legal existence apart from the partners who make it up. Cf. AGGREGATE THEORY OF PARTNERSHIP.

entrapment, *n.* **1.** A law-enforcement officer's or government agent's inducement of a person to commit a crime, by means of fraud or undue persuasion, in an attempt to later bring a criminal prosecution against that person. **2.** The affirmative defense of having been so induced. • To establish entrapment (in most states), the defendant must show that he or she would not have committed the crime but for the fraud or undue persuasion. — **entrap,** *vb.* Cf. DECOY.

entry, *n.* **1.** The act, right, or privilege of entering real property.

lawful entry. **1.** The entry onto real property by a person not in possession, under a claim or color of right, and without force or fraud. **2.** The entry of premises under a search warrant. See SEARCH.

open entry. A conspicuous entry onto real estate to take possession; an entry that is neither clandestine nor carried out by secret artifice or stratagem and that (by law in some states) is accomplished in the presence of two witnesses.

unlawful entry. **1.** The crime of entering another's property, by fraud or other illegal means, without the owner's consent. **2.** An alien's crossing of a border into a country without proper documents.

2. An item written in a record; a notation. **3.** The placement of something before the court or on the record. **4.** *Copyright.* The deposit of a title of work with the Register of Copyrights to secure its protection. **5.** *Immigration.* Any entrance of an alien into the United States, whether voluntary or involuntary. **6.** *Criminal law.* The unlawful coming into a building to commit a crime.

entry of judgment. The ministerial recording of a court's final decision, usu. by noting it in a judgment book or civil docket. Cf. RENDITION OF JUDGMENT.

enumerate (i-**n[y]oo**-mə-rayt), *vb.* To count off or designate one by one; to list. — **enumeration,** *n.*

enumerated power. See POWER.

enunciate (i-**nən**-see-ayt), *vb.* **1.** To state publicly; to announce or proclaim. **2.** To articulate or pronounce. — **enunciation,** *n.* — **enunciable,** *adj.* — **enunciator,** *n.*

en ventre sa mere (on **von**-trə sa **mair**). [Law French "in utero"] *Jargon.* (Of a fetus) in the mother's womb <child *en ventre sa mere*>. • This phrase refers to an unborn child, usually in the context of a discussion of that child's rights.

en vie (on **vee**). [Law French "in life"] Alive.

environmental effect. *Environmental law.* A natural or artificial disturbance of the physical, chemical, or biological components that make up the environment.

environmental crime. A statutory offense involving harm to the environment, such as a violation of the criminal provisions in the Clean Air Act Amendments of 1970, the Federal Water Pollution Control Act of 1972 (commonly called the Clean Water Act), or the Endangered Species Act of 1973.

environmental-impact statement. *Environmental law.* A document that the National Environmental Policy Act (42 USCA § 4332(2)(c)) requires a federal agency to produce for a major project or legislative proposal so that better decisions can be made about the positive and negative environmental effects of an undertaking. — Abbr. EIS.

environmental law. The field of law dealing with the maintenance and protection of the environment, including preventive measures such as the requirements of environmental-impact statements, as well as measures to assign liability and provide cleanup for incidents that harm the environment.

Environmental Protection Agency. A federal agency created in 1970 to coordinate governmental action to protect the environment. — Abbr. EPA.

eo instante (**ee**-oh in-**stan**-tee). [Latin] At that very instant.

E.O.M. *abbr.* End of month. • This appears as a payment term in some sales contracts.

eo nomine (**ee**-oh **nahm**-ə-nee). [Latin] By or in that name.

EPA. *abbr.* ENVIRONMENTAL PROTECTION AGENCY.

episodic criminal. See CRIMINAL.

equal-access rule. *Criminal law.* The doctrine that contraband found on a defendant's premises will not support a conviction if other persons have the same access to the premises as the defendant. • To invoke this defense successfully, the defendant must show that other persons did in fact have equal access to the premises; speculative evidence that trespassers might have come onto the premises will not bar a conviction.

Equal Access to Justice Act. A federal statute enacted in 1980 to allow the prevailing party in certain actions against the government to recover attorney's or expert-witness fees. Pub. L. No. 96–481, tit. II, 94 Stat. 2325 (codified as amended in scattered sections of 5, 15, and 28 USCA). — Abbr. EAJA.

Equal Credit Opportunity Act. A federal statute prohibiting a creditor from discriminating against an applicant on the basis of race, color, religion, national origin, age, sex, or marital status with respect to any aspect of a credit transaction. 15 USCA §§ 1691 et seq. — Abbr. ECOA.

equal degree. See DEGREE.

Equal Employment Opportunity Commission. A federal agency created under the Civil Rights Act of 1964 to end discriminatory employment practices and to promote nondiscriminatory employment programs. • The EEOC investigates alleged discriminatory employment practices and encourages mediation and other nonlitigious means of resolving employment disputes. A claimant is required to file a charge of discrimination with the EEOC before pursuing a claim under Title VII of the Civil Rights Act and certain other employment-related statutes. — Abbr. EEOC.

equal-footing doctrine. The principle that a state admitted to the Union after 1789 enters with the same rights, sovereignty, and jurisdiction within its borders as did the original 13 states.

equality before the law. The status or condition of being treated fairly according to regularly established norms of justice; esp., in British constitutional law, the notion that all persons are subject to the ordinary law of the land administered by the ordinary law courts, that officials and others are not exempt from the general duty of obedience to the law, that discretionary governmental powers must not be abused, and that the task of superintending the operation of law rests with an impartial, independent judiciary.

equalization, *n.* **1.** The raising or lowering of assessed values to achieve conformity. **2.** *Tax.* The adjustment of an assessment or tax to create a rate uniform with another.

equalization board. A local governmental agency responsible for adjusting the tax rates in different districts to ensure an equitable distribution of the tax burden. — **equalize,** *vb.*

equally divided. 1. (Of property) apportioned per capita — not per stirpes — among heirs on the testator's death. **2.** (Of a court, legislature, or other group) having the same number of votes on each side of an issue or dispute.

Equal Pay Act. A federal law mandating that all who perform substantially the same work must be paid equally. 29 USCA § 206.

equal protection. The constitutional guarantee under the 14th Amendment that the government must treat a person or class of persons the same as it treats other persons or classes in like circumstances. • In today's constitutional jurisprudence, equal protection means that legislation that discriminates must have a rational basis for doing so. And if the legislation affects a fundamental right (such as the right to vote) or involves a suspect classification (such as race), it is unconstitutional unless it can withstand strict scrutiny. See RATIONAL-BASIS TEST; STRICT SCRUTINY.

Equal Protection Clause. The 14th Amendment provision requiring the states to give similarly situated persons or classes similar treatment under the law. Cf. DUE PROCESS CLAUSE.

Equal Time Act. A federal law requiring that a broadcasting-facility licensee who permits a legally qualified candidate for public office to use the facility for broadcasting must afford an equal opportunity to all other candidates for the office. 47 USCA § 315.

equipment. The articles or implements used for a specific purpose or activity (esp. a business operation). • Under the UCC, *equipment* includes goods if (1) the goods are used in or bought for a business enterprise (including farming or a profession) or by a debtor that is a nonprofit organization or a governmental subdivision or agency, and (2) the goods are not inventory, farm products, or consumer goods. UCC § 9–109(2).

equitable (**ek**-wi-tə-bəl), *adj.* **1.** Just; conformable to principles of justice and right. **2.** Existing in equity; available or sustainable by an action in equity, or under the rules and principles of equity.

equitable-adjustment theory. The doctrine that in settling a federal contract dispute, the contracting officer should make a fair adjustment within a reasonable time before the contractor has to settle with its subcontractors, suppliers, and other creditors.

equitable defense. See DEFENSE (1).

equitable distribution. *Family law.* The division of marital property by a court in a divorce proceeding, under statutory guidelines that provide for a fair, but not necessarily equal, allocation of the property between the spouses. • Equitable distribution is applied in all the states that do not have a community-property system.

equitable ejectment. See EJECTMENT.

equitable estate. See ESTATE.

equitable estoppel. See ESTOPPEL.

equitable foreclosure. See FORECLOSURE.

equitable interest. See INTEREST (2).

equitable life estate. See ESTATE.

equitable life tenant. See LIFE TENANT.

equitable-recoupment doctrine. A principle that diminishes a party's right to recover a debt to the extent that the party holds money or property of the debtor to which the party has no right.

equitable remedy. See REMEDY.

equitable rescission. See RESCISSION.

equitable right to setoff. The right to cancel cross-demands, usu. used by a bank to take from a customer's deposit accounts the amount equal to the customer's debts that have matured and that are owed to that bank. See SETOFF.

equitable title. See TITLE (2).

equitable tolling. The doctrine that the statute of limitations will not bar a claim if the plaintiff, despite diligent efforts, did not discover the injury until after the limitations period had expired.

equitable waste. See WASTE (1).

equity, *n.* **1.** Fairness; impartiality; evenhanded dealing. **2.** The body of principles constituting what is fair and right; natural law. **3.** The recourse to principles of justice to correct or supplement the law as applied to particular circumstances. **4.** The system of law or body of principles originating in the English Court of Chancery and superseding the common and statute law (together called "law" in the narrower sense) when the two conflict. **5.** A right, interest, or remedy recognizable by a court of equity.

contravening equity (kon-trə-**veen**-ing). A right or interest that is inconsistent with or contrary to a right sought to be enforced.

countervailing equity (kown-tər-**vayl**-ing). A contrary and balancing equity, equally deserving of consideration.

latent equity (**lay**-tənt). An equitable claim or right known only by the parties for and against whom it exists, or that has been concealed from one who is interested in the subject matter.

perfect equity. An equitable title or right that, to be a legal title, lacks only the formal conveyance or other investiture that would make it cognizable at law; esp., the equity of a real-estate purchaser who has paid the full amount due but has not yet received a deed.

6. The right to decide matters in equity; equity jurisdiction. **7.** The amount by which the value of or an interest in property exceeds secured claims or liens; the difference between the value of the property and all encumbrances upon it. **8.** An ownership interest in property, esp. in a business. See OWNERS' EQUITY. **9.** A share in a publicly traded company.

equity jurisprudence. See JURISPRUDENCE.

equity of subrogation. The right of a person who is secondarily liable on a debt, and who pays the debt, to personally enforce any right that the original creditor could have pursued against the debtor, including the right to foreclose on any security held by the creditor and any right that the creditor may have to contribution from others who are liable for the debt. See SUBROGATION.

equity-of-the-statute rule. In statutory construction, the principle that a statute should be interpreted according to the legislators' purpose and intent, even if this interpretation goes beyond the literal meaning of the text. • Under this little-used rule, for example, if a statute defines jury-tampering to include a party's "giving a juror food or drink," the giving of cigars to a juror would also fall within that definition. Cf. GOLDEN RULE; MISCHIEF RULE; PLAIN-MEANING RULE.

equity participation. The inclusion of a lender in the equity ownership of a project as a condition of the lender's granting a loan.

equity pleading. See PLEADING (2).

equity term. See TERM (5).

equity to a settlement. A wife's equitable right, arising when her husband sues in equity for the reduction of her equitable estate to his own possession, to have all or part of that estate settled upon herself and her children.

equivocal (i-**kwiv**-ə-kəl), *adj.* **1.** Of doubtful character; questionable. **2.** Having more than one meaning or sense; ambiguous.

erase, *vb.* **1.** To rub or scrape out (something written); to obliterate. **2.** To obliterate (recorded material). **3.** To seal (criminal records) from disclosure. — **erasure,** *n.*

ergo (**ər**-goh *or* **air**-goh), *conj.* & *adv.* [Latin] Therefore; thus.

***Erie* doctrine** (**eer**-ee). The principle that a federal court exercising diversity jurisdiction over a case that does not involve a federal question must apply the substantive law of the state where the court sits. *Erie R.R. v. Tompkins*, 304 U.S. 64, 58 S.Ct. 817

(1938). Cf. CLEARFIELD TRUST DOCTRINE.

***Erie/Klaxon* doctrine.** See KLAXON DOCTRINE.

ERISA (ee- *or* ə-**ris**-ə). *abbr.* EMPLOYEE RETIREMENT INCOME SECURITY ACT.

erosion. The wearing away of something by action of the elements; esp., the gradual eating away of soil by the operation of currents or tides. Cf. ACCRETION; DELICTION; AVULSION (2); ALLUVION.

err (ər), *vb.* To make an error; to be incorrect or mistaken.

errant (**er**-ənt), *adj.* **1.** Fallible; incorrect; straying from what is proper <an errant judicial holding>. **2.** Traveling <a knight errant>.

errata sheet. An attachment to a deposition transcript containing the deponent's corrections upon reading the transcript and the reasons for those corrections.

erratum (i-**ray**-təm *or* i-**rah**-təm), *n.* [Latin "error"] An error that needs correction. Pl. **errata.**

erroneous judgment. See JUDGMENT.

error, *n.* **1.** A psychological state that does not conform to objective reality; a belief that what is false is true or that what is true is false; MISTAKE.

error in corpore (**kor**-pə-ree). A mistake involving the identity of a particular object, as when a party buys a horse believing it to be the one that the party had already examined and ridden, when in fact it is a different horse.

error in negotio (ni-**goh**-shee-oh). A mistake about the type of contract that the parties actually wanted to enter.

error in qualitate (kwah-lə-**tay**-tee). A mistake affecting the quality of the contractual object.

error in quantitate (kwahn-tə-**tay**-tee). A mistake that affects the amount of the contractual object.

2. A mistake of law or of fact in a court's judgment, opinion, or order.

clear error. A trial judge's decision or action that appears to a reviewing court to have been unquestionably erroneous.

clerical error. An error resulting from a minor mistake or inadvertence, esp. in writing or copying something on the record, and not from judicial reasoning or determination.

cross-error. An error brought by the party responding to a writ of error.

harmless error. An error that does not affect a party's substantive rights or the case's outcome.

invited error. An error that a party cannot complain of on appeal because the party, through conduct, encouraged or prompted the trial court to make the erroneous ruling.

manifest constitutional error. An error by the trial court that has an identifiably negative impact on the trial to such a degree that the constitutional rights of a party are compromised.

manifest error. An error that is plain and indisputable, and that amounts to a complete disregard of the controlling law or the credible evidence in the record.

plain error. An error that is so obvious and prejudicial that an appellate court should address it despite the parties' failure to raise a proper objection.

reversible error. An error that affects a party's substantive rights or the case's outcome, and thus is grounds for reversal if the party properly objected.

3. An appeal <a proceeding in error>.

escalator clause. 1. A contractual provision that increases or decreases the contract price according to changing market conditions, such as higher or lower taxes or operating costs. **2.** A provision in a divorce decree or divorce agreement providing for the automatic increase of alimony payments upon the occurrence of any of various triggering events, such as cost-of-living increases or an increase in the obligor's salary. • Escalation clauses for child support are often unenforceable.

escape, *n.* **1.** The act or an instance of breaking free from confinement, restraint, or an obligation. **2.** An unlawful departure from legal custody without the use of force. Cf. PRISON BREACH. **3.** At common law, a criminal offense committed by a peace officer who allows a prisoner to depart unlawfully from legal custody. — **escape,** *vb.*

escape clause. A contractual provision that allows a party to avoid performance under specified conditions; specif., an insurance-policy provision — usu. contained in the "other insurance" section of the policy — requiring the insurer to provide coverage only if there is no other coverage available.

escape warrant. See WARRANT.

escheat (es-**cheet**), *n.* **1.** Reversion of property (esp. real property) to the state upon the death of an owner who has neither a will nor any legal heirs. **2.** Property that has so reverted. — **escheat,** *vb.*

escrow (**es**-kroh), *n.* **1.** A legal document or property delivered by a promisor to a third party to be held by the third party for a given amount of time or until the occurrence of a condition, at which time the third party is to hand over the document or property to the promisee <the agent received the escrow two weeks before the closing date>. **2.** An account held in trust or as security <the earnest money is in escrow>. **3.** The holder of such a document, property, or deposit <the attorney performed the function of escrow>. **4.** The general arrangement under which a legal document or property is delivered to a third person until the occurrence of a condition <creating an escrow>. — **escrow,** *vb.*

escrow agreement. The instructions given to the third-party depositary of an escrow.

espionage (**es**-pee-ə-nahzh). The practice of using spies to collect information about what another government or company is doing or plans to do.

industrial espionage. One company's spying on another to steal the other company's trade secrets or other proprietary information.

Espionage Act. A federal law that criminalizes and punishes espionage, spying, and related crimes. 18 USCA §§ 793 et seq.

espousals (ə-**spow**-zəlz), *n.* A mutual promise between a man and a woman to marry one another.

esquire (**es**-kwɪr *or* e-**skwɪr**). (*usu. cap.*) A title of courtesy commonly appended after the name of a lawyer. — Abbr. Esq.

essential mistake. See MISTAKE.

establish, *vb.* **1.** To settle, make, or fix firmly; to enact permanently. **2.** To make or form; to bring about or into existence. **3.** To prove; to convince.

establishment, *n.* **1.** The act of establishing; the state or condition of being established. **2.** An institution or place of business. **3.** A group of people who are in power or who control or exercise great influence over something.

Establishment Clause. The First Amendment provision that prohibits the government from creating or favoring a particular religion. U.S. Const. amend. I. Cf. FREE EXERCISE CLAUSE.

estate. 1. The amount, degree, nature, and quality of a person's interest in land or other property. **2.** All that a person or entity owns, including both real and personal property. **3.** The property that one leaves after death; the collective assets and liabilities of a dead person.

decedent's estate. The real and personal property that a person possesses at the time of death and that passes to the heirs or testamentary beneficiaries.

residuary estate. The part of a decedent's estate remaining after payment of all debts, expenses, statutory claims, taxes, and testamentary gifts (special, general, and demonstrative) have been made.

taxable estate. A decedent's gross estate reduced by allowable deductions (such as administration costs and ESOP deductions). IRC (26 USCA) § 2051. • The taxable estate is the amount that is subject to the federal unified transfer tax at death.

4. A tract of land, esp. one affected by an easement.

concurrent estate. Ownership or possession of property by two or more persons at the same time. • In modern practice, there are three types of concurrent estates: tenancy in common, joint tenancy, and tenancy by the entirety.

contingent estate. An estate that vests only if a certain event does or does not happen. See *estate on condition*.

defeasible estate. An estate that may come to an end before its maximum duration has run by reason of the operation of a special limitation, a condition subsequent, or an executory limitation. • If an estate is defeasible by operation of a special limitation, it is called a *determinable estate*.

derivative estate. A particular interest that has been carved out of another, larger estate.

determinable estate. An estate that is defeasible by operation of a special limitation.

dominant estate. An estate that benefits from an easement. Cf. *servient estate*.

equitable estate. An estate recognized in equity, such as a trust beneficiary's interest. See EQUITY.

equitable life estate. An interest in real or personal property that lasts for the life of the holder of the estate and that is equitable as opposed to legal in its creation. • An example is a life estate held by a trust beneficiary.

estate on condition. An estate that vests, is modified, or is defeated upon the occurrence or nonoccurrence of some specified event. • While an estate on limitation can revert without any action by the grantor or the grantor's heirs, an estate on condition requires the entry of the grantor or the grantor's heirs to end the estate whenever the condition occurs.

estate on condition expressed. A contingent estate in which the condition upon which the estate will fail is stated explicitly in the granting instrument.

estate on condition implied. A contingent estate having some condition that is so inseparable from the estate's essence that it need not be expressed in words.

estate on limitation. An estate that automatically reverts to the grantor according to a provision, usu. regarding the passage of a determined time period, designated by words such as "during," "while," and "as long as." See *fee simple determinable* under FEE SIMPLE.

joint estate. Any of the following five types of estates: (1) a joint tenancy, (2) a tenancy in common, (3) an estate in coparcenary, (4) a tenancy by the entirety, or (5) an estate in partnership.

life estate. An estate held only for the duration of a specified person's life, usu. the possessor's.

life estate pur autre vie (pər **oh**-trə **vee**). A life estate for which the measuring life — the life whose duration determines the duration of the estate — is someone other than the life tenant.

next eventual estate. An estate taking effect upon an event that terminates the accumulation of undisposed rents and profits; an estate taking effect when the existing estate terminates.

possessory estate. An estate giving the holder the right to possess the property, with or without an ownership interest in the property.

servient estate (**sər**-vee-ənt). An estate burdened by an easement.

vested estate. An estate with a present right of enjoyment or a present fixed right of future enjoyment.

estate freeze. An estate-planning maneuver whereby an owner of a closely held business exchanges common stock for dividend-paying preferred stock and gives the common stock to his or her children, thus guaranteeing a pension and avoiding estate tax.

estate in lands. 1. Property that one has in lands, tenements, or hereditaments. **2.** The conditions or circumstances under which a tenant stands in relation to the leased property.

estate planning. 1. The preparation for the distribution and management of a person's estate at death through the use of wills, trusts, insurance policies, and other arrangements, esp. to reduce estate-tax liability. **2.** A branch of law that involves the arrangement of a person's estate, taking into account the laws of wills, taxes, insurance, property, and trusts.

estate tax. See TAX.

estimated tax. See TAX.

estop (e-**stop**), *vb.* To bar or prevent by estoppel. — **estoppage** (e-**stop**-ij), *n.*

estoppel (e-**stop**-əl), *n.* **1.** A bar that prevents one from asserting a claim or right that contradicts what one has said or done before or what has been legally established as true. **2.** A bar that prevents the relitigation of issues. **3.** An affirmative defense alleging good-faith reliance on a misleading representation and an injury or detrimental change in position resulting from that reliance. Cf. WAIVER (1).

equitable estoppel. **1.** A defensive doctrine preventing one party from taking unfair advantage of another when, through false language or conduct, the person to be estopped has induced another person to act in a certain way, with the result that the other person has been injured in some way. **2.** See *promissory estoppel.*

estoppel by laches. An equitable doctrine by which some courts deny relief to a claimant who has unreasonably delayed or been negligent in asserting a claim.

estoppel by silence. Estoppel that arises when a party is under a duty to speak but fails to do so.

judicial estoppel. Estoppel that prevents a party from contradicting previous declarations made during the same or a later proceeding if the change in position would adversely affect the proceeding or constitute a fraud on the court.

promissory estoppel. The principle that a promise made without consideration may nonetheless be enforced to prevent injustice if the promisor should have reasonably expected the promisee to rely on the promise and if the promisee did actually rely on the promise to his or her detriment.

quasi-estoppel. An equitable doctrine preventing one from repudiating an act or assertion if it would harm another who reasonably relied on the act or assertion.

estoppel certificate. 1. A signed statement by a party (such as a tenant or a mortgagee) certifying for another's benefit that certain facts are correct, as that a lease exists, that there are no defaults, and that rent is paid to a certain date. • A party's delivery of this statement estops that party from later claiming a different state of facts. **2.** See WAIVER OF CLAIMS AND DEFENSES.

estreat (e-**street**), *n.* A copy or duplicate of some original writing or record, esp. of a fine or amercement imposed by a court, extracted from the record, and certified to one who is authorized and required to collect it.

estreat, *vb.* To take out a forfeited recognizance from the recordings of a court and return it to the court to be prosecuted.

estrepe (e-**streep**), *vb.* **1.** To strip; to despoil; to commit waste upon an estate, as by cutting down trees or removing buildings. **2.** To injure the value of a reversionary interest by stripping or spoiling the estate. See WASTE.

estrepement (e-**streep**-mənt), *n.* A species of aggravated waste, by stripping or devastating land to the injury of the reversioner, esp. pending a suit for possession.

et al. (et **al** *or* **ahl**). *abbr.* **1.** [Latin *et alii* or *et alia*] And other persons <the office of Thomas Webb et al.>. **2.** [Latin *et alibi*] And elsewhere.

ethical, *adj.* **1.** Of or relating to moral obligations that one person owes another; esp., in law, of or relating to legal ethics. See LEGAL ETHICS. **2.** In conformity with moral norms or standards of professional conduct. Cf. UNETHICAL.

ethical consideration. (*often cap.*) An aspirational goal or principle intended to guide a lawyer's professional conduct. • A lawyer's violation of these considerations (which are contained in the Model Code of Professional Responsibility) does not necessarily subject the lawyer to discipline. Cf. DISCIPLINARY RULE.

ethical jurisprudence. See JURISPRUDENCE.

ethical wall. A screening mechanism that protects client confidences by preventing one or more lawyers within an organization from participating in any matter involving that client. — Also termed *Chinese wall.*

et seq. (et **sek**). *abbr.* [Latin *et sequentes*] And those (pages or sections) that follow <11 USCA §§ 101 et seq.>.

EU. *abbr.* EUROPEAN UNION.

euro (**yuur**-oh). The official currency of most countries in the European Union.

Eurobank. A bank that participates in the Eurocurrency market by accepting deposits and providing loans in foreign currencies.

Eurobond. An international bond issued in a country other than the one in whose currency the bond is denominated.

Eurodollar. A U.S. dollar deposited in a foreign bank and used in European money markets.

European Community. See EUROPEAN UNION.

European Court of Human Rights. The judicial body — established in 1950 and sitting at Strasbourg — of the Council of Europe. • The Convention on Human Rights of 1950, in force as of 1953, does not necessarily form part of the domestic law of member nations, nor is a member nation obliged to accept this court's jurisdiction.

European Economic Community. See EUROPEAN UNION.

European law. 1. The law of the European Union. **2.** More broadly, the law of the European Union, together with the conventions of the Council of Europe and the European Convention on Human Rights. **3.** More broadly still, all the law current in Europe, including the law of European organizations such as the Western European Union, the Benelux Economic Union, the Organization for Economic Cooperation and Development, the North Atlantic Treaty Organization, and all the bilateral and multilateral conventions in effect, as well as European customary law.

European Union. An association of European nations, with the purpose of achieving full economic unity (and eventual political union) by agreeing to eliminate barriers to the free movement of capital, goods, and labor among the member-nations. — Abbr. EU.

euthanasia (yoo-thə-**nay**-zhə), *n.* The act or practice of killing or bringing about the death of a person who suffers from an incurable disease or condition, esp. a painful one, for reasons of mercy. — **euthanasic** (yoo-thə-**nay**-zik), *adj.* See LIVING WILL; ADVANCE DIRECTIVE. Cf. *assisted suicide* under SUICIDE.

euthanize (**yoo**-thə-nɪz), *vb.* To put to death by euthanasia. • This term is used chiefly in reference to animals.

evaluative fact. See FACT.

evasive answer. A response that neither directly admits nor denies a question. • In pleading, this is considered a failure to answer. Fed. R. Civ. P. 37(3).

even date. *Jargon.* The same date. • This jargonistic phrase is sometimes used in one instrument to refer to another instrument with the same date, especially when both relate to the same transaction (such as a deed and a mortgage).

evict, *vb.* **1.** To expel (a person, esp. a tenant), from real property, usu. by legal process. **2.** *Archaic.* To recover (property or title) from a person by legal process. — **evictor,** *n.*

eviction. The act or process of legally dispossessing a person of land or rental property. See FORCIBLE ENTRY AND DETAINER. Cf. EJECTMENT.

actual eviction. A physical expulsion of a person from land or rental property.

***constructive eviction.* 1.** A landlord's act of making premises unfit for occupancy, often with the result that the tenant is compelled to leave. **2.** The inability of a land purchaser to obtain possession because of paramount outstanding title.

retaliatory eviction. An eviction — nearly always illegal — commenced in response to a tenant's complaints or involvement in activities with which the landlord does not agree.

summary eviction. An eviction accomplished through a simplified legal procedure, without the formalities of a full trial.

total eviction. An eviction that wholly deprives the tenant of any right in the premises.

evidence, *n.* **1.** Something (including testimony, documents, and tangible objects) that tends to prove or disprove the existence of an alleged fact. **2.** See *fact in evidence* under FACT. **3.** The collective mass of things, esp. testimony and exhibits, presented before a tribunal in a given dispute. **4.** The body of law regulating the burden of proof, admissibility, relevance, and weight and sufficiency of what should be admitted into the record of a legal proceeding. — **evidence,** *vb.*

admissible evidence. Evidence that is relevant and is of such a character (e.g., not unfairly prejudicial or based on hearsay) that the court should receive it.

best evidence. Evidence of the highest quality available, as measured by the nature of the case rather than the thing being offered as evidence. • The term is usually applied to writings and recordings. See BEST-EVIDENCE RULE. Cf. *secondary evidence.*

character evidence. Evidence regarding someone's personality traits; evidence of a person's moral standing in a community, based on reputation or opinion. Fed. R. Evid. 404, 405, 608. Cf. *reputation evidence.*

circumstantial evidence. **1.** Evidence based on inference and not on personal knowledge or observation. Cf. *direct evidence* (1). **2.** All evidence that is not given by testimony.

clear and convincing evidence. Evidence indicating that the thing to be proved is highly probable or reasonably certain. • This is a greater burden than preponderance of the evidence, the standard applied in most civil trials, but less than evidence beyond a reasonable doubt, the norm for criminal trials. Cf. PREPONDERANCE OF THE EVIDENCE.

competent evidence. **1.** See *admissible evidence.* **2.** See *relevant evidence.*

conclusive evidence. **1.** Evidence so strong as to overbear any other evidence to the contrary. **2.** Evidence that, though not irrebuttable, so preponderates as to oblige a fact-finder to come to a certain conclusion.

concomitant evidence. Evidence that, at the time of the act, the alleged doer of the act was present and actually did it.

conflicting evidence. Irreconcilable evidence that comes from different sources.

corroborating evidence. Evidence that differs from but strengthens or confirms other evidence (esp. that which needs support). Cf. *cumulative evidence.*

credible evidence. Evidence that is worthy of belief; trustworthy evidence.

critical evidence. Evidence strong enough that its presence could tilt a juror's mind.

cumulative evidence. Additional evidence of the same character as existing evidence and that supports a fact established by the existing evidence (esp. that which does not need further support). Cf. *corroborating evidence.*

demeanor evidence. The behavior of a witness on the witness stand, to be considered by the fact-finder on the issue of credibility.

demonstrative evidence (di-**mon**-strə-tiv). Physical evidence that one can see and inspect (such as a model or photograph) and that, while of probative value and usu. offered to clarify testimony, does not play a direct part in the incident in question. See *nonverbal testimony* under TESTIMONY. Cf. *testimonial evidence.*

derivative evidence. Evidence that is discovered as a result of illegally obtained evidence and is therefore inadmissible because of the primary taint. See EXCLUSIONARY RULE; FRUIT-OF-THE-POISONOUS-TREE DOCTRINE.

direct evidence. **1.** Evidence that is based on personal knowledge or observation and that, if true, proves a fact without inference or presumption. Cf. *circumstantial evidence*; *negative evidence.* **2.** See *original evidence* (1).

documentary evidence. Evidence supplied by a writing or other document, which must be authenticated before the evidence is admissible.

evidence-in-chief. Evidence used by a party in making its case-in-chief.

exclusive evidence. The only facts that have any probative force at all on a particular matter in issue.

exculpatory evidence (ik-**skəl**-pə-tor-ee). Evidence tending to establish a criminal defendant's innocence. See BRADY MATERIAL.

expert evidence. Evidence about a scientific, technical, or professional issue given by a person qualified to testify because of familiarity with the subject or special training in the field. Fed. R. Evid. 702–705. See DAUBERT TEST.

extrajudicial evidence. Evidence that does not come directly under judicial cognizance but nevertheless constitutes an intermediate link between judicial evidence and the fact requiring proof. • It includes all facts that are known to the tribunal only by way of inference from some form of judicial evidence. See JUDICIAL NOTICE.

extrinsic evidence. **1.** Evidence relating to a contract but not appearing on the face of the contract because it comes from other sources, such as statements between the parties or the circumstances surrounding the agreement. • Extrinsic evidence is usually not admissible to contradict or add to the terms of an unambiguous document. **2.** Evidence that is not legitimately before the court. Cf. *intrinsic evidence.*

fabricated evidence. False or deceitful evidence that is unlawfully created, usu. after the relevant event, in an attempt to avoid liability or conviction.

false evidence. See *false testimony* under TESTIMONY.

forensic evidence. Evidence used in court; esp., evidence arrived at by scientific means, such as ballistic or medical evidence.

foundational evidence. Evidence that determines the admissibility of other evidence.

habit evidence. Evidence of one's regular response to a repeated specific situation. Fed. R. Evid. 406.

illegally obtained evidence. Evidence obtained by violating a statute or a person's constitutional right, esp. the Fourth Amendment guarantee against unreasonable searches, the Fifth Amendment right to remain silent, or the Sixth Amendment right to counsel.

immaterial evidence. **1.** Evidence lacking in probative value. **2.** Evidence offered to prove a matter that is not in issue.

impeachment evidence. Evidence used to undermine a witness's credibility. Fed. R. Evid. 607–610.

incompetent evidence. Evidence that is for any reason inadmissible.

incriminating evidence. Evidence tending to establish guilt or from which a fact-trier can infer guilt.

inculpatory evidence (in-**kəl**-pə-tor-ee). Evidence showing or tending to show one's involvement in a crime.

indispensable evidence. Evidence without which a particular fact cannot be proved.

insufficient evidence. Evidence that is inadequate to prove something, so that no presumption — even a conditional one — is raised.

intrinsic evidence. **1.** Evidence brought out by the examination of the witness testifying. **2.** Evidence existing within a writing. Cf. *extrinsic evidence*.

judicial evidence. Evidence produced in court, consisting of all facts brought to the attention of or admitted into evidence before the tribunal.

legal evidence. All admissible evidence, both oral and documentary, of such a character that it reasonably and substantially proves the point rather than merely raising suspicion or conjecture.

material evidence. Evidence having some logical connection with the consequential facts or the issues. Cf. *relevant evidence*.

mathematical evidence. Loosely, evidence that establishes its conclusions with absolute certainty.

medical evidence. Evidence furnished by a doctor, nurse, or other qualified medical person testifying in a professional capacity as an expert, or by a standard treatise on medicine or surgery.

moral evidence. Loosely, evidence that depends on a belief, rather than complete and absolute proof. • Generally, moral evidence is testimonial.

multiple evidence. Evidence with probative value on more than one issue but usu. admitted into evidence for one specific purpose.

negative evidence. Evidence suggesting that an alleged fact does not exist, such as a witness's testifying that he or she did not see an event occur. • Negative evidence is generally regarded to be weaker than positive evidence, because a positive assertion that a witness saw an event is a stronger statement than an assertion that a witness did not see it. But a negative assertion will sometimes be considered positive evidence, depending on the witness's opportunity to see the event. For instance, testimony that the witness watched the entire game and saw no riot in the stands is stronger than testimony stating only that the witness did not see a riot. Cf. *direct evidence* (1).

newly discovered evidence. Evidence existing at the time of a motion or trial but then unknown to a party, who, upon later discovering it, may assert it as grounds for reconsideration or a new trial.

opinion evidence. A witness's belief, thought, or inference about a disputed fact. Fed. R. Evid. 701–705. See OPINION (3); OPINION RULE.

original evidence. **1.** A witness's statement that he or she perceived a fact in issue by one of the five senses, or that the witness was in a particular physical or mental state. Cf. HEARSAY. **2.** See *best evidence*.

parol evidence (pə-**rohl** *or* **par**-əl). **1.** Evidence given orally. **2.** See *extrinsic evidence* (1). See PAROL-EVIDENCE RULE.

partial evidence. Evidence that establishes one of a series of facts.

preappointed evidence. Evidence prescribed in advance (as by statute) for the proof of certain facts.

preliminary evidence. Evidence that is necessary to begin a hearing or trial and that may be received conditionally in anticipation of other evidence linking it to issues in the case. Fed. R. Evid. 104.

presumptive evidence. Evidence deemed true and sufficient unless discredited by other evidence.

prima facie evidence (**prɪ**-mə **fay**-shə). Evidence that will establish a fact or sustain a judgment unless contradictory evidence is produced.

privileged evidence. Evidence that is exempt from production to an opposing party (with certain limited exceptions) because it is covered by one or more statutory and common-law protections, such as the attorney–client privilege. See *privileged communication* under COMMUNICATION.

probative evidence (**proh**-bə-tiv). Evidence that tends to prove or disprove a point in issue.

proffered evidence (**prof**-ərd). **1.** Evidence that is offered to the court to obtain a ruling on its admissibility. **2.** Evidence whose admissibility depends on the existence or nonexistence of a preliminary fact.

prospectant evidence (prə-**spek**-tənt). Evidence that, before someone does an act, suggests that the person might or might not do the act. • This evidence typically falls into any of five categories: (1) moral character or disposition, (2) physical and mental capacity, (3) habit or custom, (4) emotion or motive, and (5) plan, design, or intention.

real evidence. **1.** Physical evidence (such as a knife wound) that itself plays a direct part in the incident in question. **2.** See *demonstrative evidence*.

rebuttal evidence. Evidence offered to disprove or contradict the evidence presented by an opposing party.

relevant evidence. Evidence tending to prove or disprove a matter in issue. • Relevant evidence is both probative and material and is admissible unless excluded by a specific statute or rule. Fed. R. Evid. 401–403. Cf. *material evidence*.

reputation evidence. Evidence of what one is thought by others to be. • Reputation evidence may be introduced as proof of character when character is in issue or is used circumstantially. Fed. R. Evid. 405(a). Cf. *character evidence*.

retrospectant evidence (re-trə-**spek**-tənt). Evidence that, although it occurs after an act has been done, suggests that the alleged doer of the act actually did it.

satisfactory evidence. Evidence that is sufficient to satisfy an unprejudiced mind seeking the truth.

scientific evidence. Testimony or opinion evidence that draws on technical or specialized knowledge and relies on scientific method for its evidentiary value. See DAUBERT TEST.

secondary evidence. Evidence that is inferior to the primary or best evidence and that becomes admissible when the primary or best evidence is lost or inaccessible. • Examples include a copy of a lost instrument or testimony regarding the contents of a lost document. Cf. *best evidence*.

signature evidence. Highly distinctive evidence of a person's prior bad acts. • While ordinarily inadmissible, signature evidence will be admitted if it shows, for example, that two crimes were committed through the same planning, design, scheme, or modus operandi, and in such a way that the prior act and the current act are uniquely identifiable as those of the defendant.

slight evidence. An inconsiderable or trifling quantity of evidence; esp., the small amount sufficient for a rational fact-finder to conclude that the state failed to disprove an affirmative defense beyond a reasonable doubt. See SLIGHT-EVIDENCE RULE.

state's evidence. Testimony provided by one criminal defendant — under a promise of immunity or reduced sentence — against another criminal defendant. See TURN STATE'S EVIDENCE.

substantial evidence. Evidence that a reasonable mind would accept as adequate to support a conclusion; evidence beyond a scintilla. See SUBSTANTIAL-EVIDENCE RULE.

substantive evidence (səb-stən-tiv). Evidence offered to support a fact in issue, as opposed to impeachment or corroborating evidence.

tainted evidence. Evidence that is inadmissible because it was directly or indirectly obtained by illegal means. See FRUIT-OF-THE-POISONOUS-TREE DOCTRINE.

testimonial evidence. A person's testimony offered to prove the truth of the matter asserted; esp., evidence elicited from a witness. Cf. *demonstrative evidence.*

traditionary evidence. Evidence derived from a deceased person's former statements or reputation. • Traditionary evidence is admissible to prove ancestry, ancient boundaries, or similar facts, usually when no living witnesses are available to testify.

unwritten evidence. Evidence given orally, in court or by deposition.

evidence code. A codified set of statutory provisions governing the admissibility of evidence and the burden of proof at hearings and trials.

evidence of title. The means by which the ownership of land is satisfactorily demonstrated within a given jurisdiction. See DEED.

evidentiary (ev-i-**den**-shə-ree), *adj.* **1.** Having the quality of evidence; constituting evidence; evidencing. **2.** Pertaining to the rules of evidence or the evidence in a particular case.

evidentiary fact. See FACT.

evidentiary hearing. See HEARING.

evince, *vb.* To show, indicate, or reveal.

ex. 1. Former. **2.** Without. **3.** From. **4.** (*usu. cap.*) *abbr.* Exhibit. **5.** *abbr.* Example.

exaction, *n.* **1.** The act of demanding more money than is due; extortion. **2.** A fee, reward, or other compensation arbitrarily or wrongfully demanded. — **exact,** *vb.*

examination. 1. The questioning of a witness under oath. See DIRECT EXAMINATION; CROSS-EXAMINATION. **2.** *Bankruptcy.* The questioning of a bankrupt, esp. at the first meeting of creditors, concerning such matters as the bankrupt's debts and assets. **3.** *Patents.* An inquiry made at the Patent and Trademark Office, upon application for a patent, into the alleged invention's novelty and utility, and whether it interferes with any other patented invention. **4.** PRELIMINARY HEARING. **5.** A test, such as a bar examination.

examiner. 1. One authorized to conduct an examination; esp., a person appointed by the court to administer an oath and take testimony. See MASTER (2). **2.** A patent officer responsible for determining the patentability of an invention submitted to the patent office. **3.** MEDICAL EXAMINER.

examining board. An appointed group of public officials responsible for conducting the tests required by those applying for occupational and professional licenses.

examining court. See COURT.

ex ante (eks **an**-tee), *adj.* & *adv.* [Latin "from before"] Based on assumption and prediction; subjective; prospective <from an *ex ante* perspective>. Cf. EX POST.

ex cathedra (eks kə-**thee**-drə *or* **kath**-ə-drə), *adv.* & *adj.* [Latin "from the chair"] By virtue of one's high office or position; with authority.

exception, *n.* **1.** A formal objection to a court's ruling by a party who wants to preserve the objection for appeal. • In federal courts and most state courts, the term *exception* has been superseded by *objection*.

dilatory exception (**dil**-ə-tor-ee). An exception intended to delay but not dismiss an action.

general exception. **1.** An objection pointing out a substantive defect in an opponent's pleading, such as the insufficiency of the claim or the court's lack of subject-matter jurisdiction; an objection to a pleading for want of substance. Cf. SPECIAL EXCEPTION (1). **2.** An objection in which the excepting party does not specify the grounds of the objection.

peremptory exception. A defensive pleading asserting that no legal remedy exists for the plaintiff's alleged injury, that res judicata or prescription bars the claim, or that an indispensable party has not been included in the litigation.

special exception. See SPECIAL EXCEPTION (1).

2. Something that is excluded from a rule's operation.

statutory exception. A provision in a statute exempting certain persons or conduct from the statute's operation.

3. The retention of an existing right or interest, by and for the grantor, in real property being granted to another. Cf. RESERVATION (1). — **except,** *vb.*

excess condemnation. See CONDEMNATION.

excess insurance. See INSURANCE.

excessive bail. See BAIL.

Excessive Fines Clause. The clause of the Eighth Amendment to the U.S. Constitution prohibiting the imposition of excessive fines.

excessive force. See FORCE.

excessive punishment. See PUNISHMENT.

excessive sentence. See SENTENCE.

excessive verdict. See VERDICT.

excess of jurisdiction. 1. A court's acting beyond the limits of its power, usu. in one of three ways: (1) when the court has no power to deal with the kind of matter at issue, (2) when the court has no power to deal with the particular person concerned, or (3) when the judgment or order issued is of a kind that the court has no power to issue. **2.** A court's departure from recognized and established requirements of law, despite apparent adherence to procedural form, the effect of which is a deprivation of one's constitutional right.

excess of privilege. 1. An excessive publication of a privileged statement — that is, beyond the limits of the privilege. **2.** The improper and malicious use of the privilege to publish a statement.

excess-profits tax. See TAX.

exchange, *n.* **1.** The act of transferring interests, each in consideration for the other. **2.** The payment of a debt using a bill of exchange or credit rather than money. **3.** An organization that brings together buyers and sellers of securities, commodities, and the like to promote uniformity in the customs and usages of merchants, to facilitate the speedy adjustment of business disputes, to gather and disseminate valuable commercial and economic information, and to secure to its members the benefits of cooperation in the furtherance of their legitimate pursuits. **4.** The building or hall where members of an exchange meet every business day to buy and sell for themselves, or as brokers for their customers, for present and future delivery. See SECURITIES EXCHANGE. — **exchange,** *vb.*

excise, *n.* A tax imposed on the manufacture, sale, or use of goods (such as a cigarette tax), or on an occupation or activity (such as a license tax or an attorney occupation fee). Cf. *income tax* and *property tax* under TAX.

excited utterance. A statement about a startling event made under the stress and excitement of the event. • An excited utterance may be admissible as a hearsay exception. Fed. R. Evid. 803(2). Cf. PRESENT SENSE IMPRESSION.

excludable, *adj.* (Of evidence) subject to exclusion <excludable hearsay>.

exclusion, *n.* **1.** *Tax.* An item of income excluded from gross income.

annual exclusion. The amount (such as $10,000) allowed as nontaxable gift income during the calendar year. IRC (26 USCA) § 2503.

2. *Evidence.* A trial judge's determination that an item offered as evidence may not be presented to the trier of fact (esp. the jury). **3.** *Insurance.* An insurance-policy provision that excepts certain events or conditions from coverage. — **exclude,** *vb.* — **exclusionary,** *adj.*

exclusionary hearing. See HEARING.

exclusionary rule. 1. *Evidence.* Any rule that excludes or suppresses evidence that does not satisfy a minimum standard of probative value. **2.** *Criminal procedure.* A rule that excludes or suppresses evidence obtained in violation of an accused person's constitutional rights. See FRUIT-OF-THE-POISONOUS-TREE DOCTRINE; GOOD-FAITH EXCEPTION.

exclusive agency. See AGENCY (1).

exclusive control. Under the doctrine of res ipsa loquitur, a defendant's sole management of and responsibility for the instrumentality causing harm. • Exclusive control is a prerequisite to the doctrine's applicability. See RES IPSA LOQUITUR.

exclusive-dealing arrangement. An agreement requiring a buyer to purchase all needed goods from one seller. See *requirements contract* under CONTRACT.

exclusive evidence. See EVIDENCE.

exclusive jurisdiction. See JURISDICTION.

exclusive license. See LICENSE.

exclusive possession. See POSSESSION.

ex contractu (eks kən-**trak**-t[y]oo). [Latin "from a contract"] *Jargon.* Arising from a contract <action *ex contractu*>. Cf. EX DELICTO.

exculpate (**ek**-skəl-payt *or* ek-**skəl**-payt), *vb.* To free from blame or accusation. — **exculpation** (ek-skəl-**pay**-shən), *n.* — **exculpatory** (ek-**skəl**-pə-tor-ee), *adj.* Cf. EXONERATE (1).

exculpatory clause. A contractual provision relieving a party from any liability resulting from a negligent or wrongful act. See EXEMPTION CLAUSE.

exculpatory evidence. See EVIDENCE.

exculpatory-no doctrine. *Criminal law.* The principle that a person cannot be charged with making a false statement for falsely denying guilt in response to an investigator's question. • This doctrine is based on the Fifth Amendment right against self-incrimination.

excusable, *adj.* (Of an illegal act or omission) not punishable under the specific circumstances.

excusable homicide. See HOMICIDE.

excusable neglect. See NEGLECT.

excuse (eks-**kyoos**), *n.* **1.** A reason that justifies an act or omission or that relieves a person of a duty. **2.** *Criminal law.* A defense that arises because the defendant is not blameworthy for having acted in a way that would otherwise be criminal. Cf. JUSTIFICATION (2). — **excuse** (ek-**skyooz**), *vb.* — **excusatory** (ek-**skyooz**-ə-tor-ee), *adj.*

excuss (ek-**skəs**), *vb.* To seize and detain by law.

ex delicto (eks də-**lik**-toh). [Latin "from a tort"] *Jargon.* Arising from a tort <action *ex delicto*>. Cf. IN DELICTO; EX CONTRACTU.

execute, *vb.* **1.** To perform or complete (a contract or duty). **2.** To change (as a legal interest) from one form to another. **3.** *Jargon.* To make (a legal document) valid by signing; to bring (a legal document) into its final, legally enforceable form. **4.** To put to death, esp. by legal sentence. **5.** To enforce and collect on (a money judgment).

executed, *adj.* **1.** (Of a document) that has been signed <an executed will>. **2.** That has been done, given, or performed <executed consideration>.

executed contract. See CONTRACT.

executed trust. See TRUST.

execution, *n.* **1.** The act of carrying out or putting into effect (as a court order). **2.** Validation of a written instrument, such as a contract or will, by fulfilling the necessary legal requirements. **3.** Judicial enforcement of a money judgment, usu. by seizing and selling the judgment debtor's property. **4.** A court order directing a sheriff or other officer to enforce a judgment, usu. by seizing and selling the judgment debtor's property. **5.** *Criminal law.* The carrying out of a death sentence. — **execute,** *vb.*

execution clause. The part of a deed containing the date, seal (if required), and signatures of the grantor, grantor's spouse, and witnesses.

executive, *n.* **1.** The branch of government responsible for effecting and enforcing laws; the person or persons who constitute this branch. Cf. LEGISLATURE; JUDICIARY (1).

chief executive. The head of the executive branch of a government, such as the President of the United States.

2. A corporate officer at the upper levels of management.

executive branch. The branch of government charged with administering and carrying out the law; EXECUTIVE (1). Cf. JUDICIAL BRANCH; LEGISLATIVE BRANCH.

executive immunity. See IMMUNITY (1).

executive order. An order issued by or on behalf of the President, usu. intended to direct or instruct the actions of executive agencies or government officials, or to set policies for the executive branch to follow. — Abbr. ex. ord.

executive power. *Constitutional law.* The power to see that the laws are duly executed and enforced. • Under federal law, this power is vested in the President; in the states, it is vested in the governors. The President's enumerated powers are found in the U.S. Constitution, art. II, § 2; governors' executive powers are provided for in state constitutions. The other two great powers of government are the legislative power and the judicial power.

executive privilege. See PRIVILEGE (3).

executor, *n.* **1.** (**ek**-sə-kyoo-tər) One who performs or carries out some act. **2.** (eg-**zek**-yə-tər) A person named by a testator to carry out the provisions in the testator's will. Cf. ADMINISTRATOR (1).

acting executor. One who assumes the role of executor — usu. temporarily — but is not the legally appointed executor or the executor-in-fact.

executor de son tort (də sawn [*or* son] **tor**[t]). [Law French "executor of his own wrong"] A person who, without legal authority, takes on the responsibility to act as an executor or administrator of a decedent's property, usu. to the detriment of the estate's beneficiaries or creditors.

executor lucratus (loo-**kray**-təs). An executor who has assets of the testator, the latter having become liable by wrongfully interfering with another's property.

general executor. An executor who has the power to administer a decedent's entire estate until its final settlement.

independent executor. An executor who, unlike an ordinary executor, can administer the estate with very little supervision by the probate court.

joint executor. One of two or more persons named in a will as executor of an estate.

limited executor. An executor whose appointment is restricted in some way, such as time, place, or subject matter.

special executor. An executor whose power is limited to a portion of the decedent's estate.

substituted executor. An executor appointed to act in the place of an executor who cannot or will not perform the required duties.

executory (eg-**zek**-yə-tor-ee), *adj.* **1.** Taking full effect at a future time <executory judgment>. **2.** To be performed at a future time; yet to be completed <executory contract>.

executory bequest. See BEQUEST.

executory contract. See CONTRACT.

executory devise. See DEVISE.

executory interest. A future interest, held by a third person, that either cuts off another's interest or begins after the natural termination of a preceding estate. Cf. REMAINDER.

executory judgment. See JUDGMENT.

executory limitation. See LIMITATION.

executory trust. See TRUST.

executory unilateral accord. An offer to enter a contract; OFFER (2).

exemplar (eg-**zem**-plər *or* -plahr), *n.* **1.** An ideal or typical example; a standard specimen. **2.** Nontestimonial identification evidence, such as fingerprints, voiceprints, and DNA samples. See VOICE EXEMPLAR.

exemplary, *adj.* **1.** Serving as an ideal example; commendable. **2.** Serving as a warning or deterrent; admonitory.

exemplary damages. See *punitive damages* under DAMAGES.

exemplification, *n.* An official transcript of a public record, authenticated as a true copy for use as evidence. — **exemplify,** *vb.*

exempli gratia (eg-**zem**-plɪ **gray**-shee-ə *or* ek-**sem**-plee **grah**-tee-ə). [Latin] For example; for instance. — Abbr. e.g.

exempt, *adj.* Free or released from a duty or liability to which others are held. — **exempt,** *vb.* — **exemptive,** *adj.*

exempt income. See INCOME.

exemption. 1. Freedom from a duty, liability, or other requirement. See IMMUNITY. **2.** A privilege given to a judgment debtor by law, allowing the debtor to retain certain property without liability. **3.** *Tax.* An amount allowed as a deduction from adjusted gross income, used to determine taxable income. Cf. DEDUCTION (2).

> ***dependency exemption.*** A tax exemption granted to an individual taxpayer for each dependent whose gross income is less than the exemption amount and for each child who is younger than 19 or, if a student, younger than 24.
>
> ***personal exemption.*** An amount allowed as a deduction from an individual taxpayer's adjusted gross income.

exemption clause. A contractual provision providing that a party will not be liable for damages for which that party would otherwise have ordinarily been liable. Cf. INDEMNITY CLAUSE.

exemption law. A law describing what property of a debtor cannot be attached by a judgment creditor or trustee in bankruptcy to satisfy a debt. See EXEMPT PROPERTY (1).

exempt property. 1. A debtor's holdings and possessions that, by law, a creditor cannot attach to satisfy a debt. See HOMESTEAD. **2.** Personal property that a surviving spouse is automatically entitled to receive from the decedent's estate.

exercise, *vb.* **1.** To make use of; to put into action <exercise the right to vote>. **2.** To implement the terms of; to execute <exercise the option to buy the commodities>. — **exercise,** *n.*

exercise of judgment. The use of sound discretion — that is, discretion exercised with regard to what is right and equitable rather than arbitrarily or willfully.

ex facie (eks **fay**-shə *or* -shee). [Latin "from the face"] Apparently; evidently; facially.

ex facto (eks **fak**-toh). [Latin "from a fact"] From or in consequence of a fact or action; actually; DE FACTO.

ex gratia (eks **gray**-shee-ə *or* **grah**-tee-ə). [Latin "by favor"] As a favor; not legally necessary.

ex gratia payment. A payment not legally required; esp., an insurance payment not required to be made under an insurance policy.

exhaustion of remedies. The doctrine that, if an administrative remedy is provided by statute, a claimant must seek relief first from the administrative body before judicial relief is available.

exhaustion of state remedies. The doctrine that an available state remedy must be exhausted in certain types of cases before a party can gain access to a federal court.

exhibit, *n.* **1.** A document, record, or other tangible object formally introduced as evidence in court. **2.** A document attached to and made part of a pleading, motion, contract, or other instrument.

exhibitionism, *n.* The indecent display of one's body. — **exhibitionist,** *adj.* & *n.*

exhibit list. A pretrial filing that identifies by number and description the exhibits a party intends to offer into evidence at trial.

exhumation (eks-hyoo-**may**-shən *or* eg-zyoo-), *n.* The removal from the earth of something buried, esp. a human corpse; disinterment.

exigency (ek-sə-jən-see), *n.* A state of urgency; a situation requiring immediate action.

exigent, *adj.* Requiring immediate action or aid; urgent.

exigent circumstances. See CIRCUMSTANCE.

exigent search. See SEARCH.

exile, *n.* **1.** Expulsion from a country, esp. from the country of one's origin or longtime residence; banishment. **2.** A person who has been banished. — **exile,** *vb.*

exit, *n.* **1.** A way out. See EGRESS. **2.** In a docket entry, an issuance of something (as a writ or process). • For example, *exit attachment* denotes that a writ of attachment has been issued in the case. — **exit,** *vb.*

ex officio (eks ə-**fish**-ee-oh), *adv.* & *adj.* [Latin] By virtue or because of an office; by virtue of the authority implied by office.

ex officio justice. A judge who serves on a commission or board only because the law requires the presence of a judge rather than because the judge was selected for the position.

ex officio service. A service that the law imposes on an official by virtue of the office held, such as a local sheriff's duty to perform marriage ceremonies.

exonerate (eg-**zon**-ə-rayt), *vb.* **1.** To free from responsibility. Cf. EXCULPATE. **2.** To free from encumbrances. — **exoneration,** *n.* — **exonerative** (eg-**zon**-ər-ay-tiv *or* -ə-tiv), *adj.*

exonerative fact. See FACT.

ex. ord. (*often cap.*) *abbr.* EXECUTIVE ORDER.

exordium (eg-**zor**-dee-əm). [Latin] See INTRODUCTORY CLAUSE.

ex parte (eks **pahr**-tee), *adv.* [Latin "from the part"] On or from one party only, usu. without notice to or argument from the adverse party <the judge conducted the hearing ex parte>. Cf. INTER PARTES.

ex parte, *adj.* Done or made at the instance and for the benefit of one party only, and without notice to, or argument by, any person adversely interested; of or relating to court action taken by one party without notice to the other, usu. for temporary or emergency relief <an ex parte hearing> <an ex parte injunction>.

ex parte communication. A generally prohibited communication between counsel and the court when opposing counsel is not present.

ex parte divorce. See DIVORCE.

ex parte injunction. See INJUNCTION.

ex parte motion. See MOTION.

ex parte order. See ORDER.

ex parte proceeding. See PROCEEDING.

expatriate (eks-**pay**-tree-it), *n.* An expatriated person; esp., a person who lives permanently in a foreign country.

expatriate (eks-**pay**-tree-ayt), *vb.* **1.** To withdraw (oneself) from residence in or allegiance to one's native country; to leave one's home country to live elsewhere. **2.** To banish or exile (a person). — **expatriation,** *n.*

expectancy, *n.* **1.** *Property.* An estate with a reversion, a remainder, or an executory interest. **2.** *Wills & estates.* The possibility that an heir apparent, an heir presumptive, or a presumptive next-of-kin will acquire property by devolution on intestacy, or the possibility that a presumptive legatee or devisee will acquire property by will.

expectant, *adj.* Having a relation to, or being dependent on, a contingency; CONTINGENT.

expectant heir. See HEIR.

expectation, *n.* **1.** The act of looking forward; anticipation. **2.** A basis on which something is expected to happen; esp., the prospect of receiving wealth, honors, or the like.

expectation damages. See DAMAGES.

expectation interest. See INTEREST (2).

expectation of privacy. A belief in the existence of the right to be free of governmental intrusion in regard to a particular place or thing.

expediment (ek-**sped**-ə-mənt), *n.* The whole of one's goods and chattels.

expel, *vb.* To drive out or away; to eject, esp. with force. See EJECT; EVICT.

expenditure. **1.** The act or process of paying out; disbursement. **2.** A sum paid out.

expense, *n.* An expenditure of money, time, labor, or resources to accomplish a result; esp., a business expenditure chargeable against revenue for a specific period. — **expense,** *vb.* Cf. COST (1).

accrued expense. An expense incurred but not yet paid.

business expense. An expense incurred to operate and promote a business; esp., an expenditure made to further the business in the taxable year in which the expense is incurred.

capital expense. An expense made by a business to provide a long-term benefit; a capital expenditure.

deferred expense. A cost incurred by a business when the business expects to benefit from that cost over a period beyond the current year.

educational expense. A deductible expense incurred either to maintain or improve an existing job skill or to meet a legally imposed job requirement.

extraordinary expense. An unusual or infrequent expense, such as a write-off of goodwill or a large judgment. • As used in a constitutional provision authorizing a state to incur extraordinary expenses, the term denotes an expense for the general welfare compelled by an unforeseen condition such as a natural disaster or war.

funeral expense. (*usu. pl.*) An expense necessarily and reasonably incurred in procuring the burial, cremation, or other disposition of a corpse, including the funeral or other ceremonial rite, a coffin and vault, a monument or tombstone, a burial plot and its care, and a wake.

general administrative expense. (*usu. pl.*) An expense incurred in running a business, as distinguished from an expense incurred in manufacturing or selling; overhead.

medical expense. **1.** An expense for medical treatment or healthcare, such as drug costs and health-insurance premiums. **2.** (*usu. pl.*) In civil litigation, any one of many possible medical costs that the plaintiff has sustained because of the defendant's allegedly wrongful act, including charges for visits to physicians' offices, medical procedures, hospital bills, medicine, and recuperative therapy.

moving expense. An expense incurred in changing one's residence.

operating expense. An expense incurred in running a business and producing output.

ordinary and necessary expense. An expense that is normal or usual and helpful or appropriate for the operation of a particular trade or business and that is paid or incurred during the taxable year.

organizational expense. An expense incurred while setting up a corporation or other entity.

out-of-pocket expense. An expense paid from one's own funds.

prepaid expense. An expense (such as rent, interest, or insurance) that is paid before the due date or before a service is rendered.

travel expense. An expense (such as for meals, lodging, and transportation) incurred while away from home in the pursuit of a trade or business. See TAX HOME.

expenses of administration. Expenses incurred by a decedent's representatives in administering the estate.

expenses of receivership. Expenses incurred by a receiver in conducting the business, including rent and fees incurred by the receiver's counsel and by any master, appraiser, and auditor.

expense stop. A lease provision establishing the maximum expenses to be paid by the landlord, beyond which the tenant must bear all remaining expenses.

expert, *n.* A person who, through education or experience, has developed skill or knowledge in a particular subject, so that he or she may form an opinion that will assist the fact-finder. Fed. R. Evid. 702. — **expertise** (ek-spər-**teez**), *n.* See DAUBERT TEST.

consulting expert. An expert who, though retained by a party, is not expected to be called as a witness at trial. • A consulting expert's opinions are generally exempt from the scope of discovery. Fed. R. Civ. P. 26(b)(4)(B).

impartial expert. An expert who is appointed by the court to present an unbiased opinion. Fed. R. Evid. 706.

testifying expert. An expert who is identified by a party as a potential witness at trial. • As a part of initial disclosures in federal court, a party must provide to all other parties a wide range of information about a testifying expert's qualifications and opinion, including all information that the witness considered in forming the opinion. Fed. R. Civ. P. 26(a)(2)(b).

expert evidence. See EVIDENCE.

expert witness. See WITNESS.

expiration date. The date on which an offer, option, or the like ceases to exist.

exploitation, *n.* The act of taking advantage of something; esp., the act of taking unjust advantage of another for one's own benefit. — **exploit,** *vb.* — **exploitative,** *adj.*

export, *n.* **1.** A product or service created in one country and transported to another. **2.** The process of transporting products or services to another country.

export declaration. A document — required by federal law — containing details of an export shipment.

exposé (ek-spoh-**zay**), *n.* [French] **1.** A statement or account; an explanation. • In diplomatic language, the term describes a written explanation of the reasons for a certain act or course of conduct. **2.** Exposure of discreditable matter.

expository jurisprudence. See JURISPRUDENCE.

expository statute. See STATUTE.

ex post, *adj.* [Latin "from after"] Based on knowledge and fact; objective; retrospective. Cf. EX ANTE.

ex post facto (eks pohst **fak**-toh), *adv.* [Latin "from a thing done afterward"] After the fact; retroactively.

ex post facto, *adj.* Done or made after the fact; having retroactive force or effect.

Ex Post Facto Clause. One of two clauses in the U.S. Constitution forbidding the enactment of ex post facto laws. U.S. Const. art. I, § 9, cl. 3; art. I, § 10, cl. 1.

ex post facto law. A law that applies retroactively, esp. in a way that negatively affects a person's rights, as by criminalizing an action that was legal when it was committed.

exposure. The amount of liability or other risk to which a person is subject.

express, *adj.* Clearly and unmistakably communicated; directly stated. — **expressly,** *adv.* Cf. IMPLIED.

express abrogation. The repeal of a law or provision by a later one that refers directly to it; abrogation by express provision or enactment.

express agency. See AGENCY.

express assent. See ASSENT.

express authority. See AUTHORITY (1).

express condition. See CONDITION (2).

express consent. See CONSENT.

express contract. See CONTRACT.

express covenant. See COVENANT (1).

express dedication. See DEDICATION.

expressed, *adj.* Declared in direct terms; stated in words; not left to inference or implication.

expressio unius est exclusio alterius (ek-**spres[h]**-ee-oh yoo-**nI**-əs est eks-**kloo**-zhee-oh al-tə-**rI**-əs). [Law Latin] A canon of construction holding that to express or include one thing implies the exclusion of the other, or of the alternative. • For example, the rule that "each citizen is entitled to vote" implies that noncitizens are not entitled to vote. Cf. EJUSDEM GENERIS; NOSCITUR A SOCIIS.

express malice. See MALICE.

express notice. See NOTICE.

express repeal. See REPEAL.

express republication. A testator's repeating of the acts essential to a will's valid execution, with the avowed intent of republishing the will. See REPUBLICATION (2).

express trust. See TRUST.

express waiver. See WAIVER.

express warranty. See WARRANTY (2).

expropriation, *n.* **1.** A governmental taking or modification of an individual's property rights, esp. by eminent domain; CONDEMNATION (2). Cf. APPROPRIATION. **2.** A voluntary surrender of rights or claims; the act of renouncing or divesting oneself of something previously claimed as one's own. — **expropriate,** *vb.* — **expropriator,** *n.*

expulsion, *n.* An ejectment or banishment, either through depriving a person of a benefit or by forcibly evicting a person. — **expulsive,** *adj.*

expunge (ek-**spənj**), *vb.* To erase or destroy. — **expungement** (ek-**spənj**-mənt), *n.* — **expunction** (ek-**spəngk**-shən), *n.*

expungement of record. The removal of a conviction (esp. for a first offense) from a person's criminal record.

expurgation (ek-spər-**gay**-shən), *n.* The act or practice of purging or cleansing, as by publishing a book without its obscene passages. — **expurgate** (**eks**-pər-gayt), *vb.* — **expurgator** (**eks**-pər-gay-tər), *n.*

ex rel. *abbr.* [Latin *ex relatione* "by or on the relation of"] On the relation or information of. • A suit *ex rel.* is typically brought by the government upon the application of a private party (called a *relator*) who is interested in the matter. See RELATOR (1).

extended family. See FAMILY.

extended-term insurance. See INSURANCE.

extended warranty. See WARRANTY (2).

extension, *n.* **1.** The continuation of the same contract for a specified period. Cf. RENEWAL. **2.** *Patents.* A continuation of the life of a patent for an additional statutorily allowed period. **3.** *Tax.* A period of additional time to file an income-tax return beyond its due date. **4.** A period of additional time to take an action, make a decision, accept an offer, or complete a task. — **extend,** *vb.*

extension agreement. An agreement providing additional time for the basic agreement to be performed.

extensive interpretation. See INTERPRETATION.

extenuate (ek-**sten**-yoo-ayt), *vb.* To make less severe; to mitigate. — **extenuation** (ek-sten-yoo-**ay**-shən), *n.*

external act. See ACT.

externality. (*usu. pl.*) A social or monetary consequence or side effect of one's economic activity, causing another to benefit without paying or to suffer without compensation.

negative externality. An externality that is detrimental to another, such as water pollution created by a nearby factory.

positive externality. An externality that benefits another, such as the advantage received by a neighborhood when a homeowner attractively landscapes the property.

extinct, *adj.* **1.** No longer in existence or use. **2.** (Of a debt) lacking a claimant.

extinguishment, *n.* The cessation or cancellation of some right or interest. — **extinguish,** *vb.*

extinguishment of lien. A lien's discharge by operation of law.

extirpation (ek-stər-**pay**-shən), *n.* **1.** The act of completely removing or destroying something. **2.** Damage to land intentionally done by a person who has lost the right to the land.

extortion, *n.* **1.** The offense committed by a public official who illegally obtains property under the color of office; esp., an official's collection of an unlawful fee. **2.** The act or practice of obtaining something or compelling some action by illegal means, as by force or coercion. — **extort,** *vb.* — **extortionate,** *adj.*

extra (**ek**-strə), *prep.* [Latin] Beyond; except; without; out of; additional.

extradite. 1. To surrender or deliver (a fugitive) to another jurisdiction. **2.** To obtain the surrender of (a fugitive) from another jurisdiction.

extradition (ek-strə-**dish**-ən). The official surrender of an alleged criminal by one state or nation to another having jurisdiction over the crime charged; the return of a fugitive from justice, regardless of consent, by the authorities where the fugitive resides. — **extradite** (ek-strə-dɪt), *vb.* Cf. RENDITION (2).

Extradition Clause. The clause of the U.S. Constitution providing that any accused person who flees to another state must, on request of the executive authority of the state where the crime was committed, be returned to that state. U.S. Const. art. IV, § 2, cl. 2.

extradition treaty. A treaty governing the preconditions for, and exceptions to, the surrender of a fugitive from justice by the fugitive's country of residence to another country claiming criminal jurisdiction over the fugitive.

extradition warrant. See WARRANT.

extrahazardous, *adj.* Especially or unusually dangerous.

extrajudicial, *adj.* Outside court; outside the functioning of the court system.

extrajudicial admission. See ADMISSION.

extrajudicial confession. See CONFESSION.

extrajudicial evidence. See EVIDENCE.

extrajudicial oath. See OATH.

extrajudicial statement. Any utterance made outside of court.

extralegal, *adj.* Beyond the province of law.

extraneous offense. See OFFENSE.

extraneous question. A question that is beyond or beside the point to be decided.

extraordinary circumstances. See CIRCUMSTANCE.

extraordinary expense. See EXPENSE.

extraordinary gain. See GAIN (3).

extraordinary loss. See LOSS.

extraordinary remedy. See REMEDY.

extraordinary repair. As used in a lease, a repair that is made necessary by some unusual or unforeseen occurrence that does not destroy the building but merely renders it less suited to its intended use; a repair that is beyond the usual, customary, or regular kind.

extraordinary writ. See WRIT.

extrapolate (ek-**strap**-ə-layt), *vb.* **1.** To estimate an unknown value or quantity on the basis of the known range, esp. by statistical methods. **2.** To deduce an unknown legal principle from a known case. **3.** To speculate about possible results, based on known facts. — **extrapolative** (-lay-tiv *or* -lə-tiv), **extrapolatory** (-lə-tor-ee), *adj.* — **extrapolator** (-lay-tər), *n.* — **extrapolation** (ek-strap-ə-**lay**-shən), *n.*

extraterritorial, *adj.* Beyond the geographic limits of a particular jurisdiction.

extraterritorial jurisdiction. See JURISDICTION.

extreme cruelty. See CRUELTY.

extrinsic, *adj.* From outside sources.

extrinsic evidence. See EVIDENCE.

extrinsic fraud. See FRAUD.

eye of the law. The law as a personified thinker; legal contemplation.

eyewitness. One who personally observes an event. Cf. EARWITNESS.

eyewitness identification. A naming or description by which one who has seen an event testifies from memory about the person or persons involved.

F

F. *abbr.* The first series of the *Federal Reporter*, which includes federal decisions (trial and appellate) from 1880 to 1924.

F.2d. *abbr.* The second series of the *Federal Reporter*, which includes federal appellate decisions from 1924 to 1993.

F.3d. *abbr.* The third series of the *Federal Reporter*, which includes federal appellate decisions from 1993.

FAA. *abbr.* **1.** FEDERAL AVIATION ADMINISTRATION. **2.** The Federal Arbitration Act, 9 USCA §§ 1–16.

fabricate, *vb.* To invent, forge, or devise falsely. • To fabricate a story is to create a plausible version of events that is advantageous to the person relating those events. The term is softer than *lie*. See LIE (1).

fabricated evidence. See EVIDENCE.

face, *n.* **1.** The surface of anything, esp. the front, upper, or outer part <the face of a clock>. **2.** By extension, the apparent or explicit part of a writing or record <the fraud must appear on the face of the record>. **3.** The inscribed side of a document, instrument, or judgment <the contract appeared valid on its face>.

facial, *adj.* Apparent; on the face of things; prima facie.

facial attack. A challenge to the sufficiency of a complaint, such as a motion to dismiss in federal practice.

facial challenge. See CHALLENGE (1).

facially sufficient, *adj.* (Of a document) appearing valid on its face.

facially void. See VOID.

facilitate, *vb. Criminal law.* To make the commission of a crime easier. — **facilitation,** *n.* — **facilitator,** *n.*

facsimile (fak-**sim**-ə-lee). **1.** An exact copy. **2.** FAX.

facsimile signature. See SIGNATURE.

fact. 1. Something that actually exists; an aspect of reality. **2.** An actual or alleged event or circumstance, as distinguished from its legal effect, consequence, or interpretation. **3.** An evil deed; a crime.

adjudicative fact (ə-**joo**-di-kay-tiv *or* -kə-tiv). A controlling or operative fact, rather than a background fact; a fact that concerns the parties to a judicial or administrative proceeding and that helps the court or agency determine how the law applies to those parties. Cf. *legislative fact*.

dispositive fact (dis-**poz**-ə-tiv). **1.** A fact that confers rights or causes the loss of rights. **2.** A fact that is decisive of a legal matter; evidence that definitively resolves a legal issue or controversy. See DISPOSITION.

divestitive fact (di-**ves**-tə-tiv *or* dɪ-). A fact that causes the loss of rights; an act or event modifying or extinguishing a legal relation.

evaluative fact. A fact used to assess an action as being reasonable or negligent.

evidentiary fact (ev-i-**den**-shə-ree). **1.** A fact that is necessary for or leads to the determination of an ultimate fact. **2.** A fact that furnishes evidence of the existence of some other fact. **3.** See *fact in evidence.*

exonerative fact (eg-**zon**-ər-ə-tiv *or* -ay-tiv). A divestitive fact that extinguishes a duty.

fact in evidence. A fact that a tribunal considers in reaching a conclusion; a fact that has been admitted into evidence in a trial or hearing.

fact in issue. (*usu. pl.*) A fact to be determined by a fact-trier; PROBANDUM.

impositive fact. An investitive fact that imposes duties.

investitive fact (in-**ves**-tə-tiv). A fact that confers rights.

inferential fact. A fact established by conclusions drawn from other evidence rather than from direct testimony or evidence; a fact derived logically from other facts.

judicial fact. A fact that the court accepts as proved without hearing evidence. See JUDICIAL NOTICE.

jurisdictional fact. (*usu. pl.*) A fact that must exist for a court to properly exercise its jurisdiction over a case, party, or thing. See JURISDICTIONAL-FACT DOCTRINE.

legal fact. A fact that triggers a particular legal consequence.

legislative fact. A fact that explains a particular law's rationality and that helps a court or agency determine the law's content and application. Cf. *adjudicative fact.*

material fact. A fact that is significant or essential to the issue or matter at hand.

operative fact. A fact that affects an existing legal relation, esp. a legal claim.

predicate fact (**pred**-ə-kit). A fact from which a presumption or inference arises.

primary fact. A fact that can be established by direct testimony and from which inferences are made leading to ultimate facts. See *ultimate fact.*

private fact. A fact that has not been made public. Cf. *public fact.*

probative fact (**proh**-bə-tiv). A fact in evidence used to prove an ultimate fact, such as skid marks used to show speed as a predicate to a finding of negligence.

public fact. For the purpose of an invasion-of-privacy claim, a fact that is in a public record or in the public domain. Cf. *private fact.*

ultimate fact. A fact essential to the claim or the defense.

undisputed fact. An uncontested or admitted fact, esp. one that a court has not deemed necessary to include in a finding of fact.

fact-finder. One or more persons — such as jurors in a trial or administrative-law judges in a hearing — who hear testimony and review evidence to rule on a factual issue. See FINDING OF FACT.

fact-finding. **1.** The process of taking evidence to determine the truth about a disputed point. **2.** A method of alternative dispute resolution in which an impartial third party determines and studies the facts and positions of disputing parties that have reached an impasse, with a view toward clarifying the issues and helping the parties work through their dispute.

factor, *n.* **1.** An agent or cause that contributes to a particular result. **2.** An agent who is employed to sell property for the principal and who possesses or controls the property; a person who receives and sells goods for a commission. • A factor differs from a broker because the factor possesses or controls the property. Cf. BROKER. **3.** One who buys accounts receivable at a discount. **4.** A garnishee.

factorizing process. A procedure or legal process by which a third party, rather than the creditor, attaches a debtor's property; GARNISHMENT.

factual impossibility. See IMPOSSIBILITY.

factum (fak-təm), *n.* [Latin] **1.** A fact, such as a person's physical presence in a new domicile. **2.** An act or deed, such as the due execution of a will. See *fraud in the factum* under FRAUD. **3.** A statement of facts. **4.** BRIEF (1). Pl. **facta.**

fail, *vb.* **1.** To be deficient or unsuccessful; to fall short. **2.** To become insolvent or bankrupt. **3.** To lapse.

failure. **1.** Deficiency; lack; want. **2.** An omission of an expected action, occurrence, or performance. See LAPSE (2).

failure of consideration. A situation in which a contract's basis or inducement ceases to exist or becomes worthless. • This term, unlike *consideration* per se, relates not to the formation of a contract but to its performance. See CONSIDERATION. Cf. WANT OF CONSIDERATION.

partial failure of consideration. A situation in which the contract consists of separable items of consideration and separable parts of the agreement, so that if part of the consideration fails, the appropriate part of the agreement can be apportioned to it. • The several parts of the contract are in effect treated as separate contracts, and the contract is voided only to the extent that the consideration for one part fails.

total failure of consideration. A situation in which the contract is indivisible so that a complete lack of consideration voids the contract.

failure of issue. The fact of dying without children, esp. if they would have inherited the decedent's estate.

indefinite failure of issue. A failure of issue whenever it happens, without any certain period within which it must happen.

failure-of-proof defense. The defense that a party's proof does not establish a fact essential to a claim or defense.

failure to thrive. *Family law.* **1.** A medical and psychological condition in which a child's height, weight, and motor development fall significantly below average growth rates. • Failure to thrive is sometimes asserted as a ground for alleging abuse or neglect by a parent or caregiver. **2.** A condition, occurring during the first three years of a child's life, in which the child suffers marked retardation or ceases to grow. — Abbr. FTT.

faint pleader. A false, fraudulent, or collusive manner of pleading.

fair, *adj.* **1.** Impartial; just; equitable; disinterested. **2.** Free of bias or prejudice.

fair-and-equitable requirement. *Bankruptcy.* A Bankruptcy Code standard requiring a forced, nonconsensual Chapter 11 plan (a "cramdown" plan) to provide adequately for each class of interests that has not accepted the plan. 11 USCA § 1129(b). See CRAMDOWN.

fair comment. A statement based on the writer's or speaker's honest opinion about a matter of public concern.

fair competition. See COMPETITION.

fair consideration. See CONSIDERATION.

Fair Credit Billing Act. A federal law that facilitates the correction of billing errors by credit-card companies and makes those companies more responsible for the quality of goods purchased by cardholders. 15 USCA §§ 1666–1666j.

fair-credit-reporting act. A federal or state law that regulates the keeping of credit reports and ensures the right of consumers to get and correct their credit reports.

fair-cross-section requirement. *Constitutional law.* The principle that a person's right to an impartial jury, guaranteed by the Sixth Amendment, includes a requirement that the pool of potential jurors fairly represent the composition of the jurisdiction's population. • The pool of potential jurors need not precisely match the composition of the jurisdiction. But the representation of each group must be fair — no group should be systematically excluded or underrepresented. A minimal disparity in a particular group's representation, such as an absolute disparity of 10%, will not ordinarily violate this principle unless some aggravating factor exists. See DUREN TEST; ABSOLUTE DISPARITY; COMPARATIVE DISPARITY; STATISTICAL-DECISION THEORY.

fair dealing, *n.* **1.** The conduct of business with full disclosure, usu. by a corporate officer with the corporation. **2.** A fiduciary's transacting of business so that, although the fiduciary might derive a personal benefit, all interested persons are fully apprised of that potential and of all other material information about the transaction. Cf. SELF-DEALING.

fair hearing. See HEARING.

Fair Labor Standards Act. A federal law, enacted in 1938, that regulates minimum wages, overtime pay, and the employment of minors. 29 USCA §§ 201–219. — Abbr. FLSA.

fair market value. See VALUE.

fairness doctrine. A federal law, based on an FCC rule, requiring the broadcast media to furnish a reasonable opportunity for the discussion of conflicting views on issues of public importance. • The FCC abandoned the fairness doctrine in 1987.

fair notice. See NOTICE.

fair on its face. (Of a document) having the appearance of being regular or legal and not capable of being shown to be defective without extraneous evidence.

fair play. Equity, candor, and fidelity in dealings with another.

fair play and substantial justice. The fairness requirement that a court must meet in its assertion of personal jurisdiction over a nonresident defendant to comport with due process. *International Shoe Co. v. Washington*, 326 U.S. 310, 66 S.Ct. 154 (1945). See MINIMUM CONTACTS.

fair-report privilege. A defense to liability for publishing defamatory matter from a report of an official or judicial proceeding, when the report is a full, fair, and accurate account of the proceeding.

fair-trade agreement. A commercial agreement that a seller will sell all of a producer's goods at or above a specified minimum price. • Fair-trade agreements were valid until 1975, when the Consumer Goods Pricing Act made them illegal. 15 USCA §§ 1, 45.

fair trial. A trial by an impartial and disinterested tribunal in accordance with regular procedures; esp., a criminal trial in which the defendant's constitutional and legal rights are respected.

fair use. *Copyright*. A reasonable and limited use of a copyrighted work without the author's permission, such as quoting from a book in a book review or using parts of it in a parody. 17 USCA § 107.

fair-value law. A statute allowing a credit against a deficiency for the amount that the fair market value of land exceeds the price at foreclosure.

fair warning. *Criminal law*. The requirement that a criminal statute define an offense with enough precision so that a reasonable person can know what conduct is prohibited and so that a reasonably skilled lawyer can predict what conduct falls within the statute's scope.

Faithfully Executed Clause. The clause of the U.S. Constitution providing that the President must take care that the laws are carried out faithfully. U.S. Const. art. II, § 3.

false advertising, *n.* The tortious and sometimes criminal act of distributing an advertisement that is untrue, deceptive, or misleading.

false answer. A sham answer in a pleading. See *sham pleading* under PLEADING (1).

false arrest. See ARREST.

False Claims Act. A federal statute establishing civil and criminal penalties against persons who bill the government falsely, deliver less to the government than represented, or use a fake record to decrease an obligation to the government. 18 USCA §§ 286–287; 31 USCA §§ 3729–3733. • The Act may be enforced either by the attorney general or by a private person in a qui tam action.

false evidence. See *false testimony* under TESTIMONY.

false impersonation. The crime of falsely representing oneself as another person, usu. a law-enforcement officer, for the purpose of deceiving someone. See 18 USCA §§ 912–917.

false-implication libel. See LIBEL.

false imprisonment. A restraint of a person in a bounded area without justification or consent. • False imprisonment is a common-law misdemeanor and a tort. It applies to private as well as governmental detention. Cf. *false arrest* under ARREST.

false light. *Torts.* In an invasion-of-privacy action, a plaintiff's allegation that the defendant attributed to the plaintiff views that he or she does not hold and placed the plaintiff before the public in a highly offensive and untrue manner. See INVASION OF PRIVACY.

false misrepresentation. See MISREPRESENTATION. • This phrase is redundant — *misrepresentation* includes the idea of falsity.

false pretenses. The crime of knowingly obtaining title to another's personal property by misrepresenting a fact with the intent to defraud. Cf. *larceny by trick* under LARCENY; EMBEZZLEMENT.

false report. The criminal offense of informing law enforcement about a crime that did not occur.

false return. 1. A process server's or other court official's recorded misrepresentation that process was served, that some other action was taken, or that something is true. **2.** A tax return on which taxable income is incorrectly reported or the tax is incorrectly computed. See TAX RETURN.

false statement. See STATEMENT.

false testimony. See TESTIMONY.

falsifying a record. The crime of making false entries or otherwise tampering with a public record with the intent to deceive or injure, or to conceal wrongdoing. 18 USCA §§ 1506, 2071, 2073; Model Penal Code § 224.4.

family, *n.* **1.** A group of persons connected by blood, by affinity, or by law, esp. within two or three generations. **2.** A group consisting of parents and their children. **3.** A group of persons who live together and have a shared commitment to a domestic relationship. — **familial,** *adj.* See RELATIVE.

blended family. The combined families of persons with children from earlier marriages or relationships.

extended family. **1.** The immediate family together with the collateral relatives who make up a clan. **2.** The immediate family together with collateral relatives and close family friends.

immediate family. **1.** A person's parents, spouse, children, and siblings. **2.** A person's parents, spouse, children, and siblings, as well as those of the person's spouse. • Stepchildren and adopted children are usually immediate family members. For some purposes, such as taxes, a person's immediate family may also include the spouses of children and siblings.

family allowance. See ALLOWANCE.

family arrangement. An informal agreement among family members, usu. to distribute property in a manner other than what the law provides for.

family court. See COURT.

family-expense statute. 1. A state law that permits a charge against the property of a spouse for family debts such as rent, food, clothing, and tuition. **2.** A federal tax-code provision providing that a person may not deduct expenses incurred for family, living, or personal purposes. IRC (26 USCA) § 262.

family law. 1. The body of law dealing with marriage, divorce, adoption, child custody and support, child abuse and neglect, paternity, juvenile delinquency, and other domestic-relations issues. **2.** (More broadly) the bodies of law dealing with wills and estates, property, constitutional rights, contracts, employment, and finance as they relate to families.

family leave. An unpaid leave of absence from work taken to have or care for a baby or to care for a sick family member.

family partnership. A business partnership in which the partners are related. IRC (26 USCA) § 704(e). See FAMILY-PARTNERSHIP RULES.

family-partnership rules. Laws designed to prevent the shifting of income among partners, esp. family members, who may not be dealing at arm's length.

family-purpose rule. *Torts.* The principle that a vehicle's owner is liable for injuries or damage caused by a family member's negligent driving. Cf. GUEST STATUTE.

Fannie Mae (fan-ee may). See FEDERAL NATIONAL MORTGAGE ASSOCIATION.

FAR. (*often pl.*) *abbr.* FEDERAL AVIATION REGULATION.

Farmers Home Administration. A division of the U.S. Department of Agriculture that makes mortgage loans to farmers, issues home-mortgage insurance, and funds public-works programs in rural areas and small towns. — Abbr. FmHA; FHA.

farming operation. *Bankruptcy.* A business engaged in farming, tillage of soil, dairy farming, ranching, raising of crops, poultry, or livestock, and production of poultry or livestock products in an unmanufactured state. 11 USCA § 101(21). See CHAPTER 12.

farm out, *vb.* To turn over something (such as an oil-and-gas lease) for performance by another.

FASB (faz-bee). *abbr.* FINANCIAL ACCOUNTING STANDARDS BOARD.

fast land. See LAND.

fast-tracking, *n.* A court's method of accelerating the disposition of cases in an effort to clear its docket. • For example, a judge might order that all discovery must be finished within 90 days, and that trial is set for 30 days later. — **fast-track,** *vb.* See ROCKET DOCKET.

fatal, *adj.* **1.** Of or relating to death <the decision had fatal consequences>. **2.** Providing grounds for legal invalidity <a fatal defect in the contract>.

fatal defect. See DEFECT.

fatal variance. See VARIANCE.

father. The male parent. See PARENT.

legal father. The man recognized by law as the male parent of a child. • A man is the legal father of a child if he was married to the child's natural mother when the child was born, if he has recognized or acknowledged the child, or if he has been declared the child's natural father in a paternity action.

natural father. The man who impregnated the child's natural mother.

presumed father. The man presumed to be the father of a child for any of several reasons: (1) because he was married to the child's natural mother when the child was conceived or born, (2) because the child was conceived or born during an invalid marriage, (3) because the man married the mother after the child's birth and agreed either to have his name on the birth certificate or to support the child, or (4) because the man welcomed the child into his home and held out the child as his own.

putative father (**pyoo**-tə-tiv). The alleged biological father of a child born out of wedlock.

***Fatico* hearing** (**fat**-ə-koh). *Criminal procedure.* A sentencing hearing at which the prosecution and the defense may present evidence about what the defendant's sentence should be. *United States v. Fatico*, 603 F.2d 1053 (2d Cir. 1979).

fault. An error or defect of judgment or of conduct; any deviation from prudence or duty resulting from inattention, incapacity, perversity, bad faith, or mismanagement. See NEGLIGENCE. Cf. LIABILITY.

fault-first method. A means by which to apply a settlement credit to a jury verdict, by first reducing the amount of the verdict by the percentage of the plaintiff's comparative fault, then subtracting from the remainder the amount of any settlements the plaintiff has received on the claim. See SETTLEMENT CREDIT. Cf. SETTLEMENT-FIRST METHOD.

fault of omission. Negligence resulting from a negative act.

favorite of the law. A person or status entitled to generous and preferential treatment in legal doctrine.

favoritism. Preference or selection, usu. invidious, based on factors other than merit. See NEPOTISM; PATRONAGE. Cf. DISCRIMINATION (2), (3).

fax, *n.* **1.** A method of transmitting over telephone lines an exact copy of a printing. **2.** A machine used for this transmission. **3.** The communication sent or received by this machine. — **fax,** *vb.*

FBI. *abbr.* FEDERAL BUREAU OF INVESTIGATION.

F. Cas. *abbr.* Federal Cases, a series of reported decisions (1789–1880) predating the Federal Reporter.

FCC. *abbr.* FEDERAL COMMUNICATIONS COMMISSION.

FDA. *abbr.* FOOD AND DRUG ADMINISTRATION.

f/d/b/a. *abbr.* Formerly doing business as.

FDIC. *abbr.* FEDERAL DEPOSIT INSURANCE CORPORATION.

feasance (**fee**-zənts), *n.* The doing or execution of an act, condition, or obligation. — **feasor,** *n.* Cf. MALFEASANCE; MISFEASANCE; NONFEASANCE.

feasibility standard. *Bankruptcy.* The requirement that, to obtain bankruptcy-court approval, a Chapter 11 reorganization plan must be workable and have a reasonable likelihood of success.

feasor (**fee**-zər), *n.* An actor; a person who commits an act. See TORTFEASOR.

featherbedding. A union practice designed to increase employment and guarantee job security by requiring employers to hire or retain more employees than are needed. • Featherbedding is restricted by federal law.

Fed. *abbr.* **1.** FEDERAL. **2.** FEDERAL RESERVE SYSTEM.

Fed. Cir. *abbr.* Federal Circuit. See UNITED STATES COURT OF APPEALS FOR THE FEDERAL CIRCUIT.

federal, *adj.* Of or relating to a system of associated governments with a vertical division of governments into national and regional components having different responsibilities; esp., of or relating to the national government of the United States. — Abbr. Fed.

Federal Acquisition Regulation. (*usu. pl.*) A federal regulation that governs contracting methods, requirements, and procedures with the federal government. 48 CFR ch. 1.

federal agency. See AGENCY (2).

Federal Aviation Act. A federal law establishing the Federal Aviation Agency (FAA) to be responsible for regulation of aircraft and air travel, including aircraft safety, certification of aircraft personnel, and airport development. 49 USCA §§ 44720 et seq.

Federal Aviation Administration. The federal agency charged with regulating air commerce, advancing aviation safety, promoting civil aviation and a national system of airports, achieving efficient use of navigable airspace, developing and operating a common system of air-traffic control and air navigation, and developing and implementing programs and regulations relating to environmental effects of civil aviation. — Abbr. FAA.

Federal Aviation Regulation. (*usu. pl.*) A federal regulation governing the safety, maintenance, and piloting of civil aircraft. 14 CFR ch. 1. — Abbr. FAR.

Federal Bureau of Investigation. A division of the U.S. Department of Justice charged with investigating all violations of federal laws except those specifically assigned to another federal agency. — Abbr. FBI.

federal-comity doctrine. The principle requiring federal district courts to refrain from interfering in each other's affairs.

federal common law. See COMMON LAW.

Federal Communications Commission. The federal agency that regulates interstate and foreign communications by radio, television, telephone, and telegraph, and oversees radio and television broadcasting standards, cable-television operations, two-way-radio operators, and satellite communications. — Abbr. FCC.

federal court. See COURT.

federal crime. A criminal offense under a federal statute. • Most federal crimes are codified in Title 18 of the U.S. Code.

Federal Deposit Insurance Corporation. An independent governmental agency that insures bank deposits up to a statutory amount per depositor at each participating bank. — Abbr. FDIC.

Federal Employers' Liability Act. A workers'-compensation law that provides death and disability benefits for employees of railroads engaged in interstate and foreign commerce. 45 USCA §§ 51–60. — Abbr. FELA.

Federal Energy Regulatory Commission. The agency responsible for administering the Natural Gas Act and the Natural Gas Policy Act. — Abbr. FERC.

Federal Home Loan Bank. One of a system (the federal home loan bank system) of 11 regional banks created in 1932 to supply credit for home mortgage lending by savings-and-loan institutions and to provide funds for low- to moderate-income housing programs — Abbr. FHLB.

Federal Home Loan Bank Board. A federal agency responsible for regulating federal savings-and-loan associations and the federal home loan bank system. • It was abolished in 1989, when the Office of Thrift Supervision and the Federal Housing Finance Board assumed its functions. — Abbr. FHLBB.

Federal Home Loan Mortgage Corporation. A corporation that purchases both conventional and federally insured first mortgages from members of the Federal Reserve System and other approved banks. — Abbr. FHLMC.

Federal Housing Administration. The HUD division that encourages mortgage lending by insuring mortgage loans on homes meeting the agency's standards. — Abbr. FHA. See HUD.

Federal Housing Finance Board. An independent agency that supervises the federal home-loan-bank system. • It is the successor agency to the Federal Home Loan Bank Board. — Abbr. FHFB.

Federal Insurance Contributions Act. The federal act that authorized the social-security tax on employers and employees. IRC (26 USCA) §§ 3101–3127. — Abbr. FICA.

federalism. The relationship and distribution of power between the national and regional governments within a federal system of government. Cf. OUR FEDERALISM.

Federalist Society. A national association of lawyers, law students, and others committed to conservative and libertarian viewpoints on political and social matters. • The group is based in Washington, D.C. Cf. NATIONAL LAWYERS GUILD.

Federal Judicial Code. The portion (Title 28) of the U.S. Code dealing with the organization, jurisdiction, venue, and procedures of the federal court system, as well as court officers, personnel, and the Department of Justice.

federal jurisdiction. See JURISDICTION.

Federal Kidnapping Act. A federal law punishing kidnapping for ransom or reward when the victim is transported interstate or internationally. 18 USCA § 1201.

federal land bank. One of a system of 12 regional banks created in 1916 to provide mortgage loans to farmers. • The system is now merged with federal intermediate credit banks to create the federal farm-credit system.

federal law. The body of law consisting of the U.S. Constitution, federal statutes and regulations, U.S. treaties, and federal common law. Cf. STATE LAW.

Federal Maritime Commission. A federal agency that regulates the waterborne foreign and domestic commerce of the United States. — Abbr. FMC.

Federal Mediation and Conciliation Service. An independent agency whose purpose is to prevent disruptions in the flow of interstate commerce caused by labor disputes through the use of mediation, conciliation, and voluntary arbitration. • The agency can intervene on its own motion or on the motion of a party to the dispute. 29 USCA §§ 172, 173. — Abbr. FMCS.

Federal National Mortgage Association. A corporation that is chartered by the U.S. government but privately owned and managed, and that provides a secondary mortgage market for the purchase and sale of mortgages guaranteed by the Veterans Administration and those insured under the Federal Housing Administration. — Abbr. FNMA.

federal-question jurisdiction. See JURISDICTION.

Federal Register. A daily publication in which U.S. administrative agencies publish their regulations, including proposed regulations for public comment. — Abbr. Fed. Reg.

Federal Reporter. See F.

Federal Reporter Second Series. See F.2D.

Federal Reporter Third Series. See F.3D.

Federal Reserve Board of Governors. The board that supervises the Federal Reserve System and sets national monetary and credit policy. • The board consists of seven members appointed by the President and confirmed by the Senate for 14-year terms. — Abbr. FRB.

federal reserve note. The paper currency in circulation in the United States. • The notes are issued by the Federal Reserve Banks, are effectively non-interest-bearing promissory notes payable to bearer on demand, and are issued in denominations of $1, $5, $10, $20, $50, $100, $500, $1,000, $5,000, and $10,000.

Federal Reserve System. A network of 12 central banks supervised by the Board of Governors, who are appointed by the President and confirmed by the Senate and who set the reserve requirements for the member banks, review the discount-rate actions of the regional Federal Reserve Banks, and set ceilings on the interest rates that member banks may pay. — Abbr. Fed.

Federal Rules Act. A 1934 statute granting the U.S. Supreme Court the authority to adopt rules of civil procedure for federal courts. • For the rulemaking power of federal courts today, see 28 USCA §§ 2071, 2072.

Federal Rules Decisions. See F.R.D.

Federal Rules of Appellate Procedure. The rules governing appeals to the U.S. courts of appeals from lower courts, some federal-agency proceedings, and applications for writs. — Abbr. Fed. R. App. P.; FRAP.

Federal Rules of Bankruptcy Procedure. The rules governing proceedings instituted under the Bankruptcy Code. — Abbr. Fed. R. Bankr. P.

Federal Rules of Civil Procedure. The rules governing civil actions in the U.S. district courts. — Abbr. Fed. R. Civ. P.; FRCP.

Federal Rules of Criminal Procedure. The rules governing criminal proceedings in the U.S. district courts. — Abbr. Fed. R. Crim. P.

Federal Rules of Evidence. The rules governing the admissibility of evidence at trials in federal courts. — Abbr. Fed. R. Evid.; FRE.

Federal Savings and Loan Insurance Corporation. A federal agency created in 1934 to insure deposits in savings-and-loan associations and savings banks. • When this agency became insolvent in 1989, its assets and liabilities were transferred to an insurance fund managed by the FDIC. — Abbr. FSLIC.

Federal Supplement. See F.SUPP.

Federal Supplement Second Series. See F.SUPP.2D

Federal Tort Claims Act. A statute that limits federal sovereign immunity and allows recovery in federal court for tort damages caused by federal employees, but only if the law of the state where the injury occurred would hold a private person liable for the injury. 28 USCA §§ 2671–2680. — Abbr. FTCA. See *sovereign immunity* under IMMUNITY.

Federal Trade Commission. The independent regulatory agency created in 1914 to enforce the antitrust laws and other prohibitions against false, deceptive, and unfair advertising or trade practices. — Abbr. FTC.

federal transfer. The federal district court's right to move a civil action filed there to any other district or division where the plaintiff could have brought the action originally. 28 USCA § 1404(a). See CHANGE OF VENUE.

federation. A league or union of states, groups, or peoples arranged with a strong central authority and limited regional sovereignties — though the individual states, groups, or peoples may retain rights of varying degrees. Cf. CONFEDERATION.

Fed. R. App. P. *abbr.* FEDERAL RULES OF APPELLATE PROCEDURE.

Fed. R. Bankr. P. *abbr.* FEDERAL RULES OF BANKRUPTCY PROCEDURE.

Fed. R. Civ. P. *abbr.* FEDERAL RULES OF CIVIL PROCEDURE.

Fed. R. Crim. P. *abbr.* FEDERAL RULES OF CRIMINAL PROCEDURE.

Fed. Reg. *abbr.* FEDERAL REGISTER.

Fed. R. Evid. *abbr.* FEDERAL RULES OF EVIDENCE.

fee. 1. A charge for labor or services, esp. professional services.

docket fee. A fee charged by a court for filing a claim.

franchise fee. **1.** A fee paid by a franchisee to a franchisor for franchise rights. **2.** A fee paid to the government for a government grant of a franchise, such as the one required for operating a radio or television station.

jury fee. A fee, usu. a minimal one, that a party to a civil suit must pay the court clerk to be entitled to a jury trial.

origination fee. A fee charged by a lender for preparing and processing a loan.

2. An inheritable interest in land, constituting maximal legal ownership; esp., a fee simple absolute. See FEE SIMPLE.

base fee. A fee that has some qualification connected to it and that terminates whenever the qualification terminates. • Among the base fees at common law are the fee simple subject to a condition subsequent and the conditional fee. See *fee simple determinable* under FEE SIMPLE.

feemail (**fee**-mayl). *Slang.* **1.** An attorney's fee extorted by intimidation, threats, or pressure. **2.** The act or process of extorting such a fee. Cf. BLACKMAIL; GRAYMAIL; GREENMAIL.

fee simple. An interest in land that, being the broadest property interest allowed by law, endures until the current holder dies without heirs; esp., a fee simple absolute.

fee simple absolute. An estate of indefinite or potentially infinite duration (e.g., "to Albert and his heirs").

fee simple conditional. An estate restricted to some specified heirs, exclusive of others (e.g., "to Albert and his female heirs").

fee simple defeasible (di-**fee**-zə-bəl). An estate that ends either because there are no more heirs of the person to whom it is granted or because a special limitation, condition subsequent, or executory limitation takes effect before the line of heirs runs out.

fee simple determinable. An estate that will automatically end and revert to the grantor if some specified event occurs (e.g., "to Albert and his heirs while the property is used for charitable purposes"). • The future interest retained by the grantor is called a *possibility of reverter*.

fee simple subject to a condition subsequent. An estate subject to the grantor's power to end the estate if some specified event happens (e.g., "to Albert and his heirs, upon condition that no alcohol is sold on the premises"). • The future interest retained by the grantor is called a *power of termination* (or a *right of entry*).

fee simple subject to an executory limitation. A fee simple defeasible that is subject to divestment in favor of someone other than the grantor if a specified event happens (e.g., "to Albert and his heirs, but if the property is ever used as a parking lot, then to Bob").

fee tail. An estate that is inheritable only by specified descendants of the original grantee, and that endures until its current holder dies without issue (e.g., "to Albert and the heirs of his body"). See ENTAIL; TAIL.

FELA (fee-lə). *abbr.* FEDERAL EMPLOYERS' LIABILITY ACT.

fellow-officer rule. *Criminal procedure.* The principle that an investigative stop or an arrest is valid if the law-enforcement officer lacks personal knowledge to establish reasonable suspicion or probable cause but acts on the knowledge of another officer and the collective knowledge of the law-enforcement office.

fellow-servant rule. A common-law doctrine holding that an employer is not liable for an employee's injuries caused by a negligent coworker. • This doctrine has generally been abrogated by workers'-compensation statutes.

felon, *n.* A person who has been convicted of a felony.

felonious (fə-**loh**-nee-əs), *adj.* **1.** Of, relating to, or involving a felony. **2.** Constituting or having the character of a felony. **3.** Proceeding from an evil heart or purpose; malicious; villainous. **4.** Wrongful; (of an act) done without excuse or color of right.

felonious homicide. See HOMICIDE.

felonious restraint. 1. The offense of knowingly and unlawfully restraining a person under circumstances that expose the person to serious bodily harm. Model Penal Code § 212.2(a). **2.** The offense of holding a person in involuntary servitude. Model Penal Code § 212.2(b).

felony, *n.* A serious crime usu. punishable by imprisonment for more than one year or by death. Cf. MISDEMEANOR.

***atrocious felony*.** A serious, usu. cruel felony involving personal violence. • This term is now used less frequently than the specific type of crime alleged (e.g., first-degree murder or aggravated sexual assault).

***serious felony*.** A major felony, such as burglary of a residence or an assault that causes great bodily injury. • In many jurisdictions, a defendant's prior serious-felony convictions can be used to enhance another criminal charge.

felony murder. See MURDER.

felony-murder rule. The doctrine holding that any death resulting from the commission or attempted commission of a dangerous felony is murder. Cf. MISDEMEANOR-MANSLAUGHTER RULE.

feminist jurisprudence. See JURISPRUDENCE.

fence, *n.* **1.** A person who receives stolen goods. **2.** A place where stolen goods are sold. See RECEIVING STOLEN PROPERTY. **3.** LAWFUL FENCE. — **fence,** *vb.*

FERC (fərk). *abbr.* FEDERAL ENERGY REGULATORY COMMISSION.

fertile-octogenarian rule. The legal fiction, assumed under the rule against perpetuities, that a woman can become pregnant as long as she is alive. • The case that gave rise to this fiction was *Jee v. Audley*, 1 Cox 324, 29 Eng. Rep. 1186 (ch. 1787).

feticide (**fee**-tə-sɪd). The act or an instance of killing a fetus, usu. by assaulting and battering the mother; an intentionally induced miscarriage. — **feticidal,** *adj.* Cf. INFANTICIDE (1).

fetter, *n.* (*usu. pl.*) A chain or shackle for the feet. — **fetter,** *vb.*

ff. *abbr.* And the pages following.

FHA. *abbr.* **1.** FARMERS HOME ADMINISTRATION. **2.** FEDERAL HOUSING ADMINISTRATION.

FHFB. *abbr.* FEDERAL HOUSING FINANCE BOARD.

FHLB. *abbr.* FEDERAL HOME LOAN BANK.

FHLBB. *abbr.* FEDERAL HOME LOAN BANK BOARD.

FHLMC. *abbr.* FEDERAL HOME LOAN MORTGAGE CORPORATION.

fiat (**fee**-aht *or* **fee**-at *or* **fɪ**-at *or* **fɪ**-ət), *n.* [Latin "let it be done"] **1.** An order or decree, esp. an arbitrary one. **2.** A court decree, esp. one relating to a routine matter such as scheduling.

FICA (**fɪ**-kə). *abbr.* FEDERAL INSURANCE CONTRIBUTIONS ACT.

fiduciary (fi-**d**[**y**]**oo**-shee-er-ee), *n.* **1.** One who owes to another the duties of good faith, trust, confidence, and candor <the corporate officer is a fiduciary to the shareholders>. **2.** One who must exercise a high standard of care in managing another's money or property <the beneficiary sued the fiduciary for investing in speculative securities>. — **fiduciary,** *adj.*

fiduciary bond. See BOND (2).

fiduciary relationship. A relationship in which one person is under a duty to act for the benefit of the other on matters within the scope of the relationship. • Fiduciary relationships — such as trustee–beneficiary, guardian–ward, agent–principal, and attorney–client — require the highest duty of care. Fiduciary relationships usually arise in one of four situations: (1) when one person places trust in the faithful integrity of another, who as a result gains superiority or influence over the first, (2) when one person assumes control and responsibility over another, (3) when one person has a duty to act for or give advice to another on matters falling within the scope of the relationship, or (4) when there is a specific relationship that has traditionally been recognized as involving fiduciary duties, as with a lawyer and a client or a stockbroker and a customer. Cf. SPECIAL RELATIONSHIP.

field sobriety test. See SOBRIETY TEST.

fieri facias (**fɪ**-ə-rɪ **fay**-shee-əs). [Latin "that you cause to be done"] A writ of execution that directs a marshal or sheriff to seize and sell a defendant's property to satisfy a money judgment. — Abbr. *fi. fa.*; *Fi. Fa.*

Fifteenth Amendment. The constitutional amendment, ratified in 1870, guaranteeing all citizens the right to vote regardless of race, color, or prior condition of servitude.

Fifth Amendment. The constitutional amendment, ratified with the Bill of

Rights in 1791, providing that a person cannot be (1) required to answer for a capital or otherwise infamous offense unless a grand jury issues an indictment or presentment, (2) subjected to double jeopardy, (3) compelled to engage in self-incrimination on a criminal matter, (4) deprived of life, liberty, or property without due process of law, and (5) deprived of private property for public use without just compensation.

50-percent rule. The principle that liability for negligence is apportioned in accordance with the percentage of fault that the fact-finder assigns to each party, that the plaintiff's recovery will be reduced by the percentage of negligence assigned to the plaintiff, and that the plaintiff's recovery is barred if the plaintiff's percentage of fault is 50% or more. — Also termed *modified-comparative-negligence doctrine*. Cf. PURE-COMPARATIVE-NEGLIGENCE DOCTRINE. See *comparative negligence* under NEGLIGENCE; APPORTIONMENT OF LIABILITY.

fighting words. **1.** Inflammatory speech that might not be protected by the First Amendment's free-speech guarantee because it might incite a violent response. **2.** Inflammatory speech that is pleadable in mitigation — but not in defense — of a suit for assault.

file, *n.* **1.** A court's complete and official record of a case. **2.** A lawyer's complete record of a case. **3.** A portion or section of a lawyer's case record. **4.** A case.

file, *vb.* **1.** To deliver (a legal document) to the court clerk or record custodian for placement into the official record. **2.** To commence a law suit. **3.** To record or deposit (something) in an organized retention system or container for preservation and future reference.

filing, *n.* A particular document (such as a pleading) in the file of a court clerk or record custodian.

filing fee. A sum of money required to be paid to the court clerk before a proceeding can start.

finality doctrine. The rule that a court will not judicially review an administrative agency's action until it is final. Cf. FINAL-JUDGMENT RULE.

final judgment. See JUDGMENT.

final-judgment rule. The principle that a party may appeal only from a district court's final decision that ends the litigation on the merits. • Under this rule, a party must raise all claims of error in a single appeal. 28 USCA § 1291. Cf. FINALITY DOCTRINE; INTERLOCUTORY APPEALS ACT; DEATH-KNELL DOCTRINE.

final-offer arbitration. See ARBITRATION.

final order. See ORDER.

finance lease. See LEASE.

Financial Accounting Standards Board. The independent body of accountants responsible for establishing, interpreting, and improving standards for financial accounting and reporting. — Abbr. FASB.

financial institution. A business, organization, or other entity that manages money, credit, or capital, such as a bank, credit union, savings-and-loan association, securities broker or dealer, pawnbroker, or investment company.

financial intermediary. A financial entity — usu. a commercial bank — that advances the transfer of funds between borrowers and lenders, buyers and sellers, and investors and savers.

financial-responsibility act. A state statute conditioning license and registration of motor vehicles on proof of insurance or other financial accountability.

financial-responsibility clause. A provision in an automobile insurance policy stating that the insured has at least the minimum amount of liability insurance coverage required by a state's financial-responsibility law.

financing, *n.* **1.** The act or process of raising or providing funds. **2.** Funds that are raised or provided. — **finance,** *vb.*

financing statement. A document filed in the public records to notify third parties, usu. prospective buyers and lenders, of a secured party's security interest in goods.

finder. 1. An intermediary who brings together parties for a business opportunity, such as two companies for a merger, a borrower and a financial institution, or an issuer and an underwriter of securities. • A finder differs from a broker-dealer because the finder merely brings two parties together to make their own contract, while a broker-dealer usually participates in the negotiations. See INTERMEDIARY. **2.** A person who discovers an object, often a lost or mislaid chattel.

finder's fee. The amount charged by one who brings together parties for a business opportunity.

finder's-fee contract. An agreement between a finder and one of the parties to a business opportunity.

finding of fact. A determination by a judge, jury, or administrative agency of a fact supported by the evidence in the record, usu. presented at the trial or hearing. Cf. CONCLUSION OF FACT; CONCLUSION OF LAW.

fine, *n.* **1.** An amicable final agreement or compromise of a fictitious or actual suit to determine the true possessor of land. **2.** A fee paid by a tenant to the landlord at the commencement of the tenancy to reduce the rent payments. **3.** A pecuniary criminal punishment or civil penalty payable to the public treasury. — **fine,** *vb.*

> ***excessive fine.*** **1.** *Criminal law.* A fine that is unreasonably high and disproportionate to the offense committed. • The Eighth Amendment proscribes excessive fines. **2.** A fine or penalty that seriously impairs one's earning capacity, esp. from a business.

fine print. The part of an agreement or document — usu. in small, light print that is not easily noticeable — referring to disclaimers, restrictions, or limitations.

firm, *n.* **1.** The title under which one or more persons conduct business jointly. **2.** The association by which persons are united for business purposes. See LAW FIRM.

firm bid. See BID.

First Amendment. The constitutional amendment, ratified with the Bill of Rights in 1791, guaranteeing the freedoms of speech, religion, press, assembly, and petition.

first chair, *n. Slang.* The lead attorney in court for a given case. — **first-chair,** *vb.*

first-degree murder. See MURDER.

first-degree sexual conduct. Sexual battery that involves an aggravating factor, as when the perpetrator commits an offense against a minor or when the perpetrator commits an offense in the course of committing another crime, such as a burglary.

first offender. See OFFENDER.

first-party insurance. See INSURANCE.

first-sale doctrine. *Copyright.* The rule that a copyright owner, after conveying the title to a particular copy of the protected work, loses the exclusive right to sell that copy and therefore cannot interfere with later sales or distributions by the new owner.

first taker. See TAKER.

first-to-file rule. *Civil procedure.* **1.** The principle that, when two suits are brought by the same parties, regarding the same issues, in two courts of proper jurisdiction, the court that first acquires jurisdiction usu. retains the suit, to the exclusion of the other court. • An exception exists if the first-filed suit is brought merely in anticipation of the true plaintiff's suit — as an improper attempt at forum-shopping. **2.** The doctrine allowing a party to a previously filed lawsuit to enjoin another from pursuing a later-filed action.

fixation. *Copyright.* The process or result of recording a work of authorship in tangible form so that it can be copyrighted under federal law.

fix bail, *vb.* To set the amount and terms of bail. See BAIL.

fixed cost. See COST.

fixed fee. 1. A fee that will not vary according to the amount of work done or other factor. **2.** In a construction contract, a predetermined amount that is added to costs for calculating payments due under the contract.

fixed opinion. A bias or prejudice that disqualifies a potential juror.

fixture. Personal property that is attached to land or a building and that is regarded as an irremovable part of the real property, such as a fireplace built into a home. Cf. IMPROVEMENT.

> ***tenant's fixture.*** Removable personal property that a tenant affixes to the leased property but that the tenant can detach and take away.
>
> ***trade fixture.*** Removable personal property that a tenant attaches to leased land for business purposes, such as a display counter. • Despite its name, a trade fixture is not usually treated as a fixture — that is, as irremovable.

fixture filing. The act or an instance of recording, in public real-estate records, a security interest in personal property that is intended to become a fixture. • The creditor files a financing statement in the real-property records of the county where a mortgage on the real estate would be filed. A fixture-filing financing statement must contain a description of the real estate.

FKA. *abbr.* Formerly known as. — Also spelled *F/K/A*; *fka*; *f/k/a*.

flat tax. See TAX.

flat time. See TIME.

flip mortgage. See MORTGAGE.

float, *n.* **1.** The sum of money represented by outstanding or uncollected checks. **2.** The delay between a transaction and the withdrawal of funds to cover the transaction. **3.** The amount of a corporation's shares that are available for trading on the securities market.

float, *vb.* **1.** (Of a currency) to attain a value in the international exchange market solely on the basis of supply and demand. **2.** To issue (a security) for sale on the market. **3.** To arrange or negotiate (a loan).

floating rate. See INTEREST RATE.

floodgate. (*usu. pl.*) A restraint that prevents a release of a usu. undesirable result <the new law opened the floodgates of litigation>.

floodplain. Land that is subject to floodwaters because of its level topography and proximity to a river or arroyo; esp., level land that, extending from a riverbank, is inundated when the flow of water exceeds the channel's capacity.

floor. **1.** A legislature's central meeting place where the members sit and conduct business, as distinguished from the galleries, corridors, or lobbies. **2.** The trading area where stocks and commodities are bought and sold on an exchange. **3.** The lowest limit.

floor debate. The legislative process of debating a proposed bill before an entire chamber rather than before a committee.

FLSA. *abbr.* FAIR LABOR STANDARDS ACT.

FMC. *abbr.* FEDERAL MARITIME COMMISSION.

FMCS. *abbr.* FEDERAL MEDIATION AND CONCILIATION SERVICE.

FmHA. *abbr.* FARMERS HOME ADMINISTRATION.

FNMA. *abbr.* FEDERAL NATIONAL MORTGAGE ASSOCIATION.

FOIA (foy-ə). *abbr.* FREEDOM OF INFORMATION ACT.

foiable (foy-ə-bəl), *adj. Slang.* (Of documents) subject to disclosure under the Freedom of Information Act (FOIA).

Food and Drug Administration. The federal agency within the Department of Health and Human Services established to determine safety and quality standards for foods, drugs, medical devices, cosmetics, and other household products. — Abbr. FDA.

Food, Drug, and Cosmetic Act. A 1938 federal law prohibiting the transportation in interstate commerce of adulterated or misbranded food, drugs, or cosmetics.

for account of. A form of indorsement on a note or draft introducing the name of the person entitled to receive the proceeds.

Foraker Act (for-ə-kər). The original (1900) federal law providing Puerto Rico with a civil government, but keeping it outside the U.S. customs area. See 48 USCA §§ 731–752.

forbearance, *n.* **1.** The act of refraining from enforcing a right, obligation, or debt. • Strictly speaking, *forbearance* denotes an intentional negative act, while *omission* or *neglect* is an unintentional negative act. **2.** The act of tolerating or abstaining. — **forbear,** *vb.*

forbidden departure. See DEPARTURE.

for cause. For a legal reason or ground. — **for-cause,** *adj.*

force, *n.* Power, violence, or pressure directed against a person or thing. — **force,** *vb.*

actual force. Force consisting in a physical act, esp. a violent act directed against a robbery victim.

constructive force. Threats and intimidation to gain control or prevent resistance; esp., threatening words or gestures directed against a robbery victim.

deadly force. Violent action known to create a substantial risk of causing death or serious bodily harm. Cf. *nondeadly force.*

excessive force. Unreasonable or unnecessary force under the circumstances.

irresistible force. Force that cannot be foreseen or controlled, esp. that which prevents the performance of a contractual obligation; FORCE MAJEURE.

nondeadly force. **1.** Force that is neither intended nor likely to cause death or serious bodily harm; force intended to cause only minor bodily harm. **2.** A threat of deadly force, such as displaying a knife. Cf. *deadly force.*

reasonable force. Force that is not excessive and that is appropriate for protecting oneself or one's property.

unlawful force. Force that is directed against a person without that person's consent, and that is an offense or actionable tort. Model Penal Code § 3.11.

force and effect, *n.* Legal efficacy. • The term is now generally regarded as a redundant legalism.

forced heir. See HEIR.

force majeure (fors ma-zhər). [Law French "a superior force"] An event or effect that can be neither anticipated nor controlled. • The term includes both acts of nature (e.g., floods and hurricanes) and acts of people (e.g., riots, strikes, and wars). Cf. ACT OF GOD; VIS MAJOR.

force-majeure clause. A contractual provision allocating the risk if performance becomes impossible or impracticable as a result of an event or effect that the parties could not have anticipated or controlled.

forcible detainer. 1. The wrongful retention of possession of property by one originally in lawful possession, often with threats or actual use of violence. **2.** FORCIBLE ENTRY AND DETAINER.

forcible entry. At common law, the act or an instance of violently and unlawfully taking possession of lands and tenements against the will of those entitled to possession.

forcible entry and detainer. 1. The act of violently taking and keeping possession of lands and tenements without legal authority. **2.** A quick and simple legal proceeding for regaining possession of real property from someone who has wrongfully taken, or refused to surrender, possession. See EVICTION; EJECTMENT.

foreclosure (for-**kloh**-zhər). A legal proceeding to terminate a mortgagor's interest in property, instituted by the lender (the mortgagee) either to gain title or to force a sale in order to satisfy the unpaid debt secured by the property. — **foreclose,** *vb.* Cf. REPOSSESSION.

equitable foreclosure. A foreclosure method in which the court orders the property sold, and the proceeds are applied first to pay the costs of the suit and sale and then to the mortgage debt.

judicial foreclosure. A costly and time-consuming foreclosure method by which the mortgaged property is sold through a court proceeding requiring many standard legal steps such as the filing of a complaint, service of process, notice, and a hearing.

mortgage foreclosure. A foreclosure of the mortgaged property upon the mortgagor's default.

nonjudicial foreclosure. **1.** See *power-of-sale foreclosure*. **2.** A foreclosure method that does not require court involvement.

power-of-sale foreclosure. A foreclosure process by which, according to the mortgage instrument and a state statute, the mortgaged property is sold at a nonjudicial public sale by a public official, the mortgagee, or a trustee, without the stringent notice requirements, burdens, or delays of a judicial foreclosure.

strict foreclosure. A rare procedure that gives the mortgagee title to the mortgaged property — without first conducting a sale — after a defaulting mortgagor fails to pay the mortgage debt within a court-specified period.

tax foreclosure. A public authority's seizure and sale of property for nonpayment of taxes.

foreclosure decree. 1. Generally, a decree ordering a judicial foreclosure sale. **2.** A decree ordering the strict foreclosure of a mortgage.

foreign, *adj.* **1.** Of or relating to another country <foreign affairs>. **2.** Of or relating to another jurisdiction <the Arizona court gave full faith and credit to the foreign judgment from Mississippi>. — **foreigner,** *n.*

foreign corporation. See CORPORATION.

foreign court. See COURT.

foreign divorce. See DIVORCE.

foreign document. See DOCUMENT.

foreign-earned- income exclusion. The Internal Revenue Code provision that excludes from taxation a limited amount of income earned by nonresident taxpayers outside the United States. • The taxpayer must elect between this exclusion and the foreign tax credit. IRC (26 USCA) § 911(a), (b). See *foreign tax credit* under TAX CREDIT.

foreign jurisdiction. See JURISDICTION.

foreign object. An item that appears where it does not belong; esp., an item introduced into a living body, such as a sponge that is left in a patient's body during surgery. See FOREIGN SUBSTANCE.

foreign service. See UNITED STATES FOREIGN SERVICE.

foreign substance. A substance found in a body, organism, or thing where it is not supposed to be found.

foreign tax credit. See TAX CREDIT.

forensic (fə-**ren**-sik *also* -zik), *adj.* **1.** Used in or suitable to courts of law or public debate <forensic psychiatry>. **2.** Rhetorical; argumentative <Spence's considerable forensic skills>.

forensic engineering. The use of engineering principles or analysis in a lawsuit, usu. through an expert witness's testimony.

forensic evidence. See EVIDENCE.

forensic linguistics. The science or technique that evaluates the linguistic characteristics of written or oral communications, usu. to determine identity or authorship.

forensic medicine. The branch of medicine that establishes or interprets evidence using scientific or technical facts, such as ballistics.

forensic pathology. The specific branch of medicine that establishes or interprets evidence dealing with diseases and disorders of the body, esp. those that cause death.

forensics (fə-**ren**-siks *also* -ziks). **1.** The art of argumentative discourse. **2.** The branch of law enforcement dealing with legal evidence relating to firearms and ballistics.

foreseeability, *n.* The quality of being reasonably anticipatable. • Foreseeability, along with actual causation, is an element of proximate cause in tort law. — **foreseeable,** *adj.*

forfeiture (**for**-fi-chər), *n.* **1.** The divestiture of property without compensation. **2.** The loss of a right, privilege, or property because of a crime, breach of obligation, or neglect of duty. • Title is simultaneously transferred to another, such as the government, a corporation, or a private person. **3.** Something (esp. money or property) lost or confiscated by this process; a penalty. — **forfeit,** *vb.* — **forfeitable,** *adj.*

civil forfeiture. An in rem proceeding brought by the government against property that either facilitated a crime or was acquired as a result of criminal activity.

criminal forfeiture. A governmental proceeding brought against a person as punishment for the person's criminal behavior.

4. A destruction or deprivation of some estate or right because of the failure to perform some obligation or condition contained in a contract.

forfeiture clause. A contractual provision stating that, under certain circumstances, one party must forfeit something to the other.

forgery, *n.* **1.** The act of fraudulently making a false document or altering a real one to be used as if genuine. **2.** A false or altered document made to look genuine by someone with the intent to deceive. **3.** Under the Model Penal Code, the act of fraudulently altering, authenticating, issuing, or transferring a writing without appropriate authorization. • Under the explicit terms of the code, *writing* can include items such as coins and credit cards. Model Penal Code § 224.1(1). — **forge,** *vb.* — **forger,** *n.*

form, *n.* **1.** The outer shape or structure of something, as distinguished from its substance or matter <courts are generally less concerned about defects in form than defects in substance>. **2.** Established behavior or procedure, usu. according to custom or rule <the prosecutor followed the established form in her closing argument>. **3.** A model; a sample; an example <attorneys often draft pleadings by using a form instead of starting from scratch>. **4.** The customary method of drafting legal documents, usu. with fixed words, phrases, and sentences <Jones prepared the contract merely by following the state bar's form>. **5.** A legal document with blank spaces to be filled in by the drafter <the divorce lawyer used printed forms that a secretary could fill in>.

formal agreement. See AGREEMENT.

formal law. Procedural law.

formal rulemaking. See RULEMAKING.

formbook. A book that contains sample legal documents, esp. transaction-related documents such as contracts, deeds, leases, wills, trusts, and securities disclosure documents.

former adjudication. An adjudication in a prior action that resulted in a final determination of the rights of the parties or essential fact questions, the result of which bars relitigation. • Collateral estoppel and res judicata are the two types of former adjudication. See COLLATERAL ESTOPPEL; RES JUDICATA.

former jeopardy. The fact of having previously been prosecuted for the same offense. Cf. DOUBLE JEOPARDY.

formula instruction. See JURY INSTRUCTION.

fornication, *n.* Voluntary sexual intercourse between two unmarried persons. — **fornicate,** *vb.* Cf. ADULTERY.

forswearing (for-**swair**-ing), *n.* **1.** The act of repudiating or renouncing under oath. **2.** PERJURY. — **forswear,** *vb.*

forthwith, *adv.* **1.** Immediately; without delay. **2.** Directly; promptly; within a reasonable time under the circumstances.

fortuitous event. A happening that, because it occurs only by chance or accident, the parties could not have reasonably foreseen. See FORCE MAJEURE; UNAVOIDABLE-ACCIDENT DOCTRINE.

forum, *n.* **1.** A public place, esp. one devoted to assembly or debate. **2.** A court or other judicial body; a place of jurisdiction. Pl. **forums, fora.**

forum conveniens (**for**-əm kən-**vee**-nee-enz). [Latin "a suitable forum"] The court in which an action is most appropriately brought, considering the best interests and convenience of the parties and witnesses. Cf. FORUM NON CONVENIENS.

forum non conveniens (**for**-əm non kən-**vee**-nee-enz). [Latin "an unsuitable court"] *Civil procedure*. The doctrine that an appropriate forum — even though competent under the law — may divest itself of jurisdiction if, for the convenience of the litigants and the witnesses, it appears that the action should proceed in another forum in which the action might originally have been brought.

forum-selection clause. A contractual provision in which the parties establish the place (such as the country, state, or type of court) for specified litigation between them. Cf. CHOICE-OF-LAW CLAUSE.

forum-shopping. The practice of choosing the most favorable jurisdiction or court in which a claim might be heard. • A plaintiff might engage in forum-shopping, for example, by filing suit in a jurisdiction with a reputation for high jury awards or by filing several similar suits and keeping the one with the preferred judge. Cf. JUDGE-SHOPPING.

foster, *adj.* **1.** (Of a relationship) involving parental care given by someone not related by blood <foster home>. **2.** (Of a person) giving or receiving parental care to or from someone not related by blood <foster parent> <foster child>. — **foster,** *vb.*

fosterage, *n.* **1.** The act of caring for another's child. **2.** The entrusting of a child to another. **3.** The condition of being in the care of another. **4.** The act of encouraging or promoting.

foster care. 1. A federally funded child-welfare program providing substitute care for abused and neglected children who have been removed by court order from their parents' care or for children voluntarily placed by their parents in the temporary care of the state because of a family crisis. 42 USCA §§ 670–679a. **2.** The area of social services concerned with meeting the needs of children who participate in these types of programs.

foster-care placement. The (usu. temporary) act of placing a child in a home with a person or persons who provide parental care for the child.

foster child. See CHILD.

foster parent. See PARENT.

foundation. 1. The basis on which something is supported; esp., evidence or testimony that establishes the admissibility of other evidence. **2.** A fund established for charitable, educational, religious, research, or other benevolent purposes; an endowment.

foundational evidence. See EVIDENCE.

founded on, *adj.* Having as a basis <the suit was founded on the defendant's breach of contract>.

four corners. The face of a written instrument.

four-corners rule. 1. The principle that a document's meaning is to be gathered from the entire document and not from its isolated parts. **2.** The principle that no extraneous evidence should be used to interpret an unambiguous document. Cf. PAROL-EVIDENCE RULE.

Fourteenth Amendment. The constitutional amendment, ratified in 1868, whose primary provisions effectively apply the Bill of Rights to the states by forbidding states from denying due process and equal protection and from abridging the privileges and immunities of U.S. citizenship. • The amendment also gave Congress the power to enforce these provisions, leading to legislation such as the civil rights acts.

Fourth Amendment. The constitutional amendment, ratified with the Bill of Rights in 1791, prohibiting unreasonable searches and seizures and the issuance of warrants without probable cause. See PROBABLE CAUSE.

fourth estate. The journalistic profession; the news media.

four unities. The four qualities needed to create a joint tenancy at common law — interest, possession, time, and title. See UNITY (2).

fractional, *adj.* (Of a tract of land) covering an area less than the acreage reflected on a survey; pertaining to any irregular division of land containing either more or less than the conventional amount of acreage.

frame, *vb.* **1.** To plan, shape, or construct; esp., to draft or otherwise draw up (a document). **2.** To incriminate (an innocent person) with false evidence, esp. fabricated. — **framable, frameable,** *adj.*

franchise (**fran**-chɪz), *n.* **1.** The right to vote. **2.** The right conferred by the government to engage in a specific business or to exercise corporate powers. **3.** The sole right granted by the owner of a trademark or tradename to engage in business or to sell a good or service in a certain area. **4.** The business or territory controlled by the person or entity that has been granted such a right.

franchise, *vb.* To grant (to another) the sole right of engaging in a certain business or in a business using a particular trademark in a certain area.

franchise agreement. The contract between a franchisor and franchisee establishing the terms and conditions of the franchise relationship. • State and federal laws regulate franchise agreements.

franchise fee. See FEE (1).

***Franks* hearing.** A hearing to determine whether a police officer's affidavit used to obtain a search warrant that yields incriminating evidence was based on false statements by the police officer. *Franks v. Delaware*, 438 U.S. 154, 98 S.Ct. 2674 (1978).

FRAP (frap). *abbr.* FEDERAL RULES OF APPELLATE PROCEDURE.

fratricide (**fra**-trə-sɪd *or* **fray**-). **1.** One who has killed one's brother or sister. **2.** The killing of one's brother or sister.

fraud, *n.* **1.** A knowing misrepresentation of the truth or concealment of a material fact to induce another to act to his or her detriment. • Fraud is usually a tort, but in some cases (esp. when the conduct is willful) it may be a crime. **2.** A misrepresentation made recklessly without belief in its truth to induce another person to act. **3.** A tort arising from a knowing misrepresentation, concealment of a material fact, or a reckless misrepresentation made to induce another to act to his or her detriment. **4.** Unconscionable dealing; esp., in contract law, the unfair use of the power arising out of the parties' relative positions and resulting in an unconscionable bargain. — **fraudulent,** *adj.*

actual fraud. A concealment or false representation through a statement or conduct that injures another who relies on it in acting.

bankruptcy fraud. A fraudulent act connected to a bankruptcy case; esp., any of several prescribed acts performed knowingly and fraudulently in a bankruptcy case, such as concealing assets or destroying, withholding, or falsifying documents in an effort to defeat bankruptcy-code provisions. See 18 USCA § 152.

civil fraud. **1.** FRAUD (3). **2.** *Tax.* An intentional — but not willful — evasion of taxes. • The distinction between an intentional (i.e., *civil*) and willful (i.e., *criminal*) fraud is not always clear, but *civil fraud* carries only a monetary, noncriminal penalty. Cf. *criminal fraud*; TAX EVASION.

constructive fraud. **1.** Unintentional deception or misrepresentation that causes injury to another. **2.** See *fraud in law*.

criminal fraud. Fraud that has been made illegal by statute and that subjects the offender to criminal penalties such as fines and imprisonment. • An example is the willful evasion of taxes accomplished by filing a fraudulent tax return. Cf. *civil fraud*; *larceny by trick* under LARCENY.

extrinsic fraud. **1.** Deception that is collateral to the issues being considered in the case; intentional misrepresentation or deceptive behavior outside the transaction itself (whether a contract or a lawsuit), depriving one party of informed consent or full participation. • For example, a person might engage in extrinsic fraud by convincing a litigant not to hire counsel or answer by dishonestly saying the matter will not be pursued. **2.** Deception that prevents a person from knowing about or asserting certain rights.

fraud in law. Fraud that is presumed under the circumstances, as when a debtor transfers assets and thereby impairs creditors' efforts to collect sums due.

fraud in the factum. Fraud occurring when a legal instrument as actually executed differs from the one intended for execution by the person who executes it, or when the instrument may have had no legal existence. • Compared to fraud in the inducement, fraud in the factum occurs only rarely, as when a blind person signs a mortgage when misleadingly told that it's just a letter. Cf. *fraud in the inducement*.

fraud in the inducement. Fraud occurring when a misrepresentation leads another to enter into a transaction with a false impression of the risks, duties, or obligations involved; an intentional misrepresentation of a material risk or duty reasonably relied on, thereby injuring the other party without vitiating the contract itself, esp. about a fact relating to value. Cf. *fraud in the factum*.

fraud on the court. In a judicial proceeding, a lawyer's or party's misconduct so serious that it undermines or is intended to undermine the integrity of the proceeding. • Examples are bribery of a juror and introduction of fabricated evidence.

intrinsic fraud. Deception that pertains to an issue involved in an original action. • Examples include the use of fabricated evidence, a false return of service, perjured testimony, and false receipts or other commercial documents.

mail fraud. An act of fraud using the U.S. Postal Service, as in making false representations through the mail to obtain an economic advantage. 18 USCA §§ 1341–1347.

promissory fraud. A promise to perform made when the promisor had no intention of performing the promise.

wire fraud. An act of fraud using electronic communications, as by making false representations on the telephone to obtain money. • The federal Wire Fraud Act provides that any artifice to defraud by means of wire or other electronic communications (such as radio or television) in foreign or interstate commerce is a crime. 18 USCA § 1343.

fraudulent concealment. See CONCEALMENT.

fraudulent conveyance. 1. A transfer of property for little or no consideration, made for the purpose of hindering or delaying a creditor by putting the property beyond the creditor's reach; a transaction by which the owner of real or personal property seeks to place the property beyond the reach of creditors. **2.** *Bankruptcy.* A prebankruptcy transfer or obligation made or incurred by a debtor for little or no consideration or with the actual intent to hinder, delay, or defraud a creditor. • A bankruptcy trustee may recover such a conveyance from the transferee if the requirements of 11 USCA § 548 are met.

fraudulent joinder. See JOINDER.

fraudulent misrepresentation. See MISREPRESENTATION.

FRB. *abbr.* FEDERAL RESERVE BOARD OF GOVERNORS.

FRCP. *abbr.* FEDERAL RULES OF CIVIL PROCEDURE.

F.R.D. *abbr.* Federal Rules Decisions; a series of reported federal court decisions (beginning in 1938) that construe or apply the Federal Rules of Civil, Criminal, or Appellate Procedure, or the Federal Rules of Evidence. • Also included are rule changes, ceremonial proceedings of federal courts, and articles on federal court practice and procedure.

FRE. *abbr.* FEDERAL RULES OF EVIDENCE.

Freddie Mac. See FEDERAL HOME LOAN MORTGAGE CORPORATION.

free, *adj.* **1.** Having legal and political rights; enjoying political and civil liberty. **2.** Not subject to the constraint or domination of another; enjoying personal freedom; emancipated. **3.** Characterized by choice, rather than by compulsion or constraint. **4.** Unburdened. **5.** Not confined by force or restraint. **6.** Unrestricted and unregulated. **7.** Costing nothing; gratuitous. — **freely,** *adv.*

freedom of association. The right to join with others in a common undertaking that would be lawful if pursued individually. • This right is protected by the First Amendment to the U.S. Constitution. The government may not prohibit outsiders from joining an association, but the insiders do not necessarily have a right to exclude others. Cf. RIGHT OF ASSEMBLY.

freedom of choice. 1. The liberty embodied in the exercise of one's rights. **2.** The parents' opportunity to select a school for their child in a unitary, integrated school system that is devoid of de jure segregation. **3.** The liberty to exercise one's right of privacy, esp. the right to have an abortion.

freedom of contract. The doctrine that people have the right to bind themselves legally; a judicial concept that contracts are based on mutual agreement and free choice, and thus should not be hampered by external control such as governmental interference.

freedom of expression. The freedom of speech, press, assembly, or religion as guaranteed by the First Amendment; the prohibition of governmental interference with those freedoms.

Freedom of Information Act. The federal statute that establishes guidelines for the public disclosure of documents and materials created and held by federal agencies. 5 USCA § 552. — Abbr. FOIA.

freedom of religion. The right to adhere to any form of religion or none, to practice or abstain from practicing religious beliefs, and to be free from governmental interference with or promotion of religion, as guaranteed by the First Amendment and Article VI, Section 3 of the U.S. Constitution.

freedom of speech. The right to express one's thoughts and opinions without governmental restriction, as guaranteed by the First Amendment.

freedom of the press. The right to print and publish materials without governmental intervention, as guaranteed by the First Amendment.

free enterprise. A private and consensual system of production and distribution, usu. conducted for a profit in a competitive environment that is relatively free of governmental interference. See CAPITALISM.

Free Exercise Clause. The constitutional provision (U.S. Const. amend. I) prohibiting the government from interfering in people's religious practices or forms of worship. Cf. ESTABLISHMENT CLAUSE.

freehold, *n.* **1.** An estate in land held in fee simple, in fee tail, or for term of life. **2.** The tenure by which such an estate is held. Cf. LEASEHOLD.

freeman. 1. A person who possesses and enjoys all the civil and political rights belonging to the people under a free government. **2.** A person who is not a slave.

freeze, *n.* **1.** A period when the government restricts or immobilizes certain commercial activity.

credit freeze. A period when the government restricts bank-lending.

wage-and-price freeze. A period when the government forbids the increase of wages and prices.

2. A recapitalization of a closed corporation so that the value of its existing capital is concentrated primarily in preferred stock rather than in common stock. — **freeze,** *vb.*

fresh complaint. A reasonably prompt lodging of a grievance; esp., a victim's prompt report of a sexual assault to someone trustworthy.

fresh pursuit. 1. The right of a police officer to make a warrantless search of a fleeing suspect or to cross jurisdictional lines to arrest a fleeing suspect. **2.** The right of a person to use reasonable force to retake property that has just been taken.

fresh start. *Bankruptcy.* The favorable financial status obtained by a debtor who receives a release from personal liability on prepetition debts or who reorganizes debt obligations through the confirmation and completion of a bankruptcy plan.

friendly fire. 1. A fire burning where it is intended to burn, yet capable of causing unintended damage. **2.** Military or police gunfire that injures one's own side.

friendly suit. A lawsuit in which all the parties have agreed beforehand to allow a court to resolve the issues.

friend of the court. 1. AMICUS CURIAE. **2.** In some jurisdictions, an official who investigates and advises the circuit court in domestic-relations cases involving minors.

fringe benefit. See BENEFIT.

frisk, *n.* A pat-down search to discover a concealed weapon. See STOP AND FRISK. Cf. SEARCH.

frivolous, *adj.* Lacking a legal basis or legal merit; not serious; not reasonably purposeful.

frivolous appeal. An appeal having no legal basis, usu. filed for delay to induce a judgment creditor to settle or to avoid payment of a judgment. • The Federal Rules of Appellate Procedure provide for the award of damages and costs if the appellate court determines that an appeal is frivolous. Fed. R. App. P. 38.

frivolous defense. See DEFENSE (1).

frivolous suit. A lawsuit having no legal basis, often filed to harass or extort money from the defendant.

frolic (**frol**-ik), *n. Torts.* An employee's significant deviation from the employer's business for personal reasons. • A frolic is outside the scope of employment, and thus the employer is not vicariously liable for the employee's actions. Cf. DETOUR.

front, *n.* **1.** The side or part of a building or lot that is open to view, that is the principal entrance, or that faces out to the open (as to a lake or ocean); the foremost part of something <the property's front was its most valuable attribute>. **2.** A person or group that serves to conceal the true identity or activity of the person or group in control <the political party was a front for the terrorist group>. **3.** A political association similar to a party <popular front>.

frontage (**frən**-tij). **1.** The part of land abutting a street or highway or lying between a building's front and a street or highway. **2.** The linear distance of a frontage.

frontage assessment. A municipal fee charged to a property owner for local improvements that abut a street or highway, such as sidewalks, pavements, or sewage lines.

frontager (**frən**-tij-ər), *n.* A person owning or occupying land that abuts a highway, river, seashore, or the like.

front foot. A measurement used to calculate a frontage assessment.

front-foot rule. The principle that an improvement cost is to be apportioned among several properties in proportion to their frontage, without regard to the benefits conferred on each property.

fruit-and-the-tree doctrine. *Tax.* The rule that an individual who earns income cannot assign that income to another person to avoid taxation.

fruit-of-the-poisonous-tree doctrine. *Criminal procedure.* The rule that evidence derived from an illegal search, arrest, or interrogation is inadmissible because the evidence (the "fruit") was tainted by the illegality (the "poisonous tree"). • Under this doctrine, for example, a murder weapon is inadmissible if the map showing its location and used to find it was seized during an illegal search. See EXCLUSIONARY RULE; ATTENUATION DOCTRINE; INDEPENDENT-SOURCE RULE; INEVITABLE-DISCOVERY RULE.

fruits of a crime. The proceeds acquired through criminal acts.

frustration, *n.* **1.** The prevention or hindering of the attainment of a goal, such as contractual performance.

commercial frustration. An excuse for a party's nonperformance because of some unforeseeable and uncontrollable circumstance.

self-induced frustration. A breach of contract caused by one party's action that prevents the performance. • The phrase is something of a misnomer, since *self-induced frustration* is not really a type of frustration at all but is instead a breach of contract.

temporary frustration. An occurrence that prevents performance and legally suspends the duty to perform for the duration of the event. • If the burden or circumstance is substantially different after the event, then the duty may be discharged.

2. *Contracts.* The doctrine that, if the entire performance of a contract becomes fundamentally changed without any fault by either party, the contract is considered terminated. — **frustrate,** *vb.* Cf. IMPOSSIBILITY (4); IMPRACTICABILITY; MISTAKE.

FSLIC. *abbr.* FEDERAL SAVINGS AND LOAN INSURANCE CORPORATION.

F.Supp. *abbr.* *Federal Supplement*, a series of reported decisions of the federal district courts (from 1932 to 1998), the U.S. Court of Claims (1932 to 1960), and the U.S. Customs Court (from 1949 to 1998, but renamed the Court of International Trade in 1980).

F.Supp.2d. *abbr.* The second series of the *Federal Supplement*, which includes decisions of federal district courts and the Court of International Trade from 1997 to the present.

FTC. *abbr.* FEDERAL TRADE COMMISSION.

FTCA. *abbr.* FEDERAL TORT CLAIMS ACT.

Fugitive Felon Act. A federal statute that makes it a felony to flee across state lines to avoid state-felony prosecution or confinement, or to avoid giving testimony in a state-felony case. 18 USCA § 1073.

fugitive warrant. See WARRANT.

fugue (fyoog). An abnormal state of consciousness in which one appears to function normally but on recovery has no memory of what one did while in that condition.

full age. The age of legal majority; legal age.

full blood. See BLOOD.

full court. See COURT.

Full Faith and Credit Clause. U.S. Const. art. IV, § 1, which requires states to give effect to the legislative acts, public records, and judicial decisions of other states.

full hearing. See HEARING.

full right. The union of good title with actual possession.

full-service lease. See LEASE.

full warranty. See WARRANTY (2).

fully administered. A plea by an executor or administrator that he or she has completely and legally disposed of all the assets of the estate and that the estate has no remaining assets from which a new claim could be satisfied.

function, *n.* **1.** Activity that is appropriate to a particular business or profession. **2.** Office; duty; the occupation of an office.

functional depreciation. See DEPRECIATION.

fund, *n.* **1.** A sum of money or other liquid assets established for a specific purpose.

contingent fund. **1.** A fund created by a municipality for expenses that will necessarily arise during the year but that cannot be appropriately classified under any of the specific purposes for which taxes are collected. **2.** A fund segregated by a business to pay unknown costs that may arise in the future.

fund in court. **1.** Contested money deposited with the court. See INTERPLEADER. **2.** Money deposited to pay a contingent liability.

general fund. **1.** A government's primary operating fund; a state's assets furnishing the means for the support of government and for defraying the legislature's discretionary appropriations. **2.** A nonprofit entity's assets that are not earmarked for a specific purpose.

general revenue fund. The fund out of which a municipality pays its ordinary and incidental expenses.

revolving fund. A fund whose moneys are continually expended and then replenished, such as a petty-cash fund.

sinking fund. A fund consisting of regular deposits that are accumulated with interest to pay off a long-term corporate or public debt.

unsatisfied-judgment fund. A fund established by a state to compensate persons for losses stemming from an automobile accident caused by an uninsured or underinsured motorist.

2. (*usu. pl.*) Money or other assets, such as stocks, bonds, or working capital, available to pay debts, expenses, and the like. **3.** A pool of investments owned in common and managed for a fee; mutual fund.

fund, *vb.* **1.** To furnish money to (an individual, entity, or venture), esp. to finance a particular project. **2.** To use resources in a manner that produces interest. **3.** To convert (a debt, esp. an open account) into a long-term debt that bears interest at a fixed rate.

fundamental-fairness doctrine. The rule that applies the principles of due process to a judicial proceeding. • The term is commonly considered synonymous with *due process*.

fundamental law. The organic law that establishes the governing principles of a nation or state; esp., CONSTITUTIONAL LAW. Cf. NATURAL LAW.

fundamental right. 1. A right derived from natural or fundamental law. **2.** *Constitutional law*. A significant component of liberty, encroachments of which are rigorously tested by courts to ascertain the soundness of purported governmental justifications. • A fundamental right triggers strict scrutiny to determine whether the law violates the Due Process Clause or the Equal Protection Clause of the 14th Amendment. As enunciated by the Supreme Court, fundamental rights include voting, interstate travel, and various aspects of privacy (such as marriage and contraception rights). See STRICT SCRUTINY. Cf. SUSPECT CLASSIFICATION.

fundamental term. See TERM (2).

funeral expense. See EXPENSE.

fungible (fən-jə-bəl), *adj.* Regarded as commercially interchangeable with other property of the same kind <corn and wheat are fungible goods, whereas land is not>. — **fungible,** *n.*

furlough (fər-loh). 1. A leave of absence from military or other employment duty. **2.** A brief release from prison. See STUDY RELEASE.

further assurance. See ASSURANCE.

future advance. Money secured by an original security agreement even though it is lent after the security interest has attached.

future-advance clause. A contractual term in a security agreement covering additional loaned amounts on present collateral or collateral to be acquired in the future, regardless of whether the secured party is obliged to make the advances; esp., a provision in an open-end mortgage or deed of trust allowing the borrower to borrow additional sums in the future, secured under the same instrument and by the same security. • This type of clause makes a new security agreement unnecessary when the secured creditor makes a future loan to the debtor.

future consideration. See CONSIDERATION.

future damages. See DAMAGES.

future interest. See INTEREST (2).

future performance. See PERFORMANCE.

G

GAAP (gap). *abbr.* GENERALLY ACCEPTED ACCOUNTING PRINCIPLES.

GAAS (gas). *abbr.* GENERALLY ACCEPTED AUDITING STANDARDS.

gage (gayj), *n.* A pledge, pawn, or other thing deposited as security for performance.

gag order. 1. A judge's order directing parties, attorneys, witnesses, or journalists to refrain from publicly discussing the facts of a case. • When directed to the press, such an order is generally unconstitutional under the First Amendment. **2.** A judge's order that an unruly defendant be bound and gagged during trial to prevent further interruptions.

gain, *n.* **1.** An increase in amount, degree, or value.

pecuniary gain. **1.** A gain of money or of something having monetary value. **2.** *Criminal law.* Any monetary or economic gain that serves as an impetus for the commission of an offense. See SOLICITATION .

2. Excess of receipts over expenditures or of sale price over cost. See PROFIT. **3.** *Tax.* The excess of the amount realized from a sale or other disposition of property over the property's adjusted value. IRC (26 USCA) § 1001.

capital gain. The profit realized when a capital asset is sold or exchanged. Cf. *ordinary gain*; *capital loss* under LOSS.

extraordinary gain. A gain that is both unusual and infrequent, such as the gain realized from selling a large segment of a business.

ordinary gain. A gain from the sale or exchange of a noncapital asset. Cf. *capital gain*.

recognized gain. The portion of a gain that is subject to income taxation. IRC (26 USCA) § 1001(c). See BOOT (1).

Gallagher **agreement.** A contract that gives one codefendant the right to settle with the plaintiff for a fixed sum at any time during trial and that guarantees payment of the sum regardless of the trial's outcome. *City of Tucson v. Gallagher*, 493 P.2d 1197 (Ariz. 1972). Cf. MARY CARTER AGREEMENT.

game law. A federal or state law that regulates the hunting of game, esp. one that forbids the capturing or killing of specified game either entirely or seasonally, describes the means for killing or capturing game in season, or restricts the number and type of game animals that may be killed or captured in season. 16 USCA §§ 661–667; 18 USCA §§ 41–47.

ganancial (gə-**nan**-shəl), *adj.* Of, relating to, or consisting of community property <a spouse's ganancial rights>. See COMMUNITY PROPERTY.

gang. A group of persons who go about together or act in concert, esp. for antisocial or criminal purposes.

Ganser's syndrome (**gahn**-zər *or* **gan**-sər). An abnormality characterized by the giving of irrelevant and nonsensical answers to questions. • Prisoners have been known to feign this syndrome in an attempt to obtain leniency.

GAO. *abbr.* GENERAL ACCOUNTING OFFICE.

gap-filler. A rule that supplies a contractual term that the parties failed to include in the contract. • For example, if the contract does not contain a sales price, UCC § 2–305(1) establishes the price as being a reasonable one at the time of delivery.

gap period. *Bankruptcy*. The time between the filing of an involuntary bankruptcy petition and the entry of the order for relief.

gap report. In the making of federal court rules, a report that explains any changes made by an advisory committee in the language of a proposed amendment to a procedural rule after its publication for comment.

***Garcia* hearing** (gahr-**see**-ə). *Criminal procedure*. A hearing held to ensure that a defendant who is one of two or more defendants represented by the same attorney understands (1) the risk of a conflict of interest inherent in this type of representation, and (2) that he or she is entitled to the services of an attorney who does not represent anyone else in the defendant's case. *United States v. Garcia*, 517 F.2d 272 (5th Cir. 1975). See CONFLICT OF INTEREST (2).

garnish, *vb.* [Old French *garnir* "to warn" "to prepare"] To subject (property) to garnishment; to attach (property held by a third party) in order to satisfy a debt. — **garnishable,** *adj.*

garnishee (gahr-ni-**shee**), *n.* A person or institution (such as a bank) that is indebted to or is bailee for another whose property has been subjected to garnishment.

garnisher. A creditor who initiates a garnishment action to reach the debtor's property that is thought to be held or owed by a third party (the *garnishee*).

garnishment, *n.* **1.** A judicial proceeding in which a creditor (or potential creditor) asks the court to order a third party who is indebted to or is bailee for the debtor to turn over to the creditor any of the debtor's property (such as wages or bank accounts) held by that third party. • A plaintiff initiates a garnishment action as a means of either prejudgment seizure or postjudgment collection.

> ***wrongful garnishment.*** **1.** An improper or tortious garnishment. **2.** A cause of action against a garnisher for improperly or tortiously filing a garnishment proceeding.

2. The judicial order by which such a turnover is effected. Cf. ATTACHMENT (1); SEQUESTRATION (1).

GATT (gat). *abbr.* GENERAL AGREEMENT ON TARIFFS AND TRADE.

g.b.h. *abbr.* Grievous bodily harm. See *serious bodily injury* under INJURY.

GBMI. *abbr.* GUILTY BUT MENTALLY ILL.

General Accounting Office. The federal agency that provides legal and accounting assistance to Congress, audits and investigates federal programs, and settles certain contract claims against the United States. — Abbr. GAO.

general administration. See ADMINISTRATION.

general administrative expense. See EXPENSE.

general administrator. See ADMINISTRATOR.

general agency. See AGENCY (1).

general agent. See AGENT.

General Agreement on Tariffs and Trade. A multiparty international agreement — signed originally in 1948 — that promotes international trade by lowering import duties and providing equal access to markets. • More than 130 nations are parties to the agreement. — Abbr. GATT.

general appearance. See APPEARANCE.

general assumpsit. See ASSUMPSIT.

general authority. See AUTHORITY (1).

general benefit. See BENEFIT.

general bequest. See BEQUEST.

general counsel. See COUNSEL.

general count. See COUNT.

general damages. See DAMAGES.

general denial. See DENIAL.

general deterrence. See DETERRENCE.

general devise. See DEVISE.

general exception. See EXCEPTION (1).

general executor. See EXECUTOR.

general federal common law. See COMMON LAW.

general fund. See FUND.

general guaranty. See GUARANTY.

generalia specialibus non derogant (jen-ə-**ray**-lee-ə spesh-ee-**ay**-lə-bəs non **der**-ə-gənt). [Latin "general things do not derogate from specific things"] The doctrine holding that general words in a later statute do not repeal an earlier statutory provision dealing with a special subject.

general improvement. See IMPROVEMENT.

general intangible. See INTANGIBLE.

general intent. See INTENT (1).

general issue. See ISSUE (1).

general jurisdiction. See JURISDICTION.

general jurisprudence. See JURISPRUDENCE.

general legacy. See LEGACY.

general legislation. See LEGISLATION.

generally accepted accounting principles. The conventions, rules, and procedures that define approved accounting practices at a particular time. — Abbr. GAAP.

generally accepted auditing standards. The guidelines issued by the American Institute of Certified Public Accountants establishing an auditor's professional qualities and the criteria for the auditor's examination and required reports. — Abbr. GAAS.

general malice. See MALICE.

general objection. See OBJECTION.

general occupant. See OCCUPANT.

general owner. See OWNER.

general partner. See PARTNER.

general partnership. See PARTNERSHIP.

general plea in bar. See PLEA IN BAR.

general power. See POWER.

general power of appointment. See POWER OF APPOINTMENT.

general power of attorney. See POWER OF ATTORNEY.

general prayer. See PRAYER FOR RELIEF.

general principle of law. 1. A principle widely recognized by peoples whose legal order has attained a certain level of sophistication. **2.** A principle recognized in all kinds of legal relations, regardless of the legal system to which it belongs (state law, federal law, international law, etc.).

general reference. See REFERENCE.

general retainer. See RETAINER.

general revenue fund. See FUND.

general sentence. See SENTENCE.

General Services Administration. The independent federal agency that manages the federal government's property and records. — Abbr. GSA.

general statute. See STATUTE.

general tax. See TAX.

general tenancy. See TENANCY.

general term. See TERM (5).

general traverse. See TRAVERSE.

general usage. See USAGE.

general verdict. See VERDICT.

general-verdict rule. The principle that when a general verdict is returned on multiple causes of action (or theories of recovery), it is presumed on appeal that the jury found in the prevailing party's favor on each cause of action.

general verdict with interrogatories. See VERDICT.

general warrant. See WARRANT.

general warranty. See WARRANTY (1).

general welfare. See WELFARE.

General Welfare Clause. U.S. Const. art. I, § 8, cl. 1, which empowers Congress to levy taxes and pay debts in order to provide for the country's general welfare. • The Supreme Court has broadly interpreted this clause to allow Congress to create, for example, the social-security system.

general words. Language used in deeds to convey not only the specific property described in the conveyance but also all easements, privileges, and appurtenances that may belong to the property.

generation-skipping tax. See TAX.

generation-skipping transfer. A conveyance of assets to a person more than one generation removed from the transferor, that is, a skip person. IRC (26 USCA) §§ 2601–2663. See *generation-skipping transfer tax* under TAX; *generation-skipping trust* under TRUST; SKIP PERSON.

generation-skipping transfer tax. See TAX.

generation-skipping trust. See TRUST.

generic, *adj.* **1.** Common or descriptive, and thus not eligible for trademark protection; nonproprietary <a generic name>. **2.** Not having a trademark or brand name <generic drugs>.

generic-drug law. A statute that allows pharmacists to substitute a generic drug for a brand-name drug under specified conditions. • Most states have enacted generic-drug laws to ensure that less-expensive generic drugs are available to consumers.

generic name. *Trademarks.* A term that describes something generally without designating the thing's source or creator, such as the word "car" or "sink." • Generic names cannot be protected as trademarks.

genetic mother. See *biological mother* under MOTHER.

gentlemen's agreement. An unwritten agreement that, while not legally enforceable, is secured by the good faith and honor of the parties.

gentrification, *n.* The restoration and upgrading of a deteriorated or aging urban neighborhood by middle-class or affluent persons, resulting in increased property values and often in displacement of lower-income residents. — **gentrify,** *vb.*

genuine, *adj.* **1.** (Of a thing) authentic or real; something that has the quality of what it is purported to be or to have. **2.** (Of an instrument) free of forgery or counterfeiting. UCC § 1–201(18).

genuine issue of material fact. *Civil procedure.* In the law of summary judgments, a triable, substantial, or real question of fact supported by substantial evidence. • An issue of this kind precludes entry of summary judgment.

geodetic-survey system (jee-ə-**det**-ik). A federally created land-description method consisting of nationwide marks (or *benches*) made at longitude and latitude points. • The geodetic-survey system integrates most of the real property in the United States into one unified form of measurement.

german (**jər**-mən), *adj.* Having the same parents or grandparents; closely related.

germane (jər-**mayn**), *adj.* Relevant; pertinent.

gerrymandering (**jer**-ee-man-dər-ing *or* **ger**-ee-), *n.* **1.** The practice of dividing a geographical area into electoral districts, often of highly irregular shape, to give one political party an unfair advantage by diluting the opposition's voting strength. **2.** The practice of dividing any geographical or jurisdictional area into political units (such as school districts) to give some group a special advantage. — **gerrymander,** *vb.* Cf. REAPPORTIONMENT.

gift, *n.* **1.** The act of voluntarily transferring property to another without compensation. **2.** A thing so transferred. — **gift,** *vb.*

anatomical gift. A testamentary donation of a bodily organ or organs, esp. for transplant or for medical research.

class gift. A gift to a group of persons, uncertain in number at the time of the gift but to be ascertained at a future time, who are all to take in definite proportions, the share of each being dependent on the ultimate number in the group.

completed gift. A gift that is no longer in the donor's possession and control. • Only a completed gift is taxable under the gift tax.

gift causa mortis (**kaw**-zə **mor**-tis). A gift made in contemplation of the donor's imminent death. • The three essentials are that (1) the gift must be made with a view to the donor's present illness or peril, (2) the donor must actually die from that illness or peril, without ever recovering, and (3) there must be a delivery. Even though *causa mortis* is the more usual word order in modern law, the correct Latin phrasing is *mortis causa* — hence *gift mortis causa*.

gift in trust. A gift of legal title to property that is to be used to benefit the cestui que trust (i.e., the beneficiary).

gift over. A property gift (esp. by will) that takes effect after the expiration of a preceding estate in the property (such as a life estate or fee simple determinable) <to Sarah for life, with gift over to Don in fee>.

inter vivos gift (**in**-tər **vɪ**-vohs *or* **vee**-vohs). A gift made during the donor's lifetime and delivered with the intention of irrevocably surrendering control over the property.

prenuptial gift (pree-**nəp**-shəl). A gift of property from one spouse to another before marriage. • In community-property states, prenuptial gifts are often made to preserve the property's classification as separate property.

split gift. *Tax.* A gift that is made by one spouse to a third person and that, for gift-tax purposes, both spouses treat as being made one-half by each spouse; a gift in which the spouses combine their annual gift-tax exclusions.

substitute gift. A testamentary gift to one person in place of another who is unable to take under the will for some reason.

taxable gift. A gift that, after adjusting for the annual exclusion and applicable deductions, is subject to the federal unified transfer tax. IRC (26 USCA) § 2503.

testamentary gift (tes-tə-**men**-tə-ree *or* -tree). A gift made in a will.

vested gift. An absolute gift, being neither conditional nor contingent, though its use or enjoyment might not occur until sometime in the future.

gift deed. See DEED.

gift enterprise. 1. A scheme for the distribution of items by chance among those who have purchased shares in the scheme. **2.** A merchant's scheme to induce sales for market value by giving buyers tickets that carry a chance to win a prize. See LOTTERY.

gift tax. See TAX.

Ginnie Mae (**jin**-ee **may**). See GOVERNMENT NATIONAL MORTGAGE ASSOCIATION.

gist (jist). **1.** The ground or essence (of a legal action). **2.** The main point. • This noun derives from the Law French verb *giser* "to lie."

give, *vb.* **1.** To voluntarily transfer (property) to another without compensation. **2.** To confer by a formal act. **3.** To present for another to consider. **4.** (Of a jury) to impose or award by verdict.

give, devise, and bequeath, *vb.* To transfer (property) by will <I give, devise, and bequeath all the rest, residue, and remainder of my estate to my beloved daughter Sarah>. See BEQUEST.

glass ceiling. An actual or supposed upper limit of professional advancement, esp. for women, as a result of discriminatory practices.

Glass–Steagall Act. A federal statute that protects bank depositors by restricting the securities-related business of commercial banks, specif. by prohibiting banks from owning brokerage firms or engaging in the brokerage business. 12 USCA § 378.

gloss, *n.* **1.** A note inserted between the lines or in the margin of a text to explain a difficult or obscure word in the text <this edition of Shakespeare's works is bolstered by its many glosses on Elizabethan English>. **2.** A collection of explanations; a glossary <the hornbook's copious gloss>. **3.** Pronouncements considered collectively, usu. by courts; interpretation <the statute and its judicial gloss>.

GMI. *abbr.* GUILTY BUT MENTALLY ILL.

GNMA. *abbr.* GOVERNMENT NATIONAL MORTGAGE ASSOCIATION.

go forward, *vb.* To commence or carry on with the presentation of a case in court <after the lunch recess, the judge instructed the plaintiff to go forward with its case>.

go hence without day. *Jargon.* (Of a defendant to a lawsuit) to be finished with legal proceedings without any further settings on the court's calendar. • Thus, a defendant who "goes hence without day" succeeds in getting a case finally resolved, usually by dismissal. The phrase derives from the Law French phrase *aller sans jour,* and over time defendants came to use it to request that the case against them be dismissed without the necessity of a day in court. See SINE DIE.

going-and-coming rule. 1. The principle that torts committed by an employee while commuting to or from work are generally outside the scope of employment. **2.** The principle that denies workers'-compensation benefits to an employee injured while commuting to or from work.

going concern. A commercial enterprise actively engaging in business with the expectation of indefinite continuance.

going price, *n.* The prevailing or current market value of something. See *fair market value* under VALUE.

golden rule. The principle that, in construing written instruments, a court should adhere to the grammatical and ordinary sense of the words unless that adherence would lead to some manifest absurdity; esp., in statutory construction, the principle that if a statute's literal meaning would lead to an absurd or unjust result, or even to an inconsistency within the statute itself, the statute should be interpreted in a way that avoids such a result or inconsistency. Cf. MISCHIEF RULE; PLAIN-MEANING RULE; EQUITY-OF-THE-STATUTE RULE.

golden-rule argument. A jury argument in which a lawyer asks the jurors to reach a verdict by imagining themselves or someone they care about in the place of the injured plaintiff or crime victim. • Because golden-rule arguments ask the jurors to become advocates for the plaintiff or victim and to ignore their obligation to exercise calm and reasonable judgment, these arguments are widely condemned and are considered improper in most states.

good and workmanlike. (Of a product or service) characterized by quality craftsmanship; constructed or performed in a skillful way or method.

good behavior. 1. A standard by which judges are considered fit to continue their tenure. **2.** Orderly conduct, which in the context of penal law allows a prisoner to reduce the time spent in prison. Cf. *good time* under TIME.

good cause. See CAUSE (1).

good consideration. See CONSIDERATION.

good faith, *n.* A state of mind consisting in (1) honesty in belief or purpose, (2) faithfulness to one's duty or obligation, (3) observance of reasonable commercial standards of fair dealing in a given trade or business, or (4) absence of intent to defraud or to seek unconscionable advantage. — **good-faith,** *adj.* Cf. BAD FAITH; BEST EFFORTS.

good-faith exception. *Criminal procedure.* An exception to the exclusionary rule whereby evidence obtained under a warrant later found to be invalid (esp. because it is not supported by probable cause) is nonetheless admissible if the police reasonably relied on the notion that the warrant was valid. • The good-faith exception was adopted by the Supreme Court in *United States v. Leon*, 468 U.S. 897, 104 S.Ct. 3405 (1984).

good moral character, *n.* **1.** A pattern of behavior that is consistent with the community's current ethical standards and that shows an absence of deceit or morally reprehensible conduct. **2.** A pattern of behavior conforming to a profession's ethical standards and showing an absence of moral turpitude.

goods. 1. Tangible or movable personal property other than money; esp., articles of trade or items of merchandise <goods and services>. • The sale of goods is governed by Article 2 of the UCC. **2.** Things that have value, whether tangible or not <the importance of social goods varies from society to society>.

Good Samaritan doctrine (sə-mar-i-tən). *Torts.* The principle that a person who is injured while attempting to aid another in imminent danger, and who then sues the one whose negligence created the danger, will not be charged with contributory negligence unless the rescue attempt is an unreasonable one or the rescuer acts unreasonably in performing the attempted rescue. Cf. EMERGENCY DOCTRINE; RESCUE DOCTRINE; LOST-CHANCE DOCTRINE.

good-samaritan law. A statute that exempts from liability a person (such as an off-duty physician) who voluntarily renders aid to another in imminent danger but negligently causes injury while rendering the aid.

goods and chattels (chat-əlz), *n.* Loosely, personal property of any kind; occasionally, tangible personal property only.

good time. See TIME.

good title. See TITLE (2).

govern, *vb.* (Of a precedent) to control a point in issue <the *Smith* case will govern the outcome of the appeal>.

government. 1. The structure of principles and rules determining how a state or organization is regulated. **2.** The sovereign power in a nation or state. **3.** An organization through which a body of people exercise political authority; the machinery by which sovereign power is expressed. • In this sense, the term refers collectively to the political organs of a country regardless of their function or level, and regardless of the subject matter they deal with. **4.** The executive branch of the U.S. government. **5.** The prosecutors in a given criminal case. **6.** An academic course devoted to the study of government; political science.

government agent. See AGENT.

governmental function. *Torts.* A government agency's conduct that is expressly or impliedly mandated or authorized by constitution, statute, or other law and that is carried out for the benefit of the general public. See PUBLIC-FUNCTION TEST. Cf. PROPRIETARY FUNCTION.

governmental-function theory. *Constitutional law.* A principle by which private conduct is characterized as state action, esp. for due-process and equal-protection purposes, when a private party is exercising a public function. • Under this theory, for example, a political party (which is a private entity) cannot exclude voters from primary elections on the basis of race.

governmental instrumentality. A constitutionally or legislatively created agency that is immune from certain kinds of liability, as for taxes or punitive damages.

governmental secret. Information belonging to the government and of a military or diplomatic nature, the disclosure of which would be contrary to the public interest. • Governmental secrets are privileged from disclosure. See *executive privilege* under PRIVILEGE (3).

Government National Mortgage Association. A federally owned corporation that purchases, on the secondary market, residential mortgages originated by local lenders and that issues federally insured securities backed by these mortgages. — Abbr. GNMA. — Also termed *Ginnie Mae.*

government tort. See TORT.

grab law. The various means of debt collection involving remedies outside the scope of federal bankruptcy law, such as attachment and garnishment; aggressive collection practices.

grace period. A period of extra time allowed for taking some required action (such as making payment) without incurring the usual penalty for late performance.

grade, *n. Criminal law*. An incremental step in the scale of punishments for offenses, based on a particular offense's seriousness. See DEGREE (2).

graded offense. See OFFENSE.

grading. The fixing of a criminal offense at a level of seriousness, such as first degree, second degree, or third degree (in reference to a felony), or Class A, Class B, or Class C (in reference to a misdemeanor). See DEGREE OF CRIME.

graduated lease. See LEASE.

graft, *n.* **1.** The act of taking advantage of a position of trust to gain money or property dishonestly; esp., a public official's fraudulent acquisition of public funds. **2.** Money or property gained illegally or unfairly.

grammatical interpretation. See INTERPRETATION.

grand, *adj.* Of or relating to a crime involving the theft of money or property valued more than a statutorily established amount, and therefore considered more serious than those involving a lesser amount. See *grand larceny* under LARCENY. Cf. PETTY.

grandfather, *vb.* To cover (a person) with the benefits of a grandfather clause <the statute sets the drinking age at 21 but grandfathers those who are 18 or older on the statute's effective date>.

grandfather clause. A statutory or regulatory clause that exempts a class of persons or transactions because of circumstances existing before the new rule or regulation takes effect.

grand jury. A body of (often 23) people who are chosen to sit permanently for at least a month — and sometimes a year — and who, in ex parte proceedings, decide whether to issue indictments. • If the grand jury decides that evidence is strong enough to hold a suspect for trial, it returns a bill of indictment (a *true bill*) charging the suspect with a specific crime. Cf. *petit jury* under JURY.

investigative grand jury. A grand jury whose primary function is to examine possible crimes and develop evidence not currently available to the prosecution.

runaway grand jury. A grand jury that acts essentially in opposition to the prosecution, as by perversely failing to return an indictment that the prosecution has requested.

screening grand jury. A grand jury whose primary function is to decide whether to issue an indictment.

special grand jury. A grand jury specially summoned, usu. when the regular grand jury either has already been discharged or has not been drawn; a grand jury with limited authority.

Grand Jury Clause. The clause of the Fifth Amendment to the U.S. Constitution requiring an indictment by a grand jury before a person can be tried for serious offenses.

grand-jury witness. See WITNESS.

grand larceny. See LARCENY.

grant, *n.* **1.** An agreement that creates a right of any description other than the one held by the grantor. • Examples include leases, easements, charges, patents, franchises, powers, and licenses. **2.** The formal transfer of real property. **3.** The document by which a transfer is effected; esp., DEED. **4.** The property or property right so transferred.

grant, *vb.* **1.** To give or confer (something), with or without compensation. **2.** To formally transfer (real property) by deed or other writing. **3.** To permit or agree to. **4.** To approve, warrant, or order (a request, motion, etc.).

grantback, *n.* A license-agreement provision requiring the licensee to assign or license back to the licensor any improvements that the licensee might make to a patent or other proprietary right.

grant deed. See DEED.

grantee. One to whom property is conveyed.

grantee–grantor index. See INDEX.

granting clause. The words that transfer an interest in a deed or other instrument, esp. an oil-and-gas lease.

grantor. 1. One who conveys property to another. **2.** SETTLOR (1).

grantor–grantee index. See INDEX.

grantor trust. See TRUST.

gratuitous (grə-tyoo-ə-təs), *adj.* **1.** Done or performed without obligation to do so; given without consideration <gratuitous promise>. Cf. ONEROUS (3). **2.** Done unnecessarily <gratuitous nudity>. — **gratuity,** *n.*

gratuitous bailment. See BAILMENT.

gratuitous consideration. See CONSIDERATION.

gratuitous promise. See PROMISE.

gravamen (grə-vay-mən). The substantial point or essence of a claim, grievance, or complaint.

graymail. A criminal defendant's threat to reveal classified information during the trial in the hope of forcing the government to drop the criminal charge. Cf. BLACKMAIL; GREENMAIL; FEEMAIL.

great care. See CARE.

green card. A registration card evidencing a resident alien's status as a permanent U.S. resident.

greenmail. 1. The act of buying enough stock in a company to threaten a hostile takeover and then selling the stock back to the corporation at an inflated price. **2.** The money paid for stock in the corporation's buyback. Cf. BLACKMAIL; FEEMAIL; GRAYMAIL. **3.** A shareholder's act of filing or threatening to file a derivative action and then seeking a disproportionate settlement.

grievance, *n.* **1.** An injury, injustice, or wrong that gives ground for a complaint. **2.** The complaint itself. **3.** *Labor law.* A complaint that is filed by an employee or the employee's union representative and that usu. concerns working conditions, esp. an alleged violation of a collective-bargaining agreement.

grieve, *vb.* To contest under a grievance procedure. — **grievable,** *adj.*

grift, *vb.* To obtain money illicitly by adroit use of a scam, confidence game, or other fraudulent means. — **grifter,** *n.*

gross income. See INCOME.

gross-income tax. See TAX.

gross lease. See LEASE.

gross misdemeanor. See MISDEMEANOR.

gross negligence. See NEGLIGENCE.

gross up, *vb. Slang. Tax.* To add back to a decedent's gross estate the gift taxes paid by the decedent or the decedent's estate on gifts made by the decedent or the decedent's spouse during the three-year period preceding the decedent's death. IRC (26 USCA) § 2035.

ground, *n.* The reason or point that something (as a legal claim or argument) relies on for validity <grounds for divorce>.

ground, *vb.* **1.** To provide a basis for (something, e.g., a legal claim or argument) <his complaint was grounded in common law>. **2.** To base (something, e.g., a legal principle or judicial decision) on <strict liability is grounded on public policy>.

ground lease. See LEASE.

groundless, *adj.* (Of a legal claim or argument) lacking reason or validity <groundless cause of action>. See FRIVOLOUS.

group libel. See LIBEL.

group litigation. A set of lawsuits on behalf of or against numerous persons recognized as one litigating entity, such as a civil-rights group.

growth industry. An industry or business segment that demonstrates steadily rising sales and earnings.

growth management. *Land-use planning.* The regulation of a community's rate of growth through ordinances that restrict the issuance of residential building permits. See ZONING.

GSA. *abbr.* GENERAL SERVICES ADMINISTRATION.

guarantee, *n.* **1.** The assurance that a contract or legal act will be duly carried out. **2.** GUARANTY (1). **3.** Something given or existing as security, such as to fulfill a future engagement or a condition subsequent. **4.** One to whom a guaranty is made. — **guarantee,** *vb.*

guarantee clause. 1. A provision in a contract, deed, or mortgage by which one person promises to pay the obligation of another. **2.** (*cap.*) U.S. Const. art. IV, § 4, under which the federal government ensures for the states both a republican form of government and protection from invasion or domestic violence.

guarantor. One who makes a guaranty or gives security for a debt. • While a surety's liability begins with that of the principal, a guarantor's liability does not begin until the principal debtor is in default. Cf. SURETY (1).

guarantor of collectibility. One who guarantees a debtor's solvency and is under a duty to pay only if the creditor is unable to collect from the principal debtor after exhausting all legal remedies, including demand, suit, judgment, and any supplementary proceedings.

guarantor of payment. One who guarantees payment of a negotiable instrument when it is due without the holder first seeking payment from another party. • A guarantor of payment is liable only if "payment guaranteed" or equivalent words are added to the guarantor's indorsement.

guaranty (**gar**-ən-tee), *n.* **1.** A promise to answer for the payment of some debt, or the performance of some duty, in case of the failure of another who is liable in the first instance. • The term is most common in finance and banking contexts. While a warranty relates to things (not persons), is not collateral, and need not be in writing, a guaranty is an undertaking that a person will pay or do some act, is collateral to the duty of the primary obligor, and must be in writing.

absolute guaranty. An unqualified promise that the principal will pay or perform.

conditional guaranty. A guaranty that requires the performance of some condition by the creditor before the guarantor will become liable.

contingent guaranty. A guaranty in which the guarantor will not be liable unless a specified event occurs.

continuing guaranty. A guaranty that governs a course of dealing for an indefinite time or by a succession of credits.

general guaranty. **1.** A guaranty addressed to no specific person, so that anyone who acts on it can enforce it. **2.** A guaranty for the principal's default on obligations that the principal undertakes with anyone.

guaranty of collection. A guaranty that is conditioned on the creditor's having first exhausted legal remedies against the principal debtor before suing the guarantor. See *guarantor of collectibility* under GUARANTOR.

guaranty of payment. A guaranty that is not conditioned on the creditor's exhausting legal remedies against the principal debtor before suing the guarantor. See *guarantor of payment* under GUARANTOR.

irrevocable guaranty (i-**rev**-ə-kə-bəl). A guaranty that cannot be terminated unless the other parties consent.

limited guaranty. An agreement to answer for a debt arising from a single transaction.

revocable guaranty. A guaranty that the guarantor may terminate without any other party's consent.

special guaranty. **1.** A guaranty addressed to a particular person or group of persons, who are the only ones who can enforce it. **2.** A guaranty that names a definite person as obligee and that can be accepted only by the person named.

specific guaranty. A guaranty of a single debt or obligation.

2. GUARANTEE (1).

guardian, *n.* One who has the legal authority and duty to care for another's person or property, esp. because of the other's infancy, incapacity, or disability. • A guardian may be appointed either for all purposes or for specific purposes. — **guardianship,** *n.* See WARD (1).

guardian ad litem (ad lɪ-təm). A guardian, usu. a lawyer, appointed by the court to appear in a lawsuit on behalf of an incompetent or minor party. Cf. NEXT FRIEND.

special guardian. A guardian who has special or limited powers over the ward's person or estate. • Examples are guardians who have custody of the estate but not of the person, those who have custody of the person but not of the estate, and guardians ad litem.

guest. 1. A person who is entertained or to whom hospitality is extended. **2.** A person who pays for services at an establishment, esp. a hotel or restaurant. **3.** A nonpaying passenger in a motor vehicle.

business guest. Torts. See INVITEE.

social guest. Torts. See LICENSEE (2).

guest statute. A law that bars a nonpaying passenger in a noncommercial vehicle from suing the host-driver for damages resulting from the driver's ordinary negligence. Cf. FAMILY-PURPOSE RULE.

guilt, *n.* The fact or state of having committed a wrong, esp. a crime. Cf. INNOCENCE.

guilt phase. The part of a criminal trial during which the fact-finder determines whether the defendant committed a crime. Cf. PENALTY PHASE.

guilty, *adj.* **1.** Having committed a crime; responsible for a crime. **2.** Responsible for a civil wrong, such as a tort or breach of contract. — **guiltily,** *adv.*

guilty, *n.* **1.** A plea of a criminal defendant who does not contest the charges. **2.** A jury verdict convicting the defendant of the crime charged.

guilty but mentally ill. A form of verdict in a criminal case whereby the jury rejects the defendant's insanity defense but still recommends psychiatric treatment because the defendant is mentally ill. — Abbr. GBMI; GMI. See INSANITY DEFENSE.

guilty plea. See PLEA (1).

guilty verdict. See VERDICT.

gun-control law. A statute or ordinance that regulates the sale, possession, or use of firearms. • Gun-control laws vary widely among the states, and many cities have gun-control ordinances. Federal law prohibits the illegal sale, possession, and use of firearms. 18 USCA §§ 921–930. See BRADY ACT.

H

H. *abbr.* **1.** HOUSE OF REPRESENTATIVES. **2.** House report.

habeas corpus (**hay**-bee-əs **kor**-pəs). [Law Latin "that you have the body"] A writ employed to bring a person before a court, most frequently to ensure that the party's imprisonment or detention is not illegal (*habeas corpus ad subjiciendum*). • In addition to being used to test the legality of an arrest or commitment, the writ may be used to obtain review of (1) the regularity of the extradition process, (2) the right to or amount of bail, or (3) the jurisdiction of a court that has imposed a criminal sentence.

habendum clause (hə-**ben**-dəm). **1.** The part of a deed that defines the extent of the interest being granted and any conditions affecting the grant. • The introductory words to the clause are ordinarily *to have and to hold*. **2.** An oil-and-gas lease provision that defines the lease's primary term and that usu. extends the lease for a secondary term of indefinite duration as long as oil, gas, or other minerals are being produced.

habitability. The condition of a building in which inhabitants can live free of serious defects that might harm health and safety.

habit evidence. See EVIDENCE.

had. Commenced or begun, as used in a statute providing that no legal proceeding may be *had* (usu. followed by the words *or maintained*) <no action for foreclosure may be had or maintained until the debtor has been given at least 30 days' notice>.

Hadley v. Baxendale **rule.** *Contracts.* The principle that consequential damages will be awarded for breach of contract only if, at the time of contracting, the parties contemplated that this type of damage would result from the breach. *Hadley v. Baxendale*, 9 Exch. 341 (1854). • *Hadley v. Baxendale* is best known for its impact on a nonbreaching party's ability to recover consequential damages, but the case also confirmed the principle that the nonbreaching party may recover damages that arise naturally from the breach. See DAMAGES.

Hague Academy of International Law (hayg). A center for advanced studies in international law, both public and private, aimed at facilitating the comprehensive and impartial examination of problems of international legal relations.

Hague Convention. One of a number of international conventions that address different legal issues and attempt to standardize procedures between nations.

Hague Convention on the Civil Aspects of International Child Abduction. An international convention (established in 1980) that seeks to counteract child-snatching by noncustodial parents.

Hague Convention on the Service Abroad of Judicial and Extrajudicial Documents. An international convention, convened on November 15, 1965, that dictates the formal and usu. complicated procedures for effecting service of process in a foreign country.

Hague Convention on the Taking of Evidence Abroad in Civil or Commercial Matters. An international convention, convened on October 26, 1968, that provides the formal procedures for obtaining evidence in a foreign country, such as taking a deposition abroad.

half blood. See BLOOD.

halfway house. A transitional housing facility designed to rehabilitate people who have recently left a prison or medical-care facility, or who otherwise need help in adjusting to a normal life.

hand down, *vb.* To announce or file an opinion in a case.

Hand formula. A balancing test for determining whether conduct has created an unreasonable risk of harm, first formulated by Judge Learned Hand in *United States v. Carroll Towing Co.*, 159 F.2d 169 (2d Cir. 1947). • Under this test, an actor is negligent if the burden of taking adequate precautions against the harm is outweighed by the gravity of the probable harm multiplied by the probability that the harm will occur.

hands-off agreement. A noncompete contractual provision between an employer and a former employee prohibiting the employee from using information learned during his or her employment to divert or to steal customers from the former employer.

hand up, *vb.* (Of a grand jury) to deliver an indictment to a criminal court.

handwriting. *Evidence.* **1.** A person's chirography; the cast or form of writing peculiar to a person, including the size, shape, and style of letters, and whatever gives individuality to one's writing. **2.** Something written by hand; a writing specimen. • Nonexpert opinion about the genuineness of handwriting, based on familiarity not acquired for litigation purposes, can authenticate a document. Fed. R. Evid. 901(b)(2).

hang, *vb.* (Of a jury) to be unable to reach a verdict. See *hung jury* under JURY.

hanging judge. See JUDGE.

happiness, right to pursue. The constitutional right to pursue any lawful business or activity — in any manner not inconsistent with the equal rights of others — that might yield the highest enjoyment, increase one's prosperity, or allow the development of one's faculties.

harassment (hə-**ras**-mənt *or* **har**-əs-mənt). Words, conduct, or action (usu. repeated or persistent) that, being directed at a specific person, annoys, alarms, or causes substantial emotional distress in that person and serves no legitimate purpose. — **harass** (hə-**ras** *or* **har**-əs), *vb.* See SEXUAL HARASSMENT.

harboring, *n.* The act of affording lodging, shelter, or refuge to a person, esp. a criminal or illegal alien.

hard case. A lawsuit involving equities that tempt a judge to stretch or even disregard a principle of law at issue — hence the expression, "Hard cases make bad law."

hard labor. Work imposed on prisoners as additional punishment, usu. for misconduct while in prison.

hard-look doctrine. *Administrative law.* The principle that a court should carefully review an administrative-agency decision to ensure that the decision did not result from expediency, pressure, or whim.

hardship. 1. Privation; suffering or adversity. **2.** *Zoning.* A ground for a variance under some zoning statutes if the zoning ordinance as applied to a particular property is unduly oppressive, arbitrary, or confiscatory. **3.** The severity with which a proposed construction of law would bear on a particular case, sometimes forming a basis (also known as an argument *ab inconvenienti*) against the construction. See HARD CASE.

harm, *n.* Injury, loss, or detriment.

> ***bodily harm.*** Physical pain, illness, or impairment of the body.
>
> ***physical harm.*** Any physical impairment of land, chattels, or the human body.
>
> ***social harm.*** An adverse effect on any social interest that is protected by the criminal law.

harmless error. See ERROR (2).

harmony. Agreement or accord; conformity <the decision in *Jones* is in harmony with earlier Supreme Court precedent>. — **harmonize,** *vb.*

hate crime. See CRIME.

hate speech. See SPEECH.

hazard, *n.* **1.** Danger; peril. **2.** The risk or probability of loss or injury, esp. a loss or injury covered by an insurance policy.

hazardous substance. 1. A toxic pollutant; an imminently dangerous chemical or mixture. **2.** See *hazardous waste* under WASTE (2).

hazardous waste. See WASTE (2).

hazard pay. Special compensation for work done under unpleasant or unsafe conditions.

H.B. *abbr.* See *house bill* under BILL (3).

HDC. *abbr.* HOLDER IN DUE COURSE.

headlease. A primary lease under which a sublease has been granted.

headlessor. A lessor on a lease of property that has been subleased.

head money. A tax on people who fit within a designated class; a poll tax. See *poll tax* under TAX.

headnote. A case summary that appears before the printed judicial opinion in a law report, addresses a point of law, and usu. includes the relevant facts bearing on that point of law.

headnote lawyer. See LAWYER.

head of household. 1. The primary income-provider within a family. **2.** For income-tax purposes, an unmarried or separated person (other than a surviving spouse) who provides a home for dependents for more than one-half of the taxable year.

headright. In American Indian law, a tribemember's right to a pro rata portion of income from a tribal trust fund set up under the Allotment Act of 1906.

health. 1. The state of being sound or whole in body, mind, or soul. **2.** Freedom from pain or sickness.

***public health*. 1.** The health of the community at large. **2.** The healthful or sanitary condition of the general body of people or the community en masse; esp., the methods of maintaining the health of the community, as by preventive medicine and organized care for the sick.

health law. A statute, ordinance, or code that prescribes sanitary standards and regulations for the purpose of promoting and preserving the community's health.

health-maintenance organization. A group of participating healthcare providers that furnish medical services to enrolled members of a group health-insurance plan. — Abbr. HMO. Cf. PREFERRED-PROVIDER ORGANIZATION.

hearing. 1. A judicial session, usu. open to the public, held for the purpose of deciding issues of fact or of law, sometimes with witnesses testifying. **2.** *Administrative law*. Any setting in which an affected person presents arguments to an agency decision-maker. **3.** In legislative practice, any proceeding in which legislators or their designees receive testimony about legislation that might be enacted. **4.** *Equity practice*. A trial.

adjudicatory hearing (ə-**joo**-di-kə-tor-ee). **1.** A hearing held by a juvenile court to determine whether a juvenile has engaged in delinquent conduct; a trial of a youth accused of a delinquency. See JUVENILE DELINQUENCY. Cf. *detention hearing*; *disposition hearing*. **2.** *Administrative law*. An agency proceeding in which the rights and duties of a particular person are decided after notice and an opportunity to be heard.

***detention hearing*. 1.** A hearing to determine whether an accused should be released pending trial. See *pretrial detention* under DETENTION. **2.** A hearing held by a juvenile court to determine whether a juvenile accused of delinquent conduct should be detained, continued in confinement, or released pending an adjudicatory hearing. Cf. *adjudicatory hearing*; *disposition hearing*.

***disposition hearing*.** A hearing held to determine the most appropriate form of custody or treatment for a juvenile who has been found at an adjudicatory hearing to be a juvenile delinquent or a status offender. Cf. *adjudicatory hearing*; *detention hearing*.

***evidentiary hearing*. 1.** A hearing at which evidence is presented, as opposed to a hearing at which only legal argument is presented. **2.** See ADMINISTRATIVE PROCEEDING.

***exclusionary hearing*.** A pretrial hearing conducted to review and determine the admissibility of alleged illegally obtained evidence.

***fair hearing*.** A judicial or administrative hearing conducted in accordance with due process.

full hearing. **1.** A hearing at which the parties are allowed notice of each other's claims and are given ample opportunity to present their positions with evidence and argument. **2.** See ADMINISTRATIVE PROCEEDING.

hearing de novo (dee *or* di **noh**-voh). **1.** A reviewing court's decision of a matter anew, giving no deference to a lower court's findings. **2.** A new hearing of a matter, conducted as if the original hearing had not taken place.

omnibus hearing. A hearing designed to bring judicial oversight over criminal cases at an early stage to make certain that the cases are being handled expeditiously and properly.

public hearing. A hearing that, within reasonable limits, is open to anyone who wishes to observe.

revocation hearing. *Criminal procedure.* A hearing held to determine whether a parolee should be returned to prison for violating the terms of parole.

suppression hearing. A pretrial hearing in which a criminal defendant seeks to prevent the introduction of evidence alleged to have been seized illegally.

transfer hearing. A hearing held to determine whether a juvenile alleged to have committed a delinquent act should be tried as an adult or as a juvenile.

unfair hearing. A hearing that is not conducted in accordance with due process, as when the defendant is denied the opportunity to prepare or consult with counsel.

hearsay. 1. Traditionally, testimony that is given by a witness who relates not what he or she knows personally, but what others have said, and that is therefore dependent on the credibility of someone other than the witness. • Such testimony is generally inadmissible under the rules of evidence. **2.** In federal law, a statement (either a verbal assertion or nonverbal assertive conduct), other than one made by the declarant while testifying at the trial or hearing, offered in evidence to prove the truth of the matter asserted. Fed. R. Evid. 801(c). Cf. *original evidence* under EVIDENCE.

double hearsay. A hearsay statement that contains further hearsay statements within it, none of which is admissible unless exceptions to the rule against hearsay can be applied to each level <the double hearsay was the investigation's report stating that Amy admitted to running the red light>. Fed. R. Evid. 805.

hearsay rule. The rule that no assertion offered as testimony can be received unless it is or has been open to test by cross-examination or an opportunity for cross-examination, except as provided otherwise by the rules of evidence, by court rules, or by statute. • The chief reasons for the rule are that out-of-court statements amounting to hearsay are not made under oath and are not subject to cross-examination. Fed. R. Evid. 802. Rule 803 provides 23 explicit exceptions to the hearsay rule, regardless of whether the out-of-court declarant is available to testify, and

Rule 804 provides 5 more exceptions for situations in which the declarant is unavailable to testify.

heat of passion. Rage, terror, or furious hatred suddenly aroused by some immediate provocation, usu. another person's words or actions. • At common law, the heat of passion could serve as a mitigating circumstance that would reduce a murder charge to manslaughter. Cf. COLD BLOOD; COOL BLOOD.

hedonic damages. See DAMAGES.

hedonistic utilitarianism. See UTILITARIANISM.

heeding presumption. See PRESUMPTION.

heedlessness, *n.* The quality of being thoughtless and inconsiderate; esp., conduct whereby the actor disregards the rights or safety of others. • Heedlessness is often construed to involve the same degree of fault as recklessness. — **heedless,** *adj.* See RECKLESSNESS.

heinous (hay-nəs), *adj.* (Of a crime or its perpetrator) shockingly atrocious or odious. — **heinousness,** *n.*

heir (air). **1.** A person who, under the laws of intestacy, is entitled to receive an intestate decedent's property. **2.** Loosely (in common-law jurisdictions), a person who inherits real or personal property, whether by will or by intestate succession. **3.** Popularly, a person who has inherited or is in line to inherit great wealth.

after-born heir. One born after the death of an intestate from whom the heir is entitled to inherit.

collateral heir. One who is neither a direct descendant nor an ancestor of the decedent, but whose kinship is through a collateral line, such as a brother, sister, uncle, aunt, nephew, niece, or cousin. Cf. *lineal heir.*

expectant heir. An heir who has a reversionary or remainder interest in property, or a chance of succeeding to it. See REVERSION; REMAINDER. Cf. *prospective heir.*

forced heir. A person whom the testator or donor cannot disinherit because the law reserves part of the estate for that person.

heir apparent. An heir who is certain to inherit unless he or she dies first or is excluded by a valid will. Cf. *heir presumptive.*

heir by devise. One to whom lands are given by will.

heir of the blood. An heir who succeeds to an estate because of consanguinity with the decedent, in either the ascending or descending line.

heir presumptive. An heir who will inherit if the potential intestate dies immediately, but who may be excluded if another more closely related heir is born. Cf. *heir apparent.*

heirs and assigns. A term of art formerly required to create a fee simple <A conveys Blackacre to B and his heirs and assigns>.

joint heir. **1.** A coheir. **2.** A person who is or will be an heir to both of two designated persons at the death of the survivor of them, the word *joint* being here applied to the ancestors rather than the heirs.

known heir. An heir who is present to claim an inheritance, the extent of which depends on there being no closer relative.

laughing heir. *Slang.* An heir distant enough to feel no grief when a relative dies and leaves an inheritance (generally viewed as a windfall) to the heir.

lineal heir. A person who is either an ancestor or a descendant of the decedent, such as a parent or child. Cf. *collateral heir.*

natural heir. An heir by consanguinity as distinguished from a collateral heir, an heir by adoption, or a statutory heir (such as a person's spouse).

pretermitted heir (pree-tər-**mit**-id). A child or spouse who has been omitted from a will, as when a testator makes a will naming his or her two children and then, sometime later, has two more children who are not mentioned in the will. See PRETERMITTED-HEIR STATUTE.

prospective heir. An heir who may inherit but may be excluded; an heir apparent or an heir presumptive. Cf. *expectant heir.*

hell-or-high-water clause. A clause in a personal-property lease requiring the lessee to continue to make full rent payments to the lessor even if the thing leased is unsuitable, defective, or destroyed.

hell-or-high-water rule. 1. The principle that a personal-property lessee must pay the full rent due, regardless of any claim against the lessor, unless the lessee proves unequal bargaining power or unconscionability. **2.** *Insurance.* The principle that an insured's automobile-liability policy will cover the insured while using a vehicle owned by another if the insured uses the vehicle in a manner within the scope of the permission granted.

henceforth, *adv. Jargon.* From now on <the newly enacted rule will apply henceforth>.

hereafter, *adv. Jargon.* **1.** From now on; henceforth <because of the highway construction, she will hereafter take the bus to work>. **2.** At some future time <the court will hereafter issue a ruling on the gun's admissibility>. **3.** HEREINAFTER <the exhibits hereafter referred to as Exhibit A and Exhibit B>.

hereby, *adv. Jargon.* By this document; by these very words <I hereby declare my intention to run for public office>.

hereditament (her-ə-**dit**-ə-mənt *or* hə-**red**-i-tə-mənt). **1.** Any property that can be inherited; anything that passes by intestacy. **2.** Real property; land.

hereditary succession. See SUCCESSION.

herein, *adv. Jargon.* In this thing (such as a document, section, or matter) <the due-process arguments stated herein should convince the court to reverse the judgment>.

hereinafter, *adv. Jargon.* Later in this document <the buyer agrees to purchase the property described hereinafter>.

hereof, *adv. Jargon.* Of this thing (such as a provision or document) <the conditions hereof are stated in section 3>.

hereto, *adv. Jargon.* To this document <the exhibits are attached hereto>.

heretofore, *adv. Jargon.* Up to now; before this time <a question that has not heretofore been decided>.

hereunder, *adv. Jargon.* **1.** Later in this document <review the provisions hereunder before signing the consent form>. **2.** In accordance with this document <notice hereunder must be provided within 30 days after the loss>.

herewith, *adv. Jargon.* With or in this document <enclosed herewith are three copies>.

heritable (**her**-i-tə-bəl), *adj.* INHERITABLE.

HGN test. *abbr.* HORIZONTAL-GAZE NYSTAGMUS TEST.

HHS. *abbr.* The Department of Health and Human Services, a federal agency that administers health, welfare, and income-security policies and programs, the largest of which is social security.

HIDC. *abbr.* HOLDER IN DUE COURSE.

hidden defect. See DEFECT.

hidden tax. See TAX.

high crime. See CRIME.

highest court. The court of last resort in a particular jurisdiction; a court whose decision is final and cannot be appealed because no higher court exists to consider the matter.

highest degree of care. See DEGREE OF CARE.

high–low agreement. A settlement in which a defendant agrees to pay the plaintiff a minimum recovery in return for the plaintiff's agreement to accept a maximum amount regardless of the outcome of the trial.

hijack, *vb.* **1.** To commandeer (a vehicle or airplane), esp. at gunpoint. **2.** To steal or rob from (a vehicle or airplane in transit).

hired gun. *Slang.* **1.** An expert witness who testifies favorably for the party paying his or her fee, often because of that financial relationship rather than because of the facts. **2.** A lawyer who stops at nothing to accomplish the client's goals, regardless of moral consequences.

His Honor; Her Honor. 1. A title customarily given to a judge. **2.** A title customarily given to the mayor of a city. **3.** A title given by the Massachusetts Constitution to the lieutenant governor of the commonwealth. Cf. YOUR HONOR.

historical jurisprudence. See JURISPRUDENCE.

hit-and-run statute. A law requiring a motorist involved in an accident to remain at the scene and to give certain information to the police and others involved.

hitherto, *adv. Jargon.* Until now; heretofore.

HLA test. *abbr.* A human-leukocyte-antigen test that uses a tissue-typing process to determine the probability of fatherhood. See PATERNITY TEST. Cf. DNA IDENTIFICATION.

HMO. *abbr.* HEALTH-MAINTENANCE ORGANIZATION.

hodgepodge. 1. HOTCHPOT (1). **2.** An unorganized mixture.

hodgepodge act. A statute that deals with incongruous subjects.

hold, *vb.* **1.** To possess by a lawful title <Sarah holds the account as her separate property>. **2.** (Of a court) to adjudge or decide <this court thus holds the statute to be unconstitutional>. **3.** To direct and bring about officially; to conduct according to law <we must hold an election every two years>. **4.** To keep in custody or under an obligation <I will ask the judge to hold you accountable>. **5.** To take or have an estate from another; to have an estate on condition of paying rent or performing service <James holds Hungerstream Manor under lease>. **6.** To conduct or preside at; to convoke, open, and direct the operations of <Judge Brown holds court four days a week>. **7.** To possess or occupy; to be in possession and administration of <Jones holds the office of treasurer>.

holder. 1. A person who has legal possession of a negotiable instrument and is entitled to receive payment on it. **2.** A person with legal possession of a document of title or an investment security. **3.** A person who possesses or uses property.

holder for value. A person who has given value in exchange for a negotiable instrument. • Under the UCC, examples of "giving value" include acquiring a security interest in the instrument and accepting the instrument in payment of an antecedent claim. UCC § 3–303(a).

holder in due course. A person who in good faith has given value for a negotiable instrument that is complete and regular on its face, is not overdue, and, to the possessor's knowledge, has not been dishonored. • Under UCC § 3–305, a holder in due course takes the instrument free of all claims and personal defenses, but subject to real defenses. — Abbr. HDC; HIDC.

holder in good faith. One who takes property or an instrument without knowledge of any defect in its title.

hold harmless, *vb.* To absolve (another party) from any responsibility for damage or other liability arising from the transaction; INDEMNIFY.

hold-harmless agreement. A contract in which one party agrees to indemnify the other. See INDEMNITY.

holding, *n.* **1.** A court's determination of a matter of law pivotal to its decision; a principle drawn from such a decision. Cf. OBITER DICTUM. **2.** A ruling on evidence or other questions presented at trial. **3.** (*usu. pl.*) Legally owned property, esp. land or securities.

holding charge. A criminal charge of some minor offense filed to keep the accused in custody while prosecutors take time to build a bigger case and prepare more serious charges.

holding company. See COMPANY.

holding over. A tenant's action in continuing to occupy the leased premises after the lease term has expired. See *tenancy at sufferance* under TENANCY.

holding period. *Tax.* The time during which a capital asset must be held to determine whether gain or loss from its sale or exchange is long-term or short-term.

hold order. A notation in a prisoner's file stating that another jurisdiction has charges pending against the prisoner and instructing prison officials to alert authorities in that other jurisdiction instead of releasing the prisoner.

hold out, *vb.* **1.** To represent (oneself or another) as having a certain legal status, as by claiming to be an agent or partner with authority to enter into transactions <even though he was only a promoter, Schwartz held himself out as the principal>. **2.** To refuse to yield or submit; to stand firm <Womack held out for a higher salary and better benefits>.

holdover. See HOLDING OVER.

holograph (**hol**-ə-graf), *n.* A document (such as a will or deed) that is entirely handwritten by its author. — **holographic,** *adj.* Cf. SYMBOLIC.

holographic will. See WILL.

home equity loan. See LOAN.

home rule. A state legislative provision or action allocating a measure of autonomy to a local government, conditional on its acceptance of certain terms.

homestead. The house, outbuildings, and adjoining land owned and occupied by a person or family as a residence.

business homestead. The premises on which a family's business is located.

constitutional homestead. A homestead, along with its exemption from forced sale, conferred on the head of a household by a state constitution.

probate homestead. A homestead created by a probate court from a decedent's estate for the benefit of the decedent's surviving spouse and minor children.

homestead law. A statute exempting a homestead from execution or judicial sale for debt, unless all owners, usu. a husband and wife, have jointly mortgaged the property or otherwise subjected it to creditors' claims.

homicide (**hom**-ə-sɪd), *n.* The killing of one person by another. — **homicidal,** *adj.*

criminal homicide. **1.** Homicide prohibited and punishable by law, such as murder or manslaughter. **2.** The act of purposely, knowingly, recklessly, or negligently causing the death of another human being. Model Penal Code § 210.1.

excusable homicide. **1.** Homicide resulting from a person's lawful act, committed without intention to harm another. **2.** See *justifiable homicide* (1).

felonious homicide. Homicide committed unlawfully, without legal justification or excuse. • This is the category into which murder and manslaughter fall.

homicide by abuse. Homicide in which the perpetrator, under circumstances showing an extreme indifference to human life, causes the death of the perpetrator's dependent — usu. a child or mentally retarded person.

homicide per infortunium (pər in-for-**t[y]oo**-nee-əm). [Latin "homicide by misfortune"] The unintentional killing of another while engaged in a lawful act; ACCIDENTAL KILLING.

innocent homicide. Homicide that does not involve criminal guilt.

justifiable homicide. **1.** The killing of another in self-defense when faced with the danger of death or serious bodily injury. See SELF-DEFENSE. **2.** A killing mandated or permitted by the law, such as execution for a capital crime or killing to prevent a crime or a criminal's escape.

negligent homicide. Homicide resulting from the careless performance of a legal or illegal act in which the danger of death is apparent; the killing of a human being by criminal negligence. See *criminal negligence* under NEGLIGENCE.

reckless homicide. The unlawful killing of another person with conscious indifference toward that person's life. Cf. MANSLAUGHTER.

vehicular homicide. The killing of another person by one's unlawful or negligent operation of a motor vehicle.

willful homicide. The act of intentionally causing a person's death, with or without legal justification.

Hon. *abbr.* HONORABLE.

honor, *vb.* **1.** To accept or pay (a negotiable instrument) when presented. **2.** To recognize, salute, or praise.

Honorable. A title of respect given to judges, members of the U.S. Congress, ambassadors, and the like. — Abbr. Hon.

honorarium (on-ə-**rair**-ee-əm), *n.* **1.** A payment of money or anything of value made to a person for services rendered for which fees cannot legally be or are not traditionally paid. **2.** A voluntary reward for that for which no remuneration could be collected by law; a voluntary donation in consideration of services that admit of no compensation in money. Pl. **honoraria.**

honorary trust. See TRUST.

horizontal competition. See COMPETITION.

horizontal-gaze nystagmus test. *Criminal law.* A field-sobriety test for intoxication, in which the suspect is told to focus on an object (such as a pencil) and to track its movement, usu. from side to side, by moving only the eyes. • Intoxication is indicated if the eyes jerk or twitch while tracking the object. — Abbr. HGN test.

horizontal nonprivity. See NONPRIVITY.

horizontal price-fixing. See PRICE-FIXING.

horizontal privity. See PRIVITY.

hornbook. **1.** A book explaining the basics of a given subject. **2.** A textbook containing the rudimentary principles of an area of law. Cf. CASEBOOK.

hornbook method. A method of legal instruction characterized by a straightforward presentation of legal doctrine, occasionally interspersed with questions. • The hornbook method predominates in civil-law countries, and in certain fields of law, such as procedure and evidence. Cf. CASEBOOK METHOD; SOCRATIC METHOD.

horseshedding, *n.* The instruction of a witness favorable to one's case (esp. a client) about the proper method of responding to questions while giving testimony. — **horseshed,** *vb.* Cf. SANDPAPERING.

hospiticide (hah-**spit**-ə-sɪd), *n.* A host who murders a guest.

hostage. An innocent person held captive by another who threatens to kill or harm that person if one or more demands are not met. • Hostage-taking is a federal crime. 18 USCA § 1203. Cf. KIDNAPPING.

hostile-environment sexual harassment. See SEXUAL HARASSMENT.

hostile possession. See POSSESSION.

hostile witness. See WITNESS.

hot cargo. *Labor law.* Goods produced or handled by an employer with whom a union has a dispute.

hot-cargo agreement. *Labor law.* A voluntary agreement between a union and a neutral employer by which the latter agrees to exert pressure on another employer with whom the union has a dispute, as by ceasing or refraining from handling, using, selling, transporting, or otherwise dealing in any of the products of an employer that the union has labeled as unfair. • Most agreements of this type were prohibited by the Landrum–Griffin Act of 1959. See LANDRUM–GRIFFIN ACT.

hotchpot (**hoch**-pot), *n.* **1.** The blending of items of property to secure equality of division, esp. as practiced either in cases of divorce or in cases in which advancements of an intestate's property must be made up to the estate by a contribution or by an accounting. **2.** In a community-property state, the property that falls within the community estate.

hot court. See COURT.

hot document. See DOCUMENT.

house arrest. The confinement of a person who is accused or convicted of a crime to his or her home, usu. by attaching an electronically monitored bracelet to the criminal offender.

house bill. See BILL (3).

housebreaking. The crime of breaking into a dwelling or other secured building, with the intent to commit a felony inside; BURGLARY.

houseburning. The common-law misdemeanor of intentionally burning one's own house that is within city limits or that is close enough to other houses that they might be in danger of catching fire (even though no actual damage to them may result). Cf. ARSON.

household, *n.* **1.** A family living together. **2.** A group of people who dwell under the same roof. — **household,** *adj.* Cf. FAMILY.

House of Representatives. 1. The lower chamber of the U.S. Congress, composed of 435 members — apportioned among the states on the basis of population — who are elected to two-year terms. **2.** The lower house of a state legislature. — Abbr. H.R.; H.

howsoever, *adv.* *Jargon.* In whatever way; however.

H.R. *abbr.* HOUSE OF REPRESENTATIVES.

HUD. *abbr.* The Department of Housing and Urban Development, a federal agency responsible for programs and policies that address the country's housing needs and that develop and improve neighborhoods.

husband–wife immunity. See IMMUNITY (2).

hush money. *Slang.* A bribe to suppress the dissemination of certain information; a payment to secure silence.

hybrid class action. See CLASS ACTION.

***Hydraflow* test.** A principle for deciding when an inadvertent disclosure of a privileged document is a waiver of the attorney–client privilege, whereby the court considers the reasonableness of the precautions taken to prevent the inadvertent disclosure, the number of disclosures involved, the extent of the disclosure, the promptness of any efforts to remedy the disclosure, and whether justice would be best served by permitting the disclosing party to retrieve the document. *Hydraflow, Inc. v. Enidine, Inc.*, 145 F.R.D. 626 (W.D.N.Y. 1993). Cf. STRICT TEST; LENIENT TEST.

hypothecate (hɪ-**poth**-ə-kayt), *vb.* To pledge (property) as security or collateral for a debt, without delivery of title or possession. — **hypothecation** (hɪ-poth-ə-**kay**-shən), *n.*

hypothetical-person defense. An entrapment defense in which the defendant asserts that an undercover law-enforcement officer (or person acting at the law-enforcement officer's direction) encouraged the defendant to engage in the criminal conduct either by making false representations designed to convince the defendant that the conduct was not prohibited, or by using persuasive methods that created a substantial risk that the charged offense would be committed by a person who was not otherwise inclined to commit it. See Model Penal Code § 2.13. Cf. SHERMAN–SORRELLS DOCTRINE.

hypothetical question. A trial device that solicits an expert witness's opinion based on assumptions treated as facts established by evidence.

I

IABA. *abbr.* INTER-AMERICAN BAR ASSOCIATION.

ibid. (**ib**-id). *abbr.* [Latin *ibidem*] In the same place. • This abbreviation, used in citations (mostly outside law), denotes that the reference is to a work cited immediately before, and that the cited matter appears on the same page of the same book (unless a different page is specified). Cf. ID.

ICC. *abbr.* **1.** INTERSTATE COMMERCE COMMISSION. **2.** INTERNATIONAL CRIMINAL COURT.

ICJ. *abbr.* INTERNATIONAL COURT OF JUSTICE.

id. (id). *abbr.* [Latin *idem*] The same. • *Id.* is used in a legal citation to refer to the authority cited immediately before <*id.* at 55>. Cf. IBID.

idem sonans (I-dem **soh**-nanz), *adj.* [Latin] (Of words or names) sounding the same, regardless of spelling <the names Gene and Jean are *idem sonans*>.

idem sonans, *n.* [Latin] A legal doctrine preventing a variant spelling of a name in a document from voiding the document if the misspelling is pronounced the same way as the true spelling.

identification of goods. A process that enables a buyer to obtain an identifiable (and therefore insurable) interest in goods before taking possession from the seller. • The goods are identified in any manner agreed to by the parties. UCC § 2–501.

identify, *vb.* **1.** To prove the identity of (a person or thing) <the witness identified the weapon>. **2.** To look upon as being associated (with) <the plaintiff was identified with the environmental movement>. **3.** To specify (certain goods) as the object of a contract <identify the appliances to the contract>. See IDENTIFICATION OF GOODS.

identity. 1. The identical nature of two or more things; esp., in patent law, the sameness in two devices of the function performed, the way it is performed, and the result achieved. • Under the doctrine of equivalents, infringement may be found even if the accused device is not identical to the claimed invention. See DOCTRINE OF EQUIVALENTS. **2.** *Evidence.* The authenticity of a person or thing.

identity of interests. *Civil procedure.* A relationship between two parties who are so close that suing one serves as notice to the other, so that the other may be joined in the suit. Fed. R. Civ. P. 15(c)(3).

identity of parties. *Civil procedure.* A relationship between two parties who are so close that a judgment against one prevents later action against the other because of res judicata.

i.e. *abbr.* [Latin *id est*] That is <the federal government's highest judicial

body, i.e., the Supreme Court>. Cf. E.G.

i.f.p. *abbr.* IN FORMA PAUPERIS.

ignorantia facti excusat (ig-nə-**ran**-shee-ə **fak**-tɪ ek-**skyoo**-sat *or* -zat). [Latin] Ignorance of fact is an excuse; whatever is done under a mistaken impression of a material fact is excused or provides grounds for relief.

ignorantia juris (ig-nə-**ran**-shee-ə **joor**-is). [Latin] Ignorance of law.

ignorantia juris non excusat (ig-nə-**ran**-shee-ə **joor**-is non ek-**skyoo**-sat *or* -zat). [Latin] Lack of knowledge about a legal requirement or prohibition is never an excuse to a criminal charge. • In English, the idea is commonly rendered *ignorance of the law is no excuse*.

ignoratio elenchi (ig-nə-**ray**-shee-oh e-**leng**-kɪ *or* ig-nə-**rah**-tee-oh i-**leng**-kee). [Law Latin "ignorance of the conclusion to be proved"] An advocate's misunderstanding of an opponent's position, manifested by an argument that fails to address the opponent's point; the overlooking of an opponent's counterargument. • This fallacy of logic often involves an advocate's trying to prove something that is immaterial to the point to be decided.

ignore, *vb.* **1.** To refuse to notice, recognize, or consider. **2.** (Of a grand jury) to reject (an indictment) as groundless; to no-bill (a charge).

ill, *adj.* (Of a pleading) defective, bad, or null.

illation (i-**lay**-shən). **1.** The act or process of inferring. **2.** An inference; that which is inferred.

illegal alien. See ALIEN.

illegal consideration. See CONSIDERATION.

illegal contract. See CONTRACT.

illegal entry. 1. *Criminal law.* The unlawful act of going into a building with the intent to commit a crime. **2.** *Immigration.* The unauthorized entrance of an alien into the United States by arriving at the wrong time or place, by evading inspection, or by committing fraud.

illegality. 1. An act that is not authorized by law. **2.** The state of not being legally authorized. **3.** The state or condition of being unlawful. • The affirmative defense of illegality must be expressly set forth in the response to the opponent's pleading. Fed. R. Civ. P. 8(c).

illegally obtained evidence. See EVIDENCE.

illegal rate. See INTEREST RATE.

illegitimacy. The state or condition of a child born outside a lawful marriage.

illegitimate, *adj.* **1.** (Of a child) born out of wedlock. **2.** Against the law; unlawful. **3.** Improper. **4.** Incorrectly inferred.

illegitimate child. See CHILD.

illicit (i[l]-**lis**-ət), *adj.* Illegal or improper <illicit relations>.

illicit cohabitation. See COHABITATION.

illusory (i-**loo**-sə-ree), *adj.* Deceptive; based on a false impression.

illusory contract. See CONTRACT.

illusory promise. See PROMISE.

illusory trust. See TRUST.

immaterial, *adj.* (Of evidence) tending to prove some fact that is not properly at issue; lacking any logical connection with the consequential facts. — **immateriality,** *n.* Cf. IRRELEVANT.

immaterial averment. See AVERMENT.

immaterial evidence. See EVIDENCE.

immaterial issue. See ISSUE (1).

immaterial variance. See VARIANCE.

immediate, *adj.* **1.** Occurring without delay; instant <an immediate acceptance>. **2.** Not separated by other persons or things <her immediate neighbor>. **3.** Having a direct impact; without an intervening agency <the immediate cause of the accident>. — **immediacy,** *n.* — **immediateness,** *n.*

immediate breach. See BREACH OF CONTRACT.

immediate cause. See CAUSE (1).

immediate control. *Criminal procedure.* **1.** The area within an arrestee's reach. • A police officer may conduct a warrantless search of this area to ensure the officer's safety and to prevent the arrestee from destroying evidence. **2.** Vehicular control that is close enough to allow the driver to instantly govern the vehicle's movements.

immediate death. See DEATH.

immediate family. See FAMILY.

immediate intent. See INTENT (1).

immediately-apparent requirement. *Criminal procedure.* The principle that a police officer must have probable cause to believe that an item is contraband before seizing it. • This plain-view exception to the warrant requirement was first announced in *Coolidge v. New Hampshire*, 403 U.S. 443, 91 S.Ct. 2022 (1971).

immediate possession. See POSSESSION.

immemorial (im-ə-**mor**-ee-əl), *adj.* Beyond memory or record; very old. See TIME IMMEMORIAL.

immemorial usage. See USAGE.

immigrant. A person who arrives in a country to settle there permanently; a person who immigrates. Cf. EMIGRANT.

immigration, *n.* The act of entering a country with the intention of settling there permanently. — **immigrate,** *vb.* — **immigrant,** *n.* Cf. EMIGRATION.

Immigration and Nationality Act. A comprehensive federal law regulating immigration, naturalization, and the exclusion of aliens. 8 USCA §§ 1101–1537.

Immigration and Naturalization Service. A U.S. Department of Justice agency that administers the Immigration and Nationality Act and operates the U.S. Border Patrol. — Abbr. INS.

imminent danger. See DANGER.

imminently dangerous. (Of a person, behavior, or thing) reasonably certain to place life and limb in peril. • This term is relevant in several legal contexts. For example, if a mental condition renders a person imminently dangerous to self or others, he or she may be committed to a mental hospital. And the imminently dangerous behavior of pointing a gun at someone's head could subject the actor to criminal and tort liability. Further, the manufacturer of an imminently dangerous product may be held to a strict-liability standard in tort.

immovable, *n.* (*usu. pl.*) Property that cannot be moved; an object so firmly attached to land that it is regarded as part of the land. — **immovable,** *adj.* See FIXTURE. Cf. MOVABLE.

immunity. 1. Any exemption from a duty, liability, or service of process; esp., such an exemption granted to a public official. — **immune,** *adj.*

absolute immunity. A complete exemption from civil liability, usu. afforded to officials while performing particularly important functions, such as a representative enacting legislation and a judge presiding over a lawsuit. Cf. *qualified immunity*.

congressional immunity. Either of two special immunities given to members of Congress: (1) the exemption from arrest while attending a session of the body to which the member belongs, excluding an arrest for treason, breach of the peace, or a felony, or (2) the exemption from arrest or questioning for any speech or debate entered into during a legislative session. U.S. Const. art. I, § 6, cl. 1. See SPEECH OR DEBATE CLAUSE.

constitutional immunity. Immunity created by a constitution.

diplomatic immunity. The general exemption of diplomatic ministers from the operation of local law, the exception being that a minister who is plotting against the security of the host nation may be arrested and sent out of the country.

discretionary immunity. A qualified immunity for a public official's acts, granted when the act in question required the exercise of judgment in carrying out official duties (such as planning and policy-making). 28 USCA § 2680(a).

***executive immunity.* 1.** The absolute immunity of the U.S. President or a state governor from civil damages for actions that are within the scope of official responsibilities. **2.** The qualified immunity from civil claims against lesser executive officials, who are liable only if their conduct violates clearly established constitutional or statutory rights. Cf. *executive privilege* under PRIVILEGE (1).

intergovernmental immunity. The immunity between the federal and state governments based on their independent sovereignty. See INTERGOVERNMENTAL-IMMUNITY DOCTRINE.

judicial immunity. The immunity of a judge from civil liability arising from the performance of judicial duties.

legislative immunity. The immunity of a legislator from civil liability arising from the performance of legislative duties. See *congressional immunity*.

qualified immunity. Immunity from civil liability for a public official who is performing a discretionary function, as long as the conduct does not violate clearly established constitutional or statutory rights. Cf. *absolute immunity*.

***sovereign immunity*. 1.** A government's immunity from being sued in its own courts without its consent. • Congress has waived most of the federal government's sovereign immunity. See FEDERAL TORT CLAIMS ACT. **2.** A state's immunity from being sued in federal court by the state's own citizens.

2. *Torts*. A doctrine providing a complete defense to a tort action. • Unlike a privilege, immunity does not negate the tort, and it must be raised affirmatively or it will be waived. Cf. PRIVILEGE (3).

***charitable immunity*.** The immunity of a charitable organization from tort liability.

***corporate immunity*.** A corporate officer's immunity from personal liability for a tortious act committed while acting in good faith and within the course of corporate duties.

***husband–wife immunity*.** The immunity of one spouse from a tort action by the other spouse for personal injury.

***parental immunity*. 1.** The principle that children cannot sue their parents, and that parents cannot sue their children, for tort claims. **2.** The principle that parents are not liable for damages caused by the ordinary negligence of their minor child.

3. *Criminal law*. Freedom from prosecution granted by the government in exchange for the person's testimony. • By granting immunity, the government can compel testimony — despite the Fifth Amendment right against self-incrimination — because that testimony can no longer incriminate the witness.

***pocket immunity*.** Immunity that results from the prosecutor's decision not to prosecute, instead of from a formal grant of immunity.

***testimonial immunity*.** Immunity from the use of the compelled testimony against the witness. • Any information derived from that testimony, however, is generally admissible against the witness.

***transactional immunity*.** Immunity from prosecution for any event or transaction described in the compelled testimony. • This is the broadest form of immunity.

***use immunity*.** Immunity from the use of the compelled testimony (or any information derived from that testimony) in a future prosecution against the witness. • After granting use immunity, the government can still prosecute if it shows that its evidence comes from a legitimate independent source.

immunize, *vb.* To grant immunity to.

impact rule. *Torts*. The common-law requirement that physical contact must have occurred to allow damages for negligent infliction of emotional distress.

impair, *vb.* To diminish the value of (property or a property right). • This term is commonly used in reference to diminishing the value of a contractual obligation to the point that the contract becomes invalid or a party loses the benefit of the contract. See CONTRACTS CLAUSE.

impairing the morals of a minor. The offense of an adult's engaging in sex-related acts, short of intercourse, with a minor. • Examples of this conduct are fondling, taking obscene photographs, and showing pornographic materials. Cf. CONTRIBUTING TO THE DELINQUENCY OF A MINOR; CORRUPTION OF A MINOR.

impairment, *n.* The fact or state of being damaged, weakened, or diminished. — **impair,** *vb.*

impartial, *adj.* Unbiased; disinterested.

impartial chair. 1. ARBITRATOR. **2.** A mediator.

impartial expert. See EXPERT.

impartial jury. See JURY.

impartible (im-**pahr**-tə-bəl), *adj.* Indivisible <an impartible estate>.

impeachable offense. An offense for which a public official may legally be impeached, during the first step in a two-step process that may, depending on the vote in the U.S. Senate, lead to the official's removal from office. — **impeach,** *vb.*

impeachment. 1. The act (by a legislature) of calling for the removal from office of a public official, accomplished by presenting a written charge of the official's alleged misconduct; esp., the initiation of a proceeding in the U.S. House of Representatives against a federal official, such as the President or a judge. • Congress's authority to remove a federal official stems from Article II, Section 4 of the Constitution, which authorizes the removal of an official for "Treason, Bribery, or other high Crimes and Misdemeanors." **2.** The act of discrediting a witness, as by catching the witness in a lie or by demonstrating that the witness has been convicted of a criminal offense. **3.** The act of challenging the accuracy or authenticity of evidence.

impeachment evidence. See EVIDENCE.

impeachment of verdict. A party's attack on a verdict, alleging impropriety by a member of the jury.

impediment (im-**ped**-ə-mənt). A hindrance or obstruction; esp., some fact (such as legal minority) that bars a marriage, if known beforehand, and can serve to annul the marriage if later discovered.

imperative theory of law. The theory that law consists of the general commands issued by a country or other political community to its subjects and enforced by courts with the sanction of physical force. See POSITIVE LAW. Cf. NATURAL LAW.

imperfect defense. See DEFENSE (1).

imperfect justification. See JUSTIFICATION.

imperfect self-defense. See SELF-DEFENSE.

imperfect statute. See STATUTE.

imperfect title. See TITLE (2).

impertinent matter. *Procedure.* In pleading, matter that is not relevant to the action or defense. • A federal court may strike any impertinent matter from a pleading. Fed. R. Civ. P. 12(f). Cf. SCANDALOUS MATTER.

implead, *vb.* To bring (someone) into a lawsuit; esp., to bring (a new party) into the action. Cf. INTERPLEAD.

impleader, *n.* A procedure by which a third party is brought into a lawsuit, esp. by a defendant who seeks to shift liability to someone not sued by the plaintiff. Fed. R. Civ. P. 14. Cf. INTERPLEADER; INTERVENTION (1).

implicate, *vb.* **1.** To show (a person) to be involved in (a crime, misfeasance, etc.). **2.** To be involved or affected.

implication. 1. The act of showing involvement in something, esp. a crime or misfeasance. **2.** An inference drawn from something said or observed.

necessary implication. An implication so strong in its probability that anything to the contrary would be unreasonable.

implied, *adj.* Not directly expressed; recognized by law as existing inferentially.

implied acquittal. See ACQUITTAL (1).

implied admission. See ADMISSION.

implied agency. See AGENCY (1).

implied assent. See ASSENT.

implied assumption. See ASSUMPTION.

implied authority. See AUTHORITY (1).

implied condition. See CONDITION (2).

implied consent. See CONSENT.

implied consideration. See CONSIDERATION.

implied contract. See CONTRACT.

implied covenant. See COVENANT (1).

implied covenant of good faith and fair dealing. See COVENANT (1).

implied dedication. See DEDICATION.

implied easement. See EASEMENT.

implied in fact, *adj.* Inferable from the facts of the case.

implied-in-fact contract. See CONTRACT.

implied in law, *n.* Imposed by operation of law and not because of any inferences that can be drawn from the facts of the case.

implied-in-law contract. See CONTRACT.

implied intent. See INTENT (1).

implied malice. See MALICE.

implied negative covenant. See COVENANT (1).

implied notice. See NOTICE.

implied power. See POWER.

implied promise. See PROMISE.

implied repeal. See REPEAL.

implied reservation. See RESERVATION.

implied term. See TERM (2).

implied waiver. See WAIVER.

implied warranty. See WARRANTY (2).

implied warranty of fitness for a particular purpose. See WARRANTY (2).

implied warranty of habitability. See WARRANTY (2).

implied warranty of merchantability. See WARRANTY (2).

imply, *vb.* **1.** To express or involve indirectly; to suggest. **2.** (Of a court) to impute or impose on equitable or legal grounds. **3.** To read into (a document). See *implied term* under TERM (2). — **implication,** *n.*

import, *n.* **1.** A product brought into a country from a foreign country where it originated <imports declined in the third quarter>. **2.** The process of bringing foreign goods into a country <the import of products affects the domestic economy in significant ways>. **3.** The meaning; esp., the implied meaning <the court must decide the import of that obscure provision>. **4.** Importance; significance <time will tell the relative import of Judge Posner's decisions in American law>.

imported litigation. One or more lawsuits brought in a state that has no interest in the dispute.

Import–Export Clause. U.S. Const. art. I, § 10, cl. 2, which prohibits states from taxing imports or exports. • The Supreme Court has liberally interpreted this clause, allowing states to tax imports as long as the tax does not discriminate in favor of domestic goods.

importune (im-por-**t[y]oon**), *vb.* To solicit forcefully; to request persistently, and sometimes irksomely.

impose, *vb.* To levy or exact (a tax or duty).

imposition. An impost or tax.

impositive fact. See FACT.

impossibility. 1. The fact or condition of not being able to occur, exist, or be done. **2.** A fact or circumstance that cannot occur, exist, or be done. **3.** *Contracts.* A fact or circumstance that excuses performance because (1) the subject or means of performance has deteriorated, has been destroyed, or is no longer available, (2) the method of delivery or payment has failed, (3) a law now prevents performance, or (4) death or illness prevents performance. • Increased or unexpected difficulty and expense do not usually qualify as an impossibility and thus do not excuse performance. **4.** The doctrine by which such a fact or circumstance excuses contractual performance. Cf. FRUSTRATION; IMPRACTICABILITY. **5.** *Criminal law.* A fact or circumstance preventing the commission of a crime.

factual impossibility. Impossibility due to the fact that the illegal act cannot physically be accomplished, such as trying to pick an empty pocket. • Factual impossibility is not a defense to the crime of attempt.

legal impossibility. **1.** Impossibility due to the fact that what the defendant intended to do is not illegal even though the defendant might have believed that he or she was committing a crime. • This type of legal impossibility is a defense to the crimes of attempt, conspiracy, and solicitation. **2.** Impossibility due to the fact that an element required for an attempt has not been satisfied. • This is a defense to the crime of attempt.

impossibility-of-performance doctrine. The principle that a party may be released from a contract on the ground that uncontrollable circumstances have rendered performance impossible. Cf. FRUSTRATION; IMPRACTICABILITY.

impound, *vb.* **1.** To place (something, such as a car or other personal property) in the custody of the police or the court, often with the understanding that it will be returned intact at the end of the proceeding. **2.** To take and retain possession of (something, such as a forged document to be produced as evidence) in preparation for a criminal prosecution.

impoundment. 1. The action of impounding; the state of being impounded. See IMPOUND. **2.** *Constitutional law.* The President's refusal to spend funds appropriated by Congress. • Although not authorized by the Constitution and seldom used, the impoundment power effectively gives the executive branch a line-item veto over legislative spending.

impracticability (im-prak-ti-kə-**bil**-ə-tee). *Contracts.* **1.** A fact or circumstance that excuses a party from performing an act, esp. a contractual duty, because (though possible) it would cause extreme and unreasonable difficulty. • For performance to be truly impracticable, the duty must become much more difficult or much more expensive to perform, and this difficulty or expense must have been unanticipated. **2.** The doctrine by which such a fact or circumstance excuses performance. Cf. FRUSTRATION; IMPOSSIBILITY (4).

commercial impracticability. The occurrence of a contingency whose nonoccurrence was an assumption in the contract, as a result of which one party cannot perform.

imprescriptible (im-prə-**skrip**-tə-bəl), *adj.* Not subject to prescription; not capable of being acquired by prescription. See PRESCRIPTION.

impressment (im-**pres**-mənt), *n.* **1.** The act of forcibly taking (something) for public service. **2.** A court's imposition of a constructive trust on equitable grounds. See *constructive trust* under TRUST. — **impress,** *vb.*

imprison, *vb.* To confine (a person) in prison. — **imprisonment,** *n.*

improper, *adj.* **1.** Incorrect; unsuitable or irregular. **2.** Fraudulent or otherwise wrongful.

improved land. Real property that has been developed. • The improvements may or may not enhance the value of the land.

improved value. *Real estate.* In the appraisal of property, the value of the land plus the value of any improvements.

improvement. An addition to real property, whether permanent or not; esp., one that increases its value or utility or that enhances its appearance. Cf. FIXTURE.

general improvement. An improvement whose primary purpose or effect is to benefit the public generally, though it may incidentally benefit property owners in its vicinity.

local improvement. A real-property improvement, such as a sewer or sidewalk, financed by special assessment, and specially benefiting adjacent property.

necessary improvement. An improvement made to prevent the deterioration of property.

valuable improvement. An improvement that adds permanent value to the freehold.

improvident (im-**prahv**-ə-dənt), *adj.* **1.** Lacking foresight and care in the management of property. **2.** Of or relating to a judgment arrived at by using misleading information or a mistaken assumption. — **improvidence** (im-**prahv**-ə-dənts), *n.*

impugn (im-**pyoon**), *vb.* To challenge or call into question (a person's character, the truth of a statement, etc.). — **impugnment,** *n.*

impulse, *n.* A sudden urge or inclination that prompts an unplanned action.

uncontrollable impulse. An impulse so overwhelming that it cannot be resisted. See IRRESISTIBLE-IMPULSE TEST.

impunity (im-**pyoo**-nə-tee). An exemption or protection from punishment. See IMMUNITY.

impute (im-**pyoot**), *vb.* To ascribe or attribute; to regard (usu. something undesirable) as being done, caused, or possessed by. — **imputation,** *n.* — **imputable,** *adj.*

imputed income. See INCOME.

imputed interest. See INTEREST (3).

imputed knowledge. See KNOWLEDGE (1).

imputed negligence. See NEGLIGENCE.

imputed notice. See NOTICE.

in, *prep.* Under or based on the law of <to bring an action in contract>.

in absentia (in ab-**sen**-shee-ə *or* ab-**sen**-shə). [Latin] In the absence of (someone); in (someone's) absence.

in action. (Of property) attainable or recoverable through litigation. See *chose in action* under CHOSE.

inactive case. See CASE.

inadequate consideration. See CONSIDERATION.

inadequate remedy at law. A remedy (such as money damages) that does not sufficiently correct the wrong, as a result of which an injunction may be available to the disadvantaged party. See IRREPARABLE-INJURY RULE.

inadmissible, *adj.* **1.** (Of a thing) not allowable or worthy of being admitted. **2.** (Of evidence) excludable by some rule of evidence.

inadvertence, *n.* An accidental oversight; a result of carelessness.

inadvertent discovery. *Criminal procedure.* A law-enforcement officer's unexpected finding of incriminating evidence in plain view. • Even though this type of evidence is obtained without a warrant, it can be used against the accused under the plain-view exception to the warrant requirement.

inadvertent negligence. See NEGLIGENCE.

inalienable, *adj.* Not transferable or assignable.

inalienable interest. See INTEREST (2).

inarbitrable, *adj.* **1.** (Of a dispute) not capable of being arbitrated; not subject to arbitration. **2.** Not subject to being decided.

in arrears (in ə-**reerz**), *adj.* & *adv.* **1.** Behind in the discharging of a debt or other obligation <the tenants were in arrears with the rent>. **2.** At the end of a term or period instead of the beginning <the interests, fees, and costs are payable in arrears>.

in being. Existing in life <life in being plus 21 years>. • In property law, this includes children conceived but not yet born. See LIFE IN BEING.

in blank. (Of an indorsement) not restricted to a particular indorsee. See *blank indorsement* under INDORSEMENT.

Inc. *abbr.* Incorporated.

in camera (in **kam**-ə-rə), *adv.* & *adj.* [Law Latin "in a chamber"] **1.** In the judge's private chambers. **2.** In the courtroom with all spectators excluded. **3.** (Of a judicial action) taken when court is not in session.

in camera inspection. A trial judge's private consideration of evidence.

in camera proceeding. See PROCEEDING.

in camera sitting. See SITTING.

incapacitated person. A person who is impaired by an intoxicant, by mental illness or deficiency, or by physical illness or disability to the extent that personal decision-making is impossible.

incapacitation, *n.* **1.** The action of disabling or depriving of legal capacity. **2.** The state of being disabled or lacking legal capacity. — **incapacitate,** *vb.*

incapacity. 1. Lack of physical or mental capabilities. **2.** Lack of ability to have certain legal consequences attach to one's actions. **3.** DISABILITY (1). **4.** DISABILITY (2). Cf. INCOMPETENCY.

testimonial incapacity. The lack of capacity to testify.

in capita. Individually. See PER CAPITA.

incendiary (in-**sen**-dee-er-ee), *n.* **1.** One who deliberately and unlawfully sets fire to property. **2.** An instrument (such as a bomb) or chemical agent designed to start a fire. — **incendiary,** *adj.*

incentive pay plan. A compensation plan in which increased productivity is rewarded with higher pay.

incest, *n.* Sexual relations between family members or close relatives, including children related by adoption. — **incestuous,** *adj.*

in chief. *Jargon.* **1.** Principal, as opposed to collateral or incidental. **2.** Denoting the part of a trial in which the main body of evidence is presented. See CASE-IN-CHIEF.

inchoate (in-**koh**-it), *adj.* Partially completed or imperfectly formed; just begun. — **inchoateness,** *n.* Cf. CHOATE.

inchoate instrument. See INSTRUMENT.

inchoate interest. See INTEREST (2).

inchoate offense. See OFFENSE.

incident, *adj.* Dependent upon, subordinate to, arising out of, or otherwise connected with (something else, usu. of greater importance) <the utility easement is incident to the ownership of the tract>. — **incident,** *n.*

incident, *n.* **1.** A discrete occurrence or happening <an incident of copyright infringement> **2.** A dependent, subordinate, or consequential part (of something else) <child support is a typical incident of divorce>.

incidental, *adj.* Subordinate to something of greater importance; having a minor role.

incidental authority. See AUTHORITY (1).

incidental beneficiary. See BENEFICIARY.

incidental damages. See DAMAGES.

incident of ownership. (*usu. pl.*) Any right of control that may be exercised over a transferred life-insurance policy so that the policy's proceeds will be included in a decedent's gross estate for estate-tax purposes.

incident power. See POWER.

incite, *vb.* To provoke or stir up (someone to commit a criminal act, or the criminal act itself). Cf. ABET.

incitement, *n.* **1.** The act or an instance of provoking, urging on, or stirring up. **2.** *Criminal law.* The act of persuading another person to commit a crime; SOLICITATION (2). — **inciteful,** *adj.*

inciter. A person who incites another to commit a crime; an aider or abettor.

incivism (**in**-si-viz-əm). Unfriendliness toward one's own country or its government; lack of good citizenship.

inclusionary-approach rule. The principle that evidence of a prior crime, wrong, or act is admissible for any purpose other than to show a defendant's criminal propensity as long as it is relevant to some disputed issue and its probative value outweighs its prejudicial effect.

incognito (in-kog-**nee**-toh *or* in-**kog**-ni-toh), *adj.* Without making one's name or identity known.

income. The money or other form of payment that one receives, usu. periodically, from employment, business, investments, royalties, gifts, and the like. See EARNINGS. Cf. PROFIT.

accrued income. Money earned but not yet received.

active income. **1.** Wages; salary. **2.** Income from a trade or business.

adjusted gross income. Gross income minus allowable deductions specified in the tax code.

aggregate income. The combined income of a husband and wife who file a joint tax return.

deferred income. Money received at a time later than when it was earned, such as a check received in January for commissions earned in November.

disposable income. Income that may be spent or invested after payment of taxes and other primary obligations.

dividend income. The income resulting from a dividend distribution and subject to tax.

earned income. Money derived from one's own labor or active participation; earnings from services. Cf. *unearned income* (2).

exempt income. Income that is not subject to income tax.

gross income. Total income from all sources before deductions, exemptions, or other tax reductions.

imputed income. The benefit one receives from the use of one's own property, the performance of one's services, or the consumption of self-produced goods and services.

income in respect of a decedent. Income earned by a person, but not collected before death. • This income is included in the decedent's gross estate for estate-tax purposes. For income-tax purposes, it is taxed to the estate or, if the estate does not collect the income, it is taxed to the eventual recipient.

net income. Total income from all sources minus deductions, exemptions, and other tax reductions.

ordinary income. **1.** For business-tax purposes, earnings from the normal operations or activities of a business. **2.** For individual income-tax purposes, income that is derived from sources such as wages, commissions, and interest (as opposed to income from capital gains).

other income. Income not derived from an entity's principal business, such as earnings from dividends and interest.

passive income. Income derived from a business activity over which the earner does not participate directly or have immediate control, such as copyright royalties. See PASSIVE ACTIVITY.

personal income. The total income received by an individual from all sources.

portfolio income. Income from interest, dividends, rentals, royalties, capital gains, or other investment sources.

prepaid income. Income received but not yet earned.

split income. An equal division between spouses of earnings reported on a joint tax return, allowing for equal tax treatment in community-property and common-law states.

taxable income. Gross income minus all allowable deductions and exemptions.

unearned income. **1.** Earnings from investments rather than labor. **2.** Income received but not yet earned; money paid in advance. Cf. *earned income*.

unrelated business income. Taxable income generated by a tax-exempt organization from a trade or business unrelated to its exempt purpose or activity.

income approach. A method of appraising real property based on capitalization of the income that the property is expected to generate. Cf. MARKET APPROACH; COST APPROACH.

income averaging. *Tax.* A method of computing tax by averaging a person's current income with that of preceding years.

income-basis method. A method of computing the rate of return on a security using the interest and price paid rather than the face value.

income beneficiary. See BENEFICIARY.

income-shifting. The practice of transferring income to a taxpayer in a lower tax bracket, such as a child, to reduce tax liability. • Often this is accomplished by forming a Clifford trust. See *Clifford trust* under TRUST; *kiddie tax* under TAX.

income statement. A statement of all the revenues, expenses, gains, and losses that a business incurred during a given period. Cf. BALANCE SHEET.

income tax. See TAX.

income-withholding order. A court order providing for the withholding of a person's income, usu. to enforce a child-support order.

in common. Shared equally with others, without division into separate ownership parts. See *tenancy in common* under TENANCY.

incommunicado (in-kə-myoo-ni-**kah**-doh), *adj.* [Spanish] **1.** Without any means of communication. **2.** (Of a prisoner) having the right to communicate with only a few designated people.

incommutable (in-kə-**myoot**-ə-bəl), *adj.* (Of an offense) not capable of being commuted. See COMMUTATION.

incompatibility, *n.* Conflict in personality and disposition, usu. leading to the breakup of a marriage. • Every state now recognizes some form of incompatibility as a no-fault ground for divorce. See *no-fault divorce* under DIVORCE. Cf. IRRECONCILABLE DIFFERENCES; IRRETRIEVABLE BREAKDOWN OF THE MARRIAGE.

incompetence, *n.* **1.** The state or fact of being unable or unqualified to do something. **2.** INCOMPETENCY.

incompetency, *n.* Lack of legal ability in some respect, esp. to stand trial or to testify. — **incompetent,** *adj.* Cf. INCAPACITY.

incompetent, *adj.* **1.** (Of a witness) unqualified to testify. **2.** (Of evidence) inadmissible.

incompetent evidence. See EVIDENCE.

incomplete instrument. See INSTRUMENT.

incomplete transfer. See TRANSFER.

inconclusive, *adj.* (Of evidence) not leading to a conclusion or definite result.

inconsistent, *adj.* Lacking consistency; not compatible with another fact or claim.

inconsistent defense. See DEFENSE (1).

incontestable policy. See INSURANCE POLICY.

incorporate, *vb.* **1.** To form a legal corporation <she incorporated the family business>. **2.** To combine with something else <incorporate the exhibits into the agreement>. **3.** To make the terms of another (esp. earlier) document part of a document by specific reference <the codicil incorporated the terms of the will>; esp., to apply the provisions of the Bill of Rights to the states by interpreting the 14th Amendment's Due Process Clause as encompassing those provisions.

incorporation, *n.* **1.** The formation of a legal corporation. See ARTICLES OF INCORPORATION. **2.** *Constitutional law.* The process of applying the provisions of the Bill of Rights to the states by interpreting the 14th Amendment's Due Process Clause as encompassing those provisions. **3.** INCORPORATION BY REFERENCE. — **incorporate,** *vb.*

incorporation by reference. A method of making a secondary document part of a primary document by including in the primary document a statement that the secondary document should be treated as if it were contained within the primary one.

incorporator. A person who takes part in the formation of a corporation, usu. by executing the articles of incorporation.

incorporeal (in-kor-**por**-ee-əl), *adj.* Having a conceptual existence but no physical existence; intangible. — **incorporeality,** *n.* Cf. CORPOREAL.

incorporeal ownership. See OWNERSHIP.

incorporeal possession. See POSSESSION.

incorporeal property. See PROPERTY.

incorporeal thing. See THING.

incorrigible child. See CHILD.

incorrigibility (in-kor-ə-jə-**bil**-ə-tee *or* in-kahr-). Serious or persistent misbehavior by a child, making reformation by parental control impossible or unlikely. — **incorrigible** (in-**kor**-ə-jə-bəl *or* in-**kahr**-), *adj.* Cf. JUVENILE DELINQUENCY.

increment (**in**[g]-krə-mənt), *n.* A unit of increase in quantity or value. — **incremental,** *adj.*

incriminate (in-**krim**-ə-nayt), *vb.* **1.** To accuse (someone) of a crime. **2.** To identify (oneself or another) as being involved in the commission of a crime or other wrongdoing. — **incrimination,** *n.* — **incriminatory,** *adj.* — **incriminating,** *adj.*

incriminating circumstance. See CIRCUMSTANCE.

incriminating evidence. See EVIDENCE.

incriminating statement. See STATEMENT.

inculpate (in-**kəl**-payt *or* **in**-kəl-payt), *vb.* **1.** To accuse. **2.** To implicate (oneself or another) in a crime or other wrongdoing; INCRIMINATE. — **inculpation,** *n.* — **inculpatory** (in-**kəl**-pə-tor-ee), *adj.*

inculpatory evidence. See EVIDENCE.

incur, *vb.* To suffer or bring on oneself (a liability or expense). — **incurrence,** *n.* — **incurrable,** *adj.*

in custodia legis (in kə-**stoh**-dee-ə **lee**-jis). [Latin] In the custody of the law. • The phrase is traditionally used in reference to property taken into the court's charge during pending litigation over it.

indebtedness (in-**det**-id-nis). **1.** The condition or state of owing money. **2.** Something owed; a debt.

indecency, *n.* The state or condition of being outrageously offensive, esp. in a vulgar or sexual way. • Unlike obscene material, indecent speech is protected under the First Amendment. — **indecent,** *adj.* Cf. OBSCENITY.

indecent exposure. An offensive display of one's body in public, esp. of the genitals. Cf. LEWDNESS; OBSCENITY.

indecent liberties. Improper behavior toward a child, esp. of a sexual nature.

indefeasible (in-də-**feez**-ə-bəl), *adj.* (Of a claim or right) that cannot be defeated, revoked, or lost <an indefeasible estate>.

indefinite failure of issue. See FAILURE OF ISSUE.

in delicto (in də-**lik**-toh). [Latin] *Jargon*. In fault. Cf. EX DELICTO.

indemnification (in-dem-nə-fi-**kay**-shən), *n.* **1.** The action of compensating for loss or damage sustained. **2.** The compensation so made. — **indemnificatory,** *adj.*

indemnify (in-**dem**-nə-fı), *vb.* **1.** To reimburse (another) for a loss suffered because of a third party's act or default. **2.** To promise to reimburse (another) for such a loss. **3.** To give (another) security against such a loss. See HOLD HARMLESS.

indemnitee (in-dem-nə-**tee**). One who receives indemnity from another.

indemnitor (in-**dem**-nə-tər *or* -tor). One who indemnifies another.

indemnity (in-**dem**-nə-tee), *n.* **1.** A duty to make good any loss, damage, or liability incurred by another. **2.** The right of an injured party to claim reimbursement for its loss, damage, or liability from a person who has such a duty. **3.** Reimbursement or compensation for loss, damage, or liability in tort; esp., the right of a party who is secondarily liable to recover from the party who is primarily liable for reimbursement of expenditures paid to a third party for injuries resulting from a violation of a common-law duty. — **indemnitory,** *adj.* Cf. CONTRIBUTION.

double indemnity. The payment of twice the basic benefit in the event of a specified loss, esp. as in an insurance contract requiring the insurer to pay twice the policy's face amount in the case of accidental death.

indemnity against liability. A right to indemnity that arises on the indemnitor's default, regardless of whether the indemnitee has suffered a loss.

indemnity clause. A contractual provision in which one party agrees to answer for any specified or unspecified liability or harm that the other party might incur. Cf. EXEMPTION CLAUSE.

indenture (in-**den**-chər), *n.* **1.** A formal written instrument made by two or more parties with different interests, traditionally having the edges serrated, or indented, in a zigzag fashion to reduce the possibility of forgery and to distinguish it from a deed poll. Cf. *deed poll* under DEED. **2.** A deed or elaborate contract signed by two or more parties.

independent advice. Counsel that is impartial and not given to further the interests of the person giving it.

independent agency. See AGENCY (2).

independent agent. See AGENT.

independent contractor. One who is hired to undertake a specific project but who is left free to do the assigned work and to choose the method for accomplishing it. • Unlike an employee, an independent contractor who commits a wrong while carrying out the work does not create liability for the one who did the hiring. Cf. EMPLOYEE.

independent counsel. See COUNSEL.

independent executor. See EXECUTOR.

independent intervening cause. See *intervening cause* under CAUSE (1).

independent-significance doctrine. The principle that effect will be given to a testator's disposition that is not done solely to avoid the requirements of a will.

independent-source rule. *Criminal procedure*. The rule providing — as an exception to the fruit-of-the-poisonous-tree doctrine — that evidence obtained by illegal means may nonetheless be admissible if that evidence is also obtained by legal means unrelated to the original illegal conduct. See FRUIT-OF-THE-POISONOUS-TREE DOCTRINE. Cf. INEVITABLE-DISCOVERY RULE.

indestructible trust. See TRUST.

indeterminate, *adj.* Not definite; not distinct or precise.

indeterminate conditional release. A release from prison granted once the prisoner fulfills certain conditions.

indeterminate sentence. See SENTENCE.

indeterminate sentencing. The practice of not imposing a definite term of confinement, but instead prescribing a range for the minimum and maximum term, leaving the precise term to be fixed in some other way, usu. based on the prisoner's conduct and apparent rehabilitation while incarcerated. See *indeterminate sentence* under SENTENCE.

index, *n.* **1.** An alphabetized listing of the topics or other items included in a single book or document, or in a series of volumes, usu. found at the end of the book, document, or series <index of authorities>.

grantee–grantor index. An index, usu. kept in the county recorder's office, alphabetically listing by grantee the volume and page number of the grantee's recorded property transactions.

grantor–grantee index. An index, usu. kept in the county recorder's office, alphabetically listing by grantor the volume and page number of the grantor's recorded property transactions.

tract index. An index, usu. kept in the county recorder's office, listing, by location of each parcel of land, the volume and page number of the recorded property transactions affecting the parcel.

2. A number, usu. expressed in the form of a percentage or ratio, that indicates or measures a series of observations, esp. those involving a market or the economy <cost-of-living index> <stock index>.

indexing. 1. The practice or method of adjusting wages, pension benefits, insurance, or other types of payments to compensate for inflation. **2.** The practice of investing funds to track or mirror an index of securities.

index of authorities. An alphabetical list of authorities cited in a brief, usu. with subcategories for cases, statutes, and treatises.

index offense. See OFFENSE.

indict (in-**dɪt**), *vb.* To charge (a person) with a crime by formal legal process, esp. by grand-jury presentation.

indictable offense. See OFFENSE.

indictee (in-dɪ-**tee**). A person who has been indicted; one officially charged with a crime.

indictment (in-**dɪt**-mənt), *n.* **1.** The formal written accusation of a crime, made by a grand jury and presented to a court for prosecution against the accused person. **2.** The act or process of preparing or bringing forward such a formal written accusation. Cf. INFORMATION; PRESENTMENT (2).

barebones indictment. An indictment that cites only the language of the statute allegedly violated; an indictment that does not provide a factual statement.

duplicitous indictment (d[y]oo-**plis**-ə-təs). **1.** An indictment containing two or more offenses in the same count. **2.** An indictment charging the same offense in more than one count.

joint indictment. An indictment that charges two or more people with an offense.

indictor (in-**dɪt**-ər *or* in-**dɪ**-tor). A person who causes another to be indicted.

indigency, *n.* The state or condition of a person who lacks the means of subsistence; extreme hardship or neediness; poverty. • For purposes of the Sixth Amendment right to appointed counsel, *indigency* refers to a defendant's inability to afford an attorney. — **indigent,** *adj.* — **indigent** (**in**-di-jənt), *n.* See PAUPER.

indigent defendant. A person who is too poor to hire a lawyer and who, upon indictment, becomes eligible to receive aid from a court-appointed attorney and a waiver of court costs. See IN FORMA PAUPERIS.

indirect contempt. See CONTEMPT.

indirect cost. See COST.

indirect tax. See TAX.

indispensable-element test. *Criminal law.* A common-law test for the crime of attempt, based on whether the defendant acquires control over something that is essential to the crime. • Under this test, for example, a person commits a crime by buying the explosives with which to detonate a bomb. See ATTEMPT (2).

indispensable evidence. See EVIDENCE.

indispensable party. See PARTY (2).

individual, *adj.* **1.** Existing as an indivisible entity. **2.** Of or relating to a single person or thing, as opposed to a group.

individual retirement account. A savings or brokerage account to which a person may contribute up to a specified amount of earned income each year ($2,000 under current law). • The contributions, along with any interest earned in the account, are not taxed until the money is withdrawn after a participant reaches 59½ (or before then, if a 10% penalty is paid). — Abbr. IRA. See KEOGH PLAN.

Roth IRA. An IRA in which contributions are nondeductible for tax purposes when they are made.

indivisible, *adj.* Not separable into parts <an indivisible debt>.

indorsee (in-dor-**see**). A person to whom a negotiable instrument is transferred by indorsement.

indorsement, *n.* **1.** The placing of a signature, sometimes with an additional notation, on the back of a negotiable instrument to transfer or guarantee the instrument or to acknowledge payment. **2.** The signature or notation itself. — **indorse,** *vb.*

accommodation indorsement. An indorsement to an instrument by a third party acting as surety for another party who remains primarily liable. See ACCOMMODATION PAPER.

blank indorsement. An indorsement that names no specific payee, thus making the instrument payable to the bearer and negotiable by delivery only. UCC § 3–205(b).

conditional indorsement. An indorsement that restricts the instrument in some way, as by limiting how the instrument can be paid or transferred; an indorsement giving possession of the instrument to the indorsee, but retaining title until the occurrence of some condition named in the indorsement. • Wordings that indicate this type of indorsement are "Pay to Brad Jones when he becomes 18 years of age" and "Pay to Brigitte Turner, or order, unless before payment I give you notice to the contrary." Cf. *special indorsement.*

irregular indorsement. An indorsement by a person who signs outside the chain of title and who therefore is neither a holder nor a transferor of the instrument. • An irregular indorser is generally treated as an accommodation party. See ACCOMMODATION PARTY.

qualified indorsement. An indorsement that passes title to the instrument but limits the indorser's liability to later holders if the instrument is later dishonored. • Typically, a qualified indorsement is made by writing "without recourse" or "sans recourse" over the signature. UCC § 3–415(b). See WITHOUT RECOURSE.

restrictive indorsement. An indorsement that includes a condition (e.g., "pay Josefina Cardoza only if she has worked 8 full hours on April 13") or any other language restricting further negotiation (e.g., "for deposit only").

special indorsement. An indorsement that specifies the person to receive payment or to whom the goods named by the document must be delivered. UCC § 3–205(a). Cf. *conditional indorsement.*

trust indorsement. An indorsement stating that the payee becomes a trustee for a third person (e.g., "pay Erin Ray in trust for Kaitlin Ray"); a restrictive indorsement that limits the instrument to the use of the indorser or another person.

unauthorized indorsement. An indorsement made without authority, such as a forged indorsement.

unqualified indorsement. An indorsement that does not limit the indorser's liability on the paper.

unrestrictive indorsement. An indorsement that includes no condition or language restricting negotiation.

indorser. A person who transfers a negotiable instrument by indorsement.

accommodation indorser. An indorser who acts as surety for another person.

inducement, *n.* **1.** The act or process of enticing or persuading another person to take a certain course of action. See *fraud in the inducement* under FRAUD. **2.** *Contracts.* The benefit or advantage that causes a promisor to enter into a contract. **3.** *Criminal law.* An enticement or urging of another person to commit a crime. **4.** The preliminary statement in a pleading; esp., in an action for defamation, the plaintiff's allegation that extrinsic facts gave a defamatory meaning to a statement that is not defamatory on its face, or, in a criminal indictment, a statement of preliminary facts necessary to show the criminal character of the alleged offense. Cf. INNUENDO (2); COLLOQUIUM. — **induce,** *vb.*

induction. 1. The act or process of initiating <the induction of three new members into the legal fraternity>. **2.** The act or process of reasoning from specific instances to general propositions <after looking at several examples, the group reasoned by induction that it is a very poor practice to begin a new paragraph by abruptly bringing up a new case>. — **induct,** *vb.* Cf. DEDUCTION (4).

industrial espionage. See ESPIONAGE.

ineffective assistance of counsel. See ASSISTANCE OF COUNSEL.

inequitable (in-**ek**-wi-tə-bəl), *adj.* Not fair; opposed to principles of equity.

in equity. In a chancery court rather than a court of law; before a court exercising equitable jurisdiction.

inequity (in-**ek**-wi-tee), *n.* **1.** Unfairness; a lack of equity. **2.** An instance of injustice.

inescapable peril. A danger that one cannot avoid without another's help. See LAST-CLEAR-CHANCE DOCTRINE.

in esse (in **es**-ee *also* **es**-ay). [Latin "in being"] In actual existence; IN BEING <the court was concerned only with the rights of the children *in esse*>. Cf. IN POSSE.

in evidence. Having been admitted into evidence.

inevitable-discovery rule. *Criminal procedure.* The rule providing — as an exception to the fruit-of-the-poisonous-tree doctrine — that evidence obtained by illegal means may nonetheless be admissible if the prosecution can show that the evidence would eventually have been legally obtained anyway. See FRUIT-OF-THE-POISONOUS-TREE DOCTRINE. Cf. INDEPENDENT-SOURCE RULE.

inexcusable neglect. See NEGLECT.

in extremis (in ek-**stree**-mis). [Latin "in extremity"] **1.** In extreme circumstances. **2.** Near the point of death; on one's deathbed. • Unlike *in articulo mortis*, the phrase *in extremis* does not always mean at the point of death.

in fact. Actual or real; resulting from the acts of parties rather than by operation of law. Cf. IN LAW.

infamous (**in**-fə-məs), *adj.* **1.** (Of a person) having a bad reputation. **2.** (Of conduct) that is punishable by imprisonment.

infamous crime. See CRIME.

infamous punishment. See PUNISHMENT.

infamy (**in**-fə-mee), *n.* **1.** Disgraceful repute. **2.** The loss of reputation or position resulting from a person's being convicted of an infamous crime. See *infamous crime* under CRIME.

infancy. 1. MINORITY (1). **2.** Early childhood. **3.** The beginning stages of anything.

infanticide (in-**fant**-ə-sɪd). **1.** The act of killing a newborn child, esp. by the parents or with their consent. Cf. FETICIDE. **2.** The practice of killing newborn children. **3.** One who kills a newborn child.

infect, *vb.* **1.** To contaminate <the virus infected the entire network>. **2.** To taint with crime <one part of the city has long been infected with illegal drug-dealing>. **3.** To make (a ship or cargo) liable in the seizure of contraband, which is only a part of its cargo <claiming that the single package of marijuana had infected the ship, the Coast Guard seized the entire vessel>. — **infection,** *n.* — **infectious,** *adj.*

infer, *vb.* To conclude from facts or from factual reasoning; to draw as a conclusion or inference.

inference (**in**-fər-ənts), *n.* **1.** A conclusion reached by considering other facts and deducing a logical consequence from them. **2.** The process by which such a conclusion is reached; the process of thought by which one moves from evidence to proof. — **infer,** *vb.* — **inferential,** *adj.* — **inferrer,** *n.*

inference-on-inference rule. The principle that a presumption based on another presumption cannot serve as a basis for determining an ultimate fact.

inferential fact. See FACT.

inferior court. See COURT.

infidelity. Unfaithfulness to an obligation; esp., marital unfaithfulness. Cf. ADULTERY.

infirmative hypothesis. *Criminal law.* An approach to a criminal case in which the defendant's innocence is assumed, and incriminating evidence is explained in a manner consistent with that assumption.

infirmity (in-**fər**-mə-tee), *n.* Physical weakness caused by age or disease; esp., in insurance law, an applicant's ill health that is poor enough to deter an insurance company from insuring the applicant. — **infirm,** *adj.*

in flagrante delicto (in flə-**gran**-tee də-**lik**-toh). [Latin "while the crime is ablaze"] In the very act of committing a crime or other wrong; red-handed.

inflammatory (in-**flam**-ə-tor-ee), *adj.* Tending to cause strong feelings of anger, indignation, or other type of upset; tending to stir the passions. • Evidence can be excluded if its inflammatory nature outweighs its probative value.

informal probate. See PROBATE.

informal proceeding. See PROCEEDING.

informal rulemaking. See RULEMAKING.

informant. One who informs against another; esp., one who confidentially supplies information to the police about a crime, sometimes in exchange for a reward or special treatment.

informant's privilege. See PRIVILEGE (3).

in forma pauperis (in **for**-mə **paw**-pə-ris). [Latin "in the manner of a pauper"] In the manner of an indigent who is permitted to disregard filing fees and court costs. — Abbr. *i.f.p.*

information. A formal criminal charge made by a prosecutor without a grand-jury indictment. Cf. INDICTMENT.

information and belief, on. *Jargon.* (Of an allegation or assertion) based on secondhand information that the declarant believes to be true.

information return. See TAX RETURN.

informed consent. See CONSENT.

informer. 1. INFORMANT. **2.** A private citizen who brings a penal action to recover a penalty. See COMMON INFORMER.

infra (**in**-frə), *adv. & adj.* [Latin "below"] Later in this text. • *Infra* is used as a citational signal to refer to a later-cited authority. Cf. SUPRA.

infraction, *n.* A violation, usu. of a rule or local ordinance and usu. not punishable by incarceration. — **infract,** *vb.* See VIOLATION (1).

infringement, *n. Intellectual property.* An act that interferes with one of the exclusive rights of a patent, copyright, or trademark owner. — **infringe,** *vb.* See INTELLECTUAL PROPERTY. Cf. PLAGIARISM.

in futuro (in fyə-**tyoor**-oh), *adv.* [Latin] In the future. Cf. IN PRAESENTI.

ingress (**in**-gres). **1.** The act of entering. **2.** The right or ability to enter; access. Cf. EGRESS.

ingress, egress, and regress. The right of a lessee to enter, leave, and reenter the land in question.

inhere (in-**heer**), *vb.* To exist as a permanent, inseparable, or essential attribute or quality of a thing; to be intrinsic to something.

inherent authority. See AUTHORITY (1).

inherently dangerous. Requiring special precautions at all times to avoid injury; dangerous per se. See DANGEROUS INSTRUMENTALITY.

inherent power. See POWER.

inherit, *vb.* **1.** To receive (property) from an ancestor under the laws of intestate succession upon the ancestor's death. **2.** To receive (property) as a bequest or devise. — **inheritor,** *n.*

inheritable, *adj.* **1.** (Of property) capable of being inherited. **2.** (Of a person) capable of inheriting.

inheritable obligation. See OBLIGATION.

inheritance. 1. Property received from an ancestor under the laws of intestacy. **2.** Property that a person receives by bequest or devise.

inheritance tax. See TAX.

inheritor. A person who inherits; an heir.

in-house counsel. See COUNSEL.

initial appearance. See APPEARANCE.

initial disclosure. *Civil procedure.* In federal practice, the requirement that parties make available to each other the following information without first receiving a discovery request: (1) the names, addresses, and telephone numbers of persons likely to have relevant, discoverable information, (2) a copy or description of all relevant documents, data compilations, and tangible items in the party's possession, custody, or control, (3) a damages computation, and (4) any relevant insurance agreements. Fed. R. Civ. P. 26(a)(1)(A)–(D).

initiative (i-**nish**-ee-ə-tiv *or* i-**nish**-ə-tiv). An electoral process by which a percentage of voters can propose legislation and compel a vote on it by the legislature or by the full electorate. Cf. REFERENDUM.

injunction (in-**jəngk**-shən), *n.* A court order commanding or preventing an action. • To get an injunction, the complainant must show that there is no plain, adequate, and complete remedy at law and that an irreparable injury will result unless the relief is granted. See IRREPARABLE-INJURY RULE. Cf. TEMPORARY RESTRAINING ORDER.

ex parte injunction. A preliminary injunction issued after the court has heard from only the moving party.

mandatory injunction. An injunction that orders an affirmative act or mandates a specified course of conduct. Cf. *prohibitory injunction.*

permanent injunction. An injunction granted after a final hearing on the merits. • Despite its name, a permanent injunction does not necessarily last forever.

preliminary injunction. A temporary injunction issued before or during trial to prevent an irreparable injury from occurring before the court has a chance to decide the case. • A preliminary injunction will be issued only after the defendant receives notice and an opportunity to be heard. Cf. TEMPORARY RESTRAINING ORDER.

preventive injunction. An injunction designed to prevent a loss or injury in the future. Cf. *reparative injunction.*

prohibitory injunction. An injunction that forbids or restrains an act. • This is the most common type of injunction. Cf. *mandatory injunction.*

quia-timet injunction (**kwɪ**-ə **tɪ**-mət *or* **kwee**-ə **tim**-et). [Latin "because he fears"] An injunction granted to prevent an action that has been threatened but has not yet violated the plaintiff's rights. See QUIA TIMET.

reparative injunction (ri-**par**-ə-tiv). An injunction requiring the defendant to restore the plaintiff to the position that the plaintiff occupied before the defendant committed the wrong. Cf. *preventive injunction.*

injunctive, *adj.* That has the quality of directing or ordering; of or relating to an injunction.

injuria absque damno (in-**joor**-ee-ə **abs**-kwee **dam**-noh). [Latin "injury without damage"] A legal wrong that will not sustain a lawsuit because no harm resulted from it. Cf. DAMNUM SINE INJURIA.

injury, *n.* **1.** The violation of another's legal right, for which the law provides a remedy; a wrong or injustice. See WRONG. **2.** Harm or damage. — **injure,** *vb.* — **injurious,** *adj.*

accidental injury. An injury resulting from external, violent, and unanticipated causes; esp., a bodily injury caused by some external force or agency operating contrary to a person's intentions, unexpectedly, and not according to the usual order of events.

bodily injury. Physical damage to a person's body. See *serious bodily injury.*

civil injury. Physical harm or property damage caused by breach of a contract or by a criminal offense redressable through a civil action.

continuing injury. An injury that is still in the process of being committed. • An example is the constant smoke or noise of a factory.

direct injury. **1.** An injury resulting directly from violation of a legal right. **2.** An injury resulting directly from a particular cause, without any intervening causes.

injury in fact. An actual or imminent invasion of a legally protected interest, in contrast to an invasion that is conjectural or hypothetical.

irreparable injury (i-**rep**-ər-ə-bəl). An injury that cannot be adequately measured or compensated by money and is therefore often considered remediable by injunction. See IRREPARABLE-INJURY RULE.

legal injury. Violation of a legal right.

malicious injury. **1.** An injury resulting from a willful act committed with knowledge that it is likely to injure another or with reckless disregard of the consequences. **2.** MALICIOUS MISCHIEF.

permanent injury. **1.** A completed wrong whose consequences cannot be remedied for an indefinite period. **2.** An injury to land the consequences of which will endure until the reversioner takes possession, as a result of which the reversioner has a present right of possession.

personal injury. *Torts.* **1.** In a negligence action, any harm caused to a person, such as a broken bone, a cut, or a bruise; bodily injury. **2.** Any invasion of a personal right, including mental suffering and false imprisonment.

reparable injury (**rep**-ər-ə-bəl). An injury that can be adequately compensated by money.

serious bodily injury. Serious physical impairment of the human body; esp., bodily injury that creates a substantial risk of death or that causes serious, permanent disfigurement or protracted loss or impairment of the function of any body part or organ. Model Penal Code § 210.0(3).

in kind, *adv.* **1.** In goods or services rather than money <payment in cash or in kind>. **2.** In a similar way; with an equivalent of what has been offered or received <returned the favor in kind>. — **in-kind,** *adj.* <in-kind repayment>.

in law. Existing in law or by force of law; in the contemplation of the law. Cf. IN FACT.

in-law, *n.* A relative by marriage.

in lieu of. Instead of or in place of; in exchange or return for <the creditor took a note in lieu of cash>.

in limine (in **lim**-ə-nee), *adv.* [Latin "at the outset"] Preliminarily; presented to only the judge, before or during trial. See MOTION IN LIMINE.

in-limine, *adj.* (Of a motion or order) raised preliminarily, esp. because of an issue about the admissibility of evidence believed by the movant to be prejudicial.

in loco parentis (in **loh**-koh pə-**ren**-tis), *adv.* & *adj.* [Latin "in the place of a parent"] Of, relating to, or acting as a temporary guardian or caretaker of a child, taking on all or some of the responsibilities of a parent.

inmate. A person confined in a prison, hospital, or other institution.

in mercy, *adv.* At a judge's discretion concerning punishment. • The Law Latin phrase is *in misericordia*.

innocence, *n.* The absence of guilt; esp., freedom from guilt for a particular offense. Cf. GUILT.

actual innocence. Criminal law. The absence of facts that are prerequisites for the sentence given to a defendant. Cf. CAUSE-AND-PREJUDICE RULE.

legal innocence. Criminal law. The absence of one or more procedural or legal bases to support the sentence given to a defendant. • In a petition for writ of habeas corpus or other attack on the sentence, actual innocence can sometimes be used to obtain relief from the death penalty based on errors not objected to at trial, even if the petitioner cannot meet the elements of the cause-and-prejudice rule. But legal innocence is not as readily available; failure to assert an established legal principle will not ordinarily be sufficient to satisfy the cause-and-prejudice rule or to establish the right to an exception from that rule. See CAUSE-AND-PREJUDICE RULE.

innocent, *adj.* Free from guilt; free from legal fault. Cf. NOT GUILTY (2).

innocent agent. *Criminal law.* A person who lacks the mens rea for an offense but who is tricked or coerced by the principal into committing a crime. • The principal is legally accountable for the innocent agent's actions. See Model Penal Code § 2.06(2)(a).

innocent homicide. See HOMICIDE.

innocent misrepresentation. See MISREPRESENTATION.

innocent party. See PARTY (2).

innocent spouse. *Tax.* A spouse who may be relieved of liability for taxes on income that the other spouse did not include on a joint tax return. • The innocent spouse must prove that the other spouse omitted the income, that the innocent spouse did not know and had no reason to know of the omission, and that it would be unfair under the circumstances to hold the innocent spouse liable.

innocent trespasser. See TRESPASSER.

innominate obligations. Obligations having no specific classification or name because they are not strictly contractual, delictual, or quasi-contractual. • An example is the obligation of a trustee to a beneficiary.

innuendo (in-yoo-**en**-doh). [Latin "by hinting"] **1.** An oblique remark or indirect suggestion, usu. of a derogatory nature. **2.** An explanatory word or passage inserted parenthetically into a legal document. • In criminal law, an innuendo is a statement in an indictment showing the application or meaning of matter previously expressed, the meaning of which would not otherwise be clear. In the law of defamation, an innuendo is the plaintiff's explanation of a statement's defamatory meaning when that meaning is not apparent from the statement's face. Cf. INDUCEMENT (4); COLLOQUIUM.

inoperative, *adj.* Having no force or effect; not operative.

in pais (in **pay** *or* **pays**). [Law French "in the country"] Outside court or legal proceedings. See *estoppel in pais* under ESTOPPEL.

in pari delicto (in **par**-I də-**lik**-toh), *adv.* [Latin "in equal fault"] Equally at fault.

***in pari delicto* doctrine,** *n.* [Latin] The principle that a plaintiff who has participated in wrongdoing may not recover damages resulting from the wrongdoing.

in pari materia (in **par**-I mə-**teer**-ee-ə). [Latin "in the same matter"] **1.** *adj.* On the same subject; relating to the same matter. • It is a canon of construction that statutes that are *in pari materia* may be construed together, so that inconsistencies in one statute may be resolved by looking at another statute on the same subject. **2.** *adv.* Loosely, in conjunction with.

in perpetuity (in pər-pə-**t[y]oo**-ə-tee). Forever.

in personam (in pər-**soh**-nəm), *adj.* [Latin "against a person"] Involving or determining the personal rights and interests of the parties. — **in personam,** *adv.* See *action in personam* under ACTION. Cf. IN REM.

in personam jurisdiction. See JURISDICTION.

in posse (in **pos**-ee). [Latin] Not currently existing, but ready to come into existence under certain conditions in the future; potential. Cf. IN ESSE.

in praesenti (in pri-**zen**-tI *or* pree-). [Latin] At present; right now. Cf. IN FUTURO.

inquest. 1. An inquiry by a coroner or medical examiner, sometimes with the aid of a jury, into the manner of death of a person who has died under suspicious circumstances, or who has died in prison. **2.** An inquiry into a certain matter by a jury empaneled for that purpose. **3.** The finding of such a specially empaneled jury. **4.** A proceeding, usu. ex parte, to determine, after the defendant has defaulted, the amount of the plaintiff's damages. Cf. INQUISITION.

inquest jury. See JURY.

inquiry notice. See NOTICE.

inquisition. 1. The record of the finding of the jury sworn by the coroner to inquire into a person's death. **2.** A judicial inquiry, esp. in a derogatory sense. **3.** A persistent, grueling examination conducted without regard for the examinee's dignity or civil rights. Cf. INQUEST.

inquisitorial system. A system of proof-taking used in civil law, whereby the judge conducts the trial, determines what questions to ask, and defines the scope and the extent of the inquiry. Cf. ADVERSARY SYSTEM.

in re (in **ree** *or* **ray**). [Latin "in the matter of"] (Of a judicial proceeding) not formally including adverse parties, but rather involving something (such as an estate). • The term is often used in case citations, especially in uncontested proceedings <*In re Butler's Estate*>.

in rem (in **rem**), *adj.* [Latin "against a thing"] Involving or determining the status of a thing, and therefore the rights of persons generally with respect to that thing. — **in rem,** *adv.* See *action in rem* under ACTION. Cf. IN PERSONAM.

> ***quasi in rem*** (**kway**-SI in **rem** *or* **kway**-ZI). [Latin "as if against a thing"] Involving or determining the rights of a person having an interest in property located within the court's jurisdiction. See *action quasi in rem* under ACTION.

in rem jurisdiction. See JURISDICTION.

INS. *abbr.* IMMIGRATION AND NATURALIZATION SERVICE.

insane, *adj.* Mentally deranged; suffering from one or more delusions or false beliefs that (1) have no foundation in reason or reality, (2) are not credible to any reasonable person of sound mind, and (3) cannot be overcome in a sufferer's mind by any amount of evidence or argument. See INSANITY.

insane delusion. An irrational, persistent belief in an imaginary state of facts that deprives a person of the capacity to undertake acts of legal consequence, such as making a will.

insanity, *n.* Any mental disorder severe enough that it prevents a person from having legal capacity and excuses the person from criminal or civil responsibility. • Insanity is a legal, not a medical, standard. Cf. *diminished capacity* under CAPACITY; SANITY.

> ***emotional insanity.*** Insanity produced by a violent excitement of the emotions or passions, although reasoning faculties may remain unimpaired; a passion that for a period creates complete derangement of intellect. • Emotional insanity is sometimes described as an irresistible impulse to do an act. See IRRESISTIBLE-IMPULSE TEST.

> ***temporary insanity.*** Insanity that exists only at the time of a criminal act.

insanity defense. *Criminal law.* An affirmative defense alleging that a mental disorder caused the accused to commit the crime. See MCNAGHTEN RULES; SUBSTANTIAL-CAPACITY TEST; IRRESISTIBLE-IMPULSE TEST; APPRECIATION TEST.

insecurity clause. A loan-agreement provision that allows the creditor to demand immediate and full payment of the loan balance if the creditor has reason to believe that the debtor is about to default, as when the debtor suddenly loses a significant source of income. Cf. ACCELERATION CLAUSE.

insolvency, *n.* **1.** The condition of being unable to pay debts as they fall due or in the usual course of business. **2.** The inability to pay debts as they mature. See BANKRUPTCY (2). Cf. SOLVENCY.

inspection. A careful examination of something, such as goods (to determine their fitness for purchase) or items produced in response to a discovery request (to determine their relevance to a lawsuit).

inspection right. The legal entitlement in certain circumstances to examine articles or documents, such as a consumer's right to inspect goods before paying for them.

installment, *n.* A periodic partial payment of a debt.

installment accounting method. See ACCOUNTING METHOD.

installment contract. See CONTRACT.

installment loan. See LOAN.

installment sale. A conditional sale in which the buyer makes a down payment followed by periodic payments and the seller retains title or a security interest until all payments have been received.

instance, *n.* **1.** An example or occurrence <there were 55 instances of reported auto theft in this small community last year>. **2.** The act of instituting legal proceedings <court of first instance>. **3.** Urgent solicitation or insistence <she applied for the job at the instance of her friend>.

instance, *vb.* To illustrate by example; to cite.

instant, *adj. Jargon.* This; the present (case, judgment, order, etc.); now being discussed.

instantaneous crime. See CRIME.

instantaneous death. See DEATH.

instant case. See *case at bar* under CASE.

instanter (in-**stan**-tər), *adv. Jargon.* Instantly; at once.

institutionalize, *vb.* **1.** To place (a person) in an institution. **2.** To give (a rule or practice) official sanction.

institutional litigant. An organized group that brings lawsuits not merely to win but also to bring about a change in the law or to defend an existing law.

instrument. 1. A written legal document that defines rights, duties, entitlements, or liabilities, such as a contract, will, promissory note, or share certificate. **2.** *Commercial law.* An unconditional promise or order to pay a fixed amount of money, with or without interest or other fixed charges described in the promise or order. • Under the UCC, a promise or order must meet several other specifically listed requirements to qualify as an instrument. UCC § 3–104(a). See NEGOTIABLE INSTRUMENT. **3.** A means by which something is achieved, performed, or furthered.

inchoate instrument. An unrecorded instrument that must, by law, be recorded to serve as effective notice to third parties.

incomplete instrument. A paper that, although intended to be a negotiable instrument, lacks an essential element. • An incomplete instrument may be enforced if it is subsequently completed. UCC § 3–115.

perfect instrument. An instrument (such as a deed or mortgage) that is executed and filed with a public registry.

instrumentality, *n.* **1.** A thing used to achieve an end or purpose. **2.** A means or agency through which a function of another entity is accomplished, such as a branch of a governing body.

insufficient evidence. See EVIDENCE.

insurable interest. See INTEREST (2).

insurance (in-**shuur**-ənts), *n.* **1.** An agreement by which one party (the *insurer*) commits to do something of value for another party (the *insured*) upon the occurrence of some specified contingency; esp., an agreement by which one party assumes a risk faced by another party in return for a premium payment. **2.** The amount for which someone or something is covered by such an agreement. — **insure,** *vb.*

broad-form insurance. Comprehensive insurance.

coinsurance. **1.** Insurance provided jointly by two or more insurers. **2.** Property insurance that requires the insured to bear a portion of any loss if the property is not covered up to a certain percentage of its full value. Cf. *double insurance.*

collision insurance. Automobile insurance that covers damage to the insured's vehicle, but does not cover a personal injury resulting from an accident.

comprehensive insurance. Insurance that combines coverage against many kinds of losses that may also be insured separately.

compulsory insurance. Statutorily required insurance; esp., motor-vehicle liability insurance that a state requires as a condition to registration of the vehicle.

convertible insurance. Insurance that can be changed to another form without further evidence of insurability, usu. referring to a term-life-insurance policy that can be changed to permanent insurance without a medical examination.

deposit insurance. A federally sponsored indemnification program to protect depositors against the loss of their money, up to a specified maximum, if the bank or savings-and-loan association fails or defaults.

double insurance. Insurance coverage by more than one insurer for the same interest and for the same insured. • The insured is entitled to only a single indemnity from a loss, and to recover this, the insured may either (1) sue each insurer for its share of the loss, or (2) sue one or more of the insurers for the entire amount, leaving any paying insurers to recover from the others their respective shares of the loss. Cf. *coinsurance.*

excess insurance. An agreement to indemnify against any loss that exceeds the amount of coverage under another policy. Cf. *primary insurance.*

extended-term insurance. Insurance that remains in effect after a default in paying premiums, as long as the policy has cash value to pay premiums.

first-party insurance. A policy that applies to oneself or one's own property, such as life insurance, health insurance, disability insurance, and fire insurance.

joint life insurance. Life insurance on two or more persons, payable to the survivor or survivors when one of the policyholders dies.

Lloyd's insurance. Insurance provided by insurers as individuals, rather than as a corporation. • The insurers' liability is several but not joint. See LLOYD'S OF LONDON; LLOYD'S UNDERWRITERS.

malpractice insurance (mal-**prak**-tis). An agreement to indemnify a professional person, such as a doctor or lawyer, against negligence claims.

paid-up insurance. Insurance that remains in effect even though no more premiums are due.

primary insurance. Insurance that attaches immediately on the happening of a loss; insurance that is not contingent on the exhaustion of an underlying policy. Cf. *excess insurance*.

replacement insurance. Insurance under which the value of the loss is measured by the current cost of replacing the insured property. See *replacement cost* under COST.

self-insurance. A plan under which a business sets aside money to cover any loss.

third-party insurance. See *liability insurance*.

title insurance. An agreement to indemnify against damage or loss arising from a defect in title to real property, usu. issued to the buyer of the property by the title company that conducted the title search.

unemployment insurance. A type of social insurance that pays money to workers who are unemployed for reasons unrelated to job performance.

universal life insurance. A form of term life insurance in which the premiums are paid from the insured's earnings from a money-market fund.

insurance adjuster. A person who determines the value of a loss to the insured and settles the claim against the insurer.

insurance agent. A person authorized by an insurance company to sell its insurance policies.

insurance broker. One who sells insurance policies without an exclusive affiliation with a particular insurance company. See BROKER.

insurance certificate. 1. A document issued by an insurer as evidence of insurance or membership in an insurance or pension plan. **2.** A document issued by an insurer to a shipper as evidence that a shipment of goods is covered by a marine insurance policy.

insurance commissioner. A public official who supervises the insurance business conducted in a state.

insurance company. A corporation or association that issues insurance policies.

insurance policy. 1. A contract of insurance. **2.** A document detailing such a contract.

basic-form policy. A policy that offers limited coverage against loss.

blanket policy. An agreement to indemnify all property, regardless of location.

broad-form policy. A policy that offers broad protection with few limitations.

claims-made policy. An agreement to indemnify against all claims made during a specified period, regardless of when the incidents that gave rise to the claims occurred.

closed policy. An insurance policy whose terms cannot be changed.

comprehensive general liability policy. An insurance policy, usu. obtained by a business, that covers damages that the insured becomes legally obligated to pay to a third party because of bodily injury or property damage.

concurrent policy. One of two or more insurance policies that cover the same risk.

incontestable policy. A policy containing a provision that prohibits the insurer from contesting or canceling the policy on the basis of statements made in the application.

joint life policy. A life-insurance policy that matures and becomes due upon the death of any of those jointly insured.

lapsed policy. **1.** An insurance policy on which there has been a default in premium payments. **2.** An insurance policy that, because of statutory provisions, remains in force after a default in premium payments.

limited policy. **1.** An insurance policy that specifically excludes certain classes or types of loss. **2.** See *basic-form policy.*

manuscript policy. An insurance policy containing nonstandard provisions that have been negotiated between the insurer and the insured.

master policy. An insurance policy that covers those under a group-insurance plan.

multiperil policy. An insurance policy that covers several types of losses, such as a homeowner's policy that covers losses from fire, theft, and personal injury.

open-perils policy. A property insurance policy covering all risks against loss except those specifically excluded from coverage.

standard policy. **1.** An insurance policy providing insurance that is recommended or required by state law, usu. regulated by a state agency. **2.** An insurance policy that contains standard terms used for similar insurance policies nationwide, usu. drafted by an insurance industrial association such as Insurance Services Office.

time policy. An insurance policy that is effective only during a specified period.

insurance pool. A group of several insurers that, to spread the risk, combine and share premiums and losses.

insurance rating. The process by which an insurer arrives at a policy premium for a particular risk.

insurance underwriter. 1. INSURER. **2.** An insurance-company employee who is responsible for determining whether to issue a policy and the amount to charge for the coverage provided.

insured, *n.* A person who is covered or protected by an insurance policy.

additional insured. A person who is covered by an insurance policy but who is not the primary insured.

class-one insured. In a motor-vehicle policy, the named insured and any relative residing with the named insured.

class-two insured. In a motor-vehicle policy, a person lawfully occupying a vehicle at the time of an accident.

named insured. A person designated in an insurance policy as the one covered by the policy.

insurer. One who agrees, by contract, to assume the risk of another's loss and to compensate for that loss.

quasi-insurer. A service provider who is held to strict liability in the provision of services, such as an innkeeper or a common carrier.

insuring clause. A provision in an insurance policy or bond reciting the risk assumed by the insurer or establishing the scope of the coverage.

intake, *n.* **1.** The official screening of a juvenile charged with an offense in order to determine where to place the juvenile pending formal adjudication or informal disposition. **2.** The body of officers who conduct this screening.

intake day. The day on which new cases are assigned to the courts.

intangible, *adj.* Not capable of being touched; impalpable.

intangible, *n.* Something that is not tangible; esp., an asset that is not corporeal, such as intellectual property.

general intangible. Any personal property other than goods, accounts, chattel paper, documents, instruments, investment property, rights to proceeds of written letters of credit, and money. • Some examples are goodwill, things in action, and literary rights. UCC § 9–103(b). See *intangible property* under PROPERTY.

payment intangible. A general intangible under which the account debtor's principal obligation is a monetary obligation. UCC § 9–103(d).

intangible property. See PROPERTY.

integrated bar. See BAR ASSOCIATION.

integrated contract. One or more writings constituting a final expression of one or more terms of an agreement. See INTEGRATION (2).

completely integrated contract. An integrated agreement adopted by the parties as a full and exclusive statement of the terms of the agreement.

partially integrated contract. An integrated agreement other than a completely integrated agreement.

integrated property settlement. A contract, incorporated into a divorce decree, that divides up the assets of divorcing spouses.

integration. 1. The process of making whole or combining into one. **2.** *Contracts*. The full expression of the parties' agreement, so that all earlier agreements are superseded, the effect being that neither party may later contradict or add to the contractual terms. See PAROL-EVIDENCE RULE.

complete integration. The fact or state of fully expressing the intent of the parties.

partial integration. The fact or state of not fully expressing the parties' intent, so that the contract can be changed by the admission of parol (extrinsic) evidence.

3. The incorporation of different races into existing institutions (such as public schools) for the purpose of reversing the historical effects of racial discrimination. Cf. DESEGREGATION.

integration clause. A contractual provision stating that the contract represents the parties' complete and final agreement and supersedes all informal understandings and oral agreements relating to the subject matter of the contract. See INTEGRATION (2); PAROL-EVIDENCE RULE.

integration rule. The rule that if the parties to a contract have embodied their agreement in a final document, any other action or statement is without effect and is immaterial in determining the terms of the contract.

intellectual property. 1. A category of intangible rights protecting commercially valuable products of the human intellect. • The category comprises primarily trademark, copyright, and patent rights, but also includes trade-secret rights, publicity rights, moral rights, and rights against unfair competition. **2.** A commercially valuable product of the human intellect, in a concrete or abstract form, such as a copyrightable work, a protectable trademark, a patentable invention, or a trade secret. — Abbr. IP.

intend, *vb.* **1.** To have in mind a fixed purpose to reach a desired objective; to have as one's purpose <Daniel intended to become a lawyer>. **2.** To contemplate that the usual consequences of one's act will probably or necessarily follow from the act, whether or not those consequences are desired for their own sake <although he activated the theater's fire alarm only on a dare, the jury found that Wilbur intended to cause a panic>. **3.** To signify or mean <the parties intended for the writing to supersede their earlier handshake deal>.

intended beneficiary. See BENEFICIARY.

intended to be recorded. (Of a deed or other instrument) not yet filed with a public registry, but forming a link in a chain of title.

intended-use doctrine. *Products liability*. The rule imposing a duty on a manufacturer to develop a product so that it is reasonably safe for its intended or foreseeable users. • In determining the scope of responsibility, the court considers the defendant's marketing scheme and the foreseeability of the harm.

intendment (in-**tend**-mənt). **1.** The sense in which the law understands something. **2.** A decision-maker's inference about the true meaning or intention of a legal instrument. **3.** A person's expectations when interacting with others within the legal sphere.

intent. 1. The state of mind accompanying an act, esp. a forbidden act. • While motive is the inducement to do some act, intent is the mental resolution or determination to do it. When the intent to do an act that violates the law exists, motive becomes immaterial. Cf. MOTIVE; SCIENTER; KNOWLEDGE.

constructive intent. A legal principle that actual intent will be presumed when an act leading to the result could have been reasonably expected to cause that result.

criminal intent. **1.** See MENS REA. **2.** An intent to commit an actus reus without any justification, excuse, or other defense. **3.** See *specific intent*.

general intent. The state of mind required for the commission of certain common-law crimes not requiring a specific intent or not imposing strict liability. • General intent usually takes the form of recklessness (involving actual awareness of a risk and the culpable taking of that risk) or negligence (involving blameworthy inadvertence).

immediate intent. The intent relating to a wrongful act; the part of the total intent coincident with the wrongful act itself.

implied intent. A person's state of mind that can be inferred from speech or conduct, or from language used in an instrument to which the person is a party.

intent to kill. An intent to cause the death of another; esp., a state of mind that, if found to exist during an assault, can serve as the basis for an aggravated-assault charge.

manifest intent. Intent that is apparent or obvious based on the available circumstantial evidence, even if direct evidence of intent is not available.

specific intent. The intent to accomplish the precise criminal act that one is later charged with. See SPECIFIC-INTENT DEFENSE.

testamentary intent. A testator's intent that a particular instrument function as his or her last will and testament.

transferred intent. Intent that has been shifted from the originally intended wrongful act to the wrongful act actually committed. • For example, if a person intends to kill one person but kills another, the intent may be transferred to the actual act. See TRANSFERRED-INTENT DOCTRINE.

ulterior intent. The intent that passes beyond a wrongful act and relates to the objective for the sake of which the act is done; MOTIVE. • For example, a thief's immediate intent may be to steal another's money, but the ulterior intent may be to buy food with that money.

2. A lawmaker's state of mind and purpose in drafting or voting for a measure.

original intent. The mental state of the drafters or enactors of the U.S. Constitution, a statute, or another document.

intention. The willingness to bring about something planned or foreseen; the state of being set to do something.

intentional, *adj.* Done with intention or purpose.

intentional act. See ACT.

intentional infliction of emotional distress. The tort of intentionally or recklessly causing another person severe emotional distress through one's extreme or outrageous acts. See EMOTIONAL DISTRESS. Cf. NEGLIGENT INFLICTION OF EMOTIONAL DISTRESS.

intentional tort. See TORT.

intentional wrong. See WRONG.

inter alia (**in**-tər **ay**-lee-ə *or* **ah**-lee-ə), *adv.* [Latin] Among other things.

inter alios (**in**-tər **ay**-lee-əs *or* **ah**-lee-əs), *adv.* [Latin] Among other persons.

Inter-American Bar Association. An organization of lawyers from North America, Central America, and South America whose purpose is to promote education, cooperation, and professional exchanges among lawyers from different American countries. — Abbr. IABA.

intercourse. 1. Dealings or communications, esp. between businesses, governmental entities, or the like. **2.** Physical sexual contact, esp. involving the penetration of the vagina by the penis.

interdict (in-tər-**dikt**), *vb.* To forbid or restrain.

interdiction. The act of prohibiting.

interest, *n.* **1.** Advantage or profit, esp. of a financial nature <conflict of interest>. **2.** A legal share in something; all or part of a legal or equitable claim to or right in property <right, title, and interest>.

absolute interest. An interest that is not subject to any condition.

contingent interest. An interest that the holder may enjoy only upon the occurrence of a condition precedent.

direct interest. A certain, absolute interest.

entire interest. A whole interest or right, without diminution. See FEE SIMPLE.

equitable interest. An interest held by virtue of an equitable title or claimed on equitable grounds, such as the interest held by a trust beneficiary.

expectation interest. The interest of a nonbreaching party in receiving a benefit that would have resulted if the contract had been performed. See *expectation damages* under DAMAGES; BENEFIT-OF-THE-BARGAIN RULE.

future interest. A property interest in which the privilege of possession or of other enjoyment is future and not present. Cf. *present interest.*

inalienable interest. An interest that cannot be sold or traded.

inchoate interest. A property interest that has not yet vested.

insurable interest. A legal interest in another person's life or health or in the protection of property from injury, loss, destruction, or pecuniary damage. • To take out an insurance policy, a potential insured must have an insurable interest. If a policy does not have an insurable interest as its basis, it will usually be considered a form of wagering and thus be held unenforceable.

legal interest. An interest recognized by law, such as legal title.

present interest. A property interest in which the privilege of possession or enjoyment is present and not merely future; an interest entitling the holder to immediate possession. Cf. *future interest*.

proprietary interest. The interest held by a property owner together with all appurtenant rights, such as a stockholder's right to vote the shares.

reliance interest. The interest a nonbreaching party has in recovering costs stemming from that party's reliance on the performance of the contract.

vested interest. An interest the right to the enjoyment of which, either present or future, is not subject to the happening of a condition precedent.

3. The compensation fixed by agreement or allowed by law for the use or detention of money, or for the loss of money by one who is entitled to its use; esp., the amount owed to a lender in return for the use of borrowed money. See USURY.

accrued interest. Interest that is earned but not yet paid, such as interest that accrues on real estate and that will be paid when the property is sold if, in the meantime, the rental income does not cover the mortgage payments.

add-on interest. Interest that is computed on the original face amount of a loan and that remains the same even as the principal declines. • A $10,000 loan with add-on interest at 8% payable over three years would require equal annual interest payments of $800 for three years, regardless of the unpaid principal amount. See *add-on loan* under LOAN.

compound interest. Interest paid on both the principal and the previously accumulated interest. Cf. *simple interest*.

conventional interest. Interest at a rate agreed to by the parties themselves, as distinguished from that prescribed by law. Cf. *interest as damages*.

gross interest. A borrower's interest payment that includes administrative, service, and insurance charges.

imputed interest. Interest income that the IRS attributes to a lender regardless of whether the lender actually receives interest from the borrower.

interest as damages. Interest allowed by law in the absence of a promise to pay it, as compensation for a delay in paying a fixed sum or a delay in assessing and paying damages. Cf. *conventional interest*.

prepaid interest. Interest paid before it is earned.

qualified residence interest. *Tax*. Interest paid on debt that is secured by one's home and that was incurred to purchase, build, improve, or refinance the home.

simple interest. Interest paid on the principal only and not on accumulated interest. Cf. *compound interest.*

unearned interest. Interest received by a financial institution before it is earned.

interest-analysis technique. *Conflict of laws.* A method of resolving choice-of-law questions by reviewing a state's laws and the state's interests in enforcing those laws to determine whether that state's laws or those of another state should apply.

interested party. See PARTY (2).

interested person. See PERSON.

interested witness. See WITNESS.

interest-free loan. See LOAN.

interest rate. The percentage that a borrower of money must pay to the lender in return for the use of the money, usu. expressed as a percentage of the principal payable for a one-year period.

annual percentage rate. The actual cost of borrowing money, expressed in the form of an annualized interest rate.

contract rate. The interest rate printed on the face of a bond certificate.

discount rate. **1.** The interest rate at which a member bank may borrow money from the Federal Reserve. **2.** The percentage of a commercial paper's face value paid by an issuer who sells the instrument to a financial institution. **3.** The interest rate used in calculating present value.

effective rate. The actual annual interest rate, which incorporates compounding when calculating interest, rather than the stated rate or coupon rate.

floating rate. A varying interest rate that is tied to a financial index such as the prime rate.

illegal rate. An interest rate higher than the rate allowed by law. See USURY.

legal rate. **1.** The interest rate imposed as a matter of law when none is provided by contract. **2.** The maximum interest rate, set by statute, that may be charged on a loan. See USURY.

lock rate. A mortgage-application interest rate that is established and guaranteed for a specified period.

nominal rate. The interest rate stated in a loan agreement or on a bond, with no adjustment made for inflation.

prime rate. The interest rate that a commercial bank holds out as its lowest rate for a short-term loan to its most creditworthy borrowers, usu. large corporations.

real rate. An interest rate that has been adjusted for inflation over time.

variable rate. An interest rate that varies at preset intervals in relation to the current market rate (usu. the prime rate).

interference, *n.* **1.** The act of meddling in another's affairs. **2.** An obstruction or hindrance. **3.** *Patents.* An administrative proceeding in the U.S. Patent and Trademark Office to determine which applicant is entitled to the patent when two or more applicants claim the same invention. — **interfere,** *vb.*

intergovernmental immunity. See IMMUNITY (1).

intergovernmental-immunity doctrine. *Constitutional law.* The principle that both the federal government and the states are independent sovereigns, and that neither sovereign may intrude on the other in certain political spheres. Cf. PREEMPTION.

interim-occupancy agreement. A contract governing an arrangement (called a *leaseback*) whereby the seller rents back property from the buyer. See LEASEBACK.

interim relief. See RELIEF.

interlineation (in-tər-lin-ee-**ay**-shən), *n.* **1.** The act of writing something between the lines of an earlier writing. **2.** Something written between the lines of an earlier writing. — **interline,** *vb.* Cf. INTERPOLATION.

interlocking confessions. See CONFESSION.

interlocutory (in-tər-**lok**-yə-tor-ee), *adj.* (Of an order, judgment, appeal, etc.) interim or temporary, not constituting a final resolution of the whole controversy.

interlocutory appeal. See APPEAL.

Interlocutory Appeals Act. A federal statute, enacted in 1958, that grants discretion to a U.S. court of appeals to review an interlocutory order in a civil case if the trial judge states in writing that the order involves a controlling question of law on which there is substantial ground for difference of opinion, and that an immediate appeal from the order may materially advance the termination of the litigation. 28 USCA § 1292(b).

interlocutory judgment. See JUDGMENT.

interlocutory order. See ORDER.

interloper, *n.* **1.** One who interferes without justification. **2.** One who trades illegally. — **interlope,** *vb.*

intermediary (in-tər-**mee**-dee-er-ee), *n.* A mediator or go-between; a third-party negotiator. — **intermediate** (in-tər-**mee**-dee-ayt), *vb.* Cf. FINDER.

intermediary bank. See BANK.

intermediate scrutiny. *Constitutional law.* A standard lying between the extremes of rational-basis review and strict scrutiny. • Under the standard, if a statute contains a quasi-suspect classification (such as gender or legitimacy), the classification must be substantially related to the achievement of an important governmental objective. Cf. STRICT SCRUTINY; RATIONAL-BASIS TEST.

intermediation. 1. Any process involving an intermediary. **2.** The placing of funds with a financial intermediary that reinvests the funds, such as a bank that lends the funds to others or a mutual fund that invests the funds in stocks, bonds, or other instruments.

intermittent sentence. See SENTENCE.

intern, *n.* An advanced student or recent graduate who is apprenticing to gain practical experience before entering a specific profession. — **internship,** *n.* See CLERK (3).

intern, *vb.* **1.** To segregate and confine a person or group, esp. those suspected of hostile sympathies in time of war. **2.** To work in an internship.

internal act. See ACT.

Internal Revenue Code. Title 26 of the U.S. Code, containing all current federal tax laws. — Abbr. IRC.

Internal Revenue Service. The branch of the U.S. Treasury Department responsible for administering the Internal Revenue Code and providing taxpayer education. — Abbr. IRS.

internal-security act. A statute illegalizing and controlling subversive activities of organizations whose purpose is believed to be to overthrow or disrupt the government. • In the United States, many provisions in such statutes have been declared unconstitutional. One such law was repealed in 1993. See 50 USCA § 781.

international agreement. A treaty or other contract between different countries, such as GATT or NAFTA. See GENERAL AGREEMENT ON TARIFFS AND TRADE; NORTH AMERICAN FREE TRADE AGREEMENT.

International Court of Justice. The 15-member U.N. tribunal that sits primarily at The Hague, Netherlands, to adjudicate disputes between countries that voluntarily submit cases for decision. • Appeal from the court lies only with the U.N. Security Council. — Abbr. ICJ.

international crime. *Int'l law.* A crime against international law, occurring when three conditions are satisfied: (1) the criminal norm must derive either from a treaty concluded under international law or from customary international law, and must have direct binding force on individuals without intermediate provisions of municipal law, (2) the provision must be made for the prosecution of acts penalized by international law in accordance with the principle of universal jurisdiction, so that the international character of the crime might show in the mode of prosecution itself (e.g., before the International Criminal Court), and (3) a treaty establishing liability for the act must bind the great majority of countries.

International Criminal Court. A court that was established in 1998 by the U.N. Security Council to adjudicate international crimes such as terrorism. • In the absence of any international criminal code, the court applies general principles of international criminal law. — Abbr. ICC.

International Criminal Police Organization. An international law-enforcement group founded in 1923 and headquartered in Lyons, France. • The organization gathers and shares information on transnational criminals for more than 180 member nations. — Also termed *Interpol.*

international economic law. International law relating to investment, economic relations, economic development, economic institutions, and regional economic integration.

international law. The legal principles governing the relationships between nations; more modernly, the law of international relations, embracing not only nations but also such participants as international organizations, multinational corporations, nongovernmental organizations, and even individuals (such as those who invoke their human rights or commit war crimes). See COMITY.

International Law Commission. A body created in 1948 by the United Nations for the purpose of codifying international law.

international legal community. 1. The collective body of countries whose mutual legal relations are based on sovereign equality. **2.** More broadly, all organized entities having the capacity to take part in international legal relations. **3.** An integrated organization on which a group of countries, by international treaty, confer part of their powers for amalgamated enterprise. • In this sense, the European Community is a prime example.

international organization. *Int'l law.* An association of countries, established by and operated according to multilateral treaty, whose purpose is to pursue the common aims of those countries. • Examples include the World Health Organization, the International Civil Aviation Organization, and the Organization of Petroleum Exporting Countries.

international relations. 1. World politics. **2.** Global political interaction, primarily among sovereign nations. **3.** The academic discipline devoted to studying world politics, embracing international law, international economics, and the history and art of diplomacy.

internecine (in-tər-**nee**-sin *or* in-tər-**nee**-SIN *or* in-tər-**nes**-een), *adj.* **1.** Deadly; characterized by mass slaughter. **2.** Mutually deadly; destructive of both parties. **3.** Loosely, of or relating to conflict within a group.

inter partes (in-tər **pahr**-teez), *adv.* [Latin "between parties"] Between two or more parties; with two or more parties in a transaction. — ***inter partes***, *adj.* Cf. EX PARTE.

interplea. A pleading by which a stakeholder places the disputed property into the court's registry; the plea made by an interpleader. See INTERPLEADER.

interplead, *vb.* **1.** (Of a claimant) to assert one's own claim regarding property or an issue already before the court. **2.** (Of a stakeholder) to institute an interpleader action, usu. by depositing disputed property into the court's registry to abide the court's decision about who is entitled to the property. Cf. IMPLEAD.

interpleader, *n.* **1.** A suit to determine a right to property held by a usu. disinterested third party (called a *stakeholder*) who is in doubt about ownership and who therefore deposits the property with the court to permit interested parties to litigate ownership. • Typically, a stakeholder initiates an interpleader both to determine who should receive the property and to avoid multiple liability. Fed. R. Civ. P. 22. See STAKEHOLDER (1). Cf. IMPLEADER; INTERVENTION (1). **2.** Loosely, a party who interpleads.

Interpol. See INTERNATIONAL CRIMINAL POLICE ORGANIZATION.

interpolation (in-tər-pə-**lay**-shən), *n.* The act of inserting words into a document to change or clarify the meaning. • In a negative sense, interpolation can refer to putting extraneous or false words into a document to change its meaning. — **interpolate,** *vb.* — **interpolative,** *adj.* — **interpolator,** *n.* Cf. INTERLINEATION.

interposition, *n.* The act of submitting something (such as a pleading or motion) as a defense to an opponent's claim. — **interpose,** *vb.*

interpretation, *n.* **1.** The process of determining what something, esp. the law or a legal document, means; the ascertainment of meaning.

authentic interpretation. Interpretation arrived at by asking the drafter or drafting body what the intended meaning was.

customary interpretation. Interpretation based on earlier rulings on the same subject.

extensive interpretation. A liberal interpretation that applies a statutory provision to a case not falling within its literal words.

grammatical interpretation. Interpretation that is based exclusively on the words themselves.

liberal interpretation. Interpretation according to what the reader believes the author reasonably intended, even if, through inadvertence, the author failed to think of it.

logical interpretation. Interpretation that departs from the literal words on the ground that there may be other, more satisfactory evidence of the author's true intention.

restrictive interpretation. An interpretation that is bound by a principle or principles existing outside the interpreted text. Cf. *unrestrictive interpretation.*

strict interpretation. Interpretation according to what the reader believes the author must have been thinking at the time of the writing, and no more. • Typically, this type of reading gives a text a narrow meaning.

unrestrictive interpretation. Interpretation in good faith, without reference to any specific principle. Cf. *restrictive interpretation.*

2. The understanding one has about the meaning of something. **3.** A translation, esp. oral, from one language to another. **4.** CHARACTERIZATION. — **interpret,** *vb.* — **interpretative, interpretive,** *adj.* See CONSTRUCTION (2).

interpretation clause. A legislative or contractual provision giving the meaning of words frequently used or explaining how the document as a whole is to be construed.

interpreted testimony. See TESTIMONY.

interpretivism. A doctrine of constitutional interpretation holding that judges must follow norms or values expressly stated or implied in the language of the Constitution. Cf. NONINTERPRETIVISM; ORIGINALISM.

interrogation, *n.* The formal or systematic questioning of a person; esp., intensive questioning by the police, usu. of a person arrested for or suspected of committing a crime. • The Supreme Court has held that, for purposes of the Fifth Amendment right against self-incrimination, interrogation includes not only express questioning but also words or actions that the police should know are reasonably likely to elicit an incriminating response. *Rhode Island v. Innis*, 446 U.S. 291, 100 S.Ct. 1082 (1980). — **interrogate,** *vb.* — **interrogative,** *adj.*

custodial interrogation. Police questioning of a detained person about the crime that he or she is suspected of having committed. • Miranda warnings must be given before a custodial interrogation.

investigatory interrogation. Routine, nonaccusatory questioning by the police of a person who is not in custody.

noncustodial interrogation. Police questioning of a suspect who has not been detained and can leave at will. • Miranda warnings are usually not given before a noncustodial interrogation.

interrogator (in-**ter**-ə-gay-tər). One who poses questions to another.

interrogatory (in-tə-**rog**-ə-tor-ee), *n.* A written question (usu. in a set of questions) submitted to an opposing party in a lawsuit as part of discovery.

cross-interrogatory. An interrogatory from a party who has received a set of interrogatories.

special interrogatory. A written jury question whose answer is required to supplement a general verdict. • This term is not properly used in federal practice, which authorizes interrogatories and special verdicts, but not special interrogatories. Fed. R. Civ. P. 49.

in terrorem (in te-**ror**-əm), *adv.* & *adj.* [Latin "in order to frighten"] By way of threat; as a warning.

***in terrorem* clause.** A provision designed to threaten one into action or inaction; esp., a testamentary provision that threatens to dispossess any beneficiary who challenges the terms of the will. See NO-CONTEST CLAUSE.

inter se (**in**-tər **see** *or* **say**). [Latin "between or among themselves"] (Of a right or duty) owed between the parties rather than to others.

interspousal, *adj.* Between husband and wife.

interstate, *adj.* Between two or more states or residents of different states.

interstate agreement. An agreement between states. Cf. *interstate compact* under COMPACT.

Interstate Agreement on Detainers Act. A law, originally enacted in 1956, in which the federal government, certain states, and the District of Columbia agree that a state may obtain custody of a prisoner for trial even though the prisoner is already incarcerated in another state. See UNIFORM MANDATORY DISPOSITION OF DETAINERS ACT.

interstate commerce. See COMMERCE.

Interstate Commerce Commission. The now-defunct federal agency established by the Interstate Commerce Act in 1887 to regulate surface transportation between states by certifying carriers and pipelines and by monitoring quality and pricing. — Abbr. ICC.

interstate compact. See COMPACT.

interstate income-withholding order. A court order entered to enforce a support order of a court of another state by withholding income of the defaulting person.

interstate law. 1. INTERNATIONAL LAW. **2.** The rules and principles used to determine controversies between residents of different states.

intervening cause. See CAUSE (1).

intervenor. One who voluntarily enters a pending lawsuit because of a personal stake in it.

intervention, *n.* **1.** The entry into a lawsuit by a third party who, despite not being named a party to the action, has a personal stake in the outcome. Cf. IMPLEADER; INTERPLEADER. **2.** The legal procedure by which such a third party is allowed to become a party to the litigation. — **intervene,** *vb.*

inter vivos (in-tər vɪ-vohs *or* **vee**-vohs), *adj.* [Latin "between the living"] Of or relating to property conveyed not by will or in contemplation of an imminent death, but during the conveyor's lifetime. — ***inter vivos*****,** *adv.*

inter vivos gift. See GIFT.

inter vivos transfer. See TRANSFER.

inter vivos trust. See TRUST.

intestacy (in-**tes**-tə-see). The state or condition of a person's having died without a valid will. Cf. TESTACY.

intestate (in-**tes**-tayt), *adj.* **1.** Of or relating to a person who has died without a valid will. **2.** Of or relating to the property owned by a person who died without a valid will. **3.** Of or relating to intestacy. Cf. TESTATE.

intestate, *n.* One who has died without a valid will. Cf. TESTATOR.

intestate law. A statute governing succession to the estate of a person who dies without a valid will.

intestate succession. The method used to distribute property owned by a person who dies without a valid will. Cf. TESTATE SUCCESSION.

in the course of employment. *Workers' compensation.* (Of an accident) having happened to an on-the-job employee within the scope of employment.

intimidation, *n.* Unlawful coercion; extortion. — **intimidate,** *vb.* — **intimidatory,** *adj.* — **intimidator,** *n.*

in toto (in **toh**-toh), *adv.* [Latin "in whole"] Completely; as a whole <the company rejected the offer *in toto*>.

intoxicant, *n.* A substance (esp. liquor) that deprives a person of the ordinary use of the senses or of reason.

intoxication, *n.* A diminished ability to act with full mental and physical capabilities because of alcohol or drug consumption; drunkenness. See Model Penal Code § 2.08. — **intoxicate,** *vb.*

> ***involuntary intoxication.*** The ingestion of alcohol or drugs against one's will or without one's knowledge. • Involuntary intoxication is an affirmative defense to a criminal or negligence charge.
>
> ***pathological intoxication.*** An extremely exaggerated response to an intoxicant. • This may be treat-

ed as involuntary intoxication if it is unforeseeable.

public intoxication. The appearance of a person who is under the influence of drugs or alcohol in a place open to the general public.

voluntary intoxication. A willing ingestion of alcohol or drugs to the point of impairment done with the knowledge that one's physical and mental capabilities would be impaired. • Voluntary intoxication is not a defense to a general-intent crime, but may be admitted to refute the existence of a particular state of mind for a specific-intent crime.

intrastate commerce. See COMMERCE.

intra vires (**in**-trə **vɪ**-reez), *adj.* [Latin "within the powers (of)"] Of or referring to an action taken within a corporation's or person's scope of authority. — **intra vires,** *adv.* Cf. ULTRA VIRES.

intrinsic evidence. See EVIDENCE.

intrinsic fraud. See FRAUD.

introduce into evidence. To have (a fact or object) admitted into the trial record, allowing it to be considered in the jury's or the court's decision.

introductory clause. The first paragraph of a contract, which typically begins with words such as "This Agreement is made on [date] between [parties' names]."

intromission (in-trə-**mish**-ən). **1.** The transactions of an employee or agent with funds provided by an employer or principal; loosely, dealing in the funds of another. **2.** An intermeddling with the affairs or property of another; the possession of another's property, with or without legal authority.

intrusion, *n.* **1.** A person's entering without permission. See TRESPASS. **2.** In an action for invasion of privacy, a highly offensive invasion of another person's seclusion or private life. — **intrude,** *vb.* — **intrusive,** *adj.* — **intruder,** *n.*

inure (in-**yoor**), *vb.* **1.** To take effect; to come into use <the settlement proceeds must inure to the benefit of the widow and children>. **2.** To make accustomed to something unpleasant; to habituate <abused children become inured to violence>.

invalid (in-**val**-id), *adj.* **1.** Not legally binding. **2.** Without basis in fact.

invalid (**in**-və-lid), *n.* A person who, because of serious illness or other disability, lacks the physical or mental capability of managing his or her day-to-day life.

invalid will. See WILL.

invasion of privacy. An unjustified exploitation of one's personality or intrusion into one's personal activity, actionable under tort law and sometimes under constitutional law. See RIGHT OF PRIVACY.

inveigle (in-**vay**-gəl), *vb.* To lure or entice through deceit or insincerity. — **inveiglement,** *n.*

invented consideration. See CONSIDERATION.

inventory search. See SEARCH.

inverse condemnation. See CONDEMNATION.

invest, *vb.* **1.** To supply with authority or power. **2.** To apply (money) for profit. **3.** To make an outlay of money for profit. — **investor,** *n.*

investigating magistrate. See MAGISTRATE.

investigative detention. See DETENTION.

investigative grand jury. See GRAND JURY.

investigatory interrogation. See INTERROGATION.

investment company. See COMPANY.

investment tax credit. See TAX CREDIT.

invidious discrimination (in-**vid**-ee-əs di-skrim-ə-**nay**-shən). See DISCRIMINATION.

inviolable (in-VI-ə-lə-bəl), *adj.* Safe from violation; incapable of being violated. — **inviolability** (in-VI-ə-lə-**bil**-ə-tee), *n.*

inviolate (in-VI-ə-lit), *adj.* Free from violation; not broken, infringed, or impaired.

invitation, *n. Torts.* In the law of negligence, the enticement of others to enter, remain on, or use property or its structures. — **invite,** *vb.*

invitation to negotiate. A solicitation for one or more offers, usu. as a preliminary step to forming a contract. Cf. OFFER.

invited error. See ERROR (2).

invitee (in-VI-**tee**). A person who has an express or implied invitation to enter or use another's premises, such as a business visitor or a member of the public to whom the premises are held open. • The occupier has a duty to inspect the premises and to warn the invitee of dangerous conditions. Cf. LICENSEE (2); TRESPASSER.

public invitee. An invitee who is invited to enter and remain on property for a purpose for which the property is held open to the public.

inviter. One who expressly or impliedly invites another onto the premises for business purposes. Cf. INVITEE.

involuntary, *adj.* Not resulting from a free and unrestrained choice; not subject to control by the will. — **involuntariness,** *n.*

involuntary bailment. See BAILMENT.

involuntary bankruptcy. See BANKRUPTCY.

involuntary confession. See CONFESSION.

involuntary dismissal. See DISMISSAL (1).

involuntary intoxication. See INTOXICATION.

involuntary manslaughter. See MANSLAUGHTER.

involuntary payment. See PAYMENT.

involuntary petition. See PETITION.

involuntary servitude. See SERVITUDE (2).

in witness whereof. The traditional beginning of the concluding clause (termed the *testimonium clause*) of a will or deed. See TESTIMONIUM CLAUSE.

IOU (I-oh-**yoo**). [abbr. "I owe you"] **1.** A memorandum acknowledging a debt. **2.** The debt itself.

IP. *abbr.* INTELLECTUAL PROPERTY.

ipse dixit (**ip**-see **dik**-sit). [Latin "he himself said it"] Something asserted but not proved <his testimony that she was a liar was nothing more than an *ipse dixit*>.

ipsissima verba (ip-**sis**-ə-mə **vər**-bə). [Latin "the very (same) words"] The exact words used by somebody being quoted <on its face, the *ipsissima verba* of the statute supports the plaintiff's position on the ownership issue>.

ipso facto (**ip**-soh **fak**-toh). [Latin "by the fact itself"] By the very nature of the situation <if 25% of all contractual litigation is caused by faulty drafting, then, *ipso facto*, the profession needs to improve its drafting skills>.

IRA (I-ahr-**ay** *or* I-rə). *abbr.* INDIVIDUAL RETIREMENT ACCOUNT.

IRAC (I-rak). A mnemonic acronym used mostly by law students and their writing instructors, esp. as a method of answering essay questions on law exams. • The acronym is commonly said to stand for either (1) issue, rule, application, conclusion, or (2) issue, rule, analysis, conclusion.

IRC. *abbr.* INTERNAL REVENUE CODE.

irreconcilable differences. Persistent and unresolvable disagreements between spouses, leading to the breakdown of the marriage. • These differences may be cited — without specifics — as grounds for no-fault divorce. At least 33 states have provided that irreconcilable differences are a basis for divorce. Cf. IRRETRIEVABLE BREAKDOWN OF THE MARRIAGE; INCOMPATABILITY.

irrecusable, *adj.* (Of an obligation) that cannot be avoided, although made without one's consent, as the obligation to not strike another without some lawful excuse. Cf. RECUSABLE.

irrefragable (i-**ref**-rə-gə-bəl), *adj.* Unanswerable; not to be controverted; impossible to refute.

irregular, *adj.* Not in accordance with law, method, or usage; not regular.

irregular indorsement. See INDORSEMENT.

irregular succession. See SUCCESSION.

irrelevance, *n.* **1.** The quality or state of being inapplicable to a matter under consideration. **2.** IRRELEVANCY. — **irrelevant** (i-**rel**-ə-vənt), *adj.* Cf. IMMATERIAL.

irrelevancy, *n.* **1.** Something not relevant. **2.** IRRELEVANCE.

irreparable injury. See INJURY.

irreparable-injury rule (i-**rep**-ə-rə-bəl). The principle that equitable relief (such as an injunction) is available only when no adequate legal remedy (such as monetary damages) exists.

irresistible force. See FORCE.

irresistible-impulse test. *Criminal law.* A test for insanity, holding that a person is not criminally responsible for an act if mental disease prevented that person from controlling potentially criminal conduct. See INSANITY DEFENSE; MCNAGHTEN RULES.

irretrievable breakdown of the marriage. A ground for divorce that is based on incompatibility between marriage partners and that is used in many states as the sole ground of no-fault divorce. Cf. INCOMPATIBILITY; IRRECONCILABLE DIFFERENCES.

irrevocable (i-rev-ə-kə-bəl), *adj.* Unalterable; committed beyond recall. — **irrevocability,** *n.*

irrevocable guaranty. See GUARANTY.

irrevocable offer. See OFFER.

irrevocable power of attorney. See POWER OF ATTORNEY.

irrevocable trust. See TRUST.

IRS. *abbr.* INTERNAL REVENUE SERVICE.

issuable defense. See DEFENSE (1).

issuable plea. See PLEA (3).

issue, *n.* **1.** A point in dispute between two or more parties.

collateral issue. A question or issue not directly connected with the matter in dispute.

deep issue. The fundamental issue to be decided by a court in ruling on a point of law.

general issue. **1.** A plea (often a general denial) by which a party denies the truth of every material allegation in an opposing party's pleading. **2.** The issue arising from such a plea.

immaterial issue. An issue not necessary to decide the point of law.

issue of fact. A point supported by one party's evidence and controverted by another's.

issue of law. A point on which the evidence is undisputed, the outcome depending on the court's interpretation of the law.

legal issue. A legal question, usu. at the foundation of a case and requiring a court's decision.

special issue. **1.** At common law, an issue arising from a specific allegation in a pleading. • Special issues are no longer used in most jurisdictions. **2.** See *special interrogatory* under INTERROGATORY.

ultimate issue. A not-yet-decided point that is sufficient either in itself or in connection with other points to resolve the entire case.

2. *Wills & estates.* Lineal descendants; offspring.

lawful issue. Descendants, including descendants more remote than children. See DESCENDANT; HEIR.

issue pleading. See PLEADING (2).

item. **1.** A piece of a whole, not necessarily separated. **2.** In drafting, a subpart of text that is the next smaller unit than a subparagraph. • In federal drafting, for example, "(4)" is the item in the following citation: Rule 19(a)(1)(B)(4).

itemized deduction. See DEDUCTION.

J

J. *abbr.* **1.** JUDGE. **2.** JUSTICE (2). **3.** JUDGMENT. **4.** JUS. **5.** JOURNAL.

***Jackson–Denno* hearing.** A court proceeding held outside the jury's presence, to determine whether the defendant's confession was voluntary and therefore admissible as evidence. *Jackson v. Denno*, 378 U.S. 368, 84 S.Ct. 1774 (1964).

***Jackson* standard.** *Criminal law.* The principle that the standard of review on appeal — when a criminal defendant claims that there is insufficient evidence to support the conviction — is to determine whether, after considering the evidence in the light most favorable to the prosecution, any rational trier of fact could have found the essential elements of the crime beyond a reasonable doubt. *Jackson v. Virginia*, 443 U.S. 307, 99 S.Ct. 2781 (1979).

jail, *n.* A place where persons awaiting trial or those convicted of misdemeanors are confined. — **jail,** *vb.* Cf. PRISON.

jail credit. Time spent by a criminal defendant in confinement awaiting trial. • This time is usually deducted from the defendant's final sentence (if convicted).

***James* hearing.** A court proceeding held to determine whether the out-of-court statements of a coconspirator should be admitted into evidence, by analyzing whether there was a conspiracy, whether the declarant and the defendant were part of the conspiracy, and whether the statement was made in furtherance of the conspiracy. *United States v. James*, 590 F.2d 575 (5th Cir. 1979); Fed. R. Evid. 801(d)(2)(E).

Janus-faced (jay-nəs fayst), *adj.* Having two contrasting or contradictory aspects; two-faced.

J.D. *abbr.* JURIS DOCTOR.

***Jencks* material.** *Criminal procedure.* A prosecution witness's written or recorded pretrial statement that a criminal defendant, upon filing a motion after the witness has testified, is entitled to have in preparing to cross-examine the witness. • The defense may use a statement of this kind for impeachment purposes. *Jencks v. United States*, 353 U.S. 657, 77 S.Ct. 1007 (1957); Jencks Act, 18 USCA § 3500. Cf. BRADY MATERIAL.

jeopardy. The risk of conviction and punishment that a criminal defendant faces at trial. • Jeopardy attaches in a jury trial when the jury is empaneled, and in a bench trial when the first witness is sworn. See DOUBLE JEOPARDY.

***Jewell* instruction (joo-wəl).** *Criminal procedure.* A court's instruction to the jury that the defendant can be found to have the requisite criminal mental state despite being deliberately ignorant of some of the facts surrounding the crime. *United States v. Jewell*, 532 F.2d 697 (9th Cir. 1976).

Jim Crow law. *Hist.* A law enacted or purposely interpreted to discriminate against blacks, such as a law requiring separate restrooms for blacks and whites. • Jim Crow laws are unconstitutional under the 14th Amendment.

JJ. *abbr.* **1.** Judges. **2.** Justices.

JNOV. *abbr.* Judgment *non obstante veredicto*. See *judgment notwithstanding the verdict* under JUDGMENT.

John Doe warrant. See WARRANT.

joinder, *n.* The uniting of parties or claims in a single lawsuit. — **join,** *vb.* Cf. CONSOLIDATION (3).

collusive joinder. Joinder of a defendant, usu. a nonresident, in order to have a case removed to federal court. See *manufactured diversity* under DIVERSITY OF CITIZENSHIP.

compulsory joinder. The necessary joinder of a party if either of the following is true: (1) in that party's absence, those already involved in the lawsuit cannot receive complete relief; or (2) the absence of such a party, claiming an interest in the subject of an action, might either impair the protection of that interest or leave some other party subject to multiple or inconsistent obligations. Fed. R. Civ. P. 19(a).

fraudulent joinder. The bad-faith joinder of a party, usu. a resident of the state, to prevent removal of a case to federal court.

permissive joinder. The optional joinder of parties if (1) their claims or the claims asserted against them are asserted jointly, severally, or in respect of the same transaction or occurrence, and (2) any legal or factual question common to all of them will arise. Fed. R. Civ. P. 20.

joint, *adj.* **1.** (Of a thing) common to or shared by two or more persons or entities <joint bank account>. **2.** (Of a person or entity) combined, united, or sharing with another <joint heirs>.

joint account. See ACCOUNT.

joint activity. See JOINT PARTICIPATION.

joint and mutual will. See WILL.

joint and several, *adj.* (Of liability, responsibility, etc.) apportionable either among two or more parties or to only one or a few select members of the group, at the adversary's discretion; together and in separation.

joint and several liability. See LIABILITY.

joint custody. See CUSTODY (2).

joint-defense privilege. See PRIVILEGE (3).

joint enterprise. **1.** *Criminal law.* An undertaking by two or more persons who set out to commit an offense they have conspired to commit. See CONSPIRACY. **2.** *Torts.* An undertaking by two or more persons with an equal right to direct and benefit from the endeavor, as a result of which one participant's negligence may be imputed to the others. **3.** JOINT VENTURE. **4.** A joint venture for noncommercial purposes.

joint estate. See ESTATE.

joint executor. See EXECUTOR.

joint heir. See HEIR.

joint indictment. See INDICTMENT.

joint liability. See LIABILITY.

joint life insurance. See INSURANCE.

joint life policy. See INSURANCE POLICY.

joint negligence. See NEGLIGENCE.

joint obligation. See OBLIGATION.

joint offense. See OFFENSE.

joint ownership. See OWNERSHIP.

joint participation. *Civil-rights law.* A pursuit undertaken by a private person in concert with a governmental entity or state official, resulting in the private person's performing public functions and thereby being subject to claims under the civil-rights laws. — Also termed *joint activity.* See SYMBIOTIC-RELATIONSHIP TEST; NEXUS TEST.

joint resolution. See RESOLUTION.

joint return. See TAX RETURN.

joint session. See SESSION.

joint-stock company. See COMPANY.

joint tenancy. See TENANCY.

joint tortfeasors. See TORTFEASOR.

joint trial. See TRIAL.

jointure (**joyn**-chər). **1.** *Archaic.* A woman's freehold life estate in land, made in consideration of marriage in lieu of dower and to be enjoyed by her only after her husband's death; a settlement under which a wife receives such an estate. • See DOWER. **2.** An estate in lands given jointly to a husband and wife before they marry.

joint venture. A business undertaking by two or more persons engaged in a single defined project. • The necessary elements are: (1) an express or implied agreement; (2) a common purpose that the group intends to carry out; (3) shared profits and losses; and (4) each member's equal voice in controlling the project. Cf. PARTNERSHIP; STRATEGIC ALLIANCE.

joint verdict. See VERDICT.

joint will. See WILL.

journal. **1.** A book or record, usu. kept daily, as of the proceedings of a legislature or the events of a ship's voyage. **2.** *Accounting.* In double-entry bookkeeping, a book in which original entries are recorded before being transferred to a ledger. **3.** A periodical or magazine, esp. one published for a scholarly or professional group. — Abbr. J.

journalist's privilege. See PRIVILEGE (3).

joyriding, *n.* The illegal driving of someone else's automobile without permission, but with no intent to deprive the owner of it. See Model Penal Code § 223.9. — **joyride,** *vb.* — **joyrider,** *n.*

J.P. *abbr.* JUSTICE OF THE PEACE.

J.S.D. [Law Latin *juris scientiae doctor*] *abbr.* DOCTOR OF JURIDICAL SCIENCE.

J.U.D. [Law Latin *juris utriusque doctor* "doctor of both laws"] *abbr.* A doctor of both civil and canon law.

judge, *n.* A public official appointed or elected to hear and decide legal matters in court. — Abbr. J. (and, in plural, JJ.).

associate judge. An appellate judge who is neither a chief judge nor a presiding judge.

chief judge. The judge who presides over the sessions and deliberations of a court, while also overseeing the administration of the court. — Abbr. C.J.

circuit judge. A judge who sits on a circuit court; esp., a federal judge who sits on a U.S. court of appeals. — Abbr. C.J.

county judge. A local judge having criminal or civil jurisdiction, or sometimes both, within a county.

de facto judge (di **fak**-toh). A judge operating under color of law but whose authority is procedurally defective, such as a judge appointed under an unconstitutional statute.

district judge. A judge in a federal or state judicial district.

hanging judge. Slang. A judge who is harsh with defendants, esp. those accused of capital crimes, and sometimes corruptly so.

lay judge. A judge who is not a lawyer.

municipal judge. A local judge having criminal or civil jurisdiction, or sometimes both, within a city.

presiding judge. **1.** A judge in charge of a particular court or judicial district; esp., the senior active judge on a three-member panel that hears and decides cases. **2.** A chief judge.

probate judge. A judge having jurisdiction over probate, inheritance, guardianships, and the like.

senior judge. **1.** The judge who has served for the longest time on a given court. **2.** A federal or state judge who qualifies for senior status and chooses this status over retirement.

special judge. A judge appointed or selected to sit, usu. in a specific case, in the absence or disqualification of the regular judge or otherwise as provided by statute.

trial judge. The judge before whom a case is tried. • This term is used most commonly on appeal from the judge's rulings.

visiting judge. A judge appointed by the presiding judge of an administrative region to sit temporarily on a given court, usu. in the regular judge's absence.

judge-made law. 1. The law established by judicial precedent rather than by statute. See COMMON LAW. **2.** The law that results when judges construe statutes contrary to legislative intent. See JUDICIAL ACTIVISM.

judge's chamber. See CHAMBER.

judgeship. 1. The office or authority of a judge. **2.** The period of a judge's incumbency.

judge-shopping. The practice of filing several lawsuits asserting the same claims — in a court or a district with multiple judges — with the hope of having one of the lawsuits assigned to a favorable judge and of nonsuiting or voluntarily dismissing the others. Cf. FORUM-SHOPPING.

judgment. A court's final determination of the rights and obligations of the parties in a case. • The term *judgment* includes a decree and any order from which an appeal lies. — Abbr. J. Cf. RULING; OPINION (1).

accumulative judgment. A second or additional judgment against a person who has already been convicted, the execution of which is postponed until the completion of any prior sentence.

agreed judgment. A settlement that becomes a court judgment when the judge sanctions it.

declaratory judgment. A binding adjudication that establishes the rights and other legal relations of the parties without providing for or ordering enforcement.

deferred judgment. A judgment placing a convicted defendant on probation, the successful completion of which will prevent entry of the underlying judgment of conviction.

deficiency judgment. A judgment against a debtor for the unpaid balance of the debt if a foreclosure sale or a sale of repossessed personal property fails to yield the full amount of the debt due.

dormant judgment. A judgment that has not been executed or enforced within the statutory time limit. • As a result, any judgment lien may have been lost and execution cannot be issued unless the judgment creditor first revives the judgment. See REVIVAL (1).

erroneous judgment. A judgment issued by a court with jurisdiction to issue it, but containing an improper application of law. • This type of judgment is not void, but can be corrected by a trial court while the court retains plenary jurisdiction, or in a direct appeal. See ERROR (2).

executory judgment (eg-**zek**-yə-tor-ee). A judgment that has not been carried out, such as a yet-to-be fulfilled order for the defendant to pay the plaintiff.

final judgment. A court's last action that settles the rights of the parties and disposes of all issues in controversy, except for the award of costs (and, sometimes, attorney's fees) and enforcement of the judgment.

interlocutory judgment (in-tər-**lok**-yə-tor-ee). An intermediate judgment that determines a preliminary or subordinate point or plea but does not finally decide the case.

judgment as a matter of law. A judgment rendered during a jury trial — either before or after the jury's verdict — against a party on a given issue when there is no legally sufficient basis for a jury to find for that party on that issue. • In federal practice, the term *judgment as a matter of law* has replaced both the directed verdict and the judgment notwithstanding the verdict. Fed. R. Civ. P. 50. Cf. SUMMARY JUDGMENT.

judgment in rem (in **rem**). A judgment that determines the status or condition of property and that operates directly on the property itself.

judgment nil capiat per billa (nil **kap**-ee-ət pər **bil**-ə). Judgment that the plaintiff take nothing by the bill; a take-nothing judgment in a case instituted by a bill.

judgment nil capiat per breve (nil **kap**-ee-ət pər **breev** *or* **bree**-vee). Judgment that the plaintiff take nothing by the writ; a take-nothing judgment in a case instituted by a writ.

judgment nisi (**NI**-SI). A provisional judgment that, while not final or absolute, may become final on a party's motion. See NISI.

judgment notwithstanding the verdict. A judgment entered for one party even though a jury verdict has been rendered for the opposing party. — Abbr. JNOV. See *judgment as a matter of law*.

judgment of acquittal. A judgment, rendered on the defendant's motion or the court's own motion, that acquits the defendant of the offense charged when the evidence is insufficient. See *directed verdict* under VERDICT.

judgment of conviction. The written record of a criminal judgment, consisting of the plea, the verdict or findings, the adjudication, and the sentence. Fed. R. Crim. P. 32(d)(1).

judgment of dismissal. A final determination of a case without a trial on its merits. See DISMISSAL.

judgment of nolle prosequi (**nahl**-ee **prahs**-ə-KWI). A judgment entered against a plaintiff who, after appearance but before judgment on the merits, has decided to abandon prosecution of the lawsuit. See NOLLE PROSEQUI.

judgment on the merits. A judgment based on the evidence rather than on technical or procedural grounds.

judgment on the pleadings. A judgment based solely on the allegations and information contained in the pleadings, and not on any outside matters. Fed. R. Civ. P. 12(c). See SUMMARY JUDGMENT.

judgment on the verdict. A judgment for the party receiving a favorable jury verdict.

judgment quasi in rem (**kway**-SI [*or* -ZI] in **rem**). A judgment based on the court's jurisdiction over the defendant's interest in property rather than on its jurisdiction over the defendant or the property.

judgment quod billa cassetur (kwod **bil**-ə kə-**see**-tər). Judgment that the bill be quashed. • This is a judgment for the defendant.

judgment quod breve cassetur (kwod **breev** *or* **bree**-vee kə-**see**-tər). Judgment that the writ be quashed. • This is a judgment for the defendant.

money judgment. A judgment for damages subject to immediate execution, as distinguished from equitable or injunctive relief.

nunc pro tunc judgment (**nəngk** proh **təngk**). A procedural device by which the record of a judgment is amended to accord with what the judge actually said and did, so that the record will be accurate.

personal judgment. **1.** A judgment that imposes personal liability on a defendant and that may therefore be satisfied out of any of the defendant's property within judicial reach. **2.** A judgment resulting from an action in which a court has personal jurisdiction over the parties. **3.** A judgment against a person as distinguished from a judgment against a thing, right, or status.

take-nothing judgment. A judgment for the defendant providing that the plaintiff recover nothing in damages or other relief.

voidable judgment. A judgment that, although seemingly valid, is defective in some material way; esp., a judgment that, although rendered by a court having jurisdiction, is irregular or erroneous.

void judgment. A judgment that has no legal force or effect, the invalidity of which may be asserted by any party whose rights are affected at any time and any place, whether directly or collaterally. • From its inception, a void judgment continues to be absolutely null. It is incapable of being confirmed, ratified, or enforced in any manner or to any degree.

judgment creditor. A person having a legal right to enforce execution of a judgment for a specific sum of money.

judgment debtor. A person against whom a money judgment has been entered but not yet satisfied.

judgment docket. See DOCKET (1).

judgment-proof, *adj.* (Of an actual or potential judgment debtor) unable to satisfy a judgment for money damages because the person has no property, does not own enough property within the court's jurisdiction to satisfy the judgment, or claims the benefit of statutorily exempt property.

judicator (**joo**-di-kay-tər), *n.* A person authorized to act or serve as a judge.

judicatory (**joo**-di-kə-tor-ee), *adj.* **1.** Of or relating to judgment. **2.** By which a judgment may be made; giving a decisive indication.

judicatory (**joo**-di-kə-tor-ee), *n.* **1.** A court; any tribunal with judicial authority. **2.** The administration of justice.

judicature (**joo**-di-kə-chər). **1.** The action of judging or of administering justice through duly constituted courts. **2.** JUDICIARY (3). **3.** A judge's office, function, or authority.

judicial (joo-**dish**-əl), *adj.* **1.** Of, relating to, or by the court <judicial duty>. **2.** In court <the witness's judicial confession>. **3.** Legal <the Attorney General took no judicial action>. **4.** Of or relating to a judgment <an award of judicial interest at the legal rate>. Cf. JUDICIOUS.

judicial act. See ACT.

judicial activism, *n.* A philosophy of judicial decision-making whereby judges allow their personal views about public policy, among other factors, to guide their decisions, usu. with the suggestion that adherents of this philosophy tend to find constitutional violations and are willing to ignore precedent. — **judicial activist,** *n.* Cf. JUDICIAL RESTRAINT (3).

judicial admission. See ADMISSION.

Judicial Article. Article III of the U.S. Constitution, which creates the

Supreme Court, vests in Congress the right to create inferior courts, provides for life tenure for federal judges, and specifies the powers and jurisdiction of the federal courts.

judicial bond. See BOND (2).

judicial branch. The branch of government consisting of the courts, whose function is to interpret, apply, and generally administer and enforce the laws; JUDICIARY (1). Cf. LEGISLATIVE BRANCH; EXECUTIVE BRANCH.

judicial bypass. A procedure permitting a person to obtain a court's approval for an act that would ordinarily require the approval of someone else, such as a law that requires a minor to notify a parent before obtaining an abortion but allows an appropriately qualified minor to obtain a court order permitting the abortion without parental notice.

judicial comity. See COMITY.

judicial confession. See CONFESSION.

judicial council. A regularly assembled group of judges whose mission is to increase the efficiency and effectiveness of the courts on which they sit; esp., a semiannual assembly of a federal circuit's judges called by the circuit's chief judge. 28 USCA § 332.

judicial discretion. See DISCRETION.

judicial economy. Efficiency in the operation of the courts and the judicial system; esp., the efficient management of litigation so as to minimize duplication of effort and to avoid wasting the judiciary's time and resources.

judicial-economy exception. An exemption from the final-judgment rule, by which a party may seek immediate appellate review of a nonfinal order if doing so might establish a final or nearly final disposition of the entire suit. See FINAL-JUDGMENT RULE.

judicial estoppel. See ESTOPPEL.

judicial evidence. See EVIDENCE.

judicial fact. See FACT.

judicial foreclosure. See FORECLOSURE.

judicial immunity. See IMMUNITY (1).

judicial legislation. See LEGISLATION.

judicial notice. A court's acceptance, for purposes of convenience and without requiring a party's proof, of a well-known and indisputable fact; the court's power to accept such a fact. Fed R. Evid. 201.

judicial oath. See OATH.

judicial officer. 1. A judge or magistrate. **2.** Any officer of the court, such as a bailiff or court reporter.

judicial power. 1. The authority vested in courts and judges to hear and decide cases and to make binding judgments on them; the power to construe and apply the law when controversies arise over what has been done or not done under it. **2.** A power conferred on a public officer involving the exercise of judgment and discretion in deciding questions of right in specific cases affecting personal and proprietary interests. • In this sense, the phrase is contrasted with *ministerial power*.

judicial privilege. See PRIVILEGE (3).

judicial proceeding. See PROCEEDING.

judicial question. A question that is proper for determination by the courts, as opposed to a moot question or one properly decided by the executive or legislative branch. Cf. POLITICAL QUESTION.

judicial remedy. See REMEDY.

judicial restraint. **1.** A restraint imposed by a court, as by a restraining order, injunction, or judgment. **2.** The principle that, when a court can resolve a case based on a particular issue, it should do so, without reaching unnecessary issues. **3.** A philosophy of judicial decision-making whereby judges avoid indulging their personal beliefs about the public good and instead try merely to interpret the law as legislated and according to precedent. Cf. JUDICIAL ACTIVISM.

judicial review. **1.** A court's power to review the actions of other branches or levels of government; esp., the courts' power to invalidate legislative and executive actions as being unconstitutional. **2.** The constitutional doctrine providing for this power. **3.** A court's review of a lower court's or an administrative body's factual or legal findings.

de novo judicial review. A court's nondeferential review of an administrative decision, usu. through a review of the administrative record plus any additional evidence the parties present.

judicial trustee. See TRUSTEE.

judicial writ. See WRIT.

judiciary (joo-**dish**-ee-er-ee *or* joo-**dish**-ə-ree), *n.* **1.** The branch of government responsible for interpreting the laws and administering justice. Cf. EXECUTIVE (1); LEGISLATURE. **2.** A system of courts. **3.** A body of judges. — **judiciary,** *adj.*

judicious (joo-**dish**-əs), *adj.* Well-considered; discreet; wisely circumspect. — **judiciousness,** *n.* Cf. JUDICIAL.

jump bail, *vb.* (Of an accused) to fail to appear in court at the appointed time, even after posting a bail bond and promising to appear. See BAIL-JUMPING.

junior partner. See PARTNER.

junior writ. See WRIT.

junk bond. See BOND (3).

jural (**joor**-əl), *adj.* **1.** Of or relating to law or jurisprudence; legal. **2.** Of or relating to rights and obligations.

jural act. See ACT.

jural agent. An official — someone who has the appropriate authoritative status in society to enforce or affect the society's legal system — who engages in a jural act. • Common examples include judges, legislators, and police officers acting in their official capacities. See *jural act* under ACT.

jurat (**joor**-at). [fr. Latin *jurare* "to swear"] A certification added to an affidavit or deposition stating when and before what authority the affidavit or deposition was made. • A jurat typically says "Subscribed and sworn to before me this ____ day of [month], [year]," and the officer (usually a notary public) thereby certifies three things: (1) that the person signing the document did so in the officer's presence, (2) that the signer appeared before the officer on the date indicated, and (3) that the officer administered an oath or affirmation to the signer, who swore to or affirmed the contents of the document. Cf. VERIFICATION.

jure (**joor**-ee), *adv.* [Latin] **1.** By right; in right. **2.** By law. See DE JURE.

juridical (juu-**rid**-i-kəl), *adj.* **1.** Of or relating to judicial proceedings or to the administration of justice. **2.** Of or relating to law; legal. Cf. NONJURIDICAL.

juridical day. See DAY.

juridical link. A legal relationship between members of a potential class action, sufficient to make a single suit more efficient or effective than multiple suits, as when all members of the class have been similarly affected by an allegedly illegal regulation.

jurimetrics (joor-ə-**me**-triks), *n.* The use of scientific or empirical methods, including measurement, in the study or analysis of legal matters. — **jurimetrician** (joor-ə-me-**trish**-ən), **jurimetricist** (joor-ə-**me**-trə-sist), *n.*

juris (**joor**-is). [Latin] **1.** Of law. **2.** Of right.

jurisdiction, *n.* **1.** A government's general power to exercise authority over all persons and things within its territory. **2.** A court's power to decide a case or issue a decree. **3.** A geographic area within which political or judicial authority may be exercised. **4.** A political or judicial subdivision within such an area. — **jurisdictional,** *adj.* Cf. VENUE.

ancillary jurisdiction. A court's jurisdiction to adjudicate claims and proceedings that arise out of a claim that is properly before the court. • The concept of ancillary jurisdiction has now been codified, along with the concept of pendent jurisdiction, in the supplemental-jurisdiction statute. 28 USCA § 1367. See *supplemental jurisdiction*. Cf. *pendent jurisdiction*.

anomalous jurisdiction. **1.** Jurisdiction that is not granted to a court by statute, but that is inherent in the court's authority to govern lawyers and other officers of the court, such as the power to issue a preindictment order suppressing illegally seized property. **2.** An appellate court's provisional jurisdiction to review the denial of a motion to intervene in a case, so that if the court finds that the denial was correct, then its jurisdiction disappears — and it must dismiss the appeal for want of jurisdiction — because an order denying a motion to intervene is not a final, appealable order. See ANOMALOUS-JURISDICTION RULE.

appellate jurisdiction. The power of a court to review and revise a lower court's decision. • For example, U.S. Const. art. III, § 2 vests appellate jurisdiction in the Supreme Court, while 28 USCA §§ 1291–1295 grant appellate jurisdiction to lower federal courts of appeals. Cf. *original jurisdiction*.

concurrent jurisdiction. **1.** Jurisdiction exercised simultaneously by more than one court over the same subject matter and within the same territory, with the litigant having the right to choose the court in which to file the action. **2.** Jurisdiction shared by two or more states, esp. over the physical boundaries (such as rivers or other bodies of water) between them. Cf. *exclusive jurisdiction*.

consent jurisdiction. Jurisdiction that parties have agreed to by accord, by contract, or by general appearance.

continuing jurisdiction. A court's power to retain jurisdiction over a matter after entering a judgment, allowing the court to modify its previous rulings or orders. See CONTINUING-JURISDICTION DOCTRINE.

criminal jurisdiction. A court's power to hear criminal cases.

diversity jurisdiction. A federal court's exercise of authority over a case involving parties from different states and an amount in controversy greater than a statutory minimum (now $75,000). 28 USCA § 1332. See DIVERSITY OF CITIZENSHIP; AMOUNT IN CONTROVERSY.

equity jurisdiction. At common law, the power to hear certain civil actions according to the procedure of the court of chancery, and to resolve them according to equitable rules.

exclusive jurisdiction. A court's power to adjudicate an action or class of actions to the exclusion of all other courts. Cf. *concurrent jurisdiction*.

extraterritorial jurisdiction. A court's ability to exercise power beyond its territorial limits. See LONG-ARM STATUTE.

federal jurisdiction. **1.** The exercise of federal-court authority. **2.** The area of study dealing with the jurisdiction of federal courts.

federal-question jurisdiction. The exercise of federal-court power over claims arising under the U.S. Constitution, an act of Congress, or a treaty. 28 USCA § 1331.

foreign jurisdiction. **1.** The powers of a court of a sister state or foreign country. **2.** Extraterritorial process, such as long-arm service of process.

general jurisdiction. **1.** A court's authority to hear a wide range of cases, civil or criminal, that arise within its geographic area. **2.** A court's authority to hear all claims against a defendant, at the place of the defendant's domicile or the place of service, without any showing that a connection exists between the claims and the forum state. Cf. *limited jurisdiction*; *specific jurisdiction*.

in personam jurisdiction. A court's power to bring a person into its adjudicative process; jurisdiction over a defendant's personal rights, rather than merely over property interests.

in rem jurisdiction (in **rem**). A court's power to adjudicate the rights to a given piece of property, including the power to seize and hold it. See IN REM. Cf. *personal jurisdiction*.

limited jurisdiction. Jurisdiction that is confined to a particular type of case or that may be exercised only under statutory limits and prescriptions. Cf. *general jurisdiction*.

original jurisdiction. A court's power to hear and decide a matter before any other court can review the matter. Cf. *appellate jurisdiction*.

pendent jurisdiction (**pen**-dənt). A court's jurisdiction to hear and determine a claim over which it would not otherwise have jurisdiction, based on the claim's arising from the same transaction or occurrence as another claim that is properly before the court. • Pendent jurisdiction has now been codified as supplemental jurisdiction. 28 USCA § 1367. See *supplemental jurisdiction*. Cf. *ancillary jurisdiction*.

pendent-party jurisdiction. A court's jurisdiction to adjudicate a claim against a party who is not otherwise subject to the court's jurisdiction, because the claim by or against that party arises from the same transaction or occurrence as another claim that is properly before the court. • Pendent-party jurisdiction has been a hotly debated subject, and was severely limited by the U.S. Supreme Court in *Finley v. United States*, 490 U.S. 545, 109 S.Ct. 2003 (1990). The concept is now codified in the supplemental-jurisdiction statute, and it applies to federal-question cases but not to diversity-jurisdiction cases. 28 USCA § 1367. Neither pendent-party jurisdiction nor supplemental jurisdiction may be used to circumvent the complete-diversity requirement in cases founded on diversity jurisdiction. See *supplemental jurisdiction*.

quasi-in-rem jurisdiction (**kway**-sɪ in **rem** *or* **kway**-zɪ). Jurisdiction over a person but based on that person's interest in property located within the court's territory. See *quasi in rem* under IN REM.

specific jurisdiction. Jurisdiction that stems from the defendant's having certain minimum contacts with the forum state so that the court may hear a case whose issues arise from those minimum contacts. Cf. *general jurisdiction*.

subject-matter jurisdiction. Jurisdiction over the nature of the case and the type of relief sought; the extent to which a court can rule on the conduct of persons or the status of things.

summary jurisdiction. **1.** A court's jurisdiction in a summary proceeding. **2.** The court's authority to issue a judgment or order (such as a finding of contempt) without the necessity of a trial or other process.

supplemental jurisdiction. Jurisdiction over a claim that is part of the same case or controversy as another claim over which the court has original jurisdiction. 28 USCA § 1367. See *ancillary jurisdiction*; *pendent jurisdiction*.

jurisdictional fact. See FACT.

jurisdictional limits. The geographic boundaries or the constitutional or statutory limits within which a court's authority may be exercised.

jurisdictional plea. See PLEA (3).

jurisdiction clause. 1. At law, a statement in a pleading that sets forth the court's jurisdiction to act in the case. **2.** *Equity practice.* The part of the bill intended to show that the court has jurisdiction, usu. by an averment that adequate relief is unavailable outside equitable channels.

Juris Doctor (**joor**-is **dok**-tər). Doctor of law — the law degree most commonly conferred by an American law school. — Abbr. J.D. Cf. MASTER OF LAWS; LL.B.; LL.D.

jurisprude (**joor**-is-prood), *n.* **1.** A person who makes a pretentious display of legal knowledge or who is overzealous about the importance of legal doctrine. **2.** JURISPRUDENT.

jurisprudence (joor-is-**prood**-ənts), *n.* **1.** Originally (in the 18th century), the study of the first principles of the law of nature, the civil law, and the law of nations. **2.** More modernly, the study of the general or fundamental elements of a particular legal system, as opposed to its practical and concrete details. **3.** The study of legal systems in general. **4.** Judicial precedents considered collectively. **5.** A system, body, or division of law. **6.** CASELAW.

analytical jurisprudence. A method of legal study that concentrates on the logical structure of law, the meanings and uses of its concepts, and the terms and the modes of its operation.

comparative jurisprudence. The scholarly study of the similarities and differences between the legal systems of different jurisdictions, such as between civil-law and common-law countries.

equity jurisprudence. **1.** The legal science treating the rules, principles, and maxims that govern the decisions of a court of equity. **2.** The cases and controversies that are considered proper subjects of equity. **3.** The nature and form of the remedies that equity grants.

ethical jurisprudence. The branch of legal philosophy concerned with the law from the viewpoint of its ethical significance and adequacy. • This area of study brings together moral and legal philosophy.

expository jurisprudence. The scholarly exposition of the contents of an actual legal system as it now exists or once existed.

feminist jurisprudence. A branch of jurisprudence that examines the relationship between women and law, including the history of legal and social biases against women, the elimination of those biases in modern law, and the enhancement of women's legal rights and recognition in society.

general jurisprudence. **1.** The scholarly study of the fundamental elements of a given legal system. **2.** The scholarly study of the law, legal theory, and legal systems generally.

historical jurisprudence. The branch of legal philosophy concerned with the history of the first principles and conceptions of a legal system, dealing with (1) the general principles governing the origin and development of law, and (2) the origin and development of the legal system's first principles.

jurisprudence of conceptions. The extension of a maxim or definition, usu. to a logical extreme, with relentless disregard for the consequences.

particular jurisprudence. The scholarly study of the legal system within a particular jurisdiction, the focus being on the fundamental assumptions of that system only.

positivist jurisprudence. A theory that denies validity to any law that is not derived from or sanctioned by a sovereign or some other determinate source.

sociological jurisprudence. A philosophical approach to law stressing the actual social effects of legal institutions, doctrines, and practices. See LEGAL REALISM.

jurisprudent, *n.* A person learned in the law; a specialist in jurisprudence. — **jurisprudential** (joor-is-proo-**den**-shəl), *adj.*

jurist. 1. One who has thorough knowledge of the law; esp., a judge or an eminent legal scholar. **2.** JURISPRUDENT.

juristic, *adj.* **1.** Of or relating to a jurist. **2.** Of or relating to law.

juror (**joor**-ər *also* **joor**-or). A person serving on a jury panel.

juror misconduct. See MISCONDUCT.

jury, *n.* A group of persons selected according to law and given the power to decide questions of fact and return a verdict in the case submitted to them.

advisory jury. A jury empaneled to hear a case when the parties have no right to a jury trial. • The judge may accept or reject the advisory jury's verdict.

blue-ribbon jury. A jury consisting of jurors who are the most highly educated on a given panel, sometimes used in a complex civil case (usu. by stipulation of the parties) and sometimes also for a grand jury (esp. those investigating governmental corruption). • An even more elite group of jurors, involving specialists in a technical field, is called a *blue-blue-ribbon jury.*

coroner's jury. A jury summoned by a coroner to investigate the cause of death.

grand jury. See GRAND JURY.

hung jury. A jury that cannot reach a verdict by the required voting margin.

impartial jury. A jury that has no opinion about the case at the start of the trial and that bases its verdict on competent legal evidence.

inquest jury. A jury summoned from a particular district to appear before a sheriff, coroner, or other ministerial officer and inquire about the facts concerning a death. See INQUEST.

mixed jury. A jury composed of both men and women or persons of different races.

petit jury (**pet**-ee). A jury (usu. consisting of 6 or 12 persons) summoned and empaneled in the trial of a specific case. Cf. GRAND JURY.

shadow jury. A group of mock jurors paid to observe a trial and report their reactions to a jury consultant hired by one of the litigants. • The shadow jurors, who are matched as closely as possible to the real jurors, provide counsel with information about the jury's likely reactions to the trial.

special jury. A jury chosen from a panel that is drawn specifically for that case. See STRIKING A JURY.

struck jury. A jury selected by allowing the parties to alternate in striking from a list any person whom a given party does not wish to have on the jury, until the number is reduced to the appropriate number (traditionally 12).

jury charge. 1. See JURY INSTRUCTION. **2.** A set of jury instructions.

jury duty. 1. The obligation to serve on a jury. **2.** Actual service on a jury.

jury fee. See FEE (1).

jury-fixing. The act or an instance of illegally procuring the cooperation of one or more jurors who actually influence the outcome of the trial. Cf. EMBRACERY; JURY-PACKING.

jury instruction. (*usu. pl.*) A direction or guideline that a judge gives a jury concerning the law of the case.

additional instruction. A jury charge, beyond the original instructions, that is usu. given in response to the jury's question about the evidence or some point of law.

affirmative converse instruction. An instruction presenting a hypothetical that, if true, commands a verdict in favor of the defendant. • An affirmative converse instruction usu. begins with language such as "your verdict must be for the defendant if you believe...."

affirmative instruction. An instruction that removes an issue from the jury's consideration, such as an instruction that whatever the evidence, the defendant cannot be convicted under the indictment count to which the charge is directed.

argumentative instruction. An instruction that assumes facts not in evidence, that singles out or unduly emphasizes a particular issue, theory, or defense, or that otherwise invades the jury's province regarding the weight, probative value, or sufficiency of the evidence.

cautionary instruction. **1.** A judge's instruction to the jurors to disregard certain evidence or consider it for specific purposes only. **2.** A judge's instruction for the jury not to be influenced by outside factors and not to talk to anyone about the case while the trial is in progress.

curative instruction. A judge's instruction that is intended to correct an erroneous instruction.

formula instruction. A jury charge intended to be the complete statement of the law on which the jury must base its verdict.

Jewell instruction. See JEWELL INSTRUCTION.

mandatory instruction. An instruction requiring a jury to find for one party and against the other if the jury determines that, based on a preponderance of the evidence, a given set of facts exists.

model jury instruction. A form jury charge usu. approved by a state bar association or similar group regarding matters arising in a typical case.

ostrich instruction. Criminal procedure. Slang. An instruction stating that a defendant who deliberately avoided acquiring actual knowledge can be found to have acted knowingly.

peremptory instruction. A court's explicit direction that a jury must obey, such as an instruction to return a verdict for a particular party. See *directed verdict* under VERDICT.

single-juror instruction. An instruction stating that if any juror is not reasonably satisfied with the plaintiff's evidence, then the jury cannot render a verdict for the plaintiff.

special instruction. An instruction on some particular point or question involved in the case, usu. in response to counsel's request for such an instruction.

standard instruction. A jury instruction that has been regularly used in a given jurisdiction.

jury nullification. A jury's knowing and deliberate rejection of the evidence or refusal to apply the law either because the jury wants to send a message about some social issue that is larger than the case itself or because the result dictated by law is contrary to the jury's sense of justice, morality, or fairness.

jury-packing. The act or an instance of contriving to have a jury composed of persons who are predisposed toward one side or the other. Cf. EMBRACERY; JURY-FIXING.

jury pardon. A rule that permits a jury to convict a defendant of a lesser offense than the offense charged if sufficient evidence exists to convict the defendant of either offense.

jury process. 1. The procedure by which jurors are summoned and their attendance is enforced. **2.** The papers served on or mailed to potential jurors to compel their attendance.

jury question. 1. An issue of fact that a jury decides. See QUESTION OF FACT. **2.** A special question that a court may ask a jury that will deliver a special verdict. See *special interrogatory* under INTERROGATORY.

jury trial. See TRIAL.

jury wheel. A physical device or electronic system used for storing and randomly selecting names of potential jurors.

jus (jəs *also* joos *or* yoos), *n.* [Latin "law, right"] **1.** Law in the abstract. **2.** A system of law. **3.** A legal right, power, or principle. — Abbr. J. Pl. *jura* (**joor**-ə *also* **yoor**-ə). Cf. LEX.

jus necessitatis (jəs nə-ses-i-**tay**-tis), *n.* [Latin] A person's right to do what is required for which no threat of legal punishment is a dissuasion. • This idea implicates the proverb that necessity knows no law (*necessitas non habet legem*), so that an act that would be objectively understood as necessary is not wrongful even if done with full and deliberate intention.

jus sanguinis (jəs **sang**-gwə-nis), *n.* [Latin "right of blood"] The rule that a child's citizenship is determined by the parents' citizenship. • Most nations follow this rule. Cf. JUS SOLI.

jus soli (jəs **soh**-lɪ), *n.* [Latin "right of the soil"] The rule that a child's citizenship is determined by place of birth. • This is the U.S. rule, as affirmed by the 14th Amendment to the Constitution. Cf. JUS SANGUINIS.

just, *adj.* Legally right; lawful; equitable.

just compensation. See COMPENSATION.

just deserts (di-**zərts**). What one really deserves; esp., the punishment that a person deserves for having committed a crime.

jus tertii (jəs **tər**-shee-ɪ), *n.* [Latin] **1.** The right of a third party. **2.** The doctrine that, particularly in constitutional law, courts do not decide what they do not need to decide.

justice. 1. The fair and proper administration of laws.

commutative justice (kə-**myoo**-tə-tiv *or* **kom**-yə-tay-tiv). Justice concerned with the relations between persons and esp. with fairness in the exchange of goods and the fulfillment of contractual obligations.

distributive justice. Justice owed by a community to its members, including the fair disbursement of common advantages and sharing of common burdens.

personal justice. Justice between parties to a dispute, regardless of any larger principles that might be involved.

popular justice. Demotic justice, which is usu. considered less than fully fair and proper even though it satisfies prevailing public opinion in a particular case. Cf. *social justice.*

positive justice. Justice as it is conceived, recognized, and incompletely expressed by the civil law or some other form of human law. Cf. POSITIVE LAW.

social justice. Justice that conforms to a moral principle, such as that all people are equal. Cf. *personal justice.*

substantial justice. Justice fairly administered according to rules of substantive law, regardless of any procedural errors not affecting the litigant's substantive rights; a fair trial on the merits.

2. A judge, esp. of an appellate court or a court of last resort. — Abbr. J. (and, in plural, JJ.).

associate justice. An appellate-court justice other than the chief justice.

chief justice. The presiding justice of an appellate court, usu. the highest appellate court in a jurisdiction and esp. the U.S. Supreme Court. — Abbr. C.J.

circuit justice. **1.** A justice who sits on a circuit court. **2.** A U.S. Supreme Court justice who has jurisdiction over one or more of the federal circuits, with power to issue injunctions, grant bail, or stay execution in those circuits.

justice court. See COURT.

justice ejectment. See EJECTMENT.

justice of the peace. A local judicial officer having jurisdiction over minor criminal offenses and minor civil disputes, and authority to perform routine civil functions (such as administering oaths and performing marriage ceremonies). — Abbr. J.P. Cf. MAGISTRATE.

justiciability (jə-stish-ee-ə-**bil**-ə-tee *or* jə-stish-ə-**bil**-ə-tee), *n.* The quality or state of being appropriate or suitable for review by a court. — **justiciable** (jə-**stish**-ee-ə-bəl *or* jəs-**tish**-ə-bəl), *adj.* See MOOTNESS DOCTRINE; RIPENESS. Cf. STANDING.

justifiable homicide. See HOMICIDE.

justification, *n.* **1.** A lawful or sufficient reason for one's acts or omissions. **2.** A showing, in court, of a sufficient reason why a defendant did what the prosecution charges the defendant to answer. Model Penal Code § 3.02. See *lesser-evils defense* under DEFENSE (1). **3.** A surety's proof of having enough money or credit to provide security for the party for whom it is required. — **justify,** *vb.* — **justificatory** (jəs-**ti**-fi-kə-tor-ee), *adj.*

imperfect justification. A reason or cause that is insufficient to completely justify a defendant's behavior but that can be used to mitigate criminal punishment.

justification defense. *Criminal & tort law.* A defense that arises when the defendant has acted in a way that the law does not seek to prevent. Cf. EXCUSE (2).

just title. See TITLE (2).

juvenile (joo-və-nəl *or* -nɪl), *n.* A person who has not reached the age (usu. 18) at which one should be treated as an adult by the criminal-justice system; MINOR. — **juvenile,** *adj.* — **juvenility** (joo-və-**nil**-ə-tee), *n.*

certified juvenile. A juvenile who has been certified to be tried as an adult.

juvenile court. See COURT.

juvenile delinquency. Antisocial behavior by a minor; esp., behavior that would be criminally punishable if the actor were an adult, but instead is usu. punished by special laws pertaining only to minors. Cf. INCORRIGIBILITY.

juvenile delinquent. A minor who is guilty of criminal behavior, usu. punishable by special laws not pertaining to adults. See OFFENDER.

juvenile officer. A juvenile-court employee who works with the judge to direct and develop the court's child-welfare work.

juvenile petition. See PETITION.

K

K. *abbr.* Contract.

k/a. *abbr.* Known as.

kangaroo court. See COURT.

keeper. One who has the care, custody, or management of something and who usu. is legally responsible for it.

Keogh plan (kee-oh). A tax-deferred retirement program developed for the self-employed. • This plan is also known as an *H.R. 10 plan*, after the House of Representatives bill that established the plan. See INDIVIDUAL RETIREMENT ACCOUNT.

***Ker–Frisbie* rule.** The principle that the government's power to try a criminal defendant is not impaired by the defendant's having been brought back illegally to the United States from a foreign country. *Ker v. Illinois*, 119 U.S. 436, 7 S.Ct. 225 (1886); *Frisbie v. Collins*, 342 U.S. 519, 72 S.Ct. 509 (1952).

KeyCite, *vb.* To determine the subsequent history of (a case, statute, etc.) by using the online citator of the same name to establish that the point being researched is still good law. — **KeyCiting,** *n.*

key money. 1. Payment (as rent or security) required from a new tenant in exchange for a key to the leased property. **2.** Payment made (usu. secretly) by a prospective tenant to a landlord or current tenant to increase the chance of obtaining a lease in an area where there is a housing shortage. • Key money in the first sense is a legal transaction; key money in the second sense is usually an illegal bribe that violates housing laws.

key-number system. A legal-research indexing system developed by West Publishing Company (now the West Group) to catalogue American caselaw with headnotes. • In this system, a number designates a point of law, allowing a researcher to find all reported cases addressing a particular point by referring to its number.

kickback, *n.* A return of a portion of a monetary sum received, esp. as a result of coercion or a secret agreement. Cf. BRIBERY.

kickout clause. A contractual provision allowing a party to end or modify the contract if a specified event occurs.

kiddie tax. See TAX.

kidnapping. 1. At common law, the crime of forcibly abducting a person from his or her own country and sending the person to another. **2.** The crime of seizing and taking away a person by force or fraud. — **kidnap,** *vb.* Cf. HOSTAGE.

aggravated kidnapping. Kidnapping accompanied by some aggravating factor (such as a demand for ransom or injury of the victim).

child-kidnapping. The kidnapping of a child, often without the element of force or fraud (as when someone walks off with another's baby stroller).

kidnapping for ransom. The offense of unlawfully seizing a person and then confining the person in a secret place while attempting to extort ransom.

parental kidnapping. The kidnapping of a child by one parent in violation of the other parent's custody or visitation rights.

simple kidnapping. Kidnapping not accompanied by an aggravating factor.

kin, *n.* **1.** One's relatives; family. **2.** A relative by blood, marriage, or adoption, though usu. by blood only; a kinsman or kinswoman.

kindred, *n.* **1.** One's relatives; KIN (1). **2.** Family relationship; KINSHIP.

kinship. Relationship by blood, marriage, or adoption.

***Klaxon* doctrine** (**klak**-sən). *Conflict of laws.* The principle that a federal court exercising diversity jurisdiction must apply the choice-of-law rules of the state where the court sits. • In *Klaxon Co. v. Stentor Elec. Mfg. Co.*, the Supreme Court extended the rule of *Erie v. Tompkins* to choice-of-law issues. 313 U.S. 487, 61 S.Ct. 1020 (1941). See ERIE DOCTRINE.

kleptomania (klep-tə-**may**-nee-ə), *n.* A compulsive urge to steal, esp. without economic motive. — **kleptomaniac,** *n. & adj.*

knock-and-announce rule. *Criminal procedure.* The requirement that the police knock at the door and announce their identity, authority, and purpose before entering a residence to execute an arrest or search warrant.

knock-for-knock agreement. An arrangement between insurers whereby each will pay the claim of its insured without claiming against the other party's insurance.

knock off, *vb.* **1.** To make an unauthorized copy of (another's product), usu. for sale at a substantially lower price than the original. — **knockoff,** *n.* **2.** *Slang.* To murder. **3.** *Slang.* To rob or burglarize.

know all men by these presents. *Jargon.* Take note. • This archaic form of address — a loan translation of the Latin *noverint universi per praesentes* — was traditionally used to begin certain legal documents such as bonds and powers of attorney, but in modern drafting style the phrase is generally considered deadwood.

know-how. The information, practical knowledge, techniques, and skill required to achieve some practical end, esp. in industry or technology. See TRADE SECRET.

knowing, *adj.* **1.** Having or showing awareness or understanding; well-informed. **2.** Deliberate; conscious. — **knowingly,** *adv.*

knowledge. 1. An awareness or understanding of a fact or circumstance. Cf. INTENT (1); NOTICE; SCIENTER.

actual knowledge. **1.** Direct and clear knowledge, as distinguished from constructive knowledge <the employer, having witnessed the accident, had actual knowledge of the worker's injury>. **2.** Knowledge of such information as would lead a reasonable person to inquire further <under the discovery rule, the limitations period begins to run once the plaintiff has actual knowledge of the injury>.

constructive knowledge. Knowledge that one using reasonable care or diligence should have, and therefore that is attributed by law to a given person <the court held that the partners had constructive knowledge of the partnership agreement even though none of them had read it>.

imputed knowledge. Knowledge attributed to a given person, esp. because of the person's legal responsibility for another's conduct <the principal's imputed knowledge of its agent's dealings>.

personal knowledge. Knowledge gained through firsthand observation or experience, as distinguished from a belief based on what someone else has said. • Rule 602 of the Federal Rules of Evidence requires lay witnesses to have personal knowledge of the matters they testify about. An affidavit must also be based on personal knowledge, unless the affiant makes it clear that a statement relies on "information and belief."

reckless knowledge. A defendant's belief that a prohibited circumstance may exist, regardless of which the defendant goes on to take the risk.

scientific knowledge. *Evidence.* Knowledge that is grounded on scientific methods that have been supported by adequate validation. • Four primary factors are used to determine whether evidence amounts to scientific knowledge: (1) whether it has been tested; (2) whether it has been subject to peer review and publication; (3) the known or potential rate of error; and (4) the degree of acceptance within the scientific community. See DAUBERT TEST.

superior knowledge. Knowledge greater than that had by another person, esp. so as to adversely affect that person.

2. *Archaic.* CARNAL KNOWLEDGE.

known heir. See HEIR.

L

L. *abbr.* **1.** LAW (5). **2.** LOCUS.

label, *n.* **1.** An informative logo, title, or similar marking affixed to a manufactured product. **2.** Any writing (such as a codicil) attached to a larger writing. **3.** A narrow slip of paper or parchment attached to a deed or writ in order to hold a seal.

labeling. Under the Federal Food, Drug, and Cosmetic Act, any label or other written, printed, or graphic matter that is on a product or its container, or that accompanies the product. • To come within the Act, the labeling does not need to accompany the product. It may be sent before or after delivery of the product, as long as delivery of the product and the written material are part of the same distribution program.

labor, *n.* **1.** Work of any type, including mental exertion. • The term usually refers to work for wages as opposed to profits. **2.** Workers considered as an economic unit or a political element.

labor agreement. An agreement between an employer and a union governing working conditions, wages, benefits, and grievances.

labor dispute. A controversy between an employer and its employees concerning the terms or conditions of employment, or concerning the association or representation of those who negotiate or seek to negotiate the terms or conditions of employment.

labor–management relations. The broad spectrum of activities concerning the relationship between employers and employees, both union and nonunion. See FAIR LABOR STANDARDS ACT; NATIONAL LABOR RELATIONS ACT; NATIONAL LABOR RELATIONS BOARD.

Labor–Management Relations Act. A federal statute, enacted in 1947, that regulates certain union activities, permits suits against unions for proscribed acts, prohibits certain strikes and boycotts, and provides steps for settling strikes involving national emergencies. 29 USCA §§ 141 et seq. See NATIONAL LABOR RELATIONS BOARD.

labor-relations act. A statute regulating relations between employers and employees. • Although the Labor–Management Relations Act is the chief federal labor-relations act, various states have enacted these statutes as well.

Lacey Act. A federal law, originally enacted in 1900, that permits states to enforce their own game laws against animals imported from other states or countries. 16 USCA §§ 661 et seq. See GAME LAW.

laches (**lach**-iz). [Law French "remissness; slackness"] **1.** Unreasonable delay or negligence in pursuing a right or claim — almost always an equitable one — in a way that prejudices the party against whom relief is sought. **2.** The equitable doctrine by which a court denies relief to a claimant who has unreasonably delayed or been negligent in asserting the claim, when that delay or negligence has prejudiced the party against whom relief is sought. Cf. LIMITATION (3).

lame duck. An elected official who is serving out a term after someone else has been elected as a successor.

lame-duck session. See SESSION.

land, *n.* **1.** An immovable and indestructible three-dimensional area consisting of a portion of the earth's surface, the space above and below the surface, and everything growing on or permanently affixed to it. **2.** An estate or interest in real property.

accommodation land. Land that is bought by a builder or speculator, who erects houses or improvements on it and then leases it at an increased rent.

arable land (**ar**-ə-bəl). Land that is fit for cultivation, as distinguished from swampland.

enclosed land. Land that is actually enclosed and surrounded with fences.

fast land. (*often pl.*) Land that is above the high-water mark and that, when flooded by a government project, is subjected to a governmental taking. See TAKING.

mineral land. Land that contains deposits of valuable minerals in quantities justifying the costs of extraction and using the land for mining, rather than agricultural or other purposes.

public land. Unappropriated land belonging to the federal or a state government; the general public domain.

school land. Public real estate set apart for sale or exploitation by a state to establish and fund public schools.

seated land. Land that is occupied, cultivated, improved, reclaimed, farmed, or used as a place of residence, with or without cultivation.

swamp and overflowed land. Land that, because of its boggy, marshy, fenlike character, is unfit for cultivation, requiring drainage or reclamation to render it available for beneficial use. • Such lands were granted out of the U.S. public domain to the littoral states by acts of Congress in 1850 and thereafter. 43 USCA §§ 981 et seq.

land bank. 1. A bank created under the Federal Farm Loan Act to make loans at low interest rates secured by farmland. **2.** A program in which land is retired from agricultural production for conservation or tree-cultivation purposes. See FEDERAL HOME LOAN BANK.

land boundary. The limit of a landholding, usu. described by linear measurements of the borders, by points of the compass, or by stationary markers. See BOUNDARY; LEGAL DESCRIPTION.

landed, *adj.* **1.** (Of a person) having an estate in land. **2.** (Of an estate, etc.) consisting of land.

land flip. *Real estate*. A transaction in which a piece of property is purchased for one price and immediately sold, usu. to a fictitious entity, for a much higher price, to dupe a lender or later purchaser into thinking that the property is more valuable than it actually is.

land grant. A donation of public land to an individual, a corporation, or a subordinate government.

private land grant. A land grant to a natural person.

landholder. One who possesses or owns land.

landing. 1. A place on a river or other navigable water for loading and unloading goods, or receiving and delivering passengers and pleasure boats. **2.** The termination point on a river or other navigable water for these purposes. **3.** The act or process of coming back to land after a voyage or flight.

landlocked, *adj.* Surrounded by land, often with the suggestion that there is little or no way to get in or out without crossing the land of another.

landlord. One who leases real property to another.

landlord's warrant. See WARRANT.

landlord–tenant relationship. The familiar legal relationship existing between the lessor and lessee of real estate. • The relationship is contractual, created by a lease (or agreement for lease) for a term of years, from year to year, for life, or at will, and exists when one person occupies the premises of another with the lessor's permission or consent, subordinated to the lessor's title or rights. There must be a landlord's reversion, a tenant's estate, transfer of possession and control of the premises, and (generally) an express or implied contract. See LEASE.

landmark. 1. A feature of land (such as a natural object, or a monument or marker) that demarcates the boundary of the land. **2.** A historically significant building or site. See MONUMENT.

landmark decision. A judicial decision that significantly changes existing law. • Examples are *Brown v. Board of Educ.*, 347 U.S. 483, 74 S.Ct. 686 (1954) (holding that segregation in public schools violates the Equal Protection Clause), and *Palsgraf v. Long Island R.R.*, 162 N.E. 99 (N.Y. 1928) (establishing that a defendant's duty in a negligence action is limited to plaintiffs within the apparent zone of danger — that is, plaintiffs to whom damage could be reasonably foreseen). Cf. LEADING CASE (1).

land office. A government office in which sales of public land are recorded.

land-poor, *adj.* (Of a person) owning a substantial amount of unprofitable or encumbered land, but lacking the money to improve or maintain the land or to pay the charges due on it.

Landrum–Griffin Act. A federal law, originally enacted in 1959 as the Labor–Management Reporting and Disclosure Act, designed to (1) curb corruption in union leadership and undemocratic conduct in internal union affairs, (2) outlaw certain types of secondary boycotts, and (3) prevent so-called hot-cargo provisions in collective-bargaining agreements. See HOT CARGO.

lands, *n. pl.* **1.** At common law, property less extensive than either tenements or hereditaments. **2.** By statute in some states, land including tenements and hereditaments. See HEREDITAMENT; TENEMENT.

lands, tenements, and hereditaments. Real property.

land-use planning. The deliberate, systematic development of real estate through methods such as zoning, environmental-impact studies, and the like.

language. 1. Any means of conveying or communicating ideas, esp. by human speech, written characters, or sign language. **2.** The letter or grammatical import of a document or instrument, as distinguished from its spirit.

Lanham Act (**lan**-əm). A federal trademark statute, enacted in 1946, that provides for a national system of trademark registration and protects the owner of a federally registered mark against the use of similar marks if any confusion might result. • The Lanham Act's scope is independent of and concurrent with state common law. 15 USCA §§ 1051 et seq.

lapping. An embezzlement technique by which an employee takes funds from one customer's accounts receivable and covers it by using a second customer's payment to pay the first account, then a third customer's payment to pay the second account, and so on.

lapse, *n.* **1.** The termination of a right or privilege because of a failure to exercise it within some time limit or because a contingency has occurred or not occurred. **2.** *Wills & estates.* The failure of a testamentary gift, esp. when the beneficiary dies before the testator dies. See ANTILAPSE STATUTE. Cf. ADEMPTION.

lapse, *vb.* **1.** (Of an estate or right) to pass away or revert to someone else because conditions have not been fulfilled or because a person entitled to possession has failed in some duty. See *lapsed policy* under INSURANCE POLICY. **2.** (Of a devise, grant, etc.) to become void.

lapsed devise. See DEVISE.

lapsed legacy. See LEGACY.

lapsed policy. See INSURANCE POLICY.

larcenable (**lahr**-sə-nə-bəl), *adj.* Subject to larceny.

larcenous (**lahr**-sə-nəs), *adj.* **1.** Of, relating to, or characterized by larceny. **2.** (Of a person) contemplating or tainted with larceny; thievish.

larcenous intent. A state of mind existing when a person (1) knowingly takes away the goods of another without any claim or pretense of a right to do so, and (2) intends to deprive the owner of them or to convert the goods to personal use. See LARCENY.

larceny (**lahr**-sə-nee), *n.* The unlawful taking and carrying away of someone else's personal property with the intent to deprive the possessor of it permanently.

aggravated larceny. Larceny accompanied by some aggravating factor (as when the theft is from a person).

constructive larceny. Larceny in which the perpetrator's felonious intent to appropriate the goods is construed from the defendant's conduct at the time of asportation, although a felonious intent was not present before that time.

grand larceny. Larceny of property worth more than a statutory cutoff amount, usu. $100. Cf. *petit larceny*.

larceny by trick. Larceny in which the taker misleads the rightful possessor, by misrepresentation of fact, into giving up possession of (but not title to) the goods. Cf. FALSE PRETENSES; *cheating by false pretenses* under CHEATING.

larceny from the person. Larceny in which the goods are taken directly from the person, but without violence or intimidation, the victim usu. being unaware of the taking. Cf. ROBBERY.

mixed larceny. **1.** Larceny accompanied by aggravation or violence to the person. Cf. *simple larceny*. **2.** Larceny involving a taking from a house.

petit larceny. Larceny of property worth less than an amount fixed by statute, usu. $100. Cf. *grand larceny*.

simple larceny. Larceny unaccompanied by aggravating factors; larceny of personal goods unattended by an act of violence. Cf. *mixed larceny* (1).

larger parcel. *Eminent domain.* A portion of land that is not a complete parcel, but is the greater part of an even bigger tract, entitling the owner to damages both for the parcel taken and for severance from the tract. • To grant both kinds of damages, a court generally requires the owner to show unity of ownership, unity of use, and contiguity of the land. But some states and the federal courts do not require contiguity when there is strong evidence of unity of use.

***Larrison* rule** (**lar**-ə-sən). *Criminal law.* The doctrine that a defendant may be entitled to a new trial on the basis of newly discovered evidence of false testimony by a government witness if the jury might have reached a different conclusion without the evidence and it unfairly surprised the defendant at trial. *Larrison v. United States*, 24 F.2d 82 (7th Cir. 1928).

lascivious (lə-**siv**-ee-əs), *adj.* (Of conduct) tending to excite lust; lewd; indecent; obscene.

lascivious cohabitation. See *illicit cohabitation* under COHABITATION.

last-clear-chance doctrine. *Torts.* The rule that a plaintiff who was contributorily negligent may nonetheless recover from the defendant if the defendant had the last opportunity to prevent the harm but failed to use reasonable care to do so (in other words, if the defendant's negligence is later in time than the plaintiff's).

last illness. The sickness ending in the person's death.

last-link doctrine. The rule that an attorney need not divulge nonprivileged information if doing so would reveal information protected by the attorney–client privilege, particularly if the information would provide essential evidence to support indicting or convicting the client of a crime.

last-proximate-act test. *Criminal law.* A common-law test for the crime of attempt, based on whether the defendant does the final act necessary to commit an offense (such as pulling the trigger of a gun, not merely aiming it). See ATTEMPT (2).

last will. See WILL.

last will and testament. A person's final will. See WILL.

latent (**lay**-tənt), *adj.* Concealed; dormant <a latent defect>. Cf. PATENT.

latent ambiguity. See AMBIGUITY.

latent equity. See EQUITY.

lateral departure. See DEPARTURE.

laughing heir. See HEIR.

laundering, *n.* The federal crime of transferring illegally obtained money through legitimate persons or accounts so that its original source cannot be traced. 18 USCA § 1956. — **launder,** *vb.*

laundry list. *Slang.* An enumeration of items, as in a statute or court opinion.

law. 1. The regime that orders human activities and relations through systematic application of the force of politically organized society, or through social pressure, backed by force, in such a society; the legal system <respect and obey the law>. **2.** The aggregate of legislation, judicial precedents, and accepted legal principles; the body of authoritative grounds of judicial and administrative action <the law of the land>. **3.** The set of rules or principles dealing with a specific area of a legal system <copyright law>. **4.** The judicial and administrative process; legal action and proceedings <when settlement negotiations failed, they submitted their dispute to the law>. **5.** A statute <Congress passed a law>. — Abbr. L. **6.** COMMON LAW <law but not equity>. **7.** The legal profession <she spent her entire career in law>.

law and economics. (*often cap.*) **1.** A discipline advocating the economic analysis of the law, whereby legal rules are subjected to a cost-benefit analysis to determine whether a change from one legal rule to another will increase or decrease allocative efficiency and social wealth. **2.** The field or movement in which scholars devote themselves to this discipline. **3.** The body of work produced by these scholars.

law and literature. (*often cap.*) **1.** Traditionally, the study of how lawyers and legal institutions are depicted in literature; esp., the examination of law-related fiction as sociological evidence of how a given culture, at a given time, views law. **2.** More modernly, the application of literary theory to legal texts, focusing esp. on lawyers' rhetoric, logic, and style, as well as legal syntax and semantics. **3.** The field or movement in which scholars devote themselves to this study or application. **4.** The body of work produced by these scholars.

law arbitrary. A law not found in the nature of things, but imposed by the legislature's mere will; a bill not immutable.

lawbook. A book, usu. a technical one, about the law; esp., a primary legal text such as a statute book or book that reports caselaw.

law-craft, *n.* The practice of law.

law enforcement. 1. The detection and punishment of violations of the law. • This term is not limited to the enforcement of criminal laws. For example, the Freedom of Information Act contains an exemption from disclosure for information compiled for law-enforcement purposes and furnished in confidence. That exemption is valid for the enforcement of a variety of noncriminal laws (such as national-security laws) as well as criminal laws. See 5 USCA § 552(b)(7). **2.** CRIMINAL JUSTICE (2). **3.** Police officers and other members of the executive branch of government charged with carrying out and enforcing the criminal law.

Law Enforcement Assistance Administration. A former federal agency (part of the Department of Justice) that was responsible for administering law-enforcement grants under the Omnibus Crime Control and Safe Streets Act of 1968. • It has been replaced by a variety of federal agencies, including the National Institute of Corrections and National Institute of Justice.

Law Enforcement Information Network. A computerized communications system used in some states to document drivers' license records, automobile registrations, wanted persons' files, etc.

law firm. An association of lawyers who practice law together, usu. sharing clients and profits, in a business traditionally organized as a partnership but often today as either a professional corporation or a limited-liability company.

Law French. The corrupted form of the Norman French language that arose in England in the centuries after William the Conqueror invaded England in 1066 and that was used for several centuries as the primary language of the English legal system; the Anglo-French used in medieval England in judicial proceedings, pleadings, and lawbooks.

lawful, *adj.* Not contrary to law; permitted by law. See LEGAL.

lawful admission. *Immigration.* Legal entry into the country, including under a valid immigrant visa.

lawful arrest. See ARREST.

lawful authorities. Those persons (such as the police) with the right to exercise public power, to require obedience to their lawful commands, and to command or act in the public name.

lawful dependent. See DEPENDENT.

lawful entry. See ENTRY.

lawful fence. A strong, substantial, and well-suited barrier that is sufficient to prevent animals from escaping property and to protect the property from trespassers.

lawful goods. Property that one may legally hold, sell, or export; property that is not contraband.

lawful issue. See ISSUE (2).

lawful representative. See REPRESENTATIVE.

lawgiver. 1. A legislator, esp. one who promulgates an entire code of laws. **2.** A judge with the power to interpret law. — **lawgiving,** *adj.* & *n.*

Law Latin. A corrupted form of Latin formerly used in law and legal documents, including judicial writs, royal charters, and private deeds. • It primarily consists of a mixture of Latin, French, and English words used in English sentence structures.

law list. 1. A publication compiling the names and addresses of practicing lawyers and other information of interest to the profession, such as court calendars, lawyers with specialized practices, stenographers, and the like. **2.** A legal directory such as Martindale–Hubbell. • Many states and large cities also have law lists or directories. See MARTINDALE-HUBBELL LAW DIRECTORY.

law of persons. The law relating to persons; the law that pertains to the different statuses of persons. • This is also commonly known as the *jus personarum*, a shortened form of *jus quod ad personas pertinet* ("the law that pertains to persons").

law of the case. 1. The doctrine holding that a decision rendered in a former appeal of a case is binding in a later appeal. **2.** An earlier decision giving rise to the application of this doctrine. Cf. LAW OF THE TRIAL; RES JUDICATA; STARE DECISIS.

law of the circuit. 1. The law as announced and followed by a U.S. Circuit Court of Appeals. **2.** The rule that one panel of judges on a U.S. Circuit Court of Appeals should not overrule a decision of another panel of judges on the same court. **3.** The rule that an opinion of one U.S. Circuit Court of Appeals is not binding on another circuit but may be considered persuasive.

law of the land. 1. The law in effect in a country and applicable to its members, whether the law is statutory, administrative, or case-made. **2.** Due process of law. See DUE PROCESS.

law of the place. Under the Federal Tort Claims Act, the state law applicable to the place where the injury occurred. • Under the Act, the federal government waives its sovereign immunity for specified injuries, including certain wrongful acts or omissions of a government employee causing injury that the United States, if it were a private person, would be liable for under the law of the state where the incident occurred. 28 USCA § 1346(b).

law of the trial. A legal theory or court ruling that is not objected to and is used or relied on in a trial <neither party objected to the court's jury instruction, so it became the law of the trial>. Cf. LAW OF THE CASE.

law of things. The law pertaining to things; the law that is determined by changes in the nature of things. • This is also commonly known as the *jus rerum*, a shortened form of *jus quod ad res pertinet* ("the law that pertains to things").

law practice. An attorney's professional business, including the relationships that the attorney has with clients and the goodwill associated with those relationships. Cf. PRACTICE OF LAW.

law reform. The process of, or a movement dedicated to, streamlining, modernizing, or otherwise improving a nation's laws generally or the code governing a particular branch of the law; specif., the investigation and discussion of the law on a topic (e.g., bankruptcy), usu. by a commission or expert committee, with the goal of formulating proposals for change to improve the operation of the law.

law review. 1. A journal containing scholarly articles, essays, and other commentary on legal topics by professors, judges, law students, and practitioners. • Law reviews are usually published at law schools and edited by law students. **2.** The law-student staff and editorial board of such a journal.

law school. An institution for formal legal education and training. • Graduates who complete the standard program, usually three years in length, receive a Juris Doctor (or, formerly, a Bachelor of Laws).

accredited law school. A law school approved by the state and the Association of American Law Schools, or by the state and the American Bar Association.

lawsuit, *n.* See SUIT.

law-talk, *n.* **1.** LEGALESE. **2.** Discussion that is heavily laced with lawyers' concerns and legal references.

law writer. A person who writes on legal subjects, usu. from a technical, nonpopular point of view.

lawyer, *n.* One who is licensed to practice law. — **lawyerly,** *adj.* — **lawyerlike,** *adj.* — **lawyerdom,** *n.* Cf. ATTORNEY; COUNSEL.

criminal lawyer. A lawyer whose primary work is to represent criminal defendants. • This term is rarely if ever applied to prosecutors despite their integral involvement in the criminal-justice system.

headnote lawyer. Slang. A lawyer who relies on the headnotes of judicial opinions rather than taking the time to read the opinions themselves.

transactional lawyer. A lawyer who works primarily on transactions such as licensing agreements, mergers, acquisitions, joint ventures, and the like.

lawyer, *vb.* **1.** To practice as a lawyer. **2.** To supply with lawyers. — **lawyering,** *n.*

lawyer-witness rule. The principle that an attorney who will likely be called as a fact witness at trial may not participate as an advocate in the case, unless the testimony will be about an uncontested matter or the amount of attorney's fees in the case, or if disqualifying the attorney would create a substantial hardship for the client. • The rule permits an attorney actively participating in the case to be a witness on merely formal matters but discourages testimony on other matters on behalf of a client. *Model Rules of Professional Conduct* Rule 3.7 (1987).

lay, *adj.* Not expert, esp. with reference to law or medicine; nonprofessional.

lay, *vb.* To allege or assert.

lay damages, *vb.* To allege damages, esp. in the complaint. See AD DAMNUM CLAUSE.

laying a foundation. *Evidence.* Introducing evidence of certain facts needed to render later evidence relevant, material, or competent. • For example, propounding a hypothetical question to an expert is necessary before the expert may render an opinion.

laying of the venue. A statement in a complaint naming the district or county in which the plaintiff proposes that any trial of the matter should occur. See VENUE.

lay judge. See JUDGE.

layman. 1. A person who is not a member of the clergy. **2.** A person who is not a member of a profession or an expert on a particular subject.

lay opinion testimony. See TESTIMONY.

lay witness. See WITNESS.

LC. *abbr.* LETTER OF CREDIT. — Also written L/C.

L–Claim proceeding. A hearing under the Racketeer Influenced and Corrupt Organizations Act, intended to ensure that property ordered to be forfeited belongs solely to the defendant. • A petition for an L–Claim proceeding is filed by a third party who claims an interest in the property. The purpose is not to divide the assets among competing claimants, and general creditors of the defendant are not allowed to maintain an L–Claim petition. The name refers to its legal basis in subsection *l* of RICO's penalty provision. 18 USCA § 1963(*l*)(2).

lead counsel. See COUNSEL.

leading case. 1. A judicial decision that first definitively settled an important legal rule or principle and that has since been often and consistently followed. • An example is *Miranda v. Arizona*, 384 U.S. 436, 86 S.Ct. 1602 (1966) (creating the exclusionary rule for evidence improperly obtained from a suspect being interrogated while in police custody). Cf. LANDMARK DECISION. **2.** An important, often the most important, judicial precedent on a particular legal issue. **3.** Loosely, a reported case that is cited as the dispositive authority on an issue being litigated.

leading question. A question that suggests the answer to the person being interrogated; esp., a question that may be answered by a mere "yes" or "no."

league. 1. A covenant made by nations, groups, or individuals for promoting common interests or ensuring mutual protection. **2.** An alliance or association of nations, groups, or individuals formed by such a covenant.

leakage. 1. The waste of a liquid caused by its leaking from a storage container. **2.** An allowance against duties granted by customs to an importer of liquids for losses sustained by this waste. **3.** *Intellectual property.* Loss in value of a piece of intellectual property because of unauthorized copying.

leapfrog development. An improvement of land that requires the extension of public facilities from their current stopping point, through undeveloped land that may be scheduled for future development, to the site of the improvement.

learned (**lər**-nid), *adj.* **1.** Having a great deal of learning; erudite. **2.** Well-versed in the law and its history.

learned-treatise rule. *Evidence.* An exception to the hearsay rule, by which a published text may be established as authoritative, either by expert testimony or by judicial notice. • Under the Federal Rules of Evidence, a statement contained in a published treatise, periodical, or pamphlet on sciences or arts (such as history and medicine) can be established as authoritative — and thereby admitted into evidence for the purpose of examining or cross-examining an expert witness — by expert testimony or by the court's taking judicial notice of the authoritative nature or reliability of the text. If the statement is admitted into evidence, it may be read into the trial record, but it may not be received as an exhibit. Fed. R. Evid. 803(18).

lease, *n.* **1.** A contract by which a rightful possessor of real property conveys the right to use and occupy that property in exchange for consideration, usu. rent. **2.** Such a conveyance plus all covenants attached to it. **3.** The written instrument memorializing such a conveyance and its covenants. **4.** The piece of real property so conveyed. **5.** A contract by which the rightful possessor of personal property conveys the right to use that property in exchange for consideration.

assignable lease. A lease that can be transferred by a lessee. See SUBLEASE.

commercial lease. A lease for business purposes.

community lease. A lease in which a number of lessors owning interests in separate tracts execute a lease in favor of a single lessee.

concurrent lease. A lease that begins before a previous lease ends, entitling the new lessee to be paid all rents that accrue on the previous lease after the new lease begins, and to appropriate remedies against the holding tenant.

consumer lease. **1.** A lease of goods by a person who is in the business of selling or leasing a product to someone who leases it primarily for personal or household use. UCC § 2A–103(1)(e). **2.** A residential — rather than commercial — lease.

durable lease. A lease that reserves a rent payable annually, usu. with a right of reentry for nonpayment.

finance lease. A fixed-term lease used by a business to finance capital equipment. • The lessor's service is usually limited to financing the asset, and the lessee pays maintenance costs and taxes and has the option of purchasing the asset at the end of the lease for a nominal price. Finance leases strongly resemble security agreements and are written almost exclusively by financial institutions as a way to help a commercial customer obtain an expensive capital item that the customer might not otherwise be able to afford. UCC § 2A–103(1)(g).

full-service lease. A lease in which the lessor agrees to pay all maintenance expenses, insurance premiums, and property taxes.

graduated lease. A lease in which rent varies depending on future contingencies, such as operating expenses or gross income.

gross lease. A lease in which the lessee pays a flat amount for rent, out of which the lessor pays all the expenses (such as gas, water, and electricity).

ground lease. A long-term (usu. 99–year) lease of land only.

leveraged lease. A lease that is collateral for the loan through which the lessor acquired the leased asset, and that provides the lender's only recourse for nonpayment of the debt; a lease in which a creditor provides nonrecourse financing to the lessor (who has substantial leverage in the property) and in which the lessor's net investment in the lease, apart from nonrecourse financing, declines during the early years and increases in later years.

master lease. A lease that controls later leases or subleases.

month-to-month lease. A tenancy with no written contract. • Rent is paid monthly, and usually one month's notice by the landlord or tenant is required to terminate the tenancy. See *periodic tenancy* under TENANCY.

oil-and-gas lease. A lease granting the right to extract oil and gas from a specified piece of land. • Although called a "lease," this interest is typically considered a determinable fee in the minerals rather than a grant of possession for a term of years.

sandwich lease. A lease in which the lessee subleases the property to a third party, esp. for more rent than under the original lease.

short lease. A lease of brief duration, often less than six months.

sublease. See SUBLEASE.

timber lease. A real-property lease that contemplates that the lessee will cut timber on the leased premises.

lease, *vb.* **1.** To grant the possession and use of (land, buildings, rooms, movable property, etc.) to another in return for rent or other consideration. **2.** To take a lease of; to hold by a lease.

leaseback, *n.* The sale of property on the understanding, or with the express option, that the seller may lease the property from the buyer immediately upon the sale.

leasehold, *n.* A tenant's possessory estate in land or premises, the four types being the tenancy for years, the periodic tenancy, the tenancy at will, and the tenancy at sufferance. See TENANCY. Cf. FREEHOLD.

leasehold improvements. Beneficial changes to leased property (such as a parking lot or driveway) made by or for the benefit of the lessee. • The phrase is used in a condemnation proceeding to determine the share of compensation to be allocated to the lessee.

leasehold interest. 1. LEASEHOLD; esp., for purposes of eminent domain, the lessee's interest in the lease itself, measured by the difference between the total remaining rent and the rent the lessee would pay for similar space for the same period. **2.** A lessor's or lessee's interest under a lease contract. UCC § 2A–103.

leasehold value. The value of a leasehold interest. • This term usually applies to a long-term lease when the rent paid under the lease is lower than current market rates. See LEASEHOLD INTEREST; NO-BONUS CLAUSE.

lease-purchase agreement. A rent-to-own purchase plan under which the buyer takes possession of the goods with the first payment and takes ownership with the final payment; a lease of property (esp. equipment) by which ownership of the property is transferred to the lessee at the end of the lease term. • Such a lease is usually treated as an installment sale. Under a capital lease, the lessee is responsible for paying taxes and other expenses on the property.

least-intrusive-means doctrine. A doctrine requiring the government to exhaust all other investigatory means before seeking sensitive testimony, as by compelling an attorney to testify before a grand jury on matters that may be protected by the attorney–client privilege.

least-intrusive-remedy doctrine. The rule that a legal remedy should provide the damaged party with appropriate relief, without unduly penalizing the opposing party or the jurisdiction's system, as by striking only the unconstitutional portion of a challenged statute while leaving the rest of the statute intact.

least-restrictive-means test. The rule that a law or governmental regulation, even when based on a legitimate governmental interest, should be crafted in a way that will protect individual civil liberties as much as possible, and should be only as restrictive as is necessary to accomplish a legitimate governmental purpose.

leave, *vb.* **1.** To give by will; to bequeath or devise. **2.** To depart willfully with the intent not to return.

leave no issue, *vb.* To die without a surviving child, children, or descendants. • The spouse of a deceased child is usually not issue.

leave of court. Judicial permission to follow a nonroutine procedure.

legacy (**leg**-ə-see), *n.* A gift by will, esp. of personal property and often of money. Cf. BEQUEST; DEVISE.

accumulated legacy. A legacy that has not yet been paid to a legatee.

alternate legacy. A legacy by which the testator gives the legatee a choice of one of two or more items.

conditional legacy. A legacy that will take effect or be defeated subject to the occurrence or nonoccurrence of an event.

contingent legacy. A legacy that depends on an uncertain event and thus has not vested. • An example is a legacy given to one's granddaughter "if or when she attains the age of 21."

cumulative legacies. Two or more legacies that, being given in the same will to the same person (often in similar language), are considered additional to one another and not merely a repeated expression of the same gift.

demonstrative legacy (di-**mon**-strə-tiv). A legacy paid from a particular source if that source has enough money.

general legacy. A gift of personal property that the testator intends to come from the general assets of the estate, payable in money or items indistinguishable from each other, such as shares of stock.

lapsed legacy. A legacy to a legatee who dies either before the testator dies or before the legacy is payable. See ANTILAPSE STATUTE.

pecuniary legacy (pi-**kyoo**-nee-er-ee). A legacy of a sum of money.

residuary legacy (ri-**zij**-oo-er-ee). A legacy of the estate remaining after the satisfaction of all claims and all specific, general, and demonstrative legacies.

specific legacy. A legacy of property that can be distinguished from the other property forming the testator's estate.

substitutional legacy. A legacy that replaces a different legacy already given to a legatee.

vested legacy. A legacy given in such a way that the legatee has a fixed, indefeasible right to its payment. • An example is a legacy given to one's granddaughter "when she attains the age of 21."

void legacy. A legacy that never had any legal existence.

legal, *adj.* **1.** Of or relating to law; falling within the province of law. **2.** Established, required, or permitted by law; LAWFUL. **3.** Of or relating to law as opposed to equity.

legal act. 1. Any act not condemned as illegal. **2.** An action or undertaking that creates a legally recognized obligation; an act that binds a person in some way. **3.** See *act in the law* under ACT (2). **4.** See *act of the law* under ACT (2).

legal-acumen doctrine (**lee**-gəl ə-**kyoo**-mən). The principle that if a defect in, or the invalidity of, a claim to land cannot be discovered without legal expertise, then equity may be invoked to remove the cloud created by the defect or invalidity.

legal aid. Free or inexpensive legal services provided to those who cannot afford to pay full price.

legal assistant. 1. PARALEGAL. **2.** A legal secretary.

legal-certainty test. *Civil procedure.* A test designed to establish whether the jurisdictional amount has been met. • The amount claimed in the complaint will control unless there is a "legal certainty" that the claim is actually less than the minimum amount necessary to establish jurisdiction. See AMOUNT IN CONTROVERSY.

legal citology (sI-**tol**-ə-jee). The study of citations (esp. in footnotes) and their effect on legal scholarship. — **legal citologist** (sI-**tol**-ə-jist), *n.*

legal conclusion. A statement that expresses a legal duty or result but omits the facts creating or supporting the duty or result. Cf. CONCLUSION OF LAW; CONCLUSION OF FACT; FINDING OF FACT.

legal cruelty. See CRUELTY.

legal defense. See DEFENSE (1).

legal dependent. See DEPENDENT.

legal description. A formal description of real property, including a description of any part subject to an easement or reservation, complete enough that a particular piece of land can be located and identified.

legal duty. See DUTY.

legal-elements test. *Criminal law.* A method of determining whether one crime is a lesser-included offense in relation to another crime, by examining the components of the greater crime to analyze whether a person who commits the greater crime necessarily commits the lesser one also.

legal entity. A body, other than a natural person, that can function legally, sue or be sued, and make decisions through agents. Cf. *artificial person* under PERSON.

legalese (lee-gə-**leez**). The jargon characteristically used by lawyers, esp. in legal documents. Cf. PLAIN-LANGUAGE MOVEMENT.

legal ethics. 1. The standards of minimally acceptable conduct within the legal profession, involving the duties that its members owe one another, their clients, and the courts. **2.** The study or observance of those duties. **3.** The written regulations governing those duties. See MODEL RULES OF PROFESSIONAL CONDUCT.

legal evidence. See EVIDENCE.

legal fact. See FACT.

legal father. See FATHER.

legal fiction. An assumption that something is true even though it may be untrue, made esp. in judicial reasoning to alter how a legal rule operates.

legal formalism, *n.* The theory that law is a set of rules and principles independent of other political and social institutions. — **legal formalist,** *n.* Cf. LEGAL REALISM.

legal holiday. A day designated by law as exempt from court proceedings, issuance of process, and the like.

legal impossibility. See IMPOSSIBILITY.

legal injury. See INJURY.

legal-injury rule. The doctrine that the statute of limitations on a claim does not begin to run until the claimant has sustained some legally actionable damage.

legal innocence. See INNOCENCE.

legal interest. See INTEREST (2).

legalism, *n.* **1.** Formalism carried almost to the point of meaninglessness; an inclination to exalt the importance of law or formulated rules in any area of action. **2.** A mode of expression characteristic of lawyers; a jargonistic phrase characteristic of lawyers, such as "pursuant to." — **legalistic,** *adj.*

legal issue. See ISSUE (1).

legalist, *n.* A person who views things from a legal or formalistic standpoint; esp., one who believes in strict adherence to the letter of the law rather than its spirit.

legality. 1. Strict adherence to law, prescription, or doctrine; the quality of being legal. **2.** The principle that a person may not be prosecuted under a criminal law that has not been previously published.

legalize, *vb.* **1.** To make lawful; to authorize or justify by legal sanction. **2.** To imbue with the spirit of the law; to make legalistic. — **legalization,** *n.*

legal life tenant. See LIFE TENANT.

legally determined, *adj.* (Of a claim, issue, etc.) decided by legal process.

legally incapacitated person. A person, other than a minor, who is permanently or temporarily impaired by mental illness, mental deficiency, physical illness or disability, or use of drugs or alcohol to the extent that the person lacks sufficient understanding to make or communicate responsible personal decisions or to enter into contracts.

legally inconsistent verdict. See VERDICT.

legal memory. The period during which a legal right or custom can be determined or established. Cf. TIME IMMEMORIAL (1).

legal mind. The intellect, legal capacities, and attitudes of a well-trained lawyer — often used as a personified being.

legal moralism. The theory that a government or legal system may prohibit conduct that is considered immoral.

legal opinion. See OPINION (2).

legal order. 1. Traditionally, a set of regulations governing a society and those responsible for enforcing them. **2.** Modernly, such regulations and officials plus the processes involved in creating, interpreting, and applying the regulations.

legal owner. See OWNER.

legal paternalism. The theory that a government or legal system is justified in controlling the individual affairs of the citizens. • This theory is often associated with legal positivists. See PATERNALISM; LEGAL POSITIVISM.

legal-personal representative. See REPRESENTATIVE.

legal positivism, *n.* The theory that legal rules are valid only because they are enacted by an existing political authority or accepted as binding in a given society, not because they are grounded in morality or in natural law. — **legal positivist,** *n.* See POSITIVE LAW. Cf. LOGICAL POSITIVISM.

legal possessor. One with the legal right to possess property, such as a buyer under a conditional sales contract, as contrasted with the legal owner who holds legal title. See *legal owner* under OWNER.

legal prejudice. See PREJUDICE.

legal proceeding. Any proceeding authorized by law and instituted in a court or tribunal to acquire a right or to enforce a remedy.

legal rate. See INTEREST RATE.

legal realism, *n.* The theory that law is based, not on formal rules or principles, but instead on judicial decisions that should derive from social interests and public policy. — **legal realist,** *n.* Cf. LEGAL FORMALISM.

legal remedy. See REMEDY.

legal rescission. See RESCISSION.

legal research. 1. The finding and assembling of authorities that bear on a question of law. **2.** The field of study concerned with the effective marshaling of authorities that bear on a question of law.

legal science. The field of study that, as one of the social sciences, deals with the institutions and principles that particular societies have developed (1) for defining the claims and liabilities of persons against one another in various circumstances, and (2) for peaceably resolving disputes and controversies in accordance with principles accepted as fair and right in the particular community at a given time.

legal secretary. An employee in a law office whose responsibilities include typing legal documents and correspondence, keeping records and files, and performing other duties supportive of the employer's law practice.

legal servitude. See SERVITUDE (1).

legal succession. See SUCCESSION.

legal tender. The money (bills and coins) approved in a country for the payment of debts, the purchase of goods, and other exchanges for value. See TENDER (5).

legal theory. **1.** See *general jurisprudence* under JURISPRUDENCE. **2.** The principle under which a litigant proceeds, or on which a litigant bases its claims or defenses in a case.

legal title. See TITLE (2).

legal wrong. See WRONG.

legatee (leg-ə-**tee**). **1.** One who is named in a will to take personal property; one who has received a legacy or bequest. **2.** Loosely, one to whom a devise of real property is given.

residuary legatee (ri-**zij**-oo-er-ee). A person designated to receive the residue of a decedent's estate. See *residuary estate* under ESTATE.

specific legatee. The recipient, under a will, of designated property that is transferred by the owner's death.

legislate, *vb.* **1.** To make or enact laws. **2.** To bring (something) into or out of existence by making laws; to attempt to control (something) by legislation.

legislation. **1.** The process of making or enacting a positive law in written form, according to some type of formal procedure, by a branch of government constituted to perform this process. **2.** The law so enacted. **3.** The whole body of enacted laws.

ancillary legislation. Legislation that is auxiliary to principal legislation.

general legislation. Legislation that applies to the community at large.

judicial legislation. The making of new legal rules by judges; JUDGE-MADE LAW (2).

local and special legislation. Legislation that affects only a specific geographic area or a particular class of persons.

pork-barrel legislation. Legislation that favors a particular local district by allocating funds or resources to projects (such as constructing a highway or a post office) of economic value to the district and of political advantage to the district's legislator.

subordinate legislation. **1.** Legislation that derives from any authority other than the sovereign power in a state and that therefore depends for its continued existence and validity on some superior or supreme authority. **2.** REGULATION (2).

supreme legislation. Legislation that derives directly from the supreme or sovereign power in a state and is therefore incapable of being repealed, annulled, or controlled by any other legislative authority.

4. A proposed law being considered by a legislature. **5.** The field of study concentrating on statutes.

legislative branch. The branch of government responsible for enacting laws; LEGISLATURE. Cf. EXECUTIVE BRANCH; JUDICIAL BRANCH.

legislative council. A state agency that studies legislative problems and plans legislative strategy between regular legislative sessions.

legislative counsel. A person or group charged with helping legislators fulfill their legislative duties, as by performing research, drafting bills, and the like.

legislative court. See COURT.

legislative district. See DISTRICT.

legislative districting. The process of dividing a state into territorial districts to be represented in the state or federal legislature. See APPORTIONMENT; GERRYMANDERING; REAPPORTIONMENT.

legislative-equivalency doctrine. The rule that a law should be amended or repealed only by the same procedures that were used to enact it.

legislative fact. See FACT.

legislative history. The background and events leading to the enactment of a statute, including hearings, committee reports, and floor debates.

legislative immunity. See IMMUNITY (1).

legislative intent. The design or plan that the legislature had at the time of enacting a statute.

dormant legislative intent. The intent that the legislature would have had if a given ambiguity, inconsistency, or omission had been called to the legislators' minds. — Sometimes shortened to *dormant intent*.

legislative power. *Constitutional law.* The power to make laws and to alter them at discretion; a legislative body's exclusive authority to make, amend, and repeal laws. • Under federal law, this power is vested in Congress, consisting of the House of Representatives and the Senate. A legislative body may delegate a portion of its lawmaking authority to agencies within the executive branch for purposes of rulemaking and regulation. But a legislative body may not delegate its authority to the judicial branch, and the judicial branch may not encroach on legislative duties.

legislative privilege. See PRIVILEGE (1).

legislative veto. See VETO.

legislator, *n.* One who makes laws within a given jurisdiction; a member of a legislative body. — **legislatorial** (lej-is-lə-**tor**-ee-əl), *adj.*

legislature. The branch of government responsible for making statutory laws. Cf. EXECUTIVE (1); JUDICIARY (1).

legisprudence (lee-jis-**proo**-dənts). The systematic analysis of statutes within the framework of jurisprudential philosophies about the role and nature of law.

legist (**lee**-jist). **1.** One learned or skilled in the law; a lawyer. **2.** JURIST.

legitimacy. 1. Lawfulness. **2.** The status of a person who is born within a lawful marriage or who acquires that status by later action of the parents. Cf. ILLEGITIMACY.

legitimate, *adj.* **1.** Complying with the law; lawful. **2.** Born of legally married parents. **3.** Genuine; valid. — **legitimacy,** *n.*

legitimate child. See CHILD.

legitimation, *n.* **1.** The act of making something lawful; authorization. **2.** The act or process of authoritatively declaring a person legitimate. — **legitimate,** *vb.*

lemon law. 1. A statute designed to protect a consumer who buys a substandard automobile, usu. by requiring the manufacturer or dealer either to replace the vehicle or to refund the full purchase price. **2.** By extension, a statute designed to protect a consumer who buys any product of inferior quality.

lend, *vb.* **1.** To allow the temporary use of (something), sometimes in exchange for compensation, on condition that the thing or its equivalent be returned. **2.** To provide (money) temporarily on condition of repayment, usu. with interest.

lend-lease. A mutually beneficial exchange made between friendly parties.

lenient test. The principle that the attorney–client privilege applicable to a document will be waived only by a knowing or intentional disclosure, and will not usu. be waived by an inadvertent disclosure. Cf. STRICT TEST; HYDRAFLOW TEST.

lenity (**len**-ə-tee). The quality or condition of being lenient; mercy or clemency. See RULE OF LENITY.

lessee (le-**see**). One who has a possessory interest in real or personal property under a lease; TENANT.

lesser-evils defense. See DEFENSE (1).

lesser included offense. See OFFENSE.

lessor (**les**-or *or* le-**sor**). One who conveys real or personal property by lease; LANDLORD.

lessor's interest. The present value of the future income under a lease, plus the present value of the property after the lease expires.

let, *n.* An impediment or obstruction <free to act without let or hindrance>.

let, *vb.* **1.** To allow or permit. **2.** To offer (property) for lease; to rent out. **3.** To award (a contract), esp. after bids have been submitted.

lethal injection. An injection of a deadly substance into a prisoner, done to carry out a sentence of capital punishment.

letter. 1. A written communication that is usu. enclosed in an envelope, sealed, stamped, and delivered; esp., an official written communication <an opinion letter>. **2.** (*usu. pl.*) A written instrument containing or affirming a grant of some power or right <letters testamentary>. **3.**

Strict or literal meaning <the letter of the law>. Cf. SPIRIT OF THE LAW.

letter of credit. An instrument under which the issuer (usu. a bank), at a customer's request, agrees to honor a draft or other demand for payment made by a third party (the *beneficiary*), as long as the draft or demand complies with specified conditions, and regardless of whether any underlying agreement between the customer and the beneficiary is satisfied. • Letters of credit are governed by Article 5 of the UCC. — Abbr. LC; L/C. — Often shortened to *credit*.

letter of intent. A written statement detailing the preliminary understanding of parties who plan to enter into a contract or some other agreement; a noncommittal writing preliminary to a contract. Cf. *precontract* under CONTRACT.

letter of request. A document issued by one court to a foreign court, requesting that the foreign court (1) take evidence from a specific person within the foreign jurisdiction or serve process on an individual or corporation within the foreign jurisdiction and (2) return the testimony or proof of service for use in a pending case. See Fed. R. Civ. P. 28. Pl. **letters of request.**

letter of the law. The strictly literal meaning of the law, rather than the intention or policy behind it. Cf. SPIRIT OF THE LAW.

letter ruling. *Tax.* A written statement issued by the IRS to an inquiring taxpayer, explaining the tax implications of a particular transaction.

letters. *Wills & estates.* A court order giving official authority to a fiduciary to conduct appointed tasks. • Examples are letters of administration, letters of conservatorship, letters of guardianship, and letters testamentary. Unif. Probate Code § 1–201(23). See LETTER (2).

letters of administration. A formal document issued by a probate court to appoint the administrator of an estate. See ADMINISTRATION (4). Cf. LETTERS TESTAMENTARY.

letters of administration c.t.a. Letters of administration appointing an administrator *cum testamento annexo* (with the will annexed) either because the will does not name an executor or because the named executor does not qualify. See *administration cum testamento annexo* under ADMINISTRATION.

letters of administration d.b.n. Letters of administration appointing an administrator *de bonis non* (concerning goods not yet administered) because the named executor failed to complete the estate's probate. See *administration de bonis non* under ADMINISTRATION.

letters of guardianship. A document issued by a court appointing a guardian to care for a minor's or an incapacitated adult's well-being, property, and affairs. • It defines the scope of the guardian's rights and duties, including the extent of control over the ward's education and medical issues. See GUARDIAN.

letters patent. A governmental grant of the exclusive right to use an invention or design. See PATENT (2).

letters testamentary. The instrument by which a probate court approves the appointment of an executor under a will and authorizes the executor to administer the estate. Cf. LETTERS OF ADMINISTRATION.

leverage, *n.* **1.** Positional advantage; effectiveness. **2.** The use of credit or borrowed funds (such as buying on margin) to improve one's speculative ability and to increase an investment's rate of return. **3.** The advantage obtained from using credit or borrowed funds rather than equity capital. **4.** The ratio between a corporation's debt and its equity capital. **5.** The effect of this ratio on common-stock prices.

leverage, *vb.* **1.** To provide (a borrower or investor) with credit or funds to improve speculative ability and to seek a high rate of return. **2.** To supplement (available capital) with credit or outside funds. **3.** To fund (a company) with debt as well as shareholder equity. **4.** *Antitrust.* To use power in one market to gain an unfair advantage in another market. **5.** *Insurance.* To manipulate two coverages, as by an insurer withholding settlement of one claim to influence a claim arising under another source of coverage.

leverage contract. An agreement for the purchase or sale of a contract for the future delivery of a specified commodity, usu. silver, gold, or another precious metal, in a standard unit and quantity, for a particular price, with no right to a particular lot of the commodity. • A leverage contract operates much like a futures contract, except that there is no designated contract market for leverage contracts. 7 USCA § 23(a).

leveraged buyout. See BUYOUT.

leveraged lease. See LEASE.

levy (lev-ee), *n.* **1.** The imposition of a fine or tax; the fine or tax so imposed. **2.** The legally sanctioned seizure and sale of property; the money obtained from such a sale. — **levy,** *vb.* — **leviable (lev-ee-ə-bəl),** *adj.*

wrongful levy. A levy on a third party's property that is not subject to a writ of execution.

lewdness. Gross, wanton, and public indecency that is outlawed by many state statutes; a sexual act that the actor knows will likely be observed by someone who will be affronted or alarmed by it. See Model Penal Code § 251.1. Cf. INDECENT EXPOSURE; OBSCENITY.

lex **(leks),** *n.* [Latin "law"] **1.** Law, esp. statutory law. **2.** Positive law, as opposed to natural law. • Strictly speaking, *lex* is a statute, whereas *jus* is law in general (as well as a right). **3.** A system or body of laws, written or unwritten, that are peculiar to a jurisdiction or to a field of human activity. **4.** A collection of uncodified laws within a jurisdiction. Cf. JUS.

lex domicilii **(leks dom-ə-sil-ee-ɪ).** [Latin] **1.** The law of the country where a person is domiciled. **2.** The determination of a person's rights by establishing where, in law, that person is domiciled. See Restatement (Second) of Conflict of Laws §§ 11 et seq. (1971).

lex fori **(leks for-ɪ).** [Latin] The law of the forum; the law of the jurisdiction where the case is pending. Cf. LEX LOCI (1).

lexical definition. See DEFINITION.

Lexis (**lek**-sis). An online computer service that provides access to databases of legal information, including federal and state caselaw, statutes, and secondary materials.

lex loci (**leks loh**-sɪ). [Latin] **1.** The law of the place; local law. Cf. LEX FORI. **2.** LEX LOCI CONTRACTUS.

lex loci contractus (**leks loh**-sɪ kən-**trak**-təs). [Latin] The law of the place where a contract is executed or to be performed.

lex loci delicti (**leks loh**-sɪ də-**lik**-tɪ). [Latin] The law of the place where the offense was committed. Cf. LOCUS DELICTI.

liability, *n.* **1.** The quality or state of being legally obligated or accountable; legal responsibility to another or to society, enforceable by civil remedy or criminal punishment. **2.** (*often pl.*) A financial or pecuniary obligation; DEBT. Cf. FAULT.

accomplice liability. Criminal responsibility of one who acts with another before, during, or (in some jurisdictions) after a crime. See 18 USCA § 2.

accrued liability. A debt or obligation that is properly chargeable in a given accounting period but that is not yet paid.

alternative liability. Liability arising from the tortious acts of two or more parties — when the plaintiff proves that one of the defendants has caused harm but cannot prove which one caused it — resulting in a shifting of the burden of proof to each defendant. Restatement (Second) of Torts § 433B(3) (1965).

civil liability. **1.** Liability imposed under the civil, as opposed to the criminal, law. **2.** The state of being legally obligated for civil damages.

contingent liability. A liability that will occur only if a specific event happens; a liability that depends on the occurrence of a future and uncertain event.

derivative liability. Liability for a wrong that a person other than the one wronged has a right to redress.

enterprise liability. **1.** Liability imposed on each member of an industry responsible for manufacturing a harmful or defective product, allotted by each manufacturer's market share of the industry. See *market-share liability*. **2.** Criminal liability imposed on a business (such as a corporation or partnership) for certain offenses, such as public-welfare offenses or offenses for which the legislature specifically intended to impose criminal sanctions. See Model Penal Code § 2.07. See *public-welfare offense* under OFFENSE.

joint and several liability. Liability that may be apportioned either among two or more parties or to only one or a few select members of the group, at the adversary's discretion.

joint liability. Liability shared by two or more parties.

limited liability. Liability restricted by law or contract; esp., the liability of a company's owners for nothing more than the capital they have invested in the business.

market-share liability. Liability that is imposed, usu. severally, on each member of an industry, based on each member's share of the market or respective percentage of the product that is placed on the market. See *enterprise liability*.

personal liability. Liability for which one is personally accountable and for which a wronged party can seek satisfaction out of the wrongdoer's personal assets.

primary liability. Liability for which one is directly responsible, as opposed to secondary liability.

products liability. See PRODUCTS LIABILITY.

secondary liability. Liability that does not arise unless the primarily liable party fails to honor its obligation.

several liability. Liability that is separate and distinct from another's liability, so that the plaintiff may bring a separate action against one defendant without joining the other liable parties.

strict liability. Liability that does not depend on actual negligence or intent to harm, but that is based on the breach of an absolute duty to make something safe.

vicarious liability (vɪ-**kair**-ee-əs). Liability that a supervisory party (such as an employer) bears for the actionable conduct of a subordinate or associate (such as an employee) because of the relationship between the two parties. See RESPONDEAT SUPERIOR.

liable (**lɪ**-ə-bəl *also* **lɪ**-bəl), *adj.* **1.** Responsible or answerable in law; legally obligated. **2.** (Of a person) subject to or likely to incur (a fine, penalty, etc.). See LIABILITY.

libel (**lɪ**-bəl), *n.* **1.** A defamatory statement expressed in a fixed medium, esp. writing but also a picture, sign, or electronic broadcast. See DEFAMATION. Cf. SLANDER.

false-implication libel. Libel of a public figure in a news article that creates a false implication or impression even though each statement in the article, taken separately, is true. See FALSE LIGHT; INVASION OF PRIVACY.

group libel. Libel that defames a class of persons, esp. because of their race, sex, national origin, religious belief, or the like. Cf. *hate speech* under SPEECH.

libel per quod (pər **kwod**). **1.** Libel that is actionable only on allegation and proof of special damages. **2.** Libel in which the defamatory meaning is not apparent from the statement on its face but rather must be proved from extrinsic circumstances. See INNUENDO (2).

libel per se (pər **say**). **1.** Libel that is actionable in itself, requiring no proof of special damages. **2.** Libel that is defamatory on its face, such as the statement "Frank is a thief."

2. The act of making such a statement. — **libel,** *vb.*

liberal, *adj.* **1.** (Of a condition, state, opinion, etc.) not restricted; expansive; tolerant. **2.** (Of a person or entity) opposed to conservatism; advocating expansive freedoms and individual expression. **3.** (Of an act, etc.) generous. **4.** (Of an interpretation, construction, etc.) not strict or literal; loose.

liberal construction. See CONSTRUCTION.

liberal interpretation. See INTERPRETATION.

liberty. 1. Freedom from arbitrary or undue external restraint, esp. by a government. **2.** A right, privilege, or immunity enjoyed by prescription or by grant; the absence of a legal duty imposed on a person.

natural liberty. The power to act as one wishes, without any restraint or control, unless by nature.

personal liberty. One's freedom to do as one pleases, limited only by the government's right to regulate the public health, safety, and welfare.

political liberty. A person's freedom to participate in the operation of government, esp. in the making and administration of laws.

religious liberty. Freedom — as guaranteed by the First Amendment — to express, without external control other than one's own conscience, any or no system of religious opinion and to engage in or refrain from any form of religious observance or public or private religious worship, as long as it is consistent with the peace and order of society.

Liberty Clause. The Due Process Clause in the 14th Amendment to the U.S. Constitution. See DUE PROCESS CLAUSE.

liberty interest. An interest protected by the due-process clauses of state and federal constitutions. See FUNDAMENTAL RIGHT (2).

license, *n.* **1.** A revocable permission to commit some act that would otherwise be unlawful; esp., an agreement (not amounting to a lease or profit à prendre) that it will be lawful for the licensee to enter the licensor's land to do some act that would otherwise be illegal, such as hunting game. See SERVITUDE. **2.** The certificate or document evidencing such permission. — **license,** *vb.*

bare license. A license in which no property interest passes to the licensee, who is merely not a trespasser.

exclusive license. A license that gives the licensee the exclusive right to perform the licensed act and that prohibits the licensor from granting the right to anyone else; esp., such a license of a copyright, patent, or trademark right.

license coupled with an interest. An irrevocable license conveyed with an interest in land or a chattel interest.

shrink-wrap license. A license printed on the outside of a software package to advise the buyer that by opening the package, the buyer becomes legally bound to abide by the terms of the license. • Shrink-wrap licenses usu. seek to (1) prohibit users from making unauthorized copies of the software, (2) prohibit modifications to the software, (3) limit use of the software to one computer, (4) limit the manufacturer's liability, and (5) disclaim warranties. — Also written *shrinkwrap license*. — Also termed *box-top license*; *tear-me-open license*. See POINT-AND-CLICK AGREEMENT.

licensee. 1. One to whom a license is granted. **2.** One who has permission to enter or use another's premises, but only for one's own purposes and not for the occupier's benefit. Cf. INVITEE; TRESPASSER.

bare licensee. A licensee whose presence on the premises the occupier tolerates but does not necessarily approve, such as one who takes a shortcut across another's land.

licensee by invitation. One who is expressly or impliedly permitted to enter another's premises to transact business with the owner or occupant or to perform an act benefiting the owner or occupant.

licensee by permission. One who has the owner's permission or passive consent to enter the owner's premises for one's own convenience, curiosity, or entertainment.

licentiate (lɪ-**sen**-shee-ət), *n.* One who has obtained a license or authoritative permission to exercise some function, esp. to practice a profession.

licentious (lɪ-**sen**-shəs), *adj.* Lacking or ignoring moral or legal restraint, esp. in sexual activity; lewd; lascivious. — **licentiousness,** *n.*

licit (**lis**-it), *adj.* Not forbidden by law; permitted; legal. — **licitly,** *adv.*

licitation (lis-ə-**tay**-shən). The offering for sale or bidding for purchase at an auction; esp., in civil law, an auction held to partition property held in common.

lie, *vb.* **1.** To tell an untruth; to speak or write falsely <she lied on the witness stand>. See PERJURY. Cf. FABRICATE. **2.** To have foundation in the law; to be legally supportable, sustainable, or proper <in such a situation, an action lies in tort>. **3.** To exist; to reside <final appeal lies with the Supreme Court>.

lien (leen *or* **lee**-ən), *n.* A legal right or interest that a creditor has in another's property, lasting usu. until a debt or duty that it secures is satisfied. — **lien,** *vb.* — **lienable,** *adj.* — **liened,** *adj.* Cf. PLEDGE (1).

lienholder. A person having or owning a lien.

lien of a covenant. The beginning portion of a covenant, stating the names of the parties and the character of the covenant.

lien theory. The idea that a mortgage resembles a lien, so that the mortgagee acquires only a lien on the property and the mortgagor retains both legal and equitable title unless a valid foreclosure occurs. Cf. TITLE THEORY.

life beneficiary. One who receives payments or other benefits from a trust for life.

life-care contract. An agreement in which one party is assured of care and maintenance for life in exchange for transferring property to the other party.

life estate. See ESTATE.

life estate pur autre vie. See ESTATE.

life in being. Under the rule against perpetuities, anyone alive when a future interest is created, whether or not the person has an interest in the estate. Cf. MEASURING LIFE.

life interest. An interest in real or personal property measured by the duration of the holder's or another named person's life. See *life estate* under ESTATE.

life of a writ. The effective period during which a writ may be levied. • That period usually ends on the day that the law or the writ itself provides that it must be returned to court.

life sentence. See SENTENCE.

life-sustaining procedure. A medical procedure that uses mechanical or artificial means to sustain, restore, or substitute for a vital function and that serves only or mainly to postpone death.

life tenant. A person who, until death, is beneficially entitled to land; the holder of a life estate. See *life estate* under ESTATE.

> ***equitable life tenant.*** A life tenant not automatically entitled to possession but who makes an election allowed by law to a person of that status — such as a spouse — and to whom a court will normally grant possession if security or an undertaking is given.

> ***legal life tenant.*** A life tenant who is automatically entitled to possession by virtue of a legal estate.

lift, *vb.* **1.** To stop or put an end to; to revoke or rescind <lift the stay>. **2.** To discharge or pay off (a debt or obligation) <lift a mortgage>. **3.** *Slang.* To steal <lift a purse>.

light-and-air easement. See EASEMENT.

light most favorable. The standard of scrutinizing or interpreting a verdict by accepting as true all evidence and inferences that support it and disregarding all contrary evidence and inferences.

like, *adj.* **1.** Equal in quantity, quality, or degree; corresponding exactly <like copies>. **2.** Similar or substantially similar <like character>.

like-kind exchange. An exchange of trade, business, or investment property (except inventory or securities) for property of the same kind, class, or character. IRC (26 USCA) § 1031.

like-kind property. *Tax.* Property that is of such a similar kind, class, or character to other property that a gain from an exchange of the property is not recognized for federal income-tax purposes. See LIKE-KIND EXCHANGE.

limine out (**lim**-ə-nee), *vb.* (Of a court) to exclude (evidence) by granting a motion in limine.

limit, *n.* **1.** A restriction or restraint. **2.** A boundary or defining line. **3.** The extent of power, right, or authority. — **limit,** *vb.* — **limited,** *adj.*

limitation. **1.** The act of limiting; the state of being limited. **2.** A restriction. **3.** A statutory period after which a lawsuit or prosecution cannot be brought in court. See STATUTE OF LIMITATIONS. Cf. LACHES. **4.** *Property.* The restriction of the extent of an estate; the creation by deed or devise of a lesser estate out of a fee simple. See WORDS OF LIMITATION.

conditional limitation. **1.** See *executory limitation.* **2.** A lease provision that automatically terminates the lease if a specified event occurs, such as if the lessee defaults.

executory limitation. A restriction that causes an estate to automatically end and revest in a third party upon the happening of a specified event. See *fee simple subject to an executory limitation* under FEE SIMPLE.

limitation over. An additional estate created or contemplated in a conveyance, to be enjoyed after the first estate expires or is exhausted. • An example of language giving rise to a limitation over is "to A for life, remainder to B."

special limitation. A restriction that causes an estate to end automatically and revert to the grantor upon the happening of a specified event. See *fee simple determinable* under FEE SIMPLE.

limitation-of-damages clause. A contractual provision by which the parties agree on a maximum amount of damages recoverable for a future breach of the agreement.

limitation-of-liability act. A federal or state law that limits the type of damages that may be recovered, the liability of particular persons or groups, or the time during which an action may be brought. See FEDERAL TORT CLAIMS ACT; *sovereign immunity* under IMMUNITY (1).

limitation-of-remedies clause. A contractual provision that restricts the remedies available to the parties if a party defaults. • Under the UCC, such a clause is valid unless it fails of its essential purpose or it unconscionably limits consequential damages. UCC § 2–719. Cf. LIQUIDATED-DAMAGES CLAUSE; PENALTY CLAUSE.

limited administration. See ADMINISTRATION.

limited admissibility. See ADMISSIBILITY.

limited appeal. See APPEAL.

limited company. See COMPANY.

limited divorce. See DIVORCE.

limited executor. See EXECUTOR.

limited guaranty. See GUARANTY.

limited jurisdiction. See JURISDICTION.

limited liability. See LIABILITY.

limited-liability company. See COMPANY.

limited-liability partnership. See PARTNERSHIP.

limited owner. See OWNER.

limited partner. See PARTNER.

limited partnership. See PARTNERSHIP.

limited policy. See INSURANCE POLICY.

limited power of appointment. See POWER OF APPOINTMENT.

limited-purpose public figure. See PUBLIC FIGURE.

limited warranty. See WARRANTY (2).

line, *n.* **1.** A demarcation, border, or limit. **2.** A person's occupation or business. **3.** In manufacturing, a series of closely related products. **4.** The ancestry of a person; lineage.

collateral line. A line of descent connecting persons who are not directly related to each other as ascendants or descendants, but whose relationship consists in common descent from the same ancestor.

direct line. A line of descent traced through only those persons who are related to each other directly as ascendants or descendants.

maternal line. A person's ancestry or relationship with another traced through the mother.

paternal line. A person's ancestry or relationship with another traced through the father.

lineage (**lin**-ee-əj). Ancestry and progeny; family, ascending or descending.

lineal (**lin**-ee-əl), *adj.* Derived from or relating to common ancestors, esp. in a direct line; hereditary. Cf. COLLATERAL (2).

lineal, *n.* A lineal descendant; a direct blood relative.

lineal consanguinity. See CONSANGUINITY.

lineal heir. See HEIR.

line-item veto. See VETO.

line of credit. The maximum amount of borrowing power extended to a borrower by a given lender, to be drawn upon by the borrower as needed.

lineup. A police identification procedure in which a criminal suspect and other physically similar persons are shown to the victim or a witness to determine whether the suspect can be identified as the perpetrator of the crime. Cf. SHOWUP.

link-in-chain principle. *Criminal procedure.* The principle that a criminal defendant's Fifth Amendment right against self-incrimination protects the defendant not only from answering directly incriminating questions but also from giving answers that might connect the defendant to criminal activity in the chain of evidence.

liquid, *adj.* **1.** (Of an asset) capable of being readily converted into cash. **2.** (Of a person or entity) possessing assets that can be readily converted into cash.

liquidate, *vb.* **1.** To determine by litigation or agreement the amount of (damages or indebtedness). **2.** To settle (an obligation) by payment or other adjustment. **3.** To ascertain the liabilities and distribute the assets of (an entity), esp. in bankruptcy or dissolution. **4.** To convert (a nonliquid asset) into cash. **5.** *Slang.* To get rid of (a person), esp. by killing.

liquidated, *adj.* **1.** (Of an amount or debt) settled or determined, esp. by agreement. **2.** (Of an asset or assets) converted into cash.

liquidated amount. A figure readily computed, based on an agreement's terms.

liquidated damages. See DAMAGES.

liquidated-damages clause. A contractual provision that determines in advance the measure of damages if a party breaches the agreement. • Traditionally, courts have upheld such a clause unless the agreed-on sum is deemed a penalty for one of the following reasons: (1) the sum grossly exceeds the probable damages on breach, (2) the same sum is made payable for any variety of different breaches (some major, some minor), or (3) a mere delay in payment has been listed among the events of default. Cf. LIMITATION-OF-REMEDIES CLAUSE; PENALTY CLAUSE.

liquidating partner. See PARTNER.

liquidation, *n.* **1.** The act of determining by agreement or by litigation the exact amount of something (as a debt or damages) that before was uncertain. **2.** The act of settling a debt by payment or other satisfaction. **3.** The act or process of converting assets into cash, esp. to settle debts.

liquidator. A person appointed to wind up a business's affairs, esp. by selling off its assets. See LIQUIDATION (3). Cf. RECEIVER.

lis (lis). [Latin] A piece of litigation; a controversy or dispute.

lis pendens (lis **pen**-dənz). [Latin "a pending lawsuit"] **1.** A pending lawsuit. **2.** The jurisdiction, power, or control acquired by a court over property while a legal action is pending. **3.** A notice, recorded in the chain of title to real property, required or permitted in some jurisdictions to warn all persons that certain property is the subject matter of litigation, and that any interests acquired during the pendency of the suit are subject to its outcome. Cf. PENDENTE LITE.

list, *n.* **1.** A roll or register, as of names. **2.** A docket of cases ready for hearing or trial. See CALENDAR (2); DOCKET.

list, *vb.* **1.** To set down or enter (information) in a list. **2.** To register (a security) on an exchange so that it may be publicly traded. **3.** To place (property) for sale under an agreement with a real-estate agent or broker.

listing. 1. *Real estate.* An agreement between a property owner and an agent, whereby the agent agrees to try to secure a buyer or tenant for a specific property at a certain price and terms in return for a fee or commission. **2.** *Securities.* The contract between a firm and a stock exchange by which the trading of the firm's securities on the exchange is handled. **3.** *Tax.* The creation of a schedule or inventory of a person's taxable property; the list of a person's taxable property.

listing agent. The real-estate broker's representative who obtains a listing agreement with the owner. Cf. SELLING AGENT.

list of creditors. A schedule giving the names and addresses of creditors, along with amounts owed them.

literal, *adj.* According to expressed language. • Literal performance of a condition requires exact compliance with its terms.

literary property. 1. The physical property in which an intellectual production is embodied, such as a book, screenplay, or lecture. **2.** An owner's exclusive right to possess, use, and dispose of such a production. See COPYRIGHT; INTELLECTUAL PROPERTY.

literary work. A work, other than an audiovisual work, that is expressed in words, numbers, or other symbols, regardless of the medium that embodies it. 17 USCA § 101.

litigable (lit-ə-gə-bəl), *adj.* Able to be contested or disputed in court. — **litigability,** *n.*

litigant. A party to a lawsuit.

litigation, *n.* **1.** The process of carrying on a lawsuit. **2.** A lawsuit itself. — **litigate,** *vb.* — **litigatory,** *adj.* — **litigational,** *adj.*

litigation privilege. See PRIVILEGE (1).

litigator. 1. A trial lawyer. **2.** A lawyer who prepares cases for trial, as by conducting discovery and pretrial motions, trying cases, and handling appeals.

litigious (li-**tij**-əs), *adj.* **1.** Fond of legal disputes; contentious <our litigious society>. **2.** *Archaic.* Of or relating to the subject of a lawsuit <the litigious property>. **3.** *Archaic.* Of or relating to lawsuits; litigatory <they couldn't settle the litigious dispute>. — **litigiousness,** *n.* — **litigiosity** (li-tij-ee-**os**-ə-tee), *n.*

littoral (lit-ər-əl), *adj.* Of or relating to the coast or shore of an ocean, sea, or lake. Cf. RIPARIAN.

livery (liv-ə-ree *or* **liv**-ree). The delivery of the possession of real property. Cf. DELIVERY.

living separate and apart. (Of spouses) residing in different places and having no intention of resuming marital relations.

living will. An instrument, signed with the formalities statutorily required for a will, by which a person directs that his or her life not be artificially prolonged by extraordinary measures when there is no reasonable expectation of recovery from extreme physical or mental disability. • Most states have living-will legislation. Cf. ADVANCE DIRECTIVE.

L.J. *abbr.* Law Journal.

LL.B. *abbr.* Bachelor of Laws. • This was formerly the law degree ordinarily conferred by American law schools. It is still the normal degree in British law schools. Cf. JURIS DOCTOR.

L.L.C. *abbr.* See *limited liability company* under COMPANY.

LL.D. *abbr.* Doctor of Laws — commonly an honorary law degree.

LL.M. *abbr.* MASTER OF LAWS.

Lloyd's insurance. See INSURANCE.

Lloyd's of London. 1. A London insurance mart where individual underwriters gather to quote rates and write insurance on a wide variety of risks. **2.** A voluntary association of merchants, shipowners, underwriters, and brokers formed not to write policies but instead to issue a notice of an endeavor to members who may individually underwrite a policy by assuming shares of the total risk of insuring a client.

Lloyd's underwriters. An unincorporated association of underwriters who, under a common name, engage in the insurance business through an attorney-in-fact having authority to obligate the underwriters severally, within specified limits, on insurance contracts that the attorney makes or issues in the common name.

L.L.P. *abbr.* See *limited-liability partnership* under PARTNERSHIP.

loan, *n.* **1.** An act of lending; a grant of something for temporary use. **2.** A thing lent for the borrower's temporary use; esp., a sum of money lent at interest. — **loan,** *vb.*

accommodation loan. A loan for which the lender receives no consideration in return. See ACCOMMODATION.

add-on loan. A loan in which the interest is calculated at the stated rate for the loan agreement's full term for the full principal amount, and then the interest is added to the principal before installment payments are calculated, resulting in an interest amount higher than if it were calculated on the monthly unpaid balance. See *add-on interest* under INTEREST (3).

amortized loan. A loan calling for periodic payments that are applied first to interest and then to principal, as provided by the terms of the note. See AMORTIZATION (1).

bridge loan. A short-term loan that is used to cover costs until more permanent financing is arranged.

call loan. A loan for which the lender can demand payment at any time, usu. with 24 hours' notice, because there is no fixed maturity date. Cf. *term loan.*

commercial loan. A loan that a financial institution gives to a business, generally for 30 to 90 days.

consolidation loan. A loan whose proceeds are used to pay off other individual loans, thereby creating a more manageable debt.

consumer loan. A loan that is given to an individual for family, household, personal, or agricultural purposes and that is generally governed by truth-in-lending statutes and regulations.

home equity loan. A line of bank credit given to a homeowner, using as collateral the homeowner's equity in the home. See EQUITY (7).

installment loan. A loan that is to be repaid in usu. equal portions over a specified period.

interest-free loan. Money loaned to a borrower at no charge or, under the Internal Revenue Code, with a charge that is lower than the market rate. IRC (26 USCA) § 7872.

mortgage loan. A loan secured by a mortgage or deed of trust on real property.

nonperforming loan. An outstanding loan that is not being repaid.

nonrecourse loan. A secured loan that allows the lender to attach only the collateral, not the borrower's personal assets, if the loan is not repaid.

participation loan. A loan issued by two or more lenders. See LOAN PARTICIPATION.

recourse loan. A loan that allows the lender, if the borrower defaults, not only to attach the collateral but also to seek judgment against the borrower's (or guarantor's) personal assets.

revolver loan. A single loan that a debtor takes out in lieu of several lines of credit or other loans from various creditors, and that is subject to review and approval at certain intervals.

revolving loan. A loan that is renewed at maturity.

secured loan. A loan that is secured by property or securities.

short-term loan. A loan with a due date of less than one year, usu. evidenced by a note.

signature loan. An unsecured loan based solely on the borrower's promise or signature.

term loan. A loan with a specified due date, usu. of more than one year.

loan-amortization schedule. A schedule that divides each loan payment into an interest component and a principal component. See AMORTIZATION (3).

loan commitment. A lender's binding promise to a borrower to lend a specified amount of money at a certain interest rate, usu. within a specified period and for a specified purpose (such as buying real estate). See MORTGAGE COMMITMENT.

loan for consumption. An agreement by which a lender delivers goods to a borrower who consumes them and who is obligated to return goods of the same quantity, type, and quality.

loan for exchange. A contract by which a lender delivers personal property to a borrower who agrees to return similar property, usu. without compensation for its use.

loan for use. An agreement by which a lender delivers an asset to a borrower who must use it according to its normal function or according to the agreement, and who must return the asset when finished using it.

loan participation. The coming together of multiple lenders to issue a large loan (called a *participation loan*) to one borrower, thereby reducing each lender's individual risk.

loan-receipt agreement. *Torts.* A settlement agreement by which the defendant lends money to the plaintiff interest-free, the plaintiff not being obligated to repay the loan unless he or she recovers money from other tortfeasors responsible for the same injury.

loansharking, *n.* The practice of lending money at excessive and esp. usurious rates, and often threatening or using extortion to enforce repayment. — **loan-shark,** *vb.* — **loan shark,** *n.*

lobby, *vb.* **1.** To talk with a legislator, sometimes in a luxurious setting, in an attempt to influence the legislator's vote. **2.** To support or oppose (a measure) by working to influence a legislator's vote. **3.** To try to influence (a decision-maker). — **lobbying,** *n.* — **lobbyist,** *n.*

lobbying act. A federal or state law governing the conduct of lobbyists, usu. by requiring them to register and file reports. • An example is the Federal Regulation of Lobbying Act, 12 USCA § 261.

local and special legislation. See LEGISLATION.

local chattel. Personal property that is affixed to land; FIXTURE.

local concern. An activity conducted by a municipality in its proprietary capacity.

local improvement. See IMPROVEMENT.

locality of a lawsuit. The place where a court may exercise judicial authority.

local rule. **1.** A rule based on the physical conditions of a state and the character, customs, and beliefs of its people. **2.** A rule by which an individual court supplements the procedural rules applying generally to all courts within the jurisdiction. See Fed. R. Civ. P. 83.

local usage. A practice or method regularly observed in a particular place, sometimes considered by a court in interpreting a document. UCC § 1–205(2), (3). See CUSTOM AND USAGE.

location. **1.** The specific place or position of a person or thing. **2.** The act or process of locating. **3.** *Real estate.* The designation of the boundaries of a particular piece of land, either on the record or on the land itself.

locative calls (**lok**-ə-tiv). *Property.* In land descriptions, specific descriptions that fix the boundaries of the land. See CALL (4); DIRECTORY CALLS.

Lochnerize (**lok**-nər-IZ), *vb.* To examine and strike down economic legislation under the guise of enforcing the Due Process Clause, esp. in the manner of the U.S. Supreme Court during the early 20th century. • The term takes its name from the decision in *Lochner v. New York*, 198 U.S. 45, 25 S.Ct. 539 (1905), in which the Court invalidated New York's maximum-hours law for bakers. — **Lochnerization,** *n.*

lockdown. The temporary confinement of prisoners in their cells during a state of heightened alert caused by an escape, riot, or other emergency.

lockout. **1.** An employer's withholding of work and closing of a business because of a labor dispute. **2.** Loosely, an employee's refusal to work because the employer unreasonably refuses to abide by an expired employment contract while a new one is being negotiated.

lock rate. See INTEREST RATE.

locus (**loh**-kəs). [Latin "place"] The place or position where something is done or exists. — Abbr. L. See SITUS.

locus delicti (**loh**-kəs də-**lik**-tI). [Latin "place of the wrong"] The place where an offense is committed; the place where the last event necessary to making the actor liable occurs. Cf. LEX LOCI DELICTI.

locus in quo (**loh**-kəs in **kwoh**). [Latin "place in which"] The place where something is alleged to have occurred.

locus standi (**loh**-kəs **stan**-dI *or* -dee). [Latin "place of standing"] The right to bring an action or to be heard in a given forum; STANDING.

lodestar. **1.** A guiding star; an inspiration or model. **2.** A reasonable amount of attorney's fees in a given case, usu. calculated by multiplying a reasonable number of hours worked by the prevailing hourly rate in the community for similar work, and often considering such additional factors as the degree of skill and difficulty involved in the case, the degree of its urgency, its novelty, and the like.

logical-cause doctrine. The principle that, if the plaintiff proves that an injury occurred and proves a logical cause of it, a party desiring to defeat the claim cannot succeed merely by showing that there is another imaginable cause, but must also show that the alternative cause is more probable than the cause shown by the plaintiff.

logical interpretation. See INTERPRETATION.

logical positivism. A philosophical system or movement requiring that meaningful statements be in principle verifiable. Cf. LEGAL POSITIVISM.

logical-relationship standard. *Civil procedure*. A test applied to determine whether a defendant's counterclaim is compulsory, by examining whether both claims are based on the same operative facts or whether those facts activate additional rights, otherwise dormant, for the defendant. • One of the most important factors considered is whether hearing the claims together would promote judicial economy and efficiency. Fed. R. Civ. P. 13(a).

loitering, *n.* The criminal offense of remaining in a certain place (such as a public street) for no apparent reason. — **loiter,** *vb.* Cf. VAGRANCY.

lollipop syndrome. *Family law*. A situation in which one or both parents, often in a custody battle, manipulate the child with gifts, fun, good times, and minimal discipline in an attempt to win over the child.

long-arm, *adj.* Relating to or arising from a long-arm statute.

long-arm statute. A statute providing for jurisdiction over a nonresident defendant who has had contacts with the territory where the statute is in effect.

long title. See TITLE (3).

look-through principle. A doctrine for allocating transfer-gains taxes on real estate by looking beyond the entity possessing legal title to identify the beneficial owners of the property.

loophole. An ambiguity, omission, or exception (as in a law or other legal document) that provides a way to avoid a rule without violating its literal requirements; esp., a tax-code provision that allows a taxpayer to legally avoid or reduce income taxes.

loopification, *n.* In critical legal studies, the collapse of a legal distinction resulting when the two ends of a continuum become so similar that they become indistinguishable. — **loopify,** *vb.*

looseleaf service. A type of lawbook having pages that are periodically replaced with updated pages, designed to cope with constant change and increasing bulk.

loss. 1. The failure to keep possession of something. **2.** A decrease in value; the amount by which a thing's original cost exceeds its later selling price. **3.** The amount of financial detriment caused by an insured person's death or an insured property's damage, for which the insurer becomes liable. **4.** *Tax*. The excess of a property's adjusted value over the amount realized from its sale or other disposition. IRC (26 USCA) § 1001.

actual loss. A loss resulting from the real and substantial destruction of insured property.

capital loss. The loss realized upon selling or exchanging a capital asset. Cf. *capital gain* under GAIN (3).

casualty loss. For tax purposes, the total or partial destruction of an asset resulting from an unexpected or unusual event, such as an automobile accident or a tornado.

consequential loss. A loss arising from the results of damage rather than from the damage itself. • A consequential loss is proximate when the natural and probable effect of the wrongful conduct, under the circumstances, is to set in operation the intervening cause from which the loss directly results. When the loss is not the natural and probable effect of the wrongful conduct, the loss is remote. Cf. *direct loss*.

constructive total loss. Such serious damage to the insured property that the cost of repairs would exceed the value of the thing repaired. See *total loss*.

direct loss. A loss that results immediately and proximately from an event. Cf. *consequential loss*.

extraordinary loss. A loss that is both unusual and infrequent, such as a loss resulting from a natural disaster.

net operating loss. The excess of operating expenses over revenues, the amount of which can be deducted from gross income if other deductions do not exceed gross income.

ordinary loss. *Tax.* A loss incurred from the sale or exchange of an item that is used in a trade or business.

out-of-pocket loss. The difference between the value of what the buyer paid and the market value of what was received in return.

paper loss. A loss that is realized only by selling something (such as a security) that has decreased in market value.

total loss. The complete destruction of insured property so that nothing of value remains and the subject matter no longer exists in its original form. • Generally, a loss is total if, after the damage occurs, no substantial remnant remains standing that a reasonably prudent uninsured owner, desiring to rebuild, would use as a basis to restore the property to its original condition. Cf. *constructive total loss*.

loss leader. A good or commodity sold at a very low price, usu. below cost, to attract customers to buy other items. See BAIT AND SWITCH.

loss-of-bargain rule. The doctrine that damages for a breach of a contract should put the injured party in the position it would have been in if both parties had performed their contractual duties.

loss-of-chance doctrine. A rule in some states providing a claim against a doctor who has engaged in medical malpractice that, although it does not result in a particular injury, decreases or eliminates the chance of surviving or recovering from the preexisting condition for which the doctor was consulted.

loss of consortium (kən-sor-shee-əm). **1.** A loss of the benefits that one spouse is entitled to receive from the other, including companionship, cooperation, aid, affection, and sexual relations. **2.** A similar loss of benefits that one is entitled to receive from a parent or child. See CONSORTIUM.

lost, *adj.* **1.** (Of property) beyond the possession and custody of its owner and not locatable by diligent search. **2.** (Of a person) missing.

lost-chance doctrine. 1. LOSS-OF-CHANCE DOCTRINE. **2.** A rule permitting a claim, in limited circumstances, against someone who fails to come to the aid of a person who is in imminent danger of being injured or killed. Cf. GOOD SAMARITAN DOCTRINE.

lost earning capacity. A person's diminished earning power resulting from an injury.

lost profits. A measure of damages that allows a seller to collect the profit that would have been made on the sale if the buyer had not breached. UCC § 2–708(2).

lost property. See PROPERTY.

lost-volume seller. A seller of goods who, after a buyer has breached a sales contract, resells the goods to a different buyer who would have bought identical goods from the seller's inventory even if the original buyer had not breached. • Such a seller is entitled to lost profits, rather than contract price less market price, as damages from the original buyer's breach. UCC § 2–708(2).

lost will. See WILL.

lot. 1. A tract of land, esp. one having specific boundaries or being used for a given purpose. **2.** An article that is the subject of a separate sale, lease, or delivery, whether or not it is sufficient to perform the contract. UCC §§ 2–105(5), 2A–103(1)(s). **3.** A specified number of shares or a specific quantity of a commodity designated for trading.

lot line. A land boundary that separates one tract from another.

lower chamber. See CHAMBER.

lower-of-cost-or-market method. A means of pricing or costing inventory by which inventory value is set at either acquisition cost or market cost, whichever is lower.

lowest responsible bidder. A bidder who has the lowest price conforming to the contract specifications and who is financially able and competent to complete the work, as shown by the bidder's prior performance.

L.P. See *limited partnership* under PARTNERSHIP.

Ltd. *abbr.* Limited — used in company names to indicate limited liability.

lucid interval. 1. A brief period during which an insane person regains sufficient sanity to have the legal capacity to contract and act on his or her own behalf. **2.** A period during which a person has enough mental capacity to understand the concept of marriage and the duties and obligations it imposes.

lucrative (**loo**-krə-tiv), *adj.* Profitable; remunerative.

lumping. *Criminal procedure.* The imposition of a general sentence on a criminal defendant. See *general sentence* under SENTENCE.

lump-sum payment. See PAYMENT.

luxury tax. See TAX.

lying in wait. *Criminal law.* The series of acts involved in watching, waiting for, and hiding from someone, with the intent of killing or inflicting serious bodily injury on that person.

lynch, *vb.* (Of a mob) to kill (somebody) without legal authority, usu. by hanging.

lynch law. The administration of summary punishment, esp. death, for an alleged crime, without legal authority.

M

mace-proof, *vb.* To exempt from an arrest; to secure against an arrest.

MACRS. *abbr.* MODIFIED ACCELERATED COST RECOVERY SYSTEM.

magisterial (maj-ə-**steer**-ee-əl), *adj.* Of or relating to the character, office, powers, or duties of a magistrate.

magisterial precinct. A county subdivision that defines the territorial jurisdiction of a magistrate, constable, or justice of the peace.

magistracy (**maj**-ə-strə-see). **1.** The office, district, or power of a magistrate. **2.** A body of magistrates.

magistral, *adj.* **1.** Of or relating to a master or masters. **2.** Formulated by a physician. **3.** MAGISTERIAL.

magistrate (**maj**-ə-strayt), *n.* **1.** The highest-ranking official in a government, such as the king in a monarchy, the president in a republic, or the governor in a state. **2.** A local official who possesses whatever power is specified in the appointment or statutory grant of authority. **3.** A judicial officer with strictly limited jurisdiction and authority, often on the local level and often restricted to criminal cases. Cf. JUSTICE OF THE PEACE. — **magisterial** (maj-ə-**stir**-ee-əl), *adj.*

committing magistrate. A judicial officer who conducts preliminary criminal hearings and may order that a defendant be released for lack of evidence, sent to jail to await trial, or released on bail. See *examining court* under COURT.

district-court magistrate. In some states, a quasi-judicial officer given the power to set bail, accept bond, accept guilty pleas, impose sentences for traffic violations and similar offenses, and conduct informal hearings on civil infractions.

investigating magistrate. A quasi-judicial officer responsible for examining and sometimes ruling on certain aspects of a criminal proceeding before it comes before a judge.

police magistrate. A judicial officer who has jurisdiction to try minor criminal offenses, breaches of police regulations, and similar violations.

magistrate's court. See COURT.

Magnuson–Moss Warranty Act (**mag**-nə-sən-**maws** *or* **-mos**). A federal statute requiring that a written warranty of a consumer product fully and conspicuously disclose, in plain language, the terms and conditions of the warranty, including whether the warranty is full or limited, according to standards given in the statute. 15 USCA §§ 2301–2312.

mailbox rule. 1. *Contracts.* The principle that an acceptance becomes effective — and binds the offeror — once it has been properly mailed. •

The mailbox rule does not apply, however, if the offer provides that an acceptance is not effective until received. **2.** The principle that when a pleading or other document is filed or served by mail, filing or service is deemed to have occurred on the date of mailing.

mail cover. A process by which the U.S. Postal Service provides a government agency with information on the face of an envelope or package (such as a postmark) for the agency's use in locating a fugitive, identifying a coconspirator, or obtaining other evidence necessary to solve a crime.

mail fraud. See FRAUD.

mail-order divorce. See DIVORCE.

main pot. *Tax.* A step in evaluating tax liability in which qualified transactions are compared to determine whether a net gain or loss has occurred. IRC (26 USCA) § 1231. Cf. CASUALTY POT.

maintainor. *Criminal law.* A person who meddles in someone else's litigation, by providing money or other assistance; a person who is guilty of maintenance. See MAINTENANCE (6).

maintenance, *n.* **1.** The continuation of something, such as a lawsuit. **2.** The continuing possession of something, such as property. **3.** The assertion of a position or opinion; the act of upholding a position in argument. **4.** The care and work put into property to keep it operating and productive; general repair and upkeep. **5.** Financial support given by one person to another, usu. paid as a result of a legal separation or divorce; esp., ALIMONY. • Maintenance may end after a specified time or upon the death, cohabitation, or remarriage of the receiving party. See MAINTENANCE IN GROSS.

> ***separate maintenance.*** Money paid by one married person to another for support if they are no longer living together as husband and wife.

6. Assistance in prosecuting or defending a lawsuit given to a litigant by someone who has no bona fide interest in the case; meddling in someone else's litigation. — **maintain,** *vb.* Cf. CHAMPERTY.

maintenance in gross. *Family law.* A fixed amount of money to be paid upon divorce by one former spouse to the other, in a lump sum or in installments.

majority. **1.** The status of one who has attained the age of majority (usu. 18). See *age of majority* under AGE. Cf. MINORITY (1). **2.** A number that is more than half of a total; a group of more than 50 percent. Cf. PLURALITY; MINORITY (2).

majority opinion. See OPINION (1).

majority rule. **1.** A political principle that a majority of a group has the power to make decisions that bind the group. **2.** *Corporations.* The common-law principle that a director or officer owes no fiduciary duty to a shareholder with respect to a stock transaction.

majority voting. See VOTING.

major life activity. Any activity that an average person in the general population can perform with little or no difficulty, such as seeing, hearing, sleeping, eating, walking, traveling, and working. • A person who is substantially limited in a major life activity is protected from discrimination under a variety of disability laws, most significantly the Americans with Disabilities Act and the Rehabilitation Act. 42 USCA § 12102(2); 29 USCA § 705(9)(B). See AMERICANS WITH DISABILITIES ACT.

make, *vb.* **1.** To cause (something) to exist <to make a record>. **2.** To enact (something) <to make law>. **3.** To acquire (something) <to make money on execution>. **4.** To legally perform, as by executing, signing, or delivering (a document) <to make a contract>.

maker. 1. One who frames, promulgates, or ordains (as in *lawmaker*). **2.** A person who signs a promissory note. See NOTE. Cf. COMAKER. **3.** DRAWER.

> ***accommodation maker.*** One who signs a note as a surety. See ACCOMMODATION (2); *accommodation indorser* under INDORSER.
>
> ***prime maker.*** The person who is primarily liable on a note or other negotiable instrument.

mala fides (**mal**-ə **fī**-deez), *n.* See BAD FAITH.

malapportionment, *n.* The improper or unconstitutional apportionment of a legislative district. — **malapportion,** *vb.* See APPORTIONMENT; GERRYMANDERING.

malfeasance (mal-**fee**-zənts), *n.* A wrongful or unlawful act; esp., wrongdoing or misconduct by a public official; MISFEASANCE IN PUBLIC OFFICE. — **malfeasant** (mal-**fee**-zənt), *adj.* — **malfeasor** (mal-**fee**-zər), *n.* Cf. MISFEASANCE; NONFEASANCE.

malfunction theory. *Products-liability law.* A principle permitting a products-liability plaintiff to prove that a product was defective by proving that the product malfunctioned, instead of requiring the plaintiff to prove a specific defect.

malice, *n.* **1.** The intent, without justification or excuse, to commit a wrongful act. **2.** Reckless disregard of the law or of a person's legal rights. **3.** Ill will; wickedness of heart. — **malicious,** *adj.*

> ***actual malice.*** **1.** The deliberate intent to commit an injury, as evidenced by external circumstances. Cf. *implied malice.* **2.** *Defamation.* Knowledge (by the person who utters or publishes a defamatory statement) that a statement is false, or reckless disregard about whether the statement is true.
>
> ***express malice.*** **1.** *Criminal law.* The intent to kill or seriously injure arising from a deliberate, rational mind. **2.** See *actual malice* (1). **3.** *Defamation.* The bad-faith publication of defamatory material.
>
> ***general malice.*** Malice that is necessary for any criminal conduct; malice that is not directed at a specific person. Cf. *particular malice.*
>
> ***implied malice.*** Malice inferred from a person's conduct. Cf. *actual malice* (1).
>
> ***particular malice.*** Malice that is directed at a particular person.
>
> ***transferred malice.*** Malice directed to one person or object but instead

harming another in the way intended for the first.

universal malice. The state of mind of a person who determines to take a life on slight provocation, without knowing or caring who may be the victim.

malice aforethought. The requisite mental state for common-law murder, encompassing any one of the following: (1) the intent to kill, (2) the intent to inflict grievous bodily harm, (3) extremely reckless indifference to the value of human life (the so-called "abandoned and malignant heart"), or (4) the intent to commit a dangerous felony (which leads to culpability under the felony-murder rule).

malice exception. A limitation on a public official's qualified immunity, by which the official can face civil liability for willfully exercising discretion in a way that violates a known or well-established right. See *qualified immunity* under IMMUNITY (1).

malicious, *adj.* **1.** Substantially certain to cause injury. **2.** Without just cause or excuse.

malicious act. An intentional, wrongful act performed against another without legal justification or excuse.

malicious arrest. See ARREST.

malicious injury. See INJURY.

malicious killing. An intentional killing without legal justification or excuse.

malicious mischief. The common-law misdemeanor of intentionally destroying or damaging another's property. See Model Penal Code § 220.3.

malicious motive. See MOTIVE.

malicious prosecution. 1. The institution of a criminal or civil proceeding for an improper purpose and without probable cause. **2.** The cause of action resulting from the institution of such a proceeding. Cf. ABUSE OF PROCESS; VEXATIOUS SUIT.

malpractice (mal-**prak**-tis). An instance of negligence or incompetence on the part of a professional. • To succeed in a malpractice claim, a plaintiff must also prove proximate cause and damages.

malpractice insurance. See INSURANCE.

maltreatment. Bad treatment (esp. improper treatment by a surgeon) resulting from ignorance, neglect, or willfulness. See MALPRACTICE.

malum in se (**mal**-əm in **say** *or* **see**), *n.* [Latin "evil in itself"] A crime or an act that is inherently immoral, such as murder, arson, or rape. Pl. ***mala in se***. — ***malum in se***, *adj.* Cf. MALUM PROHIBITUM.

malum prohibitum (**mal**-əm proh-**hib**-i-təm), *n.* [Latin "prohibited evil"] An act that is a crime merely because it is prohibited by statute, although the act itself is not necessarily immoral. Pl. ***mala prohibita***. — ***malum prohibitum***, *adj.* Cf. MALUM IN SE.

managing agent. See AGENT.

managing conservator. See CONSERVATOR.

mandamus (man-**day**-məs), *n.* [Latin "we command"] A writ issued by a superior court to compel a lower court or a government officer to perform mandatory or purely ministerial duties correctly. Pl. **mandamuses.** — **mandamus,** *vb.*

mandate, *n.* **1.** An order from an appellate court directing a lower court to take a specified action. **2.** A judicial command directed to an officer of the court to enforce a court order. **3.** In politics, the electorate's overwhelming show of approval for a given political platform. — **mandate,** *vb.* — **mandatory,** *adj.*

mandate rule. The doctrine that, after an appellate court has remanded a case to a lower court, the lower court must follow the decision that the appellate court has made in the case, unless new evidence or an intervening change in the law dictates a different result.

mandatory commitment. See COMMITMENT.

mandatory injunction. See INJUNCTION.

mandatory instruction. See JURY INSTRUCTION.

mandatory sentence. See SENTENCE.

mandatory statute. See STATUTE.

manifestation of intention. *Wills & estates.* The external expression of the testator's intention, as distinguished from an undisclosed intention.

manifest constitutional error. See ERROR (2).

manifest-disregard doctrine. The principle that an arbitration award will be vacated if the arbitrator knows the applicable law and deliberately chooses to disregard it, but will not be vacated for a mere error or misunderstanding of the law.

manifest error. See ERROR (2).

manifest-error-or-clearly-wrong rule. In some jurisdictions, the doctrine that an appellate court cannot set aside a trial court's finding of fact unless a review of the entire record reveals that the finding has no reasonable basis.

manifest injustice. An error in the trial court that is direct, obvious, and observable, such as a defendant's guilty plea that is involuntary or that is based on a plea agreement that the prosecution rescinds.

manifest intent. See INTENT (1).

manifest necessity. See NECESSITY.

manifest weight of the evidence. A deferential standard of review under which a verdict will be reversed or disregarded only if another outcome is obviously correct and the verdict is clearly unsupported by the evidence. Cf. WEIGHT OF THE EVIDENCE.

Mann Act. A federal law, enacted originally in 1948, that criminalizes the transportation of any person in interstate or foreign commerce for prostitution or similar sexual activities. 18 USCA § 2421.

Mansfield rule. The doctrine that a juror's testimony or affidavit about juror misconduct may not be used to challenge the verdict.

manslaughter, *n.* The unlawful killing of a human being without malice aforethought. — **manslaughter,** *vb.* Cf. MURDER.

involuntary manslaughter. Homicide in which there is no intention to kill or do grievous bodily harm, but that is committed with criminal negligence or during the commission of a crime not included within the felony-murder rule. Cf. ACCIDENTAL KILLING.

misdemeanor manslaughter. Unintentional homicide that occurs during the commission of a misdemeanor (such as a traffic violation).

voluntary manslaughter. An act of murder reduced to manslaughter because of extenuating circumstances such as adequate provocation (arousing the "heat of passion") or diminished capacity.

manufactured diversity. See DIVERSITY.

manufacturing defect. See DEFECT.

manuscript policy. See INSURANCE POLICY.

***Mapp* hearing.** *Criminal procedure*. A hearing held to determine whether evidence implicating the accused was obtained as the result of an illegal search and seizure, and should therefore be suppressed. *Mapp v. Ohio*, 367 U.S. 643, 81 S.Ct. 1684 (1961).

margin, *n.* **1.** A boundary or edge. **2.** A measure or degree of difference. **3.** PROFIT MARGIN. **4.** The difference between a loan's face value and the market value of the collateral that secures the loan. **5.** Cash or collateral required to be paid to a securities broker by an investor to protect the broker against losses from securities bought on credit. **6.** The amount of an investor's equity in securities bought on credit through a broker. — **margin,** *vb.* — **marginal,** *adj.* — **margined,** *adj.*

marginal cost. See COST.

marginal note. A brief notation, in the nature of a subheading, placed in the margin of a printed statute for ease of reference.

marginal tax rate. See TAX RATE.

marital, *adj.* Of or relating to the marriage relationship.

marital agreement. An agreement between spouses concerning the division and ownership of marital property during marriage or upon dissolution by death or divorce; esp., a premarital contract or separation agreement that is primarily concerned with dividing marital property in the event of divorce. See PRENUPTIAL AGREEMENT; POSTNUPTIAL AGREEMENT.

marital deduction. See DEDUCTION.

marital-deduction trust. See TRUST.

marital privilege. See PRIVILEGE (3).

marital property. See PROPERTY.

marital rape. See RAPE.

marital rights. Rights and incidents (such as property or cohabitation rights) arising from the marriage contract.

mariticide. 1. The murder of one's husband. **2.** A woman who murders her husband. Cf. UXORICIDE.

mark, *n.* **1.** A symbol, impression, or feature on something, usu. to identify it or distinguish it from something else. **2.** TRADEMARK (1). **3.** SERVICEMARK.

marked money. Money that bears a telltale mark so that the money can be traced, usu. to a perpetrator of a crime, as when marked money is given to a kidnapper as ransom.

market, *n.* **1.** A place of commercial activity in which goods or services are bought and sold <the farmers' market>. **2.** A geographic area or demographic segment considered as a place of demand for particular goods or services <the foreign market for microchips>. **3.** The opportunity for buying and selling goods or services; the extent of economic demand <a strong job market for accountants>. **4.** A securities or commodities exchange <the stock market closed early because of the blizzard>. **5.** The business of such an exchange; the enterprise of buying and selling securities or commodities <the stock market is approaching an all-time high>. **6.** The price at which the buyer and seller of a security or commodity agree <the market for oil is $16 per barrel>.

marketability. Salability; the probability of selling property, goods, securities, or services at specified times, prices, and terms.

marketable, *adj.* Of commercially acceptable quality; fit for sale and in demand by buyers. — **marketability,** *n.*

marketable title. See TITLE (2).

marketable-title act. A state statute providing that a person can establish good title to land by searching the public records only back to a specified time (such as 40 years ago). See *marketable title* under TITLE (2).

market approach. A method of appraising real property, by surveying the market and comparing the property to similar pieces of property that have been recently sold, and making appropriate adjustments for differences between the properties, including location, size of the property, and the dates of sale. Cf. COST APPROACH; INCOME APPROACH.

marketing defect. See DEFECT.

market-participant doctrine. The principle that, under the Commerce Clause, a state does not discriminate against interstate commerce by acting as a buyer or seller in the market, by operating a proprietary enterprise, or by subsidizing private business. • Under the Dormant Commerce Clause principle, the Commerce Clause — art. I, § 8, cl. 3 of the U.S. Constitution — disallows most state regulation of, or discrimination against, interstate commerce. But if the state is participating in the market instead of regulating it, the Dormant Commerce Clause analysis does not apply, and the state activity will generally stand. See *Dormant Commerce Clause* under COMMERCE CLAUSE.

marketplace of ideas. A forum in which expressions of opinion can freely compete for acceptance without governmental restraint.

market power. The ability to reduce output and raise prices above the competitive level — specif., above marginal cost — for a sustained period, and to make a profit by doing so. See MONOPOLIZATION. Cf. MARKET SHARE.

market share. The percentage of the market for a product that a firm supplies, usu. calculated by dividing the firm's output by the total market output. See MONOPOLIZATION. Cf. MARKET POWER.

market-share liability. See LIABILITY.

marksman. 1. A person who, not being able to write, signs documents with some kind of character or symbol. **2.** A highly skilled shooter.

***Marks* rule.** The doctrine that, when the U.S. Supreme Court issues a fractured, plurality opinion, the opinion of the justices concurring in the judgment on the narrowest grounds — that is, the legal standard with which a majority of the Court would agree — is considered the Court's holding. *Marks v. United States*, 430 U.S. 188, 97 S.Ct. 990 (1977).

mark up, *vb.* **1.** To increase (the price of goods, etc.) **2.** To revise or amend (a legislative bill, a rule, etc.). **3.** To place (a case) on the trial calendar.

markup, *n.* **1.** An amount added to an item's cost to determine its selling price. See PROFIT MARGIN. **2.** A session of a congressional committee during which a bill is revised and put into final form before it is reported to the appropriate house.

marriage, *n.* **1.** The legal union of a man and woman as husband and wife. • The essentials of a valid marriage are (1) parties legally capable of contracting to marry, (2) mutual consent or agreement, and (3) an actual contracting in the form prescribed by law. — Also termed *matrimony*.

common-law marriage. A marriage that takes legal effect, without license or ceremony, when a couple live together as husband and wife, intend to be married, and hold themselves out to others as a married couple.

covenant marriage. A special type of marriage in which the parties agree to more stringent requirements for marriage and divorce than are otherwise imposed by state law for ordinary marriages. • In the late 1990s, several states (beginning with Louisiana) passed laws providing for covenant marriages.

marriage of convenience. **1.** A marriage contracted for social or financial advantages rather than out of mutual love. **2.** Loosely, an ill-considered marriage that, at the time, is convenient to the parties involved.

plural marriage. A marriage in which one spouse is already married to someone else; a bigamous or polygamous union.

sham marriage. A purported marriage in which all the formal requirements are met or seemingly met, but in which the parties go through the ceremony with no intent of living together as husband and wife.

voidable marriage. A marriage that is initially invalid but that remains in effect unless terminated by court order.

void marriage. A marriage that is invalid from its inception, that cannot be made valid, and that can be terminated by either party without obtaining a divorce or annulment.

2. The act or ceremony so uniting them; a wedding. — **marital,** *adj.*

ceremonial marriage. A wedding that follows all the statutory requirements and that has been solemnized before a religious or civil official.

civil marriage. A wedding ceremony conducted by an official, such as a judge, or by some other authorized person — as distinguished from one solemnized by a member of the clergy.

proxy marriage. A wedding in which someone stands in for an absent bride or groom, as when one party is stationed overseas in the military.

marriage article. A premarital stipulation between spouses who intend to incorporate the stipulation in a postnuptial agreement.

marriage ceremony. The religious or civil proceeding that solemnizes a marriage.

marriage certificate. A document that is executed by the religious or civil official presiding at a marriage ceremony and filed with a public authority (usu. the county clerk) as evidence of the marriage.

marriage license. A document, issued by a public authority, that grants a couple permission to marry.

marriage of convenience. See MARRIAGE (1).

marshal, *n.* **1.** A law-enforcement officer with duties similar to those of a sheriff. **2.** A judicial officer who provides court security, executes process, and performs other tasks for the court. — **marshalship,** *n.*

United States Marshal. A federal official who carries out the orders of a federal court.

marshal, *vb.* To arrange or rank in order.

marshaling the evidence. 1. Arranging all of a party's evidence in the order that it will be presented at trial. **2.** The practice of formulating a jury charge so that it arranges the evidence to give more credence to a particular interpretation.

Martindale–Hubbell Law Directory. A series of books, published annually, containing a roster of lawyers and law firms in most cities of the United States, corporate legal departments, government lawyers, foreign lawyers, and lawyer-support providers, as well as a digest of the laws of the states, the District of Columbia, and territories of the United States, and a digest of the laws of many foreign jurisdictions, including Canada and its provinces.

Mary Carter agreement. A contract (usu. a secret one) by which one or more, but not all, codefendants settle with the plaintiff and obtain a release, along with a provision granting them a portion of any recovery from the nonparticipating codefendants. • In a Mary Carter agreement, the participating codefendants agree to remain parties to the lawsuit and, if no recovery is awarded against the nonparticipating codefendants, to pay the plaintiff a settled amount. *Booth v. Mary Carter Paint Co.*, 202 So. 2d 8 (Fla. Dist. Ct. App. 1967). Cf. GALLAGHER AGREEMENT.

masking, *n.* In critical legal studies, the act or an instance of concealing something's true nature. — **mask,** *vb.*

***Massiah* rule.** The principle that an attempt to elicit incriminating statements (usu. not during a formal interrogation) from a suspect whose right to counsel has attached but who has not waived that right violates the Sixth Amendment. *Massiah v. United States*, 377 U.S. 201, 84 S.Ct. 1199 (1964). See DELIBERATE ELICITATION.

mass murder. See MURDER.

mass tort. See TORT.

master, *n.* **1.** One who has personal authority over another's services; EMPLOYER. **2.** A parajudicial officer (such as a referee, an auditor, an examiner, or an assessor) specially appointed to help a court with its proceedings. • A master may take testimony, hear and rule on discovery disputes and other pretrial matters, compute interest, value annuities, investigate encumbrances on land titles, and the like — usually with a written report to the court. Fed. R. Civ. P. 53.

> ***special master.*** A master appointed to assist the court with a particular matter or case.
>
> ***standing master.*** A master appointed to assist the court on an ongoing basis.

master and servant. The relation between two persons, one of whom (the master) has authority over the other (the servant), with the power to direct the time, manner, and place of the services. • This relationship is similar to that of principal and agent, but that terminology applies to employments in which the employee has some discretion, while the servant is almost completely under the control of the master. Also, an agent usually acts for the principal in business relations with third parties, while a servant does not.

master lease. See LEASE.

Master of Laws. A law degree conferred on those completing graduate-level legal study, beyond the J.D. degree. — Abbr. LL.M. Cf. JURIS DOCTOR.

master plan. *Land-use planning.* A municipal plan for housing, industry, and recreation facilities, including their projected environmental impact.

master policy. See INSURANCE POLICY.

master's report. A master's formal report to a court, usu. containing a recommended decision in a case as well as findings of fact and conclusions of law.

matching principle. *Tax.* A method for handling expense deductions, by which the depreciation in a given year is matched by the associated tax benefit.

material, *adj.* **1.** Of or relating to matter; physical. **2.** Having some logical connection with the consequential facts. **3.** Of such a nature that knowledge of the item would affect a person's decision-making process; significant; essential. — **materiality,** *n.* Cf. RELEVANT.

material allegation. See ALLEGATION.

material alteration. See ALTERATION.

material breach. See BREACH OF CONTRACT.

material evidence. See EVIDENCE.

material fact. See FACT.

material misrepresentation. See MISREPRESENTATION.

material representation. See REPRESENTATION.

material terms. Contractual provisions dealing with significant issues such as subject matter, price, payment terms, quantity, quality, duration, or the work to be done.

material witness. See WITNESS.

maternal, *adj.* Of, relating to, or coming from one's mother. Cf. PATERNAL.

maternal line. See LINE.

mathematical evidence. See EVIDENCE.

***Mathews v. Eldridge* test.** *Constitutional law.* The principle for determining whether an administrative procedure provides due-process protection, by analyzing (1) the nature of the private interest that will be affected by the governmental action, (2) the risk of an erroneous deprivation through the procedure used, (3) the probable value of additional or substitute procedural safeguards, (4) the governmental function involved, and (5) the administrative burden and expense that would be created by requiring additional or substitute procedural safeguards. *Mathews v. Eldridge*, 424 U.S. 319, 96 S.Ct. 893 (1976).

matricide (**ma**-trə-sɪd), *n.* **1.** The act of killing one's own mother. **2.** One who kills his or her mother. — **matricidal,** *adj.*

matrimonial res. The marriage state. See RES.

matrimony, *n.* The act or state of being married; MARRIAGE. — **matrimonial,** *adj.*

matter, *n.* **1.** A subject under consideration, esp. involving a dispute or litigation; CASE (1). **2.** Something that is to be tried or proved; an allegation forming the basis of a claim or defense.

matter of fact. A matter involving a judicial inquiry into the truth of alleged facts.

matter of form. A matter concerned only with formalities or noncritical characteristics <the objection that the motion was incorrectly titled related to a matter of form>. Cf. *matter of substance.*

matter of law. A matter involving a judicial inquiry into the applicable law.

matter of record. A matter that has been entered on a judicial or other public record and therefore can be proved by producing that record.

matter of substance. A matter concerning the merits or critical elements, rather than mere formalities. Cf. *matter of form.*

new matter. A matter not previously raised by either party in the pleadings, usu. involving new issues with new facts to be proved.

special matter. *Common-law pleading.* Out-of-the-ordinary evidence that a defendant is allowed to enter, after notice to the plaintiff, under a plea of the general issue.

matter of course. Something done as a part of a routine process or procedure.

mature, *vb.* (Of a debt or obligation) to become due. — **maturity,** *n.* — **mature,** *adj.*

maxim (**mak**-sim). A traditional legal principle that has been frozen into a concise expression. • Examples are "possession is nine-tenths of the law" and *caveat emptor* ("let the buyer beware").

maximum medical improvement. The point at which an injured person's condition stabilizes, and no further recovery or improvement is expected, even with additional medical intervention.

maximum sentence. See SENTENCE.

may, *vb.* **1.** Is permitted to. • This is the primary legal sense — usually termed the "permissive" or "discretionary" sense. **2.** Has a possibility (to); might. Cf. CAN. **3.** Loosely, is required to; shall; must. • In dozens of cases, courts have held *may* to be synonymous with *shall* or *must*, usually in an effort to effectuate legislative intent.

mayhem (**may**-hem), *n.* **1.** The crime of maliciously injuring a person's body, esp. to impair or destroy the victim's capacity for self-defense. See BATTERY. **2.** Violent destruction. **3.** Rowdy confusion or disruption. — **maim** (for sense 1), *vb.*

May it please the court. An introductory phrase that lawyers use when first addressing a court, esp. when presenting oral argument to an appellate court.

mayor, *n.* An official who is elected or appointed as the chief executive of a city, town, or other municipality. — **mayoral** (**may**-ər-əl), *adj.*

MBE. See *Multistate Bar Examination* under BAR EXAMINATION.

***McNaghten* rules** (mik-**nawt**-ən). *Criminal law.* The doctrine that a person is not criminally responsible for an act when a mental disability prevented the person from knowing either (1) the nature and quality of the act or (2) whether the act was right or wrong. • The federal courts and most states have adopted this test in some form. *McNaghten's Case*, 8 Eng. Rep. 718 (H.L. 1843). — Also spelled *McNaughten rules*; *M'Naghten rules*; *M'Naughten rules*. See INSANITY DEFENSE.

M.D. *abbr.* **1.** Middle District, usu. in reference to U.S. judicial districts. **2.** Doctor of medicine.

meander line (mee-**an**-dər). A survey line (not a boundary line) on a portion of land, usu. following the course of a river or stream.

meaning. The sense of anything, but esp. of words; that which is conveyed (or intended to be conveyed) by a written or oral statement or other communicative act.

objective meaning. The meaning that would be attributed to an unambiguous document (or portion of a document) by a disinterested reasonable person who is familiar with the surrounding circumstances. • Parties to a contract are often held to its objective meaning, which they are deemed to have had reason to know, even if they subjectively understood or intended something else.

plain meaning. The meaning attributed to a document (usu. by a court) based on a commonsense reading of the words, giving them their ordinary sense and without reference to extrinsic indications of the author's intent. See PLAIN-MEANING RULE.

subjective meaning. The meaning that one party to a legal document attributes to it when the document is written, executed, or otherwise adopted.

measure of damages. The basis for calculating damages to be awarded to someone who has suffered an injury.

measuring life. Under the rule against perpetuities, the last beneficiary to die who was alive at the testator's death and who usu. holds a preceding interest. Cf. LIFE IN BEING.

mediate possession. See POSSESSION.

mediate powers (**mee**-dee-it). Subordinate powers incidental to primary powers, esp. as given by a principal to an agent; powers necessary to accomplish the principal task. Cf. PRIMARY POWERS.

mediation (mee-dee-**ay**-shən), *n.* A method of nonbinding dispute resolution involving a neutral third party who tries to help the disputing parties reach a mutually agreeable solution. — **mediate** (**mee**-dee-ayt), *vb.* — **mediatory** (**mee**-dee-ə-tor-ee), *adj.* — **mediator** (**mee**-dee-ay-tər), *n.* Cf. ARBITRATION.

Medicaid. A cooperative federal–state program that pays for medical expenses for those who cannot afford private medical services. • The program is authorized under the Social Security Act.

Medicaid-qualifying trust. See TRUST.

medical-emergency exception. *Criminal law.* The principle that a police officer does not need a warrant to enter a person's home if the entrance is made to render aid to someone whom the officer reasonably believes to be in need of immediate assistance.

medical evidence. See EVIDENCE.

medical examiner. A public official who investigates deaths, conducts autopsies, and helps the state prosecute homicide cases. See CORONER.

medical expense. See EXPENSE.

Medicare. A federal program — established under the Social Security Act — that provides health insurance for the elderly and the disabled.

medicolegal (med-i-koh-**lee**-gəl), *adj.* Involving the application of medical science to law. See FORENSIC MEDICINE.

medium of exchange. Any commodity generally accepted as payment in a transaction and recognized as a standard of value. See LEGAL TENDER.

meeting of the minds. *Contracts.* Actual assent by both parties to the formation of a contract. • This was required under the traditional subjective theory of assent, but modern contract doctrine requires only objective manifestations of assent. See MUTUAL ASSENT.

Megan's law (**meg**-ən *or* **may**-gən). A statute that requires sex offenders who are released from prison to register with a local board and that provides for community dissemination of information about the registrants.

membrum (**mem**-brəm), *n.* [Latin "limb"] A division of something, esp. a slip or small piece of land.

memorandum. 1. An informal written note or record outlining the terms of a transaction or contract <the memorandum indicated the developer's intent to buy the property at its appraised value>. • To satisfy the statute of frauds, a memorandum can be written in any form, but it must (1) identify the parties to the contract, (2) indicate the contract's subject matter, (3) contain the contract's essential terms, and (4) contain the signature of the party against whom enforcement is sought. See STATUTE OF FRAUDS. **2.** An informal written communication used esp. in offices <the firm sent a memorandum reminding all lawyers to turn in their timesheets>. **3.** A party's written statement of its legal arguments presented to the court, usu. in the form of a brief <memorandum of law>. Pl. **memoranda, memorandums.**

memorandum in error. A document alleging a factual error, usu. accompanied by an affidavit of proof.

memorandum opinion. See OPINION (1).

memorial, *n.* **1.** An abstract of a legal record, esp. a deed; MEMORANDUM (1). **2.** A written statement of facts presented to a legislature or executive as a petition.

menacing, *n.* An attempt to commit common-law assault. See ASSAULT.

mendacity (men-**das**-ə-tee), *n.* **1.** The quality of being untruthful. **2.** A lie; falsehood. — **mendacious** (men-**day**-shəs), *adj.*

mens (menz), *n.* [Latin] Mind; intention; will.

mensa et thoro (**men**-sə et **thor**-oh). [Latin] Bed and board. See *divorce a mensa et thoro* under DIVORCE.

mens rea (**menz ree**-ə). [Law Latin "guilty mind"] The state of mind that the prosecution, to secure a conviction, must prove that a defendant had when committing a crime; criminal intent or recklessness. Pl. ***mentes reae*** (**men**-teez **ree**-ee). See STATE OF MIND. Cf. ACTUS REUS.

mental cruelty. See CRUELTY.

mental illness. 1. A disorder in thought or mood so substantial that it impairs judgment, behavior, perceptions of reality, or the ability to cope with the ordinary demands of life. **2.** Mental disease that is severe enough to necessitate care and treatment for the afflicted person's own welfare or the welfare of others in the community.

mental reservation. One party's silent understanding or exception to the meaning of a contractual provision.

mental shock. See SHOCK.

mentition (men-**tish**-ən), *n.* [fr. Latin *mentitio* "lying"] The act of lying.

merchandise (**mər**-chən-dɪz *also* -dɪs). Goods that are bought and sold in business; commercial wares.

merchant. One whose business is buying and selling goods for profit; esp., a person or entity that holds itself out as having expertise peculiar to the goods in which it deals and is therefore held by the law to a higher standard of expertise than that of a nonmerchant. • Because the term relates solely to goods, a supplier of services is not considered a merchant.

merchantable (**mər**-chənt-ə-bəl), *adj.* Fit for sale in the usual course of trade at the usual selling prices; MARKETABLE. — **merchantability,** *n.* See *implied warranty of merchantability* under WARRANTY (2).

merchant exception. *Contracts.* An exemption from the statute of frauds making a contract between merchants enforceable if, within a reasonable time after they reach an oral agreement, a written confirmation of the terms is sent, to which the recipient does not object within ten days of receiving it. UCC § 2–201(2).

merchant's defense. The principle that a store owner will not be held liable for reasonably detaining a suspected shoplifter, to facilitate an investigation by a law-enforcement officer, if probable cause exists to suspect the detained person of wrongfully removing merchandise from the store.

mercy. Compassionate treatment, as of criminal offenders or of those in distress; esp., imprisonment, rather than death, imposed as punishment for capital murder. See CLEMENCY.

mercy rule. *Evidence.* The principle that a defendant is entitled to offer good-character evidence as a defense to a criminal charge. Fed. R. Evid. 404(a)(1).

mere right. An abstract right in property, without possession or even the right of possession.

meretricious (mer-ə-**trish**-əs), *adj.* **1.** Involving prostitution; of an unlawful sexual nature <a meretricious encounter>. **2.** (Of a romantic relationship) involving either unlawful sexual connection or lack of capacity on the part of one party <a meretricious marriage>. **3.** Superficially attractive but fake nonetheless; alluring by false show <meretricious advertising claims>.

merger. 1. The act or an instance of combining or uniting. **2.** *Contracts.* The substitution of a superior form of contract for an inferior form, as when a written contract supersedes all oral agreements and prior understandings; INTEGRATION (2). **3.** *Property.* The absorption of a lesser estate into a greater estate when both become the same person's property. **4.** *Criminal law.* The absorption of a lesser included offense into a more serious offense when a person is charged with both crimes, so that the person is not subject to double jeopardy. **5.** *Civil procedure.* The effect of a judgment for the plaintiff, which absorbs any claim that was the subject of the lawsuit into the judgment, so that the plaintiff's rights are confined to enforcing the judgment. Cf. BAR (5). **6.** The joining of the procedural aspects of law and equity. **7.** The absorption of one company (esp. a corporation) that ceases to exist into another that retains its own name and identity and acquires the assets and liabilities of the former. **8.** The blending of the rights of a creditor and debtor, resulting in the extinguishment of the creditor's right to collect the debt.

meritorious (mer-ə-**tor**-ee-əs), *adj.* **1.** (Of an act, etc.) meriting esteem or reward. **2.** (Of a case, etc.) meriting a legal victory; having legal worth.

meritorious defense. See DEFENSE (1).

merits. 1. The elements or grounds of a claim or defense; the substantive considerations to be taken into account in deciding a case, as opposed to extraneous or technical points, esp. of procedure <trial on the merits>. **2.** EQUITY (3) <on questions of euthanasia, the Supreme Court has begun to concern itself with the merits as well as the law>.

mesne (meen), *adj.* Occupying a middle position; intermediate or intervening.

messuage (**mes**-wij). A dwelling-house together with the curtilage, including any outbuildings. Cf. CURTILAGE.

metalaw (**met**-ə-law). A hypothetical set of legal principles based on the rules of existing legal systems and designed to provide a framework of agreement for these different systems.

mete out, *vb.* To dispense or measure out (justice, punishment, etc.).

metes and bounds (meets). The territorial limits of real property as measured by distances and angles from designated landmarks and in relation to adjoining properties.

migratory divorce. See DIVORCE.

mild exigency. A circumstance that justifies a law-enforcement officer's departure from the knock-and-announce rule, such as the likelihood that the building's occupants will try to escape, resist arrest, or destroy evidence. See KNOCK-AND-ANNOUNCE RULE.

militate (**mil**-ə-tayt), *vb.* To exert a strong influence. Cf. MITIGATE.

militia (mə-**lish**-ə). A body of citizens armed and trained, esp. by a state, for military service apart from the regular armed forces. • The Constitution recognizes a state's right to form a "well-regulated militia." U.S. Const. amend. II. See NATIONAL GUARD.

Militia Clause. One of two clauses of the U.S. Constitution giving Congress the power to call forth, arm, and maintain a military force to enforce compliance with its laws, suppress insurrections, and repel invasions. U.S. Const. art. I, § 8, cls. 15, 16.

***Mimms* order.** A police officer's command for a motorist to get out of the vehicle. • A *Mimms* order need not be independently justified if the initial stop was lawful. *Pennsylvania v. Mimms*, 434 U.S. 106, 98 S.Ct. 330 (1977).

mineral, *n.* Any natural inorganic matter that has a definite chemical composition and specific physical properties that give it value.

mineral district. A particular region of the country where valuable minerals are typically found and mined.

mineral entry. The right of entry on public land to mine valuable mineral deposits.

mineral land. See LAND.

mineral lode. A mineral bed of rock with definite boundaries in a general mass of a mountain; any belt of mineralized rock lying within boundaries that clearly separate it from neighboring rock.

mineral right. The right to search for, develop, and remove minerals from land or to receive a royalty based on the production of minerals. See SUBSURFACE RIGHT. Cf. SURFACE RIGHT.

mineral servitude. See SERVITUDE (1).

minimal participant. *Criminal law.* Under the federal sentencing guidelines, a defendant who is among the least culpable of a group of criminal actors, as when the defendant does not understand the scope or structure of the criminal enterprise or the actions of the other members of the group. Cf. MINOR PARTICIPANT.

minimization requirement. *Criminal law.* The mandate that police officers acting under an eavesdropping warrant must use the wiretap in a way that will intercept the fewest possible conversations that are not subject to the warrant.

minimum contacts. A nonresident defendant's forum-state connections, such as business activity or actions foreseeably leading to business activity, that are substantial enough to bring the defendant within the forum-state court's personal jurisdiction without offending traditional notions of fair play and substantial justice. *International Shoe Co. v. Washington*, 326 U.S. 310, 66 S.Ct. 154 (1945).

minimum sentence. See SENTENCE.

ministerial, *adj.* Of or relating to an act that involves obedience to instructions or laws instead of discretion, judgment, or skill <the court clerk's ministerial duties include recording judgments on the docket>.

ministerial-function test. The principle that the First Amendment bars judicial resolution of a Title VII employment-discrimination claim based on a religious preference, if the employee's responsibilities are religious in nature, as in spreading faith, supervising a religious order, and the like. 42 USCA § 2000e–1(a). See TITLE VII OF THE CIVIL RIGHTS ACT OF 1964.

minitrial. A private, voluntary, and informal form of dispute resolution in which each party's attorney presents an abbreviated version of its case to a neutral third party and to the opponent's representatives, who have settlement authority. Cf. *summary jury trial* under TRIAL.

minor, *n.* A person who has not reached full legal age; a child or juvenile.

emancipated minor. A minor who is self-supporting and independent of parental control, usu. as a result of a court order. See EMANCIPATION.

minority. 1. The state or condition of being under legal age. Cf. MAJORITY (1). **2.** A group having fewer than a controlling number of votes. Cf. MAJORITY (2). **3.** A group that is different in some respect (such as race or religious belief) from the majority and that is sometimes treated differently as a result; a member of such a group.

minor participant. *Criminal law.* Under the federal sentencing guidelines, a defendant who is less culpable for a crime than the other members of the group committing the crime, but who has more culpability than a minimal participant. Cf. MINIMAL PARTICIPANT.

mint, *n.* **1.** A government-authorized place for coining money. **2.** A large supply, esp. of money.

mintage. 1. The mint's charge for coining money. **2.** The product of minting; money.

minute book. 1. A book in which a court clerk enters minutes of court proceedings. **2.** A record of the subjects discussed and actions taken at a corporate directors' or shareholders' meeting.

***Miranda* hearing** (mə-**ran**-də). A pretrial proceeding held to determine whether the *Miranda* rule has been followed and thus whether the prosecutor may introduce into evidence the defendant's statements to the police made after arrest. See MIRANDA RULE.

***Miranda* rule.** The doctrine that a criminal suspect in police custody must be informed of certain constitutional rights before being interrogated. • The suspect must be advised of the right to remain silent, the right to have an attorney present during questioning, and the right to have an attorney appointed if the suspect cannot afford one. If the suspect is not advised of these rights or does not validly waive them, any evidence obtained during the interrogation cannot be used against the suspect at trial (except for impeachment purposes). *Miranda v. Arizona*, 384 U.S. 436, 86 S.Ct. 1602 (1966).

Mirandize (mə-**ran**-dɪz), *vb. Slang.* To read (an arrestee) rights under the *Miranda* rule. See MIRANDA RULE.

mirror-image rule. *Contracts.* The doctrine that the acceptance of a contractual offer must be positive, unconditional, unequivocal, and unambiguous, and must not change, add to, or qualify the terms of the offer; the common-law principle that for a contract to be formed, the terms of an acceptance must correspond exactly with those of the offer. • In modern commercial contexts, the mirror-image rule has been replaced by UCC § 2–207, which allows parties to enforce their agreement despite minor discrepancies between the offer and the acceptance. See BATTLE OF THE FORMS.

misadventure. 1. A mishap or misfortune. **2.** Homicide committed accidentally by a person doing a lawful act and having no intent to injure; ACCIDENTAL KILLING.

misallege, *vb.* To erroneously assert (a fact, a claim, etc.).

misapplication, *n.* The improper or illegal use of funds or property lawfully held. — **misapply,** *vb.*

misappropriation, *n.* The application of another's property or money dishonestly to one's own use. — **misappropriate,** *vb.* See EMBEZZLEMENT. Cf. APPROPRIATION; EXPROPRIATION.

miscarriage of justice. A grossly unfair outcome in a judicial proceeding, as when a defendant is convicted despite a lack of evidence on an essential element of the crime.

miscellaneous itemized deduction. See DEDUCTION.

mischarge. An erroneous jury instruction that may be grounds for reversing a verdict.

mischief (**mis**-chəf). **1.** A condition in which a person suffers a wrong or is under some hardship, esp. one that a statute seeks to remove or for which equity provides a remedy <this legislation seeks to eliminate the mischief of racially restrictive deed covenants>. **2.** Injury or damage caused by a specific person or thing <the vandals were convicted of criminal mischief>. **3.** The act causing such injury or damage <their mischief damaged the abbey>.

mischief rule. In statutory construction, the doctrine that a statute should be interpreted by first identifying the problem (or "mischief") that the statute was designed to remedy and then adopting a construction that will suppress the problem and advance the remedy. Cf. GOLDEN RULE; PLAIN-MEANING RULE; EQUITY-OF-THE-STATUTE RULE.

misconduct (mis-**kon**-dəkt). **1.** A dereliction of duty; unlawful or improper behavior.

affirmative misconduct. **1.** An affirmative act of misrepresentation or concealment of a material fact; intentional wrongful behavior. **2.** With respect to a claim of estoppel against the federal government, a misrepresentation or concealment of a material fact by a government employee — beyond a merely innocent or negligent misrepresentation.

juror misconduct. A juror's violation of the court's charge or the law, committed either during trial or in deliberations after trial, such as (1) communicating about the case with outsiders, witnesses, attorneys, bailiffs, or judges, (2) bringing into the jury room information about the case but not in evidence, and (3) conducting experiments regarding theories of the case outside the court's presence.

official misconduct. A public officer's corrupt violation of assigned duties by malfeasance, misfeasance, or nonfeasance.

wanton misconduct. An act, or a failure to act when there is a duty to do so, in reckless disregard of another's rights, coupled with the knowledge that injury will probably result.

willful and wanton misconduct. Conduct committed with an intentional or reckless disregard for the safety of others, as by failing to exercise ordinary care to prevent a known danger or to discover a danger.

willful misconduct. Misconduct committed voluntarily and intentionally.

2. An attorney's dishonesty or attempt to persuade a court or jury by using deceptive or reprehensible methods.

miscontinuance. A continuance erroneously ordered by a court.

miscreant (mis-kree-ənt). **1.** A wrongdoer. **2.** An apostate; an unbeliever.

misdate. To erroneously date (a document, etc.).

misdelivery. Delivery not according to the contractual specifications.

misdemeanant (mis-də-**mee**-nənt), *n.* A person who has been convicted of a misdemeanor.

misdemeanor (mis-di-**mee**-nər). A crime that is less serious than a felony and is usu. punishable by fine, penalty, forfeiture, or confinement (usu. for a brief term) in a place other than prison (such as a county jail). Cf. FELONY.

gross misdemeanor. A serious misdemeanor, though not a felony.

serious misdemeanor. One of a class of misdemeanors having more severe penalties than most other misdemeanors.

misdemeanor manslaughter. See MANSLAUGHTER.

misdemeanor-manslaughter rule. The doctrine that a death occurring during the commission of a misdemeanor (or sometimes a nondangerous felony) is involuntary manslaughter. Cf. FELONY-MURDER RULE.

misdescription. 1. A contractual error or falsity that deceives, injures, or materially misleads one of the contracting parties. **2.** A bailee's inaccurate identification, in a document of title, of goods received from the bailor. **3.** An inaccurate legal description of land in a deed.

misfeasance (mis-**fee**-zənts), *n.* **1.** A lawful act performed in a wrongful manner. **2.** More broadly, a transgression or trespass; MALFEASANCE. — **misfeasant,** *adj.* — **misfeasor,** *n.* Cf. NONFEASANCE.

misfeasance in public office. The tort of excessive, malicious, or negligent exercise of statutory powers by a public officer. — Also termed *malfeasance*.

misjoinder (mis-**joyn**-dər). **1.** The improper union of parties in a civil case. See JOINDER. Cf. DISJOINDER; NONJOINDER. **2.** The improper union of offenses in a criminal case.

mislaid property. See PROPERTY.

mislay, *vb.* To deposit (property, etc.) in a place not afterwards recollected; to lose (property, etc.) by forgetting where it was placed. See *mislaid property* under PROPERTY.

misleading, *adj.* (Of an instruction, direction, etc.) delusive; calculated to be misunderstood.

misnomer (mis-**noh**-mər). A mistake in naming a person, place, or thing, esp. in a legal instrument. • In federal pleading — as well as in most states — misnomer of a party can be corrected by an amendment, which will relate back to the date of the original pleading. Fed. R. Civ. P. 15(c)(3).

misperformance. A faulty attempt to discharge an obligation (esp. a contractual one). Cf. PERFORMANCE; NONPERFORMANCE.

mispleading. Pleading incorrectly. • A party who realizes that its pleading is incorrect can usually amend the pleading, as a matter of right, within a certain period, and can thereafter amend with the court's permission.

misprision (mis-**prizh**-ən). **1.** Concealment or nondisclosure of a serious crime by one who did not participate in the crime.

clerical misprision. A court clerk's mistake or fraud that is apparent from the record.

misprision of felony. Concealment or nondisclosure of someone else's felony.

misprision of treason. Concealment or nondisclosure of someone else's treason.

negative misprision. The wrongful concealment of something that should be revealed <misprision of treason>.

positive misprision. The active commission of a wrongful act <seditious conduct against the government is positive misprision>.

2. Seditious conduct against the government. **3.** An official's failure to perform the duties of public office. **4.** Misunderstanding; mistake.

misreading. An act of fraud in which a person incorrectly reads the contents of an instrument to an illiterate or blind person with the intent to deceitfully obtain that person's signature.

misrecital. An incorrect statement of a factual matter in a contract, deed, pleading, or other instrument.

misrepresentation, *n.* **1.** The act of making a false or misleading statement about something, usu. with the intent to deceive. **2.** The statement so made; an assertion that does not accord with the facts. — **misrepresent,** *vb.* Cf. REPRESENTATION (1).

fraudulent misrepresentation. A false statement that is known to be false or is made recklessly — without knowing or caring whether it is true or false — and that is intended to induce a party to detrimentally rely on it.

innocent misrepresentation. A false statement not known to be false; a misrepresentation that, though false, was not made fraudulently.

material misrepresentation. **1.** *Contracts.* A false statement that is likely to induce a reasonable person to assent or that the maker knows is likely to induce the recipient to assent. **2.** *Torts.* A false statement to which a reasonable person would attach importance in deciding how to act in the transaction in question or to which the maker knows or has reason to know that the recipient attaches some importance. See Restatement (Second) of Torts § 538 (1979).

negligent misrepresentation. A careless or inadvertent false statement in circumstances where care should have been taken.

missing-evidence rule. The doctrine that, when a party fails at trial to present evidence that the party controls and that would have been proper to present, the jury is entitled to infer that the evidence would have been unfavorable to that party.

missing person. **1.** Someone whose whereabouts are unknown and, after a reasonable time, seem to be unascertainable. **2.** Someone whose continuous and unexplained absence entitles the heirs to petition a court to declare the person dead and to divide up the person's property. See SEVEN-YEARS'-ABSENCE RULE. Cf. DISAPPEARED PERSON.

missing-witness rule. The doctrine that, when a party fails at trial to present a witness who is available only to that party and whose testimony would have been admissible, the jury is entitled to infer that the witness's testimony would have been unfavorable to that party.

mistake, *n.* **1.** An error, misconception, or misunderstanding; an erroneous belief. See ERROR. **2.** *Contracts.* The situation in which either (1) the parties to a contract did not mean the same thing, or (2) at least one party was wrong about the subject matter of the contract. • As a result, the contract may be rendered void. Cf. FRUSTRATION.

essential mistake. *Contracts.* A mistake serious enough that no real consent could have existed, so that there was no real agreement.

mistake of fact. **1.** A mistake about a fact that is material to a transaction. **2.** The defense asserting that a criminal defendant acted from an innocent misunderstanding of fact rather than from a criminal purpose.

mistake of law. **1.** A mistake about the legal effect of a known fact or situation. **2.** The defense asserting that a defendant did not understand the criminal consequences of certain conduct.

mutual mistake. **1.** A mistake in which each party misunderstands the other's intent. **2.** A mistake that is shared and relied on by both parties to a contract.

unessential mistake. *Contracts.* A mistake that does not relate to the nature of the contents of an agreement, but only to some external circumstance, so that the mistake has no effect on the validity of the agreement.

unilateral mistake. A mistake by only one party to a contract.

mistrial. 1. A trial that the judge brings to an end, without a determination on the merits, because of a procedural error or serious misconduct occurring during the proceedings. **2.** A trial that ends inconclusively because the jury cannot agree on a verdict.

misuse, *n.* **1.** *Products liability.* A defense alleging that the plaintiff used the product in an improper, unintended, or unforeseeable manner. **2.** *Patents.* The use of a patent either to improperly extend the granted monopoly to nonpatented goods or to violate antitrust laws.

misuser. An abuse of a right or office, as a result of which the person having the right might lose it. Cf. USER.

mitigate (mit-ə-gayt), *vb.* To make less severe or intense. — **mitigation,** *n.* — **mitigatory (mit-ə-gə-tor-ee),** *adj.* Cf. MILITATE.

mitigating circumstance. See CIRCUMSTANCE.

mitigation-of-damages doctrine. The principle requiring a plaintiff, after an injury or breach of contract, to use ordinary care to alleviate the effects of the injury or breach.

mitigation of punishment. *Criminal law.* A reduction in punishment due to mitigating circumstances that reduce the criminal's level of culpability, such as the existence of no prior convictions. See *mitigating circumstance* under CIRCUMSTANCE.

mixed blood. See BLOOD.

mixed jury. See JURY.

mixed larceny. See LARCENY.

mixed law. A law concerning both persons and property.

mixed nuisance. See NUISANCE.

mixed presumption. See PRESUMPTION.

mixed property. See PROPERTY.

mixed question. 1. MIXED QUESTION OF LAW AND FACT. **2.** An issue involving conflicts of foreign and domestic law.

mixed question of law and fact. An issue that is neither a pure question of fact nor a pure question of law.

***M'Naghten* rules.** See MCNAGHTEN RULES.

***M'Naughten* rules.** See MCNAGHTEN RULES.

M.O. *abbr.* MODUS OPERANDI.

mock trial. 1. A fictitious trial organized to allow law students, or sometimes lawyers, to practice the techniques of trial advocacy. **2.** A fictitious trial, arranged by a litigant's attorney, to assess trial strategy, to estimate the case's value or risk, and to evaluate the case's strengths and weaknesses. Cf. MOOT COURT.

mode. A manner of doing something.

model act. A statute drafted by the National Conference of Commissioners on Uniform State Laws and proposed as guideline legislation for the states to borrow from or adapt to suit their individual needs. Cf. UNIFORM ACT.

Model Code of Professional Responsibility. A set of ethical guidelines for lawyers, organized in the form of canons, disciplinary rules, and ethical considerations. • Published by the ABA in 1969, this code has been replaced in most states by the Model Rules of Professional Conduct.

model jury instruction. See JURY INSTRUCTION.

Model Penal Code. A proposed criminal code drafted by the American Law Institute and used as the basis for criminal-law revision by many states. — Abbr. MPC.

Model Rules of Professional Conduct. A set of ethical guidelines for lawyers, organized in the form of 52 rules — some mandatory, some discretionary — together with explanatory comments. • Published by the ABA in 1983, these rules have generally replaced the Model Code of Professional Responsibility and have been adopted as law by many states.

moderator. A presider at a meeting or assembly.

modification. 1. A change to something; an alteration. **2.** A qualification or limitation of something.

Modified Accelerated Cost Recovery System. An accounting method that is used to calculate asset depreciation and that allows for the faster recovery of costs by assigning the asset a shorter useful life than may actually be expected. • This system applies to property put into service after 1986. — Abbr. MACRS.

modified-comparative-negligence doctrine. See 50-PERCENT RULE.

modus operandi (**moh**-dəs op-ə-**ran**-dɪ *or* -dee). [Latin "a manner of operating"] A method of operating or a manner of procedure; esp., a pattern of criminal behavior so distinctive that investigators attribute it to the work of the same person. — Abbr. M.O. Pl. **modi operandi.**

moiety (**moy**-ə-tee). **1.** A half of something (such as an estate). **2.** A portion less than half; a small segment. **3.** In federal customs law, a payment made to an informant who assists in the seizure of contraband, the payment being no more than 25% of the contraband's net value (up to a maximum of $250,000). 19 USCA § 1619.

moiety act. *Criminal law.* A law providing that a portion of an imposed fine will inure to the benefit of the informant.

mole. A person who uses a long affiliation with an organization to gain access to and betray confidential information.

molestation. 1. The persecution or harassment of someone, as in the molestation of a witness. **2.** The act of making unwanted and indecent advances to or on someone, esp. for sexual gratification. — **molest,** *vb.* — **molester,** *n.*

child molestation. Any indecent or sexual activity on, involving, or surrounding a child, usu. under the age of 14. See Fed. R. Evid. 414(d).

money. 1. The medium of exchange authorized or adopted by a government as part of its currency. UCC § 1–201(24). **2.** Assets that can be easily converted to cash. **3.** Capital that is invested or traded as a commodity **4.** (*pl.*) Funds; sums of money. See MEDIUM OF EXCHANGE; LEGAL TENDER.

money demand. A claim for a fixed, liquidated sum, as opposed to a damage claim that must be assessed by a jury.

money judgment. See JUDGMENT.

monition (mə-**nish**-ən), *n.* Generally, a warning or caution; ADMONITION. — **monish** (**mon**-ish), *vb.* — **monitory** (**mon**-ə-tor-ee), *adj.*

monogamy (mə-**nog**-ə-mee), *n.* **1.** The custom prevalent in most modern cultures restricting a person to one spouse at a time. **2.** The fact of being married to only one spouse. — **monogamous,** *adj.* — **monogamist,** *n.* Cf. BIGAMY; POLYGAMY.

monopolization, *n.* The act or process of obtaining a monopoly. • In federal antitrust law, monopolization is an offense with two elements: (1) the possession of monopoly power — that is, the power to fix prices and exclude competitors — within the relevant market, and (2) the willful acquisition or maintenance of that power, as distinguished from growth or development as a consequence of a superior product, business acumen, or historical accident. *United States v. Grinnell Corp.*, 384 U.S. 563, 86 S.Ct. 1698 (1966). — **monopolize,** *vb.* — **monopolistic,** *adj.* — **monopolist,** *n.*

monopoly, *n.* **1.** Control or advantage obtained by one supplier or producer over the commercial market within a given region. **2.** The market condition existing when only one economic entity produces a particular product or provides a particular service. • The term is now commonly applied also to situations that approach but do not strictly meet this definition.

monopsony (mə-**nop**-sə-nee), *n.* A market situation in which one buyer controls the market. — **monopsonistic,** *adj.*

month-to-month lease. See LEASE.

monument, *n.* **1.** A written document or record, esp. a legal one. **2.** Any natural or artificial object that is fixed permanently in land and referred to in a legal description of the land. — **monumental,** *adj.*

moot, *adj.* **1.** *Archaic.* Open to argument; debatable. **2.** Having no practical significance; hypothetical or academic. — **mootness,** *n.*

moot, *vb.* **1.** *Archaic.* To raise or bring forward (a point or question) for discussion. **2.** To render (a question) moot or of no practical significance.

moot court. 1. A fictitious court held usu. in law schools to argue moot or hypothetical cases, esp. at the appellate level. **2.** A practice session for an appellate argument in which a lawyer presents the argument to other lawyers, who first act as judges by asking questions and who later provide criticism on the argument. Cf. MOCK TRIAL.

mootness doctrine. The principle that American courts will not decide moot cases — that is, cases in which there is no longer any actual controversy. Cf. RIPENESS.

moral certainty. Absolute certainty. See REASONABLE DOUBT.

moral evidence. See EVIDENCE.

morality. 1. Conformity with recognized rules of correct conduct. **2.** The character of being virtuous, esp. in sexual matters. **3.** A system of duties; ethics.

private morality. A person's ideals, character, and private conduct, which are not valid governmental concerns if the individual is to be considered sovereign over body and mind and if the need to protect the individual's physical or moral well-being is insufficient to justify governmental intrusion.

public morality. **1.** The ideals or general moral beliefs of a society. **2.** The ideals or actions of an individual to the extent that they affect others.

moral law. A collection of principles defining right and wrong conduct; a standard to which an action must conform to be right or virtuous.

moral necessity. See NECESSITY.

moral obligation. A duty that is based only on one's conscience and that is not legally enforceable.

moral turpitude. Conduct that is contrary to justice, honesty, or morality.

moral wrong. See WRONG.

moral-wrong doctrine. The doctrine that if a wrongdoer acts on a mistaken understanding of the facts, the law will not exempt the wrongdoer from culpability when, if the facts had been as the actor believed them to be, his or her conduct would nevertheless be immoral.

moratorium (mor-ə-**tor**-ee-əm). **1.** An authorized postponement, usu. a lengthy one, in the deadline for paying a debt or performing an obligation. **2.** The period of this delay. **3.** The suspension of a specific activity. Pl. **moratoriums, moratoria.**

moratory (**mor**-ə-tor-ee), *adj.* Of or relating to a delay; esp., of or relating to a moratorium.

Morgan presumption. A presumption that shifts the burden of proof by requiring the person against whom it operates to produce sufficient evidence to outweigh the evidence that supports the presumed fact, as in requiring a criminal defendant who was arrested while in possession of an illegal substance — and is thereby presumed to have knowingly possessed it — to produce sufficient evidence to entitle the jury to find that the defendant's evidence outweighs the evidence of knowing possession. See Edmund M. Morgan, *Instructing the Jury Upon Presumptions and Burdens of Proof*, 47 Harv. L. Rev. 59, 82–83 (1933). Cf. THAYER PRESUMPTION.

mortgage (**mor**-gij), *n.* **1.** A conveyance of title to property that is given as security for the payment of a debt or the performance of a duty and that will become void upon payment or performance according to the stipulated terms. **2.** A lien against property that is granted to secure an obligation (such as a debt) and that is extinguished upon payment or performance according to stipulated terms. **3.** An instrument (such as a deed or contract) specifying the terms of such a transaction. **4.** Loosely, the loan on which such a transaction is based. **5.** The mortgagee's rights conferred by such a transaction. **6.** Loosely, any real-property security transaction, including a deed of trust. — **mortgage,** *vb.*

mortgage certificate. A document evidencing part ownership of a mortgage.

mortgage commitment. A lender's written agreement with a borrower stating the terms on which it will lend money for the purchase of specified real property, usu. with a time limitation.

mortgage-contingency clause. A real-estate-sale provision that conditions the buyer's performance on obtaining a mortgage loan.

mortgage deed. See DEED.

mortgage discount. The difference between the mortgage principal and the amount the mortgage actually sells for; the up-front charge by a lender at a real-estate closing for the costs of financing.

mortgagee (mor-gə-**jee**). One to whom property is mortgaged; the mortgage creditor, or lender.

> ***mortgagee in possession.*** A mortgagee who takes control of mortgaged land by agreement with the mortgagor, usu. upon default of the loan secured by the mortgage.

mortgage foreclosure. See FORECLOSURE.

mortgage loan. See LOAN.

mortmain (**mort**-mayn). [French "deadhand"] The condition of lands or tenements held inalienably by an ecclesiastical or other corporation. See AMORTIZE; DEADHAND CONTROL.

mortmain statute. A law that limits gifts or other dispositions of land to corporations (esp. charitable ones) and that prohibits corporations from holding land in perpetuity.

most-favored-tenant clause. A commercial-lease provision ensuring that the tenant will be given the benefit of any negotiating concessions given to other tenants.

most-significant-relationship test. *Conflict of laws.* The doctrine that, to determine the state law to apply to a dispute, the court should determine which state has the most substantial connection to the occurrence and the parties.

mother. A woman who has given birth to, provided the egg for, or legally adopted a child. • The term is sometimes interpreted as including a pregnant woman who has not yet given birth.

biological mother. The woman who provides the egg that develops into an embryo.

birth mother. The woman who carries an embryo during the gestational period and who delivers the child.

genetic mother. See *biological mother.*

natural mother. **1.** See *birth mother.* **2.** See *biological mother.*

surrogate mother. **1.** A woman who carries out the gestational function and gives birth to a child for another; esp., a woman who agrees to provide her uterus to carry an embryo throughout pregnancy, typically on behalf of an infertile couple, and who relinquishes any parental rights she may have upon the birth of the child. **2.** A person who performs the role of a mother.

Mother Hubbard clause. A court's written declaration that any relief not expressly granted in a specific ruling or judgment is denied.

motion. **1.** A written or oral application requesting a court to make a specified ruling or order. **2.** A proposal made under formal parliamentary procedure.

calendar motion. A motion relating to the time of court appearances.

dilatory motion (**dil**-ə-tor-ee). **1.** A motion made solely for the purpose of delay. **2.** A motion that has the effect of delaying the proceedings.

ex parte motion (eks **pahr**-tee). A motion made to the court without notice to the adverse party; a motion that a court considers and rules on after hearing from fewer than all sides.

omnibus motion. A motion that makes several requests or asks for multiple forms of relief.

posttrial motion. A motion made after judgment is entered, such as a motion for new trial.

speaking motion. A motion that addresses matters not raised in the pleadings.

special motion. A motion specifically requiring the court's discretion upon hearing, as distinguished from one granted as a matter of course.

motion for a repleader. *Common-law pleading.* An unsuccessful party's posttrial motion asking that the pleadings begin anew because the issue was joined on an immaterial point.

motion for directed verdict. A party's request that the court enter judgment in its favor before submitting the case to the jury because there is no legally sufficient evidentiary foundation on which a reasonable jury could find for the other party. • Under the Federal Rules of Civil Procedure, the equivalent court paper is known as a motion for judgment as a matter of law. See MOTION FOR JUDGMENT AS A MATTER OF LAW; *directed verdict* under VERDICT.

motion for judgment as a matter of law. A party's request that the court enter a judgment in its favor before the case is submitted to the jury, or after a contrary jury verdict, because there is no legally sufficient evidentiary basis on which a jury could find for the other party. • Under the Federal Rules of Civil Procedure, a party may move for judgment as a matter of law anytime before the case has been submitted to the jury. If the motion is denied and the case is submitted to the jury, resulting in an unfavorable verdict, the motion may be renewed within ten days after entry of the judgment. This aspect of the motion replaces the court paper formerly known as a *motion for judgment notwithstanding the verdict*. Fed. R. Civ. P. 50.

motion for judgment notwithstanding the verdict. A party's request that the court enter a judgment in its favor despite the jury's contrary verdict because there is no legally sufficient evidentiary basis for a jury to find for the other party. • Under the Federal Rules of Civil Procedure, this procedure has been replaced by the provision for a motion for judgment as a matter of law, which must be presented before the case has been submitted to the jury but can be reasserted if it is denied and the jury returns an unfavorable verdict. Fed. R. Civ. P. 50. See MOTION FOR JUDGMENT AS A MATTER OF LAW.

motion for judgment of acquittal. A criminal defendant's request, at the close of the government's case or the close of all evidence, to be acquitted because there is no legally sufficient evidentiary basis on which a reasonable jury could return a guilty verdict. Fed. R. Crim. P. 29(a).

motion for judgment on the pleadings. A party's request that the court rule in its favor based on the pleadings on file, without accepting evidence, as when the outcome of the case rests on the court's interpretation of the law. Fed. R. Civ. P. 12(c).

motion for leave to appeal. A request that an appellate court review an interlocutory order that meets the standards of the collateral-order doctrine. See COLLATERAL-ORDER DOCTRINE.

motion for more definite statement. A party's request that the court require an opponent to amend a vague or ambiguous pleading to which the party cannot reasonably be required to respond. Fed. R. Civ. P. 12(e).

motion for new trial. A party's postjudgment request that the court vacate the judgment and order a new trial for a reason such as factually insufficient evidence, newly discovered evidence, or jury misconduct.

motion for protective order. A party's request that the court protect it from potentially abusive action by the other party, usu. relating to discovery, as when one party seeks discovery of the other party's trade secrets.

motion for relief from the judgment. A party's request that the court correct a clerical mistake in the judgment — that is, a mistake that results in the judgment's incorrectly reflecting the court's intentions — or relieve the party from the judgment because of such matters as (1) inadvertence, surprise, or excusable neglect, (2) newly discovered evidence that could not have been discovered through diligence in time for a motion for new trial, (3) the judgment's being the result of fraud, misrepresentation, or misconduct by the other party, or (4) the judgment's being void or having been satisfied or released. Fed. R. Civ. P. 60. Cf. MOTION TO ALTER OR AMEND THE JUDGMENT.

motion for summary judgment. A request that the court enter judgment without a trial because there is no genuine issue of material fact to be decided by a fact-finder — that is, because the evidence is legally insufficient to support a verdict in the nonmovant's favor. • In federal court and in most state courts, the movant-defendant must point out in its motion the absence of evidence on an essential element of the plaintiff's claim, after which the burden shifts to the nonmovant-plaintiff to produce evidence raising a genuine fact issue. But if a party moves for summary judgment on its own claim or defense, then it must establish each element of the claim or defense as a matter of law. Fed. R. Civ. P. 56. — Abbr. MSJ. See SUMMARY JUDGMENT.

motion in arrest of judgment. 1. A defendant's motion claiming that a substantial error appearing on the face of the record vitiates the whole proceeding and the judgment. **2.** A postjudgment motion in a criminal case claiming that the indictment is insufficient to sustain a judgment or that the verdict is somehow insufficient.

motion in limine (in **lim**-ə-nee). A pretrial request that certain inadmissible evidence not be referred to or offered at trial. • Typically, a party makes this motion when it believes that mere mention of the evidence during trial would be highly prejudicial and could not be remedied by an instruction to disregard.

motion to alter or amend the judgment. A party's request that the court correct a substantive error in the judgment, such as a manifest error of law or fact. • A motion to alter or amend the judgment is usually directed to substantive issues regarding the judgment, such as an intervening change in the law or newly discovered evidence that was not available at trial. Fed. R. Civ. P. 59(e). Cf. MOTION FOR RELIEF FROM THE JUDGMENT.

motion to compel discovery. A party's request that the court force the party's opponent to respond to the party's discovery request (as to answer interrogatories or produce documents). Fed. R. Civ. P. 37(a).

motion to dismiss. A request that the court dismiss the case because of settlement, voluntary withdrawal, or a procedural defect. • Under the Federal Rules of Civil Procedure, a plaintiff may voluntarily dismiss the case (under Rule 41(a)) or the defendant may ask the court to dismiss the case, usually based on one of the defenses listed in Rule 12(b).

motion to lift the stay. *Bankruptcy*. A party's request that the bankruptcy court alter the automatic bankruptcy stay to allow the movant to act against the debtor or the debtor's property, as when a creditor seeks permission to foreclose on a lien because its security interest is not adequately protected.

motion to quash (kwahsh). A party's request that the court nullify process or an act instituted by the other party, as in seeking to nullify a subpoena.

motion to remand. In a case that has been removed from state court to federal court, a party's request that the federal court return the case to state court, usu. because the federal court lacks jurisdiction or because the procedures for removal were not properly followed. 28 USCA § 1447(c).

motion to strike. 1. *Civil procedure*. A party's request that the court delete insufficient defenses or immaterial, redundant, impertinent, or scandalous statements from an opponent's pleading. Fed. R. Civ. P. 12(f). **2.** *Evidence*. A request that inadmissible evidence be deleted from the record and that the jury be instructed to disregard it.

motion to suppress. A request that the court prohibit the introduction of illegally obtained evidence at a criminal trial.

motion to transfer venue. A request that the court transfer the case to another district or county, usu. because the original venue is improper under the applicable venue rules or because of local prejudice. See VENUE; CHANGE OF VENUE.

motive. Something, esp. willful desire, that leads one to act. Cf. INTENT.

bad motive. A person's knowledge that an act is wrongful while the person commits the act.

malicious motive. A motive for bringing a prosecution, other than to do justice.

movable, *n.* (*usu. pl.*) Property that can be moved or displaced, such as personal goods. — **movable,** *adj.* Cf. IMMOVABLE.

movable freehold. The land a seashore owner acquires or loses as water recedes or approaches.

movant (moov-ənt). One who makes a motion to the court.

move, *vb.* **1.** To make an application (to a court) for a ruling, order, or some other judicial action. **2.** To propose under formal parliamentary procedure.

moving expense. See EXPENSE.

moving violation. An infraction of a traffic law while the vehicle is in motion.

MPC. *abbr.* MODEL PENAL CODE.

MSJ. *abbr.* MOTION FOR SUMMARY JUDGMENT.

MUD. *abbr.* See *municipal utility district* under DISTRICT.

mug book. A collection of mug shots of criminal suspects maintained by law-enforcement agencies (such as the FBI and police departments) to be used in identifying criminal offenders.

mug shot. A photograph of a person's face taken after the person has been arrested and booked.

mulct, *vb.* **1.** To punish by a fine. **2.** To deprive or divest of, esp. fraudulently.

multidistrict litigation. *Civil procedure.* Federal-court litigation in which civil actions pending in different districts and involving common fact questions are transferred to a single district for coordinated pretrial proceedings, after which the actions are returned to their original districts for trial. 28 USCA § 1407.

multifarious (məl-tə-**fair**-ee-əs), *adj.* **1.** (Of a single pleading) improperly joining distinct matters or causes of action, and thereby confounding them. **2.** Improperly joining parties in a lawsuit. **3.** Diverse; many and various. — **multifariousness,** *n.*

multilateral, *adj.* Involving more than two parties.

multipartite, *adj.* (Of a document, etc.) divided into many parts.

multiperil policy. See INSURANCE POLICY.

multiple admissibility. See ADMISSIBILITY.

multiple counts. See COUNT.

multiple evidence. See EVIDENCE.

multiple offense. See OFFENSE.

multiple sentences. See SENTENCE.

multiplicity (məl-tə-**plis**-i-tee), *n.* *Criminal procedure.* The improper charging of the same offense in several counts of the indictment or information. • Multiplicity violates the Fifth Amendment protection against double jeopardy. — **multiplicitous** (məl-tə-**plis**-i-təs), *adj.*

multiplicity of actions. The existence of two or more lawsuits litigating the same issue against the same defendant.

Multistate Bar Examination. See BAR EXAMINATION.

multital (məl-ti-təl), *adj.* Of or relating to legal relations that exist among three or more people, esp. a multitude of people. Cf. UNITAL.

municipal bond. See BOND (3).

municipal court. See COURT.

municipal judge. See JUDGE.

municipal utility district. See DISTRICT.

muniment of title. Documentary evidence of title, such as a deed or a judgment regarding the ownership of property. See CHAIN OF TITLE.

murder, *n.* The killing of a human being with malice aforethought. • See Model Penal Code § 210.2. — **murder,** *vb.* — **murderous,** *adj.* See MALICE AFORETHOUGHT. Cf. MANSLAUGHTER.

depraved-heart murder. A murder resulting from an act so reckless and careless of the safety of others that it demonstrates the perpetrator's complete lack of regard for human life.

felony murder. Murder that occurs during the commission of a dangerous felony (often limited to rape, kidnapping, robbery, burglary, and arson). See FELONY-MURDER RULE.

first-degree murder. Murder that is willful, deliberate, or premeditated, or that is committed during the course of another dangerous felony.

mass murder. A murderous act or series of acts by which a criminal kills many victims at or near the same time, usu. as part of one act or plan. Cf. *serial murder*.

murder by torture. A murder preceded by the intentional infliction of pain and suffering on the victim.

second-degree murder. Murder that is not aggravated by any of the circumstances of first-degree murder.

serial murder. A murder in which a criminal kills one of many victims over time, often as part of a pattern in which the criminal targets victims who have some similar characteristics. Cf. *mass murder*.

third-degree murder. Statutorily defined murder that is considered less heinous than first- or second-degree murder, resulting from an act that did not constitute murder at common law.

willful murder. The unlawful and intentional killing of another without excuse or mitigating circumstances.

mutation, *n.* A significant and basic alteration; esp., in property law, the alteration of a thing's status, such as from separate property to community property. — **mutate,** *vb.* — **mutational,** *adj.*

mutatis mutandis (myoo-**tay**-tis myoo-**tan**-dis). [Latin] All necessary changes having been made; with the necessary changes <what was said regarding the first contract applies *mutatis mutandis* to all later ones>.

mute, *n.* **1.** A person who cannot speak. **2.** A person (esp. a prisoner) who stands silent when required to answer or plead.

mutilation, *n.* **1.** The act or an instance of rendering a document legally ineffective by subtracting or altering — but not completely destroying — an essential part through cutting, tearing, burning, or erasing. **2.** *Criminal law.* The act of cutting off or permanently damaging a body part, esp. an essential one. — **mutilate,** *vb.* — **mutilator,** *n.* See MAYHEM.

mutual, *adj.* **1.** Generally, directed by each toward the other or others; reciprocal. **2.** (Of a condition, credit covenant, promise, etc.) reciprocally given, received, or exchanged. **3.** (Of a right, etc.) belonging to two parties; common. — **mutuality,** *n.*

mutual-agreement program. A prisoner-rehabilitation plan in which the prisoner agrees to take part in certain self-improvement activities to receive a definite parole date.

mutual assent. Agreement by both parties to a contract, usu. in the form of offer and acceptance. ● In modern contract law, mutual assent is determined by an objective standard — that is, by the apparent intention of the parties as manifested by their actions. See MEETING OF THE MINDS.

mutual combat. A consensual fight on equal terms — arising from a moment of passion but not in self-defense — between two persons armed with deadly weapons. Cf. DUEL.

mutual demands. Countering demands between two parties at the same time <a claim and counterclaim in a lawsuit are mutual demands>.

mutuality. The state of sharing or exchanging something; a reciprocation; an interchange <mutuality of obligation>.

mutuality doctrine. The collateral-estoppel requirement that, to bar a party from relitigating an issue determined against that party in an earlier action, both parties must have been in privity with one another in the earlier proceeding.

mutuality of estoppel. The collateral-estoppel principle that a judgment is not conclusively in favor of someone unless the opposite decision would also be conclusively against that person.

mutuality of obligation. The agreement of both parties to a contract to be bound in some way. See MUTUAL ASSENT.

mutuality of remedy. The availability of a remedy, esp. equitable relief, to both parties to a transaction, usu. required before either party can be granted specific performance. See SPECIFIC PERFORMANCE.

mutual mistake. See MISTAKE.

mutual promise. See PROMISE.

mutual will. See WILL.

mutuant (**myoo**-choo-ənt). The provider of property in a mutuum. See MUTUUM.

mutuary (**myoo**-choo-er-ee). The recipient of property in a mutuum. See MUTUUM.

mutuum (**myoo**-choo-əm). A transaction (sometimes referred to as a bailment) in which goods are delivered but, instead of being returned, are replaced by other goods of the same kind. • At common law such a transaction is regarded as a sale or exchange, not as a bailment, because the particular goods are not returned.

N

n.a. *abbr.* **1.** Not applicable. **2.** Not available. **3.** Not allowed.

NAFTA (**naf**-tə). *abbr.* NORTH AMERICAN FREE TRADE AGREEMENT.

naked, *adj.* (Of a legal act or instrument) lacking confirmation or validation <naked ownership of property>.

naked authority. See AUTHORITY (1).

naked confession. See CONFESSION.

naked owner. See OWNER.

naked possession. See POSSESSION.

naked possibility. See POSSIBILITY.

naked power. See POWER.

named insured. See INSURED.

name partner. See PARTNER.

nanny tax. See TAX.

Napoleonic Code. 1. (*usu. pl.*) The codification of French law commissioned by Napoleon in the 19th century, including the *Code civil* (1804), the *Code de procédure civil* (1806), the *Code de commerce* (1807), the *Code pénal* (1810), and the *Code d'instruction crimenelle* (1811). **2.** Loosely, CIVIL CODE (2).

narcoanalysis (nahr-koh-ə-**nal**-ə-sis). The process of injecting a "truth-serum" drug into a patient to induce semiconsciousness, and then interrogating the patient.

narcotic, *n.* **1.** An addictive drug, esp. an opiate, that dulls the senses and induces sleep. **2.** (*usu. pl.*) A drug that is controlled or prohibited by law. — **narcotic,** *adj.*

narrowly tailored, *adj.* (Of a content-neutral restriction on the time, place, or manner of speech in a designated public forum) being only as broad as is reasonably necessary to promote a substantial governmental interest that would be achieved less effectively without the restriction; no broader than absolutely necessary. See *designated public forum* under PUBLIC FORUM.

NASDAQ (**naz**-dak). *abbr.* NATIONAL ASSOCIATION OF SECURITIES DEALERS AUTOMATED QUOTATION SYSTEM.

National Aeronautics and Space Act. A 1958 federal statute that created the National Aeronautics and Space Administration (NASA), a civilian agency of the federal government whose functions include conducting space research, improving aeronautical travel, building manned and unmanned space vehicles, developing operational space programs, and engaging in other space activities devoted to peaceful purposes for the benefit of all humankind. 42 USCA §§ 2451–2484.

National Association of Securities Dealers Automated Quotation System. A computerized system for recording transactions and displaying price quotations for a group of actively traded securities on the over-the-counter market. — Abbr. NASDAQ.

National Bar Association. An organization of primarily African-American lawyers, founded in 1925 to promote education, professionalism, and the protection of civil rights. — Abbr. NBA.

National Conference of Commissioners on Uniform State Laws. An organization that drafts and proposes statutes for adoption by individual states, with the goal of making the laws on various subjects uniform among the states. See UNIFORM ACT; MODEL ACT.

National Guard. The U.S. militia, which is maintained as a reserve for the U.S. Army and Air Force. • Its members are volunteers, recruited and trained on a statewide basis and equipped by the federal government. A state may request the National Guard's assistance in quelling disturbances, and the federal government may order the National Guard into active service in times of war or other national emergency. See MILITIA.

National Institute of Corrections. A federal organization (established within the Bureau of Prisons) whose responsibilities include helping federal, state, and local authorities improve correctional programs, conducting research on correctional issues such as crime prevention, and conducting workshops for law-enforcement personnel, social workers, judges, and others involved in treating and rehabilitating offenders. 18 USCA §§ 4351–4353. See BUREAU OF PRISONS.

nationalization, *n.* **1.** The act of bringing an industry under governmental control or ownership. **2.** The act of giving a person the status of a citizen. See NATURALIZATION.

nationalize, *vb.* **1.** To bring (an industry) under governmental control or ownership. **2.** To give (a person) the status of a citizen. See NATURALIZATION.

National Labor Relations Act. A federal statute regulating the relations between employers and employees and establishing the National Labor Relations Board. 29 USCA §§ 151–169. • The statute is also known as the Wagner Act of 1935. It was amended by the Taft–Hartley Act of 1947 and the Landrum–Griffin Act of 1959. — Abbr. NLRA.

National Labor Relations Board. A federal agency (created by the National Labor Relations Act) that regulates employer–employee relations by establishing collective bargaining, conducting union elections, and prohibiting unfair labor practices. 29 USCA § 153. — Abbr. NLRB.

National Lawyers Guild. An association of lawyers, law students, and legal workers dedicated to promoting a left-wing political and social agenda. • Founded in 1937, it now comprises some 4,000 members. Cf. FEDERALIST SOCIETY.

National Mediation Board. A federal agency that, among other things, mediates disputes between rail and air carriers and their employees over wages and working conditions. • It was created by the Railway Labor Act. 45 USCA §§ 154–163. — Abbr. NMB.

national origin. The country in which a person was born, or from which the person's ancestors came. • This term is used in several antidiscrimination statutes, including Title VII of the Civil Rights Act of 1964, which prohibits discrimination because of an individual's "race, color, religion, sex, or national origin." 42 USCA § 2000e–2.

National Reporter System. A series of lawbooks, published by the West Group, containing every published decision of the federal and state courts in the United States. • For federal courts, the system includes the *Supreme Court Reporter*, *Federal Reporter*, *Federal Claims Reporter*, *Federal Supplement*, *Federal Rules Decisions*, *Bankruptcy Reporter*, *Military Justice Reporter*, and *Veterans Appeals Reporter*. For state courts, the system includes the *Atlantic Reporter*, *New York Supplement*, *North Eastern Reporter*, *North Western Reporter*, *Pacific Reporter*, *South Eastern Reporter*, *Southern Reporter*, and *South Western Reporter*.

National Transportation Safety Board. An independent government agency that investigates some transportation accidents, conducts safety studies, hears and rules on licensing appeals, and proposes safety guidelines and improved safety standards for the transportation industry. 49 USCA §§ 1101–1155. — Abbr. NTSB.

natural affection. The love naturally existing between close relatives, such as parent and child. • Natural affection may be valid consideration for a completed contract but insufficient to support an unperformed contract. See CONSIDERATION; *executory contract* under CONTRACT.

Natural Born Citizen Clause. The clause of the U.S. Constitution barring persons not born in the United States from the presidency. U.S. Const. art. II, § 1, cl. 5.

natural child. See CHILD.

natural consequence. Something that predictably occurs as the result of an act <plaintiff's injuries were the natural consequence of the car wreck>.

natural death. See DEATH.

natural-death act. A statute that allows a person to prepare a living will instructing a physician to withhold life-sustaining procedures if the person should become terminally ill. See ADVANCE DIRECTIVE; LIVING WILL.

natural father. See FATHER.

natural heir. See HEIR.

naturalization. The granting of citizenship to a foreign-born person under statutory authority. — **naturalize,** *vb.*

Naturalization Clause. The constitutional provision stating that every person born or naturalized in the United States is a citizen of the United States and of the state of residence. U.S. Const. amend. XIV, § 1. See JUS SOLI.

natural law. 1. A physical law of nature <gravitation is a natural law>. **2.** A philosophical system of legal and moral principles purportedly deriving from a universalized conception of human nature or divine justice rather than from legislative or judicial action; moral law embodied in principles of right and wrong

<many ethical teachings are based on natural law>. Cf. POSITIVE LAW.

natural liberty. See LIBERTY.

natural life. A person's physical life span.

natural mother. 1. See *birth mother* under MOTHER. **2.** See *biological mother* under MOTHER.

natural object. A person likely to receive a portion of another person's estate based on the nature and circumstances of their relationship.

natural person. See PERSON.

natural presumption. See PRESUMPTION.

natural servitude. See SERVITUDE (1).

natural succession. See SUCCESSION.

natural wear and tear. See WEAR AND TEAR.

N.B. *abbr.* [Latin *nota bene*] Note well; take notice — used in documents to call attention to something important.

NBA. *abbr.* NATIONAL BAR ASSOCIATION.

N.D. *abbr.* Northern District, in reference to a U.S. judicial district.

N.E. *abbr.* NORTH EASTERN REPORTER.

necessaries. 1. Things that are indispensable to living <an infant's necessaries include food, shelter, and clothing>. **2.** Things that are essential to maintaining the lifestyle to which one is accustomed <a multimillionaire's necessaries may include a chauffeured limousine and a private chef>. • The term includes whatever is reasonably needed for subsistence, health, comfort, and education, considering the person's age, station in life, and medical condition, but it excludes (1) anything purely ornamental, (2) anything solely for pleasure, (3) what the person is already supplied with, (4) anything that concerns someone's estate or business as opposed to personal needs, and (5) borrowed money.

necessary and proper, *adj.* Being appropriate and well adapted to fulfilling an objective.

Necessary and Proper Clause. The clause of the U.S. Constitution permitting Congress to make laws "necessary and proper" for the execution of its enumerated powers. U.S. Const. art. I, § 8, cl. 18. • The Supreme Court has broadly interpreted this clause to grant Congress the implied power to enact any law reasonably designed to achieve an express constitutional power. *McCulloch v. Maryland*, 17 U.S. (4 Wheat.) 316 (1819).

necessary implication. See IMPLICATION.

necessary improvement. See IMPROVEMENT.

necessary inference. A conclusion that is unavoidable if the premise on which it is based is taken to be true.

necessary party. See PARTY (2).

necessary repair. An improvement to property that is both needed to prevent deterioration and proper under the circumstances.

necessities. 1. Indispensable things of any kind. **2.** NECESSARIES.

necessitous, *adj.* Living in a state of extreme want; hard up.

necessitous circumstances. The situation of one who is very poor; extreme want.

necessity. 1. *Criminal law.* A justification defense for a person who acts in an emergency that he or she did not create and who commits a harm that is less severe than the harm that would have occurred but for the person's actions. **2.** *Torts.* A privilege that may relieve a person from liability for trespass or conversion if that person, having no alternative, harms another's property in an effort to protect life or health.

manifest necessity. *Criminal procedure.* A sudden and overwhelming emergency, beyond the court's and parties' control, that makes conducting a trial or reaching a fair result impossible and that therefore authorizes the granting of a mistrial.

moral necessity. A necessity arising from a duty incumbent on a person to act in a particular way.

physical necessity. A necessity involving an actual, tangible force that compels a person to act in a particular way.

private necessity. *Torts.* A necessity that involves only the defendant's personal interest and thus provides only a limited privilege.

public necessity. *Torts.* A necessity that involves the public interest and thus completely excuses the defendant's liability.

nee (nay), *adj.* [French] (Of a woman) born. • This term is sometimes used after a married woman's name to indicate her maiden name <Mrs. Robert Jones, nee Thatcher>. — Also spelled *née.*

negate, *vb.* **1.** To deny. **2.** To nullify; to render ineffective.

negative act. See ACT.

negative amortization. See AMORTIZATION.

negative averment. See AVERMENT.

negative condition. See CONDITION (2).

negative covenant. See COVENANT (1).

negative easement. See EASEMENT.

negative evidence. See EVIDENCE.

negative externality. See EXTERNALITY.

negative misprision. See MISPRISION.

negative plea. See PLEA (3).

negative-pledge clause. 1. A provision requiring a borrower, who borrows funds without giving security, to refrain from giving future lenders any security without the consent of the first lender. **2.** A provision, usu. in a bond indenture, stating that the issuing entity will not pledge its assets if it will result in less security to the bondholders under the indenture agreement.

negative pregnant. A denial implying its affirmative opposite by seeming to deny only a qualification of the allegation and not the allegation itself. • An example is the statement, "I didn't steal the money last Tuesday," the implication being that the theft might have happened on another day. Cf. AFFIRMATIVE PREGNANT.

negative proof. See PROOF.

negative statute. See STATUTE.

neglect, *n.* The omission of proper attention to a person or thing, whether inadvertent, negligent, or willful; the act or condition of disregarding. — **neglect,** *vb.* — **neglectful,** *adj.*

culpable neglect. Censurable or blameworthy neglect; neglect that is less than gross carelessness but more than the failure to use ordinary care.

excusable neglect. A failure — which the law will excuse — to take some proper step at the proper time (esp. in neglecting to answer a lawsuit) not because of the party's own carelessness, inattention, or willful disregard of the court's process, but because of some unexpected or unavoidable hindrance or accident or because of reliance on the care and vigilance of the party's counsel or on a promise made by the adverse party.

inexcusable neglect. Unjustifiable neglect; neglect that implies more than unintentional inadvertence.

willful neglect. Intentional neglect; deliberate neglect.

neglected child. See CHILD.

neglect hearing. A judicial hearing involving alleged child abuse or some other situation in which a child has not been properly cared for.

negligence, *n.* **1.** The failure to exercise the standard of care that a reasonably prudent person would have exercised in a similar situation; any conduct that falls below the legal standard established to protect others against unreasonable risk of harm, except for conduct that is intentionally, wantonly, or willfully disregardful of others' rights. **2.** A tort grounded in this failure, usu. expressed in terms of the following elements: duty, breach of duty, causation, and damages. Cf. *intentional tort* under TORT.

active negligence. Negligence resulting from an affirmative or positive act, such as driving through a barrier. Cf. *passive negligence.*

advertent negligence. Negligence in which the actor is aware of the unreasonable risk that he or she is creating; RECKLESSNESS.

comparative negligence. A plaintiff's own negligence that proportionally reduces the damages recoverable from a defendant. See COMPARATIVE-NEGLIGENCE DOCTRINE.

concurrent negligence. The negligence of two or more parties acting independently but causing the same damage. Cf. *joint negligence.*

contributory negligence. **1.** A plaintiff's own negligence that played a part in causing the plaintiff's injury and that is significant enough (in a few jurisdictions) to bar the plaintiff from recovering damages. • In most jurisdictions, this defense has been superseded by the doctrine of comparative negligence. See CONTRIBUTORY-NEGLIGENCE DOCTRINE; DISTRACTION DOCTRINE. **2.** *Rare.* The negligence of a third party — neither the plaintiff nor the defendant — whose act or omission played a part in causing the plaintiff's injury.

criminal negligence. Gross negligence so extreme that it is punishable as a crime.

culpable negligence. **1.** Negligent conduct that, while not intentional, involves a disregard of the consequences likely to result from one's actions. **2.** See *criminal negligence*.

gross negligence. **1.** A lack of slight diligence or care. **2.** A conscious, voluntary act or omission in reckless disregard of a legal duty and of the consequences to another party, who may typically recover exemplary damages. **3.** See *criminal negligence*.

imputed negligence. Negligence of one person charged to another; negligence resulting from a party's special relationship with another party who is originally negligent — so that, for example, a parent might be held responsible for some acts of a child.

inadvertent negligence. Negligence in which the actor is not aware of the unreasonable risk that he or she is creating, but should have foreseen and avoided it.

joint negligence. The negligence of two or more persons acting together to cause an accident. Cf. *concurrent negligence*.

negligence per se. Negligence established as a matter of law, so that breach of the duty is not a jury question. • Negligence per se usually arises from a statutory violation.

ordinary negligence. Lack of ordinary diligence; the failure to use ordinary care. • The term is most commonly used to differentiate between *negligence* and *gross negligence*.

passive negligence. Negligence resulting from a person's failure or omission in acting, such as failing to remove hazardous conditions from public property. Cf. *active negligence*.

slight negligence. The failure to exercise the great care of an extraordinarily prudent person, resulting in liability in special circumstances (esp. those involving bailments or carriers) in which lack of ordinary care would not result in liability; lack of great diligence.

subsequent negligence. The negligence of the defendant when, after the defendant's initial negligence and the plaintiff's contributory negligence, the defendant discovers — or should have discovered — that the plaintiff was in a position of danger and fails to exercise due care in preventing the plaintiff's injuries. See LAST-CLEAR-CHANCE DOCTRINE.

negligence rule. *Commercial law.* The principle that if a party's negligence contributes to an unauthorized signing or a material alteration in a negotiable instrument, that party is estopped from raising this issue against later parties who transfer or pay the instrument in good faith. • Examples of negligence include leaving blanks or spaces on the amount line of the instrument, erroneously mailing the instrument to a person with the same name as the payee, and failing to follow internal procedures designed to prevent forgeries.

negligent, *adj.* Characterized by a person's failure to exercise the degree of care that someone of ordinary prudence would have exercised in the same circumstance. **negligently,** *adv.*

negligent entrustment. The act of leaving a dangerous article (such as a gun or car) with a person who the lender knows, or should know, is likely to use it in an unreasonably risky manner.

negligent homicide. See HOMICIDE.

negligent infliction of emotional distress. The tort of causing another severe emotional distress through one's negligent conduct. • Most courts will allow a plaintiff to recover damages for emotional distress if the defendant's conduct results in physical contact with the plaintiff or, when no contact occurs, if the plaintiff is in the zone of danger. See EMOTIONAL DISTRESS; ZONE-OF-DANGER RULE. Cf. INTENTIONAL INFLICTION OF EMOTIONAL DISTRESS.

negligent misrepresentation. See MISREPRESENTATION.

negligent tort. See TORT.

negotiable, *adj.* **1.** (Of a written instrument) capable of being transferred by delivery or indorsement when the transferee takes the instrument for value, in good faith, and without notice of conflicting title claims or defenses. **2.** (Of a deal, agreement, etc.) capable of being accomplished. **3.** (Of a price or deal) subject to further bargaining and possible change. — **negotiability,** *n.* Cf. NONNEGOTIABLE; ASSIGNABLE.

negotiable instrument. A written instrument that (1) is signed by the maker or drawer, (2) includes an unconditional promise or order to pay a specified sum of money, (3) is payable on demand or at a definite time, and (4) is payable to order or to bearer. UCC § 3–104(a). • Among the various types of negotiable instruments are bills of exchange, promissory notes, bank checks, certificates of deposit, and other negotiable securities.

negotiable words. The terms and phrases that make a document a negotiable instrument. See NEGOTIABLE INSTRUMENT.

negotiated plea. See PLEA (1).

negotiation, *n.* **1.** A consensual bargaining process in which the parties attempt to reach agreement on a disputed or potentially disputed matter. • Negotiation usually involves complete autonomy for the parties involved, without the intervention of third parties. **2.** (*usu. pl.*) Dealings conducted between two or more parties for the purpose of reaching an understanding. **3.** The transfer of an instrument by delivery or indorsement whereby the transferee takes it for value, in good faith, and without notice of conflicting title claims or defenses. — **negotiate,** *vb.* — **negotiable,** *adj.* — **negotiability,** *n.* See HOLDER IN DUE COURSE.

neighbor principle. The doctrine that one must take reasonable care to avoid acts or omissions that one can reasonably foresee will be likely to injure one's neighbor. • According to this principle, *neighbor* includes all persons who are so closely and directly affected by the act that the actor should reasonably think of them when engaging in the act or omission in question.

neither party. A docket entry reflecting the parties' agreement not to continue to appear to prosecute and defend a lawsuit. • This entry is equivalent to a dismissal.

nepotism (**nep**-ə-tiz-əm), *n.* Bestowal of official favors on one's relatives, esp. in hiring. — **nepotistic** (nep-ə-**tis**-tik), *adj.*

net income. See INCOME.

net operating loss. See LOSS.

net proceeds. See PROCEEDS.

neutral, *adj.* **1.** Indifferent. **2.** (Of a judge, mediator, arbitrator, or actor in international law) refraining from taking sides in a dispute.

neutral, *n.* **1.** A person or country taking no side in a dispute. **2.** A nonpartisan arbitrator typically selected by two other arbitrators — one of whom has been selected by each side in the dispute.

neutralization. 1. The act of making something ineffective. **2.** *Evidence.* The cancellation of unexpected harmful testimony from a witness by showing, usu. by cross-examination, that the witness has made conflicting statements. • For example, a prosecutor may attempt to neutralize testimony of a state witness who offers unexpected adverse testimony. See IMPEACHMENT.

neutral principles. *Constitutional law.* Rules grounded in law, as opposed to rules based on personal interests or beliefs.

neutron-activation analysis. A method of identifying and analyzing physical evidence by measuring gamma rays emitted by a sample of material after that material has been bombarded with neutrons in a nuclear reactor. • This technique can be used, for example, to detect gunshot residue on the hand of someone who recently fired a gun. The analysis is usually expensive to perform, but most courts allow the results into evidence.

never indebted, plea of. A common-law traverse — or denial — by which the defendant in an action on a contract debt denies that an express or implied contract existed. See TRAVERSE.

new debtor. See DEBTOR.

newly discovered evidence. See EVIDENCE.

new matter. See MATTER.

new promise. See PROMISE.

new-rule principle. *Criminal procedure.* A doctrine barring federal courts from granting habeas corpus relief to a state prisoner because of a rule, not dictated by existing precedent, announced after the prisoner's conviction and sentence became final. See HABEAS CORPUS.

new ruling. *Criminal procedure.* A Supreme Court ruling not dictated by precedent existing when the defendant's conviction became final and thus not applicable retroactively to habeas cases. • For example, when the Court in *Ford v. Wainwright*, 477 U.S. 399, 106 S.Ct. 2595 (1986), ruled that the Eighth Amendment prohibits execution of insane prisoners, this new ruling was nonretroactive because it departed so widely from prior doctrine. *Teague v. Lane*,

489 U.S. 288, 109 S.Ct. 1060 (1989). See HABEAS CORPUS.

newspaper of general circulation. A newspaper that contains news and information of interest to the general public, rather than to a particular segment, and that is available to the public within a certain geographic area. • Legal notices (such as class-action notices) are often required by law to be published in a newspaper of general circulation.

new trial. A postjudgment retrial or reexamination of some or all of the issues determined in an earlier judgment. • The trial court may order a new trial by motion of a party or on the court's own initiative. Also, when an appellate court reverses the trial court's judgment, it may remand the case to the trial court for a new trial on some or all of the issues on which the reversal is based. See Fed. R. Civ. P. 59. See MOTION FOR NEW TRIAL; REMAND.

New York Stock Exchange. An unincorporated association of member firms that handle the purchase and sale of securities both for themselves and for customers. • This exchange, the dominant one in the United States, trades in only large companies having at least 1 million outstanding shares. — Abbr. NYSE.

New York Supplement. A set of regional lawbooks that, being part of the West Group's National Reporter System, contain every published decision from intermediate and lower courts of record in New York, from 1888 to date. • The first series ran from 1888 to 1937; the second series is the current one. — Abbr. N.Y.S.; N.Y.S.2d.

***New York Times* rule.** A commonsense rule of ethical conduct holding that one should not do anything arguably newsworthy — in public or in private — that one would mind having reported on the front page of a major newspaper. • In various communities, a local newspaper is substituted for the *Times*. See *actual malice* under MALICE.

next eventual estate. See ESTATE.

next friend. A person who appears in a lawsuit to act for the benefit of an incompetent or minor plaintiff, but who is not a party to the lawsuit and is not appointed as a guardian. Cf. *guardian ad litem* under GUARDIAN.

next of kin. 1. The person or persons most closely related to a decedent by blood or affinity. **2.** An intestate's heirs — that is, the person or persons entitled to inherit personal property from a decedent who has not left a will. See HEIR.

nexus. A connection or link, often a causal one. Pl. **nexuses, nexus.**

nexus test. The standard by which a private person's act is considered state action — and may give rise to liability for violating someone's constitutional rights — if the conduct is so closely related to the government's conduct that the choice to undertake it may fairly be said to be that of the state. • While similar to the symbiotic-relationship test, the nexus test focuses on the particular act complained of, instead of on the overall relationship of the parties. Still, some courts use the terms and analyses interchangeably. Cf. SYMBIOTIC-RELATIONSHIP TEST. See JOINT PARTICIPATION; STATE-COMPULSION TEST.

night. 1. The time from sunset to sunrise. **2.** Darkness; the time when a person's face is not discernible. • This definition was used in the common-law definition of certain offenses, such as burglary. **3.** Thirty minutes after sunset and thirty minutes before sunrise, or a similar definition as set forth by statute, as in a statute requiring specific authorization for night searches. **4.** Evening. Cf. DAY.

nihil dicit (**nɪ**-hil **dɪ**-sit), *n.* [Latin "he says nothing"] **1.** The failure of a defendant to answer a lawsuit. **2.** See *nihil-dicit default judgment* under DEFAULT JUDGMENT.

nihil est (**nɪ**-hil est). [Latin "there is nothing"] A form of return by a sheriff or constable who was unable to serve a writ because nothing was found to levy on. Cf. NULLA BONA.

nil (nil). [Latin] Nothing. • This word is a contracted form of *nihil.*

nil-dicit default judgment. See DEFAULT JUDGMENT.

nimmer. A petty thief; pilferer; pickpocket.

Nineteenth Amendment. The constitutional amendment, ratified in 1920, providing that a citizen's right to vote cannot be denied or abridged by the United States, or by any state within it, on the basis of sex.

ninety-day letter. Statutory notice of a tax deficiency sent by the IRS to a taxpayer. • During the 90 days after receiving the notice, the taxpayer must pay the taxes (and, if desired, seek a refund) or challenge the deficiency in tax court. IRC (26 USCA) §§ 6212, 6213. — Also written *90-day letter.* Cf. THIRTY-DAY LETTER.

Ninth Amendment. The constitutional amendment, ratified with the Bill of Rights in 1791, providing that rights listed in the Constitution must not be construed in a way that denies or disparages unlisted rights, which are retained by the people.

nisi (**nɪ**-sɪ), *adj.* [Latin "unless"] (Of a court's ex parte ruling or grant of relief) having validity unless the adversely affected party appears and shows cause why it should be withdrawn <a decree *nisi*>. See *decree nisi* under DECREE.

nisi prius (**nɪ**-sɪ **prɪ**-əs). [Latin "unless before then"] A civil trial court in which, unlike in an appellate court, issues are tried before a jury.

NLRA. *abbr.* NATIONAL LABOR RELATIONS ACT.

NLRB. *abbr.* NATIONAL LABOR RELATIONS BOARD.

NMB. *abbr.* NATIONAL MEDIATION BOARD.

NMI. *abbr.* No middle initial.

no-action letter. A letter from the staff of a governmental agency stating that if the facts are as represented in a person's request for an agency ruling, the staff will advise the agency not to take action against the person. • Typically, a no-action letter is requested from the SEC on such matters as shareholder proposals, resales of stock, and marketing techniques.

no actus reus (noh **ak**-təs **ree**-əs). A plea in which a criminal defendant either denies involvement with a crime or asserts that the harm suffered is too remote from the criminal act to be imputable to the defendant.

no-answer default judgment. See DEFAULT JUDGMENT.

no bill, *n.* A grand jury's notation that insufficient evidence exists for an indictment on a criminal charge <the grand jury returned a no bill instead of the indictment the prosecutors expected>. — **no-bill,** *vb.* <the grand jury no-billed three of the charges>. Cf. TRUE BILL.

no-bonus clause. *Landlord–tenant law.* A lease provision that takes effect upon governmental condemnation, limiting the lessee's damages to the value of any improvements to the property and preventing the lessee from recovering the difference between the lease's fixed rent and the property's market rental value. See CONDEMNATION.

no-claim, *n.* The lack of a claim. • Legal philosophers devised this term to denote the opposite of a claim.

no-confidence vote. The formal legal method by which a legislative body, by a majority vote, forces the resignation of a cabinet or ministry.

no contest. A criminal defendant's plea that, while not admitting guilt, the defendant will not dispute the charge. • This plea is often preferable to a guilty plea, which can be used against the defendant in a later civil lawsuit.

no-contest clause. A provision designed to threaten one into action or inaction; esp., a testamentary provision that threatens to dispossess any beneficiary who challenges the terms of the will.

no-duty, *n.* Liberty not to do an act.

no-duty doctrine. 1. *Torts.* The rule that a defendant who owes no duty to the plaintiff is not liable for the plaintiff's injury. **2.** The rule that the owner or possessor of property has no duty to warn or protect an invitee from known or obvious hazards.

***Noerr–Pennington* doctrine.** The principle that the First Amendment shields from liability (esp. under antitrust laws) companies that join together to lobby the government. • The doctrine derives from a line of Supreme Court cases beginning with *Eastern R.R. Presidents Conference v. Noerr Motor Freight, Inc.*, 365 U.S. 127, 81 S.Ct. 523 (1961), and *United Mine Workers v. Pennington*, 381 U.S. 657, 85 S.Ct. 1585 (1965).

no evidence. 1. The lack of a legally sufficient evidentiary basis for a reasonable fact-finder to rule in favor of the party who bears the burden of proof <there is no evidence in the record about his whereabouts at midnight>. • Under the Federal Rules of Civil Procedure, a party can move for judgment as a matter of law to claim that the other party — who bears the burden of proof — has been fully heard and has not offered sufficient evidence to prove one or more essential elements of the suit or defense. Fed. R. Civ. P. 50. Though such a contention is usually referred to as a no-evidence motion, the issue is not whether there was actually no evidence, but rather whether the evidence was sufficient for the fact-finder to be able to reasonably rule in favor of the other party. **2.** Evidence that has no value in an attempt to prove a matter in issue <that testimony is no evidence of an alibi>.

no-eyewitness rule. *Torts.* The largely defunct principle that if no direct evidence shows what a dead person did to avoid an accident, the jury may infer that the person acted with ordinary care for his or her own safety. • In a jurisdiction where the rule persists, a plaintiff in a survival or wrongful-death action can assert the rule to counter a defense of contributory negligence.

no-fault, *adj.* Of or relating to a claim that is adjudicated without any determination that a party is blameworthy <no-fault divorce>.

no-fault divorce. See DIVORCE.

no-fault insurance. See INSURANCE.

no funds. An indorsement marked on a check when there are insufficient funds in the account to cover the check.

no-knock search. See SEARCH.

no-knock search warrant. See SEARCH WARRANT.

nolens volens (**noh**-lenz **voh**-lenz), *adv.* & *adj.* [Latin] Willing or unwilling <*nolens volens*, the school district must comply with the court's injunction>.

nolition (noh-**lish**-ən). The absence of volition; unwillingness.

nolle prosequi (**nahl**-ee **prahs**-ə-kwɪ), *n.* [Latin "not to wish to prosecute"] **1.** A legal notice that a lawsuit has been abandoned. **2.** A docket entry showing that the plaintiff or the prosecution has abandoned the action.

nolle prosequi (**nahl**-ee **prahs**-ə-kwɪ), *vb.* To abandon (a suit or prosecution); to have (a case) dismissed by a *nolle prosequi* <the state *nolle prosequied* the charges against Johnson>.

nolo contendere (**noh**-loh kən-**ten**-də-ree). [Latin "I do not wish to contend"] NO CONTEST. — Often shortened to *nolo*.

NOM clause. *abbr.* See NO-ORAL-MODIFICATION CLAUSE.

nominal (**nahm**-ə-nəl), *adj.* **1.** Existing in name only <the king was a nominal figurehead because he had no power>. **2.** (Of a price or amount) trifling, esp. as compared to what would be expected <the lamp sold for a nominal price of ten cents>. **3.** Of or relating to a name or term <a nominal definition>. — **nominally,** *adv.*

nominal consideration. See CONSIDERATION.

nominal damages. See DAMAGES.

nominal partner. See PARTNER.

nominal party. See PARTY (2).

nominal rate. See INTEREST RATE.

nominal sentence. See SENTENCE.

nominate, *vb.* **1.** To propose (a person) for election or appointment <Steven nominated Jane for president>. **2.** To name or designate (a person) for a position <the testator nominated an executor, who later withdrew because he couldn't perform his duties>.

nominee. **1.** A person who is proposed for an office, position, or duty. **2.** A person designated to act in place of another, usu. in a very limited way. **3.** A party who holds bare legal title for the benefit of others or who receives and distributes funds for the benefit of others.

nomographer (nə-**mog**-rə-fər). **1.** A person who drafts laws. **2.** A person skilled in nomography.

nomography (nə-**mog**-rə-fee). **1.** The art of drafting laws. **2.** A treatise on the drafting of laws.

non (non). [Latin] Not; no. • This term negates, sometimes as a separate word and sometimes as a prefix.

nonability. 1. The lack of legal capacity, esp. to sue on one's own behalf. **2.** A plea or exception raising a lack of legal capacity.

nonacceptance. 1. The refusal or rejection of something, such as a contract offer. See REJECTION. **2.** A buyer's rejection of goods because they fail to conform to contractual specifications. See UCC § 2–601(a). **3.** A drawee's failure or refusal to receive and pay a negotiable instrument.

nonaccess. *Family law.* Absence of opportunity for sexual intercourse. • Nonaccess is often used as a defense by the alleged father in paternity cases.

nonadmission. 1. The failure to acknowledge something. **2.** The refusal to allow something, such as evidence in a legal proceeding.

nonappearance. The failure to appear in court, esp. to prosecute or defend a lawsuit. See DEFAULT; NONSUIT.

nonassertive conduct. See CONDUCT.

nonbailable, *adj.* **1.** (Of a person) not entitled to bail <the defendant was nonbailable because of a charge of first-degree murder>. **2.** (Of an offense) not admitting of bail <murder is a nonbailable offense>.

nonbillable time. An attorney's or paralegal's time that is not chargeable to a client. Cf. BILLABLE TIME.

noncapital, *adj.* (Of a crime) not involving or deserving of the death penalty <noncapital murder>.

nonclaim. A person's failure to pursue a right within the legal time limit, resulting in that person's being barred from asserting the right. See STATUTE OF LIMITATIONS.

nonclaim statute. See STATUTE.

non compos mentis (non **kom**-pəs **men**-tis), *adj.* [Latin "not master of one's mind"] **1.** Insane. **2.** Incompetent. Cf. COMPOS MENTIS.

nonconsent. 1. Lack of voluntary agreement. **2.** *Criminal law.* In the law of rape, the refusal to engage willingly in sexual intercourse. — **nonconsensual,** *adj.* See CONSENT.

nonconstitutional, *adj.* Of or relating to some legal basis or principle other than those of the U.S. Constitution or a state constitution <the appellate court refused — on nonconstitutional procedural grounds — to hear the defendant's argument about cruel and unusual punishment>. Cf. UNCONSTITUTIONAL.

nonconsumable, *n.* A thing (such as land, a vehicle, or a share of stock) that can be enjoyed without any change to its substance other than a natural diminishment over time. Cf. CONSUMABLE.

noncontractual, *adj.* Not relating to or arising from a contract <a noncontractual obligation>.

noncontributory, *adj.* **1.** Not involved in something. **2.** (Of an employee benefit plan) funded solely by the employer.

noncumulative voting. See VOTING.

noncustodial, *adj.* **1.** (Of an interrogation, etc.) not taking place while a person is in custody. **2.** Of or relating to someone, esp. a parent, who does not have sole or primary custody.

noncustodial interrogation. See INTERROGATION.

noncustodial sentence. See SENTENCE.

nondeadly force. See FORCE.

nondelegable (non-**del**-ə-gə-bəl), *adj.* (Of a power, function, etc.) not capable of being entrusted to another's care.

nondelegable duty. See DUTY.

nondelivery. A failure to transfer or convey something, such as goods. Cf. DELIVERY.

nondirection. The failure of a judge to properly instruct a jury on a necessary point of law.

nondischargeable debt. A debt (such as one for delinquent taxes) that is not released through bankruptcy.

nondisclosure. The failure or refusal to reveal something that either might be or is required to be revealed.

nondiverse, *adj.* **1.** Of or relating to similar types <the attorney's practice is nondiverse: she handles only criminal matters>. **2.** (Of a person or entity) having the same citizenship as the party or parties on the other side of a lawsuit <the parties are nondiverse because both plaintiff and defendant are California citizens>. See *diversity jurisdiction* under JURISDICTION.

nonfeasance (non-**feez**-ənts), *n.* The failure to act when a duty to act existed. — **nonfeasant,** *adj.* — **nonfeasor,** *n.* Cf. MALFEASANCE; MISFEASANCE; FEASANCE.

nonforfeitable, *adj.* Not subject to forfeiture. See FORFEITURE.

nonfundamental term. See TERM (2).

noninterpretivism, *n.* In constitutional interpretation, the doctrine holding that judges are not confined to the Constitution's text or preratification history but may instead look to evolving social norms and values as the basis for constitutional judgments. — **noninterpretivist,** *n.* Cf. INTERPRETIVISM; ORIGINALISM.

nonissuable plea. See PLEA (3).

nonjoinder. The failure to bring a person who is a necessary party into a lawsuit. Fed. R. Civ. P. 12(b)(7), 19. Cf. JOINDER; MISJOINDER; DISJOINDER.

nonjudicial day. See DAY.

nonjudicial foreclosure. See FORECLOSURE.

nonjuridical (non-juu-**rid**-i-kəl), *adj.* **1.** Not of or relating to judicial proceedings or to the administration of justice <the dispute was nonjuridical>. **2.** Not of or relating to the law; not legal <a natural person is a nonjuridical entity>. Cf. JURIDICAL.

nonjusticiable (non-jəs-**tish**-ee-ə-bəl *or* non-jəs-**tish**-ə-bəl), *adj.* Not proper for judicial determination <the

controversy was nonjusticiable because none of the parties had suffered any harm>.

nonleviable (non-**lev**-ee-ə-bəl), *adj.* (Of property or assets) exempt from execution, seizure, forfeiture, or sale, as in bankruptcy. See HOMESTEAD LAW.

nonmonetary item. An asset or liability whose price fluctuates over time (such as land, equipment, inventory, and warranty obligations).

nonmovant (non-**moov**-ənt). A litigating party other than the one that has filed the motion currently under consideration.

nonnegotiable, *adj.* **1.** (Of an agreement or term) not subject to change. **2.** (Of an instrument or note) incapable of transferring by indorsement or delivery. Cf. NEGOTIABLE.

non obstante veredicto (non ahb-**stan**-tee [*or* əb-**stan**-tee] ver-ə-**dik**-toh). [Latin] Notwithstanding the verdict. See *judgment notwithstanding the verdict* under JUDGMENT.

nonoccupant visitor. *Criminal procedure.* A person who owns, co-owns, is employed by, or is a patron of a business enterprise where a search is being conducted in accordance with a search warrant.

nonoccupational, *adj.* **1.** Not relating to one's job. **2.** Of or relating to a general-disability policy providing benefits to an individual whose disability prevents that individual from working at any occupation.

nonoccupier. One who does not occupy a particular piece of land; esp., an entrant on land who is either an invitee or a licensee. See INVITEE; LICENSEE (2).

nonparticipating, *adj.* Of or relating to not taking part in something; specif., not sharing or having the right to share in profits or surpluses.

nonpayment. Failure to deliver money or other valuables, esp. when due, in discharge of an obligation. Cf. PAYMENT (1).

nonperformance. Failure to discharge an obligation (esp. a contractual one). Cf. PERFORMANCE; MISPERFORMANCE.

nonperforming loan. See LOAN.

nonprivity (non-**priv**-ə-tee). The fact or state of not being in privity of contract with another; lack of privity. See PRIVITY (1).

horizontal nonprivity. The lack of privity occurring when the plaintiff is not a buyer within the distributive chain, but one who consumes, uses, or is otherwise affected by the goods. • For example, a houseguest who becomes ill after eating meat that her host bought from the local deli is in horizontal nonprivity with the deli.

vertical nonprivity. The lack of privity occurring when the plaintiff is a buyer within the distributive chain who did not buy directly from the defendant. • For example, someone who buys a drill from a local hardware store and later sues the drill's manufacturer is in vertical nonprivity with the manufacturer.

nonprobate, *adj.* **1.** Of or relating to some method of estate disposition apart from wills <nonprobate distribution>. **2.** Of or relating to the property so disposed <nonprobate assets>.

nonprofit corporation. See CORPORATION.

non prosequitur (non prə-**sek**-wə-tər *or* proh-). [Latin "he does not prosecute"] The judgment rendered against a plaintiff who has not pursued the case.

nonpublic forum. *Constitutional law.* Public property that is not designated or traditionally considered an arena for public communication, such as a jail or a military base. • The government's means of regulating a nonpublic forum need only be reasonable and viewpoint-neutral to be constitutional. Cf. PUBLIC FORUM.

non-purchase-money, *adj.* Not pertaining to or being an obligation secured by property obtained by a loan <non-purchase-money mortgage>.

nonrecognition provision. *Tax.* A statutory rule that allows all or part of a realized gain or loss not to be recognized for tax purposes. • Generally, this type of provision only postpones the recognition of the gain or loss. See RECOGNITION (3).

nonrecourse, *adj.* Of or relating to an obligation that can be satisfied only out of the collateral securing the obligation and not out of the debtor's other assets.

nonrecourse loan. See LOAN.

nonrenewal. A failure to renew something, such as a lease or an insurance policy.

nonresident alien. See ALIEN.

non sequitur (non **sek**-wə-tər). [Latin "it does not follow"] **1.** An inference or conclusion that does not logically follow from the premises. **2.** A remark or response that does not logically follow from what was previously said.

nonservice. The failure to serve a summons, warrant, or other process in a civil or criminal case.

nonskip person. *Tax.* A person who is not a skip person for purposes of the generation-skipping transfer tax. IRC (26 USCA) § 2613(b). See SKIP PERSON.

nonsuit, *n.* **1.** A plaintiff's voluntary dismissal of a case or of a defendant, without a decision on the merits. • Under the Federal Rules of Civil Procedure, a voluntary dismissal is equivalent to a nonsuit. Fed. R. Civ. P. 41(a). **2.** A court's dismissal of a case or of a defendant because the plaintiff has failed to make out a legal case or to bring forward sufficient evidence. — **nonsuit,** *vb.*

compulsory nonsuit. An involuntary nonsuit.

nonsupport. The failure to support a person that one is legally obliged to provide for, such as a child, spouse, or other dependent. • Nonsupport is a crime in most states, where it is often termed *criminal nonsupport.*

nonunion, *adj.* **1.** (Of a person or thing) not belonging to or affiliated with a labor union <a nonunion worker> <a nonunion contract>. **2.** (Of a position or belief) not favoring labor unions <she will not alter her nonunion stance>. **3.** (Of a product) not made by labor-union members <the equipment was of nonunion manufacture>.

nonuse. 1. The failure to exercise a right <nonuse of the easement>. **2.** The condition of not being put into service <the equipment was in nonuse>.

nonuser. The failure to exercise a right (such as a franchise or easement), as a result of which the person having the right might lose it. Cf. USER (1).

nonverbal testimony. See TESTIMONY.

no-oral-modification clause. A contractual provision stating that the parties cannot make any oral modifications or alterations to the agreement. — Abbr. NOM clause. See INTEGRATION CLAUSE.

no-pass, no-play rule. A state law requiring public-school students who participate in extracurricular activities (such as sports or band) to maintain a minimum grade-point average or else lose the privilege to participate.

no recourse. 1. The lack of means by which to obtain reimbursement from, or a judgment against, a person or entity <the bank had no recourse against the individual executive for collection of the corporation's debts>. **2.** A notation indicating that such means are lacking <the bill was indorsed "no recourse">. See *nonrecourse loan* under LOAN; WITHOUT RECOURSE.

no-retreat rule. *Criminal law.* The doctrine that the victim of a murderous assault may use deadly force in self-defense if there is no reasonable alternative to avoid the assailant's threatened harm. • A majority of American jurisdictions have adopted this rule. Cf. RETREAT RULE.

no-right, *n.* The absence of right against another in some particular respect. • A no-right is the correlative of a privilege.

norm. 1. A model or standard accepted (voluntarily or involuntarily) by society or other large group, against which society judges someone or something. • An example of a norm is the standard for right or wrong behavior. **2.** An actual or set standard determined by the typical or most frequent behavior of a group.

normal law. The law as it applies to persons who are free from legal disabilities.

normal mind. A mental capacity that is similar to that of the majority of people who can handle life's ordinary responsibilities.

normative, *adj.* Establishing or conforming to a norm or standard.

Norris–LaGuardia Act (**nor**-is lə-**gwahr**-dee-ə). A 1932 federal law that forbids federal courts from ruling on labor policy and that severely limits their power to issue injunctions in labor disputes. 29 USCA §§ 101–115.

North American Free Trade Agreement. A trilateral treaty — entered into on January 1, 1994 between the United States, Canada, and Mexico — that phases out all tariffs and eliminates many nontariff barriers (such as quotas) inhibiting the free trade of goods between the participating nations. — Abbr. NAFTA.

North Eastern Reporter. A set of regional lawbooks that, being part of the West Group's National Reporter System, contain every published decision from Illinois, Indiana, Massachusetts, New York, and Ohio, from 1885 to date. • The first series ran from 1885 to 1936; the second series is the current one. — Abbr. N.E.; N.E.2d.

North Western Reporter. A set of regional lawbooks that, being part of the West Group's National Reporter System, contain every published decision from Iowa, Michigan, Minnesota, Nebraska, North Dakota, South Dakota, and Wisconsin, from 1879 to date. • The first series ran from 1879 to 1941; the second series is the current one. — Abbr. N.W.; N.W.2d.

noscitur a sociis (**nos**-ə-tər ay [*or* ah] **soh**-shee-is). [Latin "it is known by its associates"] A canon of construction holding that the meaning of an unclear word or phrase should be determined by the words immediately surrounding it. Cf. EJUSDEM GENERIS; EXPRESSIO UNIUS EST EXCLUSIO ALTERIUS.

notarial, *adj.* Of or relating to the official acts of a notary public <a notarial seal>. See NOTARY PUBLIC.

notarial act. An official function of a notary public, such as placing a seal on an affidavit. See NOTARY PUBLIC.

notary public (**noh**-tə-ree), *n.* A person authorized by a state to administer oaths, certify documents, attest to the authenticity of signatures, and perform official acts in commercial matters, such as protesting negotiable instruments. Pl. **notaries public.** — **notarize,** *vb.* — **notarial,** *adj.*

notary seal. 1. The imprint or embossment made by a notary public's seal. **2.** A device, usu. a stamp or embosser, that makes an imprint on a notarized document.

embossed seal. **1.** A notary seal that is impressed onto a document, raising the impression above the surface. **2.** The embossment made by this seal.

rubber-stamp seal. **1.** In most states, a notary public's official seal, which is ink-stamped onto documents and is therefore photographically reproducible. **2.** The imprint made by this seal.

notation credit. A letter of credit specifying that anyone purchasing or paying a draft or demand for payment made under it must note the amount of the draft or demand on the letter. See LETTER OF CREDIT.

note, *n.* **1.** A written promise by one party (the *maker*) to pay money to another party (the *payee*) or to bearer. • A note is a two-party negotiable instrument, unlike a draft (which is a three-party instrument). Cf. DRAFT (1).

promissory note. An unconditional written promise, signed by the maker, to pay absolutely and in any event a certain sum of money either to, or to the order of, the bearer or a designated person.

2. A scholarly legal essay shorter than an article and restricted in scope, explaining or criticizing a particular set of cases or a general area of the law, and usu. written by a law student for publication in a law review. Cf. ANNOTATION. **3.** A minute or memorandum intended for later reference; MEMORANDUM (1).

note, *vb.* **1.** To notice carefully or with particularity <the defendant noted that the plaintiff seemed nervous>. **2.** To put down in writing <the court reporter noted the objection in the record>. **3.** *Archaic.* To brand <as punishment, the criminal was noted>.

not found. Words placed on a bill of indictment, meaning that the grand jury has insufficient evidence to support a true bill. See NO BILL. Cf. TRUE BILL.

not guilty. 1. A defendant's plea denying the crime charged. **2.** A jury verdict acquitting the defendant because the prosecution failed to prove the defendant's guilt beyond a reasonable doubt. Cf. INNOCENT.

***not guilty by reason of insanity.* 1.** A not-guilty verdict, based on mental illness, that usu. does not release the defendant but instead results in commitment to a mental institution. **2.** A criminal defendant's plea of not guilty that is based on the insanity defense. See INSANITY DEFENSE.

3. *Common-law pleading.* A defendant's plea denying both an act of trespass alleged in a plaintiff's declaration and the plaintiff's right to possess the property at issue. **4.** A general denial in an ejectment action.

not-guilty plea. See PLEA (1).

notice, *n.* **1.** Legal notification required by law or agreement, or imparted by operation of law as a result of some fact (such as the recording of an instrument); definite legal cognizance, actual or constructive, of an existing right or title <under the lease, the tenant must give the landlord written notice 30 days before vacating the premises>. • A person has notice of a fact or condition if that person (1) has actual knowledge of it; (2) has received a notice of it; (3) has reason to know about it; (4) knows about a related fact; or (5) is considered as having been able to ascertain it by checking an official filing or recording. **2.** The condition of being so notified, whether or not actual awareness exists <all prospective buyers were on notice of the judgment lien>. **3.** A written or printed announcement <the notice of sale was posted on the courthouse bulletin board>. Cf. KNOWLEDGE.

actual notice. Notice given directly to, or received personally by, a party.

constructive notice. Notice arising by presumption of law from the existence of facts and circumstances that a party had a duty to take notice of, such as a registered deed or a pending lawsuit; notice presumed by law to have been acquired by a person and thus imputed to that person.

direct notice. Actual notice of a fact that is brought directly to a party's attention.

due notice. Sufficient and proper notice that is intended to and likely to reach a particular person or the public; notice that is legally adequate given the particular circumstance.

express notice. Actual knowledge or notice given to a party directly, not arising from any inference, duty, or inquiry.

fair notice. **1.** Sufficient notice apprising a litigant of the opposing party's claim. **2.** The requirement that a pleading adequately apprise the opposing party of a claim. • A pleading must be drafted so that an opposing attorney of reasonable competence would be able to ascertain the nature and basic issues of the controversy and the evidence probably relevant to those issues. **3.** FAIR WARNING.

implied notice. Notice that is inferred from facts that a person had a means of knowing and that is thus imputed to that person; actual notice of facts or circumstances that, if properly followed up, would have led to a knowledge of the particular fact in question.

imputed notice. Information attributed to a person whose agent, having received actual notice of the information, has a duty to disclose it to that person. • For example, notice of a hearing may be imputed to a witness because it was actually disclosed to that witness's attorney of record.

inquiry notice. Notice attributed to a person when the information would lead an ordinarily prudent person to investigate the matter further; esp., the time at which the victim of an alleged securities fraud became aware of facts that would have prompted a reasonable person to investigate.

personal notice. Oral or written notice, according to the circumstances, given directly to the affected person.

public notice. Notice given to the public or persons affected, usu. by publishing in a newspaper of general circulation. • This notice is usually required, for example, in matters of public concern.

record notice. Constructive notice of the contents of an instrument, such as a deed or mortgage, that has been properly recorded.

notice, *vb.* **1.** To give legal notice to or of <the plaintiff's lawyer noticed depositions of all the experts that the defendant listed>. **2.** To realize or give attention to <the lawyer noticed that the witness was leaving>.

notice doctrine. The equitable doctrine that when a new owner takes an estate with notice that someone else had a claim on it at the time of the transfer, that claim may still be asserted against the new owner even if it might have been disregarded at law.

notice-of-alibi rule. *Criminal procedure.* The principle that, upon written demand from the government, a criminal defendant who intends to call an alibi witness at trial must give notice of who that witness is and where the defendant claims to have been at the time of the alleged offense. • The government is, in turn, obligated to give notice to the defendant of what witness it intends to call to rebut the alibi testimony. See Fed. R. Crim. P. 12.1.

notice of appeal. A document filed with a court and served on the other parties, stating an intention to appeal a trial court's judgment or order. • In most jurisdictions, filing a notice of appeal is the act by which the appeal is perfected. For instance, the Federal Rules of Appellate Procedure provide that an appeal is taken by filing a notice of appeal with the clerk of the district court from which the appeal is taken, and that the clerk is to send copies of the notice to all the other parties' attorneys, as well as the court of appeals. Fed. R. App. P. 3(a), (d). See APPEAL.

notice of appearance. **1.** *Procedure*. A party's written notice filed with the court or oral announcement on the record informing the court and the other parties that the party wants to participate in the case. **2.** *Bankruptcy*. A written notice filed with the court or oral announcement in open court by a person who wants to receive all pleadings in a particular case. • This notice is usually filed by an attorney for a creditor who wants to be added to the official service list. **3.** A pleading filed by an attorney to notify the court and the other parties that he or she represents one or more parties in the lawsuit.

notice of dishonor. Notice to the indorser of an instrument that acceptance or payment has been refused. • This notice — along with presentment and actual dishonor — is a condition of an indorser's secondary liability. UCC § 3–503(a).

notice of motion. Written certification that a party to a lawsuit has filed a motion or that a motion will be heard or considered by the court at a particular time. • Under the Federal Rules of Civil Procedure, the requirement that a motion be made in writing is fulfilled if the motion is stated in a written notice of the hearing on the motion. Also, the courts in most jurisdictions require all motions to include a certificate, usually referred to as a certificate of service, indicating that the other parties to the suit have been given notice of the motion's filing. Notice of any hearing or other submission of the motion must usually be provided to all parties by the party requesting the hearing or submission. Fed. R. Civ. P. 5(d), 7(b)(1); Fed. R. Civ. P. Form 19.

notice of orders or judgments. Written notice of the entry of an order or judgment, provided by the court clerk or one of the parties. • Notice of a judgment is usually provided by the clerk of the court in which the judgment was entered. If the court does not provide notice, a party is usually required to provide it. Under the Federal Rules of Civil Procedure and the Federal Rules of Criminal Procedure, the clerk is required to provide immediate notice of any order or judgment to any party to the case who is not in default. Fed. R. Civ. P. 77(d); Fed. R. Crim. P. 49(c).

notice of removal. The pleading by which the defendant removes a case from state court to federal court. • A notice of removal is filed in the federal district court in the district and division in which the suit is pending. The notice must contain a short and plain statement of the grounds for removal and must include a copy of all process, pleadings, and orders that have been served on the removing party while the case has been pending. The removing party must also notify the state court and other parties to the suit that the notice of removal has been filed. A notice of removal must be filed, if at all, within 30 days after the defendant is served with process in the suit. 28 USCA § 1446; *Murphy Bros., Inc. v. Michetti Pipe Stringing, Inc.*, 526 U.S. 344, 119 S.Ct. 1322 (1999).

notice of trial. A document issued by a court informing the parties of the date on which the lawsuit is set for trial. • While the court typically provides the notice to all parties, it may instead instruct one party to send the notice to all the others.

notice pleading. See PLEADING (2).

notice statute. A recording act providing that the person with the most recent valid claim, and who purchased without notice of an earlier, unrecorded claim, has priority. • About half the states have notice statutes. Cf. RACE STATUTE; RACE-NOTICE STATUTE.

notice to appear. A summons or writ by which a person is cited to appear in court. • This is an informal phrase sometimes used to refer to the summons or other initial process by which a person is notified of a lawsuit. The Federal Rules of Civil Procedure require the summons to state that the defendant must appear and defend within a given time and that failure to do so will result in a default judgment. Fed. R. Civ. P. 4(a). See PROCESS; SUMMONS; DEFAULT JUDGMENT; NOTICE TO PLEAD.

notice to plead. A warning to a defendant, stating that failure to file a responsive pleading within a prescribed time will result in a default judgment. • The Federal Rules of Civil Procedure require the summons to notify the defendant that failure to appear and defend within a prescribed time will result in a default judgment. Fed. R. Civ. P. 4(a). See PROCESS; SUMMONS; DEFAULT JUDGMENT; NOTICE TO APPEAR.

notice to quit. 1. A landlord's written notice demanding that a tenant surrender and vacate the leased property, thereby terminating the tenancy. **2.** A landlord's notice to a tenant to pay any back rent within a specified period (often seven days) or else vacate the leased premises.

notify, *vb.* **1.** To inform (a person or group) in writing or by any method that is understood. **2.** *Archaic.* To give notice of; to make known. See NOTICE.

notoriety. 1. The state of being generally, and often unfavorably, known and spoken of. **2.** A person in such a state.

notorious, *adj.* **1.** Generally known and spoken of, usu. unfavorably. **2.** (Of the possession of property) so conspicuous as to impute notice to the true owner. See ADVERSE POSSESSION.

notorious cohabitation. See COHABITATION.

notorious possession. See POSSESSION.

not sufficient funds. The notation of dishonor (of a check) indicating that the drawer's account does not contain enough money to cover payment. — Abbr. NSF.

novation (noh-vay-shən), *n.* The act of substituting for an old obligation a new one that either replaces an existing obligation with a new obligation or replaces an original party with a new party. ● A novation may substitute (1) a new obligation between the same parties, (2) a new debtor, or (3) a new creditor. — **novate** (noh-**vayt** *or* **noh**-vayt), *vb.* — **novatory** (**noh**-və-tor-ee), *adj.* See *substituted contract* under CONTRACT; ACCORD (1).

now comes. See COMES NOW.

noxious (**nok**-shəs), *adj.* **1.** Harmful to health; injurious. **2.** Unwholesome; corruptive.

n.r. *abbr.* **1.** New reports. **2.** Not reported.

n.s. *abbr.* New series. ● This citation form indicates that a periodical has been renumbered in a new series.

NSF. *abbr.* NOT SUFFICIENT FUNDS.

NTSB. *abbr.* NATIONAL TRANSPORTATION SAFETY BOARD.

nude, *adj.* **1.** Naked; unclothed. **2.** Lacking in consideration or in some essential particular. See NUDUM PACTUM. **3.** Mere; lacking in description.

nudum pactum (**n[y]oo**-dəm **pak**-təm). [Latin "bare agreement"] An agreement that is unenforceable as a contract because it is not "clothed" with consideration.

nugatory (**n[y]oo**-gə-tor-ee), *adj.* Of no force or effect; useless; invalid.

nuisance. 1. A condition or situation (such as a loud noise or foul odor) that interferes with the use or enjoyment of property. ● Liability might or might not arise from the condition or situation. **2.** Loosely, an act or failure to act resulting in an interference with the use or enjoyment of property. ● In this sense, the term denotes the action causing the interference, rather than the resulting condition. **3.** The class of torts arising from such conditions, acts, or failures to act when they occur unreasonably.

abatable nuisance. A nuisance so easily removable that the aggrieved party may lawfully cure the problem without notice to the liable party, such as overhanging tree branches.

absolute nuisance. **1.** Interference with a property right that a court considers fixed or invariable, such as a riparian owner's right to use a stream in its natural condition. **2.** See *nuisance per se*. **3.** Interference in a place where it does not reasonably belong, even if the interfering party is careful. **4.** Interference for which a defendant is held strictly liable for resulting harm, esp. in the nature of pollution. Cf. *qualified nuisance*.

attractive nuisance. A dangerous condition that may attract children onto land, thereby causing a risk to their safety. See ATTRACTIVE-NUISANCE DOCTRINE.

continuing nuisance. A nuisance that is either uninterrupted or frequently recurring. ● It need not be constant or unceasing, but it must occur often enough that it is almost continuous.

mixed nuisance. A condition that is both a private nuisance and a public nuisance, so that it is dangerous to the community at large but also causes particular harm to private individuals.

nuisance in fact. A nuisance existing because of the circumstances of the use or the particular location.

nuisance per se (pər **say**). Interference so severe that it would constitute a nuisance under any circumstances; a nuisance regardless of location or circumstances of use, such as a leaky nuclear-waste storage facility.

permanent nuisance. A nuisance that cannot readily be abated at reasonable expense. Cf. *temporary nuisance*.

private nuisance. A condition that interferes with a person's enjoyment of property, but does not involve a trespass.

public nuisance. An unreasonable interference with a right common to the general public, such as a condition dangerous to health, offensive to community moral standards, or unlawfully obstructing the public in the free use of public property.

qualified nuisance. A condition that, though lawful in itself, is so negligently permitted to exist that it creates an unreasonable risk of harm and, in due course, actually results in injury to another. Cf. *absolute nuisance*.

temporary nuisance. A nuisance that can be corrected by a reasonable expenditure of money or labor. Cf. *permanent nuisance*.

null, *adj.* Having no legal effect; without binding force; VOID. • The phrase *null and void* is a common redundancy.

nulla bona (**nəl**-ə **boh**-nə). [Latin "no goods"] A form of return by a sheriff or constable upon an execution when the judgment debtor has no seizable property within the jurisdiction. Cf. NIHIL EST.

nulla poena sine lege (**nəl**-ə **pee**-nə **SI**-nee **lee**-jee *or* **sin**-ay **lay**-gay). [Latin] No punishment without a law authorizing it.

nullification (nəl-i-fi-**kay**-shən), *n.* **1.** The act of making something void; specif., the action of a state in abrogating a federal law, on the basis of state sovereignty. **2.** The state or condition of being void. — **nullify,** *vb.* See JURY NULLIFICATION.

nullity (**nəl**-ə-tee). **1.** Something that is legally void. **2.** The fact of being legally void.

numerosity (n[y]oo-mər-**ahs**-ə-tee). The requirement in U.S. district courts that, for a case to be certified as a class action, the party applying for certification must show, among other things, that the class of potential plaintiffs is so large that the joinder of all of them into the suit is impracticable. See CLASS ACTION.

nunc pro tunc (**nəngk** proh **təngk** *or* **nuungk** proh **tuungk**). [Latin "now for then"] Having retroactive legal effect through a court's inherent power <the court entered a *nunc pro tunc* order to correct a clerical error in the record>.

***nunc pro tunc* judgment.** See JUDGMENT.

nuncupative (**nəng**-kyə-pay-tiv *or* nəng-**kyoo**-pə-tiv), *adj.* [fr. Latin *nuncupare* "to call by name"] Stated by spoken word; declared orally.

nuncupative will. See WILL.

nuptial (**nəp**-shəl), *adj.* Of or relating to marriage.

N.W. *abbr.* NORTH WESTERN REPORTER.

N.Y.S. *abbr.* NEW YORK SUPPLEMENT.

NYSE. *abbr.* NEW YORK STOCK EXCHANGE.

O

oath. 1. A solemn declaration, accompanied by a swearing to God or a revered person or thing, that one's statement is true or that one will be bound to a promise. • The person making the oath implicitly invites punishment if the statement is untrue or the promise is broken. The legal effect of an oath is to subject the person to penalties for perjury if the testimony is false. **2.** A statement or promise made by such a declaration. **3.** A form of words used for such a declaration. **4.** A formal declaration made solemn without a swearing to God or a revered person or thing; AFFIRMATION.

assertory oath (ə-**sər**-tə-ree). An oath by which one attests to some factual matter, rather than making a promise about one's future conduct.

corporal oath (**kor**-pər-əl). An oath made solemn by touching a sacred object, esp. the Bible.

extrajudicial oath. An oath that, although formally sworn, is taken outside a legal proceeding or outside the authority of law.

judicial oath. An oath taken in the course of a judicial proceeding, esp. in open court.

oath of calumny (**kal**-əm-nee). An oath, taken by a plaintiff or defendant, that attests to the party's good faith and to the party's belief that there is a bona fide cause of action. See CALUMNY.

oath of office. An oath taken by a person about to enter into the duties of public office, by which the person promises to perform the duties of that office in good faith.

pauper's oath. An affidavit or verification of poverty by a person requesting public funds or services. See *poverty affidavit* under AFFIDAVIT; IN FORMA PAUPERIS.

promissory oath. An oath that binds the party to observe a specified course of conduct in the future.

Oath or Affirmation Clause. The clause of the U.S. Constitution requiring members of Congress and the state legislatures, and all members of the executive or judicial branches — state or local — to pledge by oath or affirmation to support the Constitution. U.S. Const. art. VI, cl. 3.

obediential obligation. See OBLIGATION.

obiter (**oh**-bi-tər), *adv.* [Latin "by the way"] Incidentally; in passing <the judge said, obiter, that a nominal sentence would be inappropriate>.

obiter dictum (**oh**-bi-tər **dik**-təm). [Latin "something said in passing"] A judicial comment made during the course of delivering a judicial opinion, but one that is unnecessary to the decision in the case and therefore not precedential (although it may be considered persuasive). Pl. **obiter dicta** (**oh**-bi-tər **dik**-tə). See DICTUM. Cf. HOLDING (1); RATIO DECIDENDI.

object (**ob**-jekt), *n.* **1.** A person or thing to which thought, feeling, or action is directed. See NATURAL OBJECT. **2.** Something sought to be attained or accomplished; an end, goal, or purpose.

object (əb-**jekt**), *vb.* **1.** To state in opposition; to put forward as an objection. **2.** To state or put forward an objection, esp. to something in a judicial proceeding. — **objector,** *n.*

objection, *n.* A formal statement opposing something that has occurred, or is about to occur, in court and seeking the judge's immediate ruling on the point. • The party objecting must usually state the basis for the objection to preserve the right to appeal an adverse ruling.

continuing objection. A single objection to all the questions in a given line of questioning. • A judge may allow a lawyer to make a continuing objection when the judge has overruled an objection applicable to many questions, and the lawyer wants to preserve the objection for the appellate record.

general objection. An objection made without specifying any grounds in support of the objection. • A general objection preserves only the issue of relevancy.

speaking objection. An objection that contains more information (often in the form of argument) than needed by the judge to sustain or overrule it. • Many judges prohibit lawyers from using speaking objections, and sometimes even from stating the grounds for objections, because of the potential for influencing the jury.

specific objection. An objection that is accompanied by a statement of one or more grounds in support of the objection.

objection in point of law. A defensive pleading by which the defendant admits the facts alleged by the plaintiff but objects that they do not make out a legal claim.

objective, *adj.* **1.** Of, relating to, or based on externally verifiable phenomena, as opposed to an individual's perceptions, feelings, or intentions. **2.** Without bias or prejudice; disinterested. Cf. SUBJECTIVE.

objective meaning. See MEANING.

objective standard. See STANDARD.

objective theory of contract. The doctrine that a contract is not an agreement in the sense of a subjective meeting of the minds but is instead a series of external acts giving the objective semblance of agreement. Cf. SUBJECTIVE THEORY OF CONTRACT; MEETING OF THE MINDS.

object of a right. The thing in respect of which a right exists; the subject matter of a right. See SUBJECT OF A RIGHT.

obligation, *n.* **1.** A legal or moral duty to do or not do something. **2.** A formal, binding agreement or acknowledgment of a liability to pay a certain amount or to do a certain thing for a particular person or set of persons. — **obligate,** *vb.* See DUTY; LIABILITY.

absolute obligation. An obligation requiring strict fulfillment according to the terms of the engagement, without any alternatives to the obligor.

accessory obligation. An obligation that is incidental to another obligation. • For example, a mortgage to secure payment of a bond is an accessory obligation. The primary obligation is to pay the bond itself. Cf. *primary obligation* (1).

alternative obligation. An obligation that can be satisfied in two different ways, at the choice of the obligor.

conditional obligation. An obligation that depends on an uncertain event.

conventional obligation. An obligation that results from actual agreement of the parties; a contractual obligation. Cf. *obediential obligation.*

current obligation. An obligation that is presently enforceable, but not past due.

inheritable obligation. An obligation that may be enforced by a successor of the creditor or against a successor of the debtor.

***joint obligation.* 1.** An obligation that binds two or more debtors to a single performance for one creditor. **2.** An obligation that binds one debtor to a single performance for two or more creditors.

obediential obligation (ə-bee-dee-**en**-shəl). An obligation imposed on a person because of a situation or relationship, such as an obligation of parents to care for their children. Cf. *conventional obligation.*

***primary obligation.* 1.** An obligation that arises from the essential purpose of the transaction between the parties. Cf. *accessory obligation.* **2.** A fundamental contractual term imposing a requirement on a contracting party from which other obligations may arise.

secondary obligation. A duty, promise, or undertaking that is incident to a primary obligation; esp., a duty to make reparation upon a breach of contract.

simple obligation. An obligation that does not depend on an outside event; an unconditional obligation.

single obligation. An obligation with no penalty attached for nonperformance, as when one party simply promises to pay $10 to another.

statutory obligation. An obligation — whether to pay money, perform certain acts, or discharge duties — that is created by or arises out of a statute, rather than based on an independent contractual or legal relationship.

obligatory (ə-**blig**-ə-tor-ee), *adj.* **1.** Legally or morally binding. **2.** Required; mandatory. **3.** Creating or recording an obligation.

oblige (ə-**blIj**), *vb.* **1.** To bind by legal or moral duty; obligate. **2.** To bind by doing a favor or service.

obligee (ob-lə-**jee**). **1.** One to whom an obligation is owed; a promisee or creditor. **2.** *Archaic.* One who is obliged to do something; OBLIGOR (1).

obligor (ob-lə-**gor** *or* **ob**-lə-gor). **1.** One who has undertaken an obligation; a promisor or debtor. **2.** *Archaic*. One who obliges another to do something; OBLIGEE (1).

oblique (ə-**bleek**), *adj.* **1.** Not direct in descent; collateral <an oblique heir>. **2.** Indirect; circumstantial <oblique evidence>.

obloquy (**ob**-lə-kwee). **1.** Abusive or defamatory language; CALUMNY. **2.** The state or condition of being ill spoken of; disgrace or bad repute.

obnoxious, *adj.* **1.** Offensive; objectionable <obnoxious behavior>. **2.** Contrary; opposed <a practice obnoxious to the principle of equal protection under the law>. **3.** *Archaic*. Exposed to harm; liable to something undesirable <actions obnoxious to criticism>.

obscene, *adj.* Extremely offensive under contemporary community standards of morality and decency; grossly repugnant to the generally accepted notions of what is appropriate. • Under the Supreme Court's three-part test, material is legally obscene — and therefore not protected under the First Amendment — if, taken as a whole, the material (1) appeals to the prurient interest in sex, as determined by the average person applying contemporary community standards; (2) portrays sexual conduct, as specifically defined by the applicable state law, in a patently offensive way; and (3) lacks serious literary, artistic, political, or scientific value. *Miller v. California*, 413 U.S. 15, 93 S.Ct. 2607 (1973).

obscenity, *n.* **1.** The quality or state of being morally abhorrent or socially taboo, esp. as a result of referring to or depicting sexual or excretory functions. **2.** Something (such as an expression or act) that has this quality. See CONTEMPORARY COMMUNITY STANDARD. Cf. INDECENCY.

commercialized obscenity. Obscenity produced and marketed for sale to the public.

observe, *vb.* To adhere to or abide by (a law, rule, or custom).

obsolescence (ob-sə-**les**-ənts). **1.** The process or state of falling into disuse or becoming obsolete. **2.** A diminution in the value or usefulness of property, esp. as a result of technological advances. • For tax purposes, obsolescence is usually distinguished from physical deterioration. — **obsolescent,** *adj.* — **obsolete,** *adj.* Cf. DEPRECIATION.

obstruction of justice. Interference with the orderly administration of law and justice, as by giving false information to or withholding evidence from a police officer or prosecutor, or by harming or intimidating a witness or juror. • Obstruction of justice is a crime in most jurisdictions.

obtaining property by false pretenses. See FALSE PRETENSES.

obtest (ob- *or* əb-**test**), *vb.* **1.** To call to or invoke as a witness. **2.** To ask for earnestly; beseech; implore. **3.** To protest.

obviate (**ob**-vee-ayt), *vb.* **1.** To dispose of or do away with (a thing); to anticipate and prevent from arising. **2.** To make unnecessary. — **obviation,** *n.* — **obviator,** *n.*

occupancy. **1.** The act, state, or condition of holding, possessing, or residing in or on something; actual possession, residence, or tenancy, esp. of a dwelling or land. **2.** The act of taking possession of something that has no owner (such as abandoned property) so as to acquire legal ownership. See ADVERSE POSSESSION. **3.** The period or term during which one owns, rents, or otherwise occupies property. **4.** The state or condition of being occupied. **5.** The use to which property is put.

occupant. **1.** One who has possessory rights in, or control over, certain property or premises. **2.** One who acquires title by occupancy.

general occupant. A person who occupies land in the interim arising after the death of a *pur autre vie* tenant but before the death of the person who serves as the measuring life for the estate. • The *pur autre vie* tenant does not state who may occupy the land after the death of the first tenant; the land can be occupied by the first possessor of the land. Cf. CESTUI QUE VIE.

special occupant. A *pur autre vie* tenant's heir who occupies land in the interim between the death of the tenant and the death of the person who serves as the measuring life for the estate. • A special occupancy can arise when the grant to the *pur autre vie* tenant provides that possession is for the life of the tenant, then to the tenant's heirs.

occupation. **1.** An activity or pursuit in which a person is engaged; esp., a person's usual or principal work or business. **2.** The possession, control, or use of real property; OCCUPANCY. **3.** The seizure and control of a territory by military force; the condition of territory that has been placed under the authority of a hostile army. **4.** The period during which territory seized by military force is held.

occupational disease. A disease that is contracted as a result of exposure to debilitating conditions or substances in the course of employment.

occupational hazard. A danger or risk that is peculiar to a particular calling or occupation. • Occupational hazards include both accidental injuries and occupational diseases.

Occupational Safety and Health Act of 1970. A federal statute that requires employers to (1) keep the workplace free from recognized hazards that cause or are likely to cause death or serious physical harm to employees, and (2) comply with standards promulgated by the Secretary of Labor. — Abbr. OSHA (**oh**-shə).

Occupational Safety and Health Administration. A federal agency that establishes and enforces health and safety standards in various industries. • This agency, created in 1970 as part of the Labor Department, routinely conducts inspections of businesses and issues citations for noncompliance with its standards. — Abbr. OSHA.

occupation tax. See TAX.

occupying claimant. A person who claims the right under a statute to recover for the cost of improvements done to land that is later found not to belong to the person.

occurrence rule. *Civil procedure*. The rule that a limitations period begins to run when the alleged wrongful act or omission occurs, rather than when the plaintiff discovers the injury. • This rule applies, for example, to most breach-of-contract claims. See STATUTE OF LIMITATIONS. Cf. DISCOVERY RULE.

odium (**oh**-dee-əm). **1.** The state or fact of being hated. **2.** A state of disgrace, usu. resulting from detestable conduct. **3.** Hatred or strong aversion accompanied by loathing or contempt. — **odious,** *adj.*

of counsel. See COUNSEL.

of course. 1. Following the ordinary procedure <the writ was issued as a matter of course>. **2.** Naturally; obviously; clearly <we'll appeal that ruling, of course>.

offender. A person who has committed a crime.

adult offender. **1.** A person who has committed a crime after reaching the age of majority. **2.** A person who, having committed a crime while a minor, has been convicted after reaching the age of majority. **3.** A juvenile who has committed a crime and is tried as an adult rather than as a juvenile.

career offender. Under the federal sentencing guidelines, an adult who, after being convicted of two violent felonies or controlled-substance felonies, commits another such felony. U.S. Sentencing Guidelines Manual § 4B1.1.

first offender. A person who authorities believe has committed a crime but who has never before been convicted of a crime.

repeat offender. A person who has been convicted of a crime more than once; RECIDIVIST.

situational offender. A first-time offender who is unlikely to commit future crimes.

status offender. A youth who engages in conduct that — though not criminal by adult standards — is considered inappropriate enough to bring a charge against the youth in juvenile court; a juvenile who commits a status offense. Cf. *youthful offender*; JUVENILE DELINQUENT.

youthful offender. **1.** A person in late adolescence or early adulthood who has been convicted of a crime. • A youthful offender is often eligible for special programs not available to older offenders, including community supervision, the successful completion of which may lead to erasing the conviction from the offender's record. **2.** JUVENILE DELINQUENT.

offense (ə-**fents**). A violation of the law; a crime, often a minor one. See CRIME.

acquisitive offense. An offense characterized by the unlawful appropriation of another's property. • This is a generic term that refers to a variety of crimes (such as larceny) rather than a particular one.

allied offense. A crime with elements so similar to those of another that the commission of the one is automatically the commission of the other.

bailable offense. A criminal charge for which a defendant may be released from custody after providing proper security.

capital offense. A crime for which the death penalty may be imposed.

cognate offense. A lesser offense that is related to the greater offense because it shares several of the elements of the greater offense and is of the same class or category. • For example, shoplifting is a cognate offense of larceny because both crimes require the element of taking property with the intent to deprive the rightful owner of that property. Cf. *lesser included offense*.

continuing offense. A crime (such as a conspiracy) that is committed over a period of time, so that the last act of the crime controls when the statute of limitations begins to run.

cumulative offense. An offense committed by repeating the same act at different times.

divisible offense. A crime that includes one or more crimes of lesser grade. • For example, murder is a divisible offense comprising assault, battery, and assault with intent to kill.

extraneous offense. An offense beyond or unrelated to the offense for which a defendant is on trial.

graded offense. A crime that is divided into various degrees of severity with corresponding levels of punishment, such as murder (first-degree and second-degree) or assault (simple and aggravated). See DEGREE (2).

inchoate offense. A step toward the commission of another crime, the step in itself being serious enough to merit punishment. • The three inchoate offenses are attempt, conspiracy, and solicitation. The term is sometimes criticized.

index offense. One of eight classes of crimes reported annually by the FBI in the Uniform Crime Report. • The eight classes are murder (and nonnegligent homicide), rape, robbery, aggravated assault, burglary, larceny-theft, arson, and auto theft.

indictable offense. A crime that can be prosecuted only by indictment. • In federal court, such an offense is one punishable by death or by imprisonment for more than one year or at hard labor. Fed. R. Crim. P. 7(a). See INDICTMENT.

joint offense. An offense (such as conspiracy) committed by the participation of two or more persons.

lesser included offense. A crime that is composed of some, but not all, of the elements of a more serious crime and that is necessarily committed in carrying out the greater crime. • For double-jeopardy purposes, a lesser included offense is considered the "same offense" as the greater offense, so that acquittal or conviction of either offense precludes a separate trial for the other. Cf. *cognate offense*.

multiple offense. An offense that violates more than one law but that may require different proof so that an acquittal or conviction under one statute does not exempt the defendant from prosecution under another.

offense against property. A crime against another's personal property. • Although the term *crimes against property*, a common term in modern usage, includes crimes against real property, the term *offense against property* is traditionally restricted to personal property. Cf. CRIMES AGAINST PROPERTY.

offense against the habitation. A crime against another's house — traditionally either arson or burglary.

offense against the person. A crime against the body of another human being. Cf. CRIMES AGAINST PERSONS.

offense against the public health, safety, comfort, and morals. A crime traditionally viewed as endangering the whole of society.

offense against the public peace. A crime that tends to disturb the peace.

petty offense. A minor or insignificant crime. Cf. *serious offense*.

public offense. An act or omission forbidden by law.

public-welfare offense. A minor offense that does not involve moral delinquency and is prohibited only to secure the effective regulation of conduct in the interest of the community. • An example is driving a car with one brake-light missing.

same offense. **1.** For double-jeopardy purposes, the same criminal act, omission, or transaction for which the person has already stood trial. See DOUBLE JEOPARDY. **2.** For sentencing and enhancement-of-punishment purposes, an offense that is quite similar to a previous one.

separate offense. **1.** An offense arising out of the same event as another offense but containing some differences in elements of proof. • A person may be tried, convicted, and sentenced for each separate offense. **2.** An offense arising out of a different event entirely from another offense under consideration.

serious offense. An offense not classified as a petty offense and usu. carrying at least a six-month sentence. Cf. *petty offense*.

sexual offense. An offense involving unlawful sexual conduct, such as prostitution, indecent exposure, incest, pederasty, and bestiality.

status offense. **1.** See *status crime* under CRIME. **2.** A minor's violation of the juvenile code by doing some act that would not be considered illegal if an adult did it, but that indicates that the minor is beyond parental control. • Examples include running away from home, truancy, and incorrigibility. See JUVENILE DELINQUENCY.

substantive offense (**səb**-stən-tiv). A crime that is complete in itself and is not dependent on another crime for one of its elements.

summary offense. An offense (such as a petty misdemeanor) that can be prosecuted without an indictment. Cf. *indictable offense*.

unrelated offense. A crime that is independent from the charged offense.

violent offense. A crime characterized by extreme physical force, such as murder, forcible rape, and assault and battery with a dangerous weapon.

offensive collateral estoppel. See COLLATERAL ESTOPPEL.

offensive-use waiver. An exemption from the attorney–client privilege, whereby a litigant is considered to have waived the privilege by seeking affirmative relief, if the claim relies on privileged information that would be outcome-determinative and that the opposing party has no other way to obtain. Cf. AT-ISSUE WAIVER.

offer, *n.* **1.** The act or an instance of presenting something for acceptance <the prosecutor's offer of immunity>. **2.** A promise to do or refrain from doing some specified thing in the future; a display of willingness to enter into a contract on specified terms, made in a way that would lead a reasonable person to understand that an acceptance, having been sought, will result in a binding contract <she accepted the $750 offer on the Victorian armoire>. Cf. ACCEPTANCE.

irrevocable offer (i-**rev**-ə-kə-bəl). An offer that includes a promise to keep it open for a specified period, during which the offer cannot be withdrawn without the offeror's becoming subject to liability for breach of contract. • Traditionally, this type of promise must be supported by consideration to be enforceable, but under UCC § 2–205, a merchant's signed, written offer giving assurances that it will be held open — but lacking consideration — is nonetheless irrevocable for the stated period (or, if not stated, for a reasonable time not exceeding three months).

offer to all the world. An offer, by way of advertisement, of a reward for the rendering of specified services, addressed to the public at large. • As soon as someone renders the services, a contract is made.

standing offer. An offer that is in effect a whole series of offers, each of which is capable of being converted into a contract by a distinct acceptance.

3. A price at which one is ready to buy or sell; BID <she lowered her offer to $200>. **4.** ATTEMPT (2) <an offer to commit battery>. — **offer,** *vb.*

offeree (ah-fər-**ee**). One to whom an offer is made.

offering, *n.* **1.** The act of making an offer; something offered for sale. **2.** The sale of an issue of securities.

offer of compromise. An offer by one party to settle a dispute amicably (usu. by paying money) to avoid or end a lawsuit or other legal action.

offer of judgment. A settlement offer by one party to allow a specified judgment to be taken against the party. • In federal procedure (and in many states), if the adverse party rejects the offer, and if a judgment finally obtained by that party is not more favorable than the offer, then that party must pay the costs incurred after the offer was made. Fed. R. Civ. P. 68.

offer of performance. *Contracts*. One party's reasonable assurance to the other, through words or conduct, of a present ability to fulfill contractual obligations.

offer of proof. *Procedure*. A presentation of evidence for the record (but outside the jury's presence) usu. made after the judge has sustained an objection to the admissibility of that evidence, so that the evidence can be preserved on the record for an appeal of the judge's ruling. • An offer of proof, which may also be used to persuade the court to admit the evidence, consists of three parts: (1) the evidence itself, (2) an explanation of the purpose for which it is offered (its relevance), and (3) an argument supporting admissibility. Such an offer may include tangible evidence or testimony (through questions and answers, a lawyer's narrative description, or an affidavit). Fed. R. Evid. 103(a)(2).

offeror (ah-fər-**or**). One who makes an offer.

offer to all the world. See OFFER.

office practice. A law practice that primarily involves handling matters outside of court, such as negotiating and drafting contracts, preparing wills and trusts, setting up corporations and partnerships, and advising on tax or employment issues.

office practitioner. A lawyer who does not litigate; an attorney whose work is accomplished primarily in the office, without court appearances.

officer. A person who holds an office of trust, authority, or command. • In public affairs, the term refers especially to a person holding public office under a national, state, or local government, and authorized by that government to exercise some specific function. In corporate law, the term refers especially to a person elected or appointed by the board of directors to manage the daily operations of a corporation, such as a CEO, president, secretary, or treasurer. Cf. DIRECTOR (2).

officer of the court. A person who is charged with upholding the law and administering the judicial system. • Typically, *officer of the court* refers to a judge, clerk, bailiff, sheriff, or the like, but the term also applies to a lawyer, who is obliged to obey court rules and who owes a duty of candor to the court.

official misconduct. See MISCONDUCT.

official privilege. See PRIVILEGE (3).

officious intermeddler (ə-**fish**-əs). A person who confers a benefit on another without being requested or having a legal duty to do so, and who therefore has no legal grounds to demand restitution for the benefit conferred.

off point. Not discussing the precise issue at hand; irrelevant. Cf. ON POINT.

offset, *n.* Something (such as an amount or claim) that balances or compensates for something else; SET-OFF.

offset, *vb.* To balance or calculate against; to compensate for <the gains offset the losses>.

of record. 1. Recorded in the appropriate records <counsel of record>. **2.** (Of a court) that has proceedings taken down stenographically or otherwise documented <court of record>. See *court of record* under COURT.

of the essence. (Of a contractual requirement) so important that if the requirement is not met, the promisor will be held to have breached the contract and a rescission by the promisee will be justified <time is of the essence>.

oil-and-gas lease. See LEASE.

old-age and survivors' insurance. (*usu. cap.*) A system of insurance, subsidized by the federal government, that provides retirement benefits for persons who turn 65 and payments to survivors upon the death of the insured. • This was the original name for the retirement and death benefits established by the Social Security Act of 1935. As the scope of these benefits expanded, the name changed to Old Age, Survivors, and Disability Insurance (OASDI), and then to Old Age, Survivors, Disability, and Health Insurance (OASDHI). Today, the system is most often referred to as *social security*. See SOCIAL SECURITY ACT.

omission, *n.* **1.** A failure to do something; esp., a neglect of duty <the complaint alleged that the driver had committed various negligent acts and omissions>. **2.** The act of leaving something out <the contractor's omission of the sales price rendered the contract void>. **3.** The state of having been left out or of not having been done <his omission from the roster caused no harm>. **4.** Something that is left out, left undone, or otherwise neglected <the many omissions from the list were unintentional>. — **omit,** *vb.* — **omissive,** *adj.* — **omissible,** *adj.*

omnibus (**om**-ni-bəs), *adj.* Relating to or dealing with numerous objects or items at once; including many things or having various purposes.

omnibus bill. See BILL (3).

omnibus clause. 1. A provision in an automobile-insurance policy that extends coverage to all drivers operating the insured vehicle with the owner's permission. **2.** RESIDUARY CLAUSE.

omnibus hearing. See HEARING.

omnibus motion. See MOTION.

OMVI. *abbr.* Operating a motor vehicle while intoxicated. See DRIVING UNDER THE INFLUENCE.

OMVUI. *abbr.* Operating a motor vehicle while under the influence. See DRIVING UNDER THE INFLUENCE.

on all fours. *Jargon.* **1.** (Of a precedent) squarely on point (with a pending case) on both facts and law. **2.** (Of a law case) squarely on point (with a precedent) on both facts and law. Cf. WHITEHORSE CASE.

on demand. When presented or upon request for payment <this note is payable on demand>. See PAYABLE.

one-day, one-trial method. A system of summoning and using jurors whereby a person answers a jury summons and participates in the venire for one day only, unless the person is actually empaneled for a trial, in which event the juror's service lasts for the entire length of the trial.

one-person, one-vote rule. *Constitutional law.* The principle that the Equal Protection Clause requires legislative voting districts to have about the same population. *Reynolds v. Sims*, 377 U.S. 533, 84 S.Ct. 1362 (1964). See APPORTIONMENT.

onerous (**oh**-nər-əs *or* **on**-ər-əs), *adj.* **1.** Excessively burdensome or troublesome; causing hardship <onerous discovery requests>. **2.** Having or involving obligations that outweigh the advantages. <onerous property>. — **onerousness,** *n.* Cf. GRATUITOUS.

one-satisfaction rule. The principle that a plaintiff is entitled to only one recovery for a particular harm, and that the plaintiff must elect a single remedy if the jury has awarded more than one. • This rule is, for example, one of the foundations of a defendant's right to have a jury verdict reduced by the amount of any settlements the plaintiff has received from other entities for the same injury.

on or about. Approximately; at or around the time specified. • This language is used in pleading to prevent a variance between the pleading and the proof, usually when there is any uncertainty about the exact date of a pivotal event. When used in nonpleading contexts, the phrase is mere jargon.

on pain of. Or else suffer punishment for noncompliance. • This phrase usually follows a command or condition <ordered to cease operations on pain of a $2,000 fine>.

on point. Discussing the precise issue now at hand; apposite <this opinion is not on point as authority in our case>. Cf. OFF POINT.

on the brief. (Of a lawyer) having participated in preparing a given brief. • The names of all the lawyers on the brief are typically listed on the front cover.

on the merits. (Of a judgment) delivered after the court has heard and evaluated the evidence and the parties' substantive arguments.

on the pleadings. (Of a judgment) rendered for reasons that are apparent from the faces of the complaint and answer, without hearing or evaluating the evidence or the substantive arguments. See SUMMARY JUDGMENT.

onus (**oh**-nəs). **1.** A burden; a load. **2.** A disagreeable responsibility; an obligation. **3.** ONUS PROBANDI.

onus probandi (**oh**-nəs prə-**ban**-dɪ). [Latin] BURDEN OF PROOF. — Often shortened to *onus*.

op. *abbr.* (*often cap.*) **1.** OPINION (1). **2.** Opinions.

open, *adj.* **1.** Manifest; apparent; notorious. **2.** Visible; exposed to public view; not clandestine. **3.** Not closed, settled, fixed, or terminated.

open account. See ACCOUNT.

open and notorious. **1.** NOTORIOUS (2). **2.** (Of adultery) known and recognized by the public and flouting the accepted standards of morality in the community.

open bid. See BID.

open court. **1.** A court that is in session, presided over by a judge, attended by the parties and their attorneys, and engaged in judicial business. • *Open court* usually refers to a proceeding in which formal entries are made on the record. The term is distinguished from a court that is hearing evidence in camera or from a judge that is exercising merely magisterial powers. **2.** A court session that the public is free to attend.

open-end, *adj.* **1.** Allowing for future changes or additions <open-end credit plan>. **2.** Continuously issuing or redeeming shares on demand at the current net asset value <open-end investment company>.

open entry. See ENTRY.

open-fields doctrine. *Criminal procedure.* The rule permitting a warrantless search of the area outside a property owner's curtilage. • The search must exclude the home and any adjoining land (such as a yard) that is within an enclosure or otherwise protected from public scrutiny. Cf. PLAIN-VIEW DOCTRINE.

opening statement. At the outset of a trial, an advocate's statement giving the fact-finder a preview of the case and of the evidence to be presented. • Although the opening statement is not supposed to be argumentative, lawyers — purposefully or not — often include some form of argument. The term is thus sometimes referred to as *opening argument.*

open-perils policy. See INSURANCE POLICY.

open session. See SESSION.

open verdict. See VERDICT.

operating expense. See EXPENSE.

operation of law. The means by which a right or a liability is created for a party regardless of the party's actual intent <because the court didn't rule on the motion for rehearing within 30 days, it was overruled by operation of law>.

operative, *adj.* **1.** Being in or having force or effect; esp., designating the part of a legal instrument that gives effect to the transaction involved <the operative provision of the contract>. **2.** Having principal relevance; essential to the meaning of the whole <*may* is the operative word of the statute>.

operative fact. See FACT.

opinion. 1. A court's written statement explaining its decision in a given case, usu. including the statement of facts, points of law, rationale, and dicta. — Abbr. op. See DECISION. Cf. JUDGMENT; RULING.

advisory opinion. **1.** A nonbinding statement by a court of its interpretation of the law on a matter submitted for that purpose. • Federal courts are constitutionally prohibited from issuing advisory opinions by the case-or-controversy requirement. See CASE-OR-CONTROVERSY REQUIREMENT. **2.** A written statement, issued only by an administrator of an employee benefit plan, that interprets ERISA and applies it to a specific factual situation. • Only the parties named in the request for the opinion can rely on it, and its reliability depends on the accuracy and completeness of all material facts.

dissenting opinion. An opinion by one or more judges who disagree with the decision reached by the majority. — Often shortened to *dissent.*

majority opinion. An opinion joined in by more than half the judges considering a given case.

memorandum opinion. A unanimous opinion stating the decision of the court; an opinion that briefly reports the court's conclusion, usu. without elaboration because the decision follows a well-established legal principle or does not relate to any point of law.

per curiam opinion (pər **kyoor**-ee-əm). An opinion handed down by an appellate court without identifying the individual judge who wrote the opinion. — Sometimes shortened to *per curiam*.

plurality opinion. An opinion lacking enough judges' votes to constitute a majority, but receiving more votes than any other opinion.

seriatim opinions (seer-ee-**ay**-tim). A series of opinions written individually by each judge on the bench, as opposed to a single opinion speaking for the court as a whole.

slip opinion. **1.** A court opinion that is published individually after being rendered and then collectively in advance sheets before being released for publication in a reporter. • Unlike an unpublished opinion, a slip opinion can usually be cited as authority. Cf. ADVANCE SHEETS. **2.** *Archaic*. A preliminary draft of a court opinion not yet ready for publication. Cf. *unpublished opinion*.

unpublished opinion. An opinion that the court has specifically designated as not for publication. • Court rules usually prohibit citing an unpublished opinion as authority. Such an opinion is considered binding only on the parties to the particular case in which it is issued. Cf. *slip opinion*.

2. A formal expression of judgment or advice based on an expert's special knowledge; esp., a document, usu. prepared at a client's request, containing a lawyer's understanding of the law that applies to a particular case.

legal opinion. A written document in which an attorney provides his or her understanding of the law as applied to assumed facts. • A party may be entitled to rely on a legal opinion, depending on factors such as the identity of the parties to whom the opinion was addressed and the law governing these opinions.

title opinion. A lawyer's or title company's opinion on the state of title for a given piece of real property, usu. describing whether the title is clear and marketable or whether it is encumbered. See TITLE SEARCH.

3. A witness's thoughts, beliefs, or inferences about facts in dispute, as opposed to personal knowledge of the facts themselves. See *opinion evidence* under EVIDENCE.

opinion evidence. See EVIDENCE.

opinion rule. *Evidence*. The principle that a witness should testify to facts, not opinions, and that a witness's opinions are often excludable from evidence. • Traditionally, this principle is regarded as one of the important exclusionary rules in evidence law. It is based on the idea that a witness who has observed data should provide the most factual evidence possible, leaving the jury to draw inferences and conclusions from the evidence. Under this system, the witness's opinion is unnecessary. Today, opinions are admissible if rationally based on a witness's perceptions and helpful to the fact-finder.

opinion testimony. See TESTIMONY.

opponent. 1. An adverse party in a contested matter. **2.** A party that is challenging the admissibility of evidence. • In this sense, the word is an antonym of *proponent*.

opportunity. The fact that the alleged doer of an act was present at the time and place of the act.

opportunity cost. See COST.

opportunity to be heard. The chance to appear in a court or other tribunal and present evidence and argument before being deprived of a right by governmental authority. • The opportunity to be heard is a fundamental requirement of procedural due process. It ordinarily includes the right to receive fair notice of the hearing, to secure the assistance of counsel, and to cross-examine adverse witnesses. See *procedural due process* under DUE PROCESS.

oppression. 1. The act or an instance of unjustly exercising authority or power. **2.** An offense consisting in the abuse of discretionary authority by a public officer who has an improper motive, as a result of which a person is injured. • This offense does not include extortion, which is typically a more serious crime. **3.** *Contracts*. Coercion to enter into an illegal contract. See DURESS; UNCONSCIONABILITY. **4.** *Corporations*. Unfair treatment of minority shareholders (esp. in a close corporation) by the directors or those in control of the corporation. — **oppress,** *vb*. — **oppressive,** *adj*.

opt in, *vb*. To choose to participate in (something).

option, *n*. **1.** The right or power to choose; something that may be chosen <the lawyer was running out of options for settlement>. **2.** A contract made to keep an offer open for a specified period, so that the offeror cannot revoke the offer during that period <the option is valid because it is supported by consideration>. See *irrevocable offer* under OFFER. **3.** The right conveyed by such a contract <Pitts declined to exercise his first option to buy the house>. **4.** The right (but not the obligation) to buy or sell a given quantity of securities, commodities, or other assets at a fixed price within a specified time <trading stock options is a speculative business>.

option, *vb*. To grant or take an option on (something) <Ward optioned his first screenplay to the studio for $50,000>.

optional writ. See WRIT.

opt out, *vb*. To choose not to participate in (something).

O.R. *abbr*. Own recognizance; on one's own recognizance. See RECOGNIZANCE; RELEASE ON RECOGNIZANCE.

oral, *adj.* Spoken or uttered; not expressed in writing. Cf. PAROL.

oral argument. An advocate's spoken presentation before a court (esp. an appellate court) supporting or opposing the legal relief at issue.

oral deposition. See DEPOSITION.

oral will. See WILL.

order, *n.* **1.** A command, direction, or instruction. **2.** A written direction or command delivered by a court or judge.

ex parte order (eks **pahr**-tee). An order made by the court upon the application of one party to an action without notice to the other.

final order. An order that is dispositive of the entire case. See *final judgment* under JUDGMENT.

interlocutory order (in-tər-**lok**-yə-tor-ee). An order that relates to some intermediate matter in the case; any order other than a final order. See *appealable decision* under DECISION; COLLATERAL-ORDER DOCTRINE.

preclusion order. An order barring a litigant from presenting or opposing certain claims or defenses for failing to comply with a discovery order.

show-cause order. An order directing a party to appear in court and explain why the party took (or failed to take) some action or why the court should or should not grant some relief.

3. The words in a draft (such as a check) directing one person to pay money to or deliver something to a designated person. • An order should appear to be the demand of a right as opposed to the request for a favor. **4.** *Securities.* A customer's instructions to a broker about how and when to buy or sell securities.

ordered, adjudged, and decreed. Judicially commanded; formally mandated by a judge.

Order of the Coif (koyf). An honorary legal fraternity composed of a select few law students with the highest grades.

ordinance (**or**-də-nənts). An authoritative law or decree; esp., a municipal regulation.

ordinary, *adj.* **1.** Occurring in the regular course of events; normal; usual. **2.** (Of a judge) having jurisdiction by right of office rather than by delegation. **3.** (Of jurisdiction) original or immediate, as opposed to delegated.

ordinary and necessary expense. See EXPENSE.

ordinary diligence. See DILIGENCE.

ordinary gain. See GAIN (3).

ordinary income. See INCOME.

ordinary loss. See LOSS.

ordinary negligence. See NEGLIGENCE.

ordinary's court. A probate court.

ore tenus (**or**-ee **tee**-nəs *or* **ten**-əs), *adv.* & *adj.* [Latin "by word of mouth"] **1.** Orally; by word of mouth <pleading carried on ore tenus>. **2.** Made or presented orally <ore tenus evidence>.

ore tenus rule. The presumption that a trial court's findings of fact are correct and should not be disturbed unless clearly wrong or unjust.

organic law. The body of laws (as in a constitution) that define and establish a government; FUNDAMENTAL LAW.

organic statute. See STATUTE.

organizational expense. See EXPENSE.

organized crime. 1. Widespread criminal activities that are coordinated and controlled through a central syndicate. See RACKETEERING. **2.** Persons involved in these criminal activities; a syndicate of criminals who rely on their unlawful activities for income. See SYNDICATE.

original evidence. See EVIDENCE.

original intent. See INTENT (2).

originalism. *Constitutional law.* The theory that the U.S. Constitution should be interpreted according to the intent of those who drafted and adopted it. Cf. INTERPRETIVISM; NONINTERPRETIVISM.

original jurisdiction. See JURISDICTION.

original precedent. See PRECEDENT.

original title. See TITLE (2).

original writ. See WRIT.

Origination Clause. 1. The constitutional provision that all bills for increasing taxes and raising revenue must originate in the House of Representatives, not the Senate (U.S. Const. art. I, § 7, cl. 1). • The Senate may, however, amend revenue bills. **2.** A provision in a state constitution requiring that revenue bills originate in the lower house of the state legislature.

origination fee. See FEE (1).

OSHA (oh-shə). *abbr.* **1.** OCCUPATIONAL SAFETY AND HEALTH ACT OF 1970. **2.** OCCUPATIONAL SAFETY AND HEALTH ADMINISTRATION.

ostrich defense. *Slang.* A criminal defendant's claim not to have known of the criminal activities of an associate.

ostrich instruction. See JURY INSTRUCTION.

other consideration. See CONSIDERATION.

other income. See INCOME.

OUI. *abbr.* Operating under the influence. See DRIVING UNDER THE INFLUENCE.

our federalism. (*often cap.*) The doctrine holding that a federal court must refrain from hearing a constitutional challenge to state action if federal adjudication would be considered an improper intrusion into the state's right to enforce its own laws in its own courts. See ABSTENTION. Cf. FEDERALISM.

oust, *vb.* To put out of possession; to deprive of a right or inheritance.

ouster. 1. The wrongful dispossession or exclusion of someone (esp. a cotenant) from property (esp. real property). **2.** The removal of a public or corporate officer from office. Cf. EJECTMENT.

outbuilding. A detached building (such as a shed or garage) within the grounds of a main building.

outcome-determinative test. *Civil procedure.* A test used to determine whether an issue is substantive for purposes of the *Erie* doctrine by examining the issue's potential effect on the outcome of the litigation. See ERIE DOCTRINE.

out-of-court, *adj.* Not done or made as part of a judicial proceeding <an out-of-court settlement>. See EXTRAJUDICIAL.

out-of-pocket expense. See EXPENSE.

out-of-pocket loss. See LOSS.

out-of-pocket rule. The principle that a defrauded buyer may recover from the seller as damages the difference between the amount paid for the property and the actual value received. Cf. BENEFIT-OF-THE-BARGAIN RULE.

output contract. See CONTRACT.

outrageous conduct. See CONDUCT.

outstanding, *adj.* **1.** Unpaid; uncollected <outstanding debts>. **2.** Publicly issued and sold <outstanding shares>.

outstanding warrant. See WARRANT.

over, *adj.* (Of a property interest) intended to take effect after the failure or termination of a prior estate; preceded by some other possessory interest <a limitation over> <a gift over>.

overage, *n.* **1.** An excess or surplus, esp. of goods or merchandise. **2.** A percentage of retail sales paid to a store's landlord in addition to fixed rent.

overbreadth doctrine. *Constitutional law.* The doctrine holding that if a statute is so broadly written that it deters free expression, then it can be struck down on its face because of its chilling effect — even if it also prohibits acts that may legitimately be forbidden. • The Supreme Court has used this doctrine to invalidate a number of laws, including those that would disallow peaceful picketing or require loyalty oaths. Cf. VAGUENESS DOCTRINE.

overdraft. 1. A withdrawal of money from a bank in excess of the balance on deposit. **2.** The amount of money so withdrawn. — Abbr. OD; o/d. **3.** A line of credit extended by a bank to a customer (esp. an established or institutional customer) who might overdraw on an account.

overinclusive, *adj.* (Of legislation) extending beyond the class of persons intended to be protected or regulated; burdening more persons than necessary to cure the problem.

overreaching, *n.* **1.** The act or an instance of taking unfair commercial advantage of another, esp. by fraudulent means. **2.** The act or an instance of defeating one's own purpose by going too far. — **overreach,** *vb.*

overridden veto. See VETO.

override (oh-vər-**rɪd**), *vb.* To prevail over; to nullify or set aside.

override (**oh**-vər-rɪd), *n.* **1.** A commission paid to a manager on a sale made by a subordinate. **2.** A commission paid to a real-estate broker who listed a property when, within a reasonable amount of time after the expiration of the listing, the owner sells that property directly to a buyer with whom the broker had negotiated during the term of the listing. **3.** ROYALTY (2).

overrule, *vb.* **1.** To rule against; to reject <the judge overruled all of the defendant's objections>. **2.** (Of a court) to overturn or set aside (a precedent) by expressly deciding that it should no longer be controlling law

<in *Brown v. Board of Education*, the Supreme Court overruled *Plessy v. Ferguson*>. Cf. VACATE (1).

overt, *adj.* Open and observable; not concealed or secret <the conspirators' overt acts>.

overt act. *Criminal law.* **1.** An act that indicates an intent to kill or seriously harm another person and thus gives that person a justification to use self-defense. **2.** An outward act, however innocent in itself, done in furtherance of a conspiracy, treason, or criminal attempt. **3.** See ACTUS REUS.

overtry, *vb.* (Of a trial lawyer) to try a lawsuit by expending excessive time, effort, and other resources to explore minutiae, esp. to present more evidence than the fact-trier can assimilate, the result often being that the adversary gains arguing points by disputing the minutiae.

overturn, *vb.* To overrule or reverse <the court overturned a long-established precedent>.

owelty (**oh**-əl-tee). **1.** Equality as achieved by a compensatory sum of money given after an exchange of parcels of land having different values or after an unequal partition of real property. **2.** The sum of money so paid.

OWI. *abbr.* Operating while intoxicated. See DRIVING UNDER THE INFLUENCE.

owner. One who has the right to possess, use, and convey something; a proprietor. See OWNERSHIP.

adjoining owner. A person who owns land abutting another's.

beneficial owner. **1.** One recognized in equity as the owner of something because use and title belong to that person, even though legal title may belong to someone else; esp., one for whom property is held in trust. **2.** A corporate shareholder who has the power to buy or sell the shares, but who is not registered on the corporation's books as the owner.

general owner. One who has the primary or residuary title to property; one who has the ultimate ownership of property. Cf. *special owner.*

legal owner. One recognized by law as the owner of something; esp., one who holds legal title to property for the benefit of another. See TRUSTEE.

limited owner. A tenant for life; the owner of a life estate. See *life estate* under ESTATE.

record owner. A property owner in whose name the title appears in the public records.

sole and unconditional owner. *Insurance.* The owner who has full equitable title to, and exclusive interest in, the insured property.

special owner. One (such as a bailee) with a qualified interest in property. Cf. *general owner.*

owners' association. The basic governing entity for a condominium or planned unit developments. • It is usually an unincorporated association or a nonprofit corporation.

owners' equity. The aggregate of the owners' financial interests in the assets of a business entity; the capital contributed by the owners plus any retained earnings.

ownership. The collection of rights allowing one to use and enjoy property, including the right to convey it to others. • Ownership implies the right to possess a thing, regardless of any actual or constructive control. Ownership rights are general, permanent, and inheritable. Cf. POSSESSION; TITLE (1).

beneficial ownership. **1.** A beneficiary's interest in trust property. **2.** A corporate shareholder's power to buy or sell the shares, though the shareholder is not registered on the corporation's books as the owner.

contingent ownership. Ownership in which title is imperfect but is capable of becoming perfect on the fulfillment of some condition; conditional ownership.

corporeal ownership. The actual ownership of land or chattels.

incorporeal ownership. The ownership of rights in land or chattels.

joint ownership. Ownership shared by two or more persons whose interests, at death, pass to the survivor or survivors by virtue of the right of survivorship.

ownership in common. Ownership shared by two or more persons whose interests, at death, pass to the dead owner's heirs or successors.

qualified ownership. Ownership that is shared, restricted to a particular use, or limited in the extent of its enjoyment.

trust ownership. A trustee's interest in trust property.

vested ownership. Ownership in which title is perfect; absolute ownership.

oyez (**oh**-yes *or* **oh**-yez *or* **oh**-yay). [Law French] Hear ye. • The utterance *oyez, oyez, oyez* is usually used in court by the public crier to call the courtroom to order when a session begins or when a proclamation is about to be made.

P

P. *abbr.* PACIFIC REPORTER.

P.A. *abbr.* See *professional association* under ASSOCIATION.

PAC (pak). *abbr.* POLITICAL-ACTION COMMITTEE.

PACER. *abbr.* PUBLIC ACCESS TO COURT ELECTRONIC RECORDS.

Pacific Reporter. A set of regional lawbooks that, being part of the West Group's National Reporter System, contain every published decision from Alaska, Arizona, California, Colorado, Hawaii, Idaho, Kansas, Montana, Nevada, New Mexico, Oklahoma, Oregon, Utah, Washington, and Wyoming, from 1883 to date. • The first series ran from 1883 to 1931; the second series ran from 1931 to 2000; the third series is the current one. — Abbr. P.; P.2d; P.3d.

pack, *vb.* To choose or arrange (a tribunal, jurors, etc.) to accomplish a desired result <pack a jury>.

packing, *n.* A gerrymandering technique in which a dominant political or racial group minimizes minority representation by concentrating the minority into as few districts as possible. Cf. CRACKING; STACKING.

pact. An agreement between two or more parties; esp., an agreement (such as a treaty) between two or more nations or governmental entities.

paid-up insurance. See INSURANCE.

pain and suffering. Physical discomfort or emotional distress compensable as an element of damages in torts. See DAMAGES.

palimony (**pal**-ə-moh-nee). [Portmanteau word from *pal* + *alimony*] A court-ordered allowance paid by one member to the other of a couple that, though unmarried, formerly cohabited. The term originated in the press coverage of *Marvin v. Marvin*, 557 P.2d 106 (Cal. 1976). Cf. ALIMONY.

Palsgraf **rule** (**pawlz**-graf). *Torts.* The principle that negligent conduct resulting in injury will lead to liability only if the actor could have reasonably foreseen that the conduct would injure the victim. • *Palsgraf v. Long Island R.R.*, 162 N.E. 99 (N.Y. 1928).

pander, *n.* One who engages in pandering. See PIMP.

pandering (**pan**-dər-ing), *n.* **1.** The act or offense of recruiting a prostitute, finding a place of business for a prostitute, or soliciting customers for a prostitute. **2.** The act or offense of selling or distributing textual or visual material (such as magazines or videotapes) openly advertised to appeal to the recipient's sexual interest. — **pander,** *vb.*

P & L. *abbr.* Profit and loss. See INCOME STATEMENT.

panel. 1. A list of persons summoned as potential jurors. **2.** A group of persons selected for jury duty; VENIRE. **3.** A set of judges selected from a complete court to decide a specific case; esp., a group of three judges designated to sit for an appellate court.

panelation (pan-əl-**ay**-shən). The act of empaneling a jury.

panel attorney. A private attorney who represents indigent defendants at government expense.

panel-shopping. The practice of choosing the most favorable group of judges to hear an appeal.

paper. 1. Any written or printed document or instrument. **2.** A negotiable document or instrument evidencing a debt; esp., commercial documents or negotiable instruments considered as a group. See NEGOTIABLE INSTRUMENT. **3.** (*pl.*) COURT PAPERS.

paper loss. See LOSS.

paralegal, *n.* A person who assists a lawyer in duties related to the practice of law but who is not a licensed attorney. — **paralegal,** *adj.*

paralegalize, *vb. Slang.* To proofread, cite-check, and otherwise double-check the details in (a legal document).

parallel citation. See CITATION.

paramount title. See TITLE (2).

parcel, *n.* **1.** A small package or bundle. **2.** A tract of land.

parcel, *vb.* To divide and distribute (goods, land, etc.).

pardon, *n.* The act or an instance of officially nullifying punishment or other legal consequences of a crime. • A pardon is usually granted by the chief executive of a government. — **pardon,** *vb.* See CLEMENCY. Cf. COMMUTATION (2); REPRIEVE.

parens patriae (**par**-enz **pay**-tree-ee *or* **pa**-tree-I). [Latin "parent of his or her country"] **1.** The state regarded as a sovereign; the state in its capacity as provider of protection to those unable to care for themselves <the attorney general acted as *parens patriae* in the administrative hearing>. **2.** A doctrine by which a government has standing to prosecute a lawsuit on behalf of a citizen, esp. on behalf of someone who is under a legal disability to prosecute the suit <*parens patriae* allowed the state to institute proceedings>. • The state ordinarily has no standing to sue on behalf of its citizens, unless a separate, sovereign interest will be served by the suit.

parent. The lawful father or mother of someone. • In ordinary usage, the term denotes more than responsibility for conception and birth. The term commonly includes (1) either the natural father or the natural mother of a child, (2) the adoptive father or adoptive mother of a child, (3) a child's putative blood parent who has expressly acknowledged paternity, and (4) an individual or agency whose status as guardian has been established by judicial decree. In law, parental status based on any criterion may be terminated by judicial decree.

adoptive parent. A parent by virtue of legal adoption. See ADOPTION.

foster parent. An adult who, though without blood ties or legal ties, cares for and rears a child, esp. an orphaned or neglected child who might otherwise be deprived of nurture.

surrogate parent. **1.** A person who carries out the role of a parent by court appointment or the voluntary assumption of parental responsibilities. **2.** See *surrogate mother* (2) under MOTHER.

parental immunity. See IMMUNITY (2).

parental kidnapping. See KIDNAPPING.

Parental Kidnapping Prevention Act. A federal law, enacted in 1980, providing a penalty for child-kidnapping by a noncustodial parent and requiring a state to recognize and enforce a child-custody order rendered by a court of another state. 28 USCA § 1738A; 42 USCA §§ 654, 655, 663. — Abbr. PKPA. Cf. UNIFORM CHILD CUSTODY JURISDICTION ACT.

parental-liability statute. A law obliging parents to pay damages for torts (esp. intentional ones) committed by their minor children. • All states have these laws, but most limit the parents' monetary liability to about $3,000 per tort. Cf. PARENTAL-RESPONSIBILITY STATUTE.

parental-preference doctrine. The principle that a fit parent, who is willing and able to care for a minor child, should be granted custody instead of someone who is not the child's parent.

parental-responsibility statute. **1.** A law imposing criminal sanctions (such as fines) on parents whose minor children commit crimes as a result of the parents' failure to exercise sufficient control over them. **2.** PARENTAL-LIABILITY STATUTE.

parental rights. A parent's rights to make all decisions concerning his or her child, including the right to determine the child's care and custody, the right to educate and discipline the child, and the right to control the child's earnings and property. See TERMINATION OF PARENTAL RIGHTS.

parent corporation. See CORPORATION.

parentela (par-ən-**tee**-lə), *n. pl.* [Law Latin] Persons who can trace descent from a common ancestor.

parentelic method (par-ən-**tee**-lik *or* **-tel**-ik). A scheme of computation used to determine the paternal or maternal collaterals entitled to inherit when a childless intestate decedent is not survived by parents or their issue. • Under this method, the estate passes to grandparents and their issue; if there are none, to great-grandparents and their issue; and so on down each line until an heir is found.

parenticide (pə-**ren**-tə-sɪd). **1.** The act of murdering one's parent. **2.** A person who murders his or her parent.

parliamentary privilege. See PRIVILEGE (1).

parol (pə-**rohl** *or* **par**-əl), *adj.* **1.** Oral; unwritten <parol evidence>. **2.** Not under seal <parol contract>.

parol (pə-**rohl** *or* **par**-əl), *n.* An oral statement or declaration.

parol arrest. See ARREST.

parol contract. See CONTRACT.

parole (pə-**rohl**), *n.* The release of a prisoner from imprisonment before the full sentence has been served. — **parole,** *vb.* Cf. PARDON; PROBATION (1).

parole board. A governmental body that decides whether prisoners may be released from prison before completing their sentences.

parolee (pə-roh-**lee**). A prisoner who is released on parole.

parole revocation. The administrative act of returning a parolee to prison because of the parolee's failure to abide by the conditions of parole (as by committing a new offense).

parol evidence. See EVIDENCE.

parol-evidence rule. *Contracts.* The principle that a writing intended by the parties to be a final embodiment of their agreement cannot be modified by evidence that adds to, varies, or contradicts the writing. See INTEGRATION (2); MERGER (2). Cf. FOUR-CORNERS RULE.

***Parratt–Hudson* doctrine.** The principle that a state actor's random, unauthorized deprivation of someone's property does not amount to a due-process violation if the state provides an adequate postdeprivation remedy. *Parratt v. Taylor*, 451 U.S. 527, 101 S.Ct. 1908 (1984); *Hudson v. Palmer*, 468 U.S. 517, 104 S.Ct. 3194 (1984).

parricide (**par**-ə-sɪd), *n.* **1.** The act of killing a close relative, esp. a parent. **2.** One who kills such a relative. — **parricidal,** *adj.* Cf. PATRICIDE.

partial account. A preliminary accounting of an executor's or administrator's dealings with an estate.

partial breach. See BREACH OF CONTRACT.

partial defense. See DEFENSE (1).

partial evidence. See EVIDENCE.

partial failure of consideration. See FAILURE OF CONSIDERATION.

partial integration. See INTEGRATION.

partial loss. See LOSS.

partially disclosed principal. See PRINCIPAL (1).

partially integrated contract. See INTEGRATED CONTRACT.

partial release. See RELEASE.

partial summary judgment. See SUMMARY JUDGMENT.

partial verdict. See VERDICT.

particeps (**pahr**-tə-seps), *n.* [Latin] **1.** A participant. **2.** A part owner.

particeps criminis (**pahr**-tə-seps **krim**-ə-nis), *n.* [Latin "partner in crime"] **1.** An accomplice or accessory. Pl. ***participes criminis*** (pahr-**tis**-ə-peez). See ACCESSORY. **2.** The doctrine that one participant in an unlawful activity cannot recover in a civil action against another participant in the activity. • This is a civil doctrine only, having nothing to do with criminal responsibility.

participation loan. See LOAN.

particular jurisprudence. See JURISPRUDENCE.

particular malice. See MALICE.

particulars of sale. A document that describes the various features of a thing (such as a house) that is for sale.

partition, *n.* **1.** Something that separates one part of a space from another. **2.** The act of dividing; esp., the division of real property held jointly or in common by two or more persons into individually owned interests. — **partition,** *vb.* — **partible,** *adj.*

partner. 1. One who shares or takes part with another, esp. in a venture with shared benefits and shared risks; an associate or colleague. **2.** One of two or more persons who jointly own and carry on a business for profit. See PARTNERSHIP. **3.** One of two persons who are married or who live together; a spouse or companion.

general partner. A partner who ordinarily takes part in the daily operations of the business, shares in the profits and losses, and is personally responsible for the partnership's debts and liabilities.

junior partner. A partner whose participation is limited with respect to both profits and management.

limited partner. A partner who receives profits from the business but does not take part in managing the business and is not liable for any amount greater than his or her original investment. See *limited partnership* under PARTNERSHIP.

liquidating partner. The partner appointed to settle the accounts, collect the assets, adjust the claims, and pay the debts of a dissolving or insolvent firm.

name partner. A partner whose name appears in the name of the partnership <Mr. Tibbs is a name partner in the accounting firm of Gibbs & Tibbs>.

nominal partner. A person who is held out as a partner in a firm or business but who has no actual interest in the partnership.

quasi-partner. A person who joins others in an enterprise that appears to be, but is not, a partnership. • A joint venturer, for example, is a quasi-partner.

secret partner. A partner whose connection with the firm is concealed from the public.

senior partner. A high-ranking partner, as in a law firm.

silent partner. A partner who shares in the profits but who has no active voice in management of the firm and whose existence is often not publicly disclosed.

surviving partner. The partner who, upon the partnership's dissolution because of another partner's death, serves as a trustee to administer the firm's remaining affairs.

partnership. A voluntary association of two or more persons who jointly own and carry on a business for profit. • Under the Uniform Partnership Act, a partnership is presumed to exist if the persons agree to share proportionally the business's profits or losses. Cf. JOINT VENTURE; STRATEGIC ALLIANCE.

collapsible partnership. *Tax.* A partnership formed by partners who intend to dissolve it before they realize any income. See IRC (26 USCA) § 751. Cf. *collapsible corporation* under CORPORATION.

general partnership. A partnership in which all partners participate fully in running the business and share equally in profits and losses (though the partners' monetary contributions may vary).

limited-liability partnership. A partnership in which a partner is not liable for a negligent act committed by another partner or by an employee not under the partner's supervision. — Abbr. L.L.P.

limited partnership. A partnership composed of one or more persons who control the business and are personally liable for the partnership's debts (called *general partners*), and one or more persons who contribute capital and share profits but who cannot manage the business and are liable only for the amount of their contribution (called *limited partners*). — Abbr. L.P.

partnership at will. A partnership that any partner may dissolve at any time without thereby incurring liability.

partnership by estoppel. A partnership implied by law when one or more persons represent themselves as partners to a third party who relies on that representation. • A person who is deemed a partner by estoppel becomes liable for any credit extended to the partnership by the third party.

partnership agreement. A contract defining the partners' rights and duties toward one another — not the partners' relationship with third parties.

partnership association. A business organization that combines the features of a limited partnership and a close corporation. • Partnership associations are statutorily recognized in only a few states.

partner's lien. A partner's right to have the partnership property applied in payment of the partnership's debts and to have whatever is due the firm from fellow partners deducted from what would otherwise be payable to them for their shares.

part performance. 1. The accomplishment of some but not all of one's contractual obligations. **2.** A party's execution, in reliance on an opposing party's oral promise, of enough of an oral contract's requirements that a court may hold the statute of frauds not to apply. **3.** PART-PERFORMANCE DOCTRINE.

part-performance doctrine. The equitable principle by which a failure to comply with the statute of frauds is overcome by a party's execution, in reliance on an opposing party's oral promise, of an oral contract's requirements.

party. 1. One who takes part in a transaction <a party to the contract>.

party of the first part. *Archaic.* The party named first in a contract; esp., the owner or seller.

party of the second part. *Archaic.* The party named second in a contract; esp., the buyer.

2. One by or against whom a lawsuit is brought <a party to the lawsuit>.

adverse party. A party whose interests are opposed to the interests of another party to the action.

aggrieved party. A party whose personal, pecuniary, or property rights have been adversely affected by another person's actions or by a court's decree or judgment.

indispensable party. A party who, having interests that would inevitably be affected by a court's judgment, must be included in the case. • If such a party is not included, the case must be dismissed. Fed. R. Civ. P. 19(b). Cf. *necessary party*.

innocent party. A party who did not consciously or intentionally participate in an event or transaction.

interested party. A party who has a recognizable stake (and therefore standing) in a matter.

necessary party. A party who, being closely connected to a lawsuit, should be included in the case if feasible, but whose absence will not require dismissal of the proceedings. See *compulsory joinder* under JOINDER. Cf. *indispensable party*.

nominal party. A party who, having some interest in the subject matter of a lawsuit, will not be affected by any judgment but is nonetheless joined in the lawsuit to avoid procedural defects. • An example is the disinterested stakeholder in a garnishment action. Cf. *real party in interest*.

party opponent. An adversary in a legal proceeding.

party to be charged. A defendant in an action to enforce a contract falling within the statute of frauds.

prevailing party. A party in whose favor a judgment is rendered, regardless of the amount of damages awarded.

proper party. A party who may be joined in a case for reasons of judicial economy but whose presence is not essential to the proceeding. See *permissive joinder* under JOINDER.

real party in interest. A person entitled under the substantive law to enforce the right sued upon and who generally, but not necessarily, benefits from the action's final outcome. Cf. *nominal party*.

pass, *vb.* **1.** To pronounce or render an opinion, ruling, sentence, or judgment <the court refused to pass on the constitutional issue, deciding the case instead on procedural grounds>. **2.** To transfer or be transferred <title passed when the nephew received the deed>. **3.** To enact (a legislative bill or resolution) <Congress has debated whether to pass a balanced-budget amendment to the Constitution>. **4.** To approve or certify (something) as meeting specified requirements <the mechanic informed her that the car had passed inspection>. **5.** To publish, transfer, or circulate (a thing, often a forgery) <he was found guilty of passing counterfeit bills>. **6.** To forgo or proceed beyond <the case was passed on the court's trial docket because the judge was presiding over a criminal trial>.

passim (**pas**-im), *adv.* [Latin] Here and there; throughout (the cited work). • In modern legal writing, the citation signal *see generally* is preferred to *passim* as a general reference, although *passim* can be useful in a brief's index of authorities to show that a given authority is cited throughout the brief.

passing off, *n.* The act or an instance of falsely representing one's own product as that of another in an attempt to deceive potential buyers. — **pass off,** *vb.* Cf. MISAPPROPRIATION.

passive, *adj.* Not involving active participation; esp., of or relating to a business enterprise in which an investor does not have immediate control over the activity that produces income.

passive activity. *Tax.* A business activity in which the taxpayer does not materially participate and therefore does not have immediate control over the income.

passive concealment. See CONCEALMENT.

passive income. See INCOME.

passive negligence. See NEGLIGENCE.

pass-through, *adj.* (Of a seller's or lessor's costs) chargeable to the buyer or lessee.

pass-through taxation. See TAXATION.

past consideration. See CONSIDERATION.

past recollection recorded. *Evidence.* A document concerning events that a witness once knew about but can no longer remember. • The document itself is evidence and, despite being hearsay, may be admitted (or read into the record) if it was prepared or adopted by the witness when the events were fresh in the witness's memory. Fed. R. Evid. 803(5). Cf. PRESENT RECOLLECTION REFRESHED.

patent (pay-tənt), *adj.* Obvious; apparent <a patent ambiguity>. Cf. LATENT.

patent (**pat-ənt**), *n.* **1.** The governmental grant of a right, privilege, or authority. **2.** The official document so granting. See LETTERS PATENT. **3.** The exclusive right to make, use, or sell an invention for a specified period (usu. 20 years), granted by the federal government to the inventor if the device or process is novel, useful, and nonobvious. 35 USCA §§ 101–103.

patent ambiguity. See AMBIGUITY.

Patent and Copyright Clause. The constitutional provision granting Congress the authority to promote the advancement of science and the arts by establishing a national system for patents and copyrights. U.S. Const. art. I, § 8, cl. 8.

Patent and Trademark Office. The Department of Commerce agency that examines patent and trademark applications, issues patents, registers trademarks, and furnishes patent and trademark information and services to the public.

patent defect. See DEFECT.

patent pending. The designation given to an invention while the Patent and Trademark Office is processing the patent application. • No protection against infringement exists, however, unless an actual patent is granted. — Abbr. pat. pend.

paternal, *adj.* Of, relating to, or coming from one's father <paternal property>. Cf. MATERNAL.

paternalism, *n.* A government's policy or practice of taking responsibility for the individual affairs of its citizens, esp. by supplying their needs or regulating their conduct in a heavy-handed manner. — **paternalistic,** *adj.*

paternal line. See LINE.

paternity (pə-**tər**-ni-tee). The state or condition of being a father, esp. a biological one; fatherhood.

paternity suit. A court proceeding to determine whether a person is the father of a child (esp. one born out of wedlock), usu. initiated by the mother in an effort to obtain child support.

paternity test. A test, usu. involving DNA identification or tissue-typing, for determining whether a given man is the biological father of a particular child. See DNA IDENTIFICATION; HLA TEST.

pathological intoxication. See INTOXICATION.

pathology (pə-**thol**-ə-jee), *n.* The branch of medical study that examines the origins, symptoms, and nature of diseases. — **pathological** (path-ə-**loj**-i-kəl), *adj.* — **pathologist** (pə-**thol**-ə-jist), *n.*

patient–litigant exception. An exemption from the doctor–patient privilege, whereby the privilege is lost when the patient sues the doctor for negligence or malpractice.

patient's bill of rights. A general statement of patient rights voluntarily adopted by a healthcare provider or mandated by statute, covering such matters as access to care, patient dignity and confidentiality, personal safety, consent to treatment, and explanation of charges.

pat. pend. *abbr.* PATENT PENDING.

patricide (**pa**-trə-sɪd), *n.* **1.** The act of killing one's own father. **2.** One who kills his or her father. — **patricidal,** *adj.* Cf. PARRICIDE.

patrimony (**pa**-trə-moh-nee). An estate inherited from one's father or other ancestor; legacy or heritage. — **patrimonial** (pa-trə-**moh**-nee-əl), *adj.*

patron. **1.** A regular customer or client of a business. **2.** A person who protects or supports some person or thing.

patronage (**pay**-trə-nij). **1.** The giving of support, sponsorship, or protection. **2.** All the customers of a business; clientele. **3.** The power to appoint persons to governmental positions or to confer other political favors. — **patron,** *n.*

patronizing a prostitute. The offense of requesting or securing the performance of a sex act for a fee; PROSTITUTION. Cf. SOLICITATION (3).

pattern, *n.* A mode of behavior or series of acts that are recognizably consistent <a pattern of racial discrimination>.

pattern of racketeering activity. Two or more related criminal acts that amount to, or pose a threat of, continued criminal activity. See RACKETEERING.

pauper. A very poor person, esp. one who receives aid from charity or public funds; an indigent. See IN FORMA PAUPERIS.

pauper's oath. See OATH.

pawn, *n.* **1.** An item of personal property deposited as security for a debt; a pledge or guarantee. **2.** The act of depositing personal property in this manner. **3.** The condition of being held on deposit as a pledge. — **pawn,** *vb.* Cf. BAILMENT.

payable, *adj.* (Of a sum of money or a negotiable instrument) that is to be paid. • An amount may be payable without being due.

payable after sight. Payable after acceptance or protest of nonacceptance. See *sight draft* under DRAFT.

payable on demand. Payable when presented or upon request for payment; payable at any time.

payable to bearer. Payable to anyone holding the instrument.

payable to order. Payable only to a specified payee.

payee. One to whom money is paid or payable; esp., a party named in commercial paper as the recipient of the payment.

payment. 1. Performance of an obligation by the delivery of money or some other valuable thing accepted in partial or full discharge of the obligation. **2.** The money or other valuable thing so delivered in satisfaction of an obligation.

advance payment. A payment made in anticipation of a contingent or fixed future liability or obligation.

balloon payment. A final loan payment that is usu. much larger than the preceding regular payments and that discharges the principal balance of the loan. See *balloon note* under NOTE (1).

conditional payment. Payment of an obligation only on condition that something be done. • Generally, the payor reserves the right to demand the payment back if the condition is not met.

constructive payment. A payment made by the payor but not yet credited by the payee. • For example, a rent check mailed on the first of the month is a constructive payment even though the landlord does not deposit the check until ten days later.

direct payment. **1.** A payment made directly to the payee, without using an intermediary. **2.** A payment that is absolute and unconditional on the amount, the due date, and the payee.

down payment. The portion of a purchase price paid in cash (or its equivalent) at the time the sale agreement is executed. Cf. BINDER (2); EARNEST MONEY.

involuntary payment. A payment obtained by fraud or duress.

lump-sum payment. A payment of a large amount all at once, as opposed to smaller payments over time.

payment bond. See BOND (2).

payment in due course. A payment to the holder of a negotiable instrument at or after its maturity date, made by the payor in good faith and without notice of any defect in the holder's title. See HOLDER IN DUE COURSE.

payment intangible. See INTANGIBLE.

payment into court. A party's money or property deposited with a court for distribution after a proceeding according to the parties' settlement or the court's order. See INTERPLEADER.

payola (pay-**oh**-lə). An indirect and secret payment for a favor, esp. one relating to business; a bribe.

payor. One who pays; esp., a person responsible for paying a negotiable instrument. See DRAWEE.

payor bank. See BANK.

payroll tax. See TAX.

PBGC. *abbr.* PENSION BENEFIT GUARANTY CORPORATION.

P.C. *abbr.* **1.** See *professional corporation* under CORPORATION. **2.** POLITICAL CORRECTNESS.

PCR action. See POSTCONVICTION-RELIEF PROCEEDING.

P.D. *abbr.* PUBLIC DEFENDER.

peaceable possession. See POSSESSION.

peace bond. See BOND (2).

peace warrant. See WARRANT.

peculation (pek-yə-**lay**-shən), *n.* Embezzlement, esp. by a public official. — **peculate** (**pek**-yə-layt), *vb.* — **peculative** (**pek**-yə-lə-tiv), *adj.* — **peculator** (**pek**-yə-lay-tər), *n.*

peculiar-risk doctrine. The principle that an employer will be liable for injury caused by an independent contractor if the employer failed to take precautions against a risk that is peculiar to the contractor's work and that the employer should have recognized.

pecuniary (pi-**kyoo**-nee-er-ee), *adj.* Of or relating to money; monetary.

pecuniary benefit. See BENEFIT.

pecuniary bequest. See BEQUEST.

pecuniary damages. See DAMAGES.

pecuniary gain. See GAIN (1).

pecuniary legacy. See LEGACY.

pedal possession. See POSSESSION.

pederasty (**ped**-ər-as-tee), *n.* Anal intercourse between a man and a boy. — **pederast** (**ped**-ə-rast), *n.* Cf. SODOMY.

pedophilia. 1. An adult's sexual disorder consisting in the desire for sexual gratification by molesting children, esp. prepubescent children. **2.** An adult's act of child molestation. • Pedophilia can but does not necessarily involve intercourse. — **pedophile,** *n.* Cf. PEDERASTY.

Peeping Tom. A person who spies on another (as through a window), usu. to gain sexual pleasure; VOYEUR.

peer-reviewed journal. A publication whose practice is to forward submitted articles to disinterested experts who screen them for scholarly or scientific reliability, the idea being that articles actually published have already withstood expert scrutiny and comment.

peer-review organization. A government agency that monitors health-regulation compliance by private hospitals requesting public funds (such as Medicare payments).

peer-review privilege. See PRIVILEGE (3).

penal (**pee**-nəl), *adj.* Of, relating to, or being a penalty or punishment, esp. for a crime.

penal action. See ACTION.

penal bond. See BOND (2).

penal code. A compilation of criminal laws, usu. defining and categorizing the offenses and setting forth their respective punishments. See MODEL PENAL CODE.

penal statute. See STATUTE.

penal sum. The monetary amount specified as a penalty in a penal bond. See *penal bond* under BOND (2).

penalty. 1. Punishment imposed on a wrongdoer, esp. in the form of imprisonment or fine. • Though usually for crimes, penalties are also sometimes imposed for civil wrongs. **2.** Excessive liquidated damages that a contract purports to impose on a party that breaches.

civil penalty. A fine assessed for a violation of a statute or regulation.

statutory penalty. A penalty imposed for a statutory violation; esp., a penalty imposing automatic liability on a wrongdoer for violation of a statute's terms without reference to any actual damages suffered.

penalty clause. A contractual provision that assesses an excessive monetary charge against a defaulting party. • Penalty clauses are mostly unenforceable. Cf. LIQUIDATED-DAMAGES CLAUSE; LIMITATION-OF-REMEDIES CLAUSE.

penalty phase. The part of a criminal trial in which the fact-finder determines the punishment for a defendant who has been found guilty. Cf. GUILT PHASE.

pend, *vb.* (Of a lawsuit) to be awaiting decision or settlement.

pendency (**pen**-dən-see), *n.* The state or condition of being pending or continuing undecided.

pendent (**pen**-dənt), *adj.* **1.** Not yet decided; pending <a pendent action>. **2.** Of or relating to pendent jurisdiction or pendent-party jurisdiction <pendent parties>. **3.** Contingent; dependent <pendent upon a different claim>.

pendente lite (pen-**den**-tee **lı**-tee), *adv.* [Latin "while the action is pending"] During the proceeding or litigation; contingent on the outcome of litigation. Cf. LIS PENDENS.

pendent jurisdiction. See JURISDICTION.

pendent-party jurisdiction. See JURISDICTION.

pending, *adj.* Remaining undecided; awaiting decision <a pending case>.

pending, *prep.* **1.** Throughout the continuance of; during <in escrow pending arbitration>. **2.** While awaiting; until <the injunction was in force pending trial>.

penitentiary (pen-ə-**ten**-shə-ree), *n.* A correctional facility or other place of long-term confinement for convicted criminals; PRISON. — **penitentiary,** *adj.*

Pennoyer **rule** (pə-**noy**-ər). The principle that a court may not issue a personal judgment against a defendant over which it has no personal jurisdiction. *Pennoyer v. Neff*, 95 U.S. 714 (1877).

Pennsylvania rule. *Torts*. The principle that a tortfeasor who violates a statute in the process of causing an injury has the burden of showing that the violation did not cause the injury.

penology (pee-**nol**-ə-jee), *n.* The study of penal institutions, crime prevention, and the punishment and rehabilitation of criminals, including the art of fitting the right treatment to an offender. — **penological** (pee-nə-**loj**-i-kəl), *adj.* — **penologist** (pee-**nol**-ə-jist), *n.* Cf. CRIMINOLOGY.

pen register. A mechanical device that logs dialed telephone numbers by monitoring electrical impulses. Cf. WIRETAPPING.

pension. A fixed sum paid regularly to a person (or to the person's beneficiaries), esp. by an employer as a retirement benefit. Cf. ANNUITY.

Pension Benefit Guaranty Corporation. The federal agency that guarantees the payment of retirement benefits covered by private pension plans that lack sufficient assets to pay the promised benefits. — Abbr. PBGC.

penumbra (pi-**nəm**-brə), *n.* A surrounding area or periphery of uncertain extent. • In constitutional law, the Supreme Court has ruled that the specific guarantees in the Bill of Rights have penumbras containing implied rights, especially the right of privacy. Pl. **penumbras, penumbrae** (pi-**nəm**-bree). — **penumbral** (pi-**nəm**-brəl), *adj.*

peonage (**pee**-ə-nij), *n.* Illegal and involuntary servitude in satisfaction of a debt. — **peon,** *n.*

people. (*usu. cap.*) The citizens of a state as represented by the prosecution in a criminal case <*People v. Snyder*>.

people's court. 1. A court in which ordinary people can resolve small disputes. See *small-claims court* under COURT. **2.** In totalitarian countries, a group of nonlawyer citizens, often illiterate commoners, convened at the scene of a crime to pass judgment or impose punishment on the accused criminal.

per (pər), *prep.* **1.** Through; by <the dissent, per Justice Thomas>. **2.** For each; for every <55 miles per hour>. **3.** *Jargon.* In accordance with the terms of; according to <per the contract>.

per annum (pər **an**-əm), *adv.* [Latin] By, for, or in each year; annually.

per capita (pər **kap**-i-tə), *adj.* [Latin "by the head"] **1.** Divided equally among all individuals, usu. in the same class <the court will distribute the property to the descendants on a per capita basis>. Cf. PER STIRPES.

per capita with representation. Divided equally among all members of a class of takers, including those who have predeceased the testator, so that no family stocks are cut off by the prior death of a taker. • For example, if T (the testator) has three children — A, B, and C — and C has two children but predeceases T, C's children will still take C's share when T's estate is distributed.

2. Allocated to each person; possessed by each individual <the average annual per capita income has increased over the last two years>. — **per capita,** *adv.*

percipient witness. See WITNESS.

per contra (pər **kon**-trə). [Latin] On the other hand; to the contrary; by contrast.

per curiam (pər **kyoor**-ee-əm), *adv.* & *adj.* [Latin] By the court as a whole.

per curiam opinion. See OPINION (1).

per diem (pər **dɪ**-əm *or* **dee**-əm), *adv.* [Latin] By the day; for each day.

per diem, *adj.* Based on or calculated by the day <per diem interest>.

per diem, *n.* **1.** A monetary daily allowance, usu. to cover expenses. **2.** A daily fee.

perdurable (pər-**d[y]uur**-ə-bəl), *adj.* (Of an estate in land) lasting or enduring; durable; permanent.

peremptory (pər-**emp**-tə-ree), *adj.* **1.** Final; absolute; conclusive; incontrovertible <the king's peremptory order>. **2.** Not requiring any shown cause; arbitrary <peremptory challenges>.

peremptory challenge. See CHALLENGE (2).

peremptory day. See DAY.

peremptory defense. See DEFENSE (1).

peremptory exception. See EXCEPTION (1).

peremptory instruction. See JURY INSTRUCTION.

peremptory plea. See PLEA (3).

peremptory writ. See WRIT.

perfect (pər-**fekt**), *vb.* To take all legal steps needed to complete, secure, or record (a claim, right, or interest); to put in final conformity with the law <perfect a security interest> <perfect the title>.

perfect attestation clause. A provision in a testamentary instrument asserting that all actions required to make a valid testamentary disposition have been performed.

perfect defense. See DEFENSE (1).

perfected security interest. See SECURITY INTEREST.

perfect equity. See EQUITY.

perfect instrument. See INSTRUMENT.

perfection. Validation of a security interest as against other creditors, usu. by filing a statement with some public office or by taking possession of the collateral. Cf. ATTACHMENT (4).

perfect self-defense. See SELF-DEFENSE.

perfect tender. See TENDER (3).

perfect-tender rule. *Commercial law.* The principle that a buyer may reject a seller's goods if the quality, quantity, or delivery of the goods fails to conform precisely to the contract. • Although the perfect-tender rule was adopted by the UCC (§ 2–601), other code provisions — such as the seller's right to cure after rejection — have softened the rule's impact. Cf. SUBSTANTIAL-PERFORMANCE DOCTRINE.

performance, *n.* **1.** The successful completion of a contractual duty, usu. resulting in the performer's release from any past or future liability; EXECUTION (2). — **perform,** *vb.* Cf. NONPERFORMANCE; MISPERFORMANCE.

defective performance. A performance that, whether partial or complete, does not completely comply with the contract.

future performance. Performance in the future of an obligation that will become due under a contract.

substantial performance. Performance of the primary, necessary terms of an agreement. See SUBSTANTIAL-PERFORMANCE DOCTRINE.

2. The equitable doctrine by which acts consistent with an intention to fulfill an obligation are construed to be in fulfillment of that obligation, even if the party was silent on the point. **3.** A company's earnings. **4.** The ability of a corporation to maintain or increase earnings.

peril. 1. Exposure to the risk of injury, damage, or loss <the perils of litigation>. **2.** *Insurance.* The cause of a loss to person or property <insured against all perils>.

periodic tenancy. See TENANCY.

periphrasis (pə-**rif**-rə-sis), *n.* A roundabout way of writing or speaking; circumlocution. — **periphrastic** (per-ə-**fras**-tik), *adj.*

perjury (**pər**-jər-ee), *n.* The act or an instance of a person's deliberately making material false or misleading statements while under oath. — **perjure** (**pər**-jər), *vb.* — **perjured** (**pər**-jərd), *adj.* — **perjurious** (pər-**juur**-ee-əs), *adj.* — **perjuror** (**pər**-jər-ər), *n.*

perjury-trap doctrine. The principle that a perjury indictment against a person must be dismissed if the prosecution secures it by calling that person as a grand-jury witness in an effort to obtain evidence for a perjury charge, esp. when the person's testimony does not relate to issues material to the ongoing grand-jury investigation.

permanent disability. See DISABILITY (1).

permanent injunction. See INJUNCTION.

permanent injury. See INJURY.

permanent nuisance. See NUISANCE.

permanent ward. See WARD.

permission. 1. The act of permitting. **2.** A license or liberty to do something; authorization.

permissive counterclaim. See COUNTERCLAIM.

permissive joinder. See JOINDER.

permissive presumption. See PRESUMPTION.

permissive waste. See WASTE (1).

permit (**pər**-mit), *n.* A certificate evidencing permission; a license.

permit (pər-**mit**), *vb.* **1.** To consent to formally <permit the inspection to be carried out>. **2.** To give opportunity for <lax security permitted the escape>. **3.** To allow or admit of <if the law so permits>.

perpetrate, *vb.* To commit or carry out (an act, esp. a crime). — **perpetration,** *n.*

perpetrator. A person who commits a crime or offense.

perpetual statute. See STATUTE.

perpetuating testimony. The means or procedure for preserving for future use witness testimony that might otherwise be unavailable at trial.

perquisite (**pər**-kwi-zit). A privilege or benefit given in addition to one's salary or regular wages.

per quod (pər **kwod**), *adv.* & *adj.* [Latin "whereby"] Requiring reference to additional facts; (of libel or slander) actionable only on allegation and proof of special damages. See *libel per quod* under LIBEL; *slander per quod* under SLANDER.

per se (pər **say**), *adv.* & *adj.* [Latin] **1.** Of, in, or by itself; standing alone, without reference to additional facts. See *libel per se* under LIBEL. **2.** As a matter of law.

person. 1. A human being. **2.** An entity (such as a corporation) that is recognized by law as having the rights and duties of a human being. **3.** The living body of a human being.

artificial person. An entity, such as a corporation, created by law and given certain legal rights and duties of a human being; a being, real or imaginary, who for the purpose of legal reasoning is treated more or less as a human being. Cf. LEGAL ENTITY.

disabled person. A person who has a mental or physical impairment. See DISABILITY.

interested person. A person having a property right in or claim against a thing, such as a trust or decedent's estate.

natural person. A human being, as distinguished from an artificial person created by law.

person in loco parentis (in **loh**-koh pə-**ren**-tis). A person who acts in place of a parent, either temporarily (as a schoolteacher does) or indefinitely (as a stepparent does); a person who has assumed the obligations of a parent without formally adopting the child. See IN LOCO PARENTIS.

person of incidence. The person against whom a right is enforceable; a person who owes a legal duty.

person of inherence (in-**heer**-ənts). The person in whom a legal right is vested; the owner of a right.

personable, *adj.* Having the status of a legal person (and thus the right to plead in court, enter into contracts, etc.) <a personable entity>.

personal, *adj.* **1.** Of or affecting a person <personal injury>. **2.** Of or constituting personal property <personal belongings>. See IN PERSONAM.

personal action. See ACTION.

personal defense. See DEFENSE (4).

personal effects. Items of a personal character; esp., personal property owned by a decedent at the time of death.

personal exemption. See EXEMPTION.

personal holding company. See COMPANY.

personal income. See INCOME.

personal injury. See INJURY.

personality. The legal status of one regarded by the law as a person; the legal conception by which the law regards a human being or an artificial entity as a person.

personal judgment. See JUDGMENT.

personal justice. See JUSTICE (1).

personal knowledge. See KNOWLEDGE (1).

personal law. The law that governs a person's family matters, usu. regardless of where the person goes. • In common-law systems, personal law refers to the law of the person's domicile. In civil-law systems, it refers to the law of the individual's nationality (and so is sometimes called *lex patriae*).

personal liability. See LIABILITY.

personal liberty. See LIBERTY.

personal notice. See NOTICE.

personal property. See PROPERTY.

personal-property tax. See TAX.

personal recognizance. See RECOGNIZANCE.

personal replevin. See REPLEVIN.

personal representative. See REPRESENTATIVE.

personal service. 1. Actual delivery of the notice or process to the person to whom it is directed. **2.** An act done personally by an individual. • In this sense, a personal service is an economic service involving either the intellectual or manual personal effort of an individual, as opposed to the salable product of the person's skill.

personal servitude. See SERVITUDE (1).

personal tort. See TORT.

personalty (**pərs**-ən-əl-tee). Personal property as distinguished from real property. See *personal property* (4) under PROPERTY.

personal warranty. See WARRANTY (2).

person-endangering state of mind. An intent to kill, inflict great bodily injury, act in wanton disregard of an unreasonable risk, or perpetrate a dangerous felony.

per stirpes (pər **stər**-peez), *adv.* & *adj.* [Latin "by roots or stocks"] Proportionately divided among beneficiaries according to their deceased ancestor's share. Cf. PER CAPITA.

persuasion. The act of influencing or attempting to influence others by reasoned argument; the act of persuading.

persuasive precedent. See PRECEDENT.

pertinent, *adj.* Pertaining to the issue at hand; relevant.

perverse verdict. See VERDICT.

petit (**pet**-ee *or* **pet**-it), *adj.* [Law French "minor, small"] See PETTY.

petition, *n.* **1.** A formal written request presented to a court or other official body.

involuntary petition. A petition filed in a bankruptcy court by a creditor seeking to declare a debtor bankrupt.

juvenile petition. A petition filed in a juvenile court, alleging delinquent conduct by the accused. See *adjudicatory hearing* under HEARING.

voluntary petition. A petition filed with a bankruptcy court by a debtor seeking protection from creditors.

2. In some states, a lawsuit's first pleading; COMPLAINT. — **petition,** *vb.*

petitioner. A party who presents a petition to a court or other official body, esp. when seeking relief on appeal. Cf. RESPONDENT (2).

petit jury. See JURY.

petit larceny. See LARCENY.

petitory action. See ACTION.

pettifogger (**pet**-i-fog-ər), *n.* **1.** A lawyer lacking in education, ability, sound judgment, or common sense. **2.** A lawyer who clouds an issue with insignificant details. — **pettifoggery** (pet-i-**fog**-ər-ee), *n.*

petty, *adj.* Relatively insignificant or minor <a petty crime>. Cf. GRAND.

petty offense. See OFFENSE.

Philadelphia lawyer. A shrewd and learned lawyer. • This term can have positive or negative connotations today, but when it first appeared (in colonial times), it carried only a positive sense deriving from Philadelphia's position as America's center of learning and culture.

phonorecord (**foh**-noh-rek-ərd). A physical object (such as a phonographic record, cassette tape, or compact disc) from which fixed sounds can be perceived, reproduced, or otherwise communicated directly or with a machine's aid. • The term is fairly common in copyright contexts since it is defined in the U.S. Copyright Act of 1976 (17 USCA § 101).

physical cruelty. See CRUELTY.

physical custody. See CUSTODY (1), (2).

physical disability. See DISABILITY (1).

physical-facts rule. *Evidence.* The principle that oral testimony may be disregarded when it is inconsistent or irreconcilable with the physical evidence in the case.

physical harm. See HARM.

physical necessity. See NECESSITY.

physical-proximity test. *Criminal law.* A common-law test for the crime of attempt, focusing on how much more the defendant would have needed to do to complete the offense. See ATTEMPT (2).

physical shock. See SHOCK.

P.I. *abbr.* **1.** Personal injury. **2.** Private investigator.

picketing. The demonstration by one or more persons outside a business or organization to protest the entity's activities or policies and to pressure the entity to meet the protesters' demands; esp., an employees' demonstration aimed at publicizing a labor dispute and influencing the public to withhold business from the employer. Cf. BOYCOTT; STRIKE.

pickpocket. A thief who steals money or property from the person of another, usu. by stealth but sometimes by physical diversion such as bumping into or pushing the victim.

piercing the corporate veil. The judicial act of imposing personal liability on otherwise immune corporate officers, directors, and shareholders for the corporation's wrongful acts. See CORPORATE VEIL.

pignorate (**pig**-nə-rayt), *vb.* **1.** To give over as a pledge; to pawn. **2.** To take in pawn. — **pignorative,** *adj.*

pignus (**pig**-nəs), *n.* [Latin "pledge"] A bailment in which goods are delivered to secure the payment of a debt or performance of an engagement, accompanied by a power of sale in case of default. • This type of bailment is for the benefit of both parties.

pilferage (**pil**-fər-ij), *n.* **1.** The act or an instance of stealing. **2.** The item or items stolen. — **pilfer** (**pil**-fər), *vb.* See LARCENY; THEFT.

pimp, *n.* A person who solicits customers for a prostitute, usu. in return for a share of the prostitute's earnings. — **pimp,** *vb.* See PANDERING (1).

Pinkerton **rule.** *Criminal law.* The doctrine imposing liability on a conspirator for all offenses committed in furtherance of the conspiracy, even if those offenses are actually performed by coconspirators. *Pinkerton v. United States*, 328 U.S. 640, 66 S.Ct. 1180 (1946).

pinpoint citation. See CITATION.

piracy, *n.* **1.** Robbery, kidnapping, or other criminal violence committed at sea. **2.** A similar crime committed aboard a plane or other vehicle; hijacking.

> ***air piracy.*** The crime of using force or threat to seize control of an aircraft; the hijacking of an aircraft, esp. one in flight.

3. The unauthorized and illegal reproduction or distribution of materials protected by copyright, patent, or trademark law. See INFRINGEMENT. — **pirate,** *vb.* — **piratical** (pɪ-**rat**-ə-kəl), *adj.* — **pirate,** *n.*

PKPA. *abbr.* PARENTAL KIDNAPPING PREVENTION ACT.

P.L. *abbr.* PUBLIC LAW.

place of abode. A person's residence or domicile. See RESIDENCE; DOMICILE.

place of business. A location at which one carries on a business. Cf. DOMICILE (2).

place of contracting. The country or state in which a contract is entered into.

place of delivery. The place where goods sold are to be sent by the seller. • If no place is specified in the contract, the seller's place of business is usually the place of delivery. UCC § 2–308.

place of employment. The location at which work done in connection with a business is carried out; the place where some process or operation related to the business is conducted.

plagiarism (**play**-jə-riz-əm), *n.* The act or an instance of copying or stealing another's words or ideas and attributing them as one's own. — **plagiarize** (**play**-jə-rɪz), *vb.* — **plagiarist** (**play**-jə-rist), *n.* Cf. INFRINGEMENT.

plain error. See ERROR (2).

plain-feel doctrine. *Criminal procedure.* The principle that a police officer, while conducting a legal pat-down search, may seize any contraband that the officer can immediately and clearly identify, by touch but not by manipulation, as being illegal or incriminating.

plain-language law. Legislation requiring nontechnical, readily comprehensible language in consumer contracts such as residential leases or insurance policies.

plain-language movement. **1.** The loosely organized campaign to encourage legal writers and business writers to write clearly and concisely — without legalese — while preserving accuracy and precision. **2.** The body of persons involved in this campaign.

plain meaning. See MEANING.

plain-meaning rule. The rule that if a writing, or a provision in a writing, appears to be unambiguous on its face, its meaning must be determined from the writing itself without resort to any extrinsic evidence. • Though often applied, this rule is often condemned as simplistic because the meaning of words varies with the verbal context and the surrounding circumstances, not to mention the linguistic ability of the users and readers (including judges). Cf. GOLDEN RULE; MISCHIEF RULE; EQUITY-OF-THE STATUTE RULE.

plaintiff. The party who brings a civil suit in a court of law. Cf. DEFENDANT.

plaintiff in error. *Archaic.* See APPELLANT; PETITIONER.

plain-view doctrine. *Criminal procedure.* The rule permitting a police officer's warrantless seizure and use as evidence of an item seen in plain view from a lawful position or during a legal search when the officer has probable cause to believe that the item is evidence of a crime. Cf. OPEN-FIELDS DOCTRINE.

plat. **1.** A small piece of land; PLOT (1). **2.** A map describing a piece of land and its features, such as boundaries, lots, roads, and easements.

plat map. A document that gives the legal descriptions of pieces of real property by lot, street, and block number.

plea, *n.* **1.** An accused person's formal response of "guilty," "not guilty," or "no contest" to a criminal charge.

blind plea. A guilty plea made without the promise of a concession from either the judge or the prosecutor. Cf. *negotiated plea*.

guilty plea. An accused person's formal admission in court of having committed the charged offense. • A guilty plea is usually part of a plea bargain. It must be made voluntarily, and only after the accused has been informed of and understands his or her rights. A guilty plea ordinarily has the same effect as a guilty verdict and conviction after a trial on the merits.

negotiated plea. The plea agreed to by a criminal defendant and the prosecutor in a plea bargain. See PLEA BARGAIN. Cf. *blind plea*.

not-guilty plea. An accused person's formal denial in court of having committed the charged offense. • The prosecution must then prove all elements of the charged offense beyond a reasonable doubt if the defendant is to be convicted.

2. At common law, the defendant's responsive pleading in a civil action. Cf. DECLARATION (7). **3.** A factual allegation offered in a case; a pleading. Cf. DEMURRER.

anomalous plea. An equitable plea consisting in both affirmative and negative matter. • That is, it is partly confession and avoidance and partly traverse. The plea is appropriate when the plaintiff, in the bill, has anticipated the plea, and the defendant then traverses the anticipatory matters. Cf. *pure plea*.

common plea. A common-law plea in a civil action as opposed to a criminal prosecution.

dilatory plea (**dil**-ə-tor-ee). A plea that does not challenge the merits of a case but that seeks to delay or defeat the action on procedural grounds.

double plea. A plea consisting in two or more distinct grounds of complaint or defense for the same issue. Cf. *alternative pleading* under PLEADING (2); DUPLICITY (2).

issuable plea. A plea on the merits presenting a complaint to the court. Cf. *issuable defense* under DEFENSE (1).

jurisdictional plea. A plea asserting that the court lacks jurisdiction either over the defendant or over the subject matter of the case.

negative plea. A plea that traverses some material fact or facts stated in the bill.

nonissuable plea. A plea on which a court ruling will not decide the case on the merits, such as a plea in abatement.

peremptory plea. A plea that responds to the merits of the plaintiff's claim.

plea in abatement. A plea that objects to the place, time, or method of asserting the plaintiff's claim but does not dispute the claim's merits.

plea in discharge. A plea alleging that the defendant has previously satisfied and discharged the plaintiff's claim.

plea in equity. A special defense relying on one or more reasons why the suit should be dismissed, delayed, or barred. • The various kinds are (1) pleas to the jurisdiction, (2) pleas to the person, (3) pleas to the form of the bill, and (4) pleas in bar of the bill. Pleas in equity generally fall into two classes: *pure pleas* and *anomalous pleas*.

plea in estoppel. *Common-law pleading.* A plea that neither confesses nor avoids, but rather pleads a previous inconsistent act, allegation, or denial on the part of the adverse party to preclude that party from maintaining an action or defense.

plea in suspension. A plea that shows some ground for not proceeding in the suit at the present time and prays that the proceedings be stayed until that ground is removed, such as a party's being a minor or the plaintiff's being an alien enemy.

plea of privilege. A plea that raises an objection to the venue of an action. See CHANGE OF VENUE (1).

plea of release. A plea that admits the claim but sets forth a written discharge executed by a party authorized to release the claim. See RELEASE (2).

plea puis darrein continuance (**pwis dar**-ayn kən-**tin**-yoo-ənts). [Law French "plea since the last continuance"] A plea that alleges new defensive matter that has arisen during a continuance of the case and that did not exist at the time of the defendant's last pleading.

plea to the declaration. A plea in abatement that objects to the declaration and applies immediately to it.

plea to the person of the defendant. A plea in abatement alleging that the defendant has a legal disability to be sued.

plea to the person of the plaintiff. A plea in abatement alleging that the plaintiff has a legal disability to sue.

plea to the writ. A plea in abatement that objects to the writ (summons) and applies (1) to the form of the writ for a matter either apparent on the writ's face or outside the writ, or (2) to the way in which the writ was executed or acted on.

pure plea. An equitable plea that affirmatively alleges new matters that are outside the bill. • If proved, the effect is to end the controversy by dismissing, delaying, or barring the suit. A pure plea must track the allegations of the bill, not evade it or mistake its purpose. Cf. *anomalous plea*.

rolled-up plea. *Defamation*. A defendant's plea claiming that the statements complained of are factual and that, to the extent that they consist of comment, they are fair comment on a matter of public interest. See FAIR COMMENT.

special plea. A plea alleging one or more new facts rather than merely disputing the legal grounds of the action or charge. • All pleas other than general issues are special pleas. See *general issue* under ISSUE (1).

plea bargain, *n.* A negotiated agreement between a prosecutor and a criminal defendant whereby the defendant pleads guilty to a lesser offense or to one of multiple charges in exchange for some concession by the prosecutor, usu. a more lenient sentence or a dismissal of the other charges. — **plea-bargain,** *vb.* — **plea-bargaining,** *n.*

charge bargain. A plea bargain in which a prosecutor agrees to drop some of the counts or reduce the charge to a less serious offense in exchange for a plea of either guilty or no contest from the defendant.

sentence bargain. A plea bargain in which a prosecutor agrees to recommend a lighter sentence in exchange for a plea of either guilty or no contest from the defendant.

plead, *vb.* **1.** To make a specific plea, esp. in response to a criminal charge. **2.** To assert or allege in a pleading. **3.** To file or deliver a pleading.

pleader. 1. A party who asserts a particular pleading. **2.** A person who pleads in court on behalf of another.

pleading, *n.* **1.** A formal document in which a party to a legal proceeding (esp. a civil lawsuit) sets forth or responds to allegations, claims, denials, or defenses.

accusatory pleading. An indictment, information, or complaint by which the government begins a criminal prosecution.

amended pleading. A pleading that replaces an earlier pleading and that contains matters omitted from or not known at the time of the earlier pleading.

anomalous pleading. A pleading that is partly affirmative and partly negative in its allegations.

articulated pleading. A pleading that states each allegation in a separately numbered paragraph.

defective pleading. A pleading that fails to meet minimum standards of sufficiency or accuracy in form or substance.

responsive pleading. A pleading that replies to an opponent's earlier pleading. See ANSWER.

sham pleading. An obviously frivolous or absurd pleading that is made only for purposes of vexation or delay.

shotgun pleading. A pleading that encompasses a wide range of contentions, usu. supported by vague factual allegations.

supplemental pleading. A pleading that either corrects a defect in an earlier pleading or addresses facts arising since the earlier pleading was filed. • Unlike an amended pleading, a supplemental pleading merely adds to the earlier pleading and does not replace it.

2. A system of defining and narrowing the issues in a lawsuit whereby the parties file formal documents alleging their respective positions.

alternative pleading. A form of pleading whereby the pleader alleges two or more independent claims or defenses that are not necessarily consistent with each other, such as alleging both intentional infliction of emotional distress and negligent infliction of emotional distress based on the same conduct. Fed. R. Civ. P. 8(e)(2). Cf. DUPLICITY (2); *double plea* under PLEA (3).

artful pleading. A plaintiff's disguised phrasing of a federal claim as solely a state-law claim in order to prevent a defendant from removing the case from state court to federal court.

code pleading. A procedural system requiring that the pleader allege merely the facts of the case giving rise to the claim, not the legal conclusions necessary to sustain the claim. Cf. *issue pleading*.

equity pleading. The system of pleading used in courts of equity. • In most jurisdictions, rules unique to equity practice have been largely supplanted by rules of court, esp. where law courts and equity courts have merged.

issue pleading. The common-law method of pleading, the main purpose of which was to frame an issue. Cf. *code pleading*.

notice pleading. A procedural system requiring that the pleader give only a short and plain statement of the claim showing that the pleader is entitled to relief, and not a complete detailing of all the facts. Fed. R. Civ. P. 8(a).

3. The legal rules regulating the statement of the plaintiff's claims and the defendant's defenses.

pleading the Fifth. The act or an instance of asserting one's right against self-incrimination under the Fifth Amendment. See RIGHT AGAINST SELF-INCRIMINATION.

plead over, *vb.* To fail to notice a defective allegation in an opponent's pleading. See AIDER BY PLEADING OVER.

plea in abatement. See PLEA (3).

plea in bar. A plea that seeks to defeat the plaintiff's or prosecutor's action completely and permanently.

general plea in bar. A criminal defendant's plea of not guilty by which the defendant denies every fact and circumstance necessary to be convicted of the crime charged.

special plea in bar. A plea that, rather than addressing the merits and denying the facts alleged, sets up some extrinsic fact showing why a criminal defendant cannot be tried for the offense charged.

plea in discharge. See PLEA (3).

plea in equity. See PLEA (3).

plea in estoppel. See PLEA (3).

plea in reconvention. See PLEA (3).

plea in suspension. See PLEA (3).

plea of privilege. See PLEA (3).

plea of release. See PLEA (3).

plea of tender. At common law, a pleading asserting that the defendant has consistently been willing to pay the debt demanded, has offered it to the plaintiff, and has brought the money into court ready to pay the plaintiff. See TENDER.

***plea puis darrein* continuance.** See PLEA (3).

plea to the declaration. See PLEA (3).

plea to the person of the defendant. See PLEA (3).

plea to the person of the plaintiff. See PLEA (3).

plea to the writ. See PLEA (3).

plebiscite (**pleb**-ə-sɪt *or* **pleb**-ə-sit), *n.* A binding or nonbinding referendum on a proposed law, constitutional amendment, or significant public issue. — **plebiscitary** (plə-**bi**-sə-ter-ee), *adj.*

pledge, *n.* **1.** A bailment or other deposit of personal property to a creditor as security for a debt or obligation; PAWN (2). Cf. LIEN. **2.** The item of personal property so deposited; PAWN (1). **3.** Broadly, the act of providing something as security for a debt or obligation. **4.** The thing so provided. — **pledge,** *vb.* — **pledgeable,** *adj.*

plenary (**plee**-nə-ree *or* **plen**-ə-ree), *adj.* **1.** Full; complete; entire <plenary authority>. **2.** (Of an assembly) intended to have the attendance of all members or participants <plenary session>.

plenary action. See ACTION.

plenary confession. See CONFESSION.

plenary power. See POWER.

plenary session. See SESSION.

plenary suit. See SUIT.

plot, *n.* **1.** A measured piece of land; LOT (1). **2.** A plan forming the basis of a conspiracy.

plot plan. A plan that shows a proposed or present use of a plot of land, esp. of a residential area.

plottage. The increase in value achieved by combining small, undeveloped tracts of land into larger tracts of land.

plurality. A number or quantity (esp. of votes) that does not constitute a majority but is greater than any other, regardless of the margin. Cf. MAJORITY (2).

plurality opinion. See OPINION (1).

plural marriage. See MARRIAGE (1).

pluries (**pluur**-ee-eez), *n.* [Latin "many times"] A third or subsequent writ issued when the previous writs have been ineffective; a writ issued after an alias writ.

P.O. *abbr.* Post office.

pocket immunity. See IMMUNITY (3).

pocket part. A supplemental pamphlet inserted usu. into the back inside cover of a lawbook, esp. a treatise or code, to update the material in the main text until the publisher issues a new edition of the entire work. • Legal publishers frequently leave a little extra room inside their hardcover books so that pocket parts may later be added.

pocket veto. See VETO.

P.O.D. *abbr.* Pay on delivery.

poena (**pee**-nə). [Latin] Punishment; penalty.

point, *n.* **1.** A pertinent and distinct legal proposition, issue, or argument <point of error>. **2.** One percent of the face value of a loan (esp. a mortgage loan), paid up front to the lender as a service charge or placement fee <the borrower hoped for only a two-point fee on the mortgage>. See MORTGAGE DISCOUNT. **3.** A unit used for quoting stock, bond, or commodity prices <the stock closed up a few points today>.

point-and-click agreement. An electronic version of a shrink-wrap license in which a computer user agrees to the terms of an electronically displayed agreement by pointing the mouse to a particular location on the screen and then clicking. See *shrink-wrap license* under LICENSE.

point of error. An alleged mistake by a lower court asserted as a ground for appeal. See ERROR (2); WRIT OF ERROR.

point of law. A discrete legal proposition at issue in a case.

> ***reserved point of law.*** An important or difficult point of law that arises during trial but that the judge sets aside for future argument or decision so that testimony can continue.

point system. *Criminal law.* A system that assigns incremental units to traffic violations, the accumulation of a certain number within a year resulting in the automatic suspension of a person's driving privileges.

police magistrate. See MAGISTRATE.

police power. 1. The inherent and plenary power of a sovereign to make all laws necessary and proper to preserve the public security, order, health, morality, and justice. • It is a fundamental power essential to government, and it cannot be surrendered by the legislature or irrevocably transferred away from government. **2.** A state's Tenth Amendment right, subject to due-process and other limitations, to establish and enforce laws protecting the public's health, safety, and general welfare, or to delegate this right to local governments. **3.** Loosely, the power of the government to intervene in the use of privately owned property, as by subjecting it to eminent domain. See EMINENT DOMAIN.

policy. 1. The general principles by which a government is guided in its management of public affairs. See PUBLIC POLICY. **2.** A document containing a contract of insurance; INSURANCE POLICY. **3.** A type of lottery in which a bettor selects numbers to bet on and places the bet with a "policy writer."

political-action committee. An organization formed by a special-interest group to raise and contribute money to the campaigns of political candidates who the group believes will promote its interests. — Abbr. PAC.

political correctness, *n.* **1.** The inclination to avoid language and practices that might offend political sensibilities, esp. in racial or sexual matters. **2.** An instance in which a person conforms to this inclination. — Abbr. P.C. — **politically correct,** *adj.*

political liberty. See LIBERTY.

political offense. A crime directed against the security or government of a nation, such as treason, sedition, or espionage.

political question. A question that a court will not consider because it involves the exercise of discretionary power by the executive or legislative branch of government. Cf. JUDICIAL QUESTION.

political science. The branch of learning concerned with the study of the principles and conduct of government.

political subdivision. A division of a state that exists primarily to discharge some function of local government.

political trial. See TRIAL.

polity (**pol**-ə-tee). **1.** The total governmental organization as based on its goals and policies. **2.** A politically organized body or community.

polity approach. A method of resolving church-property disputes by which a court examines the structure of the church to determine whether the church is independent or hierarchical, and then resolves the dispute in accordance with the decision of the proper church-governing body.

poll, *n.* **1.** A sampling of opinions on a given topic, conducted randomly or obtained from a specified group. **2.** The act or process of voting at an election. **3.** The result of the counting of votes. **4.** (*usu. pl.*) The place where votes are cast.

poll, *vb.* **1.** To ask how each member of (a group) individually voted. **2.** To question (people) so as to elicit votes, opinions, or preferences. **3.** To receive (a given number of votes) in an election.

pollicitation. *Contracts.* The offer of a promise.

poll tax. See TAX.

polyandry (**pol**-ee-an-dree). The condition or practice of having more than one husband. Cf. POLYGYNY.

polygamy (pə-**lig**-ə-mee), *n.* The state or practice of having more than one spouse simultaneously. — **polyga-**

mous, *adj.* — **polygamist,** *n.* Cf. BIGAMY; MONOGAMY.

polygraph, *n.* A device used to evaluate veracity by measuring and recording involuntary physiological changes in the human body during interrogation. — **polygraphic,** *adj.* — **polygraphy,** *n.*

polygyny (pə-**lij**-ə-nee). The condition or practice of having more than one wife. Cf. POLYANDRY.

Ponzi scheme (pon-zee). A fraudulent investment scheme in which money contributed by later investors generates artificially high dividends for the original investors, whose example attracts even larger investments. • Money from the new investors is used directly to repay or pay interest to earlier investors, usually without any operation or revenue-producing activity other than the continual raising of new funds. Cf. PYRAMID SCHEME.

pool, *n.* **1.** An association of individuals or entities who share resources and funds to promote their joint undertaking; esp., an association of persons engaged in buying or selling commodities. **2.** A gambling scheme in which numerous persons contribute stakes for betting on a particular event (such as a sporting event).

popular justice. See JUSTICE (1).

pork-barrel legislation. See LEGISLATION.

pornography, *n.* Material (such as writings, photographs, or movies) depicting sexual activity or erotic behavior in a way that is designed to arouse sexual excitement. • Pornography is protected speech under the First Amendment unless it is determined to be legally obscene. — **pornographic,** *adj.* See OBSCENITY.

child pornography. Material depicting a person under the age of 18 engaged in sexual activity. • Child pornography is not protected by the First Amendment — even if it falls short of the legal standard for obscenity — and those directly involved in its distribution can be criminally punished.

portable business. A law practice that an attorney can take from one firm or geographic location to another, with little loss in client relationships.

port authority. A state or federal agency that regulates traffic through a port or that establishes and maintains airports, bridges, tollways, and public transportation.

portfolio. The various securities or other investments held by an investor at any given time.

portfolio income. See INCOME.

position of the United States. The legal position of the federal government in a case involving the Equal Access to Justice Act.

positive externality. See EXTERNALITY.

positive justice. See JUSTICE (1).

positive law. A system of law promulgated and implemented within a particular political community by political superiors, as distinct from moral law or law existing in an ideal community or in some nonpolitical community. • Positive law typically consists of enacted law — the codes, statutes, and regulations that are applied and enforced in the courts. Cf. NATURAL LAW.

positive misprision. See MISPRISION.

positive proof. See PROOF.

positive wrong. See WRONG.

positivism. The doctrine that all true knowledge is derived from observable phenomena, rather than speculation or reasoning. — **positivistic,** *adj.* See LEGAL POSITIVISM; LOGICAL POSITIVISM; *positivist jurisprudence* under JURISPRUDENCE.

positivist jurisprudence. See JURISPRUDENCE.

posse (**pos**-ee). [Latin] **1.** A possibility. See IN POSSE. Cf. IN ESSE. **2.** Power; ability. **3.** POSSE COMITATUS.

posse comitatus (**pos**-ee kom-ə-**tay**-təs), *n.* [Latin "power of the county"] A group of citizens who are called together to assist the sheriff in keeping the peace.

Posse Comitatus Act. A federal law that, with a few exceptions, prohibits the Army or Air Force from directly participating in civilian law-enforcement operations, as by making arrests, conducting searches, or seizing evidence.

possess, *vb.* To have in one's actual control; to have possession of. — **possessor,** *n.*

possession. 1. The fact of having or holding property in one's power; the exercise of dominion over property. **2.** The right under which one may exercise control over something to the exclusion of all others; the continuing exercise of a claim to the exclusive use of a material object. **3.** (*usu. pl.*) Something that a person owns or controls; PROPERTY (2). **4.** A territorial dominion of a state or nation. Cf. OWNERSHIP; TITLE (1).

actual possession. Physical occupancy or control over property. Cf. *constructive possession*.

bona fide possession. Possession of property by a person who in good faith does not know that the property's ownership is disputed.

constructive possession. Control or dominion over a property without actual possession or custody of it. Cf. *actual possession*.

criminal possession. The unlawful possession of certain prohibited articles, such as illegal drugs or drug paraphernalia, firearms, or stolen property.

derivative possession. Lawful possession by one (such as a tenant) who does not hold title.

exclusive possession. The exercise of exclusive dominion over property, including the use and benefit of the property.

hostile possession. Possession asserted against the claims of all others, esp. the record owner. See ADVERSE POSSESSION.

immediate possession. Possession that is acquired or retained directly or personally.

incorporeal possession. Possession of something other than a material object, such as an easement over a neighbor's land, or the access of light to the windows of a house.

mediate possession (**mee**-dee-it). Possession of a thing through someone else, such as an agent. •

In every instance of mediate possession, there is a direct possessor (such as an agent) as well as a mediate possessor (the principal).

naked possession. The mere possession of something, esp. real estate, without any apparent right or colorable title to it.

notorious possession. Possession or control that is evident to others; possession of property that, because it is generally known by people in the area where the property is located, gives rise to a presumption that the actual owner has notice of it. See ADVERSE POSSESSION.

peaceable possession. Possession (as of real property) not disturbed by another's hostile or legal attempts to recover possession. Cf. ADVERSE POSSESSION.

pedal possession. Actual possession, as by living on the land or by improving it. • This term usually appears in adverse-possession contexts.

possession in fact. Actual possession that may or may not be recognized by law. • For example, an employee's possession of an employer's property is for some purposes not legally considered possession, the term *detention* or *custody* being used instead.

possession in law. **1.** Possession that is recognized by the law either because it is a specific type of possession in fact or because the law for some special reason attributes the advantages and results of possession to someone who does not in fact possess. **2.** See *constructive possession*.

possession of a right. The continuing exercise and enjoyment of a right. • This type of possession is often unrelated to an ownership interest in property. For example, a criminal defendant possesses the right to demand a trial by jury.

scrambling possession. Possession that is uncertain because it is in dispute. • With scrambling possession, the dispute is over who actually has possession — not over whether a party's possession is lawful.

possessor. One who has possession. — **possessorial** (pos-ə-**sor**-ee-əl), *adj.*

possessory action. See ACTION.

possessory claim. Title to public land held by a claimant who has filed a declaratory statement but has not paid for the land.

possessory conservator. See CONSERVATOR.

possessory estate. See ESTATE.

possessory interest. 1. The present right to control property, including the right to exclude others, by a person who is not necessarily the owner. **2.** A present or future right to the exclusive use and possession of property.

possessory warrant. A process similar to a search warrant used by a civil plaintiff to search for and recover property wrongfully taken.

possibility. 1. An event that may or may not happen. **2.** A contingent interest in real or personal property.

naked possibility. A mere chance or expectation that a person will acquire future property. • A conveyance of a naked possibility is usually void for lack of subject matter, as in a deed conveying all rights to a future estate not yet in existence.

possibility coupled with an interest. An expectation recognized in law as an estate or interest, as occurs in an executory devise or in a shifting or springing use. • This type of possibility may be sold or assigned.

remote possibility. A limitation dependent on two or more facts or events that are contingent and uncertain; a double possibility.

possibility of reverter. A future interest retained by a grantor after conveying a fee simple determinable, so that the grantee's estate terminates automatically and reverts to the grantor if the terminating event ever occurs. • In this type of interest, the grantor transfers an estate whose maximum potential duration equals that of the grantor's own estate and attaches a special limitation that operates in the grantor's favor. See *fee simple determinable* under FEE SIMPLE. Cf. POWER OF TERMINATION.

post. [Latin] After. Cf. ANTE.

post, *vb.* **1.** To publicize or announce by affixing a notice in a public place <foreclosure notice was posted at the county courthouse>. **2.** To place in the mail <post a letter>. **3.** To make a payment or deposit; to put up <post bail>.

post-answer default judgment. See DEFAULT JUDGMENT.

postconviction-relief proceeding. A state or federal procedure for a prisoner to request a court to vacate or correct a conviction or sentence.

postdate, *vb.* To put a date on (an instrument, such as a check) that is later than the actual date. Cf. ANTEDATE; BACKDATE (1).

posterity, *n.* **1.** Future generations collectively. **2.** All the descendants of a person to the furthest generation.

post hoc (pohst hok). **1.** *adv.* After this; consequently. **2.** [Latin fr. *post hoc, ergo propter hoc* "after this, therefore because of this"] *adj.* Of or relating to the fallacy of assuming causality from temporal sequence; confusing sequence with consequence.

posthumous child. See CHILD.

posting. 1. A method of substituted service of process by displaying the process in a prominent place (such as the courthouse door) when other forms of service have failed. See SERVICE (1). **2.** A publication method, as by displaying municipal ordinances in designated localities. **3.** The act of providing legal notice, as by affixing notices of judicial sales at or on the courthouse door.

postjudgment discovery. See DISCOVERY.

postmortem, *adj.* Done or occurring after death <a postmortem examination>.

postnuptial (pohst-**nəp**-shəl), *adj.* Made or occurring during marriage <a postnuptial contract>. Cf. PRENUPTIAL.

postnuptial agreement (pohst-**nəp**-shəl). An agreement entered into during marriage to define each spouse's property rights in the event of death or divorce. • The term commonly refers to an agreement between spouses during the marriage at a time when separation or divorce is not imminent. Cf. PRENUPTIAL AGREEMENT.

postpone, *vb.* **1.** To put off to a later time. **2.** To place lower in precedence or importance; esp., to subordinate (a lien) to a later one. — **postponement,** *n.*

post-terminal sitting. A court session held after the normal term.

posttrial motion. See MOTION.

pound, *n.* A place where impounded property is held until redeemed.

poundage fee. A percentage commission awarded to a sheriff for moneys recovered under judicial process, such as execution or attachment.

pound of land. An uncertain quantity of land, usu. thought to be about 52 acres.

pour out, *vb. Slang.* To deny (a claimant) damages or relief in a lawsuit <the plaintiff was poured out of court by the jury's verdict of no liability>.

pourover trust. See TRUST.

pourover will. See WILL.

poverty affidavit. See AFFIDAVIT.

power. **1.** The ability to act or not act. **2.** Dominance, control, or influence over another. **3.** The legal right or authorization to act or not act; the ability conferred on a person by the law to alter, by an act of will, the rights, duties, liabilities, or other legal relations either of that person or of another. **4.** A document granting legal authorization. See AUTHORITY. **5.** An authority to affect an estate in land by (1) creating some estate independently of any estate that the holder of the authority possesses, (2) imposing a charge on the estate, or (3) revoking an existing estate. See POWER OF APPOINTMENT.

appendant power (ə-**pen**-dənt). **1.** A power that gives the donee a right to appoint estates that attach to the donee's own interest. **2.** A power held by a donee who owns the property interest in the assets subject to the power, and whose interest can be divested by the exercise of the power. • The power appendant is generally viewed as adding nothing to the ownership and thus is not now generally recognized as a true power.

beneficial power. A power that is executed for the benefit of the power's donee, as distinguished from a *trust power*, which is executed for the benefit of someone other than the power's donee (i.e., a trust beneficiary).

concurrent power. A political power independently exercisable by both federal and state governments in the same field of legislation.

enumerated power. A political power specifically delegated to a governmental branch by a constitution.

general power. Power that can be exercised in anyone's favor, including the agent, to affect another's interest in property; a power that authorizes the alienation of a fee to any alienee.

implied power. A political power that is not enumerated but that nonetheless exists because it is needed to carry out an express power.

incident power. A power that, although not expressly granted, must exist because it is necessary to the accomplishment of an express purpose.

inherent power. A power that necessarily derives from an office, position, or status.

naked power. The power to exercise rights over something (such as a trust) without having a corresponding interest in that thing. Cf. *power coupled with an interest*.

plenary power (**plee**-nə-ree *or* **plen**-ə-ree). Power that is broadly construed; esp., a court's power to dispose of any matter properly before it.

power coupled with an interest. A power to do some act, conveyed along with an interest in the subject matter of the power. • A power coupled with an interest is not held for the benefit of the principal, and it is irrevocable due to the agent's interest in the subject property. For this reason, some authorities assert that it is not a true agency power. Cf. *naked power*.

power in gross. A power held by a donee who has an interest in the assets subject to the power but whose interest cannot be affected by the exercise of the power. • An example is a life tenant with a power over the remainder.

power of revocation (rev-ə-**kay**-shən). A power that a person reserves in an instrument (such as a trust) to revoke the legal relationship that the person has created.

quasi-judicial power. An administrative agency's power to adjudicate the rights of those who appear before it.

quasi-legislative power. An administrative agency's power to engage in rulemaking. 5 USCA § 553.

reserved power. A political power that is not enumerated or prohibited by a constitution, but instead is reserved by the constitution for a specified political authority, such as a state government. See TENTH AMENDMENT.

special power. **1.** A power that either does not allow the entire estate to be conveyed or restricts to whom the estate may be conveyed. **2.** An agent's limited authority to perform only specific acts or to perform under specific restrictions.

spending power. The power granted to a governmental body to spend public funds; esp., the congressional power to spend money for the payment of debt and provision of the common defense and general welfare of the United States. U.S. Const. art. I, § 8, cl. 1.

taxing power. The power granted to a governmental body to levy a tax; esp., the congressional power to levy and collect taxes as a means of effectuating Congress's delegated powers. U.S. Const. art. I, § 8, cl. 1. See SIXTEENTH AMENDMENT.

power of alienation. The capacity to sell, transfer, assign, or otherwise dispose of property.

power of appointment. A power conferred on a donee by will or deed to select and determine one or more recipients of the donor's estate or income.

general power of appointment. A power of appointment by which the donee can appoint — that is, dispose of the donor's property — in favor of anyone at all, including oneself or one's own estate.

limited power of appointment. A power of appointment by which the donee can appoint to only the person or class specified in the instrument creating the power, but cannot appoint to oneself or one's own estate. — Also termed *special power of appointment*.

testamentary power of appointment (tes-tə-**men**-tə-ree *or* -tree). A power of appointment created by a will.

power-of-appointment trust. See TRUST.

power of attorney. 1. An instrument granting someone authority to act as agent or attorney-in-fact for the grantor. **2.** The authority so granted. Pl. **powers of attorney.** See ATTORNEY (1).

durable power of attorney. A power of attorney that remains in effect during the grantor's incompetency.

general power of attorney. A power of attorney that authorizes an agent to transact business for the principal.

irrevocable power of attorney (i-**rev**-ə-kə-bəl). A power of attorney that the principal cannot revoke. See *power coupled with an interest* under POWER.

special power of attorney. A power of attorney that limits the agent's authority to only a specified matter.

power-of-sale clause. A provision in a mortgage or deed of trust permitting the mortgagee or trustee to sell the property without court authority if the payments are not made.

power-of-sale foreclosure. See FORECLOSURE.

power of termination. A future interest retained by a grantor after conveying a fee simple subject to a condition subsequent, so that the grantee's estate terminates (upon breach of the condition) only if the grantor exercises the right to retake it. See *fee simple subject to a condition subsequent* under FEE SIMPLE. Cf. POSSIBILITY OF REVERTER.

PPO. *abbr.* PREFERRED-PROVIDER ORGANIZATION.

practicable, *adj.* (Of a thing) reasonably capable of being accomplished; feasible.

practice, *n.* **1.** The procedural methods and rules used in a court of law <local practice requires that an extra copy of each motion be filed with the clerk>. **2.** PRACTICE OF LAW <where is your practice?>.

practice act. A statute governing practice and procedure in courts. •

Practice acts are usually supplemented with court rules such as the Federal Rules of Civil Procedure.

practice book. A volume devoted to the procedures in a particular court or category of courts, usu. including court rules, court forms, and practice directions.

practice of law. The professional work of a duly licensed lawyer, encompassing a broad range of services such as conducting cases in court, preparing papers necessary to bring about various transactions from conveying land to effecting corporate mergers, preparing legal opinions on various points of law, drafting wills and other estate-planning documents, and advising clients on legal questions. • The term also includes activities that comparatively few lawyers engage in but that require legal expertise, such as drafting legislation and court rules. Cf. LAW PRACTICE.

> ***unauthorized practice of law.*** The practice of law by a person, typically a nonlawyer, who has not been licensed or admitted to practice law in a given jurisdiction.

practitioner. A person engaged in the practice of a profession, esp. law or medicine.

praecipe (**pree**-sə-pee *or* **pres**-ə-pee), *n.* [Latin "command"] **1.** At common law, a writ ordering a defendant to do some act or to explain why inaction is appropriate. **2.** A written motion or request seeking some court action, esp. a trial setting or an entry of judgment. — **praecipe,** *vb.*

praxis (**prak**-sis). [Greek "doing; action"] In critical legal studies, practical action; the practice of living the ethical life in conjunction and in cooperation with others.

prayer for relief. A request addressed to the court and appearing at the end of a pleading; esp., a request for specific relief or damages.

> ***general prayer.*** A prayer for additional unspecified relief, traditionally using language such as, "Plaintiff additionally prays for such other and further relief to which she may show herself to be justly entitled." • The general prayer typically follows a special prayer.
>
> ***special prayer.*** A prayer for the particular relief to which a plaintiff claims to be entitled.

prayer of process. A conclusion in a bill in equity requesting the issuance of a subpoena if the defendant fails to answer the bill.

preamble (**pree**-am-bəl), *n.* An introductory statement in a constitution, statute, or other document explaining the document's basis and objective; esp., a statutory recital of the inconveniences for which the statute is designed to provide a remedy. — **preambulary** (pree-**am**-byə-ler-ee), **preambular** (pree-**am**-byə-lər), *adj.*

preappointed evidence. See EVIDENCE.

precarious, *adj.* Dependent on the will or pleasure of another; uncertain.

precatory (**prek**-ə-tor-ee), *adj.* (Of words) requesting, recommending, or expressing a desire for action, but usu. in a nonbinding way. • An example of precatory language is "it is my wish and desire to. . . ."

precatory trust. See TRUST.

precedence (**pres**-ə-dənts *or* prə-**seed**-ənts), *n.* **1.** The act or state of going before; esp., the order or priority in place or time observed by or for persons of different statuses (such as political dignitaries) on the basis of rank during ceremonial events. **2.** The order in which persons may claim the right to administer an intestate's estate.

precedent (prə-**seed**-ənt *also* **pres**-ə-dənt), *adj.* Preceding in time or order <condition precedent>.

precedent (**pres**-ə-dənt), *n.* **1.** The making of law by a court in recognizing and applying new rules while administering justice. **2.** A decided case that furnishes a basis for determining later cases involving similar facts or issues. — **precedential,** *adj.* See STARE DECISIS.

binding precedent. A precedent that a court must follow. • For example, a lower court is bound by an applicable holding of a higher court in the same jurisdiction.

declaratory precedent. A precedent that is merely the application of an already existing legal rule.

original precedent. A precedent that creates and applies a new legal rule.

persuasive precedent. A precedent that is not binding on a court, but that is entitled to respect and careful consideration.

precedent sub silentio (səb sə-**len**-shee-oh). A legal question that was neither argued nor explicitly discussed in a judicial decision but that seems to have been silently ruled on and might therefore be treated as a precedent.

3. DOCTRINE OF PRECEDENT. **4.** A form of pleading or property-conveyancing instrument. • Precedents are often compiled in book form and used by lawyers as guides for preparing similar documents.

precept (**pree**-sept). **1.** A standard or rule of conduct; a command or principle <several legal precepts govern here>. **2.** A writ or warrant issued by an authorized person demanding another's action, such as a judge's order to an officer to bring a party before the court <the sheriff executed the precept immediately>.

précis (pray-**see** *or* **pray**-see), *n.* [French] A concise summary of a text's essential points; an abstract. Pl. **précis** (pray-**seez** *or* **pray**-seez).

preclusion order. See ORDER.

precontract. See CONTRACT.

predial (**pree**-dee-əl), *adj.* Of, consisting of, relating to, or attached to land <predial servitude>.

predicate act. Under RICO, one of two or more related acts of racketeering necessary to establish a pattern. See RACKETEER INFLUENCED AND CORRUPT ORGANIZATIONS ACT.

predicate fact. See FACT.

predictive theory of law. The view that the law is nothing more than a set of predictions about what the courts will decide in given circumstances. Cf. BAD-MAN THEORY.

predisposition. A person's inclination to engage in a particular activity; esp., an inclination that vitiates a criminal defendant's claim of entrapment.

preemption (pree-**emp**-shən), *n.* **1.** The right to buy before others. See RIGHT OF PREEMPTION. **2.** The purchase of something under this right. **3.** An earlier seizure or appropriation. **4.** The occupation of public land so as to establish a preemptive title. **5.** *Constitutional law.* The principle (derived from the Supremacy Clause) that a federal law can supersede or supplant any inconsistent state law or regulation. — **preempt,** *vb.* — **preemptive,** *adj.* See COMPLETE-PREEMPTION DOCTRINE.

preemption claimant. One who has settled on land subject to preemption, intending in good faith to acquire title to it.

preemption right. The privilege to take priority over others in claiming land subject to preemption. • The privilege arises from the holder's actual settlement of the land.

preexisting duty. See DUTY.

preexisting-duty rule. *Contracts.* The rule that if a party does or promises to do what the party is already legally obligated to do — or refrains or promises to refrain from doing what the party is already legally obligated to refrain from doing — the party has not incurred detriment.

prefer, *vb.* **1.** To put forward or present for consideration; esp. (of a grand jury), to bring (a charge or indictment) against a criminal suspect <the defendant claimed he was innocent of the charges preferred against him>. **2.** To give priority to, such as to one creditor over another <the statute prefers creditors who are first to file their claims>.

preferential rule. *Evidence.* A rule that prefers one kind of evidence to another. • It may work provisionally, as when a tribunal refuses to consider one kind of evidence until another kind (presumably better) is shown to be unavailable, or it may work absolutely, as when the tribunal refuses to consider anything but the better kind of evidence.

preferred docket. See DOCKET (2).

preferred-provider organization. A group of healthcare providers (such as doctors, hospitals, and pharmacies) that agree to provide medical services at a discounted cost to covered persons in a given geographic area. — Abbr. PPO. Cf. HEALTH-MAINTENANCE ORGANIZATION.

prehearing conference. An optional conference for the discussion of procedural and substantive matters on appeal, usu. held in complex civil, criminal, tax, and agency cases. Fed. R. App. P. 33.

prejudice, *n.* **1.** Damage or detriment to one's legal rights or claims. See *dismissal with/without prejudice* under DISMISSAL.

> ***legal prejudice.*** A condition that, if shown by a party, will usu. defeat the opposing party's action; esp., a condition that, if shown by the defendant, will defeat a plaintiff's motion to dismiss a case without prejudice.
>
> ***undue prejudice.*** The harm resulting from a fact-trier's being exposed to evidence that is persuasive but inadmissible (such as

evidence of prior criminal conduct) or that so arouses the emotions that calm and logical reasoning is abandoned.

2. A preconceived judgment formed without a factual basis; a strong bias. — **prejudice,** *vb.* — **prejudicial,** *adj.*

prejudicial publicity. Extensive media attention devoted to an upcoming civil or criminal trial.

preliminary complaint. See COMPLAINT.

preliminary evidence. See EVIDENCE.

preliminary hearing. A criminal hearing (usu. conducted by a magistrate) to determine whether there is sufficient evidence to prosecute an accused person. • If sufficient evidence exists, the case will be set for trial or bound over for grand-jury review, or an information will be filed in the trial court. Cf. ARRAIGNMENT.

preliminary injunction. See INJUNCTION.

preliminary statement. The introductory part of a brief or memorandum in support of a motion, in which the advocate summarizes the essence of what follows.

preliminary warrant. See WARRANT.

prematurity. **1.** The circumstance existing when the facts underlying a plaintiff's complaint do not yet create a live claim. Cf. RIPENESS. **2.** The affirmative defense based on this circumstance.

premeditated, *adj.* Done with willful deliberation and planning; consciously considered beforehand <a premeditated killing>.

premeditation, *n.* Conscious consideration and planning that precedes some act (such as committing a crime). — **premeditate,** *vb.* — **premeditated,** *adj.*

premise (**prem**-is), *n.* A previous statement or contention from which a conclusion is deduced. — **premise** (**prem**-is *or* pri-**mɪz**), *vb.*

premises (**prem**-ə-siz). **1.** Matters (usu. preliminary facts or statements) previously referred to in the same instrument <wherefore, premises considered, the plaintiff prays for the following relief>. **2.** A house or building, along with its grounds <smoking is not allowed on these premises>.

premises liability. A landowner's or landholder's tort liability for conditions or activities on the premises.

premium bond. See BOND (3).

prenatal tort. See TORT.

prenuptial (pree-**nəp**-shəl), *adj.* Made or occurring before marriage; premarital.

prenuptial agreement. An agreement made before marriage, usu. to resolve issues of support and property division if the marriage ends in divorce or by the death of a spouse. See SETTLEMENT (2). Cf. POSTNUPTIAL AGREEMENT.

prenuptial gift. See GIFT.

prenuptial will. See WILL.

prepaid expense. See EXPENSE.

prepaid income. See INCOME.

prepaid interest. See INTEREST (3).

prepaid legal services. An arrangement — usu. serving as an employee benefit — that enables a person to make advance payments for future legal services.

preparation. *Criminal law*. The act or process of devising the means necessary to commit a crime. Cf. ATTEMPT.

prepayment clause. A loan-document provision that permits a borrower to satisfy a debt before its due date, usu. without paying a penalty.

prepayment penalty. A charge assessed against a borrower who elects to pay off a loan before it is due.

prepetition (pree-pə-**tish**-ən), *adj.* Occurring before the filing of a petition (esp. in bankruptcy) <prepetition debts>.

preponderance (pri-**pon**-dər-ənts), *n.* Superiority in weight, importance, or influence. — **preponderate** (pri-**pon**-dər-ayt), *vb.* — **preponderant** (pri-**pon**-dər-ənt), *adj.*

preponderance of the evidence. The greater weight of the evidence; superior evidentiary weight that, though not sufficient to free the mind wholly from all reasonable doubt, is still sufficient to incline a fair and impartial mind to one side of the issue rather than the other. • This is the burden of proof in most civil trials, in which the jury is instructed to find for the party that, on the whole, has the stronger evidence, however slight the edge may be. See REASONABLE DOUBT. Cf. *clear and convincing evidence* under EVIDENCE.

prerogative (pri-**rog**-ə-tiv), *n.* An exclusive right, power, privilege, or immunity, usu. acquired by virtue of office. — **prerogative,** *adj.*

prescribable (pri-**skrɪb**-ə-bəl), *adj.* (Of a right) that can be acquired by prescription.

prescription, *n.* **1.** The effect of the lapse of time in creating and destroying rights. **2.** The acquisition of title to a thing (esp. an intangible thing such as the use of real property) by open and continuous possession over a statutory period. Cf. ADVERSE POSSESSION. **3.** The extinction of a title or right by failure to claim or exercise it over a long period. **4.** The act of establishing authoritative rules; a rule so established. — **prescribe,** *vb.* Cf. PROSCRIPTION.

prescriptive easement. See EASEMENT.

prescriptive right. A right obtained by prescription <after a nuisance has been continuously in existence for 20 years, a prescriptive right to continue it is acquired as an easement appurtenant to the land on which it exists>.

presence-of-defendant rule. The principle that a felony defendant is entitled to be present at every major stage of the criminal proceeding. Fed. R. Crim. P. 43.

presence of the court. The company or proximity of the judge or other courtroom official. • For purposes of contempt, an action is in the presence of the court if it is committed within the view of the judge or other person in court and is intended to disrupt the court's business.

presence-of-the-testator rule. The principle that a testator must be aware (through sight or other sense) that the witnesses are signing the will.

present, *adj.* **1.** Now existing; at hand <a present right to the property>. **2.** Being the one under consideration <the present appeal does not deal with that issue>. **3.** In attendance; not elsewhere <all present voted for him>.

presentation. The delivery of a document to an issuer or named person for the purpose of initiating action under a letter of credit; PRESENTMENT (3).

present case. See *case at bar* under CASE.

presentence hearing. A proceeding at which a judge or jury receives and examines all relevant information regarding a convicted criminal and the related offense before passing sentence.

presentence investigation report. A probation officer's detailed account of a convicted defendant's educational, criminal, family, and social background, conducted at the court's request as an aid in passing sentence.

present enjoyment. See ENJOYMENT.

presenting bank. See BANK.

present interest. See INTEREST (2).

presentment (pri-**zent**-mənt). **1.** The act of presenting or laying before a court or other tribunal a formal statement about a matter to be dealt with legally. **2.** A formal written accusation returned by a grand jury on its own initiative, without a prosecutor's previous indictment request. • Presentments are obsolete in the federal courts. **3.** The formal production of a negotiable instrument for acceptance or payment.

presentment for acceptance. Production of an instrument to the drawee, acceptor, or maker for acceptance. • This type of presentment may be made anytime before maturity, except that with bills payable at sight, after demand, or after sight, presentment must be made within a reasonable time.

presentment for payment. Production of an instrument to the drawee, acceptor, or maker for payment. • This type of presentment must be made on the date when the instrument is due.

presentment warranty. See WARRANTY (2).

present recollection refreshed. *Evidence.* A witness's memory that has been enhanced by showing the witness a document that describes the relevant events. • The document itself is merely a memory stimulus and is not admitted in evidence. Fed. R. Evid. 612. Cf. PAST RECOLLECTION RECORDED.

presents, *n. pl. Archaic.* The instrument under consideration. • This is usually part of the phrase *these presents*, which is part of the longer phrase *know all men by these presents* (itself a loan translation from the Latin *noverint universi per praesentes*). See KNOW ALL MEN BY THESE PRESENTS.

present sense impression. *Evidence.* One's perception of an event or condition, formed during or immediately after the fact. • A statement containing a present sense impression is admissible even if it is hearsay. Fed. R. Evid. 803(1). Cf. EXCITED UTTERANCE.

preside, *vb.* **1.** To occupy the place of authority, esp. as a judge during a hearing or trial <preside over the proceedings>. **2.** To exercise management or control <preside over the estate>.

presiding judge. See JUDGE.

presumed father. See FATHER.

presumption. A legal inference or assumption that a fact exists, based on the known or proven existence of some other fact or group of facts. • A presumption shifts the burden of production or persuasion to the opposing party, who can then attempt to overcome the presumption. See BURDEN OF PRODUCTION.

conclusive presumption. A presumption that cannot be overcome by any additional evidence or argument. Cf. *rebuttable presumption*.

conflicting presumption. One of two or more presumptions that would lead to opposite results.

heeding presumption. A rebuttable presumption that an injured product user would have followed a warning label had the product manufacturer provided one.

mixed presumption. A presumption containing elements of both law and fact.

natural presumption. A deduction of one fact from another, based on common experience.

permissive presumption. A presumption that a trier of fact is free to accept or reject from a given set of facts.

presumption of fact. A type of rebuttable presumption that may be, but as a matter of law need not be, drawn from another established fact or group of facts.

presumption of intent. A permissive presumption that a criminal defendant who intended to commit an act did so.

presumption of law. A legal assumption that a court is required to make if certain facts are established and no contradictory evidence is produced.

rebuttable presumption. An inference drawn from certain facts that establish a prima facie case, which may be overcome by the introduction of contrary evidence. Cf. *conclusive presumption*.

statutory presumption. A rebuttable or conclusive presumption that is created by statute.

presumption of death. A presumption that arises on the unexpected disappearance and continued absence of a person for an extended period, commonly seven years.

presumption of innocence. The fundamental criminal-law principle that a person may not be convicted of a crime unless the government proves guilt beyond a reasonable doubt, without any burden placed on the accused to prove innocence.

presumption of legitimacy. The presumption that the husband of a woman who gives birth is the father of the child.

presumption of natural and probable consequences. *Criminal law.* The presumption that *mens rea* may be derived from proof of the defendant's conduct.

presumption of survivorship. The presumption that one of two or more victims of a common disaster survived the others, based on the supposed survivor's youth, good health, or other reason rendering survivorship likely.

presumptive (pri-**zəmp**-tiv), *adj.* **1.** Giving reasonable grounds for belief or presumption. **2.** Based on a presumption. — **presumptively,** *adv.*

presumptive death. See DEATH.

presumptive evidence. See EVIDENCE.

presumptive sentence. See SENTENCE.

presumptive title. See TITLE (2).

pretermission (pree-tər-**mish**-ən). **1.** The condition of one who is pretermitted, as an heir of a testator. **2.** The act of omitting an heir from a will.

pretermit (pree-tər-**mit**), *vb.* **1.** To ignore or disregard purposely <the court pretermitted the constitutional question by deciding the case on procedural grounds>. **2.** To neglect or overlook accidentally <the third child was pretermitted in the will>.

pretermitted defense. See DEFENSE (1).

pretermitted heir. See HEIR.

pretermitted-heir statute. A state law that, under certain circumstances, grants an omitted heir the right to inherit a share of the testator's estate, usu. by treating the heir as though the testator had died intestate.

pretext (**pree**-tekst), *n.* A false or weak reason or motive advanced to hide the actual or strong reason or motive. — **pretextual** (pree-**teks**-choo-əl), *adj.*

pretextual arrest. See ARREST.

pretrial conference. An informal meeting at which opposing attorneys confer, usu. with the judge, to work toward the disposition of the case by discussing matters of evidence and narrowing the issues that will be tried.

pretrial detention. See DETENTION.

pretrial discovery. See DISCOVERY.

pretrial order. A court order setting out the claims and defenses to be tried, the stipulations of the parties, and the case's procedural rules, as agreed to by the parties or mandated by the court at a pretrial conference.

prevail, *vb.* **1.** To obtain the relief sought in an action; to win a lawsuit. **2.** To be commonly accepted or predominant.

prevailing party. See PARTY (2).

prevarication (pri-var-ə-**kay**-shən), *n.* The act or an instance of lying or avoiding the truth; equivocation. — **prevaricate** (pri-**var**-ə-kayt), *vb.* — **prevaricator** (pri-**var**-ə-kay-tər), *n.*

prevention doctrine. *Contracts.* The principle that each contracting party has an implied duty to not do anything that prevents the other party from performing its obligation.

preventive custody. See CUSTODY (1).

preventive detention. See DETENTION.

preventive injunction. See INJUNCTION.

preventive punishment. See PUNISHMENT.

price discrimination. The practice of offering identical or similar goods to different buyers at different prices when the costs of producing the goods are the same.

price-fixing. The artificial setting or maintenance of prices at a certain level, contrary to the workings of the free market.

horizontal price-fixing. Price-fixing among competitors on the same level, such as retailers throughout an industry.

vertical price-fixing. Price-fixing among parties in the same chain of distribution, such as manufacturers and retailers attempting to control an item's resale price.

price leadership. A market condition in which an industry leader establishes a price that others in the field adopt as their own.

price support. The artificial maintenance of prices (as of a particular commodity) at a certain level, esp. by governmental action (as by subsidy).

price war. A period of sustained or repeated price-cutting in an industry (esp. among retailers), designed to undersell competitors or force them out of business.

priest–penitent privilege. See PRIVILEGE (3).

prima facie (**prɪ**-mə **fay**-shə *or* **fay**-shee), *adv.* [Latin] At first sight; on first appearance but subject to further evidence or information <the agreement is prima facie valid>.

prima facie, *adj.* Sufficient to establish a fact or raise a presumption unless disproved or rebutted <a prima facie showing>.

prima facie case. 1. The establishment of a legally required rebuttable presumption. **2.** A party's production of enough evidence to allow the fact-trier to infer the fact at issue and rule in the party's favor.

prima facie evidence. See EVIDENCE.

prima facie tort. See TORT.

primary allegation. See ALLEGATION.

primary authority. See AUTHORITY (4).

primary beneficiary. See BENEFICIARY.

primary boycott. See BOYCOTT.

primary fact. See FACT.

primary insurance. See INSURANCE.

primary liability. See LIABILITY.

primary obligation. See OBLIGATION.

primary powers. The chief powers given by a principal to an agent to accomplish the agent's tasks. Cf. MEDIATE POWERS.

prime, *vb.* To take priority over <Watson's preferred mortgage primed Moriarty's lien>.

prime maker. See MAKER.

prime rate. See INTEREST RATE.

primogeniture (prɪ-mə-**jen**-ə-chər). **1.** The state of being the firstborn child among siblings. **2.** The common-law right of the firstborn son to inherit his ancestor's estate, usu. to the exclusion of younger siblings.

principal, *n.* **1.** One who authorizes another to act on his or her behalf as an agent. Cf. AGENT (1).

disclosed principal. A principal whose identity is revealed by the agent to a third party. • A disclosed principal is always liable on a contract entered into by the agent with the principal's authority, but the agent is usually not liable.

partially disclosed principal. A principal whose existence — but not actual identity — is revealed by the agent to a third party.

undisclosed principal. A principal whose identity is kept secret by the agent. • An undisclosed principal and the agent are both liable on a contract entered into by the agent with the principal's authority.

2. One who commits or participates in a crime. Cf. ACCESSORY (2); ACCOMPLICE (2).

principal in the first degree. The perpetrator of a crime.

principal in the second degree. One who helped the perpetrator at the time of the crime. See ABET.

3. One who has primary responsibility on an obligation, as opposed to a surety or indorser. **4.** The corpus of an estate or trust. **5.** The amount of a debt, investment, or other fund, not including interest, earnings, or profits.

principal place of business. The place of a corporation's chief executive offices, which is typically viewed as the "nerve center."

Printers Ink Statute. A model statute drafted in 1911 and adopted in a number of states making it a misdemeanor to print an advertisement that contains a false or deceptive statement.

prior, *adj.* **1.** Preceding in time or order <under this court's prior order>. **2.** Taking precedence <a prior lien>.

prior, *n. Criminal law. Slang.* A previous conviction <because the defendant had two priors, the judge automatically enhanced his sentence>.

prior-appropriation doctrine. The rule that, among the persons whose properties border on a waterway, the earliest users of the water have the right to take all they can use before anyone else has a right to it. Cf. RIPARIAN-RIGHTS DOCTRINE.

prior consistent statement. See STATEMENT.

prior inconsistent statement. See STATEMENT.

priority. 1. The status of being earlier in time or higher in degree or rank; precedence. **2.** An established right to such precedence; esp., a creditor's right to have a claim paid before other creditors of the same debtor receive payment. **3.** The doctrine that, as between two courts, jurisdiction should be accorded the court in which proceedings are first begun.

prior restraint. A governmental restriction on speech or publication before its actual expression. • Prior restraints violate the First Amendment unless the speech is obscene, is defamatory, or creates a clear and present danger to society.

prior sentence. See SENTENCE.

prior-use doctrine. The principle that, without legislative authorization, a government agency may not appropriate property already devoted to a public use.

prison. A state or federal facility of confinement for convicted criminals, esp. felons. Cf. JAIL; PENITENTIARY.

private prison. A prison that is managed by a private company, not by a governmental agency.

prison breach. A prisoner's forcible breaking and departure from a place of lawful confinement; the offense of escaping from confinement in a prison or jail. Cf. ESCAPE (2).

prison camp. A usu. minimum-security camp for the detention of trustworthy prisoners who are often employed on government projects.

prisoner at the bar. An accused person who is on trial.

privacy law. A federal or state statute that protects a person's right to be left alone or that restricts public access to personal information such as tax returns and medical records.

private, *adj.* **1.** Relating or belonging to an individual, as opposed to the public or the government. **2.** (Of a company) not having shares that are freely available on an open market. **3.** Confidential; secret.

private adoption. See ADOPTION.

private carrier. See CARRIER.

private corporation. See CORPORATION.

private fact. See FACT.

private judging. A type of alternative dispute resolution whereby the parties hire a private individual to hear and decide a case.

private land grant. See LAND GRANT.

private law. **1.** The body of law dealing with private persons and their property and relationships. Cf. PUBLIC LAW (1). **2.** See *special law* under LAW.

private morality. See MORALITY.

private necessity. See NECESSITY.

private nuisance. See NUISANCE.

private prison. See PRISON.

private property. See PROPERTY.

private reprimand. See REPRIMAND.

private seal. See SEAL.

private search. See SEARCH.

private sector. The part of the economy or an industry that is free from direct governmental control. Cf. PUBLIC SECTOR.

private servitude. See SERVITUDE (1).

private way. See WAY.

private wrong. See WRONG.

privation (prɪ-**vay**-shən). **1.** The act of taking away or withdrawing. **2.** The condition of being deprived.

privatization (prɪ-və-tə-**zay**-shən), *n.* The act or process of converting a business or industry from governmental ownership or control to private enterprise. — **privatize,** *vb.*

privilege. **1.** A special legal right, exemption, or immunity granted to a person or class of persons; an exception to a duty.

absolute privilege. A privilege that immunizes an actor from suit, no matter how wrongful the action might be, and even though it is done with an improper motive. Cf. *qualified privilege*.

deliberative-process privilege. A privilege permitting the government to withhold documents relating to policy formulation to encourage open and independent discussion among those who develop government policy.

litigation privilege. A privilege protecting the attorneys and parties in a lawsuit from defamation claims arising from statements made in the course of the suit.

parliamentary privilege. The right of a particular question, motion, or statement to take precedence over all other business before the legislative body.

privilege from arrest. An exemption from arrest, as that enjoyed by members of Congress during legislative sessions. U.S. Const. art. I, § 6, cl. 1.

qualified privilege. A privilege that immunizes an actor from suit only when the privilege is properly exercised in the performance of a legal or moral duty. Cf. *absolute privilege.*

special privilege. A privilege granted to a person or class of persons to the exclusion of others and in derogation of the common right.

testimonial privilege. A right not to testify based on a claim of privilege; a privilege that overrides a witness's duty to disclose matters within the witness's knowledge, whether at trial or by deposition.

viatorial privilege (vɪ-ə-**tor**-ee-əl). A privilege that overrides a person's duty to attend court in person and to testify.

2. An affirmative defense by which a defendant acknowledges at least part of the conduct complained of but asserts that the defendant's conduct was authorized or sanctioned by law; esp., in tort law, a circumstance justifying or excusing an intentional tort. See JUSTIFICATION (2). Cf. IMMUNITY (2). **3.** An evidentiary rule that gives a witness the option to not disclose the fact asked for, even though it might be relevant; the right to prevent disclosure of certain information in court, esp. when the information was originally communicated in a professional or confidential relationship.

accountant–client privilege. The protection afforded to a client from an accountant's unauthorized disclosure of materials submitted to or prepared by the accountant.

attorney–client privilege. The client's right to refuse to disclose and to prevent any other person from disclosing confidential communications between the client and the attorney.

doctor–patient privilege. The right to exclude from evidence in a legal proceeding any confidential communication that a patient makes to a physician for the purpose of diagnosis or treatment, unless the patient consents to the disclosure.

executive privilege. A privilege, based on the constitutional doctrine of separation of powers, that exempts the executive branch of the federal government from usual disclosure requirements when the matter to be disclosed involves national security or foreign policy.

Cf. *executive immunity* under IMMUNITY (1).

informant's privilege. The qualified privilege that a government can invoke to prevent disclosure of the identity and communications of its informants. • A party can usually overcome the privilege if it can demonstrate that the need for the information outweighs the public interest in maintaining the privilege.

joint-defense privilege. The rule that a defendant can assert the attorney–client privilege to protect a confidential communication made to a codefendant's lawyer if the communication was related to the defense of both defendants.

journalist's privilege. **1.** A reporter's protection, under constitutional or statutory law, from being compelled to testify about confidential information or sources. See SHIELD LAW (1). **2.** A publisher's protection against defamation lawsuits when the publication makes fair comment on the actions of public officials in matters of public concern. See FAIR COMMENT.

judicial privilege. *Defamation.* The privilege protecting any statement made in the course of and with reference to a judicial proceeding by any judge, juror, party, witness, or advocate.

legislative privilege. *Defamation.* The privilege protecting (1) any statement made in a legislature by one of its members, and (2) any paper published as part of legislative business.

marital privilege. **1.** The privilege allowing a defendant's spouse not to testify, and preventing another person from testifying, about confidential communications between the spouses during the marriage. **2.** The privilege allowing a spouse not to testify in a criminal case as an adverse witness against the other spouse, regardless of the subject matter of the testimony. **3.** The privilege immunizing from a defamation lawsuit any statement made between husband and wife.

official privilege. The privilege immunizing from a defamation lawsuit any statement made by one state officer to another in the course of official duty.

peer-review privilege. A privilege that protects from disclosure the proceedings and reports of a medical facility's peer-review committee, which reviews and oversees the patient care and medical services provided by the staff.

priest–penitent privilege. The privilege barring a clergy member from testifying about a confessor's communications.

psychotherapist–patient privilege. A privilege that a person can invoke to prevent the disclosure of a confidential communication made in the course of diagnosis or treatment of a mental or emotional condition by or at the direction of a psychotherapist. • The privilege can be overcome under certain conditions, as when the examination is ordered by a court.

self-critical-analysis privilege. A privilege protecting individuals and entities from divulging the results of candid assessments of their compliance with laws and regulations, to the extent that the assessments are internal, the results were intended from the outset to be confidential, and the information is of a type that would be curtailed if it were forced to be disclosed.

state-secrets privilege. A privilege that the government may invoke against the discovery of a material that, if divulged, could compromise national security.

privileged, *adj.* Not subject to the usual rules or liabilities; esp., not subject to disclosure during the course of a lawsuit <a privileged document>.

privileged communication. See COMMUNICATION.

privileged evidence. See EVIDENCE.

Privileges and Immunities Clause. The constitutional provision (U.S. Const. art. IV, § 2, cl. 1) prohibiting a state from favoring its own citizens by discriminating against other states' citizens who come within its borders.

Privileges or Immunities Clause. The constitutional provision (U.S. Const. amend. XIV, § 1) prohibiting state laws that abridge the privileges or immunities of U.S. citizens. • The clause was effectively nullified by the Supreme Court in the *Slaughter–House Cases*, 83 U.S. (16 Wall.) 36 (1873). Cf. DUE PROCESS CLAUSE; EQUAL PROTECTION CLAUSE.

privity (**priv**-ə-tee). **1.** The connection or relationship between two parties, each having a legally recognized interest in the same subject matter (such as a transaction, proceeding, or piece of property); mutuality of interest <privity of contract>.

horizontal privity. *Commercial law.* The legal relationship between a party and a nonparty who is related to the party (such as a buyer and a member of the buyer's family).

privity of blood. **1.** Privity between an heir and an ancestor. **2.** Privity between coparceners.

privity of contract. The relationship between the parties to a contract, allowing them to sue each other but preventing a third party from doing so.

privity of estate. A mutual or successive relationship to the same right in property, as between grantor and grantee or landlord and tenant.

privity of possession. Privity between parties in successive possession of real property. • The existence of this type of privity is often at issue in adverse-possession claims.

vertical privity. **1.** *Commercial law.* The legal relationship between parties in a product's chain of distribution (such as a manufacturer and a seller). **2.** Privity between one who signs a contract containing a restrictive covenant and one who acquires the property burdened by it.

2. Joint knowledge or awareness of something private or secret, esp. as implying concurrence or consent <privity to a crime>.

privy (**priv**-ee), *n. pl.* A person having a legal interest of privity in any action, matter, or property; a person who is in privity with another. Pl. **privies.**

pro (proh). [Latin] For.

probable cause. A reasonable ground to suspect that a person has committed or is committing a crime or that a place contains specific items connected with a crime. • Under the Fourth Amendment, probable cause — which amounts to more than a bare suspicion but less than evidence that would justify a conviction — must be shown before an arrest warrant or search warrant may be issued. Cf. REASONABLE SUSPICION.

probable consequence. An effect or result that is more likely than not to follow its supposed cause.

probable-desistance test. *Criminal law.* A common-law test for the crime of attempt, focusing on whether the defendant has exhibited dangerous behavior indicating a likelihood of committing the crime. See ATTEMPT (2).

probate (**proh**-bayt), *n.* **1.** The judicial procedure by which a testamentary document is established to be a valid will; the proving of a will to the satisfaction of the court.

informal probate. Probate designed to operate with minimal involvement and supervision of the probate court. • Most modern probate codes encourage this type of administration, with an independent personal representative.

small-estate probate. An informal procedure for administering small estates, less structured than the normal process and usu. not requiring the assistance of an attorney.

2. Loosely, a personal representative's actions in handling a decedent's estate. **3.** Loosely, all the subjects over which probate courts have jurisdiction.

probate, *vb.* **1.** To admit (a will) to proof. **2.** To administer (a decedent's estate). **3.** To grant probation to (a criminal); to reduce (a sentence) by means of probation.

probate code. A collection of statutes setting forth the law (substantive and procedural) of decedents' estates and trusts.

probate court. See COURT.

probate estate. A decedent's property subject to administration by a personal representative. See *decedent's estate* under ESTATE.

probate homestead. See HOMESTEAD.

probate judge. See JUDGE.

probate register. See REGISTER.

probation. 1. A court-imposed criminal sentence that, subject to stated conditions, releases a convicted person into the community instead of sending the criminal to jail or prison. Cf. PAROLE.

bench probation. Probation in which the offender agrees to certain conditions or restrictions and reports only to the sentencing judge rather than a probation officer.

shock probation. Probation that is granted after a brief stay in jail or prison. • Shock probation is intended to awaken the defendant to the reality of confinement for failure to abide by the conditions of probation. Cf. BOOT CAMP; SHOCK INCARCERATION.

2. The act of judicially proving a will. See PROBATE.

probation termination. The ending of a person's status as a probationer by (1) the routine expiration of the probationary period, (2) early termination by court order, or (3) probation revocation.

probative (**proh**-bə-tiv), *adj.* Tending to prove or disprove. • Courts can exclude relevant evidence if its probative value is substantially outweighed by the danger of unfair prejudice. Fed. R. Evid. 403. — **probativeness,** *n.*

probative evidence. See EVIDENCE.

probative fact. See FACT.

problem-oriented policing. A method that law-enforcement officers use to reduce crime by identifying and remedying the underlying causes of criminal incidents rather than merely seeking basic information (such as the identity of the perpetrator) about the crime being investigated.

pro bono (proh **boh**-noh), *adv.* & *adj.* [Latin *pro bono publico* "for the public good"] Being or involving uncompensated legal services performed esp. for the public good <took the case pro bono>.

procedural-default doctrine. The principle that a federal court lacks jurisdiction to review the merits of a habeas corpus petition if a state court has refused to review the complaint because the petitioner failed to follow reasonable state-court procedures.

procedural due process. See DUE PROCESS.

procedural law. The rules that prescribe the steps for having a right or duty judicially enforced, as opposed to the law that defines the specific rights or duties themselves. Cf. SUBSTANTIVE LAW.

procedural right. See RIGHT.

procedural unconscionability. See UNCONSCIONABILITY.

procedure. 1. A specific method or course of action. **2.** The judicial rule or manner for carrying on a civil lawsuit or criminal prosecution. See CIVIL PROCEDURE; CRIMINAL PROCEDURE.

proceeding. 1. The regular and orderly progression of a lawsuit, including all acts and events between the time of commencement and the entry of judgment. **2.** Any procedural means for seeking redress from a tribunal or agency. **3.** An act or step that is part of a larger action. **4.** The business conducted by a court or other official body; a hearing.

collateral proceeding. A proceeding brought to address an issue incidental to the principal proceeding.

competency proceeding. A proceeding to assess a person's mental capacity. • A competency hearing may be held either in a criminal context to determine a defendant's competency to stand trial or as a civil proceeding to assess whether a person should be committed to a mental-health facility.

contempt proceeding. A judicial or quasi-judicial hearing conducted to determine whether a person has committed contempt.

criminal proceeding. A proceeding instituted to determine a person's guilt or innocence or to set a convicted person's punishment; a criminal hearing or trial.

ex parte proceeding (eks **pahr**-tee). A proceeding in which not all parties are present or given the opportunity to be heard.

in camera proceeding (in **kam**-ə-rə). A proceeding held in a judge's chambers or other private place.

informal proceeding. A trial conducted in a more relaxed manner than a typical court trial, such as an administrative hearing or a trial in small-claims court.

judicial proceeding. Any court proceeding.

special proceeding. **1.** A proceeding that can be commenced independently of a pending action and from which a final order may be appealed immediately. **2.** A proceeding involving statutory or civil remedies or rules rather than the rules or remedies ordinarily available under rules of procedure; a proceeding providing extraordinary relief.

summary proceeding. A nonjury proceeding that settles a controversy or disposes of a case in a relatively prompt and simple manner. Cf. *plenary action* under ACTION.

supplementary proceeding. **1.** A proceeding held in connection with the enforcement of a judgment, for the purpose of identifying and locating the debtor's assets available to satisfy the judgment. **2.** A proceeding that in some way supplements another.

proceeds (**proh**-seedz), *n.* **1.** The value of land, goods, or investments when converted into money; the amount of money received from a sale. **2.** Something received upon selling, exchanging, collecting, or otherwise disposing of collateral. UCC § 9–306(1).

net proceeds. The amount received in a transaction minus the costs of the transaction (such as expenses and commissions).

process, *n.* **1.** The proceedings in any action or prosecution. **2.** A summons or writ, esp. to appear or respond in court. **3.** The procedure by which a contumacious defendant is compelled to plead. **4.** *Patents.* A method, operation, or series of actions intended to achieve some end or result.

process agent. See AGENT.

process server. A person authorized by law or by a court to formally deliver process to a defendant or respondent. See SERVICE (1).

procurement (proh-**kyoor**-mənt), *n.* **1.** The act of getting or obtaining something. **2.** The act of persuading or inviting another, esp. a woman or child, to have illicit sexual intercourse. — **procure,** *vb.*

procurer. One who induces or prevails upon another to do something, esp. to engage in an illicit sexual act. See PIMP.

produce (prə-**doos**), *vb.* **1.** To bring into existence; to create. **2.** To provide (a document, witness, etc.) in response to subpoena or discovery request. **3.** To yield (as revenue). **4.** To bring (oil, etc.) to the surface of the earth.

product. Something that is distributed commercially for use or consumption and that is usu. (1) tangible personal property, (2) the result of fabrication or processing, and (3) an item that has passed through a chain of commercial distribution before ultimate use or consumption. See PRODUCTS LIABILITY.

defective product. A product that is unreasonably dangerous for normal use, as when it is not fit for its intended purpose, inadequate instructions are provided for its use, or it is inherently dangerous in its design or manufacture.

product defect. See DEFECT.

production of suit. *Common-law pleading.* The plaintiff's burden to produce evidence to confirm the allegations made in the declaration.

products liability, *n.* **1.** A manufacturer's or seller's tort liability for any damages or injuries suffered by a buyer, user, or bystander as a result of a defective product. **2.** The legal theory by which liability is imposed on the manufacturer or seller of a defective product. **3.** The field of law dealing with this theory. — **product-liability,** *adj.* See LIABILITY.

strict products liability. Products liability arising when the buyer proves that the goods were unreasonably dangerous and that (1) the seller was in the business of selling goods, (2) the goods were defective when they were in the seller's hands, (3) the defect caused the plaintiff's injury, and (4) the product was expected to and did reach the consumer without substantial change in condition.

profert (**proh**-fərt). *Common-law pleading.* A declaration on the record stating that a party produces in court the deed or other instrument relied on in the pleading.

profess, *vb.* To declare openly and freely; to confess.

profession. 1. A vocation requiring advanced education and training. **2.** Collectively, the members of such a vocation.

professional, *n.* A person who belongs to a learned profession or whose occupation requires a high level of training and proficiency.

professional association. See ASSOCIATION.

professional corporation. See CORPORATION.

proffer (**prof**-ər), *vb.* To offer or tender (something, esp. evidence) for immediate acceptance. — **proffer,** *n.*

proffered evidence. See EVIDENCE.

profit, *n.* **1.** The excess of revenues over expenditures in a business transaction; GAIN (2). Cf. EARNINGS; INCOME. **2.** A servitude that gives the right to pasture cattle, dig for minerals, or otherwise take away some part of the soil; PROFIT À PRENDRE. ● A profit may be either appurtenant or in gross. See SERVITUDE.

profit à prendre (a **prawn**-drə *or* ah **prahn**-dər). [Law French "profit to take"] (*usu. pl.*) A right or privilege to go on another's land and take away something of value from its soil or from the products of its soil (as by mining, logging, or hunting). Pl. **profits à prendre.** Cf. EASEMENT.

profiteering, *n.* The taking advantage of unusual or exceptional circumstances to make excessive profits, as in the selling of scarce goods at inflated prices during war. — **profiteer,** *vb.*

pro forma (proh **for**-mə), *adj.* [Latin "for form"] **1.** Made or done as a formality. **2.** (Of an invoice or financial statement) provided in advance to describe items, predict results, or secure approval.

progeny (**proj**-ə-nee), *n. pl.* **1.** Children or descendants; offspring <only one of their progeny attended law school>. **2.** A group of successors; esp., a line of opinions succeeding a leading case <*Erie* and its progeny>.

prognosis (prog-**noh**-sis). **1.** The process of forecasting the probable outcome of a present medical condition (such as a disease). **2.** The forecast of such an outcome. Cf. DIAGNOSIS.

progressive tax. See TAX.

pro hac vice (proh hahk **vee**-chay *or* hak **vɪ**-see *also* hahk **vees**). [Latin] For this occasion or particular purpose. • The phrase usually refers to a lawyer who has not been admitted to practice in a particular jurisdiction but who is admitted there temporarily for the purpose of conducting a particular case.

prohibited degree. See DEGREE.

prohibition. 1. A law or order that forbids a certain action. **2.** An extraordinary writ issued by an appellate court to prevent a lower court from exceeding its jurisdiction or to prevent a nonjudicial officer or entity from exercising a power. **3.** (*cap.*) The period from 1920 to 1933, when the manufacture, transport, and sale of alcoholic beverages in the United States was forbidden by the 18th Amendment to the Constitution. • The 18th Amendment was repealed by the 21st Amendment.

prohibitory injunction. See INJUNCTION.

prolicide (**proh**-lə-sɪd). **1.** The killing of offspring; esp., the crime of killing a child shortly before or after birth. **2.** One who kills a child shortly before or after birth. — **prolicidal,** *adj.* Cf. INFANTICIDE.

prolixity (proh-**lik**-sə-tee). The unnecessary and superfluous stating of facts in pleading or evidence.

promise, *n.* **1.** The manifestation of an intention to act or refrain from acting in a specified manner, conveyed in such a way that another is justified in understanding that a commitment has been made; a person's assurance that the person will or will not do something. **2.** The words in a promissory note expressing the maker's intention to pay a debt. — **promise,** *vb.*

alternative promise. A contractual promise to do one of two or more things, any one of which must satisfy the promisee for the promise to qualify as consideration.

conditional promise. A promise that is conditioned on the occurrence of an event • A conditional promise is not illusory as long as the condition is not entirely within the promisor's control.

dependent promise. A promise to be performed by a party only when another obligation has first been performed by another party.

gratuitous promise. A promise made in exchange for nothing; a promise not supported by consideration.

illusory promise. A covenant cloaked in promissory terms but actually containing no commitment by the promisor. • For example, if a guarantor promises to make good on the principal debtor's obligation "as long as I think it's in my commercial interests," the promisor is not really bound.

implied promise. A promise created by law to render a person liable on a contract so as to avoid fraud or unjust enrichment.

mutual promises. Promises given simultaneously by two parties, each promise serving as consideration for the other.

new promise. A previously unenforceable promise that a promisor revives and agrees to fulfill, as when a debtor agrees to pay a creditor an amount discharged in the debtor's bankruptcy.

promise implied in fact. A promise existing by inference from the circumstances or actions of the parties. See *implied promise*.

unconditional promise. A promise that either is unqualified or requires nothing but the lapse of time to make the promise presently enforceable. • A party who makes an unconditional promise must perform that promise even though the other party has not performed according to the bargain.

promisee (prom-is-**ee**). One to whom a promise is made.

promisor (prom-is-**or**). One who makes a promise; esp., one who undertakes a contractual obligation.

promissory, *adj.* Containing or consisting of a promise <promissory note>.

promissory estoppel. See ESTOPPEL.

promissory fraud. See FRAUD.

promissory note. See NOTE.

promissory oath. See OATH.

promissory representation. See REPRESENTATION.

promoter. 1. A person who encourages or incites. **2.** A founder or organizer of a corporation or business venture; one who takes the entrepreneurial initiative in founding or organizing a business or enterprise.

promulgate (prə-**məl**-gayt *or* **prom**-əl-gayt), *vb.* **1.** To declare or announce publicly; to proclaim. **2.** To put (a law or decree) into force or effect. — **promulgation** (prom-əl-**gay**-shən *or* proh-məl-), *n.*

pronounce, *vb.* To announce formally <pronounce judgment>.

proof, *n.* **1.** The establishment or refutation of an alleged fact by evidence; the persuasive effect of evidence in the mind of a fact-finder. **2.** Evidence that determines the judgment of a court. **3.** An attested document that constitutes legal evidence.

affirmative proof. Evidence establishing the fact in dispute by a preponderance of the evidence.

conditional proof. A fact that amounts to proof as long as there is no other fact amounting to disproof.

double proof. **1.** *Evidence.* Corroborating government evidence (usu. by two witnesses) required to sustain certain convictions. **2.** *Bankruptcy.* Proof of claims by two or more creditors against the same debt.

negative proof. Proof that establishes a fact by showing that its opposite is not or cannot be true. Cf. *positive proof.*

positive proof. Direct or affirmative proof. Cf. *negative proof.*

proof beyond a reasonable doubt. Proof that precludes every reasonable hypothesis except that which it tends to support.

proof brief. See BRIEF.

proof of acknowledgment. An authorized officer's certification — based on a third party's testimony — that the signature of a person (who usu. does not appear before the notary) is genuine and was freely made.

proof of service. A document filed (as by a sheriff) in court as evidence that process has been successfully served on a party. See SERVICE (1).

pro per, *adv. & adj.* See PRO PERSONA.

pro per, *n.* See PRO SE.

proper law. *Conflict of laws.* The substantive law that, under the principles of conflicts of law, governs a transaction.

proper lookout, *n.* The duty of a vehicle operator to exercise caution to avoid collisions with pedestrians or other vehicles.

proper party. See PARTY (2).

pro persona (proh pər-**soh**-nə), *adv. & adj.* [Latin] For one's own person; on one's own behalf <a *pro persona* brief>. See PRO SE.

property. 1. The right to possess, use, and enjoy a determinate thing (either a tract of land or a chattel); the right of ownership. **2.** Any external thing over which the rights of possession, use, and enjoyment are exercised.

abandoned property. Property that the owner voluntarily surrenders, relinquishes, or disclaims. Cf. *lost property*; *mislaid property.*

common property. **1.** Property that is held jointly by two or more persons. **2.** See COMMON AREA.

distressed property. Property that must be sold because of mortgage foreclosure or because it is part of an insolvent estate.

incorporeal property. **1.** An in rem proprietary right that is not classified as corporeal property. • Incorporeal property is traditionally broken down into two classes: (1) *jura in re aliena* (encumbrances), whether over material or immaterial things, examples being leases, mortgages, and servitudes; and (2) *jura in re propria* (full ownership over an immaterial thing), examples being patents, copyrights, and trademarks. **2.** A legal right in property having no physical existence. • Patent rights, for example, are incorporeal property.

intangible property. Property that lacks a physical existence. • Examples include bank accounts, stock options, and business goodwill. Cf. *tangible property*.

lost property. Property that the owner no longer possesses because of accident, negligence, or carelessness, and that cannot be located by an ordinary, diligent search. Cf. *abandoned property*; *mislaid property*.

marital property. Property that is acquired during marriage and that is subject to distribution or division at the time of marital dissolution. • Generally, it is property acquired after the date of the marriage and before a spouse files for divorce. See COMMUNITY PROPERTY; EQUITABLE DISTRIBUTION.

mislaid property. Property that has been voluntarily relinquished by the owner with an intent to recover it later — but that cannot now be found. Cf. *abandoned property*; *lost property*.

mixed property. Property with characteristics of both real property and personal property — such as heirlooms and fixtures.

personal property. **1.** Any movable or intangible thing that is subject to ownership and not classified as real property. Cf. *real property*. **2.** *Tax.* Property not used in a taxpayer's trade or business or held for income production or collection.

private property. Property — protected from public appropriation — over which the owner has exclusive and absolute rights.

public property. State- or community-owned property not restricted to any one individual's use or possession.

qualified-terminable-interest property. Property that passes by a QTIP trust from a deceased spouse to the surviving spouse and that (if the executor so elects) qualifies for the marital deduction provided that the spouse is entitled to receive income in payments made at least annually for life and that no one has the power to appoint the property to anyone other than the surviving spouse. See *QTIP trust* under TRUST.

real property. Land and anything growing on, attached to, or erected on it, excluding anything that may be severed without injury to the land. • Real property can be either corporeal (soil and buildings) or incorporeal (easements). Cf. *personal property*.

tangible personal property. Corporeal personal property of any kind; personal property that can be seen, touched, weighed, measured, or felt, or is in any way perceptible to the senses.

tangible property. Property that has physical form and characteristics. Cf. *intangible property*.

property right. See RIGHT.

property tax. See TAX.

property tort. See TORT.

prophylactic (proh-fə-**lak**-tik), *adj.* Formulated to prevent something <a prophylactic rule>. — **prophylaxis** (proh-fə-**lak**-sis), *n.* — **prophylactic,** *n.*

propinquity (prə-**ping**-kwə-tee). The state of being near; specif., kindred or parentage <degrees of propinquity>.

proponent, *n.* **1.** A person who puts forward a legal instrument for consideration or acceptance; esp., one who offers a will for probate. **2.** A person who puts forward a proposal; one who argues in favor of something <a proponent of gun control>. — **propone** (prə-**pohn**), *vb.*

proportionality review. *Criminal law.* An appellate court's analysis of whether a death sentence is arbitrary or capricious by comparing the case in which it was imposed with similar cases in which the death penalty was approved or disapproved.

propound (prə-**pownd**), *vb.* **1.** To offer for consideration or discussion. **2.** To make a proposal. **3.** To put forward (a will) as authentic. — **propounder,** *n.*

propria persona (**proh**-pree-ə pər-**soh**-nə). [Latin] In his own person; that is, pro se.

proprietary (prə-**prı**-ə-ter-ee), *adj.* **1.** Of or relating to a proprietor <the licensee's proprietary rights>. **2.** Of, relating to, or holding as property <the software designer sought to protect its proprietary data>.

proprietary function. *Torts.* A municipality's conduct that is performed for the profit or benefit of the municipality, rather than for the benefit of the general public. Cf. GOVERNMENTAL FUNCTION.

proprietary interest. See INTEREST (2).

proprietor, *n.* An owner, esp. one who runs a business. — **proprietorship,** *n.* See SOLE PROPRIETORSHIP.

pro rata (proh **ray**-tə *or* **rah**-tə *or* **ra**-tə), *adv.* Proportionately; according to an exact rate, measure, or interest <the liability will be assessed pro rata between the defendants>. — **pro rata,** *adj.* See RATABLE.

prorate (**proh**-rayt *or* proh-**rayt**), *vb.* To divide, assess, or distribute proportionately <prorate taxes between the buyer and the seller>. — **proration,** *n.*

prorogation (proh-rə-**gay**-shən). The act of putting off to another day; esp., the discontinuance of a legislative session until its next term.

prorogue (proh-**rohg** *or* prə-), *vb.* **1.** To postpone or defer. **2.** To suspend or discontinue a legislative session.

proscribe, *vb.* To outlaw or prohibit; to forbid.

proscription, *n.* **1.** The act of prohibiting; the state of being prohibited. **2.** A prohibition or restriction. — **proscriptive,** *adj.* Cf. PRESCRIPTION.

pro se (proh **say** *or* **see**), *adv.* & *adj.* [Latin] For oneself; on one's own behalf; without a lawyer <the defendant proceeded pro se> <a pro se defendant>.

pro se, *n.* One who represents oneself in a court proceeding without the assistance of a lawyer <the third case on the court's docket involving a pro se>.

prosecute, *vb.* **1.** To commence and carry out a legal action <because the plaintiff failed to prosecute its contractual claims, the court dismissed the suit>. **2.** To institute and pursue a criminal action against (a person) <the notorious felon has been prosecuted in seven states>. **3.** To engage in; carry on <the company prosecuted its business for 12 years before going bankrupt>. — **prosecutory,** *adj.*

prosecuting witness. See WITNESS.

prosecution. 1. The commencement and carrying out of any action or scheme <the prosecution of a long, bloody war>. **2.** A criminal proceeding in which an accused person is tried <the conspiracy trial involved the prosecution of seven defendants>.

sham prosecution. A prosecution that seeks to circumvent a defendant's double-jeopardy protection by appearing to be prosecuted by another sovereignty, when it is in fact controlled by the sovereignty that already prosecuted the defendant for the same crime. See DUAL-SOVEREIGNTY DOCTRINE.

vindictive prosecution. A prosecution in which a person is singled out under a law or regulation because the person has exercised a constitutionally protected right. Cf. SELECTIVE ENFORCEMENT.

3. The government attorneys who initiate and maintain a criminal action against an accused defendant <the prosecution rests>.

prosecutor, *n.* A legal officer who represents the government in criminal proceedings. — **prosecutorial,** *adj.* See DISTRICT ATTORNEY; UNITED STATES ATTORNEY; ATTORNEY GENERAL.

special prosecutor. A lawyer appointed to investigate and, if justified, seek indictments in a particular case. See *independent counsel* under COUNSEL.

prosecutorial discretion. See DISCRETION.

prosecutorial misconduct. A prosecutor's improper or illegal act (or failure to act), esp. involving an attempt to persuade the jury to wrongly convict a defendant or assess an unjustified punishment.

prospectant evidence. See EVIDENCE.

prospective, *adj.* **1.** Effective or operative in the future <prospective application of the new statute>. Cf. RETROACTIVE. **2.** Anticipated or expected; likely to come about <prospective clients>.

prospective heir. See HEIR.

prospective statute. See STATUTE.

prospective waiver. See WAIVER.

prostitution, *n.* **1.** The act or practice of engaging in sexual activity for money or its equivalent; commercialized sex. **2.** The act of debasing. — **prostitute,** *vb.* — **prostitute,** *n.*

pro tanto (proh **tan**-toh), *adv.* & *adj.* [Latin] *Jargon.* To that extent; for so much; as far as it goes <the debt is pro tanto discharged> <a pro tanto payment>.

protected activity. Conduct that is permitted or encouraged by a statute or constitutional provision, and for which the actor may not legally be retaliated against.

protection, *n.* **1.** The act of protecting. **2.** PROTECTIONISM. **3.** COVERAGE. **4.** A document given by a notary public to sailors and other persons who travel abroad, certifying that the bearer is a U.S. citizen. — **protect,** *vb.*

protectionism. The protection of domestic businesses and industries against foreign competition by imposing high tariffs and restricting imports.

protection money. 1. A bribe paid to an officer as an inducement not to interfere with the criminal activities of the briber. **2.** Money extorted from a business owner by one who promises to "protect" the business premises, with the implied threat that if the owner does not pay, the person requesting the payment will harm the owner or damage the premises.

protective custody. See CUSTODY (1).

protective order. 1. A court order prohibiting or restricting a party from engaging in conduct (esp. a legal procedure such as discovery) that unduly annoys or burdens the opposing party or a third-party witness. **2.** RESTRAINING ORDER (1).

protective search. See SEARCH.

protective sweep. A police officer's quick and limited search — conducted after the officer has lawfully entered the premises — based on a reasonable belief that such a search is necessary to protect the officer or others from harm.

pro tem. *abbr.* PRO TEMPORE.

pro tempore (proh **tem**-pə-ree), *adv.* & *adj.* [Latin] For the time being; appointed to occupy a position temporarily <a judge pro tempore>. — Abbr. pro tem.

protest, *n.* **1.** A formal statement or action expressing dissent or disapproval. **2.** A notary public's written statement that, upon presentment, a negotiable instrument was neither paid nor accepted. Cf. NOTICE OF DISHONOR. **3.** A formal statement, usu. in writing, disputing a debt's legality or validity but agreeing to make payment while reserving the right to recover the amount at a later time. • The disputed debt is described as *under protest*. — **protest,** *vb.*

protestation (prot-ə-**stay**-shən). *Common-law pleading.* A declaration by which a party makes an oblique allegation or denial of some fact, claiming that it does or does not exist or is or is not legally sufficient, while not directly affirming or denying the fact.

provable, *adj.* Capable of being proved.

prove, *vb.* To establish or make certain; to establish the truth of (a fact or hypothesis) by satisfactory evidence.

prove up, *vb.* To present or complete the proof of (something) <deciding not to put a doctor on the stand, the plaintiff attempted to prove up his damages with medical records only>.

prove-up, *n.* The establishment of a prima facie claim. • A prove-up is necessary when a factual assertion is unopposed because even without opposition, the claim must be supported by evidence.

provided, *conj.* On the condition or understanding (that) <we will sign the contract provided that you agree to the following conditions>.

provision. 1. A clause in a statute, contract, or other legal instrument. **2.** A stipulation made beforehand. See PROVISO.

provisional, *adj.* **1.** Temporary <a provisional injunction>. **2.** Conditional <a provisional government>.

provisional exit. A prisoner's temporary release from prison for a court appearance, hospital treatment, work detail, or other purpose requiring a release with the expectation of return.

provisional remedy. See REMEDY.

proviso (prə-vɪ-zoh). **1.** A limitation, condition, or stipulation upon whose compliance a legal or formal document's validity or application may depend. **2.** In drafting, a provision that begins with the words *provided that* and supplies a condition, exception, or addition.

provocation, *n.* **1.** The act of inciting another to do something, esp. to commit a crime. **2.** Something (such as words or actions) that affects a person's reason and self-control, esp. causing the person to commit a crime impulsively. — **provoke,** *vb.* — **provocative,** *adj.*

adequate provocation. Something that would cause a reasonable person to act without self-control and lose any premeditated state of mind. See HEAT OF PASSION. Cf. SELF-DEFENSE.

proximate (**prok**-sə-mit), *adj.* **1.** Immediately before or after. **2.** Very near or close in time.

proximate cause. See CAUSE (1).

proximate consequence. A result following an unbroken sequence from some (esp. negligent) event.

proximity. The quality or state of being near in time, place, order, or relation.

proxy, *n.* **1.** One who is authorized to act as a substitute for another; esp., in corporate law, a person who is authorized to vote another's stock shares. **2.** The grant of authority by which a person is so authorized. **3.** The document granting this authority.

proxy marriage. See MARRIAGE (2).

PRP. *abbr.* Potentially responsible party.

prudent, *adj.* Circumspect or judicious in one's dealings; cautious. — **prudence,** *n.*

prudent-investor rule. *Trusts.* The principle that a fiduciary must invest in only those securities or portfolios of securities that a reasonable person would buy.

prurient (**pruur**-ee-ənt), *adj.* Characterized by or arousing inordinate or unusual sexual desire <films appealing to prurient interests>. — **prurience,** *n.* See OBSCENITY.

psychopath (sɪ-kə-path), *n.* **1.** A person with a mental disorder characterized by an extremely antisocial personality that often leads to aggressive, perverted, or criminal behavior. **2.** Loosely, a person who is mentally ill or unstable. — **psycho-**

pathic (SI-kə-**path**-ik), *adj.* — **psychopathy** (SI-**kop**-ə-thee), *n.*

psychotherapist–patient privilege. See PRIVILEGE (3).

Pub. L. *abbr.* PUBLIC LAW (2).

public, *adj.* **1.** Relating or belonging to an entire community, state, or nation. **2.** Open or available for all to use, share, or enjoy. **3.** (Of a company) having shares that are available on an open market.

public, *n.* **1.** The people of a nation or community as a whole <a crime against the public>. **2.** A place open or visible to the public <in public>.

public access to court electronic records. A computer system by which subscribers can obtain online information from the federal courts, including information from a court's docket sheet about the parties, filing, and orders in a specific case. — Abbr. PACER.

public accommodation. A business establishment that provides lodging, food, entertainment, or other services to the public; esp. (as defined by the Civil Rights Act of 1964), one that affects interstate commerce or is supported by state action.

public administration. See ADMINISTRATION.

public administrator. See ADMINISTRATOR.

publication, *n.* **1.** Generally, the act of declaring or announcing to the public. **2.** *Copyright*. The distribution of copies of a work to the public. **3.** *Defamation*. The communication of defamatory words to someone other than the person defamed. **4.** *Wills*. The formal declaration made by a testator when signing the will that it is the testator's will.

public bill. See BILL (3).

public-convenience-and-necessity standard. A common criterion used by a governmental body to assess whether a particular request or project is suitable for the public.

public corporation. See CORPORATION.

public defender. A lawyer or staff of lawyers, usu. publicly appointed, whose duty is to represent indigent criminal defendants. — Abbr. P.D.

public disclosure of private facts. The public revelation of some aspect of a person's private life without a legitimate public purpose. See INVASION OF PRIVACY.

public document. See DOCUMENT.

public domain. 1. Government-owned land. **2.** The realm of publications, inventions, and processes that are not protected by copyright or patent.

public-duty doctrine. *Torts*. The rule that a governmental entity (such as a state or municipality) cannot be held liable for an individual plaintiff's injury resulting from a governmental officer's or employee's breach of a duty owed to the general public rather than to the individual plaintiff. See SPECIAL-DUTY DOCTRINE.

public enemy. 1. A notorious criminal who is a menace to society; esp., one who seems more or less immune from successful prosecution <Public Enemy No. 1>. **2.** A social, health, or economic condition or problem that affects the public at large and is difficult to control <teenage smoking has been declared a public enemy in this country>.

public fact. See FACT.

public figure. A person who has achieved fame or notoriety or who has voluntarily become involved in a public controversy.

limited-purpose public figure. A person who, having become involved in a particular public issue, has achieved fame or notoriety in relation to that particular issue.

public forum. *Constitutional law.* Public property where people traditionally gather to express ideas and exchange views. • To be constitutional, the government's regulation of a public forum must be narrowly tailored to serve a significant government interest and must usually be limited to time, place, or manner restrictions. Cf. NONPUBLIC FORUM.

designated public forum. Public property that has not traditionally been open for public assembly and debate but that the government has opened for use by the public as a place for expressive activity, such as a public-university facility or a publicly owned theater. • The subject matter of the expression permitted in a designated public forum may be limited to accord with the character of the forum. Reasonable, content-neutral time, place, or manner restrictions are generally permissible. But any prohibition based on the content of the expression must be narrowly drawn to effectuate a compelling state interest, as with a traditional public forum.

traditional public forum. Public property that has by long tradition been used by the public for assembly and expression, such as a public street, public sidewalk, or public park. • To be constitutional, the government's content-neutral restrictions of the time, place, or manner of expression must be narrowly tailored to serve a significant government interest, and leave open ample alternative channels of communication. Any government regulation of expression that is based on the content of the expression must meet the much higher test of being necessary to serve a compelling state interest.

public-function test. In a suit under 42 USCA § 1983, the doctrine that a private person's actions constitute state action if the private person performs functions that are traditionally reserved to the state.

public health. See HEALTH.

public hearing. See HEARING.

public interest. 1. The general welfare of the public that warrants recognition and protection. **2.** Something in which the public as a whole has a stake; esp., an interest that justifies governmental regulation.

public-interest exception. The principle that an appellate court may consider and decide a moot case — although such decisions are generally prohibited — if (1) the case involves a question of considerable public importance, (2) the question is likely to arise in the future, and (3) the question has evaded appellate review.

public intoxication. See INTOXICATION.

public invitee. See INVITEE.

public land. See LAND.

public law. 1. The body of law dealing with the relations between private individuals and the government, and with the structure and operation of the government itself; constitutional law, criminal law, and administrative law taken together. Cf. PRIVATE LAW (1). **2.** A statute affecting the general public. • Federal public laws are first published in *Statutes at Large* and are eventually collected by subject in the U.S. Code. — Abbr. Pub. L.; P.L. Cf. *general law* (1) under LAW. **3.** Constitutional law.

public morality. See MORALITY.

public necessity. See NECESSITY.

public notice. See NOTICE.

public nuisance. See NUISANCE.

public offense. See OFFENSE.

public person. A sovereign government, or a body or person delegated authority under it.

public policy. 1. Broadly, principles and standards regarded by the legislature or by the courts as being of fundamental concern to the state and the whole of society. **2.** More narrowly, the principle that a person should not be allowed to do anything that would tend to injure the public at large.

public-policy limitation. *Tax.* A judicially developed principle that a person should not be allowed to deduct expenses related to an activity that is contrary to the public welfare.

public property. See PROPERTY.

public purpose. An action by or at the direction of a government for the benefit of the community as a whole.

public record. See RECORD.

public reprimand. See REPRIMAND.

public safety. The welfare and protection of the general public, usu. expressed as a governmental responsibility <Department of Public Safety>.

public-safety exception. An exception to the *Miranda* rule allowing into evidence an otherwise suppressible statement by a defendant concerning information that the police needed at the time it was made in order to protect the public. • If, for example, a victim tells the police that an assailant had a gun, and upon the suspect's arrest the police find a holster but no gun, they would be entitled immediately to ask where the gun is. The suspect's statement of the gun's location is admissible.

public seal. See SEAL.

public sector. The part of the economy or an industry that is controlled by the government. Cf. PRIVATE SECTOR.

public service. 1. A service provided or facilitated by the government for the general public's convenience and benefit. **2.** Government employment; work performed for or on behalf of the government.

public-service corporation. See CORPORATION.

public servitude. See SERVITUDE (1).

public tort. See TORT.

public utility. See UTILITY.

public verdict. See VERDICT.

public welfare. See WELFARE.

public wrong. See WRONG.

publish, *vb.* **1.** To distribute copies (of a work) to the public. **2.** To communicate (defamatory words) to someone other than the person defamed. **3.** To declare (a will) to be the true expression of one's testamentary intent. **4.** To make (evidence) available to a jury during trial. See PUBLICATION.

PUC. *abbr.* Public Utilities Commission.

PUD. See *municipal utility district* under DISTRICT.

puffing. 1. The expression of an exaggerated opinion — as opposed to a factual misrepresentation — with the intent to sell a good or service. • Puffing involves expressing opinions, not asserting something as a fact. Although there is some leeway in puffing goods, a seller may not misrepresent them or say that they have attributes that they do not possess. **2.** Secret bidding at an auction by or on behalf of a seller; BY-BIDDING.

puisne (pyoo-nee), *adj.* [Law French] Junior in rank; subordinate.

***Pullman* abstention.** See ABSTENTION.

punishable, *adj.* **1.** (Of a person) subject to a punishment <there is no dispute that Jackson remains punishable for these offenses>. **2.** (Of a crime or tort) giving rise to a specified punishment <a felony punishable by imprisonment for up to 20 years>. — **punishability,** *n.*

punishment, *n.* A sanction — such as a fine, penalty, confinement, or loss of property, right, or privilege — assessed against a person who has violated the law. — **punish,** *vb.* See SENTENCE.

corporal punishment. Physical punishment; punishment that is inflicted upon the body (including imprisonment).

cruel and unusual punishment. Punishment that is torturous, degrading, inhuman, grossly disproportionate to the crime in question, or otherwise shocking to the moral sense of the community.

cumulative punishment. Punishment that increases in severity when a person is convicted of the same offense more than once.

deterrent punishment. Punishment intended to deter others from committing crimes by making an example of the offender so that like-minded people are warned of the consequences of crime.

excessive punishment. Punishment that is not justified by the gravity of the offense or the defendant's criminal record. See *excessive fine* (1) under FINE.

infamous punishment. Punishment by imprisonment, usu. in a penitentiary. See *infamous crime* under CRIME.

preventive punishment. Punishment intended to prevent a repetition of wrongdoing by disabling the offender.

reformative punishment. Punishment intended to change the character of the offender.

retributive punishment. Punishment intended to satisfy the community's retaliatory sense of indignation that is provoked by injustice.

punitive, *adj.* Involving or inflicting punishment.

punitive damages. See DAMAGES.

punitive segregation. See SEGREGATION.

pur autre vie (pər **oh**-trə [*or* **oh**-tər] **vee**). [Law French "for another's life"] For or during a period measured by another's life <a life estate *pur autre vie*>.

purchase, *n.* **1.** The act or an instance of buying. **2.** The acquisition of real property by one's own or another's act (as by will or gift) rather than by descent or inheritance. — **purchase,** *vb.* Cf. DESCENT (1).

purchase agreement. A sales contract.

purchase money. The initial payment made on property secured by a mortgage.

purchase-money security interest. See SECURITY INTEREST.

purchase order. A document authorizing a seller to deliver goods with payment to be made later.

purchaser. 1. One who obtains property for money or other valuable consideration; a buyer.

bona fide purchaser. One who buys something for value without notice of another's claim to the item or of any defects in the seller's title; one who has in good faith paid valuable consideration for property without notice of prior adverse claims. — Abbr. BFP.

2. One who acquires real property by means other than descent or inheritance.

pure-comparative-negligence doctrine. The principle that liability for negligence is apportioned in accordance with the percentage of fault that the fact-finder assigns to each party and that a plaintiff's percentage of fault reduces the amount of recoverable damages but does not bar recovery. Cf. 50-PERCENT RULE. See *comparative negligence* under NEGLIGENCE; APPORTIONMENT OF LIABILITY.

pure plea. See PLEA (3).

pure speech. See SPEECH.

purge, *vb.* To exonerate (oneself or another) of guilt <purged the defendant of contempt>.

purport (**pər**-port), *n.* The idea or meaning that is conveyed or expressed, esp. by a formal document.

purport (pər-**port**), *vb.* To profess or claim falsely; to seem to be <the document purports to be a will, but it is neither signed nor dated>.

purported, *adj.* Reputed; rumored.

purpose. An objective, goal, or end; specif., the business activity that a corporation is chartered to engage in.

purpresture (pər-**pres**-chər). An encroachment upon public rights and easements by appropriation to private use of that which belongs to the public.

pursuant to. *Jargon.* **1.** In compliance with; in accordance with; under <she filed the motion pursuant to the

court's order>. **2.** As authorized by; under <pursuant to Rule 56, the plaintiff moves for summary judgment>. **3.** In carrying out <pursuant to his responsibilities, he ensured that all lights had been turned out>.

pursuit. 1. An occupation or pastime. **2.** The act of chasing to overtake or apprehend. See FRESH PURSUIT.

pursuit of happiness. The principle — announced in the Declaration of Independence — that a person should be allowed to pursue the person's desires (esp. in regard to an occupation) without unjustified interference by the government.

purview (pər-vyoo). 1. Scope; area of application. **2.** The body of a statute following the preamble.

putative (pyoo-tə-tiv), *adj.* Reputed; believed; supposed.

putative father. See FATHER.

put in, *vb.* To place in due form before a court; to place among the records of a court.

putting in fear. The threatening of another person with violence to compel the person to hand over property.

pyramiding inferences, rule against. *Evidence.* A rule prohibiting a factfinder from piling one inference on another to arrive at a conclusion. Cf. REASONABLE-INFERENCE RULE.

pyramid scheme. A property-distribution scheme in which a participant pays for the chance to receive compensation for introducing new persons to the scheme, as well as for when those new persons themselves introduce participants. Cf. PONZI SCHEME.

Q

Q. *abbr.* QUESTION. • This abbreviation is almost always used in deposition and trial transcripts to denote each question asked by the examining lawyer.

Q-and-A. *abbr.* QUESTION-AND-ANSWER.

q.c.f. *abbr.* QUARE CLAUSUM FREGIT.

Q.D. *abbr.* [Latin *quasi dicat*] As if he should say.

QDRO (**kwah**-droh). *abbr.* QUALIFIED DOMESTIC-RELATIONS ORDER.

Q.E.D. *abbr.* [Latin *quod erat demonstrandum*] Which was to be demonstrated or proved.

QTIP trust. See TRUST.

qua (kway *or* kwah). [Latin] In the capacity of; as <the fiduciary, qua fiduciary, is not liable for fraud, but he may be liable as an individual>.

quaere (**kweer**-ee), *vb.* [Latin] Inquire; query; examine. • This term was often used in the syllabus of a reported case to show that a point was doubtful or open to question.

qualification. 1. The possession of qualities or properties (such as fitness or capacity) inherently or legally necessary to make one eligible for a position or office, or to perform a public duty or function <voter qualification requires one to meet residency, age, and registration requirements>. **2.** A modification or limitation of terms or language; esp., a restriction of terms that would otherwise be interpreted broadly <the contract contained a qualification requiring the lessor's permission before exercising the right to sublet>. **3.** CHARACTERIZATION (1). — **qualify,** *vb.*

qualified, *adj.* **1.** Possessing the necessary qualifications; capable or competent <a qualified medical examiner>. **2.** Limited; restricted <qualified immunity>. — **qualify,** *vb.*

qualified disclaimer. See DISCLAIMER.

qualified domestic-relations order. A state-court order or judgment that relates to alimony, child support, or some other state domestic-relations matter and that (1) recognizes or provides for an alternate payee's right to receive all or part of any benefits due a participant under a pension, profit-sharing, or other retirement benefit plan, (2) otherwise satisfies § 414 of the Internal Revenue Code, and (3) is exempt from the ERISA rule prohibiting the assignment of plan benefits. — Abbr. QDRO.

qualified general denial. See DENIAL.

qualified immunity. See IMMUNITY (1).

qualified indorsement. See INDORSEMENT.

qualified nuisance. See NUISANCE.

qualified ownership. See OWNERSHIP.

qualified privilege. See PRIVILEGE (1).

qualified residence interest. See INTEREST (3).

qualified-terminable-interest property. See PROPERTY.

qualified veto. See VETO.

qualified witness. See WITNESS.

quality of estate. 1. The period when the right of enjoying an estate is conferred upon the owner, whether at present or in the future. **2.** The manner in which the owner's right of enjoyment of an estate is to be exercised, whether solely, jointly, in common, or in coparcenary.

quantitative rule. An evidentiary rule requiring that a given type of evidence is insufficient unless accompanied by additional evidence before the case is closed.

quantum (**kwon**-təm). [Latin "an amount"] The required, desired, or allowed amount; portion or share <a quantum of evidence>. Pl. **quanta** (**kwon**-tə).

quantum meruit (**kwon**-təm **mer**-oo-it). [Latin "as much as he has deserved"] **1.** The reasonable value of services; damages awarded in an amount considered reasonable to compensate a person who has rendered services in a quasi-contractual relationship. **2.** A claim or right of action for the reasonable value of services rendered. **3.** At common law, a count in an assumpsit action to recover payment for services rendered to another person. See *implied-in-law contract* under CONTRACT.

quantum valebant (**kwon**-təm və-**lee**-bant *or* -bənt). [Latin "as much as they were worth"] **1.** The reasonable value of goods and materials. **2.** At common law, a count in an assumpsit action to recover payment for goods sold and delivered to another.

quarantine. 1. The isolation of a person or animal afflicted with a communicable disease or the prevention of such a person or animal from coming into a particular area, the purpose being to prevent the spread of disease. **2.** A place where a quarantine is in force. — **quarantine,** *vb.*

quare (**kwair**-ee). [Latin] Why; for what reason; on what account. • This was used in various common-law writs, especially writs in trespass.

quare clausum fregit (**kwair**-ee **klaw**-zəm **free**-jit). [Latin] Why he broke the close. — Abbr. *qu. cl. fr.*; *q.c.f.* See *trespass quare clausum fregit* under TRESPASS.

quash (kwahsh), *vb.* **1.** To annul or make void; to terminate <quash an indictment> <quash proceedings>. **2.** To suppress or subdue; to crush out <quash a rebellion>. — **quashal** (**kwahsh**-əl), *n.*

quasi (**kway**-SI *or* **kway**-ZI *also* **kwah**-zee). [Latin "as if"] Seemingly but not actually; in some sense; resembling; nearly.

quasi-admission. See ADMISSION.

quasi-contract. See CONTRACT.

quasi-crime. See CRIME.

quasi-estoppel. See ESTOPPEL.

quasi in rem. See IN REM.

quasi-in-rem jurisdiction. See JURISDICTION.

quasi-insurer. See INSURER.

quasi-judicial, *adj.* Of, relating to, or involving an executive or administrative official's adjudicative acts.

quasi-judicial act. 1. A judicial act performed by an official who is not a judge. **2.** An act performed by a judge who is not acting entirely in a judicial capacity. See *judicial act* under ACT.

quasi-judicial power. See POWER.

quasi-legislative, *adj.* (Of an act, function, etc.) not purely legislative in nature <the administrative agency's rulemaking, being partly adjudicative, is not entirely legislative — that is, it is quasi-legislative>.

quasi-legislative power. See POWER.

quasi-partner. See PARTNER.

quasi-suspect classification. See SUSPECT CLASSIFICATION.

quasi-tort. See TORT.

quasi-trustee. See TRUSTEE.

qu. cl. fr. *abbr.* QUARE CLAUSUM FREGIT.

question. 1. A query directed to a witness. — Abbr. Q.

> ***categorical question.* 1.** LEADING QUESTION. **2.** (*often pl.*) One of a series of questions, on a particular subject, arranged in systematic or consecutive order.
>
> ***cross-question.*** A question asked of a witness during cross-examination.
>
> ***direct question.*** A question asked of a witness during direct examination.

2. An issue in controversy; a matter to be determined.

question-and-answer. 1. The portion of a deposition or trial transcript in which evidence is developed through a series of questions asked by the lawyer and answered by the witness. — Abbr. Q-and-A. **2.** The method for developing evidence during a deposition or at trial, requiring the witness to answer the examining lawyer's questions, without offering unsolicited information. **3.** The method of instruction used in many law-school classes, in which the professor asks questions of one or more students and then follows up each answer with another question. See SOCRATIC METHOD.

question of fact. 1. An issue that has not been predetermined and authoritatively answered by the law. **2.** An issue that does not involve what the law is on a given point. **3.** A disputed issue to be resolved by the jury in a jury trial or by the judge in a bench trial. See FACT-FINDER. **4.** An issue capable of being answered by way of demonstration, as opposed to a question of unverifiable opinion.

question of law. 1. An issue to be decided by the judge, concerning the application or interpretation of the law. **2.** A question that the law itself has authoritatively answered, so that the court may not answer it as a matter of discretion. **3.** An issue about what the law is on a particular point; an issue in which parties argue about, and the court must decide, what the true rule of law is. **4.** An issue that, although it may turn on a factual point, is reserved for the court and excluded from the jury; an issue that is exclusively within the province of the judge and not the jury.

quia timet (**kwɪ**-ə **tɪ**-mət *or* **kwee**-ə **tim**-et). [Latin "because he fears"] A legal doctrine that allows a person to seek equitable relief from future probable harm to a specific right or interest.

***quia-timet* injunction.** See INJUNCTION.

quick condemnation. See CONDEMNATION.

quid pro quo (**kwid** proh **kwoh**), *n.* [Latin "something for something"] A thing that is exchanged for another thing of more or less equal value; a substitute <the discount was given as a quid pro quo for the extra business>. Cf. CONSIDERATION.

quid pro quo sexual harassment. See SEXUAL HARASSMENT.

quiet enjoyment. See ENJOYMENT.

quit, *adj.* (Of a debt, obligation, or person) acquitted; free; discharged.

quit, *vb.* **1.** To cease (an act, etc.); to stop <he didn't quit stalking the victim until the police intervened>. **2.** To leave or surrender possession of (property) <the tenant received a notice to quit but had no intention of quitting the premises>.

qui tam action (kwɪ tam). [Latin *qui tam pro domino rege quam pro se ipso in hac parte sequitur* "who as well for the king as for himself sues in this matter"] An action brought under a statute that allows a private person to sue for a penalty, part of which the government or some specified public institution will receive. Often shortened to *qui tam* (Q.T.).

quitclaim, *n.* **1.** A formal release of one's claim or right. **2.** See *quitclaim deed* under DEED.

quitclaim, *vb.* **1.** To relinquish or release (a claim or right). **2.** To convey all of one's interest in (property), to whatever extent one has an interest; to execute a quitclaim deed.

quitclaim deed. See DEED.

quittance. 1. A release or discharge from a debt or obligation. **2.** The document serving as evidence of such a release. See ACQUITTANCE.

quoad hoc (**kwoh**-ad **hok**). [Latin] As to this; with respect to this; so far as this is concerned. • A prohibition *quoad hoc* is a prohibition of certain things among others, such as matters brought in an ecclesiastical court that should have been brought in a temporal court.

quod erat demonstrandum (kwod **er**-ət dem-ən-**stran**-dəm). See Q.E.D.

quod vide (kwod **vɪ**-dee *or* **vee**-day). See Q.V.

quorum, *n.* The minimum number of members (usu. a majority) who must be present for a body to transact business or take a vote. Pl. **quorums.**

quota. 1. A proportional share assigned to a person or group; an allotment <the university's admission standards included a quota for in-state residents>. **2.** A quantitative restriction; a minimum or maximum number <Faldo met his sales quota for the month>.

quotation. 1. A statement or passage that is reproduced, attributed, and cited. **2.** The amount stated as a stock's or commodity's current price.

3. A contractor's estimate for a given job. — Sometimes shortened to *quote*.

quotient verdict. See VERDICT.

quo warranto (kwoh wə-**ran**-toh *also* kwoh **wahr**-ən-toh). [Law Latin "by what authority"] **1.** A common-law writ used to inquire into the authority by which a public office is held or a franchise is claimed. **2.** An action by which the state seeks to revoke a corporation's charter.

q.v. *abbr.* [Latin *quod vide*] Which see — used in non-*Bluebook* citations for cross-referencing. Pl. **qq.v.**

R

race-notice statute. A recording law providing that the person who records first, without notice of prior unrecorded claims, has priority. Cf. RACE STATUTE; NOTICE STATUTE.

race statute. A recording act providing that the person who records first, regardless of notice, has priority. Cf. NOTICE STATUTE; RACE-NOTICE STATUTE.

race to the courthouse. 1. *Civil procedure.* The competition between disputing parties, both of whom know that litigation is inevitable, to prepare and file a lawsuit in a favorable or convenient forum before the other side files in one that is less favorable or less convenient. **2.** *Bankruptcy.* The competition among creditors to make claims on assets, usu. motivated by the advantages to be gained by those who act first in preference to other creditors.

racket, *n.* **1.** An organized criminal activity; esp., the extortion of money by threat or violence. **2.** A dishonest or fraudulent scheme or business.

racketeer, *n.* A person who engages in racketeering. — **racketeer,** *vb.*

Racketeer Influenced and Corrupt Organizations Act. A law designed to attack organized criminal activity and preserve marketplace integrity by investigating, controlling, and prosecuting persons who participate or conspire to participate in racketeering. • Enacted in 1970, the federal RICO statute applies only to activity involving interstate or foreign commerce. 18 USCA §§ 1961–1968. — Abbr. RICO.

racketeering, *n.* **1.** A system of organized crime traditionally involving the extortion of money from businesses by intimidation, violence, or other illegal methods. **2.** A pattern of illegal activity (such as bribery, extortion, fraud, and murder) carried out as part of an enterprise (such as a crime syndicate) that is owned or controlled by those engaged in the illegal activity. See 18 USCA §§ 1951–1960.

rack-rent, *n.* Rent equal to or nearly equal to the full annual value of the property; excessively or unreasonably high rent. — **rack-rent,** *vb.*

raid, *n.* **1.** A sudden attack or invasion by law-enforcement officers, usu. to make an arrest or to search for evidence of a crime. **2.** An attempt by a business or union to lure employees or members from a competitor. **3.** An attempt by a group of speculators to cause a sudden fall in stock prices by concerted selling.

railroad, *vb.* **1.** To transport by train. **2.** To send (a measure) hastily through a legislature so that there is little time for consideration and debate. **3.** To convict (a person) hastily, esp. by the use of false charges or insufficient evidence.

rainmaker, *n.* A lawyer who generates a large amount of business for a law firm, usu. through wide contacts within the business community. — **rainmaking,** *n.*

raise, *vb.* **1.** To increase in amount or value <the industry raised prices>. **2.** To gather or collect <the charity raised funds>. **3.** To bring up for discussion or consideration; to introduce or put forward <the party raised the issue in its pleading>. **4.** To create or establish <the person's silence raised an inference of consent>. **5.** To increase the stated amount of (a negotiable instrument) by fraudulent alteration <the indorser raised the check>.

raised check. See CHECK.

raising an instrument. The act of fraudulently altering a negotiable instrument, esp. a check, to increase the sum stated as being payable. See *raised check* under CHECK.

rake-off, *n.* A percentage or share taken, esp. from an illegal transaction; an illegal bribe, payoff, or skimming of profits. — **rake off,** *vb.*

Rambo lawyer. *Slang.* A lawyer, esp. a litigator, who uses aggressive, unethical, or illegal tactics in representing a client and who lacks courtesy and professionalism in dealing with other lawyers. — Often shortened to *Rambo*.

ransom, *n.* **1.** The release of a captured person or property in exchange for payment of a demanded price. **2.** Money or other consideration demanded or paid for the release of a captured person or property. See KIDNAPPING.

ransom, *vb.* **1.** To obtain the release of (a captive) by paying a demanded price. **2.** To release (a captive) upon receiving such a payment. **3.** To hold and demand payment for the release of (a captive).

rap, *n. Slang.* **1.** Legal responsibility for a criminal act <he took the rap for his accomplices>. **2.** A criminal charge <a murder rap>. **3.** A criminal conviction; esp., a prison sentence <a 20–year rap for counterfeiting>.

rape, *n.* **1.** At common law, unlawful sexual intercourse committed by a man with a woman not his wife through force and against her will. **2.** Unlawful sexual activity (esp. intercourse) with a person (usu. a female) without consent and usu. by force or threat of injury. — **rape,** *vb.* — **rapist, raper,** *n.* Cf. *sexual assault* under ASSAULT.

acquaintance rape. Rape committed by someone known to the victim, esp. by the victim's social companion.

date rape. Rape committed by a person who is escorting the victim on a social occasion. • Loosely, *date rape* is also sometimes used in reference to what is more accurately called *acquaintance rape* or *relationship rape*.

marital rape. A husband's sexual intercourse with his wife by force or without her consent.

relationship rape. Rape committed by someone with whom the victim has had a significant association, often (though not always) of a romantic nature. • This term encompasses all types of relationships, including those as family, friends, dates, cohabitants, and spouses, in which the victim has had more than brief or perfunctory interaction with another person. Thus it does not extend to those with whom the victim has had only brief encounters or a nodding acquaintance. Cf. *date rape*; *acquaintance rape*.

statutory rape. Unlawful sexual intercourse with a person under the age of consent (as defined by statute), regardless of whether it is against that person's will. • Generally, only an adult may be convicted of this crime. See *age of consent* under AGE.

rap sheet. *Slang.* A person's criminal record.

ratable (**ray**-tə-bəl), *adj.* **1.** Proportionate <ratable distribution>. **2.** Capable of being estimated, appraised, or apportioned <because hundreds of angry fans ran onto the field at the same time, blame for the goalpost's destruction is not ratable>. **3.** Taxable <the government assessed the widow's ratable estate>. See PRO RATA.

ratchet theory. *Constitutional law.* The principle that Congress — in exercising its enforcement power under the 14th Amendment — can increase, but cannot dilute, the scope of 14th Amendment guarantees as previously defined by the Supreme Court. • Thus, the enabling clause works in only one direction, like a ratchet.

rate, *n.* **1.** Proportional or relative value; the proportion by which quantity or value is adjusted <rate of inflation>. **2.** An amount paid or charged for a good or service <the rate for a business-class fare is $550>. **3.** INTEREST RATE <the rate on the loan increases by 2% after five years>. — **rate,** *vb.*

ratification, *n.* **1.** Confirmation and acceptance of a previous act, thereby making the act valid from the moment it was done. **2.** *Contracts.* A person's binding adoption of an act already completed but either not done in a way that originally produced a legal obligation or done by a third party having at the time no authority to act as the person's agent. — **ratify,** *vb.* Cf. CONFIRMATION.

ratiocination (rash-ee-os-ə-**nay**-shən), *n.* The process or an act of reasoning. — **ratiocinate** (rash-ee-**os**-ə-nayt), *vb.* — **ratiocinative** (rash-ee-**os**-ə-nay-tiv), *adj.*

ratio decidendi (**ray**-shee-oh des-ə-**den**-dɪ), *n.* [Latin "the reason for deciding"] **1.** The principle or rule of law on which a court's decision is founded <many poorly written judicial opinions do not contain a clearly ascertainable *ratio decidendi*>. **2.** The rule of law on which a later court thinks that a previous court founded its decision; a general rule without which a case must have been decided otherwise <this opinion recognizes the Supreme Court's *ratio decidendi* in the school desegregation cases>. Pl. ***rationes decidendi*** (**ray**-shee-oh-neez des-ə-**den**-dɪ). Cf. OBITER DICTUM; HOLDING.

rational-basis test. *Constitutional law.* A principle whereby a court will uphold a law as valid under the Equal Protection Clause or Due Process Clause if it bears a reasonable relationship to the attainment of some legitimate governmental objective. Cf. STRICT SCRUTINY; INTERMEDIATE SCRUTINY.

rational-choice theory. The theory that criminals engage in criminal activity when they believe that the potential benefits outweigh the risks of committing the crime. Cf. CONTROL THEORY; ROUTINE-ACTIVITIES THEORY; STRAIN THEORY.

re (ree *or* ray), *prep.* Regarding; in the matter of; IN RE. • The term is often used as a signal or introductory title announcing the subject of business correspondence.

readjustment, *n.* Voluntary reorganization of a financially troubled corporation by the shareholders themselves, without a trustee's or a receiver's intervention. — **readjust,** *vb.*

ready, willing, and able. (Of a prospective buyer) legally and financially capable of consummating a purchase.

reaffirmation, *n.* **1.** Approval of something previously decided or agreed to; renewal <the Supreme Court's reaffirmation of this principle is long overdue>. **2.** *Bankruptcy.* An agreement between the debtor and a creditor by which the debtor promises to repay a prepetition debt that would otherwise be discharged at the conclusion of the bankruptcy <the debtor negotiated a reaffirmation so that he could keep the collateral>. — **reaffirm,** *vb.*

real, *adj.* **1.** Of or relating to things (such as lands and buildings) that are fixed or immovable <real property> <a real action>. **2.** Actual; genuine; true <real authority>. **3.** (Of money, income, etc.) measured in terms of purchasing power rather than nominal value; adjusted for inflation <real wages>.

real action. See ACTION.

real defense. See DEFENSE (4).

real evidence. See EVIDENCE.

realignment (ree-ə-**lın**-mənt), *n.* The process by which a court, usu. in determining diversity jurisdiction, identifies and rearranges the parties as plaintiffs and defendants according to their ultimate interests. — **realign,** *vb.*

realization, *n.* **1.** Conversion of noncash assets into cash assets. **2.** *Tax.* An event or transaction, such as the sale or exchange of property, that substantially changes a taxpayer's economic position so that income tax may be imposed or a tax allowance granted. Cf. RECOGNITION (3). — **realize,** *vb.*

real law. The law of real property; real-estate law.

real party in interest. See PARTY (2).

real property. See PROPERTY.

real rate. See INTEREST RATE.

real things. Property that is fixed and immovable, such as lands and buildings; real property. See *real property* under PROPERTY. Cf. *chattel real* under CHATTEL.

real wrong. See WRONG.

reapportionment, *n.* Realignment of a legislative district's boundaries to reflect changes in population. • The U.S. Supreme Court has required federal reapportionment. See U.S. Const. art. I, § 2, cl. 3. — **reapportion,** *vb.* Cf. GERRYMANDERING.

reargument, *n.* The presentation of additional arguments to a court (usu. an appellate court) that has already heard initial arguments. — **reargue,** *vb.* Cf. REHEARING.

reasonable, *adj.* **1.** Fair, proper, or moderate under the circumstances <reasonable pay>. **2.** According to reason <your argument is reasonable but not convincing>. **3.** (Of a person) having the faculty of reason <a reasonable person would have looked both ways before crossing the street>. — **reasonableness,** *n.*

reasonable accommodation. 1. An action taken to adapt or adjust for a disabled person, done in a way that does not impose an undue hardship on the party taking the action. **2.** An action taken to adapt or adjust for an employee's religious need or practice, done in a way that does not impose an undue hardship on the employer.

reasonable care. See CARE.

reasonable diligence. See DILIGENCE.

reasonable doubt. The doubt that prevents one from being firmly convinced of a defendant's guilt, or the belief that there is a real possibility that a defendant is not guilty. • "Beyond a reasonable doubt" is the standard used by a jury to determine whether a criminal defendant is guilty. See Model Penal Code § 1.12. In deciding whether guilt has been proved beyond a reasonable doubt, the jury must begin with the presumption that the defendant is innocent. See BURDEN OF PERSUASION; PREPONDERANCE OF THE EVIDENCE.

reasonable force. See FORCE.

reasonable-inference rule. An evidentiary principle providing that a jury, in deciding a case, may properly consider any reasonable inference drawn from the evidence presented at trial. Cf. PYRAMIDING INFERENCES, RULE AGAINST.

reasonable medical probability. In proving the cause of an injury, a standard requiring a showing that the injury was more likely than not caused by a particular stimulus, based on the general consensus of recognized medical thought.

reasonable person. A hypothetical person used as a legal standard, esp. to determine whether someone acted with negligence. • The reasonable person acts sensibly, does things without serious delay, and takes proper but not excessive precautions. See *reasonable care* under CARE.

reasonable suspicion. A particularized and objective basis, supported by specific and articulable facts, for suspecting a person of criminal activity. See STOP AND FRISK. Cf. PROBABLE CAUSE.

reasonable time. 1. *Contracts.* The time needed to do what a contract requires to be done, based on subjective circumstances. **2.** *Commercial law.* The time during which the UCC permits a party to accept an offer, inspect goods, substitute conforming goods for rejected goods, and the like.

reasonable-use theory. *Property.* The principle that owners of riparian land may make reasonable use of their water if this use does not affect the water available to lower riparian owners.

reason to know. Information from which a person of ordinary intelligence — or of the superior intelligence that the person may have — would infer that the fact in question exists or that there is a substantial enough chance of its existence that, if the person is exercising reasonable care, the person's action would be based on the assumption of its possible existence.

rebut, *vb.* To refute, oppose, or counteract (something) by evidence, argument, or contrary proof <rebut the opponent's expert testimony>.

rebuttable presumption. See PRESUMPTION.

rebuttal, *n.* **1.** In-court contradiction of an adverse party's evidence. **2.** The time given to a party to present contradictory evidence or arguments. Cf. CASE-IN-CHIEF.

rebuttal evidence. See EVIDENCE.

rebuttal witness. See WITNESS.

rebutter. **1.** *Common-law pleading.* The defendant's answer to a plaintiff's surrejoinder; the pleading that followed the rejoinder and surrejoinder, and that might in turn be answered by the surrebutter. **2.** One who rebuts.

recall, *n.* **1.** Removal of a public official from office by popular vote. **2.** A manufacturer's request to consumers for the return of defective products for repair or replacement. **3.** Revocation of a judgment for factual or legal reasons. — **recall,** *vb.*

recant (ri-**kant**), *vb.* **1.** To withdraw or renounce (prior statements or testimony) formally or publicly <the prosecution hoped the eyewitness wouldn't recant her corroborating testimony on the stand>. **2.** To withdraw or renounce prior statements or testimony formally or publicly <under grueling cross-examination, the witness recanted>. — **recantation,** *n.*

recaption. **1.** At common law, lawful seizure of another's property for a second time to secure the performance of a duty; a second distress. See DISTRESS. **2.** Peaceful retaking, without legal process, of one's own property that has been wrongfully taken.

receipt, *n.* **1.** The act of receiving something <my receipt of the document was delayed by two days>. **2.** A written acknowledgment that something has been received <keep the receipt for the gift>. **3.** (*usu. pl.*) Something received; INCOME <post the daily receipts in the ledger>.

receipt, *vb.* **1.** To acknowledge in writing the receipt of (something, esp. money) <the bill must be receipted>. **2.** To give a receipt for (something, esp. money) <the bookkeeper receipted the payments>.

receiptor (ri-**see**-tər). A person who receives from a sheriff another's property seized in garnishment and agrees to return the property upon demand or execution.

receivable, *adj.* **1.** Capable of being admitted or accepted <receivable evidence>. **2.** Awaiting receipt of payment <accounts receivable>. **3.** Subject to a call for payment <a note receivable>.

receiver. A disinterested person appointed by a court, or by a corporation or other person, for the protection or collection of property that is the subject of diverse claims (for example, because it belongs to a bankrupt or is otherwise being litigated). Cf. LIQUIDATOR.

receivership. 1. The state or condition of being in the control of a receiver. **2.** The position or function of being a receiver appointed by a court or under a statute. **3.** A proceeding in which a court appoints a receiver.

receiving stolen property. The criminal offense of acquiring or controlling property known to have been stolen by another person. See FENCE.

reception. The adoption in whole or in part of the law of one jurisdiction by another jurisdiction.

recess (ree-ses), *n.* **1.** A brief break in judicial proceedings <the court took an hour recess for lunch>. Cf. CONTINUANCE (3). **2.** An interval between sittings of the same legislative body <Congress took a monthlong recess>. — **recess** (ri-**ses**), *vb.*

recession. A period characterized by a sharp slowdown in economic activity, declining employment, and a decrease in investment and consumer spending. Cf. DEPRESSION.

recidivism (ri-**sid**-ə-viz-əm), *n.* A tendency to relapse into a habit of criminal activity or behavior. — **recidivate** (ri-**sid**-ə-vayt), *vb.* — **recidivous,** *adj.* — **recidivist,** *adj.*

recidivist (ri-**sid**-ə-vist), *n.* One who has been convicted of multiple criminal offenses, usu. similar in nature; a repeat offender.

reciprocal (ri-**sip**-rə-kəl), *adj.* **1.** Directed by each toward the other or others; MUTUAL <reciprocal trusts>. **2.** BILATERAL <a reciprocal contract>. **3.** Corresponding; equivalent <reciprocal discovery>.

reciprocal dealing. A business arrangement in which a buyer having greater economic power than a seller agrees to buy something from the seller only if the seller buys something in return. Cf. TYING ARRANGEMENT.

reciprocity (res-ə-**pros**-i-tee). **1.** Mutual or bilateral action <the Arthurs stopped receiving social invitations from friends because of their lack of reciprocity>. **2.** The mutual concession of advantages or privileges for purposes of commercial or diplomatic relations <Texas and Louisiana grant reciprocity to each other's citizens in qualifying for in-state tuition rates>.

recital. 1. An account or description of some fact or thing <the recital of the events leading up to the accident>. **2.** A preliminary statement in a contract or deed explaining the background of the transaction or showing the existence of particular facts <the recitals in the settlement agreement should describe the underlying dispute>. — **recite,** *vb.*

reckless, *adj.* Characterized by the creation of a substantial and unjustifiable risk of harm to others and by a conscious (and sometimes deliberate) disregard for or indifference to that risk; heedless; rash. • Reckless conduct is much more than mere negligence: it is a gross deviation from what a reasonable person would do. — **recklessly,** *adv.* See RECKLESSNESS. Cf. WANTON; CARELESS.

reckless disregard. 1. Conscious indifference to the consequences (of an act). **2.** *Defamation.* Serious doubts about the truth or accuracy of a publication. • "Reckless disregard for the truth" is the standard in proving the defendant's actual malice toward the plaintiff in a libel action.

reckless driving. The criminal offense of operating a motor vehicle in a manner that shows conscious indifference to the safety of others.

reckless endangerment. The criminal offense of putting another person at substantial risk of death or serious injury. • This is a statutory, not a common-law, offense.

reckless homicide. See HOMICIDE.

reckless knowledge. See KNOWLEDGE (1).

recklessness, *n.* **1.** Conduct whereby the actor does not desire harmful consequence but nonetheless foresees the possibility and consciously takes the risk. • Recklessness involves a greater degree of fault than negligence but a lesser degree of fault than intentional wrongdoing. **2.** The state of mind in which a person does not care about the consequences of his or her actions. Cf. WANTONNESS.

reclamation (rek-lə-**may**-shən), *n.* **1.** The act or an instance of improving the value of economically useless land by physically changing the land, such as irrigating a desert. **2.** *Commercial law.* A seller's limited right to retrieve goods delivered to a buyer when the buyer is insolvent. UCC § 2–702(2). **3.** The act or an instance of obtaining valuable materials from waste materials. — **reclaim,** *vb.*

recognition, *n.* **1.** Confirmation that an act done by another person was authorized. See RATIFICATION. **2.** The formal admission that a person, entity, or thing has a particular status; esp., a nation's act in formally acknowledging the existence of another nation or national government. **3.** *Tax.* The act or an instance of accounting for a taxpayer's realized gain or loss for the purpose of income-tax reporting. Cf. NONRECOGNITION PROVISION; REALIZATION (2). **4.** An employer's acknowledgment that a union has the right to act as a bargaining agent for employees. — **recognize,** *vb.*

recognizance (ri-**kog**-nə-zənts). A bond or obligation, made in court, by which a person promises to perform some act or observe some condition, such as to appear when called, to pay a debt, or to keep the peace. • Most commonly, a recognizance takes the form of a bail bond that guarantees an unjailed criminal defendant's return for a court date <the defendant was released on his own recognizance>. See RELEASE ON RECOGNIZANCE.

personal recognizance. The release of a defendant in a criminal case in which the court takes the defendant's word that he or she will appear for a scheduled matter or when told to appear. • This type of release dispenses with the necessity of the person's posting money or having a surety sign a bond with the court. See O.R.

recognized gain. See GAIN (3).

recognizee (ri-kog-nə-**zee**). A person in whose favor a recognizance is made; one to whom someone is bound by a recognizance.

recognizor (ri-kog-nə-**zor**). A person who is obligated under a recognizance; one who is bound by a recognizance.

recollection, *n.* **1.** The action of recalling something to the mind, esp. through conscious effort. **2.** Something recalled to the mind. — **recollect,** *vb.* See PAST RECOLLECTION RECORDED; PRESENT RECOLLECTION REFRESHED.

recompense (**rek**-əm-pents), *n.* Repayment, compensation, or retribution for something, esp. an injury or loss. — **recompense,** *vb.*

reconciliation (rek-ən-sil-ee-**ay**-shən), *n.* **1.** Restoration of harmony between persons or things that had been in conflict <a reconciliation between the plaintiff and the defendant is unlikely even if the lawsuit settles before trial>. **2.** *Family law.* Voluntary resumption, after a separation, of full marital relations between spouses <the court dismissed the divorce petition after the parties' reconciliation>. **3.** *Accounting.* An adjustment of accounts so that they agree, esp. by allowing for outstanding items <reconciliation of the checking account and the bank statement>. — **reconcile** (**rek**-ən-sɪl), *vb.*

reconsideration. The action of discussing or taking something up again <legislative reconsideration of the measure>.

recontinuance. 1. Resumption or renewal. **2.** The recovery of an incorporeal hereditament that had been wrongfully deprived.

reconversion. The notional or imaginary process by which an earlier constructive conversion (a change of personal into real property or vice-versa) is annulled and the converted property is restored to its original character.

reconveyance, *n.* The restoration or return of something (esp. an estate or title) to a former owner or holder. — **reconvey,** *vb.*

record, *n.* **1.** A documentary account of past events, usu. designed to memorialize those events. **2.** Information that is inscribed on a tangible medium or that, having been stored in an electronic or other medium, is retrievable in perceivable form. UCC § 2A–102(a)(34). **3.** The official report of the proceedings in a case, including the filed papers, a verbatim transcript of the trial or hearing (if any), and tangible exhibits. See DOCKET (1).

defective record. **1.** A trial record that fails to conform to requirements of appellate rules. **2.** A flawed real-estate title resulting from a defect on the property's record in the registry of deeds.

public record. A record that a governmental unit is required by law to keep, such as land deeds kept at a county courthouse. • Public records are generally open to view by the public. Cf. *public document* under DOCUMENT.

silent record. Criminal procedure. A record that fails to disclose that a defendant voluntarily and knowingly entered a plea, waived a right to counsel, or took any other action affecting his or her rights.

recorder. 1. A municipal judge with the criminal jurisdiction of a magistrate or a police judge and sometimes also with limited civil jurisdiction. **2.** A municipal or county officer who keeps public records such as deeds, liens, and judgments.

court recorder. A court official who records court activities using electronic recording equipment, usu. for the purpose of preparing a verbatim transcript. Cf. COURT REPORTER (1).

recording act. A law that establishes the requirements for recording a deed or other property interest and the standards for determining priorities between persons claiming interests in the same property (usu. real property). • Recording acts — the three main types of which are the *notice statute*, the *race statute*, and the *race-notice statute* — are designed to protect bona fide purchasers from earlier unrecorded interests. See NOTICE STATUTE; RACE STATUTE; RACE-NOTICE STATUTE.

record notice. See NOTICE.

record on appeal. The record of a trial-court proceeding as presented to the appellate court for review. See RECORD (2).

record owner. See OWNER.

record title. See TITLE (2).

recoupment (ri-**koop**-mənt), *n.* **1.** The recovery or regaining of something, esp. expenses. **2.** The withholding, for equitable reasons, of all or part of something that is due. **3.** Reduction of a plaintiff's damages because of a demand by the defendant arising out of the same transaction. Cf. SETOFF. **4.** The right of a defendant to have the plaintiff's claim reduced or eliminated because of the plaintiff's breach of contract or duty in the same transaction. **5.** An affirmative defense alleging such a breach. — **recoup,** *vb.*

recourse (**ree**-kors *or* **ri-kors**). **1.** The act of seeking help or advice. **2.** Enforcement of, or a method for enforcing, a right. **3.** The right of a holder of a negotiable instrument to demand payment from the drawer or indorser if the instrument is dishonored. See WITH RECOURSE; WITHOUT RECOURSE. **4.** The right to repayment of a loan from the borrower's personal assets, not just from the collateral that secured the loan.

recourse loan. See LOAN.

recover, *vb.* **1.** To get back or regain in full or in equivalence <the landlord recovered higher operating costs by raising rent>. **2.** To obtain by a judgment or other legal process <the plaintiff recovered punitive damages in the lawsuit>. **3.** To obtain (a judgment) in one's favor <the plaintiff recovered a judgment against the defendant>. **4.** To obtain damages or other relief; to succeed in a lawsuit or other legal proceeding <the defendant argued that the plaintiff should not be allowed to recover for his own negligence>.

recoverable, *adj.* Capable of being recovered, esp. as a matter of law <court costs and attorney's fees are recoverable under the statute>. — **recoverability,** *n.*

recovery. 1. The regaining or restoration of something lost or taken away. **2.** The obtainment of a right to something (esp. damages) by a judgment or decree. **3.** An amount awarded in or collected from a judgment or decree.

double recovery. **1.** A judgment that erroneously awards damages twice for the same loss, based on two different theories of recovery. **2.** Recovery by a party of more than the maximum recoverable loss that the party has sustained.

recross-examination. A second cross-examination, after redirect examination. — Often shortened to *recross*. See CROSS-EXAMINATION.

rectification (rek-tə-fi-**kay**-shən), *n.* **1.** A court's equitable correction of a contractual term that is misstated; the judicial alteration of a written contract to make it conform to the true intention of the parties when, in its original form, it did not reflect this intention. • As an equitable remedy, the court alters the terms as written so as to express the true intention of the parties. **2.** A court's slight modification of words of a statute as a means of carrying out what the court is convinced must have been the legislative intent. • For example, courts engage in rectification when they read *and* as *or* or *shall* as *may*, as they frequently must do because of unfastidious drafting. — **rectify,** *vb.* See REFORMATION.

recusable (ri-**kyoo**-zə-bəl), *adj.* **1.** (Of an obligation) arising from a party's voluntary act and that can be avoided. Cf. IRRECUSABLE. **2.** (Of a judge) capable of being disqualified from sitting on a case. **3.** (Of a fact) providing a basis for disqualifying a judge from sitting on a case.

recusal (ri-**kyoo**-zəl), *n.* Removal of oneself as judge or policy-maker in a particular matter, esp. because of a conflict of interest. Cf. DISQUALIFICATION.

recusant (**rek**-yə-zənt *or* ri-**kyoo**-zənt), *adj.* Refusing to submit to an authority or comply with a command <a recusant witness>.

recuse (ri-**kyooz**), *vb.* **1.** To remove (oneself) as a judge in a particular case because of prejudice or conflict of interest <the judge recused himself from the trial>. **2.** To challenge or object to (a judge) as being disqualified from hearing a case because of prejudice or a conflict of interest <the defendant filed a motion to recuse the trial judge>.

redaction (ri-**dak**-shən), *n.* **1.** The careful editing of a document, esp. to remove confidential references or offensive material. **2.** A revised or edited document. — **redact,** *vb.* — **redactional,** *adj.*

reddendum (ri-**den**-dəm). A clause in a deed by which the grantor reserves some new thing (esp. rent) out of what had been previously granted.

redelivery. An act or instance of giving back or returning something; restitution.

redemise, *n.* An act or instance of conveying or transferring back (an estate) already demised. — **redemise,** *vb.* See DEMISE.

redemption, *n.* **1.** The act or an instance of reclaiming or regaining possession by paying a specific price. **2.** *Bankruptcy.* A debtor's right to repurchase property from a buyer who obtained the property at a forced sale initiated by a creditor. **3.** *Property.* The payment of a defaulted mortgage debt by a borrower who does not want to lose the property. — **redeem,** *vb.* — **redeemable,** *adj.* — **redemptive,** *adj.* — **redemptional,** *adj.*

statutory redemption. The statutory right of a defaulting mortgagor to recover property, within a specified period, after a foreclosure or tax sale, by paying the outstanding debt or charges. • The purpose is to protect against the sale of property at a price far less than its value.

tax redemption. A taxpayer's recovery of property taken for nonpayment of taxes, accomplished by paying the delinquent taxes and any interest, costs, and penalties.

red herring. An irrelevant legal or factual issue.

redirect examination. A second direct examination, after cross-examination, the scope ordinarily being limited to matters covered during cross-examination. — Often shortened to *redirect*. See DIRECT EXAMINATION.

redisseisin (ree-dis-**see**-zin), *n.* **1.** A disseisin by one who has already dispossessed the same person of the same estate. **2.** A writ to recover an estate that has been dispossessed by redisseisin. — **redisseise** (ree-dis-**seez**), *vb.* See DISSEISIN.

redlining, *n.* **1.** Credit discrimination (usu. unlawful discrimination) by a financial institution that refuses to make loans on properties in allegedly bad neighborhoods. **2.** The process of creating a new draft of a document showing suggested revisions explicitly alongside the text of an earlier version. — **redline,** *vb.*

redraft, *n.* A second negotiable instrument offered by the drawer after the first instrument has been dishonored. — **redraft,** *vb.*

redress (ri-**dres** *or* **ree**-dres), *n.* **1.** Relief; remedy <money damages, as opposed to equitable relief, is the only redress available>. **2.** A means of seeking relief or remedy <if the statute of limitations has run, the plaintiff is without redress>. — **redress** (ri-**dres**), *vb.* — **redressable,** *adj.*

reductio ad absurdum (ri-**dək**-shee-oh *or* ri-**dək**-tee-oh ad ab-**sər**-dəm). [Latin "reduction to the absurd"] In logic, disproof of an argument by showing that it leads to a ridiculous conclusion.

reenactment rule. In statutory construction, the principle that when re-enacting a law, the legislature implicitly adopts well-settled judicial or administrative interpretations of the law.

reentry, *n.* **1.** The act or an instance of retaking possession of land by someone who formerly held the land and who reserved the right to retake it when the new holder let it go. **2.** A landlord's resumption of possession of leased premises upon the tenant's default under the lease. — **reenter,** *vb.* See POWER OF TERMINATION.

reexamination, *n.* **1.** REDIRECT EXAMINATION <the attorney focused on the defendant's alibi during reexamination>. **2.** *Patents.* A procedure whereby a party can seek review of a patent on the basis of additional references to prior art not originally considered by the U.S. Patent Office <the alleged infringer, hoping to avoid liability, sought reexamination of the patent to narrow its scope>. — **reexamine,** *vb.*

reexecution. The equitable remedy by which a lost or destroyed deed or other instrument is restored. • Equity compels the party or parties to execute a new deed or instrument if a claimant properly proves a right under one that has been lost or destroyed.

referee. A type of master appointed by a court to assist with certain proceedings. • In some jurisdictions, referees take testimony before reporting to the court. See MASTER (2).

reference, *n.* **1.** The act of sending or directing to another for information, service, consideration, or decision; specif., the act of sending a case to a master or referee for information or decision.

general reference. A court's reference of a case to a referee, usu. with all parties' consent, to decide all issues of fact and law. • The referee's decision stands as the judgment of the court.

special reference. A court's reference of a case to a referee for decisions on specific questions of fact. • The special referee makes findings and reports them to the trial judge, who treats them as advisory only and not as binding decisions.

2. An order sending a case to a master or referee for information or decision. **3.** Mention or citation of one document or source in another document or source. — **refer,** *vb.*

reference statute. See STATUTE.

referendum. 1. The process of referring a state legislative act, a state constitutional amendment, or an important public issue to the people for final approval by popular vote. **2.** A vote taken by this method. Pl. **referendums, referenda.** Cf. INITIATIVE.

referral. The act or an instance of sending or directing to another for information, service, consideration, or decision <referral of the client to an employment-law specialist> <referral of the question to the board of directors>.

reformation (ref-ər-**may**-shən), *n.* An equitable remedy by which a court will modify a written agreement to reflect the actual intent of the parties, usu. to correct fraud or mutual mistake, such as an incomplete property description in a deed. • The actual intended agreement must usually be established by clear and convincing evidence. — **reform**, *vb.* See RECTIFICATION.

reformative punishment. See PUNISHMENT.

reformatory, *n.* A penal institution for young offenders, esp. minors.

refusal. 1. The denial or rejection of something offered or demanded. **2.** An opportunity to accept or reject something before it is offered to others; the right or privilege of having this opportunity. See RIGHT OF FIRST REFUSAL.

refute, *vb.* **1.** To prove (a statement) to be false. **2.** To prove (a person) to be wrong. Cf. REBUTTAL.

Reg. *abbr.* **1.** REGULATION. **2.** REGISTER.

reg, *n.* (*usu. pl.*) *Slang.* REGULATION (3) <review not only the tax code but also the accompanying regs>.

regard, *n.* Attention, care, or consideration.

regime (rə-**zheem** *or* ray-**zheem**). A system of rules, regulations, or government <the community-property regime>. — Also spelled *régime*.

register, *n.* **1.** A governmental officer who keeps official records <each county employs a register of deeds and wills>. See REGISTER OF THE TREASURY. Cf. REGISTRAR.

probate register. One who serves as the clerk of a probate court and, in some jurisdictions, as a quasi-judicial officer in probating estates.

register of deeds. A public official who records deeds, mortgages, and other instruments affecting real property.

2. A book in which all docket entries are kept for the various cases pending in a court. **3.** An official record or list, such as a corporation's list of the names and addresses of its shareholders. — Abbr. Reg.

register, *vb.* **1.** To enter in a public registry <register a new car>. **2.** To enroll formally <five voters registered yesterday>. **3.** To make a record of <counsel registered three objections>. **4.** (Of a lawyer, party, or witness) to check in with the clerk of court before a judicial proceeding <please register at the clerk's office before entering the courtroom>. **5.** To file (a new security issue) with the Securities and Exchange Commission or a similar state agency <the company hopes to register its securities before the end of the year>.

registered agent. See AGENT.

registered bond. See BOND (2).

registered corporation. See CORPORATION.

registered representative. See REPRESENTATIVE.

register of deeds. See REGISTER (1).

Register of the Treasury. An officer of the U.S. Treasury whose duty is to keep accounts of receipts and expenditures of public money, to record public debts, to preserve adjusted accounts with vouchers and certificates, to record warrants drawn on the Treasury, to sign and issue government securities, and to supervise the registry of vessels under federal law. 31 USCA § 161.

register of wills. A public official who records probated wills, issues letters testamentary and letters of administration, and serves generally as clerk of the probate court.

registrant. One who registers; esp., one who registers something for the purpose of securing a right or privilege granted by law upon official registration.

registrar. A person who keeps official records; esp., a school official who maintains academic and enrollment records. Cf. REGISTER (1).

regress, *n.* **1.** The act or an instance of going or coming back; return or reentry. **2.** The right or liberty of going back; reentry. — **regress** (ri-**gres**), *vb.* Cf. EGRESS; INGRESS.

regressive tax. See TAX.

regular session. See SESSION.

regular term. See TERM (5).

regulation, *n.* **1.** The act or process of controlling by rule or restriction <the federal regulation of the airline industry>. **2.** BYLAW (1) <the CEO referred to the corporate regulation>. **3.** A rule or order, having legal force, issued by an administrative agency or a local government <Treasury regulations explain and interpret the Internal Revenue Code>. — Often shortened to *reg*; *Reg.* — **regulate,** *vb.* — **regulatory,** *adj.* — **regulable,** *adj.*

rehabilitation, *n.* **1.** *Criminal law.* The process of seeking to improve a criminal's character and outlook so that he or she can function in society without committing other crimes <rehabilitation is a traditional theory of criminal punishment, along with deterrence and retribution>. Cf. DETERRENCE; RETRIBUTION (1). **2.** *Evidence.* The restoration of a witness's credibility after the witness has been impeached <the inconsistencies were explained away during the prosecution's rehabilitation of the witness>. **3.** *Bankruptcy.* The process of reorganizing a debtor's financial affairs — under Chapter 11, 12, or 13 of the Bankruptcy Code — so that the debtor may continue to exist as a financial entity, with creditors satisfying their claims from the debtor's future earnings <the corporation's rehabilitation was successful>. — **rehabilitate,** *vb.* — **rehabilitative,** *adj.*

rehearing. A second or subsequent hearing of a case or an appeal, usu. held to consider an error or omission in the first hearing. — Abbr. reh'g. Cf. REARGUMENT.

reification (ree-ə-fi-**kay**-shən), *n.* **1.** Mental conversion of an abstract concept into a material thing. **2.** *Civil procedure.* Identification of the disputed thing in a nonpersonal action and attribution of an in-state situs to it for jurisdictional purposes. **3.** *Commercial law.* Embodiment of a right to payment in a writing (such as a negotiable instrument) so that a transfer of the writing also transfers the right. — **reify** (**ree**-ə-fɪ *or* **ray**-), *vb.*

reissue. An abstractor's certificate attesting to the correctness of an abstract. • A reissue is an important precaution when the abstract comprises an original abstract brought down to a certain date and then several later continuations or extensions.

rejection. **1.** A refusal to accept a contractual offer. **2.** A refusal to accept tendered goods as contractual performance. • Under the UCC, a buyer's rejection of nonperforming goods must be made within a reasonable time after tender or delivery, and notice of the rejection must be given to the seller. — **reject,** *vb.* Cf. REPUDIATION; RESCISSION; REVOCATION.

rejoinder, *n. Common-law pleading.* The defendant's answer to the plaintiff's reply (or replication). — **rejoin,** *vb.*

relation back, *n.* **1.** The doctrine that an act done at a later time is considered to have occurred at an earlier time. • For example, in federal civil procedure, an amended pleading relates back, for purposes of the statute of limitations, to the time when the original pleading was filed. Fed. R. Civ. P. 15(c). **2.** A judicial application of that doctrine. — **relate back,** *vb.*

relationship rape. See RAPE.

relative, *n.* A person connected with another by blood or affinity; a person who is kin with another. — Also termed *relation*; *kinsman*.

blood relative. One who shares an ancestor with another.

collateral relative. A relative who is not in the direct line of inheritance, such as a cousin.

relative by affinity. Blood or adopted relatives of one's spouse. See AFFINITY.

relative-convenience doctrine. The principle that an injunction or other equitable relief may be denied if it would cause one party great inconvenience but the other party little or no inconvenience.

relative right. See RIGHT.

relator. **1.** The real party in interest in whose name a state or an attorney general brings a lawsuit. See EX REL. **2.** The applicant for a writ, esp. a writ of mandamus, prohibition, or quo warranto. **3.** A person who furnishes information on which a civil or criminal case is based; an informer.

release, *n.* **1.** Liberation from an obligation, duty, or demand; the act of giving up a right or claim to the person against whom it could have been enforced <the employee asked for a release from the noncompete agreement>. **2.** The relinquishment or concession of a right, title, or claim <Benson's effective release of the claim against Thompson's estate precluded his filing a lawsuit>. **3.** A written discharge, acquittance, or receipt <Jones signed the release before accepting the cash from Hawkins>. **4.** A written authorization or permission for publication <the newspaper obtained a release from the witness before printing his picture on the front page>. **5.** The act of conveying an estate or right to another, or of legally disposing of it <the release of the easement on February 14>. **6.** A deed or document effecting a conveyance <the legal description in the release was defective>. See *deed of release* under DEED. **7.** The action of freeing or the fact of being freed from restraint or confinement <he became a model citizen after his release from prison>. **8.** A document giving formal discharge from custody <after the sheriff signed the release, the prisoner was free to go>. — **release,** *vb.*

conditional release. **1.** A discharge from an obligation based on some condition, the failure of which defeats the release. **2.** An early discharge of a prison inmate, who is then subject to the rules and regulations of parole.

partial release. A release of a portion of a creditor's claims against property; esp., a mortgagee's release of specified parcels covered by a blanket mortgage.

study release. A program that allows a prisoner to be released for a few hours at a time to attend classes at a nearby college or technical institution. See FURLOUGH.

unconditional release. The final discharge of a prison inmate from custody.

release on recognizance. The pretrial release of an arrested person who promises, usu. in writing but without supplying a surety or posting bond, to appear for trial at a later date.

release to uses. Conveyance of property, by deed of release, by one party to another for the benefit of the grantor or a third party. See *deed of release* under DEED; USE (4).

releasor. One who releases property or a claim to another. — Also spelled *releaser*.

relegation, *n.* **1.** Banishment or exile, esp. a temporary one. **2.** Assignment or delegation. — **relegate,** *vb.*

relevant, *adj.* Logically connected and tending to prove or disprove a matter in issue; having appreciable probative value — that is, rationally tending to persuade people of the probability or possibility of some alleged fact. — **relevance, relevancy,** *n.* Cf. MATERIAL.

relevant evidence. See EVIDENCE.

reliance, *n.* Dependence or trust by a person, esp. when combined with action based on that dependence or trust. — **rely,** *vb.*

detrimental reliance. Reliance by one party on the acts or representations of another, causing a worsening of the first party's position. • Detrimental reliance may serve as a substitute for consideration and thus make a promise enforceable as a contract. See *promissory estoppel* under ESTOPPEL.

reliance damages. See DAMAGES.

reliance interest. See INTEREST (2).

relict (**rel**-ikt). A widow.

reliction (ri-**lik**-shən). **1.** A process by which a river or stream shifts its location, causing the recession of water from its bank. **2.** The alteration of a boundary line because of the gradual removal of land by a river or stream. See ACCRETION; DERELICTION.

relief. **1.** Aid or assistance given to those in need; esp., financial aid provided by the state. **2.** The redress or benefit, esp. equitable in nature (such as an injunction or specific performance), that a party asks of a court. Cf. REMEDY.

affirmative relief. The relief sought by a defendant by raising a counterclaim or cross-claim that could have been maintained independently of the plaintiff's action.

alternative relief. Judicial relief that is mutually exclusive with another form of judicial relief. • In pleading, a party may request alternative relief, as by asking for both specific performance and damages. Fed. R. Civ. P. 8(a). Cf. ELECTION OF REMEDIES.

coercive relief. Active judicial relief, either legal or equitable, that the government will enforce.

interim relief. Relief that is granted on a preliminary basis before an order finally disposing of a request for relief.

therapeutic relief. The relief, esp. in a settlement, that requires the defendant to take remedial measures as opposed to paying damages.

religion, freedom of. See FREEDOM OF RELIGION.

Religion Clause. In the Bill of Rights, the provision stating that "Congress shall make no law respecting an establishment of religion or prohibiting the free exercise thereof." U.S. Const. amend. I.

religious liberty. See LIBERTY.

relinquishment, *n.* The abandonment of a right or thing. — **relinquish,** *vb.*

relitigate, *vb.* To litigate (a case or matter) again or anew. — **relitigation,** *n.*

remainder. *Property.* **1.** In a decedent's estate, the property that is not otherwise specifically devised or bequeathed in a will. **2.** A future interest arising in a third person — that is, someone other than the creator of the estate or the creator's heirs — who is intended to take after the natural termination of the preceding estate. • For example, if a grant is "to A for life, and then to B," B's future interest is a remainder. Cf. EXECUTORY INTEREST; REVERSION; POSSIBILITY OF REVERTER.

accelerated remainder. A remainder that has passed to the remainderman, as when the gift to the preceding beneficiary fails.

alternative remainder. A remainder in which the disposition of property is to take effect only if another disposition does not take effect.

charitable remainder. A remainder, usu. from a life estate, that is given to a charity; for example, "to Jane for life, and then to the American Red Cross."

contingent remainder. A remainder that is either given to an unascertained person or made subject to a condition precedent. • An example is "to A for life, and then, if B has married before A dies, to B."

cross-remainder. A future interest that results when particular estates are given to two or more persons in different parcels of land, or in the same land in undivided shares, and the remainders of all the estates are made to vest in the survivor or survivors. • Two examples of devises giving rise to cross-remainders are (1) "to A and B for life, with the remainder to the survivor and her heirs," and (2) "Blackacre to A and Whiteacre to B, with the remainder of A's estate to B on A's failure of issue, and the remainder of B's estate to

A on B's failure of issue." If no tenants or issue survive, the remainder vests in a third party (sometimes known as the *ulterior remainderman*).

defeasible remainder. A vested remainder that will be destroyed if a condition subsequent occurs. • An example is "to A for life, and then to B, but if B ever sells liquor on the land, then to C."

indefeasible remainder. A vested remainder that is not subject to a condition subsequent.

remainder subject to open. A vested remainder that is given to one person but that may later have to be shared with others. • An example is "to A for life, and then equally to all of B's children."

vested remainder. A remainder that is given to an ascertained person and that is not subject to a condition precedent. • An example is "to A for life, and then to B."

remainder interest. The property that passes to a beneficiary after the expiration of an intervening income interest. • For example, if a grantor places real estate in trust with income to A for life and remainder to B upon A's death, then B has a remainder interest.

remainderman. A person who holds or is entitled to receive a remainder.

remand (ri-**mand** *also* **ree**-mand), *n.* **1.** The act or an instance of sending something (such as a case, claim, or person) back for further action. **2.** An order remanding a case, claim, or person.

remand (ri-**mand**), *vb.* **1.** To send (a case or claim) back to the court or tribunal from which it came for some further action <the appellate court reversed the trial court's opinion and remanded the case for new trial>. Cf. REMOVAL (2). **2.** To recommit (an accused person) to custody after a preliminary examination <the magistrate, after denying bail, remanded the defendant to custody>.

remanet (**rem**-ə-net). **1.** A case or proceeding whose hearing has been postponed. **2.** A remainder or remnant.

remediable, *adj.* Capable of being remedied, esp. by law. — **remediability,** *n.*

remedial, *adj.* **1.** Affording or providing a remedy; providing the means of obtaining redress. **2.** Intended to correct, remove, or lessen a wrong, fault, or defect. **3.** Of or relating to a means of enforcing an existing substantive right; procedural.

remedial law. 1. A law providing a means to enforce rights or redress injuries. **2.** A law passed to correct or modify an existing law; esp., a law that gives a party a new or different remedy when the existing remedy, if any, is inadequate.

remedial statute. See STATUTE.

remedies. The field of law dealing with the means of enforcing rights and redressing wrongs.

remedy, *n.* The means of enforcing a right or preventing or redressing a wrong; legal or equitable relief. — **remedy,** *vb.* Cf. RELIEF.

adequate remedy at law. A legal remedy (such as an award of damages) that provides sufficient relief to the petitioning party, thus preventing the party from obtaining equitable relief.

administrative remedy. A nonjudicial remedy provided by an administrative agency. See EXHAUSTION OF REMEDIES.

concurrent remedy. One of two or more legal actions available to redress a wrong.

cumulative remedy. A remedy available to a party in addition to another remedy that still remains in force.

equitable remedy. A nonmonetary remedy, such as an injunction or specific performance, obtained when monetary damages cannot adequately redress the injury. See IRREPARABLE-INJURY RULE.

extraordinary remedy. A remedy — such as a writ of mandamus or habeas corpus — not available to a party unless necessary to preserve a right that cannot be protected by a standard legal or equitable remedy.

judicial remedy. A remedy granted by a court; esp., a tort remedy that is either ordinary (as in an action for damages) or extraordinary (as in an equitable suit for an injunction).

legal remedy. A remedy available in a court of law, as distinguished from a remedy available only in equity.

provisional remedy. **1.** A restraining order or injunctive relief pending the disposition of an action; a temporary remedy, such as attachment, incidental to the primary action and available to a party while the action is pending. **2.** An equitable proceeding before judgment to provide for the postjudgment safety and preservation of property.

remedy over. A remedy that arises from a right of indemnification or subrogation. • For example, if a city is liable for injuries caused by a defect in a street, the city has a "remedy over" against the person whose act or negligence caused the defect.

self-help remedy. A remedy not obtained from a court, such as repossession.

specific remedy. A remedy for breach of contract whereby the injured party is awarded the very performance that was contractually promised, as when the court orders a defaulting seller of goods to deliver the specified goods to the buyer (as opposed to paying damages).

speedy remedy. A remedy (such as a restraining order) that, under the circumstances, can be pursued expeditiously before the aggrieved party has incurred substantial detriment.

substitutional remedy. A remedy for breach of contract intended to give the promisee something as a replacement for the promised performance, as when the court orders a defaulting seller of goods to pay the buyer damages (as opposed to delivering the goods).

remedy, mutuality of. See MUTUALITY OF REMEDY.

remise (ri-**mɪz**), *vb.* To give up, surrender, or release (a right, interest, etc.) <the quitclaim deed provides that the grantor remises any rights in the property>.

remission. 1. A cancellation or extinguishment of all or part of a financial obligation; a release of a debt or claim. **2.** A pardon granted for an offense. **3.** Relief from a forfeiture or penalty.

remit, *vb.* **1.** To pardon or forgive <the wife could not remit her husband's infidelity>. **2.** To abate or slacken; to mitigate <the receipt of money damages remitted the embarrassment of being fired>. **3.** To refer (a matter for decision) to some authority; esp., to send back (a case) to a lower court <the appellate court remitted the case to the trial court for further factual determinations>. See REMAND. **4.** To send or put back to a previous condition or position <a landlord's breach of a lease does not justify the tenant's refusal to pay rent; instead, the tenant is remitted to the right to recover damages>. **5.** To transmit (as money) <upon receiving the demand letter, she promptly remitted the amount due>. — **remissible** (for senses 1–4), *adj.* — **remittable** (for sense 5), *adj.*

remittance. 1. A sum of money sent to another as payment for goods or services. **2.** An instrument (such as a check) used for sending money. **3.** The action or process of sending money to another person or place.

remittee. One to whom payment is sent.

remitter. 1. The principle by which a person having two titles to an estate, and entering on it by the later or more defective title, is deemed to hold the estate by the earlier or more valid title. **2.** The act of sending back a case to a lower court. **3.** One who sends payment to someone else.

remittitur (ri-**mit**-i-tər). **1.** The process by which a court reduces or proposes to reduce the damages awarded in a jury verdict. **2.** A court's order reducing an award of damages. Cf. ADDITUR.

remittitur of record. The action of sending the transcript of a case back from an appellate court to a trial court; the notice for doing so.

remonstrance (ri-**mon**-strənts), *n.* **1.** A presentation of reasons for opposition or grievance. **2.** A formal document stating reasons for opposition or grievance. **3.** A formal protest against governmental policy, actions, or officials. — **remonstrate** (ri-**mon**-strayt), *vb.*

remote, *adj.* **1.** Far removed or separated in time, space, or relation. **2.** Slight. **3.** *Property.* Beyond the 21 years after some life in being by which a devise must vest. See RULE AGAINST PERPETUITIES.

remote cause. See CAUSE (1).

remote possibility. See POSSIBILITY.

removal, *n.* **1.** The transfer or moving of a person or thing from one location, position, or residence to another. **2.** The transfer of an action from state to federal court. — **remove,** *vb.* Cf. REMAND (1).

civil-rights removal. Removal of a case from state to federal court for any of these reasons: (1) because a person has been denied or cannot enforce a civil right in the state court, (2) because a person is being sued for performing an act under color of authority derived from a law providing for equal rights, or (3) because a person is being sued for refusing to perform an act that would be inconsistent with equal rights.

remuneration (ri-myoo-nə-**ray**-shən), *n.* **1.** Payment; compensation. **2.** The act of paying or compensating. — **remunerate,** *vb.* — **remunerative,** *adj.*

rencounter (ren-**kown**-tər). A hostile meeting or contest; a battle or combat.

render, *vb.* **1.** To transmit or deliver <render payment>. **2.** (Of a judge) to deliver formally <render a judgment>. **3.** (Of a jury) to agree on and report formally <render a verdict>. **4.** To pay as due <render an account>.

rendition, *n.* **1.** The action of making, delivering, or giving out, such as a legal decision. **2.** The return of a fugitive from one state to the state where the fugitive is accused or convicted of a crime. Cf. EXTRADITION.

rendition of judgment. The judge's oral or written ruling containing the judgment entered. Cf. ENTRY OF JUDGMENT.

rendition warrant. See WARRANT.

renege (ri-**nig** *or* ri-**neg**), *vb.* To fail to keep a promise or commitment; to back out of a deal.

renegotiation, *n.* **1.** The act or process of negotiating again or on different terms; a second or further negotiation. **2.** The reexamination and adjustment of a government contract to eliminate or recover excess profits by the contractor. — **renegotiate,** *vb.*

renewal, *n.* **1.** The act of restoring or reestablishing. **2.** The re-creation of a legal relationship or the replacement of an old contract with a new contract, as opposed to the mere extension of a previous relationship or contract. — **renew,** *vb.* Cf. EXTENSION (1); REVIVAL (1).

renounce, *vb.* **1.** To give up or abandon formally (a right or interest); to disclaim <renounce an inheritance>. **2.** To refuse to follow or obey; to decline to recognize or observe <renounce one's allegiance>.

rent, *n.* Consideration paid, usu. periodically, for the use or occupancy of property (esp. real property).

rentage. Rent or rental.

rental, *n.* **1.** The amount received as rent. **2.** The income received from rent. **3.** A record of payments received from rent. — **rental,** *adj.*

rent control. A restriction imposed, usu. by municipal legislation, on the maximum rent that a landlord may charge for rental property, and often on a landlord's power of eviction.

rents, issues, and profits. The total income or profit arising from the ownership or possession of property.

rent strike. A refusal by a group of tenants to pay rent until grievances with the landlord are heard or settled.

renunciation (ri-nən-see-**ay**-shən), *n.* **1.** The express or tacit abandonment of a right without transferring it to another. **2.** *Criminal law.* Complete and voluntary abandonment of criminal purpose — sometimes coupled with an attempt to thwart the activity's success — before a crime is committed. • Renunciation can be an affirmative defense to attempt, conspiracy, and the like. Model Penal Code § 5.01(4). **3.** *Wills & estates.* The act of waiving a right under a will and claiming instead a statutory share. See RIGHT OF ELECTION. — **renounce,** *vb.* — **renunciative, renunciatory,** *adj.*

reparable injury. See INJURY.

reparation (rep-ə-**ray**-shən). **1.** The act of making amends for a wrong. **2.** (*usu. pl.*) Compensation for an injury or wrong, esp. for wartime damages or breach of an international obligation.

reparative injunction. See INJUNCTION.

reparole. A second release from prison on parole, served under the same sentence for which the parolee served the first term of parole.

repeal, *n.* Abrogation of an existing law by legislative act. — **repeal,** *vb.*

express repeal. Repeal effected by specific declaration in a new statute.

implied repeal. Repeal effected by irreconcilable conflict between an old law and a new law.

repealing clause. A statutory provision that repeals an earlier statute.

repeat offender. See OFFENDER.

replacement cost. See COST.

replacement insurance. See INSURANCE.

replead, *vb.* **1.** To plead again or anew; to file a new pleading, esp. to correct a defect in an earlier pleading. **2.** To make a repleader.

repleader (ree-**plee**-dər). *Common-law pleading.* A court order or judgment — issued on the motion of a party who suffered an adverse verdict — requiring the parties to file new pleadings because of some defect in the original pleadings.

repleviable (ri-**plev**-ee-ə-bəl), *adj.* Capable of being replevied; recoverable by replevin. — Also spelled *replevisable* (ri-**plev**-ə-sə-bəl).

replevin (ri-**plev**-in), *n.* **1.** An action for the repossession of personal property wrongfully taken or detained by the defendant, whereby the plaintiff gives security for and holds the property until the court decides who owns it. **2.** A writ obtained from a court authorizing the retaking of personal property wrongfully taken or detained. Cf. DETINUE; TROVER.

personal replevin. At common law, an action to replevy a person out of prison or out of another's custody. • Personal replevin has been largely superseded by the writ of habeas corpus as a means of investigating the legality of an imprisonment. See HABEAS CORPUS.

replevin in cepit (in **see**-pit). An action for the repossession of property that is both wrongfully taken and wrongfully detained.

replevin in detinet (in **det**-i-net). An action for the repossession of property that is rightfully taken but wrongfully detained.

replevy, *vb.* **1.** To recover possession of (goods) by a writ of replevin. **2.** To recover (goods) by replevin.

repliant (ri-**plɪ**-ənt). A party who makes a replication (i.e., a common-law reply). — Also spelled *replicant.*

replication (rep-lə-**kay**-shən). A plaintiff's or complainant's reply to a defendant's plea or answer; REPLY (2).

reply, *n.* **1.** *Civil procedure.* In federal practice, the plaintiff's response to the defendant's counterclaim (or, by court order, to the defendant's or a third party's answer). Fed. R. Civ. P. 7(a). **2.** *Common-law pleading.* The plaintiff's response to the defendant's plea or answer. • The reply is the plaintiff's second pleading, and it is followed by the defendant's rejoinder. — **reply,** *vb.*

reply brief. See BRIEF.

report, *n.* **1.** A formal oral or written presentation of facts <according to the treasurer's report, there is $300 in the bank>. **2.** A written account of a court proceeding and judicial decision <the law clerk sent the court's report to counsel for both sides>. **3.** (*usu. pl.*) A published volume of judicial decisions by a particular court or group of courts <U.S. Reports>. Cf. ADVANCE SHEETS. **4.** (*usu. pl.*) A collection of administrative decisions by one or more administrative agencies. — **report,** *vb.*

reporter. 1. A person responsible for making and publishing a report; esp., a lawyer-consultant who prepares drafts of official or semi-official writings such as court rules or Restatements. **2.** REPORTER OF DECISIONS. **3.** REPORT (3). — Abbr. rptr.

reporter of decisions. The person responsible for publishing a court's opinions. • The reporter of decisions often has duties that include verifying citations, correcting spelling and punctuation, and suggesting minor editorial improvements before judicial opinions are released or published. — Often shortened to *reporter.*

repose (ri-**pohz**), *n.* **1.** Cessation of activity; temporary rest. **2.** A statutory period after which an action cannot be brought in court, even if it expires before the plaintiff suffers any injury. See STATUTE OF REPOSE.

repository (ri-**poz**-ə-tor-ee). A place where something is deposited or stored; a warehouse or storehouse.

repossession, *n.* The act or an instance of retaking property; esp., a seller's retaking of goods sold on credit when the buyer has failed to pay for them. — **repossess,** *vb.* Cf. FORECLOSURE.

representation, *n.* **1.** A presentation of fact — either by words or by conduct — made to induce someone to act, esp. to enter into a contract <the buyer relied on the seller's representation that the roof did not leak>. Cf. MISREPRESENTATION.

> ***affirmative representation.*** A representation asserting the existence of certain facts pertaining to a given subject matter.
>
> ***material representation.*** A representation that relates directly to the matter in issue or that actually causes an event to occur (such as a party's relying on the representation in entering into a contract).

promissory representation. A representation about what one will do in the future; esp., a representation made by an insured about what will happen during the time of coverage, stated as a matter of expectation and amounting to an enforceable promise.

2. The act or an instance of standing for or acting on behalf of another, esp. by a lawyer on behalf of a client <Clarence Darrow's representation of Mr. Scopes>. **3.** The fact of a litigant's having such a close alignment of interests with another person that the other is considered as having been present in the litigation <the named plaintiff provided adequate representation for the absent class members>. See ADEQUATE REPRESENTATION. **4.** The assumption by an heir of the rights and obligations of his or her predecessor <each child takes a share by representation>. See PER STIRPES. — **represent,** *vb.*

representative, *n.* **1.** One who stands for or acts on behalf of another <the owner was the football team's representative at the labor negotiations>. See AGENT.

accredited representative. A person with designated authority to act on behalf of another person, group, or organization, usu. by being granted that authority by law or by the rules of the group or organization.

class representative. A person who sues on behalf of a group of plaintiffs in a class action. See CLASS ACTION.

lawful representative. **1.** A legal heir. **2.** An executor or administrator. **3.** Any other legal representative.

legal-personal representative. **1.** When used by a testator referring to personal property, an executor or administrator. **2.** When used by a testator referring to real property, one to whom the real estate passes immediately upon the testator's death. **3.** When used concerning the death of a seaman, the public administrator, executor, or appointed administrator in the seaman's state of residence.

personal representative. A person who manages the legal affairs of another because of incapacity or death, such as the executor of an estate.

registered representative. A person approved by the SEC and stock exchanges to sell securities to the public.

2. A member of a legislature, esp. of the lower house <a senator and a representative attended the rally>.

representative action. 1. CLASS ACTION. **2.** DERIVATIVE ACTION (1).

representative capacity. The position of one standing or acting for another, esp. through delegated authority <an agent acting in a representative capacity for the principal>.

reprieve (ri-**preev**), *n.* Temporary postponement of the carrying out of a criminal sentence, esp. a death sentence. — **reprieve,** *vb.* Cf. COMMUTATION (2); PARDON.

reprimand, *n.* In professional responsibility, a form of disciplinary action — imposed after trial or formal charges — that declares the lawyer's conduct improper but does not limit his or her right to practice law. — **reprimand,** *vb.*

private reprimand. A reprimand that is not published but instead communicated only to the lawyer, or that is published without identifying the lawyer by name.

public reprimand. A reprimand that is published, usu. in a bar journal or legal newspaper.

republication, *n.* **1.** The act or an instance of publishing again or anew. **2.** *Wills & estates.* Reestablishment of the validity of a previously revoked will by repeating the formalities of execution or by using a codicil. — **republish,** *vb.* Cf. REVIVAL (2).

repudiate, *vb.* To reject or renounce (a duty or obligation); esp., to indicate an intention not to perform (a contract).

repudiation (ri-pyoo-dee-**ay**-shən), *n.* A contracting party's words or actions that indicate an intention not to perform the contract in the future; a threatened breach of contract. — **repudiatory** (ri-**pyoo**-dee-ə-tor-ee), *adj.* — **repudiable** (ri-**pyoo**-dee-ə-bəl), *adj.* Cf. REJECTION; RESCISSION; REVOCATION.

anticipatory repudiation. Repudiation of a contractual duty before the time for performance, giving the injured party an immediate right to damages for total breach, as well as discharging the injured party's remaining duties of performance. See *anticipatory breach* under BREACH OF CONTRACT.

total repudiation. An unconditional refusal by a party to perform the acts required by a contract.

repugnancy (ri-**pəg**-nən-see). An inconsistency or contradiction between two or more parts of a legal instrument (such as a contract or statute).

repugnant (ri-**pəg**-nənt), *adj.* Inconsistent or irreconcilable with; contrary or contradictory to <the court's interpretation was repugnant to the express wording of the statute>.

repugnant verdict. See VERDICT.

reputation, *n.* The esteem in which a person is held by others. • Evidence of reputation may be introduced as proof of character whenever character evidence is admissible. Fed. R. Evid. 405. — **reputational,** *adj.*

reputation evidence. See EVIDENCE.

request for admission. *Civil procedure.* In pretrial discovery, a party's written factual statement served on another party who must admit, deny, or object to the substance of the statement. • Ordinarily, many requests for admission appear in one document. The admitted statements — along with any statements not denied or objected to — will be treated by the court as established, and therefore do not have to be proved at trial. Fed. R. Civ. P. 36.

request for instructions. *Procedure.* During trial, a party's written request that the court instruct the jury on the law as set forth in the request. See Fed. R. Civ. P. 51.

request for production. *Procedure.* In pretrial discovery, a party's written request that another party provide specified documents or other tangible things for inspection and copying. Fed. R. Civ. P. 34.

required-records doctrine. The principle that the privilege against self-incrimination does not apply when one is being compelled to produce business records that are kept in accordance with government regulations and that involve public aspects.

requirements contract. See CONTRACT.

res (rays *or* reez *or* rez), *n.* [Latin "thing"] **1.** An object, interest, or status, as opposed to a person <jurisdiction of the res — the real property in Colorado>. **2.** The subject matter of a trust; CORPUS (2) <the stock certificate is the res of the trust>. Pl. **res.**

resale, *n.* **1.** The act of selling goods or property — previously sold to a buyer who breached the sales contract — to someone else. UCC § 2–706. **2.** A retailer's selling of goods, previously purchased from a manufacturer or wholesaler, to consumers. — **resell,** *vb.*

rescind (ri-**sind**), *vb.* **1.** To abrogate or cancel (a contract) unilaterally or by agreement. **2.** To make void; to repeal or annul. — **rescindable,** *adj.*

rescission (ri-**sizh**-ən), *n.* **1.** A party's unilateral unmaking of a contract for a legally sufficient reason, such as the other party's material breach. **2.** An agreement by contracting parties to discharge all remaining duties of performance and terminate the contract. — **rescissory** (ri-**sis**-ə-ree *or* ri-**siz-**), *adj.* Cf. REJECTION; REPUDIATION; REVOCATION.

equitable rescission. Rescission that is decreed by a court of equity.

legal rescission. Rescission that is effected by the agreement of the parties.

rescript (**ree**-skript), *n.* **1.** A judge's written order to a court clerk explaining how to dispose of a case. **2.** An appellate court's written decision, usu. unsigned, that is sent down to the trial court. **3.** A duplicate or counterpart; a rewriting.

rescue, *n.* **1.** The act or an instance of saving or freeing someone from danger or captivity. **2.** The forcible and unlawful freeing of a person from arrest or imprisonment. **3.** The forcible retaking by the owner of goods that have been lawfully distrained. Cf. REPOSSESSION. — **rescue,** *vb.*

rescue doctrine. *Torts.* The principle that a tortfeasor who negligently endangered a person is liable for injuries to someone who reasonably attempted to rescue the person in danger. Cf. EMERGENCY DOCTRINE; GOOD SAMARITAN DOCTRINE.

resentencing, *n.* The act or an instance of imposing a new or revised criminal sentence. — **resentence,** *vb.*

reservation. 1. The creation of a new right or interest (such as an easement), by and for the grantor, in real property being granted to another. Cf. EXCEPTION (3).

implied reservation. An implied easement that reserves in a landowner an easement across a portion of sold land, such as a right-of-way over land lying between the seller's home and the only exit. • An implied reservation arises only if the seller could have expressly reserved an easement, but for some reason failed to do so. See *implied easement* under EASEMENT.

2. The establishment of a limiting condition or qualification; esp., a nation's formal declaration, upon signing or ratifying a treaty, that its willingness to become a party to the treaty is conditioned on certain additional terms that will limit the effect of the treaty in some way. **3.** A tract of public land set aside for a special purpose; esp., a tract of land set aside for use by an American Indian tribe.

reserved point of law. See POINT OF LAW.

reserved power. See POWER.

resettlement, *n.* **1.** The settlement of one or more persons in a new or former place. **2.** The reopening of an order or decree for the purpose of correcting a mistake or adding an omission.

res gestae (rays **jes**-tee *also* **jes**-tɪ), *n. pl.* [Latin "things done"] The events at issue, or other events contemporaneous with them. • In evidence law, words and statements about the res gestae are usu. admissible under a hearsay exception (such as present sense impression or excited utterance). Where the Federal Rules of Evidence or state rules fashioned after them are in effect, the use of *res gestae* is now out of place. See Fed. R. Evid. 803(1), (2).

res gestae witness. See WITNESS.

residence. 1. The act or fact of living in a given place for some time <a year's residence in New Jersey>. **2.** The place where one actually lives, as distinguished from a domicile <she made her residence in Oregon>. • *Residence* usu. just means bodily presence as an inhabitant in a given place; *domicile* usu. requires bodily presence plus an intention to make the place one's home. A person thus may have more than one residence at a time but only one domicile. Sometimes, though, the two terms are used synonymously. Cf. DOMICILE. **3.** The place where a corporation or other enterprise does business or is registered to do business <Pantheon, Inc.'s principal residence is in Delaware>. **4.** A house or other fixed abode; a dwelling <a three-story residence>.

residency. 1. A place of residence, esp. an official one <the diplomat's residency>. **2.** The fact or condition of living in a given place <one year's residency to be eligible for in-state tuition>.

resident, *n.* **1.** A person who lives in a particular place. **2.** A person who has a home in a particular place. • In sense 2, a resident is not necessarily either a citizen or a domiciliary. Cf. CITIZEN; DOMICILIARY.

resident alien. See ALIEN.

residual, *adj.* Of, relating to, or constituting a residue; remaining; leftover <a residual claim> <a residual functional disability>.

residuary (ri-**zij**-oo-er-ee), *adj.* Of, relating to, or constituting a residue; residual <a residuary gift>.

residuary bequest. See BEQUEST.

residuary clause. *Wills & estates.* A testamentary clause that disposes of any estate property remaining after the satisfaction of specific bequests and devises.

residuary devise. See DEVISE.

residuary estate. See ESTATE (3).

residuary legacy. See LEGACY.

residuary legatee. See LEGATEE.

residue. 1. Something that is left over after a part has been removed or disposed of; a remainder. **2.** See *residuary estate* under ESTATE.

residuum (ri-**zij**-oo-əm). **1.** That which remains; a residue. **2.** See *residuary estate* under ESTATE. Pl. **residua** (ri-**zij**-oo-ə).

resignation, *n.* **1.** The act or an instance of surrendering or relinquishing an office, right, or claim. **2.** A formal notification of relinquishing an office or position. — **resign,** *vb.*

res integra (rays **in**-tə-grə *also* in-**teg**-rə). [Latin "an entire thing"] See RES NOVA.

res inter alios acta (rays **in**-tər **ay**-lee-ohs **ak**-tə). [Latin "a thing done between others"] **1.** *Contracts.* The common-law doctrine holding that a contract cannot unfavorably affect the rights of a person who is not a party to the contract. **2.** *Evidence.* The rule prohibiting the admission of collateral facts into evidence.

res ipsa loquitur (rays **ip**-sə **loh**-kwə-tər). [Latin "the thing speaks for itself"] *Torts.* The doctrine providing that, in some circumstances, the mere fact of an accident's occurrence raises an inference of negligence so as to establish a prima facie case.

res ipsa loquitur test (rays **ip**-sə **loh**-kwə-tər). A method for determining whether a defendant has gone beyond preparation and has actually committed an attempt, based on whether the defendant's act itself would have indicated to an observer what the defendant intended to do. See ATTEMPT.

resisting arrest. The crime of obstructing or opposing a police officer who is making an arrest.

resisting unlawful arrest. The act of opposing a police officer who is making an unlawful arrest. See Model Penal Code § 3.04(2)(a)(i).

res judicata (rays joo-di-**kay**-tə *or* -**kah**-tə). [Latin "a thing adjudicated"] **1.** An issue that has been definitively settled by judicial decision. **2.** An affirmative defense barring the same parties from litigating a second lawsuit on the same claim, or any other claim arising from the same transaction or series of transactions and that could have been — but was not — raised in the first suit. • The three essential elements are (1) an earlier decision on the issue, (2) a final judgment on the merits, and (3) the involvement of the same parties, or parties in privity with the original parties. Restatement (Second) of Judgments §§ 17, 24 (1982). Cf. COLLATERAL ESTOPPEL.

res nova (rays **noh**-və). [Latin "new thing"] **1.** An undecided question of law. **2.** A case of first impression. See *case of first impression* under CASE.

resolution. 1. A formal expression of an opinion, intention, or decision by an official body or assembly (esp. a legislature).

concurrent resolution. A resolution passed by one house and agreed to by the other. • It expresses the legislature's opinion on a subject but does not have the force of law.

joint resolution. A legislative resolution passed by both houses. • It has the force of law and is subject to executive veto.

simple resolution. A resolution passed by one house only. • It expresses the opinion or affects the internal affairs of the passing house, but it does not have the force of law.

2. Formal action by a corporate board of directors or other corporate body authorizing a particular act, transaction, or appointment. **3.** A document containing such an expression or authorization.

resolutory (ri-**zahl**-yə-tor-ee), *adj.* Operating or serving to annul, dissolve, or terminate <a resolutory clause>.

respite (**res**-pit), *n.* **1.** A period of temporary delay; an extension of time. **2.** A temporary suspension of a death sentence; a reprieve. **3.** A delay granted to a jury or court for further consideration of a verdict or appeal. — **respite,** *vb.*

respondeat ouster (ri-**spon**-dee-at **ow**-stər). [Latin "let him make further answer"] A judgment or order that a party who made a dilatory plea that has been denied must now plead on the merits.

respondeat superior (ri-**spon**-dee-at soo-**peer**-ee-ər *or* sə-peer-ee-**or**). [Law Latin "let the superior make answer"] *Torts.* The doctrine holding an employer or principal liable for the employee's or agent's wrongful acts committed within the scope of the employment or agency. See SCOPE OF EMPLOYMENT.

respondent. 1. The party against whom an appeal is taken; APPELLEE. **2.** The party against whom a motion or petition is filed. Cf. PETITIONER. **3.** At common law, the defendant in an equity proceeding.

responsibility, *n.* **1.** LIABILITY (1). **2.** *Criminal law.* A person's mental fitness to answer in court for his or her actions. See COMPETENCY. **3.** *Criminal law.* Guilt. — **responsible,** *adj.*

responsive, *adj.* Giving or constituting a response; answering <the witness's testimony is not responsive to the question>.

responsive pleading. See PLEADING (1).

rest, *vb.* (Of a litigant) to voluntarily conclude presenting evidence in a trial <after the police officer's testimony, the prosecution rested>.

Restatement. One of several influential treatises, published by the American Law Institute, describing the law in a given area and guiding its development. • Although the Restatements are frequently cited in cases and commentary, they are not binding on the courts. Restatements have been published in the following areas of law: Agency, Conflict of Laws, Contracts, Foreign Relations Law of the United States, Judgments, Law Governing Lawyers, Property, Restitution, Security, Suretyship and Guaranty, Torts, Trusts, and Unfair Competition.

restater. An author or reporter of a Restatement.

restitution, *n.* **1.** Return or restoration of some specific thing to its rightful owner or status. **2.** Compensation for benefits derived from a wrong done to another. **3.** Compensation or reparation for the loss caused to another. • In senses 2 and 3, restitution is available in tort and contract law and is sometimes ordered as a condition of probation in criminal law. — **restitutionary,** *adj.*

restitution damages. See DAMAGES.

restraining order. **1.** A court order prohibiting family violence; esp., an order restricting a person from harassing, threatening, and sometimes merely contacting or approaching another specified person. **2.** TEMPORARY RESTRAINING ORDER. **3.** A court order entered to prevent the dissipation or loss of property.

restraint, *n.* **1.** Confinement, abridgment, or limitation <a restraint on the freedom of speech>. See PRIOR RESTRAINT. **2.** Prohibition of action; holding back <the victim's family exercised no restraint — they told the suspect exactly what they thought of him>.

restraint of marriage. A condition (esp. in a gift or bequest) that nullifies the grant to which it applies if the grantee marries or remarries.

restraint on alienation. **1.** A restriction, usu. in a deed of conveyance, on a grantee's ability to sell or transfer real property; a provision that conveys an interest and that, even after the interest has become vested, prevents the owner from disposing of it at all or from disposing of it in particular ways or to particular persons. **2.** A trust provision that prohibits or penalizes alienation of the trust corpus.

restriction. **1.** A limitation or qualification. **2.** A limitation (esp. in a deed) placed on the use or enjoyment of property. See *restrictive covenant* under COVENANT (3).

restrictive covenant. See COVENANT (3).

restrictive indorsement. See INDORSEMENT.

restrictive interpretation. See INTERPRETATION.

resulting trust. See TRUST.

resulting use. See USE.

resummons. A second or renewed summons to a party or witness already summoned. See SUMMONS.

retainage (ri-**tayn**-ij). A percentage of what a landowner pays a contractor, withheld until the construction has been satisfactorily completed and all mechanic's liens are released or have expired.

retainer, *n.* **1.** A client's authorization for a lawyer to act in a case <the attorney needed an express retainer before making a settlement offer>. **2.** A fee paid to a lawyer to secure legal representation <he requires a $100,000 retainer>. — **retain,** *vb.* Cf. ATTORNEY'S FEES.

> ***general retainer.*** A retainer for a specific length of time rather than for a specific project.
>
> ***special retainer.*** A retainer for a specific case or project.

retaliatory discharge. See DISCHARGE.

retaliatory eviction. See EVICTION.

retaliatory law. A state law restraining another state's businesses — as by levying taxes — in response to similar restraints imposed by the second state on the first state's businesses.

retirement, *n.* **1.** Voluntary termination of one's own employment or career, esp. upon reaching a certain age <she traveled around the world after her retirement>. **2.** Withdrawal from action or for privacy <Carol's retirement to her house by the lake>. **3.** Withdrawal from circulation; payment of a debt <retirement of a series of bonds>. See REDEMPTION. — **retire,** *vb.*

retraction, *n.* **1.** The act of taking or drawing back <retraction of anticipatory repudiation before breach of contract>. **2.** The act of recanting; a statement in recantation <retraction of a defamatory remark>. **3.** *Wills & estates.* A withdrawal of a renunciation <because of her retraction, she took property under her uncle's will>. See RENUNCIATION (3). — **retract,** *vb.*

retreat rule. *Criminal law.* The doctrine holding that the victim of a murderous assault must choose a safe retreat instead of resorting to deadly force in self-defense, unless (1) the victim is at home or in his or her place of business (the so-called *castle doctrine*), or (2) the assailant is a person whom the victim is trying to arrest. Cf. NO-RETREAT RULE.

retrial, *n.* A new trial of an action that has already been tried. — **retry,** *vb.* See *trial de novo* under TRIAL.

retribution, *n.* **1.** *Criminal law.* Punishment imposed as repayment or revenge for the offense committed; requital. Cf. DETERRENCE; REHABILITATION (1). **2.** Something justly deserved; repayment; reward. — **retribute,** *vb.* — **retributive,** *adj.*

retributive danger. See DANGER.

retributive punishment. See PUNISHMENT.

retributivism (ri-**trib**-yə-tə-viz-əm). The legal theory by which criminal punishment is justified, as long as the offender is morally accountable, regardless of whether deterrence or other good consequences would result. • According to retributivism, a criminal is thought to have a debt to pay to society, which is paid by punishment. The punishment is also sometimes said to be society's act of paying back the criminal for the wrong done. Opponents of retributivism sometimes refer to it as "vindictive theory." Cf. *hedonistic utilitarianism* under UTILITARIANISM; UTILITARIAN-DETERRENCE THEORY.

retroactive, *adj.* (Of a statute, ruling, etc.) extending in scope or effect to matters that have occurred in the past. — **retroactivity,** *n.* Cf. PROSPECTIVE (1).

retroactive law. A legislative act that looks backward or contemplates the past, affecting acts or facts that existed before the act came into effect. • A retroactive law is not unconstitutional unless it (1) is in the nature of an ex post facto law or a bill of attainder, (2) impairs the obligation of contracts, (3) divests vested rights, or (4) is constitutionally forbidden.

retrocession. 1. The act of ceding something back (such as a territory or jurisdiction). **2.** The return of a title or other interest in property to its former or rightful owner.

retrospective evidence. See EVIDENCE.

retrospective statute. See STATUTE.

return, *n.* **1.** A court officer's bringing back of an instrument to the court that issued it; RETURN OF WRIT <a sheriff's return of citation>. **2.** A court officer's indorsement on an instrument brought back to the court, reporting what the officer did or found <a return of *nulla bona*>. See FALSE RETURN (1). **3.** TAX RETURN <file your return before April 15>. — **return,** *vb.*

return day. See DAY.

return of writ. The sheriff's bringing back a writ to the court that issued it, with a short written account (usu. on the back) of the manner in which the writ was executed. See RETURN (1).

rev'd. *abbr.* Reversed.

revenue. Gross income or receipts.

revenue bill. See BILL (3).

Revenue Procedure. An official statement by the IRS regarding the administration and procedures of the tax laws. — Abbr. Rev. Proc.

Revenue Ruling. An official interpretation by the IRS of the proper application of the tax law to a specific transaction. — Abbr. Rev. Rul.

revenue stamp. A stamp used as evidence that a tax has been paid.

reversal, *n.* **1.** An appellate court's overturning of a lower court's decision. **2.** *Securities.* A change in a security's near-term market-price trend. — **reverse,** *vb.*

reverse discrimination. See DISCRIMINATION.

reversible error. See ERROR (2).

reversion, *n.* **1.** A future interest in land arising by operation of law whenever an estate owner grants to another a particular estate, such as a life estate or a term of years, but does not dispose of the entire interest. • A reversion occurs automatically upon termination of the prior estate, as when a life tenant dies. **2.** Loosely, REMAINDER (2). — **revert,** *vb.* — **reversionary,** *adj.* Cf. POSSIBILITY OF REVERTER; REMAINDER.

reversioner. 1. One who possesses the reversion to an estate; the grantor or heir in reversion. **2.** Broadly, one who has a lawful interest in land but not the present possession of it.

reverter. See POSSIBILITY OF REVERTER.

revest, *vb.* To vest again or anew <revesting of title in the former owner>.

rev'g. *abbr.* Reversing.

review, *n.* Consideration, inspection, or reexamination of a subject or thing. — **review,** *vb.*

administrative review. **1.** Judicial review of an administrative proceeding. **2.** Review of an administrative proceeding within the agency itself.

appellate review. Examination of a lower court's decision by a higher court, which can affirm, reverse, or modify the decision.

discretionary review. The form of appellate review that is not a matter of right but that occurs only with the appellate court's permission. See CERTIORARI.

revised statute. See STATUTE.

revision, *n.* A reexamination or careful review for correction or improvement.

revival, *n.* **1.** Restoration to current use or operation; esp., the act of restoring the validity or legal force of an expired contract or dormant judgment. Cf. RENEWAL (2). **2.** *Wills & estates.* The reestablishment of the validity of a revoked will by revoking the will that invalidated the original will or in some other way manifesting the testator's intent to be bound by the earlier will. Cf. REPUBLICATION. — **revive,** *vb.*

revival statute. See STATUTE.

revivor. A proceeding to revive an action ended because of either the death of one of the parties or some other circumstance.

revocable (**rev**-ə-kə-bəl), *adj.* Capable of being canceled or withdrawn.

revocable guaranty. See GUARANTY.

revocation (rev-ə-**kay**-shən), *n.* **1.** An annulment, cancellation, or reversal, usu. of an act or power. **2.** *Contracts.* Withdrawal of an offer by the offeror. **3.** *Wills & estates.* Invalidation of a will by the testator, either by destroying the will or by executing a new one. — **revoke,** *vb.* Cf. REJECTION; REPUDIATION; RESCISSION.

revocation hearing. See HEARING.

revolving fund. See FUND.

revolving loan. See LOAN.

Rev. Proc. *abbr.* REVENUE PROCEDURE.

Rev. Rul. *abbr.* REVENUE RULING.

Rev. Stat. See *revised statutes* under STATUTE.

rezone, *vb.* To change the zoning boundaries or restrictions of (an area). See ZONING.

rhadamanthine (rad-ə-**man**-thin), *adj.* (*often cap.*) (Of a judge) rigorous and inflexible.

RICO (**ree**-koh). *abbr.* RACKETEER INFLUENCED AND CORRUPT ORGANIZATIONS ACT.

right, *n.* **1.** That which is proper under law, morality, or ethics <know right from wrong>. **2.** Something that is due to a person by just claim, legal guarantee, or moral principle <the right of liberty>. **3.** A power, privilege, or immunity secured to a person by law <the right to dispose of one's estate>. **4.** A legally enforceable claim that another will do or will not do a given act; a recognized and protected interest the violation of which is a wrong <a breach of duty that infringes one's right>. **5.** (*often pl.*) The interest, claim, or ownership that one has in tangible or intangible property <a debtor's rights in collateral> <publishing rights>.

procedural right. A right that derives from legal or administrative procedure; a right that helps in the protection or enforcement of a substantive right. Cf. *substantive right.*

property right. A right to specific property, whether tangible or intangible.

substantial right. An essential right that potentially affects the outcome of a lawsuit and is capable of legal enforcement and protection, as distinguished from a mere technical or procedural right.

substantive right (**səb**-stən-tiv). A right that can be protected or enforced by law; a right of substance rather than form. Cf. *procedural right*.

right against self-incrimination. A criminal defendant's or a witness's constitutional right — under the Fifth Amendment, but waivable under certain conditions — guaranteeing that a person cannot be compelled by the government to testify if the testimony might result in the person's being criminally prosecuted. • Although this right is most often asserted during a criminal prosecution, a person can also "plead the Fifth" in a civil, legislative, administrative, or grand-jury proceeding. See SELF-INCRIMINATION.

rightful, *adj.* **1.** (Of an action) equitable; fair <a rightful dispossession>. **2.** (Of a person) legitimately entitled to a position <a rightful heir>. **3.** (Of an office or piece of property) that one is entitled to <her rightful inheritance>.

right of action. 1. The right to bring a specific case to court. **2.** A right that can be enforced by legal action; a chose in action. Cf. CAUSE OF ACTION.

right of assembly. The constitutional right — guaranteed by the First Amendment — of the people to gather peacefully for public expression of religion, politics, or grievances. Cf. FREEDOM OF ASSOCIATION; *unlawful assembly* under ASSEMBLY.

right of election. *Wills & estates.* A surviving spouse's statutory right to choose either the gifts given by the deceased spouse in the will or a forced share or a share of the estate as defined in the probate statute. — Also termed *widow's election*. See ELECTION (2).

right of entry. 1. The right of taking or resuming possession of land or other real property in a peaceable manner. **2.** POWER OF TERMINATION. **3.** The right to go into another's real property for a special purpose without committing trespass. **4.** The right of an alien to go into a jurisdiction for a special purpose.

right of first refusal. A potential buyer's contractual right to meet the terms of a third party's offer if the seller intends to accept that offer. • For example, if Beth has a right of first refusal on the purchase of Sam's house, and if Sam intends to accept Terry's offer to buy the house for $300,000, Beth can match this offer and prevent Terry from buying it. Cf. RIGHT OF PREEMPTION.

right of possession. The right to hold, use, occupy, or otherwise enjoy a given property; esp., the right to enter real property and eject or evict a wrongful possessor.

right of preemption. A potential buyer's contractual right to have the first opportunity to buy, at a specified price, if the seller chooses to sell within the contracted period of time. Cf. RIGHT OF FIRST REFUSAL.

right of privacy. 1. The right to personal autonomy. • The U.S. Constitution does not explicitly provide for a right of privacy, but the Supreme

Court has repeatedly ruled that this right is implied in the "zones of privacy" created by specific constitutional guarantees. **2.** The right of a person and the person's property to be free from unwarranted public scrutiny or exposure. See INVASION OF PRIVACY.

right of publicity. The right to control the use of one's own name, picture, or likeness and to prevent another from using it for commercial benefit without one's consent.

right of revolution. The inherent right of a people to cast out their rulers, change their polity, or effect radical reforms in their system of government or institutions, by force or general uprising, when the legal and constitutional methods of making such changes have proved inadequate or are so obstructed as to be unavailable.

right of support. *Property*. **1.** A landowner's right to have the land supported by adjacent land and by the underlying earth. **2.** A servitude giving the owner of a house the right to rest timber on the walls of a neighboring house.

right of survivorship. A joint tenant's right to succeed to the whole estate upon the death of the other joint tenant. See SURVIVORSHIP; *joint tenancy* under TENANCY.

right-of-way. 1. A person's legal right, established by usage or by contract, to pass through grounds or property owned by another. Cf. EASEMENT. **2.** The right to build and operate a railway line or a highway on land belonging to another, or the land so used. **3.** The right to take precedence in traffic.

right to bear arms. The constitutional right of persons to own firearms.

right to counsel. A criminal defendant's constitutional right, guaranteed by the Sixth Amendment, to representation by a court-appointed lawyer if the defendant cannot afford to hire one. See ASSISTANCE OF COUNSEL.

right to die. The right of a terminally ill person to refuse life-sustaining treatment. See ADVANCE DIRECTIVE.

right-to-know act. A federal or state statute requiring businesses (such as chemical manufacturers) that produce hazardous substances to disclose information about the substances both to the community where they are produced or stored and to employees who handle them.

right to petition. The constitutional right — guaranteed by the First Amendment — of the people to make formal requests to the government, as by lobbying or writing letters to public officials.

right to pursue happiness. See HAPPINESS, RIGHT TO PURSUE.

right to travel. A person's constitutional right — guaranteed by the Privileges and Immunities Clause — to travel freely between states.

right to vote. See SUFFRAGE.

right-to-work law. A state law that prevents labor–management agreements requiring a person to join a union as a condition of employment. See SHOP.

riot, *n.* An unlawful disturbance of the peace by an assembly of usu. three or more persons acting with a common purpose in a violent or tumultuous manner that threatens or terrorizes the public. — **riot,** *vb.* — **riotous,** *adj.* Cf. *unlawful assembly* under ASSEMBLY; CIVIL COMMOTION; ROUT.

riparian (ri-**pair**-ee-ən *or* rɪ-), *adj.* Of, relating to, or located on the bank of a river or stream (or occasionally another body of water, such as a lake) <riparian land> <a riparian owner>. Cf. LITTORAL.

riparian proprietor. A landowner whose property borders on a stream or river.

riparian right. (*often pl.*) The right of a landowner whose property borders on a body of water or watercourse.

riparian-rights doctrine. The rule that owners of land bordering on a waterway have equal rights to use the water passing through or by their property. Cf. PRIOR-APPROPRIATION DOCTRINE.

ripeness, *n.* **1.** The circumstance existing when a case has reached, but has not passed, the point when the facts have developed sufficiently to permit an intelligent and useful decision to be made. **2.** The requirement that this circumstance must exist before a court will decide a controversy. — **ripen,** *vb.* — **ripe,** *adj.* See JUSTICIABILITY. Cf. MOOTNESS DOCTRINE; PREMATURITY.

risk, *n.* **1.** The chance of injury, damage, or loss; danger or hazard <many feel that skydiving is not worth the risk>. See ASSUMPTION OF THE RISK. **2.** Liability for injury, damage, or loss if it occurs <the consumer-protection statute placed the risk on the manufacturer instead of the buyer>.

risk of loss. The danger or possibility that a party will have to bear the costs and expenses for the damage, destruction, or inability to locate goods or other property.

risk-utility test. A method of imposing product liability on a manufacturer if the evidence shows that a reasonable person would conclude that the benefits of a product's particular design versus the feasibility of an alternative safer design did not outweigh the dangers inherent in the original design. Cf. CONSUMER-CONTEMPLATION TEST.

robbery, *n.* The illegal taking of property from the person of another, or in the person's presence, by violence or intimidation; aggravated larceny. — **rob,** *vb.* See LARCENY; THEFT. Cf. BURGLARY.

aggravated robbery. Robbery committed by a person who either carries a dangerous weapon — often called *armed robbery* — or inflicts bodily harm on someone during the robbery.

armed robbery. Robbery committed by a person carrying a dangerous weapon, regardless of whether the weapon is revealed or used. • Most states punish armed robbery as an aggravated form of robbery rather than as a separate crime.

simple robbery. Robbery that does not involve an aggravating factor or circumstance.

robe. (*often cap.*) The legal or judicial profession <eminent members of the robe>.

rocket docket. **1.** An accelerated dispute-resolution process. **2.** A court or judicial district known for its speedy disposition of cases. **3.** A similar administrative process, in which disputes must be decided within a specified time (such as 60 days).

roll, *n.* **1.** A record of a court's or public office's proceedings. **2.** An official list of persons and property subject to taxation.

rolled-up plea. See PLEA (3).

Roman law. **1.** The legal system of the ancient Romans, forming the basis of the modern civil law. **2.** CIVIL LAW (1).

root of title. The recorded land transaction, usu. at least 40 years old, that is used to begin a title search. See CHAIN OF TITLE; TITLE SEARCH.

Roth IRA. See INDIVIDUAL RETIREMENT ACCOUNT.

rout (rowt), *n.* The offense that occurs when an unlawful assembly makes some move toward the accomplishment of its participants' common purpose. Cf. RIOT.

routine-activities theory. The theory that criminal acts occur when (1) a person is motivated to commit the offense, (2) a vulnerable victim is available, and (3) there is insufficient protection to prevent the crime. Cf. CONTROL THEORY; RATIONAL-CHOICE THEORY; STRAIN THEORY.

royalty. **1.** A payment made to an author or inventor for each copy of a work or article sold under a copyright or patent. **2.** A share of the product or profit from real property, reserved by the grantor of a mineral lease, in exchange for the lessee's right to mine or drill on the land.

rptr. *abbr.* REPORTER.

R.S. *abbr.* See *revised statutes* under STATUTE.

rubber-stamp seal. See NOTARY SEAL.

rule, *n.* **1.** Generally, an established and authoritative standard or principle; a general norm mandating or guiding conduct or action in a given type of situation. **2.** A regulation governing a court's or an agency's internal procedures.

rule, *vb.* **1.** To command or require; to exert control <the dictator ruled the country>. **2.** To decide a legal point <the court ruled on the issue of admissibility>.

rule, the. An evidentiary and procedural rule by which all witnesses are excluded from the courtroom while another witness is testifying <invoking "the rule">.

Rulc 11. *Civil procedure.* In federal practice, the procedural rule requiring the attorney of record or the party (if not represented by an attorney) to sign all pleadings, motions, and other papers filed with the court and — by this signing — to represent that the paper is filed in good faith after an inquiry that is reasonable under the circumstances. Fed. R. Civ. P. 11.

rule against perpetuities. (*sometimes cap.*) *Property.* The common-law rule prohibiting a grant of an estate unless the interest must vest, if at all, no later than 21 years after the death of some person alive when the interest was created. • The purpose of the rule was to limit the time that title to property could be suspended out of commerce because there was no owner who had title to the property and who could sell it or exercise other aspects of ownership. If the terms of the contract or gift exceeded the time limits of the rule, the gift or transaction was void.

Rule in Shelley's Case. *Property.* The rule that if — in a single grant — a freehold estate is given to a person and a remainder is given to the person's heirs, the remainder belongs to the named person and not the heirs, so that the person is held to have a fee simple absolute.

Rule in Wild's Case. *Property.* The rule construing a grant to "A and A's children" as a fee tail if A's children do not exist at the effective date of the instrument, and as a joint tenancy if A's children do exist at the effective date.

rulemaking, *n.* The process used by an administrative agency to formulate, amend, or repeal a rule or regulation. — **rulemaking,** *adj.*

formal rulemaking. Agency rulemaking that, when required by statute or the agency's discretion, must be on the record after an opportunity for an agency hearing, and must comply with certain procedures, such as allowing the submission of evidence and the cross-examination of witnesses. Cf. *informal rulemaking.*

informal rulemaking. Agency rulemaking in which the agency publishes a proposed regulation and receives public comments on the regulation, after which the regulation can take effect without the necessity of a formal hearing on the record. Cf. *formal rulemaking.*

rule of capture. **1.** The doctrine that if the donee of a general power of appointment manifests an intent to assume control of the property for all purposes and not just for the purpose of appointing it to someone, the donee captures the property and the property goes to the donee's estate. **2.** *Property.* The principle that wild animals belong to the person who captures them, regardless of whether they were originally on another person's land.

rule of court. A rule governing the practice or procedure in a given court <federal rules of court>. See LOCAL RULE.

rule of decision. A rule, statute, body of law, or prior decision that provides the basis for deciding or adjudicating a case.

rule of four. The convention that for certiorari to be granted by the U.S. Supreme Court, four justices must vote in favor of the grant. See CERTIORARI.

rule of inconvenience. The principle of statutory interpretation holding that a court should not construe a statute in a way that will jeopardize an important public interest or produce a serious hardship for anyone, unless that interpretation is unavoidable.

rule of law. **1.** A substantive legal principle <under the rule of law known as respondeat superior, the

employer is answerable for all wrongs committed by an employee in the course of the employment>. **2.** The supremacy of regular as opposed to arbitrary power <citizens must respect the rule of law>. **3.** The doctrine that every person is subject to the ordinary law within the jurisdiction <all persons within the United States are within the American rule of law>. **4.** The doctrine that general constitutional principles are the result of judicial decisions determining the rights of private individuals in the courts <under the rule of law, Supreme Court caselaw makes up the bulk of what we call "constitutional law">. **5.** Loosely, a legal ruling; a ruling on a point of law <the *ratio decidendi* of a case is any rule of law reached by the judge as a necessary step in the decision>.

rule of lenity (**len**-ə-tee). The judicial doctrine holding that a court, in construing an ambiguous criminal statute that sets out multiple or inconsistent punishments, should resolve the ambiguity in favor of the more lenient punishment.

rule of necessity. A rule requiring a judge or other official to hear a case, despite bias or conflict of interest, when disqualification would result in the lack of any competent court or tribunal.

rule of optional completeness. The evidentiary rule providing that when a party introduces part of a writing or an utterance at trial, the opposing party may require that the remainder of the passage be read to establish the full context. Fed. R. Evid. 106.

rule of right. The source of a right; the rule that gives rise to a right.

rule of the last antecedent. An interpretative principle by which a court determines that qualifying words or phrases modify the words or phrases immediately preceding them and not words or phrases more remote, unless the extension is necessary from the context or the spirit of the entire writing. • For example, an application of this rule might mean that, in the phrase *Texas courts, New Mexico courts, and New York courts in the federal system*, the words *in the federal system* might be held to modify only *New York courts* and not *Texas courts* or *New Mexico courts*.

ruling, *n.* The outcome of a court's decision either on some point of law or on the case as a whole. — **rule,** *vb.* Cf. JUDGMENT; OPINION (1).

run, *vb.* **1.** To expire after a prescribed period <the statute of limitations had run, so the plaintiff's lawsuit was barred>. **2.** To accompany a conveyance or assignment of (land) <the covenant runs with the land>. **3.** To apply <the injunction runs against only one of the parties in the dispute>.

runaway. A person (usu. a juvenile) who has fled from the custody of legal guardians without permission and who has failed to return within a reasonable time.

runaway grand jury. See GRAND JURY.

runner. **1.** A law-office employee who delivers papers between offices and files papers in court. **2.** One who solicits personal-injury cases for a lawyer.

running account. See ACCOUNT.

S

s. *abbr.* **1.** STATUTE. **2.** SECTION (1). **3.** (*usu. cap.*) SENATE.

sabotage (**sab**-ə-tahzh), *n.* **1.** The destruction, damage, or knowingly defective production of materials, premises, or utilities used for national defense or for war. **2.** The willful and malicious destruction of an employer's property or interference with an employer's normal operations, esp. during a labor dispute. — **sabotage,** *vb.*

saboteur (sab-ə-**tər**), *n.* A person who commits sabotage.

SAET. *abbr.* SUBSTANCE-ABUSE EVALUATION AND TREATMENT.

safe-deposit box. A lockbox stored in a bank's vault to secure a customer's valuables. • It usually takes two keys (one held by the bank and one held by the customer) to open the box.

safe harbor. A provision (as in a statute or regulation) that affords protection from liability or penalty. • SEC regulations, for example, provide a safe harbor for an issuer's business forecasts that are made in good faith.

said, *adj.* Aforesaid; above-mentioned. • The adjective *said* is obsolescent in legal drafting, its last bastion being patent claims. But even in that context the word is giving way to the ordinary word *the*, which if properly used is equally precise. See AFORESAID.

salable (**say**-lə-bəl *or* **sayl**-ə-bəl), *adj.* Fit for sale in the usual course of trade at the usual selling price; MERCHANTABLE. — **salability** (say-lə-**bil**-ə-tee *or* sayl-ə-**bil**-ə-tee), *n.*

salary. An agreed compensation for services — esp. professional or semiprofessional services — usu. paid at regular intervals on a yearly basis, as distinguished from an hourly basis. • Salaried positions are usually exempt from the requirements of the Fair Labor Standards Act (on overtime and the like) but are subject to state regulation. Cf. WAGE.

sale, *n.* **1.** The transfer of property or title for a price. **2.** The agreement by which such a transfer takes place. • The four elements are (1) parties competent to contract, (2) mutual assent, (3) a thing capable of being transferred, and (4) a price in money paid or promised.

sale or exchange. 1. *Tax.* A voluntary transfer of property for value (as distinguished from a gift) resulting in a gain or loss recognized for federal tax purposes. **2.** A transfer of property; esp., a situation in which proceeds of a sale are to be vested in another estate of the same character and use.

sales agreement. A contract to transfer ownership of property from a seller to a buyer for a fixed sum. UCC § 2–106(1).

sales tax. See TAX.

salvage value. See VALUE.

same, *pron. Jargon.* The thing just mentioned or described; it or them <two days after receiving the goods, Mr. Siviglio returned same>.

same offense. See OFFENSE.

same-sex harassment. See HARASSMENT.

sanction (**sangk**-shən), *n.* **1.** Official approval or authorization <the committee gave sanction to the proposal>. **2.** A penalty or coercive measure that results from failure to comply with a law, rule, or order <a sanction for discovery abuse>.

criminal sanction. A penalty attached to a criminal conviction, such as a fine or restitution.

death-penalty sanction. Civil procedure. A court's order dismissing the suit or entering a default judgment in favor of the plaintiff because of extreme discovery abuses by a party or because of a party's action or inaction that shows an unwillingness to participate in the case. • Such a sanction is rarely ordered, and is usually preceded by orders of lesser sanctions that have not been complied with or that have not remedied the problem.

shame sanction. A criminal penalty designed to stigmatize or disgrace a convicted offender, and often to alert the public about the offender's conviction. • A shame sanction usually publicly associates the offender with the crime that he or she committed. An example is being required to post a sign in one's yard stating, "Convicted Child Molester Lives Here."

sanction, *vb.* **1.** To approve, authorize, or support <the court will sanction the trust disposition if it is not against public policy>. **2.** To penalize by imposing a sanction <the court sanctioned the attorney for violating the gag order>.

sanctionable, *adj.* (Of conduct or action) meriting sanctions; likely to be sanctioned.

sanctions tort. A means of recovery for another party's discovery abuse, whereby the judge orders the abusive party to pay a fine to the injured party for the discovery violation. • This is not a tort in the traditional sense, but rather a form of punishment that results in monetary gain for the injured party.

sanctity of contract. The principle that the parties to a contract, having duly entered into it, must honor their obligations under it.

sanctuary. 1. A safe place, esp. where legal process cannot be executed; asylum. **2.** A holy area of a religious building; esp., the area in a church where the main altar is located.

sandbagging, *n.* A trial lawyer's remaining cagily silent when a possible error occurs at trial, with the hope of preserving an issue for appeal if the court does not correct the problem. • Such a tactic does not usually preserve the issue for appeal because objections must be made promptly to alert the trial judge of the possible error.

S & L. *abbr.* SAVINGS-AND-LOAN ASSOCIATION.

sandpapering, *n. Slang.* A lawyer's general preparation of a witness before a deposition or trial. Cf. HORSESHEDDING.

sandwich lease. See LEASE.

sane, *adj.* Having a relatively sound and healthy mind; capable of reason and of distinguishing right from wrong.

sanity. The state or condition of having a relatively sound and healthy mind. Cf. INSANITY.

sanity hearing. 1. An inquiry into the mental competency of a person to stand trial. **2.** A proceeding to determine whether a person should be institutionalized.

satellite litigation. 1. One or more lawsuits related to a major piece of litigation that is being conducted in another court <the satellite litigation in state court prevented the federal judge from ruling on the issue>. **2.** Peripheral skirmishes involved in the prosecution of a lawsuit <the plaintiffs called the sanctions "satellite litigation," drummed up by the defendants to deflect attention from the main issues in the case>.

satisfaction, *n.* **1.** The giving of something with the intention, express or implied, that it is to extinguish some existing legal or moral obligation. • Satisfaction differs from performance because it is always something given as a substitute for or equivalent of something else, while performance is the identical thing promised to be done. **2.** The fulfillment of an obligation; esp., the payment in full of a debt. **3.** SATISFACTION PIECE. **4.** *Wills & estates.* The payment by a testator, during the testator's lifetime, of a legacy provided for in a will; ADVANCEMENT. **5.** *Wills & estates.* A testamentary gift intended to satisfy a debt owed by the testator to a creditor. — **satisfy,** *vb.* See ACCORD AND SATISFACTION.

satisfaction of judgment. 1. The complete discharge of obligations under a judgment. **2.** The document filed and entered on the record indicating that a judgment has been paid.

satisfaction of lien. 1. The fulfillment of all obligations made the subject of a lien. **2.** The document signed by the lienholder releasing the property subject to a lien.

satisfaction of mortgage. 1. The complete payment of a mortgage. **2.** A discharge signed by the mortgagee or mortgage holder indicating that the property subject to the mortgage is released or that the mortgage debt has been paid and the mortgage conditions have been fully satisfied.

satisfaction piece. A written statement that one party (esp. a debtor) has discharged its obligation to another party, who accepts the discharge.

satisfactory evidence. See EVIDENCE.

satisfied term. See TERM (4).

Saturday-night special. 1. A handgun that is easily obtained and concealed. **2.** *Corporations.* A surprise tender offer typically held open for a limited offering period (such as one week) to maximize pressure on a shareholder to accept. • These tender offers are now effectively prohibited by section

14(e) of the Williams Act. 15 USCA § 78n(e).

saving clause. 1. A statutory provision exempting from coverage something that would otherwise be included. • A saving clause is generally used in a repealing act to preserve rights and claims that would otherwise be lost. **2.** SEVERABILITY CLAUSE.

savings-and-loan association. A financial institution — often organized and chartered like a bank — that primarily makes home-mortgage loans but also usu. maintains checking accounts and provides other banking services. — Often shortened to S&L. Cf. BUILDING-AND-LOAN ASSOCIATION.

savings-and-loan bank. See SAVINGS-AND-LOAN ASSOCIATION.

savings bank. See BANK.

savings bond. See BOND (3).

savor, *vb.* To partake of the character of or bear affinity to (something). • In traditional legal idiom, an interest arising from land is said to "savor of the realty."

S.B. See *senate bill* under BILL (3).

SBA. *abbr.* SMALL BUSINESS ADMINISTRATION.

S.C. *abbr.* **1.** SUPREME COURT. **2.** Same case. • In former practice, when put between two citations, the abbreviation indicated that the same case was reported in both places.

scab. A person who works under conditions contrary to a union contract; esp., a worker who crosses a union picket line to replace a union worker during a strike.

scalping, *n.* **1.** The practice of selling something (esp. a ticket) at a price above face value once it becomes scarce (usu. just before a high-demand event begins). **2.** The purchase of a security by an investment adviser before the adviser recommends that a customer buy the same security. • This practice is usually considered unethical because the customer's purchase will increase the security's price, thus enabling the adviser to sell at a profit. **3.** The excessive markup or markdown on a transaction by a market-maker. • This action violates National Association of Securities Dealers guidelines. — **scalp,** *vb.*

scandalous matter. *Civil procedure.* A matter that is both grossly disgraceful (or defamatory) and irrelevant to the action or defense. • A federal court — upon a party's motion or on its own — can order a scandalous matter struck from a pleading. Fed. R. Civ. P. 12(f). Cf. IMPERTINENT MATTER.

scatter-point analysis. A method for studying the effect that minority-population changes have on voting patterns, involving a plotting of the percentage of votes that candidates receive to determine whether voting percentages increase or decrease as the percentages of voters of a particular race increase or decrease.

schedule, *n.* A written list or inventory; esp., a statement that is attached to a document and that gives a detailed showing of the matters referred to in the document <Schedule B to the title policy lists the encumbrances on the property>. — **schedule,** *vb.* — **scheduled,** *adj.*

scheme. 1. A systemic plan; a connected or orderly arrangement, esp. of related concepts <legislative scheme>. **2.** An artful plot or plan, usu. to deceive others <a scheme to defraud creditors>.

schism (**siz**-əm *or* **skiz**-əm). **1.** A breach or rupture; a division, esp. among members of a group, as of a union. **2.** A separation of beliefs and doctrines by persons of the same organized religion, religious denomination, or sect.

school land. See LAND.

scienter (sɪ-**en**-tər *or* see-), *n.* [Latin "knowingly"] **1.** A degree of knowledge that makes a person legally responsible for the consequences of his or her act or omission; the fact of an act's having been done knowingly, esp. as a ground for civil damages or criminal punishment. See KNOWLEDGE; MENS REA. **2.** A mental state consisting in an intent to deceive, manipulate, or defraud. • In this sense, the term is used most often in the context of securities fraud.

scientific evidence. See EVIDENCE.

scientific knowledge. See KNOWLEDGE (1).

scilicet (**sil**-ə-set *or* -sit). [fr. Latin *scire licet* "that you may know"] That is to say; namely; VIDELICET. • Like *videlicet*, this word is used in pleadings and other instruments to introduce a more particular statement of matters previously mentioned in general terms. It has never been quite as common, however, as *videlicet*.

scintilla (sin-**til**-ə). A spark or trace <the standard is that there must be more than a scintilla of evidence>. Pl. **scintillas** (sin-**til**-əz).

scintilla-of-evidence rule. A common-law doctrine holding that if even the slightest amount of relevant evidence exists on an issue, then a motion for summary judgment or for directed verdict cannot be granted and the issue must go to the jury. • Federal courts do not follow this rule, but some states apply it.

scire facias (sɪ-ree **fay**-shee-əs). [Law Latin "you are to make known, show cause"] A writ requiring the person against whom it is issued to appear and show cause why some matter of record should not be annulled or vacated, or why a dormant judgment against that person should not be revived.

scofflaw (**skof**-law). A person who treats the law with contempt; esp., one who avoids various laws that are not easily enforced <some scofflaws carry mannequins in their cars in order to drive in the carpool lane>.

scope note. In a law digest, an abstract appearing after a title and showing concisely what subject matter is included and what is excluded.

scope of authority. *Agency.* The reasonable power that an agent has been delegated or might foreseeably be delegated in carrying out the principal's business. See SCOPE OF EMPLOYMENT; RESPONDEAT SUPERIOR.

scope of employment. The range of reasonable and foreseeable activities that an employee engages in while carrying out the employer's business. See RESPONDEAT SUPERIOR.

S corporation. See CORPORATION.

scrambling possession. See POSSESSION.

screening grand jury. See GRAND JURY.

scrip. 1. A document that entitles the holder to receive something of value. **2.** Paper money issued for temporary use.

script. 1. An original or principal writing. **2.** Handwriting.

scrivener (**skriv-[ə]-nər**). A writer; esp., a professional drafter of contracts or other documents.

scrivener's exception. An exemption from the attorney–client privilege whereby the privilege does not attach if the attorney is retained solely to perform a ministerial task for the client, such as preparing a statutory-form deed.

scroll, *n.* **1.** A roll of paper; a list. **2.** A draft or outline to be completed at a later time. **3.** A written mark; esp., a character affixed to a signature in place of a seal.

S.Ct. *abbr.* **1.** SUPREME COURT. **2.** Supreme Court Reporter.

S.D. *abbr.* Southern District, in reference to U.S. judicial districts.

S.E. *abbr.* SOUTH EASTERN REPORTER.

seal, *n.* **1.** An impression or sign that has legal consequence when applied to an instrument. **2.** A fastening that must be broken before access can be obtained.

corporate seal. A seal adopted by a corporation for executing and authenticating its corporate and legal instruments.

private seal. A corporate or individual seal, as distinguished from a public seal.

public seal. A seal used to certify documents belonging to a public authority or government bureau.

seal, *vb.* **1.** To authenticate or execute (a document) by use of a seal. **2.** To close (an envelope, etc.) tightly. **3.** To prevent access to (a document, record, etc.).

sealed bid. See BID.

sealed-container rule. *Products liability.* The principle that a seller is not liable for a defective product if the seller receives the product from the manufacturer and sells it without knowing of the defect or having a reasonable opportunity to inspect the product.

sealed instrument. At common law and under some statutes, a legal document to which the bound party has affixed a personal seal, usu. recognized as providing indisputable evidence of the validity of the underlying obligations. • The common-law distinction between sealed and unsealed instruments has been abolished by many states. The UCC provides that the laws applicable to sealed instruments do not apply to contracts for the sale of goods or negotiable instruments. UCC § 2–203. See *contract under seal* under CONTRACT.

sealed verdict. See VERDICT.

sealing records. The act or practice of officially preventing access to particular (esp. juvenile-criminal) records, in the absence of a court order. See EXPUNGEMENT OF RECORD.

search, *n.* **1.** An examination of a person's body, property, or other area that the person would reasonably be expected to consider as private, conducted by a law-enforcement officer for the purpose of finding evidence of a crime. • Because the Fourth Amendment prohibits unreasonable searches (as well as seizures), a search cannot ordinarily be conducted without probable cause. — **search,** *vb.* Cf. FRISK.

administrative search. A search of public or commercial premises carried out by a regulatory authority to enforce compliance with health, safety, or security regulations. • The probable cause required for an administrative search is less stringent than that required for a search incident to a criminal investigation.

border search. **1.** A search conducted at the border of a country, esp. at a checkpoint, to exclude illegal aliens and contraband. **2.** Loosely, a search conducted near the border of a country.

checkpoint search. **1.** A search anywhere on a military installation. **2.** A search in which police officers set up roadblocks and stop motorists to ascertain whether the drivers are intoxicated.

consent search. A search conducted after a person with the authority to do so voluntarily waives Fourth Amendment rights. • The government has the burden to show that the consent was given freely — not under duress. *Bumper v. North Carolina*, 391 U.S. 543, 548–49, 88 S.Ct. 1788, 1792 (1968).

emergency search. A warrantless search conducted by a police officer who has probable cause and reasonably believes that, because of a need to protect life or property, there is not enough time to obtain a warrant. See EMERGENCY DOCTRINE.

exigent search (**eks-ə-jənt**). A warrantless search carried out under exigent circumstances, such as an imminent danger to human life or a risk of the destruction of evidence. See *exigent circumstances* under CIRCUMSTANCE.

inventory search. **1.** A complete search of an arrestee's person before that person is booked into jail. **2.** The search of an arrestee's impounded vehicle for the purpose of listing everything it contains. • All possessions found are typically held in police custody.

no-knock search. A search of property by police without knocking and announcing their presence and purpose before entry. • A no-knock search warrant may be issued under limited circumstances, as when a prior announcement would probably lead to the destruction of the objects searched for or would endanger the safety of the police or others.

private search. A search conducted by a private person rather than by a law-enforcement officer. • Items found during a private search are generally admissible into evidence if the person conducting the search was not acting at the direction of a law-enforcement officer.

protective search. A search of a detained suspect and the area within the suspect's immediate control, conducted to protect the arresting officer's safety (as from a concealed weapon) and often to preserve evidence. • A protective search can be conducted without a warrant. *Chimel v. California*, 395 U.S. 752, 89 S.Ct. 2034 (1969).

shakedown search. A usu. random and warrantless search for illicit or contraband material (such as weapons or drugs) in a prisoner's cell.

strip search. A search of a person conducted after that person's clothes have been removed, the purpose usu. being to find any contraband the person might be hiding.

unreasonable search. A search conducted without probable cause or other considerations that would make it legally permissible.

voluntary search. A search in which no duress or coercion was applied to obtain the defendant's consent. See *consent search*.

warranted search. A search conducted under authority of a search warrant.

warrantless search. A search conducted without obtaining a proper warrant. • Warrantless searches are permissible under exigent circumstances or when conducted incident to an arrest. See *exigent circumstances* under CIRCUMSTANCE; *protective search*.

zone search. A search of a crime scene (such as the scene of a fire or explosion) by dividing it up into sectors.

2. An examination of public documents or records for information; esp., TITLE SEARCH.

search book. A lawbook that contains no statements of the law but instead consists of lists or tables of cases, statutes, and the like, used simply to help a researcher find the law. • Most indexes, other than index-digests, are search books.

search warrant. A judge's written order authorizing a law-enforcement officer to conduct a search of a specified place and to seize evidence. See WARRANT.

anticipatory search warrant. A search warrant based on an affidavit showing probable cause that evidence of a certain crime (such as illegal drugs) will be located at a specific place in the future.

blanket search warrant. **1.** A single search warrant that authorizes the search of more than one area. **2.** An unconstitutional warrant that authorizes the seizure of everything found at a given location, without specifying which items may be seized.

no-knock search warrant. A search warrant that authorizes the police to enter premises without knocking and announcing their presence and purpose before entry because a prior announcement would probably lead to the destruction of the objects searched for or would endanger the safety of the police or others. See *no-knock search* under SEARCH.

seasonable, *adj.* Within the time agreed on; within a reasonable time <seasonable performance of the contract>.

seated land. See LAND.

sec. *abbr.* SECTION.

SEC. *abbr.* SECURITIES AND EXCHANGE COMMISSION.

Second Amendment. The constitutional amendment, ratified with the Bill of Rights in 1791, guaranteeing the right to keep and bear arms as necessary for securing freedom through a well-regulated militia.

secondary, *adj.* (Of a position, status, use, etc.) subordinate or subsequent.

secondary authority. See AUTHORITY (4).

secondary boycott. See BOYCOTT.

secondary evidence. See EVIDENCE.

secondary liability. See LIABILITY.

secondary obligation. See OBLIGATION.

second chair, *n.* A lawyer who helps the lead attorney in court, usu. by examining some of the witnesses, arguing some of the points of law, and handling parts of the voir dire, opening statement, and closing argument <the young associate was second chair for the fraud case>. — **second-chair,** *vb.*

second-degree murder. See MURDER.

second delivery. See DELIVERY.

second-look doctrine. 1. WAIT-AND-SEE PRINCIPLE. **2.** An approach that courts use to monitor the continuing effectiveness or validity of an earlier order. • For example, a family court might reconsider a waiver of alimony.

secret, *n.* **1.** Something that is kept from the knowledge of others or shared only with those concerned. See TRADE SECRET. **2.** Information that cannot be disclosed without a breach of trust; specif., information that is acquired in the attorney–client relationship and that either (1) the client has requested be kept private or (2) the attorney believes would be embarrassing or likely to be detrimental to the client if disclosed. • Under the ABA Code of Professional Responsibility, a lawyer cannot reveal a client's secret unless the client consents after full disclosure. DR 4–101. Cf. CONFIDENCE (3).

secretary of state. 1. (*usu. cap.*) The cabinet member who heads the State Department and directs foreign policy. **2.** A state government official responsible for the licensing and incorporation of businesses, the administration of elections, and other formal duties. • The secretary of state is elected in some states and appointed in others.

secrete (si-**kreet**), *vb.* To conceal or secretly transfer (property, etc.), esp. to hinder or prevent officials or creditors from finding it.

secret partner. See PARTNER.

Secret Service. A federal law-enforcement agency — organized as a division of the Treasury Department — primarily responsible for preventing counterfeiting and protecting the President and other public officials.

section. **1.** A distinct part or division of a writing, esp. a legal instrument. — Abbr. §; sec.; s. **2.** *Real estate*. A piece of land containing 640 acres, or one square mile. • Traditionally, public lands in the United States were divided into 640-acre squares, each one called a "section."

secured, *adj.* **1.** (Of a debt or obligation) supported or backed by security or collateral. **2.** (Of a creditor) protected by a pledge, mortgage, or other encumbrance of property that helps ensure financial soundness and confidence. See SECURITY.

secured bond. See BOND (3).

secured loan. See LOAN.

secured transaction. A business arrangement by which a buyer or borrower gives collateral to the seller or lender to guarantee payment of an obligation. • Article 9 of the UCC deals with secured transactions.

securities act. A federal or state law protecting the public by regulating the registration, offering, and trading of securities. See SECURITIES ACT OF 1933; SECURITIES EXCHANGE ACT OF 1934.

Securities Act of 1933. The federal law regulating the registration and initial public offering of securities, with an emphasis on full public disclosure of financial and other information. 15 USCA §§ 77a–77aa.

Securities and Exchange Commission. The federal agency that regulates the issuance and trading of securities in an effort to protect investors against fraudulent or unfair practices. • The Commission was established by the Securities Exchange Act of 1934. — Abbr. SEC.

securities exchange. **1.** A marketplace or facility for the organized purchase and sale of securities, esp. stocks. **2.** A group of people who organize themselves to create such a marketplace.

Securities Exchange Act of 1934. The federal law regulating the public trading of securities. • This law provides for the registration and supervision of securities exchanges and brokers, and regulates proxy solicitations. The Act also established the SEC. 15 USCA §§ 78a et seq.

security, *n.* **1.** Collateral given or pledged to guarantee the fulfillment of an obligation; esp., the assurance that a creditor will be repaid (usu. with interest) any money or credit extended to a debtor. **2.** A person who is bound by some type of guaranty; SURETY. **3.** The state of being secure, esp. from danger or attack. **4.** An instrument that evidences the holder's ownership rights in a firm (e.g., a stock), the holder's creditor relationship with a firm or government (e.g., a bond), or the holder's other rights (e.g., an option). • A security indicates an interest based on an investment in a common enterprise rather than direct participation in the enterprise. Under an important statutory definition, a security is any interest or instrument relating to finances. 15 USCA § 77b(1). Cf. SHARE (2); STOCK (4).

security for costs. Money, property, or a bond given to a court by a plaintiff or an appellant to secure the payment of court costs if that party loses.

security interest. A property interest created by agreement or by operation of law to secure performance of an obligation (esp. repayment of a debt). • Although the UCC limits the creation of a security interest to personal property, the Bankruptcy Code defines the term to mean "a lien created by an agreement." 11 USCA § 101(51).

perfected security interest. A security interest that has completed the statutory requirements for achieving priority over other security interests that are subject to the same requirements.

purchase-money security interest. A security interest that is created when a buyer uses the lender's money to make the purchase and immediately gives the lender security (UCC § 9–107); a security interest that is either (1) taken or retained by the seller of the collateral to secure all or part of its price or (2) taken by a person who by making advances or incurring an obligation gives value to enable the debtor to acquire rights in or the use of collateral if that value is in fact so used. • If a buyer's purchase of a boat, for example, is financed by a bank that loans the amount of the purchase price, the bank's security interest in the boat that secures the loan is a purchase-money security interest.

unperfected security interest. A security interest held by a creditor who has not established priority over any other creditor.

sedition, *n.* **1.** An agreement, communication, or other preliminary activity aimed at inciting treason or some lesser commotion against public authority. **2.** Advocacy aimed at inciting or producing — and likely to incite or produce — imminent lawless action. — **seditious,** *adj.* Cf. TREASON.

seditious conspiracy. See CONSPIRACY.

seditious speech. See SPEECH.

seduction. The offense that occurs when a man entices a woman of previously chaste character to have unlawful intercourse with him by means of persuasion, solicitation, promises, or bribes, or other means not involving force. • Many states have abolished this offense for persons over the age of legal consent.

segregation, *n.* **1.** The act or process of separating. **2.** The unconstitutional policy of separating people on the basis of color, nationality, religion, or the like. — **segregate,** *vb.* — **segregative,** *adj.*

de facto segregation. Segregation that occurs without state authority, usu. on the basis of socioeconomic factors.

de jure segregation. Segregation that is mandated or permitted by law.

punitive segregation. The act of removing a prisoner from the prison population for placement in separate or solitary confinement, usu. for disciplinary reasons.

seise (seez), *vb.* To invest with seisin or establish as a holder in fee simple; to put in possession <he became seised of half a section of farmland near Tulia>.

seisin (**see**-zin), *n.* Possession of a freehold estate in land; ownership.

seisin in deed. Actual possession of a freehold estate in land, by oneself or by one's tenant or agent, as distinguished from legal possession.

seisin in law. The right to immediate possession of a freehold estate in land, as when an heir inherits land but has not yet entered it.

seize, *vb.* **1.** To forcibly take possession of (a person or property). **2.** To place (someone) in possession. **3.** To be in possession of (property). See SEISIN; SEIZURE.

seizure, *n.* The act or an instance of taking possession of a person or property by legal right or process; esp., in constitutional law, a confiscation or arrest that may interfere with a person's reasonable expectation of privacy.

selective disclosure. The act of divulging part of a privileged communication, or one of several privileged communications, usu. because the divulged portion is helpful to the party giving the information, while harmful portions are withheld. • Such a disclosure can result in a limited waiver of the privilege for all communications on the same subject matter as the divulged portion.

selective enforcement. The practice of law-enforcement officers who use wide or even unfettered discretion about when and where to carry out certain laws; esp., the practice of singling a person out for prosecution or punishment under a statute or regulation because the person is a member of a protected group or because the person has exercised or is planning to exercise a constitutionally protected right. Cf. *vindictive prosecution* under PROSECUTION.

selective prosecution. 1. See SELECTIVE ENFORCEMENT. **2.** The practice or an instance of a criminal prosecution brought at the discretion of a prosecutor rather than as a matter of course in the normal functioning of the prosecuting authority's office. • Selective prosecution violates the Equal Protection Clause if a defendant is singled out when others similarly situated have not been prosecuted and the prosecutor's reasons for the disparate treatment are impermissible.

selective prospectivity. A court's decision to apply a new rule of law in the particular case in which the new rule is announced, but to apply the old rule in all other cases pending at the time the new rule is announced or in which the facts predate the new rule's announcement.

self-applying, *adj.* (Of a statute, ordinance, etc.) requiring no more for interpretation than a familiarity with the ordinary meanings of words.

self-authentication. See AUTHENTICATION.

self-critical-analysis privilege. See PRIVILEGE (3).

self-dealing, *n.* Participation in a transaction that benefits oneself instead of another who is owed a fiduciary duty. • For example, a corporate director might engage in self-dealing by participating in a competing business to the corporation's detriment. — **self-deal,** *vb.* Cf. FAIR DEALING.

self-defense, *n.* The use of force to protect oneself, one's family, or one's property from a real or threatened attack. • Generally, a person is justified in using a reasonable amount of force in self-defense if he or she believes that the danger of bodily harm is imminent and that force is necessary to avoid this danger. — **self-defender,** *n.* Cf. *adequate provocation* under PROVOCATION.

imperfect self-defense. The use of force by one who makes an honest but unreasonable mistake that force is necessary to repel an attack. • In some jurisdictions, such a self-defender will be charged with a lesser offense than the one committed.

perfect self-defense. The use of force by one who accurately appraises the necessity and the amount of force to repel an attack.

self-executing, *adj.* (Of an instrument) effective immediately without the need of any type of implementing action <the wills had self-executing affidavits attached>. • Legal instruments may be self-executing according to various standards. For example, treaties are self-executing under the Supremacy Clause of the U.S. Constitution (art. VI, § 2) if textually capable of judicial enforcement and intended to be enforced in that manner.

self-help, *n.* An attempt to redress a perceived wrong by one's own action rather than through the normal legal process. • The UCC and other statutes provide for particular self-help remedies (such as repossession) if the remedy can be executed without breaching the peace. UCC § 9–503.

self-help remedy. See REMEDY.

self-incrimination. The act of indicating one's own involvement in a crime or exposing oneself to prosecution, esp. by making a statement. See RIGHT AGAINST SELF-INCRIMINATION.

Self-Incrimination Clause. The clause of the Fifth Amendment to the U.S. Constitution barring the government from compelling criminal defendants to testify against themselves.

self-induced frustration. See FRUSTRATION.

self-proved will. See WILL.

self-proving affidavit. See AFFIDAVIT.

self-serving declaration. See DECLARATION.

self-settled trust. See TRUST.

self-stultification. The act or an instance of testifying about one's own deficiencies. See STULTIFY.

sell, *vb.* To transfer (property) by sale.

seller. 1. A person who sells or contracts to sell goods; a vendor. UCC § 2–103(1)(d). **2.** Generally, a person who sells anything; the transferor of property in a contract of sale.

selling agent. The real-estate broker's representative who sells the property, as opposed to the agent who lists the property for sale. Cf. LISTING AGENT.

semble (**sem**-bəl). [Law French] It seems; it would appear <semble that the parties' intention was to create a

binding agreement>. • This term is used chiefly to indicate an obiter dictum in a court opinion or to introduce an uncertain thought or interpretation.

senate. **1.** The upper chamber of a bicameral legislature. **2.** (*cap.*) The upper house of the U.S. Congress, composed of 100 members — two from each state — who are elected to six-year terms. — Abbr. S.

senate bill. See BILL (3).

senator. A person who is a member of a senate.

senatorial courtesy. **1.** The tradition that the President should take care in filling a high-level federal post (such as a judgeship) with a person agreeable to the senators from the nominee's home state, lest the senators defeat confirmation. **2.** Loosely, civility among senators.

senility. Mental feebleness or impairment caused by old age. • A senile person (in the legal sense, not the popular sense) is incompetent to enter into a binding contract or to execute a will.

senior, *adj.* **1.** (Of a debt, etc.) first; preferred, as over junior obligations. **2.** (Of a person) older than someone else. **3.** (Of a person) higher in rank or service. **4.** (Of a man) elder, as distinguished from the man's son who has the same name.

seniority. **1.** The preferential status, privileges, or rights given an employee based on the employee's length of service with an employer. • Employees with seniority may receive additional or enhanced benefit packages and obtain competitive advantages over fellow employees in layoff and promotional decisions. **2.** The status of being older or senior.

senior judge. See JUDGE.

senior partner. See PARTNER.

senior status. The employment condition of a semiretired judge who continues to perform certain judicial duties that the judge is willing and able to undertake.

sensitivity training. One or more instructional sessions for corporate managers or other employees, designed to counteract the callous treatment of others, esp. women and minorities, in the workplace.

sentence, *n.* The judgment that a court formally pronounces after finding a criminal defendant guilty; the punishment imposed on a criminal wrongdoer <a sentence of 20 years in prison>. — **sentence,** *vb.*

aggregate sentence. A sentence that arises from conviction on multiple counts in an indictment.

alternative sentence. A sentence other than incarceration. • Examples include community service and victim restitution.

concurrent sentences. Two or more sentences of jail time to be served simultaneously. • For example, if a defendant receives concurrent sentences of 5 years and 15 years, the total amount of jail time is 15 years.

conditional sentence. A sentence of confinement if the defendant fails to perform the conditions of probation.

consecutive sentences. Two or more sentences of jail time to be served in sequence. • For example, if a defendant receives consecutive sentences of 20 years and 5 years, the total amount of jail time is 25 years.

death sentence. A sentence that imposes the death penalty. See Model Penal Code § 210.6. See DEATH PENALTY.

deferred sentence. A sentence that will not be carried out if the defendant meets certain requirements, such as complying with conditions of probation.

delayed sentence. A sentence that is not imposed immediately after conviction, allowing the defendant to satisfy the court (usu. by complying with certain restrictions or conditions during the delay period) that probation is preferable to a prison sentence.

determinate sentence. A sentence for a fixed length of time rather than for an unspecified duration.

excessive sentence. A sentence that gives more punishment than is allowed by law.

general sentence. An undivided, aggregate sentence in a multicount case; a sentence that does not specify the punishment imposed for each count. • General sentences are prohibited.

indeterminate sentence. **1.** A sentence of an unspecified duration, such as one for a term of 10 to 20 years. **2.** A maximum prison term that the parole board can reduce, through statutory authorization, after the inmate has served the minimum time required by law. See INDETERMINATE SENTENCING.

intermittent sentence. A sentence consisting of periods of confinement interrupted by periods of freedom.

life sentence. A sentence that imprisons the convicted criminal for life — although in some jurisdictions the prisoner may become eligible for release on good behavior, rehabilitation, or the like.

mandatory sentence. A sentence set by law with no discretion for the judge to individualize punishment.

maximum sentence. The highest level of punishment provided by law for a particular crime.

minimum sentence. The least amount of time that a defendant must serve in prison before becoming eligible for parole.

multiple sentences. Concurrent or consecutive sentences, if a defendant is found guilty of more than one offense.

nominal sentence. A criminal sentence in name only; an exceedingly light sentence.

noncustodial sentence. A criminal sentence (such as probation) not requiring prison time.

presumptive sentence. An average sentence for a particular crime (esp. provided under sentencing guidelines) that can be raised or lowered based on the presence of mitigating or aggravating circumstances.

prior sentence. A sentence previously imposed on a criminal defendant for a different offense, whether by a guilty verdict, a guilty plea, or a *nolo contendere*.

split sentence. A sentence in which part of the time is served in confinement — to expose the offender to the unpleasantness of prison — and the rest on probation. See *shock probation* under PROBATION.

straight sentence. See *determinate sentence*.

suspended sentence. A sentence postponed so that the defendant is not required to serve time unless he or she commits another crime or violates some other court-imposed condition. • A suspended sentence, in effect, is a form of probation.

sentence bargain. See PLEA BARGAIN.

sentenced to time served. A sentencing disposition in which a criminal defendant is sentenced to jail but is credited with time served in an amount equal to the sentence handed down, resulting in the defendant's release from custody. Cf. BALANCE OF SENTENCE SUSPENDED.

sentence-package rule. *Criminal procedure*. The principle that a defendant can be resentenced on an aggregate sentence — that is, one arising from a conviction on multiple counts in an indictment — when the defendant successfully challenges part of the conviction, as by successfully challenging some but not all of the counts.

sentencing council. A panel of three or more judges who confer to determine a criminal sentence. • Sentencing by a council occurs less frequently than sentencing by a single trial judge.

sentencing guidelines. A set of standards for determining the punishment that a convicted criminal should receive, based on the nature of the crime and the offender's criminal history. • The federal government and several states have adopted sentencing guidelines in an effort to make judicial sentencing more consistent.

Sentencing Reform Act of 1984. A federal statute enacted to bring greater uniformity to punishments assessed for federal crimes by creating a committee of federal judges and other officials (the United States Sentencing Commission) responsible for producing sentencing guidelines to be used by the federal courts. 28 USCA § 994(a)(1).

Sentencing Table. A reference guide used by federal courts to calculate the appropriate punishment under the sentencing guidelines by taking into account the gravity of the offense and the convicted person's criminal history.

separable, *adj.* Capable of being separated or divided <a separable controversy>.

separable controversy. A claim that is separate and independent from the other claims being asserted in a suit. • This term is most often associated with the statute that permits an entire case to be removed to federal court if one of the claims, being separate and independent from the others, presents a federal question that is within the jurisdiction of the federal courts. 28 USCA § 1441(c).

separate, *adj.* (Of liability, cause of action, etc.) individual; distinct; particular; disconnected.

separate action. See ACTION.

separate and apart. (Of a husband and wife) living away from each other, along with at least one spouse's intent to dissolve the marriage.

separate-but-equal doctrine. The now-defunct doctrine that African-Americans could be segregated if they were provided with equal opportunities and facilities in education, public transportation, and jobs. • This rule was established in *Plessy v. Ferguson*, 163 U.S. 537, 16 S.Ct. 1138 (1896), and overturned in *Brown v. Board of Education*, 347 U.S. 483, 74 S.Ct. 686 (1954).

separate count. See COUNT.

separate examination. **1.** The private interrogation of a witness, apart from the other witnesses in the same case. **2.** The interrogation of a wife outside the presence of her husband by a court clerk or notary for the purpose of acknowledging a deed or other instrument. • This was done to ensure that the wife signed without being coerced to do so by her husband.

separate maintenance. See MAINTENANCE.

separate offense. See OFFENSE.

separate property. **1.** Property that a spouse owned before marriage or acquired during marriage by inheritance or by gift from a third party, and in some states property acquired during marriage but after the spouses have entered into a separation agreement and have begun living apart or after one spouse has commenced a divorce action. — Also termed *individual property*. Cf. COMMUNITY PROPERTY; *marital property* under PROPERTY. **2.** In some common-law states, property titled to one spouse or acquired by one spouse individually during marriage. **3.** Property acquired during the marriage in exchange for separate property (in sense 1 or sense 2).

separate return. See TAX RETURN.

separate-sovereigns rule. *Criminal procedure.* The principle that a person may be tried twice for the same offense — despite the Double Jeopardy Clause — if the prosecutions are conducted by separate sovereigns, as by the federal government and a state government or by two different states. See DOUBLE JEOPARDY.

separate trial. See TRIAL.

separation. **1.** An arrangement whereby a husband and wife live apart from each other while remaining married, either by mutual consent (often in a written agreement) or by judicial decree; the act of carrying out such an arrangement. **2.** The status of a husband and wife having begun such an arrangement, or the judgment or contract that brought the arrangement about. **3.** Cessation of a contractual relationship, esp. in an employment situation. — **separate,** *vb.*

separation agreement. An agreement between spouses in the process of a divorce or legal separation concerning alimony, property division, child custody and support, and the like.

separation of powers. The division of governmental authority into three branches — legislative, executive, and judicial — each with specified powers and duties on which neither of the other branches can encroach; the constitutional doctrine of checks and balances. Cf. DIVISION OF POWERS.

separation of witnesses. The exclusion of witnesses (other than the plaintiff and defendant) from the courtroom to prevent them from hearing the testimony of others.

sequester (si-**kwes**-tər), *n.* **1.** An across-the-board cut in government spending. **2.** A person with whom litigants deposit property being contested until the case has concluded; a sequestrator.

sequester, *vb.* **1.** To seize (property) by a writ of sequestration. **2.** To segregate or isolate (a jury or witness) during trial.

sequestration (see-kwes-**tray**-shən), *n.* **1.** The process by which property is removed from the possessor pending the outcome of a dispute in which two or more parties contend for it. Cf. ATTACHMENT (1); GARNISHMENT. **2.** The setting apart of a decedent's personal property when no one has been willing to act as a personal representative for the estate. **3.** A judicial writ commanding the sheriff or other officer to seize the goods of a person named in the writ. • This writ is sometimes issued against a civil defendant who has defaulted or has acted in contempt of court. **4.** The court-ordered seizure of a bankrupt's estate for the benefit of creditors. **5.** The freezing of a government agency's funds; SEQUESTER (1). **6.** Custodial isolation of a trial jury to prevent tampering and exposure to publicity, or of witnesses to prevent them from hearing the testimony of others.

sequestrator (see-kwes-tray-tər). **1.** An officer appointed to execute a writ of sequestration. **2.** A person who holds property in sequestration.

serendipity doctrine. *Criminal procedure.* The principle that all evidence discovered during a lawful search is eligible to be admitted into evidence at trial.

serial bond. See BOND (3).

serial murder. See MURDER.

serial violation. *Civil-rights law.* The practice by an employer of committing a series of discriminatory acts against an employee, all of which arise out of the same discriminatory intent or animus. • Such a series of discriminatory acts will usually be considered a continuing violation. Cf. SYSTEMATIC VIOLATION.

seriatim opinion. See OPINION (1).

series bond. See BOND (3).

serious felony. See FELONY.

serious misdemeanor. See MISDEMEANOR.

serious offense. See OFFENSE.

serological test (seer-ə-**loj**-ə-kəl). A blood examination to detect the presence of antibodies and antigens, as well as other characteristics, esp. as indicators of disease. • Many states require serological tests to determine the presence of venereal disease in a couple applying for a marriage license. See BLOOD TEST.

servant. A person who is employed by another to do work under the control and directions of the employer. See EMPLOYEE.

serve, *vb.* **1.** To make legal delivery of (a notice or process) <a copy of the pleading was served on all interested parties>. **2.** To present (a person) with a notice or process as required by law <the defendant was served with process>.

service, *n.* The formal delivery of a writ, summons, or other legal process or notice.

constructive service. **1.** See *substituted service.* **2.** Service accomplished by a method or circumstance that does not give actual notice.

service by publication. The service of process on an absent or nonresident defendant by publishing a notice in a newspaper or other public medium.

sewer service. Slang. The fraudulent service of process on a debtor by a creditor seeking to obtain a default judgment.

substituted service. Any method of service allowed by law in place of personal service, such as service by mail.

3. The act of doing something useful for a person or company for a fee. **4.** A person or company whose business is to do useful things for others. **5.** An intangible commodity in the form of human effort, such as labor, skill, or advice.

service, *vb.* To provide service for; specif., to make interest payments on (a debt) <service the deficit>.

service life. The period of the expected usefulness of an asset. • It may or may not coincide with the asset's depreciable life for income-tax purposes.

servicemark. A name, phrase, or other device used to identify and distinguish the services of a certain provider. • Servicemarks identify and afford protection to intangible things such as services, as distinguished from the protection already provided for marks affixed to tangible things such as goods and products. Cf. TRADEMARK (1).

servient (**sər**-vee-ənt), *adj.* (Of an estate) subject to a servitude or easement. See *servient estate* under ESTATE.

servient estate. See ESTATE.

servitude. 1. An encumbrance consisting in a right to the limited use of a piece of land without the possession of it; a charge or burden on an estate for another's benefit <the easement by necessity is an equitable servitude>. • The three types of servitudes are easements, licenses, and profits. See EASEMENT; LICENSE; PROFIT (2).

acquired servitude. A servitude that requires a special mode of acquisition before it comes into existence.

additional servitude. A servitude imposed on land taken under an eminent-domain proceeding for a different type of servitude, as when a highway is constructed on land condemned for a public sidewalk.

• A landowner whose land is burdened by an additional servitude is entitled to further compensation.

apparent servitude. *Civil law.* A predial servitude that is manifested by exterior signs or constructions, such as a roadway. Cf. *nonapparent servitude.*

legal servitude. A servitude arising from a legal limitation on a property's use.

mineral servitude. A servitude granting the right to enter another's property to explore for and extract minerals.

natural servitude. A servitude naturally appurtenant to land, requiring no special mode of acquisition. • An example is the right of land, unencumbered by buildings, to the support of the adjoining land.

personal servitude. A servitude granting a specific person certain rights in property.

private servitude. A servitude vested in a particular person. • Examples include a landowner's personal right-of-way over an adjoining piece of land or a right granted to one person to fish in another's lake.

public servitude. A servitude vested in the public at large or in some class of indeterminate individuals. • Examples include the right of the public to a highway over privately owned land and the right to navigate a river the bed of which belongs to some private person.

servitude appurtenant. A servitude that is not merely an encumbrance of one piece of land but is accessory to another piece; the right of using one piece of land for the benefit of another, such as the right of support for a building.

servitude in gross. A servitude that is not accessory to any dominant tenement for whose benefit it exists but is merely an encumbrance on a given piece of land.

urban servitude. A servitude appertaining to the building and construction of houses in a city, such as the right to light and air.

2. The condition of being a servant or slave <under the 15th Amendment, an American citizen's right to vote cannot be denied on account of race, color, or previous condition of servitude>. **3.** The condition of a prisoner who has been sentenced to forced labor <penal servitude>.

involuntary servitude. The condition of one forced to labor — for pay or not — for another by coercion or imprisonment.

session. 1. A sitting together or meeting of a court, legislature, or other deliberative body so that it can conduct business <the court's spring session>. See TERM (5). **2.** The period within any given day during which such a body is assembled and performing its duties <court is in session>.

biennial session. A legislative session held every two years. • Most state legislatures have biennial sessions, usually held in odd-numbered years.

closed session. A session to which parties not directly involved are not admitted.

joint session. The combined meeting of two legislative bodies (such as the House of Representatives and the Senate) to pursue a common agenda.

lame-duck session. A post-election legislative session in which some of the participants are voting during their last days as elected officials. See LAME DUCK.

open session. A session to which parties not directly involved are admitted.

plenary session. A meeting of all the members of a deliberative body, not just a committee.

regular session. A session that takes place at fixed intervals or specified times.

special session. A legislative session, usu. called by the executive, that meets outside its regular term to consider a specific issue or to reduce backlog.

session laws. 1. A body of statutes enacted by a legislature during a particular annual or biennial session. **2.** The softbound booklets containing these statutes.

set-aside, *n.* Something (such as a percentage of funds) that is reserved or put aside for a specific purpose.

set aside, *vb.* (Of a court) to annul or vacate (a judgment, order, etc.) <the judge refused to set aside the default judgment>.

setback, *n. Real estate.* The minimum amount of space required between a lot line and a building line <a 12-foot setback>. • Typically contained in zoning ordinances or deed restrictions, setbacks are designed to ensure that enough light and ventilation reach the property and to keep buildings from being erected too close to property lines.

set down, *vb.* To schedule (a case) for trial or hearing, usu. by making a docket entry.

setoff, *n.* **1.** A defendant's counterdemand against the plaintiff, arising out of a transaction independent of the plaintiff's claim. **2.** A debtor's right to reduce the amount of a debt by any sum the creditor owes the debtor; the counterbalancing sum owed by the creditor. — Also written *set-off.* — **set off,** *vb.* See COUNTERCLAIM; OFFSET. Cf. RECOUPMENT (3).

set out, *vb.* To recite, explain, narrate, or incorporate (facts or circumstances) <set out the terms of the contract>.

set over, *vb.* To transfer or convey (property) <to set over the land to the purchaser>.

setting, *n.* The date and time established by a court for a trial or hearing <the plaintiff sought a continuance of the imminent setting>.

special setting. A preferential setting on a court's calendar, usu. reserved for older cases or cases given priority by law, made either on a party's motion or on the court's own motion. • For example, some jurisdictions authorize a special setting for cases involving a party over the age of 70.

settlement, *n.* **1.** An agreement ending a dispute or lawsuit <the parties reached a settlement the day before trial>. **2.** Payment, satisfaction, or final adjustment <the seller shipped the goods after confirming the buyer's settlement of the account>. **3.** The conveyance of property — or of interests in property — to provide for one or more beneficiaries, usu. members of the settlor's family, in a way that differs from what the beneficiaries would receive as heirs under the statutes of descent and distribution <in marriage settlements, historically, the wife waived her right to claim dower or to succeed to her husband's property>. **4.** *Wills & estates*. The complete execution of an estate by the executor <the settlement of the tycoon's estate was long and complex>. **5.** CLOSING <the settlement on their first home is next Friday>. — **settle,** *vb.*

settlement class. See CLASS (4).

settlement credit. *Civil procedure*. A court's reduction of the amount of a jury verdict — or the effect of the verdict on nonsettling defendants — to account for settlement funds the plaintiff has received from former defendants or from other responsible parties.

settlement-first method. A means by which to apply a settlement credit to a jury verdict, by first reducing the amount of the verdict by subtracting the amount of all settlements the plaintiff has received on the claim, then reducing the remainder by the percentage of the plaintiff's comparative fault. See SETTLEMENT CREDIT. Cf. FAULT-FIRST METHOD.

settler. 1. A person who occupies property with the intent to establish a residence. • The term is usually applied to an early resident of a country or region. **2.** SETTLOR.

settle up, *vb.* To collect, pay, and turn over debts and property (of a decedent, bankrupt, or insolvent business).

settlor (set-lər). A person who makes a settlement of property; esp., one who sets up a trust.

set up, *vb.* To raise (a defense) <the defendant set up the insanity defense on the murder charge>.

Seventeenth Amendment. The constitutional amendment, ratified in 1913, transferring the power to elect U.S. senators from the state legislatures to the states' voters.

Seventh Amendment. The constitutional amendment, ratified with the Bill of Rights in 1791, guaranteeing the right to a jury trial in federal civil cases that are traditionally considered to be suits at common law and that have an amount in controversy exceeding $20.

seven-years'-absence rule. The principle that a person who has been missing without explanation for at least seven years is legally presumed dead. Cf. ENOCH ARDEN LAW.

severability clause. A provision that keeps the remaining provisions of a contract or statute in force if any portion of that contract or statute is judicially declared void or unconstitutional. See *severable contract* under CONTRACT; *severable statute* under STATUTE.

severable contract. See CONTRACT.

severable statute. See STATUTE.

several, *adj.* **1.** (Of a person, place, or thing) more than one or two but not a lot <several witnesses>. **2.** (Of liability, etc.) separate; particular; distinct, but not necessarily independent <a several obligation>. **3.** (Of things, etc.) different; various <several settlement options>.

several liability. See LIABILITY.

several-remedies rule. A procedural rule that tolls a statute of limitations for a plaintiff who has several available forums (such as a workers'-compensation proceeding and the court system) and who timely files in one forum and later proceeds in another forum, as long as the defendant is not prejudiced.

several tenancy. See TENANCY.

severalty (sev-[ə]-rəl-tee). The state or condition of being separate or distinct <the individual landowners held the land in severalty, not as joint tenants>.

severance, *n.* **1.** The act of cutting off; the state of being cut off. **2.** The separation of claims, by the court, of multiple parties either to permit separate actions on each claim or to allow certain interlocutory orders to become final. Cf. *bifurcated trial* under TRIAL. **3.** The termination of a joint tenancy, usu. by converting it into a tenancy in common. **4.** The removal of anything (such as crops or minerals) attached or affixed to real property, making it personal property rather than a part of the land. — **sever,** *vb.* — **severable,** *adj.*

sewer service. See SERVICE.

sex. 1. The sum of the peculiarities of structure and function that distinguish a male from a female organism. **2.** Sexual intercourse. **3.** SEXUAL RELATIONS (2).

sexual abuse. See ABUSE.

sexual battery. See BATTERY.

sexual harassment. A type of employment discrimination consisting in verbal or physical abuse of a sexual nature. See HARASSMENT.

hostile-environment sexual harassment. Sexual harassment in which a work environment is created where an employee is subject to unwelcome verbal or physical sexual behavior that is either severe or pervasive. • This type of harassment might occur, for example, if a group of coworkers repeatedly e-mailed pornographic pictures to a colleague who found the pictures offensive.

quid pro quo sexual harassment. Sexual harassment in which the satisfaction of a sexual demand is used as the basis of an employment decision. • This type of harassment might occur, for example, if a boss fired or demoted an employee who refused to go on a date with the boss.

sexual offense. See OFFENSE.

sexual orientation. A person's predisposition or inclination toward a particular type of sexual activity or behavior; heterosexuality, homosexuality, or bisexuality. • There has been a trend in recent years to make sexual orientation a protected class, especially in employment and hate-crime statutes.

sexual relations. 1. Sexual intercourse. **2.** Physical sexual activity that does not necessarily culminate in intercourse. • Sexual relations usually involve the touching of another's breast, vagina, penis, or anus. Both persons (the toucher and the person touched) engage in sexual relations.

S/F. *abbr.* STATUTE OF FRAUDS.

shadow jury. See JURY.

shakedown. **1.** An extortion of money using threats of violence or, in the case of a police officer, threats of arrest. **2.** See *shakedown search* under SEARCH.

shakedown search. See SEARCH.

shall, *vb.* **1.** Has a duty to; more broadly, is required to <the requester shall send notice> <notice shall be sent>. **2.** Should (as often interpreted by courts) <all claimants shall request mediation>. **3.** May <no person shall enter the building without first signing the roster>. **4.** Will (as a future-tense verb) <the debtor shall then be released from all debts>. **5.** Is entitled to <the secretary shall be reimbursed for all expenses>. • Only sense 1 is acceptable under strict standards of drafting.

sham, *n.* **1.** Something that is not what it seems; a counterfeit. **2.** A person who pretends to be something that he or she is not; a faker. — **sham,** *vb.* — **sham,** *adj.*

sham defense. See DEFENSE (1).

shame sanction. See SANCTION.

sham exception. An exception to the *Noerr–Pennington* doctrine whereby a company that petitions the government will not receive First Amendment protection or an exemption from the antitrust laws if its intent in petitioning the government is really an effort to harm its competitors rather than to obtain favorable governmental action. See NOERR–PENNINGTON DOCTRINE.

sham marriage. See MARRIAGE (1).

sham pleading. See PLEADING (1).

sham prosecution. See PROSECUTION.

sham transaction. An agreement or exchange that has no independent economic benefit or business purpose and is entered into solely to create a tax advantage (such as a deduction for a business loss). • The Internal Revenue Service is entitled to ignore the purported tax benefits of a sham transaction.

share, *n.* **1.** An allotted portion owned by, contributed by, or due to someone <each partner's share of the profits>. **2.** One of the definite number of equal parts into which the capital stock of a corporation or joint-stock company is divided <the broker advised his customer to sell the stock shares when the price reaches $29>. • A share represents an equity or ownership interest in the corporation or joint-stock company. Cf. STOCK (4); SECURITY (4).

share, *vb.* **1.** To divide (something) into portions. **2.** To enjoy or partake of (a power, right, etc.).

share draft. See DRAFT.

shareholder. One who owns or holds a share or shares in a company, esp. a corporation.

sharp, *adj.* (Of a clause in a mortgage, deed, etc.) empowering the creditor to take immediate and summary action upon the debtor's default.

sharp practice. Unethical action and trickery, esp. by a lawyer. — **sharp practitioner,** *n.*

shave, *vb.* **1.** To purchase (a negotiable instrument) at a greater than usual discount rate. **2.** To reduce or deduct from (a price).

shell corporation. See CORPORATION.

Shelley's Case, Rule in. See RULE IN SHELLEY'S CASE.

shelter doctrine. *Commercial law.* The principle that a person to whom a holder in due course has transferred commercial paper, as well as any later transferee, will succeed to the rights of the holder in due course. • As a result, transferees of holders in due course are generally not subject to defenses against the payment of an instrument. This doctrine ensures the free transferability of commercial paper. Its name derives from the idea that the transferees "take shelter" in the rights of the holder in due course.

shepardize, *vb.* **1.** (*often cap.*) To determine the subsequent history of (a case) by using *Shepard's Citators*. **2.** Loosely, to check the precedential value of (a case) by the same or similar means. — **shepardization,** *n.* — **shepardizing,** *n.*

Sherman Antitrust Act. A federal statute, passed in 1890, that prohibits direct or indirect interference with the freely competitive interstate production and distribution of goods. • This Act was amended by the Clayton Act in 1914. 15 USCA §§ 1–7. — Often shortened to *Sherman Act*.

Sherman–Sorrells **doctrine.** The principle that a defendant may claim as an affirmative defense that he or she was not disposed to commit the offense until a public official (often an undercover police officer) encouraged the defendant to do so. • This entrapment defense, which is recognized in the federal system and a majority of states, was developed in *Sherman v. United States*, 356 U.S. 369, 78 S.Ct. 819 (1958), and *Sorrells v. United States*, 287 U.S. 435, 53 S.Ct. 210 (1932). See ENTRAPMENT. Cf. HYPOTHETICAL-PERSON DEFENSE.

shield law. **1.** A statute that affords journalists the privilege not to reveal confidential sources. See *journalist's privilege* under PRIVILEGE (3). **2.** A statute that restricts or prohibits the use, in rape or sexual-assault cases, of evidence about the past sexual conduct of the victim.

shifting, *adj.* (Of a position, place, etc.) changing or passing from one to another <a shifting estate>.

shifting clause. At common law, a clause under the Statute of Uses prescribing a substituted mode of devolution in the settlement of an estate.

shifting the burden of proof. In litigation, the transference of the duty to prove a fact from one party to the other; the passing of the duty to produce evidence in a case from one side to another as the case progresses, when one side has made a prima facie showing on a point of evidence, requiring the other side to rebut it by contradictory evidence. See BURDEN OF PROOF.

shifting use. See USE.

shipment contract. See CONTRACT.

shock incarceration. Incarceration in a military-type setting, usu. for three to six months, during which the offender is subjected to strict discipline, physical exercise, and hard labor. • Upon successful completion of the program, the offender is placed on probation. Cf. *shock probation* under PROBATION.

shop, *n.* A business establishment or place of employment; a factory, office, or other place of business.

shop-book rule. *Evidence.* An exception to the hearsay rule permitting the admission into evidence of original bookkeeping records if the books' entries were made in the ordinary course of business and the books are introduced by somebody who maintains them.

shop books. Records of original entry maintained in the usual course of business by a shopkeeper, trader, or other businessperson.

shoplifting, *n.* Theft of merchandise from a store or business; specif., larceny of goods from a commercial establishment by willfully taking and concealing the merchandise with the intention of converting the goods to one's personal use without paying the purchase price. — **shoplift,** *vb.* See LARCENY.

shop-right doctrine. The principle that an employer is entitled to a nonexclusive free license to use an employee's invention that the employee developed in the course of employment while using the employer's materials.

shore. 1. Land lying between the lines of high- and low-water mark; lands bordering on the shores of navigable waters below the line of ordinary high water. **2.** Land adjacent to a body of water regardless of whether it is below or above the ordinary high-or low-water mark.

short lease. See LEASE.

short-term loan. See LOAN.

short title. See TITLE (4).

shotgun pleading. See PLEADING (1).

show, *vb.* To make (facts, etc.) apparent or clear by evidence; to prove.

show-cause order. See ORDER.

show-cause proceeding. A usu. expedited proceeding on a show-cause order.

showing, *n.* The act or an instance of establishing through evidence and argument; proof <a prima facie showing>.

show trial. A trial, usu. in a nondemocratic country, that is staged primarily for propagandistic purposes, with the outcome predetermined.

showup, *n.* A pretrial identification procedure in which a suspect is confronted with a witness to or the victim of a crime. • Unlike a lineup, a showup is a one-on-one confrontation. Cf. LINEUP.

shrinkage. The reduction in inventory caused by theft, breakage, or waste.

shrink-wrap license. See LICENSE.

shutdown. A cessation of work production, esp. in a factory.

shyster (**shɪs**-tər). A person (esp. a lawyer) whose business affairs are unscrupulous, deceitful, or unethical.

sic (sik). [Latin "so, thus"] Spelled or used as written. • *Sic*, invariably bracketed and often set in italics, is used to indicate that a preceding word or phrase in a quoted passage is reproduced as it appeared in the original document <"that case peeked [*sic*] the young lawyer's interest">.

side, *n.* **1.** The position of a person or group opposing another <the law is on our side>. **2.** Either of two parties in a transaction or dispute <both sides put on a strong case>.

sidebar. 1. A position at the side of a judge's bench where counsel can confer with the judge beyond the jury's earshot <the judge called the attorneys to sidebar>. **2.** SIDEBAR CONFERENCE <during the sidebar, the prosecutor accused the defense attorney of misconduct>. **3.** A short, secondary article within or accompanying a main story in a publication <the sidebar contained information on related topics>.

sidebar comment. An unnecessary, often argumentative remark made by an attorney or witness, esp. during a trial or deposition.

sidebar conference. 1. A discussion among the judge and counsel, usu. over an evidentiary objection, outside the jury's hearing. **2.** A discussion, esp. during voir dire, between the judge and a juror or prospective juror.

side reports. 1. Unofficial volumes of case reports. **2.** Collections of cases omitted from the official reports.

sight. A drawee's acceptance of a draft <payable after sight>. • The term *after sight* means "after acceptance."

sight draft. See DRAFT.

sign, *vb.* **1.** To identify (a record) by means of a signature, mark, or other symbol with the intent to authenticate it as an act or agreement of the person identifying it <both parties signed the contract>. **2.** To agree with or join <the commissioner signed on for a four-year term>.

signal. In the citation of legal authority, an abbreviation or notation supplied to indicate how the authority relates to the proposition. • For example, according to the *Bluebook*, the signal *See* means that the cited authority directly states or supports the proposition, while Cf. means that the cited authority supports a proposition analogous to (but in some way different from) the main proposition.

signatory (**sig**-nə-tor-ee), *n.* A party that signs a document, personally or through an agent, and thereby becomes a party to an agreement <eight countries are signatories to the treaty>. — **signatory,** *adj.*

signature. 1. A person's name or a mark written by that person or at the person's direction. **2.** *Commercial law.* A name, mark, or writing used with the intention of authenticating a document. UCC §§ 1–201(39), 3–401(b).

digital signature. A secure digital code attached to an electronically transmitted message that uniquely identifies and authenticates the sender. • Digital signatures are especially important for electronic commerce and are a key component of many electronic message-authentication schemes. Several states have passed legislation recognizing the legality of digital signatures. See E-COMMERCE.

facsimile signature. **1.** A signature that has been prepared and reproduced by mechanical or photographic means. **2.** A signature on a document that has been transmitted by a facsimile machine. See FAX.

unauthorized signature. A signature made without actual, implied, or apparent authority. • It includes a forgery. UCC § 1–201(43).

signature card. A financial-institution record consisting of a customer's signature and other information that assists the institution in monitoring financial transactions, as by comparing the signature on the record with signatures on checks, withdrawal slips, and other documents.

signature crime. See CRIME.

signature evidence. See EVIDENCE.

signature loan. See LOAN.

signed, sealed, and delivered. In a certificate of acknowledgment, a statement that the instrument was executed by the person acknowledging it.

silence, *n.* **1.** A restraint from speaking. • In criminal law, silence includes an arrestee's statements expressing the desire not to speak and requesting an attorney. **2.** A failure to reveal something required by law to be revealed. See *estoppel by silence* under ESTOPPEL. — **silent,** *adj.*

silent partner. See PARTNER.

silent record. See RECORD.

silent-witness theory. *Evidence.* A method of authenticating and admitting evidence (such as a photograph), without the need for a witness to verify its authenticity, upon a sufficient showing of the reliability of the process of producing the evidence, including proof that the evidence has not been altered.

silver-platter doctrine. *Criminal procedure.* The principle that a federal court could admit evidence obtained illegally by a state police officer as long as a federal officer did not participate in or request the search. • The Supreme Court rejected this doctrine in *Elkins v. United States*, 364 U.S. 206, 80 S.Ct. 1437 (1960).

similar happenings. *Evidence.* Events that occur at a time different from the time in dispute and are therefore usu. inadmissible except to the extent that they provide relevant information on issues that would be fairly constant, such as the control of and conditions on land on the day in question.

similiter (si-**mil**-i-tər). [Latin "similarly"] *Common-law pleading.* A party's written acceptance of an opponent's issue or argument; a set form of words by which a party accepts or joins in an issue of fact tendered by the other side.

simple, *adj.* **1.** (Of a crime) not accompanied by aggravating circumstances. Cf. AGGRAVATED (1). **2.** (Of an estate or fee) inheritable by the owner's heirs with no conditions concerning tail. **3.** (Of a contract) not made under seal.

simple agreement. See AGREEMENT.

simple battery. See BATTERY.

simple interest. See INTEREST (3).

simple kidnapping. See KIDNAPPING.

simple larceny. See LARCENY.

simple obligation. See OBLIGATION.

simple resolution. See RESOLUTION.

simple robbery. See ROBBERY.

simpliciter (sim-**plis**-i-tər), *adv.* [Latin] **1.** In a simple or summary manner; simply. **2.** Absolutely; unconditionally; per se.

simulated fact. A fabricated fact intended to mislead; a lie.

simultaneous death. See DEATH.

simultaneous-death act. See UNIFORM SIMULTANEOUS DEATH ACT.

simultaneous-death clause. A testamentary provision mandating that if the testator and beneficiary die in a common disaster, or the order of their deaths is otherwise unascertainable, the testator is presumed to have survived the beneficiary. • If the beneficiary is the testator's spouse, an express exception is often made so that the spouse with the smaller estate is presumed to have survived. See *simultaneous death* under DEATH.

sine (**sɪ**-nee *or* **sin**-ay), *prep.* [Latin] Without.

sine die (**sɪ**-nee **dɪ**-ee *or* **dɪ** *or* **sin**-ay **dee**-ay). [Latin "without day"] With no day being assigned (as for resumption of a meeting or hearing). See GO HENCE WITHOUT DAY.

sine qua non (**sɪ**-nee kway **non** *or* **sin**-ay kwah **nohn**), *n.* [Latin "without which not"] An indispensable condition or thing; something on which something else necessarily depends.

single-date-of-removal doctrine. *Civil procedure.* The principle that the deadline for removing a case from state court to federal court is 30 days from the day that any defendant receives a copy of the state-court pleading on which the removal is based. • If a later-served defendant seeks to remove a case to federal court more than 30 days after the day any other defendant received the pleading, the removal is untimely even if made within 30 days after the removing defendant received the pleading. One theory underlying this doctrine is that all defendants must consent to remove a case to federal court, and a defendant who has waited longer than 30 days to remove does not have the capacity to consent to removal. 28 USCA § 1446(b). See NOTICE OF REMOVAL.

single-juror instruction. See JURY INSTRUCTION.

single-larceny doctrine. *Criminal law.* The principle that the taking of different items of property belonging to either the same or different owners at the same time and place constitutes one act of larceny if the theft is part of one larcenous plan, as when it involves essentially one continuous act or if control over the property is exercised simultaneously. • The intent of the thief determines the number of occurrences.

single obligation. See OBLIGATION.

single original. An instrument executed singly, not in duplicate.

singular title. See TITLE (2).

sinking fund. See FUND.

sinking-fund debenture. See DEBENTURE.

sin tax. See TAX.

sit, *vb.* **1.** (Of a judge) to occupy a judicial seat <Judge Wilson sits on the trial court for the Eastern District of Arkansas>. **2.** (Of a judge) to hold court or perform official functions <is the judge sitting this week?>. **3.** (Of a court or legislative body) to hold proceedings <the U.S. Supreme Court sits from October to June>.

site plan. A proposal for the development or use of a particular piece of real property. • Some zoning ordinances require a developer to present a site plan to the city council, and to receive council approval, before certain projects may be completed.

sitting, *n.* A court session; esp., a session of an appellate court. See SESSION.

en banc sitting. A court session in which all the judges (or a quorum) participate. See EN BANC.

in camera sitting. A court session conducted by a judge in chambers or elsewhere outside the courtroom. See IN CAMERA.

situational offender. See OFFENDER.

situs (sɪ-təs). [Latin] The location or position (of something) for legal purposes, as in *lex situs,* the law of the place where the thing in issue is situated. See LOCUS.

Sixteenth Amendment. The constitutional amendment, ratified in 1913, allowing Congress to tax income.

Sixth Amendment. The constitutional amendment, ratified with the Bill of Rights in 1791, guaranteeing in criminal cases the right to a speedy and public trial by jury, the right to be informed of the nature of the accusation, the right to confront witnesses, the right to counsel, and the right to compulsory process for obtaining favorable witnesses.

S.J.D. See DOCTOR OF JURIDICAL SCIENCE.

skip person. *Tax.* A beneficiary who is more than one generation removed from the transferor and to whom assets are conveyed in a generation-skipping transfer. IRC (26 USCA) § 2613(a). See GENERATION-SKIPPING TRANSFER. Cf. NONSKIP PERSON.

skiptracing agency. A service that locates persons (such as delinquent debtors or missing heirs, witnesses, or stockholders) or missing assets (such as bank accounts).

S.L. *abbr.* **1.** Session law. See SESSION LAWS. **2.** Statute law.

slamming. The practice by which a long-distance telephone company wrongfully appropriates a customer's service from another company, usu. through an unauthorized transfer or by way of a transfer authorization that is disguised as something else, such as a form to sign up for a free vacation.

slander, *n.* **1.** A defamatory statement expressed in a transitory form, esp. speech. • Damages for slander — unlike those for libel — are not presumed and thus must be proved by the plaintiff (unless the defamation is slander per se). **2.** The act of making such a statement. — **slander,** *vb.* — **slanderous,** *adj.* See DEFAMATION. Cf. LIBEL (1).

slander per quod. Slander that does not qualify as slander per se, thus forcing the plaintiff to prove special damages.

slander per se. Slander for which special damages need not be proved because it imputes to the plaintiff any one of the following: (1) a crime involving moral turpitude, (2) a loathsome disease (such as a sexually transmitted disease), (3) conduct that would adversely affect one's business or profession, or (4) unchastity (esp. of a woman).

slanderer, *n.* One who commits slander.

slander of title. A false statement, made orally or in writing, that casts doubt on another person's ownership of property. See DISPARAGEMENT.

slayer rule. The doctrine that neither a person who kills another nor the killer's heirs can share in the decedent's estate.

slight care. See CARE.

slight diligence. See DILIGENCE.

slight evidence. See EVIDENCE.

slight-evidence rule. 1. The doctrine providing that, when there is evidence establishing the existence of a conspiracy between at least two other people, the prosecution need only offer slight evidence of a defendant's knowing participation or intentional involvement in the conspiracy to secure a conviction. • This rule was first announced in *Tomplain v. United States*, 42 F.2d 202, 203 (5th Cir. 1930). In the 1970s, the rule became widespread, but it has since been widely criticized and, in most circuits, abolished. **2.** The doctrine that only slight evidence of a defendant's participation in a conspiracy need be offered in order to admit a coconspirator's out-of-court statement under the coconspirator exception to the hearsay rule. See Fed. R. Evid. 801(d)(2)(E).

slight negligence. See NEGLIGENCE.

slip-and-fall case. 1. A lawsuit brought by a plaintiff for injuries sustained in slipping and falling, usu. on the defendant's property. **2.** Loosely, any minor case in tort.

slip law. An individual pamphlet in which a single enactment is printed immediately after its passage but before its inclusion in the general laws (such as the session laws or the *U.S. Statutes at Large*).

slip opinion. See OPINION (1).

Small Business Administration. A federal agency that assists and protects the interests of small businesses, often by making low-interest loans. — Abbr. SBA.

small-business corporation. See CORPORATION.

small-claims court. See COURT.

small-estate probate. See PROBATE.

Smith Act. A 1948 federal antisedition law that criminalizes advocating the forcible or violent overthrow of the government. 18 USCA § 2385.

smoking gun. A piece of physical or documentary evidence that conclusively impeaches an adversary on an outcome-determinative issue or destroys the adversary's credibility.

smuggling, *n.* The crime of importing or exporting illegal articles or articles on which duties have not been paid. — **smuggle,** *vb.* See CONTRABAND.

So. *abbr.* SOUTHERN REPORTER.

sober, *adj.* **1.** (Of a person) not under the influence of drugs or alcohol. **2.** (Of a person) regularly abstinent or moderate in the use of intoxicating liquors. **3.** (Of a situation, person, etc.) serious; grave. **4.** (Of facts, arguments, etc.) basic; unexaggerated. **5.** (Of a person) rational; having self-control.

sobriety checkpoint. A part of a roadway at which police officers maintain a roadblock to stop motorists and ascertain whether the drivers are intoxicated.

sobriety test. A method of determining whether a person is intoxicated. • Among the common sobriety tests are coordination tests and the use of mechanical devices to measure the blood alcohol content of a person's breath sample. See BREATHALYZER; HORIZONTAL-GAZE NYSTAGMUS TEST.

field sobriety test. A motor-skills test administered by a peace officer during a stop to determine whether a suspect has been driving while intoxicated. • The test usually involves checking the suspect's speaking ability or coordination (as by reciting the alphabet or walking in a straight line).

social contract. The express or implied agreement between citizens and their government by which individuals agree to surrender certain freedoms in exchange for mutual protection; an agreement forming the foundation of a political society.

social guest. See LICENSEE (2).

social harm. See HARM.

social justice. See JUSTICE (1).

Social Security Act. A federal law, originally established in 1935 in response to the Great Depression, creating a system of benefits, including old-age and survivors' benefits, and establishing the Social Security Administration. 42 USCA §§ 401–433. See OLD-AGE AND SURVIVORS' INSURANCE.

Social Security Administration. A federal agency created by the Social Security Act to institute a national program of social insurance. — Abbr. SSA.

society. 1. A community of people, as of a state, nation, or locality, with common cultures, traditions, and interests. **2.** An association or company of persons (usu. unincorporated) united by mutual consent, to deliberate, determine, and act jointly for a common purpose. **3.** The general love, affection, and companionship that family members share with one another.

sociological jurisprudence. See JURISPRUDENCE.

sociopath, *n.* See PSYCHOPATH. — **sociopathic,** *adj.* — **sociopathy,** *n.*

Socratic method. A technique of philosophical discussion — and of law-school instruction — by which the questioner (a law professor) questions one or more followers (the law students), building on each answer with another question, esp. an analogy incorporating the answer. • Named for the Greek philosopher Socrates (469–399 B.C.), the method is traditional in law schools, primarily because it forces students to think through issues rationally and deductively — a skill required in the practice of law. Most law professors who employ this method call on students randomly, an approach designed to teach students to think quickly, without stage fright.

SODDI defense (**sahd**-ee). *Slang*. The some-other-dude-did-it defense; a claim that somebody else committed a crime, usu. made by a criminal defendant who cannot identify the third party.

sodomy (**sod**-ə-mee), *n*. **1.** Oral or anal copulation between humans, esp. those of the same sex. **2.** Oral or anal copulation between a human and an animal; bestiality. — **sodomize,** *vb*. — **sodomitic,** *adj*. — **sodomist, sodomite,** *n*. Cf. PEDERASTY.

aggravated sodomy. Criminal sodomy that involves force or results in serious bodily injury to the victim in addition to mental injury and emotional distress. • Some laws provide that sodomy involving a minor is automatically aggravated sodomy.

SOF. *abbr*. STATUTE OF FRAUDS.

solar easement. See EASEMENT.

sole-actor doctrine. *Agency*. The rule charging a principal with knowledge of the agent's actions, even if the agent acted fraudulently.

sole and unconditional owner. See OWNER.

sole cause. See CAUSE (1).

sole custody. See CUSTODY (2).

solemnity (sə-**lem**-nə-tee). **1.** A formality (such as a ceremony) required by law to validate an agreement or action <solemnity of marriage>. **2.** The state of seriousness or solemn respectfulness or observance <solemnity of contract>.

solemnity of contract. The concept that two people may enter into any contract they wish and that the resulting contract is enforceable if formalities are observed and no defenses exist.

solemnize (**sol**-əm-nɪz), *vb*. To enter into (a marriage, contract, etc.) by a formal act, usu. before witnesses. — **solemnization** (sol-əm-ni-**zay**-shən), *n*.

solemn occasion. In some states, the serious and unusual circumstance in which the supreme court is constitutionally permitted to render advisory opinions to the remaining branches of government, as when the legislature doubts the legality of proposed legislation and a determination must be made to allow the legislature to exercise its functions. • Some factors that have been considered in determining whether a solemn occasion exists include whether an important question of law is presented, whether the question is urgent, whether the matter is ripe for an opinion, and whether the court has enough time to consider the question.

sole practitioner. A lawyer who practices law without any partners or associates. — Often shortened to *solo.*

sole proprietorship. 1. A business in which one person owns all the assets, owes all the liabilities, and operates in his or her personal capacity. **2.** Ownership of such a business.

solicitation, *n.* **1.** The act or an instance of requesting or seeking to obtain something; a request or petition. **2.** The criminal offense of urging, advising, commanding, or otherwise inciting another to commit a crime. • Solicitation is an inchoate offense distinct from the solicited crime. Under the Model Penal Code, a defendant is guilty of solicitation even if the command or urging was not actually communicated to the solicited person, as long as it was designed to be communicated. Model Penal Code § 5.02(2). Cf. ATTEMPT. **3.** An offer to pay or accept money in exchange for sex. Cf. PATRONIZING A PROSTITUTE. **4.** An attempt or effort to gain business. • The Model Rules of Professional Conduct place certain prohibitions on lawyers' direct solicitation of potential clients. — **solicit,** *vb.*

solicitor. 1. A person who seeks business or contributions from others; an advertiser or promoter. **2.** A person who conducts matters on another's behalf; an agent or representative. **3.** The chief law officer of a governmental body or a municipality. **4.** A prosecutor (in some jurisdictions, such as South Carolina). **5.** In the United Kingdom, a lawyer who consults with clients and prepares legal documents but is not generally heard in court unless specifically licensed. Cf. BARRISTER.

solicitor general. The second-highest-ranking legal officer in a government (after the attorney general); esp., the chief courtroom lawyer for the executive branch. Pl. **solicitors general.**

solidarity. The state of being jointly and severally liable (as for a debt).

solidary (sol-ə-der-ee), *adj.* (Of a liability or obligation) joint and several. See JOINT AND SEVERAL.

solitary confinement. Separate confinement that gives a prisoner extremely limited access to other people; esp., the complete isolation of a prisoner.

solo. See SOLE PRACTITIONER.

solvency, *n.* The ability to pay debts as they come due. — **solvent,** *adj.* Cf. INSOLVENCY.

somnambulism (sahm-**nam**-byə-liz-əm). Sleepwalking. • Generally, a person will not be held criminally responsible for an act performed while in this state.

somnolentia (sahm-nə-**len**-shee-ə), *n.* **1.** The state of drowsiness. **2.** A condition of incomplete sleep resembling drunkenness, during which part of the faculties are abnormally excited while the others are dormant; the combined condition of sleeping and wakefulness producing a temporary state of involuntary intoxication. • To the extent that it destroys moral agency, somnolentia may be a defense to a criminal charge.

Son-of-Sam law. A state statute that prohibits a convicted criminal from profiting by selling his or her story rights to a publisher or filmmaker. • State law usually authorizes prosecutors to seize royalties from a convicted criminal and to place the money in an escrow account for the crime victim's benefit. This type of law was first enacted in New York in 1977, in response to the lucrative book deals that publishers offered David Berkowitz, the serial killer who called himself "Son of Sam." In 1992, the U.S. Supreme Court declared New York's Son-of-Sam law unconstitutional as a content-based speech regulation, prompting many states to amend their laws in an attempt to avoid constitutionality problems. *Simon & Schuster, Inc. v. New York State Crime Victims Bd.*, 502 U.S. 105, 112 S.Ct. 501 (1992).

sororicide (sə-**ror**-ə-sɪd). **1.** The act of killing one's own sister. **2.** A person who kills his or her sister.

sound, *adj.* **1.** (Of health, mind, etc.) good; whole; free from disease or disorder. **2.** (Of property) good; marketable. **3.** (Of discretion) exercised equitably under the circumstances. — **soundness,** *n.*

sound, *vb.* **1.** To be actionable (in) <her claims for physical injury sound in tort, not in contract>. **2.** To be recoverable (in) <his tort action sounds in damages, not in equitable relief>.

source of law. Something (such as a constitution, treaty, statute, or custom) that provides authority for legislation and for judicial decisions; a point of origin for law or legal analysis.

South Eastern Reporter. A set of regional lawbooks that, being part of the West Group's National Reporter System, contain every published decision from Georgia, North Carolina, South Carolina, Virginia, and West Virginia, from 1887 to date. • The first series ran from 1887 to 1939; the second series is the current one. — Abbr. S.E.; S.E.2d.

Southern Reporter. A set of regional lawbooks that, being part of the West Group's National Reporter System, contain every published decision from Alabama, Florida, Louisiana, and Mississippi, from 1887 to date. • The first series ran from 1887 to 1941; the second series is the current one. — Abbr. So.; So.2d.

South Western Reporter. A set of regional lawbooks that, being part of the West Group's National Reporter System, contain every published decision from Arkansas, Kentucky, Missouri, Tennessee, and Texas, from 1886 to date. • The first series ran from 1886 to 1928; the second series ran from 1928 to 1999; the third series is the current one. — Abbr. S.W.; S.W.2d.; S.W.3d.

sovereign, *n.* **1.** A person, body, or state vested with independent and supreme authority. **2.** The ruler of an independent state. See SOVEREIGNTY.

sovereign immunity. See IMMUNITY (1).

sovereign people. The political body consisting of the collective number of citizens and qualified electors who possess the powers of sovereignty and exercise them through their chosen representatives.

sovereign power. The power to make and enforce laws.

sovereign right. A unique right possessed by a state or its agencies that enables it to carry out its official functions for the public benefit, as distinguished from certain proprietary rights that it may possess like any other private person.

sovereign state. 1. A state that possesses an independent existence, being complete in itself, without being merely part of a larger whole to whose government it is subject. **2.** A political community whose members are bound together by the tie of common subjection to some central authority, whose commands those members must obey.

sovereignty (sahv-[ə-]rin-tee). **1.** Supreme dominion, authority, or rule. **2.** The supreme political authority of an independent state. **3.** The state itself.

s.p. *abbr.* Same principle; same point. • This notation, when inserted between two citations, indicates that the second involves the same principles as the first.

speaking demurrer. See DEMURRER.

speaking motion. See MOTION.

speaking objection. See OBJECTION.

speaking statute. See STATUTE.

special, *adj.* **1.** Of, relating to, or designating a species, kind, or individual thing. **2.** (Of a statute, rule, etc.) designed for a particular purpose. **3.** (Of powers, etc.) unusual; extraordinary.

special administration. See ADMINISTRATION.

special administrator. See ADMINISTRATOR.

special agency. See AGENCY (1).

special appearance. See APPEARANCE.

special authority. See AUTHORITY (1).

special benefit. See BENEFIT.

special case. See *case reserved* under CASE.

special counsel. See COUNSEL.

special count. See COUNT.

special covenant against encumbrances. See COVENANT (3).

special demurrer. See DEMURRER.

special deterrence. See DETERRENCE.

special-duty doctrine. *Torts.* The rule that a governmental entity (such as a state or municipality) can be held liable for an individual plaintiff's injury when the entity owed a duty to the plaintiff but not to the general public. • This is an exception to the public-duty doctrine. The special-duty doctrine applies only when the plaintiff has reasonably relied on the governmental entity's assumption of the duty. See PUBLIC-DUTY DOCTRINE.

special exception. 1. A party's objection to the form rather than the substance of an opponent's claim, such as an objection for vagueness or ambiguity. See DEMURRER. Cf. *general exception* (1) under EXCEPTION (1). **2.** An allowance in a zoning ordinance for special uses that are considered essential and are not fundamentally incompatible with the original zoning regulations. Cf. VARIANCE (2).

special executor. See EXECUTOR.

special grand jury. See GRAND JURY.

special guaranty. See GUARANTY.

special guardian. See GUARDIAN.

special indorsement. See INDORSEMENT.

special instruction. See JURY INSTRUCTION.

special interrogatory. See INTERROGATORY.

special issue. See ISSUE (1).

special judge. See JUDGE.

special jury. See JURY.

special limitation. See LIMITATION.

special master. See MASTER.

special matter. See MATTER.

special motion. See MOTION.

special-needs analysis. *Criminal procedure*. A balancing test used by the Supreme Court to determine whether certain searches (such as administrative, civil-based, or public-safety searches) impose unreasonably on individual rights.

special occupant. See OCCUPANT.

special owner. See OWNER.

special plea. See PLEA (3).

special pleading. 1. The common-law system of pleading that required the parties to exchange a series of court papers (such as replications, rebutters, and surrebutters) setting out their contentions in accordance with hypertechnical rules before a case could be tried. • Often, therefore, cases were decided on points of pleading and not on the merits. **2.** The art of drafting pleadings under this system. **3.** An instance of drafting such a pleading. **4.** A responsive pleading that does more than merely deny allegations, as by introducing new matter to justify an otherwise blameworthy act. **5.** An argument that is unfairly slanted toward the speaker's viewpoint because it omits unfavorable facts or authorities and develops only favorable ones.

special plea in bar. See PLEA IN BAR.

special plea in error. At common law, a plea alleging some extraneous matter as a ground for defeating a writ of error (such as a release or expiration of the time within which error can be brought), to which the plaintiff in error must reply or demur.

special power. See POWER.

special power of appointment. See *limited power of appointment* under POWER OF APPOINTMENT.

special power of attorney. See POWER OF ATTORNEY.

special prayer. See PRAYER FOR RELIEF.

special privilege. See PRIVILEGE (1).

special proceeding. See PROCEEDING.

special prosecutor. See PROSECUTOR.

special reference. See REFERENCE.

special relationship. A nonfiduciary relationship having an element of trust, arising esp. when one person trusts another to exercise a reasonable degree of care and the other knows or ought to know about the reliance. Cf. FIDUCIARY RELATIONSHIP.

special-relationship doctrine. The principle that when a state assumes control over a person (as in an involuntary hospitalization or custody), the state has an affirmative duty to protect that person and may be liable for harm inflicted on the person by a third party. • This is an exception to the general principle prohibiting members of the public from suing state employees for failing to protect them from third parties. Cf. DANGER-CREATION DOCTRINE.

special retainer. See RETAINER.

special session. See SESSION.

special setting. See SETTING.

special statute. See STATUTE.

special tax. See TAX.

special term. See TERM (5).

special traverse. See TRAVERSE.

specialty. 1. See *contract under seal* under CONTRACT. **2.** *Eminent domain.* Unique property (such as a church or cemetery) that is essentially not marketable, so that its value for condemnation purposes is determined by measuring the property's reproduction cost less any depreciation.

specialty bar. See BAR ASSOCIATION.

special-use valuation. See VALUATION.

special verdict. See VERDICT.

special warranty. See WARRANTY (2).

special warranty deed. See DEED.

specification. 1. The act of making a detailed statement, esp. of the measurements, quality, materials, or other items to be provided under a contract. **2.** The statement so made. **3.** The acquisition of title to materials belonging to another person by converting those materials into a new and different form, as by changing grapes into wine, lumber into shelving, or corn into liquor. • The effect is that the original owner of the materials loses the property rights in them and is left with a right of action for their original value.

specific bequest. See BEQUEST.

specific denial. See DENIAL.

specific devise. See DEVISE.

specific guaranty. See GUARANTY.

specific intent. See INTENT (1).

specific-intent defense. *Criminal law.* A defendant's claim that he or she did not have the capacity (often supposedly because of intoxication or mental illness) to form the mental state necessary for committing the crime alleged.

specific jurisdiction. See JURISDICTION.

specific legacy. See LEGACY.

specific legatee. See LEGATEE.

specific objection. See OBJECTION.

specific performance. A court-ordered remedy that requires precise fulfillment of a legal or contractual obligation when monetary damages are inappropriate or inadequate, as when the sale of real estate or a rare article is involved. • Specific performance is an equitable remedy that lies within the court's discretion to award whenever the common-law remedy is insufficient, either because damages would be inadequate or because the damages could not possibly be established.

specific remedy. See REMEDY.

specific tax. See TAX.

spectrograph. An electromagnetic machine that analyzes sound, esp. a human voice, by separating and mapping it into elements of frequency, time lapse, and intensity (represented by a series of horizontal and vertical bar lines) to produce a final voiceprint. See VOICEPRINT.

speculation, *n.* **1.** The buying or selling of something with the expectation of profiting from price fluctuations. **2.** The act or practice of theorizing about matters over which there is no certain knowledge. — **speculate,** *vb.* — **speculative,** *adj.*

speculative damages. See DAMAGES.

speech. The expression or communication of thoughts or opinions in spoken words; something spoken or uttered. See FREEDOM OF SPEECH.

commercial speech. Communication (such as advertising and marketing) that involves only the commercial interests of the speaker and the audience, and is therefore afforded lesser First Amendment protection than social, political, or religious speech. Cf. *pure speech.*

corporate speech. Speech deriving from a corporation. • It does not lose First Amendment protection merely because of its corporate source.

hate speech. Speech that carries no meaning other than the expression of hatred for some group, such as a particular race, esp. in circumstances in which the communication is likely to provoke violence. Cf. *group libel* under LIBEL.

pure speech. Words or conduct limited in form to what is necessary to convey the idea. • This type of speech is given the greatest constitutional protection. Cf. *commercial speech*; *symbolic speech.*

seditious speech. Speech advocating the violent overthrow of government. See SEDITION.

symbolic speech. Conduct that expresses opinions or thoughts, such as flag-burning or the wearing of a black armband. • Symbolic speech does not enjoy the same degree of constitutional protection that pure speech does. Cf. *pure speech.*

Speech or Debate Clause. The clause of the U.S. Constitution giving members of Congress immunity for statements made during debate in either the House or the Senate. • This immunity is extended to other areas where it is necessary to prevent impairment of deliberations and other legitimate legislative activities, such as subpoenaing bank records for an investigation. U.S. Const. art. I, § 6, cl. 1. See *congressional immunity* under IMMUNITY (1).

speedy remedy. See REMEDY.

speedy trial. *Criminal procedure.* A trial that the prosecution, with reasonable diligence, begins promptly and conducts expeditiously. • The Sixth Amendment secures the right to a speedy trial. In deciding whether an accused has been deprived of that right, courts generally consider the length of the delay, the reason for the delay, and the prejudice to the accused.

Speedy Trial Act of 1974. A federal statute establishing time limits for carrying out the major events (such as information or indictment, arraignment, and trial commencement) in the prosecution of federal criminal cases. 18 USCA §§ 3161–3174.

spending power. See POWER.

spillover theory. The principle that a severance must be granted only when a defendant can show that trial with a codefendant would substantially prejudice the defendant's case, as when the jury might wrongly use evidence against the defendant. See BRUTON ERROR.

spirit of the law. The general meaning or purpose of the law, as opposed to its literal content. Cf. LETTER OF THE LAW.

spite fence. A fence erected solely to annoy a neighbor, as by blocking the neighbor's view or preventing the neighbor from acquiring an easement of light.

split, *vb.* To divide (a cause of action) into segments or parts.

split gift. See GIFT.

split income. See INCOME.

split-level statute. See STATUTE.

split sentence. See SENTENCE.

splitting a cause of action. Separating parts of a demand and pursuing it piecemeal; presenting only a part of a claim in one lawsuit, leaving the rest for a second suit. • This practice has long been considered procedurally impermissible.

split verdict. See VERDICT.

spoliation (spoh-lee-**ay**-shən), *n.* **1.** The intentional destruction, mutilation, alteration, or concealment of evidence, usu. a document. • If proved, spoliation may be used to establish that the evidence was unfavorable to the party responsible. **2.** The seizure of personal or real property by violent means; the act of pillaging. **3.** The taking of a benefit properly belonging to another. — **spoliate** (**spoh**-lee-ayt), *vb.* — **spoliator** (**spoh**-lee-ay-tər), *n.*

spontaneous declaration. *Evidence.* A statement that is made without time to reflect or fabricate and is related to the circumstances of the perceived occurrence. See EXCITED UTTERANCE; PRESENT SENSE IMPRESSION.

spousal abuse. See ABUSE.

spousal allowance. See ALLOWANCE.

springing use. See USE.

spurious (**spyoor**-ee-əs), *adj.* **1.** Deceptively suggesting an erroneous origin; fake <spurious trademarks>. **2.** Of doubtful or low quality <spurious goods that fell apart>.

square, *n.* **1.** A certain portion of land within a city limit. **2.** A space set apart for public use. **3.** In a government survey, an area measuring 24 by 24 miles.

squatter. 1. A person who settles on property without any legal claim or title. **2.** A person who settles on public land under a government regulation allowing the person to acquire title upon fulfilling specified conditions.

squatter's rights. The right to acquire title to real property by adverse possession, or by preemption of public lands. See ADVERSE POSSESSION.

ss. *abbr.* **1.** Sections. **2.** *Subscripsi* (i.e., signed below). **3.** Sans (i.e., without).

SSA. *abbr.* SOCIAL SECURITY ADMINISTRATION.

SSI. *abbr.* SUPPLEMENTAL SECURITY INCOME.

stacking. A gerrymandering technique in which a large political or racial group is combined in the same district with a larger opposition group. Cf. CRACKING; PACKING.

staff attorney. 1. A lawyer who works for a court, usu. in a permanent position, on matters such as reviewing motions, screening docketing statements, preparing scheduling orders, and examining habeas corpus petitions. ● Staff attorneys do not rule on motions or decide cases, but they review and research factual and legal points and then recommend proposed rulings to judges, as well as draft the orders implementing those rulings. **2.** An in-house lawyer for a corporation.

stake, *n.* **1.** Something (such as property) deposited by two or more parties with a third party pending the resolution of a dispute; the subject matter of an interpleader. **2.** An interest or share in a business venture. **3.** Something (esp. money) bet in a wager, game, or contest. **4.** A boundary marker used in land surveys.

stakeholder. 1. A disinterested third party who holds money or property, the right to which is disputed between two or more other parties. See INTERPLEADER. **2.** A person who has an interest or concern in a business or enterprise, though not necessarily as an owner. **3.** One who holds the money or valuables bet by others in a wager.

stale check. See CHECK.

stale claim. A claim that is barred by the statute of limitations or the defense of laches.

stalking. 1. The act or an instance of following another by stealth. **2.** The offense of following or loitering near another, often surreptitiously, with the purpose of annoying or harassing that person or committing a further crime such as assault or battery. ● Some statutes require that the victim reasonably feel harassed, alarmed, or distressed about personal safety or the safety of someone for whom that person is responsible. Others cover acts such as telephoning another and remaining silent during the call. Cf. CYBERSTALKING.

stamp, *n.* An official mark or seal placed on a document, esp. to indicate that a required tax (such as duty or excise tax) has been paid.

stamp tax. See TAX.

standard, *n.* **1.** A model accepted as correct by custom, consent, or authority <the standard in the industry>. **2.** A criterion for measuring acceptability, quality, or accuracy <a nice living — even by New York standards>. — **standard,** *adj.*

objective standard. A legal standard based on conduct and perceptions external to a particular person. ● In tort law, for example, the reasonable-person standard is considered an objective standard because it does not require a determination of what the defendant was thinking.

subjective standard. A legal standard peculiar to a particular person and based on the person's individual views and experiences. • In criminal law, for example, premeditation is determined by a subjective standard because it depends on the defendant's mental state.

standard deduction. See DEDUCTION.

standard-form contract. See CONTRACT.

standard instruction. See JURY INSTRUCTION.

standard of care. *Torts*. In the law of negligence, the degree of prudence that a reasonable person should exercise. See CARE (2).

standard of proof. The degree or level of proof demanded in a specific case, such as "beyond a reasonable doubt" or "by a preponderance of the evidence." See BURDEN OF PERSUASION.

standard policy. See INSURANCE POLICY.

standing, *n.* A party's right to make a legal claim or seek judicial enforcement of a duty or right. • To have standing in federal court, a plaintiff must show (1) that the challenged conduct has caused the plaintiff actual injury, and (2) that the interest sought to be protected is within the zone of interests meant to be regulated by the statutory or constitutional guarantee in question. Cf. JUSTICIABILITY.

third-party standing. Standing held by someone claiming to protect the rights of others.

standing by. 1. The awaiting of an opportunity to respond, as with assistance. **2.** Silence or inaction when there is a duty to speak or act; esp., the tacit possession of knowledge under circumstances requiring the possessor to reveal the knowledge. See *estoppel by silence* under ESTOPPEL.

Standing Committee on Rules of Practice and Procedure. A group of judges, lawyers, and legal scholars appointed by the Chief Justice of the United States to advise the Judicial Conference of the United States on possible amendments to the procedural rules in the various federal courts and on other issues relating to the operation of the federal courts. 28 USCA § 331.

standing master. See MASTER.

standing offer. See OFFER.

stand mute. 1. (Of a defendant) to refuse to enter a plea to a criminal charge. • Standing mute is treated as a plea of not guilty. **2.** (Of any party) to raise no objections.

standstill agreement. Any agreement to refrain from taking further action; esp., an agreement by which a party agrees to refrain from further attempts to take over a corporation (as by making no tender offer) for a specified period, or by which financial institutions agree not to call bonds or loans when due.

stand trial. To submit to a legal proceeding, esp. a criminal prosecution.

stare decisis (**stahr**-ee di-**sɪ**-sis *or* **stair**-ee), *n.* [Latin "to stand by things decided"] The doctrine of precedent, under which it is necessary for a court to follow earlier judicial decisions when the same points arise again in litigation. See PRECEDENT. Cf. RES JUDICATA; LAW OF THE CASE.

star paging, *n.* **1.** A method of referring to a page in an earlier edition of a book, esp. a legal source. • This method correlates the pagination of the later edition with that of the earlier (usually the first) edition. **2.** By extension, the method of displaying on a computer screen the page breaks that occur in printed documents such as law reports and law reviews. — **star page,** *n.*

stat. *abbr.* STATUTE.

state, *n.* **1.** The political system of a body of people who are politically organized; the system of rules by which jurisdiction and authority are exercised over such a body of people. **2.** An institution of self-government within a larger political entity; esp., one of the constituent parts of a nation having a federal government. **3.** (*often cap.*) The prosecution as the representative of the people.

state action. Anything done by a government; esp., in constitutional law, an intrusion on a person's rights (esp. civil rights) either by a governmental entity or by a private requirement that can be enforced only by governmental action (such as a racially restrictive covenant, which requires judicial action for enforcement).

state bar association. See BAR ASSOCIATION.

state-compulsion test. *Civil-rights law.* The rule that a state is responsible for discrimination that a private party commits while acting under the requirements of state law, as when a restaurant owner is required by state law to refuse service to minorities. *Adickes v. S.H. Kress & Co.*, 398 U.S. 144, 90 S.Ct. 1598 (1970). See SYMBIOTIC-RELATIONSHIP TEST; NEXUS TEST.

state court. See COURT.

state criminal. See CRIMINAL.

State Department. The U.S. executive department, headed by the Secretary of State, responsible for analyzing, making recommendations on, and carrying out foreign policy (including trade relations, environmental concerns, and human-rights issues), as by negotiating treaties and other international agreements, and representing the United States in the United Nations and other international organizations. 22 USCA §§ 2651–2728.

state law. A body of law in a particular state consisting of the state's constitution, statutes, regulations, and common law. Cf. FEDERAL LAW.

statement. **1.** *Evidence.* A verbal assertion or nonverbal conduct intended as an assertion. **2.** A formal and exact presentation of facts. **3.** *Criminal procedure.* An account of a person's (usu. a suspect's) knowledge of a crime, taken by the police pursuant to their investigation of the offense. Cf. CONFESSION.

consonant statement. A prior declaration of a witness, testified to by a person to whom the declaration was made and allowed into evidence only after the witness's testimony has been impeached. • This type of evidence would, but for the impeachment of the witness, be inadmissible hearsay.

false statement. **1.** An untrue statement knowingly made with the intention of misleading. See PERJURY. **2.** Any one of three distinct federal offenses: (1) falsifying or concealing a material fact by trick, scheme, or device; (2) making a false, fictitious, or fraudulent representation; and (3) making or using a false document or writing. 18 USCA § 1001.

incriminating statement. A statement that tends to establish the guilt of an accused.

prior consistent statement. A witness's earlier statement that is consistent with the witness's trial testimony. • A prior consistent statement is not hearsay if it is offered to rebut a charge that the testimony was improperly influenced or fabricated. Fed. R. Evid. 801(d)(1)(B).

prior inconsistent statement. A witness's earlier statement that conflicts with the witness's testimony at trial. • In federal practice, extrinsic evidence of an unsworn prior inconsistent statement is admissible — if the witness is given an opportunity to explain or deny the statement — for impeachment purposes only. Fed. R. Evid. 613(b). Sworn statements may be admitted for all purposes. Fed. R. Evid. 801(d)(1)(A).

sworn statement. **1.** A statement given under oath; an affidavit. **2.** A contractor-builder's listing of suppliers and subcontractors, and their respective bids, required by a lending institution for interim financing.

voluntary statement. A statement free from duress, coercion, or inducement.

Statement and Account Clause. The clause of the U.S. Constitution requiring the regular publication of the receipts and expenditures of the federal government. U.S. Const. art. I, § 9, cl. 7.

statement of facts. A party's written presentation of the facts leading up to or surrounding a legal dispute, usu. recited toward the beginning of a brief.

state of mind. 1. The condition or capacity of a person's mind; MENS REA. **2.** Loosely, a person's reasons or motives for committing an act, esp. a criminal act.

state-of-mind exception. *Evidence.* The principle that an out-of-court declaration of an existing motive is admissible, even when the declarant cannot testify in person. • This principle constitutes an exception to the hearsay rule.

state of nature. The lack of a politically organized society. • The term is a fictional construct for the period in human history predating any type of political society.

state of the art. *Products liability.* The level of pertinent scientific and technical knowledge existing at the time of a product's manufacture, and the best technology reasonably available at the time the product was sold. — **state-of-the-art,** *adj.*

state of the case. The posture of litigation as it develops, as in discovery, at trial, or on appeal.

state police. The department or agency of a state government empowered to maintain order, as by investigating and preventing crimes, and making arrests.

state police power. The power of a state to enforce laws for the health, welfare, morals, and safety of its citizens, if enacted so that the means are reasonably calculated to protect those legitimate state interests.

state secret. A governmental matter that, because it could create a threat to the national defense or diplomatic interests of the United States if revealed, is protected against disclosure by a witness in an ordinary judicial proceeding.

state-secrets privilege. See PRIVILEGE (3).

state's evidence. See EVIDENCE.

state sovereignty. The right of a state to self-government; the supreme authority exercised by each state.

states' rights. Under the Tenth Amendment, rights neither conferred on the federal government nor forbidden to the states.

state tax. See TAX.

statistical-decision theory. A method for determining whether a jury pool represents a fair cross-section of the community, by calculating whether it is statistically probable that the pool was selected by mere chance. • This method has been criticized because potential jurors are not ordinarily selected by mere chance; some are disqualified for legitimate reasons. See FAIR-CROSS-SECTION REQUIREMENT; ABSOLUTE DISPARITY; COMPARATIVE DISPARITY; DUREN TEST.

status. 1. A person's legal condition, whether personal or proprietary; the sum total of a person's legal rights, duties, liabilities, and other legal relations, or any particular group of them separately considered <the status of a landowner>. **2.** A person's legal condition regarding personal rights but excluding proprietary relations <the status of a father> <the status of a wife>. **3.** A person's capacities and incapacities, as opposed to other elements of personal status <the status of minors>. **4.** A person's legal condition insofar as it is imposed by the law without the person's consent, as opposed to a condition that the person has acquired by agreement <the status of a slave>.

status crime. See CRIME.

status offender. See OFFENDER.

status offense. See OFFENSE.

status quo (**stay**-təs *or* **stat**-əs **kwoh**). [Latin] The situation that currently exists.

status quo ante (**stay**-təs **kwoh an**-tee). [Latin] The situation that existed before something else (being discussed) occurred.

statutable (**stach**-ə-tə-bəl), *adj.* **1.** Prescribed or authorized by statute. **2.** Conformed to the legislative requirements for quality, size, amount, or the like. **3.** (Of an offense) punishable by law. See STATUTORY.

statute. A law passed by a legislative body. — Abbr. s.; stat.

affirmative statute. A law requiring that something be done; one that directs the doing of an act. Cf. *negative statute*.

codifying statute. A law that purports to be exhaustive in restating the whole of the law on a particular topic, including prior caselaw as well as legislative provisions. • Courts generally presume that a codifying statute supersedes prior caselaw. Cf. *consolidating statute*.

consolidating statute. A law that collects the legislative provisions on a particular subject and embodies them in a single statute, often with minor amendments and drafting improvements. • Courts generally presume that a consolidating statute leaves prior caselaw intact. Cf. *codifying statute*.

criminal statute. A law that defines, classifies, and sets forth punishment for one or more specific crimes. See PENAL CODE.

declaratory statute. A law enacted to clarify prior law by reconciling conflicting judicial decisions or by explaining the meaning of a prior statute.

directory statute. A law that indicates only what should be done, with no provision for enforcement. Cf. *mandatory statute*.

disabling statute. A law that limits or curbs certain rights.

enabling statute. A law that permits what was previously prohibited or that creates new powers; esp., a congressional statute conferring powers on an administrative agency to carry out various delegated tasks.

expository statute. A law enacted to explain the meaning of a previously enacted law.

general statute. A law pertaining to an entire community or all persons generally. See PUBLIC LAW (2).

imperfect statute. A law that prohibits, but does not render void, an objectionable transaction. • Such a statute provides a penalty for disobedience without depriving the violative transaction of its legal effect.

mandatory statute. A law that requires a course of action as opposed to merely permitting it. Cf. *directory statute*.

negative statute. A law prohibiting something; a law expressed in negative terms. Cf. *affirmative statute*.

nonclaim statute. **1.** STATUTE OF LIMITATIONS. **2.** A law extinguishing a claim that is not timely asserted, esp. in the context of another proceeding. • An example is a statutory deadline for a creditor to file a claim in a probate proceeding. Unlike a statute of limitations, most nonclaim statutes are not subject to tolling.

organic statute. A law that establishes an administrative agency or local government. Cf. ORGANIC LAW.

penal statute. A law that defines an offense and prescribes its corresponding fine, penalty, or punishment.

perpetual statute. A law containing no provision for repeal, abrogation, or expiration at a future time.

prospective statute. A law that applies to future events.

reference statute. A law that incorporates and adopts by reference provisions of other laws.

remedial statute. A law that affords a remedy.

retrospective statute. A law that applies to past events.

revised statutes. Laws that have been collected, arranged, and reenacted as a whole by a legislative body. — Abbr. Rev. Stat.; R.S. See CODE.

revival statute. A law that provides for the renewal of actions, of wills, and of the legal effect of documents.

severable statute. A law that remains operative in its remaining provisions even though a portion of the law is declared unconstitutional.

speaking statute. A statute to be interpreted in light of the understanding of its terms prevailing at the time of interpretation.

special statute. A law that applies only to specific individuals, as opposed to everyone.

split-level statute. A law that has connected with it officially promulgated explanatory materials, so that courts are left with two levels of documents to construe.

temporary statute. **1.** A law that specifically provides that it is to remain in effect for a fixed, limited period. **2.** A law (such as an appropriation statute) that, by its nature, has only a single and temporary operation.

validating statute. A law that is amended either to remove errors or to add provisions to conform to constitutional requirements.

statute book. A bound collection of statutes, usu. as part of a larger set of books containing a complete body of statutory law, such as the United States Code Annotated.

statute of distribution. A state law regulating the distribution of an estate among an intestate's heirs and relatives.

statute of frauds. 1. (*cap.*) An English statute enacted in 1677 declaring certain contracts judicially unenforceable (but not void) if they are not committed to writing and signed by the party to be charged. • The statute was entitled "An Act for the Prevention of Frauds and Perjuries" (29 Car. 2, ch. 3). **2.** A statute (based on the English Statute of Frauds) designed to prevent fraud and perjury by requiring certain contracts to be in writing and signed by the party to be charged. • Statutes of frauds traditionally apply to the following types of contracts: (1) a contract for the sale or transfer of an interest in land, (2) a contract that cannot be performed within one year of its making, (3) a contract for the sale of goods valued at $500 or more, (4) a contract of an executor or administrator to answer for a decedent's debt, (5) a contract to guarantee the debt or duty of another, and (6) a contract made in consideration of marriage. UCC § 2–201. — Abbr. S/F; SOF.

statute of limitations. 1. A statute establishing a time limit for suing in a civil case, based on the date when the claim accrued (as when the injury occurred or was discovered). • The purpose of such a statute is to require diligent prosecution of known claims, thereby providing finality and predictability in legal affairs and ensuring that claims will be resolved while evidence is reasonably available and fresh. **2.** A statute establishing a time limit for prosecuting a crime, based on the date when the offense occurred. Cf. STATUTE OF REPOSE.

statute of repose. A statute that bars a suit a fixed number of years after the defendant acts in some way (as by designing or manufacturing a product), even if this period ends before the plaintiff has suffered any injury. Cf. STATUTE OF LIMITATIONS.

statute of wills. A state statute providing for testamentary disposition in that jurisdiction.

Statutes at Large. An official compilation of the acts and resolutions that become law from each session of Congress, printed in chronological order.

statutory (**stach**-ə-tor-ee), *adj.* **1.** Of or relating to legislation <statutory interpretation>. **2.** Legislatively created <the law of patents is purely statutory>. **3.** Conformable to a statute <a statutory act>.

statutory agent. See AGENT.

statutory construction. **1.** The act or process of interpreting a statute. **2.** Collectively, the principles developed by courts for interpreting statutes. See CONSTRUCTION (2).

statutory crime. See CRIME.

statutory dedication. See DEDICATION.

statutory deed. See DEED.

statutory exception. See EXCEPTION (2).

statutory exposition. A statute's special interpretation of the ambiguous terms of a previous statute <the statute contained a statutory exposition of the former act>.

statutory law. The body of law derived from statutes rather than from constitutions or judicial decisions. Cf. COMMON LAW; CONSTITUTIONAL LAW.

statutory obligation. See OBLIGATION.

statutory penalty. See PENALTY.

statutory presumption. See PRESUMPTION.

statutory rape. See RAPE.

statutory redemption. See REDEMPTION.

statutory right of redemption. The right of a mortgagor in default to recover property after a foreclosure sale by paying the principal, interest, and other costs that are owed, together with any other measure required to cure the default. • This statutory right exists in many states but is not uniform. See REDEMPTION.

stay, *n.* **1.** The postponement or halting of a proceeding, judgment, or the like. **2.** An order to suspend all or part of a judicial proceeding or a judgment resulting from that proceeding. — **stay,** *vb.* — **stayable,** *adj.*

steal, *vb.* **1.** To take (personal property) illegally with the intent to keep it unlawfully. **2.** To take (something) by larceny, embezzlement, or false pretenses.

step-in-the-dark rule. *Torts.* The contributory-negligence rule that a person who enters a totally unfamiliar area in the darkness has a duty, in the absence of unusual stress, to refrain from proceeding until first ascertaining the existence of any dangerous obstacles. See *contributory negligence* under NEGLIGENCE.

stepped-up basis. See BASIS.

stet (stet), *n.* [Latin "let it stand"] **1.** An order staying legal proceedings, as when a prosecutor determines not to proceed on an indictment and places the case on a stet docket. • The term is used chiefly in Maryland. **2.** An instruction to leave a text as it stands.

stickup. An armed robbery in which the victim is threatened by the use of weapons. See *armed robbery* under ROBBERY.

sting. An undercover operation in which law-enforcement agents pose as criminals to catch actual criminals engaging in illegal acts.

stipulation (stip-yə-**lay**-shən), *n.* **1.** A material condition or requirement in an agreement; esp., a factual representation incorporated into a contract as a term <breach of the stipulation regarding payment of taxes>. • Stipulations often appear in a section of the contract called "Representations and Warranties." **2.** A voluntary agreement between opposing parties concerning some relevant point <a stipulation on the issue of liability>. • A stipulation relating to a pending judicial proceeding, made by a party to the proceeding or the party's attorney, is binding without consideration. — **stipulate** (**stip**-yə-layt), *vb.* — **stipulative** (**stip**-yə-lə-tiv), *adj.*

stipulative definition. See DEFINITION.

stirpital (**stər**-pə-təl), *adj.* Of or relating to per stirpes distribution. See PER STIRPES.

stirps (stərps), *n.* [Latin "stock"] A branch of a family; a line of descent. Pl. **stirpes** (**stər**-peez). See PER STIRPES.

stock, *n.* **1.** The original progenitor of a family; a person from whom a family is descended <George Harper, Sr. was the stock of the Harper line>. **2.** A merchant's goods that are kept for sale or trade <the car dealer put last year's models on sale to reduce its stock>. **3.** The capital or principal fund raised by a corporation through subscribers' contributions or the sale of shares <Acme's stock is worth far more today than it was 20 years ago>. **4.** A proportional part of a corporation's capital represented by the number of equal units (or shares) owned, and granting the holder the right to participate in the company's general management and to share in its net profits or earnings <Julia sold her stock in Pantheon Corporation>. See SHARE (2). Cf. SECURITY (4).

stolen property. Goods acquired by larceny, robbery, or theft.

stop, *n.* Under the Fourth Amendment, a temporary restraint that prevents a person from walking away.

stop and frisk, *n.* A police officer's brief detention, questioning, and search of a person for a concealed weapon when the officer reasonably suspects that the person has committed or is about to commit a crime. • The stop and frisk, which can be conducted without a warrant or probable cause, was held constitutional by the Supreme Court in *Terry v. Ohio*,

392 U.S. 1, 88 S.Ct. 1868 (1968). See REASONABLE SUSPICION.

stop-notice statute. A law providing an alternative to a mechanic's lien by allowing a contractor, supplier, or worker to make a claim against the construction lender and, in some instances, the owner for a portion of the undisbursed construction-loan proceeds.

stoppage, *n.* An obstruction or hindrance to the performance of something <stoppage of goods or persons in transit for inspection>.

stoppage ***in transitu*** (in **tran**-si-t[y]oo *or* **tranz**-i-t[y]oo). The right that a seller of goods has, under certain circumstances, to regain possession of those goods even after parting with them under a contract for sale. • This right traditionally applies when goods are consigned on credit from one person to another, and the consignee becomes bankrupt or insolvent before the goods arrive — in which event the consignor may direct the carrier to deliver the goods to someone other than the consignee (who can no longer pay for them).

store, *n.* **1.** A place where goods are deposited to be purchased or sold. **2.** A place where goods or supplies are stored for future use; a warehouse.

store, *vb.* To keep (goods, etc.) in safekeeping for future delivery in an unchanged condition.

straight-line depreciation method. See DEPRECIATION METHOD.

straight sentence. See *determinate sentence* under SENTENCE.

strain theory. The theory that people commit crimes to alleviate stress created by the disjunction between their station in life and the station to which society has conditioned them to aspire. Cf. ROUTINE-ACTIVITIES THEORY; CONTROL THEORY; RATIONAL-CHOICE THEORY.

strand, *n.* A shore or bank of an ocean, lake, river, or stream.

stranger. 1. One who is not a party to a given transaction. **2.** One not standing toward another in some relation implied in the context.

stranger in blood. 1. One not related by blood, such as a relative by affinity. **2.** Any person not within the consideration of natural love and affection arising from a relationship.

stratagem. A trick or deception to obtain an advantage, esp. in a military conflict.

strategic alliance. A coalition of persons in the same or complementary businesses to gain long-term financial, operational, and marketing advantages without jeopardizing competitive independence <by their strategic alliance, the manufacturer and distributor of a co-developed product shared development costs>. Cf. JOINT VENTURE; PARTNERSHIP.

straw bond. See BOND (2).

straw man. 1. A fictitious person, esp. one that is weak or flawed. **2.** A tenuous and exaggerated counterargument that an advocate puts forward for the sole purpose of disproving it. **3.** A third party used in some transactions as a temporary transferee to allow the principal parties to accomplish something that is otherwise impermissible. **4.** A person hired to post a worthless bail bond for the release of an accused.

stream-of-commerce theory. 1. The principle that a state may exercise personal jurisdiction over a defendant if the defendant places a product in the general marketplace and the product causes injury or damage in the forum state, as long as the defendant also takes other acts to establish some connection with the forum state, as by advertising there or by hiring someone to serve as a sales agent there. *Asahi Metal Indus. Co. v. Superior Court of Cal.*, 480 U.S. 102, 107 S.Ct. 1026 (1987). **2.** The principle that a person who participates in placing a defective product in the general marketplace is strictly liable for harm caused by the product. Restatement (Second) of Torts § 402A (1979).

street crime. See CRIME.

street time. See TIME.

strict, *adj.* **1.** Narrow; restricted <strict construction>. **2.** Rigid; exacting <strict statutory terms>. **3.** Severe <strict punishment>. **4.** Absolute; requiring no showing of fault <strict liability>.

strict construction. See CONSTRUCTION.

strict constructionism, *n.* The doctrinal view of judicial construction holding that judges should interpret a document or statute (esp. one involving penal sanctions) according to its literal terms, without looking to other sources to ascertain the meaning. — **strict constructionist,** *n.*

strict foreclosure. See FORECLOSURE.

strict interpretation. See INTERPRETATION.

strict liability. See LIABILITY.

strict products liability. See PRODUCTS LIABILITY.

strict scrutiny. *Constitutional law.* The standard applied to suspect classifications (such as race) in equal-protection analysis and to fundamental rights (such as voting rights) in due-process analysis. • Under strict scrutiny, the state must establish that it has a compelling interest that justifies and necessitates the law in question. See COMPELLING-STATE-INTEREST TEST; SUSPECT CLASSIFICATION; FUNDAMENTAL RIGHT. Cf. INTERMEDIATE SCRUTINY; RATIONAL-BASIS TEST.

strict test. *Evidence*. The principle that disclosure of a privileged document, even when inadvertent, results in a waiver of the attorney–client privilege regarding the document, unless all possible precautions were taken to protect the document from disclosure. Cf. LENIENT TEST; HYDRAFLOW TEST.

strike, *n.* **1.** An organized cessation or slowdown of work by employees to compel the employer to meet the employees' demands. Cf. LOCKOUT; BOYCOTT; PICKETING. **2.** The removal of a prospective juror from the jury panel <a peremptory strike>. See CHALLENGE (2). **3.** A failure or disadvantage, as by a criminal conviction <a strike on one's record>.

strike, *vb.* **1.** (Of an employee or union) to engage in a work stoppage or slowdown. **2.** To remove (a prospective juror) from a jury panel by a peremptory challenge or a challenge for cause. See *peremptory challenge* under CHALLENGE (2). **3.** To expunge, as from a record.

strike down. To invalidate (a statute); to declare void.

strike off. 1. (Of a court) to order (a case) removed from the docket. **2.** (Of an auctioneer) to announce, usu. by the falling of the hammer, that an item has been sold.

strike suit. See SUIT.

striking a jury. The selecting of a jury out of all the candidates available to serve on the jury; esp., the selecting of a special jury. See *special jury* under JURY.

strip, *n.* The act of a tenant who, holding less than the entire fee in land, spoils or unlawfully takes something from the land.

strip search. See SEARCH.

strongly corroborated. (Of testimony) supported from independent facts and circumstances that are powerful, satisfactory, and clear to the court and jury.

struck jury. See JURY.

structural alteration. See ALTERATION.

structure. 1. Any construction, production, or piece of work artificially built up or composed of parts purposefully joined together <a building is a structure>. **2.** The organization of elements or parts <the corporate structure>. **3.** A method of constructing parts <the loan's payment structure was a financial burden>.

study release. See RELEASE.

stultify, *vb.* **1.** To make (something or someone) appear stupid or foolish. **2.** To testify about one's own lack of mental capacity. **3.** To contradict oneself, as by denying what one has already alleged.

stumpage (**stəmp**-ij). **1.** The timber standing on land. **2.** The value of the standing timber. **3.** A license to cut the timber. **4.** The fee paid for the right to cut the timber.

style, *n.* A case name or designation <the style of the opinion is *Connor v. Gray*>. Cf. CAPTION (1).

s.u. *abbr.* Straight up. ● When a prosecutor writes this on a defendant's file, it usually means that the prosecutor plans to try the case — that is, not enter into a plea bargain.

suable, *adj.* **1.** Capable of being sued <a suable party>. **2.** Capable of being enforced <a suable contract>. — **suability,** *n.*

subcontract. See CONTRACT.

subcontractor. One who is awarded a portion of an existing contract by a contractor, esp. a general contractor. ● For example, a contractor who builds houses typically retains subcontractors to perform specialty work such as installing plumbing, laying carpet, making cabinetry, and landscaping — each subcontractor is paid a somewhat lesser sum than the contractor receives for the work.

subdivision, *n.* **1.** The division of a thing into smaller parts. **2.** A parcel of land in a larger development. — **subdivide,** *vb.*

subdivision map. A map that shows how a parcel of land is to be divided into smaller lots, and generally showing the layout and utilities.

subjacent (səb-**jay**-sənt), *adj.* Located underneath or below <the land's subjacent support>.

subject, *n.* **1.** One who owes allegiance to a sovereign and is governed by that sovereign's laws <the monarchy's subjects>. **2.** The matter of concern over which something is created <the subject of the statute>.

subject, *adj. Jargon.* Referred to above; having relevance to the current discussion <the subject property was then sold to Smith>.

subjection. 1. The act of subjecting someone to something <their subjection to torture was unconscionable>. **2.** The condition of a subject in a monarchy; the obligations surrounding such a person <a subject, wherever residing, owes fidelity and obedience to the Crown, while an alien may be released at will from all such ties of subjection>. **3.** The condition of being subject, exposed, or liable; liability <the defendants' subjection to the plaintiffs became clear shortly after the trial began>.

subjective, *adj.* **1.** Based on an individual's perceptions, feelings, or intentions, as opposed to externally verifiable phenomena <the subjective theory of contract — that the parties must have an actual meeting of the minds — is not favored by most courts>. **2.** Personal; individual <subjective judgments about popular music>. Cf. OBJECTIVE.

subjective meaning. See MEANING.

subjective standard. See STANDARD.

subjective theory of contract. The doctrine (now largely outmoded) that a contract is an agreement in which the parties have a subjective meeting of the minds. See MEETING OF THE MINDS. Cf. OBJECTIVE THEORY OF CONTRACT.

subject matter. The issue presented for consideration; the thing in which a right or duty has been asserted; the thing in dispute. See CORPUS (2). — **subject-matter,** *adj.*

subject-matter jurisdiction. See JURISDICTION.

subject-matter test. A method of determining whether an employee's communication with a corporation's lawyer was made at the direction of the employee's supervisors and in the course and scope of the employee's employment, so as to be protected under the attorney–client privilege, despite the fact that the employee is not a member of the corporation's control group. *Harper & Row Pubs., Inc. v. Decker*, 423 F.2d 487 (7th Cir. 1970), *aff'd per curiam by equally divided Court*, 400 U.S. 348, 91 S.Ct. 479 (1971). Cf. CONTROL-GROUP TEST.

subject of a right. 1. The owner of a right; the person in whom a legal right is vested. **2.** OBJECT OF A RIGHT.

subject to open. Denoting the future interest of a class of people when this class is subject to a possible increase or decrease in number.

sub judice (səb **joo**-di-see *also* suub **yoo**-di-kay), *adv.* [Latin "under a judge"] *Jargon.* Before the court or judge for determination; at bar <in the case sub judice, there have been no out-of-court settlements>. • Legal writers sometimes use "case sub judice" where "the present case" would be more comprehensible.

sublease, *n.* A lease by a lessee to a third party, conveying some or all of the leased property for a shorter term than that of the lessee, who retains a reversion in the lease. — **sublease,** *vb.* — **sublet,** *vb.*

sublessee. A third party who receives by lease some or all of the leased property from a lessee.

sublessor. A lessee who leases some or all of the leased property to a third party.

sublicense. A license granting a portion or all of the rights granted to the licensee under an original license.

submission, *n.* **1.** A yielding to the authority or will of another <his resistance ended in an about-face: complete submission>. **2.** A contract in which the parties agree to refer their dispute to a third party for resolution <in their submission to arbitration, they referred to the rules of the American Arbitration Association>. **3.** An advocate's argument <neither the written nor the oral submissions were particularly helpful>. — **submit,** *vb.*

submission to a finding. The admission to facts sufficient to warrant a finding of guilt.

submission to the jury. The process by which a judge gives a case to the jury for its consideration and verdict, usu. occurring after all evidence has been presented, all arguments have been completed, and all instructions have been given.

sub nomine (səb **nom**-ə-nee). [Latin] Under the name. • This phrase, typically in abbreviated form, is often used in a case citation to indicate that there has been a name change from one stage of the case to another, as in *Guernsey Memorial Hosp. v. Secretary of Health & Human Servs.*, 996 F.2d 830 (6th Cir. 1993), *rev'd sub nom. Shalala v. Guernsey Memorial Hosp.*, 514 U.S. 87, 115 S.Ct. 1232 (1995). — Abbr. *sub nom.*

subordinate (sə-**bor**-də-nit), *adj.* **1.** Placed in or belonging to a lower rank, class, or position <a subordinate lien>. **2.** Subject to another's authority or control <a subordinate lawyer>.

subordinate (sə-**bor**-də-nayt), *vb.* To place in a lower rank, class, or position; to assign a lower priority to <subordinate the debt to a different class of claims>.

subordinate debenture. See DEBENTURE.

subordinate legislation. See LEGISLATION.

suborn (sə-**born**), *vb.* **1.** To induce (a person) to commit an unlawful or wrongful act, esp. in a secret or underhanded manner. **2.** To induce (a person) to commit perjury. **3.** To obtain (perjured testimony) from another. — **subornation** (səb-or-**nay**-shən), *n.* — **suborner** (sə-**bor**-nər), *n.*

subornation of perjury. The crime of persuading another to commit perjury. — Sometimes shortened to *subornation*.

subpoena (sə-**pee**-nə), *n.* [Latin "under penalty"] A writ commanding a person to appear before a court or other tribunal, subject to a penalty for failing to comply. — Also spelled *subpena*. Pl. **subpoenas.**

alias subpoena (**ay**-lee-əs sə-**pee**-nə). A subpoena issued after an initial subpoena has failed.

subpoena ad testificandum (sə-**pee**-nə ad tes-tə-fi-**kan**-dəm). [Law Latin] A subpoena ordering a witness to appear and give testimony.

subpoena duces tecum (sə-**pee**-nə **d[y]oo**-seez **tee**-kəm *also* **doo**-səz **tay**-kəm). [Law Latin] A subpoena ordering the witness to appear and to bring specified documents or records.

subpoena, *vb.* **1.** To call before a court or other tribunal by subpoena <subpoena the material witnesses>. **2.** To order the production of (documents or other things) by subpoena duces tecum <subpoena the corporate records>. — Also spelled *subpena*.

subpoenal (sə-**pee**-nəl), *adj.* Required or done under penalty, esp. in compliance with a subpoena.

subrogate (**səb**-rə-gayt), *vb.* To substitute (a person) for another regarding a legal right or claim.

subrogation (səb-rə-**gay**-shən), *n.* **1.** The substitution of one party for another whose debt the party pays, entitling the paying party to rights, remedies, or securities that would otherwise belong to the debtor. • For example, a surety who has paid a debt is, by subrogation, entitled to any security for the debt held by the creditor and the benefit of any judgment the creditor has against the debtor, and may proceed against the debtor as the creditor would. **2.** The principle under which an insurer that has paid a loss under an insurance policy is entitled to all the rights and remedies belonging to the insured against a third party with respect to any loss covered by the policy. See EQUITY OF SUBROGATION.

subscribing witness. See WITNESS.

subscription, *n.* **1.** The act of signing one's name on a document; the signature so affixed. **2.** *Securities.* A written contract to purchase newly issued shares of stock or bonds. **3.** An oral or a written agreement to contribute a sum of money or property, gratuitously or with consideration, to a specific person or for a specific purpose. — **subscribe,** *vb.* — **subscriber,** *n.*

subsequent, *adj.* (Of an action, event, etc.) occurring later; coming after something else.

subsequent negligence. See NEGLIGENCE.

subsequent remedial measure. (*usu. pl.*) *Evidence.* An action taken after an event, which, if taken before the event, would have reduced the likelihood of the event's occurrence. • Evidence of subsequent remedial measures is not admissible to prove negligence, but it may be admitted to prove ownership, control, feasibility, or the like. Fed. R. Evid. 407.

subsidiary corporation. See CORPORATION.

subsidy, *n.* **1.** A grant, usu. made by the government, to an enterprise whose promotion is considered to be in the public interest. **2.** A specific financial contribution by a foreign government or public entity conferring a benefit on exporters to the United States. • Such a subsidy is countervailable under 19 USCA §§ 1671, 1677. — **subsidize,** *vb.*

sub silentio (səb si-**len**-shee-oh). [Latin] Under silence; without notice being taken; without being expressly mentioned (such as precedent *sub silentio*).

subsistence. Support; means of support. See NECESSARIES.

substance. 1. The essence of something; the essential quality of something, as opposed to its mere form <matter of substance>. **2.** Any matter, esp. an addictive drug <illegal substance>.

substance-abuse evaluation and treatment. A drug offender's court-ordered participation in a drug rehabilitation program. • This type of treatment is especially common in DUI cases. — Abbr. SAET.

substantial-capacity test. *Criminal law.* The Model Penal Code's test for the insanity defense, stating that a person is not criminally responsible for an act if, as a result of a mental disease or defect, the person lacks substantial capacity either to appreciate the criminality of the conduct or to conform the conduct to the law. • This test combines elements of both the *McNaghten* rules and the irresistible-impulse test by allowing consideration of both volitional and cognitive weaknesses. This test was formerly used by the federal courts and many states, but since 1984 many jurisdictions (including federal courts) — in response to the acquittal by reason of insanity of would-be presidential assassin John Hinckley — have narrowed the insanity defense and adopted a new test resembling the *McNaghten* rules, although portions of the substantial-capacity test continue to be used. Model Penal Code § 4.01. See INSANITY DEFENSE.

substantial evidence. See EVIDENCE.

substantial-evidence rule. The principle that a reviewing court should uphold an administrative body's ruling if it is supported by evidence on which the administrative body could reasonably base its decision.

substantial-factor test. *Torts.* The principle that causation exists when the defendant's conduct is an important or significant contributor to the plaintiff's injuries. Cf. BUT-FOR TEST.

substantial justice. See JUSTICE (1).

substantially justified. (Of conduct, a position, etc.) having a reasonable basis in law and in fact. • Under the Equal Access to Justice Act, a prevailing party in a lawsuit against the government will be unable to recover its attorney's fees if the government's position is substantially justified.

substantial performance. See PERFORMANCE.

substantial-performance doctrine. The equitable rule that, if a good-faith attempt to perform does not precisely meet the terms of the agreement, the agreement will still be considered complete if the essential purpose of the contract is accomplished. • Courts may allow a remedy for minimal damages caused by the deviance. Cf. PERFECT-TENDER RULE.

substantial-step test. *Criminal law.* The Model Penal Code's test for determining whether a person is guilty of attempt, based on the extent of the defendant's preparation for the crime, the criminal intent shown, and any statements personally made that bear on the defendant's actions. Model Penal Code § 5.01(1)(c). See ATTEMPT.

substantiate, *vb.* To establish the existence or truth of (a fact, etc.), esp. by competent evidence; to verify.

substantive due process. See DUE PROCESS.

substantive evidence. See EVIDENCE.

substantive law (**səb**-stən-tiv). The part of the law that creates, defines, and regulates the rights, duties, and powers of parties. Cf. PROCEDURAL LAW.

substantive offense. See OFFENSE.

substantive right. See RIGHT.

substantive unconscionability. See UNCONSCIONABILITY.

substituted basis. See BASIS.

substituted executor. See EXECUTOR.

substituted-judgment doctrine. The principle that allows a surrogate decision-maker to attempt to establish, with as much accuracy as possible, what decision an incompetent patient would make if he or she were competent to do so. • The standard of proof is by clear and convincing evidence. Generally, the doctrine is used for a person who was once competent but no longer is.

substituted service. See SERVICE.

substitute gift. See GIFT.

substitution. **1.** A designation of a person or thing to take the place of another person or thing. **2.** The process by which one person or thing takes the place of another person or thing.

substitutional, *adj.* Capable of taking or supplying the position of another <substitutional executor> <substitutional issue>.

substitutional legacy. See LEGACY.

substitutional remedy. See REMEDY.

substraction (səb-**strak**-shən), *n.* The secret misappropriation of property, esp. from a decedent's estate.

subsume (səb-**s[y]oom**), *vb.* To judge as a particular instance governed by a general principle; to bring (a case) under a broad rule. — **subsumption** (səb-**səmp**-shən), *n.*

subsurety (səb-**shuur**[-ə]-tee). A person whose undertaking is given as additional security, usu. conditioned not only on nonperformance by the principal but also on nonperformance by an earlier promisor; a surety with the lesser liability in a subsuretyship.

subsuretyship (səb-**shuur**[-ə]-tee-ship). The relation between two (or more) sureties, in which a principal surety bears the burden of the whole performance that is due from both sureties; a relationship in which one surety acts as a surety for another.

subsurface right. **1.** A landowner's right to the minerals and water below the property. **2.** A like right, held by another through grant by, or purchase from, a landowner. See MINERAL RIGHT. Cf. SURFACE RIGHT.

subterfuge (**səb**-tər-fyooj). A clever plan or idea used to escape, avoid, or conceal something <a subterfuge to avoid liability under a statute>.

subversion. The process of overthrowing, destroying, or corrupting <subversion of legal principles> <subversion of the government>.

subversive activity. A pattern of acts designed to overthrow a government by force or other illegal means.

succession, *n.* **1.** The act or right of legally or officially taking over a predecessor's office, rank, or duties. **2.** The acquisition of rights or property by inheritance under the laws of descent and distribution; DESCENT (1). — **succeed,** *vb.*

hereditary succession. Succession by the common law of descent. See DESCENT; TESTATE SUCCESSION; INTESTATE SUCCESSION.

irregular succession. Succession by special laws favoring certain persons or the state, rather than heirs (such as testamentary heirs) under the ordinary laws of descent.

legal succession. The succession established by law, usu. in favor of the nearest relation of a deceased person.

natural succession. Succession between natural persons, as in descent on the death of an ancestor.

3. The right by which one group, in replacing another group, acquires all the goods, movables, and other chattels of a corporation. **4.** The continuation of a corporation's legal status despite changes in ownership or management. — **successor,** *n.*

successional, *adj.* Of or relating to acquiring rights or property by inheritance under the laws of descent and distribution.

succession tax. See *inheritance tax* (1) under TAX.

successive tortfeasors. See TORTFEASOR.

successive-writ doctrine. *Criminal procedure.* The principle that a second or supplemental petition for a writ of habeas corpus may not raise claims that were heard and decided on the merits in a previous petition. Cf. ABUSE-OF-THE-WRIT DOCTRINE.

successor. 1. A person who succeeds to the office, rights, responsibilities, or place of another; one who replaces or follows another. **2.** A corporation that, through amalgamation, consolidation, or other assumption of interests, is vested with the rights and duties of an earlier corporation.

successor in interest. One who follows another in ownership or control of property. • A successor in interest retains the same rights as the original owner, with no change in substance.

successor trustee. See TRUSTEE.

such, *adj.* **1.** Of this or that kind <she collects a variety of such things>. **2.** *Jargon.* That or those; having just been mentioned <a newly discovered Fabergé egg will be on auction next week; such egg is expected to sell for more than $500,000>.

sudden-onset rule. The principle that medical testimony is unnecessary to prove causation of the obvious symptoms of an injury that immediately follows a known traumatic incident.

sue facts. Facts that determine whether a party should bring a lawsuit; esp., facts determining whether a shareholder-derivative action should be instituted under state law.

sue out, *vb.* To apply to a court for the issuance of (a court order or writ).

suffer, *vb.* **1.** To experience or sustain physical or emotional pain, distress, or injury <suffer damages>. **2.** To allow or permit (an act, etc.) <to suffer a default>.

sufferance (**səf**-ər-ənts *or* **səf**-rənts). **1.** Toleration; passive consent. **2.** The state of one who holds land without the owner's permission. See *tenancy at sufferance* under TENANCY. **3.** A license implied from the omission to enforce a right.

sufficiency-of-evidence test. *Criminal procedure.* **1.** The guideline for a grand jury considering whether to indict a suspect: if all the evidence presented were uncontradicted and unexplained, it would warrant a conviction by the fact-trier. **2.** A standard for reviewing a criminal conviction on appeal, based on whether enough evidence exists to justify the fact-trier's finding of guilt beyond a reasonable doubt.

sufficient consideration. See CONSIDERATION.

suffrage (**səf**-rij). **1.** The right or privilege of casting a vote at a public election. **2.** A vote; the act of voting.

suggestion, *n.* **1.** An indirect presentation of an idea; also, a direct recommendation <the client agreed with counsel's suggestion to reword the warranty>. **2.** *Procedure.* A statement of some fact or circumstance that will materially affect the further proceedings in the case <suggestion for rehearing en banc>. — **suggest** (for sense 1), *vb.*

suggestion of bankruptcy. A pleading by which a party notifies the court that the party has filed for bankruptcy and that, because of the automatic stay provided by the bankruptcy laws, the court cannot legally take further action in the case.

suggestion of death. A pleading filed by a party, or the party's representatives, by which the court is notified that a party to a suit has died.

suggestion of error. An objection made by a party to a suit, indicating that the court has committed an error or that the party wants a rehearing of a particular issue.

suicide, *n.* **1.** The act of taking one's own life.

> ***assisted suicide.*** The intentional act of providing a person with the medical means or the medical knowledge to commit suicide. Cf. EUTHANASIA.
>
> ***attempted suicide.*** An unsuccessful suicidal act.

2. A person who has taken his or her own life. — **suicidal,** *adj.*

sui generis (**s[y]oo**-ɪ *or* **soo**-ee **jen**-ə-ris). [Latin "of its own kind"] Of its own kind or class; unique or peculiar.

sui juris (**s[y]oo**-ɪ *or* **soo**-ee **joor**-is). [Latin "of one's own right; independent"] **1.** Of full age and capacity. **2.** Possessing full social and civil rights.

suit. Any proceeding by a party or parties against another in a court of law; CASE. See ACTION.

ancillary suit (**an**-sə-ler-ee). An action, either at law or in equity, that grows out of and is auxiliary to another suit and is filed to aid the primary suit, to enforce a prior judgment, or to impeach a prior decree.

blackmail suit. A suit filed by a party having no genuine claim but hoping to extract a favorable settlement from a defendant who would rather avoid the expenses and hassles of litigation.

plenary suit (**plee**-nə-ree *or* **plen**-ə-ree). An action that proceeds on formal pleadings under rules of procedure. Cf. *summary proceeding* under PROCEEDING.

strike suit. A suit (esp. a derivative action), often based on no valid claim, brought either for nuisance value or as leverage to obtain a favorable or inflated settlement.

suit for exoneration. A suit in equity brought by a surety to compel the debtor to pay the creditor. • If the debtor has acted fraudulently and is insolvent, a suit for exoneration may include further remedies to ensure that the debtor's assets are applied equitably to the debtor's outstanding obligations.

suit money. Attorney's fees and court costs allowed or awarded by a court; esp., in some jurisdictions, a husband's payment to his wife to cover her reasonable attorney's fees in a divorce action.

suitor. 1. A party that brings a lawsuit; a plaintiff or petitioner. **2.** An individual or company that seeks to take over another company.

sum certain. 1. Any amount that is fixed, settled, or exact. **2.** *Commercial law.* In a negotiable instrument, a sum that is agreed on in the instrument or a sum that can be ascertained from the document.

summary, *adj.* **1.** Short; concise <a summary account of the events on March 6>. **2.** Without the usual formalities; esp., without a jury <a summary trial>. **3.** Immediate; done without delay <the new weapon was put to summary use by the military>. — **summarily** (**səm**-ər-ə-lee *or* sə-**mair**-ə-lee), *adv.*

summary, *n.* **1.** An abridgment or brief. **2.** A short application to a court without the formality of a full proceeding.

summary eviction. See EVICTION.

summary judgment. A judgment granted on a claim about which there is no genuine issue of material fact and upon which the movant is entitled to prevail as a matter of law. • This procedural device allows the speedy disposition of a controversy without the need for trial. Fed. R. Civ. P. 56. See JUDGMENT.

partial summary judgment. A summary judgment that is limited to certain issues in a case and that disposes of only a portion of the whole case.

summary jurisdiction. See JURISDICTION.

summary jury trial. See TRIAL.

summary offense. See OFFENSE.

summary proceeding. See PROCEEDING.

summon, *vb.* To command (a person) by service of a summons to appear in court.

summons, *n.* **1.** Formerly, a writ directing a sheriff to summon a defendant to appear in court. **2.** A writ or process commencing the plaintiff's action and requiring the defendant to appear and answer. **3.** A notice requiring a person to appear in court as a juror or witness. Pl. **summonses.**

summons, *vb.* **1.** SUMMON. **2.** To request (information) by summons.

sum payable. An amount due; esp., the amount for which the maker of a negotiable instrument becomes liable and must tender in full satisfaction of the debt.

sunk cost. See COST.

sunset law. A statute under which a governmental agency or program automatically terminates at the end of a fixed period unless it is formally renewed.

sunshine committee. An official or quasi-official committee whose proceedings and work are open to public access.

sunshine law. A statute requiring a governmental department or agency to open its meetings or its records to public access.

sup. ct. *abbr.* SUPREME COURT.

Superfund. **1.** The program that funds and administers the cleanup of hazardous-waste sites through a trust fund (financed by taxes on petroleum and chemicals and a new tax on corporations) created to pay for cleanup pending reimbursement from the liable parties. **2.** The popular name for the act that established this program — the Comprehensive Environmental Response, Compensation, and Liability Act of 1980 (CERCLA). See CERCLA.

superior, *adj.* (Of a rank, office, power, etc.) higher; elevated; possessing greater power or authority; entitled to exert authority or command over another. — **superior,** *n.*

superior court. See COURT.

superior knowledge. See KNOWLEDGE (1).

superlien. A statutory lien that is superior to all existing liens and all later-filed liens on the same property. • Superliens are sometimes granted to a state's environmental-protection agency. Several states — such as Arkansas, Connecticut, Massachusetts, New Hampshire, New Jersey, and Tennessee — have enacted statutes creating superliens on property owned by a party responsible for environmental cleanup.

supersede, *vb.* **1.** To annul, make void, or repeal by taking the place of <the 1996 statute supersedes the 1989 act>. **2.** To invoke or make applicable the right of supersedeas against (an award of damages) <what is the amount of the bond necessary to supersede the judgment against her?>. — **supersession** (for sense 1), *n.*

supersedeas (soo-pər-**seed**-ee-əs), *n.* [Latin "you shall desist"] A writ or bond that suspends a judgment creditor's power to levy execution, usu. pending appeal. Pl. **supersedeases** (soo-pər-**see**-dee-əs-iz).

supersedeas bond. See BOND (2).

superseding cause. See CAUSE (1).

supervisor, *n.* **1.** One having authority over others; a manager or overseer. • Under the National Labor Relations Act, a supervisor is any individual having authority to hire, transfer, suspend, lay off, recall, promote, discharge, discipline, and handle grievances of other employees, by exercising independent judgment. **2.** The chief administrative officer of a town or county. — **supervisorial** (soo-pər-vɪ-**zor**-ee-əl), *adj.*

supervisory control. The control exercised by a higher court over a lower court, as by prohibiting the lower court from acting extrajurisdictionally and by reversing its extrajurisdictional acts. See MANDAMUS.

supplemental, *adj.* Supplying something additional; adding what is lacking <supplemental rules>.

supplemental complaint. See COMPLAINT.

supplemental jurisdiction. See JURISDICTION.

supplemental pleading. See PLEADING (1).

Supplemental Security Income. A welfare or needs-based program providing monthly income to the aged, blind, or disabled. • It is authorized by the Social Security Act. — Abbr. SSI.

supplementary proceeding. See PROCEEDING.

suppliant (**səp**-lee-ənt). One who humbly requests something; specif., the actor in a petition of right.

support, *n.* **1.** Sustenance or maintenance; esp., articles such as food and clothing that allow one to live in the degree of comfort to which one is accustomed. See MAINTENANCE (5); NECESSARIES. **2.** Basis or foundation. **3.** The right to have one's ground braced so that it does not cave in because of another landowner's actions. — **support,** *vb.*

support obligation. A secondary obligation or letter-of-credit right that supports the payment or performance of an account, chattel paper, general intangible, document, health-care-insurance receivable, instrument, or investment property. UCC § 9–102(a)(53).

support order. A court decree requiring a party in a divorce proceeding or a paternity proceeding to make payments to maintain a child or spouse, including medical, dental, and educational expenses.

support trust. See TRUST.

suppress, *vb.* To put a stop to, put down, or prohibit; to prevent (something) from being seen, heard, known, or discussed <the defendant tried to suppress the incriminating evidence>. — **suppression,** *n.* — **suppressible,** *adj.* — **suppressive,** *adj.*

suppression hearing. See HEARING.

suppression of evidence. **1.** A trial judge's ruling that evidence should be excluded because it was illegally acquired. **2.** The destruction of evidence or the refusal to give evidence at a criminal proceeding. • This is usually considered a crime. See OBSTRUCTION OF JUSTICE. **3.** The prosecution's withholding from the defense of evidence that is favorable to the defendant.

supra (s[y]oo-prə). [Latin "above"] Earlier in this text; used as a citational signal to refer to a previously cited authority. Cf. INFRA.

supra riparian (**soo**-prə ri-**pair**-ee-ən *or* rɪ-). Upper riparian; higher up the stream. • This phrase describes the estate, rights, and duties of a riparian owner whose land is situated nearer the source of a stream than the land it is compared to.

supremacy. The position of having the superior or greatest power or authority.

Supremacy Clause. The clause in Article VI of the U.S. Constitution declaring that all laws made in furtherance of the Constitution and all treaties made under the authority of the United States are the "supreme law of the land" and enjoy legal superiority over any conflicting provision of a state constitution or law. See PREEMPTION.

supreme, *adj.* (Of a court, power, right, etc.) highest; superior to all others.

supreme court. 1. (*cap.*) SUPREME COURT OF THE UNITED STATES. **2.** An appellate court existing in most states, usu. as the court of last resort. **3.** In New York, a court of general jurisdiction with trial and appellate divisions. • The Court of Appeals is the court of last resort in New York. — Abbr. S.C.; S.Ct.; Sup. Ct.

Supreme Court of Appeals. The highest court in West Virginia.

Supreme Court of the United States. The court of last resort in the federal system, whose members are appointed by the President and approved by the Senate. • The Court was established in 1789 by Article III of the U.S. Constitution, which vests the Court with the "judicial power of the United States." — Often shortened to *Supreme Court*.

Supreme Judicial Court. The highest appellate court in Maine and Massachusetts.

supreme law of the land. 1. The U.S. Constitution. **2.** Acts of Congress made according to the U.S. Constitution. **3.** U.S. treaties.

supreme legislation. See LEGISLATION.

surcharge, *vb.* **1.** To impose an additional (usu. excessive) tax, charge, or cost. **2.** To impose an additional load or burden. **3.** (Of a court) to impose a fine on a fiduciary for breach of duty.

surety (**shuur**[-ə]-tee). **1.** A person primarily liable for paying another's debt or performing another's obligation. • Although a surety is similar to an insurer, one important difference is that a surety often receives no compensation for assuming liability. A surety differs from a guarantor, who is liable to the creditor only if the debtor does not meet the duties owed to the creditor; the surety is directly liable. Cf. GUARANTOR. **2.** A formal assurance; esp., a pledge, bond, guarantee, or security given for the fulfillment of an undertaking.

surface right. A landowner's right to the land's surface and to all substances below the surface that are not defined as minerals. • The surface right is subject to the mineral owner's right to use the surface. Cf. MINERAL RIGHT; SUBSURFACE RIGHT.

Surgeon General. **1.** The chief medical officer of the U.S. Public Health Service or of a state public-health agency. **2.** The chief officer of the medical departments in the armed forces.

surmise (sər-**mɪz**), *n.* An idea based on weak evidence; conjecture.

surplusage (**sər**-pləs-ij). **1.** Redundant words in a statute or other drafted document; language that does not add meaning <the court must give effect to every word, reading nothing as mere surplusage>. **2.** Extraneous matter in a pleading <allegations that are irrelevant to the case will be treated as surplusage>.

surprise. An occurrence for which there is no adequate warning or that affects someone in an unexpected way. • In a trial, the procedural rules are designed to limit surprise — or trial by ambush — as much as possible. For example, parties in a civil case are allowed discovery to determine the essential facts of the case and the identities of possible witnesses, and to inspect relevant documents. At trial, if a party calls a witness not previously identified, the witness's testimony may be excluded if it would unfairly surprise and prejudice the other party.

surrebuttal (sər-ri-**bət**-əl). The response to the opposing party's rebuttal in a trial or other proceeding; a rebuttal to a rebuttal.

surrebutter (sər-ri-**bət**-ər). *Common-law pleading.* The plaintiff's answer of fact to the defendant's rebutter.

surrejoinder (sər-ri-**joyn**-dər). *Common-law pleading.* The plaintiff's answer to the defendant's rejoinder. See REPLICATION.

surrender, *n.* **1.** The act of yielding to another's power or control. **2.** The giving up of a right or claim; RELEASE (1). **3.** The return of an estate to the person who has a reversion or remainder, so as to merge the estate into a larger estate. **4.** *Commercial law.* The delivery of an instrument so that the delivery releases the deliverer from all liability. **5.** A tenant's relinquishment of possession before the lease has expired, allowing the landlord to take possession and treat the lease as terminated. — **surrender,** *vb.*

surrender by bail. A surety's delivery into custody of a prisoner who had been released on bail.

surrender by operation of law. An act that is an equivalent to an agreement by a tenant to abandon property and the landlord to resume possession, as when the parties perform an act so inconsistent with the landlord–tenant relationship that surrender is presumed, or when a tenant performs some act that would not be valid if the estate continued to exist.

surreptitious (sər-əp-**tish**-əs), *adj.* (Of conduct) unauthorized and clandestine; stealthily and usu. fraudulently done <surreptitious intercep-

tion of electronic communications is prohibited under wiretapping laws>.

surreptitious-entry warrant. See WARRANT.

surrogate (**sər**-ə-git), *n.* **1.** A substitute; esp., a person appointed to act in the place of another <in his absence, Sam's wife acted as a surrogate>. **2.** See *probate judge* under JUDGE. <the surrogate held that the will was valid>. — **surrogacy** (**sər**-ə-gə-see), *n.* — **surrogateship,** *n.*

surrogate mother. See MOTHER.

surrogate parent. See PARENT.

surrogate-parenting agreement. A contract between a woman and typically an infertile couple under which the woman provides her uterus to carry an embryo throughout pregnancy; esp., an agreement between a person (the intentional parent) and a woman (the surrogate mother) providing that the surrogate mother will (1) bear a child for the intentional parent, and (2) relinquish any and all rights to the child.

surrounding circumstances. The facts underlying an act, injury, or transaction — usu. one at issue in a legal proceeding.

surtax. See TAX.

surtax exemption. **1.** An exclusion of an item from a surtax. **2.** An item or an amount not subject to a surtax. See *surtax* under TAX.

surveillance (sər-**vay**-lənts), *n.* Close observation or listening of a person or place in the hope of gathering evidence. — **surveil** (sər-**vayl**), *vb.*

survey, *n.* **1.** A general consideration of something; appraisal. **2.** The measuring of a tract of land and its boundaries and contents; a map indicating the results of such measurements. **3.** A governmental department that carries out such measurements. **4.** A poll or questionnaire, esp. one examining popular opinion. — **survey,** *vb.*

survival action. A lawsuit brought on behalf of a decedent's estate for injuries or damages incurred by the decedent immediately before dying. • A survival action derives from the claim that a decedent who had survived would have had — as opposed to the claim that beneficiaries might have in a wrongful-death action. Cf. WRONGFUL-DEATH ACTION.

survival statute. A law that modifies the common law by allowing certain actions to continue in favor of a personal representative after the death of the party who could have originally brought the action; esp., a law that provides for the estate's recovery of damages incurred by the decedent immediately before death. Cf. DEATH STATUTE.

surviving, *adj.* Remaining alive; living beyond the happening of an event so as to entitle one to a distribution of property or income <surviving spouse>. See SURVIVAL ACTION.

surviving partner. See PARTNER.

survivor. **1.** One who outlives another. **2.** A trustee who administers a trust after the cotrustee has been removed, has refused to act, or has died.

survivorship. **1.** The state or condition of being the one person out of two or more who remains alive after the others die. **2.** The right of a surviving party having a joint interest with others in an estate to take the whole. See RIGHT OF SURVIVORSHIP.

suspect, *n.* A person believed to have committed a crime or offense.

suspect class. A group identified or defined in a suspect classification.

suspect classification. *Constitutional law*. A statutory classification based on race, national origin, or alienage, and thereby subject to strict scrutiny under equal-protection analysis. ● Examples of laws creating suspect classifications are those permitting only U.S. citizens to receive welfare benefits and those setting quotas for the government's hiring of minority contractors. See STRICT SCRUTINY. Cf. FUNDAMENTAL RIGHT.

> ***quasi-suspect classification.*** A statutory classification based on gender or legitimacy, and therefore subject to intermediate scrutiny under equal-protection analysis. ● Examples of laws creating quasi-suspect classifications are those that permit alimony only for women and those that provide for an all-male draft. See INTERMEDIATE SCRUTINY.

suspend, *vb.* **1.** To interrupt; postpone; defer <the fire alarm suspended the prosecutor's opening statement>. **2.** To temporarily keep (a person) from performing a function, occupying an office, holding a job, or exercising a right or privilege <the attorney's law license was suspended for violating the Rules of Professional Conduct>.

suspended sentence. See SENTENCE.

suspense. The state or condition of being suspended; temporary cessation <a suspense of judgment>.

suspension. 1. The act of temporarily delaying, interrupting, or terminating something <suspension of business operations>. **2.** The state of such delay, interruption, or termination <transfers were not allowed because of the suspension of business>. **3.** The temporary deprivation of a person's powers or privileges, esp. of office or profession <suspension of her bar license>. **4.** The temporary withdrawal from employment, as distinguished from permanent severance <suspension from teaching without pay>.

suspensory veto. See VETO.

suspicion. The imagination or apprehension of the existence of something wrong based only on slight or no evidence, without definitive proof. See REASONABLE SUSPICION.

suspicious-activity report. A form that, as of 1996, a financial institution must complete and submit to federal regulatory authorities if it suspects that a federal crime has occurred in the course of a monetary transaction. ● This form superseded two earlier forms, the criminal-referral form and the suspicious-transaction report.

suspicious character. In some states, a person who is strongly suspected or known to be a habitual criminal and therefore may be arrested or required to give security for good behavior.

suspicious-transaction report. A checkbox on IRS Form 4789 formerly (1990–1995) requiring banks and other financial institutions to report transactions that might be relevant to a violation of the Bank Secrecy Act or its regulations or that might suggest money-laundering or tax evasion. • This checkbox, like the criminal-referral form, has since been superseded by the suspicious-activity report.

sustain, *vb.* **1.** To support or maintain, esp. over a long period <enough oxygen to sustain life>. **2.** To nourish and encourage; lend strength to <she helped sustain the criminal enterprise>. **3.** To undergo; suffer <Charles sustained third-degree burns>. **4.** (Of a court) to uphold or rule in favor of <objection sustained>. **5.** To substantiate or corroborate <several witnesses sustained Ms. Sipes's allegation>. **6.** To persist in making (an effort) over a long period <he sustained his vow of silence for the last 16 years of his life>. — **sustainment,** *n.* — **sustentation,** *n.* — **sustainable,** *adj.*

S.W. *abbr.* SOUTHWESTERN REPORTER.

swamp and overflowed land. See LAND.

swear, *vb.* **1.** To administer an oath to (a person). **2.** To take an oath. **3.** To use obscene or profane language.

swearing-in, *n.* The administration of an oath to a person who is taking office or testifying in a legal proceeding. See OATH.

swearing match. A dispute in which determining a vital fact involves the credibility choice between one witness's word and another's — the two being irreconcilably in conflict and there being no other evidence. • In such a dispute, the fact-finder is generally thought to believe the more reputable witness, such as a police officer over a convicted drug-dealer.

swear out, *vb.* To obtain the issue of (an arrest warrant) by making a charge under oath <Franklin swore out a complaint against Sutton>.

sweat equity. Financial equity created in property by the owner's labor in improving the property.

sweating. *Criminal procedure.* The illegal interrogation of a prisoner by use of threats or similar means to extort information.

sweatshop. A business where the employees are overworked and underpaid in extreme conditions; esp., in lawyer lingo, a law firm that requires associates to work so hard that they barely (if at all) maintain a family or social life — though the firm may, in return, pay higher salaries.

swindle, *vb.* **1.** To cheat (a person) out of property <Johnson swindled Norton out of $1,000>. **2.** To obtain (property) from a person by cheating <Johnson swindled $1,000 out of Norton>. — **swindle,** *n.* — **swindling,** *n.*

swing vote. The vote that determines an issue when all other voting parties, such as appellate judges, are evenly split.

sworn statement. See STATEMENT.

symbiotic-relationship test. The standard by which a private person may be considered a state actor — and may be liable for violating someone's constitutional rights — if the relationship between the private person and the government is so close that they can fairly be said to be acting jointly. • Private acts by a private person do not generally create liability for violating someone's constitutional rights. But if a private person violates someone's constitutional rights while engaging in state action, the private person, and possibly the government, can be held liable. State action may be shown by proving that the private person and the state have a mutually dependent (symbiotic) relationship. The symbiotic-relationship test is strictly construed. For example, the fact that an entity receives financial support from — or is heavily regulated by — the government is probably insufficient to show a symbiotic relationship. See JOINT PARTICIPATION. Cf. STATE-COMPULSION TEST; NEXUS TEST.

symbolic, *adj.* (Of a signature) consisting of a symbol or mark. Cf. HOLOGRAPH.

symbolic delivery. See DELIVERY.

symbolic speech. See SPEECH.

syndicate (**sin**-di-kit), *n.* A group organized for a common purpose; esp., an association formed to promote a common interest, carry out a particular business transaction, or (in a negative sense) organize criminal enterprises. — **syndicate** (**sin**-di-kayt), *vb.* — **syndication** (sin-di-**kay**-shən), *n.* — **syndicator** (**sin**-di-kay-tər), *n.* See ORGANIZED CRIME.

synopsis (si-**nop**-sis), *n.* A brief or partial survey; a summary or outline; HEADNOTE. — **synopsize** (si-**nop**-SIZ), *vb.*

systematic violation. *Civil-rights law.* An employer's policy or procedure that is discriminatory against an employee. • Such a policy or procedure will usually be considered a continuing violation. So an employee's claim of unlawful discrimination will not be barred as untimely as long as some discriminatory effect of the policy or procedure occurs within the limitations period (e.g., 300 days for a Title VII claim). Cf. SERIAL VIOLATION.

T

table, *vb.* To postpone consideration of (a pending bill or proposal) with no commitment to resume consideration unless the motion to table specifies a later date or time.

table of cases. An alphabetical list of cases cited, referred to, or digested in a legal textbook, volume of reports, or digest, with references to the section, page, or paragraph where each case appears.

tabula rasa (**tab**-yə-lə **rah**-zə). [Latin "scraped tablet"] A blank tablet ready for writing; a clean slate. Pl. ***tabulae rasae*** (**tab**-yə-lee **rahs**-I).

tacit (**tas**-it), *adj.* Implied but not actually expressed; implied by silence or silent acquiescence <a tacit understanding> <a tacit admission>. — **tacitly,** *adv.*

tacit dedication. See DEDICATION.

tacking. 1. The joining of consecutive periods of possession by different persons to treat the periods as one continuous period; esp., the adding of one's own period of land possession to that of a prior possessor to establish continuous adverse possession for the statutory period. See ADVERSE POSSESSION. **2.** The joining of a junior lien with the first lien in order to acquire priority over an intermediate lien. — **tack,** *vb.*

tail, *n.* The limitation of an estate so that it can be inherited only by the fee owner's issue or class of issue. See FEE TAIL; ENTAIL.

tail female. A limitation to female heirs.

tail general. A tail limited to the issue of a particular person, but not to that of a particular couple.

tail male. A limitation to male heirs.

tail special. A tail limited to specified heirs of the donee's body.

taint, *n.* **1.** A conviction of felony. **2.** A person so convicted. See ATTAINDER.

taint, *vb.* **1.** To imbue with a noxious quality or principle. **2.** To contaminate or corrupt. **3.** To tinge or affect slightly for the worse. — **taint,** *n.*

tainted evidence. See EVIDENCE.

take, *vb.* **1.** To obtain possession or control, whether legally or illegally. **2.** To seize with authority; to confiscate or apprehend. **3.** (Of a federal or state government) to acquire (property) for public use; condemn. **4.** To acquire possession by virtue of a grant of title, the use of eminent domain, or other legal means; esp., to receive property by will or intestate succession. See TAKING. **5.** To claim one's rights under.

take back, *vb.* To revoke; to retract.

take by stealth. To steal (personal property); to pilfer or filch.

take care of. **1.** To support or look after (a person). **2.** To pay (a debt). **3.** To attend to (some matter).

take delivery. To receive something purchased or ordered; esp., to receive a commodity under a futures contract or spot-market contract, or to receive securities recently purchased.

take effect, *vb.* **1.** To become operative or executed. **2.** To be in force; to go into operation.

take-nothing judgment. See JUDGMENT.

taker, *n.* A person who acquires; esp., one who receives property by will, by power of appointment, or by intestate succession.

first taker. A person who receives an estate that is subject to a remainder or executory devise.

taker in default. A person designated by a donor to receive property under a power of appointment if the donee fails to exercise that power.

take the witness. You may now question the witness. • This phrase is a lawyer's courtroom announcement that ends one side's questioning and prompts the other side to begin its questioning. Synonymous phrases are *your witness* and *pass the witness*.

taking, *n.* **1.** *Criminal & tort law.* The act of seizing an article, with or without removing it, but with an implicit transfer of possession or control.

constructive taking. An act that does not equal an actual appropriation of an article but that does show an intention to convert it, as when a person entrusted with the possession of goods starts using them contrary to the owner's instructions.

2. *Constitutional law.* The government's actual or effective acquisition of private property either by ousting the owner and claiming title or by destroying the property or severely impairing its utility. • There is a taking of property when government action directly interferes with or substantially disturbs the owner's use and enjoyment of the property. See CONDEMNATION (2); EMINENT DOMAIN.

actual taking. A physical appropriation of an owner's property by an entity clothed with eminent-domain authority.

de facto taking (di **fak**-toh). A taking in which an entity clothed with eminent-domain power substantially interferes with an owner's use, possession, or enjoyment of property.

Takings Clause. The Fifth Amendment provision that prohibits the government from taking private property for public use without fairly compensating the owner. See EMINENT DOMAIN.

tales (**tay**-leez *or* taylz). [Latin, pl. of *talis* "such," in the phrase *tales de circumstantibus* "such of the bystanders"] **1.** A supply of additional jurors, usu. drawn from the bystanders at the courthouse, summoned to fill a panel that has become deficient in number because of juror challenges or exemptions. **2.** A writ or order summoning these jurors.

TAM. *abbr.* TECHNICAL ADVICE MEMORANDUM.

tamper, *vb.* **1.** To meddle so as to alter (a thing); esp., to make changes that are illegal, corrupting, or perverting. **2.** To interfere improperly; to meddle.

tampering, *n.* **1.** The act of altering a thing; esp., the act of illegally altering a document or product, such as written evidence or a consumer good. See Model Penal Code §§ 224.4, 241.8; 18 USCA § 1365. **2.** The act or an instance of engaging in improper or underhanded dealings, esp. in an attempt to influence. • Tampering with a witness or jury is a criminal offense. See WITNESS TAMPERING; OBSTRUCTION OF JUSTICE; EMBRACERY.

tangible, *adj.* **1.** Having or possessing physical form. **2.** Capable of being touched and seen; perceptible to the touch; capable of being possessed or realized. **3.** Capable of being understood by the mind.

tangible chattel paper. See CHATTEL PAPER.

tangible property. See PROPERTY.

tapper, *n.* **1.** A person who approaches another for money; a beggar. **2.** By extension, a thief.

tapping, *n.* See WIRETAPPING.

target witness. See WITNESS.

tax, *n.* A charge, usu. monetary, imposed by the government on persons, entities, or property to yield public revenue. • Most broadly, the term embraces all governmental impositions on the person, property, privileges, occupations, and enjoyment of the people, and includes duties, imposts, and excises. Although a tax is often thought of as being pecuniary in nature, it is not necessarily payable only in money. — **tax,** *vb.*

accrued tax. A tax that has been incurred but not yet paid or payable.

accumulated-earnings tax. A penalty tax imposed on a corporation that has retained its earnings in an effort to avoid the income-tax liability arising once the earnings are distributed to shareholders as dividends.

ad valorem tax. A tax imposed proportionally on the value of something (esp. real property), rather than on its quantity or some other measure.

alternative minimum tax. A flat tax potentially imposed on corporations and higher-income individuals to ensure that those taxpayers do not avoid all income-tax liability by using exclusions, deductions, and credits.

capital-gains tax. A tax on income derived from the sale of a capital asset. • The federal income tax on capital gains typically has a more favorable tax rate than the maximum tax rate on ordinary income. See CAPITAL GAIN.

death tax. An estate tax or inheritance tax.

direct tax. A tax that is imposed on property, as distinguished from a tax on a right or privilege. • Ad valorem and property taxes are direct taxes.

estate tax. A tax imposed on property transferred by will or by intestate succession. Cf. *inheritance tax*.

estimated tax. A tax paid quarterly by a taxpayer not subject to withholding (such as a self-employed person) based on either the previous year's tax liability or an estimate of the current year's tax liability.

excess-profits tax. **1.** A tax levied on profits that are beyond a business's normal profits. • This type of tax is usually imposed only in times of national emergency (such as war) to discourage profiteering. **2.** See *accumulated-earnings tax*.

flat tax. A tax whose rate remains fixed regardless of the amount of the tax base. • Most sales taxes are flat taxes. Cf. *progressive tax*; *regressive tax*.

general tax. **1.** A tax that returns no special benefit to the taxpayer other than the support of governmental programs that benefit all. **2.** A property tax or an ad valorem tax that is imposed for no special purpose except to produce public revenue.

generation-skipping tax. A tax on a property transfer that skips a generation. • The tax limits the use of generation-skipping techniques as a means of avoiding estate taxes.

generation-skipping transfer tax. A gift or estate tax imposed on a generation-skipping transfer or a generation-skipping trust. IRC (26 USCA) §§ 2601–2663. See DIRECT SKIP; GENERATION-SKIPPING TRANSFER; *generation-skipping trust* under TRUST; TAXABLE DISTRIBUTION; TAXABLE TERMINATION.

gift tax. A tax imposed when property is voluntarily and gratuitously transferred. • Under federal law, the gift tax is imposed on the donor, but some states tax the donee.

gross-income tax. A tax on gross receipts rather than on net profits; an income tax without allowance for expenses or deductions.

hidden tax. A tax that is paid, often unknowingly, by someone other than the person or entity on whom it is levied; esp., a tax imposed on a manufacturer or seller (such as a gasoline producer) who passes it on to consumers in the form of higher sales prices.

income tax. A tax on an individual's or entity's net income. • The federal income tax — governed by the Internal Revenue Code — is the federal government's primary source of revenue, and many states have income taxes as well. Cf. *property tax*; EXCISE.

indirect tax. A tax on a right or privilege, such as an occupation tax or franchise tax.

inheritance tax. **1.** A tax imposed on a person who inherits property from another (unlike an estate tax, which is imposed on the decedent's estate). • There is no federal inheritance tax, but some states provide for one (though it is deductible under the federal estate tax). — Sometimes termed *succession tax*. Cf. *estate tax*. **2.** Loosely, an estate tax.

kiddie tax. A federal tax imposed on a child's unearned income at the parents' tax rate if the parents' rate is higher and if the child is under 14 years of age.

luxury tax. An excise tax imposed on high-priced items that are not deemed necessities (such as cars costing more than a specified amount). Cf. *sin tax*.

nanny tax. A federal social-security tax imposed on the employer of a domestic employee if the employer pays that employee more than a specified amount in total wages in a year. • The term, which is not a technical legal phrase, was popularized in the mid-1990s, when several of President Clinton's nominees were found not to have paid the social-security tax for their nannies.

occupation tax. An excise tax imposed for the privilege of carrying on a business, trade, or profession. • For example, many states require lawyers to pay an occupation tax.

payroll tax. **1.** A tax payable by an employer based on its payroll (such as a social-security tax or an unemployment tax). **2.** A tax collected by an employer from its employees' gross pay (such as an income tax or a social-security tax). See *withholding tax*.

personal-property tax. A tax on personal property (such as jewelry or household furniture) levied by a state or local government.

poll tax. A fixed tax levied on each person within a jurisdiction. • The 24th Amendment prohibits the federal and state governments from imposing poll taxes as a condition for voting.

progressive tax. A tax structured so that the percentage of income paid in taxes increases as the taxpayer's income increases. • Most income taxes are progressive, meaning that a higher income is taxed at a higher rate. Cf. *regressive tax*; *flat tax*.

property tax. A tax levied on the owner of property (esp. real property), usu. based on the property's value. • Local governments often impose property taxes to finance school districts, municipal projects, and the like. Cf. *income tax*; EXCISE.

regressive tax. A tax structured so that the percentage of income paid in taxes decreases as the taxpayer's income increases. • A sales tax is regressive because it is more burdensome for low-income taxpayers than for high-income taxpayers. Cf. *progressive tax*; *flat tax*.

sales tax. A tax imposed on the sale of goods and services, usu. measured as a percentage of their price. See *flat tax*.

sin tax. An excise tax imposed on goods or activities that are considered harmful or immoral (such as cigarettes, liquor, or gambling). Cf. *luxury tax*.

special tax. **1.** A tax levied for a unique purpose. **2.** A tax (such as an inheritance tax) that is levied in addition to a general tax.

specific tax. A tax imposed as a fixed sum on each article or item of property of a given class or kind without regard to its value.

stamp tax. A tax imposed by requiring the purchase of a revenue stamp that must be affixed to a legal document (such as a deed or note) before the document can be recorded.

state tax. **1.** A tax — usu. in the form of a sales or income tax — earmarked for state, rather than federal or municipal, purposes. **2.** A tax levied under a state law.

succession tax. See *inheritance tax* (1).

surtax. An additional tax imposed on something being taxed or on the primary tax itself.

transfer tax. A tax imposed on the transfer of property, esp. by will, inheritance, or gift. • The federal estate-and-gift tax is sometimes referred to as the *unified transfer tax* (or the *unified estate-and-gift tax*) because lifetime gifts and death gifts are treated equally under the same tax laws.

unemployment tax. A tax imposed on an employer by state or federal law to cover the cost of unemployment insurance. • The Federal Unemployment Tax Act (FUTA) provides for a tax based on a percentage of employee earnings but allows a credit for amounts paid in state unemployment taxes.

unified estate-and-gift tax. See *transfer tax*.

unrelated-business-income tax. A tax levied on a not-for-profit organization's taxable income, such as advertising revenue from a publication.

use tax. A tax imposed on the use of certain goods that are bought outside the taxing authority's jurisdiction. • Use taxes are designed to discourage the purchase of products that are not subject to the sales tax.

value-added tax. A tax assessed at each step in the production of a commodity, based on the value added at each step by the difference between the commodity's production cost and its selling price. • A value-added tax — which is popular in several European countries — effectively acts as a sales tax on the ultimate consumer. — Abbr. VAT.

windfall-profits tax. A tax imposed on a business or industry as a result of a sudden increase in profits. • An example is the tax imposed on oil companies in 1980 for profits resulting from the Arab oil embargo of the 1970s.

withholding tax. A portion of income tax that is deducted from salary, wages, dividends, or other income before the earner receives payment. • The most common example is the income tax and social-security tax withheld by an employer from an employee's pay.

taxable, *adj.* **1.** Subject to taxation <interest earned on a checking account is taxable income>. **2.** (Of legal costs or fees) assessable <expert-witness fees are not taxable court costs>.

taxable distribution. A generation-skipping transfer from a trust to the beneficiary (i.e., the skip person) that is neither a direct skip nor a taxable termination. See GENERATION-SKIPPING TRANSFER; *generation-skipping transfer tax* under TAX; *generation-skipping trust* under TRUST; SKIP PERSON.

taxable estate. See ESTATE (3).

taxable gift. See GIFT.

taxable income. See INCOME.

taxable termination. A taxable event that occurs when (1) an interest in a generation-skipping trust property terminates (as on the death of a skip person's parent who possessed the interest), (2) no interest in the trust is held by a nonskip person, and (3) a distribution may be made to a skip person. • Before the creation of taxable terminations in 1976, a taxpayer could create a trust that paid income to a child for life, then to that child's child for life, and so on without incurring an estate or gift tax liability. See GENERATION-SKIPPING TRANSFER; *generation-skipping transfer tax* under TAX; *generation-skipping trust* under TRUST; SKIP PERSON.

taxation. The imposition or assessment of a tax; the means by which the state obtains the revenue required for its activities.

double taxation. **1.** The imposition of two taxes on the same property during the same period and for the same taxing purpose. **2.** The imposition of two taxes on one corporate profit; esp., the structure of taxation employed by Subchapter C of the Internal Revenue Code, under which corporate profits are taxed twice, once to the corporation when earned and once to the shareholders when the earnings are distributed as dividends.

pass-through taxation. The taxation of an entity's owners for the entity's income without taxing the entity itself. • Partnerships and S corporations are taxed under this method.

tax avoidance. The act of taking advantage of legally available tax-planning opportunities in order to minimize one's tax liability. Cf. TAX EVASION.

tax base. The total property, income, or wealth subject to taxation in a given jurisdiction; the aggregate value of the property being taxed by a particular tax. Cf. BASIS (2).

tax-benefit rule. The principle that if a taxpayer recovers a loss or expense that was deducted in a previous year, the recovery must be included in the current year's gross income to the extent that it was previously deducted.

tax bracket. A categorized level of income subject to a particular tax rate under federal or state law <28% tax bracket>.

tax court. **1.** TAX COURT, U.S. **2.** In some states, a court that hears appeals in nonfederal tax cases and can modify or change any valuation, assessment, classification, tax, or final order appealed from.

Tax Court, U.S. A federal court that hears appeals by taxpayers from adverse IRS decisions about tax deficiencies. • The Tax Court was created in 1942, replacing the Board of Tax Appeals. — Abbr. T.C.

tax credit. An amount subtracted directly from one's total tax liability, dollar for dollar, as opposed to a deduction from gross income. — Often shortened to *credit*. Cf. DEDUCTION (2).

child- and dependent-care tax credit. A tax credit available to a person who is employed full-time and who maintains a household for a dependent child or a disabled spouse or dependent.

earned-income credit. A refundable federal tax credit on the earned income of a low-income worker with dependent children. • The credit is paid to the taxpayer even if it exceeds the total tax liability.

foreign tax credit. A tax credit against U.S. income taxes for a taxpayer who earns income overseas and has paid foreign taxes on that income. See FOREIGN-EARNED-INCOME EXCLUSION.

investment tax credit. A tax credit intended to stimulate business investment in capital goods by allowing a percentage of the purchase price as a credit against the taxpayer's income taxes. • The Tax Reform Act of 1986 generally repealed this credit retroactively for most property placed in service after January 1, 1986.

unified estate-and-gift tax credit. A tax credit applied against the federal unified transfer tax. • The 1999 credit is $211,300, meaning that an estate worth up to $650,000 passes to the heirs free of any federal estate tax. The credit will gradually increase so that, after 2005, it will be $345,800, meaning that no federal estate tax will be due on an estate worth up to $1 million. — Often shortened to *unified credit*.

tax-deferred, *adj.* Not taxable until a future date or event <a tax-deferred retirement plan>.

tax evasion. The willful attempt to defeat or circumvent the tax law in order to illegally reduce one's tax liability. • Tax evasion is punishable by both civil and criminal penalties. Cf. TAX AVOIDANCE.

tax-exempt, *adj.* **1.** Not legally subject to taxation <a tax-exempt charity>. **2.** Bearing interest that is free from income tax <tax-exempt municipal bonds>.

tax foreclosure. See FORECLOSURE.

tax-free exchange. A transfer of property that the tax law specifically exempts from income-tax consequences. • An example is a transfer of property to a controlled corporation under IRC (26 USCA) § 351(a) and a like-kind exchange under IRC (26 USCA) § 1031(a).

tax haven. A country that imposes little or no tax on the profits from transactions carried on in that country.

tax home. A taxpayer's principal business location, post, or station. • Travel expenses are tax-deductible only if the taxpayer is traveling away from home.

tax incentive. A governmental enticement, through a tax benefit, to engage in a particular activity, such as the mortgage financing of real-estate sales.

taxing power. See POWER.

tax law. 1. The area of legal study dealing with taxation. **2.** INTERNAL REVENUE CODE.

tax liability. The amount that a taxpayer legally owes after calculating the applicable tax; the amount of unpaid taxes.

taxpayers' bill of rights. Federal legislation granting taxpayers specific rights when dealing with the Internal Revenue Service, such as the right to have representation and the right to receive written notice of a levy 30 days before enforcement.

taxpayer-standing doctrine. *Constitutional law.* The principle that a taxpayer has no standing to sue the government for allegedly misspending the public's tax money unless the taxpayer can demonstrate a personal stake and show some direct injury.

tax-preference items. Certain items that, even though deducted in arriving at taxable income for regular tax purposes, must be considered in calculating a taxpayer's alternative minimum tax. See *alternative minimum tax* under TAX.

tax rate. A mathematical figure for calculating a tax, usu. expressed as a percentage.

average tax rate. Tax liability divided by taxable income, usu. throughout a geographic area or for a particular number of years.

marginal tax rate. In a progressive-tax scheme, the rate applicable to the last dollar of income earned by the taxpayer. • This concept is useful in calculating the tax effect of receiving additional income or of claiming additional deductions. See TAX BRACKET.

tax-rate schedule. A schedule used to determine the tax on a given level of taxable income and based on a taxpayer's status (for example, married filing a joint income-tax return).

tax redemption. See REDEMPTION.

tax return. An income-tax form on which a person or entity reports income, deductions, and exemptions, and on which tax liability is calculated.

amended return. A return filed after the original return, usu. to correct an error in the original.

consolidated return. A return that reflects combined financial information for a group of affiliated corporations.

information return. A return, such as a W-2, filed by an entity to report some economic information other than tax liability.

joint return. A return filed together by spouses. • A joint return can be filed even if only one spouse had income, but each spouse is usually individually liable for the tax payment.

separate return. A return filed by each spouse separately, showing income and liability. • Unlike the spouse filing a joint return, the spouse filing a separate return is individually liable only for taxes due on his or her return.

tax shelter, *n.* A financial operation or investment strategy (such as a partnership or real-estate investment trust) that is created primarily for the purpose of reducing or deferring income-tax payments. • The Tax Reform Act of 1986 — by restricting the deductibility of passive losses — sharply limited the effectiveness of tax shelters. — **tax-sheltered,** *adj.*

tax title. See TITLE (2).

tax warrant. See WARRANT.

tax write-off. A deduction of depreciation, loss, or expense.

tax year. The period used for computing federal or state income-tax liability, usu. either the calendar year or a fiscal year of 12 months ending on the last day of a month other than December.

TBC. *abbr.* Trial before the court. See *bench trial* under TRIAL.

T-bill. *abbr.* TREASURY BILL.

T-bond. *abbr.* TREASURY BOND.

T.C. *abbr.* TAX COURT.

T.C. memo. *abbr.* A memorandum decision of the U.S. Tax Court.

teamwork. Work done by a team; esp., work by a team of animals as a substantial part of one's business, such as farming, express carrying, freight hauling, or transporting material. • In some jurisdictions, animals (such as horses) that work in teams are exempt from execution on a civil judgment.

TECA (**tee**-kə). *abbr.* TEMPORARY EMERGENCY COURT OF APPEALS.

Technical Advice Memorandum. A publication issued by the national office of the IRS, usu. at a taxpayer's request, to explain some complex or novel tax-law issue. — Abbr. TAM.

temporary administration. See ADMINISTRATION.

Temporary Emergency Court of Appeals. A special U.S. court created in 1971 with exclusive jurisdiction over appeals from federal district courts concerning price and other economic controls begun in the 1950s and 1960s. • The court consists of eight district and circuit judges appointed by the Chief Justice. Although called "temporary," the court was still active through the end of the 20th century. — Abbr. TECA.

temporary frustration. See FRUSTRATION.

temporary insanity. See INSANITY.

temporary nuisance. See NUISANCE.

temporary restraining order. A court order, usu. preserving the status quo, forbidding the opposing party from taking some action until a litigant's application for a preliminary or permanent injunction can be heard. • A temporary restraining order may sometimes be granted without notifying the opposing party in advance. — Abbr. TRO. Cf. INJUNCTION.

temporary statute. See STATUTE.

temporary total disability. See DISABILITY (1).

temporary ward. See WARD.

tenancy. 1. The possession or occupancy of land by right or title, esp. under a lease; a leasehold interest in real estate. **2.** The period of such possession or occupancy. See ESTATE.

cotenancy. A tenancy with two or more coowners who have unity of possession. • Examples are a joint tenancy and a tenancy in common.

entire tenancy. A tenancy possessed by one person, as opposed to a joint or common tenancy. See *tenancy by the entirety*.

general tenancy. A tenancy that is not of fixed duration under the parties' agreement.

joint tenancy. A tenancy with two or more coowners who take identical interests simultaneously by the same instrument and with the same right of possession. • A joint tenancy differs from a tenancy in common because each joint tenant has a right of survivorship to the other's share. (In some states, this right must be clearly expressed in the conveyance — otherwise, the tenancy will be presumed to be a tenancy in common.) See UNITY (2); RIGHT OF SURVIVORSHIP. Cf. *tenancy in common*.

periodic tenancy. A tenancy that automatically continues for successive periods — usu. month to month or year to year — unless terminated at the end of a period by notice. • A typical example is a month-to-month apartment lease. This type of tenancy originated through court rulings that, when the lessor received a periodic rent, the lease could not be terminated without reasonable notice.

several tenancy. A tenancy that is separate and not held jointly with another person.

tenancy at sufferance. A tenancy arising when a person who has been in lawful possession of property wrongfully remains as a holdover after his or her interest has expired. • A tenancy at sufferance takes the form of either a tenancy at will or a periodic tenancy. See HOLDING OVER.

tenancy attendant on the inheritance. A tenancy for a term that is vested in a trustee in trust for the owner of the inheritance.

tenancy at will. A tenancy in which the tenant holds possession with the landlord's consent but without fixed terms (as for duration or rent). • Such a tenancy may be terminated by either party upon fair notice.

tenancy by the entirety (en-tɪ-ər-tee). A joint tenancy that arises between husband and wife when a single instrument conveys realty to both of them but nothing is said in the deed or will about the character of their ownership. • This type of tenancy exists in only a few states.

tenancy for a term. A tenancy whose duration is known in years, weeks, or days from the moment of its creation.

tenancy in common. A tenancy by two or more persons, in equal or unequal undivided shares, each person having an equal right to possess the whole property but no right of survivorship. Cf. *joint tenancy*.

tenancy in gross. A tenancy for a term that is outstanding — that is, one that is unattached to or disconnected from the estate or inheritance, such as one that is in the hands of some third party having no interest in the inheritance.

tenant, *n.* **1.** One who holds or possesses lands or tenements by any kind of right or title. See TENANCY. **2.** One who pays rent for the temporary use and occupation of another's land under a lease or similar arrangement. See LESSEE.

tenantable repair. A repair that will render premises fit for present habitation. See HABITABILITY.

tenant's fixture. See FIXTURE.

tender, *n.* **1.** An unconditional offer of money or performance to satisfy a debt or obligation <a tender of delivery>. • The tender may save the tendering party from a penalty for nonpayment or nonperformance or may, if the other party unjustifiably refuses the tender, place the other party in default.

tender of delivery. A seller's putting and holding conforming goods at the buyer's disposition and giving the buyer any notification reasonably necessary to take delivery. • The manner, time, and place for tender are determined by the agreement and by Article 2 of the Uniform Commercial Code.

2. Something unconditionally offered to satisfy a debt or obligation. **3.** *Contracts.* Attempted performance that is frustrated by the act of the party for whose benefit it is to take place. • The performance may take the form of either a tender of goods or a tender of payment. Although this sense is quite similar to sense 1, it differs in making the other party's refusal part of the definition itself.

perfect tender. A seller's tender that meets the contractual terms entered into with the buyer concerning the quality and specifications of the goods sold.

4. An offer or bid put forward for acceptance <a tender for the construction contract>. **5.** Something that serves as a means of payment, such as coin, banknotes, or other circulating medium; money <legal tender>. — **tender,** *vb.*

tender of issue. *Common-law pleading.* A form attached to a traverse, by which the traversing party refers the issue to the proper mode of trial.

tender of performance. An offer to perform, usu. necessary to hold the defaulting party to a contract liable for breach.

tender-years doctrine. *Family law.* The doctrine holding that custody of very young children (usu. five years of age and younger) should generally be awarded to the mother in a divorce unless she is found to be unfit. • This doctrine has been rejected in most states and replaced by a presumption of joint custody.

tenement. 1. Property (esp. land) held by freehold; an estate or holding of land. **2.** A house or other building used as a residence.

tenement house. An apartment house; esp., a low-rent apartment building, usu. in poor condition and at best meeting only minimal safety and sanitary conditions.

tenendum (tə-**nen**-dəm). A clause in a deed designating the kind of tenure by which the things granted are to be held. Cf. HABENDUM CLAUSE (1).

Tenth Amendment. The constitutional amendment, ratified as part of the Bill of Rights in 1791, providing that any powers not constitutionally delegated to the federal government, nor prohibited to the states, are reserved for the states or the people.

1031 exchange (ten-thər-tee-wən). A like-kind exchange of property that is exempt from income-tax consequences under IRC (26 USCA) § 1031.

tenure (ten-yər), *n.* **1.** A right, term, or mode of holding lands or tenements in subordination to a superior. **2.** A status afforded to a teacher or professor as a protection against summary dismissal without sufficient cause. • This status has long been considered a cornerstone of academic freedom. **3.** More generally, the legal protection of a long-term relationship, such as employment. — **tenurial** (ten-**yuur**-ee-əl), *adj.*

term, *n.* **1.** A word or phrase; esp., an expression that has a fixed meaning in some field <term of art>. **2.** A contractual stipulation <the delivery term provided for shipment within 30 days>. See CONDITION (3).

fundamental term. **1.** A contractual provision that must be included for a contract to exist; a contractual provision that specifies an essential purpose of the contract, so that a breach of the provision through inadequate performance makes the performance not only defective but essentially different from what had been promised. **2.** A contractual provision that must be included in the contract to satisfy the statute of frauds.

implied term. A provision not expressly agreed to by the parties but instead read into the contract by a court as being implicit. • An implied term should not, in theory, contradict the contract's express terms.

nonfundamental term. Any contractual provision that is not regarded as a fundamental term.

3. (*pl.*) Provisions that define an agreement's scope; conditions or stipulations <terms of sale>. **4.** A fixed period of time; esp., the period for which an estate is granted <term of years>.

attendant term. A long period (such as 1,000 years) specified as the duration of a mortgage, created to protect the mortgagor's heirs' interest in the land by not taking back title to the land once it is paid for, but rather by assigning title to a trustee who holds the title in trust for the mortgagor and the mortgagor's heirs. • This arrangement gives the heirs another title to the property in case the interest they inherited proves somehow defective. These types of terms have been largely abolished. See *tenancy attendant on the inheritance* under TENANCY.

satisfied term. A term of years in land that has satisfied the purpose for which it was created before the term's expiration.

term for deliberating. The time given a beneficiary to decide whether to accept or reject an inheritance or other succession.

term in gross. A term that is unattached to an estate or inheritance. See *tenancy in gross* under TENANCY.

unexpired term. The remainder of a period prescribed by law or provided for in a lease.

5. The period or session during which a court conducts judicial business <the most recent term was busy indeed>. See SESSION.

additional term. A distinct, added term to a previous term.

adjourned term. A continuance of a previous or regular term but not a separate term; the same term prolonged.

equity term. The period during which a court tries only equity cases.

general term. A regular term of court — that is, the period during which a court ordinarily sits.

regular term. A term of court begun at the time appointed by law and continued, in the court's discretion, until the court lawfully adjourns.

special term. A term of court scheduled outside the general term, usu. for conducting extraordinary business.

terminable interest. An interest that may be terminated upon the lapse of time or upon the occurrence of some condition.

terminable property. Property (such as a leasehold) whose duration is not perpetual or indefinite but that is limited in time or liable to terminate on the happening of an event.

termination, *n.* **1.** The act of ending something <termination of the partnership by winding up its affairs>. **2.** The end of something in time or existence; conclusion or discontinuance <the insurance policy's termination left the doctor without liability coverage>. — **terminate,** *vb.* — **terminable,** *adj.*

termination of parental rights. *Family law.* The legal severing of a parent's rights, privileges, and responsibilities regarding his or her child. • Termination of a parent's rights frees the child to be adopted by someone else. See PARENTAL RIGHTS.

termination proceeding. An administrative action to end a person's or entity's status or relationship.

term loan. See LOAN.

term of art. 1. A word or phrase having a specific, precise meaning in a given specialty, apart from its general meaning in ordinary contexts. • Examples in law include *and his heirs* and *res ipsa loquitur*. **2.** Loosely, a jargonistic word or phrase.

term-of-art canon. In statutory construction, the principle that if a term has acquired a technical or specialized meaning in a particular context, the term should be presumed to have that meaning if used in that context.

termor (**tər**-mər). A person who holds lands or tenements for a term of years or for life.

terre-tenant (**tair** ten-ənt). **1.** One who has actual possession of land; the occupant of land. **2.** One who has an interest in a judgment debtor's land after the judgment creditor's lien has attached to the land (such as a subsequent purchaser). — Also spelled *tertenant* (**tər**-ten-ənt).

territorialism. The traditional approach to choice of law, whereby the place of injury or of contract formation determines which state's law will be applied in a case. See CHOICE OF LAW.

territory, *n.* **1.** A geographical area included within a particular government's jurisdiction; the portion of the earth's surface that is in a state's exclusive possession and control. **2.** A part of the United States not included within any state but organized with a separate legislature (such as Guam and the U.S. Virgin Islands). — **territorial,** *adj.* Cf. COMMONWEALTH (2); DEPENDENCY (1).

territory of a judge. The territorial jurisdiction of a particular court. See JURISDICTION (3).

terrorism, *n.* The use or threat of violence to intimidate or cause panic, esp. as a means of affecting political conduct. — **terrorist,** *adj.* & *n.*

terroristic threat. See THREAT.

testable, *adj.* **1.** Capable of being tested <a testable hypothesis>. **2.** Capable of making a will <an 18-year-old person is testable in this state>. **3.** Capable of being transferred by will <today virtually all property is considered testable>.

test action. See *test case* under CASE.

testacy (**tes**-tə-see), *n.* The fact or condition of leaving a valid will at one's death. Cf. INTESTACY.

testament (**tes**-tə-mənt). **1.** A will disposing of personal property. Cf. DEVISE (4). **2.** WILL (2).

testamentary (tes-tə-**men**-tə-ree *or* -tree), *adj.* **1.** Of or relating to a will or testament <testamentary intent>. **2.** Provided for or appointed by a will <testamentary guardian>. **3.** Created by a will <testamentary gift>.

testamentary capacity. See CAPACITY.

testamentary class. See CLASS (3).

testamentary gift. See GIFT.

testamentary intent. See INTENT (1).

testamentary power of appointment. See POWER OF APPOINTMENT.

testamentary trust. See TRUST.

testamentary trustee. See TRUSTEE.

testate (**tes**-tayt), *adj.* Having left a will at death <she died testate>. Cf. INTESTATE.

testate, *n.* See TESTATOR.

testate succession. The passing of rights or property by will. Cf. INTESTATE SUCCESSION.

testator (**tes**-tay-tər *also* te-**stay**-tər). A person who has made a will; esp., a person who dies leaving a will. • Because this term is usually interpreted as applying to both sexes, *testatrix* has become archaic. Cf. INTESTATE.

test case. See CASE.

testify, *vb.* **1.** To give evidence as a witness <she testified that the Ford Bronco was at the defendant's home at the critical time>. **2.** (Of a person or thing) to bear witness <the incomplete log entries testified to his sloppiness>.

testifying expert. See EXPERT.

testimonial evidence. See EVIDENCE.

testimonial immunity. See IMMUNITY (3).

testimonial incapacity. See INCAPACITY.

testimonial privilege. See PRIVILEGE (1).

testimonium clause. A provision at the end of an instrument (esp. a will) reciting the date when the instrument was signed, by whom it was signed, and in what capacity. • This clause traditionally begins with the phrase "In witness whereof." Cf. ATTESTATION CLAUSE.

testimony, *n.* Evidence that a competent witness under oath or affirmation gives at trial or in an affidavit or deposition. — **testimonial,** *adj.*

affirmative testimony. Testimony about whether something occurred or did not occur, based on what the witness saw or heard at the time and place in question. See *direct evidence* under EVIDENCE.

cumulative testimony. Identical or similar testimony by more than one witness, and usu. by several, offered by a party usu. to impress the jury with the apparent weight of proof on that party's side. • The trial court typically limits cumulative testimony.

dropsy testimony. *Slang.* A police officer's false testimony that a fleeing suspect dropped an illegal substance that was then confiscated by the police and used as probable cause for arresting the suspect. • Dropsy testimony is sometimes given when an arrest has been made without probable cause, as when illegal substances have been found through an improper search.

false testimony. Testimony that is untrue. • This term is broader than *perjury*, which has a state-of-mind element. Unlike perjury, false testimony does not denote a crime.

interpreted testimony. Testimony translated because the witness cannot communicate in the language of the tribunal.

lay opinion testimony. Evidence given by a witness who is not qualified as an expert but who testifies to opinions or inferences. • In federal court, the admissibility of this testimony is limited to opinions or inferences that are rationally based on the witness's perception and that will be helpful to a clear understanding of the witness's testimony or the determination of a fact in issue. Fed. R. Evid. 701.

nonverbal testimony. A photograph, drawing, map, chart, or other depiction used to aid a witness in testifying. • The witness need not have made it, but it must accurately represent something that the witness saw. See *demonstrative evidence* under EVIDENCE.

opinion testimony. Testimony based on one's belief or idea rather than on direct knowledge of the facts at issue. • Opinion testimony from either a lay witness or an expert witness may be allowed in evidence under certain conditions. See *opinion evidence* under EVIDENCE.

testimony de bene esse (dee **bee**-nee **es**-ee *also* day **ben**-ay **es**-ay). Testimony taken because it is in danger of being lost before it can be given at a trial or hearing, usu. because of the impending death or departure of the witness. • Such testimony is taken in aid of a pending case, while testimony taken under a bill to perpetuate testimony is taken in anticipation of future litigation. See *deposition de bene esse* under DEPOSITION.

***written testimony*. 1.** Testimony given out of court by deposition. • The recorded writing, signed by the witness, is considered testimony. **2.** In some administrative agencies and courts, direct narrative testimony that is reduced to writing, to which the witness swears at a hearing or trial before cross-examination takes place in the traditional way.

test-paper. In Pennsylvania, a paper or instrument shown to the jury as evidence.

textbook digest. A legal text whose aim is to set forth the law of a subject in condensed form, with little or no criticism or discussion of the authorities cited, and no serious attempt to explain or reconcile apparently conflicting decisions.

thalweg (tahl-vayk *or* -veg). **1.** A line following the lowest part of a (usu. submerged) valley. **2.** The middle of the primary navigable channel of a waterway, constituting the boundary between states.

Thayer presumption. A presumption that requires the party against whom the presumption operates to come forward with evidence to rebut the presumption, but that does not shift the burden of proof to that party. See James B. Thayer, *A Preliminary Treatise on Evidence* 31–44 (1898). • Most presumptions that arise in civil trials in federal court are interpreted in this way. Fed. R. Evid. 301. Cf. MORGAN PRESUMPTION.

theft, *n.* **1.** The unlawful taking and removing of another's personal property with the intent of depriving the true owner of it; larceny. **2.** Broadly, any act or instance of stealing, including larceny, burglary, embezzlement, and false pretenses. • Many modern penal codes have consolidated such property offenses under the name "theft." See LARCENY.

***theft by deception*.** The use of trickery to obtain another's property, esp. by (1) creating or reinforcing a false impression (as about value), (2) preventing one from obtaining information that would affect one's judgment about a transaction, or (3) failing to disclose, in a property transfer, a known lien or other legal impediment. Model Penal Code § 223.3.

***theft by extortion*.** Theft in which the perpetrator obtains property by threat or coercion. Model Penal Code § 223.4. See EXTORTION.

***theft of property lost, mislaid, or delivered by mistake*.** Larceny in which one obtains control of property the person knows to be lost, mislaid, or delivered by mistake (esp. in the amount of property or identity of recipient) and fails to take reasonable measures to restore the property to the rightful owner. Model Penal Code § 223.5.

theft of services. The act of obtaining services from another by deception, threat, coercion, stealth, mechanical tampering, or using a false token or device. See Model Penal Code § 223.7.

thence, *adv.* **1.** From that place; from that time. • In surveying, and in describing land by courses and distances, this word, preceding each course given, implies that the following course is continuous with the one before it <south 240 feet to an iron post, thence west 59 feet>. **2.** On that account; therefore.

thence down the river. With the meanders of a river. • This phrase appears in the field notes of patent surveyors, indicating that the survey follows a meandering river unless evidence shows that the meander line as written was where the surveyor in fact ran it. See MEANDER LINE.

theocracy (thee-**ok**-rə-see). **1.** Government of a state by those who are presumably acting under the immediate direction of God or some other divinity. **2.** A state in which power is exercised by ecclesiastics.

theory of law. The legal premise or set of principles on which a case rests.

theory-of-pleading doctrine. The principle — now outmoded — that one must prove a case exactly as pleaded. • Modern codes and rules of procedure have abolished this strict pleading-and-proof requirement. For example, Fed. R. Civ. P. 15 allows amendment of pleadings to conform to the evidence.

theory of the case. A comprehensive and orderly mental arrangement of principles and facts, conceived and constructed for the purpose of securing a judgment or decree of a court in favor of a litigant; the particular line of reasoning of either party to a suit, the purpose being to bring together certain facts of the case in a logical sequence and to correlate them in a way that produces in the decision-maker's mind a definite result or conclusion favored by the advocate. See CAUSE OF ACTION (1).

therapeutic relief. See RELIEF.

thereabout, *adv. Jargon.* Near that time or place <Schreuer was seen in Rudolf Place or thereabout>.

thereafter, *adv. Jargon.* Afterward; later <Skurry was thereafter arrested>.

thereat, *adv. Jargon.* **1.** At that place or time; there. **2.** Because of that; at that occurrence or event.

thereby, *adv.* By that means; in that way <Blofeld stepped into the embassy and thereby found protection>.

therefor, *adv. Jargon.* For it or them; for that thing or action; for those things or actions <she lied to Congress but was never punished therefor>.

therefore, *adv.* **1.** For that reason; on that ground or those grounds <a quorum was not present; therefore, no vote was taken>. **2.** To that end <she wanted to become a tax lawyer, and she therefore applied for the

university's renowned LL.M. program in tax>.

therefrom, *adv. Jargon.* From that, it, or them <Hofer had several financial obligations to Ricks, who refused to release Hofer therefrom>.

therein, *adv. Jargon.* **1.** In that place or time <the Dallas/Fort Worth metroplex has a population of about 3 million, and some 20,000 lawyers practice therein>. **2.** Inside or within that thing; inside or within those things <there were three school buses with 108 children therein>.

thereinafter, *adv. Jargon.* Later in that thing (such as a speech or document) <the book's first reference was innocuous, but the five references thereinafter were libelous per se>.

thereof, *adv. Jargon.* Of that, it, or them <although the disease is spreading rapidly, the cause thereof is unknown>.

thereon, *adv. Jargon.* On that or them <Michaels found the online reports of the cases and relied thereon instead of checking the printed books>.

thereto, *adv. Jargon.* To that or them <the jury awarded $750,000 in actual damages, and it added thereto another $250,000 in punitive damages>.

theretofore, *adv.* Up to that time <theretofore, the highest award in such a case has been $450,000>.

thereunder, *adv. Jargon.* Under that or them <on the top shelf were three books, and situated thereunder was the missing banknote> <section 1988 was the relevant fee statute, and the plaintiffs were undeniably proceeding thereunder>.

thereupon, *adv. Jargon.* **1.** Immediately; without delay; promptly <the writ of execution issued from the court, and the sheriff thereupon sought to find the judgment debtor>. **2.** THEREON. **3.** THEREFORE.

***Thibodaux* abstention** (**tib**-ə-doh). See ABSTENTION.

thief. One who steals, esp. without force or violence; one who commits theft or larceny. See THEFT.

> ***common thief.*** A thief who has been convicted of theft or larceny more than once.

thieve, *vb.* To steal; to commit theft or larceny. See THEFT.

thing. 1. A material object regarded as the subject matter of a right, whether it is a material object or not; any subject matter of ownership within the sphere of proprietary or valuable rights. • Things are divided into three categories: (1) things real or immovable, such as land, tenements, and hereditaments, (2) things personal or movable, such as goods and chattels, and (3) things having both real and personal characteristics, such as a title deed and a tenancy for a term. The civil law divided things into corporeal (*tangi possunt*) and incorporeal (*tangi non possunt*).

> ***corporeal thing.*** The subject matter of corporeal ownership; a material object.

> ***incorporeal thing.*** The subject matter of incorporeal ownership; any proprietary right apart from the right of full dominion over a material object.

2. Anything that is owned by someone as part of that person's estate or property.

Third Amendment. The constitutional amendment, ratified as part of the Bill of Rights in 1791, prohibiting the quartering of soldiers in private homes except during wartime.

third degree, *n.* The process of extracting a confession or information from a suspect or prisoner by prolonged questioning, the use of threats, or physical torture <the police gave the suspect the third degree>.

third-degree murder. See MURDER.

third party, *n.* One who is not a party to a lawsuit, agreement, or other transaction but who is somehow involved in the transaction; someone other than the principal parties. — **third-party,** *adj.* See PARTY.

third-party, *vb. Slang.* To bring (a person or entity) into litigation as a third-party defendant <seeking indemnity, the defendant third-partied the surety>.

third-party action. See ACTION.

third-party beneficiary. See BENEFICIARY.

third-party check. A check that the payee indorses to another party — for example, a customer check that the payee indorses to a supplier. • A person who takes a third-party check in good faith and without notice of a security interest can be a holder in due course.

third-party complaint. See COMPLAINT.

third-party consent. A person's agreement to official action (such as a search of premises) that affects another person's rights or interests. • To be effective for a search, third-party consent must be based on the consenting person's common authority over the place to be searched or the items to be inspected. See COMMON-AUTHORITY RULE.

third-party defendant. A party brought into a lawsuit by the original defendant.

third-party insurance. See *liability insurance* under INSURANCE.

third-party plaintiff. A defendant who files a pleading in an effort to bring a third party into the lawsuit. See *third-party complaint* under COMPLAINT.

third-party standing. See STANDING.

Thirteenth Amendment. The constitutional amendment, ratified in 1865, that abolished slavery and involuntary servitude.

30(b)(6) deposition. See DEPOSITION.

thirty-day letter. A letter that accompanies a revenue agent's report issued as a result of an Internal Revenue Service audit or the rejection of a taxpayer's claim for refund and that outlines the taxpayer's appeal procedure before the Internal Revenue Service. • If the taxpayer does not request any such procedure within the 30-day period, the IRS will issue a statutory notice of deficiency. Cf. NINETY-DAY LETTER.

threat, *n.* **1.** A communicated intent to inflict harm or loss on another or on another's property, esp. one that might diminish a person's freedom to act voluntarily or with lawful consent <a kidnapper's threats of violence>.

terroristic threat. A threat to commit any crime of violence with the purpose of (1) terrorizing another, (2) causing the evacuation of a building, place of assembly, or facility of public transportation, (3) causing serious public inconvenience, or (4) recklessly disregarding the risk of causing such terror or inconvenience. Model Penal Code § 211.3.

2. An indication of an approaching menace <the threat of bankruptcy>. **3.** A person or thing that might well cause harm <Mrs. Harrington testified that she had never viewed her husband as a threat>. — **threaten,** *vb.* — **threatening,** *adj.*

three-strikes law. A statute prescribing an enhanced sentence, esp. life imprisonment, for a repeat offender's third felony conviction. • About half the states have enacted a statute of this kind.

threshold confession. See CONFESSION.

through lot. A lot that abuts a street at each end.

throwback rule. *Tax.* **1.** In the taxation of trusts, a rule requiring that an amount distributed in any tax year that exceeds the year's distributable net income must be treated as if it had been distributed in the preceding year. • The beneficiary is taxed in the current year although the computation is made as if the excess had been distributed in the previous year. If the trust did not have undistributed accumulated income in the preceding year, the amount of the throwback is tested against each of the preceding years. IRC (26 USCA) §§ 665–668. **2.** A taxation rule requiring a sale that would otherwise be exempt from state income tax (because the state to which the sale would be assigned for apportionment purposes does not have an income tax, even though the seller's state does) to be attributed to the seller's state and thus subjected to a state-level tax. • This rule applies only if the seller's state has adopted a throwback rule.

throw out, *vb.* To dismiss (a claim or lawsuit).

tideland. Land between the lines of the ordinary high and low tides, covered and uncovered successively by the ebb and flow of those tides; land covered and uncovered by the ordinary tides.

tidewater. Water that falls and rises with the ebb and flow of the tide. • The term is not usually applied to the open sea, but to coves, bays, and rivers.

tideway. Land between high- and low-water marks.

TILA. *abbr.* Truth in Lending Act. See CONSUMER CREDIT PROTECTION ACT.

tillage (**til**-ij), *n.* A place tilled or cultivated; land under cultivation as opposed to land lying fallow or in pasture.

till-tapping. *Slang.* Theft of money from a cash register.

timber lease. See LEASE.

time. **1.** A measure of duration. **2.** A point in or period of duration at or during which something is alleged to have occurred. **3.** *Slang.* A convicted criminal's period of incarceration.

dead time. Time that does not count for a particular purpose, such as time not included in calculating an employee's wages or time not credited toward a prisoner's sentence. • The time during which a prisoner has escaped, for example, is not credited toward the prisoner's sentence.

earned time. A credit toward a sentence reduction awarded to a prisoner who takes part in activities designed to lessen the chances that the prisoner will commit a crime after release from prison. • Earned time, which is usually awarded for taking educational or vocational courses, working, or participating in certain other productive activities, is distinct from good time, which is awarded simply for refraining from misconduct. Cf. *good time.*

flat time. A prison term that is to be served without the benefit of time-reduction allowances for good behavior and the like.

good time. The credit awarded to a prisoner for good conduct, which can reduce the duration of the prisoner's sentence. Cf. GOOD BEHAVIOR; *earned time.*

street time. The time that a convicted person spends on parole or on other conditional release. • If the person's parole is revoked, this time may or may not be credited toward the person's sentence, depending on the jurisdiction and the particular conditions of that person's parole. See *dead time.*

time-bar, *n.* A bar to a legal claim arising from the lapse of a defined length of time, esp. one contained in a statute of limitations. — **time-barred,** *adj.*

time draft. See DRAFT.

time immemorial. 1. A point in time so far back that no living person has knowledge or proof contradicting the right or custom alleged to have existed since then. • At common law, that time was fixed as the year 1189. Cf. LEGAL MEMORY. **2.** A very long time.

time-place-or-mannner restriction. *Constitutional law.* A government's limitation on when, where, or how a public speech or assembly may occur, but not on the content of that speech or assembly. • As long as such restrictions are narrowly tailored to achieve a legitimate governmental interest, they do not violate the First Amendment. See PUBLIC FORUM.

time policy. See INSURANCE POLICY.

time-sharing, *n.* Joint ownership or rental of property (such as a vacation condominium) by several persons who take turns occupying the property. — **time-share,** *vb.*

timesheet. An attorney's daily record of billable and nonbillable hours, used to generate clients' bills. See BILLABLE HOUR.

timocracy (tɪ-**mok**-rə-see). **1.** An aristocracy of property; government by propertied, relatively rich people. **2.** A government in which the rulers' primary motive is the love of honor.

title. 1. The union of all elements (as ownership, possession, and custody) constituting the legal right to control and dispose of property; the legal link between a person who owns property and the property itself <no one has title to that land>. Cf. OWNERSHIP; POSSESSION. **2.** Legal evidence of a person's ownership rights in property; an instrument (such as a deed) that constitutes such evidence <record your title with the county clerk>.

absolute title. An exclusive title to land; a title that excludes all others not compatible with it. See *fee simple absolute* under FEE SIMPLE.

adverse title. A title acquired by adverse possession. See ADVERSE POSSESSION.

after-acquired title. Title held by a person who bought property from a seller who acquired title only after purporting to sell the property to the buyer. See AFTER-ACQUIRED TITLE DOCTRINE.

bad title. **1.** See *defective title*. **2.** See *unmarketable title*.

clear title. **1.** A title free from any encumbrances, burdens, or other limitations. **2.** See *marketable title*.

defeasible title. A title voidable on the occurrence of a contingency, but not void on its face.

defective title. A title that cannot legally convey the property to which it applies, usu. because of some conflicting claim to that property.

derivative title. **1.** A title that results when an already existing right is transferred to a new owner. **2.** The general principle that a transferee of property acquires only the rights held by the transferor and no more.

dormant title. A title in real property held in abeyance.

doubtful title. A title that exposes the party holding it to the risk of litigation with an adverse claimant. See *unmarketable title*.

equitable title. A title that indicates a beneficial interest in property and that gives the holder the right to acquire formal legal title. Cf. *legal title*.

good title. **1.** A title that is legally valid or effective. **2.** See *clear title* (1). **3.** See *marketable title*.

imperfect title. A title that requires a further exercise of the granting power to pass land in fee, or that does not convey full and absolute dominion.

just title. In a case of prescription, a title that the possessor received from someone whom the possessor honestly believed to be the real owner, provided that the title was to transfer ownership of the property.

legal title. A title that evidences apparent ownership but does not necessarily signify full and complete title or a beneficial interest. Cf. *equitable title*.

marketable title. A title that a reasonable buyer would accept because it appears to lack any defect and to cover the entire property that the seller has purported to sell.

original title. A title that creates a right for the first time.

paramount title. A title that is superior to another title or claim on the same property.

presumptive title. A title of the lowest order, arising out of the mere occupation or simple possession of property without any apparent right, or any pretense of right, to hold and continue that possession.

record title. A title as it appears in the public records after the deed is properly recorded.

singular title. The title by which one acquires property as a singular successor.

tax title. A title to land purchased at a tax sale.

title by descent. A title that one acquires by law as an heir of the deceased owner.

title by devise. A title created by will.

title by prescription. A title acquired by prescription. See PRESCRIPTION (2).

title defective in form. A title for which some defect appears on the face of the deed. • Title defective in form cannot be the basis of prescription.

title of entry. The right to enter upon lands.

universal title. A title acquired by a conveyance causa mortis of a stated portion of all the conveyor's property interests so that on the conveyor's death the recipient stands as a universal successor.

unmarketable title. A title that a reasonable buyer would refuse to accept because of possible conflicting interests in or litigation over the property.

3. The heading of a statute or other legal document <the title of the contract was "Confidentiality Agreement">.

long title. The full, formal title of a statute, usu. containing a brief statement of legislative purpose.

short title. The abbreviated title of a statute by which it is popularly known; a statutory nickname.

4. A subdivision of a statute or code <Title IX>. **5.** An appellation of office, dignity, or distinction <after the election, he bore the title of mayor for the next four years>.

Title VII of the Civil Rights Act of 1964. A federal law that prohibits employment discrimination and harassment on the basis of race, sex, pregnancy, religion, and national origin, as well as prohibiting retaliation against an employee who opposes illegal harassment or discrimination in the workplace. • This term is often referred to simply as Title VII. 42 USCA §§ 2000e et seq.

Title IX of the Educational Amendments of 1972. A federal statute generally prohibiting sex discrimination and harassment by educational facilities that receive federal funds. • This term is often referred to simply as Title IX. 20 USCA §§ 1681 et seq.

title company. See COMPANY.

title deed. See DEED.

title insurance. See INSURANCE.

title of right. A court decree creating, transferring, or extinguishing rights. • Examples include a decree of divorce or judicial separation, an adjudication of bankruptcy, a discharge in bankruptcy, a decree of foreclosure against a mortgagor, an order appointing or removing a trustee, and a grant of letters of administration. The judgment operates not as a remedy but as a title of right.

title opinion. See OPINION (2).

title registration. A system of registering title to land with a public registry, such as a county clerk's office. See TORRENS SYSTEM.

title retention. A form of lien, in the nature of a chattel mortgage, to secure payment of a loan given to purchase the secured item.

title search. An examination of the public records to determine whether any defects or encumbrances exist in a given property's chain of title. • A title search is typically conducted by a title company or a real-estate lawyer at a prospective buyer's or mortgagee's request.

title standards. Criteria by which a real-estate title can be evaluated to determine whether it is defective or marketable. • Many states, through associations of conveyancers and real-estate attorneys, have adopted title standards.

title theory. *Property law.* The idea that a mortgage transfers legal title of the property to the mortgagee, who retains it until the mortgage has been satisfied or foreclosed. • Only a few American states — known as *title states*, *title jurisdictions*, or *title-theory jurisdictions* — have adopted this theory. Cf. LIEN THEORY.

title transaction. A transaction that affects title to an interest in land.

T-note. *abbr.* TREASURY NOTE.

token, *n.* **1.** A sign or mark; a tangible evidence of the existence of a fact. **2.** A sign or indication of an intention to do something, as when a buyer places a small order with a vendor to show good faith with a view toward later placing a larger order.

toll, *vb.* **1.** To annul or take away <toll a right of entry>. **2.** (Of a time period, esp. a statutory one) to stop the running of; to abate <toll the limitations period>.

tolling agreement. An agreement between a potential plaintiff and a potential defendant by which the defendant agrees to extend the statutory limitations period on the plaintiff's claim, usu. so that both parties will have more time to resolve their dispute without litigation.

tolling statute. A law that interrupts the running of a statute of limitations in certain situations, as when the defendant cannot be served with process in the forum jurisdiction.

Torrens system (tor-ənz *or* tahr-ənz). A system for establishing title to real estate in which a claimant first acquires an abstract of title and then applies to a court for the issuance of a title certificate, which serves as conclusive evidence of ownership. • This system — named after Sir Robert Torrens, a 19th-century reformer of Australian land laws — has been adopted in the United States by several counties with large metropolitan areas.

tort (tort). **1.** A civil wrong for which a remedy may be obtained, usu. in the form of damages; a breach of a duty that the law imposes on everyone in the same relation to one another as those involved in a given transaction. **2.** (*pl.*) The branch of law dealing with such wrongs.

constitutional tort. A violation of one's constitutional rights by a government officer, redressable by a civil action filed directly against the officer. • A constitutional tort committed under color of state law (such as a civil-rights violation) is actionable under 42 USCA § 1983.

dignatory tort (**dig**-nə-tor-ee). A tort involving injury to one's reputation or honor. • In the few jurisdictions in which courts use the phrase *dignatory tort* (such as Maine), defamation is commonly cited as an example.

government tort. A tort committed by the government through an employee, agent, or instrumentality under its control. • The tort may or may not be actionable, depending on whether the government is entitled to sovereign immunity. A tort action against the U.S. government is regulated by the Federal Tort Claims Act, while a state action is governed by the state's tort claims act. See FEDERAL TORT CLAIMS ACT; *sovereign immunity* under IMMUNITY (1).

intentional tort. A tort committed by someone acting with general or specific intent. • Examples include battery, false imprisonment, and trespass to land. Cf. NEGLIGENCE.

mass tort. A civil wrong that injures many people. • Examples include toxic emissions from a factory, the crash of a commercial airliner, and contamination from an industrial-waste-disposal site. Cf. *toxic tort*.

negligent tort. A tort committed by failure to observe the standard of care required by law under the circumstances. See NEGLIGENCE.

personal tort. A tort involving or consisting in an injury to one's person, reputation, or feelings, as distinguished from an injury or damage to real or personal property.

prenatal tort. **1.** A tort committed against a fetus. • If born alive, a child can sue for injuries resulting from tortious conduct predating the child's birth. **2.** Loosely, any of several torts relating to reproduction, such as those giving rise to wrongful-birth actions, wrongful-life actions, and wrongful-pregnancy actions.

prima facie tort (**prɪ**-mə **fay**-shee-ee *or* -shee *or* -shə). An unjustified, intentional infliction of harm on another person, resulting in damages, by one or more acts that would otherwise be lawful. • Some jurisdictions have established this tort to provide a remedy for malicious deeds — especially in business and trade contexts — that are not actionable under traditional tort law.

property tort. A tort involving damage to property.

public tort. A minor breach of the law (such as a parking violation) that, although it carries a criminal punishment, is considered a civil offense rather than a criminal one because it is merely a prohibited act (*malum prohibitum*) and not inherently reprehensible conduct (*malum in se*). Cf. *civil wrong* under WRONG.

quasi-tort. A wrong for which a nonperpetrator is held responsible; a tort for which one who did not directly commit it can nonetheless be found liable, as when a master is held liable for a tort committed by a servant. — Also spelled *quasi tort*. See *vicarious liability* under LIABILITY; RESPONDEAT SUPERIOR.

toxic tort. A civil wrong arising from exposure to a toxic substance, such as asbestos, radiation, or hazardous waste. • A toxic tort can be remedied by a civil lawsuit (usually a class action) or by administrative action. Cf. *mass tort*.

tortfeasor (**tort**-fee-zər). One who commits a tort; a wrongdoer.

concurrent tortfeasors. Two or more tortfeasors whose simultaneous actions cause injury to a third party. • Such tortfeasors are jointly and severally liable.

consecutive tortfeasors. Two or more tortfeasors whose actions, while occurring at different times, combine to cause a single injury to a third party. • Such tortfeasors are jointly and severally liable.

joint tortfeasors. Two or more tortfeasors who contributed to the claimant's injury and who may be joined as defendants in the same lawsuit. See *joint and several liability* under LIABILITY.

successive tortfeasors. Two or more tortfeasors whose negligence occurs at different times and causes different injuries to the same third party.

tortious (**tor**-shəs), *adj.* **1.** Constituting a tort; wrongful <tortious conduct>. **2.** In the nature of a tort <tortious cause of action>.

tortious interference with contractual relations. A third party's intentional inducement of a contracting party to break a contract, causing damage to the relationship between the contracting parties.

tortious interference with prospective advantage. An intentional, damaging intrusion on another's potential business relationship, such as the opportunity of obtaining customers or employment.

tort reform. A movement to reduce the amount of tort litigation, usu. involving legislation that restricts tort remedies or that caps damages awards (esp. for punitive damages). • Advocates of tort reform argue that it lowers insurance and healthcare costs and prevents windfalls, while opponents contend that it denies plaintiffs the recovery they deserve for their injuries.

torture, *n.* The infliction of intense pain to the body or mind to punish, to extract a confession or information, or to obtain sadistic pleasure. — **torture,** *vb.*

total, *adj.* **1.** Whole; not divided; full; complete. **2.** Utter; absolute.

total breach. See BREACH OF CONTRACT.

total disability. See DISABILITY (1).

total eviction. See EVICTION.

total failure of consideration. See FAILURE OF CONSIDERATION.

totality-of-the-circumstances test. *Criminal procedure.* A standard for determining whether hearsay (such as an informant's tip) is sufficiently reliable to establish probable cause for an arrest or search warrant. • Under this test — which replaced *Aguilar–Spinelli*'s two-pronged approach — the reliability of the hearsay is weighed by focusing on the entire situation as described in the probable-cause affidavit, and not on any one specific factor. *Illinois v. Gates*, 462 U.S. 213, 103 S.Ct. 2317 (1983).

total loss. See LOSS.

total repudiation. See REPUDIATION.

Totten trust. See TRUST.

to wit (too **wit**), *adv. Archaic.* That is to say; namely <the district attorney amended the complaint to include embezzlement, to wit, "stealing money that the company had entrusted to the accused">. — Sometimes spelled *to-wit*; *towit*.

toxicant (**tok**-si-kənt), *n.* A poison; a toxic agent; any substance capable of producing toxication or poisoning.

toxicology (tok-si-**kol**-ə-jee). The branch of medicine that concerns poisons, their effects, their recognition, their antidotes, and generally the diagnosis and therapeutics of poisoning; the science of poisons. — **toxicological** (tok-si-kə-**loj**-i-kəl), *adj.*

toxic tort. See TORT.

toxic waste. See WASTE (2).

toxin, *n.* **1.** Broadly, any poison or toxicant. **2.** As used in pathology and medical jurisprudence, any diffusible alkaloidal substance — such as the ptomaines, abrin, brucin, or serpent venoms — and esp. the poisonous products of disease-producing bacteria.

tracing, *n.* **1.** The process of tracking property's ownership or characteristics from the time of its origin to the present. **2.** A mechanical copy or facsimile of an original, produced by following its lines with a pen or pencil through a transparent medium. — **trace,** *vb.*

tract. A specified parcel of land <a 40-acre tract>.

tract index. See INDEX.

trade, *n.* **1.** The business of buying and selling or bartering goods or services; COMMERCE. **2.** A transaction or swap. **3.** A business or industry occupation; a craft or profession. — **trade,** *vb.*

trade and commerce. Every business occupation carried on for subsistence or profit and involving the elements of bargain and sale, barter, exchange, or traffic.

trade association. See ASSOCIATION.

trade discount. See DISCOUNT.

trademark, *n.* **1.** A word, phrase, logo, or other graphic symbol used by a manufacturer or seller to distinguish its product or products from those of others. • The main purpose of a trademark is to guarantee a product's genuineness. In effect, the trademark is the commercial substitute for one's signature. To receive federal protection, a trademark must be (1) distinctive rather than merely descriptive, (2) affixed to a product that is actually sold in the marketplace, and (3) registered with the U.S. Patent and Trademark Office. In its broadest sense, the term *trademark* includes a servicemark. Cf. SERVICEMARK. **2.** The body of law dealing with how businesses distinctively identify their products. See LANHAM ACT.

tradename. 1. A name, style, or symbol used to distinguish a company, partnership, or business (as opposed to a product or service); the name under which a business operates. • A tradename is a means of identifying a business — or its products or services — to establish goodwill. It symbolizes the business's reputation. **2.** A trademark that was not originally susceptible to exclusive appropriation but has acquired a secondary meaning.

trade or business. *Tax.* Any business or professional activity conducted by a taxpayer with the objective of earning a profit. • If the taxpayer can show that the primary purpose and intention is to make a profit, the taxpayer may deduct certain expenses as trade-or-business expenses under the Internal Revenue Code.

trade secret. 1. A formula, process, device, or other business information that is kept confidential to maintain an advantage over competitors; information — including a formula, pattern, compilation, program, device, method, technique, or process — that (1) derives independent economic value, actual or potential, from not being generally known or readily ascertainable by others who can obtain economic value from its disclosure or use, and (2) is the subject of reasonable efforts, under the circumstances, to maintain its secrecy. • This definition states the majority view, which is found in the Uniform Trade Secrets Act. **2.** Information that (1) is not generally known or ascertainable, (2) provides a competitive advantage, (3) has been developed at the plaintiff's expense and is used continuously in the plaintiff's business, and (4) is the subject of the plaintiff's intent to keep it confidential. • This definition states the minority view, which is found in the Restatement of Torts § 757 cmt. b (1939).

trade usage. See USAGE.

tradition. 1. Past customs and usages that influence or govern present acts or practices. **2.** The delivery of an item or an estate.

traditional public forum. See PUBLIC FORUM.

traditionary evidence. See EVIDENCE.

traduce (trə-**d[y]oos**), *vb.* To slander; calumniate. — **traducement,** *n.*

traffic, *n.* **1.** Commerce; trade; the sale or exchange of such things as merchandise, bills, and money. **2.** The passing or exchange of goods or commodities from one person to another for an equivalent in goods or money. **3.** People or things being transported along a route. **4.** The passing to and fro of people, animals, vehicles, and vessels along a transportation route.

traffic, *vb.* To trade or deal in (goods, esp. illicit drugs or other contraband) <trafficking in heroin>.

transaction, *n.* **1.** The act or an instance of conducting business or other dealings. **2.** Something performed or carried out; a business agreement or exchange. **3.** Any activity involving two or more persons. — **transactional,** *adj.*

closed transaction. Tax. A transaction in which an amount realized on a sale can be established for the purpose of stating a gain or loss.

colorable transaction. A sham transaction having the appearance of authenticity; a pretended transaction <the court set aside the colorable transaction>.

transactional immunity. See IMMUNITY (3).

transactional lawyer. See LAWYER.

transaction-or-occurrence test. A test used to determine whether, under Fed. R. Civ. P. 13(a), a particular claim is a compulsory counterclaim. • Four different tests have been suggested: (1) Are the legal and factual issues raised by the claim and counterclaim largely the same? (2) Would res judicata bar a later suit on the counterclaim in the absence of the compulsory-counterclaim rule? (3) Will substantially the same evidence support or refute both the plaintiff's claim and the counterclaim? (4) Are the claim and counterclaim logically related? See *compulsory counterclaim* under COUNTERCLAIM.

transcarceration. The movement of prisoners or institutionalized mentally ill persons from facility to facility, rather than from a prison or an institution back to the community, as when a prisoner is transferred to a halfway house or to a drug-treatment facility.

transcribe, *vb.* To make a written or typed copy of (spoken material, esp. testimony).

transcript, *n.* A handwritten, printed, or typed copy of testimony given orally; esp., the official record of proceedings in a trial or hearing, as taken down by a court reporter.

transcription. 1. The act or process of transcribing. **2.** Something transcribed; a transcript.

transfer, *n.* **1.** Any mode of disposing of or parting with an asset or an interest in an asset, including the payment of money, release, lease, or creation of a lien or other encumbrance. • The term embraces every method — direct or indirect, absolute or conditional, voluntary or involuntary — of disposing of or parting with property or with an interest in property, including retention of title as a security interest and foreclosure of the debtor's equity of redemption. **2.** Negotiation of an instrument according to the forms of law. • The four methods of transfer are by indorsement, by delivery, by assignment, and by operation of law. **3.** A conveyance of property or title from one person to another.

constructive transfer. A delivery of an item — esp. a controlled substance — by someone other than the owner but at the owner's direction.

incomplete transfer. Tax. A decedent's inter vivos transfer that is not completed for federal estate-tax purposes because the decedent retains significant powers over the property's possession or enjoyment. • Because the transfer is incomplete, some or all of the property's value will be included in the transferor's gross estate. IRC (26 USCA) §§ 2036–2038.

inter vivos transfer (**in**-tər **vɪ**-vohs *or* **vee**-vohs). A transfer of property made during the transferor's lifetime.

transfer in fraud of creditors. A conveyance of property made in an attempt to prevent the transferor's creditors from making a claim to it.

transfer, *vb.* **1.** To convey or remove from one place or one person to another; to pass or hand over from one to another, esp. to change over the possession or control of. **2.** To sell or give.

transferable (trans-**fər**-ə-bəl), *adj.* Capable of being transferred, together with all rights of the original holder.

transferee liability. *Tax.* The liability of a transferee to pay taxes owed by the transferor. • This liability is limited to the value of the asset transferred. The Internal Revenue Service can, for example, force a donee to pay the gift tax when the donor who made the transfer cannot pay it. IRC (26 USCA) §§ 6901–6905.

transfer hearing. See HEARING.

transfer in fraud of creditors. See TRANSFER.

transfer of a case. The removal of a case from the jurisdiction of one court or judge to another by lawful authority. See REMOVAL (2).

transfer of venue. See CHANGE OF VENUE.

transferor. One who conveys an interest in property.

transfer payment. (*usu. pl.*) A governmental payment to a person who has neither provided goods or services nor invested money in exchange for the payment. • Examples include unemployment compensation and welfare payments.

transferred intent. See INTENT (1).

transferred-intent doctrine. The rule that if one person intends to harm a second person but instead unintentionally harms a third, the first person's criminal or tortious intent toward the second applies to the third as well. • Thus, the offender may be prosecuted for an intent crime or sued by the third person for an intentional tort. See INTENT.

transferred malice. See MALICE.

transfer tax. See TAX.

transfer warranty. See WARRANTY (2).

transient (**tran**-shənt), *adj.* Temporary; impermanent; passing away after a short time.

transient person. One who has no legal residence within a jurisdiction for the purpose of a state venue statute.

transit, *n.* **1.** The transportation of goods or persons from one place to another. **2.** Passage; the act of passing.

transitory (**tran**-sə-tor-ee *or* **tran**-zə-), *adj.* That passes from place to place; capable of passing or being changed from one place to another.

transitory wrong. See WRONG.

transmit, *vb.* **1.** To send or transfer (a thing) from one person or place to another. **2.** To communicate.

transmittal letter. A nonsubstantive letter that establishes a record of delivery, such as a letter to a court clerk advising that a particular pleading is enclosed for filing. • Lawyers have traditionally opened transmittal letters with the phrase "Enclosed please find," even though that phrasing has been widely condemned in business-writing handbooks since the late 19th century. A transmittal letter may properly begin with a range of openers as informal as "Here is" to the more formal "Enclosed is."

transportation, *n.* **1.** The movement of goods or persons from one place to another by a carrier. **2.** *Criminal law.* A type of punishment that sends the criminal out of the country to another place (usu. a penal colony) for a specified period. Cf. DEPORTATION.

trap, *n.* **1.** A device for capturing animals, such as a pitfall, snare, or machine that shuts suddenly. **2.** Any device or contrivance by which one may be caught unawares; stratagem; snare. **3.** *Torts.* An ultrahazardous hidden peril of which the property owner or occupier, but not a licensee, has knowledge. • A trap can exist even if it was not designed or intended to catch or entrap anything.

Travel Act. A federal law, enacted in 1961, that prohibits conduct intended to promote, direct, or manage illegal business activities in interstate commerce. • This statute was enacted to create federal jurisdiction over many criminal activities traditionally handled by state and local governments to help those jurisdictions cope with increasingly complex interstate criminal activity. 18 USCA § 1952.

traveled place. A place where the public has, in some manner, acquired the legal right to travel.

travel expense. See EXPENSE.

traverse (trav-ərs), *n. Common-law pleading.* A formal denial of a factual allegation made in the opposing party's pleading <Smith filed a traverse to Allen's complaint, asserting that he did not knowingly provide false information>. — **traverse (trav-ərs** *or* trə-**vərs**), *vb.* See DENIAL.

common traverse. A traverse consisting of a tender of issue — that is, a denial accompanied by a formal offer for decision of the point denied — with a denial that expressly contradicts the terms of the allegation traversed.

cumulative traverse. A traverse that analyzes a proposition into its constituent parts and traverses them cumulatively. • It amounts to the same thing as traversing the one entire proposition, since the several parts traversed must all make up one entire proposition or point.

general traverse. A denial of all the facts in an opponent's pleading.

special traverse. A denial of one material fact in an opponent's pleading; a traverse that explains or qualifies the denial. • The essential parts of a special traverse are an inducement, a denial, and a verification.

traverser, *n.* One who traverses or denies a pleading.

treason, *n.* The offense of attempting to overthrow the government of the state to which one owes allegiance, either by making war against the state or by materially supporting its enemies. — **treasonable,** *adj.* — **treasonous,** *adj.* Cf. SEDITION.

Treas. Reg. *abbr.* TREASURY REGULATION.

treasure trove. [Law French "treasure found"] Valuables (usu. gold or silver) found hidden in the ground or other private place, the owner of which is unknown. • At common law, the finder of a treasure trove was entitled to title against all except the true owner.

Treasuries. Debt obligations of the federal government backed by the full faith and credit of the government. See TREASURY BILL; TREASURY BOND; TREASURY CERTIFICATE; TREASURY NOTE.

Treasury bill. A short-term debt security issued by the federal government, with a maturity of 13, 26, or 52 weeks. • These bills — auctioned weekly or quarterly — pay interest in the form of the difference between their discounted purchase price and their par value at maturity. — Abbr. T-bill.

Treasury bond. A long-term debt security issued by the federal government, with a maturity of 10 to 30 years. • These bonds are considered risk-free, but they usually pay relatively little interest. — Abbr. T-bond.

treasury certificate. An obligation of the federal government maturing in one year and on which interest is paid on a coupon basis.

Treasury Department. A federal department — created by Congress in 1789 — whose duties include formulating and recommending financial, tax, and fiscal policies, serving as the federal government's financial agent, and manufacturing coins and currency.

Treasury note. An intermediate-term debt security issued by the federal government, with a maturity of two to ten years. • These notes are considered risk-free, but they usually pay relatively little interest. — Abbr. T-note.

Treasury Regulation. A regulation promulgated by the U.S. Treasury Department to explain or interpret a section of the Internal Revenue Code. • Treasury Regulations are binding on all taxpayers. — Abbr. Treas. Reg.

Treaty Clause. The constitutional provision giving the President the power to make treaties, with the advice and consent of the Senate. U.S. Const. art. II, § 2.

treaty power. The President's constitutional authority to make treaties, with the advice and consent of the Senate. See TREATY CLAUSE.

treble damages. See DAMAGES.

trespass (**tres**-pəs *or* **tres**-pas), *n.* **1.** An unlawful act committed against the person or property of another; esp., wrongful entry on another's real property. **2.** At common law, a legal action for injuries resulting from an unlawful act of this kind. **3.** *Archaic.* MISDEMEANOR. — **trespass,** *vb.* — **trespassory** (**tres**-pə-sor-ee), *adj.*

trespass on the case. At common law, an action to recover damages that are not the immediate result of a wrongful act but rather a later consequence. • This action was the precursor to a variety of modern-day tort claims, including negligence, nuisance, and business torts.

trespass quare clausum fregit (**kwair**-ee **klaw**-zəm **free**-jit). [Latin "why he broke the close"] **1.** A person's unlawful entry on another's land that is visibly enclosed. • This tort consists of doing any of the following without lawful justification: (1) entering upon land in the possession of another, (2) remaining on the land, or (3) placing or projecting any object upon it. **2.** At common law, an action to recover damages resulting from another's unlawful entry on one's land that is visibly enclosed. — Abbr. trespass q.c.f.

trespass to chattels. The act of committing, without lawful justification, any act of direct physical interference with a chattel possessed by another. • The act must amount to a direct forcible injury.

trespass to try title. **1.** In some states, an action for the recovery of property unlawfully withheld from an owner who has the immediate right to possession. **2.** A procedure under which a claim to title may be adjudicated.

trespass vi et armis (**vi** et **ahr**-mis). [Latin "with force and arms"] **1.** At common law, an action for damages resulting from an intentional injury to person or property, esp. if by violent means; trespass to the plaintiff's person (as in illegal assault, battery, wounding, or imprisonment) when not under color of legal process, or when the battery, wounding, or imprisonment was at first lawful, but later became excessive. **2.** See *trespass quare clausum fregit*. • In this sense, the "force" is implied by the "breaking" of the close (that is, an enclosed area), even if no real force is used.

trespasser. One who commits a trespass; one who intentionally and without consent or privilege enters another's property. • In tort law, a landholder owes no duty to unforeseeable trespassers. Cf. INVITEE; LICENSEE (2).

innocent trespasser. One who enters another's land unlawfully, but either inadvertently or believing in a right to do so.

triable, *adj.* Subject or liable to judicial examination and trial <a triable offense>.

trial. A formal judicial examination of evidence and determination of legal claims in an adversary proceeding.

bench trial. A trial before a judge without a jury. • The judge decides questions of fact as well as questions of law.

bifurcated trial. A trial that is divided into two stages, such as for guilt and punishment or for liability and damages. Cf. SEVERANCE (2).

joint trial. A trial involving two or more parties; esp., a criminal trial of two or more persons for the same or similar offenses.

jury trial. A trial in which the factual issues are determined by a jury, not by the judge.

political trial. **1.** A trial of a person for a political crime. **2.** A trial (esp. a criminal prosecution) in which either the prosecution or the defendant (or both) uses the proceedings as a platform to espouse a particular political belief. See SHOW TRIAL.

separate trial. **1.** *Criminal procedure.* The individual trial of each of several persons jointly accused of a crime. Fed. R. Crim. P. 14. **2.** *Civil procedure.* Within a single action, a distinct trial of a separate claim or issue — or of a group of claims or issues — ordered by the trial judge, usu. to conserve resources or avoid prejudice. Fed. R. Civ. P. 42(b). Cf. SEVERANCE.

summary jury trial. A settlement technique in which the parties argue before a mock jury, which then reaches a nonbinding verdict that will assist the parties in evaluating their positions. Cf. MINITRIAL.

trial de novo (dee *or* di **noh**-voh). A new trial on the entire case — that is, on both questions of fact and issues of law — conducted as if there had been no trial in the first instance.

trial on the merits. A trial on the substantive issues of a case, as opposed to a motion hearing or interlocutory matter.

trial per pais (pər **pay** *or* **pays**). [Law French "trial by the country"] Trial by jury.

trifurcated trial. A trial that is divided into three stages, such as for liability, general damages, and special damages.

trial brief. See BRIEF.

trial counsel. See COUNSEL.

trial court. See COURT.

trial de novo. See TRIAL.

trial judge. See JUDGE.

trial on the merits. See TRIAL.

trial per pais. See TRIAL.

tribunal (trɪ-**byoo**-nəl). **1.** A court or other adjudicatory body. **2.** The seat, bench, or place where a judge sits.

tributary (**trib**-yə-ter-ee), *n.* A stream flowing directly or indirectly into a river.

tribute (trib-yoot), *n.* **1.** An acknowledgment of gratitude or respect. **2.** A contribution that a sovereign raises from its subjects to defray the expenses of state. **3.** Money paid by an inferior sovereign or state to a superior one to secure the latter's friendship and protection.

trifurcated trial. See TRIAL.

trigamy (trig-ə-mee), *n.* The act of marrying a person while legally married to someone else and bigamously married to yet another.

tripartite (trɪ-**pahr**-tɪt), *adj.* Involving, composed of, or divided into three parts or elements <a tripartite agreement>.

trivial, *adj.* Trifling; inconsiderable; of small worth or importance.

TRO (tee-ahr-**oh**). *abbr.* TEMPORARY RESTRAINING ORDER.

trover (**troh**-vər). A common-law action for the recovery of damages for the conversion of personal property, the damages generally being measured by the value of the property. Cf. DETINUE; REPLEVIN.

truancy (**troo**-ən-see), *n.* The act or state of shirking responsibility; esp., willful and unjustified failure to attend school by one who is required to attend. — **truant,** *adj.* & *n.*

true and correct. *Jargon.* Authentic; accurate; unaltered <we have forwarded a true and correct copy of the expert's report>.

true bill, *n.* A grand jury's notation that a criminal charge should go before a petit jury for trial <the grand jury returned a true bill, and the state prepared to prosecute>. Cf. NO BILL.

true-bill, *vb.* To make or deliver a true bill on <the grand jury true-billed the indictment>.

true defense. See DEFENSE (1).

true verdict. See VERDICT.

trust, *n.* **1.** The right, enforceable solely in equity, to the beneficial enjoyment of property to which another person holds the legal title; a property interest held by one person (the *trustee*) at the request of another (the *settlor*) for the benefit of a third party (the *beneficiary*). • For a trust to be valid, it must involve specific property, reflect the settlor's intent, and be created for a lawful purpose. **2.** A fiduciary relationship regarding property and subjecting the person with title to the property to equitable duties to deal with it for another's benefit; the confidence placed in a trustee, together with the trustee's obligations toward the property and the beneficiary. • A trust arises as a result of a manifestation of an intention to create it. See FIDUCIARY RELATIONSHIP. **3.** The property so held; TRUST FUND. **4.** A business combination that aims at monopoly. See ANTITRUST LAW.

blind trust. A trust in which the settlor places investments under the control of an independent trustee, usu. to avoid a conflict of interest.

bypass trust. A trust into which a decedent's estate passes, so that the surviving heirs get a life estate in the trust rather than the property itself, in order to avoid estate taxes on an estate larger than the tax-credit-sheltered amount ($700,000 in 2000, increasing to $1 million after 2005). See *unified estate-and-gift tax credit* under TAX CREDIT.

charitable trust. A trust created to benefit a specific charity, specific charities, or the general public rather than a private individual or entity. • Charitable trusts are often eligible for favorable tax treatment. See CY PRES.

Clifford trust. An irrevocable trust, set up for at least ten years and a day, whereby income from the trust property is paid to the beneficiary but the property itself reverts back to the settlor when the trust expires. • This term gets its name from *Helvering v. Clifford*, 309 U.S. 331, 60 S.Ct. 554 (1940).

constructive trust. A trust imposed by a court on equitable grounds against one who has obtained property by wrongdoing, thereby preventing the wrongful holder from being unjustly enriched. • Such a trust creates no fiduciary relationship. Cf. *resulting trust*.

destructible trust. A trust that can be destroyed by the happening of an event or by operation of law.

discretionary trust. A trust in which the settlor has delegated nearly complete or limited discretion to the trustee to decide when and how much income or property is distributed to a beneficiary. • For example, a support trust operates to provide a standard for or limit on the exercise of discretion. This is perhaps the most common type of trust used in estate planning.

executed trust. A trust in which the estates and interests in the subject matter of the trust are completely limited and defined by the instrument creating the trust and require no further instruments to complete them.

executory trust (eg-**zek**-yə-tor-ee). A trust in which the instrument creating the trust is intended to be provisional only, and further conveyances are contemplated by the trust instrument before the terms of the trust can be carried out.

express trust. A trust created with the settlor's express intent, usu. declared in writing; an ordinary trust as opposed to a resulting trust or a constructive trust.

generation-skipping trust. A trust that is established to transfer (usu. principal) assets to a skip person (a beneficiary more than one generation removed from the settlor). • The transfer is often accomplished by giving some control or benefits (such as trust income) of the assets to a nonskip person, often a member of the generation between the settlor and skip person. This type of trust is subject to a generation-skipping transfer tax. IRC (26 USCA) §§ 2601 et seq. See DEEMED TRANSFEROR; GENERATION-SKIPPING TRANSFER; *generation-skipping transfer tax* under TAX; SKIP PERSON.

grantor trust. A trust in which the settlor retains control over the trust property or its income to such an extent that the settlor is taxed on the trust's income. See *Clifford trust*.

honorary trust. A trust that is legally invalid and unenforceable because it lacks a proper beneficiary. • Examples include trusts that honor dead persons, maintain cemetery plots, or benefit animals.

illusory trust. An arrangement that looks like a trust but, because of powers retained in the settlor, has no real substance and is not a completed trust.

indestructible trust. A trust that, because of the settlor's wishes, cannot be prematurely terminated by the beneficiary.

inter vivos trust (**in**-tər **vɪ**-vohs *or* **vee**-vohs). A trust that is created and takes effect during the settlor's lifetime. Cf. *testamentary trust*.

irrevocable trust (i-**rev**-ə-kə-bəl). A trust that cannot be terminated by the settlor once it is created. • In most states, a trust will be deemed irrevocable unless the settlor specifies otherwise.

marital-deduction trust. A testamentary trust created to take full advantage of the marital deduction; esp., a trust entitling a spouse to lifetime income from the trust and sufficient control over the trust to include the trust property in the spouse's estate at death.

Medicaid-qualifying trust. A trust that is deemed to have been created in an effort to reduce someone's assets so that the person may qualify for Medicaid, and that will be included as an asset for purposes of determining the person's eligibility.

pourover trust. An inter vivos trust that receives property (usu. the residual estate) from a will upon the testator's death. Cf. *pourover will* under WILL.

power-of-appointment trust. A trust, used to qualify property for the marital deduction, under which property is left in trust for the surviving spouse. • The trustee must distribute income to the spouse for life, and the power of appointment is given to the spouse or to his or her estate.

precatory trust (**prek**-ə-tor-ee). A trust that the law will recognize to carry out the wishes of the testator or grantor even though the statement in question is in the nature of an entreaty or recommendation rather than a positive command.

QTIP trust (**kyoo**-tip). A trust that is established to qualify for the marital deduction. • Under this trust, the assets are referred to as qualified-terminable-interest property, or QTIP. See *qualified-terminable-interest property* under PROPERTY.

resulting trust. A trust imposed by law when property is transferred under circumstances suggesting that the transferor did not intend for the transferee to have the beneficial interest in the property. Cf. *constructive trust.*

self-settled trust. A trust in which the settlor is also the person who is to receive the benefits from the trust, usu. set up in an attempt to protect the trust assets from creditors. • In most states, such a trust will not protect trust assets from the settlor's creditors. Restatement (Second) of Trusts § 156 (1959).

spendthrift trust. A trust that prohibits the beneficiary's interest from being assigned and also prevents a creditor from attaching that interest.

support trust. A discretionary trust in which the settlor authorizes the trustee to pay to the beneficiary as much income or principal as the trustee believes is needed for support, esp. for "comfortable support" or "support in accordance with the beneficiary's standard of living." • The beneficiary's interest can be reached by creditors for necessaries, but usually not by general creditors.

testamentary trust (tes-tə-**men**-tə-ree *or* -tree). A trust that is created by a will and takes effect when the settlor (testator) dies. Cf. *inter vivos trust.*

Totten trust. A revocable trust created by one's deposit of money in one's own name as a trustee for another. • A Totten trust is commonly used to indicate a successor to the account without having to create a will.

trustee (trəs-**tee**), *n.* **1.** One who, having legal title to property, holds it in trust for the benefit of another and owes a fiduciary duty to that beneficiary. • Generally, a trustee's duties are to convert to cash all debts and securities that are not qualified legal investments, to reinvest the cash in proper securities, to protect and preserve the trust property, and to ensure that it is employed solely for the beneficiary, in accordance with the directions contained in the trust instrument.

corporate trustee. A corporation that is empowered by its charter to act as a trustee, such as a bank or trust company.

judicial trustee. A trustee appointed by a court to execute a trust.

quasi-trustee. One who benefits from a breach of a trust to a great enough degree to become liable as a trustee.

successor trustee. A trustee who succeeds an earlier trustee, usu. as provided in the trust agreement.

testamentary trustee (tes-tə-**men**-tə-ree *or* -tree). A trustee appointed by or acting under a will; one appointed to carry out a trust created by a will.

trustee ad litem (ad **lI**-tem *or* -təm). A trustee appointed by the court.

trustee de son tort (də sawn [*or* son] **tor**[**t**]). A person who, without legal authority, administers a living person's property to the detriment of the property owner. See *constructive trust* under TRUST.

trustee ex maleficio (eks mal-ə-**fish**-ee-oh). A person who is guilty of wrongful or fraudulent conduct and is held by equity to the duty of a trustee, in relation to the subject matter, to prevent him or her from profiting from the wrongdoing.

2. *Bankruptcy.* An officer of the court who is elected by creditors or appointed by a judge to act as the representative of a bankruptcy estate. • The trustee's duties include (1) collecting and reducing to cash the assets of the estate, (2) operating the debtor's business with court approval if appropriate to preserve the value of business assets, (3) examining the debtor at a meeting of creditors, (4) filing inventories and making periodic reports to the court on the financial condition of the estate, (5) investigating the debtor's financial affairs, (6) examining proofs of claims and objecting to improper claims, (7) furnishing information relating to the bankruptcy to interested parties, and (8) opposing discharge through bankruptcy, if advisable.

trustee, *vb.* **1.** To serve as trustee. **2.** To place (a person or property) in the hands of one or more trustees. **3.** To appoint (a person) as trustee, often of a bankrupt's estate in order to restrain a creditor from collecting moneys due. **4.** To attach (the effects of a debtor) in the hands of a third person.

trust fund. The property held in a trust by a trustee; CORPUS (2).

common trust fund. A trust fund set up within a bank trust department to combine the assets of numerous small trusts to achieve greater investment diversification. • Common trust funds are regulated by state law.

trust-fund doctrine. The principle that the assets of an insolvent company, including paid and unpaid subscriptions to the capital stock, are held as a trust fund to which the company's creditors may look for payment of their claims. • The creditors may follow the property constituting this fund, and may use it to reduce the debts, unless it has passed into the hands of a bona fide purchaser without notice.

trust indorsement. See INDORSEMENT.

trustor. One who creates a trust; SETTLOR (1).

trust ownership. See OWNERSHIP.

trust receipt. 1. A pre-UCC security device — now governed by Article 9 of the Code — consisting of a receipt stating that the wholesale buyer has possession of the goods for the benefit of the financier. • Today there must usually be a security agreement coupled with a filed financing statement. **2.** A method of financing commercial transactions by which title passes directly from the manufacturer or seller to a banker or lender, who as owner delivers the goods to the dealer on whose behalf the banker or lender is acting, and to whom title ultimately goes when the banker's or lender's primary right has been satisfied.

trusty, *n.* A convict or prisoner who is considered trustworthy by prison authorities and therefore given special privileges.

truth. 1. A fully accurate account of events; factuality. **2.** *Defamation.* An affirmative defense by which the defendant asserts that the alleged defamatory statement is substantially accurate.

try, *vb.* To examine judicially; to examine and resolve (a dispute) by means of a trial.

turncoat witness. See WITNESS.

turnkey, *adj.* **1.** (Of a product) provided in a state of readiness for immediate use <a turnkey computer network>. **2.** Of, relating to, or involving a product provided in this manner <a turnkey contract>.

turnkey, *n.* A jailer; esp., one charged with keeping the keys to a jail or prison.

turn state's evidence, *vb.* To cooperate with prosecutors and testify against other criminal defendants <after hours of intense negotiations, the suspect accepted a plea bargain and agreed to turn state's evidence>.

turntable doctrine. See ATTRACTIVE-NUISANCE DOCTRINE. • This term gets its name from the enticing yet dangerous qualities of railroad turntables, which have frequently been the subject of personal-injury litigation.

TVA. *abbr.* TENNESSEE VALLEY AUTHORITY.

Twelfth Amendment. The constitutional amendment, ratified in 1804, that altered the electoral-college system by separating the balloting for presidential and vice-presidential candidates.

twelve-day rule. *Criminal procedure.* A rule in some jurisdictions requiring that a person charged with a felony be given a preliminary examination no later than 12 days after the arraignment on the original warrant.

Twentieth Amendment. The constitutional amendment, ratified in 1933, that changed (1) the date of the presidential and vice-presidential inaugurations from March 4 to January 20, and (2) the date for congressional convention from March 4 to January 3, thereby eliminating the "short session" of Congress, during which a number of lame-duck members sat.

Twenty-fifth Amendment. The constitutional amendment, ratified in 1967, that established rules of succession for the presidency and vice presidency in the event of death, resignation, or incapacity.

Twenty-first Amendment. The constitutional amendment, ratified in 1933, that repealed the 18th Amendment (which established national Prohibition) and returned the power to regulate alcohol to the states.

Twenty-fourth Amendment. The constitutional amendment, ratified in 1964, that prohibits the federal and state governments from restricting the right to vote in a federal election because of one's failure to pay a poll tax or other tax.

Twenty-second Amendment. The constitutional amendment, ratified in 1951, that prohibits a person from being elected President more than twice (or, if the person succeeded to the office with more than two years term remaining, more than once).

Twenty-seventh Amendment. The constitutional amendment, ratified in 1992, that prevents a pay raise for senators and representatives from taking effect until a new Congress convenes. • This amendment was proposed as part of the original Bill of Rights in 1789, but it took 203 years for the required three-fourths of the states to ratify it.

Twenty-sixth Amendment. The constitutional amendment, ratified in 1971, that sets the minimum voting age at 18 for all state and federal elections.

Twenty-third Amendment. The constitutional amendment, ratified in 1961, that allows District of Columbia residents to vote in presidential elections.

twist, *n.* An informant who provides testimony in exchange for leniency in sentencing, rather than for money. See INFORMANT.

two-dismissal rule. The rule that a notice of voluntary dismissal operates as an adjudication on the merits — not merely as a dismissal without prejudice — when filed by a plaintiff who has already dismissed the same claim in another court.

two-issue rule. The rule that if multiple issues were submitted to a trial jury and at least one of them is error-free, the appellate court should presume that the jury based its verdict on the proper issue — not on an erroneous one — and should therefore affirm the judgment.

two-witness rule. **1.** The rule that, to support a perjury conviction, two independent witnesses (or one witness along with corroborating evidence) must establish that the alleged perjurer gave false testimony. **2.** The rule, as stated in the U.S. Constitution, that no person may be convicted of treason without two witnesses to the same overt act — or unless the accused confesses in open court. U.S. Const. art. IV, § 2, cl. 2.

tying arrangement. *Antitrust.* **1.** A seller's agreement to sell one product or service only if the buyer also buys a different product or service. • The product or service that the buyer wants to buy is known as the *tying product* or *tying service*; the different product or service that the seller insists on selling is known as the *tied product* or *tied service*. Tying arrangements may be illegal under the Sherman or Clayton Act if their effect is too anticompetitive. **2.** A seller's refusal to sell one product or service unless the buyer also buys a different product or service. Cf. RECIPROCAL DEALING.

U

U3C. *abbr.* UNIFORM CONSUMER CREDIT CODE.

uberrimae fidei (yoo-**ber**-ə-mee **fi**-dee-I). [Latin] Of the utmost good faith.

UCC. *abbr.* **1.** UNIFORM COMMERCIAL CODE. **2.** UNIVERSAL COPYRIGHT CONVENTION.

UCCC. *abbr.* UNIFORM CONSUMER CREDIT CODE.

UCCJA. *abbr.* UNIFORM CHILD CUSTODY JURISDICTION ACT.

UCR. *abbr.* UNIFORM CRIME REPORTS.

UDITPA. *abbr.* UNIFORM DIVISION OF INCOME FOR TAX PURPOSES ACT.

UFCA. *abbr.* UNIFORM FRAUDULENT CONVEYANCES ACT.

UFTA. *abbr.* UNIFORM FRAUDULENT TRANSFER ACT.

UGMA. See UNIFORM TRANSFERS TO MINORS ACT.

ukase (yoo-**kays** *or* **yoo**-kays). A proclamation or decree, esp. of a final or arbitrary nature. • This term originally referred to a decree issued by a Russian czar.

ulterior intent. See INTENT (1).

ultimate fact. See FACT.

ultimate issue. See ISSUE (1).

ultimatum (əl-tə-**may**-təm), *n.* The final and categorical proposal made in negotiating a treaty, contract, or the like. • An ultimatum implies that a rejection might lead to a break-off in negotiation and, possibly, some other form of action. Pl. **ultimatums.**

ultra vires (**əl**-trə **VI**-reez *also* **veer**-eez), *adj.* Unauthorized; beyond the scope of power allowed or granted by a corporate charter or by law <the officer was liable for the firm's ultra vires actions>. — **ultra vires,** *adv.* Cf. INTRA VIRES.

umpire. An impartial person appointed to make an award or a final decision, usu. when a matter has been submitted to arbitrators who have failed to agree. • An arbitral submission may provide for the appointment of an umpire.

un-, *prefix.* **1.** Not <unassignable>. **2.** Contrary to; against <unconstitutional>.

unanimous (yoo-**nan**-ə-məs), *adj.* **1.** Agreeing in opinion; being in complete accord <the judges were unanimous in their approval of the recommendation>. **2.** Arrived at by the consent of all <a unanimous verdict>.

unauthorized, *adj.* Done without authority; specif. (of a signature or indorsement), made without actual, implied, or apparent authority. UCC § 1–201(43).

unauthorized practice of law. See PRACTICE OF LAW.

unauthorized signature. See SIGNATURE.

unavailability, *n.* The status or condition of not being accessible, as when a witness is dead, missing, or exempted by court order from testifying. • Unavailability is recognized under the Federal Rules of Evidence as an exclusion to the hearsay rule. Fed. R. Evid. 804.

unavoidable-accident doctrine. *Torts.* The principle that no party is liable for an accident that was unforeseeable and could not have been prevented by the exercise of reasonable care. • The modern trend is for courts to ignore this doctrine, relying instead on the basic concepts of duty, negligence, and proximate cause.

unavoidable danger. See DANGER.

unborn-widow rule. The legal fiction, assumed under the rule against perpetuities, that a beneficiary's widow is not alive at the testator's death, and thus a succeeding life estate to her voids any remainders because the interest would not vest within the perpetuities period. See RULE AGAINST PERPETUITIES.

unbroken, *adj.* Not interrupted; continuous <unbroken possession by the adverse possessor>.

unconditional, *adj.* Not limited by a condition; not depending on an uncertain event or contingency.

unconditional delivery. See DELIVERY.

unconditional discharge. See DISCHARGE.

unconditional promise. See PROMISE.

unconditional release. See RELEASE.

unconscionability (ən-kon-shə-nə-**bil**-ə-tee). **1.** Extreme unfairness. **2.** The principle that a court may refuse to enforce a contract that is unfair or oppressive because of procedural abuses during contract formation or because of overreaching contractual terms, esp. terms that are unreasonably favorable to one party while precluding meaningful choice for the other party. • Because unconscionability depends on circumstances at the time the contract is formed, a later rise in market price is irrelevant.

procedural unconscionability. Unconscionability resulting from improprieties in contract formation (such as oral misrepresentations or disparities in bargaining position) rather than from the terms of the contract itself. • This type of unconscionability suggests that there was no meeting of the minds.

substantive unconscionability. Unconscionability resulting from contract terms that are unduly harsh, commercially unreasonable, or grossly unfair given the existing circumstances.

unconscionable (ən-**kon**-shə-nə-bəl), *adj.* **1.** (Of a person) having no conscience; unscrupulous <an unconscionable used-car salesman>. **2.** (Of an act or transaction) showing no regard for conscience; affronting the sense of justice, decency, or reasonableness <the contract is void as unconscionable>. Cf. CONSCIONABLE.

unconscionable agreement. See AGREEMENT.

unconstitutional, *adj.* Contrary to or in conflict with a constitution, esp. the U.S. Constitution <the law is unconstitutional because it violates

the First Amendment's free-speech guarantee>. Cf. NONCONSTITUTIONAL.

uncontrollable impulse. See IMPULSE.

undercover agent. See AGENT.

undersigned, *n.* A person whose name is signed at the end of a document <the undersigned agrees to all these terms and conditions>.

understanding, *n.* **1.** The process of comprehending; the act of a person who understands something. **2.** One's personal interpretation of an event or occurrence. **3.** An agreement, esp. of an implied or tacit nature.

under submission. Being considered by the court; under advisement <the case was under submission in the court of appeals for more than two years>.

undertake, *vb.* **1.** To take on an obligation or task <he has undertaken to chair the committee>. **2.** To give a formal promise; guarantee <the merchant undertook that the goods were waterproof>. **3.** To act as surety for (another); to make oneself responsible for (a person, fact, or the like) <her husband undertook for her appearance in court>.

undertaking, *n.* **1.** A promise, pledge, or engagement. **2.** A bail bond.

under the influence. (Of a driver, pilot, etc.) deprived of clearness of mind and physical self-control because of drugs or alcohol. See DRIVING UNDER THE INFLUENCE.

undisclosed agency. See AGENCY (1).

undisclosed principal. See PRINCIPAL (1).

undisputed fact. See FACT.

undivided interest. An interest held under the same title by two or more persons, whether their rights are equal or unequal in value or quantity. See *joint tenancy* and *tenancy in common* under TENANCY.

undue, *adj.* **1.** *Archaic.* Not yet owed; not currently payable <an undue debt>. **2.** Excessive or unwarranted <undue burden> <undue influence>.

undue-burden test. *Constitutional law.* The Supreme Court test stating that a law regulating abortion will be struck down if it places a substantial obstacle in the path of a woman's right to obtain an abortion.

undue influence. **1.** The improper use of power or trust in a way that deprives a person of free will and substitutes another's objective. • Consent to a contract, transaction, relationship, or conduct is voidable if the consent is obtained through undue influence. **2.** *Wills & estates.* Coercion that destroys a testator's free will and substitutes another's objectives in its place. • When a beneficiary actively procures the execution of a will, a presumption of undue influence may be raised, based on the confidential relationship between the influencer and the testator. See COERCION; DURESS. Cf. DUE INFLUENCE.

undue prejudice. See PREJUDICE.

unearned income. See INCOME.

unearned interest. See INTEREST (3).

unemployment insurance. See INSURANCE.

unemployment tax. See TAX.

unencumbered (ən-in-**kəm**-bərd), *adj.* Without any burdens or impediments <unencumbered title to property>.

unenforceable, *adj.* (Of a contract) valid but incapable of being enforced. Cf. VOID; VOIDABLE.

unequal, *adj.* Not equal in some respect; uneven <unequal treatment under the law>.

unequivocal (ən-i-**kwiv**-ə-kəl), *adj.* Unambiguous; clear; free from uncertainty.

unessential mistake. See MISTAKE.

unethical, *adj.* Not in conformity with moral norms or standards of professional conduct. See LEGAL ETHICS.

unexpired term. See TERM (4).

unfair competition. 1. Dishonest or fraudulent rivalry in trade and commerce; esp., the practice of trying to palm off one's own goods or services for those of another by imitating or counterfeiting a competitor's name, brand, or distinctive characteristic. **2.** The body of law protecting the first user against an imitating or counterfeiting competitor.

unfair hearing. See HEARING.

unfair persuasion. *Contracts.* A type of undue influence in which a stronger party achieves a result by means that seriously impair the weaker party's free and competent exercise of judgment. • Unfair persuasion is a lesser form of undue influence than duress and misrepresentation. The two primary factors to be considered are the unavailability of independent advice and the susceptibility of the person persuaded. See UNDUE INFLUENCE (1).

unfair surprise. A situation in which a party, having had no notice of some action or proffered evidence, is unprepared to answer or refute it.

unfit, *adj.* **1.** Unsuitable; not adapted or qualified for a particular use or service <the buyer returned the unfit goods>. **2.** *Family law.* Morally unqualified; incompetent <the judge found her to be an unfit mother and awarded custody to the father>.

unified credit. See TAX CREDIT.

unified estate-and-gift tax. See *transfer tax* under TAX.

unified transfer tax. See *transfer tax* under TAX.

uniform act. A law drafted with the intention that it will be adopted by all or most of the states; esp., UNIFORM LAW. Cf. MODEL ACT.

Uniform Child Custody Jurisdiction Act. A 1968 model statute that sets out a standard (based on the child's residence in and connections with the state) by which a state court determines whether it has jurisdiction over a particular child-custody matter or whether it must recognize a custody decree issued by another state's court. — Abbr. UCCJA. Cf. PARENTAL KIDNAPPING PREVENTION ACT.

Uniform Commercial Code. A uniform law that governs commercial transactions, including sales of goods, secured transactions, and negotiable instruments. • This code has been adopted in some form by every state. — Abbr. UCC.

Uniform Consumer Credit Code. A uniform law designed to simplify and modernize the consumer credit and usury laws, to improve consumer understanding of the terms of credit transactions, to protect consumers against unfair practices, and the like. • This code has been adopted by only a few states. — Abbr. UCCC; U3C. See CONSUMER CREDIT PROTECTION ACT.

Uniform Controlled Substances Act. A uniform act, adopted by many states and the federal government, governing the sale, use, and distribution of drugs. 21 USCA §§ 801 et seq.

Uniform Crime Reports. A series of annual criminological studies (*Crime in the United States*) prepared by the FBI. • The reports include data on eight index offenses, statistics on arrests, and information on offenders, crime rates, and the like. — Abbr. UCR.

Uniform Deceptive Trade Practices Act. A type of Baby FTC Act that provides monetary and injunctive relief for a variety of unfair and deceptive acts, such as false advertising and disparagement. See BABY FTC ACT.

Uniform Division of Income for Tax Purposes Act. A uniform law, adopted by some states, that provides criteria to assist in assigning the total taxable income of a multistate corporation among the various states. — Abbr. UDITPA.

Uniform Divorce Recognition Act. A uniform code adopted by some states regarding full-faith-and-credit issues that arise in divorces.

Uniform Enforcement of Foreign Judgments Act. A uniform state law giving the holder of a foreign judgment the right to levy and execute as if it were a domestic judgment.

Uniform Fraudulent Conveyances Act. A model act adopted in 1918 to deal with issues arising from fraudulent conveyances by insolvent persons. • This act differentiated between conduct that was presumed fraudulent and conduct that required an actual intent to commit fraud. — Abbr. UFCA.

Uniform Fraudulent Transfer Act. A model act designed to bring uniformity among the states regarding the definition of, and penalties for, fraudulent transfers. • This act was adopted in 1984 to replace the Uniform Fraudulent Conveyances Act. — Abbr. UFTA.

Uniform Gifts to Minors Act. See UNIFORM TRANSFERS TO MINORS ACT.

Uniformity Clause. The clause of the U.S. Constitution requiring the uniform collection of federal taxes. U.S. Const. art. I, § 8, cl. 1.

uniform law. An unofficial law proposed as legislation for all the states to adopt exactly as written, the purpose being to promote greater consistency among the states. • All the uniform laws are promulgated by the National Conference of Commissioners on Uniform State Laws. For a complete collection, see *Uniform Laws Annotated*.

Uniform Mandatory Disposition of Detainers Act. A law, promulgated in 1958 and adopted by several states, requiring a state to timely dispose of any untried charges against a prisoner in that state, on the prisoner's written request. See INTERSTATE AGREEMENT ON DETAINERS ACT.

Uniform Partnership Act. A model code promulgated in 1914 to bring uniformity to state laws governing general and limited partnerships. • The act was adopted by almost all the states, but has been superseded in several of them by the Revised Uniform Partnership Act (1994). — Abbr. UPA.

Uniform Principal and Income Act. A uniform code adopted by some states governing allocation of principal and income in trusts and estates.

Uniform Reciprocal Enforcement of Support Act. A 1950 model statute (now superseded) that sought to unify the way in which interstate support matters were processed and the way in which one jurisdiction's orders were given full faith and credit in another jurisdiction. • This Act, which was amended in 1958 and 1960, was replaced in 1997 with the Uniform Interstate Family Support Act. — Abbr. URESA.

Uniform Simultaneous Death Act. A 1940 model statute creating a rule that a person must survive a decedent by at least 120 hours in order to avoid disputes caused by simultaneous deaths (as in a common disaster) or by quickly successive deaths of persons between whom property or death benefits pass on the death of one survived by the other. • In the absence of the 120-hour period of survival, each person is presumed to have survived the other for purposes of distributing their respective estates. The Act was revised in 1993 and has been adopted in some form by almost all states.

Uniform Transfers to Minors Act. A 1983 model statute providing for the transfer of property to a minor and permitting a custodian who acts in a fiduciary capacity to manage investments and apply the income from the property to the minor's support. • The Act has been adopted in most states. It was revised in 1986. — Abbr. UTMA.

unilateral (yoo-nə-**lat**-ər-əl), *adj.* One-sided; relating to only one of two or more persons or things <unilateral mistake>.

unilateral act. See ACT.

unilateral contract. See CONTRACT.

unilateral mistake. See MISTAKE.

unimproved land. 1. Land that has never been improved. **2.** Land that was once improved but has now been cleared of all buildings and structures.

unindicted conspirator. See CONSPIRATOR.

unintentional act. See ACT.

unital (yoo-nə-təl), *adj.* Of or relating to legal relations that exist between only two persons. Cf. MULTITAL.

United States Attorney. A lawyer appointed by the President to represent the federal government in civil and criminal cases in a federal judicial district. • U.S. Attorneys work under the direction of the Attorney General. Cf. DISTRICT ATTORNEY.

United States Claims Court. See UNITED STATES COURT OF FEDERAL CLAIMS.

United States Code. A multivolume published codification of federal statutory law. • In a citation, it is abbreviated as USC, as in 42 USC § 1983. — Abbr. USC.

United States Code Annotated. A multivolume publication of the complete text of the United States Code with historical notes, cross-references, and casenotes of federal and state decisions construing specific code sections. — Abbr. USCA.

United States Court of Appeals. A federal appellate court having jurisdiction to hear cases in one of the 13 judicial circuits of the United States (the First Circuit through the Eleventh Circuit, plus the District of Columbia Circuit and the Federal Circuit).

United States Court of Appeals for the Federal Circuit. The federal appellate court with jurisdiction to hear appeals in patent cases, various actions against the United States to recover damages, cases from the U.S. Court of Federal Claims, the U.S. Court of International Trade, the U.S. Court of Veterans Appeals, the Merit Systems Protection Board, and some administrative agencies. • The Court originated in the 1982 merger of the Court of Customs and Patent Appeals and the U.S. Court of Claims (although the trial jurisdiction of the Court of Claims was given to a new U.S. Claims Court). — Abbr. Fed. Cir.

United States Court of Federal Claims. A specialized federal court created under Article I of the Constitution in 1982 (with the name *United States Claims Court*) as the successor to the Court of Claims, and renamed in 1992 as the United States Court of Federal Claims. • It has original, nationwide jurisdiction to render a money judgment on any claim against the United States founded on the Constitution, a federal statute, a federal regulation, an express or implied-in-fact contract with the United States, or any other claim for damages not sounding in tort.

United States District Court. A federal trial court having jurisdiction within its judicial district. — Abbr. U.S.D.C.

United States Foreign Service. A division of the State Department responsible for maintaining diplomatic and consular offices and personnel in foreign countries. — Often shortened to *Foreign Service*.

United States Magistrate Judge. A federal judicial officer who hears civil and criminal pretrial matters and who may conduct civil trials or criminal misdemeanor trials. 28 USCA §§ 631–639.

United States Marshal. See MARSHAL.

***United States Reports*.** The official printed record of U.S. Supreme Court cases. • In a citation, it is abbreviated as U.S., as in 388 U.S. 14 (1967). — Abbr. U.S.

United States Sentencing Commission. An independent commission of the federal judiciary responsible for promulgating sentencing guidelines to be used in the federal courts. • The commission is made up of seven members (three of whom must be federal judges) appointed by the President.

unitrust. A trust from which a fixed percentage of the fair market value of the trust's assets, valued annually, is paid each year to the beneficiary.

unity, *n.* **1.** The fact or condition of being one in number; oneness. **2.** At common law, a requirement for the creation of a joint tenancy. • The four unities are interest, possession, time, and title. — **unitary,** *adj.* See *joint tenancy* under TENANCY.

unity of interest. The requirement that all joint tenants' interests must be identical in nature, extent, and duration.

unity of possession. The requirement that each joint tenant must be entitled to possession of the whole property.

unity of time. The requirement that all joint tenants' interests must vest at the same time.

unity of title. The requirement that all joint tenants must acquire their interests under the same instrument.

unity of seisin (**see**-zin). The merging of seisin in one person, brought about when the person becomes seised of a tract of land on which he or she already has an easement.

universal agent. See AGENT.

Universal Copyright Convention. An international convention, first adopted in the United States in 1955, by which signatory countries agree to give the published works of a member country the same protection as that given to works of its own citizens. — Abbr. UCC.

Universal Declaration of Human Rights. An international bill of rights approved by the United Nations in December 1948, being that body's first enumeration of human rights and fundamental freedoms. • The preamble states that "recognition of the inherent dignity and of the equal and inalienable rights of all members of the human family is the foundation of freedom, justice and peace in the world."

universal life insurance. See INSURANCE.

universal malice. See MALICE.

universal title. See TITLE (2).

unjudicial, *adj.* Not becoming of or appropriate to a judge.

unjust, *adj.* Contrary to justice; not just.

unjust enrichment. **1.** The retention of a benefit conferred by another, without offering compensation, in circumstances where compensation is reasonably expected. **2.** A benefit obtained from another, not intended as a gift and not legally justifiable, for which the beneficiary must make restitution or recompense. **3.** The area of law dealing with unjustifiable benefits of this kind.

unlawful, *adj.* **1.** Not authorized by law; illegal <in some cities, jaywalking is unlawful>. **2.** Criminally punishable <unlawful entry>. **3.** Involving moral turpitude <the preacher spoke to the congregation about the unlawful activities of gambling and drinking>. — **unlawfully,** *adv.*

unlawful act. Conduct that is not authorized by law; a violation of a civil or criminal law.

unlawful assembly. See ASSEMBLY.

unlawful detainer. See DETAINER.

unlawful-detainer proceeding. An action to return a wrongfully held tenancy (as one held by a tenant after the lease has expired) to its owner. See *unlawful detainer* under DETAINER.

unlawful entry. See ENTRY.

unlawful force. See FORCE.

unliquidated, *adj.* Not previously specified or determined.

unliquidated damages. See DAMAGES.

unmarketable title. See TITLE (2).

unnatural will. See WILL.

unperfected security interest. See SECURITY INTEREST.

unprofessional conduct. See CONDUCT.

unpublished opinion. See OPINION (1).

unqualified indorsement. See INDORSEMENT.

unrealized receivable. An amount earned but not yet received. • Unrealized receivables have no income-tax basis for cash-basis taxpayers.

unreasonable, *adj.* **1.** Not guided by reason; irrational or capricious. **2.** Not supported by a valid exception to the warrant requirement <unreasonable search and seizure>.

unreasonable compensation. See COMPENSATION.

unreasonable decision. An administrative agency's decision that is so obviously wrong that there can be no difference of opinion among reasonable minds about its erroneous nature.

unreasonable search. See SEARCH.

unrecorded, *adj.* Not recorded; esp., not filed in the public record <unrecorded deed>.

unrelated-business-income tax. See TAX.

unrelated income. See INCOME.

unrelated offense. See OFFENSE.

unresponsive answer. *Evidence.* A response from a witness (usu. at a deposition or hearing) that is irrelevant to the question asked.

unrestrictive indorsement. See INDORSEMENT.

unrestrictive interpretation. See INTERPRETATION.

unreviewable, *adj.* Incapable of being legally or judicially reviewed <the claim is unreviewable on appeal>.

unsatisfied-judgment fund. See FUND.

unsound, *adj.* **1.** Not healthy; esp., not mentally well <unsound mind>. **2.** Not firmly made; impaired <unsound foundation>. **3.** Not valid or well founded <unsound argument>.

unsworn, *adj.* Not sworn <an unsworn statement>.

untenantable (ən-**ten**-ən-tə-bəl), *adj.* Not capable of being occupied or lived in; not fit for occupancy <the city closed the untenantable housing project>.

untimely, *adj.* Too soon or too late <an untimely answer>.

unwritten evidence. See EVIDENCE.

unwritten law. Law that, although never enacted in the form of a statute or ordinance, has the sanction of custom. • The term traditionally includes caselaw.

UPA. *abbr.* UNIFORM PARTNERSHIP ACT.

upper chamber. See CHAMBER.

upward departure. See DEPARTURE.

urban renewal. The process of redeveloping urban areas by demolishing or repairing existing structures or by building new facilities in areas that have been cleared in accordance with an overall plan.

urban servitude. See SERVITUDE (1).

URESA (yə-ree-sə). *abbr.* UNIFORM RECIPROCAL ENFORCEMENT OF SUPPORT ACT.

U.S. *abbr.* **1.** United States. **2.** UNITED STATES REPORTS.

usage. A well-known, customary, and uniform practice, usu. in a specific profession or business. See CUSTOM (1). Cf. CONVENTION (3).

general usage. A usage that prevails throughout a country or particular trade or profession; a usage that is not restricted to a local area.

immemorial usage. A usage that has existed for a very long time; longstanding custom. See TIME IMMEMORIAL.

trade usage. A practice or method of dealing having such regularity of observance in a region, vocation, or trade that it justifies an expectation that it will be observed in a given transaction; a customary practice or set of practices relied on by persons conversant in, or connected with, a trade or business. • While a course of performance or a course of dealing can be established by the parties' testimony, a trade usage is usually established by expert testimony. Cf. COURSE OF DEALING; COURSE OF PERFORMANCE.

USC. *abbr.* UNITED STATES CODE.

USCA. *abbr.* UNITED STATES CODE ANNOTATED.

U.S.D.C. *abbr.* UNITED STATES DISTRICT COURT.

use (yoos), *n.* **1.** The application or employment of something; esp., a long-continued possession and employment of a thing for the purpose for which it is adapted, as distinguished from a possession and employment that is merely temporary or occasional <the neighbors complained to the city about the owner's use of the building as a dance club>. **2.** A habitual or common practice <drug use>. **3.** A purpose or end served <the tool had several uses>. **4.** A benefit or profit; esp., the right to take profits from land owned and possessed by another; the equitable ownership of land to which another person holds the legal title <cestui que use>. See CESTUI QUE USE. — **use** (yooz), *vb.*

contingent use. A use that would be a contingent remainder if it had not been limited by way of use. • An example is a transfer "to A, to the use of B for life, with the remainder to the use of C's heirs."

entire use. A use of property that is solely for the benefit of a married woman. • When used in the habendum of a trust deed for the benefit of a married woman, this phrase operates to keep her husband from taking anything under the deed.

resulting use. A use created by implication and remaining with the grantor when the conveyance lacks consideration.

shifting use. A use arising from the occurrence of a certain event that terminates the preceding use. • In the following example, C has a shifting use that arises when D makes the specified payment: "to A for the use of B, but then to C when D pays $1,000 to E." This is a type of conditional limitation. See *conditional limitation* under LIMITATION.

springing use. A use that arises on the occurrence of a future event. • In the following example, B has a springing use that vests when B marries: "to A for the use of B when B marries."

useful life. The estimated length of time that depreciable property will generate income. • Useful life is used to calculate depreciation and amortization deductions. See DEPRECIATION METHOD.

use immunity. See IMMUNITY (3).

useless-gesture exception. *Criminal procedure.* An exception to the knock-and-announce rule by which police are excused from having to announce their purpose before entering the premises to execute a warrant when it is evident from the circumstances that the authority and purpose of the police are known to those inside. See KNOCK-AND-ANNOUNCE RULE.

use plaintiff. *Common-law pleading.* A plaintiff for whom an action is brought in another's name. • For example, when the use plaintiff was an assignee ("A") of a chose in action and had to sue in someone else's name, the assignor ("B") would appear first on the petition's title: "B for the Use of A against C."

user (yooz-ər). 1. The exercise or employment of a right or property <the neighbor argued that an easement arose by his continuous user over the last 15 years>. Cf. NONUSER; MISUSER. **2.** Someone who uses a thing <the stapler's last user did not put it away>.

end user. The ultimate consumer for whom a product is designed.

user fee. A charge assessed for the use of a particular item or facility.

use tax. See TAX.

usual, *adj.* **1.** Ordinary; customary. **2.** Expected based on previous experience.

usurious (yoo-**zhuur**-ee-əs), *adj.* **1.** Practicing usury <a usurious lender>. **2.** Characterized by usury <a usurious contract>.

usurpation (yoo-sər-**pay**-shən *or* yoo-zər-**pay**-shən), *n.* The unlawful seizure and assumption of another's position, office, or authority. — **usurp** (yoo-**sərp** *or* yoo-**zərp**), *vb.*

usury (yoo-zhə-ree), *n.* **1.** Historically, the lending of money with interest. **2.** Today, the charging of an illegal rate of interest. **3.** An illegally high rate of interest. — **usurious**

(yoo-**zhuur**-ee-əs), *adj.* — **usurer** (**yoo**-zhər-ər), *n.*

utilitarian-deterrence theory. The legal theory that a person should be punished only if it is for the good of society — that is, only if the punishment would further the prevention of future harmful conduct. See *hedonistic utilitarianism* under UTILITARIANISM. Cf. RETRIBUTIVISM.

utilitarianism. A philosophy that the goal of public action should be the greatest happiness to the greatest number of people.

hedonistic utilitarianism. The theory that the validity of a law should be measured by determining the extent to which it would promote the greatest happiness to the greatest number of citizens. • Hedonistic utilitarianism generally maintains that pleasure is intrinsically good and pain intrinsically bad. Therefore, inflicting pain, as by punishing a criminal, is justified only if it results in a net increase of pleasure by deterring future harmful behavior. See UTILITARIAN-DETERRENCE THEORY. Cf. RETRIBUTIVISM.

utility. 1. The quality of serving some function that benefits society. **2.** *Patents.* Capacity to perform a function or attain a result claimed for protection as intellectual property. • In patent law, utility is one of the three basic requirements of patentability, the others being nonobviousness and novelty. **3.** A business enterprise that performs essential public service and that is subject to governmental regulation.

public utility. A company that provides necessary services to the public, such as telephones, electricity, and water. • Most utilities operate as monopolies but are subject to governmental regulation.

utter, *vb.* **1.** To say, express, or publish <don't utter another word until your attorney is present>. **2.** To put or send (a document) into circulation; esp., to circulate (a forged note) as if genuine <she uttered a counterfeit $50 bill at the grocery store>. — **utterance** (for sense 1), *n.* — **uttering** (for sense 2), *n.*

utter, *adj.* Complete; absolute; total <an utter denial>.

uttering. The crime of presenting a false or worthless instrument with the intent to harm or defraud. See FORGERY.

uxor (**ək**-sor). [Latin] Wife. — Abbr. *ux.*

uxoricide (ək-**sor**-ə-sɪd *or* əg-**zor**-). **1.** The murder of one's wife. **2.** A man who murders his wife. Cf. MARITICIDE.

V

v. *abbr.* **1.** VERSUS. — Also abbreviated *vs*. **2.** Volume. — Also abbreviated *vol*. **3.** Verb. — Also abbreviated *vb*.

VA. *abbr.* VETERANS AFFAIRS, DEPARTMENT OF.

vacant, *adj.* **1.** Empty; unoccupied. • Courts have sometimes distinguished *vacant* from *unoccupied*, holding that *vacant* means completely empty while *unoccupied* means not routinely characterized by the presence of human beings. **2.** Absolutely free, unclaimed, and unoccupied. **3.** (Of an estate) abandoned; having no heir or claimant. — The term implies either abandonment or nonoccupancy for any purpose.

vacate, *vb.* **1.** To surrender occupancy or possession; to move out or leave <the tenant vacated the premises>. **2.** To nullify or cancel; make void; invalidate <the court vacated the judgment>. Cf. OVERRULE.

vacation, *n.* **1.** The act of vacating <vacation of the court's order>. **2.** The period between one term of court and the beginning of the next; the space of time during which a court holds no sessions. **3.** Loosely, any time when a given court is not in session.

vacatur (və-**kay**-tər), *n.* [Law Latin "it is vacated"] **1.** The act of annulling or setting aside. **2.** A rule or order by which a proceeding is vacated.

vagrancy (**vay**-grən-see), *n.* The state or condition of wandering from place to place without a home, job, or means of support. • Vagrancy is generally considered a course of conduct or a manner of living rather than a single act. Cf. LOITERING.

vagrant, *adj.* **1.** Of, relating to, or characteristic of a vagrant; inclined to vagrancy. **2.** Nomadically homeless.

vagrant, *n.* **1.** At common law, anyone belonging to the several classes of idle or disorderly persons, rogues, and vagabonds. **2.** One who, not having a settled habitation, strolls from place to place; a homeless, idle wanderer. • The term often refers to one who spends time in idleness, lacking any property and without any visible means of support.

vague, *adj.* **1.** Imprecise; not sharply outlined; indistinct. **2.** (Of words) broadly indefinite; not clearly or concretely expressed; uncertain. **3.** Characterized by haziness of thought.

vagueness. 1. Uncertain breadth of meaning <the phrase "within a reasonable time" is plagued by vagueness — what is reasonable?>. • Though common in writings generally, vagueness raises due-process concerns if legislation does not provide fair notice of what is required or prohibited, so that enforcement may be arbitrary. **2.** Loosely, ambiguity. See AMBIGUITY.

vagueness doctrine. *Constitutional law.* The doctrine — based on the Due Process Clause — requiring that a criminal statute state explicitly and definitely what acts are prohibited, so as to provide fair warning and preclude arbitrary enforcement. See *void for vagueness* under VOID. Cf. OVERBREADTH DOCTRINE.

valid, *adj.* **1.** Legally sufficient; binding <a valid contract>. **2.** Meritorious <that is a valid conclusion based on the facts presented in this case>. — **validate,** *vb.* — **validation,** *n.* — **validity,** *n.*

validating statute. See STATUTE.

valuable consideration. See CONSIDERATION.

valuable improvement. See IMPROVEMENT.

valuable papers. Documents that, upon a person's death, are important in carrying out the decedent's wishes and in managing the estate's affairs. • Examples include a will, title documents, stock certificates, powers of attorney, letters to be opened on one's death, and the like.

valuation, *n.* **1.** The process of determining the value of a thing or entity. **2.** The estimated worth of a thing or entity. — **value,** *vb.* — **valuate,** *vb.*

assessed valuation. The value that a taxing authority gives to property and to which the tax rate is applied.

special-use valuation. An executor's option of valuating real property in an estate, esp. farmland, at its current use rather than for its highest potential value.

value, *n.* **1.** The monetary worth or price of something; the amount of goods, services, or money that something will command in an exchange. **2.** The significance, desirability, or utility of something. **3.** Sufficient contractual consideration. — **value,** *vb.* — **valuation,** *n.*

fair market value. The price that a seller is willing to accept and a buyer is willing to pay on the open market and in an arm's-length transaction; the point at which supply and demand intersect.

salvage value. The value of an asset after it has become useless to the owner; the amount expected to be obtained when a fixed asset is disposed of at the end of its useful life. • Salvage value is used, under some depreciation methods, to determine the allowable tax deduction for depreciation. And under the UCC, when a buyer of goods breaches or repudiates the contract of sale, the seller may, under certain circumstances, either complete the manufacture of any incomplete goods or cease the manufacture and sell the partial product for scrap or salvage value. UCC § 2–704(2). See DEPRECIATION.

value-added tax. See TAX.

value received. Consideration that has been delivered. • This phrase is commonly used in a bill of exchange or promissory note to show that it was supported by consideration.

vandal. [fr. Latin *Vandalus*, a member of the Germanic tribe known as Vandals] A malicious destroyer or defacer of works of art, monuments, buildings, or other property.

vandalism, *n.* **1.** Willful or ignorant destruction of public or private property, esp. of artistic, architectural, or literary treasures. **2.** The actions or attitudes of one who maliciously or ignorantly destroys or disfigures public or private property; active hostility to anything that is venerable or beautiful. — **vandalize,** *vb.* — **vandalistic,** *adj.*

variable cost. See COST.

variable rate. See INTEREST RATE.

variance. 1. A difference or disparity between two statements or documents that ought to agree; esp., in criminal procedure, a difference between the allegations in a charging instrument and the proof actually introduced at trial.

> ***fatal variance.*** A variance that either deprives the defendant of fair notice of the charges or exposes the defendant to the risk of double jeopardy. • A fatal variance is grounds for reversing a conviction.
>
> ***immaterial variance.*** A variance that is too slight to mislead or prejudice the defendant and is thus harmless error.

2. A license or official authorization to depart from a zoning law. Cf. SPECIAL EXCEPTION (2).

VAT. *abbr.* See *value-added tax* under TAX.

vehicular homicide. See HOMICIDE.

vel non (vel **non**). [Latin "or not"] *Jargon.* Or the absence of it (or them) <this case turns solely on the finding of discrimination vel non>.

venal (**vee**-nəl), *adj.* **1.** (Of a person) capable of being bribed. **2.** Ready to sell one's services or influence for money or other valuable consideration, usu. for base motives. **3.** Of, relating to, or characterized by corrupt bargaining. **4.** Broadly, purchasable; for sale.

vend, *vb.* **1.** To transfer to another for money or other thing of value. • The term is not commonly applied to real estate, although its derivatives (*vendor* and *vendee*) are. **2.** To make an object of trade, esp. by hawking or peddling. **3.** To utter publicly; to say or state; to publish broadly.

vendee. A purchaser, usu. of real property; a buyer.

vendetta (ven-**det**-ə), *n.* A private blood feud in which family members seek revenge on a person outside the family (often members of another family); esp., a private war in which the nearest of kin seek revenge for the slaying of a relative.

vendor. A seller, usu. of real property.

venial (**vee**-nee-əl), *adj.* (Of a transgression) forgivable; pardonable.

venire (və-**nI**-ree *or* -**neer**-ee *or* -**nIr** *or* -**neer**). **1.** A panel of persons selected for jury duty and from among whom the jurors are to be chosen. See PANEL (2). **2.** VENIRE FACIAS.

venire facias (və-**nI**-ree [*or* -**neer**-ee *or* -**nIr** *or* -**neer**] **fay**-shee-əs). A writ directing a sheriff to assemble a jury. — Often shortened to *venire.*

venire facias ad respondendum (ad ree-spon-**den**-dəm). A writ requiring a sheriff to summon a person against whom an indictment for a misdemeanor has been issued. • A warrant is now more commonly used.

venire facias de novo (dee *or* di **noh**-voh). A writ for summoning a jury panel anew because of some impropriety or irregularity in the original jury's return or verdict so that no judgment can be given on it. • The result of a new venire is a new trial. In substance, the writ is a motion for new trial, but when the party objects to the verdict because of an error in the course of the proceeding (and not on the merits), the form of motion is traditionally for a venire facias de novo. — Often shortened to *venire de novo*.

veniremember (və-**nI**-ree-mem-bər *or* və-**neer**-ee- *or* və-**neer**-). A prospective juror; a member of a jury panel.

venture. An undertaking that involves risk; esp., a speculative commercial enterprise.

venturer, *n.* **1.** One who risks something in a business enterprise. **2.** One who participates in a joint venture. See JOINT VENTURE.

venue (**ven**-yoo). [Law French "coming"] *Procedure.* **1.** The proper or a possible place for the trial of a case, usu. because the place has some connection with the events that have given rise to the case. **2.** The county or other territory over which a trial court has jurisdiction. Cf. JURISDICTION. **3.** Loosely, the place where a conference or meeting is being held. **4.** In a pleading, the statement establishing the place for trial. **5.** In an affidavit, the designation of the place where it was made.

venue facts. Facts that need to be established in a hearing to determine whether venue is proper in a given court.

veracious (və-**ray**-shəs), *adj.* Truthful; accurate.

veracity (və-**ras**-ət-ee), *n.* **1.** Truthfulness <the witness's fraud conviction supports the defense's challenge to his veracity>. **2.** Accuracy <you called into question the veracity of Murphy's affidavit>. — **veracious** (və-**ray**-shəs), *adj.*

verbal, *adj.* **1.** Of, relating to, or expressed in words. **2.** Loosely, of, relating to, or expressed in spoken words.

verbal act. See ACT.

verbal-act doctrine. The rule that utterances accompanying conduct that might have legal effect are admissible when the conduct is material to the issue and is equivocal in nature, and when the words help give the conduct its legal significance.

verdict. **1.** A jury's finding or decision on the factual issues of a case. **2.** Loosely, in a nonjury trial, a judge's resolution of the issues of a case.

chance verdict. A now-illegal verdict, arrived at by hazard or lot.

compromise verdict. A verdict reached when jurors, to avoid a deadlock, concede some issues so that other issues will be resolved in their favor.

defective verdict. A verdict that will not support a judgment because of irregularities or legal inadequacies.

directed verdict. A ruling by a trial judge taking a case from the jury because the evidence will permit only one reasonable verdict.

excessive verdict. A verdict that results from the jury's passion or prejudice and thereby shocks the court's conscience.

general verdict. A verdict by which the jury finds in favor of one party or the other, as opposed to resolving specific fact questions. Cf. *special verdict*.

general verdict with interrogatories. A general verdict accompanied by answers to written interrogatories on one or more issues of fact that bear on the verdict.

guilty verdict. A jury's finding that a defendant is guilty of the offense charged.

joint verdict. A verdict covering two or more parties to a lawsuit.

legally inconsistent verdict. A verdict in which the same element is found to exist and not to exist, as when a defendant is acquitted of one offense and convicted of another, even though the offenses arise from the same set of facts and an element of the second offense requires proof that the first offense has been committed.

open verdict. A verdict of a coroner's jury finding that the subject "came to his death by means to the jury unknown" or "came to his death at the hands of a person or persons to the jury unknown." • This verdict leaves open either the question whether any crime was committed or the identity of the criminal.

partial verdict. A verdict by which a jury finds a criminal defendant innocent of some charges and guilty of other charges.

perverse verdict. A jury verdict so contrary to the evidence that it justifies the granting of a new trial.

public verdict. A verdict delivered by the jury in open court.

quotient verdict. An improper damage verdict that a jury arrives at by totaling what each juror would award and then dividing by the number of jurors.

repugnant verdict. A verdict that contradicts itself in that the defendant is convicted and acquitted of different crimes having identical elements.

sealed verdict. A written verdict put into a sealed envelope when the jurors have agreed on their decision but court is not in session. • Upon delivering a sealed verdict, the jurors may separate. When court convenes again, this verdict is officially returned with the same effect as if the jury had returned it in open court before separating. This type of verdict is useful to avoid detaining the jurors until the next session of court.

special verdict. A verdict in which the jury makes findings only on factual issues submitted by the judge, who then decides the legal effect of the jury's verdict. Cf. *general verdict*.

split verdict. **1.** A verdict in which one party prevails on some claims, while the other party prevails on others. **2.** *Criminal law.* A verdict finding a defendant guilty on one charge but innocent on another. **3.** *Criminal law.* A verdict of guilty for one defendant and of not guilty for a codefendant.

true verdict. A verdict that is reached voluntarily — even if one or more jurors freely compromise their views — and not as a result of an arbitrary rule or order, whether imposed by the jurors themselves, the court, or a court officer.

verdict contrary to law. A verdict that the law does not authorize a jury to render because the conclusion drawn is not justified by the evidence.

verdict subject to opinion of court. A verdict that is subject to the court's determination of a legal issue reserved to the court upon the trial, so that judgment is ultimately entered depending on the court's ruling on a point of law.

verification, *n.* **1.** A formal declaration either made in the presence of an authorized officer, such as a notary public, or (in some jurisdictions) made under oath but not in the presence of such an officer, whereby one swears to the truth of the statements in the document. • Traditionally, a verification is used as a conclusion for all pleadings that are required to be sworn. Cf. ACKNOWLEDGMENT (4). **2.** An oath or affirmation that an authorized officer administers to an affiant or deponent. **3.** Loosely, ACKNOWLEDGMENT (5). **4.** See *certified copy* under COPY. **5.** CERTIFICATE OF AUTHORITY (1). **6.** Any act of notarizing. — **verify,** *vb.* — **verifier,** *n.* Cf. JURAT (1).

verity (**ver**-ə-tee). Truth; truthfulness; conformity to fact.

versus, *prep.* Against. — Abbr. v.; vs.

vertical competition. See COMPETITION.

vertical nonprivity. See NONPRIVITY.

vertical price-fixing. See PRICE-FIXING.

vertical privity. See PRIVITY.

vest, *vb.* **1.** To confer ownership of (property) upon a person. **2.** To invest (a person) with the full title to property. **3.** To give (a person) an immediate, fixed right of present or future enjoyment. — **vesting,** *n.*

vested, *adj.* Having become a completed, consummated right for present or future enjoyment; not contingent; unconditional; absolute.

vested in interest. Consummated in a way that will result in future possession and use. • Reversions, vested remainders, and any other future use or executory devise that does not depend on an uncertain period or event are all said to be vested in interest.

vested in possession. Consummated in a way that has resulted in present possession and use.

vested estate. See ESTATE.

vested gift. See GIFT.

vested interest. See INTEREST (2).

vested legacy. See LEGACY.

vested ownership. See OWNERSHIP.

vested remainder. See REMAINDER.

vestigial words (ve-**stij**-ee-əl). Statutory words and phrases that, through a succession of amendments, have been made useless or meaningless.

vesting order. A court order passing legal title in lieu of a legal conveyance.

Veterans Affairs, Department of. An independent federal agency that administers benefit programs for veterans and their families. — Abbr. VA.

veto (**vee**-toh), *n.* [Latin "I forbid"] **1.** A power of one governmental branch to prohibit an action by another branch; esp., a chief executive's refusal to sign into law a bill passed by the legislature. **2.** VETO MESSAGE. Pl. **vetoes. — veto,** *vb.*

absolute veto. An unrestricted veto that is not subject to being overridden.

legislative veto. A veto that allowed Congress to block a federal executive or agency action taken under congressionally delegated authority. • The Supreme Court held the legislative veto unconstitutional in *INS v. Chadha*, 462 U.S. 919, 103 S.Ct. 2764 (1983). See DELEGATION DOCTRINE.

line-item veto. The executive's power to veto some provisions in a legislative bill without affecting other provisions. • The U.S. Supreme Court declared the presidential line-item veto unconstitutional in 1998. See *Clinton v. City of New York*, 524 U.S. 417, 118 S.Ct. 2091 (1998).

overridden veto. A veto that the legislature has superseded by again passing the vetoed act, usu. by a supermajority of legislators. • In the federal government, a bill vetoed by the President must receive a two-thirds majority in Congress to override the veto and enact the measure into law.

pocket veto. A veto resulting from the President's failure to sign a bill passed within the last ten days of the congressional session.

qualified veto. A veto that is conclusive unless overridden by an extraordinary majority of the legislature. • This is the type of veto that the President of the United States has.

suspensory veto (sə-**spen**-sə-ree). A veto that suspends a law until the legislature reconsiders it and then allows the law to take effect if repassed by an ordinary majority.

veto message. A statement communicating the reasons for the executive's refusing to sign into law a bill passed by the legislature. — Sometimes shortened to *veto.*

veto power. An executive's conditional power to prevent an act that has passed the legislature from becoming law.

vex, *vb.* To harass, disquiet, or annoy.

vexation. The damage that is suffered as a result of another's trickery or malice.

vexatious (vek-**say**-shəs), *adj.* (Of conduct) without reasonable or probable cause or excuse; harassing; annoying.

vexatious suit. A lawsuit instituted maliciously and without good cause. Cf. MALICIOUS PROSECUTION.

vexed question. 1. A question often argued about but seemingly never settled. **2.** A question or point that has been decided differently by different tribunals and has therefore been left in doubt.

viable (vɪ-ə-bəl), *adj.* **1.** Capable of living, esp. outside the womb <a viable fetus>. **2.** Capable of independent existence or standing <a viable lawsuit>. — **viability** (vɪ-ə-**bil**-ə-tee), *n.*

viatorial privilege. See PRIVILEGE (1).

vicarious (vɪ-**kair**-ee-əs), *adj.* Performed or suffered by one person as substitute for another; indirect; surrogate.

vicarious disqualification. See DISQUALIFICATION.

vicarious liability. See LIABILITY.

vice (vɪs), *n.* **1.** A moral failing; an ethical fault. **2.** Wickedness; corruption. **3.** Broadly, any defect or failing.

vice (vɪ-see *or* vɪ-sə), *prep.* In the place of; in the stead of. • As a prefix, *vice-* (vɪs) denotes one who takes the place of.

vice president, *n.* **1.** An officer selected in advance to fill the presidency if the president dies, becomes incapacitated, resigns, or is removed from office. • The Vice President of the United States presides over the Senate and is first in line to succeed the President. **2.** A corporate officer of mid-level to high rank, usu. having charge of a department. — Also written *vice-president.* — **vice-presidential,** *adj.* — **vice presidency,** *n.*

vicinage (**vis**-ə-nij). [Law French "neighborhood"] **1.** Vicinity; proximity. **2.** The place where a crime is committed or a trial is held; the place from which jurors are to be drawn for trial; esp., the locale from which the accused is entitled to have jurors selected.

vicious propensity. An animal's tendency to endanger the safety of persons or property.

vicontiel (vɪ-**kon**-tee-əl), *adj.* Of or relating to a sheriff <vicontiel writ>. — Also spelled *vicountiel.*

victim, *n.* A person harmed by a crime, tort, or other wrong. — **victimize,** *vb.* — **victimization,** *n.*

victim-impact statement. A statement read into the record during sentencing to inform the judge or jury of the financial, physical, and psychological impact of the crime on the victim and the victim's family.

victimless crime. See CRIME.

videlicet (vi-**del**-ə-set *or* -sit). [Latin] To wit; that is to say; namely; SCILICET. • The term is used primarily to point out, particularize, or render more specific what has been previously stated in general (or occasionally obscure) language. One common function is to state the time, place, or manner when that is the essence of the matter at issue. — Abbr. *viz.* See VIZ.

vie (vee). [French] Life. • The term occurs in such Law French phrases as *cestui que vie* and *pur autre vie*.

view, *n.* **1.** The common-law right of prospect — that is, an outlook from the windows of one's house. **2.** An urban servitude that prohibits the obstruction of the outlook from a person's house. **3.** A jury's trip to inspect a place or thing relevant to the case it is considering; the act or proceeding by which a tribunal goes to observe an object that cannot be produced in court because it is immovable or inconvenient to remove. • The appropriate procedures are typically regulated by state statute. At common law, and today in many civil cases, the trial judge's presence is not required. The common practice has been for the jury to be escorted by "showers" who are commissioned for this purpose. Parties and counsel are generally permitted to attend at the judge's discretion. Cf. VIEW OF AN INQUEST. **4.** In a real action, a defendant's observation of the thing at issue to ascertain its identity and other circumstances surrounding it.

viewer. A person, usu. one of several, appointed by a court to investigate certain matters or to examine a particular locality (such as the proposed site of a new road) and to report to the court.

view of an inquest. A jury's inspection of a place or property to which an inquiry or inquest refers. Cf. VIEW (3).

vigilance. Watchfulness; precaution; a proper degree of activity and promptness in pursuing one's rights, in guarding them from infraction, and in discovering opportunities for enforcing one's lawful claims and demands.

vigilant, *adj.* Watchful and cautious; on the alert; attentive to discover and avoid danger.

vigilante (vij-ə-**lan**-tee). A person who seeks to avenge a crime by taking the law into his or her own hands. — **vigilantism** (vij-ə-**lan**-tiz-əm), *n.*

vindicate, *vb.* **1.** To clear (a person or thing) from suspicion, criticism, blame, or doubt <the DNA tests vindicated the suspect>. **2.** To assert, maintain, or affirm (one's interest) by action <the claimants sought to vindicate their rights through a class-action suit>. **3.** To defend (one's interest) against interference or encroachment <the borrower vindicated its interest in court when the lender tried to foreclose>. — **vindication,** *n.* — **vindicator,** *n.*

vindicatory part (**vin**-də-kə-tor-ee). The portion of a statute that sets forth the penalty for committing a wrong or neglecting a duty.

vindictive prosecution. See PROSECUTION.

violation, *n.* **1.** An infraction or breach of the law; a transgression. See INFRACTION. **2.** The act of breaking or dishonoring the law; the contravention of a right or duty. **3.** Rape; ravishment. **4.** Under the Model Penal Code, a public-welfare offense. • In this sense, a violation is not a crime. See Model Penal Code § 1.04(5). — **violate,** *vb.* — **violative** (vɪ-ə-lay-tiv), *adj.* — **violator,** *n.*

violence. The use of physical force, usu. accompanied by fury, vehemence, or outrage; esp., physical force unlawfully exercised with the intent to harm. • Some courts have held that violence in labor disputes is not limited to physical contact or injury, but may include picketing conducted with misleading signs, false statements, erroneous publicity, and veiled threats by words and acts.

violent, *adj.* **1.** Of, relating to, or characterized by strong physical force <violent blows to the legs>. **2.** Resulting from extreme or intense force <violent death>. **3.** Vehemently or passionately threatening <violent words>.

violent crime. See CRIME.

violent death. See DEATH.

violent offense. See OFFENSE.

vir (veer), *n.* **1.** An adult male; a man. **2.** A husband.

vires (vɪ-reez), *n.* **1.** Natural powers; forces. **2.** Granted powers, esp. when limited. See ULTRA VIRES; INTRA VIRES.

vir et uxor (**veer** et **ək**-sor). [Latin] Husband and wife.

virtual representation. A party's maintenance of an action on behalf of others with a similar interest, as a class representative does in a class action.

virtual-representation doctrine. The principle that a judgment may bind a person who is not a party to the litigation if one of the parties is so closely aligned with the nonparty's interests that the nonparty has been adequately represented by the party in court. • Under this doctrine, for instance, a judgment in a case naming only the husband as a party can be binding on his wife as well. See RES JUDICATA.

vis (vis). [Latin "power"] **1.** Any force, violence, or disturbance relating to a person or property. **2.** The force of law. • Thus *vim habere* ("to have force") is to be legally valid. Pl. ***vires.***

vis-à-vis (**veez**-ə-**vee**), *prep.* [French "face to face"] In relation to; opposite to <the creditor established a preferred position vis-à-vis the other creditors>.

visible means of support. An apparent method of earning a livelihood. • Vagrancy statutes have long used this phrase to describe those who have no ostensible ability to support themselves.

visitation (viz-ə-**tay**-shən). **1.** Inspection; superintendence; direction; regulation. **2.** *Family law.* A relative's, esp. a noncustodial parent's, period of access to a child. **3.** *Corporate law.* The process of inquiring into and correcting corporate irregularities.

visitation order. *Family law.* **1.** An order establishing the visiting times for a noncustodial parent with his or her child. **2.** An order establishing the visiting times for a child and a person with a significant relationship to the child.

visitation right. 1. *Family law.* A noncustodial parent's or grandparent's court-ordered privilege of spending time with a child or grandchild who is living with another person, usu. the custodial parent. **2.** *Int'l law.* A belligerent nation's right to go upon and search a neutral vessel to find out whether it is carrying contraband or is otherwise engaged in nonneutral service.

visiting judge. See JUDGE.

vis major (**vis may**-jər), *n.* [Latin "a superior force"] **1.** A greater or superior force; an irresistible force; FORCE

MAJEURE. **2.** A loss that results immediately from a natural cause without human intervention and that could not have been prevented by the exercise of prudence, diligence, and care.

VISTA (**vis**-tə). *abbr.* Volunteers in Service to America, a federal program established in 1964 to provide volunteers to help improve the living conditions of people in the poorest areas of the United States, its possessions, and Puerto Rico.

vital statistics. Public records — usu. relating to matters such as births, marriages, deaths, diseases, and the like — that are statutorily mandated to be kept by a city, state, or other governmental division or subdivision. • On the admissibility of vital statistics, see Fed. R. Evid. 803(9).

vitiate (**vish**-ee-ayt), *vb.* **1.** To impair; to cause to have no force or effect <the new statute vitiates any common-law argument that the plaintiffs might have>. **2.** To make void or voidable; to invalidate either completely or in part <fraud vitiates a contract>. **3.** To corrupt morally <Mr. Lawrence complains that his children were vitiated by their governess>. — **vitiation,** *n.* — **vitiator,** *n.*

viva voce (**vɪ**-və **voh**-see *also* **vee**-və), *adv.* [Law Latin "with living voice"] By word of mouth; orally. • In reference to votes, the term means a voice vote was held rather than a vote by ballot. In reference to the examination of witnesses, the term means that oral rather than written testimony was taken.

viz. (viz). *abbr.* [Latin *videlicet*] Namely; that is to say <the defendant engaged in fraudulent activities, *viz.*, misrepresenting his gross income, misrepresenting the value of his assets, and forging his wife's signature>. See VIDELICET.

voice exemplar. A sample of a person's voice used for the purpose of comparing it with a recorded voice to determine whether the speaker is the same person. • Although voiceprint identification was formerly inadmissible, the trend in recent years has been toward admissibility. See Fed. R. Evid. 901.

voiceprint. A distinctive pattern of curved lines and whorls made by a machine that measures human vocal sounds for the purpose of identifying an individual speaker. • Like fingerprints, voiceprints are thought to be unique to each person.

void, *adj.* **1.** Of no legal effect; null. • The distinction between *void* and *voidable* is often of great practical importance. Whenever technical accuracy is required, *void* can be properly applied only to those provisions that are of no effect whatsoever — those that are an absolute nullity. — **void,** *vb.* — **voidness,** *n.*

facially void. (Of an instrument) patently void upon an inspection of the contents.

void ab initio (ab i-**nish**-ee-oh). Null from the beginning, as from the first moment when a contract is entered into. • A contract is void ab initio if it seriously offends law or public policy, in contrast to a contract that is merely voidable at the election of one party to the contract.

void for vagueness**. 1.** (Of a deed or other instrument affecting property) having such an insufficient property description as to be unenforceable. **2.** (Of a penal statute) establishing a requirement or punishment without specifying what is required or what conduct is punishable, and therefore void because violative of due process. See VAGUENESS DOCTRINE.

2. VOIDABLE. • Although sense 1 above is the strict meaning of *void*, the word is often used and construed as bearing the more liberal meaning of "voidable." Cf. UNENFORCEABLE.

voidable, *adj.* Valid until annulled; esp., (of a contract) capable of being affirmed or rejected at the option of one of the parties. • This term describes a valid act that may be voided rather than an invalid act that may be ratified. — **voidability,** *n.*

voidable contract. See CONTRACT.

voidable judgment. See JUDGMENT.

voidable marriage. See MARRIAGE (1).

voidance, *n.* The act of annulling, canceling, or making void.

void contract. See CONTRACT.

void for vagueness. See VOID.

void judgment. See JUDGMENT.

void legacy. See LEGACY.

void marriage. See MARRIAGE (1).

voir dire (vwahr **deer** *also* vor **deer** *or* vor **dɪr**), *n.* [Law French "to speak the truth"] **1.** A preliminary examination of a prospective juror by a judge or lawyer to decide whether the prospect is qualified and suitable to serve on a jury. • Loosely, the term refers to the jury-selection phase of a trial. **2.** A preliminary examination to test the competence of a witness or evidence. — **voir dire,** *vb.*

vol. *abbr.* Volume.

volens (**voh**-lenz), *adj.* [Latin] Willing. See NOLENS VOLENS.

volenti non fit injuria (voh-**len**-tɪ non fit in-**joor**-ee-ə). [Law Latin "to a willing person it is not a wrong," i.e., a person is not wronged by that to which he or she consents] The principle that a person who knowingly and voluntarily risks danger cannot recover for any resulting injury. • This is the type of affirmative defense that must be pleaded under Fed. R. Civ. P. 8(c). — Often shortened to *volenti*. See ASSUMPTION OF THE RISK.

volition (və-**lish**-ən *or* voh-), *n.* **1.** The ability to make a choice or determine something. **2.** The act of making a choice or determining something. **3.** The choice or determination that someone makes. — **volitional,** *adj.*

Volstead Act (**vol**-sted). A federal statute enacted in 1919 to prohibit the manufacture, sale, or transportation of liquor. • Sponsored by Andrew Joseph Volstead of Minnesota, a famous Prohibitionist, the statute was passed under the 18th Amendment to the U.S. Constitution. When the 21st Amendment repealed the 18th Amendment in 1933, the Volstead Act was voided.

volume discount. See DISCOUNT.

voluntary, *adj.* **1.** Done by design or intention <voluntary act>. **2.** Unconstrained by interference; not impelled by outside influence <volun-

tary statement>. **3.** Without valuable consideration; gratuitous <voluntary gift>. **4.** Having merely nominal consideration <voluntary deed>. — **voluntariness,** *n.*

voluntary arbitration. See ARBITRATION.

voluntary bankruptcy. See BANKRUPTCY.

voluntary bar. See BAR ASSOCIATION.

voluntary courtesy. An act of kindness performed by one person toward another, from the free will of the doer, without any previous request or promise of reward made by the person who is the object of the act. • No promise of remuneration arises from such an act.

voluntary dismissal. See DISMISSAL (1).

voluntary exposure to unnecessary danger. An intentional act that, from the standpoint of a reasonable person, gives rise to an undue risk of harm. • The phrase implies a conscious, deliberate exposure of which one is consciously willing to take the risk.

voluntary ignorance. Willful obliviousness; an unknowing or unaware state resulting from the neglect to take reasonable steps to acquire important knowledge.

voluntary intoxication. See INTOXICATION.

voluntary manslaughter. See MANSLAUGHTER.

voluntary petition. See PETITION.

voluntary search. See SEARCH.

voluntary statement. See STATEMENT.

voluntary waste. See WASTE (1).

volunteer. 1. A voluntary actor or agent in a transaction; esp., a person who, without an employer's assent and without any justification from legitimate personal interest, helps an employee in the performance of the employer's business. **2.** The grantee in a voluntary conveyance; a person to whom a conveyance is made without any valuable consideration.

Volunteers in Service to America. See VISTA.

vote, *n.* **1.** The expression of one's preference or opinion by ballot, show of hands, or other type of communication <the Republican candidate received more votes than the Democratic candidate>. **2.** The total number of votes cast in an election <the incumbent received 60% of the vote>. **3.** The act of voting, usu. by a legislative body <the Senate postponed the vote on the gun-control bill>. — **vote,** *vb.*

voter. 1. A person who engages in the act of voting. **2.** A person who has the qualifications necessary for voting.

voting. The casting of votes for the purpose of deciding an issue.

absentee voting. Participation in an election by a qualified voter who is unable to appear at the polls on election day; the practice of allowing voters to participate in this way. Cf. *early voting.*

class voting. A method of shareholder voting by which different classes of shares vote separately on fundamental corporate changes that affect the rights and privileges of that class.

cumulative voting. A system for electing corporate directors whereby a shareholder may multiply his or her number of shares by the number of open directorships and cast the total for a single candidate or a select few candidates. • Cumulative voting enhances the ability of minority shareholders to elect at least one director.

early voting. Voting before the day of an election, esp. during a period designated for that purpose. • Unlike absentee voting, early voting does not require that the voter swear that he or she will not be able to come the polling place on election day. Cf. *absentee voting.*

majority voting. A system for electing corporate directors whereby each shareholder is allowed one vote for each director, who can win with a simple majority.

noncumulative voting. A corporate voting system in which a shareholder is limited in board elections to voting no more than the number of shares that he or she owns for a single candidate. • The result is that a majority shareholder will elect the entire board of directors.

voting group. 1. A classification of shareholders by the type of stock held for voting on corporate matters. **2.** Collectively, the shareholders falling within such a classification.

Voting Rights Act. The federal law that guarantees a citizen's right to vote, without discrimination based on race, color, or previous condition of servitude. • The U.S. Attorney General may bring suit to enforce the Act. 42 USCA §§ 1971–1974.

vouch, *vb.* **1.** To answer for (another); to personally assure <the suspect's mother vouched for him>. **2.** To call upon, rely on, or cite as authority; to substantiate with evidence <counsel vouched the mathematical formula for determining the statistical probability>.

voucher, *n.* **1.** Confirmation of the payment or discharge of a debt; a receipt. **2.** A written or printed authorization to disburse money.

vouching-in. 1. At common law, a procedural device by which a defendant may give notice of suit to a third party who may be liable over to the defendant on the subject matter of the suit, so that the third party will be bound by the court's decision. • Although this device has been largely replaced by third-party practice, it remains available under the Federal Rules of Civil Procedure. **2.** The invitation of a person who is liable to a defendant in a lawsuit to intervene and defend so that, if the invitation is denied and the defendant later sues the person invited, the latter is bound by any determination of fact common to the two lawsuits. See UCC § 2–607. **3.** IMPLEADER.

vouch over, *vb.* To cite (a person) into court in one's stead.

voyeur (voy-**yər** *also* vwah-**yər**), *n.* A person who observes something without participating; esp., one who gains sexual pleasure by secretly observing another's sexual organs or sexual acts.

voyeurism. Gratification derived from observing the sexual organs or sexual acts of others, usu. secretly. — **voyeuristic,** *adj.*

vs. *abbr.* VERSUS.

W

W-2 form. *Tax.* A statement of earnings and taxes withheld (including federal, state, and local income taxes and FICA tax) during a given tax year. • The W-2 is prepared by the employer, provided to each employee, and filed with the Internal Revenue Service. Cf. W-4 form.

W-4 form. *Tax.* A form that indicates the number of personal exemptions an employee is claiming and that is used by the employer in determining the amount of income to be withheld from the employee's paycheck for federal-income-tax purposes. Cf. W-2 form.

***Wade* hearing.** *Criminal law.* A pretrial hearing in which the defendant contests the validity of his or her out-of-court identification. • If the court finds that the identification was tainted by unconstitutional methods, the prosecution cannot use the identification and must link the defendant to the crime by other means. *United States v. Wade*, 388 U.S. 218, 87 S.Ct. 1926 (1967).

wage, *n.* (*usu. pl.*) Payment for labor or services, usu. based on time worked or quantity produced. Cf. SALARY.

wage-and-price freeze. See FREEZE.

wager, *n.* **1.** Money or other consideration risked on an uncertain event; a bet or gamble. **2.** A promise to pay money or other consideration on the occurrence of an uncertain event. — **wager,** *vb.* — **wagerer,** *n.*

waif (wayf), *n.* A stolen article that has been thrown away by a thief in flight, usu. through fear of apprehension. • At common law, if a waif was seized before the owner reclaimed it, the title vested in the Crown. Today, however, the general rule is that a waif passes to the state in trust for the true owner, who may regain it by proving ownership.

wait-and-see principle. A modification to the rule against perpetuities, under which a court may determine the validity of a contingent future interest based on whether it actually vests within the perpetuities period, rather than on whether it possibly could have vested outside the period.

waiting period. A period that must expire before some legal right or remedy can be enjoyed or enforced. • For example, many states have waiting periods for the issuance of marriage licenses or the purchase of handguns.

waive, *vb.* **1.** To abandon, renounce, or surrender (a claim, privilege, right, etc.); to give up (a right or claim) voluntarily. • Ordinarily, to waive a right one must do it knowingly — with knowledge of the relevant facts. **2.** To refrain from insisting on (a strict rule, formality, etc.); to forgo.

waiver (**way**-vər), *n.* **1.** The voluntary relinquishment or abandonment — express or implied — of a legal right or advantage <waiver of notice>. • The party alleged to have waived a right must have had both knowledge of the existing right and the intention of forgoing it. Cf. ESTOPPEL.

express waiver. A voluntary and intentional waiver.

implied waiver. A waiver evidenced by a party's decisive, unequivocal conduct reasonably inferring the intent to waive.

prospective waiver. A waiver of something that has not yet occurred, such as a contractual waiver of future claims for discrimination upon settlement of a lawsuit.

2. The instrument by which a person relinquishes or abandons a legal right or advantage <the plaintiff must sign a waiver when the funds are delivered>.

waiver by election of remedies. A defense arising when a plaintiff has sought two inconsistent remedies and by a decisive act chooses one of them, thereby waiving the other.

waiver of claims and defenses. 1. The intentional relinquishment by a maker, drawer, or other obligor under a contract of the right to assert against the assignee any claims or defenses the obligor has against the assignor. **2.** The contractual clause providing for such a waiver.

waiver of counsel. A criminal defendant's intentional relinquishment of the right to legal representation. • To be valid, a waiver of counsel must be made knowingly and intelligently.

waiver of exemption. 1. A debtor's voluntary relinquishment of the right to an exemption from a creditor's levy or sale of any part of the debtor's personal property by judicial process. **2.** The contractual clause expressly providing for such a waiver.

waiver of immunity. The act of giving up the right against self-incrimination and proceeding to testify. See IMMUNITY (3).

waiver of tort. The election to sue in quasi-contract to recover the defendant's unjust benefit, instead of suing in tort to recover damages. See *implied-in-law contract* under CONTRACT.

walk, *vb. Slang.* **1.** To be acquitted <though charged with three thefts, Robinson walked each time>. **2.** To escape any type of real punishment <despite the seriousness of the crime, Selvidge paid only $750: he walked>.

want of consideration. The lack of consideration for a contract. See CONSIDERATION. Cf. FAILURE OF CONSIDERATION.

want of jurisdiction. A court's lack of power to act in a particular way or to give certain kinds of relief. • A court may have no power to act at all, may lack authority over a person or the subject matter of a lawsuit, or may have no power to act until the prerequisites for its jurisdiction have been satisfied. See JURISDICTION.

want of prosecution. Failure of a litigant to pursue the case <dismissal for want of prosecution>. — Abbr. w.o.p.

want of repair. A defective condition, such as a condition on a highway making it unsafe for ordinary travel.

wanton (**wahn**-tən), *adj.* Unreasonably or maliciously risking harm while being utterly indifferent to the consequences. • In criminal law, *wanton* usually connotes malice (in the criminal-law sense), while *reckless* does not. Cf. RECKLESS; WILLFUL.

wanton misconduct. See MISCONDUCT.

wantonness, *n.* Conduct indicating that the actor is aware of the risks but indifferent to the results. • Wantonness usually suggests a greater degree of culpability than recklessness, and it often connotes malice in criminal-law contexts. — **wanton,** *adj.* Cf. RECKLESSNESS.

war clause. U.S. Const. art. I, § 8, cls. 11–14, giving Congress the power to declare war. See WAR POWER.

ward. 1. A person, usu. a minor, who is under a guardian's charge or protection. See GUARDIAN.

permanent ward. A ward who has been assigned a permanent guardian, the rights of the natural parents having been terminated by a juvenile court.

temporary ward. A minor who is under the supervision of a juvenile court but whose parents' parental rights have not been terminated.

ward of the state. A person who is housed by, and receives protection and necessities from, the government.

2. A territorial division in a city, usu. defined for purposes of city government. **3.** The act of guarding or protecting something or someone.

warden. A person in charge of something <game warden> <port warden>; esp., the official in charge of a prison or jail <prison warden>.

wardship. 1. Guardianship of a person, usu. a minor. **2.** The condition of being a ward.

warning. The pointing out of a danger, esp. to one who would not otherwise be aware of it. • State and federal laws (such as 21 USCA § 825) require warning labels to be placed on potentially dangerous materials, such as drugs and equipment.

war power. The constitutional authority of Congress to declare war and maintain armed forces (U.S. Const. art. I, § 8, cls. 11–14), and of the President to conduct war as commander-in-chief (U.S. Const. art. II, § 2, cl. 1).

war-powers resolution. A resolution passed by Congress in 1973 (over the President's veto) restricting the President's authority to involve the United States in foreign hostilities without congressional approval, unless the United States or one of its territories is attacked. 50 USCA §§ 1541–1548.

warrant, *n.* **1.** A writ directing or authorizing someone to do an act, esp. one directing a law enforcer to make an arrest, a search, or a seizure.

administrative warrant. A warrant issued by a judge at the request of an administrative agency. • This type of warrant is sought to conduct an administrative search. See *administrative search* under SEARCH.

arrest warrant. A warrant, issued only on probable cause, directing a law-enforcement officer to arrest and bring a person to court.

bench warrant. A warrant issued directly by a judge to a law-enforcement officer, esp. for the arrest of a person who has been held in contempt, has been indicted, has disobeyed a subpoena, or has failed to appear for a hearing or trial.

death warrant. A warrant authorizing a warden or other prison official to carry out a death sentence. • A death warrant typically sets the time and place for a prisoner's execution.

distress warrant. **1.** A warrant authorizing a court officer to distrain property. See DISTRESS. **2.** A writ allowing an officer to seize a tenant's goods for failing to pay rent due to the landlord.

escape warrant. A warrant directing a peace officer to rearrest an escaped prisoner.

extradition warrant. A warrant for the return of a fugitive from one jurisdiction to another. Cf. *rendition warrant*.

fugitive warrant. A warrant that authorizes law-enforcement officers to take into custody a person who has fled from one state to another to avoid prosecution or punishment.

general warrant. A warrant that gives a law-enforcement officer broad authority to search and seize unspecified places or persons; a search or arrest warrant that lacks a sufficiently particularized description of the person or thing to be seized or the place to be searched. • General warrants are unconstitutional because they fail to meet the Fourth Amendment's specificity requirements.

John Doe warrant. A warrant for the arrest of a person whose name is unknown. • A John Doe warrant may be issued, for example, for a person known by sight but not by name. This type of warrant is permitted in a few states, but not in federal practice.

landlord's warrant. A type of distress warrant from a landlord to seize the tenant's goods, to sell them at public sale, and to compel the tenant to pay rent or observe some other lease stipulation. See DISTRAIN; DISTRESS.

outstanding warrant. An unexecuted arrest warrant.

peace warrant. A warrant issued by a justice of the peace for the arrest of a specified person.

preliminary warrant. A warrant to bring a person to court for a preliminary hearing on probable cause.

rendition warrant. A warrant requesting the extradition of a fugitive from one jurisdiction to another. Cf. *extradition warrant*.

surreptitious-entry warrant. A warrant that authorizes a law officer to enter and observe an ongoing criminal operation (such as an illegal drug lab).

tax warrant. An official process that is issued for collecting unpaid taxes and under which property may be seized and sold.

warrant of commitment. A warrant committing a person to custody.

warrant upon indictment or information. An arrest warrant issued at the request of the prosecutor for a defendant named in an indictment or information. Fed. R. Crim. P. 9.

2. A document conferring authority, esp. to pay or receive money. **3.** An order by which a drawer authorizes someone to pay a particular sum of money to another.

warrant, *vb.* **1.** To guarantee the security of (realty or personalty, or a person) <the store warranted the safety of the customer's jewelry>. **2.** To give warranty of (title); to give warranty of title to (a person) <the seller warrants the property's title to the buyer>. **3.** To promise or guarantee <warrant payment>. **4.** To justify <the conduct warrants a presumption of negligence>. **5.** To authorize <the manager warranted the search of the premises>.

Warrant Clause. The clause of the Fourth Amendment to the U.S. Constitution requiring that warrants be issued on probable cause.

warranted arrest. See ARREST.

warranted search. See SEARCH.

warrantless arrest. See ARREST.

warrantless search. See SEARCH.

warrantor (**wor**-ən-tor *or* -tər *or* **wahr**-). A person who gives a warranty.

warranty (**wor**-ən-tee *or* **wahr**-), *n.* **1.** *Property.* A covenant by which the grantor in a deed promises to secure to the grantee the estate conveyed in the deed, and pledges to compensate the grantee with other land if the grantee is evicted by someone having better title. • The covenant is binding on the grantor's heirs. See COVENANT (3). Cf. *quitclaim deed* under DEED.

collateral warranty. A warranty that is made by a stranger to the title, and that consequently runs only to the covenantee and not to the land.

general warranty. A warranty against the claims of all persons.

special warranty. A warranty against any person's claim made by, through, or under the grantor or the grantor's heirs.

2. *Contracts.* An express or implied promise that something in furtherance of the contract is guaranteed by one of the contracting parties; esp., a seller's promise that the thing being sold is as represented or promised. • A warranty differs from a representation in four principal ways: (1) a warranty is an essential part of a contract, while a representation is usually only a collateral inducement, (2) a warranty is always written on the face of the contract, while a representation may be written or oral, (3) a warranty is conclusively presumed to be material, while the burden is on the party claiming breach to show that a representation is material, and (4) a warranty must be strictly complied with, while substantial truth is the only requirement for a representation. Cf. CONDITION.

as-is warranty. A warranty that goods are sold with all existing faults. See AS IS.

construction warranty. A warranty from the seller or building contractor of a new home that the home is free of structural, electrical, plumbing, and other defects and is fit for its intended purpose.

deceptive warranty. A warranty containing false or fraudulent representations or promises.

express warranty. A warranty created by the overt words or actions of the seller. • Under the UCC, an express warranty is created by any of the following: (1) an affirmation of fact or promise made by the seller to the buyer relating to the goods that becomes the basis of the bargain; (2) a description of the goods that becomes part of the basis of the bargain; or (3) a sample or model made part of the basis of the bargain. UCC § 2–313.

extended warranty. An additional warranty often sold with the purchase of consumer goods (such as appliances and motor vehicles) to cover repair costs not otherwise covered by a manufacturer's standard warranty, by extending either the standard-warranty coverage period or the range of defects covered.

full warranty. A warranty that fully covers labor and materials for repairs. • Under federal law, the warrantor must remedy the consumer product within a reasonable time and without charge after notice of a defect or malfunction. 15 USCA § 2304. Cf. *limited warranty*.

implied warranty. A warranty arising by operation of law because of the circumstances of a sale, rather than by the seller's express promise.

implied warranty of fitness for a particular purpose. A warranty — implied by law if the seller has reason to know of the buyer's special purposes for the property — that the property is suitable for those purposes. — Sometimes shortened to *warranty of fitness*.

implied warranty of habitability. In a residential lease, a warranty from the landlord to the tenant that the leased property is fit to live in and that it will remain so during the term of the lease.

implied warranty of merchantability. A warranty that the property is fit for the ordinary purposes for which it is used.

limited warranty. A warranty that does not fully cover labor and materials for repairs. • Under federal law, a limited warranty must be clearly labeled as such on the face of the warranty. Cf. *full warranty*.

personal warranty. A warranty arising from an obligation to pay all or part of the debt of another.

presentment warranty. An implied promise concerning the title and credibility of an instrument, made to a payor or acceptor upon presentment of the instrument for payment or acceptance. UCC §§ 3–417, 3–418, 4–207(1).

transfer warranty. **1.** An implied promise concerning the title and credibility of an instrument, made by a transferor to a transferee and, if the transfer is by indorsement, to remote transferees. UCC

§§ 3–417, 4–207. **2.** A warranty made by a transferee of a document of title upon a transfer of the document for value to the immediate transferee. UCC § 7–507.

warranty ab initio (ab i-**nish**-ee-oh). An independent subsidiary promise whose breach does not discharge the contract, but gives to the injured party a right of action for the damage sustained as a result of the breach. Cf. *warranty ex post facto*.

warranty ex post facto (eks pohst **fak**-toh). A broken condition for which the injured party could void the contract, but decides instead to continue the contract, with a right of action for the broken condition (which amounts to a breached warranty). See CONDITION (2). Cf. *warranty ab initio*.

warranty of assignment. An assignor's implied warranty that he or she (1) has the rights assigned, (2) will do nothing to interfere with those rights, and (3) knows of nothing that impairs the value of the assignment.

warranty of title. A warranty that the seller or assignor of property has title to that property, that the transfer is rightful, and that there are no liens or other encumbrances beyond those that the buyer or assignee is aware of at the time of contracting. • This warranty arises automatically whenever anyone sells goods.

written warranty. A warranty made in writing; specif., any written affirmation or promise by a supplier of a consumer product to a buyer (for purposes other than resale), forming the basis of the bargain and providing that the material or workmanship is free of defects or will be repaired or replaced free of charge if the product fails to meet the required specifications. 15 USCA § 2301.

warranty deed. See DEED.

waste, *n.* **1.** Permanent harm to real property committed by a tenant (for life or for years) to the prejudice of the heir, the reversioner, or the remainderman. • In the law of mortgages, any of the following acts by the mortgagor may constitute waste: (1) physical damage, whether intentional or negligent, (2) failure to maintain and repair, except for repair of casualty damage or damage caused by third-party acts, (3) failure to pay property taxes or governmental assessments secured by a lien having priority over the mortgage, so that the payments become delinquent, (4) the material failure to comply with mortgage covenants concerning physical care, maintenance, construction, demolition, or casualty insurance, or (5) keeping the rents to which the mortgagee has the right of possession.

ameliorating waste (ə-**meel**-yə-ray-ting). A lessee's unauthorized change to the physical character of a lessor's property — technically constituting waste, but in fact resulting in improvement of the property. • Generally, equity will not enjoin such waste.

commissive waste (kə-**mis**-iv). Waste caused by the affirmative acts of the tenant.

equitable waste. An abuse of the privilege of nonimpeachability for waste at common law, for which equity will restrain the commission of willful, destructive, malicious, or extravagant waste; esp., waste caused by a life tenant who, although ordinarily not responsible for permissive waste, flagrantly damages or destroys the property.

permissive waste. A tenant's failure to make normal repairs to property so as to protect it from substantial deterioration.

voluntary waste. Waste resulting from some positive act of destruction. See *commissive waste*.

2. Refuse or superfluous material, esp. that remaining after a manufacturing or chemical process.

hazardous waste. Waste that — because of its quantity, concentration, or physical, chemical, or infectious characteristics — may cause or significantly contribute to an increase in mortality or otherwise harm human health or the environment. 42 USCA § 6903(5).

toxic waste. Hazardous, poisonous substances, such as DDT. • Most states regulate the handling and disposing of toxic waste, and several federal statutes (such as CERCLA, 42 USCA §§ 9601–9657) regulate the use, transportation, and disposal of toxic waste.

wasting property. A right to or an interest in something that is consumed in its normal use, such as a wasting asset, a leasehold interest, or a patent right.

watercourse. A body of water flowing in a reasonably definite channel with bed and banks.

water right. (*often pl.*) The right to use water from a natural stream or from an artificial canal for irrigation, power, domestic use, and the like; RIPARIAN RIGHT.

waterscape, *n.* An aqueduct or passage for water.

way. 1. A passage or path. **2.** A right to travel over another's property. See RIGHT-OF-WAY.

private way. **1.** The right to pass over another's land. **2.** A way provided by local authorities primarily to accommodate one or more particular individuals (usu. at the individuals' expense) but also for the public's passage.

way of necessity. See *implied easement* under EASEMENT.

way-leave, *n.* **1.** A right-of-way (usu. created by an express grant) over or through land for the transportation of minerals from a mine or quarry. **2.** The royalty paid for such a right.

ways-and-means committee. A legislative committee that determines how money will be raised for various governmental purposes.

W.D. *abbr.* Western District, in reference to U.S. judicial districts.

weapon. An instrument used or designed to be used to injure or kill someone.

concealed weapon. A weapon that is carried by a person but that is not visible by ordinary observation.

dangerous weapon. An object or device that, because of the way it is used, is capable of causing serious bodily injury.

deadly weapon. Any firearm or other device, instrument, material, or substance that, from the manner in which it is used or is intended to be used, is calculated or likely to produce death. Cf. DANGEROUS INSTRUMENTALITY.

deadly weapon per se. A weapon that is deadly in and of itself or would ordinarily result in death by its use <a gun is a deadly weapon per se>.

wear and tear. Deterioration caused by ordinary use <the tenant is not liable for normal wear and tear to the leased premises>.

wedge principle. The principle that an act is wrong in a specific instance if, when raised to a general level of conduct, it would injure humanity.

weight of the evidence. The persuasiveness of some evidence in comparison with other evidence <because the verdict is against the great weight of the evidence, a new trial should be granted>. See BURDEN OF PERSUASION. Cf. MANIFEST WEIGHT OF THE EVIDENCE; PREPONDERANCE OF THE EVIDENCE.

welfare. 1. Well-being in any respect; prosperity.

general welfare. The public's health, peace, morals, and safety.

public welfare. A society's well-being in matters of health, safety, order, morality, economics, and politics.

2. A system of social insurance providing assistance to those who are financially in need, as by providing food stamps and family allowances.

corporate welfare. Governmental financial assistance given to a large company, usu. in the form of a subsidy.

welfare state. A nation in which the government undertakes various social insurance programs, such as unemployment compensation, old-age pensions, family allowances, food stamps, and aid to the blind or deaf.

well, *adv.* In a legally sufficient manner; unobjectionable <well-pleaded complaint>.

well-knowing, *adj.* Intentional <a well-knowing act or omission>. • This term was formerly used in a pleading to allege scienter. See SCIENTER.

well-pleaded complaint. See COMPLAINT.

welshing. 1. The act or an instance of evading an obligation, esp. a gambling debt. **2.** The common-law act of larceny in which one receives a deposit to be paid back with additional money depending on the outcome of an event (such as a horse race) but at the time of the deposit the depositee intends to cheat and defraud the depositor by absconding with the money. • Although this term is sometimes thought to be a slur against those hailing from Wales, etymologists have not been able to establish this connection. Authoritative dictionaries record the origin of the term as being unknown. — **welsh,** *vb.* — **welsher,** *n.*

Westlaw. A West Group database for computer-assisted legal research, providing online access to legal resources, including federal and state caselaw, statutes, regulations, and legal periodicals. — Abbr. WL.

Wharton rule (**[h]wor**-tən). The doctrine that an agreement by two or more persons to commit a particular crime cannot be prosecuted as a conspiracy if the crime could not be committed except by the actual number of participants involved. • But if an additional person participates so as to enlarge the scope of the agreement, all the actors may be charged with conspiracy.

wheel conspiracy. See CONSPIRACY.

whereabouts, *n.* The general locale where a person or thing is <her whereabouts are unknown> <the Joneses' present whereabouts is a closely guarded secret>. • As the examples illustrate, this noun, though plural in form, may be construed with either a plural or a singular verb. — **whereabouts,** *adv.* & *conj.*

whereas, *conj.* **1.** While by contrast; although <McWilliams was stopped at 10:08 p.m. wearing a green hat, whereas the assailant had been identified at 10:04 p.m. wearing a black hat>. **2.** Given the fact that; since <Whereas, the parties have found that their 1994 agreement did not adequately address incidental expenses . . .; and Whereas, the parties have now decided in an equitable sharing of those expense . . .; Now, Therefore, the parties agree to amend the 1994 agreement as follows . . .>. • In sense 2, *whereas* is used to introduce contractual recitals and the like, but modern drafters increasingly prefer a simple heading, such as "Recitals" or "Preamble," and in that way avoid the legalistic *whereases.* — **whereas** (recital or preamble), *n.*

whereat, *conj. Jargon.* **1.** At or toward which <the point whereat he was aiming>. **2.** As a result of which; whereupon <Pettrucione called Bickley a scurrilous name, whereat a fistfight broke out>.

whereby, *conj.* By which; through which; in accordance with which <the treaty whereby the warring nations finally achieved peace>.

wherefore, premises considered. *Jargon.* For all these reasons; for the reason or reasons mentioned above.

wherefrom, *conj. Jargon.* From which <the students sent two faxes to the president's office, wherefrom no reply ever came>.

wherein, *conj. Jargon.* **1.** In which; where <the jurisdiction wherein Lynn practices>. **2.** During which <they listened intently at the concert, wherein both of them became convinced that the composer's "new" work was a fraud>. **3.** How; in what respect <Fallon demanded to know wherein she had breached any duty>. — **wherein,** *adv.*

whereof, *conj. Jargon.* **1.** Of what <Judge Wald knows whereof she speaks>. **2.** Of which <citations whereof even the most responsible are far afield from the true issue>. **3.** Of whom <judges whereof only the most glowing words might be said>.

whereon, *conj. Jargon.* On which <the foundation whereon counsel bases this argument>.

whereto, *conj. Jargon.* To what place or time <at first, Campbell did not know whereto he was being taken>. — **whereto,** *adv.*

whereupon, *conj. Jargon.* **1.** WHEREON <the precedent whereupon the defense bases its argument>. **2.** Soon after and as a result of which; and then <a not-guilty verdict was announced, whereupon a riot erupted>.

wherewith, *conj. Jargon.* By means of which <the plaintiff lacked a form of action wherewith to state a compensable claim>.

whistleblower, *n.* An employee who reports employer wrongdoings to a governmental or law-enforcement agency. • Federal and state laws protect whistleblowers from employer retaliation. — **whistleblowing,** *n.*

whistleblower act. A federal or state law protecting employees from retaliation for disclosing employer wrongdoings, as during an investigation by a regulatory agency. • Federal laws containing whistleblower provisions include the Whistleblower Protection Act (5 USCA § 1211), the Occupational Safety and Health Act (29 USCA § 660), CERCLA (42 USCA § 9610), and the Air Pollution and Control Act (42 USCA § 7622).

Whiteacre. A fictitious tract of land used in legal discourse (esp. law-school hypotheticals) to discuss real-property issues. See BLACKACRE.

whitecapping. The criminal act of threatening a person — usu. a member of a minority group — with violence in an effort to compel the person either to move away or to stop engaging in a certain business or occupation. • Whitecapping statutes were originally enacted to curtail the activities of the Ku Klux Klan.

white-collar crime. A nonviolent crime usu. involving cheating or dishonesty in commercial matters. • Examples include fraud, embezzlement, bribery, and insider trading.

whitehorse case. *Slang.* A reported case with facts virtually identical to those of the instant case, so that the disposition of the reported case should determine the outcome of the instant case. Cf. ON ALL FOURS.

whole law. The law applied by a forum court in a multistate or multinational case after referring to its own choice-of-law rules.

wild deed. See DEED.

will, *n.* **1.** Wish; desire; choice <employment at will>. **2.** A document by which a person directs his or her estate to be distributed upon death <there was no mention of his estranged brother in the will>. — **will,** *vb.*

ambulatory will. A will that can be altered during the testator's lifetime.

duplicate will. A will executed in duplicate originals by a testator who retains one copy and gives the second copy to another person. • The rules applicable to wills apply to both wills, and upon application for probate, both copies must be tendered into the registry of the probate court.

holographic will (hol-ə-**graf**-ik). A will that is handwritten by the testator. • Such a will is typically unattested. Holographic wills are rooted in the civil-law tradition, having originated in Roman law and having been authorized under the Napoleonic Code. French and Spanish settlers introduced holographic wills in America, primarily in the South and West. Today they are recognized in about half the states.

invalid will. A will that fails to make an effective disposition of property.

joint and mutual will. A will executed by two or more people — to dispose of property they own separately, in common, or jointly — requiring the surviving testator to dispose of the property in accordance with the terms of the will, and showing that the devises are made in consideration of one another. • The word "joint" indicates the form of the will. The word "mutual" describes the substantive provisions.

joint will. A single will executed by two or more testators, usu. disposing of their common property by transferring their separate titles to one devisee.

last will. The most recent will of a deceased; the instrument ultimately fixing the disposition of real and personal property at the testator's death.

lost will. An executed will that cannot be found at the testator's death. • Its contents can be proved by parol evidence in many jurisdictions. The common-law presumption — still the view of the overwhelming majority of American jurisdictions — is that there is a presumption of revocation if a lost will is proved to have last been in the possession of the testator.

mutual will. (*usu. pl.*) One of two separate wills in which two persons, usu. a husband and wife, establish identical or similar testamentary provisions disposing of their estates in favor of each other. • It is also possible (though rare) for the testators to execute a single mutual will, as opposed to separate ones. And it is possible (though, again, rare) for more than two parties to execute mutual wills.

nuncupative will (**nəng**-kyə-pay-tiv *or* nəng-**kyoo**-pə-tiv). An oral will made in contemplation of imminent death from an injury recently incurred. • Nuncupative wills are invalid in most states, but in those states allowing them, the amount that may be conveyed is usually limited by statute, and they traditionally apply only to personal property.

oral will. A will made by the spoken declaration of the testator and usu. dependent on oral testimony for proof.

pourover will (**por**-oh-vər). A will giving money or property to an existing trust. Cf. *pourover trust* under TRUST.

prenuptial will (pree-**nəp**-shəl). A will executed before marriage. • At common law, marriage automatically revoked a spouse's will, but modern statutes usually provide that marriage does not revoke a will (although divorce does). Unif. Probate Code § 2–508.

self-proved will. A will proved by the testator's affidavit instead of by the live testimony of attesting witnesses.

unnatural will. A will that distributes the testator's estate to strangers rather than to the testator's relatives, without apparent reason.

will contest. *Wills & estates.* The litigation of a will's validity, usu. based on allegations that the testator lacked capacity or was under undue influence.

willful, *adj.* Voluntary and intentional, but not necessarily malicious. — Sometimes spelled *wilful.* — **willfulness,** *n.* Cf. WANTON.

willful and wanton misconduct. See MISCONDUCT.

willful blindness. Deliberate avoidance of knowledge of a crime, esp. by failing to make a reasonable inquiry about suspected wrongdoing despite being aware that it is highly probable. • A person acts with willful blindness, for example, by deliberately refusing to look inside an unmarked package after being paid by a known drug dealer to deliver it. Willful blindness creates an inference of knowledge of the crime in question. See Model Penal Code § 2.02(7).

willful homicide. See HOMICIDE.

willful misconduct. See MISCONDUCT.

willful misconduct of employee. The deliberate disregard by an employee of the employer's interests, including its work rules and standards of conduct, justifying a denial of unemployment compensation if the employee is terminated for the misconduct.

willful murder. See MURDER.

willful neglect. See NEGLECT.

willfulness. 1. The fact or quality of acting purposely or by design; deliberateness; intention. • Willfulness does not necessarily imply malice, but it involves more than just knowledge. **2.** The voluntary, intentional violation or disregard of a known legal duty.

willful wrong. See WRONG.

Wills Act. 1. STATUTE OF WILLS (1). **2.** An 1837 English statute that allowed people to dispose of every type of property interest by will and that had an elaborate set of requirements for valid execution. • Some states today continue to adhere to these stringent requirements. Cf. Unif. Probate Code § 2–502.

will substitute. A document or instrument that allows a person, upon death, to dispose of an estate in the same or similar manner as a will but without the formalities and expense of a probate proceeding. • The most common will substitutes are trusts, life-insurance plans, and retirement-benefits contracts. The creation of will substitutes has been one of the most important developments in the area of decedents' estates in the past 50 years.

windfall. An unanticipated benefit, usu. in the form of a profit and not caused by the recipient.

windfall-profits tax. See TAX.

winding up, *n.* The process of settling accounts and liquidating assets in anticipation of a partnership's or a corporation's dissolution. Cf. DISSOLU-

TION (3), (4). — **wind up,** *vb.* — **wind up,** *n.*

window-dressing. The deceptive arrangement of something, usu. facts or appearances, to make it appear more attractive or favorable. • The term is often used to describe the practice of some financial managers, especially some managers of mutual funds, to sell certain positions at the end of a quarter to make an investment's quarterly performance appear better than it actually was.

wire fraud. See FRAUD.

wiretapping, *n.* Electronic or mechanical eavesdropping, usu. done by law-enforcement officers under court order, to listen to private conversations. • Wiretapping is regulated by federal and state law. — Often shortened to *tapping*. — **wiretap,** *vb.* — **wiretap,** *n.* See BUGGING; EAVESDROPPING. Cf. PEN REGISTER.

withdrawal, *n.* **1.** The act of taking back or away; removal <withdrawal of consent>. **2.** The act of retreating from a place, position, or situation <withdrawal from the moot-court competition>. **3.** The removal of money from a depository <withdrawal of funds from the checking account>. **4.** RENUNCIATION (2) <withdrawal from the conspiracy to commit arson>. — **withdraw,** *vb.*

withdrawal of charges. The removal of charges by the one bringing them, such as a prosecutor. See NOLLE PROSEQUI.

withdrawal of counsel. An attorney's termination of his or her role in representing a party in a case. • Normally, the attorney must have the court's permission to withdraw from a case.

withdrawing a juror. The act or an instance of removing a juror, usu. to obtain a continuance in a case or, sometimes in English practice, to end the case, as when the case has settled, the parties are too anxious to proceed to verdict, or the judge recommends it because the action is not properly before the court.

withholding, *n.* **1.** The practice of deducting a certain amount from a person's salary, wages, dividends, winnings, or other income, usu. for tax purposes; esp., an employer's practice of taking out a portion of an employee's gross earnings and paying that portion to the government for income-tax and social-security purposes. **2.** The money so deducted. — **withhold,** *vb.*

withholding of evidence. The act or an instance of obstructing justice by stifling or suppressing evidence knowing that it is being sought in an official investigation or judicial proceeding. See OBSTRUCTION OF JUSTICE.

withholding tax. See TAX.

without delay. **1.** Instantly; at once. **2.** Within the time reasonably allowed by law.

without impeachment of waste. (Of a tenant) not subject to an action for waste; not punishable for waste. • This clause is inserted in a lease to give a tenant the right to take certain actions (such as cutting timber) without being held liable for waste. But a tenant cannot abuse the right and will usually be held liable for maliciously committing waste.

without notice. Lacking actual or constructive knowledge. • To be a bona fide purchaser, one must buy something "without notice" of another's claim to the item or of defects in the seller's title. To be a holder in due course, one must take a bill or note "without notice" that it is overdue, has been dishonored, or is subject to a claim. UCC § 3–302(a)(2). See *bona fide purchaser* under PURCHASER.

without prejudice, *adv.* Without loss of any rights; in a way that does not harm or cancel the legal rights or privileges of a party. See *dismissal without prejudice* under DISMISSAL (1).

without recourse. (In an indorsement) without liability to subsequent holders. • With this stipulation, one who indorses an instrument indicates that he or she has no further liability to any subsequent holder for payment.

with prejudice, *adv.* With loss of all rights; in a way that finally disposes of a party's claim and bars any future action on that claim. See *dismissal with prejudice* under DISMISSAL (1).

with recourse, *adv.* (In an indorsement) with liability to subsequent holders. • With this stipulation, one who indorses an instrument indicates that he or she remains liable to the holder for payment.

with strong hand. With force. • In common-law pleading, this term implies a degree of criminal force, especially as used in forcible-entry statutes.

witness, *n.* **1.** One who sees, knows, or vouches for something <a witness to the accident>. **2.** One who gives testimony under oath or affirmation (1) in person, (2) by oral or written deposition, or (3) by affidavit <the prosecution called its next witness>. • A witness must be legally competent to testify. — **witness,** *vb.*

accomplice witness. A witness who is an accomplice in the crime that the defendant is charged with. • A codefendant cannot be convicted solely on the testimony of an accomplice witness.

alibi witness. A witness who testifies that the defendant was in a location other than the scene of the crime at the relevant time; a witness that supports the defendant's alibi.

attesting witness. One who vouches for the authenticity of another's signature by signing an instrument that the other has signed <proof of the will requires two attesting witnesses>.

character witness. A witness who testifies about another person's character traits or community reputation. See *character evidence* under EVIDENCE.

competent witness. A witness who is legally qualified to testify. • A lay witness who has personal knowledge of the subject matter of the testimony is competent to testify. Fed. R. Evid. 601, 602.

corroborating witness. A witness who confirms or supports someone else's testimony.

credible witness. A witness whose testimony is believable.

disinterested witness. A witness who has no private interest in the matter at issue.

expert witness. A witness qualified by knowledge, skill, experience, training, or education to provide a scientific, technical, or other specialized opinion about the evidence or a fact issue. Fed. R. Evid. 702–706. See EXPERT; DAUBERT TEST.

grand-jury witness. A witness who is called to testify before a grand jury.

hostile witness. A witness who is biased against the examining party or who is unwilling to testify. • A hostile witness may be asked leading questions on direct examination. Fed. R. Evid. 611(c).

interested witness. A witness who has a direct and private interest in the matter at issue.

lay witness. A witness who does not testify as an expert and who is therefore restricted to giving an opinion or making an inference that (1) is based on firsthand knowledge, and (2) is helpful in clarifying the testimony or in determining facts. Fed. R. Evid. 701.

material witness. A witness who can testify about matters having some logical connection with the consequential facts, esp. if few others, if any, know about those matters.

percipient witness. A witness who perceived the things he or she testifies about. See EARWITNESS; EYEWITNESS.

prosecuting witness. A person who files the complaint that triggers a criminal prosecution and whose testimony the prosecution usu. relies on to secure a conviction.

qualified witness. A witness who, by explaining the manner in which a company's business records are made and kept, is able to lay the foundation for the admission of business records under an exception to the hearsay rule. Fed. R. Evid. 803(6).

rebuttal witness. A witness who contradicts or attempts to contradict evidence previously presented.

res gestae witness. A witness who, having been at the scene of an incident, can give a firsthand account of what happened. See RES GESTAE.

subscribing witness. One who witnesses the signatures on an instrument and signs at the end of the instrument to that effect.

target witness. **1.** The person who has the knowledge that an investigating body seeks. **2.** A witness who is called before a grand jury and against whom the government is also seeking an indictment.

turncoat witness. A witness whose testimony was expected to be favorable but who becomes (usu. during the trial) a hostile witness.

zealous witness (**zel**-əs). A witness who is unduly zealous or partial to one side of a lawsuit and shows bias through extreme readiness to answer questions or volunteer information advantageous to that side.

witnesseth, *vb*. *Jargon*. Shows; records. • This term, usually set in all capitals, commonly separates the preliminaries in a contract, up through the recitals, from the contractual terms themselves. Modern drafters increasingly avoid it as an antiquarian relic.

witness-protection program. A federal or state program in which a person who testifies against a criminal is assigned a new identity and relocated to another part of the country to avoid retaliation by anyone convicted as a result of that testimony. • The Federal Witness Protection Program was established by the Organized Crime Control Act of 1970 and is administered by the marshals of the U.S. Justice Department.

witness stand. The space in a courtroom, usu. a boxed area, occupied by a witness while testifying. — Often shortened to *stand*.

witness tampering. The act or an instance of obstructing justice by intimidating, influencing, or harassing a witness before or after the witness testifies. • Several state and federal laws, including the Victim and Witness Protection Act of 1982 (18 USCA § 1512), provide criminal penalties for tampering with witnesses or other persons in the context of a pending investigation or official proceeding. See OBSTRUCTION OF JUSTICE.

WL. *abbr.* WESTLAW.

wobbler. *Slang.* A crime that can be charged as either a felony or a misdemeanor.

w.o.p. *abbr.* WANT OF PROSECUTION.

words actionable in themselves. Language that is libelous or slanderous per se. See *slander per se* under SLANDER; *libel per se* under LIBEL.

words of limitation. Language in a deed or will — often nonliteral language — describing the extent or quality of an estate. • For example, under long-standing principles of property law, the phrasing "to A and her heirs" creates a fee simple in A but gives nothing to A's heirs. See LIMITATION (4).

words of procreation (proh-kree-**ay**-shən). Language in a deed essential to create an estate tail, such as an estate "to A and the heirs of his body."

words of purchase. Language in a deed or will designating the persons who are to receive the grant. • For example, the phrase "to A for life with a remainder to her heirs" creates a life estate in A and a remainder in A's heirs. See PURCHASE (2).

workfare. A system of requiring a person receiving a public-welfare benefit to earn that benefit by performing a job provided by a government agency.

work furlough (**fər**-loh). A prison-treatment program allowing an inmate to be released during the day to work in the community. See WORK-RELEASE PROGRAM.

workhouse. A jail for criminals who have committed minor offenses and are serving short sentences.

work product. Tangible material or its intangible equivalent — in unwritten or oral form — that was either prepared by or for a lawyer or prepared for litigation, either planned or in progress. • Work product is generally exempt from discovery or other compelled disclosure. The term is also used to describe the products of a party's investigation or communications concerning the subject matter of a lawsuit if made (1) to assist in the prosecution or defense of a pending suit, or (2) in reasonable anticipation of litigation.

work-product rule. The rule providing for qualified immunity of an attorney's work product from discovery or other compelled disclosure. Fed. R. Civ. P. 26(b)(3).

work-release program. A correctional program allowing a prison inmate — primarily one being readied for discharge — to hold a job outside prison. See HALFWAY HOUSE.

worth, *n.* **1.** The monetary value of a thing; the sum of the qualities that render a thing valuable and useful, expressed in the current medium of exchange. **2.** The emotional or sentimental value of something. **3.** The total wealth held by a person or entity.

worthier-title doctrine. *Property.* The doctrine that favors a grantor's intent by construing a grant as a reversion in the grantor instead of as a remainder in the grantor's heirs. See REMAINDER; REVERSION.

wounded feelings. Injuries resulting from insults, indignity, or humiliation, as distinguished from the usual mental pain and suffering consequent to physical injury.

wounding. 1. An injury, esp. one involving a rupture of the skin. **2.** An injury to feelings or reputation.

writ (rit). A court's written order, in the name of a state or other competent legal authority, commanding the addressee to do or refrain from doing some specified act.

alias writ. An additional writ issued after another writ of the same kind in the same case. • It derives its name from a Latin phrase that formerly appeared in alias writs: *sicut alias praecipimus*, meaning "as we at another time commanded." Cf. *alias execution* under EXECUTION.

alternative writ. A common-law writ commanding the person against whom it is issued either to do a specific thing or to show cause why the court should not order it to be done.

counterpart writ. A copy of an original writ, to be sent to a court in another county where a defendant is located.

extraordinary writ. A writ issued by a court exercising unusual or discretionary power. • Examples are certiorari, habeas corpus, mandamus, and prohibition.

judicial writ. Any writ issued by a court.

junior writ. A writ issued at a later time than a similar writ, such as a later writ issued by a different party or a later writ on a different claim against the same defendant.

optional writ. At common law, an original writ issued when the plaintiff seeks specific damages, such as payment of a liquidated debt. • The writ commands the defendant either to do a specified thing or to show why the thing has not been done.

original writ. A writ commencing an action and directing the defendant to appear and answer. • In the United States, this writ has been largely superseded by the summons. See SUMMONS.

peremptory writ (pər-**emp**-tə-ree). At common law, an original writ issued when the plaintiff seeks only general damages, as in an action for trespass. • The writ, which is issued only after the plaintiff gives security for costs, directs the sheriff to have the defendant appear in court.

writ of course. A writ issued as a matter of course or granted as a matter of right.

writ of detinue. A writ in an action for detinue — that is, to recover personal property. See DETINUE.

writ of ejectment. The writ in an action of ejectment for the recovery of land. See EJECTMENT.

writ of entry. A writ that allows a person wrongfully dispossessed of real property to enter and retake the property.

writ of error. A writ issued by an appellate court directing a lower court to deliver the record in the case for review. Cf. ASSIGNMENT OF ERROR.

writ of possession. A writ issued to recover the possession of land.

writ of prevention. A writ to prevent the filing of a lawsuit. See QUIA TIMET.

writ of protection. A writ to protect a witness in a judicial proceeding who is threatened with arrest.

writ of restitution. 1. The process of enforcing a civil judgment in a forcible-entry-and-detainer action or enforcing restitution on a verdict in a criminal prosecution for forcible entry and detainer. **2.** A common-law writ issued when a judgment is reversed, whereby all that was lost as a result of the judgment is restored to the prevailing party.

writ of review. A general form of process issuing from an appellate court to bring up for review the record of the proceedings in the court below; the common-law writ of certiorari.

writ of sequestration. A writ ordering that a court be given custody of something or that something not be taken from the jurisdiction, such as the collateral for a promissory note. • Such a writ is usually issued during litigation, often so that the object will be available for attachment or execution after judgment.

writ of supervisory control. A writ issued to correct an erroneous ruling made by a lower court either when there is no appeal or when an appeal cannot provide adequate relief and the ruling will result in gross injustice.

writ system. The common-law procedural system under which a plaintiff commenced an action by obtaining the appropriate type of original writ.

written law. Statutory law, together with constitutions and treaties, as opposed to judge-made law.

written testimony. See TESTIMONY.

written warranty. See WARRANTY (2).

wrong, *n.* Breach of one's legal duty; violation of another's legal right. — **wrong,** *vb.* See TORT.

civil wrong. A violation of noncriminal law, such as a tort, a breach of contract or trust, a breach of statutory duty, or a defect in performing a public duty; the breach of a legal duty treated as the subject matter of a civil proceeding. Cf. CRIME.

continuing wrong. An ongoing wrong that is capable of being corrected by specific enforcement. • An example is the nonpayment of a debt.

intentional wrong. A wrong in which the *mens rea* amounts to intention, purpose, or design.

legal wrong. An act that is a violation of the law; an act authoritatively prohibited by a rule of law.

moral wrong. An act that is contrary to the rule of natural justice.

positive wrong. A wrongful act, willfully committed.

private wrong. An offense committed against a private person and dealt with at the instance of the person injured.

public wrong. An offense committed against the state or the community at large, and dealt with in a proceeding to which the state is itself a party. • Not all public wrongs are crimes. For example, a person that breaches a contract with the government commits a public wrong, but the offense is a civil one, not a criminal one.

real wrong. An injury to the freehold.

transitory wrong. A wrong that, once committed, belongs to the irrevocable past. • An example is defamation.

willful wrong. See *intentional wrong.*

wrong of negligence. A wrong in which the *mens rea* is a form of mere carelessness, as opposed to wrongful intent.

wrong of strict liability. A wrong in which a *mens rea* is not required because neither wrongful intent nor culpable negligence is a necessary condition of responsibility.

wrongdoer, *n.* One who violates the law <both criminals and tortfeasors are wrongdoers>. — **wrongdoing,** *n.*

wrongful, *adj.* **1.** Characterized by unfairness or injustice <wrongful military invasion>. **2.** Contrary to law; unlawful <wrongful termination>. **3.** (Of a person) not entitled to the position occupied <wrongful possessor>. — **wrongfully,** *adv.*

wrongful-birth action. A lawsuit brought by parents against a doctor for failing to advise them prospectively about the risks of their having a child with birth defects.

wrongful conduct. An act taken in violation of a legal duty; an act that unjustly infringes on another's rights.

wrongful-death action. A lawsuit brought on behalf of a decedent's survivors for their damages resulting from a tortious injury that caused the decedent's death. Cf. SURVIVAL ACTION.

wrongful-death statute. A statute authorizing a decedent's personal representative to bring a wrongful-death action for the benefit of certain beneficiaries.

wrongful discharge. See DISCHARGE.

wrongful-discharge action. A lawsuit brought by an ex-employee against the former employer, alleging that the termination of employment violated a contract or was illegal.

wrongful dishonor, *n.* A refusal to accept or pay (a negotiable instrument) when it is properly presented and is payable. Cf. DISHONOR (1).

wrongful garnishment. See GARNISHMENT.

wrongful levy. See LEVY.

wrongful-life action. A lawsuit brought by or on behalf of a child with birth defects, alleging that but for the doctor-defendant's negligent advice, the parents would not have conceived the child, or if they had, they would have aborted the fetus to avoid the pain and suffering resulting from the child's congenital defects. ● Most jurisdictions reject these claims.

wrongful-pregnancy action. A lawsuit brought by a parent for damages resulting from a pregnancy following a failed sterilization.

wrong of negligence. See WRONG.

wrong of strict liability. See WRONG.

X

X. **1.** A mark serving as the signature of a person who is physically handicapped or illiterate. • The signer's name usu. appears near the mark, and if the mark is to be notarized as a signature, two signing witnesses are ordinarily required in addition to the notary public. **2.** (*usu. l.c.*) A symbol equivalent to "by" when used in giving dimensions, as in 3 x 5 inches. **3.** A mark placed on a document (such as an application) to indicate a selection, such as "yes" or "no"; esp., a mark on a ballot to indicate a vote.

XYY-chromosome defense. *Criminal law.* A defense, usu. asserted as the basis for an insanity plea, whereby a male defendant argues that his criminal behavior is due to the genetic abnormality of having an extra Y chromosome, which causes him to have uncontrollable aggressive impulses. • Most courts have rejected this defense because its scientific foundations are uncertain. See INSANITY DEFENSE.

Y

yea and nay (**yay** / **nay**). Yes and no. • In old records, this was a mere assertion and denial without the necessity of an oath.

year and a day. The common-law time limit fixed for various purposes, such as claiming rights, exemptions, or property (such as rights to wreckage or estrays), or for prosecuting certain acts — so called because a year was formerly counted to include the first and last days, meaning that a year from January 1 was December 31, so a year and a day would then mean a full year from January 1 through January 1. See YEAR-AND-A-DAY RULE.

year-and-a-day rule. *Criminal law.* The common-law principle that an act causing death is not homicide if the death occurs more than a year and a day after the act was committed.

yeas and nays. The affirmative and negative votes on a bill or resolution before a legislative body.

Yick Wo **doctrine** (yik **woh**). The principle that a law or ordinance that gives a person or entity absolute discretion to give or withhold permission to carry on a lawful business is in violation of the 14th Amendment to the U.S. Constitution. *Yick Wo v. Hopkins*, 118 U.S. 356, 6 S.Ct. 1064 (1886).

yield, *vb.* To give up, relinquish, or surrender (a right, etc.)

Younger **abstention.** See ABSTENTION.

your Honor. A title customarily used when directly addressing a judge or other high official. Cf. HIS HONOR.

Youth Correction Authority Act. A model act, promulgated by the American Law Institute in 1940, that proposed the creation of central state commissions responsible for setting up appropriate agencies that would determine the proper treatment for each youthful offender committed to the agency by the courts. • The Act is noteworthy for its emphasis on rehabilitating juvenile offenders, as opposed to punishing them.

youthful offender. See OFFENDER.

Z

zealous witness. See WITNESS.

zero-coupon bond. See BOND (3).

zero-tolerance law. A statute — esp. one dealing with specified criminal conduct — that the enacting authority claims will be enforced zealously and without exception.

zone-of-danger rule. *Torts.* The doctrine allowing the recovery of damages for negligent infliction of emotional distress if the plaintiff was both located in the dangerous area created by the defendant's negligence and frightened by the risk of harm.

zone of interests. The class or type of interests or concerns that a statute or constitutional guarantee is intended to regulate or protect. • To have standing to challenge a ruling (especially of an administrative agency), the plaintiff must show that the specific injury suffered comes within the zone of interests protected by the statute on which the ruling was based.

zone of privacy. *Constitutional law.* A range of fundamental privacy rights that are implied in the express guarantees of the Bill of Rights. See PENUMBRA; RIGHT OF PRIVACY.

zone search. See SEARCH.

zoning, *n.* The legislative division of a region, esp. a municipality, into separate districts with different regulations within the districts for land use, building size, and the like. — **zone,** *vb.*

zoning ordinance. A city ordinance that regulates the use to which land within various parts of thc city may be put. • It allocates uses to the various districts of a municipality, as by allocating residences to certain parts and businesses to other parts. A comprehensive zoning ordinance usu. regulates the height of buildings and the proportion of the lot area that must be kept free from buildings.

APPENDIX

THE CONSTITUTION OF THE UNITED STATES OF AMERICA

We the People of the United States, in Order to form a more perfect Union, establish Justice, insure domestic Tranquility, provide for the common defence, promote the general Welfare, and secure the Blessings of Liberty to ourselves and our Posterity, do ordain and establish this Constitution for the United States of America.

Article I

Section 1. All legislative Powers herein granted shall be vested in a Congress of the United States, which shall consist of a Senate and House of Representatives.

Section 2. The House of Representatives shall be composed of Members chosen every second Year by the People of the several States, and the Electors in each State shall have the Qualifications requisite for Electors of the most numerous Branch of the State Legislature.

No Person shall be a Representative who shall not have attained to the Age of twenty five Years, and been seven Years a Citizen of the United States, and who shall not, when elected, be an Inhabitant of that State in which he shall be chosen.

Representatives and direct Taxes shall be apportioned among the several States which may be included within this Union, according to their respective Numbers, which shall be determined by adding to the whole Number of free Persons, including those bound to Service for a Term of Years, and excluding Indians not taxed, three fifths of all other Persons. The actual Enumeration shall be made within three Years after the first Meeting of the Congress of the United States, and within every subsequent Term of ten Years, in such Manner as they shall by Law direct. The Number of Representatives shall not exceed one for every thirty Thousand, but each State shall have at Least one Representative; and until such enumeration shall be made, the State of New Hampshire shall be entitled to chuse three, Massachusetts eight, Rhode Island and Providence Plantations one, Connecticut five, New York six, New Jersey four, Pennsylvania eight, Delaware one, Maryland six, Virginia ten, North Carolina five, South Carolina five, and Georgia three.

When vacancies happen in the Representation from any State, the Executive Authority thereof shall issue Writs of Election to fill such Vacancies.

The House of Representatives shall chuse their Speaker and other Officers; and shall have the sole Power of Impeachment.

Section 3. The Senate of the United States shall be composed of two Senators from each State, chosen by the Legislature thereof, for six Years; and each Senator shall have one Vote.

Immediately after they shall be assembled in Consequence of the first Election, they shall be divided as equally as may be into three Classes. The Seats of the Senators of the first Class shall be vacated at the Expiration of the Second Year, of the second Class at the Expiration of the fourth Year, and of the third Class at the Expiration of the sixth Year, so that one third may be chosen every second Year; and if Vacancies happen by Resignation, or otherwise, during the Recess of the Legislature of any State, the Executive thereof may make temporary Appointments until the next Meeting of the Legislature, which shall then fill such Vacancies.

No Person shall be a Senator who shall not have attained to the Age of thirty Years, and been nine Years a Citizen of the United States, and who shall not, when elected, be an Inhabitant of that State for which he shall be chosen.

The Vice President of the United States shall be President of the Senate, but shall have no Vote, unless they be equally divided.

The Senate shall chuse their other Officers, and also a President pro tempore, in the Absence of the Vice President, or when he shall exercise the Office of President of the United States.

The Senate shall have the sole Power to try all Impeachments. When sitting for that Purpose, they shall be on Oath or Affirmation. When the President of the United States is tried, the Chief Justice shall preside: And no Person shall be convicted without the Concurrence of two thirds of the Members present.

Judgment in Cases of Impeachment shall not extend further than to removal from Office, and disqualification to hold and enjoy any Office of honor, Trust, or Profit under the United States: but the Party convicted shall nevertheless be liable and subject to Indictment, Trial, Judgment, and Punishment, according to Law.

Section 4. The Times, Places and Manner of holding Elections for Senators and Representatives, shall be prescribed in each State by the Legislature thereof; but the Congress may at any time by Law make or alter such Regulations, except as to the Places of chusing Senators.

The Congress shall assemble at least once in every Year, and such Meeting shall be on the first Monday in December, unless they shall by Law appoint a different Day.

Section 5. Each House shall be the Judge of the Elections, Returns, and Qualifications of its own Members, and a Majority of each shall constitute a Quorum to do Business; but a smaller Number may adjourn from day to day, and may be authorized to compel the Attendance of absent Members, in such Manner, and under such Penalties as each House may provide.

Each House may determine the Rules of its Proceedings, punish its Members for disorderly Behavior, and, with the Concurrence of two thirds, expel a Member.

Each House shall keep a Journal of its Proceedings, and from time to time publish the same, excepting such Parts as may in their Judgment require Secrecy; and the Yeas and Nays of the Members of either House on any question shall, at the Desire of one fifth of those Present, be entered on the Journal.

Neither House, during the Session of Congress, shall, without the Consent of the other, adjourn for more than three days, nor to any other Place than that in which the two Houses shall be sitting.

Section 6. The Senators and Representatives shall receive a Compensation for their Services, to be ascertained by Law, and paid out of the Treasury of the United States. They shall in all Cases, except Treason, Felony and Breach of the Peace, be privileged from Arrest during their Attendance at the Session of their respective Houses, and in going to and returning from the same; and for any Speech or Debate in either House, they shall not be questioned in any other Place.

No Senator or Representative shall, during the Time for which he was elected, be appointed to any civil Office under the Authority of the United States, which shall have been created, or the Emoluments whereof shall have been increased during such time; and no Person holding any Office under the United States, shall be a member of either House during his Continuance in Office.

Section 7. All Bills for raising Revenue shall originate in the House of Representatives; but the Senate may propose or concur with Amendments as on other Bills.

Every Bill which shall have passed the House of Representatives and the Senate, shall, before it become a Law, be presented to the President of the United States; If he approve he shall sign it, but if not he shall return it, with his Objections to the House in which it shall have originated, who shall enter the Objections at large on their Journal, and proceed to reconsider it. If after such Reconsideration two thirds of that House shall agree to pass the Bill, it shall be sent together with the Objections, to the other House, by which it shall likewise be reconsidered, and if approved by two thirds of that House, it shall become a Law. But in all such Cases the Votes of both Houses shall be determined by Yeas and Nays, and the Names of the Persons voting for and against the Bill shall be entered on the Journal of each House respectively. If any Bill shall not be returned by the President within ten Days (Sundays excepted) after it shall have been presented to him, the Same shall be a Law, in like Manner as if he had signed it, unless the Congress by their Adjournment prevent its Return in which Case it shall not be a Law.

Every Order, Resolution, or Vote, to Which the Concurrence of the Senate and House of Representatives may be necessary (except on a question of Adjournment) shall be presented to the President of the United States; and before the Same shall take Effect, shall be approved by him, or being disapproved by him, shall be repassed by two thirds of the Senate and House of Representatives, according to the Rules and Limitations prescribed in the Case of a Bill.

Section 8. The Congress shall have Power to lay and collect Taxes, Duties, Imposts and Excises, to pay the Debts and provide for the common Defence and general Welfare of the United States; but all Duties, Imposts and Excises shall be uniform throughout the United States;

To borrow money on the credit of the United States;

To regulate Commerce with foreign Nations, and among the several States, and with the Indian Tribes;

To establish an uniform Rule of Naturalization, and uniform Laws on the subject of Bankruptcies throughout the United States;

To coin Money, regulate the Value thereof, and of foreign Coin, and fix the Standard of Weights and Measures;

To provide for the Punishment of counterfeiting the Securities and current Coin of the United States;

To Establish Post Offices and Post Roads;

To promote the Progress of Science and useful Arts, by securing for limited Times to Authors and Inventors the exclusive Right to their respective Writings and Discoveries;

To constitute Tribunals inferior to the supreme Court;

To define and punish Piracies and Felonies committed on the high Seas, and Offenses against the Law of Nations;

To declare War, grant Letters of Marque and Reprisal, and make Rules concerning Captures on Land and Water;

To raise and support Armies, but no Appropriation of Money to that Use shall be for a longer Term than two Years;

To provide and maintain a Navy;

To make Rules for the Government and Regulation of the land and naval Forces;

To provide for calling forth the Militia to execute the Laws of the Union, suppress Insurrections and repel Invasions;

To provide for organizing, arming, and disciplining, the Militia, and for governing such Part of them as may be employed in the Service of the United States, reserving to the States respectively, the Appointment of the Officers, and the Authority of training the Militia according to the discipline prescribed by Congress;

To exercise exclusive Legislation in all Cases whatsoever, over such District (not exceeding ten Miles square) as may, by Cession of particular States and the Acceptance of Congress, become the Seat of the Government of the United States, and to exercise like Authority over all Places purchased by the Consent of the Legislature of the State in which the Same shall be, for the Erection of Forts, Magazines, Arsenals, dock-Yards, and other needful Buildings;—And

To make all Laws which shall be necessary and proper for carrying into Execution the foregoing Powers, and all other Powers vested by this Constitution in the Government of the United States, or in any Department or Officer thereof.

Section 9. The Migration or Importation of Such Persons as any of the States now existing shall think proper to admit, shall not be prohibited by the Congress prior to the Year one thousand eight hundred and eight, but a Tax or duty may be imposed on such Importation, not exceeding ten dollars for each Person.

The privilege of the Writ of Habeas Corpus shall not be suspended, unless when in Cases of Rebellion or Invasion the public Safety may require it.

No Bill of Attainder or ex post facto Law shall be passed.

No Capitation, or other direct, Tax shall be laid, unless in Proportion to the census or Enumeration herein before directed to be taken.

No Tax or Duty shall be laid on Articles exported from any State.

No Preference shall be given by any Regulation of Commerce or Revenue to the Ports of one State over those of another: nor shall Vessels bound to, or from, one State be obliged to enter, clear, or pay Duties in another.

No money shall be drawn from the Treasury, but in Consequence of Appropriations made by Law; and a regular Statement and Account of the Receipts and Expenditures of all public Money shall be published from time to time.

No Title of Nobility shall be granted by the United States: And no Person holding any Office of Profit or Trust under them, shall, without the Consent of the Congress, accept of any present, Emolument, Office, or Title, of any kind whatever, from any King, Prince, or foreign State.

Section 10. No State shall enter into any Treaty, Alliance, or Confederation; grant Letters of Marque and Reprisal; coin Money; emit Bills of Credit; make any Thing but gold and silver Coin a Tender in Payment of Debts; pass any Bill of Attainder, ex post facto Law, or Law impairing the Obligation of Contracts, or grant any Title of Nobility.

No State shall, without the Consent of the Congress, lay any Imposts or Duties on Imports or Exports, except what may be absolutely necessary for executing its inspection Laws: and the net Produce of all Duties and Imposts, laid by any State on Imports or Exports, shall be for the Use of the Treasury of the United States; and all such Laws shall be subject to the Revision and Controul of the Congress.

No State shall, without the Consent of Congress, lay any Duty of Tonnage, keep Troops, or Ships of War in time of Peace, enter into any Agreement or Compact with another State, or with a foreign Power or engage in War, unless actually invaded, or in such imminent Danger as will not admit of delay.

Article II

Section 1. The executive Power shall be vested in a President of the United States of America. He shall hold his Office during the Term of four Years, and, together with the Vice President, chosen for the same Term, be elected, as follows:

Each State shall appoint, in such Manner as the Legislature thereof may direct, a Number of Electors, equal to the whole Number of Senators and Representatives to which the State may be entitled in the Congress; but no Senator or Representative, or Person holding an Office of Trust or Profit under the United States, shall be appointed an Elector.

The Electors shall meet in their respective States, and vote by Ballot for two Persons, of whom one at least shall not be an Inhabitant of the same State with themselves. And they shall make a List of all the Persons voted for, and of the Number of Votes for each; which List they shall sign and certify, and transmit sealed to the Seat of the Government of the United States, directed to the President of the Senate. The President of the Senate shall, in the Presence of the Senate and House of Representatives, open all the Certificates, and the Votes shall then be counted. The Person having the greatest Number of Votes shall be the President, if such Number be a Majority of the whole Number of Electors appointed; and if there be more than one who have such Majority, and have an equal Number of Votes, then the House of Representatives shall immediately chuse by Ballot one of them for President; and if no Person have a Majority, then from the five highest on the List the said House shall in like Manner chuse the President. But in chusing the President, the Votes shall be taken by States, the Representation from each State having one Vote; A quorum for this Purpose shall consist of a Member or Members from two thirds of the States, and a Majority of all the States shall be necessary to a Choice. In every Case, after the Choice of the President, the Person having the greater Number of Votes of the Electors shall be the Vice President. But if there should remain two or more who have equal Votes, the Senate shall chuse from them by Ballot the Vice President.

The Congress may determine the Time of chusing the Electors, and the Day on which they shall give their Votes; which Day shall be the same throughout the United States.

No person except a natural born Citizen, or a Citizen of the United States, at the time of the Adoption of this Constitution, shall be eligible to the Office of President; neither shall any Person be eligible to that Office who shall not have attained to the Age of thirty five Years, and been fourteen Years a Resident within the United States.

In case of the removal of the President from Office, or of his Death, Resignation or Inability to discharge the Powers and Duties of the said Office, the Same shall devolve on the Vice President and the Congress may by Law provide for the Case of Removal, Death, Resignation or Inability, both of the President and Vice President, declaring what Officer shall then act as President, and such Officer shall act accordingly, until the Disability be removed, or a President shall be elected.

The President shall, at stated Times, receive for his Services, a Compensation, which shall neither be increased nor diminished during the Period for which he shall have been elected, and he shall not receive within that Period any other Emolument from the United States, or any of them.

Before he enter on the Execution of his Office, he shall take the following Oath or Affirmation: "I do solemnly swear (or affirm) that I will faithfully execute the Office of President of the United States, and will to the best of my Ability, preserve, protect and defend the Constitution of the United States."

Section 2. The President shall be Commander in Chief of the Army and Navy of the United States, and of the militia of the several States, when called into the actual Services of the United States; he may require the Opinion, in writing, of the principal Officer in each of the Executive Departments, upon any Subject relating to the Duties of their respective Offices and he shall have Power to grant Reprieves and Pardons for Offenses against the United States, except in Cases of Impeachment.

He shall have Power, by and with the Advice and Consent of the Senate, to make Treaties, provided two thirds of the Senators present concur; and he shall nominate, and by and with the Advice and Consent of the Senate, shall appoint Ambassadors, other public Ministers and Consuls, Judges of the supreme Court, and all other Officers of the United States, whose Appointments are not herein otherwise provided for, and which shall be established by Law; but the Congress may by Law vest the Appointment of such inferior Officers, as they think proper, in the President alone, in the Courts of Law, or in the Heads of Departments.

The President shall have Power to fill up all Vacancies that may happen during the Recess of the Senate, by granting Commissions which shall expire at the End of their next Session.

Section 3. He shall from time to time give to the Congress Information of the State of the Union, and recommend to their Consideration such Measures as he shall judge necessary and expedient; he may, on extraordinary Occasions, convene both Houses, or either of them, and in Case of Disagreement between them, with Respect to the Time of Adjournment, he may adjourn them to such Time as he shall think proper; he shall receive Ambassadors and other public Ministers; he shall take Care that the Laws be faithfully executed, and shall Commission all the Officers of the United States.

Section 4. The President, Vice President and all civil Officers of the United States, shall be removed from Office on Impeachment for, and Conviction of, Treason, Bribery, or other high Crimes and Misdemeanors.

Article III

Section 1. The judicial Power of the United States, shall be vested in one supreme Court, and in such inferior Courts as the Congress may from time to time ordain and establish. The Judges, both of the supreme and inferior Courts, shall hold their Offices during good Behaviour, and shall, at stated Times, receive for their Services a Compensation, which shall not be diminished during their Continuance in Office.

Section 2. The judicial Power shall extend to all Cases, in Law and Equity, arising under this Constitution, the Laws of the United States, and Treaties made, or which shall be made, under their Authority;—to all Cases affecting Ambassadors, other public Ministers and Consuls;—to all Cases of admiralty and maritime Jurisdiction;—to Controversies to which the United States shall be a Party;—to Controversies between two or more States;—between a State and Citizens of another State;—between Citizens of different States;—between Citizens of the same State claiming Lands under the Grants of different States, and between a State, or the Citizens thereof, and foreign States, Citizens or Subjects.

In all Cases affecting Ambassadors, other public Ministers and Consuls, and those in which a State shall be a Party, the supreme Court shall have original Jurisdiction. In all the other Cases before mentioned, the supreme Court shall have appellate Jurisdiction, both as to Law and Fact, with such Exceptions, and under such Regulations as the Congress shall make.

The trial of all Crimes, except in Cases of Impeachment, shall be by Jury; and such Trial shall be held in the State where the said Crimes shall have been committed; but when not committed within any State, the Trial shall be at such Place or Places as the Congress may by Law have directed.

Section 3. Treason against the United States, shall consist only in levying War against them, or, in adhering to their Enemies, giving them Aid and Comfort. No Person shall be convicted of Treason unless on the Testimony of two Witnesses to the same overt Act, or on Confession in open Court.

The Congress shall have Power to declare the Punishment of Treason, but no Attainder of Treason shall work Corruption of Blood, or Forfeiture except during the Life of the Person attainted.

Article IV

Section 1. Full Faith and Credit shall be given in each State to the public Acts, Records, and judicial Proceedings of every other State. And the Congress may by general Laws prescribe the Manner in which such Acts, Records and Proceedings shall be proved, and the Effect thereof.

Section 2. The Citizens of each State shall be entitled to all Privileges and Immunities of Citizens in the several States.

A Person charged in any State with Treason, Felony, or other Crime, who shall flee from Justice, and be found in another State, shall on demand of the executive Authority of the State from which he fled, be delivered up, to be removed to the State having Jurisdiction of the Crime.

No Person held to Service or Labour in one State, under the Laws thereof, escaping into another, shall, in Consequence of any Law or Regulation therein, be discharged from such Service or Labour, but shall be delivered up on Claim of the Party to whom such Service or Labour may be due.

Section 3. New States may be admitted by the Congress into this Union; but no new State shall be formed or erected with the Jurisdiction of any other State; nor any State be formed by the Junction of two or more States, or Parts of States, without the Consent of the Legislatures of the States concerned as well as of the Congress.

The Congress shall have Power to dispose of and make all needful Rules and Regulations respecting the Territory or other Property belonging to the United States;

and nothing in this Constitution shall be so construed as to Prejudice any Claims of the United States, or of any particular State.

Section 4. The United States shall guarantee to every State in this Union a Republican Form of Government, and shall protect each of them against Invasion; and on Application of the Legislature, or of the Executive (when the Legislature cannot be convened) against domestic Violence.

Article V

The Congress, whenever two thirds of both Houses shall deem it necessary, shall propose Amendments to this Constitution, or, on the Application of the Legislatures of two thirds of the several States, shall call a Convention for proposing Amendments, which, in either Case, shall be valid to all Intents and Purposes, as part of this Constitution, when ratified by the Legislatures of three fourths of the several States, or by Conventions in three fourths thereof, as the one or the other Mode of Ratification may be proposed by the Congress; Provided that no Amendment which may be made prior to the Year One thousand eight hundred and eight shall in any Manner affect the first and fourth Clauses in the Ninth Section of the first Article; and that no State, without its consent, shall be deprived of its equal Suffrage in the Senate.

Article VI

All Debts contracted and Engagements entered into, before the Adoption of this Constitution, shall be as valid against the United States under this Constitution, as under the Confederation.

This Constitution, and the Laws of the United States which shall be made in Pursuance thereof; and all treaties made, or which shall be made, under the Authority of the United States, shall be the supreme Law of the Land; and the Judges in every State shall be bound thereby, any Thing in the Constitution or Laws of any State to the Contrary notwithstanding.

The Senators and Representatives before mentioned, and the Members of the several State Legislatures, and all executive and judicial Officers, both of the United States and of the several States, shall be bound by Oath or Affirmation, to support this Constitution; but no religious Test shall ever be required as a Qualification to any Office or public Trust under the United States.

Article VII

The Ratification of the Conventions of nine States shall be sufficient for the Establishment of this Constitution between the States so ratifying the Same.

ARTICLES IN ADDITION TO, AND AMENDMENT OF, THE CONSTITUTION OF THE UNITED STATES OF AMERICA, PROPOSED BY CONGRESS, AND RATIFIED BY THE LEGISLATURES OF THE SEVERAL STATES PURSUANT TO THE FIFTH ARTICLE OF THE ORIGINAL CONSTITUTION.

Amendment I [1791]

Congress shall make no law respecting an establishment of religion, or prohibiting the free exercise thereof; or abridging the freedom of speech, or of the press; or the right of the people peaceably to assemble, and to petition the Government for a redress of grievances.

Amendment II [1791]

A well regulated Militia, being necessary to the security of a free State, the right of the people to keep and bear Arms, shall not be infringed.

Amendment III [1791]

No Soldier shall, in time of peace be quartered in any house, without the consent of the Owner, nor in time of war, but in a manner to be prescribed by law.

Amendment IV [1791]

The right of the people to be secure in their persons, houses, papers, and effects, against unreasonable searches and seizures, shall not be violated, and no Warrants shall issue, but upon probable cause, supported by Oath or affirmation, and particularly describing the place to be searched, and the persons or things to be seized.

Amendment V [1791]

No person shall be held to answer for a capital, or otherwise infamous crime, unless on a presentment or indictment of a Grand Jury, except in cases arising in the land or naval forces, or in the Militia, when in actual service in time of War or public danger; nor shall any person be subject for the same offence to be twice put in jeopardy of life or limb; nor shall be compelled in any criminal case to be a witness against himself, nor be deprived of life, liberty, or property, without due process of law; nor shall private property be taken for public use, without just compensation.

Amendment VI [1791]

In all criminal prosecutions, the accused shall enjoy the right to a speedy and public trial, by an impartial jury of the State and district wherein the crime shall have been committed, which district shall have been previously ascertained by law, and to be informed of the nature and cause of the accusation; to be confronted with the witnesses against him; to have compulsory process for obtaining witnesses in his favor, and to have the Assistance of Counsel for his defence.

Amendment VII [1791]

In Suits at common law, where the value in controversy shall exceed twenty dollars, the right of trial by jury shall be preserved, and no fact tried by jury, shall be otherwise re-examined in any Court of the United States, than according to the rules of the common law.

Amendment VIII [1791]

Excessive bail shall not be required, nor excessive fines imposed, nor cruel and unusual punishments inflicted.

Amendment IX [1791]

The enumeration in the Constitution, of certain rights, shall not be construed to deny or disparage others retained by the people.

Amendment X [1791]

The powers not delegated to the United States by the Constitution, nor prohibited by it to the States, are reserved to the States respectively, or to the people.

Amendment XI [1798]

The Judicial power of the United States shall not be construed to extend to any suit in law or equity, commenced or prosecuted against one of the United States by Citizens of another State, or by Citizens or Subjects of any Foreign State.

Amendment XII [1804]

The Electors shall meet in their respective states and vote by ballot for President and Vice President, one of whom, at least, shall not be an inhabitant of the same state with themselves; they shall name in their ballots the person voted for as President, and in distinct ballots the person voted for as Vice President, and they shall make distinct lists of all persons voted for as President, and of all persons voted for as Vice President, and of the number of votes for each, which lists they shall sign and certify, and transmit sealed to the seat of the government of the United States, directed to the President of the Senate;—The President of the Senate shall, in the presence of the Senate and House of Representatives, open all the certificates and the votes shall then be counted;—The person having the greatest number of votes for President, shall be the President, if such number be a majority of the whole number of Electors appointed; and if no person have such majority, then from the persons having the highest numbers not exceeding three on the list of those voted for as President, the House of Representatives shall choose immediately, by ballot, the President. But in choosing the President, the votes shall be taken by states, the representation from each state having one vote; a quorum for this purpose shall consist of a member or members from two-thirds of the states, and a majority of all the states shall be necessary to a choice. And if the House of Representatives shall not choose a President whenever the right of choice shall devolve upon them before the fourth day of March next following, then the Vice President shall act as President, as in the case of the death or other constitutional disability of the President.—The person having the greatest number of votes as Vice President, shall be the Vice President, if such number be a majority of the whole number of Electors appointed, and if no person have a majority, then from the two highest numbers on the list, the Senate shall choose the Vice President; a quorum for the purpose shall consist of two-thirds of the whole number of Senators, and a majority of the whole number shall be necessary to a choice. But no person constitutionally ineligible to the office of President shall be eligible to that of Vice President of the United States.

Amendment XIII [1865]

Section 1. Neither slavery nor involuntary servitude, except as a punishment for crime whereof the party shall have been duly convicted, shall exist within the United States, or any place subject to their jurisdiction.

Section 2. Congress shall have power to enforce this article by appropriate legislation.

Amendment XIV [1868]

Section 1. All persons born or naturalized in the United States, and subject to the jurisdiction thereof, are citizens of the United States and of the State wherein they reside. No State shall make or enforce any law which shall abridge the privileges or immunities of citizens of the United States; nor shall any State deprive any person of life, liberty, or property, without due process of law; nor deny to any person within its jurisdiction the equal protection of the laws.

Section 2. Representatives shall be apportioned among the several States according to their respective numbers, counting the whole number of persons in each State, excluding Indians not taxed. But when the right to vote at any election for the choice of electors for President and Vice President of the United States, Representatives in Congress, the Executive and Judicial officers of a State, or the members of the Legislature thereof, is denied to any of the male inhabitants of such State, being twenty-one years of age, and citizens of the United States, or in any way abridged, except for participation in rebellion, or other crime, the basis of representation therein shall be reduced in the proportion which the number of such male citizens shall bear to the whole number of male citizens twenty-one years of age in such State.

Section 3. No person shall be a Senator or Representative in Congress, or elector of President and Vice President, or hold any office, civil or military, under the United States, or under any State, who having previously taken an oath, as a member of Congress, or as an officer of the United States, or as a member of any State legislature, or as an executive or judicial officer of any State, to support the Constitution of the United States, shall have engaged in insurrection or rebellion against the same, or given aid or comfort to the enemies thereof. But Congress may by a vote of two-thirds of each House, remove such disability.

Section 4. The validity of the public debt of the United States, authorized by law, including debts incurred for payment of pensions and bounties for services in suppressing insurrection or rebellion, shall not be questioned. But neither the United States nor any State shall assume or pay any debt or obligation incurred in aid of insurrection or rebellion against the United States, or any claim for the loss or emancipation of any slave; but all such debts, obligations and claims shall be held illegal and void.

Section 5. The Congress shall have power to enforce, by appropriate legislation, the provisions of this article.

Amendment XV [1870]

Section 1. The right of citizens of the United States to vote shall not be denied or abridged by the United States or by any State on account of race, color, or previous condition of servitude.

Section 2. The Congress shall have power to enforce this article by appropriate legislation.

Amendment XVI [1913]

The Congress shall have power to lay and collect taxes on incomes, from whatever source derived, without apportionment among the several States, and without regard to any census or enumeration.

Amendment XVII [1913]

[1] The Senate of the United States shall be composed of two Senators from each State, elected by the people thereof, for six years; and each Senator shall have one vote. The electors in each State shall have the qualifications requisite for electors of the most numerous branch of the State legislatures.

[2] When vacancies happen in the representation of any State in the Senate, the executive authority of such State shall issue writs of election to fill such vacancies: Provided, that the legislature of any State may empower the executive thereof to make temporary appointments until the people fill the vacancies by election as the legislature may direct.

[3] This amendment shall not be so construed as to affect the election or term of any Senator chosen before it becomes valid as part of the Constitution.

Amendment XVIII [1919]

Section 1. After one year from the ratification of this article the manufacture, sale, or transportation of intoxicating liquors within, the importation thereof into, or the exportation thereof from the United States and all territory subject to the jurisdiction thereof for beverage purposes is hereby prohibited.

Section 2. The Congress and the several States shall have concurrent power to enforce this article by appropriate legislation.

Section 3. This article shall be inoperative unless it shall have been ratified as an amendment to the Constitution by the legislatures of the several States, as provided in the Constitution, within seven years from the date of the submission hereof to the States by the Congress.

Amendment XIX [1920]

[1] The right of citizens of the United States to vote shall not be denied or abridged by the United States or by any State on account of sex.

[2] Congress shall have power to enforce this article by appropriate legislation.

Amendment XX [1933]

Section 1. The terms of the President and Vice President shall end at noon on the 20th day of January, and the terms of Senators and Representatives at noon on the 3d day of January, of the years in which such terms would have ended if this article had not been ratified; and the terms of their successors shall then begin.

Section 2. The Congress shall assemble at least once in every year, and such meeting shall begin at noon on the 3d day of January, unless they shall by law appoint a different day.

Section 3. If, at the time fixed for the beginning of the term of the President, the President elect shall have died, the Vice President elect shall become President. If the President shall not have been chosen before the time fixed for the beginning of his term, or if the President elect shall have failed to qualify, then the Vice President elect shall act as President until a President shall have qualified; and the Congress may by law provide for the case wherein neither a President elect nor a Vice President elect shall have qualified, declaring who shall then act as President, or the manner in which one who is to act shall be selected, and such person shall act accordingly until a President or Vice President shall have qualified.

Section 4. The Congress may by law provide for the case of the death of any of the persons from whom the House of Representatives may choose a President whenever the right of choice shall have devolved upon them, and for the case of the death of any of the persons from whom the Senate may choose a Vice President whenever the right of choice shall have devolved upon them.

Section 5. Sections 1 and 2 shall take effect on the 15th day of October following the ratification of this article.

Section 6. This article shall be inoperative unless it shall have been ratified as an amendment to the Constitution by the legislatures of three-fourths of the several States within seven years from the date of its submission.

Amendment XXI [1933]

Section 1. The eighteenth article of amendment to the Constitution of the United States is hereby repealed.

Section 2. The transportation or importation into any State, Territory, or possession of the United States for delivery or use therein of intoxicating liquors, in violation of the laws thereof, is hereby prohibited.

Section 3. This article shall be inoperative unless it shall have been ratified as an amendment to the Constitution by conventions in the several States, as provided in the Constitution, within seven years from the date of the submission hereof to the States by the Congress.

Amendment XXII [1951]

Section 1. No person shall be elected to the office of the President more than twice, and no person who has held the office of President, or acted as President, for more than two years of a term to which some other person was elected President shall be elected to the office of President more than once. But this Article shall not apply to any person holding the office of President when this Article was proposed by the Congress, and shall not prevent any person who may be holding the office of President, or acting as President, during the term within which this Article becomes operative from holding the office of President or acting as President during the remainder of such term.

Section 2. This article shall be inoperative unless it shall have been ratified as an amendment to the Constitution by the legislatures of three-fourths of the several States within seven years from the date of its submission to the States by the Congress.

Amendment XXIII [1961]

Section 1. The District constituting the seat of Government of the United States shall appoint in such manner as the Congress may direct:

A number of electors of President and Vice President equal to the whole number of Senators and Representatives in Congress to which the District would be entitled if it were a State, but in no event more than the least populous state; they shall be in addition to those appointed by the states, but they shall be considered, for the purposes of the election of President and Vice President, to be electors appointed by a state; and they shall meet in the District and perform such duties as provided by the twelfth article of amendment.

Section 2. The Congress shall have power to enforce this article by appropriate legislation.

Amendment XXIV [1964]

Section 1. The right of citizens of the United States to vote in any primary or other election for President or Vice President, for electors for President or Vice President, or for Senator or Representative in Congress, shall not be denied or abridged by the United States or any State by reason of failure to pay any poll tax or other tax.

Section 2. The Congress shall have power to enforce this article by appropriate legislation.

Amendment XXV [1967]

Section 1. In the case of the removal of the President from office or of his death or resignation, the Vice President shall become President.

Section 2. Whenever there is a vacancy in the office of the Vice President, the President shall nominate a Vice President who shall take office upon confirmation by a majority vote of both Houses of Congress.

Section 3. Whenever the President transmits to the President pro tempore of the Senate and the Speaker of the House of Representatives his written declaration that he is unable to discharge the powers and duties of his office, and until he transmits to them a written declaration to the contrary, such powers and duties shall be discharged by the Vice President as Acting President.

Section 4. Whenever the Vice President and a majority of either the principal officers of the executive departments or of such other body as Congress may by law provide, transmit to the President pro tempore of the Senate and the Speaker of the House of Representatives, their written declaration that the President is unable to discharge the powers and duties of his office, the Vice President shall immediately assume the powers and duties of the office as Acting President.

Thereafter, when the President transmits to the President pro tempore of the Senate and the Speaker of the House of Representatives his written declaration that no inability exists, he shall resume the powers and duties of his office unless the Vice President and a majority of either the principal officers of the executive department or of such other body as Congress may by law provide, transmit within four days to the President pro tempore of the Senate and the Speaker of the House of Representatives their written declaration that the President is unable to discharge the powers and duties of his office. Thereupon Congress shall decide the issue, assembling within forty-eight hours for that purpose if not in session. If the Congress, within twenty-one days after receipt of the latter written declaration, or, if Congress is not in session, within twenty-one days after Congress is required to assemble, determines by two-thirds vote of both Houses that the President is unable to discharge the powers and duties of his office, the Vice President shall continue to discharge the same as Acting President; otherwise, the President shall resume the powers and duties of his office.

Amendment XXVI [1971]

Section 1. The right of citizens of the United States, who are eighteen years of age or older, to vote shall not be denied or abridged by the United States or by any State on account of age.

Section 2. The Congress shall have power to enforce this article by appropriate legislation.

Amendment XXVII [1992]

No Law, varying the compensation for the services of the Senators and Representatives, shall take effect, until an election of Representatives shall have intervened.

†